THE MATINS LECTIONARY

The Complete Readings from the Traditional Roman Breviary

Lessons from the Divine Office of Matins according to the *Breviarium Romanum* of 1954 in English

Compiled by Samuel McIlhearn

TAN Books
Gastonia, North Carolina

The Matins Lectionary: The Complete Readings from the Traditional Roman Breviary © 2026 Samuel McIlhearn

All rights reserved. With the exception of short excerpts used in critical review, no part of this work may be reproduced, transmitted, or stored in any form whatsoever, without the prior written permission of the publisher. Creation, exploitation and distribution of any unauthorized editions of this work, in any format in existence now or in the future—including but not limited to text, audio, and video—is prohibited without the prior written permission of the publisher.

All texts and artwork used herein are in the public domain

All passages from the Sacred Scriptures are taken from the *Douay-Rhiems (Challoner)* version.

All other Lessons are adapted from the Marquess of Bute translation of *The Roman Breviary* (Edinburgh, 1908)

All artwork is taken from various liturgical volumes of the 19th and early 20th Centuries.

Cover design by Jordan Avery

ISBN: 978-1-5051-3518-3
Kindle ISBN: 978-1-5051-3762-0
ePUB ISBN: 978-1-5051-3761-3

Published in the United States by
TAN Books
PO Box 269
Gastonia, NC 28053

www.TANBooks.com

Printed in India

Table of Contents

Lessons from the Office of Matins for every feast and feria of the liturgical year.

¶ The names of Scriptural books are rendered in their Latinate forms as done in the Vulgate of St. Jerome. Thus, the books of Samuel and Kings are called 1–4 Kings; the book of Sirach is called Ecclesiasticus; the Song of Songs is the Canticle of Canticles; the books of Chronicles are called 1–2 Parapolimenon.

Introduction

For centuries, the ceaseless prayer of the Catholic Church has been the *Opus Dei*: the Divine Office as chanted by monks and priests around the world. Every day, priests and religious worldwide chant or recite Psalms, Hymns, and other prayers in accordance with the rule as laid out by the Psalmist himself in Psalm 118. "Seven times a day I have given praise to thee" [Ps 118:164] and "In the night I have remembered Thy name, O Lord." [Psalm 118:55] This is the course of the Divine Office with its eight hours of prayer. The seven diurnal hours are Lauds, Prime, Terce, Sext, None, Vespers, and Compline. The nocturnal hour is called Matins.

The night hour of Matins has always been the longest of the hours, featuring as many as 18 Psalms on Sunday in the Traditional Roman Rite around the time of the Council of Trent. In addition to these Psalms, Matins alone features between three and nine readings (called Lessons) interspersed throughout the Psalms. These lessons are selections from the Sacred Scriptures, hagiographical works, and commentaries by the Church Fathers, selected for each day according to the liturgical calendar, with a certain scriptural and patristic focus for each season and feast day of the liturgical year.

The lessons at Matins are taken from either the temporal cycle—the occurring scripture in the proper of time—or from those appropriate to that day's feast: the common or proper of saints. While not the whole content of the Bible, the scriptural readings come from every book of the Bible, so one reads through the highlights of the Sacred Scriptures in a way that fits the liturgical calendar for each particular season or day. If there is a feast on a particular day, then there are six more readings after the three scriptural lessons; three are usually the life of the saint of the day or a history of or commentary on the feast, and the last three are a snippet of the day's Gospel followed by a three-part commentary by one of the Church Fathers on that Gospel passage.

Thus, every day the Church has arranged for every monk, nun, cleric, and layman who so desires to prayerfully reflect on the Scriptures, the lives of the saints, and the wisdom of the Church Fathers. At least, this was the case until 1960.

In 1960, Pope John XXIII radically reformed the Roman Breviary in order to reduce the temporal burden on secular clergy who were bound to pray the full Divine Office every day. As part of his sweeping reforms to the Divine Office, he reduced the lessons at Matins for almost every Sunday and Feast from the traditional nine down to three. Around 60% of the readings were removed: mostly hagiography and Patristic commentary. The Pope himself understood the magnitude of this loss, calling for priests to supplement what would be lost from the office in their own spiritual reading of the Church Fathers. He said in his *motu proprio*: "Furthermore, since the readings from the Fathers have also been somewhat [sic] reduced, We earnestly exhort all clerics to secure the writings of the Fathers, so rich in wisdom and piety, and to read and meditate on them constantly."

Yet, just 11 years later, the Divine Office was replaced with the Liturgy of the Hours, reducing the readings to merely two per day and abolishing the hagiographical lessons entirely. These developments have resulted in the near loss of an immense treasure: the Church's daily spiritual reading.

It wasn't just clerics who were affected by this loss; the laity, too, had frequent contact with the Divine Office in the past, even going to hear Sunday Matins in addition to the Mass. Some lay Catholics even read the Divine Office themselves, as evidenced by past translations of the Roman Breviary. The most notable of these translations is that done by John, the Marquess of Bute in 1908. The Marquess of Bute Breviary was a complete English translation of the entire Roman Breviary for use in England in 1908. This four-volume work is even to this day an invaluable resource for Catholics who wish to access the spiritual treasures of the Divine Office but lack the necessary proficiency in Latin. Unfortunately, his work is arranged according to the calendar of England in 1908, so it lacks a number of significant feasts in the life of a modern day Catholic (like the Feast of Christ the King) as well as placing some local feasts on the calendar instead of more universal ones. Additionally, the language of his translation can be rather obscure and difficult for modern readers. Finally, his work is in four volumes: rather a lot for someone who would just like to read the lessons at Matins. This singular volume, the Matins Lectionary, aims to remedy that.

The Matins Lectionary is an arrangement of all the lessons from the office of Matins as they would have been in 1954—before the reductions of John XXIII—with some minor additions for the spiritual benefit of the reader. Additions include both the pre-1950 and post-1950 versions of the lessons of the Assumption (August 15th), the addition of a lesson on Our Lady of Guadalupe (December 12th), and more. The Scriptural lessons are taken from the venerable Douay-Rheims version and the hagiographical and Patristic lessons are a revised translation of the Latin originals as based on the prior work of the Marquess of Bute. The selections from ecclesiastical documents, such as encyclicals, are revised translations of the official ones found on the Vatican website.

What was once lost to the faithful by the accidents of history and the decline of Latin literacy is available once more in this volume. It can be used as "the Church's spiritual reading," with daily scriptures, hagiography, and Patristic commentary on the Gospel of the day all according to the Traditional calendar with its multitude of saints and octaves. One can now be enriched daily by the Scriptures, the lives of the saints, and the wisdom of the Fathers as arranged in the Roman Breviary, in English.

Readers, both lay and clerical, can benefit from this lost treasure of Catholic Tradition. Each Sunday has nine lessons which, if read in the morning prior to Mass, serve as a spiritual preparation for that day's Mass: truly a benefit to all the faithful attached to the Traditional liturgy. What's more, as the calendar used to contain numerous octaves, there is ample opportunity for extended reflection on the great saints and mysteries of the faith. Spend a week meditating on St. Joseph or the Sacred Heart; let St. Thomas Aquinas enflame your love of the Holy Eucharist during the Octave of Corpus Christi. All of this, and more, is contained in this Spiritual Treasury compiled by Holy Mother Church and finally made available in the English language.

JANUARY

1: Circumcision of the Lord & Octave of the Nativity, Duplex II Class
2: Octave of St. Stephen, Simplex
3: Octave of St. John, Simplex
4: Octave of the Holy Innocents, Simplex
5: Vigil of the Epiphany, Semiduplex, Com. of St. Telesphorus Pope & Martyr
6: Epiphany of the Lord, Duplex I Class with privileged Octave of the II rank
7–10: Days within Epiph. Oct., Semiduplex
11: Day 6 within Oct. of Epiph., Semiduplex, Com. of St. Hyginus Pope & Martyr
12: Day 7 within Epiph. Oct., Semiduplex
13: Octave of the Epiphany, Major Duplex
14: St. Hilary Bishop, Confessor, & Doctor, Duplex, Com. of St. Felix Priest & Martyr
15: St. Paul the first hermit, Confessor, Duplex, Com. of St. Maurus
16: St. Marcellus I Pope & Martyr, Semiduplex
17: St. Anthony Abbot, Duplex
18: Chair of St. Peter at Rome, Major Duplex, Com. of St. Paul Apostle, & St. Prisca Virgin Martyr
19: Ss. Marius, Martha, Audifax, & Abachum Martyrs, Simplex, Com. of St. Canute, Martyr
20: Ss. Fabian Pope & Sebastian Martyrs, Duplex
21: St. Agnes, Virgin Martyr, Duplex
22: Ss. Vincent & Anastasius Martyrs, Semiduplex
23: St. Raymund of Peñafort Confessor, Semiduplex, Com. of St. Emerentiana Virgin Martyr
24: St. Timothy Bishop & Martyr, Duplex
25: Conversion of St. Paul, Major Duplex, Com. of St. Peter
26: St. Polycarp Bishop & Martyr, Duplex
27: St. John Chrysostom Bishop, Confessor, & Doctor, Duplex
28: St. Peter Nolasco Confessor, Duplex, Com. of St. Agnes Virgin Martyr
29: St. Francis de Sales Bishop, Confessor, & Doctor, Duplex
30: St. Martina Virgin Martyr, Semiduplex
31: St. John Bosco Confessor, Duplex

FEBRUARY

1: St. Ignatius Bishop & Martyr, Duplex
2: Purification of the Blessed Virgin Mary, Duplex II Class
3: St. Blaise Bishop & Martyr, Simplex
4: St. Andrew Corsini Confessor Bishop, Duplex
5: St. Agatha Virgin Martyr, Duplex
6: St. Titus Confessor Bishop, Duplex, Com. of St. Dorothy Virgin Martyr
7: St. Romuald Abbot, Duplex
8: St. John de Matha Confessor, Duplex
9: St. Cyril of Alexandria, Confessor Bishop, & Doctor, Duplex, Com. of St. Apollonia Virgin Martyr

10: St. Scholastica Virgin, Duplex
11: Apparition of the Immaculate BVM at Lourdes, Major Duplex
12: The Seven Holy Founders of the Servite Order Confessors, Duplex
13: Feria
14: St. Valentine Priest & Martyr, Simplex
15: Ss. Faustinus & Jovita Martyrs, Simplex
16–17: Ferias
18: St. Simeon Bishop & Martyr, Simplex
19–21: Ferias
22: Chair of St. Peter at Antioch, Major Duplex, Com. of St. Paul
23: St. Peter Damian Confessor, Duplex, Com. of the Vigil
24: St. Matthias Apostle, Duplex II Class [Leap Year: 25 February]
25–26: Ferias
27: St. Gabriel of Our Lady of Sorrows, Duplex [Leap Year: 28 February]
28: Feria

MARCH

1–3: Ferias
4: St. Casimir Confessor, Semiduplex, Com. of St. Lucius I Pope & Martyr
5: Feria
6: Ss. Perpetua & Felicity Martyrs, Duplex
7: St. Thomas Aquinas Confessor & Doctor, Duplex
8: St. John of God Confessor, Duplex
9: St. Frances of Rome Widow, Duplex
10: The Forty Holy Martyrs, Semiduplex
11: Feria
12: St. Gregory I Pope, Confessor, & Doctor, Duplex
13–16: Ferias
17: St. Patrick Confessor Bishop, Duplex
18: St. Cyril of Jerusalem, Confessor Bishop, & Doctor, Duplex
19: St. Joseph, Spouse of the BVM, Confessor, & Patron of the Church, Duplex I Class
20: Feria
21: St. Benedict Abbot, Major Duplex
22–23: Ferias
24: St. Gabriel the Archangel, Major Duplex
25: Annunciation of the BVM, Duplex I Class
26: Feria
27: St. John Damascene Confessor & Doctor, Duplex
28: St. John Capistran Confessor, Semiduplex
29–31: Ferias

APRIL

1: Feria
2: St. Francis of Paula Confessor, Duplex

3: Feria
4: St. Isidore Bishop, Confessor, & Doctor, Duplex
5: St. Vincent Ferrer Confessor, Duplex
6–10: Ferias
11: St. Leo I Pope, Confessor, & Doctor, Duplex
12: Feria
13: St. Hermenegild Martyr, Semiduplex
14: St. Justin Martyr, Duplex, Com. of Saints Tiburtius, Valerian & Maximus, Martyrs
15–16: Ferias
17: St. Anicetus Pope & Martyr, Simplex
18–20: Ferias
21: St. Anselm Bishop, Confessor, & Doctor, Duplex
22: Ss. Soter & Cajus Popes & Martyrs, Semiduplex
23: St. George Martyr, Semiduplex
24: St. Fidelis of Sigmaringen Martyr, Duplex
25: St. Mark Evangelist, Duplex II Class
26: Ss. Cletus & Marcellinus Popes & Martyrs, Semiduplex
27: St. Peter Canisius Confessor & Doctor, Duplex
28: St. Paul of the Cross Confessor, Duplex, Com. of St. Vitalis Martyr
29: St. Peter Martyr, Duplex
30: St. Catherine of Siena Virgin, Duplex

MAY

1: Ss. Philip & James Apostles, Duplex II Class
2: St. Athanasius, Bishop, Confessor, & Doctor, Duplex
3: Invention of the Holy Cross, Duplex II Class, Com. of Ss. Alexander, Pope, Eventius & Theodulus Martyrs, & Juvenal, Confessor Bishop
4: St. Monica Widow, Duplex
5: St. Pius V Confessor Pope, Duplex
6: St. John before the Latin Gate, Major Duplex
7: St. Stanislaus Bishop & Martyr, Duplex
8: Apparition of St. Michael, Major Duplex
9: St. Gregory Nazianzen Bishop, Confessor, & Doctor, Duplex
10: St. Antoninus Confessor Bishop, Duplex, Com. of Ss. Gordian and Epimachus Martyrs
11: Feria
12: Ss. Nereus, Achilleus, Domitilla Virgin, & Pancras Martyrs, Semiduplex
13: St. Robert Bellarmine Bishop, Confessor, & Doctor, Duplex
14: St. Boniface Martyr, Simplex
15: St. John Baptiste de la Salle Confessor, Duplex
16: St. Ubald Confessor Bishop, Semiduplex
17: St. Paschal Baylon Confessor, Duplex
18: St. Venantius Martyr, Duplex
19: St. Peter Celestine Confessor Pope, Duplex, Com. of St. Pudentiana Virgin

20: St. Bernardine of Siena Confessor, Semiduplex
21–24: Ferias
25: St. Gregory VII Confessor Pope, Duplex, Com. of St. Urban I Pope & Martyr
26: St. Philip Neri Confessor, Duplex, Com. of St. Eleutherius Pope & Martyr
27: St. Bede the Venerable Confessor & Doctor, Duplex, Com. of St. John I Pope & Martyr
28: St. Augustine of Canterbury Confessor Bishop, Duplex
29: St. Mary Magdalene de Pazzi Virgin, Semiduplex
30: St. Felix I Pope & Martyr, Simplex
31: Blessed Virgin Mary, Queen, Duplex II Class, Com. of St. Petronilla Virgin

JUNE

1: St. Angela Merici Virgin, Duplex
2: Ss. Marcellinus, Peter, & Erasmus Bishop, Martyrs, Simplex
3: Feria
4: St. Francis Caracciolo Confessor, Duplex
5: St. Boniface Bishop & Martyr, Duplex
6: St. Norbert Confessor Bishop, Duplex
7–8: Ferias
9: Ss. Primus & Felician Martyrs, Simplex
10: St. Margaret Queen, Widow, Semiduplex
11: St. Barnabas Apostle, Major Duplex
12: St. John of San Facundo Confessor, Duplex, Com. of Ss. Basilides, Cyrinus, Nabor & Nazarius Martyrs
13: St. Anthony of Padua Confessor & Doctor, Duplex
14: St. Basil the Great Bishop, Confessor, & Doctor, Duplex
15: Ss. Vitus, Modestus, & Crescentia Martyrs, Simplex
16–17: Ferias
18: St. Ephræm the Syrian Deacon, Confessor, & Doctor, Duplex, Com. of Ss. Mark & Marcellianus Martyrs
19: St. Juliana Falconieri Virgin, Duplex, Com. of Ss. Gervase & Protase Martyrs
20: St. Silverius Pope & Martyr, Simplex
21: St. Aloysius Gonzaga Confessor, Duplex
22: St. Paulinus Confessor Bishop, Duplex
23: Vigil
24: The Nativity of St. John the Baptist, Duplex I Class with common Octave
25: St. William Abbot, Duplex, Com. of Octave
26: Ss. John & Paul Martyrs, Duplex, Com. of Octave
27: Day 4 within the Octave, Semiduplex
28: St. Irenæus Bishop & Martyr, Duplex, Com. of Octave and of Vigil
29: Ss. Peter & Paul Apostles, Duplex I Class with common Octave
30: Commemoration of St. Paul Apostle, Major Duplex, Com. of St. Peter Apostle & of the Octave of St. John the Baptist

JULY

1: The Most Precious Blood of Our Lord, Duplex I Class, Com. of Octave day of St. John the Baptist
2: Visitation of the BVM, Duplex II Class, Com. of Ss. Processus & Martinian Martyrs
3: St. Leo II Confessor Pope, Semiduplex, Com. of Octave of Apostles
4: Day 4 within the Octave of Apostles, Semiduplex
5: St. Anthony Mary Zaccaria Confessor, Duplex, Com. of Octave of Apostles
6: Octave of Ss. Peter and Paul Apostles, Major Duplex
7: Ss. Cyril & Methodius Confessor Bishops, Duplex
8: St. Elizabeth Queen, Widow, Semiduplex
9: Feria
10: The Seven Holy Brothers Martyrs, Semiduplex, & Ss. Rufina & Secunda Virgins & Martyrs
11: St. Pius I Pope & Martyr, Simplex
12: St. John Gualbert Abbot, Duplex, Com. of Ss. Nabor and Felix Martyrs
13: St. Anacletus Pope & Martyr, Semiduplex
14: St. Bonaventure Bishop, Confessor, & Doctor, Duplex
15: St. Henry II Emperor, Confessor, Semiduplex
16: Our Lady of Mt. Carmel, Major Duplex
17: St. Alexius Confessor, Semiduplex
18: St. Camillus de Lellis Confessor, Duplex, Com. of St. Symphorosa & her seven Sons Martyrs
19: St. Vincent de Paul Confessor, Duplex
20: St. Jerome Emiliani Confessor, Duplex, Com. of St. Margaret Virgin Martyr
21: St. Praxedes Virgin, Simplex
22: St. Mary Magdalene Penitent, Duplex
23: St. Apollinaris Martyr, Duplex, Com. of St. Liborius Confessor Bishop
24: Vigil, Com. of St. Christina Virgin Martyr
25: St. James Apostle, Duplex II Class, Com. of St. Christopher Martyr
26: St. Anne Mother of the BVM, Duplex II Class
27: St. Pantaleon Martyr, Simplex
28: Ss. Nazarius & Celsus Martyrs, Victor I Pope & Martyr, & St. Innocent I Confessor Pope, Semiduplex
29: St. Martha Virgin, Semiduplex, Com. of Ss. Felix II Pope, Simplicius, Faustinus, & Beatrice Martyrs
30: Ss. Abdon & Sennen Martyrs, Simplex
31: St. Ignatius of Loyola Confessor, Major Duplex

AUGUST

1: St. Peter the Apostle in Chains, Major Duplex, Com. of St. Paul & the Holy Machabee Martyrs
2: St. Alphonsus Mary de Liguori Bishop, Confessor, & Doctor, Duplex, Com. of St. Stephen I Pope & Martyr

3: Invention of St. Stephen Protomartyr, Semiduplex
4: St. Dominic Confessor, Major Duplex
5: Dedication of Our Lady of the Snows, Major Duplex
6: Transfiguration of Our Lord, Duplex II Class, Com. of Ss. Sixtus II Pope, Felicissimus & Agapitus Martyrs
7: St. Cajetan Confessor, Duplex, Com. of St. Donatus Bishop & Martyr
8: Ss. Cyriacus, Largus & Smaragdus Martyrs, Semiduplex
9: St. John Vianney Confessor Priest, Duplex, Com. of the Vigil & St. Romanus Martyr
10: St. Laurence Martyr, Duplex II Class with Simple Octave
11: Ss. Tiburtius & Susanna Virgin, Martyrs, Simplex
12: St. Clare Virgin, Duplex
13: Ss. Hippolytus & Cassian Martyrs, Simplex
14: Vigil, Com. of St. Eusebius Confessor
15: Assumption of the BVM, Duplex I Class with common Octave
16: St. Joachim Father of the BVM, Confessor, Duplex II Class
17: St. Hyacinth Confessor, Duplex, Com. of the Octave of the Assumption & the Octave Day of St. Laurence
18: Day 4 within Octave of the Assumption, Semiduplex, Com. of St. Agapitus Martyr
19: St. John Eudes Confessor, Duplex, Com. of the Octave
20: St. Bernard Abbot, Confessor, & Doctor, Duplex, Com. of the Octave
21: St. Jane Frances Frémiot de Chantal Widow, Duplex, Com. of the Octave
22: Immaculate Heart of Mary, Duplex II Class, Com. of Ss. Timothy, Hippolytus Bishop, & Symphorianus Martyrs
23: St. Philip Benizi Confessor, Duplex, Com. of the Vigil
24: St. Bartholomew Apostle, Duplex II Class
25: St. Louis King, Confessor, Semiduplex
26: St. Zephyrinus Pope & Martyr, Simplex
27: St. Joseph Calasanctius Confessor, Duplex
28: St. Augustine Bishop, Confessor, & Doctor, Duplex, Com. of St. Hermes Martyr
29: Beheading of St. John the Baptist, Major Duplex, Com. of St. Sabina Martyr
30: St. Rose of St. Mary Virgin of Lima, Duplex, Com. of Ss. Felix & Adauctus Martyrs
31: St. Raymond Nonnatus Confessor, Duplex

SEPTEMBER

1: St. Giles Abbot, Simplex, Com. of the Holy Twelve Brothers Martyrs
2: St. Stephen King, Confessor, Semiduplex
3: St. Pius X Confessor Pope, Duplex
4: Feria
5: St. Laurence Justinian Confessor Bishop, Semiduplex
6–7: Ferias

8: Nativity of the BVM, Duplex II Class with simple Octave, Com. of St. Adrian Martyr
9: St. Gorgonius Martyr, Simplex
10: St. Nicholas of Tolentino Confessor, Duplex
11: Ss. Protus & Hyacinth Martyrs, Simplex
12: The Most Holy Name of Mary, Major Duplex
13: Feria
14: Exaltation of the Holy Cross, Major Duplex
15: Seven Sorrows of the BVM, Duplex II Class, Com. of St. Nicomedes Martyr
16: St. Cornelius Pope & St. Cyprian Bishop, Martyrs, Semiduplex, Com. of Ss. Euphemia Virgin, Lucy & Geminian Martyrs
17: Impression of the Holy Stigmata on St. Francis of Assisi, Confessor, Duplex
18: St. Joseph of Cupertino Confessor, Duplex
19: St. Januarius Bishop & Companions Martyrs, Duplex
20: St. Eustace & Companions Martyrs, Duplex, Com. of the Vigil
21: St. Matthew Apostle & Evangelist, Duplex II Class
22: St. Thomas of Villanova Confessor Bishop, Duplex, Com. of Ss. Maurice & Companions Martyrs
23: St. Linus Pope & Martyr, Semiduplex, Com. of St. Thecla Virgin Martyr
24: Our Lady of Ransom, Major Duplex
25: Feria
26: Ss. Cyprian & Justina Virgin, Martyrs, Simplex
27: Ss. Cosmas & Damian Martyrs, Semiduplex
28: St. Wenceslaus Duke, Martyr, Semiduplex
29: Dedication of St. Michael Archangel, Duplex I Class
30: St. Jerome Priest, Confessor, & Doctor, Duplex

OCTOBER

1: St. Remigius Confessor Bishop, Simplex
2: The Holy Guardian Angels, Major Duplex
3: St. Thérèse of the Child Jesus Virgin, Duplex
4: St. Francis of Assisi Confessor, Major Duplex
5: St. Placid & companions Martyrs, Simplex
6: St. Bruno Confessor, Duplex
7: The Most Holy Rosary of the BVM, Duplex II Class, Com. of St. Mark Confessor Pope, & Ss. Sergius, Bacchus, Marcellus & Apuleius Martyrs
8: St. Bridget Widow, Duplex
9: St. John Leonardi Confessor, Semiduplex, Com. of Ss. Dionysius Bishop, Rusticus Priest, & Eleutherius Martyrs
10: St. Francis Borgia Confessor, Semiduplex
11: The Maternity of the BVM, Duplex II Class
12: Feria
13: St. Edward King, Confessor, Semiduplex

14: St. Callistus I Pope & Martyr, Duplex
15: St. Teresa Virgin, Duplex
16: St. Hedwig Widow, Semiduplex
17: St. Margaret Mary Alacoque Virgin, Duplex
18: St. Luke Evangelist, Duplex II Class
19: St. Peter of Alcantara Confessor, Duplex
20: St. John Cantius Confessor, Duplex
21: St. Hilarion Abbot, Simplex, Com. of St. Ursula & Companions Virgins & Martyrs
22–23: Ferias
24: St. Raphael Archangel, Major Duplex
25: Ss. Chrysanthus & Daria Martyrs, Simplex
26: St. Evaristus Pope & Martyr, Simplex
27: Vigil.
28: Ss. Simon & Jude Apostles, Duplex II Class
29–30: Ferias
31: Vigil
Last Sunday in October: Our Lord Jesus Christ the King, Duplex I Class, Com. of the Sunday

NOVEMBER

1: All Saints, Duplex I Class with common Octave
2 (or 3 if 2 is a Sunday): Commemoration of All Faithful Departed, Duplex
3: Day 3 within the Octave of All Saints, Semiduplex
4: St. Charles Borromeo Confessor Bishop, Duplex, Com. of the Octave & Ss. Vitalis & Agricola Martyrs
5–7: Days within Octave of All Saints, Semiduplex
8: Octave of All Saints, Major Duplex, Com. of the Holy Four Crowned Martyrs
9: Dedication of the Archbasilica of the Most Holy Saviour, Duplex II Class, Com. of St. Theodore Martyr
10: St. Andrew Avellino Confessor, Duplex, Com. of Ss. Tryphon, Respicius, & Nympha Martyrs
11: St. Martin of Tours Confessor Bishop, Duplex, Com. of St. Mennas Martyr
12: St. Martin I Pope & Martyr, Semiduplex
13: St. Didacus Confessor, Semiduplex
14: St. Josaphat Bishop & Martyr, Duplex
15: St. Albert the Great Bishop, Confessor, & Doctor, Duplex
16: St. Gertrude Virgin, Duplex
17: St. Gregory Thaumaturgus Confessor Bishop, Semiduplex
18: Dedication of the Basilicas of Ss. Peter and Paul, Major Duplex
19: St. Elisabeth Widow, Duplex, Com. of St. Pontianus Pope & Martyr
20: St. Felix of Valois Confessor, Duplex
21: Presentation of the BVM, Major Duplex

22: St. Cecilia Virgin Martyr, Duplex
23: St. Clement I Pope & Martyr, Duplex, Com. of St. Felicitas Martyr
24: St. John of the Cross Confessor & Doctor, Duplex, Com. St. Chrysogonus Martyr
25: St. Catherine Virgin Martyr, Duplex
26: St. Sylvester Abbot, Duplex, Com. of St. Peter of Alexandria Bishop & Martyr
27–28: Ferias
29: Vigil, Commemoration of St. Saturninus
30: St. Andrew Apostle, Duplex II Class

DECEMBER

1: Feria
2: St. Bibiana Virgin Martyr, Semiduplex
3: St. Francis Xavier Confessor, Major Duplex
4: St. Peter Chrysologus Bishop, Confessor, & Doctor, Duplex, Com. of St. Barbara Virgin Martyr
5: Com. of St. Sabbas Abbot
6: St. Nicholas Confessor Bishop, Duplex
7: St. Ambrose Bishop, Confessor, & Doctor, Duplex, Com. of the Vigil
8: The Immaculate Conception of the BVM, Duplex I Class with common Octave
9: Day 2 within Octave of the Immaculate Conception, Semiduplex
10: Day 3 within Octave, Semiduplex, Com. of St. Melchiades Pope & Martyr
11: St. Damasus I Confessor Pope, Semiduplex, Com. of the Octave
12: Day 5 within the Octave, Semiduplex (Com. of Our Lady of Guadalupe)
13: St. Lucy Virgin Martyr, Duplex, Com. of the Octave
14: Day 7 within the Octave, Semiduplex
15: Octave of the Immaculate Conception, Major Duplex
16: St. Eusebius Bishop & Martyr, Semiduplex
17–19: Ferias
20: Vigil
21: St. Thomas Apostle, Duplex II Class
22–23: Ferias
24: Vigil
25: Nativity of Our Lord, Duplex I Class with privileged Octave of the III rank
26: St. Stephen Protomartyr, Duplex II class with simple Octave, Com. of the Nativity Octave
27: St. John Apostle & Evangelist, Duplex II class with simple Octave, Com. of the Nativity Octave
29: St. Thomas Bishop & Martyr, Duplex, Com. of the Nativity Octave
30: Day 6 within Nativity Octave, Semiduplex
31: St. Sylvester I Confessor Pope, Duplex, Com. of the Nativity Octave

The Matins Lectionary

Lessons from the Divine Office of Matins according to the *Breviarium Romanum* of 1954 in English

Compiled and Edited by Samuel McIlheran
United States
MMXXIV

PROPER OF TIME

ADVENT

SUNDAY I OF ADVENT

Duplex I Class

Lesson I - Isa 1:1–3

From the book of Isaias

The vision of Isaias the son of Amos, which he saw concerning Juda and Jerusalem in the days of Ozias, Joathan, Achaz, and Ezechias, kings of Juda Hear, O ye heavens, and give ear, O earth, for the Lord hath spoken. I have brought up children, and exalted them: but they have despised me. The ox knoweth his owner, and the ass his master's crib: but Israel hath not known me, and my people hath not understood.

Lesson II - Isa 1:4–6

Woe to the sinful nation, a people laden with iniquity, a wicked seed, ungracious children: they have forsaken the Lord, they have blasphemed the Holy One of Israel, they are gone away backwards. For what shall I strike you any more, you that increase transgression? the whole head is sick, and the whole heart is sad. From the sole of the foot unto the top of the head, there is no soundness therein: wounds and bruises and swelling sores: they are not bound up, nor dressed, nor fomented with oil.

Lesson III - Isa 1:7–9

Your land is desolate, your cities are burnt with fire: your country strangers devour before your face, and it shall be desolate as when wasted by enemies. And the daughter of Sion shall be left as a covert in a vineyard, and as a lodge in a garden of cucumbers, and as a city that is laid waste. Except the Lord of hosts had left us seed, we had been as Sodom, and we should have been like to Gomorrha.

Lesson IV

Sermon by St. Leo, Pope

Our Saviour Himself instructed His disciples concerning the times and seasons of the coming of the Kingdom of God and the end of the world, and He hath given the same teaching to the Church by the mouth of His Apostles. In connection with this subject then, Our Lord bids us beware lest we let our hearts grow heavy through excess of meat and drink, and worldly thoughts. Dearly beloved brethren, we know how that this warning applies particularly to us. We know that that day is coming, and though for a season we know not the very hour, yet this we know, that it is near.

Lesson V

Let every man then make himself ready against the coming of the Lord, so that He may not find him making his belly his god, or the world his chief care. Dearly beloved brethren, it is a matter of every day experience that fullness of drink dulls the keenness of the mind, and that excess of eating unnerves the strength of the will. The very stomach protests that gluttony does harm to the bodily health, unless temperance get the better of desire, and the thought of the indigestion afterward check the indulgence of the moment.

Lesson VI

The body without the soul has no desires; its sensibility comes from the same source as its movements. And it is the duty of a man with a reasonable soul to deny something to his lower nature and to keep back the outer man from things unseemly. Then will his soul, free from fleshly cravings, sit often at leisure in the palace of the mind, dwelling on the wisdom of God. There, when the roar and rattle of earthly cares are stilled, will she feed on holy thoughts and entertain herself with the expectation of the everlasting joy.

Lesson VII

From the Holy Gospel according to St. Luke (Luke 21:25–33)

In that time, Jesus said to his disciples: And there shall be signs in the sun, and in the moon, and in the stars; and upon the earth distress of nations. And so on.

Homily by Pope St. Gregory

Our Lord and Saviour wishes to find us ready at His second coming. Therefore He tells us what will be the evils of the world as it grows old, that He may wean our hearts from worldly affections. Here we read what great convulsions will go before the end, that, if we will not fear God in our prosperity, we may at least be scourged into fearing His judgment when it is at hand.

Lesson VIII

Immediately before the passage which hath just been read from the Gospel, are found the following words of our Lord, Nation shall rise against nation, and kingdom against kingdom, and great earthquakes shall be in diverse places, and pestilences and famines. Then, after a few more verses, comes today's Gospel. There shall be signs in the sun, and in the moon, and in the stars; and upon the earth distress of nations with perplexity, the sea and the waves roaring. Now some of these things are come to pass already, and we fear the others are not far off.

Lesson IX

In these our days we see nation rise against nation, and their distress over all the earth, more than we read in books has ever come to pass of old time. You know also how often we hear of earthquakes overwhelming countless cities in other parts of the world. As for pestilences, we suffer from them ourselves, with hardly any intermission. As yet we do not see signs in the sun, and in the moon, and in the stars; but the changes of seasons and climates warn us that we may look for these also before long.

Monday in Advent I

Lesson I ~ Isa 1:16–18

From the book of Isaias

Wash yourselves, be clean, take away the evil of your devices from my eyes: cease to do perversely, Learn to do well: seek judgment, relieve the oppressed, judge for the fatherless, defend the widow. And then come, and accuse me, saith the Lord: if your sins be as scarlet, they shall be made as white as snow: and if they be red as crimson, they shall be white as wool.

Lesson II ~ Isa 1:19–23

If you be willing, and will hearken to me, you shall eat the good things of the land. But if you will not, and will provoke me to wrath: the sword shall devour you because the mouth of the Lord hath spoken it. How is the faithful city, that was full of judgment, become a harlot? justice dwelt in it, but now murderers. Thy silver is turned into dross: thy wine is mingled with water. Thy princes are faithless, companions of thieves: they all love bribes, they run after rewards. They judge not for the fatherless: and the widow's comes not in to them.

Lesson III ~ Isa 1:24–28

Therefore saith the Lord the God of hosts, the mighty one of Israel: Ah! I will comfort myself over my adversaries: and I will be revenged of my enemies. And I will turn my hand to thee, and I will clean purge away thy dross, and I will take away all thy tin. And I will restore thy judges as they were before, and thy counsellors as of old. After this thou shalt be called the city of the just, a faithful city. Sion shall be redeemed in judgment, and they shall bring her back in justice. And he shall destroy the wicked, and the sinners together: and they that have forsaken the Lord, shall be consumed.

Tuesday in Advent I

Lesson I ~ Isa 2:1–3

From the book of Isaias

The word that Isaias the son of Amos saw, concerning Juda and Jerusalem. And in the last days the mountain of the house of the Lord shall be prepared on the top of mountains, and it shall be exalted above the hills, and all nations shall flow unto it. And many people shall go, and say: Come and let us go up to the mountain of the Lord, and to the house of the God of Jacob, and he will teach us his ways, and we will walk in his paths: for the law shall come forth from Sion, and the word of the Lord from Jerusalem.

Lesson II ~ Isa 2:4–6

And he shall judge the Gentiles, and rebuke many people: and they shall turn their swords into ploughshares, and their spears into sickles: nation shall not lift up sword against nation, neither shall they be exercised any more to war. O house of Jacob, come ye, and let us walk in the light of the Lord. For thou hast cast off thy people, the house of Jacob: because they are filled as in times past, and have had soothsayers as the Philistines, and have adhered to strange children.

Lesson III ~ Isa 2:7–9

Their land is filled with silver and gold: and there is no end of their treasures. And their land is filled with horses: and their chariots are innumerable. Their land also is full of idols: they have adored the work of their own hands, which their own fingers have made. And man hath bowed himself down, and man hath been debased: therefore forgive them not.

Wednesday in Advent I

Lesson I ~ Isa 3:1–4

From the book of Isaias

For behold, the sovereign the Lord of hosts shall take away from Jerusalem, and from Juda the valiant and the strong, the whole strength of bread, and the whole strength of water. The strong man, and the man of war, the judge, and the prophet, and the cunning man, and the ancient. The captain over fifty, and the honourable in countenance, and the counsellor, and the architect, and the skilful in eloquent speech. And I will give children to be their princes, and the effeminate shall rule over them.

Lesson II ~ Isa 3:5–7

And the people shall rush one upon another, and every man against his neighbour: the child shall make it tumult against the ancient, and the base against the honourable. For a man shall take hold of his brother, one of the house of his father, saying: Thou hast a garment, be thou our ruler, and let this ruin be under thy hand. In that day he shall answer, saying: I am no healer, and in my house there is no bread, nor clothing: make me not ruler of the people.

Lesson III ~ Isa 3:8–11

For Jerusalem is ruined, and Juda is fallen: because their tongue, and their devices are against the Lord, to provoke the eyes of his majesty. The shew of their countenance hath answered them: and they have proclaimed abroad their sin as Sodom, and they have not hid it: woe to their souls, for evils are rendered to them. Say to the just man that it is well, for he shall eat the fruit of his doings. Woe to the wicked unto evil: for the reward of his hands shall be given him.

Thursday in Advent I

Lesson I - Isa 4:1–3

From the book of Isaias

And in that day seven women shall take hold of one man, saying: We will eat our own bread, and wear our own apparel: only let us be called by thy name, take away our reproach. In that day the bud of the Lord shall be in magnificence and glory, and the fruit of the earth shall be high, and a great joy to them that shall have escaped of Israel. And it shall come to pass, that every one that shall be left in Sion, and that shall remain in Jerusalem, shall be called holy, every one that is written in life in Jerusalem.

Lesson II - Isa 5:1–4

I will sing to my beloved the canticle of my cousin concerning his vineyard. My beloved had a vineyard on a hill in a fruitful place. And he fenced it in, and picked the stones out of it, and planted it with the choicest vines, and built a tower in the midst thereof, and set up a winepress therein: and he looked that it should bring forth grapes, and it brought forth wild grapes. And now, O ye inhabitants of Jerusalem, and ye men of Juda, judge between me and my vineyard. What is there that I ought to do more to my vineyard, that I have not done to it? was it that I looked that it should bring forth grapes, and it hath brought forth wild grapes?

Lesson III - Isa 5:5–7

And now I will shew you what I will do to my vineyard. I will take away the hedge thereof, and it shall be wasted: I will break down the wall thereof, and it shall be trodden down. And I will make it desolate: it shall not be pruned, and it shall not be digged: but briers and thorns shall come up: and I will command the clouds to rain no rain upon it. For the vineyard of the Lord of hosts is the house of Israel: and the man of Juda, his pleasant plant: and I looked that he should do judgment, and behold iniquity: and do justice, and behold a cry.

Friday in Advent I

Lesson I - Isa 6:1–3

From the book of Isaias

In the year that king Ozias died, I saw the Lord sitting upon a throne high and elevated: and his train filled the temple. Upon it stood the seraphims: the one had six wings, and the other had six wings: with two they covered his face, and with two they covered his feet, and with two they flew. And they cried one to another, and said: Holy, holy, holy, the Lord God of hosts, all the earth is full of his glory.

Lesson II - Isa 6:4–7

And the lintels of the doors were moved at the voice of him that cried, and the house was filled with smoke. And I said: Woe is me, because I have held my peace; because I am a man of unclean lips, and I dwell in the midst of a people that hath unclean lips, and I have seen with my eyes the King the Lord of hosts. And one of the seraphims flew to me, and in his hand was a live coal, which he had taken with the tongs off the altar. And he touched my mouth, and said: Behold this hath touched thy lips, and thy iniquities shall be taken away, and thy sin shall be cleansed.

Lesson III ~ Isa 6:8–10

And I heard the voice of the Lord, saying: Whom shall I send? and who shall go for us? And I said: Lo, here am I, send me. And he said: Go, and thou shalt say to this people: Hearing, hear, and understand not: and see the vision, and know it not. Blind the heart of this people, and make their ears heavy, and shut their eyes: lest they see with their eyes, and hear with their ears, and understand with their heart, and be converted and I heal them.

Saturday in Advent I

Lesson I ~ Isa 7:1–3

From the book of Isaias

And it came to pass in the days of Achaz the son of Joathan, the son of Ozias, king of Juda, that Basin king of Syria, and Phacee the son of Romelia king of Israel, came up to Jerusalem, to fight against it: but they could not prevail over it. And they told the house of David, saying: Syria hath rested upon Ephraim, and his heart was moved, and the heart of his people, as the trees of the woods are moved with the wind. And the Lord said to Isaias: Go forth to meet Achaz, thou and Jasub thy son that is left, to the conduit in the upper pool, in the way of the fuller's field.

Lesson II ~ Isa 7:4–6

And thou shalt say to him: See thou be quiet: fear not, and let not thy heart be afraid of the two tails of these fire brands, smoking with the wrath of the fury of Rasin king of Syria, and of the son of Romelia. Because Syria hath taken counsel against thee, unto the evil of Ephraim and the son of Romelia, saying: Let us go up to Juda, and rouse it up, and draw it away to us, and make the son of Tabeel king in the midst thereof.

Lesson III ~ Isa 7:10–15

And the Lord spoke again to Achaz, saying: Ask thee a sign of the Lord thy God either unto the depth of hell, or unto the height above. And Achaz said: I will not ask, and I will not tempt the Lord. And he said: Hear ye therefore, O house of David: Is it a small thing for you to be grievous to men, that you are grievous to my God also? Therefore the Lord himself shall give you a sign. Behold a virgin shall conceive, and bear a son, and his name shall be called Emmanuel. He shall eat butter and honey, that he may know to refuse the evil, and to choose the good.

SUNDAY II OF ADVENT

Duplex II Class

Lesson I ~ Isa 11:1–4

From the book of Isaias

And there shall come forth a rod out of the root of Jesse, and a flower shall rise up out of his root.

And the spirit of the Lord shall rest upon him: the spirit of wisdom, and of understanding, the spirit of counsel, and of fortitude, the spirit of knowledge, and of godliness. And he shall be filled with the spirit of the fear of the Lord. He shall not judge according to the sight of the eyes, nor reprove according to the hearing of the ears. But he shall judge the poor with justice, and shall reprove with equity for the meek of the earth.

Lesson II - Isa 11:4–7

And he shall strike the earth with the rod of his mouth, and with the breath of his lips he shall slay the wicked. And justice shall be the girdle of his loins: and faith the girdle of his reins. The wolf shall dwell with the lamb: and the leopard shall lie down with the kid: the calf and the lion, and the sheep shall abide together, and a little child shall lead them. The calf and the bear shall feed: their young ones shall rest together: and the lion shall eat straw like the ox.

Lesson III - Isa 11:8–10

And the sucking child shall play on the hole of the asp: and the weaned child shall thrust his hand into the den of the basilisk. They shall not hurt, nor shall they kill in all my holy mountain, for the earth is filled with the knowledge of the Lord, as the covering waters of the sea. In that day the root of Jesse, who standeth for an ensign of the people, him the Gentiles shall beseech, and his sepulchre shall be glorious.

Lesson IV

From the Commentary on the Prophecies of Isaias made by St. Jerome, Priest

And there shall come forth a rod out of the stem of Jesse. From the beginning of the Book of this Prophet till the thirteenth chapter, where commences the vision, or burden of Babylon, the whole of the vision of Isaias, the son of Amoz, is one continual prophecy of Christ. We must explain it part by part, for if we were to take it all at once, the memory of the reader would be confused. According to the Jewish commentators, the rod and the flower would both relate to the Lord Himself. They take the rod to mean the scepter of His Royal dominion, and the flower the loveliness of His beauty.

Lesson V

We, however, understand that the rod out of the root of Jesse signifies the holy Virgin Mary. She was a clean stem that had as yet put forth no shoot; as we have read above: "Behold, the Virgin shall conceive and bear a son." And the flower we believe to mean the Lord our Redeemer, Who has elsewhere compared Himself to a flower: "I am a flower of the plain, and a lily of the valleys."

Lesson VI

The Spirit of the Lord then shall rest upon this flower; this flower which shall come forth from the stem and roots of Jesse by means of the Virgin Mary. And truly the

Spirit of the Lord did rest upon our Redeemer. It is written that In Him dwells all the fulness of the Divinity bodily. The Spirit was not shed on Him by measure, as it is upon the Saints. To Him we may apply the words of the Hebrew Gospel used by the Nazarenes: The whole fountain of the Holy Ghost shall be poured forth upon Him; The Lord is a spirit, and where the Spirit of the Lord is, there is liberty.

Lesson VII

From the Holy Gospel according to St. Matthew (Matt 11:2–10)

In that time, when John had heard in prison the works of Christ: sending two of his disciples he said to him: Art thou he that art to come, or look we for another? And so on.

Homily by Pope St. Gregory

The sight of so many signs and so many mighty works should have been a source of wonder, and not a stumbling-block. And yet the unfaithful found these very works a rock of offense, when they afterwards saw Him Who had worked so many miracles dying on the Cross. Hence Paul says: "We preach Christ crucified, unto the Jews a stumbling-block and unto the Gentiles foolishness." It is indeed folly in the eyes of men to say that the Author of life died for men and thus men put as a stumbling-block, to hinder them from coming to Jesus, the very thing that does oblige them the most unto Him. For the more humbling God has undergone for man's sake, the more worthy is He that man should worship Him.

Lesson VIII

"And blessed is he, whosoever shall not be offended in Me." Now what is this, but a plain mention of that time, when He afterwards humbled Himself, becoming obedient unto death, even the death of the Cross? It is as if He said: I indeed do wonderful works, but the day will come when I shall not refuse to suffer shame and evil treatment. Take heed then, you who now worship Me for the works' sake, that when I come to die, you despise Me not for My death's sake.

Lesson IX

And, as the disciples of John departed, what did Jesus say unto the multitudes concerning this same John? Let us hear. "What went you out into the wilderness to see? A reed shaken with the wind?" Here our Lord teaches not by assertion, but by negation. Now a reed is a thing so made that as soon as the wind blows upon it, it bends it over toward the opposite quarter. And the fleshly-minded man is like a human reed. As he is praised or blamed so he bends himself in the one direction or the other.

Monday in Advent II

Lesson I ~ Isa 13:1–4

From the book of Isaias

The burden of Babylon, which Isaias the son of Amos saw. Upon the dark mountain lift ye up a banner, exalt the voice, lift up the hand, and let the rulers go into the gates. I have commanded my sanctified ones, and have called my strong ones in my wrath, them that rejoice in my glory. The noise of a multitude in the mountains, as it were of many people, the noise of the sound of kings, of nations gathered together.

Lesson II - Isa 13:4–8

The Lord of hosts hath given charge to the troops of war. To them that come from a country afar off, from the end of heaven: the Lord and the instruments of his wrath, to destroy the whole land. Howl ye, for the day of the Lord is near: it shall come as a destruction from the Lord. Therefore shall all hands be faint, and every heart of man shall melt, And shall be broken. Gripings and pains shall take hold of them, they shall be in pain as a woman in labour. Every one shall be amazed at his neighbour, their countenances shall be as faces burnt.

Lesson III - Isa 13:9–11

Behold, the day of the Lord shall come, a cruel day, and full of indignation, and of wrath, and fury, to lay the land desolate, and to destroy the sinners thereof out of it. For the stars of heaven, and their brightness shall not display their light: the sun shall be darkened in his rising, and the moon shall not shine with her light. And I will visit the evils of the world, and against the wicked for their iniquity: and I will make the pride of infidels to cease, and will bring down the arrogancy of the mighty.

Tuesday in Advent II

Lesson I - Isa 14:1–2

From the book of Isaias

Her time is near at hand, and her days shall not be prolonged. For the Lord will have mercy on Jacob, and will yet choose out of Israel, and will make them rest upon their own ground: and the stranger shall be joined with them, and shall adhere to the house of Jacob. And the people shall take them, and bring them into their place: and the house of Israel shall possess them in the land of the Lord for servants and handmaids: and they shall make them captives that had taken them, and shall subdue their oppressors.

Lesson II - Isa 14:3–6

And it shall come to pass in that day, that when God shall give thee rest from thy labour, and from thy vexation, and from the hard bondage, wherewith thou didst serve before, Thou shalt take up this parable against the king of Babylon, and shalt say: How is the oppressor come to nothing, the tribute hath ceased? The Lord hath broken the staff of the wicked, the rod of the rulers, That struck the people in wrath with an incurable wound, that brought nations under in fury, that persecuted in a cruel manner.

Lesson III - Isa 14:12–15

How art thou fallen from heaven, O Lucifer, who didst rise in the morning? how art thou fallen to the earth, that didst wound the nations? And thou saidst in thy heart: I will ascend into heaven, I will exalt my throne above the stars of God, I will sit in the mountain of the covenant, in the sides of the north. I will ascend above the height of the clouds, I will be like the most High. But yet thou shalt be brought down to hell, into the depth of the pit.

Wednesday in Advent II

Lesson I ~ Isa 16:1–4

From the book of Isaias

Send forth, O Lord, the lamb, the ruler of the earth, from Petra of the desert, to the mount of the daughter of Sion. And it shall come to pass, that as a bird fleeing away, and as young ones flying out of the nest, so shall the daughters of Moab be in the passage of Arnon. Take counsel, gather a council: make thy shadow as the night in the midday: hide them that flee, and betray not them that wander about. My fugitives shall dwell with thee: O Moab, be thou a covert to them from the face of the destroyer.

Lesson II ~ Isa 16:4–6

For the dust is at an end, the wretch is consumed: he hath failed, that trod the earth under foot. And a throne shall be prepared in mercy, and one shall sit upon it in truth in the tabernacle of David, judging and seeking judgment and quickly rendering that which is just. We have heard of the pride of Moab, he is exceeding proud: his pride and his arrogancy, and his indignation is more than his strength.

Lesson III ~ Isa 16:7–8

Therefore shall Moab howl to Moab, every one shall howl: to them that rejoice upon the brick walls, tell ye their stripes. For the suburbs of Hesebon are desolate, and the lords of the nations have destroyed the vineyard of Sabama: the branches thereof have reached even to Jazer: they have wandered in the wilderness, the branches thereof are left, they are gone over the sea.

Thursday in Advent II

Lesson I ~ Isa 19:1–2

From the book of Isaias

The burden of Egypt. Behold the Lord will ascend upon a swift cloud, and will enter into Egypt, and the idols of Egypt shall be moved at his presence, and the heart of Egypt shall melt in the midst thereof. And I will set the Egyptians to fight against the Egyptians: and they shall fight brother against brother, and friend against friend, city against city, kingdom against kingdom.

Lesson II ~ Isa 19:3–6

And the spirit of Egypt shall be broken in the bowels thereof, and I will cast down their counsel: and they shall consult their idols, and their diviners, and their wizards, and soothsayers. And I will deliver Egypt into the hand of cruel masters, and a strong king shall rule over them, saith the Lord the God of hosts. And the water of the sea shall be dried up, and the river shall be wasted and dry. And the rivers shall fail: the streams of the banks shall be diminished, and be dried up. The reed and the bulrush shall wither away.

Lesson III ~ Isa 19:11–13

The princes of Tanis are become fools, the wise counsellors of Pharao have given foolish counsel: how will you say to Pharao: I am the son of the wise, the son of ancient kings? Where are now thy wise men? let them tell thee, and shew what the Lord of hosts hath purposed upon Egypt. The princes of Tanis are become fools, the princes of Memphis are gone astray, they have deceived Egypt, the stay of the people thereof.

Friday in Advent II

Lesson I ~ Isa 24:1–3

From the book of Isaias

Behold the Lord shall lay waste the earth, and shall strip it, and shall afflict the face thereof, and scatter abroad the inhabitants thereof. And it shall be as with the people, so with the priest: and as with the servant, so with his master: as with the handmaid, so with her mistress: as with the buyer, so with the seller: as with the lender, so with the borrower: as with him that calleth for his money, so with him that oweth. With desolation shall the earth be laid waste, and it shall be utterly spoiled: for the Lord hath spoken this word.

Lesson II ~ Isa 24:4–6

The earth mourned, and faded away, and is weakened: the world faded away, the height of the people of the earth is weakened. And the earth is infected by the inhabitants thereof: because they have transgressed the laws, they have changed the ordinance, they have broken the everlasting covenant. Therefore shall a curse devour the earth, and the inhabitants thereof shall sin: and therefore they that dwell therein shall be mad, and few men shall be left.

Lesson III ~ Isa 24:7–16

The vintage hath mourned, the vine hath languished away, all the merryhearted have sighed. The mirth of timbrels hath ceased, the noise of them that rejoice is ended, the melody of the harp is silent. They shall not drink wine with a song: the drink shall be bitter to them that drink it. The city of vanity is broken down, every house is shut up, no man comes in. There shall be a crying for wine in the streets: all mirth is forsaken: the joy of the earth is gone away. Desolation is left in the city, and calamity shall oppress the gates. For it shall be thus in the midst of the earth, in the midst of the people, as if a few olives, that remain, should be shaken out of the olive tree: or grapes, when the vintage is ended. These shall lift up their voice, and shall give praise: when the Lord shall be glorified, they shall make a joyful noise from the sea. Therefore glorify ye the Lord in instruction: the name of the Lord God of Israel in the islands of the sea. From the ends of the earth we have heard praises, the glory of the Just one.

Saturday in Advent II

Lesson I ~ Isa 25:1–4

From the book of Isaias

O Lord, thou art my God, I will exalt thee, and give glory to thy name: for thou hast done wonderful things, thy designs of old faithful, amen. For thou hast reduced the city to a heap, the strong city to ruin, the house of strangers, to be no city, and to be no more built up for ever. Therefore shall a strong people praise thee, the city of mighty nations shall fear thee. Because thou hast been a strength to the poor, a strength to the needy in his distress: a refuge from the whirlwind, a shadow from the heat.

Lesson II ~ Isa 25:4–7

For the blast of the mighty is like a whirlwind beating against a wall. Thou shalt bring down the tumult of strangers, as heat in thirst: and as with heat under a burning cloud, thou shalt make the branch of the mighty to wither away. And the Lord of hosts shall make unto all people in this mountain, a feast of fat things, a feast of wine, of fat things full of marrow, of wine purified from the lees. And he shall destroy in this mountain the face of the bond with which all people were tied, and the web that he began over all nations.

Lesson III ~ Isa 25:8–12

He shall cast death down headlong forever: and the Lord God shall wipe away tears from every face, and the reproach of his people he shall take away from off the whole earth: for the Lord hath spoken it. And they shall say in that day: Lo, this is our God, we have waited for him, and he will save us: this is the Lord, we have patiently waited for him, we shall rejoice and be joyful in his salvation. For the hand of the Lord shall rest in this mountain: and Moab shall be trodden down under him, as straw is broken in pieces with the wain. And he shall stretch forth his hands under him, as he that swimmeth stretcheth forth his hands to swim: and he shall bring down his glory with the dashing of his hands. And the bulwarks of thy high walls shall fall, and be brought low, and shall be pulled down to the ground, even to the dust.

SUNDAY III OF ADVENT

Duplex II Class

Lesson I ~ Isa 26:1–6

From the book of Isaias

In that day shall this canticle be sung in the land of Juda. Sion the city of our strength a saviour, a wall and a bulwark shall be set therein. Open ye the gates, and let the just nation, that keepeth the truth, enter in. The old error is passed away: thou wilt keep peace: peace, because we have hoped in thee. You have hoped in the Lord for evermore, in the Lord God mighty for ever. For he shall bring down them that dwell on high, the high city he shall lay low. He shall bring it down even to the ground, he shall pull it down even to the dust. The foot shall tread it down, the feet of the poor, the steps of the needy.

Lesson II ~ Isa 26:7–10

The way of the just is right, the path of the just is right to walk in. And in the way of thy judgments, O Lord, we have patiently waited for thee: thy name, and thy remembrance are the desire of the soul. My soul hath desired thee in the night: yea, and with my spirit within me in the morning early I will watch to thee. When thou shalt do thy judgments on the earth, the inhabitants of the world shall learn justice. Let us have pity on the wicked, but he will not learn justice: in the land of the saints he hath done wicked things, and he shall not see the glory of the Lord.

Lesson III ~ Isa 26:11–14

Lord, let thy hand be exalted, and let them not see: let the envious people see, and be confounded: and let fire devour thy enemies. Lord, thou wilt give us peace: for thou hast wrought all our works for us. O Lord our God, other lords besides thee have had dominion over us, only in thee let us remember thy name. Let not the dead live, let not the giants rise again: therefore hast thou visited and destroyed them, and hast destroyed all their memory.

Lesson IV

Sermon by St. Leo, Pope

Dearly beloved brethren, with the care which becomes us as the shepherd of your souls, we urge upon you the rigid observance of this December Fast. The month of December hath come round again, and with it this devout custom of the Church. The fruits of the year, which is drawing to a close, are now all gathered in, and we most meetly offer our abstinence to God as a sacrifice of thanksgiving. And what can be more useful than fasting, that exercise by which we draw nigh to God, make a stand against the devil, and overcome the softer enticements of sin?

Lesson V

Fasting has ever been the bread of strength. From abstinence proceed pure thoughts, reasonable desires, and healthy counsels. By voluntary mortifications the flesh dies to lust, and the soul is renewed in might. But since fasting is not the only mean whereby we get health for our souls, let us add to our fasting works of mercy. Let us spend in good deeds what we take from indulgence. Let our fast become the banquet of the poor.

Lesson VI

Let us defend the widow and serve the orphan; let us comfort the afflicted and reconcile the estranged; let us take in the wanderer and succor the oppressed; let us clothe the naked and cherish the sick. And may every one of us that shall offer to the God of all goodness this Advent sacrifice of fasting and alms be by Him fitted to receive an eternal reward in His heavenly kingdom! We fast on Wednesday and Friday; and there is likewise a Vigil on Saturday at the Church of St. Peter, that by his good prayers we may the more effectually obtain what we ask for, through our Lord Jesus Christ, Who with the

Father and the Holy Ghost, lives and reigns, God, world without end. Amen.

Lesson VII

From the Holy Gospel according to St. John (John 1:19–28)

In that time were sent from Jerusalem priests and Levites to John, to ask him: Who art thou? And so on.

Homily by Pope St. Gregory

Dearly beloved brethren, the first thing which strikes us in today's Gospel is the lowly-mindedness of John. He was so great that it was thought he might be the Christ; yet he soberly chose rather to seem only what he really was, than to let the belief of men invest him with a dignity which did not belong to him; "for he confessed, and denied not, but confessed, I am not the Christ," at the same time he would not deny what he was in reality; and thus his very truth-speaking made him a member of Him Whose title he would not by falsehood take. In that he arrogated not to himself the name of Christ, he became a member of Christ. While he humbly strove to confess his own weakness, he earned by his simplicity a part in the grandeur of his Master.

Lesson VIII

In considering this subject we find an apparent contradiction between one of John's statements, and the saying of our Redeemer recorded in another part of the Gospel. When His disciples asked our Lord regarding the coming of Elias, He answered: "Elias is come already, and they knew him not, but have done unto him whatsoever they liked." And if you will receive it, this that is, John is Elias. But when John was asked if he was Elias, he answered: "I am not." How comes it then, dearly beloved brethren, that we find the Truth Itself asserting what the prophet of the Truth denied? It must evidently be that our Lord meant one thing and John another, when the Lord said, This is, and John, I am not. For how can he be the prophet of truth, if he speak not according to the word of Him Who is the Eternal Truth?

Lesson IX

Let us then more minutely examine these words, and we shall find that there is no real contradiction. When the Angel announced to Zachary the coming birth of John he said He shall go before Him in the spirit and power of Elias. As the old Elias will come again before the Second Advent of the Lord, so did John, as the new Elias, go before the First Advent, in the spirit and power of Elias. As the old Elias will be the Fore-runner of the Judge, so the new Elias was the Forerunner of the Saviour. John then was Elias in spirit, but not in person; and our Lord asserts of the spirit what John denies of the person.

Monday in Advent III

Lesson I ~ Isa 28:1–3

From the book of Isaias

Woe to the crown of pride, to the drunkards of Ephraim, and to the fading flower the glory of his joy, who were on the head of the fat valley, staggering with wine. Behold the Lord is mighty and strong, as a storm of hail: a destroying whirlwind, as the violence of many waters overflowing, and sent forth upon a spacious land. The crown of pride of the drunkards of Ephraim shall be trodden under feet.

Lesson II ~ Isa 28:4–7

And the fading flower the glory of his joy, who is on the head of the fat valley, shall be as a hasty fruit before the ripeness of autumn: which when he that seeth it shall behold, as soon as he taketh it in his hand, he will eat it up. In that day the Lord of hosts shall be a crown of glory, and a garland of joy to the residue of his people: And a spirit of judgment to him that sitteth in judgment, and strength to them that return out of the battle to the gate. But these also have been ignorant through wine, and through drunkenness have erred: the priest and the prophet have been ignorant through drunkenness, they are swallowed up with wine, they have gone astray in drunkenness, they have not known him that seeth, they have been ignorant of judgment.

Lesson III ~ Isa 28:16–18

Therefore thus saith the Lord God: Behold I will lay a stone in the foundations of Sion, a tried stone, a corner stone, a precious stone, founded in the foundation. He that believeth, let him not hasten. And I will set judgment in weight, and justice in measure: and hail shall overturn the hope of falsehood: and waters shall overflow its protection. And your league with death shall be abolished, and your covenant with hell shall not stand: when the overflowing scourge shall pass, you shall be trodden down by it.

Tuesday in Advent III

Lesson I ~ Isa 30:18–20

From the book of Isaias

The Lord waiteth that be may have mercy on you: and therefore shall he be exalted sparing you: because the Lord is the God of judgment: blessed are all they that wait for him. For the people of Sion shall dwell in Jerusalem: weeping thou shalt not weep, he will surely have pity on thee: at the voice of thy cry, as soon as he shall hear, he will answer thee. And the Lord will give you spare bread, and short water: and will not cause thy teacher to flee away from thee any more, and thy eyes shall see thy teacher.

Lesson II ~ Isa 30:22–25

And thou shalt defile the plates of thy graven things of silver, and the garment of thy molten things of gold, and shalt cast them away as the uncleanness of a menstruous woman. Thou shalt say to it: Get thee hence. And rain shall be given to thy seed, wheresoever thou shalt sow in the land: and the bread of the corn of the land shall be most plentiful, and fat. The lamb in that day shall feed at large in thy possession: And thy oxen, and the ass colts that till the ground, shall eat mingled provender as it was winnowed in the floor. And there shall be upon every high mountain, and upon every elevated hill rivers of running waters in the day of the slaughter of many, when the tower shall fall.

Lesson III ~ Isa 30:26–28

And the light of the moon shall be as the light of the sun, and the light of the sun shall be sevenfold, as the light of seven days: in the day when the Lord shall bind up the wound of his people, and shall heal the stroke of their wound. Behold the name of the Lord comes from afar, his wrath burneth, and is heavy to bear: his lips are filled with indignation, and his tongue as a devouring fire. His breath as a torrent overflowing even to the midst of the neck, to destroy the nations unto nothing, and the bridle of error that was in the jaws of the people.

Ember Wednesday in Advent

Lesson I

From the Holy Gospel according to St. Luke (Luke 1:26–38)

At that time the angel Gabriel was sent from God into a city of Galilee, called Nazareth, To a virgin espoused to a man whose name was Joseph, of the house of David; and the virgin's name was Mary. And so on.

Homily by St. Ambrose, Bishop

The mysteries of God are unsearchable, and it is especially declared by a Prophet, that a man can hardly know His counsels. Nevertheless, some things have been revealed to us, and we may gather from some of the words and works of the Lord our Saviour, that there was a special purpose of God, in the fact that she who was chosen to be the mother of the Lord was espoused to a man. Why did not the power of the Highest overshadow her before she was so espoused? Perhaps it was lest any might blasphemously say that she had conceived in fornication the Holy One.

Lesson II

And the angel came in unto her. Let us learn from this Virgin how to bear ourselves, let us learn her modesty, let us learn by her devout utterance, above all let us learn by the holy mystery enacted. It is the part of a maiden to be timid, to avoid the advances of men, and to shrink from men's addresses. Would that our women would learn from the example of modesty here set before us. She upon whom the stare of men had never been fixed was alone in her chamber, and was found only by an angel. There was neither companion nor witness there, that what passed might not be debased in gossip and the angel saluted her.

Lesson III

The message of God to the Virgin was a mystery, which it was not lawful for the mouth of men, but only of angels, to utter. For the first time on earth the words are spoken "The Holy Ghost shall come upon thee." The holy maiden hears, and believes. At length she says "Behold the handmaid of the Lord be it unto me according to thy word." Here is an example of lowliness, here is a pattern of true devotion. At the very moment that she is told she is chosen to be the mother of the Lord she at once declares herself His handmaid. The knowledge that she was Mother of God caused in the heart of Mary only an act of humility.

Thursday in Advent III

Lesson I ~ Isa 33:1–2

From the book of Isaias

Woe to thee that spoilest, shalt not thou thyself also be spoiled? and thou that despisest, shalt not thyself also be despised? when thou shalt have made an end of spoiling, thou shalt be spoiled: when being wearied thou shalt cease to despise, thou shalt be despised. O Lord, have mercy on us: for we have waited for thee: be thou our arm in the morning, and our salvation in the time of trouble.

Lesson II ~ Isa 33:3–6

At the voice of the angel the people fled, and at the lifting up thyself the nations are scattered. And your spoils shall be gathered together as the locusts are gathered, as when the ditches are full of them. The Lord is magnified, for he hath dwelt on high: he hath filled Sion with judgment and justice. And there shall be faith in thy times: riches of salvation, wisdom and knowledge: the fear of the Lord is his treasure.

Lesson III ~ Isa 33:14–17

The sinners in Sion are afraid, trembling hath seized upon the hypocrites. Which of you can dwell with devouring fire? which of you shall dwell with everlasting burnings? He that walketh in justices, and speaketh truth, that casteth away avarice by oppression, and shaketh his hands from all bribes, that stoppeth his ears lest he hear blood, and shutteth his eyes that he may see no evil. He shall dwell on high, the fortifications of rocks shall be his highness: bread is given him, his waters are sure. His eyes shall see the king in his beauty, they shall see the land far off.

Ember Friday in Advent

Lesson I

From the Holy Gospel according to St. Luke (Luke 1:39–47)

In that time, Mary, rising up, went into the hill country with haste into a city of Juda. And she entered into the house of Zachary, and saluted Elizabeth. And so on.

Homily by St. Ambrose, Bishop

When any one asks another for credence, he is bound to give some reasonable ground. And so the Angel, when he announced to Mary the counsel of God, gave, as a proof, the conception of Elizabeth, then aged and barren, that Mary might perceive, by this example, that with God nothing is impossible. When the holy Virgin had heard it, she arose and went to visit her cousin. She did not go to see if what she had heard was true, because she did not believe God, or because she knew not who the messenger had been, or yet because she doubted the fact adduced in proof. She went joyfully as one who has received a mercy in answer to his vow goes to pay the same. She went with devotion, as a godly person goes to execute a religious duty. She went into the hill country in joyful haste. And is it not something that she went up into the hills? God was already in her womb, and her feeling bore her continually upward. The grace of the Holy Spirit knows no slow working.

Lesson II

Godly women will learn from the example of the Mother of God to take a tender care of their kinswomen who are with child. In pursuance of this charity, Mary, who had hitherto remained alone at home, was not deterred by her maidenly shyness from entering on a public journey; she faced for this end the hardships of mountain travel; and encountered with a sense of duty the weary length of the way. The Virgin left her home, and went into the hill country with haste, unmindful of the trouble, and remembering only the office to which her cousinly love prompted her, in spite of the delicacy of her sex. Maidens will learn from her not to idle about from house to house, to loiter in the streets, nor to take part in conversations in public. Mary, as she was hasteful to pass through the public roads, so was she slow again to enter on them; she abode with her cousin about three months.

Lesson III

As the modesty of Mary is a pattern for the imitation of all maidens, so also is her humility. She went to see Elizabeth, like one cousin going to visit another, and as the younger to the elder. Not only did she first go, but she first saluted Elizabeth. Now, the purer a virgin is, the humbler ought she to be. She will know how to submit herself to her elders. She that professes chastity ought to be a very mistress of humility. Lowly-mindedness is at once the very ground in which devotion grows, and the first and principal rule of its teaching. In this act of the Virgin then we see the greater going to visit and to succor the lesser: Mary to Elizabeth, Christ to John.

Ember Saturday in Advent

Lesson I

From the Holy Gospel according to St. Luke (Luke 3:1–6)

In the fifteenth year of the reign of Tiberius Caesar, Pontius Pilate being governor of Judea. And so on.

Homily by Pope St. Gregory

The date, at which the Forerunner of our Redeemer entered on his public office of preaching, is indicated to us by the name of the ruler of the Roman Commonwealth, and by those of the princes of Palestine. The time of his preaching is indicated by these names, because he came as the Forerunner of Him Who was to be the Redeemer of some Jews and many Gentiles. Moreover, in the enumeration of these worldly monarchs there is a foreshadowing of the fact that the Gentiles were about to be gathered into one, and the Jews to be scattered abroad in punishment of their unbelief; in the whole heathen Commonwealth we find the title of one Emperor, but in the small kingdom of Judaea are mentioned four masters.

Lesson II

The blessed voice of the Saviour itself has said, "Every kingdom divided against itself is brought to desolation." And we may well look for the ruin of the Jewish state when we see it divided among so many rulers. We observe likewise that the names of the reigning priests as well as kings are given. The Evangelist Luke has left on record the chiefs both of the monarchy and of the priesthood who held office when John the Baptist began to preach, because John preached Him Who is at once our Priest and our King.

Lesson III

And he came into all the country about Jordan, preaching the baptism of repentance for the remission of sins. It is evident from these words that John the Baptist not only preached, but also administered the baptism of repentance, and yet that baptism of repentance which he gave, was not really a baptism for the remission of sins. For there is only one baptism for the remission of sins, and that is our Christian baptism. It is worthy of note here that the words used are, preaching the baptism of repentance for the remission of sins, for he himself owned that his baptism was not the true baptism that washes away sin. Even as the Eternal Word of God made Flesh was greater than the preacher that went before Him, so was His holy baptism, by which our sins are washed away, far greater than that baptism of repentance which the Forerunner preached, and which could never wash away sin.

SUNDAY IV OF ADVENT

Duplex II Class

Lesson I - Isa 35:1–7

From the book of Isaias

The land that was desolate and impassable shall be glad, and the wilderness shall rejoice, and shall flourish like the lily. It shall bud forth and blossom, and shall rejoice with joy and praise: the glory of Libanus is given to it: the beauty of Carmel, and Saron, they shall see the glory of the Lord, and the beauty of our God. Strengthen ye the feeble hands, and confirm the weak knees. Say to the fainthearted: Take courage, and fear not: behold your God will bring the revenge of recompense: God himself will come and will save you. Then shall the eyes of the blind be opened, and the ears of the deaf shall be unstopped. Then shall the lame man leap as a hart, and the tongue of the dumb shall be free: for waters are broken out in the desert, and streams in the wilderness. And that which was dry land, shall become a pool, and the thirsty land springs of water.

Lesson II - Isa 35:7–10

In the dens where dragons dwell before, shall rise up the verdure of the reed and the bulrush. And a path and a way shall be there, and it shall be called the holy way: the unclean shall not pass over it, and this shall be unto you a straight way, so that fools shall not err therein. No lion shall be there, nor shall any mischievous beast go up by it, nor be found there: but they shall walk there that shall be delivered. And the redeemed of the Lord shall return, and shall come into Sion with praise, and everlasting joy shall be upon their heads: they shall obtain joy and gladness, and sorrow and mourning shall flee away.

Lesson III ~ Isa 41:1–4

Let the islands keep silence before me, and the nations take new strength: let them come near, and then speak, let us come near to judgment together. Who hath raised up the just one from the east, hath called him to follow him? he shall give the nations in his sight, and he shall rule over kings: he shall give them as the dust to his sword, as stubble driven by the wind, to his bow. He shall pursue them, he shall pass in peace, no path shall appear after his feet. Who hath wrought and done these things, calling the generations from the beginning? I the Lord, I am the first and the last.

Lesson IV

Sermon by St. Leo, Pope

Dearly beloved brethren, if we study attentively the history of the creation of our race, we shall find that man was made in the image of God, that his ways also might be an imitation of the ways of his Maker. This is the natural, real, and highest dignity to which we are capable of attaining, that the goodness of the Divine nature should have a reflection in us, as in a glass. As a mean of reaching this dignity, we are daily offered the grace of our Saviour, for as in the first Adam all men are fallen, so in the Second Adam can all men be raised up again.

Lesson V

Our restoration from the consequences of Adam's fall is sheer mercy of God, and nothing else; we should not have loved Him unless He had first loved us, and scattered the darkness of our ignorance by the light of His truth. This the Lord promised by the mouth of Isaias, where He says: "I will bring the blind by a way that they knew not, and I will lead them in paths that they have not known I will make darkness light before them, and crooked things straight. These things will I do unto them and not forsake them." And again: "I was found of them that sought Me not; I was made manifest unto them that asked not after Me."

Lesson VI

And we know from the Apostle John how God fulfilled His promise. "We know that the Son of God is come, and has given us an understanding, that we may know Him That is True, and be in Him That is True, even in His Son." And again: "Let us therefore love God, because He first loved us." For His great love then wherewith he has loved us, God renews His likeness in us. And, moreover, in order that He may find in us the reflection of His goodness, He gives us that whereby to work along with Himself (Who works all in all), lighting, as it were, candles in our dark minds, and kindling in us the fire of His love, to make us love not Himself only, but likewise in Him whatsoever He loves.

Lesson VII

From the Holy Gospel according to St. Luke (Luke 3:1–6)

In the fifteenth year of the reign of Tiberius Caesar, Pontius Pilate being governor of Judea. And so on.

Homily by Pope St. Gregory

John said unto the multitude, that came forth to be baptized of him: "O generation of vipers, who hath warned you to flee from the wrath to come?" The wrath to come in one sense signifies the great vengeance of the Latter Day; the sinner that repents not of his sin now will have no means whereby to flee from punishment then. Let us remark that addressing evil children copying the example of evil parents, the Baptist calls them a generation of vipers in that they were envious at the righteous and persecuted them; that they repaid evil for evil; that they hunted out ways of harming their neighbors, in all these things following the pattern of carnal parents, the prophet likens them to a venomous brood hatched from a venomous stock.

Lesson VIII

We also have sinned, we have fallen into wicked habits. What must we do, if we would flee from the wrath to come? Let us hear John. "Bring forth fruits worthy of repentance." In which words let us remark that the Friend of the Bridegroom demands not only fruits of repentance, but fruits worthy of repentance. The former are one thing, and the latter another. In considering then what are fruits worthy of repentance, we may remark that if we had done nothing unlawful we might have had free use of things which are lawful, and been able to sanctify ourselves without abstaining from indulgence in the things of the world.

Lesson IX

But if any one, for example, has fallen into fornication, or perhaps, into what is much worse, adultery, he ought to make up for his lawless pleasure by abstaining in some degree from lawful enjoyments. He that has sinned less is not bound to mortify himself as much as he that has sinned more, nor he that is innocent like him that is guilty. Let every one hearing these words bring forth fruits worthy of repentance, proceed to judge himself by his own conscience, and the more he perceives that he has sinned, the greater penance let him do.

Monday in Advent IV

Lesson I ~ Isa 41:8–10

From the book of Isaias

But thou Israel, art my servant, Jacob whom I have chosen, the seed of Abraham my friend: In whom I have taken thee from the ends of the earth, and from the remote parts thereof have called thee, and said to thee: Thou art my servant, I have chosen thee, and have not cast thee away. Fear not, for I am with thee: turn not aside, for I am thy God: I have strengthened thee, and have helped thee, and the right hand of my just one hath upheld thee.

Lesson II ~ Isa 41:11–13

Behold all that fight against thee shall be confounded and ashamed, they shall be as nothing, and the men shall perish that strive against thee. Thou shalt seek them, and shalt not find the men that resist thee: they shall be as nothing: and as a thing consumed the men that war against thee. For I am the Lord thy God, who take thee by the hand, and say to thee: Fear not, I have helped thee.

Lesson III ~ Isa 41:14–16

Fear not, thou worm of Jacob, you that are dead of Israel: I have helped thee, saith the Lord: and thy Redeemer the Holy One of Israel. I have made thee as a new thrashing wain, with teeth like a saw: thou shall thrash the mountains, and break them in pieces: and shalt make the hills as chaff. Thou shalt fan them, and the wind shall carry them away, and the whirlwind shall scatter them: and thou shalt rejoice in the Lord, in the Holy One of Israel thou shalt be joyful.

Tuesday in Advent IV

Lesson I ~ Isa 42:1–4

From the book of Isaias

Behold my servant, I will uphold him: my elect, my soul delighteth in him: I have given my spirit upon him, he shall bring forth judgment to the Gentiles. He shall not cry, nor have respect to person, neither shall his voice be heard abroad. The bruised reed he shall not break, and smoking flax he shall not quench: he shall bring forth judgment unto truth. He shall not be sad, nor troublesome, till he set judgment in the earth: and the islands shall wait for his law.

Lesson II ~ Isa 42:5–7

Thus saith the Lord God that created the heavens, and stretched them out: that established the earth, and the things that spring out of it: that giveth breath to the people upon it, and spirit to them that tread thereon. I the Lord have called thee in justice, and taken thee by the hand, and preserved thee. And I have given thee for a covenant of the people, for a light of the Gentiles: That thou mightest open the eyes of the blind, and bring forth the prisoner out of prison, and them that sit in darkness out of the prison house.

Lesson III ~ Isa 42:10–13

Sing ye to the Lord a new song, his praise is from the ends of the earth: you that go down to the sea, and all that are therein: ye islands, and ye inhabitants of them. Let the desert and the cities thereof be exalted: Cedar shall dwell in houses: ye inhabitants of Petra, give praise, they shall cry from the top of the mountains. They shall give glory to the Lord, and shall declare his praise in the islands. The Lord shall go forth as a mighty man, as a man of war shall he stir up zeal: he shall shout and cry: he shall prevail against his enemies.

Wednesday in Advent IV

Lesson I ~ Isa 51:1–3

From the book of Isaias

Give ear to me, you that follow that which is just, and you that seek the Lord: look unto the rock whence you are hewn, and to the hole of the pit from which you are dug out. Look unto Abraham your father, and to Sara that bore you: for I called him alone, and blessed him, and multiplied him. The Lord therefore will comfort Sion, and will comfort all the ruins thereof: and he will make her desert as a place of pleasure, and her wilderness as the garden of the Lord. Joy and gladness shall be found therein, thanksgiving, and the voice of praise.

Lesson II ~ Isa 51:4–6

Hearken unto me, O my people, and give ear to me, O my tribes: for a law shall go forth from me, and my judgment shall rest to be a light of the nations. My just one is near at hand, my saviour is gone forth, and my arms shall judge the people: the islands shall look for me, and shall patiently wait for my arm. Lift up your eyes to heaven, and look down to the earth beneath: for the heavens shall vanish like smoke, and the earth shall be worn away like a garment, and the inhabitants thereof shall perish in like manner: but my salvation shall be for ever, and my justice shall not fail.

Lesson III ~ Isa 51:7–8

Hearken to me, you that know what is just, my people who have my law in your heart: fear ye not the reproach of men, and be not afraid of their blasphemies. For the worm shall eat them up as a garment: and the moth shall consume them as wool: but my salvation shall be for ever, and my justice from generation to generation.

Thursday in Advent IV

Lesson I ~ Isa 64:1–4

From the book of Isaias

That thou wouldst rend the heavens, and wouldst come down: the mountains would melt away at thy presence. They would melt as at the burning of fire, the waters would burn with fire, that thy name might be made known to thy enemies: that the nations might tremble at thy presence. When thou shalt do wonderful things, we shall not bear them: thou didst come down, and at thy presence the mountains melted away. From the beginning of the world they have not heard, nor perceived with the ears: the eye hath not seen, O God, besides thee, what things thou hast prepared for them that wait for thee.

Lesson II ~ Isa 64:5–7

Thou hast met him that rejoiceth, and doth justice: in thy ways they shall remember thee: behold thou art angry, and we have sinned: in them we have been always, and we shall be saved. And we are all become as one unclean, and all our justices as the rag of a menstruous woman: and we have all fallen as a leaf, and our iniquities, like the wind, have taken us away. There is none that calleth upon thy name: that riseth up, and taketh hold of thee: thou hast hid thy face from us, and hast crushed us in the hand of our iniquity.

Lesson III ~ Isa 64:8–11

And now, O Lord, thou art our father, and we are clay: and thou art our maker, and we all are the works of thy hands. Be not very angry, O Lord, and remember no longer our iniquity: behold, see we are all thy people. The city of thy sanctuary is become a desert, Sion is made a desert, Jerusalem is desolate. The house of our holiness, and of our glory, where our fathers praised thee, is burnt with fire, and all our lovely things are turned into ruins.

Friday in Advent IV

Lesson I ~ Isa 66:5–8

From the book of Isaias

Hear the word of the Lord, you that tremble at his word: Your brethren that hate you, and cast you out for my name's sake, have said: Let the Lord be glorified, and we shall see in your joy: but they shall be confounded. A voice of the people from the city, a voice from the temple, the voice of the Lord that rendereth recompense to his enemies. Before she was in labour, she brought forth; before her time came to be delivered, she brought forth a man child. Who hath ever heard such a thing? and who hath seen the like to this? shall the earth bring forth in one day? or shall a nation be brought forth at once, because Sion hath been in labour, and hath brought forth her children?

Lesson II ~ Isa 66:9–12

Shall not I that make others to bring forth children, myself bring forth, saith the Lord? shall I, that give generation to others, be barren, saith the Lord thy God? Rejoice with Jerusalem, and be glad with her, all you that love her: rejoice for joy with her, all you that mourn for her. That you may suck, and be filled with the breasts of her consolations: that you may milk out, and flow with delights, from the abundance of her glory. For thus saith the Lord: Behold I will bring upon her as it were a river of peace, and as an overflowing torrent the glory of the Gentiles, which you shall suck; you shall be carried at the breasts, end upon the knees they shall caress you.

Lesson III ~ Isa 66:13–18

As one whom the mother caresseth, so will I comfort you, and you shall be comforted in Jerusalem. You shall see and your heart shall rejoice, and your bones shall flourish like an herb, and the hand of the Lord shall be known to his servants, and he shall be angry with his enemies. For behold the Lord will come with fire, and his chariots are like a whirlwind, to render his wrath in indignation, and his rebuke with flames of fire. For the Lord shall judge by fire, and by his sword unto all flesh, and the slain of the Lord shall be many. They that were sanctified, and thought themselves clean in the gardens behind the gate within, they that did eat swine's flesh, and the abomination, and the mouse: they shall be consumed together, saith the Lord. But I know their works, and their thoughts: I come that I may gather them together with all nations and tongues: and they shall come and shall see my glory.

Vigil of the Nativity of the Lord

Vigil

Lesson I

From the Holy Gospel according to St. Matthew (Matt 1:18–21)

When as his mother Mary was espoused to Joseph, before they came together, she was found with child, of the Holy Ghost. And so on.

Homily by St. Jerome, Priest

Why was the Lord conceived of an espoused virgin rather than of a free one? First, for the sake of the genealogy of Mary, which we have obtained by that of Joseph. Secondly, because she was thus saved from being stoned by the Jews as an adulteress. Thirdly, that Himself and His mother might have a guardian on their journey into Egypt. To these, Ignatius, the martyr of Antioch, has added a fourth reason: namely, that the birth might take place unknown to the devil, who would naturally suppose that Mary had conceived by Joseph.

Lesson II

"Before they came together, she was found with child of the Holy Ghost." She was found, that is, by Joseph, but by no one else. He had already almost a husband's privilege to know all that concerned her. "Before they came together." This does not imply that they ever did come together; the Scripture merely shows the absolute fact that up to this time they had not done so.

Lesson III

"Then Joseph her husband, being a just man, and not willing to make her a public example, was minded to put her away privily." If any man be joined to a fornicatress they become one body; and according to the law they that are privy to a crime are thereby guilty. How then can it be that Joseph is described as a just man, at the very time he was compounding the criminality of his espoused? It must have been that he knew her to be pure, and yet understood not the mystery of her pregnancy, but, while he wondered at that which had happened, was willing to hold his peace.

CHRISTMASTIDE

December 25 ~ NATIVITY OF THE LORD

Duplex I Class

Lesson I ~ Isa 9:1–6

At the first time the land of Zabulon, and the land of Nephtali was lightly touched: and at the last the way of the sea beyond the Jordan of the Galilee of the Gentiles was heavily loaded. The people that walked in darkness, have seen a great light: to them that dwelt in the region of the shadow of death, light is risen. Thou hast multiplied the nation, and hast not increased the joy. They shall rejoice before thee, as they that rejoice in the harvest, as conquerors rejoice after taking a prey, when they divide the spoils. For the yoke of their burden, and the rod of their shoulder, and the sceptre of their oppressor thou hast overcome, as in the day of Median. For every violent taking of spoils, with tumult, and garment mingled with blood, shall be burnt, and be fuel for the fire. For a child is born to us, and a son is given to us, and the government is upon his shoulder: and his name shall be called, Wonderful, Counsellor, God the Mighty, the Father of the world to come, the Prince of Peace.

Lesson II ~ Isa 40:1–8

Be comforted, be comforted, my people, saith your God. Speak ye to the heart of Jerusalem, and call to her: for her evil is come to an end, her iniquity is forgiven: she hath received of the hand of the Lord double for all her sins. The voice of one crying in the desert: Prepare ye the way of the Lord, make straight in the wilderness the paths of our God. Every valley shall be exalted, and every mountain and hill shall be made low, and the crooked shall become straight, and the rough ways plain. And the glory of the Lord shall be revealed, and all flesh together shall see, that the mouth of the Lord hath spoken. The voice of one, saying: Cry. And I said: What shall I cry? All flesh is grass, and all the glory thereof as the flower of the field. The grass is withered, and the flower is fallen, because the spirit of the Lord hath blown upon it. Indeed the people is grass: The grass is withered, and the flower is fallen: but the word of our Lord endureth for ever.

Lesson III - Isa 52:1–6

Arise, arise, put on thy strength, O Sion, put on the garments of thy glory, O Jerusalem, the city of the Holy One: for henceforth the uncircumcised, and unclean shall no more pass through thee. Shake thyself from the dust, arise, sit up, O Jerusalem: loose the bonds from off thy neck, O captive daughter of Sion. For thus saith the Lord: You were sold gratis, and you shall be redeemed without money. For thus saith the Lord God: My people went down into Egypt at the beginning to sojourn there: and the Assyrian hath oppressed them without any cause at all. And now what have I here, saith the Lord: for my people is taken away gratis. They that rule over them treat them unjustly, saith the Lord, and my name is continually blasphemed all the day long. Therefore my people shall know my name in that day: for I myself that spoke, behold I am here.

Lesson IV

Sermon by St. Leo, Pope

Dearly beloved brethren, Unto us is born this day a Saviour. Let us rejoice. It would be unlawful to be sad today, for today is Life's Birthday; the Birthday of that Life Which, for us dying creatures, takes away the sting of death, and brings the bright promise of the eternal gladness hereafter. It would be unlawful for any man to refuse to partake in our rejoicing. All men have an equal share in the great cause of our joy, for, since our Lord, Who is the destroyer of sin and of death, finds that all are bound under the condemnation, He is come to make all free. Rejoice, O thou that art holy, thou drawest nearer to thy crown! Rejoice, O thou that art sinful, thy Saviour offers thee pardon! Rejoice also, O thou Gentile, God calls thee to life! For the Son of God, when the fulness of the time was come, which had been fixed by the unsearchable counsel of God, took upon Him the nature of man, that He might reconcile that nature to Him Who made it, and so the devil, the inventor of death, is met and beaten in that very flesh which has been the field of his victory.

Lesson V

When our Lord entered the field of battle against the devil, He did so with a great and wonderful fairness. Being Himself the Almighty, He laid aside His uncreated Majesty to fight with our cruel enemy in our weak flesh. He brought against him the very shape, the very nature of our mortality, yet without sin. His birth however was not a birth like other births for no other is born pure, nay, not the little child whose life endures but a day on the earth. To His birth alone the throes of human passion had not contributed, in His alone no consequence of sin had had part. For His Mother was chosen a Virgin of the kingly lineage of David, and when she was to grow heavy with the sacred Child, her soul had already conceived Him before her body. She knew the counsel of God announced to her by the Angel, lest the unwonted events should alarm her. The future Mother of God knew what was to be wrought in her by the Holy Ghost, and that her modesty was absolutely safe.

Lesson VI

Therefore, dearly beloved brethren, let us give thanks to God the Father, through His Son, in the Holy Ghost: Who, for His great love wherewith He loved us, has had mercy on us and, even when we were dead in sins, has quickened us together with Christ, that in Him we might be a new creature, and a new workmanship. Let us then put off the old man with his deeds; and, having obtained a share in the Sonship of Christ, let us renounce the deeds of the flesh. Learn, O Christian, how great thou art, who hast been made partaker of the Divine nature, and fall not again by corrupt conversation into the beggarly elements above which thou art lifted. Remember Whose Body it is Whereof thou art made a member, and Who is its Head. Remember that it is He That has delivered thee from the power of darkness and has translated thee into God's light, and God's kingdom.

Lesson VII

From the Holy Gospel according to St. Luke (Luke 2:1–14)

At that time, it came to pass that there went out a decree from Caesar Augustus, that the whole world should be enrolled. And so on.

Homily by Pope St. Gregory

By God's mercy we are to say three Masses today, so that there is not much time left for preaching; but at the same time the occasion of the Lord's Birthday itself obliges me to speak a few words. I will first ask why, when the Lord was to be born, the world was enrolled? Was it not to herald the appearing of Him by Whom the elect are enrolled in the book of life? Whereas the Prophet says of the reprobate: "Let them be blotted out of the book of the living, and not be written with the righteous." Then, the Lord is born in Bethlehem. Now the name Bethlehem signifies the House of Bread, and thus it is the birth-place of Him Who has said: "I am the Living Bread, Which came down from heaven." We see then that this name of Bethlehem was prophetically given to the place where Christ was born, because it was there that He was to appear in the flesh by Whom the souls of the faithful are fed unto life eternal. He was born, not in His Mother's house, but away from home. And this is a mystery, showing that this our mortality into which He was born was not the home of Him Who is begotten of the Father before the ages.

Lesson VIII

From the holy Gospel according to St. Luke (Luke 2:15–20)

At that time, the shepherds said one to another: Let us go over to Bethlehem, and let us see this word that is come to pass, which the Lord hath showed to us. And so on.

Homily by St. Ambrose, Bishop

Behold the beginning of the Church. Christ is born, and the shepherds watch; shepherds, to gather together the scattered sheep of the Gentiles, and to lead them into the fold of Christ, that they might no longer be a prey to the ravages of spiritual wolves in the night of this world's darkness. And that shepherd is wide awake, whom the Good Shepherd stirs up. The flock then is the people, the night is the world, and the shepherds are the Priests. And perhaps he is a shepherd to whom it is said: "Be watchful and strengthen," for God has ordained as the shepherds of His flock not Bishops only, but also Angels.

Lesson IX

From the holy Gospel according to St. John (John 1:1–14)

In the beginning was the Word, and the Word was with God, and the Word was God. The same was in the beginning with God. And so on.

Homily by St. Augustine, Bishop

Lest thou shouldest think all things mean, as thou art accustomed to think of things human, hear and digest this: The Word was God. Now perhaps there will come forward some Arian unbeliever, and say that the Word of God was a creature. How can the Word of God be a creature, when it was by the Word that all creatures were made? If He be a creature, then there must have been some other Word, not a creature, by which He was made. And what Word is that? If thou sayest that it was by the word of the Word Himself that He was made, I tell thee that God had no other, but One Only-begotten Son. But if thou say not that it was by the word of the Word Himself that He was made, thou art forced to confess that. He by Whom all things were made was not Himself made at all. Believe the Gospel.

December 26 ~ St. Stephen the Protomartyr

Duplex II Class

Lesson I ~ Acts 6:1–6

From the Acts of Apostles

And in those days, the number of the disciples increasing, there arose a murmuring of the Greeks against the Hebrews, for that their widows were neglected in the daily ministration. Then the twelve calling together the multitude of the disciples, said: It is not reason that we should leave the word of God, and serve tables. Wherefore, brethren, look ye out among you seven men of good reputation, full of the Holy Ghost and wisdom, whom we may appoint over this business. But we will give ourselves continually to prayer, and to the ministry of the word. And the saying was liked by all the multitude. And they chose Stephen, a man full of faith, and of the Holy Ghost, and Philip, and Prochorus, and Nicanor, and Timon, and Parmenas, and Nicolas, a proselyte of Antioch. These they set before the apostles; and they praying, imposed hands upon them.

Lesson II ~ Acts 6:7–10; 7:54

And the word of the Lord increased; and the number of the disciples was multiplied in Jerusalem exceedingly: a great multitude also of the priests obeyed the faith. And Stephen, full of grace and fortitude, did great wonders and signs among the people. Now there arose some of that which is called the synagogue of the Libertines, and of the Cyrenians, and of the Alexandrians, and of them that were of Cilicia and Asia, disputing with Stephen. And they were not able to resist the wisdom and the spirit that spoke. Now hearing these things, they were cut to the heart, and they gnashed with their teeth at him.

Lesson III ~ Acts 7:55–59

But he, being full of the Holy Ghost, looking up steadfastly to heaven, saw the glory of God, and Jesus standing on the right hand of God. And he said: Behold, I see the heavens opened, and the Son of man standing on the right hand of God. And they crying out with a loud voice, stopped their ears, and with one accord ran violently upon him. And casting him forth without the city, they stoned him; and the witnesses laid down their garments at the feet of a young man, whose name was Saul. And they stoned Stephen, invoking, and saying: Lord Jesus, receive my spirit. And falling on his knees, he cried with a loud voice, saying: Lord, lay not this sin to their charge. And when he had said this, he fell asleep in the Lord.

Lesson IV

Sermons by St. Fulgentius, Bishop

Yesterday we were celebrating the birth in time of our Eternal King; today we celebrate the victory, through suffering, of one of His soldiers. Yesterday our King was pleased to come forth from His royal palace of the Virgin's womb, clothed in a robe of flesh, to visit the world; today His soldier, laying aside the tabernacle of the body, enters in triumph into the heavenly palaces. The One, preserving unchanged that glory of the Divinity which He had before the world was, girded Himself with the form of a servant, and entered the arena of this world to fight sin; the other takes off the garments of this corruptible body, and enters into the heavenly mansions, where he will reign for ever. The One comes down veiled in flesh; the other goes up clothed in a robe of glory, red with blood.

Lesson V

The One comes down amid the jubilation of angels; the other goes up amid the stoning of the Jews. Yesterday the holy angels were singing, "Glory to God in the highest;" today there is joy among them, for they receive Stephen into their company. Yesterday the Lord came forth from the Virgin's womb; today His soldier is delivered from the prison of the body. Yesterday

Christ was for our sakes wrapped in swaddling bands; today He girds Stephen with a robe of immortality. Yesterday the new-born Christ lay in a narrow manger; today Stephen enters victorious into the boundless heavens. The Lord came down alone that He might raise many up; our King humbled Himself that He might set His soldiers in high places.

Lesson VI

Why brethren, it behooves us to consider with what arms Stephen was able, amid all the cruelty of the Jews, to remain more than conqueror, and worthily to attain to so blessed a triumph. Stephen, in that struggle which brought him to the crown whereof his name is a prophecy, had for armor the love of God and man, and by it he remained victorious on all hands. The love of God strengthened him against the cruelty of the Jews; and the love of his neighbor made him pray even for his murderers. Through love he rebuked the wandering, that they might be corrected; through love he prayed for them that stoned him, that they might not be punished. By the might of his love he overcame Saul his cruel persecutor; and earned for a comrade in heaven, the very man who had done him to death upon earth.

Lesson VII

From the Holy Gospel according to St. Matthew (Matt 23:34–39)

At that time, Jesus said to the scribes and pharisee: I send to you prophets, and wise men, and scribes: and some of them you will put to death and crucify. And so on,

Homily by St. Jerome, Priest

We have already remarked that the Lord's words, "Fill ye up the measure of your fathers," refer in the first place to Himself, Whom the Jews afterwards put to death. In a secondary sense it may likewise be applied to His disciples, of whom He says, "Behold, I send unto you Prophets, and wise men, and Scribes." Here observe that, according to the Apostle writing to the Corinthians, there are diversities of gifts among Christ's followers. Some are Prophets of that which is to come; some are wise men, who know the due season for rebuke and exhortation; some are Scribes learned in the law. And of these they stoned Stephen, slew Paul with the sword, crucified Peter, and scourged the Disciples mentioned in the Acts of the Apostles.

Lesson VIII

It is a subject of dispute among commentators who is meant by Zacharias the son of Barachias. We read of several persons of the name of Zacharias. But here, in order to prevent any mistake, it is particularly said, "Whom you slew between the temple and the altar." I have read various opinions in various places upon this question, and I will give each. First, some hold that Zacharias the son of Barachias is the eleventh of the twelve Minor Prophets; and this opinion is supported by the father's name. But the Bible nowhere tells us that this Prophet was slain between the temple and the altar; and it is hardly possible that he can have been, for in his time it could scarcely be said that even the ruins of the temple were in existence. Secondly, others maintain that this Zacharias was Zachary, the father of John the Baptist. This interpretation is derived from the dreams of the Apocryphal Gospels, wherein it is asserted that he was martyred for preaching Christ's coming.

Lesson IX

A third school will have it that this Zacharias, the son of Barachias, was that Zacharias of whom we read, that he was slain by Joash, king of Judah, between the temple and the altar. Against this it is to be remarked, that that Zacharias was not the son of Barachias, but of Jehoiada the priest; whence it is written, "Joash remembered not the kindness which Jehoiada his father had done to him." The question therefore arises, if this opinion be true, why, the name and manner of death both agreeing with this explanation, Zacharias is called the son, not of Jehoiada, but of Barachias. In Hebrew, Barachias signifies the Blessed of the Lord, and Jehoiada proves his Righteousness. In the Gospel used by the Nazarenes the name of Jehoiada is used instead of Barachias.

December 27 - St. John the Apostle

Duplex II Class

Lesson I - 1 John 1:1–5

From the first letter of St. John the Apostle

That which was from the beginning, which we have heard, which we have seen with our eyes, which we have looked upon, and our hands have handled, of the word of life: For the life was manifested; and we have seen and do bear witness, and declare unto you the life eternal, which was with the Father, and hath appeared to us: That which we have seen and have heard, we declare unto you, that you also may have fellowship with us, and our fellowship may be with the Father, and with his Son Jesus Christ. And these things we write to you, that you may rejoice, and your joy may be full. And this is the declaration which we have heard from him, and declare unto you: That God is light, and in him there is no darkness.

Lesson II - 1 John 1:6–10

If we say that we have fellowship with him, and walk in darkness, we lie, and do not the truth. But if we walk in the light, as he also is in the light, we have fellowship one with another, and the blood of Jesus Christ his Son cleanseth us from all sin. If we say that we have no sin, we deceive ourselves, and the truth is not in us. If we confess our sins, he is faithful and just, to forgive us our sins, and to cleanse us from all iniquity. If we say that we have not sinned, we make him a liar, and his word is not in us.

Lesson III - 1 John 2:1–5

My little children, these things I write to you, that you may not sin. But if any man sin, we have an advocate with the Father, Jesus Christ the just: And he is the propitiation for our sins: and not for ours only, but also for those of the whole world. And by this we know that we have known him, if we keep his commandments. He who saith that he knoweth him, and keepeth not his commandments, is a liar, and the truth is not in him. But he that keepeth his word, in him in very deed the charity of God is perfected.

Lesson IV

From the Book on Ecclesiastical writers, written by St. Jerome, Priest

The Apostle John whom Jesus loved was a son of Zebedee, and brother of the Apostle James, who was beheaded by Herod soon after our Lord suffered. He was the last of the Evangelists to write his Gospel, which he published at the request of the Bishops of Asia, against Cerinthus and other heretics, and particularly against the then spreading doctrine of the Ebionites, who asserted that Christ had had no existence before Mary. It was therefore needful for the Evangelist to declare His Eternal and Divine Generation.

Lesson V

In the fourteenth year after Nero, Domitian stirred up the second persecution, and John was exiled to the island of Patmos, where he wrote his Apocalypse, which has been explained by Justin the Martyr and Irenæus. When Domitian was killed, the Senate annulled all his acts, on account of his savage cruelty, and the Apostle returned to Ephesus, during the reign of Nerva. He remained at Ephesus until the time of Trajan, and founded and governed all the Churches of Asia. There, in an extreme old age, he died, in the sixty-eighth year after the Lord's passion, and was buried near the city.

Lesson VI

The Blessed Evangelist John lived at Ephesus down to an extreme old age, and, at length, when he was with difficulty carried to the Church, and was not able to exhort the congregation at length, he was used simply to say at each meeting, My little children, love one another. At last the disciples and brethren were weary with hearing these words continually, and asked him: Master, why do you ever say this only? Whereto he replied to them: It is the commandment of the Lord, and if this only be done, it is enough.

Lesson VII

From the Holy Gospel according to St. John (John 21:19–24)

In that time Jesus said to Peter: Follow me. Peter turning about, saw that disciple whom Jesus loved following. And so on.

Homily by St. Augustine, Bishop

The Church knows of two different lives, which God has revealed and blessed: one is the life of faith, the other the life of knowledge; one the life of this pilgrimage, the other the life of the eternal mansions; one the life of work, the other the life of rest; one the life of the journey, the other the life of home; one the life of action, the other the life of contemplation. The one eschews evil and does good; the other has no evil to eschew, and only an exceeding good to enjoy. The one strives with the enemy, the other has no enemies, and reigns.

Lesson VIII

The one succors the needy; the other is where there are no needy to succor. The one forgives them that trespass against it, that its own trespasses may be forgiven; the other neither has trespasses to forgive nor to be forgiven. The one is chastened with evil, lest it be exalted above measure by good; the other enjoys such a fulness of grace that it feels no evil, and cleaves so firmly unto the Highest Good, that it has no temptation to pride.

Lesson IX

Therefore the one is good, but still sorrowful; the other is better and perfectly blessed. And of these two lives there are types, of the one in the Apostle Peter, of the other in John. The one labors here even unto the end, and finds its end hereafter; the other stretches out into the hereafter, and in eternity finds no end. Therefore is it said unto the one, Follow Me; but of the other, "If I will that he tarry till I come, what is that to thee? Follow thou Me." What is the meaning of these words? who can know? who can understand? what is it? is it Follow thou Me, imitating Me in the bearing of earthly sorrow; let him tarry till I come again, bringing the everlasting reward?

December 28 ~ Holy Innocents

Duplex II Class

Lesson I ~ Jer 31:15–17

From the book of Jeremias

Thus saith the Lord: A voice was heard on high of lamentation, of mourning, and weeping, of Rachel weeping for her children, and refusing to be comforted for them, because they are not. Thus saith the Lord: Let thy voice cease from weeping, and thy eyes from tears: for there is a reward for thy work, saith the Lord: and they shall return out of the land of the enemy. And here is hope for thy last end, saith the Lord: and the children shall return to their own borders.

Lesson II ~ Jer 31:18–20

Hearing I heard Ephraim when he went into captivity: thou hast chastised me, and I was instructed, as a young bullock unaccustomed to the yoke. Convert me, and I shall be converted, for thou art the Lord my God. For after thou didst convert me, I did penance: and after thou didst shew unto me, I struck my thigh: I am confounded and ashamed, because I have borne the reproach of my youth. Surely Ephraim is an honourable son to me, surely he is a tender child: for since I spoke of him, I will still remember him.

Lesson III ~ Jer 31:21–23

Set thee up a watchtower, make to thee bitterness: direct thy heart into the right way, wherein thou hast walked: return, O virgin of Israel, return to these thy cities. How long wilt thou be dissolute in deliciousness, O wandering daughter? for the Lord hath created a new thing upon the earth: A woman shall compass a man. Thus saith the Lord of hosts, the God of Israel: As yet shall they say this word in the land of Juda, and in the cities thereof, when I shall bring back their captivity: The Lord bless thee, the beauty of justice, the holy mountain.

Lesson IV

Sermon by St. Augustine, Bishop

Dearly beloved brethren, today we keep the birthday of those children, who, as we are informed by the Gospel, were massacred by the savage King Herod. Therefore let earth rejoice with exceeding joy, for she is the mother of these heavenly soldiers, and of this numerous host. The love of the vile Herod could never have crowned these blessed ones as his hatred has. For the Church testifies by this holy solemnity, that whereas iniquity did specially abound against these little saints, so much the more were heavenly blessings poured out upon them.

Lesson V

Blessed art thou, O Bethlehem in the land of Judah, which hast suffered the cruelty of King Herod in the slaughter of thy children; who art found worthy to offer at once to God a whole white-robed army of guileless martyrs! Surely, it is well to keep their birthday, even that blessed birthday which gave them from earth to heaven, more blessed than the day that brought them out of their mother's womb. Scarcely had they entered on the life that now is, when they obtained that glorious life which is to come.

Lesson VI

We praise the death of other martyrs because it was the crowning act of an undaunted and persistent testimony; but these were crowned at once. He That makes an end to this present life, gave to them at its very gates that eternal blessedness which we hope for at its close. They whom the wickedness of Herod tore from their mothers' breasts are rightfully called the flowers of martyrdom; hardly had these buds of the Church shown their heads above the soil, in the winter of unbelief, when the frost of persecution nipped them.

Lesson VII

From the Holy Gospel according to St. Matthew (Matt 2:13–18)

At that time, an angel of the Lord appeared in sleep to Joseph, saying: Arise, and take the child and his mother, and fly into Egypt: and be there until I shall tell thee. And so on.

Homily by St. Jerome, Priest

He took the young Child, and His mother, and fled into Egypt, by night and in darkness; and the darkness of that night was a figure of the darkness of ignorance in which they left the unbelievers from whom they fled. But when they returned into Judaea, we learn not from the Gospel that it was by night, or in darkness; which is an image of that light which will lighten the Jews, when, at the end of the world, they shall receive back the faith, which now enlightens the Gentiles, even as Judaea received Christ returning from Egypt.

Lesson VIII

That it might be fulfilled which was spoken of the Lord by the Prophet, saying "Out of Egypt have I called My Son." Those who go about to deny the authority of the Hebrew Scriptures, ask where any such passage is to be found in the Septuagint. But, although they find it not there, I tell them that the fact of its being written in the Prophet Osee can be proved by the texts which I have lately published.

Lesson IX

Then was fulfilled that which was spoken by Jeremias the Prophet, saying; "In Rama was there a voice heard, weeping and great mourning; Rachel weeping for her children." The child of Rachel was Benjamin, and Bethlehem is not a town belonging to his tribe. We must therefore seek another reason why Rachel should weep for the children of Judah, to whom Bethlehem belongs, as for her own. The plain answer is that she is buried at Ephratha close to Bethlehem, and she is called Mother on account of the resting-place of her earthly tabernacle being there. It is possible also that she is called Mother because the tribes of Judah and Benjamin were joined together, and Herod slew not only all the children that were in Bethlehem, but also in all the coasts thereof.

December 29 - St. Thomas of Canterbury

Bishop & Martyr - Duplex

Lesson I - Rom 1:1–7

Beginning of the letter of St. Paul the Apostle to the Romans

Paul, a servant of Jesus Christ, called to be an apostle, separated unto the gospel of God, Which he had promised before, by his prophets, in the holy Scriptures, Concerning his Son, who was made to him of the seed of David, according to the flesh, Who was predestinated the Son of God in power, according to the spirit of sanctification, by the resurrection of our Lord Jesus Christ from the dead; By whom we have received grace and apostleship for obedience to the faith, in all nations, for his name; Among whom are you also the called of Jesus Christ: To all that are at Rome, the beloved of God, called to be saints. Grace to you, and peace from God our Father, and from the Lord Jesus Christ.

Lesson II - Rom 1:8–12

First I give thanks to my God, through Jesus Christ, for you all, because your faith is spoken of in the whole world. For God is my witness, whom I serve in my spirit in the gospel of his Son, that without ceasing I make a commemoration of you; Always in my prayers making request, if by any means now at length I may have a prosperous journey, by the will of God, to come unto you. For I long to see you, that I may impart unto you some spiritual grace, to strengthen you: That is to say, that I may be comforted together in you, by that which is common to us both, your faith and mine.

Lesson III ~ Rom 1:13–19

And I would not have you ignorant, brethren, that I have often purposed to come unto you (and have been hindered hitherto), that I might have some fruit among you also, even as among other Gentiles. To the Greeks and to the barbarians, to the wise and to the unwise, I am a debtor; So (as much as is in me) I am ready to preach the gospel to you also that are at Rome. For I am not ashamed of the gospel. For it is the power of God unto salvation to every one that believeth, to the Jew first, and to the Greek. For the justice of God is revealed therein, from faith unto faith, as it is written: The just man liveth by faith. For the wrath of God is revealed from heaven against all ungodliness and injustice of those men that detain the truth of God in injustice: Because that which is known of God is manifest in them. For God hath manifested it unto them.

Lesson IV

Thomas was born in London, and succeeded Theobald in the Archbishopric of Canterbury. He had previously filled with great distinction the office of Lord Chancellor, and showed an indomitable firmness in his duty as Primate. When Henry II, King of England, in an assembly of the Bishops and great men of his realm, endeavored to pass laws detrimental to the advantage and dignity of the Church, he opposed himself so steadily to the king's wishes, that, neither promises nor threats availing to shake him, he was about to be cast into prison had he not made good his escape in time. The whole of his kinsfolk without regard to age or sex, his friends, and his advisers were then banished from the kingdom, and those who were able, were bound by an oath to make their way to the presence of Thomas, in the hope that though careless of his own sufferings, he might yield at the sight of their misery. But neither flesh and blood, nor the pleadings of natural affection could make him swerve from the line of his pastoral duty.

Lesson V

He betook himself to Pope Alexander III, by whom he was graciously received, and who committed him to the care of the Cistercians at Pontigni. As soon as this came to the knowledge of King Henry, he sent threatening letters to the monks in order to drive Thomas from this shelter. The saint was unwilling that the Cistercian Order should suffer on his account, and therefore voluntarily withdrew from Pontigni, and accepted the invitation of Louis VII, King of France, to go to his court. He remained here, until his banishment was recalled at the intercession of the Pope and of the King of France, and he returned to England amid great public joy. He was quietly continuing the work of a faithful shepherd of souls, when certain calumniators denounced him to the king as a plotter against the crown and the public peace. Henry, deceived by these libels, cried out that it was hard that one priest should never let him have quiet in his kingdom.

Lesson VI

Some wicked servants of the king, hearing his words, and thinking to do him pleasure, betook themselves to Canterbury to rid him of the Archbishop. They entered the cathedral in the evening as Thomas was proceeding to assist at Vespers. The clergy in attendance on him, conscious of the attempt about to be made, wished to bolt the doors. But the saint caused them to be again opened, saying, "The Church of God is not to be made a castle, and for the cause of God's Church I am willing to die." He then said to his murderers, "I charge you in the name of the Almighty God to hurt none of my people." With these words he fell on his knees, and commended himself to God, to the Blessed Virgin Mary, to St. Denis, and to the other holy Patrons of the Church of Canterbury. He presently offered his sacred head for the stroke of death, and received it from the swords of those wicked men with the same constancy with which he had withstood the commands of the unrighteous king. The murderers pulled out his brains and strewed them all about the floor of the Church. He testified on the 29th day of December, in the year of our Lord 1170, and, being afterwards honored with many miracles, was canonized by Pope Alexander III.

Lesson VII

From the Holy Gospel according to St. John (John 10:11–16)

In that time Jesus said to the pharisees: I am the good shepherd. The good shepherd giveth his life for his sheep. And so on.

Homily by St. John Chrysostom

Dearly beloved brethren, the Bishops of the Church hold a great office, an office that needs much that wisdom and strength whereof Christ has given us an example. We must learn of Him to lay down our lives for the sheep and never to leave them; and to fight bravely against the wolf. This is the difference between the true shepherd and the hireling. The one leaves the sheep and seeks his own safety, but the other thinks not of his own safety, so that he may watch over the sheep. Christ then having given us the pattern of a good shepherd, warns us against two enemies; first, the thief that comes not but to kill and to steal, and, secondly, the hireling that stands by, and defends not them that are committed to his charge.

Lesson VIII

Ezechiel has said of old: Woe be to the shepherds of Israel! Do they not feed themselves? Should not the shepherds feed the flocks? But they did the contrary, a great wickedness and the root of many evils. Therefore, he says, they brought not back that which was gone astray neither did they search for that which was lost neither did they bind up that which was broken, nor strengthen that which was sick; for they fed themselves, and not the flock. And Paul has the same in other words, where he says: All seek their own, not the things which are Jesus Christ's.

Lesson IX

Christ shows Himself very different from either the thief or the hireling; whereas the thief comes to destroy, He came that they might have life, and that they might have it more abundantly. The hireling flees, but He lays down His life for the sheep, that the sheep perish not. When then the Jews went about to kill Him, He ceased not to teach; He gave not up them that believed in Him, but stood steadfast and died. Wherefore He has good title to often say, "I am the Good Shepherd." It was but a little while, and He showed us how He could lay down His life for the sheep. And if it appears not as yet how they have life, and have it more abundantly (but it shall appear, in the world which is to come), we may well be persuaded of the truth of the second promise, we who have seen the fulfillment of the first.

December 30 ~ Day 5 within the Octave of the Nativity of the Lord

Semiduplex

Lesson I ~ Rom 2:1–4

From the letter of St. Paul the Apostle to the Romans

Wherefore thou art inexcusable, O man, whosoever thou art that judgest. For wherein thou judgest another, thou condemnest thyself. For thou dost the same things which thou judgest. For we know that the judgment of God is, according to truth, against them that do such things. And thinkest thou this, O man, that judgest them who do such things, and dost the same, that thou shalt escape the judgment of God? Or despisest thou the riches of his goodness, and patience, and longsuffering? Knowest thou not, that the benignity of God leadeth thee to penance?

Lesson II ~ Rom 2:5–8

But according to thy hardness and impenitent heart, thou treasurest up to thyself wrath, against the day of wrath, and revelation of the just judgment of God. Who will render to every man according to his works. To them indeed, who according to patience in good work, seek glory and honour and incorruption, eternal life: But to them that are contentious, and who obey not the truth, but give credit to iniquity, wrath and indignation.

Lesson III ~ Rom 2:9–13

Tribulation and anguish upon every soul of man that worketh evil, of the Jew first, and also of the Greek. But glory, and honour, and peace to every one that worketh good, to the Jew first, and also to the Greek. For there is no respect of persons with God. For whosoever have sinned without the law, shall perish without the law; and whosoever have sinned in the law, shall be judged by the law. For not the hearers of the law are just before God, but the doers of the law shall be justified.

Lesson IV

Sermon by St. Leo the Pope

In any day of the year, dearly beloved, whenever we make our meditations, we are mindful of the birth from a Virgin Mother of our Lord and Saviour. Whenever our souls are uplifted in the worship of our Maker, whether we sigh in supplication, rejoice in praise, or offer sacrifice, there is nothing which we more frequently or more confidently set our minds upon than the fact that God, the Son of God, begotten of the co-eternal Father, was also born by a human birth. But on this day his Nativity, which is to be adored both in heaven and on earth, is brought before us as at no other time. For today it is as though a new and radiant light is shining forth in the heavens, in such a way that the brightness of this wondrous mystery is perceived even by our senses. And not only do we call to mind what the Angel Gabriel said to the awe-stricken Mary, but in some sort we seem even to be present at that colloquy when she conceived of the Holy Ghost. And we marvel both at the promise made to her, and at her faith in that promise.

Lesson V

For as of today the Maker of the world was brought forth from a virginal womb, and he who made all things became the Son of her whom he had made. As of today the Word of God appeared in a garment of flesh, and that which was never beheld by men's eyes can now be even touched by their hands. As of today the shepherds learned from angelic voices that a Saviour was born in substance of our flesh and soul. And this same angelic message was a pattern to the pastors of the Lord's flock to preach the Gospel on this day, and to do it in such a way that we too may say with the heavenly hosts: Glory to God in the highest, and on earth peace to men of good will.

Lesson VI

Verily the greatness of the gift bestowed upon us demands a reverence worthy of its splendor. For, as the blessed Apostle says, we have received, not the spirit of the world, but the Spirit which is of God, that we may know the things that are given us from God. And him we can devoutly worship only by offering to him that which he bestows. And in the treasury of the Lord's bounty, what can we find so appropriate to the honor of the present Feast, as that peace which at the birth of the Lord was first proclaimed by the angelic choir? For peace it is which brings forth the children of God. Peace it is also which is the nurse of affection, the mother of unity, the rest of the blessed, and our eternal home. Peace it is whose proper work and special benefit is to join unto God those whom it separates from the world.

Lesson VII

From the Holy Gospel according to St. Luke (Luke 2:15–20)

In that time, the shepherds said one to another: Let us go over to Bethlehem, and let us see this word that is come to pass, which the Lord hath shewed to us. And they came with haste. And so on.

Homily by St. Ambrose, Bishop

The shepherds came with haste. This is how every one comes who is really earnestly seeking Christ. The shepherds believed the angel. Wilt thou not believe Father, Son, and Holy Ghost, Angels, Prophets, and Apostles? Here also remark how carefully every word in the Scripture is chosen. They came with haste to see this Word. A Word, indeed; the Word of God. He that saw the Lord's Flesh, saw the Word, that is, God the Son.

Lesson VIII

Because the office of a shepherd is low, think not lowly of the example of their faith. Verily, that which is poorest in learning is richest in faith. The Lord seeks not for schools crowded with wise men, but for a people of a single heart unused to overlay and to disguise what they learn by vain and superfluous adornments. He will have straightforwardness rather than vainglory.

Lesson IX

Think not lowly either of the shepherds' words. The shepherds strengthen the faith even of Mary; the shepherds lead God's people to His worship. For, all they that heard it, wondered at those things which were told them by the shepherds. But Mary kept all these things and pondered them in her heart. Let us learn the modesty of the Holy Virgin, that modesty of speech as of body, whereby she laid up in her heart the evidences of her faith.

December 31 ~ St. Sylvester I

Pope & Confessor ~ Duplex

Lesson I ~ Rom 3:19–22

From the letter of St. Paul the Apostle to the Romans

Now we know, that what things soever the law speaks, it speaketh to them that are in the law; that every mouth may be stopped, and all the world may be made subject to God. Because by the works of the law no flesh shall be justified before him. For by the law is the knowledge of sin. But now without the law the justice of God is made manifest, being witnessed by the law and the prophets. Even the justice of God, by faith of Jesus Christ, unto all and upon all them that believe in him: for there is no distinction:

Lesson II ~ Rom 3:23–26

For all have sinned, and do need the glory of God. Being justified freely by his grace, through the redemption, that is in Christ Jesus, Whom God hath proposed to be a propitiation, through faith in his blood, to the shewing of his justice, for the remission of former sins, Through the forbearance of God, for the shewing of his justice in this time; that he himself may be just, and the justifier of him, who is of the faith of Jesus Christ.

Lesson III ~ Rom 3:27–31

Where is then thy boasting? It is excluded. By what law? Of works? No, but by the law of faith. For we account a man to be justified by faith, without the works of the law. Is he the God of the Jews only? Is he not also of the Gentiles? Yes, of the Gentiles also. For it is one God, that justifieth circumcision by faith, and uncircumcision through faith. Do we, then, destroy the law through faith? God forbid: but we establish the law.

Lesson IV

Sylvester was a Roman by birth, and his father's name was Rufinus. He was brought up from a very early age under a Priest named Cyrinus, of whose teaching and example he was a diligent learner. In his thirtieth year he was ordained Priest of the Holy Roman Church by Pope Marcellinus. In the discharge of his duties he became a model for all the clergy, and, after the death of Melchiades, he succeeded him on the Papal throne, in the year of our Lord 314, during the reign of Constantine, who had already by public decree proclaimed peace to the Church of Christ. Hardly had he undertaken the government of the Church when he betook himself to stir up the Emperor to protect and propagate the religion of Christ. Constantine was fresh from his victory over his enemy Maxentius, on the Eve whereof the sign of the Cross had been revealed to him wreathed in light upon the sky; and there was an old story in the Church of Rome that it was Sylvester who caused him to recognize the images of the Apostles, administered to him holy Baptism, and cleansed him from the leprosy of misbelief.

Lesson V

The godly Emperor had already granted to Christ's faithful people permission to build public churches, and by the advice of Sylvester he himself set them the example. He built many Basilicas, and magnificently adorned them with holy images, and gifted them with gifts and endowments. Among these there were, besides others, the Church of Christ the Saviour near the Lateran Palace; that of St. Peter upon the Vatican Mount; that of St. Paul upon the road to Ostia; that of St. Lawrence in Verus' field; that of the Holy Cross at the Sessorian hall; that of St. Peter and St. Marcellinus upon the Lavican Way; and that of St. Agnes upon the road to Mentana. Under this Pope was held the first Council of Nicæa, presided over by the Papal Legates in the Presence of Constantine and three hundred and eighteen Bishops, where the holy and Catholic Faith was declared, and Arius and his followers condemned; which Council was finally confirmed by the Pope, at the request of all the assembled Fathers, in a synod held at Rome, where Arius was again condemned. This Pope issued many useful ordinances for the Church of God. He reserved to Bishops the right of consecrating the Holy Chrism; ordered Priests to anoint with Chrism the heads of the newly baptized; settled the officiating dress of Deacons as a dalmatic and a linen maniple; and forbade the consecration of the Sacrament of the Altar on anything but a linen corporal.

Lesson VI

Sylvester is likewise said to have ordained that all persons taking Holy Orders should remain awhile in each grade before being promoted to a higher; that laymen should not go to law against the clergy; and that the clergy themselves were not to plead before civil tribunals. He decreed that the first and seventh days of the week should be called respectively the Lord's Day and the Sabbath, and the others, Second Day, Third Day, and so on. In this he confirmed the use of the word *Feria* for the weekdays, the which use had already begun in the Church. This word signifies a holiday, and points to the duty of the clergy ever to lay aside all worldly labour, and leave themselves free to continually do the work of the Lord. The heavenly wisdom with which he ruled the Church of God, was joined in him to a singular holiness of life, and an inexhaustible tenderness towards the poor; in which matter he ordained that the wealthy clergy should each relieve a certain number of needy persons; and he also made arrangements for supplying the consecrated virgins with the necessaries of life. He lived as Pope twenty-one years, ten months and one day, and was buried in the cemetery of Priscilla on the Salarian Way. He held seven Advent ordinations, and made forty-two Priests, twenty-five Deacons, and sixty-five Bishops of various sees.

Lessons VII–IX from the Common of Supreme Pontiffs (Homily by St. Leo)

Sunday within the Octave of the Nativity of Our Lord

Semiduplex

Lessons I–III come from those on whichever day within the Octave the Sunday happens to fall (i.e. Dec 29th is Day 5). Subsequent lessons are as follows—instead of Lessons IV–VIII from whatever feast this Sunday impedes. Lesson IX is taken from that of any impeded feast.

Lesson IV

Sermon by St. Leo, Pope

Dearly beloved brethren, the greatness of God's work, in its breadth and height, passes the power of man's utterance; and, therefore, when we must needs not keep silence, we find it hard to know what to say. The words of the Prophet: Who shall declare His generation? Look not only to the Divine, but also to the human birth of Jesus Christ, the Son of God. Faith believes, but words cannot explain how the two natures were joined in one Person, and therein we find that we shall never lack matter of praise in Him Whose abundance ever outruns the power of our expression.

Lesson V

Therefore, let us rejoice that this mystery of mercy is greater than we can ever speak; and let us feel that it is good for us to fail if we try to express the height and depth of redeeming love. He comes nearest to the knowledge of the truth, who, the farther he advances, sees all the more clearly that he can never overtake that whereafter he searches. For he that imagines therein that he has ever attained unto the goal, has not found that which he seeks, but has altogether missed.

Lesson VI

But lest we should be confounded at the weakness of our mortality, we have help in the words of the Prophets and Evangelists; and they are able so to inflame and teach us that we may see the Birth of the Lord, wherein the Word was made Flesh, not so much as a thing past but as a thing present. The proclamation of the angel to the shepherds who watched their flocks by night, rings in our ears also; and for this end are we appointed to rule the Lord's flock, that we may ever keep in our heart the word revealed from heaven, and say unto you, as we do this day: "Behold, I bring you good tidings of great joy, which shall be to all people; for unto you is born this day, in the city of David, a Saviour, Which is Christ the Lord!"

Lesson VII

From the Holy Gospel according to St. Luke (Luke 2:33–40)

In that time, his father and mother were wondering at those things which were spoken concerning him. And so on.

Homily by St. Ambrose, Bishop

We see that God's abounding grace is poured forth on all by the birth of the Lord, and that the gift of prophecy is not denied to the righteous, but to the unbelieving. Simeon prophesies that our Lord Jesus Christ is set for the fall and rising again of many in Israel, setting forth that the just and the unjust reap different fruits from the coming of the Saviour; so will it be with us; according to our individual works, the True and Just Judge will apportion to us punishment or reward.

Lesson VIII

"See, a sword shall pierce through thine own soul also." We have no record or tradition that Mary left this world by suffering a violent death, and the material sword can pierce the body only, and not the soul. Wherefore here we see the wisdom of Mary in that she was not ignorant of the heavenly mysteries. For, the word of God is quick, and powerful, and sharper than any two-edged sword, piercing even to the dividing asunder of soul and spirit, and of the joints and marrow, and is a discerner of the thoughts and intents of the heart for all things are naked and opened unto the eyes of the Son of God, from Whom also the secret things of our conscience are not hidden.

Lesson IX

There had been a triple prophecy; the prophecy of Simeon had followed the prophecy of the virgin, and the prophecy of the wife; those, namely, of Mary and Elizabeth. And now ought the widow also to prophesy, that no sex nor state might be wanting. And Anna is brought before us with such a title from her widowhood and her life, that we may well believe that she received the grace to announce the Advent of the Redeemer. In our exhortation addressed to widows we have already treated of her gifts at length, and, as we have much matter before us, we will not now again enter on the subject.

January 1 ~ Circumcision of the Lord

Duplex II Class

Lesson I ~ Rom 4:1–8

From the letter of St. Paul the Apostle to the Romans

What shall we say then that Abraham hath found, who is our father according to the flesh. For if Abraham were justified by works, he hath whereof to glory, but not before God. For what saith the Scripture? Abraham believed God, and it was reputed to him unto justice. Now to him that worketh, the reward is not reckoned according to grace, but according to debt. But to him that worketh not, yet believeth in him that justifieth the ungodly, his faith is reputed to justice, according to the purpose of the grace of God. As David also termeth the blessedness of a man, to whom God reputeth justice without works: Blessed are they whose iniquities are forgiven, and whose sins are covered. Blessed is the man to whom the Lord hath not imputed sin.

Lesson II ~ Rom 4:9–12

This blessedness then, doth it remain in the circumcision only, or in the uncircumcision also? For we say that unto Abraham faith was reputed to justice. How then was it reputed? When he was in circumcision, or in uncircumcision? Not in circumcision, but in uncircumcision. And he received the sign of circumcision, a seal of the justice of the faith, which he had, being uncircumcised; that he might be the father of all them that believe, being uncircumcised, that unto them also it may be reputed to justice: And might be the father of circumcision; not to them only, that are of the circumcision, but to them also that follow the steps of the faithful, that is in the uncircumcision of our father Abraham.

Lesson III ~ Rom 4:13–17

For not through the law was the promise to Abraham, or to his seed, that he should be heir of the world; but through the justice of faith. For if they who are of the law be heirs, faith is made void, the promise is made of no effect. For the law worketh wrath. For where there is no law, neither is there transgression. Therefore is it of faith, that according to grace the promise might be firm to all the seed; not to that only which is of the law, but to that also which is of the faith of Abraham, who is the father of us all, As it is written: I have made thee a father of many nations, before God, whom he believed, who quickeneth the dead; and calleth those things that are not, as those that are.

Lesson IV

Sermon by St. Leo, Pope

Dearly beloved brethren, whosoever will keep truly and honor piously this day's festival, it is necessary for him neither to think falsely of the Lord's Incarnation, nor poorly of the Lord's Divinity. For as there is danger, on the one hand, of denying the truth of Christ's participation of our nature, so is there no less danger, on the other, of doing insult to the equality of His glory with the glory of the Father. Wherefore, when we draw near to understand the mystery of Christ's Birth, wherein He was born of the Virgin Mary, we must leave the clouds of earthly imagination behind and pierce the fog of human wisdom with the eye of enlightened faith.

Lesson V

The authority on which we believe is the authority of God Himself; the teaching which we follow is the teaching of God Himself. Wherefore whether we lend the ear of our mind to the testimony of the Law, or to the revelations of the Prophets, or to the full pealing of the Gospel trumpet, that is true, which John the Son of Thunder, uttered when he was filled with the Holy Ghost and said: "In the beginning was the Word, and the Word was with God, and the Word was God. The Same was in the beginning with God. All things were made by Him, and without Him was not anything made." True also is his witness when he says: "The Word was made Flesh, and dwelt among us, and we beheld His glory, the glory as of the Only-begotten of the Father."

Lesson VI

The Person of the Son of God therefore remains unchanged and one, though He has two natures, keeping His own and taking ours. He appears as man to be the restorer of men, but abides all the while in His immutable Divinity. That Divinity which He shares with the Father was not a whit the less Almighty, nor did the form of a servant touch the form of God to derogate from it. The Most High and Everlasting Being, bending down for man's salvation, took the Manhood into His glory; He ceased not to be That which He is from everlasting. Hence we see the Only-begotten Son of God in one place confessing that the Father is greater than He, and in another declaring that He and the Father are One. This is an evident proof of the distinction of His two natures, and the unity of His Person; for He is inferior to the Father as touching His Manhood, and yet equal to the Father as touching His Divinity, and yet, though He be God and Man, He is not two, but One Christ.

Lesson VII

From the Holy Gospel according to St. Luke (Luke 2:21)

In that time, after eight days were accomplished, that the child should be circumcised, his name was called Jesus. And so on.

Homily by St. Ambrose, Bishop

So the Child is circumcised. This is the Child of Whom it is said:

Unto us a Child is born, unto us a Son is given. Made under the law to redeem them that were under the law. To present Him to the Lord. In my Commentary on Isaias I have already explained what is meant by being presented to the Lord in Jerusalem, and therefore I will not enter into the subject again. He that is circumcised in heart gains the protection of God, for the eyes of the Lord are upon the righteous. You will see that as all the ceremonies of the old law were types of realities in the new, so the circumcision of the body signified the cleansing of the heart from the guilt of sin.

Lesson VIII

But since the body and mind of man remain yet infected with a proneness to sin, the circumcision of the eighth day is also a type of that complete cleansing from sin which we shall have at the resurrection. This ceremony was also performed in obedience to the commandment of God: "Every male that openeth the womb shall be called holy unto the Lord." These words were written with especial reference to the delivery of the Blessed Virgin. Truly He That opened her womb was holy, for He was altogether without spot, and we may gather that the law was written specially for Him from the words of the Angel: "That Holy Thing Which shall be born of thee, shall be called the Son of God."

Lesson IX

Among all that are born of women the Lord Jesus Christ stood alone in holiness. Fresh from His immaculate Birth, He felt no contagion from human corruption, and His heavenly Majesty drove it away. If we are to follow the letter and say that every male that opens the womb is holy, how shall we explain that so many have been unrighteous? Was Achab holy? Were the false prophets holy? Were they holy on whom Elias justly called down fire from heaven? But He to Whom the sacred commandment of the law of God is mystically directed is the Holy One of Israel; Who also alone has opened the secret womb of His holy Virgin-bride the Church, filling her with a sinless fruitfulness to give birth to Christian souls.

Holy Name of Jesus
~Sunday Jan 2–5~

Duplex II Class

This Sunday falls between Jan 2nd and January 5th. The Lessons are proper.

Lesson I ~ Acts 3:1–8

From the Acts of the Apostles

Now Peter and John went up into the temple at the ninth hour of prayer. And a certain man who was lame from his mother's womb, was carried: whom they laid every day at the gate of the temple, which is called Beautiful, that he might ask alms of them that went into the temple. He, when he had seen Peter and John about to go into the temple, asked to receive an alms. But Peter with John fastening his eyes upon him, said: Look upon us. But he looked earnestly upon them, hoping that he should receive something of them. But Peter said: Silver and gold I have none; but what I have, I give thee: In the name of Jesus Christ of Nazareth, arise, and walk. And taking him by the right hand, he lifted him up, and forthwith his feet and soles received strength. And he leaping up, stood, and walked, and went in with them into the temple, walking, and leaping, and praising God.

Lesson II ~ Acts 3:9–16

And all the people saw him walking and praising God. And they knew him, that it was he who sat begging alms at the Beautiful gate of the temple: and they were filled with wonder and amazement at that which had happened to him. And as he held Peter and John, all the people ran to them to the porch which is called Solomon's, greatly wondering. But Peter seeing, made answer to the people: Ye men of Israel, why wonder you at this? or why look you upon us, as if by our strength or power we had made this man to walk? The God of Abraham, and the God of Isaac, and the God of Jacob, the God of our fathers, hath glorified his Son Jesus, whom you indeed delivered up and denied before the face of Pilate, when he judged he should be released. But you denied the Holy One and the Just, and desired a murderer to be granted unto you. But the author of life you killed, whom God hath raised from the dead, of which we are witnesses. And in the faith of his name, this man, whom you have seen and known, hath his name strengthened; and the faith which is by him, hath given this perfect soundness in the sight of you all.

Lesson III ~ Acts 4:5–12

And it came to pass on the morrow, that their princes, and ancients, and scribes, were gathered together in Jerusalem; And Annas the high priest, and Caiphas, and John, and Alexander, and as many as were of the kindred of the high priest. And setting them in the midst, they asked: By what power, or by what name, have you done this? Then Peter, filled with the Holy Ghost, said to them: Ye princes of the people, and ancients, hear: If we this day are examined concerning the good deed done to the infirm man, by what means he hath been made whole: Be it known to you all, and to all the people of Israel, that by the name of our Lord Jesus Christ of Nazareth, whom you crucified, whom God hath raised from the dead, even by him this man standeth here before you whole. This is the stone which was rejected by you the builders, which is become the head of the corner. Neither is there salvation in any other. For there is no other name under heaven given to men, whereby we must be saved.

Lesson IV

Sermon by St. Bernard, Abbot

It is not idly that the Holy Ghost likens the Name of the Bridegroom to oil, when He makes the Bride say to the Bridegroom: "thy Name is as oil poured forth." Oil indeed gives light, meat, and unction. It feedes fire, it nourishes the flesh, it soothes pain; it is light, food, and healing. Behold, Thus also is the Name of the Bridegroom. To preach it is to give light; to think of it is to feed the soul; to call on it is to win grace and unction. Let us take it point by point. What, thinkest thou, has made the light of faith so suddenly and so brightly to shine in the whole world but the preaching of the Name of Jesus? Is it not in the light of this Name that God has called us into His marvelous light, even that light wherewith we being enlightened and in His light seeing light Paul saith truly of us: "You were sometimes darkness, but now are you light in the Lord."

Lesson V

This is the Name which the Apostle was commanded to bear before Gentiles, and kings, and the children of Israel, the Name which he bore as a light to enlighten his people, crying everywhere "The night is far spent, the day is at hand; let us therefore cast off the works of darkness, and let us put on the armor of light, let us walk honestly as in the daylight." He pointed out to all that candle set upon a candlestick, preaching in every place Jesus and Him crucified. How did that Name shine forth and dazzle every eye that beheld it, when it came like lightning out of the mouth of Peter to give bodily strength to the feet of the lame man, and to clear the sight of many a blind soul? Cast he not fire when he said: In the Name of Jesus Christ of Nazareth, rise up and walk?

Lesson VI

The Name of Jesus is not a Name of light only, but it is meat also. Dost thou ever call it to mind, and remain unstrengthened? Is there anything like it to enrich the soul of him that thinks of it? What is there like it to restore the weakened senses, to fortify strength, to give birth to good lives and pure affections? The soul is fed on husks if that whereon it feeds lacks seasoning with this salt. If thou writest, thou hast no meaning for me if I read not of Jesus there. If thou preach, or dispute, thou hast no meaning for me if I hear not of Jesus there. The mention of Jesus is honey in the mouth, music in the ear, and gladness in the heart. It is our healing too. Is any sorrowful among us? Let the thought of Jesus come into his heart, and spring to his mouth. Behold, when the day of that Name begins to break, every cloud will flee away, and there will be a great calm. Does anyone fall into sin? Does anyone draw nigh to a hopeless death? And if he but call on the life-giving Name of Jesus, will he not draw the breath of a new life again?

Lesson VII

From the Holy Gospel according to St. Luke (Luke 2:21)

In that time: when eight days were accomplished, that the child should be circumcised, his name was called Jesus, which was called by the angel, before he was conceived in the womb. And so on.

Homily by St. Bernard, Abbot

Behold a mystery, great and full of wonder! The Child is circumcised, and His Name is called Jesus. Why are these two things thus mentioned together? It would seem that circumcision should rather be for the saved than for the Saviour; that the Saviour ought rather to be Circumciser than circumcised. But behold here the Mediator between God and men, how even from His childhood He joins the things of the Highest to the things of the lowest, the things of God to the things of men. He is born of a woman, but her womb is made fruitful without the loss of the flower of her virginity. He is wrapped in swaddling-bands, but these swaddling-bands are a theme for the jubilation of angels. He is laid in a manger, but a bright star stands in heaven over the place. So also in His circumcision, the ceremony gave proof of the reality of the Manhood which He had taken, and that Name which is above every name proclaimed the glory of His Blessed Majesty. As very son of Abraham He underwent circumcision; He assumed the Name of Jesus as very Son of God.

Lesson VIII

For Jesus bears not that Name as others have borne it before Him, as a vain and empty title. It is not in Him the shadow of a great Name, but the very meaning of that Name. That His Name was revealed from heaven is attested by the Evangelist where it is written: Which was so named of the Angel before He was conceived in the womb. After Jesus was born, men called Him Jesus, but angels called Him Jesus, before He was conceived in the womb. The One Lord is the Saviour of angels and of men; of men, since His Incarnation; of angels, from the beginning of their creation. His Name, says the Evangelist, was called Jesus, which was so named of the Angel before He was conceived in the womb. In the mouth therefore of two or three witnesses is every word established; and that word whereof the Prophet spoke as cut short, is set forth at length in the Gospel: the Word made Flesh.

Lesson IX is taken from the last of whatever feast this Sunday impedes between January 2nd-5th. See below for said feasts.

January 2 – Octave of St. Stephen

Lesson I – Rom 5:1–5

From the letter of St. Paul the Apostle to the Romans

Being justified therefore by faith, let us have peace with God, through our Lord Jesus Christ: By whom also we have access through faith into this grace, wherein we stand, and glory in the hope of the glory of the sons of God. And not only so; but we glory also in tribulations, knowing that tribulation worketh patience; And patience trial; and trial hope; And hope confoundeth not: because the charity of God is poured forth in our hearts, by the Holy Ghost, who is given to us.

Lesson II ~ Rom 5:6–9

For why did Christ, when as yet we were weak, according to the time, die for the ungodly? For scarce for a just man will one die; yet perhaps for a good man some one would dare to die. But God commendeth his charity towards us; because when as yet we were sinners, according to the time, Christ died for us; much more therefore, being now justified by his blood, shall we be saved from wrath through him.

Lesson III

Sermon by St. Augustine

Christ, the Captain of the Martyrs, has first suffered for us, leaving us an example that we should follow His steps. And truly, Blessed Stephen followed them, when, having confessed Christ, he was stoned to death by the Jews, and obtained the crown which his name had foreshown. For the meaning of the Greek name *Stephanos* is a crown. Already he had a crown for his name, a foreshadowing of the martyr's palm which he bears in heaven. When they stoned him, he did not rejoice at the thought that God would take vengeance on his persecutors. On the contrary, he prayed that they might be forgiven.

January 3 ~ Octave of St. John

Lesson I ~ Rom 6:1–5

From the letter of St. Paul the Apostle to the Romans

What shall we say, then? shall we continue in sin, that grace may abound? God forbid. For we that are dead to sin, how shall we live any longer therein? Know you not that all we, who are baptized in Christ Jesus, are baptized in his death? For we are buried together with him by baptism into death; that as Christ is risen from the dead by the glory of the Father, so we also may walk in newness of life. For if we have been planted together in the likeness of his death, we shall be also in the likeness of his resurrection.

Lesson II ~ Rom 6:6–11

Knowing this, that our old man is crucified with him, that the body of sin may be destroyed, to the end that we may serve sin no longer. For he that is dead is justified from sin. Now if we be dead with Christ, we believe that we shall live also together with Christ: Knowing that Christ rising again from the dead, dieth now no more, death shall no more have dominion over him. For in that he died to sin, he died once; but in that he liveth, he liveth unto God: So do you also reckon, that you are dead to sin, but alive unto God, in Christ Jesus our Lord.

Lesson III

From a treatise by St. Augustine, Bishop

Of the Four Evangelists, or, rather, the Four Writers of the one Gospel, the holy Apostle John hath not unworthily been compared by spiritual writers to an eagle, because of the lofty and glorious flight of his teaching, soaring above the other three; a flight that raises not himself alone, but also the hearts of all whosoever will hear him. The other three writers walk with the Lord upon earth, as with a man, and enlarge little upon His Divinity; but John, as though it had wearied him to walk upon earth, in the very first words of his writing, rises not above the earth only, or above the firmament and the heavens, but above every angel, and above every power of things unseen, and flies directly to Him by Whom all things were made, saying "In the beginning was the Word, and the Word was with God, and the Word was God."

January 4 ~ Octave of Holy Innocents

Lesson I ~ Rom 7:1–3

From the letter of St. Paul the Apostle to the Romans

Know you not, brethren, for I speak to them that know the law, that the law hath dominion over a man, as long as it liveth? For the woman that hath a husband, whilst her husband liveth is bound to the law. But if her husband be dead, she is loosed from the law of her husband. Therefore, whilst her husband liveth, she shall be called an adulteress, if she be with another man: but if her husband be dead, she is delivered from the law of her husband; so that she is not an adulteress, if she be with another man.

Lesson II ~ Rom 7:4–6

Therefore, my brethren, you also are become dead to the law, by the body of Christ; that you may belong to another, who is risen again from the dead, that we may bring forth fruit to God. For when we were in the flesh, the passions of sins, which were by the law, did work in our members, to bring forth fruit unto death. But now we are loosed from the law of death, wherein we were detained; so that we should serve in newness of spirit, and not in the oldness of the letter.

Lesson III

Sermon by St. Augustine, Bishop

The Lord is born, and sorrow breaks out, not in heaven but on earth; to mothers is proclaimed lamentation, to angels joy, to children translation. God is born, and innocence must be offered up to Him Who comes to condemn the malice of the world. The Lamb that takes away the sins of the world is come to be crucified, and the tender flock is brought to the sacrifice. But the mothers will lament over them whose inarticulate bleating is silenced for ever. Let us turn a look on this great martyrdom, this heart-rending sorrow. The sword is drawn, though there is no offense to punish, only jealousy shrieking for Him Who is born, and does no violence. And here are mothers weeping over the lambs of the flock. In Ramah was there a voice heard, weeping and great mourning, which shall be returned hereafter, but they are pledges taken without being given, impounded without being entrusted.

January 5 ~ Vigil of the Epiphany

Semiduplex

Lesson I ~ Rom 8:1–4

From the letter of St. Paul the Apostle to the Romans

There is now therefore no condemnation to them that are in Christ Jesus, who walk not according to the flesh. For the law of the spirit of life, in Christ Jesus, hath delivered me from the law of sin and of death. For what the law could not do, in that it was weak through the flesh; God sending his own Son, in the likeness of sinful flesh and of sin, hath condemned sin in the flesh; That the justification of the law might be fulfilled in us, who walk not according to the flesh, but according to the spirit.

Lesson II ~ Rom 8:5–9

For they that are according to the flesh, mind the things that are of the flesh; but they that are according to the spirit, mind the things that are of the spirit. For the wisdom of the flesh is death; but the wisdom of the spirit is life and peace. Because the wisdom of the flesh is an enemy to God; for it is not subject to the law of God, neither can it be. And they who are in the flesh, cannot please God. But you are not in the flesh, but in the spirit, if so be that the Spirit of God dwell in you.

Lesson III ~ Rom 8:9–11

Now if any man have not the Spirit of Christ, he is none of his. And if Christ be in you, the body indeed is dead, because of sin; but the spirit liveth, because of justification. And if the Spirit of him that raised up Jesus from the dead, dwell in you; he that raised up Jesus Christ from the dead, shall quicken also your mortal bodies, because of his Spirit that dwelleth in you.

Lesson IV

Sermon by St. Augustine, Bishop.

Our Lord Jesus Christ, dearest brethren, who in eternity is the Creator of all things, was as at this time born of a mother and became our Saviour. It was as at this time that he willed to be born for us in earthly time, so as to lead us to the Father's eternity. God is made man, that man may be made as God. That man may eat Angels' food, the Lord of Angels was as on this day made man.

Lesson V

Now is fulfilled that prophecy: "Drop down, ye heavens, from above, and let the skies pour down righteousness: let the earth open, and bring forth a Saviour." He who made all things is therefore himself made, that those who are lost may be found. It is even as man is made to testify of himself in the Psalms: "Before I was humbled, I went wrong." Man sinned and became guilty. God is born man, that the guilty may be delivered. Man fell, but God descended. Man fell miserably, God descended mercifully. Man fell by pride, God descended with grace.

Lesson VI

O my brethren, what a miracle! what a wonder! The laws of nature are changed concerning man: God is born, a Virgin conceives without a husband; the Word of God is wed to one who knows no man; she is at once Mother and Virgin. A Mother yet inviolate: a Virgin having a Son; knowing no man, ever sealed, yet not unfruitful. For he alone was born without sin. He alone was born without human embrace, begotten not of the will of the flesh, but of the obedience of the mind.

Lesson VII

From the Holy Gospel according to St. Matthew (Matt 2:19–23)

In that time: When Herod was dead, behold an angel of the Lord appeared in sleep to Joseph in Egypt, Saying: Arise, and take the child and his mother, and go into the land of Israel. And so on.

Homily by St. Jerome, Priest

From the words which are used in this passage of the Gospel, we may understand that there were others beside Herod which sought the young Child's life probably the Priests and Scribes. And he Joseph arose, and took the young Child and His Mother. It is not written, He took his wife and child, but he took the young Child and His Mother; whence it is clear that the holy Evangelist wills to imply that Joseph was not the father, but the Guardian of Jesus, not the husband, but the Betrothed of Mary.

Lesson VIII

"But when he heard that Archelaus did reign in Judea, in the room of his father Herod, he was afraid to go there." There are some persons so grossly ignorant of history that they confuse themselves over the two Herods, as if the one mentioned here were the same who afterwards set our Lord at nought during His Passion, and they cannot understand how he should now be said to be dead. The Herod who was made friends with Pilate over Christ's death, was the son of the Herod who massacred the infants of Bethlehem, and the brother of Archelaus.

Lesson IX

"He shall be called a Nazarene." The Evangelist, in quoting these words, says that they were spoken by the Prophets (Plural). If he had been citing any one precise passage he would have said by the Prophet, in the Singular. But he is citing the sense of the Prophets, and not any individual passage in any of their writings. He seems to refer to the fact that in Hebrew the word Nazarene signifies holy, and that Christ is the Holy One of God is the common declaration of all the Scriptures.

EPIPHANYTIDE

January 6 ~ EPIPHANY OF THE LORD

Duplex I Class

Lesson I ~ Isa 55:1–4

From the book of Isaias

All you that thirst, come to the waters: and you that have no money make haste, buy, and eat: come ye, buy wine and milk without money, and without any price. Why do you spend money for that which is not bread, and your labour for that which doth not satisfy you? Hearken diligently to me, and eat that which is good, and your soul shall be delighted in fatness. Incline your ear and come to me: hear and your soul shall live, and I will make an everlasting covenant with you, the faithful mercies of David. Behold I have given him for a witness to the people, for a leader and a master to the Gentiles.

Lesson II ~ Isa 60:1–6

Arise, be enlightened, O Jerusalem: for thy light is come, and the glory of the Lord is risen upon thee. For behold darkness shall cover the earth, and a mist the people: but the Lord shall arise upon thee, and his glory shall be seen upon thee. And the Gentiles shall walk in thy light, and kings in the brightness of thy rising. Lift up thy eyes round about, and see: all these are gathered together, they are come to thee: thy sons shall come from afar, and thy daughters shall rise up at thy side. Then shalt thou see, and abound, and thy heart shall wonder and be enlarged, when the multitude of the sea shall be converted to thee, the strength of the Gentiles shall come to thee. The multitude of camels shall cover thee, the dromedaries of Madian and Epha: all they from Saba shall come, bringing gold and frankincense: and shewing forth praise to the Lord.

Lesson III ~ Isa 61:10–11; 62:1

I will greatly rejoice in the Lord, and my soul shall be joyful in my God: for he hath clothed me with the garments of salvation: and with the robe of justice he hath covered me, as a bridegroom decked with a crown, and as a bride adorned with her jewels. For as the earth bringeth forth her bud, and as the garden causeth her seed to shoot forth: so shall the Lord God make justice to spring forth, and praise before all the nations. For Sion's sake I will not hold my peace, and for the sake of Jerusalem, I will not rest till her just one come forth as brightness, and her saviour be lighted as a lamp.

Lesson IV

Sermon by St. Leo, Pope

Dearly beloved brethren, rejoice in the Lord; again I say, rejoice. But a few days are past since the solemnity of Christ's Birth, and now the glorious light of His Manifestation is breaking upon us. On that day the Virgin brought Him forth, and on this the world knew Him. The Word made Flesh was pleased to reveal Himself by degrees to those for whom He had come. When Jesus was born He was manifested indeed to the believing, but hidden from His enemies. Already indeed the heavens declared the glory of God, and their sound went out into all lands, when the Herald Angels appeared to tell to the shepherds the glad tidings of a Saviour's Birth; and now the guiding star leads the wise men to worship Him, that from the rising of the sun to the going down thereof, the Birth of the true King may be known abroad; that through those wise men the kingdoms of the east might learn the great truth, and the Roman empire remain no more in darkness.

Lesson V

The very cruelty of Herod, when he strove to crush at His birth this King Whom he alone feared, was made a blind means to carry out this dispensation of mercy. While the tyrant with horrid guilt sought to slay the little Child he did not know amid an indiscriminate slaughter of innocents, his infamous act served to spread wider abroad the heaven-told news of the Birth of the Lord. Thus were these glad tidings loudly proclaimed, both by the novelty of their story, and the iniquity of their enemies. Then was the Saviour borne into Egypt, that nation, of a long time hardened in idolatry, might by the mysterious virtue which went out of Him, even when His presence was unknown, be prepared for the saving light so soon to dawn on them, and might receive the Truth as a wanderer even before they had banished falsehood.

Lesson VI

Dearly beloved brethren, we recognize in the wise men who came to worship Christ, the first-fruits of that dispensation to the Gentiles wherein we also are called and enlightened. Let us then keep this Feast with grateful hearts, in thanksgiving for our blessed hope, whereof it commemorates the dawn. From that worship paid to the new-born Christ is to be dated the entry of us Gentiles upon our heirship of God and coheirship with Christ. Since that joyful day the Scriptures which testify of Christ have lain open for us as well as for the Jews. Yea, their blindness rejected that Truth, Which, since that day, has shed Its bright beams upon all nations. Let all observance, then, be paid to this most sacred day, whereon the Author of our salvation was made manifest, and as the wise men fell down and worshipped Him in the manger, so let us fall down and worship Him enthroned Almighty in heaven. As they also opened their treasures and presented unto Him mystic and symbolic gifts, so let us strive to open our hearts to Him, and offer Him from thence some worthy offering.

Lesson VII

From the Holy Gospel according to St. Matthew (Matt 2:1–12)

When Jesus therefore was born in Bethlehem of Juda, in the days of king Herod, behold, there came wise men from the east to Jerusalem, saying: Where is he that is born king of the Jews? And so on.

Homily by Pope St. Gregory

Dearly beloved brethren, do you hear from the Gospel lesson how, when the King of heaven was born, the king of earth was troubled? The heights of heaven are opened and the depths of earth are stirred. Let us now consider the question, why, when the Redeemer was born, an angel brought the news to the shepherds of Judea, but a star led the wise men of the East to worship Him. It seems as if the Jews as reasonable creatures received a revelation from a reasonable being, that is, an angel, but the Gentiles without, being as brutes, are roused not by a voice, but by a sign, that is, a star. Hence Paul has it: a sign, not to them that believe, but to them that believe not; for prophesying serves not for them that believe not, but for them which believe. So the prophesying, that is, of the angel was given to them that believed, and the sign to them that believed not.

Lesson VIII

Thus also we remark that afterwards the Redeemer was preached among the Gentiles not by Himself, but by His Apostles, even as, when a little Child, He is shown to them, not by the voice of angels, but merely by the vision of a star. When He Himself had begun to speak He was made known to us by speakers, but when He lay silent in the manger, by that silent testimony in heaven. But whether we consider the signs which accompanied His birth or His death, this thing is wonderful, namely, the hardness of heart of the Jews, who would not believe in Him either for prophesying or for miracles.

Lesson IX

All things which He had made, bore witness that their Maker was come. Let me reckon them after the manner of men. The heavens knew that He was God, and sent a star to shine over where He lay. The sea knew it, and bore Him up when He walked upon it. The earth knew it, and quaked when He died. The sun knew it, and was darkened. The rocks and walls knew it, and rent at the hour of His death. Hell knew it, and gave up the dead that were in it. And yet up to this very hour the hearts of the unbelieving Jews will not acknowledge that He to Whom all nature testified is their God, and, being more hardened than the rocks, refuse to be rent by repentance.

Sunday within the Octave of the Epiphany of the Lord ~The Holy Family~

Major Duplex

Lesson I ~ Col 3:12–16

From the letter of St. Paul the Apostle to the Colossians

Put ye on therefore, as the elect of God, holy, and beloved, the bowels of mercy, benignity, humility, modesty, patience: Bearing with one another, and forgiving one another, if any have a complaint against another: even as the Lord hath forgiven you, so do you also. But above all these things have charity, which is the bond of perfection: And let the peace of Christ rejoice in your hearts, wherein also you are called in one body: and be ye thankful. Let the word of Christ dwell in you abundantly, in all wisdom: teaching and admonishing one another in psalms, hymns, and spiritual canticles, singing in grace in your hearts to God.

Lesson II ~ Col 3:17–21

All whatsoever you do in word or in work, do all in the name of the Lord Jesus Christ, giving thanks to God and the Father by him. Wives, be subject to your husbands, as it behoveth in the Lord. Husbands, love your wives, and be not bitter towards them. Children, obey your parents in all things: for this is well pleasing to the Lord. Fathers, provoke not your children to indignation, lest they be discouraged.

Lesson III ~ Col 3:22–25; 4:1–2

Servants, obey in all things your masters according to the flesh, not serving to the eye, as pleasing men, but in simplicity of heart, fearing God. Whatsoever you do, do it from the heart, as to the Lord, and not to men: Knowing that you shall receive of the Lord the reward of inheritance. Serve ye the Lord Christ. For he that doth wrong, shall receive for that which he hath done wrongfully: and there is no respect of persons with God. Masters, do to your servants that which is just and equal: knowing that you also have a master in heaven. Be instant in prayer; watching in it with thanksgiving:

Lesson IV

From the Apostolic Letters of Pope Leo XIII *Neminem fugit*

When God in his mercy determined to accomplish the work of man's renewal, which same had so many long ages awaited, he appointed and ordained this work in such a way that its very beginning might show to the world the august spectacle of a Family which was known to be divinely constituted; that therein all men might behold a perfect model, as well of domestic life as of every virtue and pattern of holiness: for such indeed was the Holy Family of Nazareth. There in secret dwelt the Sun of Righteousness, until the time when he should shine out in full splendor in the sight of all nations. There Christ, our God and Saviour, lived with his Virgin Mother, and with that most holy man Joseph, who held to him the place of father. No one can doubt that in this Holy Family was displayed every virtue which can be called forth by an ordinary home life, with its mutual services of charity, its holy intercourse, and its practices of godly piety, since the Holy Family was destined to be a pattern to all others. For that very reason was it established by the merciful designs of Providence, namely, that every Christian, in every walk of life and in every place, might easily, if he would but give heed to it, have before him a motive and a pattern for the good life.

Lesson V

To all fathers of families, Joseph is verily the best model of paternal vigilance and care. In the most holy Virgin Mother of God, mothers may find an excellent example of love, modesty, resignation of spirit, and the perfecting of faith. And in Jesus, who was subject to his parents, the children of the family have a divine pattern of obedience which they can admire, reverence, and imitate. Those who are of noble birth may learn, from this Family of royal blood, how to live simply in times of prosperity, and how to retain their dignity in times of distress. The rich may learn that moral worth is to be more highly esteemed than wealth. Artisans, and all such as are bitterly grieved by the narrow and slender means of their families, if they would but consider the sublime holiness of the members of this domestic fellowship, cannot fail to find some cause for rejoicing in their lot, rather than for being merely dissatisfied with it. In common with the Holy Family, they have to work and to provide for the daily wants of life. Joseph had to engage in trade in order to live; even the divine hands labored at an artisan's calling. It is not to be wondered at that the wealthiest men, if truly wise, have been willing to cast away their riches, and to embrace a life of poverty with Jesus, Mary, and Joseph.

Lesson VI

From the foregoing it is evident how natural and fitting it was that devotion to the Holy Family should in due time have grown up amongst Catholics; and once begun, that it should spread far and wide. Proof of this lies first in the sodalities instituted under the invocation of the Holy Family; then in the unique honors bestowed upon it; and above all, by the privileges and favors granted to this devotion by our predecessors to stimulate fervor and piety in its regard. This devotion was already held in great esteem in the seventeenth century. Widely propagated in Italy, France, and Belgium, it spread over almost the whole of Europe; thence, crossing the wide ocean, through Canada it made is way in the Americas, and finding favor there, became very flourishing. Indeed, among Christian families, nothing more salutary nor efficacious can be imagined than the example of the Holy Family, where are to be found all domestic virtues in perfection and completeness. When Jesus, Mary, and Joseph are invoked in the home, charity is likely to be maintained in the family through their example and heavenly entreaty; a good influence is thus exerted over conduct; the practice of virtue is thus incited; and thus the hardships which are everywhere wont to harass mankind, are both mitigated and made easier to bear. To increase devotion to the Holy Family, Pope Leo XIII prescribed that Christian families should be consecrated thereto. Benedict XV extended the Mass and Office to the whole Church.

Lesson VII

From the Holy Gospel according to St. Luke (Luke 2:42–52)

And when he was twelve years old, they going up into Jerusalem, according to the custom of the feast, And having fulfilled the days, when they returned, the child Jesus remained in Jerusalem; and his parents knew it not. And so on.

Homily by St. Bernard, Abbot

"And he was subject unto them." Who was subject? And to whom? God to man! God, I repeat, to whom the Angels are subject, whom the Principalities and Powers do obey, was subject to Mary; and not only to Mary, but to Joseph also for Mary's sake. Marvel, therefore, both at God and man, and choose that which gives greater wonder, whether it be the most loving condescension of the Son, or the exceeding great dignity of his Mother. Both amaze us, both are marvelous. That God should obey a woman is lowliness without parallel, that woman should rule over God, an elevation beyond comparison. In praise of virgins it is sung of them alone, that "they follow the Lamb whithersoever he goeth." Of what praise do you judge that woman to be worthy who is thus placed before the Lamb of God?

Lesson VIII

Learn, O man, to obey! Learn, O earth, to be subject! Learn, O dust, to submit! The Evangelist speaking of thy Creator says: "And he was subject unto them." And there is no doubt that this shows us that God was subject to Mary and Joseph. Shame on you, you proud entities of dust and ashes! God abases himself, and dost thou, O creature sprung from the earth, exalt thyself? God makes himself subject to man, and dost thou, who art always so eager to lord it over men, set up thyself to lord it over thy Creator? For as often as I desire pre-eminency over men, so often do I strive to excel God. For of him it was said: "And he was subject unto them." If thou disdainest, O man, to follow the example of man, at least thou canst follow thy Creator without dishonour. If thou canst not, perchance, follow him wheresoever he goes, deign at least to follow him in this thing wherein he has emptied himself, and made himself of no reputation, for the sake of such as thou.

Lesson IX

If thou canst not enter upon the lofty paths of virginity, at least follow God by the most safe road of humility. If any turn aside from this straight way, though they be virgins, they do not "follow the Lamb," if the truth be told, "whithersoever he goeth." The humble man, though stained with sin, follows the Lamb; the virgin, though proud, also follows; but neither of these two follows "whithersoever he goeth." The former cannot attain unto the purity of the Lamb, for he is without spot; the latter deigns not to descend to his meekness, who was dumb, not before the shearer, but before the murderer. Yet the sinner who follows in humility has chosen a more saving way than the proud man who follows in virginity; for the humble one makes satisfaction, and is cleansed of his impurity, but the proud one's chastity is stained by his pride.

January 7 - Day 2 within the Octave of the Epiphany of the Lord

Semiduplex

Lesson I - Rom 9:1–5

From the letter of St. Paul the Apostle to the Romans

I speak the truth in Christ, I lie not, my conscience bearing me witness in the Holy Ghost: That I have great sadness, and continual sorrow in my heart. For I wished myself to be an anathema from Christ, for my brethren, who are my kinsmen according to the flesh, Who are Israelites, to whom belongeth the adoption as of children, and the glory, and the testament, and the giving of the law, and the service of God, and the promises: Whose are the fathers, and of whom is Christ, according to the flesh, who is over all things, God blessed for ever. Amen.

Lesson II - Rom 9:6–10

Not as though the word of God hath miscarried. For all are not Israelites that are of Israel: Neither are all they that are the seed of Abraham, children; but in Isaac shall thy seed be called: That is to say, not they that are the children of the flesh, are the children of God; but they, that are the children of the promise, are accounted for the seed. For this is the word of promise: According to this time will I come; and Sara shall have a son. And not only she. But when Rebecca also had conceived at once, of Isaac our father.

Lesson III - Rom 9:11–16

For when the children were not yet born, nor had done any good or evil that the purpose of God, according to election, might stand, Not of works, but of him that calleth, it was said to her: The elder shall serve the younger. As it is written: Jacob I have loved, but Esau I have hated. What shall we say then? Is there injustice with God? God forbid. For he saith to Moses: I will have mercy on whom I will have mercy; and I will shew mercy to whom I will shew mercy. So then it is not of him that willeth, nor of him that runneth, but of God that sheweth mercy.

Lesson IV

Sermon by St. Augustine, Bishop

Wise men came from the East to worship the Virgin's Son. This is the event which we this day commemorate, the occasion in honor of which this sermon is preached.

On them that day first broke in gladness, which year by year, now comes round to us for celebration. They were the first-fruits of that Gentile Church whereof we are the in-gathering. To us the voice of Apostles, to them a star, as a voice from heaven, proclaimed the advent of a Saviour; and to us the voice of the Apostolic preachers is also as a voice from heaven, a heaven declaring the glory of God.

Lesson V

Great is the mystery! While He lay in the manger, He drew to Himself wise men from the East; while He was unknown in the stable, He was recognized in the heavens; and, being recognized in the heavens, made Himself known in the stable. So this day is called in the Greek *Epiphaneia*, which is, being interpreted, Manifestation. Wherein is manifested both the greatness and the lowliness of Him Whose greatness was attested in the stars of heaven, and Who, being sought on earth, is found so lowly that there is no room for Him in the inn. And yet, though to be found in fashion as a little Child wrapped in swaddling clothes, He is the object of worship to the wise men and of terror to the godless.

Lesson VI

Now Herod feared when he heard from the wise men of Him Whom they sought, and of Whose birth they knew by the witness of a star. What will be the fearful judgment-seat of Him, Who, even as a Suckling, struck terror into haughty kings? How much wiser is the thought of those kings who seek Christ like the wise men, to worship Him, than of those who seek Him, like Herod, to slay Him! who seek to put Him to that same death, which He came to suffer from His enemies for their own salvation, and which, by His death, He hath trodden down! Kings will do well to fear Him Who now sits at the right hand of the Father, and Whom Herod feared when He hung upon His mother's breast.

Lesson VII

From the Holy Gospel according to St. Matthew (Matt 2:1–12)

When Jesus therefore was born in Bethlehem of Juda, in the days of king Herod, behold, there came wise men from the east to Jerusalem. Saying, Where is he that is born king of the Jews? And so on.

Homily by Pope St. Gregory

When Herod knew of the birth of our King, he betook himself to his cunning wiles, and lest he should be deprived of an earthly kingdom he desired the wise men to search diligently for the young Child, and when they had found Him, to bring him word again. He said that he also might come and worship Him, but, in reality, that, when he had found Him, he might put Him to death. But, behold, of how light weight is the malice of man, when it is tried against the counsel of God. It is written There is no wisdom, nor understanding, nor counsel, against the Lord. So the star which the wise men saw in the East, still led them on; they found the new-born King, and presented unto Him gifts; then they were warned in a dream that they should not return to Herod. And as it came to pass that when Herod sought Jesus and could not find Him, even so is it with hypocrites who, while they make pretense to seek the Lord to worship Him, find Him not.

Lesson VIII

It is as well to know that it is one of the opinions of the Priscillianist heretics that every man is born under the influence of a star; and, to confirm this notion, they bring forward the instance of the star of Bethlehem, which appeared when the Lord was born; and which they call His star, that is, the star ruling over His fate or destiny. But if we consider the words of the Gospel concerning this star, they are: "It went before, till it came and stood over where the young Child was." Whence we see that it was not the young Child Who followed the star, but the star which followed the young Child, as if to show that the young Child ruled the star, instead of the star ruling Him.

Lesson IX

But I pray that the hearts of the faithful may ever be free from the thought that anything rules their destiny. In this world there is but One Who rules the destiny of man, even He Who made man; neither was man made for the stars, but the stars for man; and if we say that they rule his destiny, we set them above him for whose service they were made. When Jacob came out of his mother's womb, and his hand took hold on his elder brother Esau's heel, he could not have done so unless this his first movement had been behind his brother, and, nevertheless, such was not in after life the position of those two brethren whom their mother brought forth at one birth.

January 8 ~ Day 3
within the Octave of the
Epiphany of the Lord

Semiduplex

Lesson I ~ Rom 12:1–3

From the letter of St. Paul the Apostle to the Romans

I beseech you therefore, brethren, by the mercy of God, that you present your bodies a living sacrifice, holy, pleasing unto God, your reasonable service. And be not conformed to this world; but be reformed in the newness of your mind, that you may prove what is the good, and the acceptable, and the perfect will of God. For I say, by the grace that is given me, to all that are among you, not to be more wise than it behoveth to be wise, but to be wise unto sobriety, and according as God hath divided to every one the measure of faith.

Lesson II ~ Rom 12:4–8

For as in one body we have many members, but all the members have not the same office: So we being many, are one body in Christ, and every one members one of another. And having different gifts, according to the grace that is given us, either prophecy, to be used according to the rule of faith; Or ministry, in ministering; or he that teacheth, in doctrine; He that exhorteth, in exhorting; he that giveth, with simplicity; he that ruleth, with carefulness; he that sheweth mercy, with cheerfulness.

Lesson III ~ Rom 12:9–16

Let love be without dissimulation. Hating that which is evil, cleaving to that which is good. Loving one another with the charity of brotherhood, with honour preventing one another. In carefulness not slothful. In spirit fervent. Serving the Lord. Rejoicing in hope. Patient in tribulation. Instant in prayer. Communicating to the necessities of the saints. Pursuing hospitality. Bless them that persecute you: bless, and curse not. Rejoice with them that rejoice; weep with them that weep. Being of one mind one towards another. Not minding high things, but consenting to the humble. Be not wise in your own conceits.

Lesson IV

Sermon by St. Augustine, Bishop

Many kings of the Jews had been born, and died, but which of them was sought after by wise men to worship him? Not one. For not one had been proclaimed by the voice of heaven. Let us not also pass by the fact that the enlightenment of the wise men stands in strong contrast to the blindness of the Jews. The first came from far to find Him Whom, being born in their midst, the second knew not.

Lesson V

The wise men found the young Child among those who denied Him. These holy pilgrims came and worshipped the yet silent Christ in the land whose inhabitants, after He grew up and worked miracles, crucified Him. They worshipped in that tiny Body the God Whom, amid great signs and wonders, the Jews would not spare even as a man. They who saw the Star which shone at His birth, put it to more profit than they who saw the sun veiled at His death.

Lesson VI

The star which led the wise men towards the place where the new-born God dwelt with His Virgin Mother, ceased to shine when it came to the city of Jerusalem, while they were inquiring of the Jews where Christ should be born. The Jews answered them according to the testimony of the Divine Scriptures In Bethlehem of Judah for thus it is written "And thou Bethlehem in the land of Judah, art not the least among the princes of Judah, for out of thee shall come a Governor, that shall rule My people Israel." What else are we to understand that God's Providence would here signify, than that there should remain among the Jews those Divine Writings only, whereby the Gentiles are enlightened, while they themselves remain dark?

Lesson VII

From the Holy Gospel according to St. Matthew (Matt 2:1–12)

When Jesus therefore was born in Bethlehem of Juda, in the days of king Herod, behold, there came wise men from the east to Jerusalem. Saying, Where is he that is born king of the Jews? And so on.

Homily by Pope St. Gregory

The wise men brought gold, frankincense, and myrrh. Gold is the fitting gift to a King, frankincense is offered in sacrifice to God, and with myrrh are embalmed the bodies of the dead. By the gifts, therefore, which they presented unto Him, the wise men set forth three things concerning Him unto Whom they offered them; by the gold, that He was King; by the frankincense, that He was God; and by the myrrh, that He was to die. There are some heretics who believe Him to be God but confess not His Kingly dominion over all things; these offer unto Him frankincense, but refuse Him gold. There are some others who admit that He is King, but deny that He is God; these present unto Him gold, but will not give Him frankincense.

Lesson VIII

There are some other heretics who profess that Christ is both God and King, but not that He took a dying nature; these offer Him gold and frankincense, but not myrrh for the Manhood. Let us, however, present gold unto the new-born Lord, acknowledging His universal Kingship; let us offer unto Him frankincense, confessing that He Who hath been made manifest unto us in time, is God before time was; let us give unto Him myrrh, believing that He Who cannot suffer as touching His Divinity, was made capable of death as touching the manhood which He shares with us.

Lesson IX

There is also another signification in this gold, frankincense, and myrrh. Gold is a type of wisdom; as says Solomon: "In the mouth of the wise abideth a treasure to be desired." Frankincense, which is burnt in honor of God, is a figure of prayer; witness the words of the Psalmist: "Let my prayer be set forth as incense before thee." By myrrh is represented the putting to death of the body; as where the holy Church says of her laborers who strive for God even unto death: "My hands dropped with myrrh."

January 9 ~ Day 4 within the Octave of the Epiphany of the Lord

Semiduplex

Lesson I ~ Rom 13:1–4

From the letter of St. Paul the Apostle to the Romans

Let every soul be subject to higher powers: for there is no power but from God: and those that are, are ordained of God. Therefore he that resisteth the power, resisteth the ordinance of God. And they that resist, purchase to themselves damnation. For princes are not a terror to the good work, but to the evil. Wilt thou then not be afraid of the power? Do that which is good: and thou shalt have praise from the same. For he is God's minister to thee, for good. But if thou do that which is evil, fear: for he beareth not the sword in vain.

Lesson II ~ Rom 13:4–7

For he is God's minister: an avenger to execute wrath upon him that doth evil. Wherefore be subject of necessity, not only for wrath, but also for conscience' sake. For therefore also you pay tribute. For they are the ministers of God, serving unto this purpose. Render therefore to all men their dues. Tribute, to whom tribute is due: custom, to whom custom: fear, to whom fear: honour, to whom honour.

Lesson III ~ Rom 13:8–10

Owe no man any thing, but to love one another. For he that loveth his neighbour hath fulfilled the law. For: Thou shalt not commit adultery: Thou shalt not kill: Thou shalt not steal: Thou shalt not bear false witness: Thou shalt not covet. And if there be any other commandment, it is comprised in this word: Thou shalt love thy neighbour as thyself. The love of our neighbour worketh no evil. Love therefore is the fulfilling of the law.

Lesson IV

Sermon by St. Leo, Pope

Dearly beloved brethren, we have but lately celebrated that day whereon the inviolate virginity of Blessed Mary gave to man a Saviour. And now the venerable solemnity of the Epiphany gives us a continuance of joy. So that by the nearness of these two holy Feasts, the freshness of our gladness and the quickening of our faith has no time wherein to die away. And truly it concerns the salvation of all men, that the Mediator between God and men is already made manifest before leaving the humble city of His birth.

Lesson V

It is true that the Lord chose the nation of Israel, and in that nation one family, whence to take upon Him that nature which He shares with all mankind, but, at the same time, He would not that the narrow walls of His Mother's house should imprison within them all the brightness of His appearing, and, as He was pleased to be born for all, so willed He to be forthwith made manifest to all. Three wise men in the East, therefore, saw a new and brilliant star, which, by excelling all others in brightness and beauty, attracted the eyes and thoughts of all beholders and thereby it became at once evident that some new and great event had befallen.

Lesson VI

Then He Who had given the sign, gave understanding to those that saw it; and having given to them to understand that He was born, He gave them the grace to seek Him; and, being sought by them, was pleased to be found. The three wise men followed the guiding of the heavenly light, and, with their eyes firmly fixed upon the glory that went before them, were so led by the light of grace as to obtain the knowledge of truth. They, knowing that He was born a King, sought Him in the Royal City; but He Who had taken upon Him the form of a servant, and came not to judge but to be judged, had chosen Bethlehem for His birth, and Jerusalem for His Suffering.

Lesson VII

From the Holy Gospel according to St. Matthew (Matt 2:1–12)

When Jesus therefore was born in Bethlehem of Juda, in the days of king Herod, behold, there came wise men from the east to Jerusalem. Saying, Where is he that is born king of the Jews? And so on.

Homily by Pope St. Gregory

The wise men teach us a great lesson in that they departed into their own country another way. That which they did, being warned of God in a dream, we ought to do. Our country is heaven; and, when we have once known Jesus, we can never get there by returning on the way wherein we walked before we knew Him. We have left our country far, by the way of pride, and disobedience, and worldliness, and forbidden indulgence we must seek that heavenly Fatherland by tears, by subjection, by contempt of the things which are seen, and by curbing the fleshly appetites.

Lesson VIII

Let us then depart into our own country another way. They that have by enjoyment put themselves away from it, must seek it again by sorrow. Therefore, my dearly beloved brethren, it behooves us to be ever fearful and watch, having continually before the eyes of our heart, on the one hand, the guilt of our doings, and, on the other, the judgment at the latter day. It behooves us to think how that awful Judge will surely come, Whose judgment is hanging over us, and has not yet fallen; the wrath to come is before sinners, and has not yet smitten them and the Judge yet tarries in order that, when He comes, there may haply be less to condemn.

Lesson IX

Let us afflict ourselves for our faults with weeping, and, with the Psalmist, let us come before His Presence with thanksgiving. Let us take heed that we be not fooled by the appearance of earthly happiness, or seduced by the vanity of earthly pleasure. For the Judge is at hand, even He That says "Woe unto you that laugh now, for you shall mourn and weep." Hence also Solomon says: "Even in laughter the heart is sorrowful; and the end of that mirth is heaviness." And again: "I said of laughter, It is mad; and of mirth, What doeth it?" And yet again: "The heart of the wise is in the house of mourning, but the heart of fools is in the house of mirth."

January 10 – Day 5 within the Octave of the Epiphany of the Lord

Semiduplex

Lesson I – Rom 14:1–4

From the letter of St. Paul the Apostle to the Romans

Now him that is weak in faith, take unto you: not in disputes about thoughts. For one believeth that he may eat all things: but he that is weak, let him eat herbs. Let not him that eateth, despise him that eateth not: and he that eateth not, let him not judge him that eateth. For God hath taken him to him. Who art thou that judgest another man's servant? To his own lord he standeth or falleth. And he shall stand: for God is able to make him stand.

Lesson II - Rom 14:5–8

For one judgeth between day and day: and another judgeth every day: let every man abound in his own sense. He that regardeth the day, regardeth it unto the Lord. And he that eateth, eateth to the Lord: for he giveth thanks to God. And he that eateth not, to the Lord he eateth not, and giveth thanks to God. For none of us liveth to himself; and no man dieth to himself. For whether we live, we live unto the Lord; or whether we die, we die unto the Lord. Therefore, whether we live, or whether we die, we are the Lord's.

Lesson III - Rom 14:9–13

For to this end Christ died and rose again; that he might be Lord both of the dead and of the living. But thou, why judgest thou thy brother? or thou, why dost thou despise thy brother? For we shall all stand before the judgment seat of Christ. For it is written: As I live, saith the Lord, every knee shall bow to me, and every tongue shall confess to God. Therefore every one of us shall render account to God for himself. Let us not therefore judge one another any more. But judge this rather, that you put not a stumblingblock or a scandal in your brother's way.

Lesson IV

Sermon by St. Maximus, Bishop

Dearly beloved brethren, we are instructed by the tradition of the Fathers, that we have to keep holiday on this solemnity in honor of several joyful events. We are taught that on this day, our Lord Christ was, first, manifested to the Gentiles by the leading of a star; secondly, that being bidden to a marriage, He turned water into wine; and, thirdly, that He received baptism from John, whereby He hallowed the waters of the Jordan, and cleansed him that baptized Him.

Lesson V

Which of these events was the greatest? He knows by Whose Will they came to pass; for us it is needful to believe and doubt not that whatever was wrought was wrought for us. For to the Gentiles is given a hope of worshipping that Very God of Very God, to adore Whom the Chaldaeans were led by the rays of a glorious star. So also He That by His Will changed water into wine, has given us to drink of the cup of His Blood of the New Testament; and the Lamb of God baptized in the Jordan has hallowed for us that saving Fountain wherein we are born again.

Lesson VI

Therefore, my brethren, as we have lately celebrated with gladness the Festival of our Saviour's birth, so now it behooves us with all earnestness to keep holy in His honor, this the birthday of His wonderworking. And, verily, these three anniversaries are rightly on one day preached to us, who acknowledge the unspeakable mystery of the Trinity under the name of one God. By these miracles the Lord Christ our Redeemer willed to manifest to men some of the power of that Divinity, Which in Him lay hidden under the Manhood.

Lesson VII

From the Holy Gospel according to St. Matthew (Matt 2:1–12)

When Jesus therefore was born in Bethlehem of Juda, in the days of king Herod, behold, there came wise men from the east to Jerusalem. Saying, Where is he that is born king of the Jews? And so on.

Homily by St. Jerome, Priest

"We have seen His star in the East." In order that the Jews might be confounded by hearing from the Gentiles of the birth of Christ, the star rose in the East. They knew that it would come, by the prophecy of Balaam, whose successors they were. See the Book of Numbers. The star led the wise men to Judea, that the Priests, having it demanded of them where Christ should be born, might have no power to plead that they knew not of His coming.

Lesson VIII

And they said unto him, "In Bethlehem of Judea." This is a mistake of copyists. In our opinion, what the Evangelist wrote must have been, not of Judea, but of Judah. Thus it is in the Hebrew text. Nor is there any town called Bethlehem among any other people, that this should be called of Judea to distinguish it. But it is fitly distinguished as of Judah, because there is in Judea another Bethlehem, namely, the one in Galilee. See the Book of Josue the son of Nun. Finally, the passage cited, which is in the prophet Micheas, has: "But thou, Bethlehem of Judah."

Lesson IX

And treasures they presented unto Him gifts, gold, and frankincense, and myrrh. The mystic meaning of these gifts is thus neatly expressed by Juvencus the Priest, To God made man, born Israel's King, Frankincense, myrrh, and gold they bring. And being warned of God in a dream that they should not return to Herod, they departed into their own country another way. They who had presented unto the Lord gifts, were honored by receiving a warning, not from an Angel, but from God Himself; whereas even Joseph was warned only by an Angel. They departed into their own country another way, that they might not be brought into contact with the unbelief of the Jews.

January 11 – Day 6 within the Octave of the Epiphany of the Lord

Semiduplex

Lesson I – Rom 15:1–4

From the letter of St. Paul the Apostle to the Romans

Now we that are stronger, ought to bear the infirmities of the weak, and not to please ourselves. Let every one of you please his neighbour unto good, to edification. For Christ did not please himself, but as it is written: The reproaches of them that reproached thee, fell upon me. For what things soever were written, were written for our learning: that through patience and the comfort of the Scriptures, we might have hope.

Lesson II ~ Rom 15:5–11

Now the God of patience and of comfort grant you to be of one mind one towards another, according to Jesus Christ: That with one mind, and with one mouth, you may glorify God and the Father of our Lord Jesus Christ. Wherefore receive one another, as Christ also hath received you unto the honour of God. For I say that Christ Jesus was minister of the circumcision for the truth of God, to confirm the promises made unto the fathers. But that the Gentiles are to glorify God for his mercy, as it is written: Therefore will I confess to thee, O Lord, among the Gentiles, and will sing to thy name. And again he saith: Rejoice, ye Gentiles, with his people. And again: Praise the Lord, all ye Gentiles; and magnify him, all ye people.

Lesson III ~ Rom 15:12–16

And again Isaias saith: There shall be a root of Jesse; and he that shall rise up to rule the Gentiles, in him the Gentiles shall hope. Now the God of hope fill you with all joy and peace in believing; that you may abound in hope, and in the power of the Holy Ghost. And I myself also, my brethren, am assured of you, that you also are full of love, replenished with all knowledge, so that you are able to admonish one another. But I have written to you, brethren, more boldly in some sort, as it were putting you in mind: because of the grace which is given me from God. That I should be the minister of Christ Jesus among the Gentiles; sanctifying the gospel of God, that the oblation of the Gentiles may be made acceptable and sanctified in the Holy Ghost.

Lesson IV

Sermon by St. Fulgentius, Bishop

The same God Who in the Old Testament had commanded the first-fruits to be offered to Himself, being born as a man, Himself consecrated to His own worship the first-fruits of the nations. The Shepherds were the first-fruits of the Jews, and the wise men of the Gentiles. The first came from near at hand, the second from afar. Where is He, say they, that is born King of the Jews? Herod, the king of the Jews, had already had children. Archelaus was born in a palace, Christ at an inn; Archelaus was laid in a silver cradle, Christ in a manger. And yet the wise men sought, not Archelaus, but Christ; they did not even name him that was born in a palace, but when they found Him That lay in a manger, they fell down and worshipped Him.

Lesson V

Who is the King of the Jews? The Poor and the Rich, the Lowly and the Exalted One. Who is the King of the Jews? He Who, being carried at the breast, is adored as the Eternal; He Who lies tiny in the manger, and is He Whom the heavens cannot contain; He Who is humbly wrapped in swaddling clothes, and is more glorious than all the stars. Why art thou troubled, O Herod? He that is born King of the Jews comes not by carnal warfare to conquer other kings, but by a marvelous working, by dying, to subdue them to Himself. He is not born to be thy successor, but that the world may faithfully believe in Him. He comes, not that He may fight in the flesh, but that He may conquer through the suffering of death.

Lesson VI

The little Child, Whom the wise men call the King of the Jews, is the Maker and Lord of Angels. If thou fearest Him at His birth, thou hast more reason to fear Him as the Almighty Judge. Fear Him, not as a pretender to thy kingdom, but fear Him as Him Who will pass a most just sentence of condemnation on thee because thou hast not believed in Him. Go, said Herod, and bring me word again, that I may come and worship Him also. We know thy cunning lying, thy godless unbelief, thine iniquitous treachery. The blood of the innocents which thou didst cruelly shed, is witness to us of what thou wouldst have done to Him.

Lesson VII

From the Holy Gospel according to St. Matthew (Matt 2:1–12)

When Jesus therefore was born in Bethlehem of Juda, in the days of king Herod, behold, there came wise men from the east to Jerusalem. Saying, Where is he that is born king of the Jews? And so on.

Homily by St. Ambrose, Bishop

What are the gifts of the faithful and true? Gold to our King, frankincense to our God, and myrrh to Him Who died for us. The first is that whereof are made the royal honors of kings, the second is that mystic offering which is used in the worship of the Divine Power, and the third is that wherewith we pay respect to the dead, whose bodies it keeps from corruption. My brethren, let us who hear and read these things, make offering out of what treasures we have albeit we have it in earthen vessels. If we confess that all that we have, we have, not from ourselves, but from Christ, how much more should we confess that whatever we have is not our own, but Christ's?

Lesson VIII

The wise men out of their treasures presented unto Him gifts. Wilt thou know how pleasing to Him they were? The star appeared to them, but disappeared when it came near Herod. Then it appeared to them again, leading them on the way that led to Christ. This star then was the way, and we know that Christ calls Himself the Way. And truly also in the mystery of His Incarnation He is called a Star; as it is written There shall come forth a Star out of Jacob, and a Man shall rise out of Israel. Where Christ is, there is a

Star; yea, He is Himself the bright and morning Star. And the light that leads to Jesus is His own.

Lesson IX

Remark another point. The wise men came by one way and departed by another. They that had seen Christ, knew Christ, and they departed better than they came. There are two ways, the one which leads to destruction, the other which leads to the kingdom; the one is the way of sin, which leads to Herod; the other is Christ, the true Way, Who leads us home to the fatherland, from that journeying here whereof it is said: "My soul hath long dwelt as an exile."

January 12 ~ Day 7 within the Octave of the Epiphany of the Lord

Semiduplex

If Saturday before the feast of the Holy Family, Lessons I–IX are as follows.

Otherwise, Lessons I–III are taken from the occurring weekday after the Epiphany, starting with Monday after the Feast of the Holy Family, and IV–IX are as follows.

Lesson I ~ 1 Cor 1:1–3

From the first letter of St. Paul the Apostle to the Corinthians

Paul, called to be an apostle of Jesus Christ by the will of God, and Sosthenes a brother, To the church of God that is at Corinth, to them that are sanctified in Christ Jesus, called to be saints, with all that invoke the name of our Lord Jesus Christ, in every place of theirs and ours. Grace to you, and peace from God our Father, and from the Lord Jesus Christ.

Lesson II ~ 1 Cor 1:4–9

I give thanks to my God always for you, for the grace of God that is given you in Christ Jesus, That in all things you are made rich in him, in all utterance, and in all knowledge; As the testimony of Christ was confirmed in you, So that nothing is wanting to you in any grace, waiting for the manifestation of our Lord Jesus Christ. Who also will confirm you unto the end without crime, in the day of the coming of our Lord Jesus Christ. God is faithful: by whom you are called unto the fellowship of his Son Jesus Christ our Lord.

Lesson III ~ 1 Cor 1:10–13

Now I beseech you, brethren, by the name of our Lord Jesus Christ, that you all speak the same thing, and that there be no schisms among you; but that you be perfect in the same mind, and in the same judgment. For it hath been signified unto me, my brethren, of you, by them that are of the house of Chloe, that there are contentions among you. Now this I say, that every one of you saith: I indeed am of Paul; and I am of Apollo; and I am of Cephas; and I of Christ. Is Christ divided? Was Paul then crucified for you? or were you baptized in the name of Paul?

Lesson IV

Sermon by St. Leo, Pope

Tis meet and right, dearly beloved brethren, yea, it is our bounden duty and godly service, to rejoice with full hearts upon those days which more especially set forth before us the workings of God's mercy; and to have in honorable memory those things that were done for our salvation. Hereto are we called by the seasons of the year which continually return, and notably by this present, which, after but a short time has passed since that day whereon the Coeternal Son of God was born of a Virgin, brings now the Feast of the Epiphany, hallowed by the Manifestation of the Lord.

Lesson V

In this said Manifestation the good Providence of God has appointed a strong bulwark to our faith. For now, while in solemn worship we call to mind how the childhood of the Saviour was adored in its first infancy, we receive from the original Scriptures the doctrine that Christ was born with the very nature of man. For this is that which makes of sinners saints, even to believe that in Our one and the same Lord Jesus Christ there is true Divinity and true Manhood: true Divinity as He, being in the form of God, is equal to the Father from everlasting to everlasting and very Manhood, wherein He, taking upon Him the form of a servant, has in these latter days been born Man.

Lesson VI

For the strengthening of this our faith, which we profess in the face of every false doctrine, the mercy of God has made it come to pass that one of those peoples who dwell in the uttermost parts of the East, and excel in the skill of reading the stars, should see the sign of the birth of that Child Who was to reign over all Israel. There appeared to the eyes of wise men a new star of such passing beauty, as wrought in the minds of all that saw it the persuasion that the event, which is announced, was of an importance not to be neglected.

Lesson VII

From the Holy Gospel according to St. Matthew (Matt 2:1–12)

When Jesus therefore was born in Bethlehem of Juda, in the days of king Herod, behold, there came wise men from the east to Jerusalem. Saying, Where is he that is born king of the Jews? And so on.

Homily by St. John Chrysostom

"The wise men entering into the house, they found the child with Mary his mother, and falling down they adored him: and opening their treasures, they offered him gifts; gold, frankincense, and myrrh." But what was it that induced them to worship? For neither was the Virgin conspicuous, nor the house distinguished, nor was any other of the things which they saw apt to amaze or attract them. Yet they not only worship, but also open their treasures, and offer gifts; and gifts, not as to a man, but as to God. For the frankincense and the myrrh were a symbol of this. What then was their inducement? That which wrought upon them to set out from home and to come so long a journey; and this was both the star, and the illumination wrought of God in their mind, guiding them little by little to the more perfect knowledge.

Lesson VIII

For, surely, had it not been so, all that was in sight being ordinary, they would not have shown so great honor. Therefore none of the outward circumstances was great in that instance, but it was a manger, and a shed, and a mother in poor estate; to set before your eyes, naked and bare, those wise men's love of wisdom, and to prove to you, that not as mere man they approached Him, but as a God, and Benefactor. Wherefore neither were they offended by any of what they saw outwardly, but even worshipped and brought gifts; gifts not only free from Judaical grossness, in that they sacrificed not sheep and calves, but also coming near to the self-devotion of the Church, for it was knowledge and obedience and love that they offered unto Him.

Lesson IX

"And having received an answer in sleep that they should not return to Herod, they went back another way into their country." See from this also their faith, how they were not offended, but are docile, and considerate; neither are they troubled, nor reason with themselves, saying, And yet, if this Child be great, and has any might, what need of flight, and of a clandestine retreat? And wherefore can it be, that when we have come openly and with boldness, and have stood against so great a people, and against a king's madness, the angel sends us out of the city as runaways and fugitives? But none of these things did they either say or think. For this most especially belongs to faith, not to seek an account of what is enjoined, but merely to obey the commandments laid upon us.

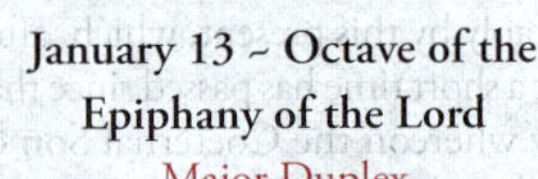

January 13 ~ Octave of the Epiphany of the Lord

Major Duplex

Lessons I–III are taken from the occurring weekday after the Epiphany, starting with Monday after the Feast of the Holy Family, and IV–IX are as follows.

Lesson IV

Sermon by St. Gregory Nazianzen

I am not able to restrain the outbursts of my happiness. I feel changed and elated. I forget my own lowliness while I undertake and try to discharge the office of the great John. It is true that I am not the Forerunner, but at least I come from the desert. Christ is enlightened, or rather, He enlightens us with His own light. Christ is baptized; let us go down with Him into the water, that we may come up with Him.

Lesson V

John is baptizing. Jesus comes. He comes that He may make holy him who baptizes Him; He comes to bury the old Adam in the waters; He comes to hallow the blessed flood of Jordan. He Who is Flesh and Spirit comes to open for all that should ever be baptized that power of generation whereby new peoples are constantly begotten of water and the Holy Ghost. The Baptist will not receive Him. Jesus strives with him. "I," says John, "have need to be baptized of thee." Thus speaks the candle to the Sun, the voice to the Word.

Lesson VI

Jesus came up out of the water, having, in a manner, washed the whole world, and brought it up with Him. And He saw the heavens opened not divided, even those heavens which Adam had once shut upon himself and us his descendants, when the cherub's fiery sword barred the gates of Paradise. And the Holy Spirit bore witness, witness unto Him Who is of One Substance with Himself. And witness was given from Heaven, unto Him that came down from heaven.

Lesson VII

From the Holy Gospel according to St. John (John 1:29–34)

At that time, John saw Jesus coming to him, and he saith: Behold the Lamb of God, behold him who taketh away the sin of the world. And so on.

Homily by St. Augustine, Bishop

John knew Jesus even before He came to be baptized of him in Jordan, as we perceive by the words "I have need to be baptized of thee, and comest Thou to me?" Behold, how he knew that He was the Lord, how he knew that He was the Son of God! How do we prove that he knew that He it was Who should baptize with the Holy Ghost? Before the Lord came to the river, when many betook themselves to John to be baptized of him, the Baptist said: "I indeed baptize you with water but One Mightier than I comes; the latchet of Whose shoes I am not worthy to unloose He shall baptize you with the Holy Ghost and with fire." Behold, John knew this also.

Lesson VIII

Yet John says: "I knew Him." Now, how are we to explain this without calling John a liar? and God forbid that we should ever even think anything of the kind. Was it not that when the Dove descended on Christ, John then, for the first time, knew Him to have that peculiar attribute, that, whosoever should baptize with His Baptism, whether they were themselves just or unjust, the virtue of the Sacrament should proceed, not from them, but from Him on Whom lingered the Dove; so that He is the real Baptizer in every Christian Baptism until the end of time, and it is in this sense that it is said of Him the Same is He Which baptizes with the Holy Ghost. Whether it be Peter, or Paul, or Judas, that performs the ceremony, the real Baptizer and effectual Worker is Christ. For if the holiness of the baptism depended on the holiness of the particular officiator, no two baptisms would be exactly alike, and every one would be supposed to be more or less regenerated according as the minister who baptized him was more or less of a saint.

Lesson IX

Now, my brethren, understand me. The saints themselves, those good men who appertain to the Dove, those good men whose portion is in Jerusalem, those good men in the Church, of whom the Apostle says: "the Lord knoweth them that are His;" these good men differ one from another by diversities of graces, and are not all of the same worthiness. Some are holier than others, and some are better than others. Supposing then for the sake of argument that A is baptized by B, a righteous saint, and C is baptized by D who is less worthy in the sight of God, who has attained only a lower degree in godliness, who is not so chaste, and whose life is not so good as B's, yet A and C receive just the same thing. And how is this, unless it be that it is Christ Himself Who is the effectual Baptizer?

What follows are the Lessons for the occurring weekdays after the Epiphany, the reckoning of which begins after the Feast of the Holy Family. The days of January 8–12 that fall *after* the Feast of the Holy Family get Lessons I–III from here.

For the remainder of Epiphanytide, Lessons IV–IX (if not provided) are taken from the Common or Proper of the Saints on their feast days.

Monday I after the Octave of the Epiphany

Lesson I ~ 1 Cor 2:1–5

From the first letter of St. Paul the Apostle to the Corinthians

And I, brethren, when I came to you, came not in loftiness of speech or of wisdom, declaring unto you the testimony of Christ. For I judged not myself to know anything among you, but Jesus Christ, and him crucified. And I was with you in weakness, and in fear, and in much trembling. And my speech and my preaching was not in the persuasive words of human wisdom, but in shewing of the Spirit and power; That your faith might not stand on the wisdom of men, but on the power of God.

Lesson II ~ 1 Cor 2:6–9

Howbeit we speak wisdom among the perfect: yet not the wisdom of this world, neither of the princes of this world that come to nought; But we speak the wisdom of God in a mystery, a wisdom which is hidden, which God ordained before the world, unto our glory Which none of the princes of this world knew; for if they had known it, they would never have crucified the Lord of glory. But, as it is written: That eye hath not seen, nor ear heard, neither hath it entered into the heart of man, what things God hath prepared for them that love him.

Lesson III ~ 1 Cor 2:10–13

But to us God hath revealed them, by this Spirit. For the Spirit searcheth all things, yea, the deep things of God. For what man knoweth the things of a man, but the spirit of a man that is in him? So the things also that are of God no man knoweth, but the Spirit of God. Now we have received not the spirit of this world, but the Spirit that is of God; that we may know the things that are given us from God. Which things also we speak, not in the learned words of human wisdom; but in the doctrine of the Spirit, comparing spiritual things with spiritual.

Tuesday I after the Octave of the Epiphany

Lesson I ~ 1 Cor 5:1–5

From the first letter of St. Paul the Apostle to the Corinthians

It is absolutely heard, that there is fornication among you, and such fornication as the like is not among the heathens; that one should have his father's wife. And you are puffed up; and have not rather mourned, that he might be taken away from among you, that hath done this deed. I indeed, absent in body, but present in spirit, have already judged, as though I were present, him that hath so done, In the name of our Lord Jesus Christ, you being gathered together, and my spirit, with the power of our Lord Jesus; To deliver such a one to Satan for the destruction of the flesh, that the spirit may be saved in the day of our Lord Jesus Christ.

Lesson II ~ 1 Cor 5:6–8

Your glorying is not good. Know you not that a little leaven corrupteth the whole lump? Purge out the old leaven, that you may be a new paste, as you are unleavened. For Christ our pasch is sacrificed. Therefore let us feast, not with the old leaven, nor with the leaven of malice and wickedness; but with the unleavened bread of sincerity and truth.

Lesson III ~ 1 Cor 5:9–11

I wrote to you in an epistle, not to keep company with fornicators. I mean not with the fornicators of this world, or with the covetous, or the extortioners, or the servers of idols; otherwise you must needs go out of this world. But now I have written to you, not to keep company, if any man that is named a brother, be a fornicator, or covetous, or a server of idols, or a railer, or a drunkard, or an extortioner: with such a one, not so much as to eat.

Wednesday I after the Octave of the Epiphany

Lesson I ~ 1 Cor 6:1–6

From the first letter of St. Paul the Apostle to the Corinthians

Dare any of you, having a matter against another, go to be judged before the unjust, and not before the saints Know you not that the saints shall judge this world And if the world shall be judged by you, are you unworthy to judge the smallest matters Know you not that we shall judge angels how much more things of this world If therefore you have judgments of things pertaining to this world, set them to judge, who are the most despised in the church. I speak to your shame. Is it so that there is not among you any one wise man, that is able to judge between his brethren But brother goeth to law with brother, and that before unbelievers.

Lesson II ~ 1 Cor 6:7–11

Already indeed there is plainly a fault among you, that you have lawsuits one with another. Why do you not rather take wrong? Why do you not rather suffer yourselves to be defrauded? But you do wrong and defraud, and that to your brethren. Know you not that the unjust shall not possess the kingdom of God? Do not err: neither fornicators, nor idolaters, nor adulterers, Nor the effeminate, nor liers with mankind, nor thieves, nor covetous, nor drunkards, nor railers, nor extortioners, shall possess the kingdom of God. And such some of you were; but you are washed, but you are sanctified, but you are justified in the name of our Lord Jesus Christ, and the Spirit of our God.

Lesson III ~ 1 Cor 6:12–18

All things are lawful to me, but all things are not expedient. All things are lawful to me, but I will not be brought under the power of any. Meat for the belly, and the belly for the meats; but God shall destroy both it and them: but the body is not for fornication, but for the Lord, and the Lord for the body. Now God hath both raised up the Lord, and will raise us up also by his power. Know you not that your bodies are the members of Christ Shall I then take the members of Christ, and make them the members of a harlot God forbid. Or know you not, that he who is joined to a harlot, is made one body For they shall be, saith he, two in one flesh.

Thursday I after the Octave of the Epiphany

Lesson I ~ 1 Cor 7:1–4

From the first letter of St. Paul the Apostle to the Corinthians

Now concerning the thing whereof you wrote to me: It is good for a man not to touch a woman. But for fear of fornication, let every man have his own wife, and let every woman have her own husband. Let the husband render the debt to his wife, and the wife also in like manner to the husband. The wife hath not power of her own body, but the husband. And in like manner the husband also hath not power of his own body, but the wife.

Lesson II ~ 1 Cor 7:5–9

Defraud not one another, except, perhaps, by consent, for a time, that you may give yourselves to prayer; and return together again, lest Satan tempt you for your incontinency. But I speak this by indulgence, not by commandment. For I would that all men were even as myself: but every one hath his proper gift from God; one after this manner, and another after that. But I say to the unmarried, and to the widows: It is good for them if they so continue, even as I. But if they do not contain themselves, let them marry. For it is better to marry than to be burnt.

Lesson III ~ 1 Cor 7:10–14

But to them that are married, not I but the Lord commandeth, that the wife depart not from her husband. And if she depart, that she remain unmarried, or be reconciled to her husband. And let not the husband put away his wife. For to the rest I speak, not the Lord. If any brother hath a wife that believeth not, and she consent to dwell with him, let him not put her away. And if any woman hath a husband that believeth not, and he consent to dwell with her, let her not put away her husband. For the unbelieving husband is sanctified by the believing wife; and the unbelieving wife is sanctified by the believing husband: otherwise your children should be unclean; but now they are holy.

Friday I after the Octave of the Epiphany

Lesson I ~ 1 Cor 13:1–3

From the first letter of St. Paul the Apostle to the Corinthians

If I speak with the tongues of men, and of angels, and have not charity, I am become as sounding brass, or a tinkling cymbal. And if I should have prophecy and should know all mysteries, and all knowledge, and if I should have all faith, so that I could remove mountains, and have not charity, I am nothing. And if I should distribute all my goods to feed the poor, and if I should deliver my body to be burned, and have not charity, it profiteth me nothing.

Lesson II ~ 1 Cor 13:4–10

Charity is patient, is kind: charity envieth not, dealeth not perversely; is not puffed up; Is not ambitious, seeketh not her own, is not provoked to anger, thinketh no evil; Rejoiceth not in iniquity, but rejoiceth with the truth; Beareth all things, believeth all things, hopeth all things, endureth all things. Charity never falleth away: whether prophecies shall be made void, or tongues shall cease, or knowledge shall be destroyed. For we know in part, and we prophesy in part. But when that which is perfect is come, that which is in part shall be done away.

Lesson III ~ 1 Cor 13:11–13

When I was a child, I spoke as a child, I understood as a child, I thought as a child. But, when I became a man, I put away the things of a child. We see now through a glass in a dark manner; but then face to face. Now I know in part; but then I shall know even as I am known. And now there remain faith, hope, and charity, these three: but the greatest of these is charity.

Saturday I after the Octave of the Epiphany

Lesson I ~ 1 Cor 16:1–4

From the first letter of St. Paul the Apostle to the Corinthians

Now concerning the collections that are made for the saints, as I have given order to the churches of Galatia, so do ye also. On the first day of the week let every one of you put apart with himself, laying up what it shall well please him; that when I come, the collections be not then to be made. And when I shall be with you, whomsoever you shall approve by letters, them will I send to carry your grace to Jerusalem. And if it be meet that I also go, they shall go with me.

Lesson II ~ 1 Cor 16:5–9

Now I will come to you, when I shall have passed through Macedonia. For I shall pass through Macedonia. And with you perhaps I shall abide, or even spend the winter:

that you may bring me on my way whithersoever I shall go. For I will not see you now by the way, for I trust that I shall abide with you some time, if the Lord permit. But I will tarry at Ephesus until Pentecost. For a great door and evident is opened unto me: and many adversaries.

Lesson III ~ 1 Cor 16:10–14

Now if Timothy come, see that he be with you without fear, for he worketh the work of the Lord, as I also do. Let no man therefore despise him, but conduct ye him on his way in peace: that he may come to me. For I look for him with the brethren. And touching our brother Apollo, I give you to understand, that I much entreated him to come unto you with the brethren: and indeed it was not his will at all to come at this time. But he will come when he shall have leisure. Watch ye, stand fast in the faith, do manfully, and be strengthened.

Sunday II after the Octave of the Epiphany

If this or subsequent Sundays after the Epiphany are impeded by Septuagesima Sunday, their Lessons are omitted.

Lesson I ~ 2 Cor 1:1–5

From the second letter of St. Paul the Apostle to the Corinthians

Paul, an apostle of Jesus Christ by the will of God, and Timothy our brother: to the church of God that is at Corinth, with all the saints that are in all Achaia: Grace unto you and peace from God our Father, and from the Lord Jesus Christ. Blessed be the God and Father of our Lord Jesus Christ, the Father of mercies, and the God of all comfort. Who comforteth us in all our tribulation; that we also may be able to comfort them who are in all distress, by the exhortation wherewith we also are exhorted by God. For as the sufferings of Christ abound in us: so also by Christ doth our comfort abound.

Lesson II ~ 2 Cor 1:6–7

Now whether we be in tribulation, it is for your exhortation and salvation: or whether we be comforted, it is for your consolation: or whether we be exhorted, it is for your exhortation and salvation, which worketh the enduring of the same sufferings which we also suffer. That our hope for you may be steadfast: knowing that as you are partakers of the sufferings, so shall you be also of the consolation.

Lesson III ~ 2 Cor 1:8–11

For we would not have you ignorant, brethren, of our tribulation, which came to us in Asia, that we were pressed out of measure above our strength, so that we were weary even of life. But we had in ourselves the answer of death, that we should not trust in ourselves, but in God who raiseth the dead. Who hath delivered and doth deliver us out of so great dangers: in whom we trust that he will yet also deliver us. You helping withal in prayer for us: that for this gift obtained for us, by the means of many persons, thanks may be given by many in our behalf.

Lesson IV

Sermon of St. John Chrysostom

As I listen intently to the reading of St. Paul's Epistles, often two or three times a week whenever we commemorate the holy martyrs, I am filled with joy, delighting in the sound of that spiritual trumpet. And as I recognize the voice of a friend, I am roused, and enkindled with love so that I almost seem to see him present, and to hear him speaking. But nevertheless I am grieved, and am troubled, that all do not know this great man as he deserves to be known. Indeed, many are so ignorant that they do not even know how many epistles he wrote. But this ignorance is not due to a want of intelligence on their part, but because they will not carefully study the writings of this great man.

Lesson V

For what we know, if we know anything, we do not know it owing to any superlative talent or penetration, but, being strongly drawn towards this great man, we never cease from reading his works. For so it is that those who love any one usually know better than others what he has done, because they take the trouble to learn all about him. The blessed Paul himself shows that this is so, when he says to the Philippians: "As it is meet for me to think this for you all: for that I have you in my heart; and in my bands, and in the defence and confirmation of the gospel."

Lesson VI

And if you also will diligently attend to the reading, you will have no need of other instruction. Most true are those words of Christ: "Seek and you shall find: knock and it shall be opened unto you." For the rest, since many of those who are assembled here are charged with the care of a wife, and with providing for a family, and with the upbringing of children, and therefore cannot devote themselves wholly to this study; let them at least bestir themselves to receive what others have gathered; showing as much eagerness in listening to what is said about him as in acquiring wealth. For though it is unseemly to demand from you no more than this, yet it is to be wished that you do this at least.

Lesson VII

From the Holy Gospel according to St. John (John 2:1–11)

At that time, there was a marriage in Cana of Galilee: and the mother of Jesus was there. And Jesus also was invited, and his disciples, to the marriage. And so on.

Homily by St. Augustine, Bishop

Even setting aside any mystical interpretation, the fact that the Lord was pleased to be asked, and to go to a marriage, shows plainly enough that He is the Author and Blesser of marriage. There were yet to be those of whom the Apostle has warned us as forbidding to marry; who say that marriage is a bad thing in itself, and a work of the devil. Yet we read in the Gospel that when the Lord was asked, Is it lawful for a man to put away his wife for every cause? He answered that it was not lawful, except it were for fornication. In which answer you will remember that He used these words: "What God hath joined together, let not man put asunder."

Lesson VIII

They who are well instructed in the Catholic religion know that God is the Author and Blesser of marriage; and that, whereas joining together in marriage is of God, divorce is of the devil. But it is lawful for a man to put away his wife in case of fornication, For by not keeping a wife's faith to her husband she herself has first willed not to be wife. They also who have made a vow of their virginity to God and have thereby attained to a higher degree of honor and holiness in the Church, are not unmarried, for they are a special part of the marriage of the whole Church, which is the Bride of Christ.

Lesson IX

And for this cause, therefore, did the Lord, on being invited, come to the marriage, to confirm conjugal chastity, and to show forth the sacrament of marriage. For the bridegroom in that marriage, to whom it was said, "Thou hast kept the good wine until now," represented the person of the Lord. For the good wine—namely, the gospel—Christ has kept until now.

Monday II after the Octave of the Epiphany

Lesson I - 2 Cor 3:1–3

From the second letter of St. Paul the Apostle to the Corinthians

Do we begin again to commend ourselves? Or do we need (as some do) epistles of commendation to you, or from you? You are our epistle, written in our hearts, which is known and read by all men: Being manifested, that you are the epistle of Christ, ministered by us, and written not with ink, but with the Spirit of the living God; not in tables of stone, but in the fleshly tables of the heart.

Lesson II - 2 Cor 3:4–8

And such confidence we have, through Christ, towards God. Not that we are sufficient to think any thing of ourselves, as of ourselves: but our sufficiency is from God. Who also hath made us fit ministers of the new testament, not in the letter, but in the spirit. For the letter killeth, but the spirit quickeneth. Now if the ministration of death, engraven with letters upon stones, was glorious; so that the children of Israel could not steadfastly behold the face of Moses, for the glory of his countenance, which is made void: How shall not the ministration of the spirit be rather in glory?

Lesson III - 2 Cor 3:9–14

For if the ministration of condemnation be glory, much more the ministration of justice aboundeth in glory. For even that which was glorious in this part was not glorified, by reason of the glory that excelleth. For if that which is done away was glorious, much more that which remaineth is in glory. Having therefore such hope, we use much confidence: And not as Moses put a veil upon his face, that the children of Israel might not steadfastly look on the face of that which is made void. But their senses were made dull. For, until this present day, the selfsame veil, in the reading of the old testament, remaineth not taken away (because in Christ it is made void).

Tuesday II after the Octave of the Epiphany

Lesson I - 2 Cor 5:1–4

From the second letter of St. Paul the Apostle to the Corinthians

For we know, if our earthly house of this habitation be dissolved, that we have a building of God, a house not made with hands, eternal in heaven. For in this also we groan, desiring to be clothed upon with our habitation that is from heaven. Yet so that we be found clothed, not naked. For we also, who are in this tabernacle, do groan, being burdened; because we would not be unclothed, but clothed upon, that that which is mortal may be swallowed up by life.

Lesson II - 2 Cor 5:6–10

Therefore having always confidence, knowing that, while we are in the body, we are absent from the Lord. (For we walk by faith, and not by sight.) But we are confident, and have a good will to be absent rather from the body, and to be present with the Lord. And therefore we labour, whether absent or present, to please him. For we must all be manifested before the judgement seat of Christ, that every one may receive the proper things of the body, according as he hath done, whether it be good or evil.

Lesson III - 2 Cor 5:11–15

Knowing therefore the fear of the Lord, we use persuasion to men; but to God we are manifest. And I trust also that in your consciences we are manifest. We commend not ourselves again to you, but give you occasion to glory in our behalf; that you may have somewhat to answer them who glory in face, and not in heart. For whether we be transported in mind, it is to God; or whether we be sober, it is for you. For the charity of Christ presseth us: judging this, that if one died for all, then all were dead. And Christ died for all; that they also who live, may not now live to themselves, but unto him who died for them, and rose again.

Wednesday II after the Octave of the Epiphany

Lesson I - 2 Cor 7:1–3

From the second letter of St. Paul the Apostle to the Corinthians

Having therefore these promises, dearly beloved, let us cleanse ourselves from all defilement of the flesh and of the spirit, perfecting sanctification in the fear of God. Receive us. We have injured no man, we have corrupted no man, we have overreached no man. I speak not this to your condemnation. For we have said before, that you are in our hearts, to die together, and to live together.

Lesson II - 2 Cor 7:4–7

Great is my confidence for you, great is my glorying for you. I am filled with comfort: I exceedingly abound with joy in all our tribulation. For also when we were come into Macedonia, our flesh had no rest, but we suffered all tribulation; combats without, fears within. But God, who comforteth the humble, comforted us by the coming of Titus. And not by his coming only, but also by the consolation, wherewith he was comforted in you, relating to us your desire, your mourning, your zeal for me, so that I rejoiced the more.

Lesson III - 2 Cor 7:8–10

For although I made you sorrowful by my epistle, I do not repent; and if I did repent, seeing that the same epistle (although but for a time) did make you sorrowful; Now I am glad: not because you were made sorrowful; but because you were made sorrowful unto penance. For you were made sorrowful according to God, that you might suffer damage by us in nothing. For the sorrow that is according to God worketh penance, steadfast unto salvation; but the sorrow of the world worketh death.

Thursday II after the Octave of the Epiphany

Lesson I - 2 Cor 10:1–3

From the second letter of St. Paul the Apostle to the Corinthians

Now I Paul myself beseech you, by the mildness and modesty of Christ, who in presence indeed am lowly among you, but being absent, am bold toward you. But I beseech you, that I may not be bold when I am present, with that confidence wherewith I am thought to be bold, against some, who reckon us as if we walked according to the flesh. For though we walk in the flesh, we do not war according to the flesh.

Lesson II - 2 Cor 10:4–7

For the weapons of our warfare are not carnal, but mighty to God unto the pulling down of fortifications, destroying counsels, And every height that exhalteth itself against the knowledge of God, and bringing into captivity every understanding unto the obedience of Christ; And having in readiness to revenge all disobedience, when your obedience shall be fulfilled. See the things that are according to outward appearance. If any man trust to himself, that he is Christ's, let him think this again with himself, that as he is Christ's, so are we also.

Lesson III - 2 Cor 10:8–12

For if also I should boast somewhat more of our power, which the Lord hath given us unto edification, and not for your destruction, I should not be ashamed. But that I may not be thought as it were to terrify you by epistles (For his epistles indeed, say they, are weighty and strong; but his bodily presence is weak, and his speech contemptible), Let such a one think this, that such as we are in word by epistles, when absent, such also we will be indeed when present. For we dare not match, or compare ourselves with some, that commend themselves; but we measure ourselves by ourselves, and compare ourselves with ourselves.

Friday II after the Octave of the Epiphany

Lesson I ~ 2 Cor 12:1–4

From the second letter of St. Paul the Apostle to the Corinthians

If I must glory (it is not expedient indeed): but I will come to visions and revelations of the Lord. I know a man in Christ above fourteen years ago (whether in the body, I know not, or out of the body, I know not; God knoweth), such a one caught up to the third heaven. And I know such a man (whether in the body, or out of the body, I know not: God knoweth): That he was caught up into paradise, and heard secret words, which it is not granted to man to utter.

Lesson II ~ 2 Cor 12:5–9

For such an one I will glory; but for myself I will glory nothing, but in my infirmities. For though I should have a mind to glory, I shall not be foolish; for I will say the truth. But I forbear, lest any man should think of me above that which he seeth in me, or any thing he heareth from me. And lest the greatness of the revelations should exalt me, there was given me a sting of my flesh, an angel of Satan, to buffet me. For which thing thrice I besought the Lord, that it might depart from me. And he said to me: My grace is sufficient for thee; for power is made perfect in infirmity.

Lesson III ~ 2 Cor 12:9–11

Gladly therefore will I glory in my infirmities, that the power of Christ may dwell in me. For which cause I please myself in my infirmities, in reproaches, in necessities, in persecutions, in distresses, for Christ. For when I am weak, then am I powerful. I am become foolish: you have compelled me. For I ought to have been commended by you: for I have no way come short of them that are above measure apostles, although I be nothing.

Saturday II after the Octave of the Epiphany

Lesson I ~ 2 Cor 13:1–4

From the second letter of St. Paul the Apostle to the Corinthians

Behold, this is the third time I am coming to you: In the mouth of two or three witnesses shall every word stand. I have told before, and foretell, as present, and now absent, to them that sinned before, and to all the rest, that if I come again, I will not spare. Do you seek a proof of Christ that speaketh in me, who towards you is not weak, but is mighty in you? For although he was crucified through weakness, yet he liveth by the power of God. For we also are weak in him: but we shall live with him by the power of God towards you.

Lesson II - 2 Cor 13:5–9

Try your own selves if you be in the faith; prove ye yourselves. Know you not your own selves, that Christ Jesus is in you, unless perhaps you be reprobates? But I trust that you shall know that we are not reprobates. Now we pray God, that you may do no evil, not that we may appear approved, but that you may do that which is good, and that we may be as reprobates. For we can do nothing against the truth; but for the truth. For we rejoice that we are weak, and you are strong. This also we pray for, your perfection.

Lesson III - 2 Cor 13:10–13

Therefore I write these things, being absent, that, being present, I may not deal more severely, according to the power which the Lord hath given me unto edification, and not unto destruction. For the rest, brethren, rejoice, be perfect, take exhortation, be of one mind, have peace; and the God of peace and of love shall be with you. Salute one another with a holy kiss. All the saints salute you. The grace of our Lord Jesus Christ, and the charity of God, and the communication of the Holy Ghost be with you all. Amen.

Sunday III after the Octave of the Epiphany

If this or subsequent Sundays after the Epiphany are impeded by Septuagesima Sunday, their Lessons are omitted.

Lesson I - Gal 1:1–5

From the letter of St. Paul the Apostle to the Galatians

Paul, an apostle, not of men, neither by man, but by Jesus Christ, and God the Father, who raised him from the dead, And all the brethren who are with me, to the churches of Galatia. Grace be to you, and peace from God the Father, and from our Lord Jesus Christ, Who gave himself for our sins, that he might deliver us from this present wicked world, according to the will of God and our Father: To whom is glory for ever and ever. Amen.

Lesson II - Gal 1:6–10

I wonder that you are so soon removed from him that called you into the grace of Christ, unto another gospel. Which is not another, only there are some that trouble you, and would pervert the gospel of Christ. But though we, or an angel from heaven, preach a gospel to you besides that which we have preached to you, let him be anathema. As we said before, so now I say again: If any one preach to you a gospel, besides that which you have received, let him be anathema. For do I now persuade men, or God? Or do I seek to please men? If I yet pleased men, I should not be the servant of Christ.

Lesson III - Gal 1:11–14

For I give you to understand, brethren, that the gospel which was preached by me is not according to man. For neither did I receive it of man, nor did I learn it; but by the revelation of Jesus Christ. For you have heard of my conversation in time past in the Jews' religion: how that, beyond measure, I persecuted the church of God, and wasted it. And I made progress in the Jews' religion above many of my equals in my own nation, being more abundantly zealous for the traditions of my fathers.

Lesson IV

From the Exposition of the Epistle to the Galatians by St. Augustine, Bishop

The reason of the Apostle's writing to the Galatians was this that they might understand that the grace of God had worked in them that they were no longer under the law. For when the grace of the Gospel was preached to them, there had not been wanting to them some of them of the circumcision, Christians indeed in name, but who had not yet apprehended that great benefit of grace, and desiring still to be bound with burdens of the law, burdens which the Lord God had laid not upon such as serve righteousness but upon such as serve sin, laying, that is to say, upon the unrighteous a righteous law, whereby their unrighteousness was made manifest, not taken away. For there is not anything which takes away sin, save only the grace of faith which works by love.

Lesson V

The men of the circumcision would have the Galatians, who were under grace, to be under the burdens of the law, persuading them that the Gospel profited them nothing, unless they should be circumcised, and take on them the other outward observances of the Jews' religion. Whence the Galatians began to have doubts of the Apostle Paul, by whom the Gospel had been preached to them, as one that held not the doctrine of the other Apostles, who compelled the Gentiles to come under the law.

Lesson VI

The same question is discussed in the Epistle to the Romans, but with this difference in that case the Apostle puts an end to the discussion, and stills the strife which had arisen between the Jewish and the Gentile converts, in consequence of the Jews holding that they had earned the knowledge of the Gospel as a reward for their observance of the law, and refusing the same knowledge to the uncircumcised, as to men who had done nothing to deserve it; and the Gentiles, on the contrary, maintaining that they were superior to the Jews, in that they were not the murderers of the Lord. Now, in this Epistle to the Galatians, the Apostle addresses himself to those who were troubled by the authority claimed by them who were of the circumcision, and sought to bring into subjection to the law them who were of the uncircumcision.

Lesson VII

From the Holy Gospel according to St. Matthew (Matt 8:1–13)

At that time, when Jesus was come down from the mountain, great multitudes followed him: And behold a leper came and adored him. And so on.

Homily by St. Jerome, Priest

When the Lord was come down from the mountain, great multitudes followed Him. They were not able to follow Him when He went up. And first there came a leper. This poor creature's disease had prevented him from hearing the Saviour's long sermon on the Mount. Let it be noted that he is the first person specially named as being healed. The second was the Centurion's servant; the third was Peter's wife's mother, who was sick of a fever at Capharnaum; the fourth were they who were brought unto Christ as being troubled with evil spirits, from whom He by His word cast out the evil spirits, at the same time that He healed all that were sick.

Lesson VIII

And, behold, there came a leper, and worshipped Him, saying—Properly after preaching and doctrine comes occasion for a sign, that the power of the miracle might confirm in the hearers the truth of the teaching that had gone before.—"Lord, if Thou wilt, Thou canst make me clean." He that begs the Lord to have the will, doubts not that He has the power. And Jesus put forth His hand, and touched him, saying: "I will; be thou clean." As soon as the Lord put forth His Hand, the leprosy departed. Let us remark how lowly and unbragging is the Lord's language. The leper had said, "If Thou wilt;" the Lord answered, "I will." The leper, "Thou canst make me clean;" the Lord, "Be thou clean." Most Latin readers, misled by the identity of form in that language between the Present Infinitive Active and the Second Person Singular Present Imperative Passive of the Verb, read Christ's answer as if it were, "I will to make thee clean." This is wrong. The sentences are separate. First comes the expression of volition, "I will," then the command, "Be thou clean."

Lesson IX

And Jesus said to him: "See to it that you tell no one." And in fact, why was it necessary to boast with his words over something that he was revealing with his body? "But go, show thyself to the priest and offer the gift which Moses prescribeth as a testimony to them." He sent him to the priest for several reasons. First, for humility's sake, that he might be seen to defer to the priests. For there was a precept in the Law that those who had been cleansed of leprosy were to offer gifts to the priests. Second, so that those who saw that the leper had been cleansed might either believe in the Savior, or not believe. If they believed, they would be saved; if they refused to believe, they would be without excuse. A concurrent reason is so that he would not seem to be breaking the Law.

Monday III after the Octave of the Epiphany

Lesson I - Gal 3:1–6

From the letter of St. Paul the Apostle to the Galatians

O senseless Galatians, who hath bewitched you that you should not obey the truth, before whose eyes Jesus Christ hath been set forth, crucified among you? This only would I learn of you: Did you receive the Spirit by the works of the law, or by the hearing of faith? Are you so foolish, that, whereas you began in the Spirit, you would now be made perfect by the flesh? Have you suffered so great things in vain? If it be yet in vain. He therefore who giveth to you the Spirit, and worketh miracles among you; doth he do it by the works of the law, or by the hearing of the faith? As it is written: Abraham believed God, and it was reputed to him unto justice.

Lesson II - Gal 3:7–10

Know ye therefore, that they who are of faith, the same are the children of Abraham. And the Scripture, foreseeing, that God justifieth the Gentiles by faith, told unto Abraham before: In thee shall all nations be blessed. Therefore they that are of faith, shall be blessed with faithful Abraham. For as many as are of the works of the law, are under a curse. For it is written: Cursed is every one, that abideth not in all things, which are written in the book of the law to do them.

Lesson III - Gal 3:11–14

But that in the law no man is justified with God, it is manifest: because the just man liveth by faith. But the law is not of faith: but, He that doth those things, shall live in them. Christ hath redeemed us from the curse of the law, being made a curse for us: for it is written: Cursed is every one that hangeth on a tree: That the blessing of Abraham might come on the Gentiles through Christ Jesus: that we may receive the promise of the Spirit by faith.

Tuesday III after the Octave of the Epiphany

Lesson I - Gal 5:1–5

From the letter of St. Paul the Apostle to the Galatians

Stand fast, and be not held again under the yoke of bondage. Behold, I Paul tell you, that if you be circumcised, Christ shall profit you nothing. And I testify again to every man circumcising himself, that he is a debtor to the whole law. You are made void of Christ, you who are justified in the law: you are fallen from grace. For we in spirit, by faith, wait for the hope of justice.

Lesson II - Gal 5:6–10

For in Christ Jesus neither circumcision availeth any thing, nor uncircumcision: but faith that worketh by charity. You did run well, who hath hindered you, that you should not obey the truth?

This persuasion is not from him that calleth you. A little leaven corrupteth the whole lump. I have confidence in you in the Lord: that you will not be of another mind: but he that troubleth you, shall bear the judgment, whosoever he be.

Lesson III ~ Gal 5:11–17

And I, brethren, if I yet preach circumcision, why do I yet suffer persecution? Then is the scandal of the cross made void. I would they were even cut off, who trouble you. For you, brethren, have been called unto liberty: only make not liberty an occasion to the flesh, but by charity of the spirit serve one another. For all the law is fulfilled in one word: Thou shalt love thy neighbour as thyself. But if you bite and devour one another; take heed you be not consumed one of another. I say then, walk in the spirit, and you shall not fulfil the lusts of the flesh. For the flesh lusteth against the spirit: and the spirit against the flesh; for these are contrary one to another: so that you do not the things that you would.

Wednesday III after the Octave of the Epiphany

Lesson I ~ Eph 1:1–4

Beginning of the letter of St. Paul the Apostle to the Ephesians

Paul, an apostle of Jesus Christ, by the will of God, to all the saints who are at Ephesus, and to the faithful in Christ Jesus. Grace be to you, and peace from God the Father, and from the Lord Jesus Christ. Blessed by the God and Father of our Lord Jesus Christ, who hath blessed us with spiritual blessings in heavenly places, in Christ: As he chose us in him before the foundation of the world, that we should be holy and unspotted in his sight in charity.

Lesson II ~ Eph 1:5–10

Who hath predestinated us unto the adoption of children through Jesus Christ unto himself: according to the purpose of his will: Unto the praise of the glory of his grace, in which he hath graced us in his beloved son. In whom we have redemption through his blood, the remission of sins, according to the riches of his grace, Which hath superabounded in us in all wisdom and prudence, That he might make known unto us the mystery of his will, according to his good pleasure, which he hath purposed in him, In the dispensation of the fulness of times, to re-establish all things in Christ, that are in heaven and on earth, in him.

Lesson III ~ Eph 1:11–14

In whom we also are called by lot, being predestinated according to the purpose of him who worketh all things according to the counsel of his will. That we may be unto the praise of his glory, we who before hoped Christ: In whom you also, after you had heard the word of truth (the gospel of your salvation); in whom also believing, you were signed with the holy Spirit of promise, Who is the pledge of our inheritance, unto the redemption of acquisition, unto the praise of his glory.

Thursday III after the Octave of the Epiphany

Lesson I - Eph 4:1–6

From the letter of St. Paul the Apostle to the Ephesians

I therefore, a prisoner in the Lord, beseech you that you walk worthy of the vocation in which you are called, With all humility and mildness, with patience, supporting one another in charity. Careful to keep the unity of the Spirit in the bond of peace. One body and one Spirit; as you are called in one hope of your calling. One Lord, one faith, one baptism. One God and Father of all, who is above all, and through all, and in us all.

Lesson II - Eph 4:7–10

But to every one of us is given grace, according to the measure of the giving of Christ. Wherefore he saith: Ascending on high, he led captivity captive; he gave gifts to men. Now that he ascended, what is it, but because he also descended first into the lower parts of the earth? He that descended is the same also that ascended above all the heavens, that he might fill all things.

Lesson III - Eph 4:11–15

And he gave some apostles, and some prophets, and other some evangelists, and other some pastors and doctors, For the perfecting of the saints, for the work of the ministry, for the edifying of the body of Christ: Until we all meet into the unity of faith, and of the knowledge of the Son of God, unto a perfect man, unto the measure of the age of the fulness of Christ; That henceforth we be no more children tossed to and fro, and carried about with every wind of doctrine by the wickedness of men, by cunning craftiness, by which they lie in wait to deceive But doing the truth in charity, we may in all things grow up in him who is the head, even Christ:

Friday III after the Octave of the Epiphany

Lesson I - Eph 5:1–4

From the letter of St. Paul the Apostle to the Ephesians

Be ye therefore followers of God, as most dear children; And walk in love, as Christ also hath loved us, and hath delivered himself for us, an oblation and a sacrifice to God for an odour of sweetness. But fornication, and all uncleanness, or covetousness, let it not so much as be named among you, as becomes saints: Or obscenity, or foolish talking, or scurrility, which is to no purpose; but rather giving of thanks.

Lesson II - Eph 5:5–8

For know you this and understand, that no fornicator, or unclean, or covetous person (which is a serving of idols), hath inheritance in the kingdom of Christ and of God. Let no man deceive you with vain words. For because of these things comes the anger of God upon the children of unbelief. Be ye not therefore partakers with them. For you were heretofore darkness, but now light in the Lord. Walk then as children of the light.

Lesson III - Eph 5:9–14

For the fruit of the light is in all goodness, and justice, and truth; Proving what is well pleasing to God: And have no fellowship with the unfruitful works of darkness, but rather reprove them. For the things that are done by them in secret, it is a shame even to speak of. But all things that are reproved, are made manifest by the light; for all that is made manifest is light. Wherefore he saith: Rise thou that sleepest, and arise from the dead: and Christ shall enlighten thee.

Saturday III after the Octave of the Epiphany

Lesson I - Eph 6:1–4

From the letter of St. Paul the Apostle to the Ephesians

Children, obey your parents in the Lord, for this is just. Honour thy father and thy mother, which is the first commandment with a promise: That it may be well with thee, and thou mayest be long lived upon earth. And you, fathers, provoke not your children to anger; but bring them up in the discipline and correction of the Lord.

Lesson II - Eph 6:5–9

Servants, be obedient to them that are your lords according to the flesh, with fear and trembling, in the simplicity of your heart, as to Christ: Not serving to the eye, as it were pleasing men, but, as the servants of Christ doing the will of God from the heart, With a good will serving, as to the Lord, and not to men. Knowing that whatsoever good thing any man shall do, the same shall he receive from the Lord, whether he be bond, or free. And you, masters, do the same things to them, forbearing threatenings, knowing that the Lord both of them and you is in heaven; and there is no respect of persons with him.

Lesson III - Eph 6:10–13

Finally, brethren, be strengthened in the Lord, and in the might of his power. Put you on the armour of God, that you may be able to stand against the deceits of the devil. For our wrestling is not against flesh and blood; but against principalities and power, against the rulers of the world of this darkness, against the spirits of wickedness in the high places. Therefore take unto you the armour of God, that you may be able to resist in the evil day, and to stand in all things perfect.

Sunday IV after the Octave of the Epiphany

If this or subsequent Sundays after the Epiphany are impeded by Septuagesima Sunday, their Lessons are omitted.

Lesson I - Phil 1:1–7

Beginning of the letter of St. Paul the Apostle to the Philippians

Paul and Timothy, the servants of Jesus Christ; to all the saints in

Christ Jesus, who are at Philippi, with the bishops and deacons. Grace be unto you, and peace from God our Father, and from the Lord Jesus Christ. I give thanks to my God in every remembrance of you, Always in all my prayers making supplication for you all, with joy; For your communication in the gospel of Christ from the first day until now. Being confident of this very thing, that he, who hath begun a good work in you, will perfect it unto the day of Christ Jesus. As it is meet for me to think this for you all, for that I have you in my heart; and that in my bands, and in the defence and confirmation of the gospel, you all are partakers of my joy.

Lesson II - Phil 1:8–14

For God is my witness, how I long after you all in the bowels of Jesus Christ. And this I pray, that your charity may more and more abound in knowledge, and in all understanding: That you may approve the better things, that you may be sincere and without offence unto the day of Christ, Filled with the fruit of justice, through Jesus Christ, unto the glory and praise of God. Now, brethren, I desire you should know, that the things which have happened to me, have fallen out rather to the furtherance of the gospel: So that my bands are made manifest in Christ, in all the court, and in all other places; And many of the brethren in the Lord, growing confident by my bands, are much more bold to speak the word of God without fear.

Lesson III - Phil 1:15–18

Some indeed, even out of envy and contention; but some also for good will preach Christ. Some out of charity, knowing that I am set for the defence of the gospel. And some out of contention preach Christ not sincerely: supposing that they raise affliction to my bands. But what then? So that by all means, whether by occasion, or by truth, Christ be preached: in this also I rejoice, yea, and will rejoice.

Lesson IV

From the Book of Morals written by Pope St. Gregory

We refresh the body lest it should grow too weak and fail us; we chasten it by abstinence, lest it should wax gross, and become lord over us; we strengthen it with exercise, lest it perish by disuse; and straightway we give it rest, lest it faint through weariness; we succor it with raiment, lest the cold should blight it; and we strip it of the raiment wherewith we have clothed it, lest the heat should afflict it. In all these so many offices what do we but serve the corruptible? Upon what is all this care spent but upon that over which hangs the doom of weakness and change?

Lesson V

Therefore says Paul well: "For the creature was made subject to vanity, not willingly, but by reason of Him Who hath subjected the same in hope because the creature itself also shall be delivered from the bondage of corruption into the glorious liberty of the children of God." The creature was made subject to vanity, not willingly for when man had of his own free will abdicated his state of unchangeable blessedness, the just sentence of death was passed upon him, and whether he willed or not, he became subject to the state of change and corruption. But the creature itself also shall be delivered from the bondage of corruption when it shall rise again incorruptible and be made partaker of the glory of the children of God.

Lesson VI

Where, then, the elect are still subject to sorrow, being yet bound by the sentence of corruption; but when we shall have put off this corruptible we shall be loosed from that sentence, and shall sorrow no more. For though we earnestly desire to appear before God, we are still hindered by the burden of this dying body. Rightly then are we called prisoners, since we are not free to go where we will, that is to say, to God; and rightly did the prisoner Paul, yearning after the things which are eternal, and still weighed down with the burden of this corruptible form, rightly did he cry out "I have a desire to depart and to be with Christ." He would not have felt this keenness if he had not felt himself bound down.

Lesson VII

From the Holy Gospel according to St. Matthew (Matt 8:23–27)

At that time, when Jesus entered into the boat, his disciples followed him: And behold a great tempest arose in the sea, so that the boat was covered with waves, but he was asleep. And so on.

Homily by St. Jerome, Priest

The fifth sign that He did was when He took ship at Capharnaum, and commanded the winds and the sea the sixth, when, in the country of the Gerasenes, He suffered the devils to enter into the swine the seventh, when, as He came into His own city, He cured the paralytic lying on a bed. The first paralytic that He cured was the centurion's servant.

Lesson VIII

But He was asleep; and His disciples came to Him, and awoke Him, saying "Lord, save us." There is a type of this in the history of Jonas, who, when the storm arose, was lying fast asleep, and whom the sailors woke to help them; who also saved the sailors by commanding them to throw him into the sea, being, as we know, a figure of Christ's Passion. "Then He arose and rebuked the winds and the sea." From these words we understand that all things, which have been made, are sentient to their Maker. All things which He rebukes or commands hear His voice. This is not the error of the heretics who will have it that everything is alive, but part of the majesty of the Creator, Who makes to feel Him things which we cannot make to feel us.

Lesson IX

Then the men were amazed and said: What sort of man is this that even the winds and the sea obey him? It is not the disciples but the sailors and the others who were in the boat who were amazed. But if someone is contentious and wants those who were amazed to be the disciples, we shall respond that they are rightly called men, for they did not yet know the power of the Savior.

Monday IV after the Octave of the Epiphany

Lesson I - Phil 4:1–3

From the letter of St. Paul the Apostle to the Philippians

Therefore, my dearly beloved brethren, and most desired, my joy and my crown; so stand fast in the Lord, my dearly beloved. I beg of Evodia, and I beseech Syntyche, to be of one mind in the Lord. And I entreat thee also, my sincere companion, help those women who have laboured with me in the gospel, with Clement and the rest of my fellow labourers, whose names are in the book of life.

Lesson II - Phil 4:4–7

Rejoice in the Lord always; again, I say, rejoice. Let your modesty be known to all men. The Lord is nigh. Be nothing solicitous; but in every thing, by prayer and supplication, with thanksgiving, let your petitions be made known to God. And the peace of God, which surpasseth all understanding, keep your hearts and minds in Christ Jesus.

Lesson III - Phil 4:8–10

For the rest, brethren, whatsoever things are true, whatsoever modest, whatsoever just, whatsoever holy, whatsoever lovely, whatsoever of good fame, if there be any virtue, if any praise of discipline, think on these things. The things which you have both learned, and received, and heard, and seen in me, these do ye, and the God of peace shall be with you. Now I rejoice in the Lord exceedingly, that now at length your thought for me hath flourished again, as you did also think; but you were busied.

Tuesday IV after the Octave of the Epiphany

Lesson I - Col 1:1–8

Beginning of the letter of St. Paul the Apostle to the Colossians

Paul, an apostle of Jesus Christ, by the will of God, and Timothy, a brother, To the saints and faithful brethren in Christ Jesus, who are at Colossa. Grace be to you and peace from God our Father, and from the Lord Jesus Christ. We give thanks to God, and the Father of our Lord Jesus Christ, praying always for you. Hearing your faith in Christ Jesus, and the love which you have towards all the saints. For the hope that is laid up for you in heaven, which you have heard in the word of the truth of the gospel, Which is come unto you, as also it is in the whole world, and bringeth forth fruit and groweth, even as it doth in you, since the day you heard and knew the grace of God in truth. As you learned of Epaphras, our most beloved fellow servant, who is for you a faithful minister of Christ Jesus; Who also hath manifested to us your love in the spirit.

Lesson II - Col 1:9–12

Therefore we also, from the day that we heard it, cease not to pray for you, and to beg that you may be filled with the knowledge of his will, in all wisdom, and spiritual understanding: That you may walk worthy of God, in all things pleasing; being fruitful in every good work, and increasing in the knowledge of God: Strengthened with all might, according to the power of his glory, in all patience and longsuffering with joy, Giving thanks to God the Father, who hath made us worthy to be partakers of the lot of the saints in light:

Lesson III - Col 1:13–18

Who hath delivered us from the power of darkness, and hath translated us into the kingdom of the Son of his love, In whom we have redemption through his blood, the remission of sins; Who is the image of the invisible God, the firstborn of every creature: For in him were all things created in heaven and on earth, visible and invisible, whether thrones, or dominations, or principalities, or powers: all things were created by him and in him. And he is before all, and by him all things consist. And he is the head of the body, the church, who is the beginning, the firstborn from the dead.

Wednesday IV after the Octave of the Epiphany

Lesson I - Col 3:12–15

From the letter of St. Paul the Apostle to the Colossians

Put ye on therefore, as the elect of God, holy, and beloved, the bowels of mercy, benignity, humility, modesty, patience: Bearing with one another, and forgiving one another, if any have a complaint against another: even as the Lord hath forgiven you, so do you also. But above all these things have charity, which is the bond of perfection: And let the peace of Christ rejoice in your hearts, wherein also you are called in one body: and be ye thankful.

Lesson II - Col 3:16–21

Let the word of Christ dwell in you abundantly, in all wisdom: teaching and admonishing one another in psalms, hymns, and spiritual canticles, singing in grace in your hearts to God. All whatsoever you do in word or in work, do all in the name of the Lord Jesus Christ, giving thanks to God and the Father by him. Wives, be subject to your husbands, as it behoveth in the Lord. Husbands, love your wives, and be not bitter towards them. Children, obey your parents in all things: for this is well pleasing to the Lord. Fathers, provoke not your children to indignation, lest they be discouraged.

Lesson III - Col 3:22–25; 4:1–2

Servants, obey in all things your masters according to the flesh, not serving to the eye, as pleasing men, but in simplicity of heart, fearing God. Whatsoever you do, do it from the heart, as to the Lord, and not to men: Knowing that you shall receive of the Lord the reward of inheritance. Serve ye the Lord Christ. For he that doth wrong, shall receive for that which he hath done wrongfully: and there is no respect of persons with God. Masters, do to your servants that which is just and equal: knowing that you also have a master in heaven. Be instant in prayer; watching in it with thanksgiving:

Thursday IV after the Octave of the Epiphany

Lesson I - 1 Thess 1:1–5

Beginning of the first letter of St. Paul the Apostle to the Thessalonians

Paul and Sylvanus and Timothy: to the church of the Thessalonians, in God the Father, and in the Lord Jesus Christ. Grace be to you and peace. We give thanks to God always for you all; making a remembrance of you in our prayers without ceasing, Being mindful of the work of your faith, and labour, and charity, and of the enduring of the hope of our Lord Jesus Christ before God and our Father: Knowing, brethren beloved of God, your election: For our gospel hath not been unto you in word only, but in power also, and in the Holy Ghost, and in much fulness, as you know what manner of men we have been among you for your sakes.

Lesson II - 1 Thess 1:6–10

And you became followers of us, and of the Lord; receiving the word in much tribulation, with joy of the Holy Ghost: So that you were made a pattern to all that believe in Macedonia and in Achaia. For from you was spread abroad the word of the Lord, not only in Macedonia, and in Achaia, but also in every place, your faith which is towards God, is gone forth, so that we need not to speak any thing. For they themselves relate of us, what manner of entering in we had unto you; and how you turned to God from idols, to serve the living and true God. And to wait for his Son from heaven (whom he raised up from the dead), Jesus, who hath delivered us from the wrath to come.

Lesson III - 1 Thess 2:1–6

For yourselves know, brethren, our entrance in unto you, that it was not in vain: But having suffered many things before, and been shamefully treated (as you know) at Philippi, we had confidence in our God, to speak unto you the gospel of God in much carefulness. For our exhortation was not of error, nor of uncleanness, nor in deceit: But as we were approved by God that the gospel should be committed to us: even so we speak, not as pleasing men, but God, who proveth our hearts. For neither have we used, at any time, the speech of flattery, as you know; nor taken an occasion of covetousness, God is witness: Nor sought we glory of men, neither of you, nor of others. Whereas we might have been burdensome to you, as the apostles of Christ: but we became little ones in the midst of you, as if a nurse should cherish her children.

Friday IV after the Octave of the Epiphany

Lesson I - 1 Thess 4:1–5

From the first letter of St. Paul the Apostle to the Thessalonians

For the rest therefore, brethren, we pray and beseech you in the Lord Jesus, that as you have received from us, how you ought to walk, and to please God, so also you would walk, that you may abound the more. For you know what precepts I have given to you by the Lord Jesus. For this is the will of God, your sanctification; that you should abstain from fornication; That every one of you should know how to possess his vessel in sanctification and honour: Not in the passion of lust, like the Gentiles that know not God:

Lesson II ~ 1 Thess 4:6–8

And that no man overreach, nor circumvent his brother in business: because the Lord is the avenger of all these things, as we have told you before, and have testified. For God hath not called us unto uncleanness, but unto sanctification. Therefore, he that despiseth these things, despiseth not man, but God, who also hath given his holy Spirit in us.

Lesson III ~ 1 Thess 4:9–11

But as touching the charity of brotherhood, we have no need to write to you: for yourselves have learned of God to love one another. For indeed you do it towards all the brethren in all Macedonia. But we entreat you, brethren, that you abound more: And that you use your endeavour to be quiet, and that you do your own business, and work with your own hands, as we commanded you: and that you walk honestly towards them that are without; and that you want nothing of any man's.

Saturday IV after the Octave of the Epiphany

Lesson I ~ 2 Thess 1:1–5

Beginning of the second letter of St. Paul the Apostle to the Thessalonians

Paul, and Sylvanus, and Timothy, to the church of the Thessalonians in God our Father, and the Lord Jesus Christ. Grace unto you, and peace from God our Father, and from the Lord Jesus Christ. We are bound to give thanks always to God for you, brethren, as it is fitting, because your faith groweth exceedingly, and the charity of every one of you towards each other, aboundeth: So that we ourselves also glory in you in the churches of God, for your patience and faith, and in all your persecutions and tribulations, which you endure, For an example of the just judgment of God, that you may be counted worthy of the kingdom of God, for which also you suffer.

Lesson II ~ 2 Thess 1:6–12

Seeing it is a just thing with God to repay tribulation to them that trouble you: And to you who are troubled, rest with us when the Lord Jesus shall be revealed from heaven, with the angels of his power: In a flame of fire, giving vengeance to them who know not God, and who obey not the gospel of our Lord Jesus Christ. Who shall suffer eternal punishment in destruction, from the face of the Lord, and from the glory of his power: When he shall come to be glorified in his saints, and to be made wonderful in all them who have believed;

because our testimony was believed upon you in that day. Wherefore also we pray always for you; that our God would make you worthy of his vocation, and fulfill all the good pleasure of his goodness and the work of faith in power; That the name of our Lord Jesus may be glorified in you, and you in him, according to the grace of our God, and of the Lord Jesus Christ.

Lesson III ~ 2 Thess 2:1–4

And we beseech you, brethren, by the coming of our Lord Jesus Christ, and of our gathering together unto him: That you be not easily moved from your sense, nor be terrified, neither by spirit, nor by word, nor by epistle, as sent from us, as if the day of the Lord were at hand. Let no man deceive you by any means, for unless there come a revolt first, and the man of sin be revealed, the son of perdition, Who opposeth, and is lifted up above all that is called God, or that is worshipped, so that he sitteth in the temple of God, shewing himself as if he were God.

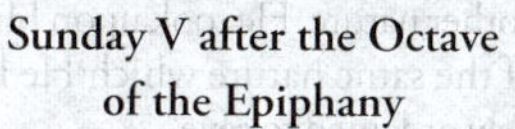

Sunday V after the Octave of the Epiphany

If this or subsequent Sundays after the Epiphany are impeded by Septuagesima Sunday, their Lessons are omitted.

Lesson I ~ 1 Tim 1:1–4

Beginning of the letter of St. Paul the Apostle to Timothy

Paul, an apostle of Jesus Christ, according to the commandment of God our Saviour, and of Christ Jesus our hope: To Timothy, his beloved son in faith. Grace, mercy, and peace from God the Father, and from Christ Jesus our Lord. As I desired thee to remain at Ephesus when I went into Macedonia, that thou mightest charge some not to teach otherwise, Not to give heed to fables and endless genealogies: which furnish questions rather than the edification of God, which is in faith.

Lesson II ~ 1 Tim 1:5–11

Now the end of the commandment is charity, from a pure heart, and a good conscience, and an unfeigned faith. From which things some going astray, are turned aside unto vain babbling: Desiring to be teachers of the law, understanding neither the things they say, nor whereof they affirm. But we know that the law is good, if a man use it lawfully: Knowing this, that the law is not made for the just man, but for the unjust and disobedient, for the ungodly and for sinners, for the wicked, and defiled, for patricides and matricides, for manslayers, For fornicators, for them who defile themselves with mankind, for menstealers, for liars, for perjured persons, and whatever other thing is contrary to sound doctrine, Which is according to the gospel of the glory of the blessed God, which hath been committed to my trust.

Lesson III ~ 1 Tim 1:12–16

I give thanks to him who hath strengthened me, even to Christ Jesus our Lord, for that he hath counted me faithful, putting me in the ministry; Who before was a blasphemer, and a persecutor, and contumelious. But I obtained the mercy of God, because I did it ignorantly in unbelief. Now the grace of our Lord hath abounded exceedingly with faith and love, which is in Christ Jesus. A faithful saying, and worthy of all acceptation, that Christ Jesus came into this world to save sinners, of whom I am the chief. But for this cause have I obtained mercy: that in me first Christ Jesus might shew forth all patience, for the information of them that shall believe in him unto life everlasting.

Lesson IV

Sermon by St. Augustine, Bishop

This is a saying made for man, and worthy of all acceptance, that Christ Jesus came into this world to save sinners. Listen to the words of the Gospel: "The Son of man is come to seek, and to save that which was lost." If man had not been lost, the Son of man would not have come. Wherefore, man had been lost; God came, being made Man, and man was found; man had perished by his own free will, God-made-Man came by grace which sets free.

Lesson V

Dost thou ask how free will avails to evil? Call to mind a sinner: Dost thou ask what God-made-Man avails to help? Consider in Him the grace which sets free. There is no example which so shows what avails the free will of man, when it is taken possession of by pride to use it without God's help; of evil is there no greater and plainer example than the first man. The first man fell, and where had he been if the second Man had not come? As the first was man, so was the second Man, and therefore is this saying a saying made for man.

Lesson VI

Neither is there any example which so shows what avails the tenderness of the grace and the abundance of the Omnipotence of God, as the Man That is the Mediator between God and men, the Man Christ Jesus. For what do we say, my brethren? I speak to them that have been bred up in the Catholic Church, or who have been reconciled to that Church. We know and hold that the Mediator between God and men, the Man Christ Jesus, as touching upon His Manhood, is of the same nature as we. For our flesh is not of one nature, and His Flesh of another nature, neither our soul of one nature and His Soul of another nature. He took upon Himself the same nature which He had freely ordained to save.

Lesson VII

From the Holy Gospel according to St. Matthew (Matt 13:24–30)

At that time, Jesus said to the people a parable: The kingdom of heaven is likened to a man that sowed good seeds in his field. And so on.

Homily by St. Augustine, Bishop

When the Shepherds of the Church wax careless, and since the Apostles sleep the sleep of death, the devil comes and sows them whom the Lord calls a seed of evildoers. Now, are these seed of evildoers the heretics, or Catholics of bad lives? It is possible to call even the heretics a seed of evildoers because they have sprung up from the seed of the Gospel, and been begotten in the Name of Christ, though afterwards they have turned after crooked ways and lying doctrines.

Lesson VIII

But whereas it is written that they were sown in the midst of the wheat, we ought haply to understand that they are of one communion with the righteous. Nevertheless, forasmuch as the Lord says, "The field is the world" (and not, the Church), we may well understand that the seed of evildoers are the heretics, since in this world they are mingled together with the good, not in one common Communion, but only under one common name of Christian. But they which are of one faith with the good seed, and yet are themselves worthless, may more fitly be likened to straw than to tares, since the straw springs from one soil and one root with the good ear.

Lesson IX

However, as touching the net cast into the sea, and enclosing a great multitude of fishes both bad and good, we may well understand that by the bad are meant Catholics of bad lives. For the sea is one thing whereby we may understand to be signified the world; and the net another, which seems to signify our faith, or the Communion of one Church. Between heretics and sinful Catholics there is this difference, that heretics believe a lie, and sinful Catholics believe the truth, but live not as they believe.

Monday V after the Octave of the Epiphany

Lesson I - 1 Tim 3:1–7

From the first letter of St. Paul the Apostle to Timothy

A faithful saying: if a man desire the office of a bishop, he desireth a good work. It behoveth therefore a bishop to be blameless, the husband of one wife, sober, prudent, of good behaviour, chaste, given to hospitality, a teacher, Not given to wine, no striker, but modest, not quarrelsome, not covetous, but One that ruleth well his own house, having his children in subjection with all chastity. But if a man know not how to rule his own house, how shall he take care of the church of God? Not a neophyte: lest being puffed up with pride, he fall into the judgment of the devil. Moreover he must have a good testimony of them who are without: lest he fall into reproach and the snare of the devil.

Lesson II - 1 Tim 3:8–13

Deacons in like manner chaste, not double tongued, not given to much wine, not greedy of filthy lucre: Holding the mystery of faith in a pure conscience. And let these also first be proved: and so let them minister, having no crime. The women in like manner chaste, not slanderers, but sober, faithful in all things. Let deacons be the husbands of one wife: who rule well their children, and their own houses. For they that have ministered well, shall purchase to themselves a good degree, and much confidence in the faith which is in Christ Jesus.

Lesson III ~ 1 Tim 3:14–16; 4:1

These things I write to thee, hoping that I shall come to thee shortly. But if I tarry long, that thou mayest know how thou oughtest to behave thyself in the house of God, which is the church of the living God, the pillar and ground of the truth. And evidently great is the mystery of godliness, which was manifested in the flesh, was justified in the spirit, appeared unto angels, hath been preached unto the Gentiles, is believed in the world, is taken up in glory. Now the Spirit manifestly saith, that in the last times some shall depart from the faith, giving heed to spirits of error, and doctrines of devils.

Tuesday V after the Octave of the Epiphany

Lesson I ~ 2 Tim 1:1–5

Beginning of the second letter of St. Paul the Apostle to Timothy

Paul, an apostle of Jesus Christ, by the will of God, according to the promise of life, which is in Christ Jesus. To Timothy my dearly beloved son, grace, mercy, and peace, from God the Father, and from Christ Jesus our Lord. I give thanks to God, whom I serve from my forefathers with a pure conscience, that without ceasing, I have a remembrance of thee in my prayers, night and day. Desiring to see thee, being mindful of thy tears, that I may be filled with joy, Calling to mind that faith which is in thee unfeigned, which also dwelt first in thy grandmother Lois, and in thy mother Eunice, and I am certain that in thee also.

Lesson II ~ 2 Tim 1:6–9

For which cause I admonish thee, that thou stir up the grace of God which is in thee, by the imposition of my hands. For God hath not given us the spirit of fear: but of power, and of love, and of sobriety. Be not thou therefore ashamed of the testimony of our Lord, nor of me his prisoner: but labour with the gospel, according to the power of God, Who hath delivered us and called us by his holy calling, not according to our works, but according to his own purpose and grace, which was given us in Christ Jesus before the times of the world.

Lesson III ~ 2 Tim 1:10–13

But is now made manifest by the illumination of our Saviour Jesus Christ, who hath destroyed death, and hath brought to light life and incorruption by the gospel: Wherein I am appointed a preacher, and an apostle, and teacher of the Gentiles. For which cause I also suffer these things: but I am not ashamed. For

I know whom I have believed, and I am certain that he is able to keep that which I have committed unto him, against that day. Hold the form of sound words, which thou hast heard of me in faith, and in the love which is in Christ Jesus.

Wednesday V after the Octave of the Epiphany

Lesson I ~ 2 Tim 3:1–5

From the second letter of St. Paul the Apostle to Timothy

Know also this, that, in the last days, shall come dangerous times. Men shall be lovers of themselves, covetous, haughty, proud, blasphemers, disobedient to parents, ungrateful, wicked, Without affection, without peace, slanderers, incontinent, unmerciful, without kindness, Traitors, stubborn, puffed up, and lovers of pleasures more than of God: Having an appearance indeed of godliness, but denying the power thereof. Now these avoid.

Lesson II ~ 2 Tim 3:6–9

For of these sort are they who creep into houses, and lead captive silly women laden with sins, who are led away with diverse desires: Ever learning, and never attaining to the knowledge of the truth. Now as Jannes and Mambres resisted Moses, so these also resist the truth, men corrupted in mind, reprobate concerning the faith. But they shall proceed no farther; for their folly shall be manifest to all men, as theirs also was.

Lesson III ~ 2 Tim 3:10–13

But thou hast fully known my doctrine, manner of life, purpose, faith, longsuffering, love, patience, Persecutions, afflictions: such as came upon me at Antioch, at Iconium, and at Lystra: what persecutions I endured, and out of them all the Lord delivered me. And all that will live godly in Christ Jesus, shall suffer persecution. But evil men and seducers shall grow worse and worse: erring, and driving into error.

Thursday V after the Octave of the Epiphany

Lesson I ~ Titus 1:1–4

From the letter of St. Paul the Apostle to Titus

Paul, a servant of God, and an apostle of Jesus Christ, according to the faith of the elect of God and the acknowledging of the truth, which is according to godliness: Unto the hope of life everlasting, which God, who lieth not, hath promised before the times of the world: But hath in due times manifested his word in preaching, which is committed to me according to the commandment of God our Saviour: To Titus my beloved son, according to the common faith, grace and peace from God the Father, and from Christ Jesus our Saviour.

Lesson II ~ Titus 1:5–9

For this cause I left thee in Crete, that thou shouldest set in order the things that are wanting, and shouldest ordain priests in every city, as I also appointed thee: If any be without crime, the husband of one wife, having faithful children, not accused of riot, or unruly. For a bishop must be without crime, as the steward of God: not proud, not subject to anger, not given to wine, no striker, not greedy of filthy lucre: But given to hospitality, gentle, sober, just, holy, continent: Embracing that faithful word which is according to doctrine, that he may be able to exhort in sound doctrine, and to convince the gainsayers.

Lesson III ~ Titus 1:10–15

For there are also many disobedient, vain talkers, and seducers: especially they who are of the circumcision: Who must be reproved, who subvert whole houses, teaching things which they ought not, for filthy lucre's sake. One of them a prophet of their own, said, The Cretians are always liars, evil beasts, slothful bellies. This testimony is true. Wherefore rebuke them sharply, that they may be sound in the faith; Not giving heed to Jewish fables and commandments of men, who turn themselves away from the truth. All things are clean to the clean: but to them that are defiled, and to unbelievers, nothing is clean: but both their mind and their conscience are defiled.

Friday V after the Octave of the Epiphany

Lesson I ~ Titus 2:15;3:1–2

From the letter of St. Paul the Apostle to Titus

These things speak, and exhort and rebuke with all authority. Let no man despise thee. Admonish them to be subject to princes and powers, to obey at a word, to be ready to every good work. To speak evil of no man, not to be litigious, but gentle: shewing all mildness towards all men.

Lesson II ~ Titus 3:3–7

For we ourselves also were some time unwise, incredulous, erring, slaves to diverse desires and pleasures, living in malice and envy, hateful, and hating one another. But when the goodness and kindness of God our Saviour appeared: Not by the works of justice, which we have done, but according to his mercy, he saved us, by the laver of regeneration, and renovation of the Holy Ghost; Whom he hath poured forth upon us abundantly, through Jesus Christ our Saviour: That, being justified by his grace, we may be heirs, according to hope of life everlasting.

Lesson III ~ Titus 3:8–11

It is a faithful saying: and these things I will have thee affirm constantly: that they, who believe in God, may be careful to excel in good works. These things are good and profitable unto men. But avoid foolish questions, and genealogies, and contentions, and strivings about the law. For they are unprofitable and vain. A man that is a heretic, after the first and second admonition, avoid: Knowing that he, that is such an one, is subverted, and sinneth, being condemned by his own judgment.

Saturday V after the Octave of the Epiphany

Lesson I ~ Phlm 1:1–6

Beginning of the letter of St. Paul the Apostle to Philemon

Paul, a prisoner of Christ Jesus, and Timothy, a brother: to Philemon, our beloved and fellow labourer; And to Appia, our dearest sister, and to Archippus, our fellow soldier, and to the church which is in thy house: Grace to you and peace from God our Father, and from the Lord Jesus Christ. I give thanks to my God, always making a remembrance of thee in my prayers. Hearing of thy charity and faith, which thou hast in the Lord Jesus, and towards all the saints: That the communication of thy faith may be made evident in the acknowledgment of every good work, that is in you in Christ Jesus.

Lesson II ~ Phlm 1:7–11

For I have had great joy and consolation in thy charity, because the bowels of the saints have been refreshed by thee, brother. Wherefore though I have much confidence in Christ Jesus, to command thee that which is to the purpose: For charity sake I rather beseech, whereas thou art such a one, as Paul an old man, and now a prisoner also of Jesus Christ. I beseech thee for my son, whom I have begotten in my bands, Onesimus, Who hath been heretofore unprofitable to thee, but now is profitable both to me and thee, whom I have sent back to thee.

Lesson III ~ Phlm 12–19

And do thou receive him as my own bowels. Whom I would have retained with me, that in thy stead he might have ministered to me in the bands of the gospel: But without thy counsel I would do nothing: that thy good deed might not be as it were of necessity, but voluntary. For perhaps he therefore departed for a season from thee, that thou mightest receive him again for ever: Not now as a servant, but instead of a servant, a most dear brother, especially to me: but how much more to thee both in the flesh and in the Lord? If therefore thou count me a partner, receive him as myself. And if he hath wronged thee in any thing, or is in thy debt, put that to my account. I Paul have written it with my own hand.

Sunday VI after the Octave of the Epiphany

If this or subsequent Sundays after the Epiphany are impeded by Septuagesima Sunday, their Lessons are omitted.

Lesson I ~ Heb 1:1–4

Beginning of the letter of St. Paul the Apostle to the Hebrews

God, who, at sundry times and in diverse manners, spoke in times past to the fathers by the prophets, last of all, In these days hath spoken to us by his Son, whom he hath appointed heir of all things, by whom also he made the world. Who being the brightness of his glory, and the figure of his substance, and upholding all things by the word of his power, making purgation of sins, sitteth on the right hand of the majesty on high. Being made so much better than the angels, as he hath inherited a more excellent name than they.

Lesson II ~ Heb 1:5–9

For to which of the angels hath he said at any time, Thou art my Son, to day have I begotten thee? And again, I will be to him a Father, and he shall be to me a Son? And again, when he bringeth in the first begotten into the world, he saith: And let all the angels of God adore him. And to the angels indeed he saith: He that maketh his angels spirits, and his ministers a flame of fire. But to the Son: thy throne, O God, is for ever and ever: a sceptre of justice is the sceptre of thy kingdom. Thou hast loved justice, and hated iniquity: therefore God, thy God, hath anointed thee with the oil of gladness above thy fellows.

Lesson III ~ Heb 1:10–14

And: Thou in the beginning, O Lord, didst found the earth: and the works of thy hands are the heavens. They shall perish, but thou shalt continue: and they shall all grow old as a garment. And as a vesture shalt thou change them, and they shall be changed: but thou art the selfsame, and thy years shall not fail. But to which of the angels said he at any time: Sit on my right hand, until I make thy enemies thy footstool? Are they not all ministering spirits, sent to minister for them, who shall receive the inheritance of salvation?

Lesson IV

Sermon by St. Athanasius, Pope

If the heretics had but known the person, the matter, and the times of the Apostle who spoke, they would never have spoken of Divinity as if It were human, nor borne themselves so wickedly, and withal so foolishly against Christ. It will be permitted to us to return, and to take again the first words of the Lesson. The Apostle then saith "God, Who at sundry times and in diverse manners, spoke in time past unto the fathers by the Prophets, hath in these last days spoken unto us by His Son" and again, a little farther on: "When the Son had purged our sins, He sat down on the right hand of the Majesty on high being made so much better than the angels as He hath by inheritance obtained a more excellent name than they." The Apostle here expressly names the times wherein God has spoken unto us by His Son, and wherein His Same Son has purged our sins; for when had He spoken unto us by His Son, when did the Son purge our sins, or when was He born a Man, but since God spoke unto the Fathers by the Prophets, namely, in these last days?

Lesson V

The Apostle, about to enter on the subject of the Word's human dispensation and the last days, naturally mentions first that God had not up to those days been silent, but had spoken unto the fathers by the Prophets and, after the Prophets had discharged their office, and the law had been given by the ministry of angels, that the Son also came down unto us to minister and then he adds, being made so much better than the angels, to show that as the Son differs from a servant, so is the ministry of the Son better than the duty and office of servants.

Lesson VI

The Apostle, therefore, seeing the difference between the new ministry and the old, makes very bold in writing and speaking to the Jews. For this cause, therefore, he does not compare the details of the two ministries and then come to the general conclusion that the new was greater or more honorable than the old (lest any should understand that the two ministries were of the same kind, and that the conclusion that the new is better is arrived at by comparing the degrees in each of things which they had in common), but he says that the Son was made better, to distinguish at once and completely the nature of the Son from the nature of things created.

Lesson VII

From the Holy Gospel according to St. Matthew (Matt 13:31–32)

At that time, Jesus said to to the people a parable: The kingdom of heaven is like to a grain of mustard seed, which a man took and sowed in his field. And so on.

Homily by St. Jerome, Priest

The kingdom of heaven is the proclamation of the Gospel, and that knowledge of the Scriptures, which leads unto life, and whereof it is said to the Jews: The kingdom of God shall be taken from you, and given to a nation bringing forth the fruits thereof. Therefore is this kingdom like to a grain of mustard-seed, which a man took and sowed in his field. By the man that sowed it in his field, many understand to be meant the Saviour, because He is the Sower That sows in the souls of believers; others understand every man that sows good seed in his own field, that is, in himself and in his own heart.

Lesson VIII

Who is he that sows, but our own mind and soul, which take the grain from preaching, and by nourishing it in the soil, cause it to sprout in the field of our own breast? The preaching of the Gospel is the least of all doctrines. He that preaches for his first lesson, God made man, Christ dead, and the stumbling-block of the Cross, receives at first but little credit. Compare such teaching as this with the doctrines of the Philosophers, with their books, their magnificent eloquence, and their rounded sentences, and thou shalt see how the grain of the Gospel, when it is sown, is the humblest of all seeds.

Lesson IX

But when the doctrines of men grow up, there is therein nothing piercing, nothing healthy, nothing life-giving. The plant is drooping, and delicate, and soft. There are herbs and grass whereof it may truly be said that the grass withers and the flower fades.

But the grain of Gospel seed, though, when it was sown, it seemed to be the least of all seeds, when once it is rooted in the soul of man, or in the whole world, grows not into an herb, but becomes a tree so that the birds of the air (whereby we may understand, either the souls of believers, or the powers bound to the service of God), come and lodge in the branches thereof. I consider that the branches of the Gospel tree, which grows from the grain of mustard-seed, are the diverse developments of doctrine, on which the birds above mentioned find resting-places.

Monday VI after the Octave of the Epiphany

Lesson I ~ Heb 3:1–4

From the letter of St. Paul the Apostle to the Hebrews

Wherefore, holy brethren, partakers of the heavenly vocation, consider the apostle and high priest of our confession, Jesus: Who is faithful to him that made him, as was also Moses in all his house. For this man was counted worthy of greater glory than Moses, by so much as he that hath built the house, hath greater honour than the house. For every house is built by some man: but he that created all things, is God.

Lesson II ~ Heb 3:5–8

And Moses indeed was faithful in all his house as a servant, for a testimony of those things which were to be said: But Christ as the Son in his own house: which house are we, if we hold fast the confidence and glory of hope unto the end. Wherefore, as the Holy Ghost saith: To day if you shall hear his voice, Harden not your hearts, as in the provocation; in the day of temptation in the desert,

Lesson III ~ Heb 3:12–16

Take heed, brethren, lest perhaps there be in any of you an evil heart of unbelief, to depart from the living God. But exhort one another every day, whilst it is called to day, that none of you be hardened through the deceitfulness of sin. For we are made partakers of Christ: yet so, if we hold the beginning of his substance firm unto the end. While it is said, To day if you shall hear his voice, harden not your hearts, as in that provocation. For some who heard did provoke: but not all that came out of Egypt by Moses.

Tuesday VI after the Octave of the Epiphany

Lesson I ~ Heb 4:1–3

From the letter of St. Paul the Apostle to the Hebrews

Let us fear therefore lest the promise being left of entering into his rest, any of you should be thought to be wanting. For unto us also it hath been declared, in like manner as unto them. But the word of hearing did not profit them, not being mixed with faith of those things they heard. For we, who have believed, shall enter into rest; as he said: As I have sworn in my wrath; If they shall enter into my rest; and this indeed when the works from the foundation of the world were finished.

Lesson II ~ Heb 4:4–7

For in a certain place he spoke of the seventh day thus: And God rested the seventh day from all his works. And in this place again: If they shall enter into my rest. Seeing then it remaineth that some are to enter into it, and they, to whom it was first preached, did not enter because of unbelief: Again he limiteth a certain day, saying in David, To day, after so long a time, as it is above said: To day if you shall hear his voice, harden not your hearts.

Lesson III ~ Heb 4:8–12

For if Jesus had given them rest, he would never have afterwards spoken of another day. There remaineth therefore a day of rest for the people of God. For he that is entered into his rest, the same also hath rested from his works, as God did from his. Let us hasten therefore to enter into that rest; lest any man fall into the same example of unbelief. For the word of God is living and effectual, and more piercing than any two edged sword; and reaching unto the division of the soul and the spirit, of the joints also and the marrow, and is a discerner of the thoughts and intents of the heart.

Wednesday VI after the Octave of the Epiphany

Lesson I ~ Heb 6:1–3

From the letter of St. Paul the Apostle to the Hebrews

Wherefore leaving the word of the beginning of Christ, let us go on to things more perfect, not laying again the foundation of penance from dead works, and of faith towards God, Of the doctrine of baptisms, and imposition of hands, and of the resurrection of the dead, and of eternal judgment. And this will we do, if God permit.

Lesson II ~ Heb 6:4–6

For it is impossible for those who were once illuminated, have tasted also the heavenly gift, and were made partakers of the Holy Ghost, Have moreover tasted the good word of God, and the powers of the world to come, And are fallen away: to be renewed again to penance, crucifying again to themselves the Son of God, and making him a mockery.

Lesson III ~ Heb 6:7–10

For the earth that drinketh in the rain which comes often upon it, and bringeth forth herbs meet for them by whom it is tilled, receiveth blessing from God. But that which bringeth forth thorns and briers, is reprobate, and very near unto a curse, whose end is to be burnt. But, my dearly beloved, we trust better things of you, and nearer to salvation; though we speak thus. For God is not unjust, that he should forget your work, and the love which you have shewn in his name, you who have ministered, and do minister to the saints.

Thursday VI after the Octave of the Epiphany

Lesson I ~ Heb 7:1–3

From the letter of St. Paul the Apostle to the Hebrews

For this Melchisedech was king of Salem, priest of the most high

God, who met Abraham returning from the slaughter of the kings, and blessed him: To whom also Abraham divided the tithes of all: who first indeed by interpretation, is king of justice: and thèn also king of Salem, that is, king of peace: Without father, without mother, without genealogy, having neither beginning of days nor end of life, but likened unto the Son of God, continueth a priest for ever.

Lesson II - Heb 7:4–6

Now consider how great this man is, to whom also Abraham the patriarch gave tithes out of the principal things. And indeed they that are of the sons of Levi, who receive the priesthood, have a commandment to take tithes of the people according to the law, that is to say, of their brethren: though they themselves also came out of the loins of Abraham. But he, whose pedigree is not numbered among them, received tithes of Abraham, and blessed him that had the promises.

Lesson III - Heb 7:7–12

And without all contradiction, that which is less, is blessed by the better. And here indeed, men that die, receive thithes: but there he hath witness, that he liveth. And (as it may be said) even Levi who received tithes, paid tithes in Abraham: For he was yet in the loins of his father, when Melchisedech met him. If then perfection was by the Levitical priesthood (for under it the people received the law), what further need was there that another priest should rise according to the order of Melchisedech, and not be called according to the order of Aaron? For the priesthood being translated, it is necessary that a translation also be made of the law.

Friday VI after the Octave of the Epiphany

Lesson I - Heb 11:1–4

From the letter of St. Paul the Apostle to the Hebrews

Now faith is the substance of things to be hoped for, the evidence of things that appear not. For by this the ancients obtained a testimony. By faith we understand that the world was framed by the word of God; that from invisible things visible things might be made. By faith Abel offered to God a sacrifice exceeding that of Cain, by which he obtained a testimony that he was just, God giving testimony to his gifts; and by it he being dead yet speaketh.

Lesson II - Heb 11:5–7

By faith Henoch was translated, that he should not see death; and he was not found, because God had translated him: for before his translation he had testimony that he pleased God. But without faith it is impossible to please God. For he that cometh to God, must believe that he is, and is a rewarder to them that seek him. By faith Noe, having received an answer concerning those things which as yet were not seen, moved with fear, framed the ark for the saving of his house, by the which he condemned the world; and was instituted heir of the justice which is by faith.

Lesson III ~ Heb 1:8–10

But to the Son: thy throne, O God, is for ever and ever: a sceptre of justice is the sceptre of thy kingdom. Thou hast loved justice, and hated iniquity: therefore God, thy God, hath anointed thee with the oil of gladness above thy fellows. And: Thou in the beginning, O Lord, didst found the earth: and the works of thy hands are the heavens.

Saturday VI after the Octave of the Epiphany

Lesson I ~ Heb 13:1–4

From the letter of St. Paul the Apostle to the Hebrews

Let the charity of the brotherhood abide in you. And hospitality do not forget; for by this some, being not aware of it, have entertained angels. Remember them that are in bands, as if you were bound with them; and them that labour, as being yourselves also in the body. Marriage honourable in all, and the bed undefiled. For fornicators and adulterers God will judge.

Lesson II ~ Heb 13:5–8

Let your manners be without covetousness, contented with such things as you have; for he hath said: I will not leave thee, neither will I forsake thee. So that we may confidently say: The Lord is my helper: I will not fear what man shall do to me. Remember your prelates who have spoken the word of God to you; whose faith follow, considering the end of their conversation, Jesus Christ, yesterday, and to day; and the same for ever.

Lesson III ~ Heb 13:9–12

Be not led away with various and strange doctrines. For it is best that the heart be established with grace, not with meats; which have not profited those that walk in them. We have an altar, whereof they have no power to eat who serve the tabernacle. For the bodies of those beasts, whose blood is brought into the holies by the high priest for sin, are burned without the camp. Wherefore Jesus also, that he might sanctify the people by his own blood, suffered without the gate.

SEPTUAGESIMATIDE

SEPTUAGESIMA SUNDAY

~3 Weeks before Lent~

Duplex II Class

Lesson I ~ Gen 1:1–8

Beginning of the book of Genesis

In the beginning God created heaven, and earth. And the earth was void and empty, and darkness was upon the face of the deep; and the spirit of God moved over the waters. And God said: Be light made. And light was made. And God saw the light that it was good; and he divided the light from the darkness. And he called the light Day, and the darkness Night; and there was evening and morning one day. And God said: Let there be a firmament made amidst the waters: and let it divide the waters from the waters. And God made a firmament, and divided the waters that were under the firmament, from those that were above the firmament, and it was so. And God called the firmament, Heaven; and the evening and morning were the second day.

Lesson II ~ Gen 1:9–19

God also said: Let the waters that are under the heaven, be gathered together into one place: and let the dry land appear. And it was so done. And God called the dry land, Earth; and the gathering together of the waters, he called Seas. And God saw that it was good. And he said: Let the earth bring forth the green herb, and such as may seed, and the fruit tree yielding fruit after its kind, which may have seed in itself upon the earth. And it was so done. And the earth brought forth the green herb, and such as yieldeth seed according to its kind, and the tree that beareth fruit having seed each one according to its kind. And God saw that it was good. And the evening and the morning were the third day. And God said: Let there be lights made in the firmament of heaven, to divide the day and the night, and let them be for signs, and for seasons, and for days and years: To shine in the firmament of heaven, and to give light upon the earth. And it was so done. And God made two great lights: a greater light to rule the day; and a lesser light to rule the night: and the stars. And he set them in the firmament of heaven to shine upon the earth. And to rule the day and the night, and to divide the light and the darkness. And God saw that it was good. And the evening and morning were the fourth day.

Lesson III ~ Gen 1:20–26

God also said: Let the waters bring forth the creeping creature having life, and the fowl that may fly over the earth under the firmament of heaven. And God created the great whales, and every living and moving creature, which the waters brought forth, according to their kinds, and every winged fowl according to its kind. And God saw that it was good. And he blessed them, saying: Increase and multiply, and fill the waters of the sea: and let the birds be multiplied upon the earth. And the evening and morning were the fifth day. And God said: Let the earth bring forth the living creature in its kind, cattle and creeping things, and beasts of the earth, according to their kinds. And it was so done. And God made the beasts of the earth according to their kinds, and cattle, and every thing that creepeth on the earth after its kind. And God saw that it was good. And he said: Let us make man to our image and likeness: and let him have dominion over the fishes of the sea, and the fowls of the air, and the beasts, and the whole earth, and every creeping creature that moveth upon the earth.

Lesson IV

From the Handbook by St. Augustine, Bishop

The Lord threatened man with the punishment of death, in case he sinned. Thus did He gift him with free will, while He yet kept His lordship over him, and helped him with the dread of destruction. And so He put him in that happy garden, under the very shadow of the tree of life, in that good place from whence, had he kept his righteousness, he might have passed to a better one. But the first man sinned, and was banished from Eden, and infected all his descendants with the disease of sin, poisoning their very root, and bringing upon all that sentence of death and damnation, which he had earned for himself. So that all that descend by fleshly generation from Adam, and from the guilty woman, who was the cause of his sin and the partaker of his punishment, derive from them original sin; whereby they are drawn through a way of diverse sins and sorrows, towards that final ruin which they shall share with the rebel angels who are at once their corrupters, their lords, and their comrades.

Lesson V

So by one man sin entered into the world, and death by sin (and so death passed upon all men), in whom all have sinned. By the world the Apostle signified in this place all mankind. Thus, then, has the matter stood. The damned mass of humanity lay in misery, or rather wallowed in it, and fell from bad to worse, till it joined the company of the sinning angels, and both together suffered the deserved punishment of their vile treason.

Lesson VI

So the wrath of God appertained whatever sin man, through the blind and untamed sting of his flesh, willingly commits, and whatever punishment, declared and open, he unwillingly suffers. There is, indeed, no pause in that goodness of the Creator whereby He gives even to the traitor angels life and strength (which if He gave not, they would be annihilated), and whereby He forms the seed of men, though they come of a corrupt and condemned stock, quickens them, strengthens and fits their limbs for the changing seasons of their life, extends their knowledge in diverse places, and gives them whereon to live. It has been His will rather to draw good out of evil, than to suffer that there should be no evil.

Lesson VII

From the Holy Gospel according to St. Matthew (Matt 20:1–16)

In that time, Jesus said to his disciples: The kingdom of heaven is like to a householder, who went out early in the morning to hire labourers into his vineyard. And so on.

Homily by Pope St. Gregory

We hear that the kingdom of heaven is like unto a man that is a householder, which went out early in the morning, to hire laborers into his vineyard. Who indeed is more justly to be likened to a householder than our Maker, Who is the Head of the household of faith, bearing rule over them whom He has made, and being Master of His chosen ones in the world, as a Master over those that are in his house? He it is That has the Church for a vineyard, a vineyard that ceases not to bring forth branches of the True Vine, from righteous Abel to the last of the elect that shall be born in the world.

Lesson VIII

This householder, then, for the cultivation of his vineyard, goes out early in the morning, and at the third hour, and the sixth hour, and the ninth hour, and the eleventh hour, to hire laborers into his vineyard. Thus the Lord, from the beginning to the end of the world, ceases not to gather together preachers for the instruction of His faithful people. The early morning of the world was from Adam until Noe; the third hour from Noe until Abraham; the sixth hour from Abraham until Moses; the ninth hour from Moses until the coming of the Lord; the eleventh hour from the coming of the Lord until the end of the world. At this eleventh hour are sent forth as preachers the Holy Apostles, who have received full wages, albeit they be come in late.

Lesson IX

For the cultivation of His vineyard (that is, the instruction of His people), the Lord has never ceased to send into it laborers. First, by the Fathers, then, by the Prophets and Teachers of the Law, and lastly, by the Apostles He has dressed and tended the lives of His people, as the owner of a vineyard dresses and tends it by means of workmen. Whoever in whatever degree joined to a right faith the teaching of righteousness, was so far one of God's laborers in God's vineyard. By the laborers at early morning, and at the third hour, the sixth hour, and the ninth hour, may be understood God's ancient people, the Hebrews, who strove to worship Him with a right faith in company with His chosen ones from the very beginning of the world, and thus continually labored in His vineyard. And now, at the eleventh hour, it is said unto the Gentiles also "Why stand ye here all the day idle?"

Monday in Septuagesima

Lesson I ~ Gen 1:27–31

From the book of Genesis

And God created man to his own image: to the image of God he created him: male and female he created them. And God blessed them, saying: Increase and multiply, and fill the earth, and subdue it, and rule over the fishes of the sea, and the fowls of the air, and all living creatures that move upon the earth. And God said: Behold I have given you every herb bearing seed upon the earth, and all trees that have in themselves seed of their own kind, to be your meat: And to all the beasts of the earth, and to every fowl of the air, and to all that move upon the earth, and wherein there is life, that they may have to feed upon. And it was so done. And God saw all the things that he had made, and they were very good. And the evening and morning were the sixth day.

Lesson II ~ Gen 2:1–6

So the heavens and the earth were finished, and all the furniture of them. And on the seventh day God ended his work which he had made: and he rested on the seventh day from all his work which he had done. And he blessed the seventh day, and sanctified it: because in it he had rested from all his work which God created and made. These are the generations of the heaven and the earth, when they were created, in the day that the Lord God made the heaven and the earth: And every plant of the field before it spring up in the earth, and every herb of the ground before it grew: for the Lord God had not rained upon the earth; and there was not a man to till the earth. But a spring rose out the earth, watering all the surface of the earth.

Lesson III ~ Gen 2:7–10

And the Lord God formed man of the slime of the earth: and breathed into his face the breath of life, and man became a living soul. And the Lord God had planted a paradise of pleasure from the beginning: wherein he placed man whom he had formed. And the Lord God brought forth of the ground all manner of trees, fair to behold, and pleasant to eat of: the tree of life also in the midst of paradise: and the tree of knowledge of good and evil. And a river went out the place of pleasure to water paradise, which from thence is divided into four heads.

Tuesday in Septuagesima

Lesson I - Gen 2:15–18

From the book of Genesis

And the Lord God took man, and put him into the paradise for pleasure, to dress it, and keep it. And he commanded him, saying: Of every tree of paradise thou shalt eat: But of the tree of knowledge of good and evil, thou shalt not eat. for in what day soever thou shalt eat of it, thou shalt die the death. And the Lord God said: It is not good for man to be alone: let us make him a help like unto himself.

Lesson II - Gen 2:19–20

And the Lord God having formed out of the ground all the beasts of the earth, and all the fowls of the air, brought them to Adam to see what he would call them: for whatsoever Adam called any living creature the same is its name. And Adam called all the beasts by their names, and all the fowls of the air, and all the cattle of the field: but for Adam there was not found a helper like himself.

Lesson III - Gen 2:21–24

Then the Lord God cast a deep sleep upon Adam: and when he was fast asleep, he took one of his ribs, and filled up flesh for it. And the Lord God built the rib which he took from Adam into a woman: and brought her to Adam. And Adam said: This now is bone of my bones, and flesh of my flesh; she shall be called woman, because she was taken out of man. Wherefore a man shall leave father and mother, and shall cleave to his wife: and they shall be two in one flesh.

Wednesday in Septuagesima

Lesson I - Gen 3:1–7

From the book of Genesis

Now the serpent was more subtle than any of the beasts of the earth which the Lord God made. And he said to the woman: Why hath God commanded you, that you should not eat of every tree of paradise? And the woman answered him, saying: Of the fruit of the trees that are in paradise we do eat: But of the fruit of the tree which is in the midst of paradise, God hath commanded us that we should not eat; and that we should not touch it, lest perhaps we die. And the serpent said to the woman: No, you shall not die the death. For God doth know that in what day soever you shall eat thereof, your eyes shall be opened: and you shall be as Gods, knowing good and evil. And the woman saw that the tree was good to eat, and fair to the eyes, and delightful to behold: and she took of the fruit thereof, and did eat, and gave to her husband who did eat. And the eyes of them both were opened.

Lesson II - Gen 3:7–13

When they perceived themselves to be naked, they sewed together fig leaves, and made themselves aprons.

And when they heard the voice of the Lord God walking in paradise at the afternoon air, Adam and his wife hid themselves from the face of the Lord God, amidst the trees of paradise. And the Lord God called Adam, and said to him: Where art thou? And he said: I heard thy voice in paradise; and I was afraid, because I was naked, and I hid myself. And he said to him: And who hath told thee that thou wast naked, but that thou hast eaten of the tree whereof I commanded thee that thou shouldst not eat? And Adam said: The woman, whom thou gavest me to be my companion, gave me of the tree, and I did eat. And the Lord God said to the woman: Why hast thou done this? And she answered: The serpent deceived me, and I did eat.

Lesson III - Gen 3:14–20

And the Lord God said to the serpent: Because thou hast done this thing, thou art cursed among all cattle, and the beasts of the earth: upon thy breast shalt thou go, and earth shalt thou eat all the days of thy life. I will put enmities between thee and the woman, and thy seed and her seed: she shall crush thy head, and thou shalt lie in wait for her heel. To the woman also he said: I will multiply thy sorrows, and thy conceptions: in sorrow shalt thou bring forth children, and thou shalt be under thy husband's power, and he shall have dominion over thee. And to Adam he said: Because thou hast hearkened to the voice of thy wife, and hast eaten of the tree, whereof I commanded thee that thou shouldst not eat, cursed is the earth in thy work; with labour and toil shalt thou eat thereof all the days of thy life. Thorns and thistles shall it bring forth to thee; and thou eat the herbs of the earth. In the sweat of thy face shalt thou eat bread till thou return to the earth, out of which thou wast taken: for dust thou art, and into dust thou shalt return. And Adam called the name of his wife Eve: because she was the mother of all the living.

Thursday in Septuagesima

Lesson I - Gen 4:1–7

From the book of Genesis

And Adam knew Eve his wife: who conceived and brought forth Cain, saying: I have gotten a man through God. And again she brought forth his brother Abel. And Abel was a shepherd, and Cain a husbandman. And it came to pass after many days, that Cain offered, of the fruits of the earth, gifts to the Lord. Abel also offered of the firstlings of his flock, and of their fat: and the Lord had respect to Abel, and to his offerings. But to Cain and his offerings he had no respect: and Cain was exceedingly angry, and his countenance fell. And the Lord said to him: Why art thou angry? and why is thy countenance fallen? If thou do well, shalt thou not receive? but if ill, shall not sin forthwith be present at the door? but the lust thereof shall be under thee, and thou shalt have dominion over it.

Lesson II - Gen 4:8–12

And Cain said to Abel his brother: Let us go forth abroad. And when they were in the field, Cain rose up against his brother Abel, and slew him. And the Lord said to Cain: Where is thy brother Abel? And he answered, I know not: am I my brother's keeper? And he said to him: What hast thou done? the voice of thy brother's blood crieth to me from the earth. Now, therefore, cursed shalt thou be upon the earth, which hath opened her mouth and received the blood of thy brother at thy hand, When thou shalt till it, it shall not yield to thee its fruit: a fugitive and vagabond shalt thou be upon the earth.

Lesson III - Gen 4:13–16

And Cain said to the Lord: My iniquity is greater than that I may deserve pardon. Behold thou dost cast me out this day from the face of the earth, and I shall be hidden from thy face, and I shall be a vagabond and a fugitive on the earth: everyone, therefore, that findeth me, shall kill me. And the Lord said to him: No, it shall not be so: but whosoever shall kill Cain, shall be punished sevenfold. And the Lord set a mark upon Cain, that whosoever found him should not kill him. And Cain went out from the face of the Lord, and dwelt as a fugitive on the earth, at the east side of Eden.

Friday in Septuagesima

Lesson I - Gen 4:17–22

From the book of Genesis

And Cain knew his wife, and she conceived, and brought forth Henoch: and he built a city, and called the name thereof by the name of his son Henoch. And Henoch begot Irad, and Irad begot Maviael, and Maviael begot Mathusael, and Mathusael begot Lamech: Who took two wives: the name of the one was Ada, and the name of the other was Sella. And Ada brought forth Jabel: who was the father of such as dwell in tents, and of herdsmen. And his brother's name was Jubal; he was the father of them that play upon the harp and the organs. Sella also brought forth Tubalcain, who was a hammerer and artificer in every work of brass and iron. And the sister of Tubalcain was Noema.

Lesson II - Gen 4:23–26

And Lamech said to his wives Ada and Sella: Hear my voice, ye wives of Lamech, hearken to my speech: for I have slain a man to the wounding of myself, and a stripling to my own bruising. Sevenfold vengeance shall be taken for Cain: but for Lamech seventy times sevenfold. Adam also knew his wife again: and she brought forth a son, and called his name Seth, saying: God hath given me another seed, for Abel whom Cain slew. But to Seth also was born a son, whom he called Enos; this man began to call upon the name of the Lord.

Lesson III - Gen 5:1–5

This is the book of the generation of Adam. In the day that God created man, he made him to the likeness of God. He created them male and female; and blessed them: and called their name Adam, in the day when they were created. And Adam lived a hundred and thirty years, and begot a son to his own image and likeness, and called his name Seth. And the days of Adam, after he begot Seth, were eight hundred years: and he begot sons and daughters. And all the time that Adam lived came to nine hundred and thirty years, and he died.

Saturday in Septuagesima

Lesson I ~ Gen 5:15–21

From the book of Genesis

And Malaleel lived sixty-five years, and begot Jared. And Malaleel lived after he begot Jared, eight hundred and thirty years, and begot sons and daughters. And all the days of Malaleel were eight hundred and ninety-five years, and he died. And Jared lived a hundred and sixty-two years, and begot Henoch. And Jared lived after he begot Henoch, eight hundred years, and begot sons and daughters. And all the days of Jared were nine hundred and sixty-two years, and he died. And Henoch lived sixty-five years, and begot Mathusala.

Lesson II ~ Gen 5:22–27

And Henoch walked with God: and lived after he begot Mathusala, three hundred years, and begot sons and daughters. And all the days of Henoch were three hundred and sixty-five years. And he walked with God, and was seen no more: because God took him. And Mathusala lived a hundred and eighty-seven years, and begot Lamech. And Mathusala lived after he begot Lamech, seven hundred and eighty-two years, and begot sons and daughters. And all the days of Mathusala were nine hundred and sixty-nine years, and he died.

Lesson III ~ Gen 5:28–31

And Lamech lived a hundred and eighty-two years, and begot a son. And he called his name Noe, saying: This same shall comfort us from the works and labours of our hands on the earth, which the Lord hath cursed. And Lamech lived after he begot Noe, five hundred and ninety-five years, and begot sons and daughters. And all the days of Lamech came to seven hundred and seventy-seven years, and he died.

SEXAGESIMA SUNDAY

~2 Weeks before Lent~

Duplex II Class

Lesson I ~ Gen 5:31; 6:1–4

From the book of Genesis

Noe, when he was five hundred years old, begot Sem, Cham, and Japheth. And after that men began to be multiplied upon the earth, and daughters were born to them, The sons of God seeing the daughters of men, that they were fair, took to themselves wives of all which they chose. And God said: My spirit shall not remain in man for ever, because he is flesh, and his days shall be a hundred and twenty years. Now giants were upon the earth in those days. For after the sons of God went in to the daughters of men, and they brought forth children, these are the mighty men of old, men of renown.

Lesson II - Gen 6:5–8

And God seeing that the wickedness of men was great on the earth, and that all the thought of their heart was bent upon evil at all times, It repented him that he had made man on the earth. And being touched inwardly with sorrow of heart, He said: I will destroy man, whom I have created, from the face of the earth, from man even to beasts, from the creeping thing even to the fowls of the air, for it repenteth me that I have made them. But Noe found grace before the Lord.

Lesson III - Gen 6:9–15

These are the generations of Noe: Noe was a just and perfect man in his generations, he walked with God. And he begot three sons, Sem, Cham, and Japheth. And the earth was corrupted before God, and was filled with iniquity. And when God had seen that the earth was corrupted (for all flesh had corrupted its way upon the earth), He said to Noe: The end of all flesh is come before me, the earth is filled with iniquity through them, and I will destroy them with the earth. Make thee an ark of timber planks: thou shalt make little rooms in the ark, and thou shalt pitch it within and without. And thus shalt thou make it: The length of the ark shall be three hundred cubits: the breadth of it fifty cubits, and the height of it thirty cubits.

Lesson IV

From the Book upon Noe's Ark by St. Ambrose, Bishop

We read that the Lord was angry. It is in the thoughts, that is to say, in the knowledge of God, that man being put on earth and weighted with the body cannot be without sin, for earth is the home of temptations, and the flesh is a bait for corruption. Yet man had a reasonable soul, and his soul had power to control his body; and, being so made, he made no struggle to keep himself from falling into that from whence he would not return. God's thoughts are not as man's thoughts; in Him there is no such thing as change of mind, no such thing as to be angry and then cool down again. These things are written that we may know the bitterness of our sins, whereby we have earned the Divine wrath. To such a degree had iniquity grown that God, Who by His nature cannot be moved by anger, or hatred, or any passion whatsoever, is represented as provoked to anger.

Lesson V

And God threatened that He would destroy man. He said: "I will destroy man, whom I have created, from the face of the earth; both man and beast, and the creeping thing, and the fowls of the air." What harm had the animals done? For man's use had they been created, and, when man was wiped away, they were of use no longer. And there is a higher reason. Man is a living soul, capable of reason, who may be described as a living animal, subject to death, and endowed with reason. When then the highest animal is gone, why should the lower branches remain? Why should anything be saved alive, when righteousness, the basis of salvation, is to be no more?

Lesson VI

But more effectually to condemn the rest of men, and to manifest the goodness of God, it is written that Noe found grace in the eyes of the Lord. Here we learn also that the sin of his neighbor casts no shadow on the righteous, when he is kept as a stock from whence the whole race are to spring. He is praised, not because he was of a noble race, but because he was a just man and perfect. The stock of a just man yields men of just souls; for virtues, like blood, are hereditary. Among men are some families illustrious for honorable pedigrees, and so there are also races of souls whose beauty is the splendor of virtues.

Lesson VII

From the Holy Gospel according to St. Luke (Luke 8:4–15)

At that time: When much people were gathered together, and were come to Jesus out of every city, he spoke by a parable. A sower went out to sow his seed. And so on.

Homily by Pope St. Gregory

Dearly beloved brethren, the passage from the Holy Gospel which you have just heard, needs not so much that I should explain it, as that I should seek to enforce its lesson. The Truth Himself has explained it, and, after that, it befits not man's frailty to fritter away His exposition by any further comment. But there is, in that very explanation by the Lord, something which it behooves us well to weigh. If it were but we who bade you believe that by the seed is signified the word; by the field, the world; by the birds, the devils; and by the thorns, riches, you would perchance doubt of the truth of our explanation. Therefore, the Lord Himself has vouchsafed to give this explanation, and that, not for this parable only, but that you may know in what manner to interpret others, whereof He has not given the meaning.

Lesson VIII

Beginning His explanation, the Lord says that He speaks in parables. Hereby He does certify us, when our weakness would unveil to you the hidden meaning of His words. If I spoke of myself, who would believe me when I say that riches are thorns? Thorns prick, but riches lull to rest. And yet riches are indeed thorns, for the anxiety they bring is a ceaseless pricking to the minds of their owners, and, if they lead into sin, they are thorns which bloodily tear the soul. But we understand from another Evangelist that in this place the Lord speaks not of riches themselves but of the deceitfulness of riches.

Lesson IX

Those riches are deceitful riches which can be ours only for a little while; those riches are deceitful riches which cannot relieve the poverty of our souls. They are the only true riches which make us rich in virtues. If then, dearly beloved brethren, you seek to be rich, earnestly desire the true riches. If you would be truly honorable, strive after the kingdom of heaven. If you love the bravery of titles, hasten to have your names written down at Court above, where Angels are. Take to heart the Lord's words which your ear hears. The food of the soul is the word of God when the stomach is sick it throws up again the food which is put into it, and so is the soul sick when a man hears and digests not in his memory the Word of God. And if any man cannot keep his food, that man's life is in desperate case.

Monday in Sexagesima

Lesson I - Gen 7:1–4

From the book of Genesis

And the Lord said to him: Go in thou and all thy house into the ark: for thee I have seen just before me in this generation. Of all clean beasts take seven and seven, the male and female. But of the beasts that are unclean two and two, the male and female. Of the fowls also of the air seven and seven, the male and the female: that seed may be saved upon the face of the whole earth. For yet a while, and after seven days, I will rain upon the earth forty days and forty nights; and I will destroy every substance that I have made, from the face of the earth.

Lesson II - Gen 7:5; 7:10–12

And Noe did all things which the Lord had commanded him. And after seven days were passed, the waters of the flood overflowed the earth. In the six hundreth year of the life of Noe in the second month, in the seventeenth day of the month, all the fountains of the great deep were broken up, and the flood gates of heaven were open: And the rain fell upon the earth forty days and forty nights.

Lesson III - Gen 7:13–14; 7:17

In the selfsame day Noe, and Sem, and Cham, and Japheth his sons: his wife, and the three wives of his sons with them, went into the ark: They and every beast according to its kind, and all the cattle in their kind, and every thing that moveth upon the earth according to its kind, and every fowl according to its kind. And the flood was forty days upon the earth, and the waters increased, and lifted up the ark on high from earth.

Tuesday in Sexagesima

Lesson I - Gen 8:1–4

From the book of Genesis

And God remembered Noe, and all the living creatures, and all the cattle which were with him in the ark, and brought a wind upon the earth, and the waters were abated. The fountains also of the deep, and the flood gates of heaven were shut up, and the rain from heaven was restrained. And the waters returned from off the earth going and coming: and they began to be abated after a hundred and fifty days. And the ark rested in the seventh month, the seven and twentieth day of the month, upon the mountains of Armenia.

Lesson II - Gen 8:5–9

And the waters were going and decreasing until the tenth month:

for in the tenth month, the first day of the month, the tops of the mountains appeared. And after that forty days were passed, Noe, opening the window of the ark which he had made, sent forth a raven: Which went forth and did not return, till the waters were dried up upon the earth. He sent forth also a dove after him, to see if the waters had now ceased upon the face of the earth. But she, not finding where her foot might rest, returned to him into the ark.

Lesson III - Gen 8:10–13

And having waited yet seven other days, he again sent forth the dove out of the ark. And she came to him in the evening, carrying a bough of an olive tree, with green leaves, in her mouth. Noe therefore understood that the waters were ceased upon the earth. And he stayed yet other seven days: and he sent forth the dove, which returned not any more unto him. Therefore in the six hundredth and first year, the first month, the first day of the month, the waters were lessened upon the earth.

Wednesday in Sexagesima

Lesson I - Gen 8:15–19
From the book of Genesis

And God spoke to Noe, saying: Go out of the ark, thou and thy wife, thy sons, and the wives of thy sons with thee. All livings things that are with thee of all flesh, as well in fowls as in beasts, and all creeping things that creep upon the earth, bring out with thee, and go ye upon the earth: increase and multiply upon it. So Noe went out, he and his sons: his wife, and the wives of his sons with him. And all living things, and cattle, and creeping things that creep upon the earth, according to their kinds, went out of the ark.

Lesson II - Gen 8:20–22

And Noe built an altar unto the Lord: and taking of all cattle and fowls that were clean, offered holocausts upon the altar. And the Lord smelled a sweet savour, and said: I will no more curse the earth for the sake of man: for the imagination and thought of man's heart are prone to evil from his youth: therefore I will no more destroy every living soul as I have done. All the days of the earth, seedtime and harvest, cold and heat, summer and winter, night and day, shall not cease.

Lesson III - Gen 9:1–6

And God blessed Noe and his sons. And he said to them: Increase and multiply, and fill the earth. And let the fear and dread of you be upon all the beasts of the earth, and upon all the fowls of the air, and all that move upon the earth: all the fishes of the sea are delivered into your hand. And every thing that moveth and liveth shall be meat for you: even as the green herbs have I delivered them all to you: Saving that flesh with blood you shall not eat. For I will require the blood of your lives at the hand of every beast, and at the hand of man, at the hand of every man, and of his brother, will I require the life of man. Whosoever shall shed man's blood, his blood shall be shed: for man was made to the image of God.

Thursday in Sexagesima

Lesson I ~ Gen 9:12–15

From the book of Genesis

And God said: This is the sign of the covenant which I will give between me and you, and to every living soul that is with you, for perpetual generations. I will set my bow in the clouds, and it shall be the sign of a covenant between me, and between the earth. And when I shall cover the sky with clouds, my bow shall appear in the clouds: And I will remember my covenant with you, and with every living soul that beareth flesh: and there shall no more be waters of a flood to destroy all flesh.

Lesson II ~ Gen 9:20–23

And Noe, a husbandman, began to till the ground, and planted a vineyard. And drinking of the wine was made drunk, and was uncovered in his tent. Which when Cham the father of Chaanan had seen, to wit, that his father's nakedness was uncovered, he told it to his two brethren without. But Sem and Japheth put a cloak upon their shoulders, and going backward, covered the nakedness of their father: and their faces were turned away, and they saw not their father's nakedness.

Lesson III ~ Gen 9:24–29

And Noe awaking from the wine, when he had learned what his younger son had done to him, He said: Cursed be Chaanan, a servant of servants, shall he be unto his brethren. And he said: Blessed be the Lord God of Sem, be Chanaan his servant. May God enlarge Japheth, and may he dwell in the tents of Sem, and Chanaan be his servant. And Noe lived after the flood three hundred and fifty years: And all his days were in the whole nine hundred and fifty years: and he died.

Friday in Sexagesima

Lesson I ~ Gen 10:1–6

From the book of Genesis

These are the generations of the sons of Noe: Sem, Cham, and Japheth: and unto them sons were born after the flood. The sons of Japheth: Gomer, and Magog, and Madai, and Javan, and Thubal, and Mosoch, and Thiras. And the sons of Gomer: Ascenez and Riphath and Thogorma. And the sons of Javan: Elisa and Tharsis, Cetthim, and Dodanim. By these were divided the islands of the Gentiles in their lands, every one according to his tongue and their families in their nations. And the sons of Cham: Chus, and Mesram, and Phuth, and Chanaan.

Lesson II ~ Gen 11:1–4

And the earth was of one tongue, and of the same speech. And when they removed from the east, they found a plain in the land of Sennaar, and dwelt in it. And each one said to his neighbour: Come, let us make brick, and bake them of stones, and slime instead of mortar. And they said: Come, let us make a city and a tower, the top whereof may reach to heaven: and let us make our name famous before we be scattered abroad into all lands.

Lesson III ~ Gen 11:5–8

And the Lord came down to see the city and the tower, which the children of Adam were building. And he said: Behold, it is one people, and all have one tongue: and they have begun to do this, neither will they leave off from their designs, till they accomplish them in deed. Come ye, therefore, let us go down, and there may not understand one another's speech. And so the Lord scattered them from that place into all lands, and they ceased to build the city.

Saturday in Sexagesima

Lesson I ~ Gen 11:10–15

From the book of Genesis

These are the generations of Sem: Sem was a hundred years old when he begot Arphaxad, two years after the flood. And Sem lived after he begot Arphaxad, five hundred years, and begot sons and daughters. And Arphaxad lived thirty-five years, and begot Sale. And Arphaxad lived after he begot Sale, three hundred and three years; and begot sons and daughters. Sale also lived thirty years, and begot Heber. And Sale lived after he begot Heber, four hundred and three years; and begot sons and daughters.

Lesson II ~ Gen 11:16–23

And Heber lived thirty-four years, and begot Phaleg. And Heber lived after he begot Phaleg, four hundred and thirty years: and begot sons and daughters. Phaleg also lived thirty years, and begot Reu. And Phaleg lived after he begot Reu, two hundred and nine years, and begot sons and daughters. And Reu lived thirty-two years, and begot Sarug. And Reu lived after he begot Sarug, two hundred and seven years, and begot sons and daughters. And Sarug lived thirty years, and begot Nachor. And Sarug lived after he begot Nachor, two hundred years: and begot sons and daughters.

Lesson III ~ Gen 11:24–30

And Nachor lived nine and twenty years, and begot Thare. And Nachor lived after he begot Thare, a hundred and nineteen years, and begot sons and daughters. And Thare lived seventy years, and begot Abram, and Nachor, and Aran. And these are the generations of Thare: Thare begot Abram, Nachor, and Aran. And Aran begot Lot. And Aran died before Thare his father, in the land of his nativity in Ur of the Chaldees. And Abram and Nachor married wives: the name of Abram's wife was Sarai: and the name of Nachor's wife, Melcha, the daughter of Aran, father of Melcha and father of Jescha. And Sarai was barren, and had no children.

QUINQUAGESIMA SUNDAY

~1 Week before Lent~

Duplex II Class

Lesson I ~ Gen 12:1–6

From the book of Genesis

And the Lord said to Abram: Go forth out of thy country, and from thy kindred, and out of thy father's house, and come into the land which I shall show thee. And I will make of thee a great nation, and I will bless thee, and magnify thy name, and thou shalt be blessed. I will bless them that bless thee, and curse them that curse thee, and in thee shall all the kindred of the earth be blessed: So Abram went out as the Lord had commanded him, and Lot went with him: Abram was seventy-five years old when he went forth from Haran. And he took Sarai his wife, and Lot his brother's son, and all the substance which they had gathered, and the souls which they had gotten in Haran: and they went out to go into the land of Chanaan. And when they were come into it, Abram passed through the country into the place of Sichem, as far as the noble vale: now the Chanaanite was at that time in the land.

Lesson II ~ Gen 12:7–13

And the Lord appeared to Abram, and said to him: To thy seed will I give this land. And he built there an altar to the Lord, who had appeared to him. And passing on from thence to a mountain, that was on the east side of Bethel, he there pitched his tent, having Bethel on the west, and Hai on the east; he built there also an altar to the Lord, and called upon his name. And Abram went forward, going, and proceeding on to the south. And there came a famine in the country; and Abram went down into Egypt, to sojourn there: for the famine was very grievous in the land. And when he was near to enter into Egypt, he said to Sarai his wife: I know that thou art a beautiful woman: And that when the Egyptians shall see thee, they will say: She is his wife: and they will kill me, and keep thee. Say, therefore, I pray thee, that thou art my sister: that I may be well used for thee, and that my soul may live for thy sake.

Lesson III ~ Gen 12:14–19

And when Abram was come into Egypt, the Egyptians saw the woman that she was very beautiful. And the princes told Pharao, and praised her before him: and the woman was taken into the house of Pharao. And they used Abram well for her sake. And he had sheep and oxen, and he asses, and men servants and maid servants, and she asses, and camels. But the Lord scourged Pharao and his house with most grievous stripes for Sarai, Abram's wife. And Pharao called Abram, and said to him: What is this that thou hast done to me? Why didst thou not tell me that she was thy wife? For what cause didst thou say, she was thy sister, that I might take her to my wife? Now, therefore, there is thy wife, take her, and go thy way.

Lesson IV

From the Book upon the Patriarch Abraham, by St. Ambrose

Abraham was truly a great man, illustrious as an example of many virtues; one the like of whom the day-dreams of Philosophy have not been able to produce. That which she imagines is less than that which he did; his simple truth and faith were something grander than her lying rounded periods. Let us then consider what this man's loyalty was.

For that virtue is first to be taken which was the source of all the others, and thus this was the first which God called for from him, when He said: "Get thee out of thy country, and from thy kindred, and from thy father's house." It would have been enough to have said, "Get thee out of thy country," for there were his kindred, and there his father's house.

Lesson V

But He gave the details of his sacrifice one by one, that He might see whether he loved Him, lest also he should begin rashly, or should seek to evade the heavenly commandment. But as the whole of the precept was plainly set forth, lest anything should be unconsidered, so also were the rewards set forth, lest the burden should seem hopeless. He was tried as one that is strong, he was roused as one that is true, he was called as one that is righteous; and he departed loyally as the Lord had spoken unto him. And Lot went forth with him. That saying of the Seven Wise Men of Greece is much spoken of: "Follow God." But this did Abraham before the Seven Wise Men were thought of; he followed God, and went out of his own land.

Lesson VI

But, forasmuch as Abraham had before had another country, namely, the land of the Chaldees, from whence went forth Terah the father of Abraham, and came unto Haran, and forasmuch as he to whom it had been said, "Get thee out from thy kindred," took Lot, his brother's son, with him, let us consider whether this "Get thee out of thy country" signifies not "get thee out of this earthly dwelling," namely, our body, from which Paul came forth, who said, "Our conversation is in heaven."

Lesson VII

From the Holy Gospel according to St. Luke (Luke 18:31–43)

In that time, Jesus took unto him the twelve, and said to them: Behold, we go up to Jerusalem, and all things shall be accomplished which were written by the prophets concerning the Son of man. And so on.

Homily by Pope St. Gregory

Our Redeemer, foreseeing that the minds of His disciples would be troubled by His suffering, told them long before both of the pains of that suffering, and of the glory of His rising again, to the end that, when they should see Him die as He had prophesied, they might not doubt that He was likewise to rise again. But, since His disciples were yet carnal, and could not receive the words telling of this mystery, He wrought a miracle before them. A blind man received his sight before their eyes, that if they could not receive heavenly things by words, they might be persuaded of heavenly things by deeds.

Lesson VIII

But, dearly beloved brethren, we must so take the miracles of our Lord and Saviour, as believing both that they were actually wrought, and that they have some mystic interpretation for our instruction. For in His works, power speaks one thing and mystery again another. Behold here, for instance. We know not historically who this blind man was, but we do know of what he was mystically the figure. Mankind is blind, driven out from Eden in the persons of his first parents, knowing not the light of heaven, and suffering the darkness of condemnation. But, nevertheless, through the coming of his Redeemer, he is enlightened, so that now he sees by hope already the gladness of inward light, and walks by good works in the path of life.

Lesson IX

One must note that as Jesus drew to Jericho a blind man received his sight. Now, this name Jericho, being interpreted, signifies the city of the moon and in Holy Scripture the moon is used as a figure of our imperfect flesh, of whose gradual corruption her monthly waning is a type. As, therefore, our Maker draws nigh to Jericho, a blind man receives his sight. While the Divinity takes into itself our weak manhood, man receives again the light which he had lost. By God's suffering in the Manhood, man is raised up toward God. This blind man is also well described as sitting by the wayside begging, for the Truth says: "I am the Way."

Monday in Quinquagesima

Lesson I - Gen 13:1–6

From the book of Genesis

And Abram went up out of Egypt, he and his wife, and all that he had, and Lot with him, into the south. And he was very rich in possession of gold and silver. And he returned by the way that he came, from the south to Bethel, to the place where before he had pitched his tent between Bethel and Hai: In the place of the altar which he had made before; and there he called upon the name of the Lord. But Lot also, who was with Abram, had flocks of sheep, and herds of beasts, and tents. Neither was the land able to bear them, that they might dwell together: for their substance was great, and they could not dwell together.

Lesson II - Gen 13:7–11

Whereupon also there arose a strife between the herdsmen of Abram and of Lot. And at that time the Chanaanite and the Pherezite dwelled in that country. Abram therefore said to Lot: Let there be no quarrel, I beseech thee, between me and thee, and between my herdsmen and thy herdsmen: for we are brethren. Behold the whole land is before thee: depart from me I pray thee: if thou wilt go to the left hand, I will take the right: if thou choose the right hand, I will pass to the left. And Lot, lifting up his eyes, saw all the country about the Jordan, which was watered throughout, before the Lord destroyed Sodom and Gomorrha, as the paradise of the Lord, and like Egypt as one cometh to Segor. And Lot chose to himself the country about the Jordan, and he departed from the east.

Lesson III - Gen 13:11–16

And they were separated one brother from the other. Abram dwelt in the land of Chanaan; and Lot abode in the towns that were about the Jordan, and dwelt in Sodom. And the men of Sodom were very wicked, and sinners before the face of the Lord, beyond measure. And the Lord said to Abram, after Lot was separated from him: Lift up thy eyes, and look from the place wherein thou now art, to the north and to the south, to the east and to the west. All the land which thou seest, I will give to thee, and to thy seed for ever. And I will make thy seed as the dust of the earth.

Tuesday in Quinquagesima

Lesson I - Gen 14:8–12

From the book of Genesis

And the king of Sodom, and the king of Gomorrha, and the king of Adama, and the king of Seboim, and the king of Bala, which is Segor, went out: and they set themselves against them in battle array in the woodland vale: To wit, against Chodorlahomor king of the Elamites, and Thadal king of nations, and Amraphel king of Sennaar, and Arioch king of Pontus: four kings against five. Now the woodland vale had many pits of slime. And the king of Sodom, and the king of Gomorrha turned their backs and were overthrown there: and they that remained fled to the mountain. And they took all the substance of the Sodomites, and Gomorrhites, and all their victuals, and went their way: And Lot also, the son of Abram's brother, who dwelt in Sodom, and his substance.

Lesson II - Gen 14:13–16

And behold one that had escaped told Abram the Hebrew, who dwelt in the vale of Mambre the Amorrhite, the brother of Escol, and the brother of Aner: for these had made league with Abram. Which when Abram had heard, to wit, that his brother Lot was taken, he numbered of the servants born in his house, three hundred and eighteen well appointed: and pursued them to Dan. And dividing his company, he rushed upon them in the night: and defeated them, and pursued them as far as Hoba, which is on the left hand of Damascus. And he brought back all the substance, and Lot his brother, with his substance, the women also the people.

Lesson III - Gen 14:17–20

And the king of Sodom went out to meet him, after he returned from the slaughter of Chodorlahomor, and of the kings that were with him in the vale of Save, which is the king's vale. But Melchisedech the king of Salem, bringing forth bread and wine, for he was the priest of the most high God, Blessed him, and said: Blessed be Abram by the most high God, who created heaven and earth. And blessed be the most high God, by whose protection the enemies are in thy hands. And he gave him the tithes of all.

Ash Wednesday

Lesson I

From the Holy Gospel according to St. Matthew (Matt 6:16–21)

In that time Jesus said to his disciples: And when you fast, be not as the hypocrites, sad. For they disfigure their faces, that they may appear unto men to fast. And so on.

Homily by St. Augustine, Bishop

It is evident that by these precepts we are bidden to seek for inner gladness, lest, by running after that reward which is without, we should become conformed to the fashion of this world, and should so lose the promise of that blessing which is all the truer and more stable that it is inward, that blessing wherein God has chosen us to be conformed to the likeness of His Son. In this chapter we will principally consider the fact that vainglory finds a ground for its exercise in struggling poverty as much as in worldly distinction and display; and this development is the most dangerous, because it entices under pretense of being the serving of God.

Lesson II

He that is characterized by unbridled indulgence in luxury or in dress, or any other display, is by these very things easily shown to be a follower of worldly vanities, and deceives no one by putting on a hypocritical mask of godliness. But those professors of Christianity, who turn all eyes on themselves by an eccentric show of groveling and dirtiness, not suffered by necessity but by their own choice, of them we must judge by their other works whether their conduct really proceeds from the desire of mortification by giving up unnecessary comfort, or is only the means of some ambition. The Lord bids us beware of wolves in sheep's clothing, but "by their fruits," says He, "ye shall know them."

Lesson III

The test is when, by diverse trials, such persons lose those things which under the cover of seeming unworldliness they have either gained or sought to gain. Then must it needs appear whether they be wolves in sheep's clothing, or indeed sheep in their own. But that hypocrites do the contrary makes it no duty of a Christian to shine before the eyes of men with a display of needless luxury the sheep need not to lay aside their own clothing because wolves sometimes falsely assume it.

Thursday after Ashes

Lesson I

From the Holy Gospel according to St. Matthew (Matt 8:5–13)

At that time, when Jesus had entered into Capharnaum, there came to him a centurion, beseeching him and saying: Lord, my servant lieth at home sick of the palsy, and is grieviously tormented. And so on.

Homily by St. Augustine, Bishop

Let us consider whether Matthew and Luke are at one as touching this centurion's servant. Matthew says: "There came unto Him a centurion, beseeching Him, and saying: 'Lord, my servant lieth at home sick, of the palsy.'" This seems to differ from what Luke says, namely: "And when he heard of Jesus, he sent unto Him the elders of the Jews, beseeching Him that He would come and heal his servant. And when they came to

Jesus, they besought him instantly, saying: 'That he was worthy for whom He should do this; for he loveth our nation, and he hath built us a synagogue.'" Then Jesus went with them; and when He was now not far from the house, the centurion sent friends to Him, saying unto Him: "Lord, trouble not thyself; for I am not worthy that Thou shouldest enter under my roof."

Lesson II

If it were done thus, how is Matthew truthful, when he says that the centurion came unto Him, seeing that, in fact, he sent his friends? We must then look well into this, and we shall see that Matthew only made use of a common form of speech. Now, we use to say of a man that he comes to a place even though he be not already come: whence also we say, He arrived close; or He arrived long way off, that is, to that place to which he would come; yea, we speak of that coming, toward which he tends, as though it had already taken place, when he that should be come-at does not yet see him that comes, but is come-at for him by friends so to obtain his favor, which is needful for him that would come to him. And so much does this manner of speaking hold, that they are commonly said to come-at a great man (who is beyond their personal reach), who, by means of suitable persons, succeed in laying before him such things as they desire.

Lesson III

Therefore it is not strange that Matthew should make use of the common short phrase, and say of the centurion, who reached the Lord's sympathies by means of friends, that he came unto Him. Also we need not lightly pass by the mystic depth which underlies the words of this holy Evangelist. It is written in the Psalms: "Draw near unto Him and be enlightened." Thus did the centurion in faith draw near unto Jesus, and the Lord so praised him that He said: "I have not found so great faith, no, not in Israel." Of him of whom these words were spoken, the Evangelist deems it wiser to say that he had found his way to Jesus; that he had got to Christ, than that they came, through whom he sent his message unto Him.

Friday after Ashes

Lesson I

From the Holy Gospel according to St. Matthew (Matt 5:43–48; 6:1–4)

In that time, Jesus said to his disciples: You have heard that it hath been said, Thou shalt love thy neighbour, and hate thy enemy. And so on.

Homily by St. Jerome, Priest

But I say unto you: "Love your enemies, do good to them that hate you." There are many who judge of the commandments of the Lord by their own weakness, and not by the strength of His Saints; and so deem Him to have commanded things impossible. These are they who think that not to hate their enemies is all that they are able to do; and that to command us to love them is to command more than man's nature can bear. It behooves them to know that this which Christ commands is not impossible, albeit perfect. This is what David did in respect of Saul and Absalom; the martyr Stephen also prayed for his enemies, even while they were stoning him; and Paul could wish that himself were accursed from Christ for his persecutors. And this, Jesus Himself did, as well as taught, when He said: "Father, forgive them for they know not what they do."

Lesson II

"That you may be the children of your Father Which is in heaven." If he that does the commandments of God becomes a son of God, then he is not a son by nature but by his own choice. "Therefore when thou doest thine alms, do not sound a trumpet before thee, as the hypocrites do in the synagogues, and in the streets, that they may have glory of men." He that sounds a trumpet before him when he does alms, is a hypocrite. He that disfigures his face when he fasts, to the end that he may show the emptiness of his belly in his looks, he also is a hypocrite.

Lesson III

He that prays in the synagogues and in the corners of the streets that he may be seen of men, is a hypocrite. From all which, we gather that a hypocrite is one which does anything that he may have glory of men. To me also it seems that he which says unto his brother: "Let me pull out the mote out of thine eye," that he also is a hypocrite; for he proposes to take upon him that office for vainglory's sake, that he himself may appear righteous. Therefore the Lord says unto him: "Thou hypocrite, first cast out the beam out of thine own eye." Thus we see that it is, not the doing of good, but the motive which moves us to do good, which will meet with reward from God; and, if thou stray but a little from the right way, it is of small moment whether thou wander to the right hand or to the left, when once thou hast lost the straight path.

Saturday after Ashes

Lesson I

From the Holy Gospel according to St. Mark (Mark 6:47–56)

In that time when it was late, the ship was in the midst of the sea, and Jesus himself alone on the land. And so on.

Homily by St. Bede the Venerable, Priest

The toil of the disciples in rowing, and the wind contrary to them, is a figure of the diverse toils of the Holy Church, as, amid the waves of a world that fights against her, and the stormy blasts of unclean spirits, she labors to reach the rest of her Fatherland above as a shore safe for her anchor. Here also it is well said that the ship was in the midst of the sea, and He alone on the land; for sometimes it comes to pass that the Church is, by the great pressure of the Gentiles, not only so afflicted, but also befouled, that it seems as though, if it were possible, her Redeemer had for the time forsaken her.

Lesson II

Whence it is that there comes that cry of hers, when she is taken amid the waves, and the winds of temptations that break upon her, and with piteous entreaty she calls on Him to protect her: "Why standest Thou afar off, O Lord, why hidest Thou thyself in times of trouble?" And then, in the verses that follow, she tells Him what says the enemy that persecuted her, saying: "For he hath said in his heart God hath forgotten; He hideth His face, He will never see it."

Lesson III

Truly, He forgets not the prayer of the poor, neither turns His face away from any that put his trust in Him; yea, rather, to him whosoever is striving with the enemy, He gives help to conquer, and, whosoever conquers, to him He gives an everlasting crown. For the which reason also it is here said plainly "He saw them toiling in rowing." The Lord sees them that are toiling in the sea, albeit He Himself is on the land. Although He seem for a moment to tarry in aiding the distressed, nevertheless the look of His love is strengthening them all the while, lest they should faint and sometimes He sets them free, even by an open deliverance, conquering all their adversaries for them, as when He walked upon the swelling of the waves, and stilled them.

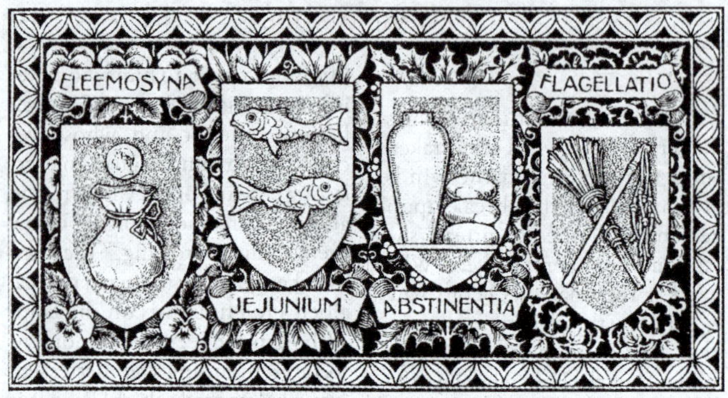

LENT

SUNDAY I OF LENT

Duplex I Class

Lesson I - 2 Cor 6:1–10

From the second letter of St. Paul the Apostle to the Corinthians

And we helping do exhort you, that you receive not the grace of God in vain. For he saith: In an accepted time have I heard thee; and in the day of salvation have I helped thee. Behold, now is the acceptable time; behold, now is the day of salvation. Giving no offence to any man, that our ministry be not blamed: But in all things let us exhibit ourselves as the ministers of God, in much patience, in tribulation, in necessities, in distresses, In stripes, in prisons, in seditions, in labours, in watchings, in fastings, In chastity, in knowledge, in longsuffering, in sweetness, in the Holy Ghost, in charity unfeigned, In the word of truth, in the power of God; by the armour of justice on the right hand and on the left; By honour and dishonour, by evil report and good report; as deceivers, and yet true; as unknown, and yet known; As dying, and behold we live; as chastised, and not killed; As sorrowful, yet always rejoicing; as needy, yet enriching many; as having nothing, and possessing all things.

Lesson II - 2 Cor 6:11–16

Our mouth is open to you, O ye Corinthians, our heart is enlarged. You are not straitened in us, but in your own bowels you are straitened. But having the same recompense (I speak as to my children), be you also enlarged. Bear not the yoke with unbelievers. For what participation hath justice with injustice? Or what fellowship hath light with darkness? And what concord hath Christ with Belial? Or what part hath the faithful with the unbeliever? And what agreement hath the temple of God with idols? For you are the temple of the living God; as God saith: I will dwell in them, and walk among them; and I will be their God, and they shall be my people.

Lesson III - 2 Cor 7:4–9

I am filled with comfort: I exceedingly abound with joy in all our tribulation. For also when we were come into Macedonia, our flesh had no rest, but we suffered all tribulation; combats without, fears within. But God, who comforteth the humble, comforted us by the coming of Titus. And not by his coming only, but also by the consolation, wherewith he was comforted in you, relating to us your desire, your mourning, your zeal for me, so that I rejoiced the more. For although I made you sorrowful by my epistle, I do not repent; and if I did repent, seeing that the same epistle (although but for a time) did make you sorrowful; Now I am glad: not because you were made sorrowful; but because you were made sorrowful unto penance.

Lesson IV

Sermon by St. Leo, Pope

Dearly beloved brethren, I am to preach to you the holiest and the greatest of Fasts; and with what words can I more fitly begin than with those words of the Apostle, in whom Christ spoke, which have just been read? "Behold, now is the acceptable time! Behold, now is the day of salvation!" It is true that there are no times which are not rich with God's gifts; His grace does ever give us an entry unto His mercy; nevertheless, more especially at this time is it fitting that the minds of all men be earnestly stirred up to make progress in things spiritual, and to be nerved by a trust in God stronger than ever; for now the anniversary of that day on which we were redeemed is drawing near, and thereby moving us to work all godliness, to the end that we may be able to celebrate with clean minds and bodies that mystery which exceeds all others, the mystery of the Lord's sufferings.

Lesson V

Mysteries so great demand sustained earnestness, and continuous worship, if we would ever abide in the sight of God, such as it is fitting that He should find us on the Feast of the Passover. But since few have the strength to do thus, and the frailty of the body rebels against such hardness, while the diverse actions of this life distract us with their cares, it necessarily befalls that the dust of earth befouls the hearts even of the godly. To meet this befoulment therefore, and to restore the cleanness of our souls, it is provided by the healthful institution of God, that we should be purged by an exercise of forty days, wherein godly works may redeem the misspending of our other time, and purifying fasts rid us of the same.

Lesson VI

Therefore, dearly beloved brethren, as we are now about to enter upon these mystic days, the end of whose most holy ordinance is the cleansing both of our souls and bodies, let us take heed that we be obedient unto the command of the Apostle, putting far away from us every defilement of flesh and spirit, ordering the strife which there is between the two substances whereof we are compounded; that the soul, which is ordained under the rule of God, and which it befits under His rule to rule the body, may enjoy the fulness of her lordship; giving no offense to any so that we may give no cause to such as revile us. For if our ways during the Fast agree not with the purity of perfect temperance, the reproaches of the unbelievers will be just, and our sins will arm the tongues of the ungodly to the harming of our religion. The sum of our Fast stands not only in abstaining from meats; neither is it profitable to deny food to the body, if the mind be not bridled from iniquity.

Lesson VII

From the Holy Gospel according to St. Matthew (Matt 4:1–11)

In that time, Jesus was led by the spirit into the desert, to be tempted by the devil. And when he had fasted forty days and forty nights, afterwards he was hungry. And so on.

Homily by Pope St. Gregory

Some persons are accustomed to question what Spirit it was of which Jesus was led up into the wilderness, on account of the words a little farther on "Then the devil taketh Him up into the holy city" and again "The devil taketh Him up into an exceeding high mountain." But in truth, and without any searching, we may very fitly take it that we are to believe it was the Holy Ghost Who led Him up into the wilderness; His own Spirit led Him where the evil spirit found Him to tempt Him. When however it is said that He, God and man, was taken up by the devil either into an exceeding high mountain or into the holy city, the mind shrinks from believing, and the ears of man tingle to hear it. Yet these things we know not to be incredible, when we consider certain other things concerning Him.

Lesson VIII

In truth, the devil is the head of all the wicked, and every wicked man is a member of this body, of which the devil is the head. Was not Pilate a limb of Satan? Were not the Jews that persecuted, and the soldiers that crucified Christ, likewise limbs of Satan? Is it then strange that He should allow Himself to be led up into a mountain by the head, Who allowed Himself to be crucified by the members? Therefore it is not unworthy of our Redeemer, Who came to be slain, that He was willing to be tempted. It was right that He should thus overcome our temptations by His own, even as He came to conquer our death by His own.

Lesson IX

We ought to know that temptation works through three forms. There is, first, the suggestion; then the delectation; lastly, the consent. When we are tempted, it often happens that we fall into delectation, and even into consent, because in the sinful flesh of which we are begotten, we carry in ourselves matter to favor the attack. But God, when He took Flesh in the womb of the Virgin, and came into the world without sin, did so without having in Himself anything of this lusting of the flesh against the spirit. It was possible therefore for Him to be tempted in the first stage, namely suggestion; but there was nothing in His Mind in which delectation could fix its teeth. And thus all the temptation which He endured from the devil was without, and none within Him.

Monday I in Lent

Lesson I

From the Holy Gospel according to St. Matthew (Matt 25:31–46)

In that time, Jesus said to his disciples: When the Son of man shall come in his majesty, and all the angels with him, then shall he sit upon the seat of his majesty. And all nations shall be gathered together before him. And so on.

Homily by St. Augustine, Bishop

If, without keeping the commandments, it be possible to attain unto life by faith only, how can it be true that the Lord will say to such as He shall have set on His left hand "Depart from Me, you cursed, into everlasting fire, prepared for the devil and his angels?" He rebukes them, not because they have not believed in Him, but because they have not wrought good works. Yea, lest any man should promise himself life eternal by faith only (and faith, if it hath not works, is dead), the Lord says that He will gather together all nations, nations who have lived mingled together in the same countries, that we may seem to hear them which have believed indeed in Him, but have not wrought good works (as though that their dead faith could, being alone, lead them into life eternal), that we may seem to hear such crying unto Him, "Lord, when saw we thee suffering such and such things, and did not minister unto thee?"

Lesson II

If they shall go into everlasting fire who have not done works of mercy, shall not they go who have taken their neighbor's goods? Or shall not they go who have outraged the temple of God in their own selves, and so been merciless to themselves? As if works of mercy could avail anything without love, contrary to the words of the Apostle: "Though I bestow all my goods to feed the poor, and have not charity, it profiteth me nothing." And what manner of love to his neighbor has he who loves him as himself and loves not himself? Remember that he that loves iniquity hates his own soul.

Lesson III

Neither dare we say here that by which some delude themselves, namely, that the fire indeed is everlasting, but that they will not burn therein everlastingly. Such men say that they whose faith is dead will pass through that everlasting fire, and that they are those to whom it is promised that they themselves shall be saved, yet so as by fire. So that, though the fire itself be everlasting, the burning of the damned therein, that is, the work of the fire upon them, will not be everlasting. As though the Lord were answering this beforehand, the last words of His Sermon are "And these shall go away into everlasting punishment, but the righteous into life eternal." As the fire, so shall the burning be; and the Truth bids us know that they shall burn therein who have lacked, not faith, but good works.

Tuesday I in Lent

Lesson I

From the Holy Gospel according to St. Matthew (Matt 21:10–17)

In that time, when Jesus was come into Jerusalem, the whole city was moved, saying: Who is this? And so on.

Homily by St. Bede the Venerable, Priest

The same thing which the Lord showed in a figure by cursing the barren fig-tree, He afterwards more plainly put before us by casting the desecrators out of the temple. The tree herself had not sinned by bearing no fruit when the Lord was hungry, for the time of figs was not yet come, but those Priests had sinned who were carrying on worldly business in the Lord's house, and who neglected to bring forth that fruit of godliness which they owed, and which the Lord was hungry to find in them. The Lord made the fig-tree to wither away under His curse, that all men who saw it, and all men who hear of it, might know that they will be condemned by the judgment of God if they content themselves with the talk of godliness, without the solid fruit of good works even as that barren fig-tree was clothed only with a rustling garb of green leaves.

Lesson II

But because the buyers and sellers understood not the parable of the barren fig-tree, the Lord brought upon them the stroke of the punishment that they had deserved, and cast out the traffickers in earthly things from that house, wherein it had been commanded that nothing should be done save the work of God, sacrifices and prayers offered up to Him, and His word read, taught, and sung. And yet it may be believed that nothing was being sold or bought in the temple save such things as were needful for the service thereof, as we read in another place, that when Jesus went into the temple He found those that sold oxen and sheep and doves, and all these things were doubtless there for no other end but to be offered to God in that His holy house, and were sold by the natives to those worshippers who came from a distance, to be so used.

Lesson III

If, therefore, the Lord would not have to be sold in the temple, even such things as He willed should be offered therein, with what anger, do you suppose, would He visit such as He might find laughing or gossiping there, or yielding to any other sin? If the Lord suffer not to be carried on in His house such worldly business as may be freely done elsewhere, how much more shall such things as ought never to be done anywhere, draw down the anger of God if they be done in His own holy house. Lastly, the Holy Ghost came down upon the Lord in the shape of a dove, and by doves therefore may be signified the gifts of that Holy Spirit. They, then, to this day sell doves in the temple of God, who take money in the Church for the laying on of their hands, whereby the Holy Ghost is given from heaven.

Ember Wednesday in Lent

Lesson I

From the Holy Gospel according to St. Matthew (Matt 12:38–50)

In that time, some of the scribes and Pharisees answered him, saying: Master, we would see a sign from thee. Who answering said to them: An evil and adulterous generation seeketh a sign. And so on.

Homily by St. Ambrose, Bishop

After the condemnation of the Jewish people, the mystery of the Church is plainly declared in the figures of the repentant Ninevites, and of the Queen of the South. Like that Queen, the Church comes from the uttermost parts of the earth, to hear the wisdom of the true Solomon, the Prince of Peace. A Queen she is, and a Queen of one indivisible realm, wrought into one body out of all nations, however diverse and distant.

Lesson II

And thus comes that great mystery of Christ and the Church, a mystery more excellent now in the fulness of truth, than in the ancient type. For there they had in Solomon only a type of that which Christ is now in His own Person. And the Church is of two classes, whereof the one knows not how to sin, and the other sins no more. To wash away sin is the work of repentance, to eschew it that of wisdom.

Lesson III

Lastly, the sign of the Prophet Jonas, as it was a figure of the Lord's sufferings, was also a witness to the gravity of those sins which the Jews committed. At the same time, we see in these words of the Lord a declaration at once of His power, and of His love; for, by turning our eyes on the Ninevites, He shows us a way of escape, while He sets before us the horror of what will otherwise be our punishment. Even the Jews need not cease to hope for pardon, if only they would repent.

Thursday I in Lent

Lesson I

From the Holy Gospel according to St. Matthew (Matt 15:21–28)

In that time, Jesus went from thence, and retired into the coasts of Tyre and Sidon. And so on.

Homily by St. Jerome, Priest

Christ leaves the Scribes and Pharisees who had spoken falsely against Him, and goeth into the coasts of Tyre and Sidon, that He may heal the Tyrians and Sidonians. But a woman of Canaan comes to Him out of the land He had left, and cries to Him to give health to her daughter. Remark that the case of the daughter of this woman of Canaan is the fifteenth case of healing. "Have mercy on me, O Lord,

Thou Son of David!" She knew that He was to be called Son of David because she was come out of His own country, and had left the errors of the Tyrians and Sidonians when she changed her home and her faith.

Lesson II

"My daughter is grievously vexed with a devil." I think that the daughter of this woman of Canaan (whom the Lord at length delivered), was a figure of the souls of such as now believe, but were once grievously vexed by the devil, knowing not Him Who made them, and bowing down to stocks and stones. But He answered not a word not because He was puffed up with the pride of the Pharisees, or shared the high looks of the Scribes, but that He might fulfill His own word that He had spoken, saying: "Go not into the way of the Gentiles, and into any city of the Samaritans enter ye not." He would not give an occasion to such as spoke falsely against Him, and He kept back perfect salvation from the Gentiles until such time as He should have suffered and risen again.

Lesson III

And His disciples came and besought Him, saying: "Send her away; for she crieth after us." The disciples, knowing not as yet the mysterious things of the Lord, said this, either because they were moved with compassion and so interceded for this Canaanite woman, whom another Evangelist calls a Syrophoenician, or because she was crying out that the Lord was a hard, instead of a merciful physician, and they desired to be rid of her clamor. But He answered and said: "I am not sent but unto the lost sheep of the house of Israel." Not that He was not sent unto the Gentiles, but because it was to Israel in the first instance that He was sent, whom refusing the Gospel, He might justly pass away from, and go to the Gentiles.

Ember Friday in Lent

Lesson I

From the Holy Gospel according to St. John (John 5:1–15)

In that time was a festival day of the Jews, and Jesus went up to Jerusalem. And so on.

Homily by St. Augustine, Bishop

Let us see what is mystically signified by that one infirm man whom alone the Lord, keeping to a mysterious unity, chose out of so many sufferers, to be the subject of His healing power. He found in him a certain number of years of sickness. He had had an infirmity thirty and eight years. How this number is proper rather to weakness than to health, will now be the subject of a few careful remarks. I bespeak your attention; the Lord will be present, that I may speak fitly, and you may understand. The number forty is put before us as hallowed, and, in a way, perfect. I think that your love knows this God's Scriptures often and; often witness it. You well know that a Fast of this number of days is hallowed. Moses fasted forty days. Elias did the same. And our Lord and Saviour Jesus Christ Himself fasted this number of days complete. Moses represents the Law, Elias the Prophets, and the Lord the Gospel. And therefore these three appeared on the Mount of the Transfiguration. There the Lord showed Himself to His disciples with His Face shining as the sun, and His raiment glistering; and He stood between Moses and Elias; as it were, the Gospel receiving testimony, on the one hand from the Law, and, on the other, from the Prophets.

Lesson II

Whether, therefore, it be in the Law, or in the Prophets, or in the Gospel, the number of forty is recommended to us for Fast-days. The great and general Fast is this to abstain from the iniquity of the world, and her forbidden pleasures. This is the perfect Fast, that, denying ungodliness, and worldly lusts, we should live soberly, righteously, and godly in this present world. After such a Fast, what is the Feast that follows? Hear what the Apostle says in continuation: "Looking for that blessed hope, and the glorious appearing of our great God and Saviour Jesus Christ." We, then, make our pilgrimage in this world a Lent, by living good lives, and abstaining from her iniquities and her forbidden pleasures. But at the end of this lifelong Lent there will be an Easter indeed. We look for that blessed hope, and the glorious appearing of our great God and Saviour Jesus Christ. When that hope is realized, when that faith is swallowed up in knowledge, then indeed shall we receive every man a penny. Indeed, it is true that every laborer in the vineyard will get his wages. Witness that Gospel which I believe you have not forgotten, and which it is not my business to quote again as if you were ignorant children. Now, the word used in the original for this penny which the laborers received is *denarion*. And the derivation of the word *denarion* is the numeral *decem*, ten. There are forty days in Lent, and if we add ten, we get fifty. So do we toil in fasting for the forty days of Lent before Easter, and, then, when we have, as it were, received our reward, we keep holiday for the fifty days of Eastertide.

Lesson III

Remember how I remarked, that the man healed by our Lord at the pool of Bethesda had had an infirmity thirty-eight years. I wish to explain why this number of thirty-eight is proper rather to weakness than to health. Love is the fulfilling of the law: to the fulfilling of the law belongs in every work the number forty. But in love we have given us two precepts "Thou shalt love the Lord thy God with all thy heart, and with all thy soul, and with all thy mind. This is the first and great commandment. And the second is like unto it: Thou shalt love thy neighbour as thyself. On these two commandments hang all the law and the prophets." When the widow gave all she had for an offering to God she gave two mites; the innkeeper received two pence wherewith to cure him that had fallen among thieves; Jesus abode for two days among the Samaritans that He might establish them in love. When, then, anything good is spoken of as two, the two great divisions of love are the chief mystic interpretation. If, then, the law is fulfilled in the number forty, and it is not fulfilled if there be lacking the two precepts of love, what wonder is it that he was infirm who lacked two of forty?

Ember Saturday in Lent

Lesson I

From the Holy Gospel according to St. Matthew (Matt 17:1–9)

In that time, Jesus taketh unto him Peter and James, and John his brother, and bringeth them up into a high mountain apart: And he was transfigured before them. And so on.

Homily by Pope St. Leo

Dearly beloved brethren, the continuation of the Holy Gospel which, entering in by our bodily ears, has knocked at the door of our inner mind, calls us to understand a great mystery. This, by the grace of God, we shall the more readily do, if we return to consider what has been told us just before. The Saviour of mankind, even Jesus Christ, laying the foundations of that faith whereby the ungodly are called to righteousness and the dead to life, instilled into the minds of His disciples, both by the voice of His teaching and the wonder of His works, that they should believe Him, the one Christ, to be both the Only-begotten Son of God and the Son of man. Had they believed Him one of these and not the other, it had availed them nothing to salvation; and the danger was equally great of holding the Lord Jesus Christ to be God without the Manhood, or Man only without the Divinity, since we are constrained to acknowledge that He is perfect God and perfect Man, and that as there is in the Divinity perfect Manhood, so there is in the Manhood perfect Divinity.

Lesson II

To strengthen, therefore, the saving knowledge of this faith, the Lord had asked His disciples what, among the differing opinions of men, was their own belief and judgment as to Who He was. Then did the Apostle Peter, by the revelation of That Father Who is above all, rising above fleshly things, yea, outstripping the thoughts of men, then did he fix the eyes of his mind upon the Son of the living God, and confess the glory of the Divinity, for he looked not on the substance of the flesh and blood only. And in all the exaltation of this faith so well did he please God, that he was gifted with that joyous blessing, the hallowed establishment of that impregnable rock, whereon the Church being founded, should prevail against the gates of hell and the laws of death; neither, when anything is to be bound or loosed, is any bound or loosed in heaven, otherwise than as the judgment of Peter hath bound or loosed it upon earth.

Lesson III

But, dearly beloved brethren, it behoved that the height of this understanding, which the Lord praised, should rest upon a foundation, and that foundation, the mystery of the lower nature, lest the faith of the Apostle, carried away by the glorious acknowledgment of the Divinity in Christ, should deem it unworthy and unnatural for the impassible God to take into Himself the frailty of our nature; and should thus believe that in Christ the Manhood had been so glorified as to be no longer able to suffer pain, or be dissolved in death. And therefore it was that, when the Lord said how that He must go up unto Jerusalem, and suffer many things of the elders and chief priests, and scribes, and be killed, and rise again the third day, and the blessed Peter, bright with heavenly illumination, and still glowing from the passionate acknowledgment of the Divine Sonship, by a natural, and, as seemed to him, a godly shrinking, could not bear the mention of mockery and insult and a cruel death, he was corrected by the merciful rebuke of Jesus, and moved rather to desire to be a partaker in the sufferings of his Master.

SUNDAY II OF LENT

Duplex I Class

Lesson I ~ Gen 27:1–10

From the book of Genesis

Now Isaac was old, and his eyes were dim, and he could not see: and he called Esau, his elder son, and said to him: My son? And he answered: Here I am. And his father said to him: Thou seest that I am old, and know not the day of my death. Take thy arms, thy quiver, and bow, and go abroad: and when thou hast taken some thing by hunting, Make me savoury meat thereof, as thou knowest I like, and bring it, that I may eat: and my soul may bless thee before I die. And when Rebecca had heard this, and he was gone into the field to fulfill his father's commandment, She said to her son Jacob: I heard thy father talking with Esau thy brother, and saying to him: Bring me of thy hunting, and make me meats that I may eat, and bless thee in the sight of the Lord, before I die. Now, therefore, my son, follow my counsel: And go thy way to the flock, bring me two kids of the best, that I may make of them meat for thy father, such as he gladly eateth: Which when thou hast brought in, and he hath eaten, he may bless thee before he die.

Lesson II ~ Gen 27:11–20

And he answered her: Thou knowest that Esau my brother is a hairy man, and I am smooth. If my father shall feel me, and perceive it, I fear lest he will think I would have mocked him, and I shall bring upon me a curse instead of a blessing. And his mother said to him: Upon me be this curse, my son: only hear thou my voice, and go, fetch me the things which I have said. He went, and brought, and gave them to his mother. She dressed meats, such as she knew his father liked. And she put on him very good garments of Esau, which she had at home with her: And the little skins of the kids she put about his hands, and covered the bare of his neck. And she gave him the savoury meat, and delivered him bread that she had baked. Which when he had carried in, he said: My father? But he answered: I hear. Who art thou, my son? And Jacob said: I am Esau thy firstborn: I have done as thou didst command me: arise, sit, and eat of my venison, that thy soul may bless me. And Isaac said to his son: How couldst thou find it so quickly, my son? He answered: It was the will of God, that what I sought came quickly in my way.

Lesson III - Gen 27:21–29

And Isaac said: Come hither, that I may feel thee, my son, and may prove whether thou be my son Esau, or not. He came near to his father, and when he had felt him, Isaac said: The voice indeed is the voice of Jacob; but the hands are the hands of Esau. He said: Art thou my son Esau? He answered: I am. Then he said: Bring me the meats of thy hunting, my son, that my soul may bless thee. And when they were brought, and he had eaten, he offered him wine also, which after he had drunk, He said to him: Come near me, and give me a kiss, my son. He came near, and kissed him. And immediately as he smelled the fragrant smell of his garments, blessing him, he said: Behold the smell of my son is as the smell of a plentiful field, which Lord hath blessed. God give thee the dew of heaven, and of the fatness of the earth, abundance of corn and wine. And let peoples serve thee, and tribes worship thee: be thou lord of thy brethren, and let they mother's children bow down before thee. Cursed be he that curseth thee: and let him that blesseth thee be filled with blessings.

Lesson IV

From the Book against Lying, by St. Augustine, Bishop

If we consider faithfully and carefully what it was that Jacob did by the advice of his mother, and wherein he seems to have deceived his father, it will appear that it is not a lie, but an allegory. If we denounce this as a lie, then must we also give the name of lies to even all parables, and to every figure devised to set forth the nature of anything, which is not to be taken in its literal sense, but in which one thing is to be understood under the name of another. And this be far from us. Whosoever should do this, would bring the charge of falsehood against very many figures of speech, including that one called metaphor to which would, by such reasoning, be given the name of a lie.

Lesson V

The deep meaning is given; but what is considered is the lie because men do not understand the way in which that signification, which is a truth, is set forth but the falsehood is plainly expressed, and believed. That we may understand this more plainly by taking some points in illustration, consider with me what Jacob did. It is certain that he covered his limbs with the skins of goats. If we consider his object in point of fact, we shall find that it was to lie, because he did this that he might be thought to be he who he was not. But if we consider this his deed in that deep typical sense which it undoubtedly possesses, we find that by the goat-skins are represented sins, and by him who covered himself therewith Him Who bore not His own sins, but the sins of others.

Lesson VI

It is impossible to apply the term a "lie" to that mystic aspect of this transaction in which it was true and such an aspect there is, not only in the acts, but in the words. When Isaac said to Jacob: "Who art thou, my son" and Jacob answered: "I am Esau, thy first-born," if we take this in its sense relative to the two brothers, it will be apparent that it was a lie. If, however, we look at it relatively to that for the sake of which these words and deeds were written down, we shall see that Christ is here signified in His mystic body, the Church. Concerning her (the younger covenant), He saith (to them of the older covenant): "Ye shall see Abraham, and Isaac, and Jacob, and all the Prophets in the kingdom of God, and you yourselves thrust out. And they shall come from the east, and from the west, and from the north, and from the south, and shall sit down in the kingdom of God. And, behold, there are last which shall be first, and there are first which shall be last." Thus did the younger take away the title and inheritance from the elder, and acquire it to himself.

Lesson VII

From the Holy Gospel according to St. Matthew (Matt 17:1–9)

At that time, Jesus taketh unto him Peter and James, and John his brother, and bringeth them up into a high mountain apart: And he was transfigured before them. And so on.

Homily by Pope St. Leo

Jesus took Peter, and James, and John his brother, and brought them up into an exceeding high mountain apart, and manifested forth the brightness of His glory. Hitherto, though they understood that there was in Him the Majesty of God, they knew not the power of that Body which veiled the Divinity. And therefore He had individually and markedly promised to some of the disciples that had stood by Him that they should "not taste of death till they had seen the Son of Man coming in His kingdom," that is, in the kingly splendor which is the right of the Manhood taken into God and which He willed to make visible to those three men. This it was that they saw, for the unspeakable and unapproachable vision of the Divinity Himself which will be the everlasting life of the pure in heart, can no man, who is still burdened with a dying body, see and live.

Lesson VIII

When the Father says: "This is My beloved Son, in Whom I am well pleased; hear ye Him" did they not plainly hear Him say: "This is My Son, Whose it is to be of Me and with Me without all time. For neither is He That begets before

Him That is begotten, neither He That is begotten, after Him That begets Him. This is My Son between Whom and Me, to be God is not a point of difference, to be Almighty a point of separation, nor to be Eternal a point of distinction. This is My Son not by adoption, but My very Own; not created from, or of another substance, or out of nothing, but begotten of Me not of another nature, and made like unto Me, but of Mine own Being, born of Me, equal unto Me."

Lesson IX

"This is My Son by Whom all things were made, and without Whom was not anything made that was made, Who makes likewise all things whatsoever I make and what things soever I do He does likewise, inseparably and indifferently. This is My Son Who thought it not robbery, nor has taken it by violence, to be equal with Me, but, abiding still in the form of My glory, that He may fulfill Our common decree for the restoration of mankind, has bowed the unchangeable Divinity even to the form of a servant. Him therefore in Whom I am in all things well pleased, by Whose preaching I am manifested, and by Whose lowliness I am glorified, Him instantly hear ye. For He is the Truth and the Life, My Power, and My Wisdom."

Monday II in Lent

Lesson I

From the Holy Gospel according to St. John (John 8:21–29)

In that time, Jesus said to the multitude of Jews: I go, and you shall seek me, and you shall die in your sin. And so on.

Homily by St. Augustine, Bishop

The Lord spoke unto the Jews, saying: I go My way. For, to the Lord Christ, death was a departure to that place from whence He had come, and from whence He had never departed. I go My way, says He, and you shall seek Me not from love, but from hatred. Yea after He had withdrawn Himself from the sight of men, two classes sought Him, even they that loved, and they that hated Him; the one because they longed for His presence, the other because they were eager to hunt Him down. In the Psalms, the Lord Himself says by His Prophet: "Refuge failed me, and no man cared for my soul." And again He said in another Psalm: "Let them be confounded and put to shame that seek after my soul."

Lesson II

Thus does He blame them that seek not, and condemn such as seek. Yea, it is a good thing to seek the soul of Christ as the disciples sought it; and an evil thing to seek it as the Jews sought it; the first sought it to possess, the second to destroy it. What then does He bid us know will be the reward of such as seek it evilly in a perverse heart? You shall seek Me, and lest you think that you shall do well so to seek Me, I tell you that you shall die in your sins. To seek Christ with bad intent, is as much as to die in sin, for it is to hate Him through Whom alone we can be saved.

Lesson III

Whereas men whose hope is in God ought to return good even for evil; those men returned evil for good. The Lord therefore told them beforehand, and, because He knew it, He let them know their coming end, how that they should die in their sins. Then He said farther "Whither I go, you cannot come." This He said in another place to His disciples, but He never said to them: You shall die in your sins. What said He? The same words as to the Jews: "Whither I go, you cannot come." Yet, to the disciples, these words only deferred, they cut not away hope for they, though for a little while they could not come whither He was to go, were yet in the end to go there. Not so they, to whom He foretold and said: "Ye shall die in your sins."

Tuesday II in Lent

Lesson I

From the Holy Gospel according to St. Matthew (Matt 23:1–12)

At that time, Jesus spoke to the multitudes and to his disciples, saying: The scribes and the Pharisees have sitten on the chair of Moses. All things therefore whatsoever they shall say to you, observe and do: but according to their works do ye not; for they say, and do not. And so on.

Homily by St. Jerome, Priest

Was there ever man gentler and kinder than the Lord? The Pharisees tempted Him; their craft was confounded, and, in the words of the Psalmist, "The arrows of babes have pierced them," and nevertheless, because of the dignity of their priesthood and name, He exhorts the people to be subject to them by doing according to their words, though not according to their works. By the words "Moses' seat" we are to understand the teaching of the law. Thus also must we mystically take: "Sitteth in the seat of the scornful," and likewise, "overthrew the seats of them that sold doves," to describe doctrine.

Lesson II

How they bind heavy burdens, and grievous to be borne, and lay them on men's shoulders, but they themselves will not move them with one of their fingers. This is generally directed against all teachers who command things hard, and themselves do not even things easy. But it is to be remarked that the shoulders, the fingers, and the binding of the burdens, have a spiritual interpretation. But all their works they do for to be seen of men. Whosoever therefore does anything for to be seen of men, the same is, so far, a Scribe and a Pharisee.

Lesson III

They make broad their phylacteries, and enlarge the borders of their garments. And love the uppermost rooms at feasts, and the chief seats in the synagogues, and greetings in the markets, and to be called of men, Rabbi. Woe to us miserable sinners who have inherited the vices of the Pharisees! When the Lord had given the commandments of the law to

Moses He added afterwards "Thou shalt bind them for a sign upon thine hand, and they shall be as frontlets between thine eyes." The sense of these words is: "My Law shall be in thine hand to order whatsoever thou doest, and ever before thine eyes that thou mayest meditate therein day and night." But the Pharisees, by a bad interpretation, were accustomed to write on pieces of parchment the Decalogue of Moses, that is, the Ten Words of the Law, and to tie these pieces of parchment, plaited in a peculiar manner, on their foreheads, so as to make a sort of crown round their heads, which projected in front of their eyes, and always moved before them.

Wednesday II in Lent

Lesson I

From the Holy Gospel according to St. Matthew (Matt 20:17–28)

In that time, Jesus, going up to Jerusalem, took the twelve disciples apart, and said to them: Behold we go up to Jerusalem, and the Son of man shall be betrayed to the chief priests and the scribes, and they shall condemn him to death. And so on.

Homily by St. Ambrose, Bishop

Consider what it was that the mother of Zebedee's children came to Christ desiring, with, and for her sons. She was a mother, who, longing for the honor of her sons, preferred a request immoderate, and yet pardonable. She was a mother who, albeit stricken in years and comfortless, at an age when she had sore need of the strength of her offspring to help and keep her, was yet so earnest in godliness and motherly love, that she had rather suffer the loss of her sons, that they might gain the reward of following Christ still, as we read they had already done, when, at the first call of the Lord, they left their nets and their father.

Lesson II

She, then, yielding to the intensity of her motherly love, besought the Saviour, saying, "Grant that these my two sons may sit, the one at thy right hand and the other at thy left hand, in thy kingdom." Although it was a mistake, it was a mistake of love. For a mother's love knows no moderation. Yet, although it was a greedy prayer, that was a pardonable greed, which hungered, not for riches, but for grace. Neither was that request shameless which sought, not her own good, but her children's. Remember that she was a mother. Think how that she was a mother.

Lesson III

Christ took into His consideration that mother's love of hers, which made her sons' reward the comfort of her own old age, and which could bear the loss of her loved ones, broken as she was by a mother's yearnings. Consider also that she was a woman, that is, of the weaker sex, to which the Lord had not yet given strength by His Passion. Consider, I say, that she was an heiress of Eve, and weakened by that transmission of the unbridled covetousness of the first woman, which the Lord had not yet disarmed by His Blood, even that craving for undue dignity, wherewith all our natures are imbued, and which Christ's Bloodshedding had not yet washed away. She erred indeed, but the mistake was an inherited weakness.

Thursday II in Lent

Lesson I

From the Holy Gospel according to St. Luke (Luke 16:19–31)

In that time, Jesus said to the pharisees: There was a certain rich man, who was clothed in purple and fine linen; and feasted sumptuously every day. And so on.

Homily by Pope St. Gregory

Whom, dearly beloved brethren, whom are we to understand as signified by that rich man which was clothed in purple and fine linen, and fared sumptuously every day, whom, I ask, are we to understand, but the Jewish people, who had all the outward life of religious ordinances, and who turned the treasure of the law they had received to show and not to use? What but the herd of the Gentiles is figured in Lazarus, full of sores? Whosoever turns himself to God and is not ashamed to confess his sin, has his sores on the skin, for in a sore on the skin breaks out the corruption which is drawn from within.

Lesson II

What is, then, the confession of our sins but the breaking out of our sores? The corrupt matter of sin is healthily opened in confession, instead of remaining in the mind to rot it. Open sores on the skin bring the poisonous matter to the surface, and when we confess our sins, what do we but open up the evil that there is lurking in us? But Lazarus desired to be fed with the crumbs which fell from the rich man's table, and no man gave unto him; even so did that proud people scorn to admit a Gentile to the knowledge of their law.

Lesson III

The teaching of the law moved them to pride, and not to love, as though they swelled with self-importance at the thought of their riches, and the words which some Gentiles caught of their knowledge were as crumbs falling from their sumptuous table. On the other hand, the dogs came and licked the sores of the beggar that was laid at their gate. Sometimes in Holy Writ, under the figure of dogs, preachers are understood. A dog's tongue heals the sore which it licks, and so do holy teachers, when we confess our sins, and they speak to us, mollify by their tongues the sores of our souls.

Friday II in Lent

Lesson I

From the Holy Gospel according to St. Matthew (Matt 21:33–46)

In that time, Jesus said to the multitude of Jews and the chief priests: Hear ye another parable. There was a man a householder, who planted a vineyard, and made a hedge round about it. And so on.

Homily by St. Ambrose, Bishop

Many derive diverse spiritual meanings from the term vineyard, but Isaias gives us to know that the vineyard of the Lord of Sabaoth is the house of Israel. Who but God planted that vineyard? He it was that let it out to husbandmen, and went into a far country; not that the Lord, Who is everywhere present, moves from place to place; but because He is nigh unto them that seek Him, and from such as regard Him not He stands afar off. For a long time He tarried away, lest He might seem to ask too early for the fruits of His vineyard. For where kindness is greatest, there ingratitude is worst.

Lesson II

Therefore it is well written in Matthew, for our instruction, that "He hedged it round about," that is, He girded it with the fortifications of His own Divine protection, that it might not easily lie open to the ravages of spiritual wild beasts. "And digged a wine-press in it." What sense are we to put upon the wine-press, unless it be that the Psalms are here described under that title, because in them the mysteries of the Lord's Passion flow over like new wine, working under the power of the Holy Ghost? Whence also, they upon whom the Holy Ghost was outpoured were deemed to be drunken. God therefore dug a wine-press, whereinto the reasonable grapes of inward fruitfulness poured their spiritual richness.

Lesson III

"And built a tower" that is, He raised up the good structure of the Law. And so this His vineyard, thus fortified, furnished, and garnished, He gave over to the Jews. And when the time of the fruit drew near, He sent His servants to the husbandmen. Well does He call it the time of the fruit, not the time of the ingathering. For the Jews yielded Him no fruit; the Lord had no ingathering from that vineyard of which He said: "When I looked that it should bring forth grapes, it brought forth wild grapes." Not that wine that makes glad the heart of man, not with the new wine of the spirit, reeked that wine-press, but with the blood of the Prophets, brutally shed.

Saturday II in Lent

Lesson I

From the Holy Gospel according to St. Luke (Luke 15:11–32)

In that time, Jesus said to the pharisees and scribes in parable: A certain man had two sons: And the younger of them said to his father: Father, give me the portion of substance that falleth to me. And so on.

Homily by St. Ambrose, Bishop

Thou seest how that the heavenly goods are given to such as seek them. Neither ought thou to think the father to blame, because he gave to his younger son. In the kingdom of God there is no age of weakness, neither does faith wax infirm with years. He, surely, who asked, deemed himself of sufficient age. And would that he had not left his father! then had he been ignorant of the obstacle of his age! But after that he had left his father's house, and had gone into a far country, he began to be in want. Well is he said to have wasted his substance, who hath cut himself off from the Church!

Lesson II

He took his journey into a far country. No man can go farther than to abandon his own better self, to leave not his country but his morals, and, as it were, in a hideous fever of lust after the world, to divorce himself from the ties that bind him to holy things. Yea, he that turns his back on Christ, banishes himself from his Fatherland and becomes a citizen of the world. But we are no more strangers and foreigners, but fellow-citizens with the saints, and of the household of God, since we who sometimes were afar off, are made nigh by the Blood of Christ. Let us not envy the pleasures of them who remain in the far country. We too have once been there, but, as says Isaias, "they that dwelt in the land of the shadow of death, upon them hath the light shined." And that far country is the land of the shadow of death.

Lesson III

But we to whom the Lord Christ is the breath of life, are alive under the shadow of Christ. And therefore it is that the Church says "I sat down under His shadow with great delight." The prodigal son by riotous living wasted all the gifts of nature. Take warning, O thou who art made in the image and likeness of God, lest thou waste the same by brutish wallowing. Thou art the work of God; say not to a stock: Thou art my father, lest thou grow into the likeness of a stock, as it is written: "They that make them are like unto them."

SUNDAY III OF LENT

Duplex I Class

Lesson I ~ Gen 37:2–10

From the book of Genesis

And these are his generations: Joseph, when he was sixteen years old, was feeding the flock with his brethren, being but a boy: and he was with the sons of Bala and of Zelpha his father's wives and he accused his brethren to his father of a most wicked crime. Now Israel loved Joseph above all his sons, because he had him in his old age: and he made him a coat of diverse colours. And his brethren seeing that he was loved by his father, more than all his sons, hated him, and could not speak peaceably to him. Now it fell out also that he told his brethren a dream, that he had dreamed: which occasioned them to hate him the more. And he said to them: Hear my dream which I dreamed. I thought we were binding sheaves in the field: and my sheaf arose as it were, and stood, and your sheaves standing about, bowed down before my sheaf. His brethren answered Shalt thou be our king? or shall we be subject to thy dominion? Therefore this matter of his dreams and words ministered nourishment to their envy and hatred. He dreamed also another dream, which he told his brethren, saying: I saw in a dream, as it were the sun, and the moon, and eleven stars worshipping me. And when he had told this to his father and brethren, his father rebuked him, and said: What meaneth this dream that thou hast dreamed? shall I and thy mother, and thy brethren worship thee upon the earth?

Lesson II ~ Gen 37:11–20

His brethren therefore envied him: but his father considered the thing with himself. And when his brethren abode in Sichem feeding their father's flocks, Israel said to him thy brethren feed the sheep in Sichem: come, I will send thee to them. And when he answered: I am ready: he said to him: Go, and see if all things be well with thy brethren, and the cattle: and bring me word again what is doing. So being sent from the vale of Hebron, he came to Sichem: And a man found him there wandering in the field, and asked what he sought. But he answered: I seek my brethren; tell me where they feed the flocks. And the man said to him: They are departed from this place: for I heard them say: Let us go to Dothain. And Joseph went forward after his brethren, and found them in Dothain. And when they saw him afar off, before he came nigh them, they thought to kill him. And said one to another: Behold the dreamer comes. Come, let us kill him, and cast him into some old pit and we will say Some evil beast hath devoured him: and then it shall appear what his dreams avail him.

Lesson III ~ Gen 37:21–28

And Ruben hearing this, endeavoured to deliver him out of their hands, and said: Do not take away his life, nor shed his blood: but cast him into this pit, that is in the wilderness, and keep your hands harmless: now he said this, being desirous to deliver him out of their hands and to restore him to his father. And as soon as he came to his brethren, they forthwith stript him of his outside coat, that was of diverse colours: And cast him into an old pit, where there was no water. And sitting down to eat bread, they saw some Ismaelites on their way coming from Calaad, with their camels, carrying spices, and balm, and myrrh to Egypt. And Juda said to his brethren: What will it profit us to kill our brother, and conceal his blood? It is better that he be sold to the Ismaelites, and that our hands be not defiled: for he is our brother and our flesh. His brethren agreed to his words. And when the Madianite merchants passed by, they drew him out of the pit, and sold him to the Ismaelites, for twenty pieces of silver: and they led him into Egypt.

Lesson IV

From the Book upon Saint Joseph by St. Ambrose, Bishop

The lives of the saints are the models for the lives of others. This is one of the reasons why we have been given the wise tale of the Scriptures, that while, by reading therein, we come to know Abraham, and Isaac, and Jacob, and others of the righteous, we may follow them in that path of innocence which is opened to us for our imitation by their virtuous lives. Of them I have often treated, and today the story of the holy Joseph comes before me. In that story there are patterns of many virtues, but chiefly is he glorious on account of his clean living. Right is it then that you who have learnt in Abraham the devotedness of a faith that nothing could daunt, in Isaac the transparency of an upright soul, in Jacob a wonderful patience of spirit in great travails, should now turn from their worthy deeds, to see the bright example of Joseph's self-control.

Lesson V

The holy Joseph is put before us as a pattern of chastity. Modesty shines in his manners and in his deeds, and a certain loveliness, which is found with chastity, shines there also. Hence his parents loved him more than their other children. But this love caused him to be the object of an envy, which we need not pass by, and upon this the whole story turns. Yet, at the same time, we learn how that just man was not swayed by any desire to avenge his own sufferings, neither repaid evil for evil. Whence also David says "If I have rewarded evil."

Lesson VI

In what would Joseph have been worthy to be chosen before others, if he had harmed them which harmed him, and loved them which loved him? For this so many do. But it is a wonder if one do that which the Saviour teaches and love his enemy. Well, then, may we wonder at him who did this before the Gospel came; who, being injured, spared; being assailed, forgave; being sold, returned no evil; but repaid insult with favor. We, from the Gospel, have been taught to do all this, and we cannot. Let us also, then, learn how that there was envy even among some of the holy (Patriarchs), that we may follow the example of the patience (wherewith others of them bore it); and let us feel that they were not men of another and higher nature than ours, but only more heedful; that they were not sinless, but that they repented. But if the passion of envy scorched even some of the holy race, how much more need is there for the sinful to take heed lest it set fire to them?

Lesson VII

From the Holy Gospel according to St. Luke (Luke 11:14–28)

At that time, Jesus was casting out a devil, and the same was dumb: and when he had cast out the devil, the dumb spoke: and the multitudes were in admiration at it. And so on.

Homily by St. Bede the Venerable, Priest

We read in Matthew that the devil, by which this poor creature was possessed, was not only dumb, but also blind; and that, when he was healed by the Lord, he saw as well as spoke. Three miracles, therefore, were performed on this one man; the blind saw, the dumb spoke, and the possessed was delivered. This mighty work was then indeed wrought carnally, but it is still wrought spiritually in the conversion of believers, when the devil is cast out of them, so that their eyes see the light of faith, and the lips, that before were dumb, are opened that their mouth may show forth the praise of God. But some of them said: He casts out devils through Beelzebub, the chief of the devils. These some were not of the multitude, but liars among the Pharisees and Scribes, as we are told by the other Evangelist.

Lesson VIII

While the multitude, who were less instructed, wondered ever at the works of the Lord, the Pharisees and Scribes, on the other hand, denied the facts when they could, and when they were not able, twisted them by an evil interpretation, and asserted that the works of God were the works of an unclean spirit. And others, tempting Him, sought of Him a sign from heaven. They would have had Christ either to call down fire from heaven like Elias or, like Samuel to have made thunder roll, and lightning flash, and rain fall at midsummer. And yet and if he had so done, they had been still able to explain away these signs also, as being the natural result of some unusual, though, till that moment, unremarked state of the atmosphere. O thou, who stubbornly deniest that which thine eye sees, thine hand holds, and thy sense perceives, what wilt thou say to a sign from heaven? Surely thou wilt say that the magicians in Egypt also wrought diverse signs from heaven.

Lesson IX

But He, knowing their thoughts, said unto them: Every kingdom divided against itself is brought to desolation, and a house divided against a house falls. He answered not their words, but their thoughts; as though He would compel them to believe in the power of Him Who sees the secrets of the heart. But if every kingdom divided against itself is brought to desolation, then have not the Father, the Son, and the Holy Ghost a divided kingdom, since His is a kingdom that, without all contradiction, shall never be brought to desolation by any shock, but abides unchanged and unchangeable for ever. "If Satan also be divided against himself, how shall his kingdom stand? Because you say that I cast out devils by Beelzebub." In saying this, He sought to draw from their own mouth a confession that they had chosen for themselves to be part of that devil's kingdom, which, if it be divided against itself, cannot stand.

Monday III in Lent

Lesson I

From the Holy Gospel according to St. Luke (Luke 4:23–30)

At that time, Jesus said to the pharisees: Doubtless you will say to me this similitude: Physician, heal thyself: as great things as we have heard done in Capharnaum, do also here in thy own country. And so on.

Homily by St. Ambrose, Bishop

Here we have a display of a spite not very common. Their hatred of Christ, and their desire to find grounds for that hatred in what in Him appealed for their love, had made them forget their local friendliness to a fellow-citizen. By this example as well as by God's declaration, thou mayest learn that thou wilt wait in vain to be helped of His mercy, whilst thou art envious of the spiritual good of thy neighbor. Yea, the Lord turns Him away from the envious, and will not show the mighty works of His power to such as are bitter against His gifts to others. The example of Himself which God has been pleased to set before us is that of His doings in the Flesh, and it is by these His doings which He suffered to be seen, that we are taught touching those which are unseen.

Lesson II

The Saviour then does not lightly excuse Himself that He had wrought none of His mighty works in His own country, lest perchance any should there learn to think lightly of our duty to love our Fatherland. Neither was it possible that He Who loved all, should not love His own countrymen; they it was who failed in that love because of their very envy. "I tell you of a truth, many widows were in Israel in the days of Elias." The days of Elias not that the said days belonged to Elias, but either because those were the days when Elias lived and worked; or, else, this is a mystic phrase, meaning that Elias by his works made many souls to awake spiritually from the night of sin to the day of grace, and turn to the Lord. In this latter sense that holy Prophet was a means whereby heaven was opened to those who looked to the eternal and mysterious things of God; it again was shut, and there was a famine, when there were no means of knowing God through outward ordinances. This subject, however, I have treated before at full length, when I was writing on the subject of widows.

Lesson III

"And many lepers were in Israel in the days of Eliseus the Prophet, and none of them was cleansed, saving Naaman the Syrian." By these words of the Lord our great Physician, we are plainly taught and urged to put our trust in the Adorable God, since we see that none was healed, or cleansed from bodily plague, save him who took a religious means to regain health. For the blessings of God are not given to them who close their eyes in sleep, but to them that look to Him. We have remarked in our other book, that the widow to whom Elias was sent was a type of the Church. And next after the Church follows the people. Yea, the Gentiles were a people foreigners by birth, leprous, and covered with plague-spots, till they were baptized in the stream of the mystic Jordan; but from the sacramental waters they rise, lepers no more, but cleansed in body and soul, a glorious virgin Church, not having spot, or wrinkle, or any such thing.

Tuesday III in Lent

Lesson I

From the Holy Gospel according to St. Matthew (Matt 18:15–22)

At that time, Jesus saith to his disciples: But if thy brother shall offend against thee, go, and rebuke him between thee and him alone. And so on.

Homily by St. Augustine, Bishop

Why tell him his fault? Because he has hurt thee by trespassing against thee? God forbid. If thou tell him his fault because thou lovest thyself, thou dost nothing. But if thou tell it him because thou lovest him, then dost exceedingly well. Hear now, in the words of the Gospel itself, for love of whom, thou oughtest to do it, of thyself, or of him. The Lord says: "If he shall hear thee, thou hast gained thy brother. Therefore it behoveth thee to do it for his sake, that thou mayest gain him; since, if thou so do, haply thou mayest gain him; whereas, if thou do it not, he may haply perish." Why then are there so many who reckon lightly of a trespass against their brother, and say "I have done no great offense, for I have trespassed only against my fellow man?" Deem it not light; thou hast trespassed, though it be against thy fellow man.

Lesson II

Wouldest thou know that thy trespass against thy brother has destroyed thee? If he against whom thou hast trespassed tell thee thy fault between himself and thee alone, and thou hear him, he has gained thee. Gained thee! And what signify those words, if it be not that thou, if thou be not gained, shalt perish? For if thou shouldest not otherwise perish, in what sense can he be said to gain thee? Therefore let no man deem it a light thing when he trespasses against his brother. For the Apostle Paul says in a certain place: "When you sin so against the brethren, and wound their weak conscience, you sin against Christ." We are all members of Christ. How dost thou not trespass against Christ, when thou trespassest against one of His members?

Lesson III

Let no man therefore say "I have not trespassed against God, but only against my brother;" that is, "I have trespassed against my fellowman; and so the sin is light, if any at all." And perchance thou wilt argue that it is light, because it is quickly mended; thou hast trespassed against thy brother, but thou art able to make satisfaction, and be right again; thou hast done the deadly thing quickly, and quickly canst thou find a remedy. O my brethren, which of us can hope for the kingdom of heaven, when we remember that the Gospel says: "Whosoever shall say to his brother: Thou fool, shall be in danger of hell fire?" It is a thought full of dread; but, lo! the remedy: "If thou bring thy gift to the altar, and there rememberest that thy brother hath aught against thee, leave there thy gift before the altar, and go thy way; first be reconciled to thy brother, and then come and offer thy gift." God is not wrathful that thou tarry or ever thou offer thy gift; for God seeks thyself more than thy gift.

Wednesday III in Lent

Lesson I

From the Holy Gospel according to St. Matthew (Matt 15:1–20)

At that time, scribes and Pharisees came to Jesus from Jerusalem, saying:

Why do thy disciples transgress the tradition of the ancients? And so on.

Homily by St. Jerome, Priest

The stupidity of the Pharisees and Scribes is something extraordinary. They rebuke the Son of God because He does not observe the traditions and commandments of men, for they wash not their hands when they eat bread. It behooves us to cleanse not the hands of the body but the hands of the soul, namely, our works, that we may do the commandments of God. But He answered and said unto them "Why do you also transgress the commandment of God by your tradition?" He meets here their false accusation with a true one. "How," says He, "do you, who pass over the commandments of God, in order to keep to the traditions of men, hold that My disciples are to be rebuked, because they deem the tradition of the elders of little moment in comparison with the doing of what they know to be the Laws of God?"

Lesson II

Now God commanded, saying: "Honor thy father and mother; and: He that curses father or mother, let him die the death. But you say: Whosoever shall say to his father or his mother: It is a gift, by whatsoever thou mightest be profited by me; and honor not his father or his mother, he shall be free." The word 'honor' is used in Scripture, not so much in the sense of paying salutations and services, as in that of giving alms and gifts. Honor widows, says the Apostle, which are widows indeed. And here 'honor' signifies support. So again: Let the Priests that rule well be counted worthy of double honor, especially they who labour in the word and doctrine. For the Scripture says: "Thou shalt not muzzle the ox that treads out the corn" and "The laborer is worthy of his reward."

Lesson III

The Lord being mindful of the helplessness, or age, or poverty of parents, had commanded their children to honor them even by giving them the necessaries of life. The Scribes and Pharisees, scrupling not to make of none effect this most benign law, and bringing in ungodliness under the very form of godliness, taught, for the benefit of unnatural children, that if any one vowed to God, Who is our very Father in heaven, whatsoever he was bound to give to his parents, the duty of discharging his debt to his heavenly Father ought to come before that which he owed to his earthly father; or, at least, that parents in such case incurred the guilt of sacrilege by taking for themselves what they knew had been made a gift to God. And so parents were left helpless, and the offerings of such children, under pretense of being given to God and His temple, became the gain of the Priests.

Thursday III in Lent

Lesson I

From the Holy Gospel according to St. Luke (Luke 4:38)

At that time Jesus arose out of the synagogue, and entered into

Simon's house. And Simon's wife's mother was taken with a great fever. And so on.

Homily by St. Ambrose, Bishop

Behold here how long-suffering is the Lord our Redeemer! Neither moved to anger against them, nor sickened at their guilt, nor outraged by their attacks, did He leave the Jews' country. Nay, forgetting their iniquity, and mindful only of His mercy, He strove to soften their hard and unbelieving hearts, sometimes by His teaching, and sometimes by freeing some of them, and sometimes by healing them. St. Luke does well to tell us first of the man who was delivered from an unclean spirit, and then of the healing of a woman. The Lord indeed came to heal both sexes, but that must be healed first which was created first, and then must not she be passed by whose first sin arose rather from fickleness of heart than from depraved will.

Lesson II

That the Lord began to heal on the Sabbath-day shows in a figure how that the new creation begins where the old creation ended. It shows, moreover, that the Son of God, Who is come not to destroy the law but to fulfill the law, is not under the law but above the law. Neither was it by the law, but by the Word, that the world was created, as it is written "By the Word of the Lord were the heavens made." The law, then, is not destroyed, but fulfilled, in the Redemption of fallen man. Whence also the Apostle says: "Put off, concerning the former conversation, the old man, which is corrupt according to the deceitful lusts and be renewed in the spirit of your mind and put on the new man, which after God is created in righteousness and true holiness."

Lesson III

It was well that He began to heal on the Sabbath, that He might show Himself to be the Creator, weaving in one with another of His works, and continuing that which He had already begun, even as a workman repairing a house begins not to take down that which is old from the foundations, but from the roof. Thus does the Lord begin to lay to His hand again in that place whence last He has lifted it; then He begins which after God is created in righteousness and true holiness with things lesser, that He may go on to things greater. Even men are able to deliver other men from evil spirits, albeit with the word of God to command the dead to rise again is for God's power alone. Perchance, also, this woman, the mother-in-law of Simon and Andrew, was a type of our nature, stricken down with the great fever of sin, and burning with unlawful lusts after diverse objects. Nor would I say that the passion which rages in the mind is a lesser fire than that fever which burns the body. Covetousness, and lust, and uncleanness, and vain desires, and strivings, and anger, these be our fevers.

Friday III in Lent

Lesson I

From the Holy Gospel according to St. John (John 4:5–42)

At that time, Jesus comes therefore to a city of Samaria, which is called Sichar, near the land which Jacob gave to his son Joseph. And so on.

Homily by St. Augustine, Bishop

Now begin the mysteries. It is not in vain that Jesus grows tired; for it is not for nothing that the power of God is wearied. It is not for nothing that He is wearied Who Himself gives Rest to all them that are weary and heavy-laden. It is not for nothing that He is wearied Whose absence prostrates us, and Whose presence makes us to be strong. Jesus, therefore, being wearied with His journey, sat thus on the well about the sixth hour. All these things hint at something, they want to indicate something: they urge us to knock. Let us knock, then, and O may He open to me and to you, He Who has spoken to us those words "Knock, and it shall be opened unto you."

Lesson II

It is for thy sake that Jesus was wearied with His journey. We find the strength of Jesus, and we find Jesus weak; yea, strong and weak. Strong, for "In the beginning was the Word, and the Word was with God, and the Word was God, the Same was in the beginning with God." Wouldest thou know again how that the Son of God is strong? All things were made by Him, and without Him was nothing made; and they were made without effort. What then is stronger than He by Whom all things were effortlessly made? Wouldest thou know His weakness? "The Word was made Flesh and dwelt among us." Christ, strong, made thee; Christ, weak, redeemed thee. Christ, strong, made all things out of nothing; Christ, weak, so did that what was made perished not. His strength has made us, and His weakness saved us.

Lesson III

He then, being Himself made weak, is strength to all such as are weak, gathering them together, to use His own figure, even as a hen gathers her chickens under her wings. O Jerusalem, Jerusalem! how often would I have gathered thy children together, even as a hen gathers her chickens under her wings, and you would not! Consider now, my brethren, in what bondage is a hen to her chickens. There is no other bird in whom motherhood is unmistakeable. We watch the sparrows building their nests under our eyes; we see swallows, and storks, and pigeons building theirs every day. But, unless we actually see them in their nests, we know not whether they have little ones or not. But the hen's motherhood is so much a part of herself, that even if at the minute we see not her children, the chickens following after her, nevertheless we see by her ways if she be a mother.

Saturday III in Lent

Lesson I

From the Holy Gospel according to St. John (John 8:1–11)

In that time, Jesus went unto Mount Olivet. And early in the morning he came again into the temple. And so on.

Homily by St. Augustine, Bishop

Jesus went unto the Mount of Olives, even unto that fruitful Mount, that anointing Mount, that Mount of Chrism. Where else was fitting for Christ to teach if not on the Mount of Olives? For the word Christ is derived from *Chrisma*, and *Chrisma* is the Greek for ointment. He has anointed us that we may be able to wrestle with the devil. And, early in the morning, He came again into the temple; and all the people came unto Him; and He sat down, and taught them and no man laid hands on Him, because He was not yet pleased to suffer. And now listen how His enemies tried the Lord's meekness.

Lesson II

And the Scribes and Pharisees brought unto Him a woman taken in adultery; and when they had set her in the midst, they say unto Him: Master, this woman was taken in adultery, in the very act. Now, Moses in the law commanded that such should be stoned; but what sayest Thou? This they said, tempting Him, that they might have to accuse Him. Of what could they accuse Him? Had they taken Him in any sin? Or was the woman said to have anything to do with Him?

Lesson III

We must understand, my brethren, that there was a wonderful gentleness in the Lord. They knew that He was most mild and most gentle. Of Him indeed it had been said of old time: "Gird thy sword upon thy thigh, O most Mighty! In thy comeliness and thy beauty go forward, fare prosperously, and reign, because of truth, and meekness, and righteousness." And He came bringing truth as one that teaches, meekness as one that delivers, and righteousness as one that knows. Because of these it was that the Prophet declared in the Holy Ghost, that He was to reign. Whenever He spoke, truth shone forth; whenever He spared His enemies, meekness was made glorious. And His enemies, racked with envy and hatred by His truth and His meekness, laid a stumbling-block for His righteousness.

SUNDAY IV OF LENT

Duplex I Class

Lesson I - Exod 3:1–6

From the book of Exodus

Now Moses fed the sheep of Jethro his father in law, the priest of Madian: and he drove the flock to the inner parts of the desert, and came to the mountain of God, Horeb. And the Lord appeared to him in a flame of fire out of the midst of a bush: and he saw that the bush was on fire and was not burnt. And Moses said: I will go and see this great sight, why the bush is not burnt. And when the Lord saw that he went forward to see, he called to him out of the midst of the bush, and said: Moses, Moses. And he answered: Here I am. And he said: Come not nigh hither, put off the shoes from thy feet: for the place whereon thou standest is holy ground. And he said: I am the God of thy father, the God of Abraham, the God of Isaac, and the God of Jacob. Moses hid his face: for he durst not look at God.

Lesson II ~ Exod 3:7–10

And the Lord said to him: I have seen the affliction of my people in Egypt, and I have heard their cry because of the rigour of them that are over the works: And knowing their sorrow, I am come down to deliver them out of the hands of the Egyptians, and to bring them out of that land into a good and spacious land, into a land that floweth with milk and honey, to the places of the Chanaanite, and Hethite, and Amorrhite, and Pherezite, and Hevite, and Jebusite. For the cry of the children of Israel is come unto me: and I have seen their affliction, wherewith they are oppressed by the Egyptians. But come, and I will send thee to Pharao, that thou mayst bring forth my people, the children of Israel out of Egypt.

Lesson III ~ Exod 3:11–15

And Moses said to God: Who am I that I should go to Pharao, and should bring forth the children of Israel out of Egypt? And he said to him: I will be with thee: and this thou shalt have for a sign, that I have sent thee: When thou shalt have brought my people out of Egypt, thou shalt offer sacrifice to God upon this mountain. Moses said to God: Lo, I shall go to the children of Israel, and say to them: The God of your fathers hath sent me to you. If they should say to me: What is his name? what shall I say to them? God said to Moses: I AM WHO AM. He said: Thus shalt thou say to the children of Israel: HE WHO IS, hath sent me to you. And God said again to Moses: Thus shalt thou say to the children of Israel: The Lord God of your fathers, the God of Abraham, the God of Isaac, and the God of Jacob, hath sent me to you: This is my name for ever, and this is my memorial unto all generations.

Lesson IV

Sermon by St. Basil the Great

We know that it was with and by fasting that Moses went up into the Mount, for he had not dared to go up to that smoking summit, nor to have entered that darkness, except he had been made strong by a Fast. It was with fasting that he received the commandments, written by the finger of God upon tables of stone. Upon the mountain, that Fast made interest with Him Whose law was given unto it; but below, gluttony was leading the people to the worship of idols and polluting them. It is written "The people sat down to eat and to drink, and rose up to play." That one fit of drunken frenzy, on the part of the people, made void and ineffective all the toil and patience of the forty days, during the which the servant of God had fasted and prayed unceasingly. To the Fast had been given those tables of stone inscribed with the finger of God; the Feast's work was to break them, by the hand of the most holy prophet, who deemed a nation of drunkards a nation unworthy to receive law from God.

Lesson V

In a moment of time, that people, who had by great wonders been taught to worship God, were, by gluttony, dropped back into the cesspool of Egyptian idolatry. Such things if thou wilt consider, thou shalt see that the tendency of fasting is toward God, and that that of feasting is toward hell. What was it that degraded Esau, and made him a slave to his brother? Was it not that one dish of pottage for which he sold his birthright? Was it not prayer when joined to fasting that gave Samuel to his mother? What made the mighty Samson invincible? Was it not the fast during the which he was conceived in his mother's womb? The fast it was which made him to be conceived; the fast, which fed him; the fast, which made a man of him, even as the Angel of the Lord commanded his mother, saying: "She may not eat of anything that comes of the vine, neither let her drink wine or strong drink." Fasting is the mother of prophets, the strength and stay of mighty men.

Lesson VI

It is fasting which gives wisdom to lawgivers; fasting which is the trustiest keeper of the soul, and the safest companion for the body. It is fasting which is strength and armor to mighty men; fasting which makes supple them which run and which wrestle. It is fasting which makes a man strong to strive against temptation, and which is to godliness as a fenced city; even fasting, whose fellow is sobriety, and her work temperance. It is fasting which makes men to wax valiant in fight; fasting which teaches to rest in time of peace. Fasting makes a Nazarite to be holy, and a priest perfect. Without a fast it is unlawful to touch the Sacrifice, not only in that mystic and true worship of God which now is, but also according to the law, in those sacrifices which were offered of old time as figures of the true. It was fasting which opened the eyes of Elias to look upon the visions of God, even as it is written, that when he had fasted forty days and forty nights he was in the mount of God, even Horeb, and he was made able, so far as man may be made able, to see God. Even so also was Moses in that Mount forty days and forty nights, fasting, at what time he again received the Law. Unless the Ninevites had fasted, both man and beast, herd and flock, they had not escaped from the ruin that hung over them. In the wilderness some fell; and who were they? Yea, they were such as lusted after flesh-meat.

Lesson VII

From the Holy Gospel according to St. John (John 6:1–15)

In that time, Jesus went over the sea of Galilee, which is that of

Tiberias. And a great multitude followed him, because they saw the miracles which he did on them that were diseased. And so on.

Homily by St. Augustine, Bishop

The miracles which our Lord Jesus Christ did were the very works of God, and they enlighten the mind of man by means of things which are seen, that he may know more of God. God is Himself of such a Substance as eye cannot see, and the miracles, by the which He rules the whole world continually, and satisfies the need of everything that He has made, have by use become so common, that scarcely any will vouchsafe to see that there are wonderful and amazing works of God in every grain of seed of grass. According to His mercy He kept some works to be done in their due season, according to the common course and order of nature, that men might wonder in seeing not the things that are greater but rather the unusual which they have seen every day.

Lesson VIII

Or it is a greater miracle to govern the whole universe, than to satisfy five thousand men with five loaves of bread; and yet no man marvels at it. At the feeding of the five thousand, men marvel, not because it is a greater miracle than the other, but because it is rarer. For Who is He Who now feeds the whole world, but He Who, from a little grain that is sown, makes the fulness of the harvest? God works in both cases in one and the same manner. He Who of the sowing makes to come the harvest, is He Who of the five barley loaves in His Hands made bread to feed five thousand men; for Christ's are the Hands which are able to do both the one and the other. He Who multiplies the grains of corn multiplied the loaves, only not by committing them to the earth whereof He is the Maker.

Lesson IX

This miracle, then, is brought to bear upon our bodies, that our souls may thereby be quickened; shown to our eyes, to give food to our understanding; that, through His works which we see, we may marvel at that God Whom we cannot see, and, being roused up to believe, and purified by believing, we may long to see Him, yea, may know by things which are seen Him Who is Unseen. Nor yet does it suffice for us to see only this meaning in Christ's miracles. Let us ask of the miracles themselves what they have to tell us concerning Christ for, truly they have a tongue of their own if only we will understand it. For, because Christ is the Word of God, therefore the work of the Word is a Word for us.

Monday IV in Lent

Lesson I

From the Holy Gospel according to St. John (John 2:13–25)

In that time, the pasch of the Jews was at hand, and Jesus went up to Jerusalem. And he found in the temple them that sold oxen and sheep and doves. And so on.

Homily by St. Augustine, Bishop

What hear we now, my brethren? Behold, that temple was still but a figure, and the Lord drove out therefrom all them that sought their own, even them that were come to deal in merchandise. And what was it that they sold there? Only such things as were needful to men for the sacrifices that then were. For your love knows that, because of that people's carnal-mindedness and the stoniness of their hearts, there were commanded unto them such sacrifices as these, to hold them back thereby from idolatry and there, accordingly, they offered up oxen, and sheep, and doves. This you have read, and know.

Lesson II

It was no great sin, therefore, if they sold in the temple that which was bought to be offered in the temple and yet He drove them out. If, then, the Lord drove out of His temple them which sold such things as are lawful and right (for to buy and sell is lawful, if only it be done honestly), and suffered not the house of prayer to be made a house of merchandise, what would He have done if He had found drunken men there?

Lesson III

If the house of God must not be a house of merchandise, must it be a house in which to drink? And yet, when we say this, men gnash upon us with their teeth. But we find consolation in remembering that so far we are even as the Psalmist, who says: "They gnashed upon me with their teeth." Yea, we have also learnt to listen to words that heal us, though really, the lashes that are made at His word are really made at Christ. "Lashes," says He, "were heaped upon Me; and they knew not what they did." He was lashed by the scourges of the Jews, and He is lashed still by the blasphemies of false Christians; they heap lashes upon the Lord their God; and know not what they do. As for us, we will do that which He has helped us to do; "But as for me, when they troubled me, my clothing was sackcloth, and I humbled my soul with fasting."

Tuesday IV in Lent

Lesson I

From the Holy Gospel according to St. John (John 7:14–31)

In that time, about the midst of the feast, Jesus went up into the temple, and taught. And the Jews wondered. And so on.

Homily by St. Augustine, Bishop

He Who had gone up unto the Feast, not openly but in secret, the Same taught and spoke openly, and no man laid hands upon Him. That He had hid Himself was for example's sake; that He manifested Himself was to show His power. And when He taught, the Jews marveled. As seems to my mind, they all marveled, but not all were converted. And wherefore did they marvel? Because many of them knew where He was born, and how He had been brought up. They had never seen Him learn letters; but they heard Him dispute concerning the law, and allege the testimony of the same, as no man could do who had not read it; and no man can read unless he learns; and therefore they marveled. But their marveling was unto the Teacher an occasion for the revealing of higher truth.

Lesson II

For when they marveled and whispered, the Lord said a certain deep thing, yea, a thing worthy of very careful thought and discussion. And what was this thing which the Lord gave for an answer to such as marveled that He knew letters, having never learned? Jesus answered them and said: "My doctrine is not Mine, but His That sent Me." Here is the first depth, for He seems in these few words to enunciate a contradiction. He says not: "This doctrine is not Mine" but: "My doctrine is not Mine." O how is it thine? If it be thine, wherefore sayest Thou that it is not thine? For Thou sayest: "My doctrine is not Mine."

Lesson III

Let us then carefully regard what this same holy Evangelist says in the beginning of his Gospel, and we shall find there wherewith to loose the knot of this difficulty. There it is written: "In the beginning was the Word, and the Word was with God, and the Word was God." What is the doctrine of the Father but the Word of the Father? If Christ therefore be the Word of the Father, He is the doctrine of the Father. But a Word cannot be of no one, but must needs, if it be a Word, have some one whose word it is. Christ therefore says that His doctrine is Himself, and therefore not His, forasmuch as He is the Word of the Father. And what hast thou that is so much thine own as thyself? Or what is there that is so little thine own as thyself, if that which thou art is another's?

Wednesday IV in Lent

Lesson I

From the Holy Gospel according to St. John (John 9:1–38)

At that time, Jesus, passing by, saw a man, who was blind from his birth. And so on.

Homily by St. Augustine, Bishop

Dread and wondrous are all the things which our Lord Jesus Christ did, both His works and His words; the works, because He wrought them; the words, because they are deep. If, therefore, we consider the meaning of this work of His, we see that that man which was blind from his birth was a figure of mankind. This spiritual blindness was the consequence of the sin of the first man, from whom we all inherit by birth, not death only, but depravity also. For if blindness be unbelief, and faith, light, whom, when Christ came, did He find faithful? Since, the Apostle who had himself been born of the race of which the Prophets came, says: "We also were by nature children of wrath, even as others." And if children of wrath, then children also of vengeance, children of damnation, children of hell. And wherefore so by nature, unless it were that the sin of the first man had made all his descendants to be born in sin, in that they partook of his nature? If, then, our nature bring sin with it, all men, according to the spirit, are born blind.

Lesson II

The Lord came; and what did He do? He set before us a great mystery. Jesus spat on the ground, and made clay of the Spittle for the Word was made flesh. And He anointed the eyes of the blind man with the clay but yet that man saw not. He was anointed, indeed, but yet still he saw not. And He said unto him: "Go, wash in the Pool of Siloam." Now, it was the duty of the Evangelist to impress upon us the name of this Pool, and therefore he says Siloam, which is, by interpretation, Sent. You, my brethren, know Who is signified where it is written: "He that shall be Sent." Yea, He it is, Who, if He had not been sent, we had never been sent loose out of the prison of sin. The blind man went his way therefore, and washed his eyes in that Pool, which is, by interpretation, Sent; in other words, he was baptized in Christ. When, therefore, he had figuratively been baptized in Him Whom the Father hath Sent into the world, he came seeing. When he was anointed, he was perchance made a figure of a Catechumen.

Lesson III

We have heard this great mystery. Ask of a man: Art thou a Christian? He answers thee: I am not. Then, if thou ask him: Art thou a pagan then, or a Jew? And he still says unto thee, Nay, and thou say: Art thou then a Catechumen, though not yet one of the faithful? and he says, Yea, a Catechumen, then there thou seest a man anointed, but not yet washed. With what has he been anointed? Ask of him, and he will tell thee. Ask of him in Whom he believes, and, being a Catechumen, he will say: In Christ. But, behold, I speak before both Faithful and Catechumens. What said I touching the Spittle and the clay? I said "for the Word was made flesh." This the Catechumens hear, but it is not enough for them to be anointed; they must make haste to the washing, if they would have their eyes opened.

Thursday IV in Lent

Lesson I

From the Holy Gospel according to St. Luke (Luke 7:11–16)

At that time, Jesus went into a city that is called Naim; and there went with him his disciples, and a great multitude. And so on.

Homily by St. Ambrose, Bishop

The history which we here read in the Holy Gospel has specially two gracious lessons for us, the one from the literal, the other from the mystic interpretation thereof. According to the letter then, we see how quickly the compassion of God was aroused by the sorrow of this mother, who was a widow, a widow broken down by nursing her only son, or by the bitterness of her grief for his death. She was a widow also whose worshipful conversation is borne witness to by this, that, much people of the city was with her. Mystically however, this widow encompassed by the multitude was something more than a poor woman whose tears won from the Lord the resurrection of her young and only son; for she is a type of our holy Mother the Church, who calls back her young children to life from the pursuit of deathly vanities, and soul-slaying honors, by bidding them look on those tears which she sheds for such as they, and which it is unlawful for her to shed for them of whom she knows that they will rise again.

Lesson II

This man, then, being dead, was carried out on a bier to the grave by four bearers, even as the sinner is borne to destruction by the four elements of which he is composed. But there was hope in his latter end, from this: that which he was carried upon was of wood, and wood, albeit it had profited us little before, is become everything to us now since Jesus touched it, being a figure of that gibbet, the Cross, which was made thereof, and wherefrom salvation flows unto all people. When, therefore, the horrid bearers of the corpse heard the commandment of God, they stood still, and carried no farther him who was dead through the fatal course of a material nature. And is not our case even as that of the widow's son, when we lie, as it were, lifeless, in our spiritual coffin, that is, in the last bed of our soul's death, consumed by the fever of unbridled lust, or frozen by cold-heartedness, or with our whole manliness sapped by some degrading habit of this earthly body, or starved by a spiritual lockjaw that shuts our mouth to the bright food of our soul? These, and such as these, are they which carry us out to burial.

Lesson III

But even at the last hour, when the hope of life has been utterly extinguished, and the bodies of the dead are lying by the side of the grave, by the word of God those carcasses live again, yea, arise and speak. Then does Jesus deliver the son to his mother, for Jesus calls him out of the grave, and delivers him from death. O, what is the grave of the soul but a bad life? Sinner! thy grave is unbelief, and thy throat is a sepulchre! Even so is it written: "Their throat is an open sepulchre, whereout breathe their pestilential words." Lo! Christ makes thee free from that grave! If only thou wilt hear the word of God, thou shalt yet arise from that sepulchre! Yea, though thy sin be exceeding weighty, so that the tears of thine own sorrow cannot wash it away, let thy Mother the Church weep for thee, that longing Mother who weeps for every one of her children as though he were the only son of his mother, and she was a widow. Believe me, her spiritual anguish is keen like the anguish of nature, when she sees her children dead in sin, and carried out to be buried for ever.

Friday IV in Lent

Lesson I

From the Holy Gospel according to St. John (John 11:1–45)

At that time, there was a certain man sick, named Lazarus, of Bethania, of the town of Mary and Martha her sister. And so on.

Homily by St. Augustine, Bishop

You remember that in our last reading we learnt how that the Lord escaped out of the hands of them which took up stones to stone Him, and went away again beyond Jordan, into the place where John first baptized. While, then, the Lord still tarried there, Lazarus was sick at Bethany, which was a town near to Jerusalem. It was that Mary which anointed the Lord with ointment, and wiped His Feet with her hair, whose brother Lazarus was sick. Therefore his sisters sent unto Him. We know already whither it was that they sent, for we know where Jesus was: He was gone away again beyond Jordan. His sisters sent unto Him, saying: "Lord, behold, he whom Thou lovest is sick," in order that, if He so pleased, He might come and free him from his sickness. But Jesus healed not, that He might afterward resuscitate.

Lesson II

What therefore sent his sisters to say? "Lord, behold, he whom Thou lovest is sick" and no more. They said not: "Come," for Jesus loved him; and to tell Him that he was sick was enough. They dared not to say: "Come, and heal him," they dared not to say: "Speak the word where Thou art, and it shall be done here." And why should they not have said this if they had the faith which won the Centurion so much praise? He had said: "Lord, I am not worthy that Thou shouldest come under my roof; but speak the word only, and my servant shall be healed." But they said none of these things, only: "Lord, behold, he whom Thou lovest is sick. It is enough that Thou shouldest know it. Thou art not one that lovest and leavest."

Lesson III

But some man will say: How shall Lazarus be a type of the sinner, and yet the Lord so love him? Let such a one hear the words of the same Lord, which He said: "I am not come to call the righteous, but sinners." For if God had not loved sinners, He had not come down from heaven to earth. When Jesus heard that, He said: "This sickness is not unto death, but for the glory of God, that the Son of God might be glorified thereby." Such a glorification is no increase of majesty for Him, but of profit for us. He therefore means to say: "This sickness is not unto death, but for the working of a miracle which, being wrought, if men will thereby believe in Christ, they shall escape the real death." Note especially how the Lord does in this place declare Himself to be God, as it were by implication, for the sake of some which say that He is not the Son of God.

Saturday IV in Lent

Lesson I

From the Holy Gospel according to St. John (John 8:12–20)

At that time, Jesus spoke to the multitude of Jews saying: I am the light of the world: he that followeth me, walketh not in darkness, but shall have the light of life. And so on.

Homily by St. Augustine, bishop

I take it that these words of the Lord: "I am the Light of the world" are sufficiently clear to all men who have eyes which see that Light. At the same time, such men as have no eyes except those which are in their bodies, are surprised to find our Lord Jesus Christ saying, "I am the Light of the world." And that we might not want somebody to say, "Is our Lord Jesus Christ, then, the same sun that rises and sets every day?" There have actually been heretics who did say it. The Manichæans believed that that sun which we see with our bodily eyes, and to see which is plain and common to beasts as well as men, was the Lord Christ.

Lesson II

But the right faith of the Catholic Church condemns such comment, and recognizes in it a doctrine of devils. And as it is her practice not only to brand errors by the difference of her own Creed, but also to remove them, if possible, by way of argument, let us take up arms against this error, which the Holy Church has, from the very beginning, anathematized. God forbid that we should believe that our Lord Jesus Christ is this sun whose apparent movement is to rise every day in the East, and set every day in the West; which when we see no more, night comes over us; and whose rays are sometimes intercepted by clouds and which has some law of motion of its own whereby it describes an orbit. The planet is not the same thing as our Lord Jesus Christ. Our Lord Jesus Christ is not that created sun, but He by Whom that sun was created; for all things were made by Him, and without Him was not anything made that was made.

Lesson III

He is therefore the Light by Whom the material light was made. Him may we love, Him may we long to know, after Him may we thirst; to Him may His own beams one day lead us, and in Him may we so live that we shall never die! For He, even He, and none other, He is that Light of Whom the Prophet that was given of old time sang in the Psalms, when he said: "For with thee is the fountain of life, and in thy Light shall we see light." Remember likewise what the word of God's ancient saints says of such Light: "O Lord, Thou preservest man and beast! How excellent is thy loving-kindness, O God!"

PASSIONTIDE

PASSION SUNDAY

Duplex I Class

Lesson I ~ Jer 1:1–6

Beginning of the book of the Prophet Jeremias

The words of Jeremias the son of Helcias, of the priests that were in Anathoth, in the land of Benjamin. The word of the Lord which came to him in the days of Josias the son of Amon king of Juda, in the thirteenth year of his reign. And which came to him in the days of Joakim the son of Josias king of Juda, unto the end of the eleventh year of Sedecias the son of Josias king of Juda, even unto the carrying away of Jerusalem captive, in the fifth month. And the word of the Lord came to me, saying: Before I formed thee in the bowels of thy mother, I knew thee: and before thou camest forth out of the womb, I sanctified thee, and made thee a prophet unto the nations. And I said: Ah, ah, ah, Lord God: behold, I cannot speak, for I am a child.

Lesson II ~ Jer 1:7–13

And the Lord said to me: Say not: I am a child: for thou shalt go to all that I shall send thee: and whatsoever I shall command thee, thou shalt speak. Be not afraid at their presence: for I am with thee to deliver thee, saith the Lord. And the Lord put forth his hand, and touched my mouth: and the Lord said to me: Behold I have given my words in thy mouth: Lo, I have set thee this day over the nations, and over the kingdoms, to root up, and pull down, and to waste, and to destroy, and to build, and to plant. And the word of the Lord came to me, saying: What seest thou, Jeremias? And I said: I see a rod watching. And the Lord said to me: Thou hast seen well: for I will watch over my word to perform it. And the word of the Lord came to me a second time, saying: What seest thou? I see a boiling caldron, and the face thereof from the face of the north.

Lesson III ~ Jer 1:14–19

And the Lord said to me: from the north shall an evil break forth upon all the inhabitants of the land. For behold I will call together all the families of the kingdoms of the north: saith the Lord: and they shall come, and shall set every one his throne in the entrance of the gates of Jerusalem, and upon all the walls thereof round about, and upon all the cities of Juda, And I will pronounce my judgements against them, touching all their wickedness, who have forsaken me, and have sacrificed to strange gods, and have adored the work of their own hands. Thou therefore gird up thy loins, and arise, and speak to them all that I command thee. Be not afraid at their presence for I will make thee not to fear their countenance. For behold I have made thee this day a fortified city, and a pillar of iron, and a wall of brass, over all the land, to the kings of Juda, to the princes thereof, and to the priests, and to the people of the land. And they shall fight against thee, and shall not prevail: for I am with thee, saith the Lord, to deliver thee.

Lesson IV

Sermon by St. Leo, Pope

Dearly beloved brethren, we know that of all the solemn Feasts which are kept by Christians the Passover is the chief. The ordinances of the whole rest of the year are ordered to the end of preparing us to come to this one in worthy and right manner. But these days, which now are, are they which ought most especially to stir up a godly mind in us, seeing that they are those which are nearest to that most glorious mystery of God's mercy. In these days, the holy Apostles, taught by the Holy Ghost, ordered the chiefest store of Fasting, that we, sharing His Cross with Christ, might, albeit we are what we are, in Him, do some of the same things which He did for our sakes, and so realize the saying of the Apostle: "If we suffer with Him, we shall be also glorified together." He that is partaker of the sufferings of the Lord has a sure and certain hope of that blessedness which He has promised unto us.

Lesson V

Dearly beloved brethren, there is no man to whom the state of the age in which he lives denies a share in this glory of partaking, first the sufferings, and then the triumph and joy of Christ. It is not as though this time of peace were barren in occasions of valor. The Apostle gives us this warning: "All that will live godly in Christ Jesus shall suffer persecution." And therefore, as long as godliness is watchful, persecution will never be asleep. The Lord Himself says in one of His own exhortations "He that takes not his cross, and follows after Me, is not worthy of Me." And we must not doubt that these words of Christ apply not only to His immediate disciples, to whom He spoke them, but belong to all the faithful and to the whole Church, who, whosoever be the believers of whom she is for the time composed on earth, hears in these words the way to be saved which her Lord has appointed for them.

Lesson VI

As then, it is the duty of the whole body of the Church to live godly, so is it her right at all times to be bearing her Master's Cross, and that not only in her general body, but individually in the person of each one of her members, who differ every one from another in the way in which they have to carry it and the shape in which it is laid upon them. The one common name for all their carrying of the Cross is persecution, but the manner of his wrestling is special to each; and there is often more danger in the ambush than in the pitched field of battle. Blessed Job, who had tried both the goods and the ills of this world, said: "Is not the life of man upon earth a warfare?" The attack upon the faithful soul arrays itself not alone in bodily torture and punishment; yea, when the limbs are sound enough, fearful is the ravage that threatens us when the lusts of the flesh unman us. But when the flesh lusts against the spirit, and the spirit against the flesh, the reasonable mind finds her reinforcement in the helpful Cross of Christ, and though she be lured by foul cravings, yet refuses to give her consent, for God makes her pure thoughts to tremble for fear of Him.

Lesson VII

From the Holy Gospel according to St. John (John 8:46–59)

At that time, Jesus said to the multitude of Jews: Which of you shall convince me of sin? If I say the truth to you, why do you not believe me? And so on.

Homily by Pope St. Gregory

Dearly beloved brethren, consider the gentleness of God. He came to take away sins, and He says: Which of you convinces Me of sin? He Who, through the might of His Divinity, was able to justify sinners, was contented to show by argument that He was not Himself a sinner. But exceedingly dreadful is that which follows. "He that is of God hears God's words; you, therefore, hear them not, because you are not of God." If, then, whosoever is of God hears God's words, and whosoever is not of Him cannot hear His words, let each one ask himself if he, in the ear of his heart, hears God's words, and understands Whose words they are? The Truth commands us to long for a Fatherland in heaven, to bridle the lusts of the flesh, to turn away from the glory of the world, to seek no man's goods, and to give away our own.

Lesson VIII

Let each of you, therefore, think within himself if this voice of God is heard in the ear of his heart, and if he knows already if he is of God. For there are some whom it pleases not to hear the commandments of God even with their bodily ears. And there are some who receive the same with their bodily ears, but whose heart is far from them. And there are also some who hear the words of God with joy, so that they are moved thereby even to tears; but when their fit of weeping is past they turn again to iniquity. They do not hear the words of God, who despise to do them. Therefore, dearly beloved brethren, call up your own life before your mind's eye, and then ponder with trembling those awful words which the mouth of the Truth spoke. "You therefore hear them not, because you are not of God."

Lesson IX

The Truth speaks these words concerning the reprobate; but the reprobate make manifest the same thing concerning themselves, by their evil works. Thus immediately follows: "Then answered the Jews, and said unto Him: Say we not well that Thou art a Samaritan, and hast a devil?" But let us hear what the Lord said to this insult. "I have not a devil, but I honor My Father, and you do dishonor Me." The Lord said: "I have not a devil," but He did not say: "I am not a Samaritan," for in a sense a Samaritan He was indeed, since the word Samaritan, in the Hebrew tongue, signifies, being interpreted, a Watcher, and the Lord is that Watcher, of Whom the Psalmist says that unless He keep the city, other watchman keep vigil in vain. He also is that Watchman unto Whom cries Isaias: "Watchman, what of the night? Watchman, what of the night?" Therefore the Lord said: "I have not a devil," but not "I am not a Samaritan." Of the two things brought against Him He denied one; but by His silence, admitted the other.

Monday in Passion Week

Lesson I

From the Holy Gospel according to St. John (John 7:32–39)

At that time, the rulers and Pharisees sent ministers to apprehend him. And so on.

Homily by St. Augustine, Bishop

How could they take Him until such time as He willed to be taken? If, then, they could not take Him until He willed to be taken, were they sent to watch His teaching? Then said Jesus unto them "Yet a little while am I with you, what you now seek to do, you shall do; but not yet, for I will not so yet. And why will I not so yet? Because yet a little while am I with you, and then I go unto Him that sent Me I must fulfill that which I am sent to do, and so go to suffer."

Lesson II

"You shall seek Me, and shall not find Me, and where I am thither you cannot come." In these words He foretold already His rising again from the dead. While He was with them they would not know Him; and afterwards they sought Him, when they saw that a multitude already believed in Him. For great signs were wrought also when the Lord rose again, and ascended up into heaven. Then were great signs again wrought through the Disciples, that is, through them by Him Who works the same directly also by Himself, according as He had said unto them: "Without Me you can do nothing." When that lame man that was laid daily at the Beautiful Gate of the Temple stood up at the voice of Peter and walked, and all the people were filled with wonder, Peter bade them know that it was not by his own power that he had made him to walk, but by the power of Him Whom they had killed. And when they heard this, many were pricked in their heart, and said: What shall we do?

Lesson III

Nor did they see that they were burdened with the guilt of an exceedingly great sin, in that they had killed Him Whom it was their duty to worship and adore, and for that guilt they knew of no propitiation. Yea, their sin was indeed exceedingly great; and the consideration of it made them to despair for those whom the Lord, when He hung upon the Cross, had been willing to pray, as it is written. Then said Jesus: "Father, forgive them, for they know not what they do." At that hour He had seen among many aliens some that were His Own; for them He asked forgiveness, while yet He suffered at their hand, nor considered that they were putting Him to death, but only that He was dying for them.

Tuesday in Passion Week

Lesson I

From the Holy Gospel according to St. John (John 7:1–13)

At that time: Jesus walked in Galilee; for he would not walk in Judea, because the Jews sought to kill him. And so on.

Homily by St. Augustine, Bishop

In this chapter of the Gospel, my brethren, our Lord Jesus Christ has much commended Himself unto our faith, as touching His Manhood. At the same time, His words and works were always such as to give us to believe that He is both God and Man, yea, that God Who made us, and that Man Who has sought us, yea, God the Son, Who, as touching His Divinity, is always with the Father and, as touching His Manhood, has been with us in time. For He had not sought the work of His hands unless He had been made His own work. Keep this well in mind, and let your hearts never forget it, namely, that Christ was not made Man so as to cease to be God. He Who made the Manhood, took It into that Divinity Which is His from everlasting to everlasting.

Lesson II

While therefore He lay hid in the Manhood, we must not think that He had suffered any lessening of power, but that He was giving example to our weakness. When He willed it, He was taken; when He willed it, He was put to death. But, since He was to have members, that is, His faithful people, who would not have that power over their lives which He, our God, had over His, He hid Himself, He concealed Himself, as if it were to escape being put to death, to show what should be done by those His members in whom He should dwell.

Lesson III

Christ is not the Head of His Church in such sense that He is not in her Body; but the whole Christ is in the Head, and the whole Christ is in the Body. Then, that which His members are is Himself, though That Which He is, That are not therefore His members. For if His members had not been indeed His Own, how had He said unto Saul: "Why persecutest thou Me?" since Saul was not persecuting Him in Himself, but in His members, that is, in His faithful ones which were upon earth. He said not: "Why persecutest thou My holy ones," nor: "My servants," no, nor yet did He call them by that more honorable name "My brethren," but, "Why persecutest thou Me?"; that is, the members of My Body, whose Head I am.

Wednesday in Passion Week

Lesson I

From the Holy Gospel according to St. John (John 10:22–38)

In that time, it was the feast of the dedication at Jerusalem: and it was winter. And Jesus walked in the temple, in Solomon's porch. And so on.

Homily by St. Augustine

The Greek word *Enkainia*, used by the Evangelist, signifies the Feast of the Dedication of the Temple. The derivation thereof is *kainon*, which is, being interpreted, new; and the Dedication of anything new is thence called *Enkainia*. The use of this word is still preserved among ourselves; if any man put on his new coat for the first time he is said to *encæniare*. It was the use of the Jews to keep solemn holiday upon the Anniversary of the Dedication of the Temple, and this was the Feast-day which was being observed when the Lord spoke the words which have been read.

Lesson II

"It was winter. And Jesus walked in the Temple in Solomon's Porch. Then came the Jews round about Him, and said unto Him How long dost Thou make us to doubt? If Thou be the Christ, tell us plainly. They sought not to know the truth, but to have whereof to accuse Him." It was winter, and they were cold; for they were slow to draw near to God's fire. If to believe is to draw near thereto, then he which believes draws near thereto and he which denies, goes away therefrom. The feet of the soul, by which it moves, are the affections thereof.

Lesson III

They were frozen with want of love, and at the same time on fire with thirst to do injury. They stood afar off, and yet came near; for though they drew not near by faith, they were eager to persecute. They sought to hear the Lord say "I am the Christ;" and perchance they knew somewhat concerning Christ, as touching His Manhood, for the Prophets had prophesied of Christ. But the Divinity of Christ even some heretics do not see witnessed either in the Prophets or in the Gospel; how much less the Jews, as long as the veil is upon their heart.

Thursday in Passion Week

Lesson I

From the Holy Gospel according to St. Luke (Luke 7:36–50)

In that time, one of the Pharisees desired him to eat with him. And he went into the house of the Pharisee, And so on.

Homily by Pope St. Gregory

When I think of the repentance of Mary Magdalene I feel nearer to weeping than to say otherwise. Is there indeed any man, however stony his heart, who is not somewhat moved to follow the example of her repentance by the tears of that poor sinful woman? She weighed what she did, and willed not to moderate what she would do. She came unbidden among the guests, and obtruded her tears upon the banquet. You may hence gather her sorrow, that she was content to weep at a feast.

Lesson II

We believe that this woman, of whom Luke says that she was a woman in the city, which was a sinner, and whom John names Mary, was the same as she of whom it is written in Mark that the Lord had cast out of her seven devils. And what signify seven devils but all manner of sin? For even as seven days do represent all time, so does the number seven stand for all. Therefore is it said that Mary had seven devils, because she was full of all sin.

Lesson III

But see how she realized the depth of her own filthiness, and came to be washed to the Well of Mercy, before all them which were bidden to the feast. The bitterness of her inward shame made her esteem it a light thing to be despised outwardly. At what then do we marvel, my brethren? That she came, or that the Lord welcomed her? Or would it be truer for me to say that He drew her to Him and welcomed her when she came? for His mercy inwardly drew her, and, when she came, His gentleness openly welcomed her.

Seven Sorrows of the Blessed Virgin Mary

~Friday in Passion Week~

Major Duplex

Lesson I ~ Isa 53:1–5

From the book of the Prophet Isaias

Who hath believed our report? and to whom is the arm of the Lord revealed? And he shall grow up as a tender plant before him, and as a root out of a thirsty ground: there is no beauty in him, nor comeliness: and we have seen him, and there was no sightliness, that we should be desirous of him: Despised, and the most abject of men, a man of sorrows, and acquainted with infirmity: and his look was as it were hidden and despised, whereupon we esteemed him not. Surely he hath borne our infirmities and carried our sorrows: and we have thought him as it were a leper, and as one struck by God and afflicted. But he was wounded for our iniquities, he was bruised for our sins: the chastisement of our peace was upon him, and by his bruises we are healed.

Lesson II ~ Isa 53:6–9

All we like sheep have gone astray, every one hath turned aside into his own way: and the Lord hath laid on him the iniquity of us all. He was offered because it was his own will, and he opened not his mouth: he shall be led as a sheep to the slaughter, and shall be dumb as a lamb before his shearer, and he shall not open his mouth. He was taken away from distress, and from judgment: who shall declare his generation? because he is cut off out of the land of the living: for the wickedness of my people have I struck him. And he shall give the ungodly for his burial, and the rich for his death: because he hath done no iniquity, neither was there deceit in his mouth.

Lesson III ~ Isa 53:10–12

And the Lord was pleased to bruise him in infirmity: if he shall lay down his life for sin, he shall see a long-lived seed, and the will of the Lord shall be prosperous in his hand. Because his soul hath laboured, he shall see and be filled: by his knowledge shall this my just servant justify many, and he shall bear their iniquities. Therefore will I distribute to him very many, and he shall divide the spoils of the strong, because he hath delivered his soul unto death, and was reputed with the wicked: and he hath borne the sins of many, and hath prayed for the transgressors.

Lessons IV–VI from those of September 15: The Seven Sorrows of the Blessed Virgin Mary (Sermon by St. Bernard)

Lesson VII

From the Holy Gospel according to St. John (John 19:25–27)

In that time stood by the cross of Jesus, his mother, and his mother's sister, Mary of Cleophas, and Mary Magdalene. And so on.

Homily by St. Augustine, Bishop

This is that hour whereof Jesus, when He was about to turn water into wine, had said unto His Mother: "Woman, what have I to do with thee? Mine hour is not yet come." He had spoken of this hour, which then was not yet come, wherein, being about to die, it should be His duty to acknowledge her of whom He had been born in a mortal Body. Then, since He was about to do the works of God, He thrust from Him, as though He knew her not, her who was His Mother, not in that nature whereby He is equal to the Father, but in that whereby He is inferior to the Father. But now, since He is suffering the pains of Man, He cares, with a Man's love, for her of whom He has been made Man. And herein He gives us a lesson. He does that which He would have us to do. The Good Master, by His Own example, commands that among His disciples, dutiful children should support their parents, as even did that Tree whereupon His dying Limbs were nailed, even that Tree was to be a pulpit for His teaching.

Lesson VIII

And of this teaching by Jesus Crucified comes that which the Apostle Paul commands where he says, "If any provide not for his own, and specially for those of his own house, he hath denied the faith, and is worse than an infidel." But what is so much of a man's own house, as children are of their parents'? and parents of their children's? Of this most healthy law the Master of the Saints was pleased Himself to give an example, when, being God, He treated not as His handmaid her of whom He was the Maker and the Lord, but, being also Man, gave another to be as a son in His stead, to her of whom as Man He had been made, and whom He was leaving.

Lesson IX - I–III of the Feria

From the holy Gospel according to St. John (John 11:47–54)

The chief priests therefore, and the Pharisees, gathered a council, and said: What do we, for this man doth many miracles? If we let him alone so, all will believe in him; and the Romans will come, and take away our place and nation. And so on.

Homily by St. Augustine, Bishop

The chief Priests and the Pharisees took counsel together, but "Let us believe in Him" was not one of the suggestions offered. Those lost creatures thought much more how they might hurt and undo Him, than how they might save themselves from perishing. And yet they were afraid, and took counsel together, and said: "What should we do? For this Man does many miracles. If we let Him thus alone, all men will believe in Him; and the Romans shall come and take away both our place and our nation." They were afraid of losing temporal things, but they gave no thought to eternal life, and so they lost both.

For, after the Lord had suffered and been glorified, first came the Romans, and took away both their place and nation, prevailing against them and leading them away captive, and secondly there followed them of which is written "But the children of the kingdom shall be cast out into outer darkness." But their fear was that, if all men should believe in Christ, none would remain to defend the city of God and His Temple against the Romans, since they deemed that Christ's teaching was against the Temple itself, and against the laws of their fathers.

And one of them, named Ca'iphas, being the High Priest that same year, said unto them: "Ye know nothing at all, nor consider that it is expedient for us that one man should die for the people, and that the whole nation perish not." And this he spoke not of himself but, being High Priest that year, he prophesied. Here we will learn that bad men are enabled by the spirit of prophecy to foretell the future; which at the same time, the Evangelist attributes to an ordinance of God, namely, that he was the High Priest.

Saturday in Passion Week

Lesson I

From the Holy Gospel according to St. John (John 12:10–36)

In that time, the chief priests thought to kill Lazarus also: Because many of the Jews, by reason of him, went away, and believed in Jesus. And so on.

Homily by St. Augustine, Bishop

When they saw Lazarus who had been raised from the dead, and knew that the miracle which the Lord had worked was so great, spread about by so many witnesses, and so plain and manifest that it could neither be concealed nor denied, see here what then they made up: "But the chief Priests consulted that they might put Lazarus also to death." What stupidity of thought, what blindness of cruelty is here! If the Lord Christ had raised up again a man who had died a natural death, could He not also raise up one that had died by violence? Would killing Lazarus paralyze the Lord? But if you consider that there is a difference between a man dead of disease, and a man killed, behold, the Lord has raised up both; for He first raised up Lazarus who had died a natural death, and then Himself after a violent one.

Lesson II

"On the next day much people that were come to the feast, when they heard that Jesus was coming to Jerusalem, took branches of palm-trees, and went forth to meet Him, and cried Hosanna! Blessed is He That comes in the Name of the Lord, the King of Israel!" Palm branches are glorious boughs which tell of victory; yea, the Lord was now ready by His Own Death to trample down death, and to carry the victorious banner of His Cross in triumph over the devil, the prince of death. The cry with which He was greeted, namely *Hosanna*, has not, as we are assured by some who are acquainted with the Hebrew language, any meaning in particular, but is a shout after the manner of interjections, as they are called, just as in Latin when we lament we say *Heu*, or when we are pleased, *Vah*.

Lesson III

These were the shouts of applause with which the crowd greeted Him, "Hosanna! Blessed is He That comes in the Name of the Lord, the King of Israel!" What inward torture must the jealousy of the Jewish leaders have caused them, when they heard that great multitude hailing Christ as their King! But, for the Lord, what was it to be King of Israel? To the Eternal King what mattered it to become a King of men? And Christ is not King of Israel in the sense of monarchs who exact tribute, or arm hosts with steel to conquer enemies that are seen. But King of Israel He is, as He Who is Lord of our intellect, a Ruler Whose power shall never wane, and Who opens a Kingdom in heaven to all such as place in Him their faith, their hope, and their love.

HOLY WEEK

PALM SUNDAY

Duplex I Class

Lesson I ~ Jer 2:12–17

From the book of the Prophet Jeremias

Be astonished, O ye heavens, at this, and ye gates thereof, be very desolate, saith the Lord. For my people have done two evils. They have forsaken me, the fountain of living water, and have digged to themselves cisterns, broken cisterns, that can hold no water. Is Israel a bondman, or a homeborn slave? why then is he become prey? The lions have roared upon him, and have made a noise, they have made his land a wilderness: his cities are burnt down and there is none to dwell in them. The children also of Memphis, and of Taphnes have deflowered thee, even to the crown of the head. Hath not this been done to thee, because thou hast forsaken the Lord thy God at that time, when he led thee by the way?

Lesson II ~ Jer 2:18–22

And now what hast thou to do in the way of Egypt, to drink the troubled water? And what hast thou to do with the way of the Assyrians, to drink the water of the river? Thy own wickedness shall reprove thee, and thy apostasy shall rebuke thee. Know thou, and see that it is an evil and a bitter thing for thee, to have left the Lord thy God, and that my fear is not with thee, saith the Lord the God of hosts. Of old time thou hast broken my yoke, thou hast burst my bands, and thou saidst: I will not serve. For on every high hill, and under every green tree thou didst prostitute thyself. Yet I planted thee a chosen vineyard, all true seed: how then art thou turned unto me into that which is good for nothing, O strange vineyard? Though thou wash thyself with nitre, and multiply to thyself the herb borith, thou art stained in thy iniquity before me, saith the Lord God.

Lesson III ~ Jer 2:29–32

Why will you contend with me in judgement? you have all forsaken me, saith the Lord. In vain have I struck your children, they have not received correction: your sword hath devoured your prophets, your generation is like a ravaging lion. See ye the word of the Lord: Am I become a wilderness to Israel, or a lateward springing land? why then have my people said: We are revolted, we will come to thee no more. Will a virgin forget her ornament, or a bride her stomacher? but my people hath forgotten me days without number.

Lesson IV

Sermon by St. Leo, Pope

Dearly beloved brethren, the jubilant and triumphal day which ushers in the commemoration of the Lord's Passion is come; even that day for which we have longed so much, and for whose yearly coming the whole world may well look. Shouts of spiritual exultation are ringing, and suffer not that we should be silent. It is indeed hard to preach often on the same Festival, and that always fittingly and rightly, but a Priest is not free, when we celebrate so great and mysterious an outpouring of God's mercy, to leave his faithful people without the service of a discourse. Nay, that his subject-matter is unspeakable should in itself make him eloquent, since where enough can never be said, there must always need be something to say. Let man's weakness, then, fall down before the glory of God, and acknowledge herself ever too feeble to unfold all the works of His mercy. We may jade our emotions, break down in our understanding, and fail in our speech; it is good for us, that even what we truly feel in presence of the Divine Majesty is but little.

Lesson V

For when the Prophet says: "Seek the Lord and be strong; seek His face evermore," let no man thence conclude that he will ever have found all that he seeks, lest he which has ceased to come near should cease to be near. But among all the works of God which foil and weary the steadfast gaze of man's wonder, what is there that does at once so ravish and so exceed the power of our mind's eye as do the sufferings of the Saviour? He it was Who, to loose man from the bands wherewith he had bound himself by the first death-dealing transgression, spared to bring against the rage of the devil the power of the Divine Majesty, and met him with the weakness of our lowly nature. For if our proud and cruel enemy had been able to know the counsel of God's mercy, it had been his task rather to have softened the minds of the Jews into gentleness, than to have inflamed them with unrighteous hatred; and so lost the service of all his slaves, by pursuing for his Debtor the One That owed him nothing.

Lesson VI

But his own hate dug a pitfall for him; he brought upon the Son of God that death which is become life to all the sons of men. He shed that innocent Blood, Which has reconciled the world unto God, and become at once the price of our redemption and the cup of our salvation. The Lord has received that which according to the purpose of His Own good pleasure He has chosen. He has let fall on Him the hands of bloody men, but while they were bent only on their own sin, they were servants ministering to the Redeemer's work. And such was His tenderness even for His murderers that His prayer to His Father from the Cross, as concerning them, was not that He might be avenged upon them, but that they might be forgiven.

Lesson VII

From the Holy Gospel according to St. Matthew (Matt 21:1–9)

At that time, when Jesus drew nigh to Jerusalem, and were come to Bethphage, unto mount Olivet, then Jesus sent two disciples, Saying to them: And so on.

Homily by St. Ambrose, Bishop

Beautiful is the type, when the Lord, about to leave the Jews, and to take up His abode in the hearts of the Gentiles, goes up into the Temple; a figure of His going to the true Temple wherein He is worshipped, not in the deadness of the letter, but in spirit and in truth, even that Temple of God whereof the foundations are laid, not in buildings of stone, but in faith. He leaves behind Him those who hate Him, and chooses for Himself those as will love Him. And therefore He comes unto the Mount of Olives that He may plant upon the heights of grace those young olive-branches, whose Mother is the Jerusalem which is above. Upon this mountain stands He, the Heavenly Husbandman, that all they which be planted in the House of the Lord may be able each one to say: "But I am like a fruitful olive-tree in the House of God."

Lesson VIII

And perchance that mountain does signify Christ Himself. For what other is there that bears such fruit of olives as He does, not rich with store of loaded branches, but spiritually fruitful with the fullness of the Gentiles? He also it is on Whom we go up, and unto Whom we go up; He is the Door; He is the Way; He is He Which is opened and Which opens; He is He upon Whom knocks whosoever enters in, and to Whom they that have entered in, do worship. A figure also was it that the disciples went into a village, and that there they found an ass tied and a colt with her; neither could they be loosed, save at the command of the Lord. It was the hand of His Apostles which loosed them. He whose work and life are like theirs will have such grace as was theirs. Be thou also such as they, if thou wouldest loose them that are bound.

Lesson IX

Now, let us consider who they were, who, being convicted of transgression, were banished from their home in the Garden of Eden into a village, and in this thou wilt see how Life called back again them whom death had cast out. For this reason, we read in Matthew that there were tied both an ass and her colt; thus, as man was banished from Eden in a member of either sex, so is it in animals of both sexes that his recall is figured.

The she-ass is a type of our sinful Mother Eve, and the colt of the multitude of the Gentiles; and it was upon the colt that Christ took His seat. And thus it is well written of the colt, that thereon never yet had man sat, for no man before Christ ever called the Gentiles into the Church which statement thou hast in Mark also: "Whereon never man sat."

Monday in Holy Week

Lesson I

From the Holy Gospel according to St. John (John 12:1–9)

Six days before the pasch, Jesus came to Bethania, where Lazarus had been dead, whom Jesus raised to life.

Homily by St. Augustine, Bishop

There they made Him a supper and Lazarus was one of them that sat at the table lest men should deem that it was but by an ocular delusion that they had seen him arise from the dead. He lived therefore, spoke, and ate; to the manifestation of the truth, and the confusion of the unbelieving Jews. Jesus, then, sat down to meat with Lazarus and others, and Martha, being one of Lazarus' sisters, served. But Mary, Lazarus' other sister, took a pound of ointment of spikenard, very costly, and anointed the Feet of Jesus, and wiped His Feet with her hair; and the house was filled with the odor of the ointment. We have now heard that which was done; let us search out the mystic meaning thereof.

Lesson II

Whatsover thou art that will be a faithful soul, seek with Mary to anoint the Feet of the Lord with costly ointment. This ointment was a figure of justice, and therefore is there said to have been a pound thereof, a pound being a weight used in scales. The word *pistikes* used by the Evangelist as the name of this ointment, we must believe to be that of some place, from which this costly perfume was imported. Neither is this name meaningless for us, but agrees well with our mystic interpretation, since *Pistis* is the Greek word which signifies Faith, and whosoever will do justice must know that: The just shall live by faith. Anoint therefore the Feet of Jesus by thy good life, following in the marks which those Feet of the Lord have traced. Wipe His Feet likewise with thy hair; that is, if thou have anything which is not needful to thee, give it to the poor; and then thou hast wiped the Feet of Jesus with thy hair, that is, with that which thou needest not, and which is therefore like to thee as is thy hair, being a needless outgrowth to the body. Here thou hast what to do with that which thou needest not. To thee it is needless, but the Lord's Feet have need of it; yea, the Feet which the Lord has on earth are sorely needy.

Lesson III

For of whom save of His members, will He say at the latter day:

"Inasmuch as you have done it unto one of the least of these My brethren, you have done it unto Me." That is, you have spent nothing save that which you needed not, but you have ministered unto My Feet. And the house was filled with the odor of the ointment. That is, the fragrance of your good example fills the world; for this odor is a figure of reputation. They which are called Christians, and yet live bad lives, cast a slur on Christ and it is even such as they unto whom it is said: "The Name of God is blasphemed among the Gentiles through you." But if, through such, the Name of God be blasphemed, through the godly is the Name of the Lord praised. Hearken to the Apostle: In every place, "we are unto God a sweet savor of Christ, in them that are saved, and in them that perish."

Tuesday in Holy Week

Lesson I ~ Jer 11:15–20

From the book of Jeremias

What is the meaning that my beloved hath wrought much wickedness in my house? shall the holy flesh take away from thee thy crimes, in which thou hast boasted? The Lord called thy name, a plentiful olive tree, fair, fruitful, and beautiful: at the noise of a word, a great fire was kindled in it and the branches thereof are burnt. And the Lord of hosts that planted thee, hath pronounced evil against thee: for the evils of the house of Israel, and the house of Juda, which they have done to themselves, to provoke me, offering sacrifice to Baalim. But thou, O Lord, hast shewn me, and I have known: then thou shewedst me their doings. And I was as a meek lamb, that is carried to be a victim: and I knew not that they had devised counsels against me, saying: Let us put wood on his bread, and cut him off from the land of the living, and let his name be remembered no more. But thou, O Lord of Sabaoth, who judgest justly, and triest the reins and hearts, let me see thy revenge on them: for to thee I have revealed my cause.

Lesson II ~ Jer 12:1–4

Thou indeed, O Lord, art just, if I plead with thee, but yet I will speak what is just to thee: Why doth the way of the wicked prosper: why is it well with all them that transgress, and do wickedly? Thou hast planted them, and they have taken root: they prosper and bring forth fruit: thou art near in their mouth, and far from their reins. And thou, O Lord, hast known me, thou hast seen me, and proved my heart with thee: gather them together as sheep for a sacrifice, and prepare them for the day of slaughter. How long shall the land mourn, and the herb of every field wither for the wickedness of them that dwell therein? The beasts and the birds are consumed: because they have said: He shall not see our last end.

Lesson III ~ Jer 12:7–11

I have forsaken my house, I have left my inheritance: I have given my dear soul into the land of her enemies. My inheritance is become to me as a lion in the wood: it hath cried out against me, therefore have I hated it. Is my inheritance to me as a speckled bird? Is it as a bird died throughout? come ye, assemble yourselves, all the beasts of the earth, make haste to devour. Many pastors have destroyed my vineyard, they have trodden my portion under foot: they have changed my delightful portion into a desolate wilderness. They have laid it waste, and it hath mourned for me. With desolation is all the land made desolate; because there is none that considereth in the heart.

Wednesday in Holy Week

Lesson I ~ Jer 17:13–18

From the book of Jeremias

O Lord, the hope of Israel: all that forsake thee shall be confounded: they that depart from thee, shall be written in the earth: because they have forsaken the Lord, the vein of living waters. Heal me, O Lord, and I shall be healed: save me, and I shall be saved, for thou art my praise. Behold they say to me: Where is the word of the Lord? let it come. And I am not troubled, following thee for my pastor, and I have not desired the day of man, thou knowest. That which went out of my lips, hath been right in thy sight. Be not thou a terror unto me, thou art my hope in the day of affliction. Let them be confounded that persecute me, and let not me be confounded: let them be afraid, and let not me be afraid: bring upon them the day of affliction, and with a double destruction, destroy them.

Lesson II ~ Jer 18:13–18

Therefore thus saith the Lord: Ask among the nations: Who hath heard such horrible things, as the virgin of Israel hath done to excess? Shall the snow of Libanus fail from the rock of the field? or can the cold waters that gush out and run down, be taken away? Because my people have forgotten me, sacrificing in vain, and stumbling in their ways, in ancient paths, to walk by them in a way not trodden: That their land might be given up to desolation, and to a perpetual hissing: every one that shall pass by it, shall be astonished, and wag his head. As a burning will I scatter them before the enemy: I will shew them the back, and not the face, in the day of their destruction. And they said: Come, and let us invent devices against Jeremias: for the law shall not perish from the priest, nor counsel from the wise, nor the word from the prophet: come, and let us strike him with the tongue, and let us give no heed to all his words.

Lesson III ~ Jer 18:19–23

Give heed to me, O Lord, and hear the voice of my adversaries. Shall evil be rendered for good, because they have digged a pit for my soul? Remember that I have stood in thy sight, to speak good for them, and turn away thy indignation from them. Therefore deliver up their children to famine, and bring them into the hands of the sword: let their wives be bereaved of children and widows: and let their husbands be slain by death: let their young men be stabbed with the sword in battle. Let a cry be heard out of their houses: for thou shalt bring the robber upon them suddenly: because they have digged a pit to take me, and have hid snares for my feet. But thou, O Lord, knowest all their counsel against me unto death: forgive not their iniquity, and let not their sin be blotted out from thy sight: let them be overthrown before thy eyes, in the time of thy wrath do thou destroy them.

MAUNDY THURSDAY

Lesson I ~ Lam 1:1–5

Beginning of the Lamentations of the Prophet Jeremias

Aleph. How doth the city sit solitary that was full of people! how is the mistress of the Gentiles become as a widow: the princes of provinces made tributary! Beth. Weeping she hath wept in the night, and her tears are on her cheeks: there is none to comfort her among all them that were dear to her: all her friends have despised her, and are become her enemies. Ghimel. Juda hath removed her dwelling place because of her affliction, and the greatness of her bondage: she hath dwelt among the nations, and she hath found no rest: all her persecutors have taken her in the midst of straits. Daleth. The ways of Sion mourn, because there are none that come to the solemn feast: all her gates are broken down: her priests sigh: her virgins are in affliction, and she is oppressed with bitterness. He. Her adversaries are become her lords, her enemies are enriched: because the Lord hath spoken against her for the multitude of her iniquities: her children are led into captivity: before the face of the oppressor. Jerusalem, Jerusalem, return to the Lord thy God.

Lesson II ~ Lam 1:6–9

Vau. And from the daughter of Sion all her beauty is departed: her princes are become like rams that find no pastures: and they are gone away without strength before the face of the pursuer. Zain. Jerusalem hath remembered the days of her affliction, and prevarication of all her desirable things which she had from the days of old, when her people fell in the enemy's hand, and there was no helper: the enemies have seen her, and have mocked at her sabbaths. Heth. Jerusalem hath grievously sinned, therefore is she become unstable: all that honoured her have despised her, because they have seen her shame: but she sighed and turned backward. Teth. Her filthiness is on her feet, and she hath not remembered her end: she is wonderfully cast down, not having a comforter: behold, O Lord, my affliction, because the enemy is lifted up. Jerusalem, Jerusalem, return to the Lord thy God.

Lesson III ~ Lam 1:10–14

Jod. The enemy hath put out his hand to all her desirable things: for she hath seen the Gentiles enter into her sanctuary, of whom thou gavest commandment that they should not enter into thy church. Caph. All her people sigh, they seek bread: they have given all their precious things for food to relieve the soul: see, O Lord, and consider, for I am become vile. Lamed. O all ye that pass by the way, attend, and see if there be any sorrow like to my sorrow: for he hath made a vintage of me, as the Lord spoke in the day of his fierce anger. Mem. From above he hath sent fire into my bones, and hath chastised me: he hath spread a net for my feet, he hath turned me back: he hath made me desolate, wasted with sorrow all the day long. Nun. The yoke of my iniquities hath watched: they are folded together in his hand, and put upon my neck: my strength is weakened: the Lord hath delivered me into a hand out of which I am not able to rise. Jerusalem, Jerusalem, return to the Lord thy God.

Lesson IV

From the Treatise of St. Augustine, Bishop, Upon the Psalms

"Give ear to my prayer, O God, and despise not my supplication: attend unto me and hear me." These are the words of a man travailing, anxious, and troubled. He prays in the midst of much suffering, longing to be rid of his affliction. Our part is to see what that his affliction was, and when he has told us, to acknowledge that we also suffer therefrom; that so partaking in his trouble, we may take part also in his exercise. Wherein mourned he? Wherein was he troubled? "In my exercise," he says, "I am troubled." He says that his affliction was by evil men; and this suffering which came upon him at the hands of wicked men he has called his exercise. Think not that wicked men are in this world for nothing, or that God doth no good with them. Every wicked man liveth, either to repent, or to exercise the righteous.

Lesson V

Would to God that they which now exercise us were converted and exercised with us! Yet, while they are as they are, and exercise us, we will not hate them: for we know not of any one of them whether he will endure to the end in his sin. Yea, oftentimes, when thou deemest that thou hatest thine enemy, he whom thou hatest is thy brother, and thou knowest it not. The Holy Scriptures show us that the devil and his angels are already damned unto everlasting fire, and therefore of their repentance it befits us to despair; but of theirs only. These are they against whom we wrestle within; the wrestling to which the Apostle stirs us up where he says: "We wrestle not against flesh and blood (that is, not against men whom we see), but against principalities, against powers, against the rulers of the darkness of this world." He says not "the rulers of this world," lest perchance thou shouldest deem that devils are the lords of heaven and earth; what he doth say is, "rulers of the darkness of this world," of that world which they love who love the world, of that world wherein the ungodly and unrighteous do prosper, of that world of which the Gospel says: "And the world knew Him not."

Lesson VI

"We have seen iniquity and strife in the city." Behold, the glory of the Cross. That Cross which was the object of the insults of God's enemies, is established now above the brows of kings. The effect has shown the measure of its power: it has conquered the world, not by the sword, but by its wood. The enemies of God thought the Cross a fitting object of insult and ridicule, yea, they stood before it, wagging their heads and saying: "If He be the Son of God, let Him come down from the Cross!" And He stretched forth His Hands unto a disobedient and gainsaying people. If he is just which lives by faith, he is unjust that has not faith. Therefore where is written iniquity we may understand unbelief. The Lord therefore says that He saw iniquity and strife in the city, and that He stretched forth His Hands unto that disobedient and gainsaying people, and, disobedient and gainsaying as they were, He was hungry for their salvation, and said: "Father, forgive them, for they know not what they do."

Lesson VII ~ 1 Cor 11:17–22

From the first letter of blessed Apostle Paul to the Corinthians

Now this I ordain: not praising you, that you come together not for the better, but for the worse. For first of all I hear that when you come together in the church, there are schisms among you; and in part I believe it. For there must be also heresies: that they also, who are approved, may be made manifest among you. When you come therefore together into one place, it is not now to eat the Lord's supper. For every one taketh before his own supper to eat. And one indeed is hungry and another is drunk. What, have you not houses to eat and to drink in? Or despise ye the church of God; and put them to shame that have not? What shall I say to you? Do I praise you? In this I praise you not.

Lesson VIII ~ 1 Cor 11:23–26

For I have received of the Lord that which also I delivered unto you, that the Lord Jesus, the same night in which he was betrayed, took bread. And giving thanks, broke, and said: Take ye, and eat: this is my body, which shall be delivered for you: this do for the commemoration of me. In like manner also the chalice, after he had supped, saying: This chalice is the new testament in my blood: this do ye, as often as you shall drink, for the commemoration of me. For as often as you shall eat this bread, and drink the chalice, you shall show the death of the Lord, until he come.

Lesson IX ~ 1 Cor 11:27–34

Therefore whosoever shall eat this bread, or drink the chalice of the Lord unworthily, shall be guilty of the body and of the blood of the Lord. But let a man prove himself: and so let him eat of that bread, and drink of the chalice. For he that eateth and drinketh unworthily, eateth and drinketh judgment to himself, not discerning the body of the Lord. Therefore are there many infirm and weak among you, and many sleep. But if we would judge ourselves, we should not be judged. But whilst we are judged, we are chastised by the Lord, that we be not condemned with this world. Wherefore, my brethren, when you come together to eat, wait for one another. If any man be hungry, let him eat at home; that you come not together unto judgment. And the rest I will set in order, when I come.

✠

GOOD FRIDAY

Lesson I ~ Lam 2:8–11

From the Lamentations of the Prophet Jeremias

Heth. The Lord hath purposed to destroy the wall of the daughter of Sion: he hath stretched out his line, and hath not withdrawn his hand from destroying: and the bulwark hath mourned, and the wall hath been destroyed together. Teth. Her gates are sunk into the ground: he hath destroyed, and broken her bars: her king and her princes are among the Gentiles: the law is no more, and her prophets have found no vision from the Lord. Jod. The ancients of the daughter of Sion sit upon the ground, they have held their peace: they have sprinkled their heads with dust, they are girded with haircloth, the virgins of Jerusalem hang down their heads to the ground. Caph. My eyes have failed with weeping, my bowels are troubled: my liver is poured out upon the earth, for the destruction of the daughter of my people, when the children, and the sucklings, fainted away in the streets of the city. Jerusalem! Jerusalem! Return unto the Lord thy God.

Lesson II ~ Lam 2:12–15

Lamed. They said to their mothers: Where is corn and wine? when they fainted away as the wounded in the streets of the city: when they breathed out their souls in the bosoms of their mothers. Mem. To what shall I compare thee? or to what shall I liken thee, O daughter of Jerusalem? to what shall I equal thee, that I may comfort thee, O virgin daughter of Sion? for great as the sea is thy destruction: who shall heal thee? Nun. thy prophets have seen false and foolish things for thee: and they have not laid open thy iniquity, to excite thee to penance: but they have seen for thee false revelations and banishments. Samech. All they that passed by the way have clapped their hands at thee: they have hissed, and wagged their heads at the daughter of Jerusalem, saying: Is this the city of perfect beauty, the joy of all the earth? Jerusalem! Jerusalem! Return unto the Lord thy God.

Lesson III ~ Lam 3:1–9

Aleph. I am the man that see my poverty by the rod of his indignation. Aleph. He hath led me, and brought me into darkness, and not into light. Aleph. Only against me he hath turned, and turned again his hand all the day. Beth. My skin and my flesh he hath made old, he hath broken my bones. Beth. He hath built round about me, and he hath compassed me with gall and labour. Beth. He hath set me in dark places as those that are dead for ever. Ghimel. He hath built against me round about, that I may not get out: he hath made my fetters heavy. Ghimel. Yea, and when I cry, and entreat, he hath shut out my prayer. Ghimel. He hath shut up my ways with square stones, he hath turned my paths upside down Jerusalem! Jerusalem! Return unto the Lord thy God.

Lesson IV

From the Treatise of St. Augustine, Bishop, Upon the Psalms

"Thou hast hidden me from the secret counsel of the wicked, from the insurrection of the workers of iniquity." Now let us fix our eyes upon our Head. Many martyrs have suffered such things as He suffered, but God's hiding of His suffering servants is not so well seen in the Martyrs, as it is in the Captain of the Martyrs. And it is in Him that we best see how it fared with them. He was hidden from the secret counsel of the wicked; hidden by God, being Himself God; hidden, according to the Manhood, by God the Son, and the very Manhood, Which is taken into God the Son; because He is the Son of man, and He is the Son of God; Son of God, as being in the form of God; Son of man, as having taken upon Him the form of a servant; having the power to lay down his life and to take it up again. What, then, were his enemies able do to Him? They killed the Body, but they were not able to kill the Soul. Consider this very earnestly. It would had been a small thing for the Lord to preach to the Martyrs by His word, if He had not also emboldened them by His example.

Lesson V

We know what secret counsel was that of the wicked Jews, and what insurrection was that of the workers of iniquity. Of what iniquity? For they willed the murder of our Lord Jesus Christ. "Many good works," says He, "have I showed you; for which of those works you go about to kill Me?" He had borne with all their weaknesses: He had healed all their diseases: He had preached unto them the kingdom of heaven: He was not silent about their vices, that they might instead displease them, rather than the Physician Who cured them. And now at last, without gratitude for all the tenderness of His healing love, like men raging in a high delirium, throwing themselves madly on the Physician, Who had come to cure them, they took counsel together how they might kill Him, as if to see if He were a Man and could die, or Something more than a man, and That would not let Himself die. In the Wisdom of Solomon we recognize their words: "Let us condemn Him with a shameful death. Let us examine Him; for, by His own saying He shall be respected. If He be the Son of God, let Him help Him."

Lesson VI

"They whetted their tongue like a sword." The Jews cannot say: "We did not murder Christ," albeit they gave Him over to Pilate His judge, that they themselves might seem free of His death. For when Pilate said unto them, "Take Him and kill Him," they answered, "It is not lawful for us to put any man to death." They could throw the blame of their sin upon a human judge; but did they deceive God, the Great Judge? In that which Pilate did, he was their accomplice, but in comparison with them, he had far the lesser sin. Pilate strove as far as he could, to deliver Him out of their hands; for which reason also he scourged Him and brought Him forth to them. He scourged not the Lord for cruelty's sake, but in the hope that; he might so slake their wild thirst for blood: that, perchance, even they might be touched with compassion, and cease to lust for His death when they saw What He was after the flagellation. Even this effort he made! But when Pilate saw that he could not prevail, but that rather a tumult was made, you know how he took water and washed his hands before the multitude saying: "I am innocent of the blood of this Just Person." And yet he delivered Him to be crucified! But if he were guilty who did it against his will, were they innocent; who goaded him on to it? No. Pilate gave sentence against Him and commanded Him to be crucified. But you, O you Jews, you also are His murderers! Wherewith? With your tongue, whetted like a sword. And when? But when you cried, "Crucify Him! Crucify Him!"

Lesson VII - Heb 4:11–15

From the letter of St. Paul the Apostle to the Hebrews

Let us hasten therefore to enter into that rest; lest any man fall into the same example of unbelief. For the word of God is living and effectual, and more piercing than any two edged sword; and reaching unto the division of the soul and the spirit, of the joints also and the marrow, and is a discerner of the thoughts and intents of the heart. Neither is there any creature invisible in his sight: but all things are naked and open to his eyes, to whom our speech is. Having therefore a great high priest that hath passed into the heavens, Jesus the Son of God: let us hold fast our confession. For we have not a high priest, who can not have compassion on our infirmities: but one tempted in all things like as we are, without sin.

Lesson VIII - Heb 4:16; 5:1–3

Let us go therefore with confidence to the throne of grace: that we may obtain mercy, and find grace in seasonable aid. For every high priest taken from among men, is ordained for men in the things that appertain to God, that he may offer up gifts and sacrifices for sins: Who can have compassion on them that are ignorant and that err: because he himself also is compassed with infirmity. And therefore he ought, as for the people, so also for himself, to offer for sins.

Lesson IX ~ Heb 5:4–10

Neither doth any man take the honour to himself, but he that is called by God, as Aaron was. So Christ also did not glorify himself, that he might be made a high priest: but he that said unto him: Thou art my Son, this day have I begotten thee. As he saith also in another place: Thou art a priest for ever, according to the order of Melchisedech. Who in the days of his flesh, with a strong cry and tears, offering up prayers and supplications to him that was able to save him from death, was heard for his reverence. And whereas indeed he was the Son of God, he learned obedience by the things which he suffered: And being consummated, he became, to all that obey him, the cause of eternal salvation. Called by God a high priest according to the order of Melchisedech.

✠

HOLY SATURDAY

Lesson I ~ Lam 3:22–30

From the Lamentations of the Prophet Jeremias

Heth. The mercies of the Lord that we are not consumed: because his commiserations have not failed. Heth. They are new every morning, great is thy faithfulness. Heth. The Lord is my portion, said my soul: therefore will I wait for him. Teth. The Lord is good to them that hope in him, to the soul that seeketh him. Teth. It is good to wait with silence for the salvation of God. Teth. It is good for a man, when he hath borne the yoke from his youth. Jod. He shall sit solitary, and hold his peace: because he hath taken it up upon himself. Jod. He shall put his mouth in the dust, if so be there may be hope. Jod. He shall give his cheek to him that striketh him, he shall be filled with reproaches. Jerusalem! Jerusalem! Return unto the Lord thy God.

Lesson II ~ Lam 4:1–8

Aleph. How is the gold become dim, the finest colour is changed, the stones of the sanctuary are scattered in the top of every street? Beth. The noble sons of Sion, and they that were clothed with the best gold: how are they esteemed as earthen vessels, the work of the potter's hands? Ghimel. Even the sea monsters have drawn out the breast, they have given suck to their young: the daughter of my people is cruel, like the ostrich in the desert. Daleth. The tongue of the sucking child hath stuck to the roof of his mouth for thirst: the little ones have asked for bread, and there was none to break it unto them. He. They that were fed delicately have died in the streets; they that were brought up in scarlet have embraced the dung. Vau. And the iniquity of the daughter of my people is made greater than the sin of Sodom, which was overthrown in a moment, and hands took nothing in her. Jerusalem! Jerusalem! Return unto the Lord thy God.

Lesson III ~ Lam 5:1–11

Remember, O Lord, what is come upon us: consider and behold our reproach. Our inheritance is turned to aliens: our houses to strangers. We are become orphans without a father: our mothers are as widows. We have drunk our water for money: we have bought our wood. We were dragged by the necks, we were weary and no rest was given us. We have given our hand to Egypt, and to the Assyrians, that we might be satisfied with bread. Our fathers have sinned, and are not: and we have borne their iniquities. Servants have ruled over us: there was none to redeem us out of their hand. We fetched our bread at the peril of our lives, because of the sword in the desert. Our skin was burnt as an oven, by reason of the violence of the famine. They oppressed the women in Sion, and the virgins in the cities of Juda. Jerusalem! Jerusalem! Return unto the Lord thy God.

Lesson IV

From the Treatise of St. Augustine, Bishop, Upon the Psalms

"Man shall come to a deep heart: and God shall be exalted." They had said, "Who shall see them?" They had searched out iniquities; they had accomplished a diligent search. And Man attained even unto their counsels, for the Lord, as Man, suffered Himself to be taken. For He would not have been taken at all, unless He had been a Man, or seen, unless He had been a Man, or smitten, unless He had been a Man, or crucified, unless He had been a Man, or have died, unless He had been a Man. Man therefore, He attained unto all those sufferings, which had had nothing in Him unless He had been a Man. But if He had not been Man, man had not been redeemed. And the Lord as Man attained to thoughts that were very deep, yea, secret; showing the Manhood to the eyes of men, and keeping the Divinity within; veiling the form of God, according to Which He is Equal to the Father, and manifesting the form of a servant, according to which He is inferior to the Father.

Lesson V

How far did the accomplishment of their diligent search reach? Even to the setting a watch of soldiers at the sepulchre to guard the Lord even after He was dead and buried. For they said unto Pilate: "that deceiver:" This was the term by which they designated the Lord Jesus Christ, and the remembrance that He was so named is a sweet consolation to us His servants, when we are called deceivers. So they said unto Pilate, "that deceiver said, while He was yet alive: After three days I will rise again. Command therefore that the sepulchre be made sure until the third day, lest His disciples come and steal Him away, and say unto the people: He is risen again from the dead: so the last error shall be worse than the first. Pilate said unto them: you have a watch; go your way; make it as sure as you can. So they went and made the sepulchre sure, sealing the stone, and setting a watch."

Lesson VI

So they went, and made the sepulchre sure, sealing the stone, and setting a watch and behold, there was a great earthquake, and the Lord arose. So great wonders were wrought about the sepulchre that the very soldiers, which were put to guard it, were witnesses thereto, if only they would have told the truth. But the same love of money which had made a slave of that disciple who was a companion of Christ, made slaves also of the soldiers that were put to watch His sepulchre. Some of the watch came into the city, and showed unto the chief-priests all the things that were done: and when they were assembled with the elders, and had taken counsel, they gave large money unto the soldiers, saying: "Say ye, His disciples came by night and stole Him away while we slept." Truly, their diligent search had been accomplished and ended before this. What didst thou say, O wretched cunning? Wast thou indeed so utterly void of the light of godly wisdom, and confounded in the bottomless pit of thine own falsehood as to tell them to say: "His disciples came by night, and stole Him away while we slept?" Part of the testimony of thine eyewitnesses was that they were asleep at the time: thou thyself wast asleep not to be able to see that on their own testimony, their testimony must have been worthless.

Lesson VII ~ Heb 9:11–14

From the letter of blessed Apostle Paul to the Hebrews

But Christ, being come a high priest of the good things to come, by a greater and more perfect tabernacle not made with hand, that is, not of this creation: Neither by the blood of goats, or of calves, but by his own blood, entered once into the holies, having obtained eternal redemption. For if the blood of goats and of oxen, and the ashes of a heifer being sprinkled, sanctify such as are defiled, to the cleansing of the flesh: How much more shall the blood of Christ, who by the Holy Ghost offered himself unspotted unto God, cleanse our conscience from dead works, to serve the living God?

Lesson VIII ~ Heb 9:15–18

And therefore he is the mediator of the new testament: that by means of his death, for the redemption of those transgressions, which were under the former testament, they that are called may receive the promise of eternal inheritance. For where there is a testament, the death of the testator must of necessity come in. For a testament is of force, after men are dead: otherwise it is as yet of no strength, whilst the testator liveth. Whereupon neither was the first indeed dedicated without blood.

Lesson IX ~ Heb 9:19–22

For when every commandment of the law had been read by Moses to all the people, he took the blood of calves and goats, with water, and scarlet wool and hyssop, and sprinkled both the book itself and all the people, Saying: This is the blood of the testament, which God hath enjoined unto you. The tabernacle also and all the vessels of the ministry, in like manner, he sprinkled with blood. And almost all things, according to the law, are cleansed with blood: and without shedding of blood there is no remission.

PASCHALTIDE

EASTER SUNDAY

Duplex I Class

Lesson I

From the Holy Gospel according to St. Mark (Mark 16:1–7)

And when the sabbath was past, Mary Magdalen, and Mary the mother of James, and Salome, bought sweet spices, that coming, they might anoint Jesus. And what follows.

Homily by St. Gregory, Pope

Dearly beloved brethren, you have heard the deed of the holy women which had followed the Lord; how that they brought sweet spices to His sepulchre, and, now that He was dead, having loved Him while He was yet alive, they followed Him with careful tenderness still. But the deed of these holy women does point to something which needs to be done in the holy Church. And it behooves us well to give ear to what they did, that we may afterward consider with ourselves what we must do likewise after their example. We also, who believe in Him That was dead, do come to His sepulchre bearing sweet spices, when we seek the Lord with the savor of good living, and the fragrant report of good works. Those women, when they brought their spices, saw a vision of Angels, and, truly, those souls whose godly desires do move them to seek the Lord with the savor of good lives, do see the countrymen of our Fatherland which is above.

Lesson II

It behooves us to mark what this means: that they saw the Angel sitting on the right side. For what signifies the left, but this present life? or the right, but life everlasting? Whence also it is written in the Canticle of Canticles: "His left hand is under my head, and His right hand doth embrace me." Since, therefore, our Redeemer had passed from the corruption of this present life, the Angel which told that His undying life was come, sat, as became him, on the right side. They saw him clothed in a white garment, for he was herald of the joy of this our great solemnity, and the glistering whiteness of his raiment told of the brightness of this holy Festival of ours. Of ours, said I? or of his? But if we will speak the truth, we must acknowledge that it is both his and ours. The Resurrection of our Redeemer is a Festival of gladness for us, for it bids us know that we shall not die for ever; and for Angels also it is a festival of gladness, for it bids them know that we are called to fulfill their number in heaven.

Lesson III

Therefore, in His and our Festival the Angel appeared in white raiment. For as the Lord, rising again from the dead, leads us unto the mansions above, He repairs the breaches of the heavenly Fatherland. But what does this mean, that the Angel said unto the women which came to the sepulchre: "Fear not?" Is it not as though he had said openly: "Let them fear which love not the coming of the heavenly countrymen; let them be afraid who are so laden by fleshly lusts, that they have lost all hope ever to be joined to their company. But as for you, why fear you, who, when you see us, see but your fellow countrymen?" Hence also Matthew, writing of the guise of the Angel, says: "His countenance was like lightning, and His raiment white as snow." The lightning speaks of fear and great dread, the snow of the soft brilliancy of rejoicing.

EASTER MONDAY

Duplex I Class

Lesson I

From the Holy Gospel according to St. Luke (Luke 24:13–35)

And behold, two of them went, the same day, to a town which was sixty furlongs from Jerusalem, named Emmaus. And so forth.

Homily by Pope St. Gregory

Dearly beloved brethren, you hear how that while two of His disciples walked together in the way, not believing in His Resurrection, but talking together concerning Him, the Lord manifested Himself unto them, yet held their eyes that they should not know Him. This holding of their bodily eyes, wrought by the Lord, was a figure of the spiritual veil which was yet upon the eyes of their heart. For in their heart they loved yet doubted: even as the Lord drew near to them outwardly, but showed not Who He was. To them that spoke together of Him, He revealed His immediate presence; but from them that doubted, He hid the knowledge of His Person.

Lesson II

He spoke to them; He rebuked the hardness of their heart; He expounded unto them in all the Scriptures the things concerning Himself: and, nevertheless, seeing that He was yet a stranger to faith in their hearts, He made as though He would have gone further. These words "He made as though" would here seem to mean He feigned, but He Who is simple Truth does nothing with feigning: He only showed Himself to them in bodily manners, as He was towards them spiritually; but they were put to the proof whether, though they loved Him not yet as their God, they could love Him at least as a wayfarer.

Lesson III

But since it was impossible that they with whom Truth walked should be loveless, they called Him, as a wayfarer, to their hospitality. But why say we that they asked Him, when it is written: "And they constrained Him?" From their example we learn that we ought not only to bid, but also to urge wayfarers to our hospitable entertainment. They laid a table therefore, and set before Him bread and meat; and that God Whom they had not known in the expounding of the Holy Scripture, they knew in the breaking of bread. In hearing the commandments of God they were not enlightened, but they were enlightened in the doing of them: as it is written: "Not the hearers of the law are just before God, but the doers of the law shall be justified." Whosoever therefore will understand that which he hears, let him make haste to practice in his works that which he has already been able to hear. Behold, the Lord was not known while He spoke, but He was contented to be known when He broke bread.

EASTER TUESDAY

Duplex I Class

Lesson I

From the Holy Gospel according to St. Luke (Luke 24:36–47)

At that time: Now whilst they were speaking these things, Jesus stood in the midst of them, and saith to them: Peace be to you; it is I, fear not. And so forth.

Homily by St. Ambrose, Bishop

We see here the marvelous nature of the Lord's glorified Body. It could enter unseen, and then become seen. It could easily be touched, but Its nature is hard to understand. The disciples were affrighted, and supposed that they had seen a spirit. And therefore the Lord, that He might show us the evidence of His Resurrection, said: "Handle Me, and see; for a spirit has not flesh and bones as you see Me have." Therefore it was not by being in a disembodied state, but by the peculiar qualities of the risen and glorified Body that He had passed through closed doors. For that which is touched or handled is a body.

Lesson II

We shall all rise again with our bodies. But it is sown a natural body; it is raised a spiritual body. The spiritual body is the finer, and the natural body is the grosser, yet weighed down by earthly corruption. Was not That a real Body, wherein remained those marks of His Wounds, those holes of the nail-prints, which the Lord bade His disciples to handle? Hereby, also, He has not only strengthened our faith, but also sharpened our devotion, since we know that it has been His will to carry to heaven those Wounds which He bore for our sake, and wherewith He would not make away; but plainly shows to His Eternal Father the price of our freedom. It is as marked with these Wounds and embracing the trophy of our salvation that the Father has said to Him, "Sit Thou at My right Hand:" and it is, marked with their wounds like Him, that He has shown us that the Martyrs, whose

Crown He is, are and will be with Him there.

Lesson III

And now, since our Lesson from Luke here fails, let us have recourse to John, and consider how that, according to him, then the disciples rejoiced when they saw the Lord, and received the grace of faith. According to Luke, He upbraided them for their unbelief, but according to John He said also, "Receive the Holy Ghost." Luke, not John, has, "Tarry in the city of Jerusalem, until you be endued with power from on high." Indeed, to me it seems as though the one Evangelist had busied himself with the greater and higher matters, and the other with the narrative, and such things as are more human: the one with the course, the other with the essence, of history. For as it is impossible to doubt the word of him who testifies of these things, and who saw these things, and concerning whom we know that his testimony is true, so is it sinful to think of negligence or falsehood as attaching to the other, even Luke, who earned to himself to be an Evangelist, albeit he was not an Apostle, and therefore we hold that both are truthful, neither are they at variance one with the other, either in the difference of the words they use, or in the sacredness of their characters as Evangelists. For though Luke says that at the first the Apostles believed not, yet he shows that afterward they believed: and although, if we regard only the first fact, the Evangelists seem divergent one from the other, yet, when we consider what comes afterward, we see that they are at one.

Easter Wednesday

Semiduplex

Lesson I

From the Holy Gospel according to St. John (John 21:1–14)

At that time: After this, Jesus showed himself again to the disciples at the sea of Tiberias. And he showed himself after this manner. There were together Simon Peter, and Thomas, who is called Didymus, And so forth.

Homily by Pope St. Gregory

Dearly beloved brethren, the portion of the Holy Gospel which has but now been read in your ears, knocks loudly at the door of your heart with a certain question, the answer whereto calls for thought. This same question is: Why did Peter, who had before his conversion been a fisherman, why did he, after his conversion, again go a-fishing? since the Truth has said: "No man, having put his hand to the plough, and looking back, is fit for the kingdom of God?" Why did Peter return to that which he had left? But only examine the matter with discretion and it may be clearly seen that the trade which was harmless before his conversion, did not become harmful because he had been converted.

Lesson II

We know that Peter had been a fisherman, and Matthew a publican, and that Peter after his conversion went back to his fishing, but Matthew did not return to tax collecting. It is one thing to seek a livelihood by fishing, and another to amass money by farming of taxes. There are many kinds of business in which it is difficult or impossible to be engaged without committing sin. Therefore, to those things which lead to sin it is necessary that, after conversion, the soul may not run back.

Lesson III

It may likewise be asked why, when the disciples were toiling in the sea, the Lord, after His Resurrection, stood on the shore, whereas, before His Resurrection, He had walked on the waves before them all. The reason of this is quickly known if we will think of the end which it then served. The sea is a figure of this present world, tossed to and fro by changing fortune, and continually ebbing and flowing with the diverse tides of life. The stability of the shore is an image of the never-ending rest of the eternal home. The disciples therefore, for that they were yet tossed to and fro upon the waves of a dying life, were toiling in the sea; but He our Redeemer, Who had already laid aside that which in this body is subject to corruption, and had risen again from the dead, He stood upon the shore.

Easter Thursday

Semiduplex

Lesson I

From the Holy Gospel according to St. John (John 20:11–18)

At that time: But Mary stood at the sepulchre without, weeping. Now as she was weeping, she stooped down, and looked into the sepulchre. And so forth.

Homily by Pope St. Gregory

Mary Magdalene, a woman in the city who was a sinner, loving the truth, washed away by her tears the stains of her sins, and the word of the Truth was fulfilled which He spoke: "Her sins, which are many, are forgiven: for she loved much." She that had remained cold while she sinned, became burning when she loved. For after that she had been to the Sepulchre, and had not found there the Body of the Lord, and had believed that It had been taken away, and had told His disciples who came and saw, and thought it was even as the woman had said. And of these things it is written forthwith: "Then the disciples went away again unto their own home but Mary stood without at the sepulchre, weeping."

Lesson II

In connection with this matter, we ought to ponder what great store of love there was in that woman's heart, who, when even His disciples were gone away, could not tear herself from the grave of the Lord. She sought Him Whom she had not found there, and as she sought, she wept, and the fire of love in her heart yearned after Him, Who she believed had been taken away. And so it came to pass that she, who had lingered to seek Him, was the only one who then saw Him, since the back-bone of a good work is endurance, and the voice of the Truth

Himself has said: "He that endureth to the end shall be saved."

Lesson III

As Mary wept there, she stooped down and looked into the Sepulchre. It was but a little while and she had seen how the Sepulchre was empty, and had told that the Lord was taken away. Why then should she stoop down and look in again? But she loved Him so well, that one look was not enough; the energy of her affection constrained her to search again and again. She began by searching and not finding; but she endured in her search, and, behold, it came to pass that she found. And this was done that our own longings for Christ's presence might be taught to expand, and know that as they expand they will meet with Him to Whom they aspire.

Easter Friday

Semiduplex

Lesson I

From the Holy Gospel according to St. Matthew (Matt 28:16–20)

At that time: And the eleven disciples went into Galilee, unto the mountain where Jesus had appointed them. And so forth.

Homily by St. Jerome, Priest

After His Resurrection Jesus was seen on a mountain in Galilee, and there He was worshipped; and, albeit some doubted, their doubts have led to a further establishing of our faith. Then He showed Himself more openly unto Thomas, and made him handle the Side That was pierced with the spear, and the Hands wherein were the holes of the nails. And Jesus came and spoke unto them, saying: "All power is given unto Me in heaven and in earth." Yea, all power is given unto Him Who but a little while before had been crucified, and buried in the grave, and had lain among the dead, but Who also had risen again. Power is given unto Him in heaven and in earth, that He Who of everlasting had been King of heaven, might have a Monarchy on earth also, through the faith of them which believe in Him.

Lesson II

"Go therefore and teach all nations, baptizing them in the Name of the Father, and of the Son, and of the Holy Ghost." First, they teach all nations; then, they wash with water them whom they have taught. For it is impossible for the body to receive the Sacrament of Baptism, unless the mind first receive the truth of the faith. And they are baptized In the Name of the Father, and of the Son, and of the Holy Ghost for, even as the Divinity of the Father, and of the Son, and of the Holy Ghost, is all One, so is the one grace of Baptism the gift of all the Three Divine Persons: and the Name of the Trinity is the Name of One God.

Lesson III

"Teaching them to observe all things whatsoever I have commanded you." The order of the

Lord's commands to the Apostles is markedly this. First, to teach all nations; secondly, to make them partake in the Sacrament of the faith; thirdly, when they had believed and been baptized, to teach them what to observe. And lest we should think that He commanded things light and few, He has said: "All things whatsoever I have commanded you," so that all who have believed and been baptized in the Name of the Trinity are bound to observe all things whatsoever He has commanded. "And, lo, I am with you always, even unto the end of the world." He Who promises that He will be with His disciples even unto the end of the world, does give them thereby to know that they will be always conquerors, and that He will never fail any who believe in Him.

White Saturday

Semiduplex

Lesson I

From the Holy Gospel according to St. John (John 20:1–9)

And on the first day of the week, Mary Magdalene comes early, when it was yet dark, unto the sepulchre. And so forth.

Homily by Pope St. Gregory

Dearly beloved brethren, the portion of the Holy Gospel which has just now been read in your ears, is exceedingly simple on the face of it, which is its historical sense; but the mystic sense, which underlies that other, requires from us a little searching. Mary Magdalene came unto the Sepulchre when it was yet dark. The historic sense tells us what was the hour of day; the mystic sense, the state of her understanding who sought. Mary Magdalene sought for Him, by Whom all things were made, and Whom she had seen die according to the flesh; she sought for Him, I say, in the grave, and finding Him not, she believed that He had been stolen away. Yea, it was yet dark, when she came unto the sepulchre. Then she ran and told the disciples, but they who had loved Him most, namely Peter and John, did outrun the others.

Lesson II

So they ran both together, but John did outrun Peter, and came first to the Sepulchre, but yet took he not upon himself to go in first. Then comes Peter following him, and went in. What, my brethren, what did the racing of these Apostles signify? Can we believe that the description given by the deepest of the Evangelists is without a mystic interpretation? By no means. John had never told how that he did outrun Peter, and yet went not into the Sepulchre, if he had not believed that his hesitation veiled some mystery. What signifies John but the Synagogue? or Peter the Church?

Lesson III

Neither must you take it as strange that the elder Apostle should represent the Church, and the younger the Synagogue: for although the Synagogue was first to worship God, yet the herd of Gentiles is in the world older than the Synagogue, as witnesses Paul where he says: "That was not first which is spiritual, but that which is natural." By Peter, then, who was the elder, is signified the Church of the Gentiles; and by John, who was the younger, the Synagogue of the Jews. They run both of them together, for from the time of her birth until now, and so will it be until the end, the Church of the Gentiles has run in a parallel road and common road with the Synagogue, albeit not with equal understandings. The Synagogue came first to the Sepulchre, but she has not yet entered in; for, though she has received the commandments of the law, and has heard the Prophets tell of the Incarnation and Passion of the Lord, she refuses to believe in Him Who died for her.

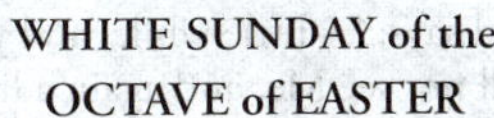

WHITE SUNDAY of the OCTAVE of EASTER

Duplex I Class

Lesson I - Col 3:1–7

From the letter of St. Paul the Apostle to the Colossians

Therefore, if you be risen with Christ, seek the things that are above; where Christ is sitting at the right hand of God: Mind the things that are above, not the things that are upon the earth. For you are dead; and your life is hid with Christ in God. When Christ shall appear, who is your life, then you also shall appear with him in glory. Mortify therefore your members which are upon the earth; fornication, uncleanness, lust, evil concupiscence, and covetousness, which is the service of idols. For which things the wrath of God comes upon the children of unbelief, In which you also walked some time, when you lived in them.

Lesson II - Col 3:8–13

But now put you also all away: anger, indignation, malice, blasphemy, filthy speech out of your mouth. Lie not one to another: stripping yourselves of the old man with his deeds, And putting on the new, him who is renewed unto knowledge, according to the image of him that created him. Where there is neither Gentile nor Jew, circumcision nor uncircumcision, Barbarian nor Scythian, bond nor free. But Christ is all, and in all. Put ye on therefore, as the elect of God, holy, and beloved, the bowels of mercy, benignity, humility, modesty, patience: Bearing with one another, and forgiving one another, if any have a complaint against another: even as the Lord hath forgiven you, so do you also.

Lesson III - Col 3:14–17

But above all these things have charity, which is the bond of perfection: And let the peace of Christ rejoice in your hearts, wherein also you are called in one body: and be ye thankful. Let the word of Christ dwell in you abundantly, in all wisdom: teaching and admonishing one another in psalms, hymns, and spiritual canticles, singing in grace in your hearts to God. All whatsoever you do in word or in work, do all in the name of the Lord Jesus Christ, giving thanks to God and the Father by him.

Lesson IV

Sermon by St. Augustine

The Feast of this day is the end of the Paschal solemnity, and therefore it is today that the Newly-Baptized put off their white garments: but, though they lay aside the outward mark of washing in their raiment, the mark of that washing in their souls remains unto eternity. Now are the days of the Passover, that is, of God's Passing-over our iniquity by His pardon and remission; and therefore our first duty is so to sanctify the mirth of these holy days, that our bodily recreation may be taken without defilement to our spiritual cleanness. Let us strive that our relaxation may be sober and our freedom holy, holding ourselves carefully aloof from anything like excess, drunkenness, or lechery. Let us try so to keep in our souls their Lenten cleansing, so that whatever we have not yet acquired by our bodily abstinence, we may still seek by purity of mind.

Lesson V

This discourse concerns all them which are committed unto my spiritual charge; but, nevertheless, since the first happy week of your Sacramental life draws this day to a close, I address myself especially to you who are the new sprouts of holiness, to you, who have but a little while been born again of water and the Holy Ghost, to you, O holy generation to you, O new creation, to you, the excellency of my dignity, and the fruit of my labour, my brethren dearly beloved and longed for, my joy and my crown, all you who now stand so fast in the Lord. To you I address the words of the Apostle: "Behold! the night is past! the day is come! Cast off therefore the works of darkness, and put on the armour of light. Let us walk honestly, as in the day; not in rioting and drunkenness, not in chambering and wantonness, not in strife and envying: but put on the Lord Jesus Christ."

Lesson VI

"We have," says Peter, "a more sure word of Prophecy, whereunto you do well that you take heed, as unto a light that shines in a dark place, until the day dawn, and the day-star arise in your hearts." Let your loins therefore be girded about, and your lights burning in your hands, and you yourselves like unto men that wait for their lord, when he will return from the wedding. Behold, the days come, whereof the Lord says: "A little while, and you shall not see Me, and again a little while and you shall see Me." Now is the hour whereof He said: "Ye shall weep and lament, but the world shall rejoice." That is to say, this present life, wherein we walk as strangers and pilgrims, far away from Him Who is our Home, this present life is very full of trials. "But," the Lord says, "I will see you again, and your heart shall rejoice, and your joy no man taketh from you."

Lesson VII

From the Holy Gospel according to St. John (John 20:19–31)

At that time: Now when it was late that same day, the first of the week, and the doors were shut, where the disciples were gathered together, for fear of the Jews, Jesus came and stood in the midst, and said to them: Peace be to you. And so forth.

Homily by Pope St. Gregory

When we hear this passage of the Gospel read, a question straightway knocks at the door of our mind. How was it that the Body of the Risen Lord was a real Body, if It was able to pass through closed doors into the assembly of His disciples? But we ought to know that the works of God are no more wonderful when they can be understood by man's reason, and faith has lost her worth when her subject-matter is the subject-matter of human demonstration. Nevertheless, those very works of our Redeemer which are in themselves impossible to be understood, must be considered in connection with other of His works, that we may be led to believe in things wonderful by means of things more wonderful still. That Body of the Lord, Which came into the assembly of the disciples through closed doors, was the Same, Which at Its birth had become manifest to the eyes of men by passing out of the cloister of the Virgin's womb without breaking the seal thereof. What wonder is it if that Body Which had come out of the Virgin's womb without opening it, coming so to die, now that It was risen again from the dead and endowed forever with undying life, what wonder is it, I say, if that Body passed through closed doors?

Lesson VIII

But since the beholders doubted the reality of that Body Which they saw, He showed unto them His Hands and His Side, and allowed them to handle that Same Flesh Which had just passed through the closed doors. In this there were two strange things manifested; yea, things which, according to our understanding, are contrary to one another. His Risen Body was incorruptible and yet palpable. For whatever can be touched, must needs be subject to corruption; and whatever is not subject to corruption, cannot be touched. But, in a way altogether wonderful and incomprehensible, our Redeemer after His Resurrection revealed Himself in a Body at once palpable and incorruptible: revealed Himself in an incorruptible Body, that we might learn to seek a similar glorification; and in a palpable Body, for the strengthening of our faith. He revealed Himself in a Body at once incorruptible and palpable, that He might thereby make manifest the fact that His Risen Body was unaltered in nature, albeit transfigured in glory.

Lesson IX

Then said Jesus to them again: "Peace be to you. As the Father hath sent Me, I also send you" that is, as My Father, Who is God, has sent Me, Who am God, even so do I, Who am Man, send you, who are men. The Father sent the Son, Whom He appointed to be made Man for the redemption of man. Him He willed to send into the world to suffer, albeit He Whom He sent to suffer was the

Son of His love. The Lord sends His chosen Apostles into the world, not to be happy in the world, but, as He had Himself been sent, to suffer. As the Father loves the Son and yet sends Him to suffer, even so does the Lord love His disciples, albeit He sends them into the world to suffer therein; and therefore it is well said: "As the Father hath sent Me, I also send you;" that is, while I send you into the wild storm of persecution, I love you all the same, I love you, yea, I love you with a love like that wherewith the Father loves Me, Who sent Me into the world to bear agony therein.

Monday I after Easter

Lesson I ~ Acts 1:1–8

Beginning of the Acts of the Apostles

The former treatise I made, O Theophilus, of all things which Jesus began to do and to teach, Until the day on which, giving commandments by the Holy Ghost to the apostles whom he had chosen, he was taken up. To whom also he showed himself alive after his passion, by many proofs, for forty days appearing to them, and speaking of the kingdom of God. And eating together with them, he commanded them, that they should not depart from Jerusalem, but should wait for the promise of the Father, which you have heard (saith he) by my mouth. For John indeed baptized with water, but you shall be baptized with the Holy Ghost, not many days hence. They therefore who were come together, asked him, saying: Lord, wilt thou at this time restore again the kingdom to Israel? But he said to them: It is not for you to know the times or moments, which the Father hath put in his own power: But you shall receive the power of the Holy Ghost coming upon you, and you shall be witnesses unto me in Jerusalem, and in all Judea, and Samaria, and even to the uttermost part of the earth.

Lesson II ~ Acts 1:9–14

And when he had said these things, while they looked on, he was raised up: and a cloud received him out of their sight. And while they were beholding him going up to heaven, behold two men stood by them in white garments. Who also said: Ye men of Galilee, why stand you looking up to heaven? This Jesus who is taken up from you into heaven, shall so come, as you have seen him going into heaven. Then they returned to Jerusalem from the mount that is called Olivet, which is nigh Jerusalem, within a sabbath day's journey. And when they were come in, they went up into an upper room, where abode Peter and John, James and Andrew, Philip and Thomas, Bartholomew and Matthew, James of Alpheus, and Simon Zelotes, and Jude the brother of James. All these were persevering with one mind in prayer with the women, and Mary the mother of Jesus, and with his brethren.

Lesson III ~ Acts 1:15–26

In those days Peter rising up in the midst of the brethren, said (now the number of persons together was about a hundred and twenty): Men, brethren, the Scripture must needs be fulfilled, which the Holy Ghost spoke before by the mouth of David concerning Judas, who was the leader of them that apprehended Jesus: Who was numbered with us, and had obtained part of this ministry. And he indeed hath possessed a field of the reward of iniquity, and being hanged, burst asunder in the midst: and all his bowels gushed out. And it became known to all the inhabitants of Jerusalem: so that the same field was called in their tongue, Haceldama, that is to say, The field of blood. For it is written in the book of Psalms: Let their habitation become desolate, and let there be none to dwell therein. And his bishopric let another take. Wherefore of these men who have companied with us all the time that the Lord Jesus came in and went out among us, Beginning from the baptism of John, until the day wherein he was taken up from us, one of these must be made a witness with us of his resurrection. And they appointed two, Joseph, called Barsabas, who was surnamed Justus, and Matthias. And praying, they said: Thou, Lord, who knowest the hearts of all men, show whether of these two thou hast chosen, To take the place of this ministry and apostleship, from which Judas hath by transgression fallen, that he might go to his own place. And they gave them lots, and the lot fell upon Matthias, and he was numbered with the eleven apostles.

Tuesday I after Easter

Lesson I ~ Acts 2:1–8

From the Acts of the Apostles

And when the days of the Pentecost were accomplished, they were all together in one place: And suddenly there came a sound from heaven, as of a mighty wind coming, and it filled the whole house where they were sitting. And there appeared to them parted tongues as it were of fire, and it sat upon every one of them: And they were all filled with the Holy Ghost, and they began to speak with diverse tongues, according as the Holy Ghost gave them to speak. Now there were dwelling at Jerusalem, Jews, devout men, out of every nation under heaven. And when this was noised abroad, the multitude came together, and were confounded in mind, because that every man heard them speak in his own tongue. And they were all amazed, and wondered, saying: Behold, are not all these, that speak, Galileans? And how have we heard, every man our own tongue wherein we were born?

Lesson II ~ Acts 2:14–21

But Peter standing up with the eleven, lifted up his voice, and spoke to them: Ye men of Judea, and all you that dwell in Jerusalem, be this known to you, and with your ears receive my words. For these are not drunk, as you suppose, seeing it is but the third hour of the day: But this is that which was spoken of by the prophet Joel: And it shall come to pass, in the last days, saith the Lord, I will pour out of my Spirit upon all flesh: and your sons and your daughters shall prophesy, and your young men shall see visions, and your old men shall dream dreams. And upon my servants indeed, and upon my handmaids will I pour out in those days of my spirit, and they shall prophesy. And I will show wonders in the heaven above, and signs on the earth beneath: blood and fire, and vapour of smoke. The sun shall be turned into darkness, and the moon into blood, before the great and manifest day of the Lord come. And it shall come to pass, that whosoever shall call upon the name of the Lord, shall be saved.

Lesson III - Acts 2:22–27

Ye men of Israel, hear these words: Jesus of Nazareth, a man approved of God among you, by miracles, and wonders, and signs, which God did by him, in the midst of you, as you also know: This same being delivered up, by the determinate counsel and foreknowledge of God, you by the hands of wicked men have crucified and slain. Whom God hath raised up, having loosed the sorrows of hell, as it was impossible that he should be holden by it. For David saith concerning him: I foresaw the Lord before my face: because he is at my right hand, that I may not be moved. For this my heart hath been glad, and any tongue hath rejoiced: moreover my flesh also shall rest in hope. Because thou wilt not leave my soul in hell, nor suffer thy Holy One to see corruption.

Wednesday I after Easter

Lesson I - Acts 3:1–6

From the Acts of the Apostles

Now Peter and John went up into the temple at the ninth hour of prayer. And a certain man who was lame from his mother's womb, was carried: whom they laid every day at the gate of the temple, which is called Beautiful, that he might ask alms of them that went into the temple. He, when he had seen Peter and John about to go into the temple, asked to receive an alms. But Peter with John fastening his eyes upon him, said: Look upon us. But he looked earnestly upon them, hoping that he should receive something of them. But Peter said: Silver and gold I have none; but what I have, I give thee: In the name of Jesus Christ of Nazareth, arise, and walk.

Lesson II - Acts 3:7–11

And taking him by the right hand, he lifted him up, and forthwith his feet and soles received strength. And he leaping up, stood, and walked, and went in with them into the temple, walking, and leaping, and praising God. And all the people saw him walking and praising God. And they knew him, that it was he who sat begging alms at the Beautiful gate of the temple: and they were filled with wonder and amazement at that which had happened to him. And as he held Peter and John, all the people ran to them to the porch which is called Solomon's, greatly wondering.

Lesson III - Acts 3:12–16

But Peter seeing, made answer to the people: Ye men of Israel, why wonder you at this? or why look you upon us, as if by our strength or power we had made this man to walk? The God of Abraham, and the

God of Isaac, and the God of Jacob, the God of our fathers, hath glorified his Son Jesus, whom you indeed delivered up and denied before the face of Pilate, when he judged he should be released. But you denied the Holy One and the Just, and desired a murderer to be granted unto you. But the author of life you killed, whom God hath raised from the dead, of which we are witnesses. And in the faith of his name, this man, whom you have seen and known, hath his name strengthened; and the faith which is by him, hath given this perfect soundness in the sight of you all.

Thursday I after Easter

Lesson I ~ Acts 5:1–6

From the Acts of the Apostles

But a certain man named Ananias, with Saphira his wife, sold a piece of land, And by fraud kept back part of the price of the land, his wife being privy thereunto: and bringing a certain part of it, laid it at the feet of the apostles. But Peter said: Ananias, why hath Satan tempted thy heart, that thou shouldst lie to the Holy Ghost, and by fraud keep part of the price of the land? Whilst it remained, did it not remain to thee? and after it was sold, was it not in thy power? Why hast thou conceived this thing in thy heart? Thou hast not lied to men, but to God. And Ananias hearing these words, fell down, and gave up the ghost. And there came great fear upon all that heard it. And the young men rising up, removed him, and carrying him out, buried him.

Lesson II ~ Acts 5:7–11

And it was about the space of three hours after, when his wife, not knowing what had happened, came in. And Peter said to her: Tell me, woman, whether you sold the land for so much? And she said: Yea, for so much. And Peter said unto her: Why have you agreed together to tempt the Spirit of the Lord? Behold the feet of them who have buried thy husband are at the door, and they shall carry thee out. Immediately she fell down before his feet, and gave up the ghost. And the young men coming in, found her dead: and carried her out, and buried her by her husband. And there came great fear upon the whole church, and upon all that heard these things.

Lesson III ~ Acts 5:12–16

And by the hands of the apostles were many signs and wonders wrought among the people. And they were all with one accord in Solomon's porch. But of the rest no man durst join himself unto them; but the people magnified them. And the multitude of men and women who believed in the Lord, was more increased: Insomuch that they brought forth the sick into the streets, and laid them on beds and couches, that when Peter came, his shadow at the least, might overshadow any of them, and they might be delivered from their infirmities. And there came also together to Jerusalem a multitude out of the neighboring cities, bringing sick persons, and such as were troubled with unclean spirits; who were all healed.

Friday I after Easter

Lesson I - Acts 8:9–13

From the Acts of the Apostles

There was therefore great joy in that city. Now there was a certain man named Simon, who before had been a magician in that city, seducing the people of Samaria, giving out that he was some great one: To whom they all gave ear, from the least to the greatest, saying: This man is the power of God, which is called great. And they were attentive to him, because, for a long time, he had bewitched them with his magical practices. But when they had believed Philip preaching of the kingdom of God, in the name of Jesus Christ, they were baptized, both men and women. Then Simon himself believed also; and being baptized, he adhered to Philip. And being astonished, wondered to see the signs and exceeding great miracles which were done.

Lesson II - Acts 8:14–19

Now when the apostles, who were in Jerusalem, had heard that Samaria had received the word of God, they sent unto them Peter and John. Who, when they were come, prayed for them, that they might receive the Holy Ghost. For he was not as yet come upon any of them; but they were only baptized in the name of the Lord Jesus. Then they laid their hands upon them, and they received the Holy Ghost. And when Simon saw, that by the imposition of the hands of the apostles, the Holy Ghost was given, he offered them money, Saying: Give me also this power, that on whomsoever I shall lay my hands, he may receive the Holy Ghost.

Lesson III - Acts 8:19–24

But Peter said to him: Keep thy money to thyself, to perish with thee, because thou hast thought that the gift of God may be purchased with money. Thou hast no part nor lot in this matter. For thy heart is not right in the sight of God. Do penance therefore for this thy wickedness; and pray to God, that perhaps this thought of thy heart may be forgiven thee. For I see thou art in the gall of bitterness, and in the bonds of iniquity. Then Simon answering, said: Pray you for me to the Lord, that none of these things which you have spoken may come upon me.

Saturday I after Easter

Lesson I - Acts 10:1–8

From the Acts of the Apostles

And there was a certain man in Caesarea, named Cornelius, a centurion of that which is called the Italian band; A religious man, and fearing God with all his house, giving much alms to the people, and always praying to God. This man saw in a vision manifestly, about the ninth hour of the day, an angel of God coming in unto him, and saying to him: Cornelius. And he, beholding him, being seized with fear, said: What is it, Lord? And he said to him: thy prayers and thy alms are ascended for a memorial in the sight of God. And now send men to Joppe, and call hither one

Simon, who is surnamed Peter: He lodgeth with one Simon a tanner, whose house is by the sea side. He will tell thee what thou must do. And when the angel who spoke to him was departed, he called two of his household servants, and a soldier who feared the Lord, of them that were under him. To whom when he had related all, he sent them to Joppe.

Lesson II ~ Acts 10:9–17

And on the next day, whilst they were going on their journey, and drawing nigh to the city, Peter went up to the higher parts of the house to pray, about the sixth hour. And being hungry, he was desirous to taste somewhat. And as they were preparing, there came upon him an ecstasy of mind. And he saw the heaven opened, and a certain vessel descending, as it were a great linen sheet let down by the four corners from heaven to the earth: Wherein were all manner of fourfooted beasts, and creeping things of the earth, and fowls of the air. And there came a voice to him: Arise, Peter; kill and eat. But Peter said: Far be it from me; for I never did eat any thing that is common and unclean. And the voice spoke to him again the second time: That which God hath cleansed, do not thou call common. And this was done thrice; and presently the vessel was taken up into heaven. Now, whilst Peter was doubting within himself, what the vision that he had seen should mean, behold the men who were sent from Cornelius, inquiring for Simon's house, stood at the gate.

Lesson III ~ Acts 10:34–41

And Peter opening his mouth, said: In very deed I perceive, that God is not a respecter of persons. But in every nation, he that feareth him, and worketh justice, is acceptable to him. God sent the word to the children of Israel, preaching peace by Jesus Christ: he is Lord of all. You know the word which hath been published through all Judea: for it began from Galilee, after the baptism which John preached, Jesus of Nazareth: how God anointed him with the Holy Ghost, and with power, who went about doing good, and healing all that were oppressed by the devil, for God was with him. And we are witnesses of all things that he did in the land of the Jews and in Jerusalem, whom they killed, hanging him upon a tree. Him God raised up the third day, and gave him to be made manifest, Not to all the people, but to witnesses preordained by God, even to us, who did eat and drink with him after he arose again from the dead.

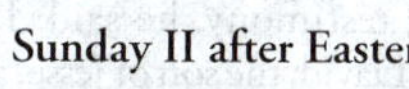

Sunday II after Easter

Semiduplex

Lesson I ~ Acts 13:13–20

From the Acts of the Apostles

Now when Paul and they that were with him had sailed from Paphos, they came to Perge in Pamphylia. And John departing from them, returned to Jerusalem. But they passing through Perge, came to Antioch in Pisidia: and entering into the synagogue on the sabbath day, they sat down. And after the reading of the law and the prophets, the rulers of the synagogue sent to them, saying: Ye men, brethren, if you have any word of exhortation to make to the people, speak. Then Paul rising up, and with his hand bespeaking silence, said: Ye men of Israel, and you that fear God, give ear. The God of the people of Israel chose our fathers, and exalted the people when they were sojourners in the land of Egypt, and with a high arm brought them out from thence, And for the space of forty years endured their manners in the desert. And destroying seven nations in the land of Chanaan, divided their land among them, by lot, As it were, after four hundred and fifty years: and after these things, he gave unto them judges, until Samuel the prophet.

Lesson II ~ Acts 13:21–25

And after that they desired a king: and God gave them Saul the son of Cis, a man of the tribe of Benjamin, forty years. And when he had removed him, he raised them up David to be king: to whom giving testimony, he said: I have found David, the son of Jesse, a man according to my own heart, who shall do all my wills. Of this man's seed God according to his promise, hath raised up to Israel a Saviour, Jesus: John first preaching, before his coming, the baptism of penance to all the people of Israel. And when John was fulfilling his course, he said: I am not he, whom you think me to be: but behold, there comes one after me, whose shoes of his feet I am not worthy to loose.

Lesson III ~ Acts 13:26–33

Men, brethren, children of the stock of Abraham, and whosoever among you fear God, to you the word of this salvation is sent. For they that inhabited Jerusalem, and the rulers thereof, not knowing him, nor the voices of the prophets, which are read every sabbath, judging him have fulfilled them. And finding no cause of death in him, they desired of Pilate, that they might kill him. And when they had fulfilled all things that were written of him, taking him down from the tree, they laid him in a sepulchre. But God raised him up from the dead the third day: Who was seen for many days, by them who came up with him from Galilee to Jerusalem, who to this present are his witnesses to the people. And we declare unto you, that the promise which was made to our fathers, This same God hath fulfilled to our children, raising up Jesus, as in the second psalm also is written: Thou art my Son, this day have I begotten thee.

Lesson IV

Sermon by St. Leo, Pope

Dearly beloved brethren, the days which passed between the Resurrection and the Ascension of the Lord, wore not idly by, but in them were established great Sacraments, and great Mysteries were revealed. In them was abolished the terror of that fearful death, and it was shown that not the soul only, but the body also, will not die eternally. In them the breathing of the Lord on His Apostles shed upon them the Holy

Ghost, and the Blessed Apostle Peter, being given the keys of the kingdom of heaven, was chosen out of the rest to receive the chief care of the Lord's fold.

Lesson V

It was during those days, that as two of His disciples were walking together, the Lord Himself joined them, and made Himself One of three companions. Then, to clear away all shadow of doubt from our mind, He rebuked the slowness of such as still feared and trembled. Their hearts enlightened by faith, caught the flame; and, whereas they had earlier been cold, they glowed again as the Lord opened to them the Scriptures. In the breaking of bread their eyes were opened, and they knew Him. And, O, how much happier were they with their eyes opened, and gazing upon the glorification of our nature in His Person, than were the first father and mother of our race, upon whom their own transgression had brought shame!

Lesson VI

Amid these and other miracles, while the disciples were still troubled with fearful thoughts, the Lord manifested Himself in the midst of them, and said: "Peace be to you." And lest their reason should be deceived by the vain imaginations which lurked in their hearts (for they thought that What they saw was a spirit, and not Flesh), He rebuked thoughts so inconsistent with the truth; and pointed out to the eyes of the doubters the marks of crucifixion which still remained in His Hands and His Feet, and bade them handle Him more closely. Those open Wounds made by the nails and spear in His Body remain ever open to close the wounds in unbelievers' hearts: that we may hold, not with doubtful faith, but with most firm and absolute knowledge, that the Manhood Which lay in the grave is the Same Which now sits at the right hand of God the Father.

Lesson VII

From the Holy Gospel according to St. John (John 10:11–16)

At that time, Jesus said unto the Pharisees: I am the Good Shepherd. The Good Shepherd giveth His life for His sheep. And so on.

Homily by Pope St. Gregory

Dearly beloved brethren, you have heard from the Holy Gospel what is at once your instruction and our danger. Behold, how He Who, not by the varying gifts of nature, but of the very essence of His being, is Good, behold how He says: "I am the Good Shepherd." And then He says what is the character of His goodness, even of that goodness of His which we must strive to copy: "The Good Shepherd giveth His life for the Sheep." As He had foretold, even so He did; as He had commanded, so He gave an example. The Good Shepherd gave His life for the sheep, and made His Own Body and His Own Blood to be our Sacramental Food, pasturing upon His Own Flesh the sheep whom He had bought.

Lesson VIII

He, by despising death, has shown us how to do likewise; He has set before us the mould wherein it befits us to be cast. Our first duty is to freely and tenderly spend our outward things for His sheep, but lastly, if need be, to serve the same by our death also. From the light offering of the first, we go on to the stern offering of the last, and, if we be ready to give our life for the sheep, why should we scruple to give our substance, seeing how much more is the life than meat?

Lesson IX

And some there be which love the things of this world better than they love the sheep; and such as they no longer deserve to be called shepherds. These are they of whom it is written: "But he that is a hireling, and not the shepherd, whose own the sheep are not, seeth the wolf coming, and leaveth the sheep, and fleeth." He is not a shepherd but a hireling which feeds the Lord's sheep, not because he loves their souls, but because he does gain earthly wealth thereby. He that takes a shepherd's place, but seeks not gain of souls, that same is but a hireling; such a one is ever ready for creature comforts, he loves his pre-eminence, he grows sleek upon his income, and he likes well to see men bow down to him.

Monday II after Easter

Lesson I ~ Acts 15:5–12

From the Acts of the Apostles

But there arose some of the sect of the Pharisees that believed, saying: They must be circumcised, and be commanded to observe the law of Moses. And the apostles and ancients assembled to consider of this matter. And when there had been much disputing, Peter, rising up, said to them: Men, brethren, you know, that in former days God made choice among us, that by my mouth the Gentiles should hear the word of the gospel, and believe. And God, who knoweth the hearts, gave testimony, giving unto them the Holy Ghost, as well as to us; And put no difference between us and them, purifying their hearts by faith. Now therefore, why tempt you God to put a yoke upon the necks of the disciples, which neither our fathers nor we have been able to bear? But by the grace of the Lord Jesus Christ, we believe to be saved, in like manner as they also. And all the multitude held their peace; and they heard Barnabas and Paul telling what great signs and wonders God had wrought among the Gentiles by them.

Lesson II ~ Acts 15:13–21

And after they had held their peace, James answered, saying: Men, brethren, hear me. Simon hath related how God first visited to take of the Gentiles a people to his name. And to this agree the words of the prophets, as it is written: After these things I will return, and will rebuild the tabernacle of David, which is fallen down; and the ruins thereof I will rebuild, and I will set it up: That the residue of men may seek after the Lord, and all nations upon whom my name is invoked, saith the Lord, who doth these things. To the Lord was his own work known from the beginning of the world. For which cause I judge that they, who from among the Gentiles are converted to God, are not to be disquieted. But that we write unto them, that they refrain themselves from the pollutions of idols, and from fornication, and from things strangled, and from blood. For Moses of old time hath in every city them that preach him in the synagogues, where he is read every sabbath.

Lesson III ~ Acts 15:22–29

Then it pleased the apostles and ancients, with the whole church, to choose men of their own company, and to send to Antioch, with Paul and Barnabas, namely, Judas, who was surnamed Barsabas, and Silas, chief men among the brethren. Writing by their hands: The apostles and ancients, brethren, to the brethren of the Gentiles that are at Antioch, and in Syria and Cilicia, greeting. Forasmuch as we have heard, that some going out from us have troubled you with words, subverting your souls; to whom we gave no commandment: It hath seemed good to us, being assembled together, to choose out men, and to send them unto you, with our well beloved Barnabas and Paul: Men that have given their lives for the name of our Lord Jesus Christ. We have sent therefore Judas and Silas, who themselves also will, by word of mouth, tell you the same things. For it hath seemed good to the Holy Ghost and to us, to lay no further burden upon you than these necessary things: That you abstain from things sacrificed to idols, and from blood, and from things strangled, and from fornication; from which things keeping yourselves, you shall do well. Fare ye well.

Tuesday II after Easter

Lesson I ~ Acts 17:22–27

From the Acts of the Apostles

But Paul standing in the midst of the Areopagus, said: Ye men of Athens, I perceive that in all things you are too superstitious. For passing by, and seeing your idols, I found an altar also, on which was written: To the unknown God. What therefore you worship, without knowing it, that I preach to you: God, who made the world, and all things therein; he, being Lord of heaven and earth, dwelleth not in temples made with hands; Neither is he served with men's hands, as though he needed any thing; seeing it is he who giveth to all life, and breath, and all things: And hath made of one, all mankind, to dwell upon the whole face of the earth, determining appointed times, and the limits of their habitation. That they should seek God, if happily they may feel after him or find him, although he be not far from every one of us:

Lesson II ~ Acts 17:28–33

For in him we live, and move, and are; as some also of your own poets said: For we are also his offspring. Being therefore the offspring of God, we must not suppose the divinity to be like unto gold, or silver, or stone, the graving of art, and device of man.

And God indeed having winked at the times of this ignorance, now declareth unto men, that all should every where do penance. Because he hath appointed a day wherein he will judge the world in equity, by the man whom he hath appointed; giving faith to all, by raising him up from the dead. And when they had heard of the resurrection of the dead, some indeed mocked, but others said: We will hear thee again concerning this matter. So Paul went out from among them.

Lesson III ~ Acts 17:34; 18:1–4

But certain men adhering to him, did believe; among whom was also Dionysius, the Areopagite, and a woman named Damaris, and others with them. After these things, departing from Athens, he came to Corinth. And finding a certain Jew, named Aquila, born in Pontus, lately come from Italy, with Priscilla his wife (because that Claudius had commanded all Jews to depart from Rome), he came to them. And because he was of the same trade, he remained with them, and wrought (now they were tentmakers by trade). And he reasoned in the synagogue every sabbath, bringing in the name of the Lord Jesus; and he persuaded the Jews and the Greeks.

Patronage of St. Joseph
~Wednesday II after Easter~

Duplex I Class

Lesson I ~ Gen 39:1–6

From the book of Genesis

And Joseph was brought into Egypt, and Putiphar an eunuch of Pharao, chief captain of the army, an Egyptian, bought him of the Ismaelites, by whom he was brought. And the Lord was with him, and he was a prosperous man in all things: and he dwelt in his master's house, Who knew very well that the Lord was with him, and made all that he did to prosper in his hand. And Joseph found favour in the sight of his master, and ministered to him: and being set over all by him, he governed the house committed to him, and all things that were delivered to him: And the Lord blessed the house of the Egyptian for Joseph's sake, and multiplied all his substance, both at home, and in the fields. Neither knew he any other thing, but the bread which he ate. And Joseph was of a beautiful countenance, and comely to behold.

Lesson II ~ Gen 41:37–43

The counsel pleased Pharao and all his servants. And he said to them: Can we find such another man, that is full of the spirit of God? He said therefore to Joseph: Seeing God hath shown thee all that thou hast said, can I find one wiser and one like unto thee? Thou shalt be over my house, and at the commandment of thy mouth all the people shall obey: only in the kingly throne will I be above thee. And again Pharao said to Joseph: Behold, I have appointed thee over the whole land of Egypt. And he took his ring from his own hand, and gave it into his hand: and he put upon him a robe of silk, and put a chain of gold about his neck. And he made him go up into his second chariot, the crier proclaiming that all should bow their knee before him, and that they should know he was made governor over the whole land of Egypt.

Lesson III - Gen 41:44–49

And the king said to Joseph: I am Pharao; without thy commandment no man shall move hand or foot in all the land of Egypt. And he turned his name, and called him in the Egyptian tongue, The saviour of the world. And he gave him to wife Aseneth the daughter of Putiphare priest of Heliopolis. Then Joseph went out to the land of Egypt: (Now he was thirty years old when he stood before king Pharao) and he went round all the countries of Egypt. And the fruitfulness of the seven years came: and the corn being bound up into sheaves was gathered together into the barns of Egypt. And all the abundance of grain was laid up in every city. And there was so great abundance of wheat, that it was equal to the sand of the sea, and the plenty exceeded measure.

Lesson IV

Sermon by St. Bernardine of Siena.

When any special favors are conferred upon a reasonable being, it is the common rule that whenever the grace of God elects so and so for such and such a grace, or for such and such a high post of duty, the person so elected receives all the gifts of grace which be needful for him in that state of life whereunto he is called, and receives them abundantly. Of this there is an excellent instance in the case of the holy Joseph, the so-called father of our Lord Jesus Christ, and the real husband of her who is Queen of the world and Lady of Angels. He had been elected by the Eternal Father to be the faithful nurse and warder of His two chief treasures, that is, His Son, and Joseph's own Wife. This duty Joseph faithfully discharged, and consequently the Lord has said to him: "Well done, thou good and faithful servant enter thou into the joy of thy Lord."

Lesson V

This man Joseph, if we compare him with the Universal Church of Christ, is he not that elect and chosen one, through whom and under whom Christ is orderly and honestly brought into the world? If, then, the Holy Universal Church be under a debt to the Virgin Mother, because it is through her that she has been made to receive Christ, next to Mary she owes love and worship to Joseph. Joseph is the key of the Old Testament, in whose person the noble structure of Patriarchs and Prophets reaches her completion and realizes her promises. He is the only one of them who actually enjoyed in full fruition what God had been pleased to promise before to them. It is, therefore, with good reason that we see a type of him in that Patriarch Joseph who stored up corn for the people. But the second Joseph has a more excellent dignity than the first, seeing that the first only gave to the Egyptians bread for the body, but the second was the watchful guardian for all the elect of that Living Bread Which came down from heaven, of Which whosoever eats will never die.

Lesson VI

There can be no doubt that Christ still treats Joseph in heaven with that familiarity, honor, and most high condescension which He paid him, like a Son to a father, while He walked among men; nay, rather, He has now crowned and completed those habits. We may very reasonably suspect that it was with a peculiar meaning that Christ said "Enter thou into the joy of thy Lord." The joy of being blessed for ever enters into the heart of man, but when the Lord said, "Enter thou into joy," He probably meant mystically to bid him realize a joy which should not be within him only, but outside him also, above him, and below him, and all round about him, and overflowing him as it were a great bottomless pit of joy to swallow him up altogether. Therefore, O thou blessed Joseph! remember us! In thy helpful prayers, make intercession for us with Him Who vouchsafed to be supposedly thy Son! Likewise, obtain some pity for us from that most blessed Maiden who was thy wife, and the Mother of Him, Who, with the Father and the Holy Ghost, lives and reigns, God, world without end. Amen.

Lesson VII

From the Holy Gospel according to St. Luke (Luke 3:21)

At that time: When all the people were baptized, it came to pass, that Jesus also being baptized and praying, the heaven was opened. And so on.

Homily by St. Augustine, Bishop

"And Jesus Himself began to be about thirty years of age, being (as was supposed) the Son of Joseph." These words, "as was supposed," were evidently here written for the correction of such as might think that the Lord was the Son of Joseph, in the same sense as other men are called the children of their fathers. Those who find any trouble in the fact that the ancestors reckoned downward by Matthew from David to Joseph, are other than those reckoned upward by Luke from Joseph to David, such, I say, as are troubled by this, may get over it by supposing that Joseph had two fathers; one, that is, who begat him, and another who adopted him. The custom of adopting children, whereby those who have none of their own surround themselves with a family, is very ancient even among the people of God. Hence, Luke is understood to have included in his Gospel, under the name of father of Joseph, that not of the father by whom he was begotten but of him by whom he was adopted, and it is the ancestors of this adoptive father who are reckoned up as far as David.

Lesson VIII

Thus since we are bound to believe that what each of the Evangelists said was true, Matthew as well as Luke; and therefore that one of them names the father who begat, and the other the father who adopted Joseph; we naturally suppose that the Evangelist who names the adoptive father was he who abstains from using the term "beget." Matthew begins: "Abraham begat Isaac; and Isaac begat Jacob," and so on, always with the use of this word "begat," till he comes to: "and Jacob begat Joseph." By the word which he uses he does sufficiently indicate that the genealogy which he is giving is that of him who begat.

Lesson IX

Luke says Joseph was the son of Heli, not that Joseph was begotten of Heli; but even if he had said the latter, it would not have troubled this interpretation of ours, that one Evangelist names the natural, and the other the adoptive father of Joseph. It is not an outrageous thing to say that one who adopts another has begotten him, albeit he has done it, not carnally, but by love. Even so has God given to us the power to become His sons, albeit He has not begotten us of His Own Nature and Substance, as He has His Only-Begotten Son, but only reckons us, in His love, among His children.

Day 2 in the Octave of St. Joseph

~ Thursday II after Easter ~

Semiduplex

Lesson I ~ Acts 24:10–16

From the Acts of the Apostles

Then Paul answered (the governor making a sign to him to speak): Knowing that for many years thou hast been judge over this nation, I will with good courage answer for myself. For thou mayest understand, that there are yet but twelve days, since I went up to adore in Jerusalem: And neither in the temple did they find me disputing with any man, or causing any concourse of the people, neither in the synagogues, nor in the city: Neither can they prove unto thee the things whereof they now accuse me. But this I confess to thee, that according to the way, which they call a heresy, so do I serve the Father and my God, believing all things which are written in the law and the prophets: Having hope in God, which these also themselves look for, that there shall be a resurrection of the just and unjust. And herein do I endeavour to have always a conscience without offence toward God, and towards men.

Lesson II ~ Acts 24:17–21

Now after many years, I came to bring alms to my nation, and offerings, and vows. In which I was found purified in the temple: neither with multitude, nor with tumult. But certain Jews of Asia, who ought to be present before thee, and to accuse, if they had any thing against me: Or let these men themselves say, if they found in me any iniquity, when standing before the council, Except it be for this one voice only that I cried, standing among them, Concerning the resurrection of the dead am I judged this day by you.

Lesson III ~ Acts 24:22–27

And Felix put them off, having most certain knowledge of this way, saying: When Lysias the tribune shall come down, I will hear you. And he commanded a centurion to keep him, and that he should be easy, and that he should not prohibit any of his friends to minister unto him. And after some days, Felix, coming with Drusilla his wife, who was a Jew, sent for Paul, and heard of him the faith, that is in Christ Jesus. And as he treated of justice, and chastity, and of the judgment to come, Felix being terrified, answered: For this time, go thy way: but when I have a convenient time, I will send for thee. Hoping also withal, that money should be given him by Paul; for which cause also oftentimes sending for him, he spoke with him. But when two years were ended, Felix had for successor Portius Festus. And Felix being willing to show the Jews a pleasure, left Paul bound.

Lesson IV

Sermon by St. Bernardine of Siena

The marriage between Mary and Joseph was a real marriage, for it was contracted under divine inspiration. Now in marriage there is so close a union of souls that the bridegroom and the bride are said to be one person, for which reason marriage is like unto the very perfection of unity. Hence how can any discerning mind think that the Holy Spirit would unite, in a union of this intimacy, a mind such as the Virgin's, with the soul of a man who had not within him the operation of a godliness like unto hers? Wherefore I believe that this Joseph was holy, the chastest of men and a virgin, completely humble, burning with a passion of charity towards God, and full of the highest graces of contemplation. And since the Virgin knew that he was given her by the Holy Spirit to be her spouse, and the faithful guardian of her virginity, and to share besides in devoted love and affectionate care towards that One who was in the divinest fashion the very offspring of God; therefore I believe that she sincerely loved Saint Joseph with all the affection of her heart.

Lesson V

Now Joseph was most ardent in his love for Christ. For who, I ask, would deny that Christ, whether as a child or as a grown man, would most deeply inspire ineffable affection, and the peculiar joys which he alone could give? And what would be the effect on one who held him in his arms, and conversed at will with him? And besides all this, who can reckon the bliss of receiving from the Christ Child those gazes of filial love? or his words spoken as a devoted son? or the giving of his trustful embraces? O how sweet were the kisses that Joseph received from him! O how sweet to hear little One lisp the name of father, and how delightful to feel his gentle caresses! Think again how often (when the little Jesus was growing bigger, and was wearied with much walking on the journeys which they made) Joseph must have been filled with compassion, and so carried him at rest in his bosom. For Joseph bore towards Jesus all the fullness of an adoptive love, as to a most dear son, given to him by the Holy Ghost in his Virgin bride.

Lesson VI

Hence it was that a most prudent Mother, who knew the devotion of Joseph to Jesus, said to her Son, when she found him in the temple: "Son, why hast thou thus dealt with us? behold, thy father and I have sought thee sorrowing." In order to understand this, we must note that Christ has within himself, as it were, two savors, sweetness and bitterness. And since the most holy Joseph was in a wonderful manner (as we shall see) a partaker of these two savors, therefore the Blessed Virgin does bestow upon him in a special sense the title of Father of Christ. This is the only place where we read that she did call Saint Joseph the father of Jesus, doubtless because the bitterness of sorrow which he felt at the loss of Jesus showed the fatherly affection which he bore him. For if according to human laws, which are approved by God, a man can adopt as his son the child of another family, how much more truly ought the Son of God to be called the Son of Joseph. For he was given to this Joseph by his most holy Spouse, in the wonderful mystery of a virginal marriage. And so it is also to be believed that in Joseph there were the two savors of Jesus, sweetness and bitterness, which were manifested as the sweetness of paternal love, and the bitterness of his compassion, towards his beloved Jesus.

Lesson VII

From the Holy Gospel according to St. Luke (Luke 3:21–23)

At that time: When all the people were baptized, it came to pass, that Jesus also being baptized and praying, the heaven was opened. And so on.

Homily by St. Augustine, Bishop

Joseph cannot be denied the name of father of Christ, merely because he did not beget him by marital union. For he would have been called the father of any child whom he adopted, even if the child were not the issue of his wife, but from another family. It is true that Christ was supposed to be the son of Joseph in another sense; namely, in that of having been actually begotten by Joseph according to the flesh. But this supposition was made only by those from whom Mary's virginity was concealed. It is of this that Luke says: "And Jesus himself began to be about thirty years of age, being (as was supposed) the son of Joseph." However, Luke shows no hesitation in giving the name of parent, not only to Mary, but also to Joseph, when in another place he says: "And the child grew, and waxed strong in spirit, filled with wisdom: and the grace of God was upon him: Now his parents went every year to Jerusalem, at the Feast of Passover."

Lesson VIII

But lest anyone should think that by the word Parents there is here to understood Mary and her forbears only, we must take into account what Luke records earlier, And Joseph and his mother marveled at those things which were spoken of him. Since, therefore, Luke witnesses that Christ was born, not by the begetting of Joseph, but of the Virgin Mary, how can he call Joseph the father of Jesus, except in the sense that Joseph was a real husband to Mary by virtue of the true bond of marriage, saving only that there never was any carnal intercourse between them? And yet, on account of this bond of marriage, Joseph was the father of Jesus in a much closer sense (seeing that the Christ Child was born of his wife) than if Joseph had adopted Jesus from another family. Hence, also, if anyone could prove that Mary did not trace her origin from David, the same reasoning by which Joseph is called the father of Christ would be sufficient reason for giving Christ the name, Son of David.

Lesson IX

Luke gives the genealogy, not at the beginning of his Gospel, but after the account of the Baptism of Christ. And he gives it, not in the descending order, but in the ascending, more as if he were pointing to Christ as Priest, making atonement for sins. This was the occasion when the voice spoke in testimony from heaven. And also at this time John himself gave testimony, saying: "Behold the Lamb of God, which taketh away the sin of the world." By thus beginning with Jesus and tracing back, Luke passes up through Abraham and eventually comes to God, to whom we are reconciled after purification and atonement. Rightly then does Luke give the origin by adoption, for through adoption and faith in the Son of God we become God's sons. In this fashion, Luke shows clearly enough why he names Joseph as the son of Heli; that is, not because Joseph was begotten by Heli, but because he was adopted by him. For Luke calls Adam himself the son of God, and this because he was made by God, being set in the paradise of Eden as a son by virtue of the grace which afterwards he lost in sinning.

Day 3 in the Octave of St. Joseph

~ Friday II after Easter ~

Semiduplex

Lesson I ~ Acts 25:1–5

From the Acts of the Apostles

Now when Festus was come into the province, after three days, he went up to Jerusalem from Caesarea. And the chief priests, and principal men of the Jews, went unto him against Paul: and they besought him, Requesting favour against him, that he would command him to be brought to Jerusalem, laying wait to kill him in the way. But Festus answered: That Paul was kept in Caesarea, and that he himself would very shortly depart thither. Let them, therefore, saith he, among you that are able, go down with me, and accuse him, if there be any crime in the man.

Lesson II ~ Acts 25:6–8

And having tarried among them no more than eight or ten days, he went down to Caesarea, and the next day he sat in the judgment seat; and commanded Paul to be brought. Who being brought, the Jews stood about him, who were come down from Jerusalem, objecting many and grievous causes, which they could not prove; Paul making answer for himself: Neither against the law of the Jews, nor against the temple, nor against Caesar, have I offended in any thing.

Lesson III ~ Acts 25:9–12

But Festus, willing to show the Jews a pleasure, answering Paul, said: Wilt thou go up to Jerusalem, and there be judged of these things before me? Then Paul said: I stand at Caesar's judgment seat, where I ought to be judged. To the Jews I have done no injury, as thou very well knowest. For if I have injured them, or have committed any thing worthy of death, I refuse not to die. But if there be none of these things whereof they accuse me, no man may deliver me to them: I appeal to Caesar. Then Festus having conferred with the council, answered: Hast thou appealed to Caesar? To Caesar shalt thou go.

Lesson IV

Sermon by St. John Chrysostom

It was the custom in ancient times for betrothed brides to dwell in the houses of their bridegrooms. And it would seem that Mary thus dwelt with her Spouse. And herein we find answer to the question: Why did not the virgin conception take place before Mary was wed? In order that the mystery might be hid in the meantime, and that the Virgin might escape all danger of evil suspicion. For Joseph had the best right to be moved by jealousy. Yet we see that he not only refrained from sending away his Espoused, or branding her with infamy, but that he received her as his own, and did cherish her after she conceived. And verily, it is evident that he would never have kept her in his house, or ministered to all her needs, if he had not clearly come to know that she had conceived by the operation of the Holy Ghost.

Lesson V

"Joseph her husband, being a just man, and not willing publicly to expose her, was minded to put her away privately." After the Evangelist has told us that she was with child, of the Holy Ghost and not of any sexual commerce, Luke brings testimony from another source to confirm the statement. For lest anyone should say: And how can this be proved? who saw it? who ever heard of any such thing having happened? and lest you might think that a disciple had invented this tale to please his Master, the Evangelist thus brings forth the grief of Joseph, and what he did thereafter, to confirm the story, as if to say: If you will not believe me, or if you hold my testimony in suspicion, at least believe the husband.

Lesson VI

He says: "Joseph her husband, being a just man." To be just, as the word is here used, implies that full growth of righteousness which comes from the habitual service of God. Being therefore a just man (that is, a worthy and good man), "he was minded to put her away privately." Thus the Evangelist records the grief of this just man before he knew the secret of the virgin conception, lest thou shouldst have doubts concerning what happened after he knew that secret. And certainly if Mary had been such as suspicion would make her out to be, she would have deserved not only to be denounced, but to be punished by the authority of the Law. But Joseph was not only unwilling to condemn her, but even to denounce her. Herein thou dost see an instance of a man full of spiritual understanding, and free from the tyranny of suspicion. But was this a matter of mere suspicion, seeing that the very swelling of her body seemed to prove a fact? Nonetheless, this man was so pure, and free from that kind of jealousy, that he would not cause the Virgin even the slightest grief. And although he lived under the Law, his spiritual understanding was above the Law. For now that the reign of grace was approaching, it was fitting that there should be a shining example of a more sublime spirituality than was common under the Law.

Lesson VII

From the Holy Gospel according to St. Luke (Luke 3:21–23)

At that time: When all the people were baptized, it came to pass, that Jesus also being baptized and praying, the heaven was opened. And so on.

Homily by St. Augustine, Bishop

The words uttered from heaven over the river Jordan: "This is my beloved Son, in whom I am well pleased:" were said also on the Mount of the Transfiguration. Now these words should not be understood to imply that he was not the Son of God before the voice from heaven was heard. For we know that he who received the form of a servant from the Virgin's womb, being in the form of God, thought it not robbery to be equal with God. Indeed, the same Apostle Paul clearly declares elsewhere: "But when the fulness of the time was come, God sent forth his Son, made of a Woman, made under the Law, that he might redeem them that were under the Law, that we might receive the adoption of sons." He therefore is the Son of God, who is according to his divinity the Lord of David, and at the same time according to the flesh the Son of David, and of the seed of David.

Lesson VIII

Except it were profitable to believe this, the same Apostle would not have exhorted Timothy so earnestly, saying: "Remember that Jesus Christ, of the seed of David, is risen again from the dead, according to my Gospel." Why then should any follower of the holy Gospel be troubled concerning this; to wit, that Christ, who was born of the Virgin without cohabitation with Joseph, has his line of descent traced by the Evangelist Matthew through Joseph rather than through Mary; or again, that because of Joseph's descent from David, the Evangelist should call Christ the Son of David? For we know good reasons for this. The first is that the genealogy of her husband would be preferred to hers as a matter of honor to the male sex. For even though he was not joined to her in cohabitation, he was not on that account any the less her husband, since Matthew himself witnesses that Mary was called the wife of Joseph by the Angel, and yet he also says that she had conceived by the Holy Ghost.

Lesson IX

Note that one and the same narrator both makes and approves all these statements: to wit, that Joseph was the husband of Mary; that the Mother of Christ was a Virgin; that Christ was of the seed of David; and that Joseph was in the line of Christ's ancestors from David. From all this we perceive several other reasons for the giving of Joseph's genealogy: to wit, that Mary was not without blood-relationship to David; and that in consideration of their union as souls, according to the due order of sex, she was not falsely given the title of Joseph's wife; and that Joseph, chiefly on account of his dignity as a man, was not to be separated from the line of their common genealogy, lest he should appear as separated from that Woman, to whom the affection of his soul bound him.

Day 4 in the Octave of St. Joseph

~ Saturday II after Easter ~

Semiduplex

Lesson I ~ Acts 28:16–20

From the Acts of the Apostles

And when we were come to Rome, Paul was suffered to dwell by himself, with a soldier that kept him. And after the third day, he called together the chief of the Jews. And when they were assembled, he said to them: Men, brethren, I, having done nothing against the people, or the custom of our fathers, was delivered prisoner from Jerusalem into the hands of the Romans; Who, when they had examined me, would have released me, for that there was no cause of death in me; But the Jews contradicting it, I was constrained to appeal unto Caesar; not that I had any thing to accuse my nation of. For this cause therefore I desired to see you, and to speak to you. Because that for the hope of Israel, I am bound with this chain.

Lesson II ~ Acts 28:21–24

But they said to him: We neither received letters concerning thee from Judea, neither did any of the brethren that came hither, relate or speak any evil of thee. But we desire to hear of thee what thou thinkest; for as concerning this sect, we know that it is every where contradicted. And when they had appointed him a day, there came very many to him unto his lodgings; to whom he expounded, testifying the kingdom of God, and persuading them concerning Jesus, out of the law of Moses and the prophets, from morning until evening. And some believed the things that were said; but some believed not.

Lesson III ~ Acts 28:25–31

And when they agreed not among themselves, they departed, Paul speaking this one word: Well did the Holy Ghost speak to our fathers by Isaias the prophet, Saying: Go to this people, and say to them: With the ear you shall hear, and shall not understand; and seeing you shall see, and shall not perceive. For the heart of this people is grown gross, and with their ears have they heard heavily, and their eyes they have shut; lest perhaps they should see with their eyes, and hear with their ears, and understand with their heart, and should be converted, and I should heal them. Be it known therefore to you, that this salvation of God is sent to the Gentiles, and they will hear it. And when he had said these things, the Jews went out from him, having much reasoning among themselves. And he remained two whole years in his own hired lodging; and he received all that came in to him, Preaching the kingdom of God, and teaching the things which concern the Lord Jesus Christ, with all confidence, without prohibition.

Lesson IV

Sermon by St. John Chrysostom

"Joseph, thou son of David, fear not to take unto thee Mary thy wife." But what is it to take? Undoubtedly, to maintain, and that in his own house. For he had already sent her away in his mind. But now the Angel commands: Her whom thou wouldst send away, maintain; her, do thou, and not her parents, maintain, for God joins her to thee; her, God verily joins to thee, not in the sacred commerce of marriage, but in the fellowship of a common home; and her, God joins to thee through the ministry of my words. Just as Christ himself later entrusted her to the care of his disciple, so now the Angel gives her to her spouse; in such manner that she may have the consolation of his company without other conjugal rights. By this means her confinement would be explained in a worthier and more honorable way, and suspicion would be allayed. It is as though the Angel said: Not only was she not dishonored by an unlawful embrace, but indeed she is fruitful in a manner above nature and usage; therefore grieve not at the happy confinement of thy Bride, but break forth into greater joy! For that which is conceived in her is of the Holy Ghost.

Lesson V

"And she shall bring forth a Son, and thou shalt call his Name Jesus." That is: Think not that the ministry of this great dispensation, because it is of the Holy Ghost, is a thing apart from thee. For even thought thou hast no part in his generation, since the Virgin remains inviolate, yet do I readily grant thee this, namely; that thine are all the rights of a father, insofar as they obscure not the dignity of the Virgin; thou shalt certainly give the new-born his Name; thou shalt be the first to call him by his Name. For even though he who is born is not thy son, nonetheless thou shalt show him the care and solicitude of a parent; and therefore I unite thee to him by this immediate giving of the Name. But, lest anyone might think from this that Joseph was the begetter of

Christ, the Angel was first careful to say: "She shall bring forth a Son." He does not say: "She shall bear thee a son:" but makes his statement in an undetermined and indefinite way. For Mary did not bear a son to Joseph, but brought forth Christ to the whole world.

Lesson VI

Therefore the Evangelist relates that the Angel brought his Name from heaven, so that thus might be shown how wonderful was his birth, seeing that he himself taught his Name to Joseph by an Angel sent from God. For this Name, which verily contains a thousand treasures of good, was not given without meaning. Therefore the Angel does himself interpret it, thereby consoling Joseph's grief with good hopes; and thus also inviting him to believe these words. For we are easily summoned to that which is pleasant, and give prompt credence unto good tidings. Wherefore the Angel said: "He shall save his people from their sins." This also shows the novelty of the gift. For he announces that this people are to be saved, not indeed from external wars, nor from the swords of barbarians, but from what is far greater than these: From their sins. And no mere man could ever accomplish this.

Lesson VII

From the Holy Gospel according to St. Luke (Luke 3:21–23)

At that time: When all the people were baptized, it came to pass, that Jesus also being baptized and praying, the heaven was opened. And so on.

Homily by St. Augustine, Bishop

No one should be troubled at the words: "As was supposed, the son of Joseph." For it was no more than a supposition, seeing that Christ was not the son of Joseph by nature. Albeit, it was so supposed because Mary who was espoused to her husband Joseph, gave Christ birth. And so, referring to Joseph as father, it is written: "Is not this the carpenter's son?" We have already discussed why the Lord of salvation chose to be born of a Virgin. We have also discussed why she was an espoused Virgin when her conception took place; and why it took place at the time of the enrollment for taxing. Hence it is not fitting to explain why Christ had a working-man for his father. For thereby is figured Christ's divine Father, who as Maker of all things, framed the world. Even though human and divine matters be not equal to each other, yet is this figure a complete one. Christ's Father works by fire and by breathing on things. Yea, like a good carpenter of the soul, he chips away our defects. Promptly does he lay his axe to the barren trees and hew them down. Skillful is he in correcting whatever is built scantily, and in buttressing whatever is to be built magnificently. He tempers the hardness of hearts as with fire, and with his gentle Breath. And by his diverse workings he forms the quality of the human race.

Lesson VIII

We might wonder why the genealogy of Joseph, rather than of Mary, is given (since Mary conceived Christ by the Holy Ghost, and Joseph had not part in the Lord's conception), were it not that the Holy Scripture teaches us how it was the custom to trace descent on the male side. For in this fashion the person of the man is set forth as pre-eminent, and his dignity maintained, even as it is usually done in the Senate and the other high places of the state. And how unseemly it would have been to have passed over the lineage of the father, and to have given that of the mother, since the doing of such would have appeared to proclaim to all the people in the world that Christ had no father. It is a world-wide custom to trace the genealogy of a family in the male line. Therefore, be not perplexed that the lineage of Joseph is given. Forasmuch as Christ was born in the flesh, he was bound to follow this custom of the flesh. And he who came into the world had to be enrolled for taxing in the worldly manner, the more so that Joseph's descent was the same as Mary's.

Lesson IX

But some explanation is required as to why Saint Matthew reckons Christ's descent from Abraham forward, whilst Saint Luke traces the same from Christ backward to the creation of Adam by God. By this, Luke would have us understand that Christ's lineage should be traced to God, because God was Christ's true Progenitor, both as his Father whereof he was begotten, and as the Author, in the laver of baptism, of the mystical gift of the Spirit. Wherefore Luke does not begin his Gospel with the reckoning of Christ's lineage, but records it after the account of the baptism, thereby showing forth in baptism the working of God, the Author of all things. Thus also Luke asserts that Christ came forth from God according to a certain rule of orderliness. For he weaves all things together to prove that Christ is by nature, by grace, and in the flesh, the Son of God. But what more evident proof of Christ's divine descent could we have than what Luke gives? For before the Evangelist reckons the genealogy of Christ, he gives the words of the Father himself: "This is my beloved Son, in whom I am well pleased."

Sunday III after Easter

~ within the Octave of St. Joseph ~

Semiduplex

Lesson I ~ Apoc 1:1–6

Beginning of the book of the Apocalypse of St. John the Apostle

The Revelation of Jesus Christ, which God gave unto him, to make known to his servants the things which must shortly come to pass: and signified, sending by his angel to his servant John, who hath given testimony to the word of God, and the testimony of Jesus Christ, what things soever he hath seen. Blessed is he, that readeth and heareth the words of this prophecy; and keepeth those things which are written in it; for the time is at hand. John to the seven churches which are in Asia. Grace be unto you and peace from him that is, and that was, and that is to come, and from the seven spirits which are before his throne, And from Jesus Christ, who is the faithful witness, the first begotten of the dead, and the prince of the kings of the earth, who hath loved us, and washed us from our sins in his own blood, And hath made us a kingdom, and priests to God and his Father, to him be glory and empire for ever and ever. Amen.

Lesson II ~ Apoc 1:7–11

Behold, he comes with the clouds, and every eye shall see him, and they also that pierced him. And all the tribes of the earth shall bewail themselves because of him. Even so. Amen. I am Alpha and Omega, the beginning and the end, saith the Lord God, who is, and who was, and who is to come, the Almighty. I John, your brother and your partner in tribulation, and in the kingdom, and patience in Christ Jesus, was in the island, which is called Patmos, for the word of God, and for the testimony of Jesus. I was in the spirit on the Lord's day, and heard behind me a great voice, as of a trumpet, Saying: What thou seest, write in a book, and send to the seven churches which are in Asia, to Ephesus, and to Smyrna, and to Pergamus, and to Thyatira, and to Sardis, and to Philadelphia, and to Laodicea.

Lesson III ~ Apoc 1:12–19

And I turned to see the voice that spoke with me. And being turned, I saw seven golden candlesticks: And in the midst of the seven golden candlesticks, one like to the Son of man, clothed with a garment down to the feet, and girt about the paps with a golden girdle. And his head and his hairs were white, as white wool, and as snow, and his eyes were as a flame of fire, And his feet like unto fine brass, as in a burning furnace. And his voice as the sound of many waters. And he had in his right hand seven stars. And from his mouth came out a sharp two edged sword: and his face was as the sun shineth in his power. And when I had seen him, I fell at his feet as dead. And he laid his right hand upon me, saying: Fear not. I am the First and the Last, And alive, and was dead, and behold I am living for ever and ever, and have the keys of death and of hell. Write therefore the things which thou hast seen, and which are, and which must be done hereafter.

Lesson IV

Sermon from St. Augustine, Bishop

During these Holy Days in commemoration of the Lord's resurrection, we purpose to preach, so far as he will empower us, the doctrine of the resurrection of the body. For this is the Faith: the gift of resurrection, which was bestowed upon the flesh of our Lord Jesus Christ, is what is promised to us, for it was first made manifest in him that we might know what to hope for ourselves. What he has thus promised would come to us at last, he willed not only to foretell but to demonstrate. Those who were present at that time (even though they were terrified and affrighted, and supposed they had seen a spirit), handled him, and saw that a spirit would not have flesh and bones, such as they saw him to have. Thus he spoke to them, not only in words which they could hear, but in a body which they could see; as if it had not been enough to show himself to their sight, but must needs even offer himself to be touched and handled.

Lesson V

For he said: Why are you troubled? and why do thoughts arise in your hearts? For they supposed that they had seen a spirit. Therefore he added: Behold my hands and my feet, that it is I myself; handle me and see; for a spirit hath not flesh and bones, as you see me have. Of course, men have disputed this evidence; for what else could men do, seeing that they are wise only according to man's wisdom, which thus permits them to dispute concerning God in spite of what God has shown them of himself. He is God, they are men. But God knows the thoughts of man, that they are but vain.

Lesson VI

To carnal men, the one rule of understanding is his ordinary experience; seeing is believing. What men are accustomed to see, that they credit; what they are not accustomed to see, that they deem incredible. But God often works wonders (that is, things contrary to what we are accustomed), because he is God. Every day many men are born that previously had no existence at all; and this is a greater miracle than that a few, who did exist, have been raised from the dead. Yet this wonder is not recognized as such; on the contrary, it is disregarded because man is accustomed to it. Christ rose again from the dead; that is a fact. He had a body: he took flesh, he hung upon the cross, he gave up the ghost; his flesh was laid in the tomb. After that, he showed his flesh as alive again, he lived again the flesh. Why wonder, why deny it? God wrought this.

Lesson VII

From the Holy Gospel according to St. John (John 16:16–22)

At that time, Jesus said to his disciples: A little while, and now you shall not see me; and again a little while, and you shall see me: because I go to the Father. And so on.

Homily by St. Augustine, Bishop

This "little while" is the whole duration of this present world. In the same sense this same Evangelist says in his Epistle: "It is the last time." The words, "because I go to the Father," refer to the first clause of the text, namely, "A little while and you shall not see Me," and not to the latter clause, that is, "and again a little while, and you shall see Me." By His going to the Father He was about to bring it to pass that they should see Him no more. And thus it was that He said, not that He was about to die, and that after His death they should not see Him until He rose again, but that He was going to the Father, which He did when, after that He was risen again and had manifested Himself to them for forty days, He ascended up into heaven.

Lesson VIII

But now, to them which were looking on Him in the Body, He says: "A little while, and you shall not see Me," a little while, and they who now saw Him clad in a dying nature, should see Him so no more, because He was about to go to the Father. But He says: "And again a little while, and you shall see Me," and these words are a promise to the Universal Church, just as are those others: "Lo, I am with you always, even unto the consummation of the world." Our Lord delays not His promised coming. Again a little while, and we shall see Him. We shall see Him. And, O, when we shall see Him, then we shall beg, we shall ask no more; for no desire will be unsatisfied, and no riddle unsolved.

Lesson IX

This little while seems a very long while to us now, while as it is still going on, but when it is over we shall feel indeed how truly it is but a little while. Therefore, may our rejoicing never be like the rejoicing of that world whereof it is said: "The world shall rejoice." A woman when she is in labor has sorrow, and yet, while hitherto our gladness is still coming to the birth through throes of sorrow, let us not be altogether sorrowful, but, as the Apostle has it: "Rejoicing in hope: patient in tribulation. A woman, when she is in travail hath sorrow, because her hour is come: but as soon as she is delivered of the child, she remembereth no more the anguish, for joy that a man is born into the world." And so will it be with us. And with that let me end my discourse. The next passage is one of extreme difficulty; nor is it possible to treat it briefly, if (with the will of God), it is to be treated satisfactorily.

Day 6 in the Octave of St. Joseph

~ Monday III after Easter ~

Semiduplex

Lesson I ~ Apoc 2:1–7

From the book of the Apocalypse of St. John the Apostle

Unto the angel of the church of Ephesus write: These things saith he, who holdeth the seven stars in his right hand, who walketh in the midst of the seven golden candlesticks: I know thy works, and thy labour, and thy patience, and how thou canst not bear them that are evil, and thou hast tried them, who say they are apostles, and are not, and hast found them liars: And thou hast patience, and hast endured for my name, and hast not fainted. But I have somewhat against thee, because thou hast left thy first charity. Be mindful therefore from whence thou art fallen: and do penance, and do the first works. Or else I come to thee, and will move thy candlestick out of its place, except thou do penance. But this thou hast, that thou hatest the deeds of the Nicolaites, which I also hate. He, that hath an ear, let him hear what the Spirit saith to the churches: To him, that overcomes, I will give to eat of the tree of life, which is in the paradise of my God.

Lesson II ~ Apoc 2:8–11

And to the angel of the church of Smyrna write: These things saith the First and the Last, who was dead, and is alive: I know thy tribulation and thy poverty, but thou art rich: and thou art blasphemed by them that say they are Jews and are not, but are the synagogue of Satan. Fear none of those things which thou shalt suffer. Behold, the devil will cast some of you into prison that you may be tried: and you shall have tribulation ten days. Be thou faithful until death: and I will give thee the crown of life. He, that hath an ear, let him hear what the Spirit saith to the churches: He that shall overcome, shall not be hurt by the second death.

Lesson III ~ Apoc 2:12–17

And to the angel of the church of Pergamus write: These things, saith he, that hath the sharp two edged sword: I know where thou dwellest, where the seat of Satan is: and thou holdest fast my name, and hast not denied my faith. Even in those days when Antipas was my faithful witness, who was slain among you, where Satan dwelleth. But I have against thee a few things: because thou hast there them that hold the doctrine of Balaam, who taught Balac to cast a stumbling-block before the children of Israel, to eat, and to commit fornication: So hast thou also them that hold the doctrine of the Nicolaites. In like manner do penance: if not, I will come to thee quickly, and will fight against them with the sword of my mouth. He, that hath an ear, let him hear what the Spirit saith to the churches: To him that overcomes, I will give the hidden manna, and will give him a white counter, and in the counter, a new name written, which no man knoweth, but he that receiveth it.

Lesson IV

Sermon by St. Bernard, Abbot

Mary was espoused to Joseph, or rather, as says the Evangelist Luke: "To a man whose name was Joseph." He is called a man, not because he was her husband, but because he was a person of manliness. And again, the same is said by the Evangelist Matthew, to wit: "Joseph the husband of Mary:" and: "Joseph her man:" for he rightly calls Joseph by this title of manliness, for so Joseph was expected to be, that his virtuous manhood might be given in marriage to Mary. And we must conclude that he is here called what he was, a man; and further, that he was called her man because it was necessary that he should be publicly accepted as her man. And likewise, he was found worthy to be called the father of the Saviour, not that he was, but that he was publicly accepted as such, as the Evangelist himself saith: "And Jesus himself began to be about thirty years of age, being (as it was supposed) the son of Joseph."

Lesson V

Without doubt, good and faithful was this Joseph who espoused the Mother of the Saviour. Yea, I say unto you, he is that faithful and wise servant whom the Lord hath made ruler over his household. For the Lord appointed him to be the comfort of his Mother, the keeper of his own body, and, in a word, his chief and most trusty helper on earth in the carrying out the eternal counsels. Add to this that he is said to have been of the house of David, as he verily was. For this Joseph was a true son of a race of kings, noble in descent, nobler yet in mind. A true son of David, not so much according to the flesh as in faith, holiness, and devotion. Whom, like another David, the Lord found to be a man after his own heart, to whom he therefore safely entrusted the most hold and hidden secret of his heart. To whom also, like another David, he showed the uncertain and hidden things of his wisdom, and granted that he should not be ignorant of a mystery which was known to none of the princes of this world.

Lesson VI

Lastly, there was given to him not only to see and hear him whom many kings desired to see yet saw not, and to hear yet heard not, but even to carry him in his arms, to kiss him with his lips, to clothe him and to guard him. We must believe that Mary too, like Joseph, was descended from the house of David. For she would not have been espoused to a man of the house of David, if she had not herself been of the house of David. Both therefore were of the house of David. But in Mary the truth, which the Lord had sworn to David, was fulfilled; whereas to Joseph it was therefore given to know and bear witness unto the fulfillment of the promise.

Lesson VII

From the Holy Gospel according to St. Luke (Luke 3:21–23)

At that time: When all the people were baptized, it came to pass, that Jesus also being baptized and praying, the heaven was opened. And so on.

Homily by St. Ambrose, Bishop

That Matthew should trace the lineage of Christ through Solomon, and Luke through Nathan, would seem to indicate that the one desires to show the royalty of Christ's descent, and the other the priestliness thereof. We need not infer from this that one is more accurate than the other. On the contrary, each agrees with the other, with an equal good faith and veracity. For he was indeed, according to the flesh, of both a royal and a priestly family, a King sprung from kings, a Priest from priests. But the voice from heaven is speaking of divine things rather than of human. So then, as it is written: "The King shall rejoice in God:" that is, in God's strength, from which come to him the judgments of his royal Father; and likewise, he is that Priest of whom it is written: "Thou art a Priest for ever after the order of Melchisedech."

Lesson VIII

Therefore both Evangelists keep well within the truth. For Matthew does establish descent through the kings; whereas Luke, by tracing through the priests the lineage transmitted to Christ from God, manifests his more sacred origin. And from this we perceive the significance of the symbol used for this Evangelist; namely, the sacrificial calf, for everywhere he brings forth the mystery of the sacrificial priesthood. Nor need it surprise us that Luke gives many more generations from Abraham to Christ than does Matthew, since we can recognize that the line of descent is led through different persons. It may be that some lived long lives, whilst persons of the other line died young. For we are used to seeing many old men living with their grandchildren, and others dying soon after the birth of their children.

Lesson IX

We notice also a further difference. Saint Matthew says that Jacob, the son of Mathan, was the father of Joseph. Whereas Luke says that Joseph, to whom Mary was espoused, was the son of Heli, and that Heli was the son of Mathat. How then could Joseph have had two fathers, that is Heli and Jacob? Perchance he is called the son of two men, because one was his father according to nature, whereas the other became his father according to the Law. The particulars of the Law regarding the raising up of seed to a dead brother were not understood by the Jewish people as a promise to us that the seed of the dead should be perpetuated forever. But insofar as they read it only according to the letter, they failed to grasp its revelation of spiritual truth. For the living brother that raised up seed unto his dead brother, is not to be considered a brother after the flesh, but only according to the purity of his motives. And on that account, perchance we read: "But no man may deliver his brother, nor make agreement unto God for him (for it cost more to redeem their souls, so that he must let that alone for ever): yea, though he live long, and see not the grave." For the man Christ Jesus was not our natural brother, but the Mediator between God and man, whereby he has engendered in us the grace of the resurrection unto perpetual life.

Day 7 in the Octave of St. Joseph

~ Tuesday III after Easter ~

Semiduplex

Lesson I ~ Apoc 4:1–5

From the book of the Apocalypse of St. John the Apostle

After these things I looked, and behold a door was opened in heaven, and the first voice which I heard, as it were, of a trumpet speaking with me, said: Come up hither, and I will shew thee the things which must be done hereafter. And immediately I was in the spirit: and behold there was a throne set in heaven, and upon the throne one sitting. And he that sat, was to the sight like the jasper and the sardine stone; and there was a rainbow round about the throne, in sight like unto an emerald. And round about the throne were four and twenty seats; and upon the seats, four and twenty ancients sitting, clothed in white garments, and on their heads were crowns of gold. And from the throne proceeded lightnings, and voices, and thunders; and there were seven lamps burning before the throne, which are the seven spirits of God.

Lesson II ~ Apoc 4:6–8

And in the sight of the throne was, as it were, a sea of glass like to crystal; and in the midst of the throne, and round about the throne, were four living creatures, full of eyes before and behind. And the first living creature was like a lion: and the second living creature like a calf: and the third living creature, having the face, as it were, of a man: and the fourth living creature was like an eagle flying. And the four living creatures had each of them six wings; and round about and within they are full of eyes. And they rested not day and night, saying: Holy, holy, holy, Lord God Almighty, who was, and who is, and who is to come.

Lesson III ~ Apoc 4:9–11

And when those living creatures gave glory, and honour, and benediction to him that sitteth on the throne, who liveth for ever and ever; The four and twenty ancients fell down before him that sitteth on the throne, and adored him that liveth for ever and ever, and cast their crowns before the throne, saying: Thou art worthy, O Lord our God, to receive glory, and honour, and power: because thou hast created all things; and for thy will they were, and have been created.

Lesson IV

Sermon by St. Bernard, Abbot

It is written: "Joseph, her husband, being a just man, and not willing to make her a public example, was minded to put her away privately." Being a just man, he was rightly unwilling to expose her. For as he would not have been a just man if he had connived at known guilt, so he would have been even less just if he had condemned proven innocence. "Being a just man," therefore, "and not willing to make her a public example, he was minded to put her away privately." Why did he wish to put her away? On this point hear, not my opinion, but that of the Fathers. Perchance Joseph wished to put her away for the same reason of reverence that made Peter seek to put away the Lord, when he said: "Depart from me, for I am a sinful man, O Lord:" just as the centurion also sought to keep the Lord away from his house, when he said: "Lord, I am not worthy that thou shouldst come under my roof."

Lesson V

In like manner Joseph may have held himself to be sinful and unworthy, in such a way that he thought he ought no longer to enjoy the familiar companionship of her whose marvelous dignity filled him with awe. Perchance he saw and trembled at the unmistakeable signs of the divine presence; and, since he could not fathom the mystery, he was minded to put her away. Peter trembled at the greatness of the divine power. The Centurion trembled at the presence of the divine Majesty. Joseph too, being but a man, was filled with awe at the strangeness of this mystery. Dost thou wonder that Joseph judged himself unworthy of the companionship of this pregnant Virgin, when thou hearest that Saint Elizabeth too was filled with reverence and trembling at her presence? For she said: "Whence is this to me, that the Mother of my Lord should come to me?"

Lesson VI

And so Joseph was minded to put her away. But why privately, and not publicly? Lest perhaps enquiry should be made about this separation, and he should be asked for reasons. What should a just man reply to a stiff-necked people, a faithless and perverse generation? If he were to have said what he thought, and what he had proved, concerning her purity, would not all the cruel and unbelieving amongst the Jews have soon laughed him to scorn, and stoned her to death? How would they have believed in the Truth lying silent in her womb, when they afterwards despised the Truth preaching in the temple? What would they have done to him before his appearance in the flesh, when afterwards they laid impious hands on him in spite of his signs and wonders? The just man, therefore, was right in wishing to put her away privately, lest he should be thought to lie, or to defame an innocent woman.

Lesson VII

From the Holy Gospel according to St. Luke (Luke 3:21–23)

At that time: When all the people were baptized, it came to pass, that Jesus also being baptized and praying, the heaven was opened. And so on.

Homily by St. John Damascene

Matthew begins his Gospel with the words: "The book of the generation of Jesus Christ, the son of David, the son of Abraham." But he does not stop here. In fact, he continues his genealogy down to the very Spouse of the Virgin. Luke, on the other hand, after relating the manifestation of the Saviour at his baptism, makes a digression in his account, and writes thus: "And Jesus himself began to be about thirty years of age, being (as was supposed) the son of Joseph, which was the son of Heli, which was the son of Mathat:" and so on, in an ascending line, going up even to Seth: which was the son of Adam, which was the Son of God. Thus after reckoning up Joseph's genealogy in this fashion, we are shown clearly at the same time how Mary, the Virgin Mother of God, was herself also of the same lineage as Joseph. For the Mosaic Law straitly forbade marriages between the different tribes, in order that the hereditary rights of one tribe might not pass into another.

Lesson VIII

Note that there was good reason for these following things: namely, that the birth of Christ by the power of the Holy Ghost was kept secret from the people; and that Joseph stood to Jesus in the place of a father; and that on that account, as was truly fitting, he was counted the father of the Child. Otherwise, it would have seemed that the Child had no father, because he had no recorded descent from his father's side. Wherefore it was of the utmost importance that the Evangelists should record Joseph's lineage. Had they not done so, but had given the Child's lineage on his mother's side, they would have done unseemly, and gone contrary to the usage of divine Scripture. It was therefore fitting that they should give the lineage of Joseph from David, for the reason which we have already given of the kinship between her and her husband. They thereby attest that the Virgin Mary was of the lineage of David.

Lesson IX

It is indeed clear to all that Joseph was endowed with righteousness, and led a life in accordance with the Law. Therefore, living by what the Law prescribed, he certainly would not marry a wife sprung from any other but his own tribe. If, then, Joseph belonged to the tribe of Judah, and came of the seed and family of David, is it not a matter of course that Mary should come from the same? Whence it is that her husband's descent is recorded. For if, according to the Apostle's saying, "the head of the woman is the man," does it not follow in consequence that when the descent of the head is registered, that of the body in included in that of the head? I think it is therefore clearly shown that the Evangelists purposely chronicle Joseph's genealogy, so that, in consequence, it would be understood that the Virgin was also sprung of the family of David; thereby implying the surpassing wonder that it was the Christ, before all ages the Son of God, who was born of her.

Octave Day of St. Joseph

~ Wednesday III after Easter ~

Major Duplex

Lesson I ~ Apoc 5:1–7

From the book of the Apocalypse of St. John the Apostle

And I saw in the right hand of him that sat on the throne, a book written within and without, sealed with seven seals. And I saw a strong angel, proclaiming with a loud voice: Who is worthy to open the book, and to loose the seals thereof? And no man was able, neither in heaven, nor on earth, nor under the earth, to open the book, nor to look on it. And I wept much, because no man was found worthy to open the book, nor to see it. And one of the ancients said to me: Weep not; behold the lion of the tribe of Juda, the root of David, hath prevailed to open the book, and to loose the seven seals thereof. And I saw: and behold in the midst of the throne and of the four living creatures, and in the midst of the ancients, a Lamb standing as it were slain, having seven horns and seven eyes: which are the seven Spirits of God, sent forth into all the earth. And he came and took the book out of the right hand of him that sat on the throne.

Lesson II ~ Apoc 5:8–10

And when he had opened the book, the four living creatures, and the four and twenty ancients fell down before the Lamb, having every one of them harps, and golden vials full of odours, which are the prayers of saints: And they sung a new canticle, saying: Thou art worthy, O Lord, to take the book, and to open the seals thereof; because thou wast slain, and hast redeemed us to God, in thy blood, out of every tribe, and tongue, and people, and nation. And hast made us to our God a kingdom and priests, and we shall reign on the earth.

Lesson III ~ Apoc 5:11–14

And I beheld, and I heard the voice of many angels round about the throne, and the living creatures, and the ancients; and the number of them was thousands of thousands, Saying with a loud voice: The Lamb that was slain is worthy to receive power, and divinity, and wisdom, and strength, and honour, and glory, and benediction. And every creature, which is in heaven, and on the earth, and under the earth, and such as are in the sea, and all that are in them: I heard all saying: To him that sitteth on the throne, and to the Lamb, benediction, and honour, and glory, and power, for ever and ever. And the four living creatures said: Amen. And the four and twenty ancients fell down on their faces, and adored him that liveth for ever and ever.

Lesson IV

Sermon by St. Augustine, Bishop

The Angel did not speak falsely when he said to Joseph: "Fear not to take unto thee Mary thy wife." She is called wife because of the mutual confidence established between them at the time of her espousal, although he had not known her carnally, nor was he ever so to do. And the name of wife was not lost or rendered untrue because there had not been any carnal intercourse, and would not be in the future. She was, in fact, The Virgin; and therefore she was holier and a more wonderful source of joy to her husband just because she became a mother without a man's intervention. Thus he knew her to be like unto himself in faithfulness, unlike him as regards her offspring. On account of his faithful union, both of them merited the name of Christ's parents. And not only is she called his Mother, but he also is called his father, as being the husband of his Mother, not according to the flesh, but according to the spirit. But even though he was a father only in spirit, whilst she was Mother according to the flesh, yet they both were the parents of his humility, not of his glory; of his infirmity, not of his divinity.

Lesson V

For the Gospel does not lie when it says: "And Joseph and his Mother marvelled at those things which were spoken of him." And in another place: "His parents went to Jerusalem every year." And a little further on: "And his Mother said unto him; Son, why hast thou done so to us? Behold thy father and I have sought thee sorrowing." But, to show that apart from them, he had a Father who begat him without a mother, he answered them: "How is it that you sought me? Did you not know that I must be about my father's business?" And to the contrary, lest anyone might think that by these words he denied his parents, the Evangelist immediately adds: "And they understood not the saying which he spoke unto them; and he went down with them, and came to Nazareth, and was subject unto them." To whom was he subject but to his parents? And who was thus subject but Jesus Christ, who, being in the form of God, thought it not robbery to be equal to God?

Lesson VI

Why therefore was he subject to them who were so far below the form of God, except that he humbled himself, taking upon himself the form of a servant, of which form they were the parents? But truly, neither of them would have attained unto the parenthood of this form of a servant, except they had become respectively husband and wife, albeit without any carnal intercourse. And hence, when the ancestors of Christ are recounted in direct line of succession, the genealogy was fittingly traced down to Joseph. Otherwise, it would have been a slur upon the male sex, which is to be accorded the greater dignity. At the same time the truth did not suffer, for both Joseph and Mary were of the seed of David, from which it was prophesied that Christ should come. Note how thus all the good things of marriage are found in these parents of Christ: offspring, fidelity, the marriage bond. The offspring we know, was the Lord Jesus himself; their fidelity is proved because there was no adultery; the marriage bond, because there was no divorce.

Lesson VII

From the Holy Gospel according to St. Luke (Luke 3:21–23)

At that time: When all the people were baptized, it came to pass, that Jesus also being baptized and praying, the heaven was opened. And so on.

Homily by St. Augustine, Bishop

The day of his baptism is, as it were, a second birthday of the Saviour. For we know that he was born with signs and wonders like to those of his baptism, and that in the latter is a great mystery like to his birth. For God says: "This is my beloved Son, in whom I am well pleased." This second birth is indeed more glorious than the first. For then, he was born in silence, and without witnesses. Now, the Lord is baptized with a proclamation of his divinity. Then, Joseph, who was thought to be his father, denied that he was. Now, his true Father, who was not believed to be so, proclaims himself so to be. Then the Mother was enduring suspicion, because no father was acknowledged. Now she that bore him is honored because the Divinity makes him known as his Son.

Lesson VIII

I say that the second birth was more glorious than the first. For, now the God of majesty proclaims himself as his father. Then the carpenter Joseph was so accounted. And although it was the Holy Ghost through whom the Lord was born and baptized, yet the Father, whose voice was heard from heaven, is greater than the father who labored on earth. Therefore Joseph the workman on earth was thought to be the father of the Lord and Saviour. But God, the true Father of our Lord Jesus Christ, is also a workman, and cannot be excluded from those who work at the carpenter's trade.

Lesson IX

For he is the artificer who has wrought the fabric of this world with power not only wondrous but ineffable. Like a wise architect has he erected the heavens on high; he has laid the foundations of the earth; he has constrained the sea within its beaches. He is the artificer who, in due measure, lowers the pinnacles of pride and brings to the surface the bedrock of humility. He is the artificer who does chip off the unnecessary substance in our behavior, and preserves whatever is useful. He is the artificer whose axe, as John the Baptist warns us, is laid to the root of our tree. So every tree, which measures not up to his standard of due growth, is cut down at the roots, and used as fuel for the fire. But that which measures up rightly, according to his rule and standard, is squared and fitted by his divine workmanship.

Thursday III after Easter

Lesson I - Apoc 15:1–4

From the book of the Apocalypse of St. John the Apostle

And I saw another sign in heaven, great and wonderful: seven angels having the seven last plagues. For in them is filled up the wrath of God. And I saw as it were a sea of glass mingled with fire, and them that had overcome the beast, and his image, and the number of his name, standing on the sea of glass, having the harps of God: And singing the canticle of Moses, the servant of God, and the canticle of the Lamb, saying: Great and wonderful are thy works, O Lord God Almighty; just and true are thy ways, O King of ages. Who shall not fear thee, O Lord, and magnify thy name? For thou only art holy: for all nations shall come, and shall adore in thy sight, because thy judgments are manifest.

Lesson II - Apoc 15:5–8

And after these things I looked; and behold, the temple of the tabernacle of the testimony in heaven was opened: And the seven angels came out of the temple, having the seven plagues, clothed with clean and white linen, and girt about the breasts with golden girdles. And one of the four living creatures gave to the seven angels seven golden vials, full of the wrath of God, who liveth for ever and ever. And the temple was filled with smoke from the majesty of God, and from his power; and no man was able to enter into the temple, till the seven plagues of the seven angels were fulfilled.

Lesson III ~ Apoc 16:1–6

And I heard a great voice out of the temple, saying to the seven angels: Go, and pour out the seven vials of the wrath of God upon the earth. And the first went, and poured out his vial upon the earth, and there fell a sore and grievous wound upon men, who had the character of the beast; and upon them that adored the image thereof. And the second angel poured out his vial upon the sea, and there came blood as it were of a dead man; and every living soul died in the sea. And the third poured out his vial upon the rivers and the fountains of waters; and there was made blood. And I heard the angel of the waters saying: Thou art just, O Lord, who art, and who wast, the Holy One, because thou hast judged these things: For they have shed the blood of saints and prophets, and thou hast given them blood to drink; for they are worthy.

Friday III after Easter

Lesson I ~ Apoc 19:1–5

From the book of the Apocalypse of St. John the Apostle

After these things I heard as it were the voice of much people in heaven, saying: Alleluia. Salvation, and glory, and power is to our God. For true and just are his judgments, who hath judged the great harlot which corrupted the earth with her fornication, and hath revenged the blood of his servants, at her hands. And again they said: Alleluia. And her smoke ascendeth for ever and ever. And the four and twenty ancients, and the four living creatures fell down and adored God that sitteth upon the throne, saying: Amen; Alleluia. And a voice came out from the throne, saying: Give praise to our God, all ye his servants; and you that fear him, little and great.

Lesson II ~ Apoc 19:6–10

And I heard as it were the voice of a great multitude, and as the voice of many waters, and as the voice of great thunders, saying, Alleluia: for the Lord our God the Almighty hath reigned. Let us be glad and rejoice, and give glory to him; for the marriage of the Lamb is come, and his wife hath prepared herself. And it is granted to her that she should clothe herself with fine linen, glittering and white. For the fine linen are the justifications of saints. And he said to me: Write: Blessed are they that are called to the marriage supper of the Lamb. And he saith to me: These words of God are true. And I fell down before his feet, to adore him. And he saith to me: See thou do it not: I am thy fellow servant, and of thy brethren, who have the testimony of Jesus. Adore God. For the testimony of Jesus is the spirit of prophecy.

Lesson III - Apoc 19:11–16

And I saw heaven opened, and behold a white horse; and he that sat upon him was called faithful and true, and with justice doth he judge and fight. And his eyes were as a flame of fire, and on his head were many diadems, and he had a name written, which no man knoweth but himself. And he was clothed with a garment sprinkled with blood; and his name is called, the Word of God. And the armies that are in heaven followed him on white horses, clothed in fine linen, white and clean. And out of his mouth proceedeth a sharp two edged sword; that with it he may strike the nations. And he shall rule them with a rod of iron; and he treadeth the winepress of the fierceness of the wrath of God the Almighty. And he hath on his garment, and on his thigh written: King of Kings, and Lord of Lords.

Saturday III after Easter

Lesson I - Apoc 22:1–7

From the book of the Apocalypse of St. John the Apostle

And he showed me a river of water of life, clear as crystal, proceeding from the throne of God and of the Lamb. In the midst of the street thereof, and on both sides of the river, was the tree of life, bearing twelve fruits, yielding its fruits every month, and the leaves of the tree were for the healing of the nations. And there shall be no curse any more; but the throne of God and of the Lamb shall be in it, and his servants shall serve him. And they shall see his face: and his name shall be on their foreheads. And night shall be no more: and they shall not need the light of the lamp, nor the light of the sun, because the Lord God shall enlighten them, and they shall reign for ever and ever. And he said to me: These words are most faithful and true. And the Lord God of the spirits of the prophets sent his angel to show his servants the things which must be done shortly. And, Behold I come quickly. Blessed is he that keepeth the words of the prophecy of this book.

Lesson II - Apoc 22:8–12

And I, John, who have heard and seen these things. And after I had heard and seen, I fell down to adore before the feet of the angel, who showed me these things. And he said to me: See thou do it not: for I am thy fellow servant, and of thy brethren the prophets, and of them that keep the words of the prophecy of this book. Adore God. And he saith to me: Seal not the words of the prophecy of this book: for the time is at hand. He that hurteth, let him hurt still: and he that is filthy, let him be filthy still: and he that is just, let him be justified still: and he that is holy, let him be sanctified still. Behold, I come quickly; and my reward is with me, to render to every man according to his works.

Lesson III - Apoc 22:13–21

I am Alpha and Omega, the first and the last, the beginning and the end. Blessed are they that wash their robes in the blood of the Lamb: that they may have a right to the tree of life, and may enter in by the gates into the city. Without are dogs, and sorcerers, and unchaste, and murderers, and servers of idols, and every one that loveth and maketh a lie. I Jesus have sent my angel, to testify to you these things in the churches. I am the root and stock of David, the bright and morning star. And the spirit and the bride say: Come. And he that heareth, let him say: Come. And he that thirsteth, let him come: and he that will, let him take the water of life, freely. For I testify to every one that heareth the words of the prophecy of this book: If any man shall add to these things, God shall add unto him the plagues written in this book. And if any man shall take away from the words of the book of this prophecy, God shall take away his part out of the book of life, and out of the holy city, and from these things that are written in this book. He that giveth testimony of these things, saith, Surely I come quickly: Amen. Come, Lord Jesus. The grace of our Lord Jesus Christ be with you all. Amen.

Sunday IV after Easter

Semiduplex

Lesson I - Jas 1:1–6

Beginning of the Catholic Epistle of St. James the Apostle

James the servant of God, and of our Lord Jesus Christ, to the twelve tribes which are scattered abroad, greeting. My brethren, count it all joy, when you shall fall into diverse temptations; Knowing that the trying of your faith worketh patience. And patience hath a perfect work; that you may be perfect and entire, failing in nothing. But if any of you want wisdom, let him ask of God, who giveth to all men abundantly, and upbraideth not; and it shall be given him. But let him ask in faith, nothing wavering.

Lesson II - Jas 1:6–11

For he that wavereth is like a wave of the sea, which is moved and carried about by the wind. Therefore let not that man think that he shall receive any thing of the Lord. A double minded man is inconstant in all his ways. But let the brother of low condition glory in his exaltation: And the rich, in his being low; because as the flower of the grass shall he pass away. For the sun rose with a burning heat, and parched the grass, and the flower thereof fell off, and the beauty of the shape thereof perished: so also shall the rich man fade away in his ways.

Lesson III - Jas 1:12–16

Blessed is the man that endureth temptation; for when he hath been proved, he shall receive a crown of life, which God hath promised to them that love him. Let no man, when he is tempted, say that he is tempted by God. For God is not a tempter of evils, and he tempteth no man. But every man is tempted by his own concupiscence, being drawn away and allured. Then when concupiscence hath conceived, it bringeth forth sin. But sin, when it is completed, begetteth death. Do not err, therefore, my dearest brethren.

Lesson IV

From the exposition by St. Cyprian, Bishop & Martyr, on the good of patience

In speaking of patience, beloved brethren, and in preaching on its benefits and advantages, how can I better begin than by pointing out the fact that now, just for you to listen to me, I see that patience is necessary, as you could not even do this, namely, listening and learning, without patience. For only then is the word of God and way of salvation effectively learned, if one listens with patience to what is being said. Dearly beloved brethren, there are diverse paths of heavenly wisdom, wherein we are invited to walk, if we would reach in the end the reward which God has prepared to crown hope and faith; but I find no path more useful toward life nor more sure toward glory than this: that while we humbly strive, in all fear and godliness, to obey the commandments of the Lord, we should set our chiefest guard in an unceasing watch over our patience. The philosophers also say that they take this path, but their patience is as much a sham as their wisdom is a cheat, for who can be wise or patient who knows nothing of God's wisdom or God's patience?

Lesson V

But as for us, dearly beloved brethren, we are the real philosophers, whose wisdom lies not in words but in deeds, and is manifested not in dress but in the truth. We are they whose knowledge has the inward consciousness, not the idle boasting, of strength. We are not speakers of high-sounding words, but our lives. Yea, God is Himself the Source, the Fountain, and the Greatness of patience, and it befits man to love what is beloved of God. That good thing which he loves is commended unto him by God's Majesty. If God be our Lord and Father, let us follow after the example of our Lord and Father's patience, since it is the duty of servants to be obedient, and of sons to not be degenerate.

Lesson VI

By our patience God draws us toward Himself, and keeps us His Own. Patience does soothe anger, bridle the tongue, govern the mind, keep peace, set rules of self-control, break the onset of lust, still the swelling of temper, put out the fire begotten of hatred, make the rich meek, and relieve the need of the poor. Patience guards in virgins their blessed wholeness, in widows their careful purity, in such as be married their single-hearted love one toward the other. Patience teaches the prosperous to be humble, the unfortunate to be brave, and all to be gentle when they are wronged and insulted. Patience makes a man soon to forgive them that trespass against him, and if he have trespassed against any, long and humbly to ask his pardon. Patience fights down temptations, bears persecution, and endures unto the end in suffering and in uplifting of our testimony. Patience is the moat that guards the stout foundations of the castle of our faith.

Lesson VII

From the Holy Gospel according to St. John (John 16:5–14)

At that time, Jesus said unto His disciples: I go My way to Him That sent Me, and none of you asketh Me: Whither goest Thou? And so on.

Homily by St. Augustine, Bishop

The Lord Jesus told His disciples what things they should suffer after that He was gone away from them, and then He said: "These things I said not unto you at the beginning, because I was with you; but now I go My way to Him That sent Me." Let us first see whether it had been that He had not told them before this what they were to suffer in time coming. That He had done so amply before the night of the last Supper, is testified by the three first Evangelists, but it was when that Supper was ended that, according to John, He said: "These things I said not unto you at the beginning, because I was with you."

Lesson VIII

Are we then to try and loose the knot of this difficulty by asserting that, according to these three Evangelists, it was on the eve of the Passion, albeit before the Supper, that He had said these things unto them, and therefore not at the beginning, when He was with them, but when He was about to leave them, and go His way to the Father? And in this way we might reconcile the truthfulness of what this Evangelist says here "These things I said not unto you at the beginning" with the truthfulness of the other three. But this explanation is rendered impossible by the Gospel according to Matthew, who tells us how that the Lord spoke to His Apostles concerning their sufferings to come, not only when He was on the point of eating the Passover with them, but at the very beginning, when the names of the twelve are first given, and they were sent forth to do the work of God.

Lesson IX

It would seem then that when He said: "These things I said not unto you at the beginning, because I was with you," He meant by "these things," not the sufferings which they were to bear for His sake, but His promise of the Comforter Who should come to them, and testify while they suffered. This Comforter then, or Advocate (for the Greek word *Parakletos* will bear either interpretation), would be needful to them when they saw Christ no more, and therefore it was that Christ spoke not of Him "at the beginning" while He Himself was with His disciples, because His visible Presence was then their sufficient comfort.

Monday IV after Easter

Lesson I ~ Jas 1:17–20

From the Catholic Epistle of St. James the Apostle

Every best gift, and every perfect gift, is from above, coming down from the Father of lights, with whom there is no change, nor shadow of alteration. For of his own will hath he begotten us by the word of truth, that we might be some beginning of his creatures. You know, my dearest brethren. And let every man be swift to hear, but slow to speak, and slow to anger. For the anger of man worketh not the justice of God.

Lesson II ~ Jas 1:21–24

Wherefore casting away all uncleanness, and abundance of naughtiness, with meekness receive the ingrafted word, which is able to save your souls. But be ye doers of the word, and not hearers only, deceiving your own selves. For if a man be a hearer of the word, and not a doer, he shall be compared to a man beholding his own countenance in a glass. For he beheld himself, and went his way, and presently forgot what manner of man he was.

Lesson III ~ Jas 1:25–27

But he that hath looked into the perfect law of liberty, and hath continued therein, not becoming a forgetful hearer, but a doer of the work; this man shall be blessed in his deed. And if any man think himself to be religious, not bridling his tongue, but deceiving his own heart, this man's religion is vain. Religion clean and undefiled before God and the Father, is this: to visit the fatherless and widows in their tribulation: and to keep one's self unspotted from this world.

Tuesday IV after Easter

Lesson I ~ Jas 2:1–4

From the Catholic Epistle of St. James the Apostle

My brethren, have not the faith of our Lord Jesus Christ of glory with respect of persons. For if there shall come into your assembly a man having a golden ring, in fine apparel, and there shall come in also a poor man in mean attire, And you have respect to him that is clothed with the fine apparel, and shall say to him: Sit thou here well; but say to the poor man: Stand thou there, or sit under my footstool: Do you not judge within yourselves, and are become judges of unjust thoughts?

Lesson II ~ Jas 2:5–9

Hearken, my dearest brethren: hath not God chosen the poor in this world, rich in faith, and heirs of the kingdom which God hath promised to them that love him? But you have dishonoured the poor man. Do not the rich oppress you by might? and do not they draw you before the judgment seats? Do not they blaspheme the good name that is invoked upon you? If then you fulfill the royal law, according to the Scriptures, Thou shalt love thy neighbour as thyself; you do well. But if you have respect to persons, you commit sin, being reproved by the law as transgressors.

Lesson III ~ Jas 2:10–13

And whosoever shall keep the whole law, but offend in one point, is become guilty of all. For he that said, Thou shalt not commit adultery, said also, Thou shalt not kill. Now if thou do not commit adultery, but shalt kill, thou art become a transgressor of the law. So speak ye, and so do, as being to be judged by the law of liberty. For judgment without mercy to him that hath not done mercy. And mercy exalteth itself above judgment.

Wednesday IV after Easter

Lesson I - Jas 2:14–17

From the Catholic Epistle of St. James the Apostle

What shall it profit, my brethren, if a man say he hath faith, but hath not works? Shall faith be able to save him? And if a brother or sister be naked, and want daily food: And one of you say to them: Go in peace, be ye warmed and filled; yet give them not those things that are necessary for the body, what shall it profit? So faith also, if it have not works, is dead in itself.

Lesson II - Jas 2:18–22

But some man will say: Thou hast faith, and I have works: show me thy faith without works; and I will show thee, by works, my faith. Thou believest that there is one God. Thou dost well: the devils also believe and tremble. But wilt thou know, O vain man, that faith without works is dead? Was not Abraham our father justified by works, offering up Isaac his son upon the altar? Seest thou, that faith did co-operate with his works; and by works faith was made perfect?

Lesson III - Jas 2:23–26

And the Scripture was fulfilled, saying: Abraham believed God, and it was reputed to him to justice, and he was called the friend of God. Do you see that by works a man is justified; and not by faith only? And in like manner also Rahab the harlot, was not she justified by works, receiving the messengers, and sending them out another way? For even as the body without the spirit is dead; so also faith without works is dead.

Thursday IV after Easter

Lesson I - Jas 3:1–3

From the Catholic Epistle of St. James the Apostle

Be ye not many masters, my brethren, knowing that you receive the greater judgment. For in many things we all offend. If any man offend not in word, the same is a perfect man. He is able also with a bridle to lead about the whole body. For if we put bits into the mouths of horses, that they may obey us, and we turn about their whole body.

Lesson II - Jas 3:4–6

Behold also ships, whereas they are great, and are driven by strong winds, yet are they turned about with a small helm, whithersoever the force of the governor willeth. Even so the tongue is indeed a little member, and boasteth great things. Behold how small a fire kindleth a great wood. And the tongue is a fire, a world of iniquity.

Lesson III - Jas 3:6–10

The tongue is placed among our members, which defileth the whole body, and inflameth the wheel of our nativity, being set on fire by hell. For every nature of beasts, and of birds, and of serpents, and of the rest, is tamed, and hath been tamed, by the nature of man: But the tongue no man can tame, an unquiet evil, full of deadly poison. By it we bless God and the Father: and by it we curse men, who are made after the likeness of God. Out of the same mouth proceedeth blessing and cursing. My brethren, these things ought not so to be.

Friday IV after Easter

Lesson I - Jas 4:1–4

From the Catholic Epistle of St. James the Apostle

From whence are wars and contentions among you? Are they not hence, from your concupiscences, which war in your members? You covet, and have not: you kill, and envy, and can not obtain. You contend and war, and you have not, because you ask not. You ask, and receive not; because you ask amiss: that you may consume it on your concupiscences. Adulterers, know you not that the friendship of this world is the enemy of God? Whosoever therefore will be a friend of this world, becomes an enemy of God.

Lesson II - Jas 4:5–10

Or do you think that the Scripture saith in vain: To envy doth the spirit covet which dwelleth in you? But he giveth greater grace. Wherefore he saith: God resisteth the proud, and giveth grace to the humble. Be subject therefore to God, but resist the devil, and he will fly from you. Draw nigh to God, and he will draw nigh to you. Cleanse your hands, ye sinners: and purify your hearts, ye double minded. Be afflicted, and mourn, and weep: let your laughter be turned into mourning, and your joy into sorrow. Be humbled in the sight of the Lord, and he will exalt you.

Lesson III - Jas 4:11–15

Detract not one another, my brethren. He that detracteth his brother, or he that judgeth his brother, detracteth the law, and judgeth the law. But if thou judge the law, thou art not a doer of the law, but a judge. There is one lawgiver, and judge, that is able to destroy and to deliver. But who art thou that judgest thy neighbour? Behold, now you that say: Today or tomorrow we will go into such a city, and there we will spend a year, and will traffic, and make our gain. Whereas you know not what shall be on the morrow. For what is your life? It is a vapour which appeareth for a little while, and afterwards shall vanish away. For that you should say: If the Lord will, and if we shall live, we will do this or that.

Saturday IV after Easter

Lesson I - Jas 5:1–6

From the Catholic Epistle of St. James the Apostle

Go to now, ye rich men, weep and howl in your miseries, which shall come upon you. Your riches are corrupted: and your garments are moth-eaten. Your gold and silver is cankered: and the rust of them shall be for a testimony against you, and shall eat your flesh like fire. You have stored up to yourselves wrath against the last days. Behold the hire of the labourers, who have reaped down your fields, which by fraud has been kept back by you, crieth: and the cry of them hath entered into the ears of the Lord of Sabaoth. You have feasted upon earth: and in riotousness you have nourished your hearts, in the day of slaughter. You have condemned and put to death the Just One, and he resisted you not.

Lesson II ~ Jas 5:7–11

Be patient therefore, brethren, until the coming of the Lord. Behold, the husbandman waiteth for the precious fruit of the earth: patiently bearing till he receive the early and latter rain. Be you therefore also patient, and strengthen your hearts: for the coming of the Lord is at hand. Grudge not, brethren, one against another, that you may not be judged. Behold the judge standeth before the door. Take, my brethren, for an example of suffering evil, of labour and patience, the prophets, who spoke in the name of the Lord. Behold, we account them blessed who have endured. You have heard of the patience of Job, and you have seen the end of the Lord, that the Lord is merciful and compassionate.

Lesson III ~ Jas 5:12–16

But above all things, my brethren, swear not, neither by heaven, nor by the earth, nor by any other oath. But let your speech be, yea, yea: no, no: that you fall not under judgment. Is any of you sad? Let him pray. Is he cheerful in mind? Let him sing. Is any man sick among you? Let him bring in the priests of the church, and let them pray over him, anointing him with oil in the name of the Lord. And the prayer of faith shall save the sick man: and the Lord shall raise him up: and if he be in sins, they shall be forgiven him. Confess therefore your sins one to another: and pray one for another, that you may be saved. For the continual prayer of a just man availeth much.

✠

Sunday V after Easter

Semiduplex

Lesson I ~ 1 Pet 1:1–5

Beginning of the first letter of St. Peter the Apostle

Peter, an apostle of Jesus Christ, to the strangers dispersed through Pontus, Galatia, Cappadocia, Asia, and Bithynia, elect, According to the foreknowledge of God the Father, unto the sanctification of the Spirit, unto obedience and sprinkling of the blood of Jesus Christ: Grace unto you and peace be multiplied. Blessed be the God and Father of our Lord Jesus Christ, who according to his great mercy hath regenerated us unto a lively hope, by the resurrection of Jesus Christ from the dead, Unto an inheritance incorruptible, and undefiled, and that can not fade, reserved in heaven for you, Who, by the power of God, are kept by faith unto salvation, ready to be revealed in the last time.

Lesson II ~ 1 Pet 1:6–12

Wherein you shall greatly rejoice, if now you must be for a little time made sorrowful in diverse temptations: That the trial of your faith (much more precious than gold which is tried by the fire) may be found unto praise and glory and honour at the appearing of Jesus Christ: Whom having not seen, you love: in whom also now, though you see him not, you believe: and believing shall rejoice with joy unspeakable and glorified; Receiving the end of your faith, even the salvation of your souls. Of which salvation the prophets have inquired and diligently searched, who prophesied of the grace to come in you. Searching what or what manner of time the Spirit of Christ in them did signify: when it foretold those sufferings that are in Christ, and the glories that should follow: To whom it was revealed, that not to themselves, but to you they ministered those things which are now declared to you by them that have preached the gospel to you, the Holy Ghost being sent down from heaven, on whom the angels desire to look.

Lesson III ~ 1 Pet 1:13–21

Wherefore having the loins of your mind girt up, being sober, trust perfectly in the grace which is offered you in the revelation of Jesus Christ, As children of obedience, not fashioned according to the former desires of your ignorance: But according to him that hath called you, who is holy, be you also in all manner of conversation holy: Because it is written: You shall be holy, for I am holy. And if you invoke as Father him who, without respect of persons, judgeth according to every one's work: converse in fear during the time of your sojourning here. Knowing that you were not redeemed with corruptible things as gold or silver, from your vain conversation of the tradition of your fathers: But with the precious blood of Christ, as of a lamb unspotted and undefiled, Foreknown indeed before the foundation of the world, but manifested in the last times for you, Who through him are faithful in God, who raised him up from the dead, and hath given him glory, that your faith and hope might be in God.

Lesson IV

From the Book written by St. Ambrose, Bishop, on faith in the Resurrection.

Since it was impossible that the Wisdom of God could die, and that which could not die could not rise from the dead, He took to Himself Flesh Which could die, that That Whose nature it was to die might die, and rise again. Neither was it possible that the resurrection of the dead should come otherwise than by man, "for since by man came death, by Man came also the resurrection of the dead." Man He rose since Man He died, Man was revived but God did the reviving. Man then, according to the Flesh, God now over all things. For now we know Christ no longer after the Flesh, but we owe it to the Flesh that we know Him as "become the First-fruits of them that slept" and the "Firstborn of the dead."

Lesson V

The first-fruits are of the same kind and nature as the other fruits, and they are brought as an offering to God to win His blessing, a holy offering made on behalf of all. Christ then is the First-fruits of them that sleep. But is He the First-fruits of only His own loved ones that fall asleep in Him, and lie as it were untouched by death, wrapt in a sweet slumber? Or is He the First-fruits of all the dead? But "as in Adam all die, even so in Christ shall all be made alive." So that, as in Adam were the first-fruits of the death wherein all die, even so in Christ were the first-fruits of the resurrection, wherein all rise again. But let no man be hopeless, neither let it be a grief to the righteous to remember that to rise again will be common to all men, when he looks for that day wherein the harvest of his life will nobly realize itself. All shall rise again, "but," as says the Apostle, "every man in his own order." The harvest of God's mercy will be for all, but in reward one man shall differ from another.

Lesson VI

I tell you how grievous an outrage against God it is not to believe in the resurrection. If we shall not rise again, then Christ died in vain, then Christ is not risen. For if He rose not for us, then He is plainly not risen, for He would have had no reason to rise again. In Him rose the world, in Him rose the heavens, in Him rose the earth. For there shall be "a new heaven, and a new earth." He needed not to rise for Himself, Whom the bands of death held not. For although He died as Man, yet was He free in the netherworld itself. Wouldest thou hear how free? "I am as a man that hath no strength, free among the dead." And well free was He, able to take up his life again at will, even as it is written: "Destroy this Temple, and in three days I will raise it up." And well free was He Who descended into hell only to redeem others therefrom.

Lesson VII

From the Holy Gospel according to St. John (John 16:23–30)

At that time, Jesus said unto His disciples: Amen, Amen, I say unto you: Whatsoever you shall ask the Father in My Name, He will give it you. And so on.

Homily by St. Augustine, Bishop

We have now to consider these words of the Lord: "Amen, Amen, I say unto you, Whatsoever you shall ask the Father in My Name, He will give it you." It has already been said in the earlier part of this discourse of the Lord, for the sake of some who ask the Father in Christ's Name and receive not, that whatsoever is asked, which tends not to salvation, is not asked in the Name of the Saviour. By the words "In My Name" we must not understand the vocalization of letters and syllables, but the meaning of what is said, the honest and true meaning.

Lesson VIII

Therefore, whosoever thinks of Christ as he ought not to think of the Only Son of God, such a one does not ask anything in Christ's Name, although he do actually utter letters and syllables to that effect, because by these sounds he means not the Real Christ, but a fancied being who has no existence except in the speaker's imagination. But on the other hand, whosoever thinks of Christ as he ought to think, the same asks in Christ's Name, and receives, provided only it be nothing against his own everlasting salvation but if it is good for him to receive, he receives. Some things are not given at once, but kept over till a more fitting season. Such is the true interpretation of the words "He will give it you" namely, that those things will be given which are good for them to ask. All the Saints also are heard when they ask for themselves, but not necessarily when they ask for their friends, or their enemies, or others, even as it is written, not simply "He will give it" but "He will give it you."

Lesson IX

Hitherto says the Lord, have you asked nothing in My Name? "Ask, and you shall receive, that your joy may be full." This their joy, whereof He says that it shall be full, is to be understood not of fleshly but of spiritual joy and when that joy is so great that it can be increased no more, then shall it without doubt be full. Whatsoever therefore we ask for the fulfilling of this joy (that is, if we thereby mean grace, if we ask for that life which is the really blessed one), that is a thing which it is right to ask in Christ's Name. If we ask anything else than this, we ask nothing, although we do actually ask something, because all things are nothing in comparison with this.

Rogation Monday – V after Easter

Lesson I

From the Holy Gospel according to St. Luke (Luke 11:5–13)

At that time Jesus said unto His disciples Which of you shall have a friend, and shall go unto him at midnight, and say unto him Friend, lend me three loaves. And so on.

Homily by St. Ambrose, Bishop

We gather from this commandment, among other things, that we ought to pray, not only by day, but also by night. Thou seest how that he which arose at midnight to ask three loaves of his friend, and endured in supplication, was not disappointed of that which he sought. Of what are these three loaves a figure, but of that our Mysterious Bread Which comes down from heaven? Thou seest that if thou lovest the Lord thy God, thou mayest win His bounty, not only for thyself, but for others likewise. And who can deserve more to be called our "Friend" than He Which gave His Own Body for us?

Lesson II

From this Friend it was that David asked bread at midnight, and received it, as he says "At midnight I rise to give thanks unto thee." Even thus did he obtain those loaves of spiritual nourishment which he still sets before us for our refreshment. How he asked it, we know from that he says "Every night wash I my bed [with tears]." He knew that there was no fear of waking

Him Who sleeps not. Therefore let us keep in mind the things which are written for our learning, and be instant in prayer both by day and by night, to ask pardon of our sins.

Lesson III

If David, who was such a Saint, and whose time was so taken up by the cares of a kingdom, praised the Lord seven times a day, and was always present with godly zeal at the morning and evening sacrifice, what ought we to do (who so much more ought to pray, as the weakness of our body and mind do so much oftener make us fall), that we, wearied with this pilgrimage, and worn out by the gradual waning of our earthly day, and the changes of life, that we, I say, may not be starved of that life-giving Bread Which strengthens man's heart? The Lord teaches us to be watchful, all of us, and not only at midnight, but always. For He comes in the evening, and the second watch, and in the third watch, and sees fit to knock. Blessed indeed are those servants whom the Lord, when He comes, shall find watching.

Rogation Tuesday ~ V after Easter

Lesson I ~ 1 Pet 4:1–7

From the first letter of St. Peter the Apostle

Christ therefore having suffered in the flesh, be you also armed with the same thought: for he that hath suffered in the flesh, hath ceased from sins: That now he may live the rest of his time in the flesh, not after the desires of men, but according to the will of God. For the time past is sufficient to have fulfilled the will of the Gentiles, for them who have walked in riotousness, lusts, excess of wine, revellings, banquetings, and unlawful worshipping of idols. Wherein they think it strange, that you run not with them into the same confusion of riotousness, speaking evil of you. Who shall render account to him, who is ready to judge the living and the dead. For, for this cause was the gospel preached also to the dead: that they might be judged indeed according to men, in the flesh; but may live according to God, in the Spirit. But the end of all is at hand.

Lesson II ~ 1 Pet 4:7–11

Be prudent therefore, and watch in prayers. But before all things have a constant mutual charity among yourselves: for charity covereth a multitude of sins. Using hospitality one towards another, without murmuring, As every man hath received grace, ministering the same one to another: as good stewards of the manifold grace of God. If any man speak, let him speak, as the words of God. If any man minister, let him do it, as of the power, which God administereth: that in all things God may be honoured through Jesus Christ: to whom is glory and empire for ever and ever. Amen.

Lesson III ~ 1 Pet 4:12–17

Dearly beloved, think not strange the burning heat which is to try you, as if some new thing happened to you; But if you partake of the sufferings of Christ, rejoice that when his glory shall be revealed, you may also be glad with exceeding joy. If you be reproached for the name of Christ, you shall be blessed: for that which is of the honour, glory, and power of God, and that which is his Spirit, resteth upon you. But let none of you suffer as a murderer, or a thief, or a railer, or a coveter of other men's things. But if as a Christian, let him not be ashamed, but let him glorify God in that name. For the time is, that judgment should begin at the house of God.

Rogation Wednesday & Vigil of the Ascension

Lesson I

From the Holy Gospel according to St. John (John 17:1–11)

At that time, Jesus lifted up His Eyes to heaven, and spoke these words: Father, the hour is come; glorify thy Son. And so on.

Homily by St. Augustine, Bishop

Our Lord, the Only-begotten and co-eternal Son of the Father, was able, if needed, in and from the form of a servant, to pray in silence, but He thus manifested Himself in prayer, remembering that He is our Teacher. Thus He made known unto us the prayer which He made for us since He was so great a Master that, not only His discourse to them, but His prayer to the Father for them, is edifying to His disciples. And if it was so for them who were there to hear, truly it is so for us also, for whose instruction it has been written down.

Lesson II

Wherefore, by these words: "Father, the hour is come, glorify thy Son," He shows that all time, and all whatsoever He does, or allows to be done, and the season wherein He will do or allow it, is alike ordained of Him Who is Himself not subject to time. Yea, all things which were then to come, or are yet to come now, have the reason why they should be, in the Wisdom of God, Which is Itself independent of all time. "The hour is come." We must not believe that that hour was brought on by the march of destiny, but was by ordination of God. No stars decreed irresistibly that the time was come for Christ to suffer; God forbid that the revolutions of His planets should force death on Him Who made them.

Lesson III

Come think that the glorification of the Son by the Father was that "He spared Him not, but delivered Him up for us all." But if we say that He was glorified by suffering, how much more shall we say that He was glorified by rising again While He suffered? His humility was more manifested than His glory, as witnesses the Apostle, where he says: "He humbled Himself, and became obedient unto death, even the death of the cross" Then he adds regarding His glorification: "Wherefore God also hath highly exalted Him, and given Him a Name which is above every name, that at the Name of Jesus every knee should bow, of things in heaven, and things in earth, and things under the earth and that every tongue should confess that our Lord Jesus Christ is in the glory of God the Father." This is the glorification of our Lord Jesus Christ, that glorification whose first rays dawned on the Resurrection morn.

ASCENSIONTIDE

ASCENSION THURSDAY

Duplex I Class

Lesson I ~ Acts 1:1–5

Beginning of the Acts of the Apostles

The former treatise I made, O Theophilus, of all things which Jesus began to do and to teach, Until the day on which, giving commandments by the Holy Ghost to the apostles whom he had chosen, he was taken up. To whom also he showed himself alive after his passion, by many proofs, for forty days appearing to them, and speaking of the kingdom of God. And eating together with them, he commanded them, that they should not depart from Jerusalem, but should wait for the promise of the Father, which you have heard (saith he) by my mouth. For John indeed baptized with water, but you shall be baptized with the Holy Ghost, not many days hence.

Lesson II ~ Acts 1:6–9

They therefore who were come together, asked him, saying: Lord, wilt thou at this time restore again the kingdom to Israel? But he said to them: It is not for you to know the times or moments, which the Father hath put in his own power: But you shall receive the power of the Holy Ghost coming upon you, and you shall be witnesses unto me in Jerusalem, and in all Judea, and Samaria, and even to the uttermost part of the earth. And when he had said these things, while they looked on, he was raised up: and a cloud received him out of their sight.

Lesson III ~ Acts 1:10–14

And while they were beholding him going up to heaven, behold two men stood by them in white garments. Who also said: Ye men of Galilee, why stand you looking up to heaven? This Jesus who is taken up from you into heaven, shall so come, as you have seen him going into heaven. Then they returned to Jerusalem from the mount that is called Olivet, which is nigh Jerusalem, within a sabbath day's journey. And when they were come in, they went up into an upper room, where abode Peter and John, James and Andrew, Philip and Thomas, Bartholomew and Matthew, James of Alpheus, and Simon Zelotes, and Jude the brother of James. All these were persevering with one mind in prayer with the women, and Mary the mother of Jesus, and with his brethren.

Lesson IV

Sermon by St. Leo, Pope

After the blessed and glorious Resurrection of our Lord Jesus Christ, wherein the Divine Power raised up in three days the true Temple of God Which the iniquity of the Jews had destroyed, God was pleased to ordain, by His Most Sacred Will, and in His Providence for our instruction and the profit of our souls, a season of forty days: the season which, dearly beloved brethren, ends on this day. During that season the bodily Presence of the Lord still lingered on earth, that the reality of the fact of His having risen again from the dead might be armed with all needful proofs. The death of Christ had troubled the hearts of many of His disciples. Their thoughts were sad when they remembered His agony upon the Cross, His giving up of the Ghost, and the laying in the grave of His lifeless Body, and a sort of hesitation had begun to weigh on them.

Lesson V

Hence the most blessed Apostles and all the disciples, who had been fearful at the finishing on the Cross, and doubtful of the trustworthiness of the resurrection, were so strengthened by the clear demonstration of the fact, that, when they saw the Lord going up into the height of heaven, they sorrowed not, nay they were even filled with great joy. And, in all verity, it was a great and unspeakable cause for joy to see the Manhood, in the presence of that the multitude of believers, exalted above all creatures even heavenly, rising above the ranks of the angelic armies and speeding Its glorious way where the most noble of the Archangels lie far behind, to rest no lower than that place where high above all principality and power, It takes Its seat at the right hand of the Eternal Father, Sharer of His throne, and Partaker of His glory, and still of the very human nature which the Son has taken upon Him.

Lesson VI

Therefore, dearly beloved brethren, let us also rejoice with worthy joy, for the Ascension of Christ is exaltation for us, and where the glory of the Head of the Church is passed in, there is the hope of the body of the Church called on to follow. Let us rejoice with exceeding great joy, and give God glad thanks. This day is not only the possession of Paradise made sure unto us, but in the Person of our Head we are actually begun to enter into the heavenly mansions above. Through the unspeakable goodness of Christ we have gained more than ever we lost by the envy of the devil. We, whom our venomous enemy thrust from our first happy home, we, being made of one body with the Son of God, have by Him been given a place at the right hand of the Father with Whom He lives and reigns, in the unity of the Holy Ghost, God, world without end. Amen.

Lesson VII

From the Holy Gospel according to St. Mark (Mark 16:14–20)

At that time, Jesus appeared unto the eleven disciples as they sat at meat, and upbraided them with their unbelief and hardness of heart, because they believed not them which had seen Him after He was risen. And so on.

Homily by Pope St. Gregory

I may be allowed to say that the disciples' slowness to believe that the Lord had indeed risen from the dead, was not so much their weakness as our strength. In consequence of their doubts, the fact of the Resurrection was demonstrated by many infallible proofs. These proofs we read and acknowledge. What then assures our faith, if not their doubt? For my part, I put my trust in Thomas, who doubted long, much more than in Mary Magdalene, who believed at once. Through his doubting, he came actually to handle the holes of the Wounds, and thereby closed up any wound of doubt in our hearts.

Lesson VIII

Now confirm to our minds the trustworthiness of the fact that our Lord did indeed rise again from the dead, it is well for us to remark one of the statements of Luke: "Eating together with them, He commanded them that they should not depart from Jerusalem." And a little afterward: "While they beheld, He was taken up, and a cloud received Him out of their sight." Consider these words, note well these mysteries. After "eating together with them He was taken up." He ate and ascended: that the fact of His eating might show the reality of the Body in Which He went up. But Mark tells us that before the Lord ascended into heaven, He upbraided His disciples; for their unbelief and hardness of heart. From this I know not why we should gather, but that the Lord then upbraided His disciples, for whom He was about to be parted in the body, to the end that the words which He spoke unto them as He left them might be the deeper imprinted on their hearts.

Lesson IX

When then, He had rebuked the hardness of their heart, what command did He give them? Let us hear. "Go into all the world and preach the Gospel to every creature." Was the Holy Gospel, then my brethren, to be preached to things insensate, or to brute beasts, that the Lord said to His disciples: "Preach the Gospel to every creature"? Nay, but by the words "every creature" we must understand man, in whom are combined qualities of all creatures. Being he has in common with stones, life in common with trees, feeling in common with beasts, understanding in common with angels. If, then, man has something in common with every creature, man is to a certain extent every creature. The Gospel, then, if it be preached to man only, is preached to every creature.

Friday within the Octave of the Ascension

Semiduplex

Lesson I ~ 2 Pet 1:1–4

Beginning of the second letter of St. Peter the Apostle

Simon Peter, servant and apostle of Jesus Christ, to them that have obtained equal faith with us in the justice of our God and Saviour Jesus Christ. Grace to you and peace be accomplished in the knowledge of God and of Christ Jesus our Lord: As all things of his divine power which appertain to life and godliness, are given us, through the knowledge of him who hath called us by his own proper glory and virtue. By whom he hath given us most great and precious promises: that by these you may be made partakers of the divine nature: flying the corruption of that concupiscence which is in the world.

Lesson II ~ 2 Pet 1:5–9

And you, employing all care, minister in your faith, virtue; and in virtue, knowledge; And in knowledge, abstinence; and in abstinence, patience; and in patience, godliness; And in godliness, love of brotherhood; and in love of brotherhood, charity. For if these things be with you and abound, they will make you to be neither empty nor unfruitful in the knowledge of our Lord Jesus Christ. For he that hath not these things with him, is blind, and groping, having forgotten that he was purged from his old sins.

Lesson III ~ 2 Pet 1:10–15

Wherefore, brethren, labour the more, that by good works you may make sure your calling and election. For doing these things, you shall not sin at any time. For so an entrance shall be ministered to you abundantly into the everlasting kingdom of our Lord and Saviour Jesus Christ. For which cause I will begin to put you always in remembrance of these things: though indeed you know them, and are confirmed in the present truth. But I think it meet as long as I am in this tabernacle, to stir you up by putting you in remembrance. Being assured that the laying away of this my tabernacle is at hand, according as our Lord Jesus Christ also hath signified to me. And I will endeavour, that you frequently have after my decease, whereby you may keep a memory of these things.

Lesson IV

Sermon by St. Leo, Pope

Dearly beloved brethren, that mysterious thing, our salvation, which the Maker of the universe thought worth purchasing with His Own Precious Blood, was aimed at by Him, in the dispensation of His humility, from the hour wherein He was born according to the flesh, till the moment when, at the end of the Passion, He cried on the Cross: "It is finished." Although from under the form of a servant many marks of His Divinity shone forth, yet, as a whole, the work of those three-and-thirty years was to manifest the verity of the Manhood Which the Son of God had taken into Himself. But when the suffering was all over, and the bands of death were broken (that death which had lost all his power by seeking to bind Him Who knew no sin), then was weakness changed into strength, mortality into immortality, insult into that glory which the Lord Jesus Christ, on so many occasions, made manifest by so many and infallible proofs, until the day came when that triumphant procession of victory, which He had led from the realms of shattered death, followed Him with unimaginable pomp into the heavens.

Lesson V

On the solemn Feast of the Passover the cause of our joy was that Christ was risen again. This day we rejoice because He is ascended up into heaven. We call to mind and justly celebrate that day whereon our lowly nature was, in the Person of Christ, borne up high above all the heavenly armies, above all the circles of Angels, beyond the heights of all the Powers, even to where Christ is sitting on the right hand of the Father. Our foundations are laid, and our house is built upon this succession of the works of God and His grace is made more wonderful by this, that, though the visible Object of worship is removed from among men, the faith of the Church does not grow weak, nor her hope wavering, nor her love cold.

Lesson VI

It is the backbone of a strong mind and the eye of a trusty soul, to believe unhesitatingly that which is not seen with the bodily eyes, and to centre all love where there can be no experimental knowledge. This it is which is the only thing we can have of godliness for how could a man be justified through faith, if the saving objects were objects of sight? There was a man who would not believe in the Resurrection of Christ until he had examined by sight, and touched the marks of the Passion in the Divine Body, and the Lord said to him "Because thou hast seen Me, thou hast believed blessed are they that have not seen, and yet have believed."

Lesson VII

From the Holy Gospel according to St. Mark (Mark 16:14–20)

At that time, Jesus appeared unto the eleven disciples as they sat at meat, and upbraided them with their unbelief and hardness of heart, because they believed not them which had seen Him after He was risen. And so on.

Homily by Pope St. Gregory

"He that believeth, and is baptized, shall be saved but he that believeth not shall be damned." Perchance some man will say within himself: "I have already believed, and therefore I shall be saved." Thou hast said well, if thou showest thy faith by thy works. He alone has a true faith whose life does not belie his confession. Hence it is that Paul says, regarding some who were falsely faithful: "They profess that they know God but in works they deny Him." And John likewise says: "He that saith, I know Him and keepeth not His commandments, is a liar."

Lesson VIII

Once, then, it so stands, it is to our lives we must look for proof of the reality of our faith. Then only are we truly Christ's faithful people when our works are the fulfillment of our profession. The day whereon we were baptized we bound ourselves to renounce all the works of the old enemy, and all his pomps. Therefore let every one of you now turn his inward eye upon his own behavior, and if, since his baptism, he has kept that promise which he made before it, let him know that he is in very truth one of Christ's faithful ones and let him rejoice.

Lesson IX

But if he has utterly broken his promise, if he has fallen away to work iniquity, and to lust after the pomps of the world, let us see if he now knows how to weep over his backsliding. By the merciful Judge that man is not punished as a perjurer who in the end tells the truth, even though he has first lied. Because Almighty God does, in His tender kindness, so receive our contrition, that, in His judgment, He declares us not guilty of that which we have done amiss.

Saturday within the Octave of the Ascension

Semiduplex

Lesson I - 2 Pet 3:1–7

From the second letter of St. Peter the Apostle

Behold this second epistle I write to you, my dearly beloved, in which I stir up by way of admonition your sincere mind: That you may be mindful of those words which I told you before from the holy prophets, and of your apostles, of the precepts of the Lord and Saviour. Knowing this first, that in the last days there shall come deceitful scoffers, walking after their own lusts, Saying: Where is his promise or his coming? for since the time that the fathers slept, all things continue as they were from the beginning of the creation. For this they are wilfully ignorant of, that the heavens were before, and the earth out of water, and through water, consisting by the word of God. Whereby the world that then was, being overflowed with water, perished. But the heavens and the earth which are now, by the same word are kept in store, reserved unto fire against the day of judgment and perdition of the ungodly men.

Lesson II - 2 Pet 3:8–13

But of this one thing be not ignorant, my beloved, that one day with the Lord is as a thousand years, and a thousand years as one day. The Lord delayeth not his promise, as some imagine, but dealeth patiently for your sake, not willing that any should perish, but that all should return to penance. But the day of the Lord shall come as a thief, in which the heavens shall pass away with great violence, and the elements shall be melted with heat, and the earth and the works which are in it, shall be burnt up. Seeing then that all these things are to be dissolved, what manner of people ought you to be in holy conversation and godliness? Looking for and hasting unto the coming of the day of the Lord, by which the heavens being on fire shall be dissolved, and the elements shall melt with the burning heat? But we look for new heavens and a new earth according to his promises, in which justice dwelleth.

Lesson III - 2 Pet 3:14–18

Wherefore, dearly beloved, waiting for these things, be diligent that you may be found before him unspotted and blameless in peace. And account the longsuffering of our Lord, salvation; as also our most dear brother Paul, according to the wisdom given him, hath written to you: As also in all his epistles, speaking in them of these things; in which are certain things hard to be understood, which the unlearned and unstable wrest, as they do also the other Scriptures, to their own destruction. You therefore, brethren, knowing these things before, take heed, lest being led aside by the error of the unwise, you fall from your own steadfastness. But grow in grace, and in the knowledge of our Lord and Saviour Jesus Christ. To him be glory both now and unto the day of eternity. Amen.

Lesson IV

Sermon by St. Leo, Pope

And so the seen Presence of our Redeemer in the Body was changed for an unseen Presence in the Sacraments, and hearing was given to the Church in place of seeing, that her faith, rightly so called, might be the more victorious and steadfast and that teaching, which the hearts of all her children are called on to hear, is a teaching enlightened by rays from heaven. This faith, strengthened by the Ascension of the Lord, and established by the gift of the Holy Ghost, neither bonds, nor imprisonment, nor exile, nor famine, nor fire, nor savage beasts, nor those forms of death, fine-wrought in cruelty, wherein they that persecute us are well skilled, have been able to scare. For this faith there have striven throughout the whole world, even unto the out-pouring of their blood, not men only, but women also, not little lads only, but tender maidens. This is the faith which hath cast out devils, healed diseases, raised the dead.

Lesson V

Hence even the blessed Apostles themselves, who had been comforted by so many miracles and taught by so many discourses, were sickened by the horrors of their Lord's Passion, and received but doubtfully the assurance of His Resurrection, till after the Lord's Ascension and then fared on so bravely, that all that had been fearful to them before became joyful then. The reason was that they had lifted up all their mind to think of the Divinity of Him Who sits at the right hand of the Father. They asked no longer for a seen Presence, when their spiritual eye had caught the fact that, even as, when He had come down to earth, He had not left His Father, so now that He was gone up into heaven, He had not left His disciples. So then it was, dearly beloved brethren, that the Son of man more excellently and more sacredly revealed Himself as the Son of God, when He had withdrawn Himself again into that glory which He had with the Father before the world was. In some unspeakable way He began to be more present in His Divinity, when He removed Himself farther from us in His Manhood.

Lesson VI

Then it was that a better instructed faith began intellectually to approach the idea of a Son equal to the Father, and no longer need to handle in Christ the bodily Matter, Which is of a nature in which He is inferior to the Father since, Its nature still remaining in the glorified Body, the faith of believers was summoned to that place where the Only-Begotten Son, Who is equal to the Father, is felt, not by the application of a bodily hand, but by the effort of a spiritual-minded intellect. Hence it was that after His Resurrection, when Mary Magdalene (in whom was there represented the Person of the whole Church), wished to handle the Lord, He said: "Touch Me not, for I am not yet ascended to My Father," that is, "I will no more that thy nearness to Me should be a nearness of body to Body, nor that thine experience of Me should henceforward be one proceeding from fleshly experiment for that, I appoint thee a higher world, I make ready for thee a nobler form of it than this after that I have ascended to My Father, a time will come when thou shalt indeed touch Me, but after a manner more perfect, more real than this, even a time when thou shalt lay hold on that which thou touchest not now, and believe that which thou seest not now."

Lesson VII

From the Holy Gospel according to St. Mark (Mark 16:14–20)

At that time, Jesus appeared unto the eleven disciples as they sat at meat, and upbraided them with their unbelief and hardness of heart, because they believed not them which had seen Him after He was risen. And so on.

Homily by Pope St. Gregory

"And these signs shall follow them that believe In My Name they shall cast out devils they shall speak with new tongues they shall take up serpents and if they drink any deadly thing, it shall not hurt them they shall lay hands on the sick, and they shall recover." My brethren, these signs do not follow us. Do we, then, not believe? Nay. The truth is, these things were needful when the Church was young. That she might grow by the increase of the faithful, she needed to be nourished with miracles. Even so we, when we plant a young tree, continually water and tend it till we see that it has taken firm root in the earth but when once it has taken firm root, it can grow of itself. Hence, Paul says of tongues: "Tongues are for a sign, not to them that believe, but to them that believe not."

Lesson VIII

We have a deeper matter of thought touching these signs and mighty works. It is the work of the holy Church to do every day spiritually that which the Apostles then did carnally. When her Priests, armed with the power of exorcism, lay their hands upon believers, and command evil spirits to dwell no longer in their souls, what is it they do but cast out devils? When Christ's faithful people themselves give up the language of their old life, and speak the wonderful works of God, the glory and power of their Maker, telling of them with all their strength, what is it they do then but speak with new tongues? When either the one or the other does by his exhortation charm the wickedness out of his neighbor's heart, what is it he does but take up serpents?

Lesson IX

When they hear the voice of temptation inviting to deadly sin, but are not drawn thereby to work iniquity, do they not then drink a deadly thing, and it does not hurt them? As often as they see their neighbor fainting in well-doing, and run to help him with all their might, so that their example braces the feeble life of the waverer, what do they but lay hands on the sick and they recover? And indeed, such miracles as these are the greatest miracles, which are spiritual: the greatest, for they bring health, not to the dying body, but to the immortal soul.

Sunday within the Octave of the Ascension

Semiduplex

Lesson I ~ 1 John 1:1–5

Beginning of the first letter of St. John the Apostle

That which was from the beginning, which we have heard, which we have seen with our eyes, which we have looked upon, and our hands have handled, of the word of life: For the life was manifested; and we have seen and do bear witness, and declare unto you the life eternal, which was with the Father, and hath appeared to us: That which we have seen and have heard, we declare unto you, that you also may have fellowship with us, and our fellowship may be with the Father, and with his Son Jesus Christ. And these things we write to you, that you may rejoice, and your joy may be full. And this is the declaration which we have heard from him, and declare unto you: That God is light, and in him there is no darkness.

Lesson II ~ 1 John 1:6–10

If we say that we have fellowship with him, and walk in darkness, we lie, and do not the truth. But if we walk in the light, as he also is in the light, we have fellowship one with another, and the blood of Jesus Christ his Son cleanseth us from all sin. If we say that we have no sin, we deceive ourselves, and the truth is not in us. If we confess our sins, he is faithful and just, to forgive us our sins, and to cleanse us from all iniquity. If we say that we have not sinned, we make him a liar, and his word is not in us.

Lesson III ~ 1 John 2:1–6

My little children, these things I write to you, that you may not sin. But if any man sin, we have an advocate with the Father, Jesus Christ the just: And he is the propitiation for our sins: and not for ours only, but also for those of the whole world. And by this we know that we have known him, if we keep his commandments. He who saith that he knoweth him, and keepeth not his commandments, is a liar, and the truth is not in him. But he that keepeth his word, in him in very deed the charity of God is perfected; and by this we know that we are in him. He that saith he abideth in him, ought himself also to walk, even as he walked.

Lesson IV

Sermon by St. Augustine, Bishop

Dearly beloved brethren, our Saviour is gone up from us into heaven, but let us not be troubled on earth. Let only our heart be there with Him, and we shall have peace here. Let us in heart thither ascend with Christ in the meanwhile, and when that glad day which He has promised comes, our body will follow. But we must know, my brethren, that there are some things that cannot ascend with Christ: pride cannot, nor covetousness, nor brutishness; no one of our diseases can ascend thither where our Healer is. And, therefore, if we would follow our Healer, we must needs leave our diseases and sins behind us. All such things tie us down, as it were, with bands, and hamper us in the meshes of a net of sins but, with God's help, we will say with the Psalmist: "Let us break their bands asunder," that we may be able honestly to say to the Lord: "Thou hast loosed my bonds, I will offer to thee the sacrifice of thanksgiving."

Lesson V

The Resurrection of the Lord is our hope, the Ascension of the Lord is our glorification. Today we keep the solemn holiday of the Ascension. If, therefore, our keeping of this holiday is to be a right, faithful, earnest, holy, godly keeping, we must in mind likewise ascend, and lift up our hearts unto the Lord. When we ascend we must not be high-minded, nor flatter ourselves with our good works, as though they were our own. We must lift up our hearts unto the Lord. When man's heart is lifted up, but not unto the Lord, such lifting-up is pride. To lift up the heart unto the Lord is to make the Most High our Refuge. Behold, my brethren, a great wonder. God is high, but if thou art lifted up He flees from thee, whereas, if thou humblest thyself, He comes down to thee. Wherefore? "The Lord is high, yet hath He respect unto the lowly but the proud He knoweth from afar." To the lowly He has respect, that He may raise them up; the proud He knows from afar, that He may thrust them down.

Lesson VI

Christ arose again, to give us hope that this mortal will yet put on immortality. He has assured against a hopeless death, and against the thought that death ends life. We were troubled eyen as touching the soul but Christ, arising from the grave, has assured to us the resurrection of the body also. Believe therefore, that thou mayest be made pure. First it behooves thee to believe, if by faith thou wouldest in the end worthily see God. And dost thou will to see God? Give ear to His own words "Blessed are the pure in heart, for they shall see God." Think first, then, how to purify thine heart; take from it whatsoever thou seest in it which displeases God.

Lesson VII

From the Holy Gospel according to St. John (John 15:26–27; 16:1–4)

At that time, Jesus said unto His disciples: When the Comforter is come, Whom I will send unto you from the Father, even the Spirit of truth, Which proceeds from the Father, He shall testify of Me. And so on.

Homily by St. Augustine, Bishop

The Lord Jesus, in that discourse which He addressed to His disciples after the Last Supper, when He was on the very eve of the Passion, when He was, as it were, about to go away and leave them in His bodily Presence, albeit in His spiritual Presence, He is with us always even unto the end of the world, in that discourse He exhorted them to bear patiently the persecution of wicked men, of whom He speaks as "the world," out of which world, nevertheless, He says that He has chosen even His disciples themselves, that they might know that it was by the grace of God that they were what they were, whereas it was by their own sins that they had been what they had been.

Lesson VIII

"If they have persecuted Me, they will also persecute you." Here He clearly points to the Jews, the persecutors both of Himself and of His disciples, so that we see that they which persecute His holy ones are as much citizens of the world of damnation as they which persecuted Himself. He says: "They know not Him That sent Me," and yet again, "They have hated both Me and My Father," that is to say, both the Sender and the Sent, the meaning of which words we have already treated in other discourses and with that He comes to the words "That the word might be fulfilled that is written in their law: 'They hated Me without a cause.' "

Lesson IX

Then says the Lord, as though in continuation "But when the Comforter is come, Whom I will send unto you from the Father, even the Spirit of truth, Which proceeds from the Father, He shall testify of Me. And you also shall bear witness, because you have been with Me from the beginning." What connection has this with the words: "Now have they both seen and hated both Me and My Father but that the word might be fulfilled that is written in their law 'They hated Me without a cause.' " Is it that when the Comforter is come, even the Spirit of truth, He will confound by irrefutable testimony them who have both seen and hated both God the Son and God the Father? Yea, indeed, some there were who had seen and still hated, whom the testimony of the Comforter converted to the faith which works by love.

Monday within the Octave of the Ascension

Semiduplex

Lesson I ~ 1 John 3:1–6

From the first letter of St. John the Apostle

Behold what manner of charity the Father hath bestowed upon us, that we should be called, and should be the sons of God. Therefore the world knoweth not us, because it knew not him. Dearly beloved, we are now the sons of God; and it hath not yet appeared what we shall be. We know, that, when he shall appear, we shall be like to him: because we shall see him as he is. And every one that hath this hope in him, sanctifieth himself, as he also is holy. Whosoever committeth sin committeth also iniquity; and sin is iniquity. And you know that he appeared to take away our sins, and in him there is no sin. Whosoever abideth in him, sinneth not; and whosoever sinneth, hath not seen him, nor known him.

Lesson II ~ 1 John 3:7–12

Little children, let no man deceive you. He that doth justice is just, even as he is just. He that committeth sin is of the devil: for the devil sinneth from the beginning. For this purpose, the Son of God appeared, that he might destroy the works of the devil. Whosoever is born of God, committeth not sin: for his seed abideth in him, and he can not sin, because he is born of God. In this the children of God are manifest, and the children of the devil. Whosoever is not just, is not of God, nor he that loveth not his brother. For this is the declaration, which you have heard from the beginning, that you should love one another. Not as Cain, who was of the wicked one, and killed his brother. And wherefore did he kill him? Because his own works were wicked: and his brother's just.

Lesson III ~ 1 John 3:13–18

Wonder not, brethren, if the world hate you. We know that we have passed from death to life, because we love the brethren. He that loveth not, abideth in death. Whosoever hateth his brother is a murderer. And you know that no murderer hath eternal life abiding in himself. In this we have known the charity of God, because he hath laid down his life for us: and we ought to lay down our lives for the brethren. He that hath the substance of this world, and shall see his brother in need, and shall shut up his bowels from him: how doth the charity of God abide in him? My little children, let us not love in word, nor in tongue, but in deed, and in truth.

Lesson IV

Sermon by St. John Chrysostom

Then Christ went up into heaven; He offered unto the Father the First-fruits of our nature, and the Father marveled at the offering, seeing the Majesty of the Priest and the Spotlessness of the oblation. He received the Sacrifice into His Own hands, He made It to sit upon His Throne, nay, more, He gave It a place at His Own Right Hand. Let us ask what nature was His Who heard the words: "Sit Thou at My right hand," what nature was His to Whom God said "Be Thou Partaker of My Throne?" It was the same nature as was his who heard the sentence "Dust thou art, and unto dust shalt thou return." Archangels beheld our nature upon the Throne of the Lord, refulgent with eternal glory.

Lesson V

It was not enough of glory for Him to be exalted above the heavens, nor to be ranked with angels but He was exalted above the heavens, He went up above the Cherubim, He ascended beyond the Seraphim, neither found He His rank beneath the Throne of the Lord of lords. Behold how high the heaven is above the earth, and the earth above hell, how high above the heaven is the heaven of heavens, how high above the heaven of heavens the Angels, above the Angels the Higher Powers, and above the Higher Powers the Throne of the Lord. Above all these has One of our nature been exalted, so that man, which had fallen so low that there was no farther fall for him, is now in place so high, that there is thence no ascending.

Lesson VI

Paul also, dwelling on this, says: "He That descended is the Same also That ascended up far above all heavens," even as he had said: "Now, that He ascended, what is it but that He also descended first into the lower parts of the earth." Learn hence Who it was That ascended, and with what nature He was exalted. And with this thought I wish to bring my sermon to an end. From the thought of that glorified Manhood let us learn with amazement what the goodness of God is that goodness which has crowned with an honor higher than which is none, and a glory greater than which is none, a Person Sharer of our nature, even That Person Which this day has taken the place which is His of right, above all things other than Himself.

Lesson VII

From the Holy Gospel according to St. Mark (Mark 16:14–20)

At that time, Jesus appeared unto the eleven disciples as they sat at meat, and upbraided them with their unbelief and hardness of heart because they believed not them which had seen Him after He was risen. And so on.

Homily by Pope St. Gregory

"So then, after the Lord Jesus had spoken unto them, He was received up into heaven, and sat on the right hand of God." We learn in the Old Testament that Elias was taken up into heaven. But this word "heaven" may mean either the terrestrial atmosphere, or the space external to the sphere of this planet. Of these the atmosphere closely surrounds the earth, and we call the birds "the fowls of the heaven," because we see them fly therein. It was only up into this that Elias was taken, that he might be carried off suddenly into some part of the earth, to us unknown, and there live in profound peace of body and soul, until the end of the world, when he will return and pay the debt of nature. For him, therefore, death waits but is not escaped. But our Redeemer made it not to wait for Him, but conquered it, and by rising again shattered it, and by His Ascension showed forth the glory of His Resurrection.

Lesson VIII

We must mark also, how that Elias was taken up in a chariot, as though to show plainly that for a mere man some outward help was needful. This help was given to him by Angels, as plainly appears, since it was impossible for one whom a weak nature yet weighed down earthward, to fly up even into the atmosphere. But of our Redeemer we read not that He was borne up in a chariot, or by Angels, since He by Whom all things were made, clearly rose above all things by His Own Power. He returned unto Him with Whom He was, and whither He returned, there He abode, for albeit as touching His Manhood He ascended up into heaven, yet, as touching His Divinity, He still comprehended both heaven and earth.

Lesson IX

But as the sale of Joseph by his brethren was a type of the sale of Christ, so were the translations of Henoch and Elias types of His Ascension. The Lord therefore had had forerunners and witnesses of His Ascension, the one before the Law, the other under the Law, that Himself might one day come, Who was able indeed to pass into the heavens. Hence also there is some difference to be observed in the manner wherein each was translated. Henoch was seen no more, for God took him; Elias was carried up by a whirlwind into heaven. He That came after them was not taken up, nor carried up, but went up through space by His Own Power.

Tuesday within the Octave of the Ascension

Semiduplex

Lesson I ~ 1 John 4:1–6

From the first letter of St. John the Apostle

Dearly beloved, believe not every spirit, but try the spirits if they be of God: because many false prophets are gone out into the world. By this is the spirit of God known. Every spirit which confesseth that Jesus Christ is come in the flesh, is of God: And every spirit that dissolveth Jesus, is not of God: and this is Antichrist, of whom you have heard that he comes, and he is now already in the world. You are of God, little children, and have overcome him. Because greater is he that is in you, than he that is in the world. They are of the world: therefore of the world they speak, and the world heareth them. We are of God. He that knoweth God, heareth us. He that is not of God, heareth us not. By this we know the spirit of truth, and the spirit of error.

Lesson II - 1 John 4:7–14

Dearly beloved, let us love one another, for charity is of God. And every one that loveth, is born of God, and knoweth God. He that loveth not, knoweth not God: for God is charity. By this hath the charity of God appeared towards us, because God hath sent his only begotten Son into the world, that we may live by him. In this is charity: not as though we had loved God, but because he hath first loved us, and sent his Son to be a propitiation for our sins. My dearest, if God hath so loved us; we also ought to love one another. No man hath seen God at any time. If we love one another, God abideth in us, and his charity is perfected in us. In this we know that we abide in him, and he in us: because he hath given us of his spirit. And we have seen, and do testify, that the Father hath sent his Son to be the Saviour of the world.

Lesson III - 1 John 4:15–21

Whosoever shall confess that Jesus is the Son of God, God abideth in him, and he in God. And we have known, and have believed the charity, which God hath to us. God is charity: and he that abideth in charity, abideth in God, and God in him. In this is the charity of God perfected with us, that we may have confidence in the day of judgment: because as he is, we also are in this world. Fear is not in charity: but perfect charity casteth out fear, because fear hath pain. And he that feareth, is not perfected in charity. Let us therefore love God, because God first hath loved us. If any man say, I love God, and hateth his brother; he is a liar. For he that loveth not his brother, whom he seeth, how can he love God, whom he seeth not? And this commandment we have from God, that he, who loveth God, love also his brother.

Lesson IV

Sermon by St. Maximus, Bishop

My holy brethren, you remember that I have likened the Saviour to that eagle, about which it is written in the Book of Psalms, "thy youth is renewed like the eagle's." There are many points of likeness. The eagle rises above ground, wings his way aloft, and mounts skyward; even so did the Saviour rise from the depth of the grave, mount up unto the exalted mansions of Paradise, and enter the heights of heaven. The eagle leaves below him the foul mists of earth, flies above, and drinks in health from a purer air; even so did the Lord leave below Him the filthy slough of sinners on earth, and rejoice Himself with the honesty of a purer life, when He soared again into His Own holy home.

Lesson V

In all ways, therefore, is the Saviour aptly likened to an eagle. But what can we make of this, that the eagle is a bird of prey, oft-times a plunderer. Even in this he is like to the Saviour. He bore off His prey, when He carried off from the jaws of hell to heaven the Manhood Which He had swooped to take to Himself, yea, when He led captive to a higher home him whom He had delivered from the mastership of another lord, namely the devil, even as it is written in the Prophet, "Thou hast ascended on high, Thou hast led captivity captive, Thou hast received gifts among men."

Lesson VI

"Thou hast ascended on high, Thou hast led captivity captive." O how nobly does the Prophet paint the Triumph of the Lord! We hear how that of old time, when kings marched in triumph, the procession of prisoners walked before the chariot of their conqueror. Lo, the Lord enters the heavens, not after, but amid a most glorious band of captives. That band are not led before His chariot, but themselves bear up their Saviour. In some mystic sense, when the Son of God bore to heaven the Son of man, captivity both led and was led.

Lesson VII

From the Holy Gospel according to St. Mark (Mark 16:14–20)

At that time, Jesus appeared unto the eleven disciples as they sat at meat, and upbraided them with their unbelief and hardness of heart because they believed not them which had seen Him after He was risen. And so on.

Homily by Pope St. Gregory

We must ponder the meaning of these words of Mark, "He sat on the right hand of God," and how that Stephen said, "Behold, I see the heavens opened, and the Son of man standing on the right hand of God." Why does Mark say that He sat, whereas Stephen testifies that he saw Him standing? But you know, my brethren, that to sit is for him that judges, to stand, for him that fights or helps.

Lesson VIII

Since therefore, our Redeemer is ascended up into heaven, and even now is Judge of all, beside that at the end of the world He will so come, therefore does Mark say that He sits where He has gone up, because we look for Him, after that His glorious Ascension, that He will come again at the end to be our Judge. But Stephen, while yet he was in the throes of the battle, saw Him That was helping him standing. Stephen on earth was overcoming the unbelief of his persecutors, but it was the grace of Him That is in heaven that fought in him all the while.

Lesson IX

"And they went forth and preached everywhere, the Lord working with them, and confirming the word with signs following." What are we to see in this, what are we to remember, but that obedience followed commandment, and signs obedience? But now, since, by the will of God, we have lightly run over our reading from the Gospel, it remains that we should say somewhat by way of reflection on this great Festival.

Wednesday within the Octave of the Ascension

Semiduplex

Lesson I ~ 2 John 1:1–5

Beginning of the second letter of St. John the Apostle

The ancient to the lady Elect, and her children, whom I love in the truth, and not I only, but also all they that have known the truth, For the sake of the truth which dwelleth in us, and shall be with us for ever. Grace be with you, mercy, and peace from God the Father, and from Christ Jesus the Son of the Father; in truth and charity. I was exceeding glad, that I found of thy children walking in truth, as we have received a commandment from the Father. And now I beseech thee, lady, not as writing a new commandment to thee, but that which we have had from the beginning, that we love one another.

Lesson II ~ 2 John 1:6–9

And this is charity, that we walk according to his commandments. For this is the commandment, that, as you have heard from the beginning, you should walk in the same: For many seducers are gone out into the world, who confess not that Jesus Christ is come in the flesh: this is a seducer and an antichrist. Look to yourselves, that you lose not the things which you have wrought: but that you may receive a full reward. Whosoever revolteth, and continueth not in the doctrine of Christ, hath not God. He that continueth in the doctrine, the same hath both the Father and the Son.

Lesson III ~ 2 John 1:10–13

If any man come to you, and bring not this doctrine, receive him not into the house nor say to him, God speed you. For he that saith unto him, God speed you, communicateth with his wicked works. Having more things to write unto you, I would not by paper and ink: for I hope that I shall be with you, and speak face to face: that your joy may be full. The children of thy sister Elect salute thee.

Lesson IV

Sermon by St. Gregory, Bishop of Nyssa.

The very thought of this day's Festival is great enough in itself, but the Prophet David has much inflamed our joyful enthusiasm by the Psalms. This noble Prophet has, as it were, gone out of himself, as though the body were a weight duller than his spirit could bear. He joins company with the Powers of heaven, and tells what they said when they went with the Lord heavenward, and cried in tones of command to those Angels who work on earth, and by whose heralding the Birth of the Incarnate One had been proclaimed "Lift up your gates, O you princes, and be you lifted up, you everlasting doors, and the King of glory shall come in."

Lesson V

He Who contains all things is everywhere, but for the sake of them which receive Him, He is pleased to make Himself a local

Presence which has bounds. Not only did He become a Man among men, but when conversing among Angels, He allows that title also to be given Him. The gatekeepers therefore ask "Who is this King of glory?" and it is answered them that He is "The Lord, strong and mighty, the Lord, mighty in battle," the Lord Whose work it had been to fight him who held mankind in bondage, and to "destroy him that had the power of death, that is, the devil" that now that dark enemy was trampled down, the race of men might claim freedom and peace.

Lesson VI

The keepers run to the gates, and bid the doors unfold, that the Lord may enter in to take again the glory which He had there among them before. But when they see Him, clad in the likeness of sinful flesh, they know Him not, even Him Who is red in His apparel, because that He has trodden Alone the winepress of human pain, and the blood is sprinkled upon His garments. Therefore they cry again to their fellows that bear Him company: "Who is this King of glory?" And they answer them no more: "The Lord, strong and mighty, the Lord mighty in battle" but "The Lord of hosts, the Lord Whose Own are become the kingdoms of the world, the Lord Who has made Himself the Head of all things, the Lord Who has made all things new." He is the King of glory!

Lesson VII

From the Holy Gospel according to St. Mark (Mark 16:14–20)

At that time, Jesus appeared unto the eleven disciples as they sat at meat, and upbraided them with their unbelief and hardness of heart because they believed not them which had seen Him after He was risen. And so on.

Homily by Pope St. Gregory

The first question we have to ask is why we read that Angels appeared at the time of the Birth of the Lord, but we read not that they appeared in white apparel whereas, when the Lord ascended into heaven, it is written that the angels which appeared were clad in white. "While they beheld, He was taken up, and a cloud received Him out of their sight. And while they looked steadfastly toward heaven, as He went up, behold, two men stood by them in white apparel." White raiment is an outward sign of solemn inward joy. That the occasion of God-made-Man entering into heaven was a great Festival for Angels, is the reason which we see why angels are specially named as robed in white at His Ascension, and not at His Birth. At the Birth of the Lord the Divinity was manifested veiled under the form of a servant, but at His Ascension the Manhood was seen exalted and white vestments are more apt to exaltation than humiliation.

Lesson VIII

Therefore were the angels bound to appear in white apparel at the

Ascension; at His Birth, He Who thought it not robbery to be equal with God was seen in the form in which He had humbled Himself; at His Ascension, the Manhood Which He had taken into God was seen glorified. Again, dearly beloved brethren, we must remember today, how that Christ has "blotted out the hand-writing that was against us," and reversed the sentence which doomed us to corruption. That same nature to which it was said, "Dust thou art, and unto dust shalt thou return," that same nature is His Who has this day ascended up into heaven. It is because of this ascension of our flesh that blessed Job, by a figure, calls the Lord a bird. The Jews could not understand the Mystery of the Ascension, and in view of this their unbelief, blessed Job said mystically "He knew not the path of the bird."

Lesson IX

The name of a bird is well given to the Lord, Who bodily soared up into heaven. And the path of that Bird knows no man who believes not in the Ascension into heaven. It is of this glorious occasion that the Psalmist says: "Who hast set thy glory above the heavens," and again "God is ascended with jubilee and the Lord with the sound of a trumpet." And yet again he says "Thou hast ascended on high, Thou hast led captivity captive." When Christ ascended up on high, He led captivity captive because by His Own incorruptibility He swallowed up our corruptibility. "He gave gifts unto men," because by sending the Spirit from above, He gave "to one, the word of wisdom to another, the word of knowledge to another, the working of miracles to another, the gifts of healing; to another, diverse kinds of tongues to another, the interpretation of tongues."

Octave Day of the Ascension

Major Duplex

Lesson I ~ Eph 4:1–8

From the letter of St. Paul the Apostle to the Ephesians

I therefore, a prisoner in the Lord, beseech you that you walk worthy of the vocation in which you are called, With all humility and mildness, with patience, supporting one another in charity. Careful to keep the unity of the Spirit in the bond of peace. One body and one Spirit; as you are called in one hope of your calling. One Lord, one faith, one baptism. One God and Father of all, who is above all, and through all, and in us all. But to every one of us is given grace, according to the measure of the giving of Christ. Wherefore he saith: Ascending on high, he led captivity captive; he gave gifts to men.

Lesson II ~ Eph 4:9–14

Now that he ascended, what is it, but because he also descended first into the lower parts of the earth? He that descended is the same also that ascended above all the heavens, that he might fill all things. And he gave some apostles, and some prophets, and other some evangelists, and other some pastors and doctors, For the perfecting of the saints, for the work of the ministry, for the edifying of the body of Christ: Until we all meet into the unity of faith, and of the knowledge of the Son of God, unto a perfect man, unto the measure of the age of the fulness of Christ; That henceforth we be no more children tossed to and fro, and carried about with every wind of doctrine by the wickedness of men, by cunning craftiness, by which they lie in wait to deceive.

Lesson III - Eph 4:15–21

But doing the truth in charity, we may in all things grow up in him who is the head, even Christ: From whom the whole body, being compacted and fitly joined together, by what every joint supplieth, according to the operation in the measure of every part, maketh increase of the body, unto the edifying of itself in charity. This then I say and testify in the Lord: That henceforward you walk not as also the Gentiles walk in the vanity of their mind, Having their understanding darkened, being alienated from the life of God through the ignorance that is in them, because of the blindness of their hearts. Who despairing, have given themselves up to lasciviousness, unto the working of all uncleanness, unto the working of all uncleanness, unto covetousness. But you have not so learned Christ; If so be that you have heard him, and have been taught in him.

Lesson IV

Sermon by St. Augustine, Bishop

Dearly beloved brethren, all the wonderful works which our Lord Jesus Christ did in this world, under the weakness of our nature, are profitable for us when He exalted His Manhood above the stars, He showed that heaven may open for a believer and while He, the Conqueror of death, went up into the heavenly mansions, He showed to him that overcomes, whither he also may follow. Therefore, the Ascension of the Lord is the seal of the Catholic Faith, which assures in us the hope of the gift which is yet to come to us, from a miracle whereof we already feel the fruits. Thus let everyone that is faithful, having already received so much, learn to hope for that which is promised, on the ground of that which he knows to have been given, and hold the goodness of God in times which have been, and times which now are, as a sure pledge of the same in times to come.

Lesson V

An earthly Body, then, is now lifted up above the heights of heaven. The Bones, Which but a little while before had lain within the narrow walls of the grave, have made their entry among the angelic hosts. Human nature has been given a place in the lap of immortality and therefore the Apostle whose account we have heard read, says "When He had spoken these things, while they beheld, He was taken up." While thou hearest these words, "taken up," thou must understand thereby the ministry of the angelic army whereby this Festival reveals to us the Mystery of Him who is both God and Man. United in One Person, we see Divine Power in Him who lifted up, and in Him Who was lifted up true Man.

Lesson VI

Therefore are utterly to be loathed those pestiferous teachings of Eastern falsehood, those brand-new inventions of ungodliness which dare to assert that He Who in One Person is both Son of God and Son of Man, has but one nature. On the one hand, if a man say that Christ is not Partaker of the Divine nature, he has denied the glory of his Maker. On the other, he who says that the Manhood is not of the nature of man, has denied the mercy of his Saviour. As touching these points, it is well-nigh impossible for an Arian to believe that the Gospel writers are any better than liars, since they distinctly assert in some places that the Son of God is equal, and, in others, that He is inferior, to the Father. Further, if a man be given over to this soul-slaying delusion of believing that our Saviour has only one nature, he must of necessity admit either that it was only God, or that it was only man who was crucified. But it was not so. If He had been of no nature but the Divine, He could not have suffered, and if He had been of no nature but the human, He could not have conquered death.

Lesson VII

From the Holy Gospel according to St. Mark (Mark 16:14–20)

At that time, Jesus appeared unto the eleven disciples as they sat at meat, and upbraided them with their unbelief and hardness of heart because they believed not them which had seen Him after He was risen. And so on.

Homily by Pope St. Gregory

The Prophet Habacuc also has spoken of the glory of Christ's Ascension in the words "The sun was lifted up on high, and the moon stood still in her habitation," Who is here signified by the Sun, if not the Saviour or by the Moon, if not the Church? Until the Lord was withdrawn from her sight (that is, by His Ascension), His Holy Church was pale before the hostile glare of the world, but after He was ascended, she waxed stronger, and distinctly shed forth the beams of that faith which had hitherto dwelt hiddenly in her. "The sun was lifted up, and the moon stood still in her habitation" when the Lord was gone away into heaven, His holy Church waxed stronger in her enlightening power.

Lesson VIII

Hence it is that Solomon has put into the mouth of the, (same) Church the words: "Behold, He comes leaping upon the mountains, skipping upon the hills!" These hills are his lofty and noble achievements. "Behold, He comes leaping upon the mountains." When He came to redeem us, He came, if I may so say, in leaps. My dearly beloved brethren, would you know what His leaps were? From heaven he leapt into the womb of the Virgin, from the womb into the manger, from the manger on to the Cross, from the Cross into the grave, and from the grave up to heaven. Lo, how the Truth made manifest in the Flesh did leap for our sakes, that He might draw us to run after Him for this end did He "rejoice, as a strong man to run a race," that we might passionately say: "Draw us after Thee; we will run after the savor of Thine ointments."

Lesson IX

Therefore, dearly beloved brethren, it behooves us in heart and mind thither to ascend, where we believe Him to have already ascended bodily. Let us fly earthly lusts: for us, who have a Father in heaven, let nothing be sweet below! And very much must we keep in our minds this thought, that He Which ascended up in peace, will return in dreadful Majesty; and will require from us with justice an account of our keeping of those commandments which He gave us in mercy. Let no man therefore reckon lightly this season which is given unto us that we may repent ourselves, nor be reckless touching the state of his soul; our Redeemer will be all the sterner, when He comes to judgment, as He has been wondrously long-suffering before.

Friday after the Octave of the Ascension

Lesson I - 3 John 1:1–4

Beginning of the third letter of St. John the Apostle

The ancient to the dearly beloved Gaius, whom I love in truth. Dearly beloved, concerning all things I make it my prayer that thou mayest proceed prosperously, and fare well as thy soul doth prosperously. I was exceedingly glad when the brethren came and gave testimony to the truth in thee, even as thou walkest in the truth. I have no greater grace than this, to hear that my children walk in truth.

Lesson II - 3 John 1:5–10

Dearly beloved, thou dost faithfully whatever thou dost for the brethren, and that for strangers, Who have given testimony to thy charity in the sight of the church: whom thou shalt do well to bring forward on their way in a manner worthy of God. Because, for his name they went out, taking nothing of the Gentiles. We therefore ought to receive such, that we may be fellow helpers of the truth. I had written perhaps to the church: but Diotrephes, who loveth to have the preeminence among them, doth not receive us. For this cause, if I come, I will advertise his works which he doth, with malicious words prating against us. And as if these things were not enough for him, neither doth he himself receive the brethren, and them that do receive them he forbiddeth, and casteth out of the church.

Lesson III - 3 John 1:11–14

Dearly beloved, follow not that which is evil, but that which is good. He that doth good, is of God: he that doth evil, hath not seen God. To Demetrius testimony is given by all, and by the truth itself, yea and we also give testimony: and thou knowest that our testimony is true. I had many things to write unto thee: but I would not by ink and pen write to thee. But I hope speedily to see thee, and we will speak mouth to mouth. Peace be to thee. Our friends salute thee. Salute the friends by name.

Lesson IV

Sermon by St. Augustine, Bishop

Dearly beloved brethren, if the Flesh wherein our Saviour trampled down the devil had not been of our nature, He would indeed have exercised Himself, but He would not have conquered for us. If the Body wherein He rose from the grave had not been of our nature, His Resurrection would not have affected our state. Whoso asserts this, that Christ has but one nature, he does not understand why Christ took Flesh upon Him; he confounds the order, and makes void the benefit of the Incarnation. If the Flesh wherein our Healer came was not sharer in human nature, then all that by His Birth He took from man would have been degradation. O, may such dangerous dreams be far from our thoughts! What He took is ours, what He gave is His. I testify that the first Adam, who fell, and the second Adam, Who rose from the dead, are both of the same human nature of which I am. I testify that What lay in the grave, and What ascended into heaven, is of the same human nature of which I am.

Lesson V

It was therefore just because His Body was of our nature, that Christ's Death has quickened us, His Resurrection raised us up, His Ascension sanctified us. It was just because His Body was of our nature, that His Presence in the heavenly kingdoms is a pledge that we also shall one day be there. Let us therefore strive, dearly beloved brethren, since the Lord has on this day gone up on high in a Body of our nature, to ascend ourselves as far as we can thither in hope, to follow Him with our heart. Let us ascend to Him in love, and speed keeping pace with love, even by our very sins and passions. If every one of us would strive to get above them, and accustom himself to tread on them, he might make of even them a stepping-stone to mount to higher things. Such things lift us up if they are underneath us.

Lesson VI

We make our vices a ladder if we tread them down. With the Author of goodness there ascended no spite with the Son of the Virgin, no lust or sensuality. I say vices do not follow to heaven the Father of perfection, sin the Holy One of God, neither weakness nor disease the Divine Healer. If therefore we would enter into the kingdom of that Healer, we must first take heed to our sores. We must so order and guard in us the mutual relations of our soul and body, that the soul, the nobler part of man, may not be dragged down to hell by her groveling companion, but may rather, being herself of a nature more glorious, bear with her to heaven at the last a sanctified body, by the help of Him Who lives and reigns for ever and ever. Amen.

Lesson VII

From the Holy Gospel according to St. John (John 15:26–27; 16:1–4)

At that time, Jesus said unto His disciples: When the Comforter is come, whom I will send unto you from the Father, even the Spirit of truth, Which proceedeth from the Father, He shall testify of Me. And so on.

Homily by St. Augustine, Bishop

Upon the day of Pentecost the Holy Ghost came down upon a congregation of a hundred and twenty men, among whom were all the Apostles. These men, after they had been filled with the Spirit, began to speak with the tongues of all nations, and many of the bystanders, amazed at the marvel, when they saw in the discourse of Peter how great and how Divine a witness was borne to the fact that the Christ, Whom they had murdered, and Whom they reckoned among the dead, had risen again and was alive, many of these bystanders were pricked in their heart and were converted. They received pardon from that noble Blood, Which they had so sacrilegiously and so brutally shed, seeing that that Blood had redeemed even Its Own out-pourers.

Lesson VIII

The Blood of Christ "Which is shed for many for the remission of sins" was so effectually shed, that It could remit even the very sin that shed It. Toward this looked the Lord when He said "They hated Me without a cause, but when the Comforter is come, Whom I will send unto you from the Father, He shall testify of Me." This was as though He had said They have hated Me and slain Me while they see Me, but when they shall see Me no more, the Comforter shall bear such testimony of Me, as will compel them to believe in Me. "And you also," says He, "shall bear witness, because you have been with Me from the beginning," the Holy Ghost shall bear witness, and you also shall bear witness. "Because you have been with Me from the beginning," you are able to speak that you do know, which you do not now, while as yet the fulness of the Spirit is not come upon you.

Lesson IX

He shall testify of Me and you also shall bear witness when the love of God is shed abroad in your hearts by the Holy Ghost Which shall be given unto you, and makes you unashamed to lift up your testimony. This love had not been so shed abroad in Peter's heart when he was frightened by the questioning of the maidservant, and could not bear witness to the truth, but broke his promise, and was driven by strong fear to deny Christ thrice. "There is no such fear in love; but perfect love casteth out fear." Before the Passion of the Lord, Peter's slavish fear was questioned by a bondwoman but after the Resurrection of the Lord, his free love was asked by the very Prince of freedom, and therefore the first questioning shook him, but under the second he was at peace; at the first he denied Him Whom he had loved, at the second he loved Him Whom he had denied. But, even so, his love was weak and narrow, until the Holy Ghost had strengthened and widened it.

Vigil of Pentecost

Vigil

Lesson I ~ Jude 1:1–4

Beginning of the letter of St. Jude the Apostle

Jude, the servant of Jesus Christ, and brother of James: to them that are beloved in God the Father, and preserved in Jesus Christ, and called. Mercy unto you, and peace, and charity be fulfilled. Dearly beloved, taking all care to write unto you concerning your common salvation, I was under a necessity to write unto you: to beseech you to contend earnestly for the faith once delivered to the saints. For certain men are secretly entered in (who were written of long ago unto this judgment), ungodly men, turning the grace of our Lord God into riotousness, and denying the only sovereign Ruler, and our Lord Jesus Christ.

Lesson II ~ Jude 1:5–8

I will therefore admonish you, though ye once knew all things, that Jesus, having saved the people out of the land of Egypt, did afterwards destroy them that believed not: And the angels who kept not their principality, but forsook their own habitation, he hath reserved under darkness in everlasting chains, unto the judgment of the great day. As Sodom and Gomorrha, and the neighbouring cities, in like manner, having given themselves to fornication, and going after other flesh, were made an example, suffering the punishment of eternal fire. In like manner these men also defile the flesh, and despise dominion, and blaspheme majesty.

Lesson III ~ Jude 1:9–13

When Michael the archangel, disputing with the devil, contended about the body of Moses, he durst not bring against him the judgment of railing speech, but said: The Lord command thee. But these men blaspheme whatever things they know not: and what things soever they naturally know, like dumb beasts, in these they are corrupted. Woe unto them, for they have gone in the way of Cain: and after the error of Balaam they have for reward poured out themselves, and have perished in the contradiction of Core. These are spots in their banquets, feasting together without fear, feeding themselves, clouds without water, which are carried about by winds, trees of the autumn, unfruitful, twice dead, plucked up by the roots, Raging waves of the sea, foaming out their own confusion; wandering stars, to whom the storm of darkness is reserved for ever.

Lesson IV

From the Treatise upon the Creed, addressed to Catechumens by St. Augustine, Bishop

We are yet the unborn offspring of a great Mother. Our Holy Mother the Church has by the most sacred sign of the Cross received you into her womb, and from thence she is now just about to bring you forth, as she has already brought forth your brethren, with thrills of spiritual joy. But until, through the washing of regeneration, she brings you forth into true light, she feeds you in her womb with such food as becomes your condition, and in gladness matures her children for the glad moment of her delivery. This Mother is not stricken by the doom of Eve, to bring forth children in sorrow, and they themselves more often weeping than laughing. Rather does your spiritual Mother annul the sentence of your earthly Eve, who by disobedience endowed her offspring with death; the Church, by obedience, gives them newness of life. All the mystic prayers and ceremonies which have been and are still being performed over you by the ministry of the servants of God, exorcisms, prayers, spiritual songs, onbreathings, haircloth, prostrations, baring of the feet, the dread which you feel, albeit so safe, all these things, I say unto you, are the nourishment which you are ever drawing from your Mother while yet you are in her womb, that at the baptismal birth she may be able to present you strong and laughing babes unto Christ.

Lesson V

We have also received the Creed, which is the shield of the travailing Mother against the venom of the dragon. In the Apocalypse of the Apostle John it is written "And the dragon stood before the woman which was ready to be delivered, for to devour her child as soon as it was born." That this dragon is the devil you all know. You know likewise that by the woman is signified the Virgin Mary, who, herself a Virgin, bore our Virgin Head, and who is revealed unto us as a type of the Holy Church, in that, even as Mary, though she bore a Son, remained a Virgin, so the Church does in all times give birth to all her members, and yet is ever presented a chaste virgin to Christ. I have undertaken, with the help of the Lord, to expound every clause of the Creed, that I may bring home to your understandings what each contains. Your hearts are ready, for the enemy has been shut out of your hearts.

Lesson VI

We have made profession of renouncing the enemy. At the moment of that profession it was not before men only, but in the presence of God and His Angels that you said: "I do renounce him." Renounce him, not only in your words but in your ways, not only with your voices but with your lives, not only with your lips but in your works. Know you well that the wrestling which you have undertaken is a strife with an enemy who is subtle, and old, and patient. Now that you have once renounced him, let him never again find in you his works; never again give him the right to bring you into bondage. O Christian thou wilt be caught and exposed, if thou dost one thing and profess another, if thou art faithful in name, and makest it to be evident by thy works that thou hast broken the faith pledged by this promise: if some while thou goest into a church to pray, and after to the shows to join in applauding obscenities. What hast thou to do any more with the pomps of the devil, which thou hast renounced?

Lesson VII

From the Holy Gospel according to St. John (John 14:15–21)

At that time, Jesus said unto His disciples: If ye love Me, keep My commandments. And I will pray the Father, and He shall give you another Comforter. And so on.

Homily by St. Augustine, Bishop

By these words of the Lord, "I will pray the Father, and He shall give you another Comforter," He does imply that Himself is a Comforter. The Greek word used, namely *Parakletos*, signifies also an Advocate, and is used in that sense where it is written "We have an Advocate (*Parakleton*) with the Father, Jesus Christ the Righteous." "Even the Spirit of truth, Whom the world cannot receive," because as we read elsewhere, "the carnal mind is enmity against God; for it is not subject to the law of God, neither indeed can it be" as we may say plainly nothing can make unrighteousness righteous. By "the world," in this place, we must understand the lovers of the world, a love which comes not of the Father. And therefore it is that this love of the world, which we strive to lessen and to destroy in ourselves, is contrary to "the love of God, which is shed abroad in our hearts by the Holy Ghost which is given unto us."

Lesson VIII

The world, therefore, cannot receive Him because it neither sees Him nor knows Him. For to love the world is to lack those spiritual eyes, which are able to see Him Who is invisible, the Holy Ghost. "But you know Him," says the Lord to His disciples, "for He shall dwell with you, and shall be in you." He will be in them so to dwell in them, not dwell in them so to be in them; for one must first be in a place before one dwell there. But lest the Apostles should think that the words, "He shall dwell with you," signified that He should visibly abide with them for a while, as do guests in the houses of men, the Lord says in explanation: "He shall be in you."

Lesson IX

Therefore is He seen That is invisible. If He were not in us we could have in us no knowledge of Him but He is seen in us, as we see our conscience. We see the faces of other men, but we cannot see our Own; but of consciences we see none save that within ourselves. But our conscience is never elsewhere but within us, whereas the Holy Ghost may be without us as well as within us. He is given to be within us, and, unless He be within us, we can neither see nor know Him, either within or without us. Then, after that He had promised the Holy Ghost, the Lord, lest they should deem that He was to give them that other Comforter instead of Himself, and that He Himself was to be no longer with them, said also "I will not leave you orphans, I will come to you." Therefore, although the Son of God has made us by adoption sons of His Own Father, and has willed that the Same Who is His Father by nature should be our Father by grace, nevertheless, He shows that He Himself has toward us a love as of a Father, where He says "I will not leave you orphans."

WHITSUNTIDE

PENTECOST SUNDAY or WHITSUN

Duplex I Class

Lesson I

From the Holy Gospel according to St. John (John 14:13–31)

At that time, Jesus said unto His disciples: If a man love Me, He will keep My word, and My Father will love him, and We will come unto him, and make Our abode with him. And so on.

Homily by Pope St. Gregory

Dearly beloved brethren, our best way will be to run briefly through the words which have been read from the Holy Gospel, and thereafter rest for a while quietly gazing upon the solemn subject of this great Festival. This is the day whereon "suddenly there came a sound from heaven," and the Holy Ghost descended upon the Apostles, and, for fleshly minds, gave them minds wherein the love of God was shed abroad and, while without "there appeared unto them cloven tongues, like as of fire, and it sat upon each of them," within, their hearts were enkindled. While they received the visible presence of God in the form of fire, the flames of His love enwrapped them. The Holy Ghost Himself is love whence it is that John says "God is love." Whosoever therefore loves God with all his soul, already has obtained Him Whom he loves, for no man is able to love God, if He has not gained Him Whom he loves.

Lesson II

But, behold, now, if I shall ask any one of you whether he loves God, he will answer with all boldness and quietness of spirit: "I do love him." But at the very beginning of this day's continuation of the Gospel, you have heard what the Truth says: "If a man love Me, he will keep My word." The test, then, of love, is whether it is showed by works. Hence the same John has said in his Epistle: "If a man say, I love God, and keepeth not His commandments, He is a liar." Then do we indeed love God, and keep His commandments, if we deny ourselves the gratification of our appetites. Whosoever still wanders after unlawful desires, such a one plainly loves not God, for he says "Nay" to that which God wills.

Lesson III

"And My Father will love him, and We will come unto him, and make Our abode with him." O my dearly beloved brethren, think what a dignity is that, to have God abiding as a guest in our heart! Surely if some rich man or some powerful friend were to come into our house, we would hasten to have our whole house cleaned, lest, perchance, when he came in, he should see aught to displease his eye. So let him that would make his mind an abode for God, cleanse it from all the filth of works of iniquity. Lo, again, what says the Truth: "We will come unto him, and make Our abode with him." There are some hearts whereunto God comes but makes not His abode, therein with a certain pricking they feel His Presence, but in time of temptation they forget that which has pricked them and so they turn again to work unrighteousness, even as though they had never repented.

Monday within the Octave of Pentecost

Duplex I Class

Lesson I

From the Holy Gospel according to St. John (John 3:16–21)

At that time, Jesus said unto Nicodemus: God so loved the world that He gave His Only-begotten Son, that whosoever believeth in Him should not perish, but have everlasting life. And so on.

Homily by St. Augustine, Bishop

The Physician comes that, as often as in him lies, he may heal the sick man. He is his own destroyer who will not keep the commandments of the Physician. Into the world came the Saviour. Why is He called the Saviour of the world, but because He came "into the world not to condemn the world, but that the world through Him might be saved"? If thou willest not be saved through Him, thou wilt be condemned of thyself. And why say I that thou wilt be condemned? Because it is written: "He that believeth in Him is not condemned." What then canst thou hope that He will say of "him that believeth not," but that He will be condemned? And indeed He does say farther: "He that believeth not is condemned already." He is condemned already, though the condemnation be not yet openly pronounced.

Lesson II

He is condemned already, for "the Lord knoweth them that are His." He knows them for whom is laid up the crown, and likewise them that are reserved unto the fire. His eye sees in the field of the world the distinction of the wheat and of the straw, of the good corn and of the tares. "He that believeth not is condemned already." And why?

"Because he hath not believed in the Name of the Only-begotten Son of God. And this is the condemnation that light is come into the world, and men loved darkness rather than light, because their deeds were evil." "Because their deeds were evil," but, my brethren, is there one man of whom God finds that his works are good? No, not one. God finds all works to be evil. How then do we hear that some there be who do truth, and come to the light? For these words come after: "But he that does truth, comes to the light."

Lesson III

But the Lord says: "They loved darkness rather than light." And here He makes the great point. There are many who have loved their sins, there are many who have confessed their sins, and he that confessed and denounces his sin is working already with God. God denounces thy sins, and if thou denounce them likewise, then dost thou join thyself with God in His act. The man and the sinner are two different things. God made the man, and the man made the sinner. Put away thy work, and God will save His. Thou art bound to hate in thyself thine own work, and to love God's work. When thine own works begin to displease thee, then is it that thou beginnest to do well, because thou denouncest thine own evil works. The first thing to do, if thou wouldest do good works, is to acknowledge thine evil ones.

Tuesday within the Octave of Pentecost

Duplex I Class

Lesson I

From the Holy Gospel according to St. John (John 10:1–10)

At that time: Jesus said unto the Pharisees: Amen, amen, I say unto you, he that entereth not by the door into the sheep-fold, but climbeth up some other way, the same is a thief and a robber but he that entereth by the door is the shepherd of the sheep. And so on.

Homily by St. Augustine, Bishop

In the words of the Gospel which are this day read, the Lord has spoken unto us in similitudes regarding His flock and the Door whereby entry is made into their fold. The Pagans therefore may say, "We have good lives," but if they enter not in the Door, what does that profit them whereof they make their boast? Good life is profitable to a man if it lead unto life everlasting, but if he does not have life everlasting, what shall his good life profit him? Neither indeed can it be truly said that they live good lives, who are either so blinded as not to know, or so puffed up as to despise, the end of a good life. And no man can have a true and certain hope of life everlasting, unless he know the true Life, Which is Christ, and enter in by that Door into the sheepfold.

Lesson II

There are many such, who try to persuade men to live good lives but not to be Christians. These are they who would fain "climb up some other way," "for to kill and to destroy," and are not as the Good Shepherd, Who is come to keep and to save. There have been philosophers who have treated many subtle questions of right and wrong, who have been the authors of many distinctions and definitions, who have completed many exceedingly clever arguments, who have filled many books, and have proclaimed their own wisdom with braying trumpets. These dared to say to men: "Follow us embrace our school of thought, and you will find therein the secret of a happy life." But these were not of them who enter in by the Door; they came not but for to steal, and to kill, and to destroy.

Lesson III

Touching these, what shall I say? Behold, the Pharisees themselves read of Christ, and therefore talked of Christ they looked for His coming, and when He came, they knew Him not. They boasted that they themselves were among the Seers, that is, of the wise ones, and they denied Christ, and entered not in by the Door. Therefore they, if they led away any, led them away only to kill and to destroy, not to free them. So much for them. Now let us see if all they who boast the name of Christian enter in by the Door. Some there are, and their number cannot be reckoned, who not only boast that they themselves are among the Seers but would gladly appear as though their hearts were enlightened by Christ, yet these are heretics.

Ember Wednesday in the Octave of Pentecost

Semiduplex

Lesson I

From the Holy Gospel according to St. John (John 6:44–52)

At that time, Jesus said unto the multitudes of the Jews: No man can come to Me, except the Father, Which hath sent me, draw him. And so on.

Homily by St. Augustine, Bishop

Think not that thou art drawn against thy will; the soul is drawn, not willingly only, but lovingly. Neither must we be afraid lest men who are great weighers of words, and very far from understanding the things of God, should catch us up upon this Gospel doctrine of the Holy Scriptures, and should say to us: How can my faith be willing if am drawn? I answer: Thou art not drawn as touching thy will, but by pleasure. And, now, what is being drawn by pleasure? Delight thyself in the Lord, and He shall give thee the desires of thy heart. There is pleasure in that heart to which the Bread That came down from heaven is sweet. The poet is allowed to say His special pleasure draws each, but pleasure, which so draws, is not a necessity, not a bond, but a delight how much more strongly, may we say that men are drawn to Christ, who delight in truth, who delight in blessedness, who delight in righteousness, who delight in life everlasting, since truth and blessedness, and righteousness and everlasting life are all to be found in Christ? Or have the bodily senses pleasure, and the spiritual senses none? If the spiritual sense have no pleasures, wherefore is it written: "And the children of men shall put their trust under the shadow of thy wings. They shall be abundantly satisfied with the fatness of thy house, and Thou shalt make them drink of the river of thy pleasures. For with thee is the fountain of life, and in thy light shall we see light?"

Lesson II

Give me a lover, and he will catch my meaning; give me one who longs, give me a hungerer, give me a wanderer in this desert, athirst and gasping for the fountains of the eternal Fatherland; give me such a one, and he will catch my meaning. If I talk to some cold creature, he will not. Such cold creatures were they of whom it is written: "The Jews then murmured at Him because He said, 'I am the Bread Which came down from heaven.' And they said: 'Is not this Jesus the son of Joseph, whose father and Mother we know? How is it then that He saith: I came down from heaven?' Jesus therefore answered and said unto them: 'Murmur not among yourselves. No man can come to Me, except the Father, Which hath sent Me, draw him.'" But why speaks Christ of them whom the Father draws, since He Himself draws. Why was it His will to say: "No man can come to Me except the Father draw him?" If we are to be drawn, let us be drawn by Him to Whom one that loved much said: "Draw me, we will run after the savor of thy good ointments." But let us consider, my brethren, what He meant, and understand it as well as we can. The Father draws to the Son them who believe in the Son, because they are persuaded that He has God to His Father. God the Father begets to Himself a coequal Son; and whosoever is persuaded, and realizes unto himself by faith and thinks that He in Whom he believes is equal to the Father, him the Father is drawing unto the Son.

Lesson III

Arius, who believed that the Son was made, was not one of them whom the Father draws since whosoever believes not that the Father is a Father by the begetting of a coequal Son, such a one knows not the Father. What sayest thou, O Arius? What sayest thou, O thou heretic? What is thy profession? What is Christ? He is not, says Arius, Himself True God. Then, O Arius, the Father has not drawn thee; thou hast not understood His dignity as a Father, to Whom thou deniest His Son. Thou dost deny the existence of the Son of God, the Father draws thee not, and thou art not drawn to the Son, since the Son of whom thou speakest is another son [existing only in thine imagination], and not the really existent Son. Photinus said: "Christ is a mere man, and not God at all." He who uttered those words was not one of them whom the Father draws. But whom has the

Father drawn? The Father drew him who said: "Thou art the Christ, the Son of the living God." Show a sheep a green bough, and thou drawest him. Let a boy see some nuts, and he is drawn by them. As they run, they are drawn, drawn by taste, drawn without bodily hurt, drawn by a line bound to their heart. If, then, among earthly things, such as be sweet and pleasant draw such as love them, as soon as they see them, so that it is truth to say, His special pleasure draws each, does not that Christ, Whom the Father has revealed, draw? What stronger object of love can a soul have than the Truth?

Thursday within the Octave of Pentecost

Semiduplex

Lesson I

From the Holy Gospel according to St. Luke (Luke 9:1–6)

At that time: Jesus called His twelve disciples together, and gave them power and authority over all devils, and to cure diseases. And so on.

Homily by St. Ambrose, Bishop

We learn from the commandments of the Gospel what manner of men they ought to be who preach the glad tidings of the kingdom of God: "Take nothing for your journey neither staves nor scrip, neither bread neither money." Thus let the Apostle, destitute of earthly help and panoplies, in faith deem himself able to do all the more, as he needs all the less. Such as please may also put upon these words a spiritual interpretation in that a man may be said to lay as the encumbrances of the body, not only by abdicating power, and casting away riches, but also by denying the very body itself its pleasures. The first general commandment given to the Apostles about their manners was to be bringers of peace, and to be no gadders about, but keepers of the laws of guests. To wander from house to house, and to abuse the rights of hospitality, are things alien to a preacher of the kingdom of heaven.

Lesson II

But as the kindness of hospitality is to be met with courtesy, so also is it said "Whosoever will not receive you, when you go out of that city, shake off the very dust from your feet, for a testimony against them." Hereby is it taught that hospitality meets with a good reward, since not only do we bring peace to such as receive us, but also, if they be shadowed by some earthly vanities, these defects are taken away, where enter the feet of them that bear the glad tidings of Apostolic preaching. It is well written in Matthew: "Into whatsoever city or town you shall enter, inquire who in it is worthy and there abide till you go thence" thus avoiding any possible need of going from house to house. But no such selection is commanded to him that gives hospitality, lest his hospitality itself should be lessened while he picks his guests.

Lesson III

This passage, taken according to the plain meaning, is a sacred commandment touching the religious duty of hospitality, but its heavenly words likewise hint at a mystery. When the house is chosen, it is asked if the master thereof be worthy. Let us see if this be not perchance a figure of the Church, and her Master, Christ. What worthier house can the Apostolic preacher enter, than the Holy Church? Or what host is more preferable before all others, than Christ, Whose use it is to wash the feet of His guests: Who suffers not that any whom He receives into His house should dwell there with foul feet, but, defiled as they are by their former wanderings, does vouchsafe to cleanse them whole and entire? He Alone is He, from Whose house no man ought ever to go forth, nor change His roof for any other shelter, for unto Him it is well said "Lord, to whom shall we go? Thou hast the words of eternal life, and we believe."

Ember Friday in the Octave of Pentecost

Semiduplex

Lesson I

From the Holy Gospel according to St. Luke (Luke 5:17–26)

At that time, it came to pass on a certain day, as Jesus sat and taught, that there were Pharisees, and Doctors of the law sitting by, which were come out of every town in Galilee, and Judaea and Jerusalem and the power of the Lord was present to heal them. And so on.

Homily by St. Ambrose, Bishop

"And, behold, men brought in a bed a man which was taken with a palsy." The healing of this paralytic was not idle, nor its fruits limited to himself. The Lord healed him, or ever he could ask, not because of the entreaties of others, but for example's sake. He gave a pattern to be followed, and sought not the intercession of prayer. In the presence of the Pharisees and doctors of the law, which were come out of every town of Galilee, and Judaea, and Jerusalem, many sick folk were healed, but among them is specially described the healing of this paralytic. First of all, as we have before said, every sick man ought to engage his friends to offer up prayers for his recovery, that so the tottering framework of this our life, and the distorted feet of our works, may be righted by the healing power of the word from heaven.

Lesson II

Here ought therefore to be advisers, who should rouse up the minds of the sick to higher things, since when the body becomes languid with sickness, the mind is apt to follow its example. With the help of such friends he can be brought and laid on the ground before the Feet of Jesus, and seem worthy of a glance from the Lord for the Lord looks upon such as lie lowly before Him, "for He hath regarded the lowliness of His handmaiden." "And when He saw their faith, He said unto him: Man, thy sins are forgiven thee." Great is the Lord, Who for the sake of some forgives the sins of others, Who tries some and pardons the wanderings of others. Why should thine equal, O man, avail not with thee, if a slave have won power to intercede, and right to obtain, with God?

Lesson III

O Thou that judgest, learn to forgive; thou that art sick, to pray. If thou doubt of the pardon of thy sins, because of their grievousness, get thee to the Church, that she may pray for thee, and that the Lord, accepting her countenance, may grant to her petitions what He refuses to thine. And although we are bound to accept this history as one of fact, and to believe that the body of the paralytic was healed yet remember thou also his inward cure, unto whom his sins were forgiven. The Jews said: "Who can forgive sins but God alone?" And in these words they confessed the Divinity of Him Who forgave the sins of the paralytic, and themselves condemned their own unbelief in Him Whose work they acknowledged, but Whose Person they denied.

Ember Saturday within the Octave of Pentecost

Semiduplex

Lesson I

From the Holy Gospel according to St. Luke (Luke 4:38)

At that time Jesus arose out of the synagogue, and entered into Simon's house. And Simon's wife's mother was taken with a great fever. And so on.

Homily by St. Ambrose, Bishop

Behold here how long-suffering is the Lord our Redeemer! Neither moved to anger against them, nor sickened at their guilt, nor outraged by their attacks, did He leave the Jews' country. Nay, forgetting their iniquity, and mindful only of His mercy, He strove to soften their hard and unbelieving hearts, sometimes by His teaching, and sometimes by freeing some of them, and sometimes by healing them. St. Luke does well to tell us first of the man who was delivered from an unclean spirit, and then of the healing of a woman. The Lord indeed came to heal both sexes, but that must be healed first which was created first, and then must not she be passed by whose first sin arose rather from fickleness of heart than from depraved will.

Lesson II

That the Lord began to heal on the Sabbath-day shows in a figure how that the new creation begins where the old creation ended. It shows, moreover, that the Son of God, Who is come not to destroy the law but to fulfill the law, is not under the law but above the law. Neither was it by the law, but by the Word, that the world was created, as it is written: "By the Word of the Lord were the heavens made." The law, then, is not destroyed, but fulfilled, in the Redemption of fallen man. Whence also the Apostle says: "Put off, concerning the former conversation, the old man, which is corrupt according to the deceitful lusts and be renewed in the spirit of your mind and put on the new man, which after God is created in righteousness and true holiness."

Lesson III

It was well that He began to heal on the Sabbath, that He might show Himself to be the Creator, weaving in one with another of His works, and continuing that which He had already begun, even as a workman, being to repair a house, begins not to take down that which is old from the foundations, but from the roof. Thus does the Lord begin to lay to His hand again, in that place whence last He has lifted it then He begins with things lesser, that He may go on to things greater. Even men are able to deliver other men from evil spirits, albeit with the word of God to command the dead to rise again is for God's power alone. Perchance, also, this woman, the mother-in-law of Simon and Andrew, was a type of our nature, stricken down with the great fever of sin, and burning with unlawful lusts after diverse objects. Nor would I say that the passion which rages in the mind is a lesser fire than that fever which burns the body. Covetousness, and lust, and uncleanness, and vain desires, and strivings, and anger; these be our fevers.

✠

TIME THROUGHOUT THE YEAR OR AFTER PENTECOST

TRINITY SUNDAY

Duplex I Class

Lesson I ~ Isa 6:1–4

From Isaias the Prophet

In the year that king Ozias died, I saw the Lord sitting upon a throne high and elevated: and his train filled the temple. Upon it stood the seraphims: the one had six wings, and the other had six wings: with two they covered his face, and with two they covered his feet, and with two they hew. And they cried one to another, and said: Holy, holy, holy, the Lord God of hosts, all the earth is full of his glory. And the lintels of the doors were moved at the voice of him that cried, and the house was filled with smoke.

Lesson II ~ Isa 6:5–8

And I said: Woe is me, because I have held my peace; because I am a man of unclean lips, and I dwell in the midst of a people that hath unclean lips, and I have seen with my eyes the King the Lord of hosts. And one of the seraphims flew to me, and in his hand was a live coal, which he had taken with the tongs off the altar. And he touched my mouth, and said: Behold this hath touched thy lips, and thy iniquities shall be taken away, and thy sin shall be cleansed. And I heard the voice of the Lord, saying: Whom shall I send? and who shall go for us? And I said: Lo, here am I, send me.

Lesson III ~ Isa 6:9–12

And he said: Go, and thou shalt say to this people: Hearing, hear, and understand not: and see the vision, and know it not. Blind the heart of this people, and make their ears heavy, and shut their eyes: lest they see with their eyes, and hear with their ears, and understand with their heart, and be converted and I heal them. And I said: How long, O Lord? And he said: Until the cities be wasted without inhabitant, and the houses without man, and the land shall be left desolate. And the Lord shall remove men far away, and she shall be multiplied that was left in the midst of the earth.

Lesson IV

From the Book on the Faith, addressed to Peter by St. Fulgentius, Bishop

The Faith which the holy Patriarchs and Prophets received from God before His Son was made Flesh, the Faith which the holy Apostles heard from the Lord Himself when Present in the Flesh, the Faith which the same Apostles learnt by the teaching of the Holy Ghost not only to preach by word of mouth, but also to leave behind them in their writings for the healthful instruction of all that should come after, that Faith teaches that the Trinity, that is to say, the Father, the Son, and the Holy Ghost, is but One God. But we could not truly call the Father, the Son, and the Holy Ghost a Trinity, if One and the Selfsame Person were named Father, Son, and Holy Ghost.

Lesson V

Nor if as the Being of the Father, the Son, and the Holy Ghost is One Being, so were there but One Person, then were it untrue to say that God is a Trinity. On the other hand, if, as the Persons of the Father, the Son, and the Holy Ghost are distinguished One from Another by that which is proper to Each, so were They diverse by difference of nature, then were it untrue to say that God is One. But since concerning the nature of the One True God, Who is a Trinity, it is the Truth to say that God is One, and the Truth to say that God is a Trinity, therefore the True God is a Trinity in Persons, and a Unity in nature.

Lesson VI

Through this Oneness of nature All That is the Father is in the Son and the Holy Ghost, All That is the Son is in the Father and the Holy Ghost, and All That is the Holy Ghost is in the Father and the Son. Of the Father, the Son, and the Holy Ghost, None is without Other, None is before Other, None is Greater than Other, None is Mightier than Other. The Father, as touching the One Divine Nature, is neither before nor greater than the Son and the Holy Ghost neither is it possible that the Eternity and Infinity of the Son, whether as before or greater, should be before or greater than the Eternity and Infinity of the Spirit.

Lesson VII

From the Holy Gospel according to St. Matthew (Matt 28:18–20)

At that time, Jesus said unto His disciples: All power is given unto Me in heaven and in earth. Go ye, therefore, and teach all nations, baptizing them in the Name of the Father, and of the Son, and of the Holy Ghost. And so on.

Homily by St. Gregory Nazianzen

Who among Catholics does not know that the Father is really a Father, the Son really a Son, and the Holy Ghost really a Holy Ghost, even as the Lord Himself says unto His Apostles: "Go and baptize all nations in the Name of the Father, and of the Son, and of the Holy

Ghost." This is that Perfect Trinity Who is but One being, and of Whom therefore we testify that His Substance is one. For we make no division in God, as divisions are made in bodies, but we believe, that, according to the power of the Divine Nature, Which is not in matter, the Persons named have a real existence, and we testify that God is One.

Lesson VIII

We do not say, as some have dreamt, that the Begetting of the Son of God is an outgrowing from one part to another part neither do we say that He is the Word in the sense of a mere sound uttered by a voice, but we do believe that these three Names and the Persons meant by them are all of only One Being, One Majesty, and One Power. And therefore we testify that God is one, because this Unity of His Majesty forbids that we should use the Plural form of speech and say, "Gods." It is Catholic language to say, "Father and Son," but we cannot and must not say that the Father and the Son are two gods. And that, not because the Son of God is not by Himself God; yea, He is True God from True God but because we know that the Son of God is not from elsewhere, but from the One Father Himself, and therefore we say that God is One. This is the doctrine which Prophets and Apostles have delivered; this is the doctrine which the Lord Himself taught when He said: "I and the Father are One," that is, He meant, as regards the one Divine Being, but as regards Persons, "We are distinct."

Lesson IX—Commemoration of Sunday I after Pentecost

From the Holy Gospel according to St. Luke (Luke 6:36–42)

At that time: Jesus said unto His disciples Be merciful, as your Father also is merciful. And so on.

Homily by St. Augustine, Bishop

There are two works of mercy which free us, and which the Lord Himself has briefly named in the Gospel: "Forgive, and you shall be forgiven give, and it shall be given unto you." "Forgive, and you shall be forgiven," such is the promise of pardon. "Give, and it shall be given unto you," such is the promise of favor. As touching forgiveness thou hast trespasses which thou wouldest gladly have forgiven, and them which have trespassed against thee, whom thou canst forgive. As touching favor, there are beggars that beg from thee, and thou art a beggar to God. When we pray, we are all beggars to God, standing at the door of the Great Householder, yea, falling down on our knees, and beseeching Him to give us somewhat and that somewhat is God Himself. What does a beggar ask of thee? Bread. And what dost thou ask of God but that Christ Who says: "I am the Living Bread Which came down from heaven?" If you will to be forgiven, forgive. If you will to be pardoned, pardon. If you will to receive, "give, and it shall be given unto you."

Monday I after the Octave of Pentecost

Lesson I ~ 1 Kings 1:1–3

Beginning of the first book of Kings

There was a man of Ramathaim-sophim, of mount Ephraim, and his name was Elcana, the son of Jeroham, the son of Eliu, the son of Thohu, the son of Suph, an Ephraimite: And he had two wives, the name of one was Anna, and the name of the other Phenenna. Phenenna had children: but Anna had no children. And this man went up out of his city upon the appointed days, to adore and to offer sacrifice to the Lord of hosts in Silo. And the two sons of Heli, Ophni and Phinees, were there priests of the Lord.

Lesson II ~ 1 Kings 1:4–8

Now the day came, and Elcana offered sacrifice, and gave to Phenenna his wife, and to all her sons and daughters, portions: But to Anna he gave one portion with sorrow, because he loved Anna. And the Lord had shut up her womb. Her rival also afflicted her, and troubled her exceedingly, insomuch that she upbraided her, that the Lord had shut up her womb: And thus she did every year, when the time returned that they went up to the temple of the Lord: and thus she provoked her: but Anna wept, and did not eat. Then Elcana her husband said to her: Anna, why weepest thou? and why dost thou not eat? And why dost thou afflict thy heart? Am not I better to thee than ten children?

Lesson III ~ 1 Kings 1:9–11

So Anna arose after she had eaten and drunk in Silo: And Heli the priest sitting upon a stool, before the door of the temple of the Lord: As Anna had her heart full of grief, she prayed to the Lord, shedding many tears, And she made a vow, saying: O Lord, of hosts, if thou wilt look down on the affliction of thy servant, and wilt be mindful of me, and not forget thy handmaid, and wilt give to thy servant a man child: I will give him to the Lord all the days of his life, and no razor shall come upon his head.

Tuesday I after the Octave of Pentecost

Lesson I ~ 1 Kings 1:12–18

From first book of Kings

And it came to pass, as she multiplied prayers before the Lord, that Heli observed her mouth. Now Anna spoke in her heart, and only her lips moved, but her voice was not heard at all. Heli therefore thought her to be drunk, And said to her: How long wilt thou, be drunk? digest a little the wine, of which thou hast taken too much. Anna answering, said: Not so, my lord: for I am an exceeding unhappy woman, and have drunk neither wine nor any strong drink, but I have poured out my soul before the Lord. Count not thy handmaid for one of the daughters of Belial: for out of the abundance of my sorrow and grief have I spoken till now. Then Heli said to her: Go in peace: and the God of Israel grant thee thy petition, which thou hast asked of him. And she said: Would to God thy handmaid may find grace in thy eyes.

Lesson II ~ 1 Kings 1:18–22

So the woman went on her way, and ate, and her countenance was no more changed. And they rose in the morning, and worshipped before the Lord: and they returned, and came into their house at Ramatha. And Elcana knew Anna his wife: and the Lord remembered her. And it came to pass when the time was come about, Anna conceived and bore a son, and called his name Samuel: because she had asked him of the Lord. And Elcana her husband went up, and all his house, to offer to the Lord the solemn sacrifice, and his vow. But Anna went not up: for she said to her husband: I will not go till the child be weaned, and till I may carry him, that he may appear before the Lord, and may abide always there.

Lesson III ~ 1 Kings 1:23–28

And Elcana her husband said to her: Do what seemeth good to thee, and stay till thou wean him: and I pray that the Lord may fulfill his word. So the woman stayed at home, and gave her son suck, till she weaned him. And after she had weaned him, she carried him with her, with three calves, and three bushels of flour, and a bottle of wine, and she brought him to the house of the Lord in Silo. Now the child was as yet very young: And they immolated a calf, and offered the child to Heli. And Anna said: I beseech thee, my lord, as thy soul liveth, my lord: I am that woman who stood before thee here praying to the Lord. For this child did I pray, and the Lord hath granted me my petition, which I asked of him. Therefore I also have lent him to the Lord all the days of his life, he shall be lent to the Lord. And they adored the Lord there.

Wednesday I after the Octave of Pentecost

Lesson I ~ 1 Kings 2:12–14

From first book of Kings

Now the sons of Heli were children of Belial, not knowing the Lord, Nor the office of the priests to the people: but whosoever had offered a sacrifice, the servant of the priest came, while the flesh was in boiling, with a flesh-hook of three teeth in his hand, And thrust it into the kettle, or into the cauldron, or into the pot, or into the pan: and all that the flesh-hook brought up, the priest took to himself. Thus did they to all Israel that came to Silo.

Lesson II ~ 1 Kings 2:15–17

Also before they burnt the fat, the servant of the priest came, and said to the man that sacrificed: Give me flesh to boil for the priest: for I will not take of thee sodden flesh, but raw. And he that sacrificed said to him: Let the fat first be burnt today according to the custom, and then take as much as thy soul desireth. But he answered and said to him: Not so: but thou shalt give it me now, or else I will take it by force. Wherefore the sin of the young men was exceeding great before the Lord:

because they withdrew men from the sacrifice of the Lord.

Lesson III ~ 1 Kings 2:18–21

But Samuel ministered before the face of the Lord: being a child girded with a linen ephod. And his mother made him a little coat, which she brought to him on the appointed days, when she went up with her husband, to offer the solemn sacrifice. And Heli blessed Elcana and his wife: and he said to him: The Lord give thee seed of this woman, for the loan thou hast lent to the Lord. And they went to their own home. And the Lord visited Anna, and she conceived, and bore three sons and two daughters: and the child Samuel became great before the Lord.

CORPUS CHRISTI

Duplex I Class

Lesson I ~ 1 Cor 11:20–22

From the first letter of St. Paul the Apostle to the Corinthians

When you come therefore together into one place, it is not now to eat the Lord's supper. For every one taketh before his own supper to eat. And one indeed is hungry and another is drunk. What, have you not houses to eat and to drink in? Or despise ye the church of God; and put them to shame that have not? What shall I say to you? Do I praise you? In this I praise you not.

Lesson II ~ 1 Cor 11:23–26

For I have received of the Lord that which also I delivered unto you, that the Lord Jesus, the same night in which he was betrayed, took bread. And giving thanks, broke, and said: Take ye, and eat: this is my body, which shall be delivered for you: this do for the commemoration of me. In like manner also the chalice, after he had supped, saying: This chalice is the new testament in my blood: this do ye, as often as you shall drink, for the commemoration of me. For as often as you shall eat this bread, and drink the chalice, you shall show the death of the Lord, until he come.

Lesson III ~ 1 Cor 11:27–32

Therefore whosoever shall eat this bread, or drink the chalice of the Lord unworthily, shall be guilty of the body and of the blood of the Lord. But let a man prove himself: and so let him eat of that bread, and drink of the chalice. For he that eateth and drinketh unworthily, eateth and drinketh judgment to himself, not discerning the body of the Lord. Therefore are there many infirm and weak among you, and many sleep. But if we would judge ourselves, we should not be judged. But whilst we are judged, we are chastised by the Lord, that we be not condemned with this world.

Lesson IV

Sermon by St. Thomas Aquinas

The immeasurable benefits, which the goodness of God has bestowed on Christian people, have conferred on them also a dignity beyond all price. "For what nation is there so great, who hath gods so nigh unto them, as the Lord, our God, is unto us?" The Only-begotten Son of God, being pleased to make us "partakers of the Divine nature," took our nature upon Him, being Himself made Man that He might make men gods. And all, as much of ours as He took, He applied to our salvation. On the Altar of the Cross He offered up His Body to God the Father as a sacrifice for our reconciliation; He shed His Blood as the price whereby He redeems us from wretchedness and bondage, and the washing whereby He cleanses us from all sin. And for a noble and abiding memorial of that so great work of His goodness, He has left unto His faithful ones His very Same Body for Food, and His very Same Blood for Drink, to be fed upon under the appearance of bread and wine.

Lesson V

O how precious and admirable a banquet! How health-giving and filled with all sweetness! For what could be more precious than this Supper? Therein there is put before us for meat, not, as of old time, the flesh of bulls and of goats, but Christ Himself, our very God. Can anything be more marvelous than this Sacrament? For therein, bread and wine are substantially converted into the Body and Blood of Christ; and therefore Christ, perfect God and Man, is contained under the species of a morsel of bread and wine. His faithful eat Him, but He is not mangled; nay, when this Sacrament is broken, in each broken piece thereof remains whole Christ Himself, Perfect God and Perfect Man. The Accidents [of Bread and Wine: All the sensible qualities thereof], however, subsist therein without subject [for they are no longer Bread and Wine according to their Substances]. And thus room is left for faith; Christ Who has a visible Form, is here taken and received not only invisibly, but seeming to be bread and wine, and the senses which judge by sight, are rendered immune from deception.

Lesson VI

Nothing is more salutary than this Sacrament, by which sins are purged away, strength is renewed, and the soul is fed upon the fatness of spiritual gifts. It is offered in the Church both for the living and dead, so that it may benefit all, which is instituted for the salvation of all. No one suffices to express the delicacy of this kind of sacrament, through which spiritual sweetness is tasted in its source, and the memory of the most excellent charity, which Christ showed in his Passion, is recalled. Whereby, so that the immensity of this kind of charity might be impressed more profoundly on the hearts of the faithful, at the last supper, when, having celebrated the Passover with His disciples, He was about to leave this world and return to the Father, He instituted this sacrament as an eternal remembrance of His Passion, the fulfillment of ancient precursors, the greatest miracle He ever wrought, and sole solace to those saddened by his absence.

Lesson VII

From the Holy Gospel according to St. John (John 6:56–59)

At that time: Jesus said unto the multitudes of the Jews: My Flesh is meat indeed, and My Blood is drink indeed. And so on.

Homily by St. Augustine, Bishop

By use of meat and drink men would fain that "they shall hunger no more, neither thirst any more," and yet there is but one Meat and one Drink, Which does work in them that feed thereon that "this corruptible must put on incorruption, and this mortal put on immortality," namely communion with that general assembly and Church of God's holy children, who are "kept in perfect peace," and are "all one," fully and utterly. And therefore it is, as men of God before our time have taken it, that our Lord Jesus Christ has set before us His Body and His Blood in the likeness of things which, from being many, are reduced into one. Into one are confected many grains, and into the other flow the juice of many grapes. And now He gives us to know how that which He spoke comes to pass, and how indeed "this Man can give us His Flesh to eat," and His Blood to drink.

Lesson VIII

"He that eateth My Flesh, and drinketh My Blood, dwelleth in Me, and I in him." To dwell in Christ, therefore, and to have Him dwelling in us, is to "eat of that Bread and drink of that Cup," and he which dwells not in Christ, and in whom Christ dwells not, doubtlessly eats not spiritually His Flesh nor drink His Blood, although he do carnally and visibly press the Sacrament with his teeth but, rather, he "eateth and drinketh damnation to himself," because he dares to draw nigh filthily to that secret and holy thing of Christ, whereunto none draws nigh worthily, save he which is pure, even he which is of them concerning whom it is said: "Blessed are the pure in heart, for they shall see God."

Lesson IX

"As the living Father hath sent Me, and I live by the Father, so he that eateth Me, even he shall live by Me." This is as though He said: The Father has sent Me into the world, and I have emptied Myself. I have My life from the Father, as One That is greater than I. He that eats Me, even he, by thereby taking part in Me, shall live by Me. It is as having humbled Myself that I live by the Father, but he that eats Me, him will I raise up, and so he shall live by Me. It is said "I live by the Father" that is to say, He is of the Father, not the Father of Him, and yet not so, but that the Father and the Son are co-equal together. Also it is said "So he that eateth Me, even he shall live by Me," whereby He shows the gracious work towards His people of Him Who is the "one Mediator between God and man," and not that He Which is eaten and he which eats Him are co-equal together.

Friday within the Octave of Corpus Christi

Semiduplex

Lesson I - 1 Kings 2:27–29

From first book of Kings

And there came a man of God to Heli, and said to him: Thus saith the Lord: Did I not plainly appear to thy father's house, when they were in Egypt in the house of Pharao? And I chose him out of all the tribes of Israel to be my priest, to go up to my altar, and burn incense to me, and to wear the ephod before me: and I gave to thy father's house of all the sacrifices of the children of Israel. Why have you kicked away my victims, and my gifts which I commanded to be offered in the temple: and thou hast rather honoured thy sons than me, to eat the firstfruits of every sacrifice of my people Israel?

Lesson II - 1 Kings 2:30–33

Wherefore thus saith the Lord the God of Israel: I said indeed that thy house, and the house of thy father should minister in my sight, for ever. But now saith the Lord: Far be this from me: but whosoever shall glorify me, him will I glorify: but they that despise me, shall be despised. Behold the days come: and I will cut off thy arm, and the arm of thy father's house, that there shall not be an old man in thy house. And thou shalt see thy rival in the temple, in all the prosperity of Israel, and there shall not be an old man in thy house for ever. However I will not altogether take away a man of thee from my altar: but that thy eyes may faint and thy soul be spent: and a great part of thy house shall die when they come to man's estate.

Lesson III - 1 Kings 2:34–36

And this shall be a sign to thee, that shall come upon thy two sons, Ophni and Phinees: In one day they shall both of them die. And I will raise me up a faithful priest, who shall do according to my heart, and my soul, and I will build him a faithful house, and he shall walk all days before my anointed. And it shall come to pass, that whosoever shall remain in thy house, shall come that he may be prayed for, and shall offer a piece of silver, and a roll of bread, and shall say: Put me, I beseech thee, to somewhat of the priestly office, that I may eat a morsel of bread.

Lesson IV

Sermon by St. Thomas Aquinas

It serves well therefore to the edifying of the faithful to make memorial of the institution of so salutary and so wonderful a Sacrament, that we may worship the unspeakable way by the which the Divine Presence dwells within in this visible Sacrament; and may praise the power of God whereby in this Sacrament are wrought so many wonders, yea, and also give God some of those thanks which we owe unto Him for this so health-giving gift of His loving kindness. It is true that on the Day of the Supper, when it is known to have been that He ordained this Sacrament, at the solemn celebration of the Mass the memory of the institution thereof is more particularly mentioned, nevertheless all the remaining worship of this same day is concerned with Christ's suffering, around whose veneration the Church at that time is occupied.

Lesson V

But, that the faithful might celebrate with a whole Festal Office all to itself the institution of this so great Sacrament, Urban IV, Roman Pontiff, being touched with love toward this said Sacrament, piously decreed that the memory of the said institution should be celebrated by all the faithful upon the Fifth Day after the Octave of Pentecost. From one end of the year to the other we use this Sacrament to our souls' health, and we more particularly celebrate the institution thereof at that season wherein the Holy Ghost taught the hearts of the disciples to acknowledge the mysteries thereof. For, at the same time, this sacrament began to be frequented by the faithful.

Lesson VI

And, moreover, to the end that on the aforesaid Thursday, and the following octave, the memory of this same saving Institution might be the more honorably celebrated, and the Feast thereby be held in more excellent worship, the aforesaid Roman Pontiff, after the manner of the distributions of material goods which in Cathedral Churches are given to such as come to the singing or saying of the Canonical Hours by night and day, has out of his Apostolic bounty granted spiritual rewards to all such as in their own persons are present in the Church at the diverse Canonical Hours during all this Festival, thereby to stir up the faithful to come to the keeping of this great Feast in greater eagerness and numbers.

Lesson VII

From the Holy Gospel according to St. John (John 6:56–59)

At that time: Jesus said unto the multitudes of the Jews: My Flesh is meat indeed, and My Blood is drink indeed. And so on.

Homily by St. Augustine, Bishop

We have heard from the Gospel the words of the Lord which follow. To your ears and understandings we owe a discourse on these also, and today it fits very well, for it is upon that Body of the Lord, Which He professes Himself that He "will give for the life of the world," "that a man may eat thereof and not die." He has made manifest how He gives, and What is His Gift, where He says: "He that eateth My Flesh and drinketh My Blood, dwelleth in Me and I in him." The sign to show whether a man has or has not eaten that Flesh and drunk that Blood, is whether or not he dwells in Christ and Christ in him, whether or not he is a guest of Christ and Christ of his, whether or not he so cleaves unto Christ, that Christ be not parted from him.

Lesson VIII

This has He taught, and warned us, by words of deep meaning, to be in His Body as members whose Head is He, eating His Flesh, and cleaving always to His Unity. "Many of His disciples when they had heard this. went back, and walked no more with Him" for they understood not by Flesh any flesh other than such as they themselves were made of. The Apostle says, and very true it is: "To be carnally minded is death." The Lord gives us His Flesh to eat, and to understand it carnally is death. He then says: "Whoso eateth My Flesh is life"; therefore, we must not think of His Flesh carnally, like those of whom it is written: "Many of His disciples" (not His enemies) "when they heard this, said 'This is a hard saying who can hear it?'"

Lesson IX

If His disciples took His words for a hard saying, how did His enemies take them? And, nevertheless, it was thus fitting to speak them even if all men were not to understand them. A Divine mystery ought to make us thoughtful, not repel us; and yet, when the Lord Jesus Christ spoke thus in mystery, many of His disciples went back and walked no more with Him. They believed not that He was speaking of some great thing, and covering some grace with these words. They understood as they pleased, even after the manner of men, that Jesus was able, or that Jesus meant, to give that Flesh wherewith the Word is clothed, as if in slices to them that believe in Him. And they said "This is a hard saying who can hear it?"

Saturday within the Octave of Corpus Christi

Semiduplex

Lesson I ~ 1 Kings 3:1–7

From first book of Kings

Now the child Samuel ministered to the Lord before Heli, and the word of the Lord was precious in those days, there was no manifest vision. And it came to pass one day when Heli lay in his place, and his eyes were grown dim, that he could not see: Before the lamp of God went out, Samuel slept in the temple of the Lord, where the ark of God was. And the Lord called Samuel. And he answered: Here am I. And he ran to Heli and said: Here am I: for thou didst call me. He said: I did not call: go back and sleep. And he went and slept. And the Lord called Samuel again. And Samuel arose and went to Heli, and said: Here am I: for thou calledst me. He answered: I did not call thee, my son: return and sleep. Now Samuel did not yet know the Lord, neither had the word of the Lord been revealed to him.

Lesson II ~ 1 Kings 3:8–12

And the Lord called Samuel again the third time. And he arose up and went to Heli. And said: Here am I: for thou didst call me. Then Heli understood that the Lord called the child, and he said to Samuel: Go, and sleep: and if he shall call thee any more, thou shalt say: Speak, Lord, for thy servant heareth. So Samuel went and slept in his place. And the Lord came and stood: and he called, as he had called the other times: Samuel, Samuel. And Samuel said: Speak, Lord, for thy servant heareth. And the Lord said to Samuel: Behold I do a thing in Israel: and whosoever shall hear it, both his ears shall tingle. In that day I will raise up against Heli all the things I have spoken concerning his house: I will begin, and I will make an end.

Lesson III ~ 1 Kings 3:15–20

And Samuel slept till morning, and opened the doors of the house of the Lord. And Samuel feared to tell the vision to Heli. Then Heli called Samuel, and said: Samuel, my son. And he answered: Here am I. And he asked him: What is the word that the Lord hath spoken to thee? I beseech thee hide it not from me. May God do so and so to thee, and add so and so, if thou hide from me one word of all that were said to thee. So Samuel told him all the words, and did not hide them from him. And he answered: It is the Lord: let him do what is good in his sight. And Samuel grew, and the Lord was with him, and not one of his words fell to the ground. And all Israel from Dan to Bersabee, knew that Samuel was a faithful prophet of the Lord.

Lesson IV

Sermon by St. John Chrysostom

Dearly beloved brethren, it behooves us to learn the miracle of the Mysteries, what the Gift is, why It was given, and what is the use thereof. "We, being many, are one body," "We are members of His Body, of His Flesh, and of His Bones." Only the initiated will now understand what I say. That this union may take place, not by love only, but verily and indeed, we ought to mingle our own with His Flesh. And this is done by eating that Food Which He has given unto us, being fain to manifest that exceedingly great love which He bears towards us. To this end He has mingled Himself with us, and infused His Body into our bodies, that we may be one together, like as the limbs of a man and his head are all of one body. Such union do they long for who love much.

Lesson V

When we come back from that Table we ought to be like so many lions breathing fire, dreadful to the devil. Our thoughts ought to be concentrated on our Great Head and the love which He shows us. Many fathers and mothers there are who give their children to others to nurse, but I, says the Lord to His children, I am not so, but I feed you with Mine Own Flesh, and join Myself to you, fain that you all should be sons of noble blood now, and giving you a noble hope of that which you shall be hereafter. I was content to become your Brother, I for your sakes have taken unto Me Flesh and Blood, and that Flesh and Blood wherein I am become your Brother, the Same give I in turn unto you.

Lesson VI

Let us then, dearly beloved brethren, take good heed to ourselves, as unto the holders of so great mercies, and when any foul word springs to our lips, or we feel anger taking possession of us, or the sting of any other sinful passion, let us call to mind of What we have been counted worthy, and let that remembrance still the unruly motion. As often as we take that Body, as often as we taste that Blood, let us think how that we feed on Him Who is sitting on high, adored of Angels, at the right hand of the Eternal Power. Ah me, how many a way is open to us whereby we may be saved! He has made us His; He has given His Body to us and we still are not turned away from evil.

Lesson VII

From the Holy Gospel according to St. John (John 6:56–59)

At that time: Jesus said unto the multitudes of the Jews: My Flesh is meat indeed, and My Blood is drink indeed. And so on.

Homily by St. Augustine, Bishop

I have said, my brethren, that what the Lord has set before us, in eating of His Flesh and drinking of His Blood, is that we should dwell in Him, and He in us. We dwell in Him when we are His members, and He dwells in us when we are His temple. But the bond whereby we are made His members is unity and what is the cause of unity but love? And whence is this love of God? Ask the Apostle. "The love of God," says he, "is shed abroad in our hearts by the Holy Ghost, Which is given unto us."

Lesson VIII

So "it is the spirit that quickeneth." It is the spirit that makes lively the limbs, nor is the vivifying power of the spirit shed through any limbs but such as remain in union with the body whose the spirit is. The spirit that thou hast in thee, O man, and whereby thou art a man, does that spirit shed life through any limb cut off from thy flesh? By "spirit," I mean soul. The soul quickens no limb but such as remain attached to the body. Cut one off, and the soul quickens it no more, for it is separate from the unity of thy body.

Lesson IX

These things I say, that we may love unity and dread division. For there is nothing which a Christian ought so much to dread, as to be cut off from the Body of Christ. If he be cut off from the Body of Christ, he is no longer a member of Christ, and the Spirit of Christ no longer quickens him. "Now, if any man," says the Apostle, "have not the Spirit of Christ, he is none of His." "It is the Spirit that quickeneth; the flesh profiteth nothing. The words that I speak unto you, they are spirit and they are life." "Spirit and life," what means this? It is to be taken spiritually. Hast thou taken it spiritually? Then the words the Lord spoke, unto thee are spirit and they are life. Hast thou taken it carnally? Then the words of the Lord are still indeed spirit and life but not for thee.

Sunday II after Pentecost

~ within the Octave of Corpus Christi ~

Semiduplex

Lesson I ~ 1 Kings 4:1–3

From first book of Kings

And it came to pass in those days, that the Philistines gathered themselves together to fight: and Israel went out to war against the Philistines, and camped by the Stone of help. And the Philistines came to Aphec, And put their army in array against Israel. And when they had joined battle, Israel turned their backs to the Philistines, and there was slain in that fight here and there in the fields about four thousand men. And the people returned to the camp: and the ancients of Israel said: Why hath the Lord defeated us today before the Philistines? Let us fetch unto us the ark of the covenant of the Lord from Silo, and let it come in the midst of us, that it may save us from the hand of our enemies.

Lesson II ~ 1 Kings 5:4–11

So the people sent to Silo, and they brought from thence the ark of the covenant of the Lord of hosts sitting upon the cherubims: and the two sons of Heli, Ophni and Phinees, were with the ark of the covenant of God. And when the ark of the covenant of the Lord was come into the camp, all Israel shouted with a great shout, and the earth rang again. And the Philistines heard the noise of the shout, and they said: What is this noise of a great shout in the camp of the Hebrews? And they understood that the ark of the Lord was come into the camp.

Lesson III ~ 1 Kings 4:7–11

And the Philistines were afraid, saying: God is come into the camp. And sighing, they said: Woe to us: for there was no such great joy yesterday and the day before: Woe to us. Who shall deliver us from the hand of these high gods? these are the gods that struck Egypt with all the plagues in the desert. Take courage and behave like men, ye Philistines: lest you come to be servants to the Hebrews, as they have served you: take courage and fight. So the Philistines fought, and Israel was overthrown, and every man fled to his own dwelling: and there was an exceeding great slaughter; for there fell of Israel thirty thousand footmen. And the ark of God was taken: and the two sons of Heli, Ophni and Phinees, were slain.

Lesson IV

Sermon by St. John Chrysostom

His Word says: "This is My Body." This we confess, and believe, and, with spiritual eyes, do see. Christ has not left unto us Himself in sensible form and yet He left Himself unto us in sensible things which all men may understand. Thus also is it in baptism: namely, through a sensible thing, water, a gift is conferred unto them which they can grasp only inwardly, that is, generation and renewal. If we were incorporeal, then these things would be given us nakedly and invisibly, but since we are here made up of souls and bodies, there are given unto our souls gifts which they can grasp, in outward signs which our bodies may perceive. How many there be which say: I would like to see His comely presence, His Face, His garments, even His shoes? Behold, thou dost see and touch Him, yea, thou dost feed upon Him. And wouldest thou behold His raiment? Lo, He has given unto thee not only to behold it, but to feed upon it, and handle it, and take it into thyself.

Lesson V

Therefore, let none dare draw near with squeamishness or carelessness. Let all be fiery, all fervent, all excited. To the Jews it was commanded: "And thus shall you eat it with your loins girded, your shoes on your feet, and your staff in your hand and you shall eat it in haste; it is the Lord's Passover." But thou needest to be more watchful than they. They were just about to travel to Palestine, and therefore they bore the guise of travelers; but the journey that lies before thee is to heaven. And therefore it befits thee in all things to be on thy guard, for the punishment of him that eats or drinks unworthily is no light one. Bethink thee how thou art indignant against him which betrayed, and them that crucified the Lord; look to it well, therefore, that thou also be not "Guilty of the Body and Blood of the Lord." As for them, they slew His Most Holy Body but thou, after all that He has done for thee, dost thrust Him into thy polluted soul. For His love it was not enough to be made Man, to be buffeted, and to be crucified; He has also mingled Himself with us, by making us His Body, and that not only by faith, but verily and indeed.

Lesson VI

Can anything be purer than he, who eats of this great Sacrifice, ought to be? Can a sunbeam be more noble than that hand, which breaks this Flesh, ought to be? That mouth, which is filled with that spiritual fire? That tongue, which is reddened by that Blood so tremendous? Think upon what honor thou art worthy, what table thou dost enjoy. That, whereupon the Angels fear to look nor dare to gaze upon steadfastly because of the blinding glory that shines therefrom, upon This we feed, with This we become one, and are made one body of Christ, and one flesh. "Who can utter the mighty acts of the Lord; who can show forth all His praise?" Where is the shepherd which feeds his flock with his own blood? And why should I say shepherd? Many mothers there be, who after all the pains of travail, give their own little ones to strangers to nurse. But this Himself He did not suffer, but feeds us with His Own Blood, and binds us to Himself through all.

Lesson VII

From the Holy Gospel according to St. Luke (Luke 14:16–24)

At that time: Jesus spoke unto the Pharisees this parable: A certain man made a great supper, and bade many. And so on.

Homily by Pope St. Gregory

Dearly beloved brethren, between the delights of the body and the delights of the mind there is this difference: that the delights of the body, when we lack them, raise up a great hunger after them, and when we devour them, straightway our fullness works loathing in us. But about the delights of the mind we are loathing while as yet we lack them, and when we fill ourselves with them, then we hunger after them, and the more, hungering, we feed thereon, the more are we hungry thereafter. In the bodily delights, the hunger is keener than the fullness, but in the spiritual the fullness is keener than the hunger. In the bodily, hunger engenders fullness, and fullness engenders loathing of the spiritual, hunger indeed engenders fullness, but fullness engenders hunger.

Lesson VIII

Spiritual delights, in the very eating, do stir up the keenness of hunger in the mind which they fill, for, the more we taste their sweetness, the better we know how well they deserve to be loved and, if we taste them not, we cannot love them, for we know not how sweet they are. And who can love that whereof he knows nothing? Hence says the Psalmist "O taste and see that the Lord is good," that is, as it were, "If you taste not, you shall not see His goodness but let your heart once taste the bread of life, and then indeed, having tasted and proved His sweetness, you shall be able to love Him." But these were the delights which man lost when he sinned in Eden, and when he had shut his own mouth against the sweet bread whereof if any man eat he shall live for ever; he forsook paradise.

Lesson IX

And we that, from the first man, are born under the afflictions of this pilgrimage, are come into the world smitten with loathing. We know not what we ought to want, and the disease of our loathing grows worse, as our soul draws itself further away from that bread of sweetness. We are no longer hungry after inward delights, since we have lost the use of feeding on them. And so in our loathing we starve, and the sickness of long famishing makes prey of our health. We will not eat of that inward sweetness which is made ready for us, and being enamored only of things outward we sink into the wretchedness of loving starvation.

Monday within the Octave of Corpus Christi

Semiduplex

Lesson I ~ 1 Kings 5:1–5

From first book of Kings

And the Philistines took the ark of God, and carried it from the

Stone of help into Azotus. And the Philistines took the ark of God, and brought it into the temple of Dagon, and set it by Dagon. And when the Azotians arose early the next day, behold Dagon lay upon his face on the ground before the ark of the Lord: and they took Dagon, and set him again in his place. And the next day again, when they rose in the morning, they found Dagon lying upon his face on the earth before the ark of the Lord: and the head of Dagon, and both the palms of his hands were cut off upon the threshold: And only the stump of Dagon remained in its place.

Lesson II ~ 1 Kings 5:6–8

And the hand of the Lord was heavy upon the Azotians, and he destroyed them, and afflicted Azotus and the coasts thereof with emerods. And in the villages and fields in the midst of that country, there came forth a multitude of mice, and there was the confusion of a great mortality in the city. And the men of Azotus seeing this kind of plague, said: The ark of the God of Israel shall not stay with us: for his hand is heavy upon us, and upon Dagon our god. And sending, they gathered together all the lords of the Philistines to them, and said: What shall we do with the ark of the God of Israel? And the Gethrites answered: Let the ark of the God of Israel be carried about.

Lesson III ~ 1 Kings 5:8–12

And they carried the ark of the God of Israel about. And while they were carrying it about, the hand of the Lord came upon every city with an exceeding great slaughter: and he smote the men of every city, both small and great, and they had emerods in their secret parts. And the Gethrites consulted together, and made themselves seats of skins. Therefore they sent the ark of God into Accaron. And when the ark of God was come into Accaron, the Accaronites cried out, saying: They have brought the ark of the God of Israel to us, to kill us and our people. They sent therefore and gathered together all the lords of the Philistines: and they said: Send away the ark of the God of Israel, and let it return into its own place, and not kill us and our people. For there was the fear of death in every city, and the hand of God was exceeding heavy.

Lesson IV

Sermon by St. John Chrysostom

In this mysterious Sacrament Christ mingles Himself with all and each of His faithful ones. They are His children, and He nurses them Himself, and gives them not over unto another, herein again assuring us that the Flesh He has taken unto Himself is ours. We then, who have been deemed worthy to be treated with such love and such honor, let us be wakeful. See you not how eagerly the sucklings seize on the breasts, how readily they fix their mouths on the paps? Let us, with like eagerness, draw nigh to that Table, and suck at that spiritual Cup. Yea, let us prize that gracious Food as the suckling does its mother's breast, and hold it the great woe of life to be cut off from that Banquet. Here there are set before us no works of man's power. He That worked at that Last Supper works the same here still. As for us Priests, we hold the place of His ministers, but He Which hallows and changes is Christ Himself. Hither let there draw nigh no Judas, nor covetous one; this is no Table for him. But he which is Christ's disciple, let him come, for the Lord says "I will keep the Passover with My disciples." This is that Passover Table; and it is all Christ's. What is wrought there is not partially Christ's work and partially man's work, but it is all His work and not another's.

Lesson V

Let there draw nigh neither brutal, nor cruel, nor merciless, in good sooth, none unclean. I speak to all that take that Holy Communion, and to you also, O you that do administer the same. To you now I turn my speech, to warn you with how great care that Gift is to be given. No slight vengeance is that which awaits you if you admit for a partaker at the Lord's Table the sinner whose guiltiness you know. At your hands will his blood be required. If a man be a General, a Governor, a crowned Monarch, yet if he come there unworthily, forbid him. Thou hast greater power than he. To this end has God exalted you to the honor you hold, that you may judge in such matters. This office is your dignity, this is your strength, this is all your crown, this, and not the going about in white robes and glittering vestments. And thou, O layman, when thou seest the Priest making the oblation, think not that He Which is then the real Worker is such a Priest as thou seest, but know of a surety that it is Christ's Hand Which is stretched out, albeit unseen by thee.

Lesson VI

Let us hear, all of us, both Priests and laymen, let us hear What Food it is whereof we are made worthy. Let us hear, I say, and let us quake. The Lord satisfies us with His Own holy Flesh, setting Himself slain before us. What excuse therefore shall we have, if, being so fed as we are, we sin as we do? If, eating of the Lamb, we are still wolves? If, pastured as the sheep of the flock, we raven like lions? This mysterious Sacrament forbids unto us not only outrage, but any of the least enmity; it is the Mystery of peace. Upon the Jews God laid it to make by solemn festivals a yearly commemoration of His mercies unto them, but upon thee to do this in remembrance of His love to thee, day by day. To this Table then let there draw nigh no Judas Iscariot, no Simon Magus. These men fell through covetousness; therefore let us fly that bottomless pit.

Lesson VII

From the Holy Gospel according to St. John (John 6:56–59)

At that time: Jesus said unto the multitudes of the Jews: My Flesh is meat indeed, and My Blood is drink indeed. And so on.

Homily by St. Augustine, Bishop

"This is the bread which comes down from heaven." By "this bread" the Lord here signifies both the manna, and That Which we receive at the Altar of God. Both these are, as it were, Sacramental signs, differing indeed somewhat in their outward and visible part, but pointing to the Same Thing signified. Hear what the Apostle says: "Moreover, brethren, I would not that you should be ignorant how that all our fathers were under the cloud, and all passed through the sea, and were all baptized unto Moses in the cloud and in the sea, and did all eat the same spiritual meat." This meat was the same spiritually but not really; they ate manna we eat Something else. Spiritually they ate What we eat; but our fathers not their fathers; unto whom we are like not unto whom they are like. And it is added "And did all drink the same Spiritual drink." They drank one thing, and we drank Another, the difference being in the outer show, the sameness in that the Same Thing is pointed to by both. And what was that Same Drink? "They drank of the spiritual Rock that followed them, and that Rock was Christ." Him did bread and rock alike signify. The Rock was a figure, but by the Word and in the Flesh there is the very Christ Himself. And how came they to drink of that rock? "Moses lift up his hand, and with his rod he smote the rock twice, and the water came out abundantly." These two strokes of the rod upon the rock are a figure of the two beams whereof the Cross was made.

Lesson VIII

Christ's faithful ones discern the Lord's Body while they remain watchful members of His Body. They remain members of His Body as long as they will to live according to His Spirit. The Spirit of Christ gives life to nothing but the body of Christ. Now, my brethren, understand what I am going to say. Thou art a man, and hast a body and a spirit. By spirit I mean the soul, which causes thee to be a man at all. Thou art a man, made up of soul and body. Thy spirit is unseen, thy body seen. Tell me, which of them is it which gives animation to the other? Does thy spirit derive animation from thy body, or thy body from thy spirit? Every one who lives will answer, for if any one cannot answer this, I know not if he be alive. What will whosoever has life answer? "Verily, it is my spirit which animates my body." Wilt thou then live by the Spirit of Christ? Be of the Body of Christ.

Lesson IX

Is it not my spirit which does animate my body? My spirit does animate my body, and thy spirit does animate thy body. The Body of Christ lives not save by the Spirit of Christ. Hence it is that the Apostle Paul says, about this Bread: "We, being many, are one bread, and one body, for we are all partakers of that one Bread." O what a Sacrament of love! O what a seal of union! O what a bond of charity! He that wills to live has a place where to live, and from whence to live. Let him come near, let him believe, let him enter into that Body, that he may be quickened. Let him not sever himself from the fit joining-together of all the members; let him not be as a putrefying limb that needs to be cut off, nor a mis-shapen limb, a cause to blush. Let him be beautiful, and useful, and healthy. Let him cleave unto the body; let him live by God to God. Let him labour now on earth, that he may reign hereafter in heaven.

Tuesday within the Octave of Corpus Christi

Semiduplex

Lesson I - 1 Kings 6:1–3

From first book of Kings

Now the ark of God was in the land of the Philistines seven months. And the Philistines called for the priests and the diviners, saying: What shall we do with the ark of the Lord? tell us how we are to send it back to its place? And they said: If you send back the ark of the God of Israel, send it not away empty, but render unto him what you owe for sin, and then you shall be healed: and you shall know why his hand departeth not from you.

Lesson II - 1 Kings 6:6–10

Why do you harden your hearts, as Egypt and Pharao hardened their hearts? did not he, after he was struck, then let them go, and they departed? Now therefore take and make a new cart: and two kine that have calved, on which there hath come no yoke, tie to the cart, and shut up their calves at home. And you shall take the ark of the Lord, and lay it on the cart, and the vessels of gold, which you have paid him for sin, you shall put into a little box, at the side thereof: and send it away that it may go. And you shall look: and if it go up by the way of his own coasts towards Bethsames, then he hath done us this great evil: but if not, we shall know that it is not his hand hath touched us, but it hath happened by chance. They did therefore in this manner.

Lesson III - 1 Kings 6:12–15

And the kine took the straight way that leadeth to Bethsames, and they went along the way, lowing as they went: and turned not aside neither to the right hand nor to the left: and the lords of the Philistines followed them as far as the borders of Bethsames. Now the Bethsamites were reaping wheat in the valley: and lifting up their eyes they saw the ark, and rejoiced to see it. And the cart came into the field of Josue a Bethsamite, and stood there. And there was a great stone, and they cut in pieces the wood of the cart, and laid the kine upon it a holocaust to the Lord. And the Levites took down the ark of God.

Lesson IV

From the Letter written to Caecilius by the Holy Martyr Cyprian

In the deed of the Priest Melchisedech we see a type of the Sacrament of the Lord's Sacrifice. For thus it is written in the writings of God: "And Melchisedech King of Salem brought forth bread and wine for he was the Priest of the Most High God and he blessed Abraham." That Melchisedech was a type of Christ, the Holy Ghost Himself does testify in the Psalms, where the First Person of the Holy Trinity, even the Father, is set before us as saying unto the Second Person, that is, the Son "Before the daystar have I begotten thee. Thou art a Priest for ever, after the order of Melchisedech." And verily that sameness of order comes of this sacrifice, and proceeds from this, that Melchisedech was the Priest of the Most High God that he offered bread and wine and that he blessed Abraham.

Lesson V

What Priest of the Most High God is there, more so than our Lord Jesus Christ: He Who has made an offering unto God the Father, and the same offering that Melchisedech made, bread and wine, that is to say, His Own Flesh and His Own Blood. And, as touching Abraham, that ancient blessing was spoken likewise by fore-knowledge upon us. For if Abraham believed God and it was accounted to him for righteousness, verily, whosoever believes God and lives by faith, the same is found righteous, and is shown unto us that he is already blessed in faithful Abraham, and justified as the Apostle Paul proves where he says: "Abraham believed God and it was accounted unto him for righteousness. Know you therefore that they which are of faith, the same are the children of Abraham." And the Scripture, foreseeing that God would justify the heathen through faith, preached before the Gospel unto Abraham, saying "In thee shall all nations be blessed."

Lesson VI

In Genesis, therefore, in order that the Priest Melchisedech might in due order pronounce the blessing upon Abraham, there was first offered a typical sacrifice, consisting of bread and wine. This was the offering which our Lord Jesus Christ completed and fulfilled when He offered up bread and a cup of wine mingled with water. This fulfillment by Him Who came to fulfill, utterly satisfied the truth of the image which had gone before. The Holy Ghost does by Solomon also clearly foreshadow, albeit in a parable, the Lord's Sacrifice, pointing to the victim slain, and the bread and the wine, and the Altar likewise, and the Apostles as it is written "Wisdom hath built herself a house, she hath hewn her out seven pillars. She hath slain her victims, mingled her wine, and set forth her table. She hath sent her maids to invite to the tower, and to the walls of the city: Whosoever is a little one, let him come to me. And to the unwise she said: Come, eat my bread, and drink the wine which I have mingled for you."

Lesson VII

From the Holy Gospel according to St. John (John 6:56–59)

At that time: Jesus said unto the multitudes of the Jews: My Flesh is meat indeed, and My Blood is drink indeed. And so on.

Homily by St. Augustine, Bishop

"Not as your fathers did eat manna, and are dead." Why did they eat and die? Because they believed only that which they saw, and that which they saw not they understood not. Therefore were they your fathers, because you are like unto them. Does this death, my brethren, mean that death which is outward and bodily? And do not we also die, who eat of that Bread Which comes down from heaven? That death died they, and so shall we also, as far, as I have said, as is meant that death which is outward and bodily.

Lesson VIII

But the death whereof the Lord does sound the alarm, the death that their fathers died, is another death than that which is outward and bodily. Moses ate manna, Aaron ate manna, Phineas ate manna, many ate manna in whom the Lord was well pleased and these are not dead. Why? Because they understood spiritually that outward bread, spiritually hungered thereafter, spiritually tasted thereof, and spiritually were satisfied therewith. So also do we this day feed on a visible food, but the Sacrament is one thing, and the grace of the Sacrament is another.

Lesson IX

"Whosever eateth and drinketh unworthily eateth and drinketh damnation to himself." Doesn't the Apostle say: "He eateth and drinketh judgement to himself?" Was not the morsel of the Lord poison to Judas? And yet he took it. And when he had eaten it, the enemy entered in and possessed him. Not because what he ate was evil, but because he, being evil, dared to eat that which was good. Look to it well, then, brethren, that you take spiritually the Bread Which comes down from heaven. Bring innocence with you to the Altar. Though your sins be daily, let them not be deadly. Before you draw near to the Altar, think well what it is that you say "Forgive us our trespasses, as we forgive them that trespass against us." "For, if you forgive men their trespasses, your heavenly Father will also forgive you;" and you may draw near boldly, for unto you It is Bread, and not poison.

Wednesday within the Octave of Corpus Christi

Semiduplex

Lesson I ~ 1 Kings 6:19–21; 7:1

From first book of Kings

But he slew of the men of Bethsames, because they had seen the ark of the Lord: and he slew of the people seventy men, and fifty thousand of the common people. And the people lamented, because the Lord had smitten the people with a great slaughter. And the men of Bethsames said: Who shall be able to stand before the Lord this holy God? and to whom shall he go up from us? And they sent messengers to the inhabitants of Cariathiarim, saying: The Philistines have brought back the ark of the Lord, come ye down and fetch it up to you. So they came as they were bidden, the men of Cariathiarim, and brought back the ark with them, housing it with a certain Abinadab in Gabaa; and they set apart his son Eleazar to keep watch over the Lord's ark.

Lesson II ~ 1 Kings 7:2–4

And it came to pass, that from the day the ark of the Lord abode in Cariathiarim days were multiplied (for it was now the twentieth year), and all the house of Israel rested following the Lord. And Samuel spoke to all the house of Israel, saying: If you turn to the Lord with all your heart, put away the strange gods from among you, Baalim and Astaroth: and prepare your hearts unto the Lord, and serve him only, and he will deliver you out of the hand of the Philistines. Then the children of Israel put away Baalim and Astaroth, and served the Lord only.

Lesson III ~ 1 Kings 7:5–8

And Samuel said: Gather all Israel to Masphath, that I may pray to the Lord for you. And they gathered together to Masphath: and they drew water, and poured it out before the Lord, and they fasted on that day, and they said there: We have sinned against the Lord. And Samuel judged the children of Israel in Masphath. And the Philistines heard that the children of Israel were gathered together to Masphath, and the lords of the Philistines went up against Israel. And when the children of Israel heard this, they were afraid of the Philistines. And they said to Samuel: Cease not to cry to the Lord our God for us, that he may save us out of the hand of the Philistines.

Lesson IV

From the Book upon the Sacraments written by St. Ambrose, Bishop

Who invented the Sacraments but the Lord Jesus? The Sacraments came down from heaven, for all counsel is from heaven. Nevertheless, it was a great and wonderful work of God when He rained down manna upon His people, and the people labored not yet were fed. Perchance, thou sayest Here, it is my bread which is used. But that bread is bread only till the Sacramental words are spoken at the Consecration; instead of bread, there comes to be the Body of Christ. This, therefore, let us establish. How comes it that that which was bread becomes the Body of Christ? Through the Consecration. And in what words and in Whose language does the Consecration take place? In those of the Lord Jesus. All the other things which are said, the ascription of praise to God (in the Preface), the prayer for the people, for kings, and for others which forms the first part of the Canon, these are put in the mouth of the Priest. But when that point is reached when this worshipful Sacrament is to be consecrated, then the Priest uses no more his own words, but Christ's.

Lesson V

It is the word of Christ, therefore, Which does the needful work in this Sacrament. And what is the word of Christ? It is the word of Him at Whose bidding all things were made. The Lord commanded, and the heavens were created. The Lord commanded, and the earth was formed. The Lord commanded, and the seas were made. The Lord commanded, and all creatures sprang into being. Thou seest, then, how mightily working a word is the word of Christ. If, then, the word of Christ has such power that it can make that to be which has never been, how does it appear greater that it makes one thing to be changed into Another? There was once no heaven, there was once no sea, there was once no earth. But hear him who says: "He spoke, and it was done. He commanded, and it stood fast." If, then, I am to answer thee, I tell thee that before the Consecration it is not the Body of Christ, but after the Consecration it is the Body of Christ, for Himself "hath spoken, and it is done He hath commanded, and it standeth fast."

Lesson VI

And now I come back to my text. It is indeed a great and worshipful fact that manna was rained down upon the Jews but, think thou, which was the more great and worshipful, the manna from heaven or the Body of Christ: "the Body of that Same Christ by Whom the heavens were made?" And, again the fathers "did eat manna, and are dead." He that eats of this Bread, it is unto him "the remission of sins," and "he shall never die." Therefore it is not idly that, when thou art receiving, thou sayest "Amen" testifying in thine heart that That Which thou art taking is the Body of Christ. The Priest says unto thee: "The Body of Christ" and thou answerest: "Amen" that is to say, "It is true." What then thy tongue confesses, let thine heart hold to.

Lesson VII

From the Holy Gospel according to St. John (John 6:56–59)

At that time: Jesus said unto the multitudes of the Jews: My Flesh is meat indeed, and My Blood is drink indeed. And so on.

Homily by St. Hilary, Bishop

When we speak concerning the things of God, we must not speak after the manner of men, nor after the manner of the world. Let us read those things which are written, and understand those things which we read and then let us act as having a perfect faith. We shall speak but folly and godlessness if we speak concerning the natural truth of Christ in use and have not learnt at Christ's School how we should speak. He Himself says "My Flesh is meat indeed, and My Blood is drink indeed. He that eateth My Flesh and drinketh My Blood, dwelleth in Me, and I in him." There is here no room left for doubt as to What is His Flesh and what is His Blood.

Lesson VIII

Now we know by the declaration of the Lord Himself and by our Faith, the reality of His Flesh and Blood. And when we eat the One and drink the Other, They work effectually in us to make us dwell in Him and He in us. Is not this a reality? Surely it befalls them not to find it true, who deny that Christ Jesus is Truly God. He is in us by means of His Flesh, and we are in Him when that which we are is with Him in God. That we dwell in Him through that Sacrament wherein His Flesh and Blood are given unto us, He Himself does testify, where He says "Yet a little while, and the world seeth Me no more but you see Me because I live you shall live also. For I am in My Father, and you in Me, and I in you."

Lesson IX

But that this union in us is a real one, He testifies thus: "He that eateth My Flesh and drinketh My Blood, dwelleth in Me, and I in him." For no one dwells in Him in whom He does not dwell, since he which receives has but received that Flesh of (the same nature as) his own, which Christ has taken into Himself. The mystery of this perfect union He had taught before, when He said: "As the living Father hath sent Me, and I live by the Father, so, he that eateth Me, even he shall live by Me." He therefore lives by the Father, and, as He lives by the Father, so shall we live by Him.

Octave Day of Corpus Christi

~Thursday II after Pentecost~

Major Duplex

Lesson I ~ 1 Kings 8:4–6

From first book of Kings

Then all the ancients of Israel being assembled, came to Samuel to Ramatha. And they said to him: Behold thou art old, and thy sons walk not in thy ways: make us a king, to judge us, as all nations have. And the word was displeasing in the eyes of Samuel, that they should say: Give us a king, to judge us. And Samuel prayed to the Lord.

Lesson II ~ 1 Kings 8:7–9

And the Lord said to Samuel: Hearken to the voice of the people in all that they say to thee. For they have not rejected thee, but me, that I should not reign over them. According to all their works, they have done from the day that I brought them out of Egypt until this day: as they have forsaken me, and served strange gods, so do they also unto thee. Now therefore hearken to their voice: but yet testify to them, and foretell them the right of the king, that shall reign over them.

Lesson III ~ 1 Kings 8:10–14

Then Samuel told all the words of the Lord to the people that had desired a king of him, And said: This will be the right of the king, that shall reign over you: He will take your sons, and put them in his chariots, and will make them his horsemen, and his running footmen to run before his chariots, And he will appoint of them to be his tribunes, and centurions, and to plough his fields, and to reap his corn, and to make him arms and chariots. Your daughters also he will take to make him ointments, and to be his cooks, and bakers. And he will take your fields, and your vineyards, and your best oliveyards, and give them to his servants.

Lesson IV

Sermon by the Blessed Patriarch of Jerusalem Cyril.

The teaching of the blessed Paul seems of itself enough instruction for you concerning those Divine Mysteries, whereof, if you be made worthy, you become therein, so to speak, of one Body and of one Blood with Christ. Paul says that our Lord Jesus Christ, "the same night in which He was betrayed, took bread and, when He had given thanks, He broke it, and gave it unto His disciples, saying Take, eat this is My Body. After the same manner also He took the chalice," and gave thanks, and said: Take this and drink it, this is My Blood. Since therefore it is He Who has definitely stated and said, regarding that Bread "This is My Body," who will dare any longer to doubt that It is so? And since it is He again that has absolutely affirmed and said, regarding that chalice "This is My Blood" who is he that will doubt any longer, or say that It is not His Blood?

Lesson V

At the beginning of His ministry, at Cana in Galilee, the Lord turned water into wine, a thing which has some qualities in common with blood, and shall we deem Him less worthy that we should believe Him, when He turns wine into Blood? When He was bidden to that marriage wherein two were made one flesh, He did the beginning of His miracles to the amazement of all men; and shall we less surely hold that He has given us His Body and Blood to be our meat and drink, or take them with weaker faith that they are indeed His Body and His Blood Under the appearance of bread? He gives unto us His Body, and under the appearance of wine, His Blood; and when thou shalt come to receive, it is on the Body and Blood of Christ that thou wilt feed, being made a partaker of His Body and of His Blood. Thus indeed it is that we become Christbearers, namely, by carrying about Christ in our bodies, when we receive His Body and Blood into our own frames. Thus, as the blessed Peter has it, we are "partakers of the Divine nature."

Lesson VI

Christ once said, in conversing with the Jews "Except you eat the Flesh of the Son of Man, and drink His Blood, you have no life in you." But they took not spiritually that which He said, and "from that time many of His disciples went back, and walked no more with Him." They thought that He had bidden them to eat flesh. The Old Testament also had Showbread, but this Old Testament bread was now to have an end. The bread of the New Testament is "the Bread Which comes down from heaven," the cup of the New Testament, the Cup of Salvation, that Bread and that Cup Which hallow both souls and bodies. Wherefore I will have thee to understand that the Bread and Wine whereunto thou art to come, are not mere common bread or mere common wine for they are the Body and the Blood of Christ. Even if thy senses do indeed deny this fact, yet let faith make thee right sure of it. Judge not the Thing by the taste thereof, but let faith assure thee beyond all doubt thou art partaking of the Body and Blood of Christ.

Lesson VII

From the Holy Gospel according to St. John (John 6:56–59)

At that time: Jesus said unto the multitudes of the Jews: My Flesh is meat indeed, and My Blood is drink indeed. And so on.

Homily by St. Cyril, Pope of Alexandria.

"He that eateth My Flesh and drinketh My Blood," says the Lord, "dwelleth in Me, and I in him." If a man take two pieces of wax and melt them, and pour the one into the other, they necessarily mingle; so also, he that receives the Body and Blood of the Lord does become so joined with the Lord that he is to be found in Christ and Christ in him. Another comparison thou wilt find in Matthew. The Lord there says "The kingdom of heaven is like unto leaven which a woman took, and hid in three measures of meal," because, as Paul says, "a little leaven leavens the whole lump." So also does a little of this Blessing draw the whole man unto Itself, and fill him with Its grace and thus does Christ dwell in us, and we in Christ.

Lesson VIII

As for ourselves, if we would win life everlasting; if we would that the Giver of immortality should dwell in us, let us run freely to receive this Blessing, and let us beware that the devil succeed not in laying a stumbling-block in our way, in the shape of a mistaken reverence. Thou rightly sayest, and we know well, how that it is written "Whosoever shall eat this Bread and drink this Cup of the Lord unworthily, eateth and drinketh damnation to himself." I therefore examine myself and find myself unworthy. And I ask thee, who cites these words to me, who shall ever be found worthy? When wilt thou be such a one as may be worthy to be offered to Christ? If by sin thou art unworthy, and thou ceasest not to sin, for, as the Psalmist has it, "Who can understand his errors?" then shalt thou for ever lack this means of life and sanctification.

Lesson IX

Therefore, I counsel thee to betake thee to godly thoughts, and to live carefully and holily, and so to receive that Blessing a Blessing which, believe me, does banish, not death only, but all diseases likewise. For when Christ dwells in us, He stills the law of death in our members, which wars against the law of our mind, He gives strength to godliness, He turns to calm the turbulent surging of our mind, He cures them which are sick, He raises up them which are fallen, and, like the Good Shepherd, Which gives His life for the sheep, He prevails that the sheep perish not.

THE MOST SACRED HEART OF OUR LORD JESUS CHRIST

Duplex I Class

Lesson I ~ Jer 24:5–7

From Jeremias the Prophet

Thus saith the Lord the God of Israel: Like these good figs, so will I regard the captives of Juda, whom I have sent forth out of this place into the land of the Chaldeans, for their good. And I will set my eyes upon them to be pacified, and I will bring them again into this land: and I will build them up, and not pull them down: and I will plant them, and not pluck them up. And I will give them a heart to know me, that I am the Lord: and they shall be my people, and I will be their God: because they shall return to me with their whole heart.

Lesson II ~ Jer 30:18–19; 30:21–24

Thus saith the Lord: Behold I will bring back the captivity of the pavilions of Jacob, and will have pity on his houses, and the city shall be built in her high place, and the temple shall be founded according to the order thereof. And out of them shall come forth praise, and the voice of them that play: And their leader shall be of themselves: and their prince shall come forth from the midst of them: and I will bring him near, and he shall come to me: for who is this that setteth his heart to approach to me, saith the Lord? And you shall be my people: and I will be your God. Behold the whirlwind of the Lord, his fury going forth, a violent storm, it shall rest upon the head of the wicked. The Lord will not turn away the wrath of his indignation, till he have executed and performed the thought of his heart: in the latter days you shall understand these things.

Lesson III ~ Jer 31:1–3; 31:31–33

At that time, saith the Lord, I will be the God of all the families of Israel, and they shall be my people. Thus saith the Lord: The people that were left and escaped from the sword, found grace in the desert: Israel shall go to his rest. The Lord hath appeared from afar to me. Yea I have loved thee with an everlasting love, therefore have I drawn thee, taking pity on thee. Behold the days shall come, saith the Lord, and I will make a new covenant with the house of Israel, and with the house of Juda: Not according to the covenant which I made with their fathers, in the day that I took them by the hand to bring them out of the land of Egypt: the covenant which they made void, and I had dominion over them, saith the Lord. But this shall be the covenant that I will make with the house of Israel, after those days, saith the Lord: I will give my law in their bowels, and I will write it in their heart: and I will be their God, and they shall be my people.

Lesson IV

Among the wonderful developments of sacred teaching and piety, by which the plans of the divine Wisdom are daily made clear to the Church, hardly any is more manifest than the triumphant progress made by the devotion of the most Sacred Heart of Jesus. Very often indeed, during the course of past ages, Fathers, Doctors, and Saints have celebrated our Redeemer's love: and they have said that the wound opened in the side of Christ was the hidden fountain of all graces. Moreover, from the Middle Ages onward, when the faithful began to show a more tender piety towards the most sacred Humanity of the Saviour, contemplative souls became accustomed to penetrate through that wound almost to the very Heart itself, wounded for the love of men. And from that time, this form of contemplation became so familiar to all persons of saintly life, that there was no country or religious order in which, during this period, witnesses to it were not to be found. Finally, during recent centuries, and most especially at that period when heretics, in the name of a false piety, strove to discourage Christians from receiving the most Holy Eucharist, the veneration of the most Sacred Heart began to be openly practiced, principally through the exertions of St. John Eudes, who is by no means unworthily called the founder of the liturgical worship of the Sacred Hearts of Jesus and Mary.

Lesson V

But in order to establish fully and entirely the worship of the most Sacred Heart of Jesus, and to spread the same throughout the whole world, God himself chose as his instrument a most humble virgin from the order of the Visitation, St. Margaret Mary Alacoque, who even in her earliest years already had a burning love for the Sacrament of the Eucharist, and to whom Christ the Lord had very many times appeared, and was pleased to make known the riches and the desires of his divine Heart. The most famous of these apparitions was that in which Jesus revealed himself to her in prayer before the blessed Sacrament, showed her his most Sacred Heart, and, complaining that in return for his unbounded love, he met with nothing but outrages and ingratitude from mankind, he ordered her to concern herself with the establishment of a new feast, on the Friday after the Octave of Corpus Christi, on which his Heart should be venerated with due honor, and that the insults offered him by sinners in the Sacrament of love should be expiated by worthy satisfaction. But there is no one who knows not how many and how great were the obstacles which the handmaid of God experienced, in carrying out the commands of Christ; but, endowed with strength by the Lord himself, and actively aided by her pious spiritual directors, who exerted themselves with an almost unbelievable zeal, up to the time of her death she never ceased faithfully to carry out the duty entrusted to her by heaven.

Lesson VI

At length, in the year 1765, the Supreme Pontiff Clement XIII approved the Mass and Office in honor of the most Sacred Heart of Jesus; and Pius IX extended the feast to the universal Church. From then on, the worship of the most Sacred Heart, like an overflowing river, washing away all obstacles, has poured itself forth over all the earth, and, at the dawn of the new century, Leo XIII, having proclaimed a jubilee, decided to dedicate the whole human race to the most Sacred Heart. This consecration was actually carried out with solemn rites in all the churches of the Catholic world, and brought about a great increase of this devotion, leading not only nations but even private families to it, who in countless numbers dedicated themselves to the Divine Heart, and submitted themselves to its royal sway. Lastly, the Sovereign Pontiff Pius XI, in order that, by its solemnity, the feast might answer more fully to the greatly widespread devotion of the Christian people, raised the feast of the most Sacred Heart of Jesus to the rite of a Duplex of the first class, with an octave; and moreover, that the violated rights of Christ, the supreme King and most loving Lord, might be repaired, and that the sins of the nations might be bewailed, he ordered that annually, on that same feast-day, there should be recited an expiatory form of prayer in all the churches of the Christian world.

Lesson VII

From the Holy Gospel according to St. John (John 19:31–37)

At that time: The Jews, because it was the Preparation, that the bodies should not remain upon the cross on the Sabbath Day, for that Sabbath Day was a high day, besought Pilate that their legs might broken, and that they might be taken away. And so on.

Homily by St. Bonaventure, Bishop

In order that the Church might be taken out of the side of Christ, in his deep sleep on the Cross, and that the Scripture might be fulfilled which says: "They shall look on him whom they pierced:" it was divinely ordained that one of the soldiers should pierce his sacred side with a spear, and open it. Then forthwith there came flowing out blood and water, which was the price of our salvation, pouring forth from its mountain-source, in sooth, from the secret places of his Heart, to give power to the Sacraments of the Church, to bestow the life of grace, and to be as a saving drink of living waters, flowing up to life eternal for those who were already quickened in Christ. Arise, then, O soul beloved of Christ. Cease not thy vigilance, place there thy lips, and drink the waters from the fount of salvation.

Lesson VIII

Because we are now come to the sweet Heart of Jesus, and because it is good for us to be here, let us not too soon turn away therefrom. O how good and joyful a thing it is to dwell in this Heart. What a good treasure, what a precious pearl, is thy Heart, O most excellent Jesu, which we have found hidden in the pit which has been dug in this field, namely, in thy body. Who would cast away such a pearl? Nay, rather, for this same I would give all my pearls. I will sell all my thoughts and affections, and buy the same for myself, turning all my thoughts to the Heart of the good Jesus, and without fail it will support me. Therefore, O most sweet Jesu, finding this Heart that is thine and mine, I will pray to thee, my God: admit my prayers into the shrine of hearkening: and draw me even more altogether into thy Heart.

Lesson IX

For to this end was thy side pierced, that an entry might be open unto us. To this end was thy Heart wounded, that in it we might be able to dwell secure from alarms from without. And it was wounded none the less on this account that, because of the visible wound, we may perceive the wound of love which is invisible. How could this fire of love better shine forth than for him to permit that not only his body, but that even his Heart, should be wounded with the spear? Who would not love that Heart so wounded? Who would not, in return, love one who is so loving? Who would not embrace one so chaste? Wherefore let us who are in the flesh love in return, as much as we can, him who so loves, embrace our wounded one, whose hands and feet, side and Heart, have been pierced by wicked husbandmen; and let us pray that he may deign to bind our hearts, still hard and impenitent, with the chain of his love, and wound them with the dart thereof.

Saturday within the Octave of the Sacred Heart

Semiduplex

Lesson I ~ 1 Kings 9:1–4

From first book of Kings

Now there was a man of Benjamin whose name was Cis, the son of Abiel, the son of Seror, the son of Bechorath, the son of Aphia, the son of a man of Jemini, valiant and strong. And he had a son whose name was Saul, a choice and goodly man, and there was not among the children of Israel a goodlier person than he: from his shoulders and upward he appeared above all the people. And the asses of Cis, Saul's father, were lost: and Cis said to his son Saul: Take one of the servants with thee, and arise, go, and seek the asses. And when they had passed through mount Ephraim, And through the land of Salisa, and had not found them, they passed also through the land of Salim, and they were not there: and through the land of Jemini, and found them not.

Lesson II - 1 Kings 9:5–8

And when they were come to the land of Suph, Saul said to the servant that was with him: Come, let us return, lest perhaps my father forget the asses, and be concerned for us. And he said to him: Behold there is a man of God in this city, a famous man: all that he saith, comes certainly to pass. Now therefore let us go thither, perhaps he may tell us of our way, for which we are come. And Saul said to his servant: Behold we will go: but what shall we carry to the man of God? the bread is spent in our bags: and we have no present to make to the man of God, nor any thing at all. The servant answered Saul again, and said: Behold there is found in my hand the fourth part of a sicle of silver, let us give it to the man of God, that he may tell us our way.

Lesson III - 1 Kings 9:14–17

And they went up into the city. And when they were walking in the midst of the city, behold Samuel was coming out over against them, to go up to the high place. Now the Lord had revealed to the ear of Samuel the day before Saul came, saying: Tomorrow about this same hour I will send thee a man of the land of Benjamin, and thou shalt anoint him to be ruler over my people Israel: and he shall save my people out of the hand of the Philistines: for I have looked down upon my people, because their cry is come to me. And when Samuel saw Saul, the Lord said to him: Behold the man, of whom I spoke to thee, this man shall reign over my people.

Lesson IV

From the Encyclical Letter of Pope Pius XI - *Miserentíssimus Redémptor*

Among all other proofs of the infinite kindness of our Redeemer, this one is especially conspicuous, that, as the love of the Christian believers grew cold, he, Divine Love itself, was proposed to be honored by a special devotion, and that the rich treasures of his goodness were thrown wide open by means of that form of worship with which we honor the most Sacred Heart of Jesus, "in whom are hid all the treasures of wisdom and knowledge." For, as formerly God wished to give light to the human race as they came out of Noe's ark by the signal of a treaty of friendship, "a bow appearing in the clouds," so, in those most troublous times of a more recent age, when that most subtle of heresies, Jansenism, was everywhere creeping in, an enemy of the love of God and of piety, preaching that God was not so much to be loved as a father, as to be feared as an unrelenting judge, the most kind Jesus manifested unto the nations his most Sacred Heart, borne on high like unto a banner of peace and love, an augury of certain victory in battle.

Lesson V

Because Our predecessor, Leo XIII, of happy memory, desiring to obtain the advantages of such a great devotion to the most Sacred Heart of Jesus, in his Encyclical Letter *Annum Sacrum* most fittingly did not hesitate to proclaim: "When the

Church, in the early period of her history, was oppressed by the yoke of the Caesars, a cross appeared in the heavens to a youthful emperor, which was at the same time both the sign and the cause of that most complete victory, which was soon to follow. Behold this day another most auspicious and most holy sign presented to our eyes: that is to say, the most Sacred Heart of Jesus, with a Cross set upon it, shining forth among flames of a most brilliant radiance. In this, all our hopes are to be placed; from this, the salvation of mankind is to be asked for and to be awaited."

Lesson VI

And it is indeed justly so; for in this most auspicious sign and in that which follows from it, is there not contained the highest model of piety of the whole of religion, and therefore the rule of the more perfect life, inasmuch as it leads our minds the more easily to a deeper knowledge of Christ the Lord, and to a more vehement love of him, and moves our souls more effectually to a more exact imitation of him? Therefore, no one will be surprised, that Our predecessors have continuously vindicated this most approved form of devotion from the accusations of objectors, that they have extolled it with the highest praises, and have promoted it with the most ardent zeal, according as considerations of the period and of affairs in general have demanded. And it has come to pass by the providence of God, that the devout affection of Christ's faithful people towards the most Sacred Heart of Jesus obtains daily a great increase.

Lesson VII

From the Holy Gospel according to St. John (John 19:31–37)

At that time: The Jews, because it was the Preparation, that the bodies should not remain upon the cross on the Sabbath Day, for that Sabbath Day was a high day, besought Pilate that their legs might broken, and that they might be taken away. And so on.

Homily by St. John Chrysostom

See you not how mighty is the Truth? Through the zeal of the Jews the prophecy is fulfilled. And more than one prophecy was fulfilled. For when the soldiers came and broke the legs of the others, they broke not the legs of Christ. But yet these soldiers, to please the Jews, pierced his side with a lance, and treated his body contumeliously. O wicked and accursed crime! But be not troubled, beloved, or downcast. They indeed did it in ill-will, but they unwittingly contended for the truth, as verily the prophecy foretold: "They shall look on him whom they have pierced." And more than this, the evil deed served as a demonstration even afterwards to those who were without faith, such as Thomas and others like him. This ineffable mystery was also consummated to another end: "Forthwith came there out blood and water." Neither causelessly nor by mere chance did these fountains flow, but because the Church was founded with Water and Blood.

Lesson VIII

This is well-known to those who have been initiated, namely, to all who have been regenerated by the Water, and nourished with the Flesh and Blood, so that when thou dost approach to the awesome cup, thou shouldst come as if thou wert about to drink from this very side of Christ. "And he that saw it bore record, and his record is true:" as though to say: "Not from others have I heard it, but I myself was present, and saw it, and therefore my record of it is true." Truly indeed does he thus speak. For he speaks to us as of an insult, and not as of something great and wonderful, else thou mightest doubt his testimony; but he (thus shutting the mouth of heretics, and foretelling future mysteries, and mindful of the treasure to be contained in them), does enumerate one by one the events as they took place. These things were done that the Scriptures should be fulfilled: "A bone of him shall not be broken." For even though this was written concerning the lamb which the Jews used for their Passover, nevertheless this lamb was a figure which came first to show forth the reality yet to come, wherein the prophecy was to be perfectly fulfilled; and that is why the Evangelist quotes the passage as a prophecy.

Lesson IX

Since the testimony he himself bears might not everywhere be held worthy of belief, he cites Moses, to intimate that this thing was not done by chance, but had already long ago been foretold in writing. By Moses it was said: "A bone of him shall not be broken." And again he rests his faith on the same Prophet: "These things I have said," says he, "that you may learn how great is the resemblance between the figure and the reality." See what great care he takes, that what appears as disgraceful and ignominious may be believed. For that the body should be treated with contempt by the soldier, was far worse than its crucifixion. "But nevertheless," says he, "I have both said these things, and have said them most emphatically, that you may believe." Let no one, therefore, deny credence to these things, nor in shame tamper with our beliefs. For those things which seem to be the most dishonoring, are in fact our greatest pride.

Sunday III after Pentecost

~ within the Octave of the Sacred Heart ~

Semiduplex

Lesson I ~ 1 Kings 9:18–21

From first book of Kings

And Saul came to Samuel in the midst of the gate and said: Tell me, I pray thee, where is the house of the seer? And Samuel answered Saul, saying: I am the seer, go up before me to the high place, that you may eat with me today, and I will let thee go in the morning: and tell thee all that is in thy heart. And as for the asses, which were lost three days ago, be not solicitous, because they are found. And for whom shall be all the best things of Israel? Shall they not be for thee and for all thy father's house? And Saul answering, said: Am not I a son of Jemini of the least tribe of Israel, and my kindred the last among all the families of the tribe of Benjamin? Why then hast thou spoken this word to me?

Lesson II ~ 1 Kings 9:22–25

Then Samuel taking Saul and his servant, brought them into the parlour, and gave them a place at the head of them that were invited. For there were about thirty men. And Samuel said to the cook: Bring the portion, which I gave thee, and commanded thee to set it apart by thee. And the cook took up the shoulder, and set it before Saul. And Samuel said: Behold what is left, set it before thee, and eat: because it was kept of purpose for thee, when I invited the people. And Saul ate with Samuel that day. And they went down from the high place into the town, and he spoke with Saul upon the top of the house: and he prepared a bed for Saul on the top of the house, and he slept.

Lesson III ~ 1 Kings 9:26–27; 10:1

And when they were risen in the morning, and it began now to be light, Samuel called Saul on the top of the house, saying: Arise, that I may let thee go. And Saul arose: and they went out both of them, to wit, he and Samuel. And as they were going down in the end of the city, Samuel said to Saul: Speak to the servant to go before us, and pass on: but stand thou still a while, that I may tell thee the word of the Lord. And Samuel took a little vial of oil and poured it upon his head, and kissed him, and said: Behold, the Lord hath anointed thee to be prince over his inheritance, and thou shalt deliver his people out of the hands of their enemies, that are round about them. And this shall be a sign unto thee, that God hath anointed thee to be prince.

Lesson IV

From the Encyclical Letter of Pope Pius XI ~ *Miserentíssimus Redémptor*

Among the various devotions paid to the Sacred Heart, the one foremost in importance and interest is assuredly the Act of Consecration, whereby we give to the divine Heart of Jesus both ourselves and all that is ours; in recognition of the truth that all we have comes unto us out of the infinite charity of the eternal Deity. But it is expedient that any attempt of ours at self-consecration be accompanied with the purpose of making expiation (otherwise called reparation) to the most Sacred Heart of Jesus. In consecration, the predominant intention may be said to be the purpose to repay (as it were) the love of the Creator by the love of us his creatures. But since Love Uncreated is passed over by human forgetfulness, and dishonored by the sins of mankind, we should endeavor to repair such outrages; and the performance of this duty is ordinarily known as reparation.

Lesson V

If we are, for the aforesaid reasons, to undertake both of those practices, we must recognize that we are impelled to the duty of reparation by the most powerful motives of justice and love: of justice, in order to expiate the injury done to God by our sins, and to re-establish through penance the divine order which was violated by them; of love, in order to suffer together with Christ (who patiently endured all possible dishonor), so that we may offer him some solace in return for his sufferings. For it is our duty to do more than honor God by the worship of adoration, whereby we adore his infinite Majesty, or by means of prayer, when we recognize his supreme dominion over us, or by acts of thanksgiving, when we praise his infinite generosity towards us. Because we are sinners, burdened with many offenses, we must also make satisfaction to the offended justice of God, because of the numberless sins, offenses and negligences we have committed. Wherefore, we must add to the act of consecration, by which we offer ourselves to God, and become thereby, as it were, sacred unto God by reason of the holiness which naturally flows from an act of consecration, as the Angelic Doctor teaches. We must add the act of reparation, by means of which all our faults are blotted out, lest perchance the sanctity of Infinite Justice spurn our arrogant unworthiness, and look upon the gift of ourselves as something to be rejected rather than accepted.

Lesson VI

All men are under obligation to make reparation; for our souls are disfigured, as the Christian faith teaches, by original sin as a result of the pitiable fall of Adam. We are also subject to passions, whereby we are corrupted in a truly sad state, and have thus made ourselves worthy of everlasting condemnation. It is true that the proud philosophers of this world deny the aforesaid truths, and in their place do raise up again the ancient heresy of Pelagius: which taught that in human nature there is a certain innate goodness wherewith, by our own powers, we are raised up to ever higher levels of perfection; but such false theories, born of human pride, have been condemned by the Apostle in his saying that all men are by nature the children of wrath. As a matter of fact, from the very beginning of the creation of the world, mankind recognized, in one way or another, the obligation of making reparation, impelled thereto, as by a natural instinct, in an endeavor to placate God by offering public sacrifices unto him.

Lesson VII

From the Holy Gospel according to St. Luke (Luke 15:1–10)

At that time: the publicans and sinners drew near unto him to hear him. And so on.

Homily by Pope St. Gregory

You have heard, my brethren, from the Gospel which has but now been read, how that the publicans and sinners drew near unto our Redeemer, and how He received them, not only to converse, but also to eat with Him. And when the Pharisees and Scribes saw it, they murmured. From this learn that true righteousness is merciful and false righteousness is contemptuous, albeit that the righteous also often feel moved with just indignation at sinners. But it is one thing to feel thus indignant through pride, and another to feel so through love of law.

Lesson VIII

The righteous indeed look down upon sinners, and yet, as not despising them; they abandon them, and yet, as not without hope; they fight against them, and yet, as loving them all the while; for if they be bound to chasten them grievously as touching the outer man, yet is it through charity which offers sweetness to their inner man. In their hearts they prefer before themselves them whom they are correcting; they hold as better than themselves them whom they judge. And thus doing, they watch by carefulness over them, which are committed unto their charge, and, by humility, over themselves.

Lesson IX

On the other hand, they whose exaltation comes of a false righteousness, look down upon their neighbor, but are softened by no mercy toward his misery, and are all the more sinful, because they perceive not that they themselves are sinners. Of such were those Pharisees who judged the Lord because He received sinners, and, in the dryness of their own heart, rebuked the very Fountain of mercy. They were sick of so desperate a sickness that they knew not of themselves that they were sick; but, that they might know that they were so, the Heavenly Physician applied to them His tender ointments, and, by means of a gracious parable, lanced the boil of their pride of heart.

Monday within the Octave of the Sacred Heart

Semiduplex

Lesson I ~ 1 Kings 10:17–19

From first book of Kings

And Samuel called together the people to the Lord in Maspha: And he said to the children of Israel: Thus saith the Lord the God of Israel: I brought up Israel out of Egypt, and delivered you from the hand of the Egyptians, and from the hand of all the kings who afflicted you. But you this day have rejected your God, who only hath saved you out of all your evils and your tribulations: and you have said: Nay: but set a king over us. Now therefore stand before the Lord by your tribes, and by your families.

Lesson II ~ 1 Kings 10:20–24

And Samuel brought to him all the tribes of Israel, and the lot fell on the tribe of Benjamin. And he brought the tribe of Benjamin and the kindreds thereof, and the lot fell upon the kindred of Metri, and it came to Saul the son of Cis. They sought him therefore and he was not found. And after this they consulted the Lord whether he would come thither. And the Lord answered: Behold he is hidden at home. And they ran and fetched him thence: and he stood in the midst of the people, and he was higher than any of the people from the shoulders and upward. And Samuel said to all the people: Surely you see him whom the Lord hath chosen, that there is none like him among all the people. And all the people cried and said: God save the king.

Lesson III - 1 Kings 10:25–27

And Samuel told the people the law of the kingdom, and wrote it in a book, and laid it up before the Lord: and Samuel sent away all the people, every one to his own house. Saul also departed to his own house in Gabaa: and there went with him a part of the army, whose hearts God had touched. But the children of Belial said: Shall this fellow be able to save us? And they despised him, and brought him no presents, but he dissembled as though he heard not.

Lesson IV

From the Encyclical Letter of Pope Pius XI - *Miserentissimus Redémptor*

No effort on our part could have availed for the expiation of human sin, if the Son of God had not assumed human nature in order to redeem men from their sins. This truth the Saviour of mankind has made known in the words of the Psalmist: "Sacrifice and offering thou wouldest not, but a body hast thou prepared me; in burnt offerings and sacrifices for sin thou hast had no pleasure; then said I, Lo, I come." Surely he has borne our griefs, and carried our sorrows: he was wounded for our transgressions, he was bruised for our iniquities: who his own self bore our sins in his body on the Tree; and blotting out the handwriting of ordinances that was against us, which same was contrary to us, he took it out of the way, nailing it to his Cross: that we, being dead unto sins, should live unto righteousness. But although this plenteous redemption of Christ was more than sufficient to satisfy for all our offenses, nevertheless (due to the wondrous dispensation of the divine Wisdom, whereby in our own flesh we may fill up that which is behind of the afflictions of Christ for his body's sake, which is the Church), we can, and in fact, we should, add our own acts of praise and satisfaction to those acts of praise and satisfaction which Christ, in the name of sinners, presented to God.

Lesson V

However, we must always remember this, to wit: The expiatory value of our acts is dependent upon the Bloody Sacrifice of Christ; which same is presented bloodlessly on our altars, without intermission. Note that in both the Unbloody and the Bloody Sacrifice, the Victim is one and the same. He that offered himself on the Cross is the very same that offers himself by means of our ministerial priesthood; the only difference being the manner in which the Sacrifice is made; for which reason there must be conjoined to the august Sacrifice of the Holy Eucharist an act of immolation from the priests and the faithful, whereby they offer up themselves, also, to be a reasonable, holy, and living sacrifice, acceptable unto God. With this in mind, Saint Cyprian dared to affirm that the Sacrifice of the Lord is not complete so far as our sanctification is concerned until our personal offerings and sacrifices are brought into union with his passion. To which end we have been given apostolic admonition: That we should always bear about in the body of the dying of the Lord Jesus; and thereby, buried with him by Baptism unto death, not only can we crucify the flesh with its affections and lusts, thus escaping the corruption that is in the world through lust, but also thereby the life of Jesus can be made manifest in our bodies; and so, having been made partakers of Christ in his holy and eternal priesthood, we should offer both gifts and sacrifices for sins.

Lesson VI

And note who they are that be partakers in the mysteries of such a priesthood, and in the duty of offering sacrifices and satisfaction to God; not only they who have been ordained as ministers of such sacrifices, to wit, to offer unto the divine Name in every place a pure offering, from the rising of the sun even unto the going down of the same, but also all others who are Christians; which same by the Prince of the Apostles are called, and rightly so, a chosen generation, a royal priesthood, who are to offer sacrifices for sin, not only for themselves but for all mankind, and this in much the same way as every priest and high priest taken from among men is ordained for men in the things that appertain to God.

Lesson VII

From the Holy Gospel according to St. John (John 19:31–37)

At that time: The Jews, because it was the Preparation, that the bodies should not remain upon the cross on the Sabbath Day, for that Sabbath Day was a high day, besought Pilate that their legs might broken, and that they might be taken away. And so on.

Homily by St. Lawrence Justinian, Bishop

"But when they came to Jesus, and saw that he was dead already, they broke not his legs, but one of the soldiers with a spear pierced his side, and forthwith came there out blood and water." Truly this is a great and unheard-of wonder, that from a lifeless body should gush out blood and water! And thereby we are constrained to believe that God willed to set forth the great mystery, namely, the unity between Christ and the Church. Consider how formerly a figure of this spiritual union was given us in the Scriptures, where we are told that, from the side of Adam as he slept, one of his ribs was taken, wherefrom was formed Eve, the mother of us all, which same is understood to be a type of the Church. For thereby the Holy Ghost signified that there was to be a true and spiritual Adam, fashioned by the same Paraclete, from whose side, while he slept on the Cross, the Church would be formed, a beautiful spouse radiant with youth, that is, without spot or wrinkle, or any such thing.

Lesson VIII

For the blood and water are the Sacraments of the Church, whereby the whole body of the Church is washed and sanctified. Certain it is that in the laver of regenerating water (the same which was consecrated by the death of Christ), the Church is cleansed from original sin. And not only is purification given thereby, but entrance to the heavenly kingdom is also made. Both these things are done at one and the same time, nor does one avail for salvation without the other; for no one can take unto himself the inheritance of the blessedness which is to come without the Sacrament of Baptism and the remission of sins. This truth is confessed all the world over by holy Mother Church, and confirmed by manifold testimonies in the Word of God. Moreover, he too bore witness, who saw the water and blood flow forth from the side of Christ, and his testimony is true. Now this is John the Apostle and Evangelist who was loved with an exceedingly great love by the Lord.

Lesson IX

Verily, all these things were done that the Scriptures might be fulfilled, which say: "A bone of him shall not be broken:" which was in obedience to the Lord's commandment to Moses, that in the sacrifice of the Passover (wherein was celebrated the offering up of the lamb), no bone should be broken. Wherefrom, when this ancient prototype was fulfilled in the most innocent Lamb (the Lord Jesus himself), obedience to the ancient command was also fulfilled. For in no way were his legs broken, after the manner of what was done to the two malefactors hanging with him; but his side alone was opened, that another Scripture might be fulfilled, which says: "They shall look upon him whom they have pierced." Moreover, the Lord willed to retain the marks of the Wounds in his body, thereby to incite the devotion of the elect, and also be an unanswerable testimony of damnation to the reprobate. And so all things were consummated in Christ, which had been long before declared by the oracles of the Prophets, that the Catholic faith might be strengthened both in itself and against the errors of the heretics.

Tuesday within the Octave of the Sacred Heart

Semiduplex

Lesson I ~ 1 Kings 12:1–5

From first book of Kings

And Samuel said to all Israel: Behold I have hearkened to your voice in all that you said to me, and have made a king over you. And now the king goeth before you: but I am old and greyheaded: and my sons are with you: having then conversed with you from my youth unto this day, behold here I am. Speak of me before the Lord, and before his anointed, whether I have taken any man's ox, or ass: If I have wronged any man, if I have oppressed any man, if I have taken a bribe at any man's hand: and I will despise it this day, and will restore it to you. And they said: Thou hast not wronged us, nor oppressed us, nor taken ought at any man's hand. And he said to them: The Lord is witness against you, and his anointed is witness this day, that you have not found any thing in my hand. And they said: He is witness.

Lesson II ~ 1 Kings 12:6–9

And Samuel said to the people: It is the Lord, who made Moses and Aaron, and brought our fathers out of the land of Egypt. Now therefore stand up, that I may plead in judgment against you before the Lord, concerning all the kindness of the Lord, which he hath shown to you, and to your fathers: How Jacob went into Egypt, and your fathers cried to the Lord: and the Lord sent Moses and Aaron, and brought your fathers out of Egypt: and made them dwell in this place. And they forgot the Lord their God, and he delivered them into the hands of Sisara, captain of the army of Hasor, and into the hands of the Philistines, and into the hand of the king of Moab, and they fought against them.

Lesson III ~ 1 Kings 12:10–14

But afterwards they cried to the Lord, and said: We have sinned, because we have forsaken the Lord, and have served Baalim and Astaroth: but now deliver us from the hand of our enemies, and we will serve thee. And the Lord sent Jerobaal, and Badan, and Jephte, and Samuel, and delivered you from the hand of your enemies round about, and you dwelt securely. But seeing that Naas king of the children of Ammon was come against you, you said to me: Nay, but a king shall reign over us: whereas the Lord your God was your king. Now therefore your king is here, whom you have chosen and desired: Behold the Lord hath given you a king. If you will fear the Lord, and serve him, and hearken to his voice, and not provoke the mouth of the Lord: then shall both you, and the king who reigneth over you, be followers of the Lord your God.

Lesson IV

From the Encyclical Letter of Pope Pius XI ~ *Miserentíssimus Redémptor*

According to that degree of perfection wherewith our oblation and our sacrifice do correspond to the Sacrifice of our Lord, that is to say, to the extent that we have immolated love of self and its passions, and thereby have crucified our flesh in that mystical crucifixion concerning which the Apostle wrote, in that same degree shall we gather the fruits of propitiation and expiation for ourselves and for others. For a wondrous bond joins all the faithful unto Christ, namely, that bond which unites the Head with the members of the body, which is to say, the Communion of the Saints, a bond full of mystery in which we as Catholics do nevertheless verily believe. By virtue of this bond, individuals and nations are not only united the one with the other, but likewise with the Head itself, which is Christ: from whom the whole body, fitly joined together and compacted by that which every joint supplies, according to the working in due measure of each several part, makes increase of the body unto the building up of itself in love. This verily was the prayer which Christ Jesus himself, the Mediator between God and man, made at the time of his death: "I in them, and thou in me, that they may be perfected into one."

Lesson V

Therefore, even as our effort at consecration manifests and strengthens our union with Christ, so our practice of expiation (by purifying us from sins) is the beginning of such union; wherefrom our participation in the sufferings of Christ is the means of perfecting such union; and the offering which we make to him of our sacrifices for the welfare of our brethren brings such union to its final consummation. Now this is precisely the design of the mercy of Jesus, when he unveils to the gaze of mankind his Heart, surrounded by the emblems of his passion, and aflame with the Fire of Love, namely: that we (on the one hand, perceiving the unlimited malice of sin, and on the other, filled with a knowledge of the infinite love of him who is The Reparator), may detest sin more heartily, and substitute for it a burning love for him. And verily, the spirit of expiation or of reparation has always played a chief part in the devotion to the most Sacred Heart of Jesus, and reparation is most consonant with the origin, nature, efficacy and particular practices of this special devotion, a fact confirmed by history and the customs of the faithful, by the sacred liturgy, and by the official documents of the Supreme Pontiffs.

Lesson VI

Inasmuch as, when Christ revealed himself to the sight of Margaret Mary, though he then insisted on the immensity of his love, at the same time, with sorrowful manner, he grieved over the great number of horrible outrages heaped upon him by the ingratitude of mankind; he used then these words, words which should be engraved on the hearts of all pious souls so as never to be forgotten by them: "Behold that Heart which has so loved men; the same which has heaped upon them so many benefits; in return for whose infinite love no gratitude is to be found; but instead comes unto it forgetfulness, indifference, outrages; and all such things do come at times even from souls that are bound closely thereunto by the bonds of a very special love."

Lesson VII

From the Holy Gospel according to St. John (John 19:31–37)

At that time: The Jews, because it was the Preparation, that the bodies should not remain upon the cross on the Sabbath Day, for that Sabbath Day was a high day, besought Pilate that their legs might broken, and that they might be taken away. And so on.

Homily by St. Bernardine of Siena

John continues: "One of the soldiers with a spear pierced his side, and forthwith came there out blood and water." O Love, thou that canst dissolve all things, how thou didst flow forth from our Beloved, for the sake of our redemption! In order that this thy flood of love might spread everywhere, the great firmament was rent above us, even the heights of the Heart of Jesus, which the cruel spear did not fail to pierce to its innermost abyss. And forthwith came there out blood and water. Blood for redemption flowed out, but also water for cleansing; whence the Church was formed from the side of Christ, that she might know herself ever to be the sole-beloved one of Christ, and that she might understand how greatly sin displeases him, as she sees his divine blood flow forth from the God-Man, both in life and in death. For if the divine blood be shed for us, then we cost not a little.

Lesson VIII

The water flowed not forth intermingled with the blood. For if it had so done, it could not have been perceived by simple folk. And perchance all the blood flowed forth from that divine body, as a sign that all his love was poured out, after which a watery humor came forth. Verily this was a token of a profound mystery, indeed, that from one and the same body came forth first the price of our redemption amongst all peoples. For many waters may be taken to signify many peoples; yet all who belong to the Christian Faith, are one people in the Faith, so that they are not as many waters; rather they are as one stream of water, and as such did flow from the side of Christ, as says the Apostle in the tenth chapter of the former Epistle to the Corinthians: "For we being many are one bread, and one body: for we are all partakers of that one bread and one cup." And again, in the fourth chapter of Ephesians, he says: "One God, one faith, one baptism."

Lesson IX

Nevertheless, it is especially deserving of our attention that the side of Christ is said to have been pierced, not wounded, since a wound cannot properly be said to be inflicted except on a living body. For John the Evangelist says: "One of the soldiers with a spear pierced his side:" that through this side thus opened, we might become aware of the love of his Heart, even unto death, and that we might enter into that unutterable love of his, through the same channel whereby it came unto us. Let us draw near then to his Heart, a deep Heart, a hidden Heart, a Heart thinking of all, a Heart knowing all, a Heart loving, yea, even aflame with love. Let us also recognize at least in the vehemence of his love that the gate is open; with our hearts made like unto his, let us enter into that secret place, hidden from all eternity, but now in death revealed, as it were, through the open side; for the opening of his side is a figure of the opening of the eternal temple, where is consummated the everlasting happiness of every creature.

Wednesday within the Octave of the Sacred Heart

Semiduplex

Lesson I ~ 1 Kings 13:1–4

From first book of Kings

Saul was a child of one year when he began to reign, and he reigned two years over Israel. And Saul chose him three thousand men of Israel: and two thousand were with Saul in Machmas, and in mount Bethel: and a thousand with Jonathan in Gabaa of Benjamin, and the rest of the people he sent back every man to their dwellings. And Jonathan smote the garrison of the Philistines which was in Gabaa. And when the Philistines had heard of it, Saul sounded the trumpet over all the land, saying: Let the Hebrews hear. And all Israel heard this report: Saul hath smitten the garrison of the Philistines: and Israel took courage against the Philistines. And the people were called together after Saul to Galgal.

Lesson II ~ 1 Kings 13:5–8

The Philistines also were assembled to fight against Israel, thirty thousand chariots, and six thousand horsemen, and a multitude of people besides, like the sand on the sea shore for number. And going up they camped in Machmas at the east of Bethaven. And when the men of Israel saw that they were straitened (for the people were distressed), they hid themselves in caves, and in thickets, and in rocks, and in dens, and in pits. And some of the Hebrews passed over the Jordan into the land of Gad and Galaad. And when Saul was yet in Galgal, all the people that followed him were greatly afraid. And he waited seven days according to the appointment of Samuel, and Samuel came not to Galgal, and the people slipt away from him.

Lesson III ~ 1 Kings 13:9–14

Then Saul said: Bring me the holocaust, and the peace offerings. And he offered the holocaust. And when he had made an end of offering the holocaust, behold Samuel came: and Saul went forth to meet him and salute him. And Samuel said to him: What hast thou done? Saul answered: Because I saw that the people slipt from me, and thou wast not come according to the days appointed, and the Philistines were gathered together in Machmas, I said: Now will the Philistines come down upon me to Galgal, and I have not appeased the face of the Lord. Forced by necessity, I offered the holocaust. And Samuel said to Saul: Thou hast done foolishly, and hast not kept the commandments of the Lord thy God, which he commanded thee. And if thou hadst not done thus, the Lord would now have established thy kingdom over Israel for ever. But thy kingdom shall not continue. The Lord hath sought him a man according to his own heart: and him hath the Lord commanded to be prince over his people, because thou hast not observed that which the Lord commanded.

Lesson IV

From the Encyclical Letter of Pope Pius XI - *Miserentíssimus Redémptor*

But in what sense can it be said that our expiatory practices can give consolation to Christ, since he is now reigning in heavenly joy? We answer in the words of Saint Augustine (from a passage entirely appropriate to this subject): "Give me a lover, and he will feel the truth of what I say. Every soul which is on fire with the love of God, if it but turns its thoughts to the past, does in its meditation perceive and contemplate Christ suffering for mankind; afflicted by grief in the midst of sorrows endured for us men and for our salvation; almost overcome by afflictions, vexations, and reproaches; yea, bruised by our sins; with whose stripes we are healed." And devout souls will have an appreciation in proportion to their understanding of these mysteries, if they perceive that the sins and crimes of men (no matter when committed) were the real reason why the Son of God was condemned to death, and that sins committed in this present are able in some way to cause the death of Christ, renewing as they do, the cause of that selfsame death, with its sufferings and agonies, which was accomplished on the Cross; for every sin must be said to renew, in some fashion, the Lord's passion, concerning which we read in the Scriptures: "They crucify themselves the Son of God afresh, and put him to an open shame."

Lesson V

And since in the agony in the Garden the soul of Christ became sorrowful even unto death, in view of our own future sins which were foreseen by him, there can be no doubt that at the same time he was in some way consoled, through the provision of our acts of reparation, when the Angel from heaven appeared unto him to comfort him in the sorrows of his Heart, which was so bowed down with weariness and grief. And so, even at this present time, we can and we ought to console, in a mystical but nonetheless real manner, that most Sacred Heart: which is being wounded continually by the sins of thankless men. It is in this sense, namely, that Christ is grieved over his abandonment by his friends that we are accustomed to interpret the holy liturgy whenever we say in the words of the Psalmist: "Thy rebuke hath broken my Heart; I am full of heaviness; I looked for some to have pity on me, but there was no man, neither found I any to comfort me."

Lesson VI

To the foregoing we should add that the expiatory passion of Christ is renewed, and in a certain manner continued, in his mystical body, which is the Church. In this connection, once more the words of Saint Augustine are appropriate: "Christ suffered all that he needed to suffer; nothing at all is lacking in the number of his sufferings; therefore his sufferings are completed in him as the Head; but there remains even yet the sufferings of Christ to be endured in the body." Which truth verily the Lord Jesus himself made known, at the time that Saul was breathing out threats and slaughter against the disciples, to whom the Lord said: "I am Jesus whom thou persecutest." By these words he plainly affirmed that persecutions visited on the Church are in reality directed against the Head of the Church. It is therefore fitting that Christ, thus still suffering in his mystical body, should desire to have us as sharers in his own work of expiation, even as our own need moves us to desire and seek union with him. And since we are the body of Christ, and members of his very flesh and bones, whatever the Head must suffer all the members of the body must suffer together with him.

Lesson VII

From the Holy Gospel according to St. John (John 19:31–37)

At that time: The Jews, because it was the Preparation, that the bodies should not remain upon the cross on the Sabbath Day, for that Sabbath Day was a high day, besought Pilate that their legs might broken, and that they might be taken away. And so on.

Homily by St. Peter Canisius, Priest

Have all diligence to turn over in thy mind this matter: namely, That he, who is God over all, endured with unutterable charity, a most bitter death on the Cross, in the exceeding anguish of his Heart, whilst the whole world mocked him! And this he did for thee, who art but a paltry little worm! Meditate on the boundless generosity which Christ the Preserver manifested to all his own people. For at one time, standing in the midst of the people, he cried out: "If any man thirst, let him come to me and drink;" thereby showing how ready he was to welcome everyone, and help him in his every need. Consider how freely he gives thee to drink of his Heart's precious blood, considering that his sacred side was set open, wherefrom he poured forth whatever blood was still left in his body.

Lesson VIII

And so that I may not be utterly ungrateful, often I call up before mine eyes those perennial fountains of gifts and of all good things, since from them that most sweet promise stands out: "Ye shall draw waters with joy out of the founts of the Saviour, and you shall say in that day: Praise ye the Lord." There will I flee, to those thrice-blest holes in the rock which can never be demolished; there will I build for myself a most durable nest, holding nothing better, in all sorrows and perils that befall me, than to think on the wounds of the Lord.

Lesson IX

Therefore in every trial do thou flee quickly to the lovable Heart of Christ, and call to mind his goodness and charity, setting them in contrast to thine own vileness, malice, unfaithfulness, and pride.

For consider how great was the charity of Christ in inviting all men unto himself: "Come unto me, all you that travail and are heavy laden, and I will refresh you." It is with this intent that he offers himself to us, ready and desirous, out of love for us, to carry the burdens of each and all! Cast then thy sins into the abyss of his charity, and straightway thou shalt find thyself lightened of thy load.

Thursday within the Octave of the Sacred Heart

Semiduplex

Lesson I ~ 1 Kings 14:6–11

From first book of Kings

And Jonathan said to the young man that bore his armour: Come, let us go over to the garrison of these uncircumcised, it may be the Lord will do for us, because it is easy for the Lord to save either by many, or by few. And his armourbearer said to him: Do all that pleaseth thy mind: go whither thou wilt, and I will be with thee wheresoever thou hast a mind. And Jonathan said: Behold we will go over to these men. And when we shall be seen by them, If they shall speak thus to us: Stay till we come to you: let us stand still in our place, and not go up to them. But if they shall say: Come up to us: let us go up, because the Lord hath delivered them into our hands, this shall be a sign unto us. So both of them discovered themselves to the garrison of the Philistines: and the Philistines said: Behold the Hebrews come forth out of the holes wherein they were hid.

Lesson II ~ 1 Kings 14:12–15

And the men of the garrison spoke to Jonathan, and to his armourbearer, and said: Come up to us, and we will show you a thing. And Jonathan said to his armourbearer: Let us go up, follow me: for the Lord hath delivered them into the hands of Israel. And Jonathan went up creeping on his hands and feet, and his armourbearer after him. And some fell before Jonathan, others his armourbearer slew as he followed him. And the first slaughter which Jonathan and his armourbearer made, was of about twenty men, within half an acre of land, which a yoke of oxen is wont to plough in a day. And there was a miracle in the camp, through the fields: yea and all the people of their garrison, who had gone out to plunder, were amazed, and the earth trembled: and it happened as a miracle from God.

Lesson III ~ 1 Kings 14:16–20

And the watchmen of Saul, who were in Gabaa of Benjamin looked, and behold a multitude overthrown, and fleeing this way and that. And Saul said to the people that were with him: Look, and see who is gone from us. And when they had sought, it was found that Jonathan and his armourbearer were not there. And Saul said to Achias: Bring the ark of the Lord. (For the ark of God was there that day with the children of Israel.) And while Saul spoke to the priest, there arose a great uproar in the camp of the Philistines: and it increased by degrees, and was heard more clearly. And Saul said to the priest: Draw in thy hand. Then Saul and all the people that were with him, shouted together, and they came to the place of the fight: and behold every man's sword was turned upon his neighbour, and there was a very great slaughter.

Lesson IV

From the Encyclical Letter of Pope Pius XI - *Miserentíssimus Redémptor*

Anyone who will use his eyes and mind, if he but think of this world, whereof it is truly said: "The whole world lies in wickedness:" can see how urgent, especially in these our own times, is the need for expiation or atonement. For there come to our ears from every side the cries of nations, whose rulers or governments have actually risen up, and conspired together, against the Lord, and against his Church. Nor is that other sight less sad, to wit, that even among the faithful (washed as they are by Baptism in the blood of the spotless Lamb, and enriched by his grace), we find so many of every station in life who are ignorant of divine things, and poisoned by false doctrine; and who do live a sinful life, far from their Father's house; without the light of the true Faith; without the joy of a hope in the future life; deprived of the strength and comfort which come with the Spirit of Love; so that it may be said of them quite truthfully: "They sit in darkness and in the shadow of death."

Lesson V

To the aforesaid accumulation of evils must be added the sloth and indifference of many of his followers, who are like unto the disciples that fled from him or slept. These are such as are not firmly rooted in the Faith, and have therefore shamefully abandoned Christ at a time when he is burdened with sorrows and attacked by the hosts of Satan. And others of his followers are like unto Judas the traitor, in that they walk in the footsteps of perfidy. These are such as approach the Sacrament of the Altar with sacrilegious boldness, or even go over to the camp of the enemy. And we are therefore moved to think that now is come the hour of which our Lord prophesied: "Because iniquity shall abound, the love of the many shall grow cold." If those who remain faithful on fire with love at the sufferings of Christ will but meditate on these considerations, it is unthinkable that they will do other than strive with greater zeal to expiate both their own faults and the faults of others; and that they will thus seek to make reparation for the dishonor done to Christ; and so they will be filled with zeal for the eternal salvation of souls.

Lesson VI

Surely we shall do well to apply to this our own age what the Apostle wrote: "Where sin abounded, grace did much more abound." For even though the sinfulness of man does greatly increase, by the grace of the Holy Spirit there does also increase in number those of both sexes who most cheerfully do endeavor to make satisfaction to the divine Heart for the numerous injuries heaped thereupon; moreover, they even cheerfully offer themselves as victims for sin. Verily, anyone that considers in a spirit of love all the revelation which has come into his mind up to this time, if he have impressed such things on the fleshly tablets of his own heart, as it were, cannot but abhor and flee sin as the greatest of all evils. Such a one will therefore offer himself wholly and completely to the will of God, and by constant prayer, willing penances, and the patient endurance of all the ills that befall him will endeavor to repair the injuries done to the Majesty of God. In a word, he will so organize his life that all things in it may be motivated by the spirit of reparation.

Lesson VII

From the Holy Gospel according to St. John (John 19:31–37)

At that time: The Jews, because it was the Preparation, that the bodies should not remain upon the cross on the Sabbath Day, for that Sabbath Day was a high day, besought Pilate that their legs might broken, and that they might be taken away. And so on.

Homily by St. Cyril of Alexandria

The blessed Evangelist does not record these things as if they were evidence of some godliness amidst all the savage cruelty which Jewry had manifested. Rather, by them he does show how foolishly and ignorantly a gnat can be carefully strained out, and a camel swallowed, as Christ himself had before said. For we perceive that they made light of most grievous and awful crimes, while they took careful and anxious pains to observe mere trivialities; with such inconsistency they did in both things display their ignorance, as can be readily shown. For lo! they put Christ to death while they give honor to the Great Sabbath. Thus, with incredible insolence, they make a show of reverence for the Law concerning the Sabbath, whose very Author they so dishonor.

Lesson VIII

They pretend to show special reverence for that Great Sabbath Day—they who have put to death the Lord of that great day! And thereupon they earnestly beseech a favor worthy of such folk alone, namely, That the legs of the crucified ones may be broken! And thereby was inflicted an intolerable pain, a bitterer misfortune than death itself, on men who were already well nigh at the point of death! The Evangelist says: "Then came the soldiers and broke the legs of the first, and of the other which was crucified with him." Thus it appears that the soldiers who went in answer to this request were laboring under a frenzy of cruelty like to that of Jewry itself, and therefore they broke the legs of the two thieves whom they found yet alive. But when they came to Jesus, whose head was bowed, they concluded that he was dead already, so that it was useless to go to the trouble of breaking his legs. But to make quite certain that he was dead indeed, they did pierce his side with a spear. And forthwith there came out blood and water: a figure of the mystical Banquet and of holy Baptism, and also the first-fruits of the same.

Lesson IX

And from these things which came to pass, the most wise Evangelist proves to his hearers that this is the Christ, who was long ago foretold by holy Scripture; for all that happened does agree with what was prophesied through God concerning him. And so, according to the Scriptures, not a bone of him was broken, and he was pierced with the soldier's lance. The Evangelist does certainly say that the one who saw this thing was the same disciple that gave testimony concerning these things, and that he knew that his testimony was true, by this expression meaning not another, but himself.

Octave Day of the Sacred Heart

Major Duplex

Lesson I - 1 Kings 15:1–3

From first book of Kings

And Samuel said to Saul: The Lord sent me to anoint thee king over his People Israel: now therefore hearken thou unto the voice of the Lord: Thus saith the Lord of hosts: I have reckoned up all that Amalec hath done to Israel: I how he opposed them in the way when they came up out of Egypt. Now therefore go, and smite Amalec, and utterly destroy all that he hath: spare him not, nor covet any thing that is his: but slay both man and woman, child and suckling, ox and sheep, camel and ass.

Lesson II - 1 Kings 15:4–8

So Saul commanded the people, and numbered them as lambs: two hundred thousand footmen, and ten thousand of the men of Juda. And when Saul was come to the city of Amalec, he laid ambushes in the torrent. And Saul said to the Cinite: Go, depart and get ye down from Amalec: lest I destroy thee with him. For thou hast shown kindness to all the children of Israel, when they came up out of Egypt. And the Cinite departed from the midst of Amalec. And Saul smote Amalec from Hevila, until thou comest to Sur, which is over against Egypt. And he took Agag the king of Amalec alive: but all the common people he slew with the edge of the sword.

Lesson III - 1 Kings 15:9–11

And Saul and the people spared Agag and the best of the flocks of sheep and of the herds, and the garments and the rams, and all that was beautiful, and would not destroy them: but every thing that was vile and good for nothing, that they destroyed. And the word of the Lord came to Samuel, saying: It repenteth me that I have made Saul king: for he hath forsaken me, and hath not executed my commandments. And Samuel was grieved, and he cried unto the Lord all night.

Lesson IV

Sermon by St. Bernard, Abbot

For us who are so frail and weak, where is to be found a sure and certain place of abiding safety, or of everlasting rest? Where except in the Wounds of the Saviour? There alone I may dwell safely. There alone I may find a safety as great as his mighty power to save. The world may rage around me; the body may weigh me down; the devil may lay snares for me; but if I hide me there I cannot fall, for I am founded on the firm Rock. If I have committed a great sin; if my conscience is sore troubled; I will not despair, for I have always in remembrance the Wounds of the Lord. For in all truth: "He was wounded for our transgressions." And there is no sin so deadly that it cannot be remitted through Christ's death. If then I keep in remembrance a remedy so powerful and efficacious, I cannot in this present life be terrified by any evil, no matter how malignant.

Lesson V

But as for me, since mercies thus abound, I take unto myself whatever is lacking in me; yea, I take it unto myself with confidence; I take it unto myself from the compassion of the Lord, with whom every kind of mercy abounds. For openings are not wanting, through which these mercies may flow forth. They have pierced his hands and his feet; yea, and his side too they have pierced with a spear. It is through these clefts that I am permitted to suck honey from the Rock, and oil out of the flinty Rock, and to taste and see how gracious the Lord is. His thoughts are thoughts of peace, and I knew it not. For who has known the mind of the Lord? or who has been his counsellor? But the nail which did pierce has become unto me a key which does unlock, so that the will of the Lord is set open unto me. How could I, with such an opening, do other than to see his will? For the nails cry aloud, and the Wounds speak, saying the truth: To wit, that God is in Christ reconciling the world unto himself.

Lesson VI

The iron entered into his soul, and came nigh unto his Heart, that he might truly know compassion for my infirmities. The secrets of his Heart lie open through the Wounds of his body. Thus is that great mystery of love laid open: there lie open the bowels of the mercy of our God, whereby the Dayspring from on high has visited us. But why should not the bowels of mercy lie open through the wounds? For in what has it appeared more clearly than in thy wounds, that thou, O Lord, art sweet and gentle, and of great mercy? For greater pity has no man, than that a man lay down his life for those who were doomed and condemned to death. From this pity of the Lord is all my merit. I am not entirely destitute of merit, so long as he is not wanting in compassion. And if the mercies of the Lord are from eternity unto eternity, I also will sing the mercies of the Lord forever.

Lesson VII

From the Holy Gospel according to St. John (John 19:31–37)

At that time: The Jews, because it was the Preparation, that the bodies should not remain upon the cross on the Sabbath Day, for that Sabbath Day was a high day, besought Pilate that their legs might broken, and that they might be taken away. And so on.

Homily by St. Augustine, Bishop

"But when they came to Jesus, and saw that he was dead already, they broke not his legs: but one of the soldiers with a spear opened his side, and forthwith came there out blood and water." Note that the Evangelist makes use of a word of special significance. He says not: "Penetrated his side:" nor yet: "Wounded:" nor any other thing; but rather: "Opened:" that thereby in a sense the door of life might be thrown open, from whence the Sacraments of the Church have flowed forth, without which there is no entrance into the life which is the only true life. For that blood was shed for the remission of sins; and that water has brought into being the life-giving flagon, the same which is both the laver of Baptism and the cup that gives refreshment to them that thirst. All this was announced long before, to wit, when Noe was commanded to make a door in the side of the ark, through which might enter all living creatures which were not destined to perish in the flood; and this same is a figure of the Church.

Lesson VIII

Another figure is also to be found in the first woman. For she was made out of the side of the first man whilst he slept a deep sleep; and she was called: Life: or as it may be interpreted: The Mother of all living. Thus was indicated the great good which was later to come to pass, even before the great evil of transgression had come into being. Here, in the Gospel, the second Adam is shown as bowing his head, and sleeping his deep sleep upon the Cross, that a bride might be formed for him out of that which came forth from his side as he slept. What a death, whereby the dead are raised anew to life! How clean and cleansing is this blood! What is more salutary than this wound! "And he that saw it," says he, "bore record, and his record is true: and he knoweth that he saith true, that you might believe." He said not: "That you might know;" but: "That you might believe." For he knows, who has seen, that he who has not seen might believe his record. And believing belongs more to the nature of faith than seeing.

Lesson IX

From the Scriptures he gives two testimonies, one for each of the things which he has recorded as having been done. To the words: "When they came to Jesus, and saw that he was dead already, they broke not his legs:" belongs the testimony: "A bone of him shall not be broken:" which comes from the Mosaic injunction laid upon the Jews, who were commanded by the Old Law to celebrate the Passover by the sacrifice of a lamb, which was a foreshadowing of the passing of Christ, whence we have the passage: "Christ our Passover is sacrificed for us:" concerning which the Prophet Isaias also foretold: "He is brought as a lamb to the slaughter." To the words: "One of the soldiers with a spear pierced his side:" belongs the other testimony: "They shall look on him whom they pierced:" which same is a promise of the coming of Christ in that selfsame flesh wherein he was afterwards crucified.

Saturday III after the Octave of Pentecost

Lesson I ~ 1 Kings 16:1–3

From first book of Kings

And the Lord said to Samuel. How long wilt thou mourn for Saul, whom I have rejected from reigning over Israel? fill thy horn with oil, and come, that I may send thee to Isai the Bethlehemite: for I have provided me a king among his sons. And Samuel said: How shall I go? for Saul will hear of it, and he will kill me. And the Lord said: Thou shalt take with thee a calf of the herd, and thou shalt say: I am come to sacrifice to the Lord. And thou shalt call Isai to the sacrifice, and I will show thee what thou art to do, and thou shalt anoint him whom I shall show to thee.

Lesson II ~ 1 Kings 16:4–7

Then Samuel did as the Lord had said to him. And he came to Bethlehem, and the ancients of the city wondered, and meeting him, they said: Is thy coming hither peaceable? And he said: It is peaceable: I am come to offer sacrifice to the Lord, be ye sanctified, and come with me to the sacrifice. And he sanctified Isai and his sons, and called them to the sacrifice. And when they were come in, he saw Eliab, and said: Is the Lord's anointed before him? And the Lord said to Samuel: Look not on his countenance, nor on the height of his stature: because I have rejected him, nor do I judge according to the look of man: for man seeth those things that appear, but the Lord beholdeth the heart.

Lesson III ~ 1 Kings 16:8–11

And Isai called Abinadab, and brought him before Samuel. And he said: Neither hath the Lord chosen this. And Isai brought Samma, and he said of him: Neither hath the Lord chosen this. Isai therefore brought his seven sons before Samuel: and Samuel said to Isai: The Lord hath not chosen any one of these. And Samuel said to Isai: Are here all thy sons? He answered: There remaineth yet a young one, who keepeth the sheep. And Samuel said to Isai: Send, and fetch him, for we will not sit down till he come hither.

Sunday IV after Pentecost

Semiduplex

Lesson I ~ 1 Kings 17:1–7

From first book of Kings

Now the Philistines gathering together their troops to battle, assembled at Socho of Juda, and camped between Socho and Azeca in the borders of Dommim. And

Saul and the children of Israel being gathered together came to the valley of Terebinth, and they set the army in array to fight against the Philistines. And the Philistines stood on a mountain on the one side, and Israel stood on a mountain on the other side: and there was a valley between them. And there went out a man baseborn from the camp of the Philistines named Goliath, of Geth, whose height was six cubits and a span: And he had a helmet of brass upon his head, and he was clothed with a coat of mail with scales, and the weight of his coat of mail was five thousand sicles of brass: And he had greaves of brass on his legs, and a buckler of brass covered his shoulders. And the staff of his spear was like a weaver's beam, and the head of his spear weighed six hundred sicles of iron: and his armourbearer went before him.

Lesson II ~ 1 Kings 17:8–11

And standing he cried out to the bands of Israel, and said to them: Why are you come out prepared to fight? Am not I a Philistine, and you the servants of Saul? Choose out a man of you, and let him come down and fight hand to hand. If he be able to fight with me, and kill me, we will be servants to you: but if I prevail against him, and kill him, you shall be servants, and shall serve us. And the Philistine said: I have defied the bands of Israel this day: Give me a man, and let him fight with me hand to hand. And Saul and all the Israelites hearing these words of the Philistine were dismayed, and greatly afraid.

Lesson III ~ 1 Kings 17:12–16

Now David was the son of that Ephrathite of Bethlehem Juda before mentioned, whose name was Isai, who had eight sons, and was an old man in the days of Saul, and of great age among men. And his three eldest sons followed Saul to the battle: and the names of his three sons that went to the battle, were Eliab the firstborn, and the second Abinadab, and the third Samma. But David was the youngest. So the three eldest having followed Saul, David went, and returned from Saul, to feed his father's flock at Bethlehem. Now the Philistine came out morning and evening, and presented himself forty days.

Lesson IV

Sermon by St. Augustine, Bishop

The children of Israel faced their enemies for forty days. These forty days, by reason of the four Seasons of the year, and of the four parts of the globe, are a figure of this present life, during which the Christian world ceases not to be arrayed in battle against the devil and his angels, as it were against Goliath and the army of the Philistines. Neither can they hope to overcome him, were it not for the true David, that is, Christ, with His staff, that is, with the Mystery of His Cross. For before Christ came, my dearly beloved brethren, the devil was at large. But when Christ came, He did to him what is written in the Gospel, where it is said "How can one enter into a strong man's house, and spoil his goods, except he first bind the strong man?" Christ therefore came, and bound the devil.

Lesson V

But some man will say: If he is bound, why is he still so powerful? It is quite true, my dearly beloved brethren, that he is very powerful but his lordship is over the lukewarm and the careless, and such as fear not God in truth. He is chained up like a dog, and can only bite those who are such suicidal fools as to go within the length of his tether. Look you, my brethren, what a dolt a man must be who gets himself bitten by a dog that is chained up. Let not the desires and lusts of the world draw thee within reach of him, and he will not be able to get at thee. He can bark, he can whine, but he can only bite those who are willing to be bitten. He assails us not by violence but by persuasion; he asks, not seizes, our consent.

Lesson VI

David, then, came, and found the Jewish people set in battle array against the devil and since there was no one who dared to go to single combat, he, who was a type of Christ, sallied out to the battle, took his staff in his hand, and went forth against Goliath. In him was a shadow of a substance which is in Christ. Christ, the true David, when He went forth to fight against the spiritual Goliath, that is to say, against the devil, went forth bearing His Cross. You see, my brethren, in what part it was that David smote Goliath: it was upon that forehead whereon the Cross had never been traced. And as the staff of David was a figure of the Cross of Christ, so was the stone wherewith the giant was smitten a figure of the Lord Himself.

Lesson VII

From the Holy Gospel according to St. Luke (Luke 5:1–11)

At that time: As the people pressed upon Jesus, to hear the word of God, He stood by the lake of Gennesareth. And so on.

Homily by St. Ambrose, Bishop

When the Lord wrought so many works of healing, neither time nor place could restrain the people from seeking health. Evening came, and they still followed Him. He went down to the lake, and they still pressed upon Him, and therefore He entered into Peter's ship. This is that ship, which spiritually up to this very hour, according to the expression of Matthew, "is buffeted by tempests," but still, according to Luke, "is filled with fishes," this signifying, that, for a while, the Church is presently to labor, but, hereafter, it shall be to rejoice. The fishes are they which swim in the troublous waters of human life. In this ship also spiritually does Christ, for His disciples, still sleep, and still command; for He sleeps for the lukewarm, and watches for the perfect.

Lesson VIII

Fear not, then, for the ship where wisdom steers, false teaching is not known, and faith swells the sails. How shall she be troubled, whose Lord is Himself the Church's sure Foundation? It is where faith is weak that there is fear; where love is perfect, there there is safety. To many it is commanded to loose their nets, but to Peter only to "Launch out into the deep," that is, into the depths of doctrine. What indeed is there so deep, as to gaze upon the depth of all riches, to recognize the Son of God, and to take up the confession of His Divine generation? This is a thing which the mind is not able to grasp by the searchings of man's reason, but which is embraced by a hearty faith.

Lesson IX

It is not given unto me to know how He was born, yet I may not be ignorant that He was born at all. What the order of His generation was, I know not, but the Source of His generation I acknowledge. None has beheld the Begetting of the Son of God by the Father, but the Church has stood by to hear the Father testify that this is His beloved Son. If we believe not God, whom shall we believe? For whatsoever we believe comes either by sight or by hearing; sight is oftentimes deceived, but "faith comes by hearing."

Monday IV after the Octave of Pentecost

Lesson I - 1 Kings 17:25–26

From first book of Kings

And some one of Israel said: Have you seen this man that is come up, for he is come up to defy Israel. And the man that shall slay him, the king will enrich with great riches, and will give him his daughter, and will make his father's house free from tribute in Israel. And David spoke to the men that stood by him, saying: What shall be given to the man that shall kill this Philistine, and shall take away the reproach from Israel? for who is this uncircumcised Philistine, that he should defy the armies of the living God?

Lesson II - 1 Kings 17:31–33

And the words which David spoke were heard, and were rehearsed before Saul. And when he was brought to him, he said to him: Let not any man's heart be dismayed in him: I thy servant will go, and will fight against the Philistine. And Saul said to David: Thou art not able to withstand this Philistine, nor to fight against him: for thou art but a boy, but he is a warrior from his youth.

Lesson III - 1 Kings 17:34–36

And David said to Saul: thy servant kept his father's sheep, and there came a lion, or a bear, and took a ram out of the midst of the flock: And I pursued after them, and struck them, and delivered it out of their mouth: and they rose up against me, and I caught them by the throat, and I strangled and killed them. For I thy servant have killed both a lion and a bear: and this uncircumcised Philistine shall be also as one of them. I will go now, and take away the reproach of the people: for who is this uncircumcised Philistine, who hath dared to curse the army of the living God?

Tuesday IV after the Octave of Pentecost

Lesson I ~ 1 Kings 17:38–40

From first book of Kings

And Saul clothed David with his garments, and put a helmet of brass upon his head, and armed him with a coat of mail. And David having girded his sword upon his armour, began to try if he could walk in armour: for he was not accustomed to it. And David said to Saul: I cannot go thus, for I am not used to it. And he laid them off, And he took his staff, which he had always in his hands: and chose him five smooth stones out of the brook, and put them into the shepherd's scrip, which he had with him, and he took a sling in his hand, and went forth against the Philistine.

Lesson II ~ 1 Kings 17:41–46

And the Philistine came on, and drew nigh against David, and his armour-bearer before him. And when the Philistine looked, and beheld David, he despised him. For he was a young man, ruddy, and of a comely countenance. And the Philistine said to David: Am I a dog, that thou comest to me with a staff? And the Philistine cursed David by his gods. And he said to David: Come to me, and I will give thy flesh to the birds of the air, and to the beasts of the earth. And David said to the Philistine: Thou comest to me with a sword, and with a spear, and with a shield: but I come to thee in the name of the Lord of hosts, the God of the armies of Israel, which thou hast defied. This day, and the Lord will deliver thee into my hand, and I will slay thee, and take away thy head from thee: and I will give the carcasses of the army of the Philistines this day to the birds of the air, and to the beasts of the earth: that all the earth may know that there is a God in Israel.

Lesson III ~ 1 Kings 17:48–51

And when the Philistine arose and was coming, and drew nigh to meet David, David made haste, and ran to the fight to meet the Philistine. And he put his hand into his scrip, and took a stone, and cast it with the sling, and fetching it about struck the Philistine in the forehead: and the stone was fixed in his forehead, and he fell on his face upon the earth. And David prevailed over the Philistine, with a sling and a stone, and he struck, and slew the Philistine. And as David had no sword in his hand, He ran, and stood over the Philistine, and took his sword, and drew it out of the sheath, and slew him, and cut off his head. And the Philistines seeing that their champion was dead, fled away.

Wednesday IV after the Octave of Pentecost

Lesson I ~ 1 Kings 18:6–8

From first book of Kings

Now when David returned, after be slew the Philistine, the women came out of all the cities of Israel, singing and dancing, to meet king Saul, with timbrels of joy, and cornets. And the women sung as they played, and they said: Saul slew his thousands, and David his ten thousands. And Saul was exceeding angry, and this word was displeasing in his eyes, and he said: They have given David ten thousands, and to me they have given but a thousand; what can he have more but the kingdom?

Lesson II ~ 1 Kings 18:9–13

And Saul did not look on David with a good eye from that day and forward. And the day after the evil spirit from God came upon Saul, and he prophesied in the midst of his house. And David played with his hand as at other times. And Saul held a spear in his hand, And threw it, thinking to nail David to the wall: and David stept aside out of his presence twice. And Saul feared David, because the Lord was with him, and was departed from himself. Therefore Saul removed him from him, and made him a captain over a thousand men, and he went out and came in before the people.

Lesson III ~ 1 Kings 18:14–17

And David behaved wisely in all his ways, and the Lord was with him. And Saul saw that he was exceeding prudent, and began to beware of him. But all Israel and Juda loved David, for he came in and went out before them. And Saul said to David: Behold my elder daughter Merob, her will I give thee to wife: only be a valiant man, and fight the battles of the Lord. Now Saul said within himself: Let not my hand be upon him, but let the hands of the Philistines be upon him.

Thursday IV after the Octave of Pentecost

Lesson I ~ 1 Kings 19:1–3

From first book of Kings

And Saul spoke to Jonathan his son and to all his servants, that they should kill David. But Jonathan the son of Saul loved David exceedingly. And Jonathan told David, saying: Saul my father seeketh to kill thee: wherefore look to thyself, I beseech thee, in the morning, and thou shalt abide in a secret place and shalt be hid. And I will go out and stand beside my father in the field where thou art: and I will speak of thee to my father, and whatsoever I shall see, I will tell thee.

Lesson II ~ 1 Kings 19:4–6

And Jonathan spoke good things of David to Saul his father: and said to him: Sin not, O king, against thy servant, David, because he hath not sinned against thee, and his works are very good towards thee. And he put his life in his hand, and slew the Philistine, and the Lord wrought great salvation for all Israel. Thou sawest it and didst rejoice. Why therefore wilt thou sin against innocent blood by killing David, who is without fault? And when Saul heard this he was appeased with the words of Jonathan, and swore: As the Lord liveth he shall not be slain.

Lesson III ~ 1 Kings 19:8–10

And the war began again, and David went out and fought against the Philistines, and defeated them with a great slaughter, and they fled from his face. And the evil spirit from the Lord came upon Saul, and he sat in his house, and held a spear in his hand: and David played with his hand. And Saul endeavoured to nail David to the wall with his spear. And David slipt away out of the presence of Saul: and the spear missed him, and was fastened in the wall, and David fled and escaped that night.

Friday IV after the Octave of Pentecost

Lesson I ~ 1 Kings 20:1–2

From first book of Kings

But David fled from Najoth, which is in Ramatha, and came and said to Jonathan: What have I done? what is my iniquity, and what is my sin against thy father, that he seeketh my life? And he said to him: God forbid, thou shalt not die: for my father will do nothing great or little, without first telling me: hath then my father hid this word only from me? no, this shall not be.

Lesson II ~ 1 Kings 20:3–4

And he swore again to David. And David said: thy father certainly knoweth that I have found grace in thy sight, and he will say: Let not Jonathan know this, lest he be grieved. But truly as the Lord liveth, and thy soul liveth, there is but one step (as I may say) between me and death. And Jonathan said to David: Whatsoever thy soul shall say to me, I will do for thee.

Lesson III ~ 1 Kings 20:5–7

And David said to Jonathan: Behold tomorrow is the new moon, and I according to custom am wont to sit beside the king to eat: let me go then that I may be hid in the field till the evening of the third day. If thy father look and inquire for me, thou shalt answer him: David asked me that he might run to Bethlehem his own city: because there are solemn sacrifices there for all his tribe. If he shall say, It is well: thy servant shall have peace: but if he be angry, know that his malice is come to its height.

Saturday IV after the Octave of Pentecost

Lesson I ~ 1 Kings 21:1–3

From first book of Kings

And David came to Nobe to Achimelech the priest: and Achimelech was astonished at David's coming. And he said to him: Why art thou alone, and no man with thee? And David said to Achimelech the priest: The king hath commanded me a business, and said: Let no man know the thing for which thou art sent by me, and what manner of commands I have given thee: and I have appointed my servants to such and such a place. Now therefore if thou have any thing at hand, though it were but five loaves, give me, or whatsoever thou canst find.

Lesson II ~ 1 Kings 21:4–6

And the priest answered David, saying: I have no common bread at hand, but only holy bread, if the young men be clean, especially from women? And David answered the priest, and said to him: Truly, as to what concerneth women, we have refrained ourselves from yesterday and the day before, when we came out, and the vessels of the young men were holy. Now this way is defiled, but it shall also be sanctified this day in the vessels. The priest therefore gave him hallowed bread: for there was no bread there, but only the loaves of proposition, which had been taken away from before the face of the Lord, that hot loaves might be set up.

Lesson III ~ 1 Kings 21:7–9

Now a certain man of the servants of Saul was there that day, within the tabernacle of the Lord: and his name was Doeg, an Edomite, the chiefest of Saul's herdsmen. And David said to Achimelech: Hast thou here at hand a spear, or a sword? for I brought not my own sword, nor my own weapons with me, for the king's business required haste. And the priest said: Lo, here is the sword of Goliath the Philistine whom thou slewest in the valley of Terebinth, wrapped up in a cloth behind the ephod: if thou wilt take this, take it, for here is no other but this. And David said: There is none like that, give it me.

✠

Sunday V after Pentecost

Semiduplex

Lesson I ~ 2 Kings 1:1–4

From second book of Kings

Now it came to pass, after Saul was dead, that David returned from the slaughter of the Amalecites, and abode two days in Siceleg. And on the third day, there appeared a man who came out of Saul's camp, with his garments rent, and dust strewed on his head: and when he came to David, he fell upon his face, and adored. And David said to him: From whence comest thou? And he said to him: I am fled out of the camp of Israel. And David said unto him: What is the matter that is come to pass? tell me. He said: The people are fled from the battle, and many of the people are fallen and dead: moreover Saul and Jonathan his son are slain.

Lesson II ~ 2 Kings 1:5–10

And David said to the young man that told him: How knowest thou that Saul and Jonathan his son, are dead? And the young man that told him, said: I came by chance upon mount Gelboe, and Saul leaned upon his spear: and the chariots and horsemen drew nigh unto him, And looking behind him, and seeing me, he called me. And I answered, Here am I. And he said to me: Who art thou? And I said to him: I am an Amalecite. And he said to me: Stand over me, and kill me: for anguish is come upon me, and as yet my whole life is in me. So standing over him, I killed him: for I knew that he could not live after the fall: and I took the diadem that was on his head, and the bracelet that was on his arm and have brought them hither to thee, my lord.

Lesson III ~ 2 Kings 1:11–15

Then David took hold of his garments and rent them, and likewise all the men that were with him. And they mourned, and wept, and fasted until evening for Saul, and for Jonathan his son, and for the people of the Lord, and for the house of Israel, because they were fallen by the sword. And David said to the young man that told him: Whence art thou? He answered: I am the son of a stranger of Amalee. David said to him: Why didst thou not fear to put out thy hand to kill the Lord's anointed? And David calling one of his servants, said: Go near and fall upon him. And he struck him so that he died.

Lesson IV

From the Book of Morals by Pope St. Gregory

Thus was it that David, who rewarded no evil to them that did evil to him, when Saul and Jonathan had fallen in battle, cursed the mountains of Gilboa, saying: "Ye mountains of Gilboa, let there be no dew, neither let there be rain upon you, nor fields of offerings;" for there the shield of the mighty is vilely cast away, the shield of Saul, as though he had not been anointed with oil. Why was it that Jeremias, when he saw that his preaching was thrown away upon his hearers, cursed and said "Cursed be the man who brought tidings to my father, saying: A man-child is born unto thee?"

Lesson V

What had the mountains of Gilboa to do with the death of Saul, that they should be condemned to have dew fall on them no more, nor rain, but should wither away, barren of the green glory of the springtime? But this word Gilboa signified bubbling fountain, and the death of Saul, the Anointed of God, is a type of the death of our Anointed Mediator. Thus we find in the mountains of Gilboa no unfit image of the proud hearts of the Jews, which had their spring in earthly desires, and took part in the death of the Anointed Saviour. And since among them their Anointed Monarch met His death, the dew of grace is upon them no more.

Lesson VI

And well is it said of them: "Let there be upon you no fields of offerings." The proud minds of the Hebrews bear yet no offering. Since the coming of their Redeemer, the most part of them remain still without belief in Him, and refuse to follow the promise of their ancient faith. The Holy Church has borne for her first-born, holy unto the Lord, a multitude of the Gentiles, and will, but in the end of the world, embrace such Jews as she then shall find, and present them as the last gatherings of her harvest.

Lesson VII

From the Holy Gospel according to St. Matthew (Matt 5:20–24)

At that time, Jesus said unto His disciples: Unless your righteousness shall exceed the righteousness of the Scribes and Pharisees, you shall in no case enter into the kingdom of heaven. And so on.

Homily by St. Augustine, Bishop

"Thou shalt not kill," is of the righteousness of the Pharisees; "Thou shalt not be angry with thy brother without a cause," is of the righteousness of them which shall enter into the kingdom of heaven. The least therefore is: "Thou shalt not kill, and whosoever shall break this commandment, he shall be called the least in the kingdom of heaven." But whosoever shall do it, and not kill, he is not therefore great, and fit for the kingdom of heaven; albeit he has risen a step; but he will have gotten farther, if he be not angry with his brother without a cause, which if he do, he will be the farther off from manslaughter. Wherefore, He Who teaches us that we are not to be angry without cause, destroys not the law, "Thou shalt not kill," but rather fulfills and increases it, making us not only to be free of the sin of outward killing, but also clean of anger within.

Lesson VIII

On sins of this kind there are diverse steps. First, there is the swelling feeling of anger. When this feeling appears in a man's heart, he keeps it. Then the inward disturbance wrings forth words of indignation, not themselves meaning anything, but showing the trouble of him who is provoked. And this is something more than anger kept covered under silence. Next, this audible outburst of indignation may contain direct and open reviling of him who has roused it. And it cannot be doubted that this is something more than an empty cry of anger.

Lesson IX

Behold here the three degrees of guilt open respectively to the judgment, to the council, and to hellfire. In the judgment, there is still place for defense. In the council, albeit this too is, in a sense, a judgment, yet we may suppose this distinction from the judgment proper, that the council pronounces sentence, not as the result of a trial whereat the accused is present, but as the result of a consultation among the judges, to what punishment he is to be sentenced of whom it is already established that he is guilty. When we get to hell-fire, there remains no longer any doubt about condemnation as in the judgment, and no longer any doubt about sentence as in the council. In hellfire the condemnation and the pain of he who is condemned are alike certain.

Monday V after the Octave of Pentecost

Lesson I ~ 2 Kings 2:1–4

From second book of Kings

And after these things David consulted the Lord, saying: Shall I go up into one of the cities of Juda? And the Lord said to him: Go up. And David said: Whither shall I go up? And he answered him: Into Hebron. So David went up, and his two wives, Achinoam the Jezrahelitess, and Abigail the wife of Nabal of Carmel: And the men also that were with him, David brought up every man with his household: and they abode in the towns of Hebron. And the men of Juda came, and anointed David there, to be king over the house of Juda.

Lesson II ~ 2 Kings 2:4–7

And it was told David, that the men of Jabes Galaad had buried

Saul. David therefore sent messengers to the men of Jabes Galaad, and said to them: Blessed be you to the Lord, who have shown this mercy to your master Saul, and have buried him. And now the Lord surely will render you mercy and truth, and I also will, requite you for this good turn, because you have done this thing. Let your hands be strengthened, and be ye men of valour: for although your master Saul be dead, yet the house of Juda hath anointed me to be their king.

Lesson III - 2 Kings 2:8–11

But Abner the son of Ner, general of Saul's army, took Isboseth the son of Saul, and led him about through the camp? And made him king over Galaad, and, over Gessuri, and over Jezrahel, and over Ephraim, and over Benjamin, and over all Israel. Isboseth the son of Saul was forty years old when he began to reign over, Israel, and he reigned two years: and only the house of Juda followed David. And the number of the days that David abode, reigning in Hebron over the house of Juda, was seven years and six months.

Tuesday V after the Octave of Pentecost

Lesson I - 2 Kings 3:6–10

From second book of Kings

Now while there was war between the house of Saul and the house of David, Abner the son of Ner ruled the house of Saul. And Saul had a concubine named Respha, the daughter of Aia. And Isboseth said to Abner: Why didst thou go in to my father's concubine? And he was exceedingly angry for the words of Isboseth, and said: Am I a dog's head against Juda this day, who have shown mercy to the house of Saul thy father, and to his brethren and friends, and have not delivered thee into the hands of David, and hast thou sought this day against me to charge me with a matter concerning a woman? So do God to Abner, and more also, unless as the Lord hath sworn to David, so I do to him, That the kingdom be translated from the house of Saul, and the throne of David be set up over Israel, and over Juda from Dan to Bersabee.

Lesson II - 2 Kings 3:12–16

Abner therefore sent messengers to David for himself, saying: Whose is the land? and that they should say: Make a league with me, and my hand shall be with thee: and I will bring all Israel to thee. And he said: Very well: I will make a league with thee: but one thing I require of thee, saying: Thou shalt not see my face before thou bring Michol the daughter of Saul: and so thou shalt come, and see me. And David sent messengers to Isboseth the son of Saul, saying: Restore my wife Michol, whom I espoused to me for a hundred foreskins of the Philistines. And Isboseth sent, and took her from her husband Phaltiel, the son of Lais. And her husband followed her, weeping as far as Bahurim: and Abner said to him: Go and return. And he returned.

Lesson III ~ 2 Kings 3:17–21

Abner also spoke to the ancients of Israel, saying: Both yesterday and the day before you sought for David that he might reign over you. Now then do it: because the Lord hath spoken to David, saying: By the hand of my servant David I will save my people Israel from the hands of the Philistines, and of all their enemies. And Abner spoke also to Benjamin. And he went to speak to David in Hebron all that seemed good to Israel, and to all Benjamin. And he came to David in Hebron with twenty men: and David made a feast for Abner, and his men that came with him. And Abner said to David: I will rise, that I may gather all Israel unto thee, my lord the king.

Wednesday V after the Octave of Pentecost

Lesson I ~ 2 Kings 4:5–8

From second book of Kings

And the sons of Remmon the Berothite, Rechab and Baana coming, went into the house of Isboseth in the heat of the day: and he was sleeping upon his bed at noon. And the doorkeeper of the house, who was cleansing wheat, was fallen asleep. And they entered into the house secretly taking ears of corn, and Rechab and Baana his brother stabbed him in the groin, and fled away. For when they came into the house, be was sleeping upon his bed in a parlour, and they struck him and killed him: and taking away his head they went off by the way of the wilderness, walking all night. And they brought the head of Isboseth to David to Hebron: and they said to the king: Behold the head of Isboseth the son of Saul thy enemy who sought thy life: and the Lord hath revenged my lord the king this day of Saul, and of his seed.

Lesson II ~ 2 Kings 4:9–12

But David answered Rechab, and Baana his brother, the sons of Remmon the Berothite, and said to them: As the Lord liveth, who hath delivered my soul out of all distress, The man that told me, and said: Saul is dead, who thought he brought good tidings, I apprehended, and slew him in Siceleg, who should have been rewarded for his news. How much more now when wicked men have slain an innocent man in his own house, upon his bed, shall I not require his blood at your hand, and take you away from the earth? And David commanded his servants and they slew them: and cutting off their hands and feet, hanged them up over the pool in Hebron: but the head of Isboseth they took and buried in the sepulchre of Abner in Hebron.

Lesson III ~ 2 Kings 5:1–7

Then all the tribes of Israel came to David in Hebron, saying: Behold we are thy bone and thy flesh. Moreover yesterday also and the day before, when Saul was king over us, thou wast he that did lead out and bring in Israel: and the Lord said to thee: Thou shalt feed my people Israel, and thou shalt be prince over Israel. The ancients also of Israel came to the king to Hebron, and king David made a league with them in Hebron before the Lord: and they anointed David to be king over Israel. David was thirty years old when he began to reign, and he reigned forty years. In Hebron he reigned over Juda seven years and six months: and in Jerusalem he reigned three and thirty years over all Israel and Juda. And the king and all the men that were with him went to Jerusalem to the Jebusites the inhabitants of the land: and they said to David: Thou shalt not come in hither unless thou take away the blind and the lame that say: David shall not come in hither. But David took the castle of Sion, the same is the city of David.

Thursday V after the Octave of Pentecost

Lesson I - 2 Kings 6:1–3

From second book of Kings

And David again gathered together all the chosen men of Israel, thirty thousand. And David arose and went, with all the people that were with him of the men of Juda to fetch the ark of God, upon which the name of the Lord of hosts is invoked, who sitteth over it upon the cherubims. And they laid the ark of God upon a new cart: and took it out of the house of Abinadab, who was in Gabaa: and Oza, and Ahio, the sons of Abinadab, drove the new cart.

Lesson II - 2 Kings 6:4–7

And when they had taken it out of the house of Abinadab, who was in Gabaa, Ahio having care of the ark of God went before the ark. But David and all Israel played before the Lord on all manner of instruments made of wood, on harps and lutes and timbrels and cornets and cymbals. And when they came to the floor of Nachon, Oza put forth his hand to the ark of God, and took hold of it: because the oxen kicked and made it lean aside. And the indignation of the Lord was enkindled against Oza, and he struck him for his rashness: and he died there before the ark of God.

Lesson III - 2 Kings 6:8–12

And David was grieved because the Lord had struck Oza, and the name of that place was called: The striking of Oza, to this day. And David was afraid of the Lord that day, saying: How shall the ark of the Lord come to me? And he would not have the ark of the Lord brought in to himself into the city of David: but he caused it to be carried into the house of Obededom the Gethite. And the ark of the Lord abode in the house of Obededom the Gethite three months: and the Lord blessed Obededom, and all his household. And it was told king David, that the Lord had blessed Obededom, and all that he had, because of the ark of God. So David went, and brought away the ark of God out of the house of Obededom into the city of David with joy. And there were with David seven choirs, and calves for victims.

Friday V after the Octave of Pentecost

Lesson I ~ 2 Kings 7:4–6

From second book of Kings

But it came to pass that night, that the word of the Lord came to Nathan, saying: Go, and say to my servant David: Thus saith the Lord: Shalt thou build me a house to dwell in? Whereas I have not dwelt in a house from the day that I brought the children of Israel out of the land of Egypt even to this day: but have walked in a tabernacle, and in a tent.

Lesson II ~ 2 Kings 7:7–11

In all the places that I have gone through with all the children of Israel, did ever I speak a word to any one of the tribes of Israel, whom I commanded to feed my people Israel, saying: Why have you not built me a house of cedar? And now thus shalt thou speak to my servant David: Thus saith the Lord of hosts: a I took thee out of the pastures from following the sheep to be ruler over my people Israel: And I have been with thee wheresoever thou hast walked, and have slain all thy enemies from before thy face: and I have made thee a great man, like unto the name of the great ones that are on the earth. And I will appoint a place for my people Israel, and I will plant them, and they shall dwell therein, and shall be disturbed no more: neither shall the children of iniquity afflict them any more as they did before, From the day that I appointed judges over my people Israel: and I will give thee rest from all thy enemies. And the Lord foretelleth to thee, that the Lord will make thee a house.

Lesson III ~ 2 Kings 7:12–17

And when thy days shall be fulfilled, and thou shalt sleep with thy fathers, I will raise up thy seed after thee, which shall proceed out of thy bowels, and I will establish his kingdom. He shall build a house to my name, and I will establish the throne of his kingdom for ever. I will be to him a father, and he shall be to me a son: and if he commit any iniquity, I will correct him with the rod of men, and with the stripes of the children of men. But my mercy I will not take away from him, as I took it from Saul, whom I removed from before my face. And thy house shall be faithful, and thy kingdom for ever before thy face, and thy throne shall be firm for ever. According to all these words and according to all this vision, so did Nathan speak to David.

Saturday V after the Octave of Pentecost

Lesson I ~ 2 Kings 11:1–4

From second book of Kings

And it came to pass at the return of the year, at the time when kings go forth to war, that David sent Joab and his servants with him, and all Israel, and they spoiled the children of Ammon, and besieged Rabba: but David remained in Jerusalem. In the mean time it happened that David arose from his bed after noon, and walked upon the roof of the king's house: and he saw from the roof of his house a woman washing herself, over against him: and the woman was very beautiful. And the king sent, and inquired who the woman was. And it was told him, that she was Bethsabee the daughter of Eliam, the wife of Urias the Hethite.

Lesson II ~ 2 Kings 11:5–11

And she returned to her house having conceived. And she sent and told David, and said: I have conceived. And David sent to Joab, saying: Send me Urias the Hethite. And Joab sent Urias to David. And Urias came to David. And David asked how Joab did, and the people, and how the war was carried on. And David said to Urias: Go into thy house, and wash thy feet. And Urias went out from the king's house, and there went out after him a mess of meat from the king. But Urias slept before the gate of the king's house, with the other servants of his lord, and went not down to his own house. And it was told David by some that said: Urias went not to his house. And David said to Urias: Didst thou not come from thy journey? why didst thou not go down to thy house? And Urias said to David: The ark of God and Israel and Juda dwell in tents, and my lord Joab and the servants of my lord abide upon the face of the earth: and shall I go into my house, to eat and to drink, and to sleep with my wife? By thy welfare and by the welfare of thy soul I will not do this thing.

Lesson III ~ 2 Kings 11:12–17

Then David said to Urias: Tarry here today, and tomorrow I will send thee away. Urias tarried in Jerusalem that day and the next. And David called him to eat and to drink before him, and he made him drunk: and he went out in the evening, and slept on his couch with the servants of his lord, and went not down into his house. And when the morning was come, David wrote a letter to Joab: and sent it by the hand of Urias, Writing in the letter: Set ye Urias in the front of the battle, where the fight is strongest: and leave ye him, that he may be wounded and die. Wherefore as Joab was besieging the city, he put Urias in the place where he knew the bravest men were. And the men coming out of the city, fought against Joab, and there fell some of the people of the servants of David, and Urias the Hethite was killed also.

Sunday VI after Pentecost

Semiduplex

Lesson I ~ 2 Kings 12:1–4

From second book of Kings

And the Lord sent Nathan to David: and when he was come to him, he said to him: There were two men in one city, the one rich, and the other poor. The rich man had exceeding many sheep and oxen. But the poor man had nothing at all but one little ewe lamb, which he had bought and nourished up, and which had grown up in his house together with his children, eating of his bread, and drinking of his cup, and sleeping in his bosom: and it was unto him as a daughter. And when a certain stranger was come to the rich man, he spared to take of his own sheep and oxen, to make a feast for that stranger, who was come to him, but took the poor man's ewe, and dressed it for the man that was come to him.

Lesson II ~ 2 Kings 12:5–9

And David's anger being exceedingly kindled against that man, he said to Nathan: As the Lord liveth, the man that hath done this is a child of death. He shall restore the ewe fourfold, because he did this thing, and had no pity. And Nathan said to David: Thou art the man. Thus saith the Lord the God of Israel: I anointed thee king over Israel, and I delivered thee from the hand of Saul, And gave thee thy master's house and thy master's wives into thy bosom, and gave thee the house of Israel and Juda: and if these things be little, I shall add far greater things unto thee. Why therefore hast thou despised the word of the Lord, to do evil in my sight? Thou hast killed Urias the Hethite with the sword, and hast taken his wife to be thy wife, and hast slain him with the sword of the children of Ammon.

Lesson III ~ 2 Kings 12:10–16

Therefore the sword shall never depart from thy house, because thou hast despised me, and hast taken the wife of Urias the Hethite to be thy wife. Thus saith the Lord: Behold, I will raise up evil against thee out of thy own house, and I will take thy wives before thy eyes I and give them to thy neighhour, and he shall lie with thy wives in the sight of this sun. For thou didst it secretly: but I will do this thing in the sight of all Israel, and in the sight of the sun. And David said to Nathan: I have sinned against the Lord. And Nathan said to David: The Lord also hath taken away thy sin: thou shalt not die. Nevertheless, because thou hast given occasion to the enemies of the Lord to blaspheme, for this thing, the child that is born to thee, shall surely die. And Nathan returned to his house. The Lord also struck the child which the wife of Urias had borne to David, and his life was despaired of. And David besought the Lord for the child: and David kept a fast, and going in by himself lay upon the ground.

Lesson IV

From the Book On
the Defense of David by
St. Ambrose, Bishop

In how many things does each one of us transgress every hour? And nevertheless not one of all us common men thinks it well to confess his sin. Yet that strong and great King would not suffer the acknowledgment of his iniquity to remain, even for a moment, hidden in his own heart. With eager confession and bitter sorrow, he admitted that he had sinned against the Lord. Which of you will easily find me now some honored and wealthy person, who will not take it ill if I rebuke him for a fault whereof he is guilty? But David, amid the splendors of a throne and the certainty of Divine revelations, when he was rebuked by one of his subjects for his grievous transgression, was not roused to anger, but contrarily, acknowledged his sin with groans and affliction.

Lesson V

The heartfelt sorrow of David moved the Lord to compassion, so that Nathan said "Because thou hast repented, the Lord also hath put away thy sin." The instant gift of pardon declares the depth of the King's repentance, which was able to obtain the forgiveness of so grievous a transgression. Other men, when they be rebuked of Priests, do but aggravate the heinousness of their sins by the seeking to deny or to excuse them, and thereby make deeper their fall by means of that which should have helped them up. But the saints of the Lord want to fight a good fight of godliness unto the end and to finish their course by saving their souls, howbeit, they may perchance have fallen like other men, through man's weakness rather than through lust for iniquity, arise more eager to go on than before. Shame goads them on to fly at higher things; so that not only is it deemed to have brought no obstacle to them, but rather to have accumulated an incentive to speed.

Lesson VI

David sinned; and so oftentimes do other kings. David repented with groaning and tears; and so do not oftentimes other kings. He admitted his guilt; he implored forgiveness; he cast himself down upon the ground, and there wept over his crime; he fasted; he prayed; by publishing his sorrow he left an everlasting witness of his acknowledgment. What private men blush to do, the King was not ashamed to own. They who are answerable to law are bold to deny their crimes, and too haughty to ask pardon. Not so he, though he could be held before no earthly judgment-seat. That he sinned was a matter flowing from his nature; that he asked for pardon, his own repentance. To fall is common to all men, but his confession was his own. To transgress thusly was nature; to efface his guilt, greatness.

Lesson VII

From the Holy Gospel according to St. Mark (Mark 8:1–9)

In those days, the multitude being very great, and having nothing to eat, Jesus called His disciples unto Him, and saith unto them: I have compassion on the multitude, because they have now been with Me for three days, and have nothing to eat. And so on.

Homily by St. Ambrose, Bishop

After that woman, who is a type of the Church, was healed of the issue of blood; the Lord had sent His disciples to preach the kingdom of God. His heavenly tenderness gave food. But consider who they were unto whom He gave it. He gave it not to such as dwell at ease, not to men in cities, not to such as sit in places of worldly splendor, but to men seeking Christ in a desert place. Such as are not given to disdain are they whom Christ receives, and unto whom the Word of God speaks, not of earthly things, but of the kingdom of God. And if any bear in them the running sores of fleshly passion, He heals them.

Lesson VIII

And then it came to pass that, as He had healed them that had need of healing, He fed their hunger with spiritual meat. Thus it is that no man takes Christ's meat, unless he be first healed, and they, that are bidden to the supper, are first cured by the invitation. The lame receive the power to walk, that they may be able to come; the blind cannot see the door of the house of the Lord, unless light be given them.

Lesson IX

Everywhere is preserved the order of the Sacraments. The sinful soul is first healed by the remission of sins, and afterward is filled at the Table of the Lord albeit this multitude now present is of such as do not yet feed on those strong meats, nor pasture their starving spirits upon the Body and Blood of Christ, as do they of a manlier faith. To use the words of Paul, I have fed you with milk and not with meat, for hitherto you were not able to bear it, neither yet now are you able. The five loaves are, as it were, your milk; the stronger meat will be the Body of Christ; the more generous cup, the Blood of the Lord.

Monday VI after the Octave of Pentecost

Lesson I ~ 2 Kings 13:22–25

From second book of Kings

But Absalom spoke not to Amnon neither good nor evil: for Absalom hated Amnon because he had ravished his sister Thamar. And it came to pass after two years, that the sheep of Absalom were shorn in Baalhasor, which is near Ephraim: and Absalom invited all the king's sons: And he came to the king, and said to him: Behold thy servant's sheep are shorn. Let the king, I pray, with his servants come to his servant. And the king said to Absalom: Nay, my son, do not ask that we should all come, and be chargeable to thee. And when he pressed him, and he would not go, he blessed him.

Lesson II ~ 2 Kings 13:26–29

And Absalom said: If thou wilt not come, at least let my brother Amnon, I beseech thee, come with us. And the king said to him: It is not necessary that he should go with thee. But Absalom pressed him, so that he let Amnon and all the king's sons go with him. And Absalom made a feast as it were the feast of a king. And Absalom had commanded his servants, saying: Take notice when Amnon shall be drunk with wine, and when I shall say to you: Strike him, and kill him, fear not: for it is I that command you: take courage, and be valiant men. And the servants of Absalom did to Amnon as Absalom had commanded them. And all the king's sons arose and got up every man upon his mule, and fled.

Lesson III ~ 2 Kings 13:30–34

And while they were yet in the way, a rumour came to David, saying: Absalom hath slain all the king's sons, and there is not one of them left. Then the king rose up, and rent his garments: and fell upon the ground, and all his servants, that stood about him, rent their garments. But Jonadab the son of Semmaa David's brother answering, said: Let not my lord the king think that all the king's sons are slain: Amnon only is dead, for he was appointed by the mouth of Absalom from the day that he ravished his sister Thamar. Now therefore let not my lord the king take this thing into his heart, saying: All the king's sons are slain: for Amnon only is dead. But Absalom fled away.

Tuesday VI after the Octave of Pentecost

Lesson I ~ 2 Kings 14:4–7

From second book of Kings

And when the woman of Thecua was come in to the king, she fell before him upon the ground, and worshipped, and said: Save me, O king. And the king said to her: What is the matter with thee? She answered: Alas, I am a widow woman: for my husband is dead. And thy handmaid had two sons: and they quarrelled with each other in the field, and there was none to part them: and the one struck the other, and slew him. And behold the whole kindred rising against thy handmaid, saith: Deliver him that hath slain his brother, that we may kill him for the life of his brother, whom he slew, and that we may destroy the heir: and they seek to quench my spark which is left, and will leave my husband no name, nor remainder upon the earth.

Lesson II ~ 2 Kings 14:10–14

And the king said: If any one shall say ought against thee, bring him to me, and be shall not touch thee any more. And she said: Let the king remember the Lord his God, that the next of kin be not multiplied to take revenge, and that they may not kill my son. And he said: As the Lord liveth, there shall not one hair of thy son fall to the earth. Then the woman said: Let thy handmaid speak one word to my lord the king. And he said: Speak. And the woman said: Why hast thou thought such a thing against the people of God, and why hath the king spoken this word, to sin, and not bring home again his own exile? We all die, and like waters that return no more, we fall down into the earth: neither will God have a soul to perish, but recalleth, meaning that he that is cast off should not altogether perish.

Lesson III ~ 2 Kings 14:19–21

And the king said: Is not the hand of Joab with thee in all this? The woman answered, and said: By the health of thy soul, my lord, O king, it is neither on the left hand, nor on the right, in all these things which my lord the king hath spoken: for thy servant Joab, he commanded me, and he put all these words into the mouth of thy handmaid. That I should come about with this form of speech, thy servant Joab, commanded this: but thou, my lord, O king, art wise, according to the wisdom of an angel of God, to understand all things upon earth. And the king said to Joab: Behold I am appeased and have granted thy request: Go therefore and fetch back the boy Absalom.

Wednesday VI after the Octave of Pentecost

Lesson I ~ 2 Kings 15:1–3

From second book of Kings

Now after these things Absalom made himself chariots, and horsemen, and fifty men to run before him. And Absalom rising up early stood by the entrance of the gate, and when any man had business to come to the king's judgment, Absalom called him to him, and said: Of what city art thou? He answered, and said: thy servant is of such a tribe of Israel. And Absalom answered him: thy words seem to me good and just. But there is no man appointed by the king to hear thee.

Lesson II ~ 2 Kings 15:3–6

And Absalom said: O that they would make me judge over the land, that all that have business might come to me, that I might do them justice. Moreover when any man came to him to salute him, he put forth his hand, and took him, and kissed him. And this he did to all Israel that came for judgment, to be heard by the king, and he enticed the hearts of the men of Israel.

Lesson III ~ 2 Kings 15:7–10

And after forty years, Absalom said to king David: Let me go, and pay my vows which I have vowed to the Lord in Hebron. For thy servant made a vow, when he was in Gessur of Syria, saying: If the Lord shall bring me again into Jerusalem I will offer sacrifice to the Lord. And king David said to him: Go in peace. And he arose, and went to Hebron. And Absalom sent spies into all the tribes of Israel, saying: As soon as you shall hear the sound of the trumpet, say ye: Absalom reigneth in Hebron.

Thursday VI after the Octave of Pentecost

Lesson I ~ 2 Kings 15:13–15

From second book of Kings

And there came a messenger to David, saying: All Israel with their whole heart followeth Absalom. And David said to his servants, that were with him in Jerusalem: Arise and let us flee: for we shall not escape else from the face of Absalom: make haste to go out, lest he come and overtake us, and bring ruin upon us, and smite the city with the edge of the sword. And the king's servants said to him: Whatsoever our lord the king shall command, we thy servants will willingly execute.

Lesson II ~ 2 Kings 15:16–18

And the king went forth, and all his household on foot: and the king left ten women his concubines to keep the house: And the king going forth and all Israel on foot, stood afar off from the house: And all his servants walked by him, and the bands of the Cerethi, and the Phelethi, and all the Gethites, valiant warriors, six hundred men who had followed him from Geth on foot, went before the king.

Lesson III ~ 2 Kings 15:19–20

And the king said to Ethai the Gethite: Why comest thou with us? return and dwell with the king, for thou art a stranger, and art come out of thy own place. Yesterday thou camest, and today shalt thou be forced to go forth with us? but I shall go whither I am going: return thou, and take back thy brethren with thee, and the Lord will show thee mercy, and truth, because thou hast shown grace and fidelity.

Friday VI after the Octave of Pentecost

Lesson I ~ 2 Kings 16:5–8

From second book of Kings

And king David came as far as Bahurim: and behold there came out from thence a man of the kindred of the house of Saul named Semei, the son of Gera, and coming out he cursed as he went on, And he threw stones at David, and at all the servants of king David: and all the people, and all the warriors walked on the right, and on the left side of the king. And thus said Semei when he cursed the king: Come out, come out, thou man of blood, and thou man of Belial. The Lord hath repaid thee for all the blood of the house of Saul: because thou hast usurped the kingdom in his stead, and the Lord hath given the kingdom into the hand of Absalom thy son: and behold thy evils press upon thee, because thou art a man of blood.

Lesson II ~ 2 Kings 16:9–10

And Abisai the son of Sarvia said to the king: Why should this dead dog curse my lord the king? I will go, and cut off his head. And the king said: What have I to do with you, ye sons of Sarvia? Let him alone and let him curse: for the Lord hath bid him curse David: and who is he that shall dare say, why hath he done so?

Lesson III ~ 2 Kings 16:11–12

And the king said to Abisai, and to all his servants: Behold my son, who came forth from my bowels, seeketh my life: how much more now a son of Jemini? let him alone that he may curse as the Lord hath bidden him. Perhaps the Lord may look upon my affliction, and the Lord may render me good for the cursing of this day.

Saturday VI after the Octave of Pentecost

Lesson I ~ 2 Kings 18:6–8

From second book of Kings

So the people went out into the field against Israel and the battle was fought in the forest of Ephraim. And the people of Israel were defeated there by David's army, and a great slaughter was made that day of twenty thousand men. And the battle there was scattered over the face of all the country, and there were many more of the people whom the forest consumed, than whom the sword devoured that day.

Lesson II ~ 2 Kings 18:9–12

And it happened that Absalom met the servants of David, riding on a mule: and as the mule went under a thick and large oak, his head stuck in the oak: and while he hung between the heaven and the earth, the mule on which he rode passed on. And one saw this and told Joab, saying: I saw Absalom hanging upon an oak. And Joab said to the man that told him: If thou sawest him, why didst thou not stab him to the ground, and I would have given thee ten sicles of silver, and belt? And he said to Joab: If thou wouldst have paid down in my hands a thousand pieces of silver, I would not lay my hands upon the king's son: for in our hearing he king charged thee, and Abisai, and Ethai, saying: Save me the boy Absalom.

Lesson III ~ 2 Kings 18:14–17

And Joab said: Not as thou wilt, but will set upon him in thy sight. So he took three lances in his hand, and thrust them into the heart of Absalom: and whilst he yet panted for life, sticking on the oak, Ten young men, armourbearers of Joab, ran up, and striking him slew him. And Joab sounded the trumpet, and kept back the people from pursuing after Israel in their flight, being willing to spare he multitude. And they took Absalom, and cast him into a great pit in the forest, and they laid an exceeding great heap of stones upon him: but all Israel fled to their own dwellings.

✠

Sunday VII after Pentecost

Semiduplex

Lesson I ~ 3 Kings 1:1–4

Beginning of the third book of Kings

Now king David was old, and advanced in years: and when he was covered with clothes, he was not warm. His servants therefore said to him: Let us seek for our lord the king, a young virgin, and let her stand before the king, and cherish him, and sleep in his bosom, and warm our lord the king. So they sought a beautiful young woman in all the coasts of Israel, and they found Abisag a Sunamitess, and brought her to the king. And the damsel was exceeding beautiful, and she slept with the king: and served him, but the king did not know her.

Lesson II ~ 3 Kings 1:5–8

And Adonias the son of Haggith exalted himself, saying: I will be king. And he made himself chariots and horsemen, and fifty men to run before him. Neither did his father rebuke him at any time, saying: Why hast thou done this? And he also was very beautiful, the next in birth after Absalom. And he conferred with Joab the son of Sarvia, and with Abiathar the priest, who furthered Adonias's side. But Sadoc the priest, and Banaias the son of Joiada, and Nathan the prophet, and Semei, and Rei, and the strength of David's army was not with Adonias.

Lesson III ~ 3 Kings 1:11–15

And Nathan said to Bethsabee the mother of Solomon: Hast thou not heard that Adonias the son of Haggith reigneth, and our lord David knoweth it not? Now then come, take my counsel and save thy life, and the life of thy son Solomon. Go, and get thee in to king David, and say to him: Didst not thou, my lord O king, swear to me thy handmaid, saying: Solomon thy son shall reign after me, and he shall sit on my throne? why then doth Adonias reign? And while thou art yet speaking there with the king, I will come in after thee, and will fill up thy words. So Bethsabee went in to the king into the chamber.

Lesson IV

From the Epistle written to Nepotian by St. Jerome, Priest

Then David, who had once been a man of war, was seventy years old, the chill of old age came upon him, and he could get no heat. So they sought out for him throughout all the coasts of Israel Abisag the Sunamite, to sleep with the king and to warm his aged body. Who is this Sunamite, wife and yet virgin, so hot that she could heat the chilly, so holy that her warmth provoked him not to lust? Let Solomon the Wise explain his father's enjoyment, and the "Peaceful One" tell of the warrior's embraces. "Get wisdom, get understanding, forget it not, neither decline from the words of my mouth, forsake her not, and she shall preserve thee love her, and she shall keep thee. Wisdom is the principal thing; therefore, get wisdom and with all thy getting, get understanding. Exalt her, and she shall promote thee. Honor her, and she shall embrace thee, and shall give to thine head an ornament of grace. She shall compass thee like a crown of delights."

Lesson V

In old men almost all the powers of the body become weakened, and while wisdom only is increasing, all things else beside wisdom fail. Then fails strength for fasting, for watching, for "*chameuniae*" (that is, sleeping on the floor), for wandering hither and thither, for receiving strangers, for defending the poor, for instance and constancy in prayer, for visiting the sick, for that work with the hands whence alms are given. I need not treat of this with long talk, but, in short, when the body is broken down, all the works of the body become enfeebled.

Lesson VI

Nor do I say, on the other hand, that wisdom, which in many old men drivels into second childhood, is weak, or wanting in such of the young and stout as win knowledge by work and earnest study, by holiness of life and instancy of prayer to the Lord Jesus; but this I do say, that the more spiritual faculties have to go through in youth many struggles with the body, and that, what with violent provocations to vice, and what with the sensual ticklings of the flesh, they are apt to be smothered like fire among green wood, and not able to blaze forth in all their brightness. But when old age comes upon them, who have spent their youth in acquiring sound knowledge, and have meditated in the law of the Lord day and night, it has this effect on them, to make them more learned by their increased years, more experienced by constant use, more wise through the advance of time and, in short, does offer them the rich harvest of their past diligence.

Lesson VII

From the Holy Gospel according to St. Matthew (Matt 7:15–21)

At that time, Jesus said unto His disciples: Beware of false prophets, which come to you in sheep's clothing, but inwardly they are ravening wolves. And so on.

Homily by St. Hilary, Bishop

The Lord here warns us that we must rate the worth of soft words and seeming meekness, by the fruits which they that manifest such things bring forth in their works, and that we should look, in order to see what a man is, not at his professions, but at his deeds. For there are many in whom sheep's clothing is but a mask to hide wolfish ravening. But "Do men gather grapes of thorns, or figs of thistles? Even so, every good tree bringeth forth good fruit, but a corrupt tree bringeth forth evil fruit." Thus, the Lord teaches us, is it with men also; evil men bring not forth good fruits, and hereby are we to know them. Lip-service alone wins not the kingdom of heaven, nor is every one that says unto Christ: "Lord, Lord," an heir thereof.

Lesson VIII

What use is there in calling the Lord, Lord? Would He not be Lord all the same, whether or not we called Him so? What holiness is there in this ascription of a name, when the true way to enter into the kingdom of heaven is to do the will of our Father, Who is in heaven? "Many will say to Me in that day: Lord, Lord, have we not prophesied in thy Name?" Already here does the Lord rebuke the deceit of the false prophets, and the feigning of the hypocrites, who take glory to themselves because of the power of their words, their prophesying in teaching, their casting out of devils, and such-like mighty works.

Lesson IX

Because of all these things they promised unto themselves that they shall enter into the kingdom of heaven as though in their words and works any good thing were their own, and not all the mighty working of that God upon Whom they call, since reading brings knowledge of doctrine, and the Name of Christ drives out devils. That which is needed on our part to win that blessed eternity, that of our own which we must give, is to will to do right, to turn away from all evil, to obey with our whole heart the commandments laid on us from heaven, and so to become the friends of God. It should be ours rather to do God's will, than to boast of God's power. And we must put off from us and thrust away such as are by their wicked works already estranged from His friendship.

Monday VII after the Octave of Pentecost

Lesson I ~ 3 Kings 1:28–31

From third book of Kings

And King David answered and said: Call to me Bethsabee. And when she was come in to the king, and stood before him, The king swore and said: As the Lord liveth, who hath delivered my soul out of all distress, Even as I swore to thee by the Lord the God of Israel, saying: Solomon thy son shall reign after me, and he shall sit upon my throne in my stead, so will I do this day. And Bethsabee bowing with her face to the earth worshipped the king, saying: May my lord David live for ever.

Lesson II ~ 3 Kings 1:32–35

King David also said: Call me Sadoc the priest, and Nathan the prophet, and Banaias the son of Joiada. And when they were come in before the king, He said to them: Take with you the servants of your lord, and set my son Solomon upon my mule: and bring him to Gihon. And let Sadoc the priest, and Nathan the prophet anoint him there king over Israel: and you shall sound the trumpet, and shall say: God save king Solomon. And you shall come up after him, and he shall come, and shall sit upon my throne, and he shall reign in my stead: and I will appoint him to be ruler over Israel, and over Juda.

Lesson III ~ 3 Kings 1:38–40

So Sadoc the priest, and Nathan the prophet went down, and Banaias the son of Joiada, and the Cerethi, and Phelethi: and they set Solomon upon the mule of king David, and brought him to Gihon. And Sadoc the priest took a horn of oil out of the tabernacle, and anointed Solomon: and they sounded the trumpet, and all the people said: God save king Solomon. And all the multitude went up after him, and the people played with pipes, and rejoiced with a great joy, and the earth rang with the noise of their cry.

Tuesday VII after the Octave of Pentecost

Lesson I ~ 3 Kings 2:1–4

From third book of Kings

And the days of David drew nigh that he should die, and he charged his son Solomon, saying: I am going the way of all flesh: take thou courage, and show thyself a man. And keep the charge of the Lord thy God, to walk in his ways, and observe his ceremonies, and his precepts, and judgments, and testimonies, as it is written in the law of Moses: that thou mayest understand all thou dost, and whithersoever thou shalt turn thyself: That the Lord may confirm his words, which he hath spoken of me, saying: If thy children shall take heed to their ways, and shall walk before me in truth, with all their heart, and with all their soul, there shall not be taken away from thee a man on the throne of Israel.

Lesson II ~ 3 Kings 2:5–6

Thou knowest also what Joab the son of Sarvia hath done to me, what he did to the two captains of the army of Israel, to Abner the son of Ner, and to Amasa the son of Jether: whom he slew, and shed the blood of war in peace, and put the blood of war on his girdle that was about his loins, and in his shoes that were on his feet. Do therefore according to thy wisdom, and let not his hoary head go down to hell in peace.

Lesson III ~ 3 Kings 2:7–9

But show kindness to the sons of Berzellai the Galaadite, and let them eat at thy table: for they met me when I fled from the face of Absalom thy brother. Thou hast also with thee Semei the son of Gera the son of Jemini of Bahurim, who cursed me with a grievous curse, when I went to the camp: but because he came down to meet me when I passed over the Jordan, and I swore to him by the Lord, saying: I will not kill thee with a sword: Do not thou hold him guiltless. But thou art a wise man, and knowest what to do with him, and thou shalt bring down his grey hairs with blood to hell.

Wednesday VII after the Octave of Pentecost

Lesson I ~ 3 Kings 3:5–6

From third book of Kings

And the Lord appeared to Solomon in a dream by night, saying: Ask what thou wilt that I should give thee. And Solomon said: Thou hast shown great mercy to thy servant David my father, even at, he walked before thee in truth, and justice, and an upright heart with thee: and thou hast kept thy great mercy for him, and hast given him a son to sit on his throne, as it is this day.

Lesson II ~ 3 Kings 3:7–9

And now, O Lord God, thou hast made thy servant king instead of David my father: and I am but a child, and know not how to go out and come in. And thy servant is in the midst of the people which thou hast chosen, an immense people, which cannot be numbered nor counted for multitude. Give therefore to thy servant an understanding heart, to judge thy people, and discern between good and evil. For who shall be able to judge this people, thy people which is so numerous?

Lesson III ~ 3 Kings 3:10–13

And the word was pleasing to the Lord that Solomon had asked such a thing. And the Lord said to Solomon: Because thou hast asked this thing, and hast not asked for thyself long life or riches, nor the lives of thy enemies, but hast asked for thyself wisdom to discern judgment, Behold I have done for thee according to thy words, and have given thee a wise and understanding heart, insomuch that there hath been no one like thee before thee, nor shall arise after thee. Yea and the things also which thou didst not ask, I have given thee: to wit riches and glory, as that no one hath been like thee among the kings in all days heretofore.

Thursday VII after the Octave of Pentecost

Lesson I ~ 3 Kings 4:21–24

From third book of Kings

And Solomon had under him all the kingdoms from the river to the land of the Philistines, even to the border of Egypt: and they brought him presents, and served him, all the days of his life. And the provision of Solomon for each day was thirty measures of fine flour, and three-score measures of meal, Ten fat oxen and twenty out of the pastures, and a hundred rams, besides venison of harts, roes, and buffles, and fatted fowls. For he had all the country which was beyond the river, from Thaphsa to Gazan, and all the kings of those countries: and he had peace on every side round about.

Lesson II ~ 3 Kings 4:25–29

And Juda and Israel dwelt without any fear, every one under his vine, and under his fig tree, from Dan to Bersabee, all the days of Solomon. And Solomon had forty thousand stalls of chariot horses, and twelve thousand for the saddle. And the foresaid governors of the king fed them: and they furnished the necessaries also for king Solomon's table, with great care in their time. They brought barley also and straw for the horses, and beasts, to the place where the king was, according as it was appointed them. And God gave to Solomon wisdom and understanding exceeding much, and largeness of heart as the sand that is on the sea shore.

Lesson III ~ 3 Kings 4:30–34

And the wisdom of Solomon surpassed the wisdom of all the Orientals, and of the Egyptians, And he was wiser than all men: wiser than Ethan the Ezrahite, and Heman, and Chalcol, and Dorda the sons of Mahol, and he was renowned in all nations round about. Solomon also spoke three thousand parables: and his poems were a thousand and five. And he treated about trees from the cedar that is in Libanus, unto the hyssop that comes out of the wall: and he discoursed of beasts, and of fowls, and of creeping things, and of fishes. And they came from all nations to hear the wisdom of Solomon, and from all the kings of the earth, who heard of his wisdom.

Friday VII after the Octave of Pentecost

Lesson I ~ 3 Kings 5:1–4

From third book of Kings

And Hiram king of Tyre sent his servants to Solomon: for he heard that they had anointed him king in the room of his father: for Hiram had always been David's friend. And Solomon sent to Hiram, saying: Thou knowest the will of David my father, and that he could not build a house to the name of the Lord his God, because of the wars that were round about him, until the Lord put them under the soles of his feet. But now the Lord my God hath given me rest round about: and there is no adversary nor evil occurrence.

Lesson II ~ 3 Kings 5:5–6

Wherefore I purpose to build a temple to the name of the Lord my God, as the Lord spoke to David my father, saying: my son, whom I will set upon the throne in thy piece, he shall build a house to my name. Give orders therefore that thy servants cut me down cedar trees out of Libanus, and let my servants be with thy servants: and I will give thee the hire of thy servants whatsoever thou wilt ask, for thou knowest how there is not among my people a man that has skill to hew wood like to the Sidonians.

Lesson III ~ 3 Kings 5:7–9

Now when Hiram had heard the words of Solomon, he rejoiced exceedingly, and said: Blessed be the Lord God this day, who hath given to David a very wise son over this numerous people. And Hiram sent to Solomon, saying: I have heard all thou hast desired of me: and I will do all thy desire concerning cedar trees, and fir trees. My servants shall bring them down from Libanus to the sea: and I will put them together in floats in the sea, and convey them to the place, which thou shalt signify to me; and will land them there, and thou shalt receive them: and thou shalt allow me necessaries, to furnish food for my household.

Saturday VII after the Octave of Pentecost

Lesson I ~ 3 Kings 7:51; 8:1–2

From third book of Kings

And Solomon finished all the work that he made in the house of the Lord, and brought in the things that David his father had dedicated, the silver and the gold, and the vessels, and laid them up in the treasures of the house of the Lord. Then all the ancients of Israel with the princes of the tribes, and the heads of the families of the children of Israel were assembled to king Solomon in Jerusalem: that they might carry the ark of the covenant of the Lord out of the city of David, that is, out of Sion. And all Israel assembled themselves to king Solomon on the festival day in the month of Ethanim, the same is the seventh month.

Lesson II ~ 3 Kings 8:3–7

And all the ancients of Israel came, and the priests took up the ark, And carried the ark of the Lord, and the tabernacle of the covenant, and all the vessels of the sanctuary, that were in the tabernacle: and the priests and the Levites carried them. And king Solomon, and all the multitude of Israel, that were assembled unto him went with him before the ark, and they sacrificed sheep and oxen that could not be counted or numbered. And the priests brought in the ark of the covenant of the Lord into its place, into the oracle of the temple, into the holy of holies under the wings of the cherubims. For the cherubims spread forth their wings over the place of the ark, and covered the ark, and the staves thereof above.

Lesson III ~ 3 Kings 8:9–12

Now in the ark there was nothing else but the two tables of stone, which Moses put there at Horeb, when the Lord made a covenant with the children of Israel, when they came out of the land of Egypt. And it came to pass, when the priests were come out of the sanctuary, that a cloud filled the house of the Lord, And the priests could not stand to minister because of the cloud: for the glory of the Lord had filled the house of the Lord. Then

Solomon said: The Lord said that he would dwell in a cloud.

Following the practice of the Church since the 6th Century AD, Lessons for the following Sundays and weeks after Pentecost are to be replaced by those of the Sundays and weeks in August, etc **if** this be the Sunday closest to August 1st.

The first Sunday of each month is that which occurs closest to the first calendar day of the month, *even if it be before the 1st of that month.*

✠

Sunday VIII after Pentecost

Semiduplex

Lesson I ~ 3 Kings 9:1–5

From the third book of Kings

And it came to pass when Solomon had finished the building of the house of the Lord, and the king's house, and all that he desired, and was pleased to do, That the Lord appeared to him the second time, as he had appeared to him in Gabaon. And the Lord said to him: I have heard thy prayer and thy supplication, which thou hast made before me: I have sanctified this house, which thou hast built, to put my name there for ever, and my eyes and my heart shall be there always. And if thou wilt walk before me, as thy father walked, in simplicity of heart, and in uprightness: and wilt do all that I have commanded thee, and wilt keep my ordinances and my judgments, I will establish the throne of thy kingdom over Israel for ever, as I promised David thy father, saying: There shall not fail a man of thy race upon the throne of Israel.

Lesson II ~ 3 Kings 9:6–9

But if you and your children revolting shall turn away from following me, and will not keep my commandments, and my ceremonies, which I have set before you, but will go and worship strange gods, and adore them: I will take away Israel from the face of the land which I have given them; and the temple which I have sanctified to my name, I will cast out of my sight; and Israel shall be a proverb, and a byword among all people. And this house shall be made an example of: every one that shall pass by it, shall be astonished, and shall hiss, and say: Why hath the Lord done thus to this land, and to this house: And they shall answer: Because they forsook the Lord their God, who brought their fathers out of the land of Egypt, and followed strange gods, and adored them, and worshipped them: therefore hath the Lord brought upon them all this evil.

Lesson III ~ 3 Kings 9:10–14

And when twenty years were ended after Solomon had built the two houses, that is, the house of the Lord, and the house of the king (Hiram the king of Tyre furnishing Solomon with cedar trees and fir trees, and gold according to all he had need of), then Solomon gave Hiram twenty cities in the land of Galilee. And Hiram came out of Tyre, to see the towns which Solomon had given him, and they pleased him not, And he said: Are these the cities which thou hast given me, brother? And he called them the land of Chabul, unto this day. And Hiram sent to king Solomon a hundred and twenty talents of gold.

Lesson IV

From *The City of God* by St. Augustine, Bishop

Things which were then still to come were in a certain manner imagined in Solomon, who built the temple, who had that peace which his name implies (for the name Solomon signifies "the Peaceful One") and who, at the beginning of his reign, was marvelously praiseworthy. By these things he foreshadowed in his own person, though he set not forth with his mouth, our Lord Christ. Thus are some things written of Solomon which are, as it were, things written concerning Christ, the Holy Scripture in this way, by giving the history of things past, prophesying all the while of things to come.

Lesson V

Nor besides the books of the Divine history wherein his reign is recorded, the 71st Psalm is superscribed with his name. In this Psalm are many things which cannot suit him, but are most clearly applicable to the Lord Christ, thus showing that Solomon was, as it were, a shadowy figure cast before, of that which was afterwards revealed in very truth in the Person of Christ.

Lesson VI

Without going into the rest, I may say that it is known what were the limits of Solomon's dominions, and yet in that Psalm we read: "He shall have dominion also from sea to sea, and from the river unto the ends of the earth." This we see fulfilled in Christ. It was from the river, that is, from His Baptism by John in Jordan, that He began His assumption of dominion, for then it was when John bore testimony unto Him that His disciples began to acknowledge Him, calling Him, not Master only, but Lord.

Lesson VII

From the Holy Gospel according to St. Luke (Luke 16:1–9)

At that time, Jesus spoke this parable unto His disciples: There was a certain rich man, which had a steward and the same was accused unto him that he had wasted his goods. And so on.

Homily by St. Jerome, Priest

The lord commended the unjust steward, because he had done wisely though wickedly. The lord, although himself defrauded by it, could not but praise the shrewdness of his dishonest servant, because he had cheated him with profit to himself. How much more will our Master Christ, Who is above any defrauding by us, and is Himself the Great Forgiver, praise us if we win a blessing from Him by dealing indulgently with those who are to believe in Him?

Lesson VIII

After this parable the Lord says: "Make to yourselves friends of the mammon of unrighteousness." This word "mammon" is not Hebrew but a Syriac word, signifying ill-gotten gains. If then even ill-gotten gains can be well used unto justice, how much more can they who, like the Apostles, are "stewards of the mysteries of God," those true and blameless riches, how much more can they profit themselves, even everlastingly, by their right use of them?

Lesson IX

Therefore it is immediately written: "He that is faithful in that which is least, that is to say, in bodily things, is faithful also in much that is to say, in spiritual things." "And he that is unjust in the least," that is to say, by not giving to his needy brother aid of those things which are needful for the body, and which God has made for all men, such a one is unjust also in much, that is to say: he will deal out spiritual things unfairly, this to one and that to another, and not according to their true spiritual needs. "If therefore," says the Lord, "ye have not been faithful in the use of earthly riches which pass away, who will commit to your trust the true and abiding riches," that is, the spiritual riches of the word of God?

Monday VIII after the Octave of Pentecost

Lesson I ~ 3 Kings 10:1–3

From third book of Kings

And the queen of Saba, having; heard of the fame of Solomon in the name of the Lord, came to try him with hard questions. And entering into Jerusalem with a great train, and riches, and camels that carried spices, and an immense quantity of gold, and precious stones, she came to king Solomon, and spoke to him all that she had in her heart. And Solomon informed her of all the things she proposed to him: there was not any word the king was ignorant of, and which he could not answer her.

Lesson II ~ 3 Kings 10:4–7

And when the queen of Saba saw all the wisdom of Solomon, and the house which he had built, And the meat of his table, and the apartments of his servants, and the order of his ministers, and their apparel, and the cupbearers, and the holocausts, which he offered in the house of the Lord: she had no longer any spirit in her, And she said to the king: The report is true, which I heard in my own country, Concerning thy words, and concerning thy wisdom. And I did not believe them that told me, till I came myself, and saw with my own eyes, and have found that the half hath not been told me: thy wisdom and thy works, exceed the fame which I heard.

Lesson III ~ 3 Kings 10:8–11

Blessed are thy men, and blessed are thy servants, who stand before thee always, and hear thy wisdom. Blessed be the Lord thy God, whom thou hast pleased, and who hath set thee upon the throne of Israel, because the Lord hath loved Israel for ever, and hath appointed thee king, to do judgment and justice. And she gave the king a hundred and twenty talents of gold, and of spices a very great store, and precious stones: there was brought no more such abundance of spices as these which the queen of Saba gave to king Solomon. The navy also of Hiram, which brought gold from Ophir, brought from Ophir great plenty of thyine trees, and precious stones.

Tuesday VIII after the Octave of Pentecost

Lesson I ~ 3 Kings 11:1–4

From third book of Kings

And king Solomon loved many strange women besides the daughter of Pharao, and women of Moab, and of Ammon, and of Edom, and of Sidon, and of the Hethites: Of the nations concerning which the Lord said to the children of Israel: You shall not go in unto them, neither shall any of them come in to yours: for they will most certainly turn away your heart to follow their gods. And to these was Solomon joined with a most ardent love. And he had seven hundred wives as queens, and three hundred concubines: and the women turned away his heart. And when he was now old, his heart was turned away by women to follow strange gods: and his heart was not perfect with the Lord his God, as was the heart of David his father.

Lesson II ~ 3 Kings 11:5–8

But Solomon worshipped Astarthe the goddess of the Sidonians, and Moloch the idol of the ammonites. And Solomon did that which was not pleasing before the Lord, and did not fully follow the Lord, as David his father. Then Solomon built a temple for Chamos the idol of Moab, on the hill that is over against Jerusalem, and for Moloch the idol of the children of Ammon. And he did in this manner for all his wives that were strangers, who burnt incense, and offered sacrifice to their gods.

Lesson III ~ 3 Kings 11:9–12

And the Lord was angry with Solomon, because his mind was turned away from the Lord the God of Israel, who had appeared to him twice, And had commanded him concerning this thing, that he should not follow strange gods: but he kept not the things which the Lord commanded him. The Lord therefore said to Solomon: Because thou hast done this, and hast not kept my covenant, and my precepts, which I have commanded thee, I will divide and rend thy kingdom, and will give it to thy servant. Nevertheless in thy days I will not do it, for David thy father's sake: but I will rend it out of the hand of thy son.

Wednesday VIII after the Octave of Pentecost

Lesson I ~ 3 Kings 11:26–28

From third book of Kings

Jeroboam also the son of Nabat an Ephrathite of Sareda, a servant of Solomon, whose mother was named Sarua, a widow woman, lifted up his hand against the king. And this is the cause of his rebellion against him, for Solomon built Mello, and filled up the breach of the city of David his father. And Jeroboam was a valiant and mighty man: and Solomon seeing him a young man ingenious and industrious, made him chief over the tributes of all the house of Joseph.

Lesson II ~ 3 Kings 11:29–31

So it came to pass at that time, that Jeroboam went out of Jerusalem, and the prophet Ahias the Silonite, clad with a new garment, found him in the way: and they two were alone in the field. And Ahias taking his new garment, wherewith he was clad, divided it into twelve parts: And he said to Jeroboam: Take to thee ten pieces: for thus saith the Lord the God of Israel: Behold I will rend the kingdom out of the hand of Solomon, and will give thee ten tribes.

Lesson III ~ 3 Kings 11:40–43

Solomon therefore sought to kill Jeroboam: but he arose, and fled into Egypt to Sesac the king of Egypt, and was in Egypt till the death of Solomon. And the rest of the words of Solomon, and all that he did, and his wisdom: behold they are all written in the book of the words of the days of Solomon. And the days that Solomon reigned in Jerusalem over all Israel, were forty years. And Solomon slept with his fathers, and was buried in the city of David his father, and Roboam his son reigned in his stead.

Thursday VIII after the Octave of Pentecost

Lesson I ~ 3 Kings 12:1–5

From third book of Kings

And Roboam went to Sichem: for thither were all Israel come together to make him king. But Jeroboam the son of Nabat, who was yet in Egypt, a fugitive from the face of king Solomon, hearing of his death, returned out of Egypt. And they sent and called him: and Jeroboam came, and all the multitude of Israel, and they spoke to Roboam, saying: Thy father laid a grievous yoke upon us: now therefore do thou take off a little of the grievous service of thy father, and of his most heavy yoke, which he put upon us, and we will serve thee. And he said to them: Go till the third day, and come to me again.

Lesson II ~ 3 Kings 12:5–8

And when the people was gone, King Roboam took counsel with the old men, that stood before Solomon his father while he yet lived, and he said: What counsel do you give me, that I may answer this people? They said to him: If thou wilt yield to this people today, and condescend to them, and grant their petition, and wilt speak gentle words to them, they will be thy servants always. But he left the counsel of the old men, which they had given him, and consulted with the young men, that had been brought up with him, and stood before him.

Lesson III - 3 Kings 12:13–16

And the king answered the people roughly, leaving the counsel of the old men, which they had given him, And he spoke to them according to the counsel of the young men, saying: My father made your yoke heavy, but I will add to your yoke: my father beat you with whips, but I will beat you with scorpions. And the king condescended not to the people: for the Lord was turned away from him, to make good his word, which he had spoken in the hand of Ahias the Silonite, to Jeroboam the son of Nabat. Then the people seeing that the king would not hearken to them, answered him, saying: What portion have we in David? or what inheritance in the son of Isai? Go home to thy dwellings, O Israel, now David look to thy own house. So Israel departed to their dwellings.

Friday VIII after the Octave of Pentecost

Lesson I - 3 Kings 14:5–6

From third book of Kings

And the Lord said to Ahias: Behold the wife of Jeroboam comes in, to consult thee concerning her son that is sick: thus and thus shalt thou speak to her. So when she was coming in, and made as if she were another woman, Ahias heard the sound of her feet coming in at the door, and said: Come in, thou wife of Jeroboam: why dost thou feign thyself to be another? But I am sent to thee with heavy tidings.

Lesson II - 3 Kings 14:7–9

Go, and tell Jeroboam: Thus saith the Lord the God of Israel: Forasmuch as I exalted thee from among the people, and made thee prince over my people Israel: And rent the kingdom away from the house of David, and gave it to thee, and thou hast not been as my servant David, who kept my commandments, and followed me with all his heart, doing that which was well pleasing in my sight: But hast done evil above all that were before thee, and hast made thee strange gods and molten gods, to provoke me to anger, and hast cast me behind thy back.

Lesson III - 3 Kings 14:10–12

Therefore behold I will bring evils upon the house of Jeroboam, and will cut of from Jeroboam him that pisseth against the wall, and him that is shut up, and the last in Israel: and I will sweep away the remnant of the house of Jeroboam, as dung is swept away till all be clean. Them that shall die of Jeroboam in the city, the dogs shall eat: and them that shall die in the field, the birds of the air shall devour: for the Lord hath spoken it. Arise thou therefore, and go to thy house: and when thy feet shall be entering into the city, the child shall die.

Saturday VIII after the Octave of Pentecost

Lesson I - 3 Kings 18:21–22

From third book of Kings

And Elias coming to all the people, said: How long do you halt between two sides? if the Lord be God, follow him: but if Baal, then follow him. And the people did not answer him a word. And Elias said again to the people: I only remain a prophet of the Lord: but the prophets of Baal are four hundred and fifty men.

Lesson II ~ 3 Kings 18:23–24

Let two bullocks be given us, and let them choose one bullock for themselves, and cut it in pieces and lay it upon wood, but put no fire under: and I will dress the other bullock, and lay it on wood, and put no fire under it. Call ye on the names of your gods, and I will call on the name of my Lord: and the God that shall answer by fire, let him be God. And all the people answering said: A very good proposal.

Lesson III ~ 3 Kings 18:25–27

Then Elias said to the prophets of Baal: Choose you one bullock and dress it first, because you are many: and call on the names of your gods, but put no fire under. And they took the bullock which he gave them, and dressed it: and they called on the name of Baal from morning even till noon, saying: O Baal, hear us. But there was no voice, nor any that answered: and they leaped over the altar that they had made. And when it was now noon, Elias jested at them, saying: Cry with a louder voice: for he is a God, and perhaps he is talking, or is in an inn, or on a journey, or perhaps he is asleep, and must be awaked.

Following the practice of the Church since the 6th Century AD, Lessons for the following Sundays and weeks after Pentecost are to be replaced by those of the Sundays and weeks in August, etc **if** this be the Sunday closest to August 1st.

The first Sunday of each month is that which occurs closest to the first calendar day of the month, *even if it be before the 1st of that month.*

Sunday IX after Pentecost

Semiduplex

Lesson I ~ 4 Kings 1:1–4

Beginning of the fourth book of Kings

And Moab rebelled against Israel, after the death of Achab. And Ochozias fell through the lattices of his upper chamber which he had in Samaria, and was sick: and he sent messengers, saying to them: Go, consult Beelzebub, the god of Accaron, whether I shall recover of this my illness. And an angel of the Lord spoke to Elias the Thesbite, saying: Arise, and go up to meet the messengers of the king of Samaria, and say to them: Is there not a God in Israel, that ye go to consult Beelzebub the god of Accaron? Wherefore thus saith the Lord: From the bed, on which thou art gone up, thou shalt not come down, but thou shalt surely die.

Lesson II ~ 4 Kings 1:4–6

And Elias went away. And the messengers turned back to Ochozias. And he said to them: Why are you come back? But they answered him: A man met us, and said to us: Go, and return to the king, that sent you, and you shall say to him: Thus saith the Lord: Is it because there was no God in Israel that thou sendest to Beelzebub the god of Accaron? Therefore thou shalt not come down from the bed, on which thou art gone up, but then shalt surely die.

Lesson III - 4 Kings 1:7–10

And he said to them: What manner of man was he who met you, and spoke these words? But they said: A hairy man with a girdle of leather about his loins. And he said: It is Elias the Thesbite. And he sent to him a captain of fifty, and the fifty men that were under him. And he went up to him, and as he was sitting on the top of a hill, said to him: Man of God, the king hath commanded that thou come down. And Elias answering, said to the captain of fifty: If I be a man of God, let fire come down from heaven, and consume thee, and thy fifty. And there came down fire from heaven, and consumed him, and the fifty that were with him.

Lesson IV

Sermon by St. Augustine, Bishop

Dearly beloved brethren, in the Lessons which are now being read to us day by day, I have often warned you that we must not follow the deathful letter, to the abandonment of the life-giving spirit. For it is thus that the Apostle says: "The letter killeth, but the spirit giveth life." If we will understand only the plain meaning of the letter, we shall get little or no edification from our readings in the Divine Scriptures. All those things whereof we hear were types and images of things.

Lesson V

The Blessed Elias was a type of the Lord our Saviour. Just as Elias was rejected by the Jews, so was even the true Elias, our Lord, rejected and despised by the same Jews. Elias went away out of his own country, and Christ has left the synagogue. Elias went into the desert, and Christ has come into the world. Elias, when he was in the desert, was fed by ravens, and Christ in the desert of this world is comforted by the faith of the Gentiles.

Lesson VI

For the ravens which, at the command of the Lord, ministered unto Elias, were a type of the flock of Gentiles. Wherefore also it is said for the Gentile Church: "I am black, but beautiful, O you daughters of Jerusalem!" Why is the Church black but beautiful? She is black by nature, but beautiful by grace. Why is she black by nature? Because: "Behold, I was conceived in iniquities, and in sin did my mother conceive me." Why is she beautiful? "Sprinkle me with hyssop, and I shall be clean wash me, and I shall be whiter than snow."

Lesson VII

From the Holy Gospel according to St. Luke (Luke 19:41–47)

At that time: When Jesus was come near to Jerusalem, He beheld the city, and wept over it, saying If thou hadst known, even thou, at least in this thy day, the things which belong unto thy peace! but now they are hid from thine eyes. And so on.

Homily by Pope St. Gregory

No man that has read the history of the destruction of Jerusalem by the Roman Princes Vespasian and Titus, can be ignorant that it was of that destruction that the Lord spoke when He wept over the ruin of the city. It is these Princes that are pointed at where it is said "For the days shall come upon thee that thine enemies shall cast a trench about thee." The truth of what follows: "They shall not leave in thee one stone upon another" is even now fulfilled in the change of site of the city, which has been re-built round about that place outside the gates where the Lord was crucified, while the ancient city has been, as I am told, uprooted from the very foundations.

Lesson VIII

What the sin of Jerusalem was which brought upon her the punishment of this destruction, we find written after: "Because thou knewest not the time of thy visitation." The Maker of men, through the mystery of His Incarnation, was pleased to visit her, but she remembered not to fear and to love Him. Hence also the Prophet Jeremias, rebuking the hardness of man's heart, calls the birds of the air to testify against it, saying "The stork in the heaven knoweth her appointed time and the turtle, and the swallow, and the crane, observe the time of their coming but my people know not the judgment of the Lord."

Lesson IX

The Saviour wept over the ruin of the unfaithful city, while she herself as yet knew not that it was coming. "If thou hadst known," said He, even thou and we may understand Him to have meant thou wouldest thyself have wept, in place of making merry as thou now dost, knowing not what hangs over thee. And hence He says farther: "at least in this thy day, the things which belong unto thy peace." While she was giving herself up to fleshly pleasures, and casting no look ahead upon coming sorrows, she had still for a day in her power the things which might have brought unto her peace.

Monday IX after the Octave of Pentecost

Lesson I - 4 Kings 2:5–7

From fourth book of Kings

The sons of the prophets that were at Jericho, came to Eliseus, and said to him: Dost thou know that this day the Lord will take away thy master from thee? And he said: I also know it: hold your peace. And Elias said to him: Stay here, because the Lord hath sent me as far as the Jordan. And he said: As the Lord liveth, and as thy soul liveth, I will not leave thee; and they two went on together, And fifty men of the sons of the prophets followed them, and stood in sight at a distance: but they two stood by the Jordan.

Lesson II ~ 4 Kings 2:8–10

And Elias took his mantle and folded it together, and struck the waters, and they were divided hither and thither, and they both passed over on dry ground. And when they were gone over, Elias said to Eliseus: Ask what thou wilt have me to do for thee, before I be taken away from thee. And Eliseus said: I beseech thee that in me may be thy double spirit. And he answered: Thou hast asked a hard thing: nevertheless if thou see me when I am taken from thee, thou shalt have what thou hast asked: but if thou see me not, thou shalt not have it.

Lesson III ~ 4 Kings 2:11–13

And as they went on, walking and talking together, behold a fiery chariot, and fiery horses parted them both asunder: and Elias went up by a whirlwind into heaven. And Eliseus saw him, and cried: My father, my father, the chariot of Israel, and the driver thereof. And he saw him no more: and he took hold of his own garments, and rent them in two pieces. And he took up the mantle of Elias, that fell from him: and going back, he stood upon the bank of the Jordan.

Tuesday IX after the Octave of Pentecost

Lesson I ~ 4 Kings 3:6–9

From fourth book of Kings

And king Joram went out that day from Samaria, and mustered all Israel. And he sent to Josaphat king of Juda, saying: The king of Moab is revolted from me, come with me against him to battle. And he answered: I will come up: he that is mine, is thine: my people, thy people: and my horses, thy horses. And he said: Which way shall we go up? But he answered: By the desert of Edom. So the king of Israel, and the king of Juda, and the king of Edom went, and they fetched a compass of seven days' journey, and there was no water for the army, and for the beasts, that followed them.

Lesson II ~ 4 Kings 3:10–13

And the king of Israel said: Alas, alas, alas, the Lord hath gathered us three kings together, to deliver us into the hands of Moab! And Josaphat said: Is there not here a prophet of the Lord, that we may beseech the Lord by him? And one of the servants of the king of Israel answered: Here is Eliseus the son of Saphat, who poured water on the hands of Elias. And Josaphat said: The word of the Lord is with him. And the king of Israel, and Josaphat king of Juda, and the king of Edom went down to him. And Eliseus said to the king of Israel: What have I to do with thee? go to the prophets of thy father, and thy mother.

Lesson III ~ 4 Kings 3:13–18

And the king of Israel said to him: Why hath the Lord gathered together these three kings, to deliver them into the hands of Moab? And Eliseus said to him: As the Lord of hosts liveth, in whose sight I stand, if I did not reverence the face of Josaphat king of Juda, I would not have hearkened to thee, nor looked on thee. But now bring me hither a minstrel. And when the minstrel played, the hand of the Lord came upon him, and he said: Thus saith the Lord: Make the channel of this torrent full of ditches. For thus saith the Lord: You shall not see wind, nor rain: and yet this channel shall be filled with waters, and you shall drink, you and your families, and your beasts. And this is a small thing in the sight of the Lord: moreover he will deliver also Moab into your hands.

Wednesday IX after the Octave of Pentecost

Lesson I - 4 Kings 4:1–4

From fourth book of Kings

Now a certain woman of the wives of the prophets cried to Eliseus, saying: thy servant my husband is dead, and thou knowest that thy servant was one that feared God, and behold the creditor is come to take away my two sons to serve him. And Eliseus said to her: What wilt thou have me to do for thee? Tell me, what hast thou in thy house? And she answered: I thy handmaid have nothing in my house but a little oil, to anoint me. And he said to her: Go, borrow of all thy neighbours empty vessels not a few. And go in, and shut thy door, when thou art within, and thy sons: and pour out thereof into all those vessels: and when they are full take them away.

Lesson II - 4 Kings 4:5–10

So the woman went, and shut the door upon her, and upon her sons: they brought her the vessels, and she poured in. And when the vessels were full, she said to her son: Bring me yet a vessel. And he answered: I have no more. And the oil stood. And she came, and told the man of God. And he said: Go, sell the oil, and pay thy creditor: and thou and thy sons live of the rest. And there was a day when Eliseus passed by Sunam: now there was a great woman there, who detained him to eat bread; and as he passed often that way, he turned into her house to eat bread. And she said to her husband: I perceive that this is a holy man of God, who often passeth by us. Let us therefore make him a little chamber, and put a little bed in it for him, and a table, and a stool, and a candlestick, that when he comes to us, he may abide there.

Lesson III - 4 Kings 4:11–17

Now there was a certain day when he came and turned in to the chamber, and rested there. And he said to Giezi his servant Call this Sunamitess. And when he had called her, and she stood before him, He said to his servant: Say to her Behold thou hast diligently served us in all things, what wilt thou have me to do for thee? hast thou any business, and wilt thou that I speak to the king, or to the general of the army? And she answered: I dwell in the midst of my own people. And he said: What will she then that I do for her? And Giezi said: Do not ask, for she hath no son, and her husband is old. Then he bid him call her: And when she was called, and stood before the door. He said to her: At this time, and this same hour, if life accompany, thou shalt have a son in thy womb. But she answered: Do not, I beseech thee, my lord, thou man of God, do not lie to thy handmaid. And the woman conceived, and brought forth a son in the time, and at the same hour, that Eliseus had said.

Thursday IX after the Octave of Pentecost

Lesson I - 4 Kings 6:24–27

From fourth book of Kings

And it came to pass after these things, that Benadad king of Syria gathered together all his army, and went up, and besieged Samaria. And there was a great famine in Samaria: and so long did the siege continue, till the head of an ass was sold for fourscore pieces of silver, and the fourth part of a cabe of pigeon's dung, for five pieces of silver. And as the king of Israel was passing by the wall, a certain woman cried out to him, saying: Save me, my lord O king. And he said: If the Lord doth not save thee, how can I save thee? out of the barnfloor, or out of the winepress?

Lesson II - 4 Kings 6:27–32

And the king said to her: What aileth thee? And she answered: This woman said to me: Give thy son, that we may eat him today, and we will eat my son tomorrow. So we boiled my son, and ate him. And I said to her on the next day: Give thy son that we may eat him. And she hath hid her son. When the king heard this, he rent his garments, and passed by upon the wall. And all the people saw the haircloth which he wore within next to his flesh. And the king said: May God do so and so to me, and may he add more, if the head of Eliseus the son of Saphat shall stand on him this day. But Eliseus sat in his house, and the ancients sat with him.

Lesson III - 4 Kings 6:32–33; 7:1

So he sent a man before: and before that messenger came, he said to the ancients: Do you know that this son of a murderer hath sent to cut off my head? Look then, when the messenger shall come, shut the door, and suffer him not to come in: for behold the sound of his master's feet is behind him. While he was yet speaking to them, the messenger appeared who was coming to him. And he said: Behold, so great an evil is from the Lord: what shall I look for more from the Lord? And Eliseus said: Hear ye the word of the Lord: Thus saith the Lord: Tomorrow about this time a bushel of fine flour shall be sold for a stater, and two bushels of barley for a stater, in the gate of Samaria.

Friday IX after the Octave of Pentecost

Lesson I - 4 Kings 8:1–3

From fourth book of Kings

And Eliseus spoke to the woman, whose son he had restored to life, saying: Arise, and go thou and thy household, and sojourn wheresoever thou canst find: for the Lord hath exiled a famine, and it shall come upon the land seven years. And she arose, and did according to the word of the man of God: and going with her household, she sojourned in the land of the Philistines many days. And when the seven years were ended, the woman returned out of the land of the Philistines, and she went forth to speak to the king for her house, and for her lands.

Lesson II ~ 4 Kings 8:4–6

And the king talked with Giezi, the servant of the man of God, saying: Tell me all the great things that Eliseus hath done. And when he was telling the king how he had raised one dead to life, the woman appeared, whose son he had restored to life, crying to the king for her house, and her lands. And Giezi said: My lord O king, this is the woman, and this is her son, whom Eliseus raised to life. And the king asked the woman: and she told him. And the king appointed her an eunuch, saying: Restore her all that is hers, and all the revenues of the lands, from the day that she left the land, to this present.

Lesson III ~ 4 Kings 8:7–10

Eliseus also came to Damascus, and Benadad king of Syria was sick: and they told him, saying: The man of God is come hither. And the king said to Hazael: Take with thee presents, and go to meet the man of God, and consult the Lord by him, saying: Can I recover of this my illness? And Hazael went to meet him, taking with him presents, and all the good things of Damascus, the burdens of forty camels. And when he stood before him, he said: thy son Benadad the king of Syria hath sent me to thee, saying: Can I recover of this my illness? And Eliseus said to him: Go tell him: Thou shalt recover: but the Lord hath shown me that he shall surely die.

Saturday IX after the Octave of Pentecost

Lesson I ~ 4 Kings 9:1–5

From fourth book of Kings

And Eliseus the prophet called one of the sons of the prophets, slid said to him: Gird up thy loins, and take this little bottle of oil in thy hand, and go to Ramoth Galaad. And when thou art come thither, thou shalt see Jehu the son of Josaphat the son of Namsi: and going in thou shalt make him rise up from amongst his brethren, and carry him into an inner chamber. Then taking the little bottle of oil, thou shalt pour it on his head, and shalt say: Thus saith the Lord: I have anointed thee king over Israel. And thou shalt open the door and flee, and shalt not stay there. So the young man, the servant of the prophet, went awry to Ramoth Galaad, And went in thither: and behold the captains of the army were sitting: and he said: I have a word to thee, O prince. And Jehu said: Unto whom of us all? And he said: To thee, O prince.

Lesson II ~ 4 Kings 9:6–10

And he arose, and went into the chamber: and he poured the oil upon his head, and said: Thus saith the Lord God of Israel: I have anointed thee king over Israel, the people of the Lord. And thou shalt cut off the house of Achab thy master, and I will revenge the blood of my servants the prophets, and the blood of all the servants of the Lord at the hand of Jezabel. And I will destroy all the house of Achab, and I will cut off from Achab him that pisseth against the well, and him that is shut up, and the meanest in Israel. And I will make the house of Achab like the house of Jeroboam the son of Nabat, and like the house of Baasa the son of Ahias. And the dogs shall eat Jezabel in the field of Jezrahel, and there shall be no one to bury her. And he opened the door and fled.

Lesson III ~ 4 Kings 9:11–13

Then Jehu went forth to the servants of his lord: and they said to him: Are all things well? why came this mad man to thee? And he said to them: You know the man, and what he said. But they answered: It is false, but rather do thou tell us. And he said to them: Thus and thus did he speak to me: and he said: Thus saith the Lord: I have anointed thee king over Israel. Then they made haste and taking every man his garment laid it under his feet, after the manner of a judgment seat, and they sounded the trumpet, and said: Jehu is king.

Following the practice of the Church since the 6th Century AD, Lessons for the following Sundays and weeks after Pentecost are to be replaced by those of the Sundays and weeks in August, etc **if** this be the Sunday closest to August 1st.

The first Sunday of each month is that which occurs closest to the first calendar day of the month, *even if it be before the 1st of that month.*

Sunday X after Pentecost

Semiduplex

Lesson I ~ 4 Kings 9:29–34

From the fourth book of Kings

In the eleventh year of Joram the son of Achab, Ochozias reigned over Juda, And Jehu came into Jezrahel. But Jezabel hearing of his coming in, painted her face with stibic stone, and adorned her head, and looked out of a window At Jehu coming in at the gate, and said: Can there be peace for Zambri, that hath killed his master? And Jehu lifted up his face to the window, and said: Who is this? And two or three eunuchs bowed down to him. And he said to them: Throw her down headlong: and they threw her down, and the wall was sprinkled with her blood, and the hoofs of the horses trod upon her. And when he was come in, to eat, and to drink, he said: Go, and see after that cursed woman, and bury her: because she is a king's daughter.

Lesson II ~ 4 Kings 9:35–37; 10:1–3

And when they went to bury her, they found nothing but the skull, and the feet, and the extremities of her hands. And coming back they told him. And Jehu said: It is the word of the Lord, which he spoke by his servant Elias the Thesbite, saying: In the field of Jezrahel the dogs shall eat the flesh of Jezabel,

And the flesh of Jezabel shall be as dung upon the face of the earth in the field of Jezrahel, so that they who pass by shall say: Is this that same Jezabel? And Achab had seventy sons in Samaria: so Jehu wrote letters, and sent to Samaria, to the chief men of the city, and to the ancients, and to them that brought up Achab's children, saying: As soon as you receive these letters, ye that have your master's sons, and chariots, and horses, and fenced cities, and armour, Choose the best, and him that shall please you most of your master's sons, and set him on his father's throne, and fight for the house of your master.

Lesson III - 4 Kings 10:4–7

But they were exceedingly afraid, and said: Behold two kings could not stand before him, and how shall we be able to resist? Therefore the overseers of the house, and the rulers of the city, and the ancients, and the tutors sent to Jehu, saying: We are thy servants, whatsoever thou shalt command us we will do, neither will we make us a king: do thou all that pleaseth thee. And he wrote letters the second time to them, saying: If you be mine, and will obey me, take the heads of the sons of your master, and come to me to Jezrahel by tomorrow this time. Now the king's sons, being seventy men, were brought up with the chief men of the city. And when the letters came to them, they took the king's sons, and slew seventy persons, and put their heads in baskets, and sent them to him to Jezrahel.

Lesson IV

Sermon by St. John Chrysostom

Let us not dream that we are ourselves to be held less guilty, when we find that we have not been alone in sin. On the contrary, such fellowship adds to our punishment. The serpent was more heavily punished than Eve, and Eve than Adam, and Jezebel suffered more than Achab, who took the vineyard of Naboth. She it had been that planned the whole matter, and opened the way for her husband's crime. Even so thou also, who shalt have caused another's perdition, shalt suffer more grievously than shall they, whom thou hast ruined. Since, for a man to commit sin himself is less wicked than to lead others into sin.

Lesson V

If, therefore, we should see others sinning, let us not only not help them, but let us do what lies in us to draw them out of the bottomless pit of destruction, lest we should suffer as accomplices in their trespass. Let our memory never forget that right awful judgment-seat, the river of fire, the chains that can never be unlocked, the darkness that cannot be pierced, the sound of teeth gnashing, the deadly worm. But thou sayest God is good. Are then all these things but idle words? Is there no punishment for the rich man who gives no heed to Lazarus? Does the bridegroom open to the foolish virgins the door of the marriage-chamber? They that have denied to Christ the necessaries of life, are they not to depart from Him into everlasting fire, prepared for the devil and his angels? The man that comes in to the marriage-supper, not having a wedding garment, shall he, or shall he not, be bound hand and foot, and taken away, and cast into outer darkness? The servant that has no compassion on his fellow-servant, which owes him a hundred pence, shall he, or shall he not, be delivered to the tormentors? Isn't it said, concerning such as commit adultery, that their worm dies not and their fire is not quenched?

Lesson VI

But these are perhaps only threats on God's part, no doubt, sayest thou. I ask thee: How darest thou say such a thing out loud, and deliver this judgment from thine own imagining? Indeed, I can prove to thee, from the things which God has done, that thou art wrong. If thou wilt not believe for things to come, at least believe for things past. Of them at least it cannot be said that they are nought but threats and mere words, for they have happened, and actually been realized in fact. Who was He which brought in a great flood, until the whole land was standing water, and our whole race perished, save eight persons? Who was He which rained upon Sodom brimstone and fire out of heaven? Who was He which overthrew all the host of Egypt in the Red Sea? Who was He which sent out a fire and consumed them that were of the faction of Abiram? Who was He which sent a pestilence upon Israel, because David had sinned, and, from the morning even to the time appointed, there died of the people seventy thousand men? Was it not God, and none other, Which brought upon them all these things, and more also?

Lesson VII

From the Holy Gospel according to St. Luke (Luke 18:9–14)

At that time: Jesus spoke this parable unto certain which trusted in themselves that they were righteous, and despised others: Two men went up into the Temple to pray, the one a Pharisee, and the other a publican. And so on.

Homily by St. Augustine, Bishop

The Pharisee might at least have said: "I am not as many men are." But what means "other men"? All other men except himself. "I," said he, "am righteous; others are sinners." "I am not as other men are, extortioners, unjust, adulterers," and then he took occasion, from the neighborhood of the publican, to plume himself "or even," quotes he, "as this publican." "I am alone," he thought, "that publican is one of the others. My own righteousness makes the gulf between me and the wicked, such as he is."

Lesson VIII

"I fast twice in the week; I give tithes of all that I possess." If we look in his prayer to find what he went to the Temple to pray to God for, we shall find nothing. He went up to pray, but his prayer was not a request of anything from God, but a glorification of himself. It was little enough not to pray to God, but he also glorified himself and despised his neighbor. But the publican stood afar off and yet drew nigh to God. Self-knowledge bade him keep at a distance, but his earnestness made him close. The publican stood afar off, but the Lord was at hand to hear him.

Lesson IX

"Though the Lord be high, yet hath He respect unto the lowly" but the proud, such as was this Pharisee, "He knoweth afar off." He knows the proud, all the same, but they are afar off from Him. Consider now the lowliness of the publican. It was not only that he stood afar off, but "he would not lift up so much as his eyes unto heaven." He looked carefully, lest he should look up, he dared not to lift up his eyes unto heaven. Self-knowledge kept him down, though hope raised him up. Consider again, how that he "smote upon his breast." He afflicted himself, and therefore the Lord had compassion upon his acknowledgment of guilt. "He smote upon his breast, saying Lord, be merciful to me a sinner." Hearken here to a prayer and wonder that when the sinner remembers, God forgets.

Monday X after the Octave of Pentecost

Lesson I - 4 Kings 11:1–3

From fourth book of Kings

And Athalia the mother of Ochozias seeing that her son was dead, arose, and slew all the royal seed. But Josaba the daughter of king Joram, sister of Ochozias, took Joas the son of Ochozias, and stole him from among the king's sons that were slain, out of the bedchamber with his nurse: and hid him from the face of Athalia, so that he was not slain. And he was with her six years hid in the house of the Lord. And Athalia reigned over the land.

Lesson II - 4 Kings 11:4–7

And in the seventh year Joiada sent, and taking the centurions and the soldiers, brought them in to him into the temple of the Lord, and made a covenant with them: and taking an oath of them in the house of the Lord, showed them the king's son: And he commanded them, saying: This is the thing that you must do: Let a third part of you go in on the sabbath, and keep the watch of the king's house. And let a third part be at the gate of Sur: and let a third part be at the gate behind the dwelling of the shieldbearers: and you shall keep the watch of the house of Messa. But let two parts of you, all that go forth on the sabbath, keep the watch of the house of the Lord about the king.

Lesson III - 4 Kings 11:9–12

And the centurions did according to all things that Joiada the priest had commanded them: and taking every one their men, that went in on the sabbath, with them that went out on the sabbath, came to Joiada the priest. And he gave them the spears, and the arms of king David, which were in the house of the Lord. And they stood having every one their weapons in their hands, from the right side of the temple, unto the left side of the altar, and of the temple, about the king. And he brought forth the king's son, and put the diadem upon him, and the testimony: and they made him king, and anointed him: and clapping their hands. they said, God save the king.

Tuesday X after the Octave of Pentecost

Lesson I ~ 4 Kings 12:1–3

From fourth book of Kings

In the seventh year of Jehu Joas began to reign: and he reigned forty years in Jerusalem. The name of his mother was Sebia of Bersabee. And Joas did that which was right before the Lord all the days that Joiada the priest taught him. But yet he took not away the high places: for the people still sacrificed and burnt incense in the high places.

Lesson II ~ 4 Kings 12:4–5

And Joas said to the priests: O All the money of the sanctified things, which is brought into the temple of the Lord by those that pass, which is offered for the price of a soul, and which of their own accord, and of their own free heart they bring into the temple of the Lord: Let the priests take it according to their order, and repair the house, wheresoever they shall see any thing that wanteth repairing.

Lesson III ~ 4 Kings 12:6–8

Now till the three and twentieth year of king Joas, the priests did not make the repairs of the temple. And king Joas called Joiada the high priest and the priests, saying to them: Why do you not repair the temple? Take you therefore money no more according to your order, but restore it for the repairing of the temple. And the priests were forbidden to take any more money of the people, and to make the repairs of the house.

Wednesday X after the Octave of Pentecost

Lesson I ~ 4 Kings 13:14–17

From fourth book of Kings

Now Eliseus was sick of the illness whereof he died: and Joas king of Israel went down to him, and wept before him, and said: O my father, my father, the chariot of Israel and the guider thereof. And Eliseus said to him: Bring a bow and arrows. And when he had brought him a bow, and arrows, He said to the king of Israel: Put thy hand upon the bow. And when he had put his hand, Eliseus put his hands over the king's hands, And said: Open the window to the east. And when he had opened it, Eliseus said: Shoot an arrow. And he shot. And Eliseus said: The arrow of the Lord's deliverance, and the arrow of the deliverance from Syria: and thou shalt strike the Syrians in Aphec, till thou consume them.

Lesson II ~ 4 Kings 13:18–20

And he said: Take the arrows. And when he had taken them, he said to him: Strike with an arrow upon the ground. And he struck three times and stood still. And the man of God was angry with him, and said: If thou hadst smitten five or six or seven times, thou hadst smitten Syria even to utter destruction: but now three times shalt thou smite it. And Eliseus died, and they buried him. And the rovers from Moab came into the land the same year.

Lesson III ~ 4 Kings 13:21, 24–25

And some that were burying a man, saw the rovers, and cast the body into the sepulchre of Eliseus. And when it had touched the bones of Eliseus, the man came to life, and stood upon his feet. And Hazael king of Syria died, and Benadad his son reigned in his stead. Now Joas the son of Joachaz, took the cities out of the hand of Benadad, the son of Hazael, which he had taken out of the hand of Joachaz his father by war, three times did Joas beat him, and he restored the cities to Israel.

Thursday X after the Octave of Pentecost

Lesson I ~ 4 Kings 17:6–9

From fourth book of Kings

And in the ninth year of Osee, the king of the Assyrians took Samaria, and carried Israel away to Assyria: and he placed them in Hala and Habor by the river of Gozan, in the cities of the Medes. For so it was that the children of Israel had sinned against the Lord their God, who brought them out of the land of Egypt, from under the hand of Pharao king of Egypt, and they worshipped strange gods. And they walked according to the way of the nations which the Lord had destroyed in the sight of the children of Israel and of the kings of Israel: because they had done in like manner. And the children of Israel offended the Lord their God with things that were not right: and built them high places in all their cities from the tower of the watchmen to the fenced city.

Lesson II ~ 4 Kings 17:13–15

And the Lord testified to them in Israel and in Juda by the hand of all the prophets and seers, saying: Return from your wicked ways, and keep my precepts, and ceremonies, according to all the law which I commanded your fathers: and as I have sent to you in the hand of my servants the prophets. And they hearkened not, but hardened their necks like to the neck of their fathers, who would not obey the Lord their God. And they rejected his ordinances and the covenant that he made with their fathers, and the testimonies which he testified against them: and they followed vanities, and acted vainly: and they followed the nations that were round about them, concerning which the Lord had commanded them that they should not do as they did.

Lesson III ~ 4 Kings 17:18–21

And the Lord was very angry with Israel, and removed them from his sight, and there remained only the tribe of Juda. But neither did Juda itself keep the commandments of the Lord their God: but they walked in the errors of Israel, which they had wrought. And the Lord cast off all the seed of Israel, and afflicted them and delivered them into the hand of spoilers, till he cast them away from his face: Even from that time, when Israel was rent from the house of David, and made Jeroboam son of Nabat their king: for Jeroboam separated Israel from the Lord, and made them commit a great sin.

Friday X after the Octave of Pentecost

Lesson I ~ 4 Kings 17:21–23

From fourth book of Kings

Jeroboam separated Israel from the Lord, and made them commit a great sin. And the children of Israel walked in all the sins of Jeroboam, which he had done: and they departed not from them, Till the Lord removed Israel from his face, as he had spoken in the hand of all his servants the prophets: and Israel was carried away out of their land to Assyria, unto this day.

Lesson II ~ 4 Kings 17:24–25

And the king of the Assyrians brought people from Babylon, and from Cutha, and from Avah, and from Emath, and from Sepharvaim: and placed them in the cities of Samaria instead of the children of Israel: and they possessed Samaria, and dwelt in the cities thereof. And when they began to dwell there, they feared not the Lord: and the Lord sent lions among them, which killed them.

Lesson III ~ 4 Kings 17:26–27

And it was told the king of the Assyrians, and it was said: The nations which thou hast removed, and made to dwell in the cities of Samaria, know not the ordinances of the God of the land: and the Lord hath sent lions among them: and behold they kill them, because they know not the manner of the God of the land. And the king of the Assyrians commanded, saying: Carry thither one of the priests whom you brought from thence captive, and let him go, and dwell with them: and let him teach them the ordinances of the God of the land.

Saturday X after the Octave of Pentecost

Lesson I ~ 4 Kings 18:1–5

From fourth book of Kings

In the third year of Osee the son of Ela king of Israel, reigned Ezechias the son of Achaz king of Juda. He was five and twenty years old when he began to reign: and he reigned nine and twenty years in Jerusalem: the name of his mother was Abi the daughter of Zacharias. And he did that which was good before the Lord, according to all that David his father had done. He destroyed the high places, and broke the statues in pieces, and cut down the groves, and broke the brazen serpent, which Moses had made: for till that time the children of Israel burnt incense to it: and he called its name Nohestan. He trusted in the Lord the God of Israel.

Lesson II - 4 Kings 18:5–8

So that after him there was none like him among all the kings of Juda, nor any of them that were before him: And he stuck to the Lord, and departed not from his steps, but kept his commandments, which the Lord commanded Moses. Wherefore the Lord also was with him, and in all things, to which he went forth, he behaved himself wisely. And he rebelled against the king of the Assyrians, and served him not. He smote the Philistines as far as Gaza, and all their borders, from the tower of the watchmen to the fenced city.

Lesson III - 4 Kings 18:9–12

In the fourth year of king Ezechias, which was the seventh year of Osee the son of Ela king of Israel, Salmanasar king of the Assyrians came up to Samaria, and besieged it, And took it. For after three years, in the sixth year of Ezechias, that is, in the ninth year of Osee king of Israel, Samaria was taken: And the king of the Assyrians carried away Israel into Assyria, and placed them in Hale, and in Habor by the rivers of Gozan in the cities of the Medes: Because they hearkened not to the voice of the Lord their God, but transgressed his covenant: all that Moses the servant of the Lord commanded, they would not hear nor do.

Following the practice of the Church since the 6th Century AD, Lessons for the following Sundays and weeks after Pentecost are to be replaced by those of the Sundays and weeks in August, etc **if** this be the Sunday closest to August 1st.

The first Sunday of each month is that which occurs closest to the first calendar day of the month, *even if it be before the 1st of that month.*

Sunday XI after Pentecost

Semiduplex

Lesson I - 4 Kings 20:1–3

From the fourth book of Kings

In those days Ezechias was sick unto death: and Isaias the son of Amos the prophet came and said to him: Thus saith the Lord God: Give charge concerning thy house, for thou shalt die, and not live. And he turned his face to the wall, and prayed to the Lord, saying: I beseech thee, O Lord, remember how I have walked before thee in truth, and with a perfect heart, and have done that which is pleasing before thee. And Ezechias wept with much weeping.

Lesson II - 4 Kings 20:4–7

And before Isaias was gone out of the middle of the court, the word of the Lord came to him, saying: Go back, and tell Ezechias the captain of my people: Thus saith the Lord the God of David thy father: I have heard thy prayer, and I have seen thy tears: and behold I have healed thee; on the third day thou shalt go up to the temple of the Lord. And I will add to thy days fifteen years: and I will deliver thee and this city out of the hand of the king of the

Assyrians, and I will protect this city for my own sake, and for David my servant's sake. And Isaias said: Bring me a lump of figs. And when they had brought it, and laid it upon his boil. he was healed.

Lesson III ~ 4 Kings 20:8–11

And Ezechias had said to Isaias: What shall be the sign that the Lord will heal me, and that I shall go up to the temple of the Lord the third day? And Isaias said to him: This shall be the sign from the Lord, that the Lord will do the word which he hath spoken: Wilt thou that the shadow go forward ten lines, or that it go back so many degrees? And Ezechias said: It is an easy matter for the shadow to go forward ten lines: and I do not desire that this be done, but let it return back ten degrees. And Isaias the prophet called upon the Lord, and he brought the shadow ten degrees backwards by the lines, by which it had already gone down in the dial of Achaz.

Lesson IV

The Lesson is taken from the Exposition of the Prophet Isaias written by St Jerome, Priest

Lest the heart of Ezechias should be puffed up by his strange and unlooked for triumphs, and by his victory when he was but a prisoner, he was visited by bodily weakness, and told that he was to die; that he might betake himself to the Lord, and turn Him from carrying out the sentence. We read of a like case in the history of the Prophet Jonas. And in regard to the threat made against David when punishments were foretold which were not brought to pass. This is not because God is a Being capable of changing His mind, but because He wills mankind to know Him, how "He is gracious and merciful, slow to anger, and of great kindness, and repents Him of evil." Ezechias turned his face unto the wall, not being able to go up to the Temple. This may either mean that he turned towards the wall of the Temple, near which Solomon had built a palace, or simply, that he turned his face to the wall, so as not to parade his tears before his attendants.

Lesson V

Having been told that he was about to die, he prayed not for life and many years, but left it to God to do as in His good judgment He was pleased to will. He knew how this had pleased God on the part of Solomon. So, when he betook him to the Lord, he only made mention of his works, how he had walked before Him in truth, and with a perfect heart. Happy is he whose conscience in the hour of affliction can assure him of good works. Yea, "blessed are the pure in heart, for they shall see God." It is indeed written in another place: "Who can say, I have made my heart clean, I am pure from my sin?" How then could Ezechias say that he had walked with a perfect heart? But the answer is, that by this is meant that he had destroyed the idols, opened the doors of the Temple, broken in pieces the brazen serpent, and done the rest of the things whereof the Scripture makes mention.

Lesson VI

"And Ezechias wept with much weeping." He had then no children, and it seemed as though the promise which God had made unto David was about to fail in his own death. It is written that "Manassas was twelve years old when he began to reign," whence it is evident that Ezechias begat him not till after three years of his new lease of life. Sorely therefore wept he, when all hope was torn from him that the Messiah should spring from his seed. Others again remark that he wept sorely, since death terrifies sometimes even the saints, since they know not what sentence is about to be pronounced upon them, and what place shall be allotted them in the inscrutable judgment.

Lesson VII

From the Holy Gospel according to St. Mark (Mark 7:31–37)

At that time: Jesus, departing from the coasts of Tyre and Sidon, came unto the sea of Galilee, through the midst of the coasts of Decapolis. And so on.

Homily by Pope St. Gregory

What signifies it that when God, the Maker of all, would heal a deaf and dumb man, "He put His Fingers into his ears, and He spit, and touched his tongue?" What is figured by the Fingers of the Redeemer but the gifts of the Holy Ghost? Hence it is written in another place that after He had cast out an evil spirit, He said: "If I with the finger of God cast out devils, no doubt the kingdom of God is come upon you." Which words are thus given by another Evangelist: "If I cast out devils by the Spirit of God, then the kingdom of God is come unto you." By setting these two passages together we see that the Spirit is called the Finger. For our Lord, then, to put His Fingers into the deaf man's ears was by the gift of the Holy Spirit to enlighten his dark mind unto obedience.

Lesson VIII

What signifies it also that "He spit and touched his tongue?" We receive spittle out of the Redeemer's mouth upon our tongues when we receive wisdom to speak God's truth. Spittle is a secretion of the head which flows into the mouth. And so, that wisdom, which is Himself, the great Head of His Church, as soon as it has touched our tongue, does straightaway take the form of preaching. "And looking up to heaven, He sighed," not that He had any need to sigh, Who gave whatsoever He asked, but that He was eager to teach us to look up and sigh toward Him Whose throne is in heaven, confessing our need, that our ears should be opened by the gift of the Holy Spirit, and our tongue loosed by the spittle of our Saviour's Mouth, that is, by knowledge of His Divine Word, before we can use it to preach to others.

Lesson IX

"And He said unto him: *Ephphatha*—that is: Be opened. And straightway his ears were opened, and the string of his tongue was loosed." Herein we must remark the command, "Be opened" was addressed to the deaf ears, but the tongue also was immediately loosed. Just so, when the ears of a man's heart have been opened to learn the obedience of faith, the string of his tongue also is thereupon loosed, that he may exhort others to do the good things which he himself does. It is well added: "And he spoke plainly." He only does well to preach obedience to others who has first learnt himself to obey.

Monday XI after the Octave of Pentecost

Lesson I - 4 Kings 22:1–5

From fourth book of Kings

Josias was eight years old when he began to reign: he reigned one and thirty years in Jerusalem: the name of his mother was Idida, the daughter of Hadaia, of Besecath. And he did that which was right in the sight of the Lord, and walked in all the ways of David his father: he turned not aside to the right hand, or to the left. And in the eighteenth year of king Josias, the king sent Saphan the son of Assia, the son of Messulam, the scribe of the temple of the Lord, saying to him: Go to Helcias the high priest, that the money may be put together which is brought into the temple of the Lord, which the doorkeepers of the temple have gathered of the people. And let it be given to the workmen by the overseers of the house of the Lord: and lot them distribute it to those that work in the temple of the Lord, to repair the temple.

Lesson II - 4 Kings 22:8–10

And Helcias the high priest said to Saphan the scribe: I have found the book of the law in the house of the Lord: and Helcias gave the book to Saphan, and he read it. And Saphan the scribe came to the king, and brought him word again concerning that which he had commanded, and said: thy servants have gathered together the money that was found in the house of the Lord, and they have given it to be distributed to the workmen, by the overseers of the works of the temple of the Lord. And Saphan the scribe told the king, saying: Helcias the priest hath delivered to me a book.

Lesson III - 4 Kings 22:10–13

And when Saphan had read it before the king, And the king had heard the words of the law of the Lord, he rent his garments. And he commanded Helcias the priest, and Ahicam the son of Saphan, and Achobor the son of Micha, and Saphan the scribe, and Asaia the king's servant, saying: Go and consult the Lord for me, and for the people, and for all Juda, concerning the words of this book which is found: for the great wrath of the Lord is kindled against us, because our fathers have not hearkened to the words of this book, to do all that is written for us.

Tuesday XI after the Octave of Pentecost

Lesson I - 4 Kings 23:2–3

From fourth book of Kings

And the king went up to the temple of the Lord, and all the men of Juda, and all the inhabitants of

Jerusalem with him, the priests and the prophets, and all the people both little and great: and in the hearing of them all he read all the words of the book of the covenant, which was found in the house of the Lord. And the king stood upon the step: and made a covenant with the Lord, to walk after the Lord, and to keep his commandments, and his testimonies and his ceremonies, with all their heart, and with all their soul, and to perform the words of this covenant, which were written in that book: and the people agreed to the covenant.

Lesson II - 4 Kings 23:4–5

And the king commanded Helcias the high priest, and the priests of the second order, and the doorkeepers, to cast out of the temple of the Lord all the vessels that had been made for Baal, and for the grove, and for all the host of heaven: and he burnt them without Jerusalem in the valley of Cedron, and he carried the ashes of them to Bethel. And he destroyed the soothsayers, whom the kings of Juda had appointed to sacrifice in the high places in the cities of Juda, and round about Jerusalem: them also that burnt incense to Baal, and to the sun, and to the moon, and to the twelve signs, and to all the host of heaven.

Lesson III - 4 Kings 23:6–8

And he caused the grove to be carried out from the house of the Lord without Jerusalem to the valley of Cedron, and he burnt it there, and reduced it to dust, and cast the dust upon the graves of the common people. He destroyed also the pavilions of the effeminate, which were in the house of the Lord, for which the women wove as it were little dwellings for the grove. And he gathered together all the priests out of the cities of Juda: and he defiled the high places, where the priests offered sacrifice, from Gabaa to Bersabee: and he broke down the altars of the gates that were in the entering in of the gate of Josue governor of tile city, which was on the left hand of the gate of the city.

Wednesday XI after the Octave of Pentecost

Lesson I - 4 Kings 23:24–26

From fourth book of Kings

Moreover the diviners by spirits, and soothsayers, and the figures of idols, and the uncleannesses, and the abominations, that had been in the land of Juda, and Jerusalem, Josias took away: that he might perform the words of the law, that were written in the book which Helcias the priest had found in the temple of the Lord. There was no king before him like unto him, that returned to the Lord with all his heart, and with all his soul, and with ail his strength, according to all the law of Moses: neither after him did there arise any like him. But yet the Lord turned not away from the wrath of his great indignation, wherewith his anger was kindled against Juda: because of the provocations, wherewith Manasses had provoked him.

Lesson II ~ 4 Kings 23:27–30

And the Lord said: I will remove Juda also from before my face, as I have removed Israel: and I will cast off this city Jerusalem, which I chose, and the house, of which I said: My name shall be there. Now the rest of the acts of Josias, and all that he did, are they not written in the book of the words of the days of the kings of Juda? In his days Pharao Nechao king of Egypt went up against the king of Assyria to the river Euphrates: and king Josias went to meet him: and was slain at Mageddo, when he had seen him. And his servants carried him dead from Mageddo: and they brought him to Jerusalem, and buried him in Iris own sepulchre.

Lesson III ~ 4 Kings 23:30–34

And the people of the land took Joachaz the son of Josias: and they anointed him, and made him king in his father's stead. Joachaz was three and twenty years old when he began to reign, and he reigned three months in Jerusalem: the name of his mother was Amital, the daughter of Jeremias of Lobna. And he did evil before the Lord, according to all that his fathers had done. And Pharao Nechao bound him at Rebla, which is in the land of Emath, that he should not reign in Jerusalem: and he set a fine upon the land, of a hundred talents of silver, and a talent of gold. And Pharao Nechao made Eliacim the son of Josias king in the room of Josias his father: and turned his name to Joakim. And he took Joachaz away and carried him into Egypt, and he died there.

Thursday XI after the Octave of Pentecost

Lesson I ~ 4 Kings 23:36–37; 24:1

From fourth book of Kings

Joakim was five and twenty years old when he began to reign: and he reigned eleven years in Jerusalem: the name of his mother was Zebida the daughter of Phadaia of Ruma. And he did evil before the Lord according to all that his fathers had done. In his days Nabuchodonosor king of Babylon came up, and Joakim became his servant three years: then again he rebelled against him.

Lesson II ~ 4 Kings 24:2–4

And the Lord sent against him the rovers of the Chaldees, and the rovers of Syria, and the rovers of Moab, and the rovers of the children of Ammon: and he sent them against Juda, to destroy it, according to the word of the Lord, which he had spoken by his servants the prophets. And this came by the word of the Lord against Juda, to remove them from before him for all the sins of Manasses which he did. And for the innocent blood that he shed, filling Jerusalem with innocent blood: and therefore the Lord would not be appeased.

Lesson III ~ 4 Kings 24:5–7

But the rest of the acts of Joakim, and all that he did, are they not written in the book of the words of the days of the kings of Juda? And Joakim slept with his fathers: And Joachin his son reigned in his stead. And the king of Egypt came not again any more out of his own country: for the king of Babylon had taken all that had belonged to the king of Egypt, from the river of Egypt, unto the river Euphrates.

Friday XI after the Octave of Pentecost

Lesson I ~ 4 Kings 24:8–11

From fourth book of Kings

Joachin was eighteen years old when he began to reign, a and he reigned three months in Jerusalem: the name of his mother was Nohesta the daughter of Elnathan of Jerusalem. And he did evil before the Lord, according to all that his father had done. At that time the servants of Nabuchodonosor king of Babylon came up against Jerusalem, and the city was surrounded with their forts. And Nabuchodonosor king of Babylon came to the city with his servants to assault it.

Lesson II ~ 4 Kings 24:12–14

And Joachin king of Juda went out to the king of Babylon, he and his mother, and his servants, and his nobles, and his eunuchs: and the king of Babylon received him in the eighth year of his reign. And he brought out from thence all the treasures of the house of the Lord, and the treasures of the king's house: and he cut in pieces all the vessels of gold which Solomon king of Israel had made in the temple of the Lord, according to the word of the Lord. And he carried away all Jerusalem, and all the princes, and all the valiant men of the army, to the number of ten thousand into captivity: and every artificer and smith: and none were left, but the poor sort of the people of the land.

Lesson III ~ 4 Kings 24:15–17

And he carried away Joachin into Babylon, and the king's mother, and the king's wives, and his eunuchs: and the judges of the land he carried into captivity from Jerusalem into Babylon. And all the strong men, seven thousand, and the artificers, and the smiths a thousand, all that were valiant men and fit for war: and the king of Babylon led them captives into Babylon. And he appointed Matthanias his uncle in his stead: and called his name Sedecias.

Saturday XI after the Octave of Pentecost

Lesson I ~ 4 Kings 24:18–20; 25:1–3

From fourth book of Kings

Sedecias was one and twenty years old when he began to reign, and he reigned eleven years in Jerusalem: the name of his mother was Amital, the daughter of Jeremias of Lobna. And he did evil before the Lord, according to all that Joakim had done. For the Lord was angry against Jerusalem and against Juda, till he cast them out from his face: and Sedecias revolted from the king of Babylon. And it came to pass in the ninth year of his reign, in the tenth month, the tenth day of the month, that Nabuchodonosor king of Babylon came, he and all his army against Jerusalem: and they surrounded it: and raised works round about it. And the city was shut up and besieged till the eleventh year of king Sedecias, The ninth day of the month: and a famine prevailed in the city, and there was no bread for the people of the land.

Lesson II ~ 4 Kings 25:4–7

And a breach was made into the city: and all the men of war fled in the night between the two walls by the king's garden (now the Chaldees besieged the city round about), and Sedecias fled by the way that leadeth to the plains of the wilderness. And the army of the Chaldees pursued after the king, and overtook him in the plains of Jericho: and all the warriors that were with him were scattered, and left him: So they took the king, and brought him to the king of Babylon to Reblatha, and he gave judgment upon him. And he slew the sons of Sedecias before his face, and he put out his eyes, and bound him with chains, and brought him to Babylon.

Lesson III ~ 4 Kings 25:8–13

In the fifth month, the seventh day of the month, that is, the nineteenth year of the king of Babylon, came Nabuzardan commander of the army, a servant of the king of Babylon, into Jerusalem. And he burnt the house of the Lord, and the king's house, and the houses of Jerusalem, and every house he burnt with fire. And all the army of the Chaldees, which was with the commander of the troops, broke down the walls of Jerusalem round about. And Nabuzardan the commander of the army, carried away the rest of the people that remained in the city, and the fugitives that had gone over to the king of Babylon, and the remnant of the common people. But of the poor of the land he left some dressers of vines and husbandmen. And the pillars of brass that were in the temple of the Lord, and the bases, and the sea of brass which was in the house of the Lord, the Chaldees broke in pieces, and carried all the brass of them to Babylon.

Following the practice of the Church since the 6th Century AD, Lessons I–VI for the following Sundays after Pentecost are taken entirely from those of the Sundays in August, September, October, and November.

The first Sunday of each month is that which occurs closest to the first calendar day of the month, *even if it be before the 1st of that month.*

Lessons VII–IX are yet taken from the proper Sundays after Pentecost, as provided in the next section.

LESSONS VII–IX FOR THE REMAINING SUNDAYS AFTER PENTECOST

Sunday XII after the Octave of Pentecost

Semiduplex

Lesson VII

From the Holy Gospel according to St. Luke (Luke 10:23–37)

At that time, Jesus said unto His disciples: Blessed are the eyes which see the things that you see. For I tell you that many prophets and kings have desired to see those things which you see, and have not seen them. And so on.

Homily by St. Bede the Venerable, Priest

Blessed were the eyes not of Scribes and Pharisees, which saw but the Body of the Lord, but those eyes, eyes blessed indeed, which were able to see those things whereof it is written "Thou hast hid these things from the wise and prudent, and hast revealed them unto babes." Blessed are the eyes of those little ones unto whom it seems good in the eyes of the Son to reveal Himself and the Father also. Abraham rejoiced to see the day of Christ and he saw it, and was glad. Isaias, and Micheas, and many among the Prophets, saw the glory of the Lord, wherefore also are they called Seers, but all of them beheld it and hailed it afar off, seeing as through a glass, darkly.

Lesson VIII

Otherwise were the Apostles, who saw the Lord face to Face, eating with Him, and learning from Him by asking whatsoever they liked. For them there was no need to be taught by Angels, or the shifting fabric of visions. They whom Luke does call Prophets and kings, Matthew names as "Prophets and righteous men." Righteous men are indeed mighty kings, who know how to rule over their own rebellious temptations, instead of falling under them to become their slaves.

Lesson IX

"And, behold, a certain lawyer stood up, and tempted Him, saying Master, what shall I do to inherit eternal life?" This lawyer, who stood up to ask the Lord a tempting question concerning eternal life, took the subject of his asking, as I think, from the words which the Lord had just uttered, when He said "Rejoice, because your names are written in heaven." But his attempt was proof of the truth of that which the Lord immediately added "I thank thee, O Father, Lord of heaven and earth, that Thou hast hid these things from the wise and prudent, and hast revealed them unto babes!"

Sunday XIII after the Octave of Pentecost

Semiduplex

Lesson VII

From the Holy Gospel according to St. Luke (Luke 17:11–19)

It came to pass, as Jesus went to Jerusalem, that He passed through the midst of Samaria and Galilee. And, as He entered into a certain village, there met Him ten men that were lepers. And so on.

Homily by St. Augustine, Bishop

The ten lepers "lifted up their voices and said: Jesus, Master, have mercy on us. And when He saw them, He said unto them: Go, show yourselves unto the Priests. And it came to pass that, as they went, they were cleansed." Question: why did the Lord send them unto the Priests, that, as they went, they might be cleansed? Lepers were the only class among those upon whose bodies He worked mercy, whom we find that He sent unto the Priests. It is written in another place that He said to a leper whom He had cleansed: "Go, and show thyself to the Priest, and offer for thy cleansing according as Moses commanded, for a testimony unto them." We ask then, of what leprosy was a type, whereof they that were ridded were called, not "healed," but "cleansed." It is a disease which does first appear in the skin, but destroys not immediately the strength, nor the use of feeling and the limbs.

Lesson VIII

The lepers, therefore, we may not absurdly suppose such to be figured as have not the knowledge of the true faith, but do show forth diverse-colored teachings of error. They hide not their witlessness, but do use all such wit as they have to make it manifest, and proclaim it in high-sounding phrases. There is no false doctrine that hasn't some truth mixed up with it. A man's discourse then, with some truths in it unequally mingled with falsehoods, and all confounded in one mass, is like to the body of one that is stricken with leprosy, whereon all manner of foul colors do appear in this and that place along with the true color of skin.

Lesson IX

Such men as these are banished out of the walls of the Church, to the end that haply when they stand afar off they may lift up their voices and cry to Christ for pardon, just as those ten men that were lepers, which stood afar off, outside the village, lifted up their voices and said "Jesus, Master, have mercy on us." That they styled Him Master, by which title I know not if any besought the Lord for bodily healing, I think does sufficiently show that leprosy signifies false doctrine, whereof the Good Master does cleanse us.

Sunday XIV after the Octave of Pentecost

Semiduplex

Lesson VII

From the Holy Gospel according to St. Matthew (Matt 6:24–33)

At that time, Jesus said unto His disciples: No man can serve two masters. And so on.

Homily by St. Augustine, Bishop

"No man can serve two masters," and this is further explained "for either he will hate the one, and love the other; or he will sustain the one, and despise the other." These words we ought carefully to weigh, for the Lord shows straightaway who be the two masters of whom we have choice: "You cannot serve God and Mammon." Mammon is a term which the Hebrews are said to use for riches. It is also a Carthaginian word; for the Punic for "gain" is "mammon."

Lesson VIII

He which serves mammon, serves that evil one who has perversely chosen to be lord of these earthly things, and is called by the Lord "the prince of this world." Of these two masters, either a man will hate the one and love the other, that is God or he will hold to the one and despise the other. He which serves mammon holds to a hard and destroying master, for he, led captive by his lust, is sold a slave to the devil and he (the devil) does not love him. Is there any man that loves the devil? And yet there be some that hold to him.

Lesson IX

"Therefore, I say unto you, Take no thought for your life, what you shall eat, or what you shall drink; nor yet for your body, what you shall put on," lest, albeit such idle things are not sought yet the seeking for even needful things should divide the heart and our intention should be corrupted when we do something mercifully: that is, lest, when we would seem to be seeking another's good, it should be profit to ourselves, rather than benefit to him; and therefore we seem not to ourselves to sin, because we would seek not idle things, but the rather things which are needful.

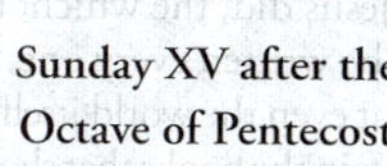

Sunday XV after the Octave of Pentecost

Semiduplex

Lesson VII

From the Holy Gospel according to St. Luke (Luke 7:11–16)

At that time: Jesus went into a city called Naim and His disciples went with Him, and much people. And so on.

Homily by St. Augustine, Bishop

That her son was called again to life was the joy of that widowed mother; that souls of men are every day called to life is the joy of our Mother the Church. He was dead in body, they have been dead in mind. His death was outward, and was outwardly bewailed; theirs inward. Death has been neither mourned for nor seen. But He has sought for them, He Who has seen that they are dead, and He only has seen that they are dead, He Who has been able to make them alive. If He had not come to raise the dead, the Apostle had not said: "Awake, thou that sleepest, and arise from the dead, and Christ shall give thee light."

Lesson VIII

We find written how the Lord raised from the dead three persons visibly, but thousands invisibly. But how many might they have been whom He raised visibly? Who knows? For all the things which He did are not written. John says thus: "There are also many other things which Jesus did, the which, if they should be written every one, I suppose that even the world itself could not contain the books that should be written." There were then, doubtless, many more raised to life, but it is not meaningless that three are recorded. For our Lord Jesus Christ has willed that those things which He did carnally, we should understand also spiritually. He worked not miracles only for the sake of working wonders, but that His works might be at once wonderful to them that beheld, and true to them that understand them.

Lesson IX

Even as one that looks upon a scroll fairly written, and knows not how to read therein, praises the hand of the old scribe when he sees the beauty of the points, but what it says, what those points mean, he knows not, and praises by the eye, without understanding by the mind, and as, on the other hand, he that can not only gaze on it, as can all men, but also can read it, praises the penmanship, and catches the sense likewise, which the unlearned cannot do even so, there were some that saw the miracles which Christ did, and understood not what they meant, nor what they, as it were, hinted to such as did understand them, and these only marveled to see them wrought. And other some there were which saw the works, and marveled, and understood them, and profited by them. And it is as these last that we ought to be in the school of Christ.

Sunday XVI after the Octave of Pentecost

Semiduplex

Lesson VII

From the Holy Gospel according to St. Luke (Luke 14:1–11)

At that time: As Jesus went into the house of one of the chief Pharisees, to eat bread on the Sabbath-day, they watched Him. And, behold, there was a certain man before Him, which had the dropsy. And so on.

Homily by St. Ambrose, Bishop

Now is healed this man sick of the dropsy, in whom too much watery matter had nearly drowned the functions of life, and quenched the fire of understanding. Here a lesson is given in humility, when it is forbidden to the guests at a marriage feast to go and sit down unasked in the highest room, albeit the Lord spoke gently, that the teaching of courtesy might forestall a harsh rebuke, reason prevails by way of persuasion, and the desires are bent to follow the instruction. And upon this, as next-door neighbor, comes courtesy, which is so called by the Lord, when it is shown to the poor and weak, since to show it to them from whom we are to receive anything, is but a movement of self-interest.

Lesson VIII

Lastly, as to a soldier that has served his full time, is apportioned a reward for esteeming lightly of riches so he only can inherit the kingdom of God, whose soul is not given to seek after lower ends, and who purchases not to himself earthly possessions whereas the Lord says: "Sell that thou hast, and follow Me." Neither can he gain it that buys oxen, beasts which Eliseus slew and gave unto the people. Neither can he win it who has married a wife and therefore cannot come, for "he that is unmarried cares for the things that belong to the Lord, how he may please the Lord but he that is married cares for the things that are of the world, how he may please his wife." Not that this is to be taken for blame of marriage, but only that virginity is the more honorable way, since "the unmarried woman" and the widow "cares for the things of the Lord, that she may be holy both in body and in spirit."

Lesson IX

But in all fairness, having thus spoken concerning widows, let us betake ourselves again among the married, and join with them in entertaining the opinion which is held by so many, that there are only three classes of men who are shut out from the great supper named in the gospel, three classes which are the Heathens, the Jews, and Heretics. And therefore it is that the Apostle warns us that we "walk not as other Gentiles walk," in malice and bitterness, and uncleanness, and covetousness, and so have no entry into the kingdom of Christ, since "no unclean person, nor covetous man, who is an idolater, hath any inheritance in the kingdom of Christ and of God."

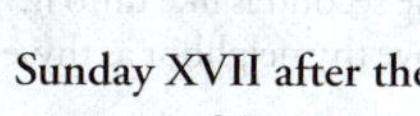

Sunday XVII after the Octave of Pentecost

Semiduplex

Lesson VII

From the Holy Gospel according to St. Matthew (Matt 22:34–46)

At that time, the Pharisees came unto Jesus, and one of them, which was a lawyer, asked Him a question, tempting Him, saying: Master, which is the great commandment in the Law? And so on.

Homily by St. John Chrysostom

When the Pharisees had heard that Christ had put the Sadducees to silence, they gathered themselves together for a fresh attack just when it behooved them to be quiet; they willed to contend and so they put forward one of themselves who professed skill in the law, not wishing to learn, but to lay a snare. This person therefore proposed the question: "Which is the great commandment in the law?" The first and great commandment is: "Thou shalt love the Lord thy God," but they expected that He would make some exception or addition to this in His Own case, since He made Himself God. With this expectation they asked Him the question, but what said Christ? To show that they had adopted this course, because they were loveless, and sick with envy, He answered: "Thou shalt love the Lord thy God with all thy heart, and with all thy soul, and with all thy mind. This is the first and great commandment. And the second is like unto it: Thou shalt love thy neighbor as thyself."

Lesson VIII

Why is this second commandment like unto the first? Because the first is the second's source and sanction. "For every one that doeth evil hateth the light, neither comes to the light." And again: "The fool hath said in his heart There is no God" and there follows: "They are corrupt, and become abominable in their works." And yet again: "The love of money is the root of all evil which while some coveted after, they have erred from the faith." And yet once more: "If ye love Me, keep My commandments," of which commandments the head and root is "Thou shalt love the Lord thy God and thy neighbor as thyself."

Lesson IX

If therefore, to love God is to love our neighbor (also, it is written: "Simon, son of Jonas, lovest thou Me? Feed My sheep"), and if "love is the fulfilling of the law," justly does the Lord say that "on these two commandments hang all the law and the Prophets." And even as when, before this, being interrogated about the Resurrection, He answered them more than they asked, so, now, being interrogated concerning the first and great commandment, He answers them of His own accord, about that second one also, which is little lower than the first, for "the second is like unto it." Herein He would have them understand that it was hatred that stirred them up to question Him. For "Charity," says the Apostle, "envieth not."

Sunday XVIII after the

Octave of Pentecost

Semiduplex

Lesson VII

From the Holy Gospel according to St. Matthew (Matt 9:1–8)

At that time: Jesus entered into a ship, and passed over, and came into His own city. And so on.

Homily by St. Peter Chrysologus

This day's reading has shown us an instance of how Christ, in those things which He did as Man, worked deep works of God, and by things which were seen, wrought things which were not seen. The Evangelist says Jesus "entered into a ship, and passed over, and came into His Own city." Was not This He Who had once parted the waves hither and thither, and made the dry ground appear at the bottom of the sea, so that His people Israel passed dry-shod between masses of water standing still, as through a hollow glen in a mountain? Was not This He Who made the depths of the sea solid under the feet of Peter, so that the watery path offered a firm way for human footsteps?

Lesson VIII

Therefore He then denied Himself a similar service from the sea, but crossed over that narrow lake at the cost of a voyage aboard a ship "He entered into a ship, and passed over." What wonder, brethren? Christ came to take our weakness upon Him, that He might make us partakers of His strength; to seek the things of men, that He might give to men the things of God; to receive insults, that He might bestow honors; to bear weariness, that He might grant rest; for the physician that is himself beset by no frailties knows not how to treat the frailties of others, nor he that is not weak with the weak, how to make the weak strong.

Lesson IX

Therefore, if Christ had abode still in His strength, He had in no way been a fellow of men if in Him Flesh had not run the way of flesh, then had it been idle for Him to have taken Flesh at all. "He entered into a ship, and passed over, and came into His Own city." The Lord, the Maker of the world, and of all things that are therein, having been pleased for our sakes to prison Himself in our flesh, began to have a human home, and to be a citizen of a Jewish city: Himself the Father of all, to have parents and all, that His love might invite, His charity draw, His tenderness bind, His gentleness persuade them whom His Kingship had scared, His awfulness scattered, and His power terrified out of His dominion.

Sunday XIX after the Octave of Pentecost

Semiduplex

Lesson VII

From the Holy Gospel according to St. Matthew (Matt 22:1–14)

At that time, Jesus spoke by parables unto the chief priests and Pharisees, and said: The kingdom of heaven is like unto a certain king, which made a marriage for his son. And so on.

Homily by Pope St. Gregory

I remember that I have often said that, in the Holy Gospel, the Church as she now is, is called the kingdom of heaven, for the kingdom of heaven is indeed the assembly of the righteous. The Lord has said by the mouth of His Prophet: "The heaven is My throne." Solomon says: "The throne of wisdom is the soul of the righteous." And Paul says that Christ is the power of God and the wisdom of God. From these passages we may clearly gather that if wisdom be God, and wisdom's throne be the soul of the righteous, and God's throne be the heaven, then the soul of the righteous is heaven. Hence also the Psalmist says, speaking of holy preachers: "The heavens declare the glory of God."

Lesson VIII

The kingdom of heaven, therefore, is the Church of the righteous, even of them whose hearts seek not for anything upon earth, but who sigh so continually after the things which are above, that God already reigns in them as He does in heaven. Let it then be said, "The kingdom of heaven is like unto a certain king, which made a marriage for his son." You already understand, my loving friends, who is that Royal Father of a Royal Son. It is indeed no other than He to Whom the Psalmist says: "Give the King thy judgments, O God, and thy righteousness unto the King's son." Which made a marriage for his son. God the Father made a marriage for God the Son, when He wedded Him to the manhood in the womb of the Virgin, when He willed that He Who is God before all ages, should in the end of the ages become Man.

Lesson IX

The marriage union is the union of two persons, but God forbid that we should imagine that the One Person of our Redeemer Jesus Christ, Who is both God and Man, is formed by a union of a human person with a Divine Person. We profess concerning Him that He is of and in two natures, but we shrink from the blasphemy of saying that He is compounded of two persons. It will therefore be clearer and safer to say that the marriage which the Father made for His Royal Son was the wedding of Him, through the mystery of the Incarnation, to His mystic Bride the Holy Church. The womb of the Virgin Mother was the marriage chamber in which this union took place. Hence it is that the Psalmist says: "In the sun hath He set His tabernacle, Who is as a bridegroom coming out of his chamber."

Sunday XX after the Octave of Pentecost

Semiduplex

Lesson VII

From the Holy Gospel according to St. John (John 4:46–53)

At that time: There was a certain nobleman, whose son was sick at Capharnaum. And so on.

Homily by Pope St. Gregory

My brethren, the passage from the Holy Gospel, which you have just now heard, stands in need of no explanation. But lest I should seem to pass the same by in idle silence, I will say something thereupon, but rather by way of exhortation than of explanation. Indeed, there seems to me to be but one point which calls for explanation, and that point is this: Why was it that when the nobleman went unto the Lord, and besought Him that He would come down and heal his son, Jesus said unto him: "Except you see signs and wonders, you will not believe"? The very fact that he had come to beseech Christ to heal his son, puts it beyond all doubt that this nobleman believed. If he had not believed Him to be a Saviour, he would not have asked Him to save his son. Why then did Jesus say unto him: "Except you see signs and wonders, you will not believe," since he was one who had not seen, and yet had believed?

Lesson VIII

But bethink you what was his prayer, and then shall you understand clearly wherein his faith was shaky. He "besought Him that He would come down and heal his son." He asked for the bodily presence of Him Who is spiritually always present everywhere. He therefore believed not enough in Christ, for he thought that He could not heal unless He were bodily present. Had his faith been perfect, he would doubtless have known that God is everywhere.

Lesson IX

This was therefore a grievously imperfect faith, in attributing the virtue not to Christ's Majesty, but to His bodily presence. Thus it was that his faith was still unsound, even while he was asking for his son's health. For, though he believed concerning Him unto Whom he came that He was mighty to save, yet he thought also that at that moment He was absent from his dying child. But the Lord, being asked to go, showed that, wherever He is called on, He is there, and being He Who, by a simple act of will, brought all things into being, gave health by a simple command.

Sunday XXI after the Octave of Pentecost

Semiduplex

Lesson VII

From the Holy Gospel according to St. Matthew (Matt 18:23–35)

At that time, Jesus spoke unto His disciples this parable: The kingdom of heaven is likened unto a certain king, which would take account of his servants. And so on.

Homily by St. Jerome, Priest

It is a way much in use with the Syrians, and especially with the inhabitants of Palestine, to illustrate their discourse with parables, that what their hearers may not be able to catch so easily when spoken plainly, they may lay hold on by way of comparisons and examples. Thus it was that the Lord, by an allegory about a Royal master and a servant who owed him ten thousand talents, and who obtained by entreaty forgiveness of the debt, taught Peter how it was his duty to forgive his fellow-servants their comparatively trifling offenses. For if that Royal master so readily forgave his servant his debt of ten thousand talents, should not his servants much more forgive lesser debts unto their fellows?

Lesson VIII

Let put this more clearly, let us take a case. If one of us were to commit adultery, or murder, or sacrilege, our sin, great like a debt of ten thousand talents, it would be forgiven us in answer to prayer, if we also from our heart forgive our brethren their trespasses against us. But if we refuse to forgive a slight, and keep up unceasing enmity because of an unkind word, how just does it appear that we should be cast into prison, and entail on ourselves, by the example of our own deeds, that our great debt should not be forgiven unto us?

Lesson IX

"So likewise shall My heavenly Father do also unto you, if you from your hearts forgive not every one his brother their trespasses." God's awful purpose can be turned and changed but if we will not forgive unto our brethren small things, God will not forgive us great things. And if we forgive them, it must be from our hearts. Any one can say: "I have nothing against such-a-one, he knows what he has done, and God will judge him for it; I do not care what he does, I have forgiven him." But the Lord makes His sentence clear, and destroys such a mockery of peace as this, where He says: "So likewise shall My heavenly Father do also unto you, if you from your hearts forgive not every one his brother their trespasses."

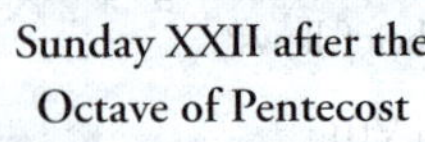

Sunday XXII after the Octave of Pentecost

Semiduplex

Lesson VII

From the Holy Gospel according to St. Matthew (Matt 22:15–21)

At that time: The Pharisees went and took counsel how they might entangle Jesus in His talk. And so on.

Homily by St. Hilary, Bishop

The Pharisees had oftentimes been put to confusion, and were not able to find any ground to accuse Him out of anything that He had hitherto said or done. His words and works are, of necessity, faultless, but still, from spite, they set themselves to seek in every direction for some cause to accuse Him. He was calling all to turn away from the corruptions of the world, and the superstitious practices of devotion invented by men, and to fix their hopes upon the kingdom of heaven. They therefore arranged a question calculated to entrap Him into an offense against civil government, namely: "Is it lawful to give tribute unto Caesar or not?"

Lesson VIII

But Jesus perceived their wickedness, for in truth there is nothing hidden in the heart of man but what God sees, "and said Why tempt ye Me, you hypocrites? Show Me the tribute-money. And they brought unto Him a penny. And He saith unto them: Whose is this image and superscription? They say unto Him Caesar's. Then saith He unto them: Render therefore unto Caesar the things which are Caesar's, and unto God the things that are God's." How wonderful is this answer? How perfect the fulfillment of the Divine Law herein prescribed! So beautifully does He here strike the balance between caring not for the things of the world, on the one hand, and the offense of injuring Caesar, on the other, that He proves the perfect freedom of minds, however devoted to God, to discharge all human cares and duties, by commanding them to render unto Caesar the things which are Caesar's.

Lesson IX

If we have nothing which is Caesar's, then we have nothing which we are bound to render unto him. But if we are concerned with the things which are his, if we are entrusted by him with the use of delegated power, if we are subject to him as paid servants to take care of property which is not our own, there can be no dispute but that it is our duty to render unto Caesar the things which are Caesar's. But unto God all of us are bound always to render the things that are God's, that is to say, our body, soul, and will. These are things which we hold from Him, and whereof He is the Author and Maker. It is therefore simply just that they, who acknowledge that they owe to Him their being and creation, should render to Him all that they are.

Sunday XXIII after the Octave of Pentecost

Semiduplex

Lesson VII

From the Holy Gospel according to St. Matthew (Matt 9:18–26)

At that time: While Jesus spoke these things unto the multitudes, behold, there came a certain ruler, and worshipped Him, saying Lord, my daughter is even now dead. And so on.

Homily by St. Jerome, Priest

The eighth miracle took place upon the occasion when a certain ruler, desiring not to be kept out of the mystery of the true circumcision, besought Christ to recall his daughter to life. But a woman, which was diseased with an issue of blood, thrust herself in, and her cure occupies the eighth place, so that the resurrection of the ruler's daughter is postponed and made the ninth in enumeration even as it is written in the Psalms: "Ethiopia shall soon stretch forth her hands unto God." And again: "Blindness in part is happened to Israel, until the fullness of the Gentiles is come in and so all Israel shall be saved."

Lesson VIII

"And, behold, a woman, which was diseased with an issue of blood for twelve years, came behind Him and touched the hem of His garment." In the Gospel according to Luke it is written that the ruler's daughter was about twelve years of age. Note therefore that this woman, who typifies the Gentiles, had been diseased for the same time that the Jewish nation, typified by the ruler's daughter, had been living in faith. We see not clearly the hideousness of evil, until we compare it with good.

Lesson IX

This woman with the issue of blood came not to the Lord in a house or in a city, for such as she were by the Law banished out of cities, but in the way, as He walked so that the Lord healed one, even while He was on the road to heal another. Whence also the Apostles said: "It was necessary that the word of God should first have been spoken to you but, seeing you put it from you, and judge yourselves unworthy of everlasting life, lo, we turn to the Gentiles."

Sunday XXIV and the Final of those after the Octave of Pentecost

Semiduplex

Lesson VII

From the Holy Gospel according to St. Matthew (Matt 24:15–35)

At that time, Jesus said unto his disciples: When you shall see the abomination of desolation, spoken of by Daniel the Prophet, stand in the Holy Place (whoso reads, let him understand). And so on.

Homily by St. Jerome, Priest

This injunction to whoso reads, to understand, shows that there is here something mysterious. In Daniel we read as follows: "And in the midst of the week the sacrifice and the oblations shall be taken away and in the temple there shall be the abomination of desolation, even until the consummation of the time and a consummation shall be given to the desolation." It is of this same thing that the Apostle speaks, when he says that a man of iniquity, even an adversary, shall be exalted against whatsoever is called God, or is worshipped so that he shall even dare to stand in the temple of God, and to show himself as God whose coming shall, according to the working of Satan, destroy and banish away from God all who shall receive him.

Lesson VIII

This prophecy may be understood either (first) simply of Antichrist, (secondly) of the statue of Caesar, which Pilate set up in the Temple, or (thirdly) of the statue of Hadrian on horse-back, which has stood, even until our own day, upon the site of the Holy of Holies. In the Scriptures of the Old Testament "abomination" is a word very often used for an idol, and the farther title "of desolation" is added to identify an idol erected upon the site of the desolate and ruined temple.

Lesson IX

But we may also understand by the abomination of desolation, any bad doctrine and when we see such a thing get a standing in the Holy Place, that is, in the Church, and showing itself that it is God, that is, pretending that it is His revealed truth, then will be the time when it will be our duty to flee from Judea into the mountains, that is to say, to leave the letter, which passes away, and all guise of Jewish superstition, and to get us unto the everlasting hills, from whence God does wondrously cause His light to shine forth. Then will it be our duty to find ourselves under a roof and in a house, wherethrough the fiery darts of the wicked one can never pierce to smite us, and not to come down to take anything out of the house of our old conversation, or to have regard unto those things which are behind but rather to sow in the field of the spiritual Scriptures, that we may reap thereof a bountiful harvest neither to have two coats, that thing forbidden to Apostles.

OCCURRING SCRIPTURES & PATRISTIC COMMENTARIES FOR THE REMAINING SUNDAYS AND WEEKDAYS AFTER PENTECOST

SUNDAYS OF AUGUST

Sunday I of August

Lesson I ~ Prov 1:1–6

Begun are the Proverbs of Solomon

The parables of Solomon, the son of David, king of Israel. To know wisdom, and instruction, To understand the words of prudence: and to receive the instruction of doctrine, justice, and judgment, and equity: To give subtilty to little ones, to the young man knowledge and understanding. A wise man shall hear and shall be wiser: and he that understandeth, shall possess governments. He shall understand a parable, and the interpretation, the words of the wise, and their mysterious sayings.

Lesson II ~ Prov 1:7–14

The fear of the Lord is the beginning of wisdom. Fools despise wisdom and instruction. My son, hear the instruction of thy father, and forsake not the law of thy mother: That grace may be added to thy head, and a chain of gold to thy neck. My son, if sinners shall entice thee, consent not to them. If they shall say: Come with us, let us lie in wait for blood, let us hide snares for the innocent without cause: Let us swallow him up alive like hell, and whole as one that goeth down into the pit. We shall find all precious substance, we shall fill our houses with spoils. Cast in thy lot with us, let us all have one purse.

Lesson III ~ Prov 1:15–19

My son, walk not thou with them, restrain thy foot from their paths. For their feet run to evil, and make haste to shed blood. But a net is spread in vain before the eyes of them that have wings. And they themselves lie in wait for their own blood, and practise deceits against their own souls. So the wage of every covetous man destroy the souls of the possessors.

Lesson IV

From the Treatise of
St. Ambrose, Bishop, upon the
118th Psalm.

The Prophet says that "the fear of the Lord is the beginning of wisdom." And what is the first act of wisdom but to renounce the world, since to love the things of the world is folly? So indeed says the Apostle "The wisdom of this world is foolishness with God." But the very fear of the Lord itself is useless, nay, harmful, if it be not according to knowledge. The Jews have a truly fervent zeal for God, but since they have not knowledge, their very zeal and fear do cause them to do things contrary to God's will. That they circumcise their children, that they keep holy the Sabbath-Day, shows how they fear the Lord, but knowing not the spiritual meaning of the Law, they circumcise the body and not the heart.

Lesson V

But why should I speak of Jews? There are those among ourselves who have the fear of God, but not according to knowledge, and set up hard ordinances which the weakness of man is not able to bear. They fear God in this, that they seem to themselves to be looking to discipline, and to be enforcing the practice of godliness, but they lack knowledge in that they feel not for the weakness of nature, nor consider whether a thing can or cannot be done. Let not then the fear of God be unreasonable. True wisdom begins with the fear of God, neither is it spiritual wisdom without the fear of God, but neither ought the fear of God to be without wisdom.

Lesson VI

Holy fear is the foundation of all good instruction. Just as a statue is set up upon a pedestal, and thereby receives both beauty and strength, even so does it become the word of God to be set forth based upon a holy fear, and it is in the heart of him that fears that it gets the firmest root, even a home wherefrom it drops not, neither do the fowls of the air come and carry it away, as from the heart of him that is careless and deceiving.

Lessons VII, VIII, & IX from the *Sermons for After Pentecost* Section

Monday I of August

Lesson I - Prov 3:1–6

From the Proverbs of Solomon

My son, forget not my law, and let thy heart keep my commandments. For they shall add to thee length of days, and years of life and peace. Let not mercy and truth leave thee, put them about thy neck, and write them in the tables of thy heart: And thou shalt find grace and good understanding before God and men. Have confidence in the Lord with all thy heart, and lean not upon thy own prudence. In all thy ways think on him, and he will direct thy steps.

Lesson II - Prov 3:7–10

Be not wise in thy own conceit: fear God, and depart from evil: For it shall be health to thy navel, and moistening to thy bones. Honour the Lord with thy substance, and give him of the first of all thy fruits: And thy barns shall be filled with abundance, and thy presses shall run over with wine.

Lesson III - Prov 3:11–15

My son, reject not the correction of the Lord: and do not faint when thou art chastised by him: For whom the Lord loveth, he chastiseth: and as a father in the son he pleaseth himself. Blessed is the man that findeth wisdom and is rich in prudence: The purchasing thereof is better than the merchandise of silver, and her fruit than the chiefest and purest gold: She is more precious than all riches: and all the things that are desired, are not to be compared with her.

Tuesday I of August

Lesson I - Prov 5:1–6

From the Proverbs of Solomon

My son, attend to my wisdom, and incline thy ear to my prudence.

That thou mayst keep thoughts, and thy lips may preserve instruction. Mind not the deceit of a woman. For the lips of a harlot are like a honeycomb dropping, and her throat is smoother than oil. But her end is bitter as wormwood, and sharp as a two-edged sword. Her feet go down into death, and her steps go in as far as hell. They walk not by the path of life, her steps are wandering, and unaccountable.

Lesson II ~ Prov 5:7–13

Now therefore, my son, hear me, and depart not from the words of my mouth. Remove thy way far from her, and come not nigh the doors of her house. Give not thy honour to strangers, and thy years to the cruel. Lest strangers be filled with thy strength, and thy labours be in another man's house, And thou mourn it the last, when thou shalt have spent thy flesh and thy body, and say: Why have I hated instruction, and my heart consented not to reproof, And have not heard the voice of them that taught me, and have not inclined my ear to masters?

Lesson III ~ Prov 5:20–23

Why art thou seduced, my son, by a strange woman, and art cherished in the bosom of another? The Lord beholdeth the ways of man, and considereth all his steps. His own iniquities catch the wicked, and he is fast bound with the ropes of his own sins. He shall die, because he hath not received instruction, and in the multitude of his folly he shall be deceived.

Wednesday I of August

Lesson I ~ Prov 8:1–6

From the Proverbs of Solomon

Doth not wisdom cry aloud, and prudence put forth her voice? Standing in the top of the highest places by the way, in the midst of the paths. Beside the gates of the city, in the very doors she speaketh, saying: O ye men, to you I call, and my voice is to the sons of men. O little ones, understand subtilty, and ye unwise, take notice. Hear, for I will speak of great things: and my lips shall be opened to preach right things.

Lesson II ~ Prov 8:7–11

My mouth shall meditate truth, and my lips shall hate wickedness. All my words are just, there is nothing wicked nor perverse in them. They are right to them that understand, and just to them that find knowledge. Receive my instruction, and not money: choose knowledge rather than gold. For wisdom is better than all the most precious things: and whatsoever may be desired cannot be compared to it.

Lesson III ~ Prov 8:12–17

I wisdom dwell in counsel, and am present in learned thoughts. The fear of the Lord hateth evil: I hate arrogance, and pride, and every wicked way, and a mouth with a double tongue. Counsel and equity is mine, prudence is mine, strength is mine. By me kings reign, and lawgivers decree just things, By me princes rule, and the mighty decree justice. I love them that love me: and they that in the morning early watch for me, shall find me.

Thursday I of August

Lesson I ~ Prov 10:1–5

From the Proverbs of Solomon

A wise son maketh the father glad: but a foolish son is the sorrow of his mother. Treasures of wickedness shall profit nothing: but justice shall deliver from death. The Lord will not afflict the soul of the just with famine, and he will disappoint the deceitful practices of the wicked. The slothful hand hath wrought poverty: but the hand of the industrious getteth riches. He that trusteth to lies feedeth the winds: and the same runneth after birds that fly away. He that gathered in the harvest is a wise son: but he that snorteth in the summer, is the son of confusion.

Lesson II ~ Prov 10:6–10

The blessing of the Lord is upon the head of the just: but iniquity covereth the mouth of the wicked. The memory of the just is with praises: and the name of the wicked shall rot. The wise of heart receiveth precepts: a fool is beaten with lips. He that walketh sincerely, walketh confidently: but he that perverteth his ways, shall be manifest. He that winketh with the eye shall cause sorrow: and the foolish in lips shall be beaten.

Lesson III ~ Prov 10:11–16

The mouth of the just is a vein of life: and the mouth of the wicked covereth iniquity. Hatred stirreth up strifes: and charity covereth all sins. In the lips of the wise is wisdom found: and a rod on the back of him that wanteth sense. Wise men lay up knowledge: but the mouth of the fool is next to confusion. The substance of a rich man is the city of his strength: the fear of the poor is their poverty. The work of the just is unto life: but the fruit of the wicked, unto sin.

Friday I of August

Lesson I ~ Prov 14:1–5

From the Proverbs of Solomon

A wise woman buildeth her house: but the foolish will pull down with her hands that also which is built. He that walketh in the right way, and feareth God, is despised by him that goeth by an infamous way. In the mouth of a fool is the rod of pride: but the lips of the wise preserve them. Where there are no oxen, the crib is empty: but where there is much corn, there the strength of the ox is manifest. A faithful witness will not lie: but a deceitful witness uttereth a lie.

Lesson II ~ Prov 14:6–11

A scorner seeketh wisdom, and findeth it not: the learning of the wise is easy. Go against a foolish man, and he knoweth not the lips of prudence. The wisdom of a. discreet man is to understand his way: and the imprudence of fools erreth. A fool will laugh at sin, but among the just grace shall abide. The heart that knoweth the bitterness of his own soul, in his joy the stranger shall not intermeddle. The house of the wicked shall be destroyed: but the tabernacles of the just shall flourish.

Lesson III ~ Prov 14:12–16

There is a way which seemeth just to a man: but the ends thereof lead to death. Laughter shall be mingled with sorrow, and mourning taketh hold of the end of joy. A fool shall be filled with his own ways, and the good man shall be above him. The innocent believeth every word: the discreet man considereth his steps. No good shall come to the deceitful son: but the wise servant shall prosper in his dealings, and his way shall be made straight. A wise man feareth and declineth from evil: the fool leapeth over and is confident.

Saturday I of August

Lesson I ~ Prov 16:1–5

From the Proverbs of Solomon

It is the part of man to prepare the soul: and of the Lord to govern the tongue. All the ways of a man are open to his eyes: the Lord is the weigher of spirits. Lay open thy works to the Lord: and thy thoughts shall be directed. The Lord hath made all things for himself: the wicked also for the evil day. Every proud man is an abomination to the Lord: though hand should be joined to hand, he is not innocent.

Lesson II ~ Prov 16:5–9

The beginning of a good way is to do justice; and this is more acceptable with God, than to offer sacrifices. By mercy and truth iniquity is redeemed: and by the fear of the Lord men depart from evil. When the ways of man shall please the Lord, he will convert even his enemies to peace. Better is a little with justice, than great revenues with iniquity. The heart of man disposeth his way: but the Lord must direct his steps.

Lesson III ~ Prov 16:10–15

Divination is in the lips of the king, his mouth shall not err in judgment. Weight and balance are judgments of the Lord: and his work all the weights of the bag. They that act wickedly are abominable to the king: for the throne is established by justice. Just lips are the delight of kings: he that speaketh right things shall be loved. The wrath of a king is as messengers of death: and the wise man will pacify it. In the cheerfulness of the king's countenance is life: and his clemency is like the latter rain.

Sunday II of August

Lesson I ~ Eccl 1:1–7

Beginning of the book of Ecclesiastes

The words of Ecclesiastes, the son of David, king of Jerusalem. Vanity of vanities, said Ecclesiastes vanity of vanities, and all is vanity. What hath a man more of all his labour, that he taketh under the sun? One generation passeth away, and another generation comes: but the earth standeth for ever. The sun riseth, and goeth down, and returneth to his place: and there rising again, Maketh his round by the south, and turneth again to the north: the spirit goeth forward surveying all places round about, and returneth to his circuits. All the rivers run into the sea, yet the sea doth not overflow: unto the place from whence the rivers come, they return, to flow again.

Lesson II ~ Eccl 1:8–11

All things are hard: man cannot explain them by word. The eye is not filled with seeing, neither is the ear filled with hearing. What is it that hath been? the same thing that shall be. What is it that hath been done? the same that shall be done. Nothing under the sun is new, neither is any man able to say: Behold this is new: for it hath already gone before in the ages that were before us. There is no remembrance of former things: nor indeed of those things which hereafter are to come, shall there be any remembrance with them that shall be in the latter end.

Lesson III ~ Eccl 1:12–17

I Ecclesiastes was king over Israel in Jerusalem, And I proposed in my mind to seek and search out wisely concerning all things that are done under the sun. This painful occupation hath God given to the children of men, to be exercised therein. I have seen all things that are done under the sun, and behold all is vanity, and vexation of spirit. The perverse are hard to be corrected, and the number of fools is infinite. I have spoken in my heart, saying: Behold I am become great, and have gone beyond all in wisdom, that were before me in Jerusalem: and my mind hath contemplated many things wisely, and I have learned. And I have given my heart to know prudence, and learning, and errors, and folly: and I have perceived that in these also there was labour, and vexation of spirit.

Lesson IV

Sermon by St. John Chrysostom

While Solomon was given up to the lust of the world, he deemed the same a great and noble pursuit, and expended thereon great labour and care. He built magnificent palaces, he heaped up gold in plenty, he gathered together choirs of singers, and all sorts of servants to minister to the luxury of his table and of his fare. He sought enjoyment for his heart from the charm of gardens and of fair bodies. In short, he gave himself up to the study of all kinds of pleasure and recreation.

Lesson V

But when he came to himself again, and was once more able, as it were, out of that dark pit, to look upon the light of true wisdom, he uttered that saying so high, so worthy of heaven, "Vanity of vanities; all is vanity." And you also, if ever you will shake yourselves clear of your debasing habit, will utter this cry, and a higher cry than this, as you turn from your untimely indulgences.

Lesson VI

The ages that had rolled before the time of Solomon had not left to his own so precious an inheritance of wisdom as those which have preceded us have left to us; the old law did not forbid these indulgences, nor pronounce it folly to enjoy other idle luxuries and yet, even with matters so, we can see how low, how worthless, such things be. We, verily, are called to a higher life, we ascend to a nobler peak, and brace ourselves in a manlier school: and what other are we bidden to strive for than the life like that of the spiritual and bodiless powers?

Lessons VII, VIII, & IX from the *Sermons for After Pentecost* Section

Monday II of August

Lesson I ~ Eccl 2:1–4

From the book of Ecclesiastes

I said in my heart: I will go, and abound with delights, and enjoy good things. And I saw that this also was vanity. Laughter I counted error: and to mirth I said: Why art thou vainly deceived? I thought in my heart, to withdraw my flesh from wine, that I might turn my mind to wisdom, and might avoid folly, till I might see what was profitable for the children of men: and what they ought to do under the sun, all the days of their life. I made me great works, I built me houses, and planted vineyards.

Lesson II ~ Eccl 2:7–9

I got me menservants, and maidservants, and had a great family: and herds of oxen, and great flocks of sheep, above all that were before me in Jerusalem: I heaped together for myself silver and gold, and the wealth of kings, and provinces: I made me singing men, and singing women, and the delights of the sons of men, cups and vessels to serve to pour out wine: And I surpassed in riches all that were before me in Jerusalem: my wisdom also remained with me.

Lesson III ~ Eccl 2:10–11

And whatsoever my eyes desired, I refused them not: and I withheld not my heart from enjoying every pleasure, and delighting itself in the things which I had prepared: and esteemed this my portion, to make use of my own labour. And when I turned myself to all the works which my hands had wrought, and to the labours wherein I had laboured in vain, I saw in all things vanity, and vexation of mind, and that nothing was lasting under the sun.

Tuesday II of August

Lesson I ~ Eccl 3:1–8

From the book of Ecclesiastes

All things have their season, and in their times all things pass under heaven. A time to be born and a time to die. A time to plant, and a time to pluck up that which is planted. A time to kill, and a time to heal. A time to destroy, and a time to build. A time to weep, and a time to laugh. A time to mourn, and a time to dance. A time to scatter stones, and a time to gather. A time to embrace, and a time to be far from embraces. A time to get, and a time to lose. A time to keep, and a time to cast away. A time to rend, and a time to sew. A time to keep silence, and a time to speak. A time of love, and a time of hatred. A time of war, and a time of peace.

Lesson II ~ Eccl 3:9–13

What hath man more of his labour? I have seen the trouble, which God hath given the sons of men to be exercised in it. He hath made all things good in their time, and hath delivered the world to their consideration, so that man cannot find out the work which God hath made from the beginning to the end. And I have known that there was no better thing than to rejoice, and to do well in this life. For every man that eateth and drinketh, and seeth good of his labour, this is the gift of God.

Lesson III ~ Eccl 3:14–17

I have learned that all the works which God hath made, continue for ever: we cannot add any thing, nor take away from those things which God hath made that he may be feared. That which hath been made, the same continueth: the things that shall be, have already been: and God restoreth that which is past. I saw under the sun in the place of judgment wickedness, and in the place of justice iniquity. And I said in my heart: God shall judge both the just and the wicked, and then shall be the time of every thing.

Wednesday II of August

Lesson I ~ Eccl 4:1–4

From the book of Ecclesiastes

I turned myself to other things, and I saw the oppressions that are done under the sun, and the tears of the innocent, and they had no comforter; and they were not able to resist their violence, being destitute of help from any. And I praised the dead rather than the living: And I judged him happier than them both, that is not yet born, nor hath seen the evils that are done under the sun. Again I considered all the labours of men, and I remarked that their industries are exposed to the envy of their neighhour: so in this also there is vanity, and fruitless care.

Lesson II ~ Eccl 4:5–8

The fool foldeth his hands together, and eateth his own flesh, saying: Better is a handful with rest, than both hands full with labour, and vexation of mind. Considering I found also another vanity under the sun: There is but one, and he hath not a second, no child, no brother, and yet he ceaseth not to labour, neither are his eyes satisfied with riches, neither doth he reflect, saying: For whom do I labour, and defraud my soul of good things? in this also is vanity, and a grievous vexation.

Lesson III ~ Eccl 4:9–13

It is better therefore that two should be together, than one: for they have the advantage of their society: If one fall he shall be supported by the other: woe to him that is alone, for when he falleth, he hath none to lift him up. And if two lie together, they shall warm one another: how shall one alone be warmed? And if a man prevail against one, two shall withstand him: a threefold cord is not easily broken. Better is a child that is poor and wise, than a king that is old and foolish, who knoweth not to foresee for hereafter.

Thursday II of August

Lesson I ~ Eccl 5:1–4

From the book of Ecclesiastes

Speak not any thing rashly, and let not thy heart be hasty to utter a word before God. For God is in heaven, and thou upon earth: therefore let thy words be few. Dreams follow many cares: and in many words shall be found folly. If thou hast vowed any thing to God, defer not to pay it: for an unfaithful and foolish promise displeaseth him: but whatsoever thou hast vowed, pay it. And it is much better not to vow, than after a vow not to perform the things promised.

Lesson II ~ Eccl 5:5–8

Give not thy mouth to cause thy flesh to sin: and say not before the angel: There is no providence: lest God be angry at thy words, and destroy all the works of thy hands. Where there are many dreams, there are many vanities, and words without number: but do thou fear God. If thou shalt see the oppressions of the poor, and violent judgments, and justice perverted in the province, wonder not at this matter: for he that is high hath another higher, and there are others still higher than these: Moreover there is the king that reigneth over all the land subject to him.

Lesson III ~ Eccl 5:9–13

A covetous man shall not be satisfied with money: and he that loveth riches shall reap no fruit from them: so this also is vanity. Where there are great riches, there are also many to eat them. And what doth it profit the owner, but that he seeth the riches with his eyes? Sleep is sweet to a labouring man, whether he eat little or much: but the fulness of the rich will not suffer him to sleep. There is also another grievous evil, which I have seen under the sun: riches kept to the hurt of the owner. For they are lost with very great affliction: he hath begotten a son, who shall be in extremity of want.

Friday II of August

Lesson I ~ Eccl 6:1–2

From the book of Ecclesiastes

There is also another evil, which I have seen under the sun, and that frequent among men: A man to whom God hath given riches, and substance, and honour, and his soul wanteth nothing of all that he desireth: yet God doth not give him power to eat thereof, but a stranger shall eat it up. This is vanity and a great misery.

Lesson II ~ Eccl 6:3–6

If a man beget a hundred children, and live many years, and attain to a great age, and his soul make no use of the goods of his substance, and he be without burial: of this man I pronounce, that the untimely born is better than he. For he came in vain, and goeth to darkness, and his name shall be wholly forgotten. He hath not seen the sun, nor known the distance of good and evil: Although he lived two thousand years, and hath not enjoyed good things.

Lesson III ~ Eccl 6:6–9

Do not all make haste to one place? All the labour of man is for his mouth, but his soul shall not be filled. What hath the wise man more than the fool? and what the poor man, but to go thither, where there is life? Better it is to see what thou mayst desire, than to desire that which thou canst not know. But this also is vanity, and presumption of spirit.

Saturday II of August

Lesson I ~ Eccl 7:1–3

From the book of Ecclesiastes

What needeth a man to seek things that are above him, whereas he knoweth not what is profitable for him in his life, in all the days of his pilgrimage, and the time that passeth like a shadow? Or who can tell him what shall be after him under the sun? A good name is better than precious ointments: and the day of death than the day of one's birth. It is better to go to the house of mourning, than to the house of feasting: for in that we are put in mind of the end of all, and the living thinketh what is to come.

Lesson II ~ Eccl 7:4–9

Anger is better than laughter: because by the sadness of the countenance the mind of the offender is corrected. The heart of the wise is where there is mourning, and the heart of fools where there is mirth. It is better to be rebuked by a wise man, than to be deceived by the flattery of fools. For as the crackling of thorns burning under a pot, so is the laughter of a fool: now this also is vanity. Oppression troubleth the wise, and shall destroy the strength of his heart. Better is the end of a speech than the beginning. Better is the patient man than the presumptuous.

Lesson III ~ Eccl 7:11–14

Say not: What thinkest thou is the cause that former times were better than they are now? for this manner of question is foolish. Wisdom with riches is more profitable, and bringeth more advantage to them that see the sun. For as wisdom is a defence, so money is a defence: but learning and wisdom excel in this, that they give life to him that possesseth them. Consider the works of God, that no man can correct whom he hath despised.

Sunday III of August

Lesson I ~ Wis 1:1–4

Beginning of the book of Wisdom

Love justice, you that are the judges of the earth. Think of the Lord in goodness, and seek him in simplicity of heart. For he is found by them that tempt him not: and he showeth himself to them that have faith in him. For perverse thoughts separate from God: and his power, when it is tried, reproveth the unwise: For wisdom will not enter into a malicious soul, nor dwell in a body subject to sins.

Lesson II - Wis 1:5–8

For the Holy Spirit of discipline will flee from the deceitful, and will withdraw himself from thoughts that are without understanding, and he shall not abide when iniquity comes in. For the spirit of wisdom is benevolent, and will not acquit the evil speaker from his lips: for God is witness of his reins, and he is a true searcher of his heart, and a hearer of his tongue. For the spirit of the Lord hath filled the whole world: and that, which containeth all things, hath knowledge of the voice. Therefore he that speaketh unjust things cannot be hid, neither shall the chastising judgment pass him by.

Lesson III - Wis 1:9–11

For inquisition shall be made into the thoughts of the ungodly: and the hearing of his words shall come to God, to the chastising of his iniquities. For the ear of jealousy heareth all things, and the tumult of murmuring shall not be hid. Keep yourselves therefore from murmuring, which profiteth nothing, and refrain your tongue from detraction, for an obscure speech shall not go for nought: and the mouth that belieth, killeth the soul.

Lesson IV

From the Book of St. Ambrose, Bishop, "On Offices."

Great is the glory of justice. She lives for others rather than for herself. By her our commonwealth and fellowship are helped. She holds such a preeminence that all things are subject unto her judgment. She helps others. She gives wealth. She refuses not to labour. She takes upon herself the dangers of others. Who would not desire to hold this castle of power and courage, if the covetousness of our first parents had not weakened and distorted the strength of our nerve? But so it is, that, while we are fain to increase wealth, to put by money, to add lands to our possessions, or to make show of our abundance, we put off the image of justice, and lose charity toward our brethren.

Lesson V

Yet how much justice there is may be known from this, that there is exempt therefrom no place, person, or time, nay, she has to do even as regards enemies: for if one be agreed with his enemy of a certain place or day for battle, it should be deemed unjust to fall on him beforehand at another place or time. For it is a very different thing, whether one get the better of another in a hard fight, or by skill, or by accident. If, therefore, in war justice has place, how much more is she to be observed in time of peace?

Lesson VI

Honor is the foundation of justice. The thoughts in the hearts of just men are honorable thoughts and when the just man accuses himself, it is honor that brings him to that just deed. Then is his justice made manifest by his honorable avowal. The Lord says by Isaias "Behold, I lay in Sion a foundation-stone"; that is to say, He gives Christ unto the Church to be her foundation. Christ is the true honor for all men, and the Church is as it were a figure of justice, being a commonwealth wherein all have rights, and which prays as one, and works as one, and suffers as one. Whosoever denies himself, the same is just, and worthy of Christ. Therefore also Paul says "Other foundation can no man lay than that is laid, which is Jesus Christ," and upon that foundation is it, that every building of justice must be raised. For the spirit of Christ is the true spirit of honor which is the foundation whereon justice rests.

Lessons VII, VIII, & IX from the *Sermons for After Pentecost* Section

Monday III of August

Lesson I ~ Wis 3:1–6

From the book of Wisdom

But the souls of the just are in the hand of God, and the torment of death shall not touch them. In the sight of the unwise they seemed to die: and their departure was taken for misery: And their going away from us, for utter destruction: but they are in peace. And though in the sight of men they suffered torments, their hope is full of immortality. Afflicted in few things, in many they shall be well rewarded: because God hath tried them, and found them worthy of himself. As gold in the furnace he hath proved them, and as a victim of a holocaust he hath received them, and in time there shall be respect had to them.

Lesson II ~ Wis 3:7–11

The just shall shine, and shall run to and fro like sparks among the reeds. They shall judge nations, and rule over people, and their Lord shall reign for ever. They that trust in him, shall understand the truth: and they that are faithful in love shall rest in him: for grace and peace is to his elect. But the wicked shall be punished according to their own devices: who have neglected the just, and have revolted from the Lord. For he that rejecteth wisdom, and discipline, is unhappy: and their hope is vain, and their labours without fruit, and their works unprofitable.

Lesson III ~ Wis 5:16–21

But the just shall live for evermore: and their reward is with the Lord, and the care of them with the most High. Therefore shall they receive a kingdom of glory, and a crown of beauty at the hand of the Lord: for with his right hand he will cover them, and with his holy arm he will defend them. And his zeal will take armour, and he will arm the creature for the revenge of his enemies. He will put on justice as a breastplate, and will take true judgment instead of a helmet. He will take equity for an invincible shield: And he will sharpen his severe wrath for a spear, and the whole world shall fight with him against the unwise.

Tuesday III of August

Lesson I ~ Wis 6:1–5

From the book of Wisdom

Wisdom is better than strength, and a wise man is better than a strong man. Hear therefore, ye kings, and understand: learn, ye that are judges of the ends of the earth. Give ear, you that rule the people, and that please yourselves in multitudes of nations:

For power is given you by the Lord, and strength by the most High, who will examine your works, and search out your thoughts: Because being ministers of his kingdom, you have not judged rightly, nor kept the law of justice, nor walked according to the will of God.

Lesson II - Wis 6:6–9

Horribly and speedily will he appear to you: for a most severe judgment shall be for them that bear rule. For to him that is little, mercy is granted: but the mighty shall be mightily tormented. For God will not except any man's person, neither will he stand in awe of any man's greatness: for he made the little and the great, and he hath equally care of all. But a greater punishment is ready for the more mighty.

Lesson III - Wis 6:10–13

To you, therefore, O kings, are these my words, that you may learn wisdom, and not fall from it. For they that have kept just things justly, shall be justified: and they that have learned these things, shall find what to answer. Covet ye therefore my words, and love them, and you shall have instruction. Wisdom is glorious, and never fadeth away, and is easily seen by them that love her, and is found by them that seek her.

Wednesday III of August

Lesson I - Wis 7:1–6

From the book of Wisdom

I myself also am a mortal man, like all others, and of the race of him, that was first made of the earth, and in the womb of my mother I was fashioned to be flesh. In the time of ten months I was compacted in blood, of the seed of man, and the pleasure of sleep concurring. And being born I drew in the common air, and fell upon the earth, that is made alike, and the first voice which I uttered was crying, as all others do. I was nursed in swaddling clothes, and with great cares. For none of the kings had any other beginning of birth. For all men have one entrance into life, and the like going out.

Lesson II - Wis 7:7–10

Wherefore I wished, and understanding was given me: and I called upon God, and the spirit of wisdom came upon me: And I preferred her before kingdoms and thrones, and esteemed riches nothing in comparison of her. Neither did I compare unto her any precious stone: for all gold in comparison of her, is as a little sand, and silver in respect to her shall be counted as clay. I loved her above health and beauty, and chose to have her instead of light: for her light cannot be put out.

Lesson III - Wis 7:11–14

Now all good things came to me together with her, and innumerable riches through her hands, And I rejoiced in all these: for this wisdom went before me, and I knew not that she was the mother of them all. Which I have learned without guile, and communicate without envy, and her riches I hide not. For she is an infinite treasure to men! which they that use, become the friends of

God, being commended for the gift of discipline.

Thursday III of August

Lesson I - Wis 9:13–19

From the book of Wisdom

For who among men is he that can know the counsel of God? or who can think what the will of God is? For the thoughts of mortal men are fearful, and our counsels uncertain. For the corruptible body is a load upon the soul, and the earthly habitation presseth down the mind that museth upon many things. And hardly do we guess aright at things that are upon earth: and with labour do we find the things that are before us. But the things that are in heaven, who shall search out? And who shall know thy thought, except thou give wisdom, and send thy Holy Spirit from above: And so the ways of them that are upon earth may be corrected, and men may learn the things that please thee? For by wisdom they were healed, whosoever have pleased thee, O Lord, from the beginning.

Lesson II - Wis 10:1–5

She preserved him, that was first formed by God the father of the world, when he was created alone, And she brought him out of his sin, and gave him power to govern all things. But when the unjust went away from her in his anger, he perished by the fury wherewith he murdered his brother. For whose cause, when water destroyed the earth, wisdom healed it again, directing the course of the just by contemptible wood. Moreover when the nations had conspired together to consent to wickedness, she knew the just, and preserved him without blame to God, and kept him strong against the compassion for his son.

Lesson III - Wis 10:6–9

She delivered the just man who fled from the wicked that were perishing, when the fire came down upon Pentapolis: Whose land for a testimony of their wickedness is desolate, and smoketh to this day, and the trees bear fruits that ripen not, and a standing pillar of salt is a monument of an incredulous soul. For regarding not wisdom, they did not only slip in this, that they were ignorant of good things, but they left also unto men a memorial of their folly, so that in the things in which they sinned, they could not so much as lie hid. But wisdom hath delivered from sorrow them that attend upon her.

Friday III of August

Lesson I - Wis 13:1–3

From the book of Wisdom

But all men are vain, in whom there is not the knowledge of God: and who by these good things that are seen, could not understand him that is, neither by attending to the works have acknowledged who was the workman: But have imagined either the fire, or the wind, or the swift air, or the circle of the stars, or the great water, or the sun and moon, to be the gods that rule the world. With whose beauty, if they, being delighted, took them to be gods: let them know how much the

Lord of them is more beautiful than they: for the first author of beauty made all those things.

Lesson II ~ Wis 13:4–7

Or if they admired their power and their effects, let them understand by them, that he that made them, is mightier than they: For by the greatness of the beauty, and of the creature, the creator of them may be seen, so as to be known thereby. But yet as to these they are less to be blamed. For they perhaps err, seeking God, and desirous to find him. For being conversant among his works, they search: and they are persuaded that the things are good which are seen.

Lesson III ~ Wis 13:8–10

But then again they are not to be pardoned. For if they were able to know so much as to make a judgment of the world: how did they not more easily find out the Lord thereof? But unhappy are they, and their hope is among the dead, who have called gods the works of the hands of men, gold and silver, the inventions of art, and the resemblances of beasts, or an unprofitable stone the work of an ancient hand.

Saturday III of August

Lesson I ~ Wis 15:1–3

From the book of Wisdom

But thou, our God, art gracious and true, patient, and ordering all things in mercy. For if we sin, we are thine, knowing thy greatness: and if we sin not, we know that we are counted with thee. For to know thee is perfect justice: and to know thy justice, and thy power, is the root of immortality.

Lesson II ~ Wis 15:4–6

For the invention of mischievous men hath not deceived us, nor the shadow of a picture, a fruitless labour, a graven figure with diverse colours, The sight whereof enticeth the fool to lust after it, and he loveth the lifeless figure of a dead image. The lovers of evil things deserve to have no better things to trust in, both they that make them, and they that love them, and they that worship them.

Lesson III ~ Wis 15:7–8

The potter also tempering soft earth, with labour fashioneth every vessel for our service, and of the same clay he maketh both vessels that are for clean uses, and likewise such as serve to the contrary: but what is the use of these vessels, the potter is the judge. And of the same clay by a vain labour he maketh a god: he who a little before was made of earth himself, and a little after returneth to the same out of which he was taken, when his life which was lent him shall be called for again.

Sunday IV of August

Lesson I ~ Ecclus 1:1–5

Beginning of the book of Ecclesiasticus

All wisdom is from the Lord God, and hath been always with

him, and is before all time. Who hath numbered the sand of the sea, and the drops of rain, and the days of the world? Who hath measured the height of heaven, and the breadth of the earth, and the depth of the abyss? Who hath searched out the wisdom of God that goeth before all things? Wisdom hath been created before all things, and the understanding of prudence from everlasting. The word of God on high is the fountain of wisdom, and her ways are everlasting commandments.

Lesson II ~ Ecclus 1:6–10

To whom hath the root of wisdom been revealed, and who hath known her wise counsels? To whom hath the discipline of wisdom been revealed and made manifest? and who hath understood the multiplicity of her steps? There is one most high Creator Almighty, and a powerful king, and greatly to be feared, who sitteth upon his throne, and is the God of dominion. He created her in the Holy Ghost, and saw her, and numbered her, and measured her. And he poured her out upon all his works, and upon all flesh according to his gift, and hath given her to them that love him.

Lesson III ~ Ecclus 1:11–16

The fear of the Lord is honour, and glory, and gladness, and a crown of joy. The fear of the Lord shall delight the heart, and shall give joy, and gladness, and length of days. With him that feareth the Lord, it shall go well in the latter end, and in the day of his death he shall be blessed. The love of God is honourable wisdom. And they to whom she shall show herself love her by the sight, and by the knowledge of her great works. The fear of the Lord is the beginning of wisdom, and was created with the faithful in the womb, it walketh with chosen women, and is known with the just and faithful.

Lesson IV

From the Book of Morals, written by Pope St. Gregory

Some there are who are careless concerning their true life, greedy of the things which pass away, but as to the things which are eternal, either understand them not, or, understanding them, holding them to be but of little moment they feel no sorrow, nor know how to take wise advice and, in forgetfulness of the heavenly possessions which they have lost, they deem themselves (alas, poor wretches) happy in their goods. They lift not up their eyes to the light of truth for which they were created; no keen desire ever makes them to cast a longing look toward the everlasting Fatherland. Leaving alone the chief end for which they were made, they fix their affections upon the exile which they are enduring, instead of upon their home, and make merry in the blindness which they are suffering, as though it were glorious daylight.

Lesson V

But, on the other hand, the understandings of the elect, while they apprehend the things which pass away, perceive them to be indeed nothings, and work towards grasping the true end to which they were created, and since nothing outside God satisfies them, their thought, wearied by the intensity of speculation, finds rest in the hope for, and the contemplation of, their Maker. They are eager to take their place among the citizens above, and each one of them, although still placed in the world as concerns his body, does yet in heart and mind ascend above the world. They bemoan the hardships of the exile which they are enduring, and rouse themselves by the constant pricking of their love, to look to their Fatherland above. When therefore such a one sees with grief that by sin he has lost an eternal inheritance, he finds this healthy counsel, to reckon but lightly the things of time through which he is passing, and as his wise course that he has chosen, to leave be these perishing things, grows riper, the deeper grows his sorrow that he has not yet attained unto the things which endure.

Lesson VI

We must also realize that they who are headlong in their courses, feel not sorrow of heart. They that live without thought, who leave themselves recklessly to the guidance of events, escape the weariness of thought. He that orders his life by prudent consideration, looks carefully around him before each thing that he does, and, like a man that before advancing on an uncertain way tries the ground with his foot, so he takes thought beforehand, lest some sudden and evil thing should happen to him; he considers whether that which he has a mind to do is not forbidden to him by caution, whether he be not too hasty about things which were better put off to another season, lest evil should overcome him by open attack upon his lusts, or even good undo him by the in-bringing of vainglory.

Lessons VII, VIII, & IX from the *Sermons for After Pentecost* Section

Monday IV of August

Lesson I ~ Ecclus 1:22–26

From the book of Ecclesiasticus

The fear of the Lord is a crown of wisdom, filling up peace and the fruit of salvation: And it hath seen, and numbered her: but both are the gifts of God. Wisdom shall distribute knowledge, and understanding of prudence: and exalteth the glory of them that hold her. The root of wisdom is to fear the Lord: and the branches thereof are longlived. In the treasures of wisdom is understanding, and religiousness of knowledge: but to sinners wisdom is an abomination.

Lesson II ~ Ecclus 1:27–33

The fear of the Lord driveth out sin; For he that is without fear, cannot be justified: for the wrath of his high spirits is his ruin. A patient man shall bear for a time, and afterwards joy shall be restored to him. A good understanding will hide his words for a time, and the lips of many shall declare his wisdom. In the treasures of wisdom is the signification of discipline: But the worship of God is an abomination to a sinner. Son, if thou desire wisdom, keep justice, and God will give her to thee.

Lesson III ~ Ecclus 1:34–40

For the fear of the Lord is wisdom and discipline: and that which is agreeable to him, Is faith, and meekness: and he will fill up his treasures. Be not incredulous to the fear of the Lord: and come not to him with a double heart. Be not a hypocrite in the sight of men, and let not thy lips be a stumblingblock to thee. Watch over them, lest thou fall, and bring dishonour upon thy soul, And God discover thy secrets, and cast thee down in the midst of the congregation. Because thou camest to the Lord wickedly, and thy heart is full of guile and deceit.

Tuesday IV of August

Lesson I ~ Ecclus 2:1–3

From the book of Ecclesiasticus

Son, when thou comest to the service of God, stand in justice and in fear, and prepare thy soul for temptation. Humble thy heart, and endure: incline thy ear, and receive the words of understanding: and make not haste in the time of clouds. Wait on God with patience: join thyself to God, and endure, that thy life may be increased in the latter end.

Lesson II ~ Ecclus 2:4–6

Take all that shall be brought upon thee: and in thy sorrow endure, and in thy humiliation keep patience. For gold and silver are tried in the fire, but acceptable men in the furnace of humiliation. Believe God, and he will recover thee: and direct thy way, and trust in him. Keep his fear, and grow old therein.

Lesson III ~ Ecclus 2:7–12

Ye that fear the Lord, wait for his mercy: and go not aside from him, lest ye fall. Ye that fear the Lord, believe him: and your reward shall not be made void. Ye that fear the Lord, hope in him: and mercy shall come to you for your delight. Ye that fear the Lord, love him, and your hearts shall be enlightened. My children behold the generations of men: and know ye that no one hath hoped in the Lord, and hath been confounded. For who hath continued in his commandment, and hath been forsaken? or who hath called upon him, and he despised him?

Wednesday IV of August

Lesson I ~ Ecclus 3:1–4

From the book of Ecclesiasticus

The sons of wisdom are the church of the just: and their generation, obedience and love. Children, hear the judgment of your father, and so do that you may be saved. For God hath made the father honourable to the children: and seeking the judgment of the mothers, hath confirmed it upon the children. He that loveth God, shall obtain pardon for his sins by prayer, and shall refrain himself from them, and shall be heard in the prayer of days.

Lesson II ~ Ecclus 3:5–8

And he that honoureth his mother is as one that layeth up a treasure. He that honoureth his father shall have joy in his own children, and in the day of his prayer he shall be heard. He that honoureth his father shall enjoy a long life: and he that obeyeth the father, shall be a comfort to his mother. He that feareth the Lord, honoureth his parents, and will serve them as his masters that brought him into the world.

Lesson III ~ Ecclus 3:9–13

Honour thy father, in work and word, and all patience, That a blessing may come upon thee from him, and his blessing may remain in the latter end. The father's blessing establisheth the houses of the children: but the mother's curse rooteth up the foundation. Glory not in the dishonour of thy father: for his shame is no glory to thee. For the glory of a man is from the honour of his father, and a father without honour is the disgrace of the son.

Thursday IV of August

Lesson I ~ Ecclus 3:22–26

From the book of Ecclesiasticus

Seek not the things that are too high for thee, and search not into things above thy ability: but the things that God hath commanded thee, think on them always, and in many of his works be not curious. For it is not necessary for thee to see with thy eyes those things that are hid. In unnecessary matters be not over curious, and in many of his works thou shalt not be inquisitive. For many things are shown to thee above the understanding of men. And the suspicion of them hath deceived many, and hath detained their minds in vanity.

Lesson II ~ Ecclus 3:27–30

A hard heart shall fear evil at the last: and he that loveth danger shall perish in it. A heart that goeth two ways shall not have success, and the perverse of heart shall be scandalized therein. A wicked heart shall be laden with sorrows, and the sinner will add sin to sin. The congregation of the proud shall not be healed: for the plant of wickedness shall take root in them, and it shall not be perceived.

Lesson III ~ Ecclus 3:31–34

The heart of the wise is understood in wisdom, and a good ear will hear wisdom with all desire. A wise heart, and which hath understanding, will abstain from sins, and in the works of justice shall have success. Water quencheth a flaming fire, and alms resisteth sins: And God provideth for him that showeth favour: he remembereth him afterwards, and in the time of his fall he shall find a sure stay.

Friday IV of August

Lesson I ~ Ecclus 4:1–4

From the book of Ecclesiasticus

Son, defraud not the poor of alms, and turn not away thy eyes from the poor. Despise not the hungry soul: and provoke not the poor in his want. Afflict not the heart of the needy, and defer not to give to him that is in distress. Reject not the petition of the afflicted: and turn not away thy face from the needy.

Lesson II - Ecclus 4:5–7

Turn not away thy eyes from the poor for fear of anger: and leave not to them that ask of thee to curse thee behind thy back. For the prayer of him that curseth thee in the bitterness of his soul, shall be heard, for he that made him will hear him. Make thyself affable to the congregation of the poor, and humble thy soul to the ancient, and bow thy head to a great man.

Lesson III - Ecclus 4:8–11

Bow down thy ear cheerfully to the poor, and pay what thou owest, and answer him peaceable words with mildness. Deliver him that suffereth wrong out of the hand of the proud: and be not fainthearted in thy soul. In judging be merciful to the fatherless as a father, and as a husband to their mother. And thou shalt be as the obedient son of the most High, and he will have mercy on thee more than a mother.

Saturday IV of August

Lesson I - Ecclus 4:23–28

From the book of Ecclesiasticus

Son, observe the time, and fly from evil. For thy soul be not ashamed to say the truth. For there is a shame that bringeth sin, and there is a shame that bringeth glory and grace. Accept no person against thy own person, nor against thy soul a lie. Reverence not thy neighbour in his fall, And refrain not to speak in the time of salvation. Hide not thy wisdom in her beauty.

Lesson II - Ecclus 4:29–32

For by the tongue wisdom is discerned: and understanding, and knowledge, and learning by the word of the wise, and steadfastness in the works of justice. In nowise speak against the truth, but be ashamed of the lie of thy ignorance. Be not ashamed to confess thy sins, but submit not thyself to every man for sin. Resist not against the face of the mighty, and do not strive against the stream of the river.

Lesson III - Ecclus 4:33–36

Strive for justice for thy soul, and even unto death fight for justice, and God will overthrow thy enemies for thee. Be not hasty in thy tongue: and slack and remiss in thy works. Be not as a lion in thy house, terrifying them of thy household, and oppressing them that are under thee. Let not thy hand be stretched out to receive, and shut when thou shouldst give.

Sunday V of August

(If not the Sunday closest to Sept 1)

Lesson I - Ecclus 5:1–5

From the book of Ecclesiasticus

Set not thy heart upon unjust possessions, and say not: I have enough to live on: for it shall be of no service in the time of vengeance and darkness. Follow not in thy strength the desires of thy heart: And say not: How mighty am I? and who shall bring me under for my deeds?

for God will surely take revenge. Say not: I have sinned, and what harm hath befallen me? for the most High is a patient rewarder. Be not without fear about sin forgiven, and add not sin upon sin.

Lesson II - Ecclus 5:6–11

And say not: The mercy of the Lord is great, he will have mercy on the multitude of my sins. For mercy and wrath quickly come from him, and his wrath looketh upon sinners. Delay not to be converted to the Lord, and defer it not from day to day. For his wrath shall come on a sudden, and in the time of vengeance he will destroy thee. Be not anxious for goods unjustly gotten: for they shall not profit thee in the day of calamity and revenge. Winnow not with every wind, and go not into every way: for so is every sinner proved by a double tongue.

Lesson III - Ecclus 5:12–16

Be steadfast in the way of the Lord, and in the truth of thy judgment, and in knowledge, and let the word of peace and justice keep with thee. Be meek to hear the word, that thou mayst understand: and return a true answer with wisdom. If thou have understanding, answer thy neighbour: but if not, let thy hand be upon thy mouth, lest thou be surprised in an unskillful word, and be confounded. Honour and glory is in the word of the wise, but the tongue of the fool is his ruin. Be not called a whisperer, and be not taken in thy tongue, and confounded.

Lesson IV

Sermon by St. John Chrysostom

Tarry not in turning to the Lord, yea, defer not thy repentance from day to day; for thou knowest not what the morrow may bring forth. In delay there is danger and terror, but where there is no delay, there health is safe and secure. Live well then, and, then, however young thou diest, thou wilt die safely; and if thou come to old age thou wilt depart without vexation or trouble; and thou wilt have a double happiness, in that thou wilt be leaving all the evils of life, and in that thou hast lived well. Say not: "There will be a time ripe for repentance." For such words as these do greatly rouse the anger of God.

Lesson V

He has promised thee eternal ages, and thou willest not to work in this present life, which is so short and so fleeting. Dost thou so idly and loosely carry thyself, as though the life for which thou seekest were a shorter life than this? Do not daily feastings, daily gluttonies, daily uncleanness, shows, and riches bear witness to the undying nature of sinful cravings? Think it well over, that as often as thou dost commit uncleanness, thou dost damn thyself? For this is the nature of sin, as soon as it is committed, the Judge's sentence is uttered.

Lesson VI

Hast thou been drunk? Hast thou overeaten? Hast thou stolen?

Stop, and turn back; thank the goodness of God, that He has not taken thee away in the midst of thy sins. Seek not more time wherein to commit iniquity. Many have they been who have perished suddenly, in the midst of bad and vicious lives, and have gone away to manifest damnation; have fear lest the same thing befall thee. But, thou sayest, "they have been many to whom God has given time, and they have been to confession in their old age." What then? Is that a proof that it will be given to thee? Perchance, sayest thou. Why sayest thou, Perchance? Does it happen sometimes? Think that it is of thy soul thou art considering. Look at it the other way, and say: "What if it be not given?" But, sayest thou, and what if it be? May it be so! It is true; it is among His gifts, but nevertheless, this is the safer and the better way.

Lessons VII, VIII, & IX from the *Sermons for After Pentecost* Section

Monday V of August

Lesson I ~ Ecclus 7:1–5

From the book of Ecclesiasticus

Do no evils, and no evils shall lay hold of thee. Depart from the unjust, and evils shall depart from thee. My son, sow not evils in the furrows of injustice, and thou shalt not reap them sevenfold. Seek not of the Lord a pre-eminence, nor of the king the seat of honour. Justify not thyself before God, for he knoweth the heart: and desire not to appear wise before the king.

Lesson II ~ Ecclus 7:6–10

Seek not to be made a judge, unless thou have strength enough to extirpate iniquities: lest thou fear the person of the powerful, and lay a stumblingblock for thy integrity. Offend not against the multitude of a city, neither cast thyself in upon the people, Nor bind sin to sin: for even in one thou shalt not be unpunished. Be not fainthearted in thy mind: Neglect not to pray, and to give alms.

Lesson III ~ Ecclus 7:11–15

Say not: God will have respect to the multitude of my gifts, and when I offer to the most high God, he will accept my offerings. Laugh no man to scorn in the bitterness of his soul: for there is one that humbleth and exalteth, God who seeth all. Devise not a lie against thy brother: neither do the like against thy friend. Be not willing to make any manner of lie: for the custom thereof is not good. Be not full of words in a multitude of ancients, and repeat not the word in thy prayer.

Tuesday V of August

Lesson I ~ Ecclus 10:1–5

From the book of Ecclesiasticus

A wise judge shall judge his people, and the government of a prudent man shall be steady. As the judge of the people is himself, so also are his ministers: and what manner of man the ruler of a city is, such also are they that dwell therein. An unwise king shall be the ruin of his people: and cities shall be inhabited through the prudence of the rulers. The power of the earth is in the hand of God, and in his time he will raise up a profitable ruler over it. The prosperity of man is in the hand of God, and upon the person of the scribe he shall lay his honour.

Lesson II - Ecclus 10:6–10

Remember not any injury done thee by thy neighbour, and do thou nothing by deeds of injury. Pride is hateful before God and men: and all iniquity of nations is execrable. A kingdom is translated from one people to another, because of injustices, and wrongs, and injuries, and diverse deceits. But nothing is more wicked than the covetous man. Why is earth and ashes proud? There is not a more wicked thing than to love money: for such a one setteth even his own soul to sale: because while he liveth he hath cast away his bowels.

Lesson III - Ecclus 10:11–16

All power is of short life. A long sickness is troublesome to the physician. The physician cutteth off it short sickness: so also a king is today, and tomorrow he shall die. For when a man shall die, he shall inherit serpents, and beasts, and worms. The beginning of the pride of man, is to fall off from God: Because his heart is departed from him that made him: for pride is the beginning of all sin: be that holdeth it, shall be filled with maledictions, and it shall ruin him in the end. Therefore hath the Lord disgraced the assemblies of the wicked, and hath utterly destroyed them.

Wednesday V of August

Lesson I - Ecclus 13:1–6

From the book of Ecclesiasticus

He that toucheth pitch, shall be defiled with it: and he that hath fellowship with the proud, shall put on pride. He shall take a burden upon him that hath fellowship with one more honourable than himself. And have no fellowship with one that is richer than thyself. What agreement shall the earthen pot have with the kettle? for if they knock one against the other, it shall be broken. The rich man hath done wrong, and yet he will fume: but the poor is wronged and must hold his peace. If thou give, he will make use of thee: and if thou have nothing, he will forsake thee. If thou have any thing, he will live with thee, and will make thee bare, and he will not be sorry for thee.

Lesson II - Ecclus 13:9–15

Humble thyself to God, and wait for his hands. Beware that thou be not deceived Into folly, and be humbled. Be not lowly in thy wisdom, lest being humbled thou be deceived into folly. If thou be invited by one that is mightier, withdraw thyself: for so he will invite thee the more. Be not troublesome to him, lest thou be put back: and keep not far from him, lest thou be forgotten. Affect not to speak with him as an equal: and believe not his many words: for by much talk he will sift thee, and smiling will examine thee concerning thy secrets. His cruel mind will lay up thy words: and he will not spare to do thee hurt, and to cast thee into prison.

Lesson III ~ Ecclus 13:16–22

Take heed to thyself, and attend diligently to what thou hearest: for thou walkest in danger of thy ruin. When thou hearest those things, see as it were in sleep, and thou shalt awake. Love God all thy life, and call upon him for thy salvation. Every beast loveth its like: so also every man him that is nearest to himself. All flesh shall consort with the like to itself, and every man shall associate himself to his like. If the wolf shall at any time have fellowship with the lamb, so the sinner with the just. What fellowship hath a holy man with a dog, or what part hath the rich with the poor?

Thursday V of August

Lesson I ~ Ecclus 14:1–5

From the book of Ecclesiasticus

Blessed is the man that hath not slipped by a word out of his mouth, and is not pricked with the remorse of sin. Happy is he that hath had no sadness of his mind, and who is not fallen from his hope. Riches are not comely for a covetous man and a niggard, and what should an envious man do with gold? He that gathereth together by wronging his own soul, gathereth for others, and another will squander away his goods in rioting. He that is evil to himself, to whom will he be good? and he shall not take pleasure in his goods.

Lesson II ~ Ecclus 14:6–10

There is none worse than he that envieth himself, and this is the reward of his wickedness: And if he do good, he doth it ignorantly, and unwillingly: and at the last he discovereth his wickedness. The eye of the envious is wicked: and he turneth away his face, and despiseth his own soul. The eye of the covetous man is insatiable in his portion of iniquity: he will not be satisfied till he consume his own soul, drying it up. An evil eye is towards evil things: and he shall not have his fill of bread, but shall be needy and pensive at his own table.

Lesson III ~ Ecclus 14:11–17

My son, if thou have any thing, do good to thyself, and offer to God worthy offerings. Remember that death is not slow, and that the covenant of hell hath been shown to thee: for the covenant of this world shall surely die. Do good to thy friend before thou die, and according to thy ability, stretching out thy hand give to the poor. Defraud not thyself of the good day, and let not the part of a good gift overpass thee. Shalt thou not leave to others to divide by lot thy sorrows and labours? Give and take, and justify thy soul. Before thy death work justice: for in hell there is no finding food.

Friday V of August

Lesson I ~ Ecclus 21:1–5

From the book of Ecclesiasticus

My son, hast thou sinned? do so no more: but for thy former sins also pray that they may be forgiven thee. Flee from sins as from the face of a serpent: for if thou comest near them, they will take hold of thee. The teeth thereof are the teeth of a lion, killing the souls of men. All iniquity is like a two-edged sword, there is no remedy for the wound thereof. Injuries and wrongs will waste riches: and the house that is very rich shall be brought to nothing by pride: so the substance of the proud shall be rooted out.

Lesson II ~ Ecclus 21:6–10

The prayer out of the mouth of the poor shall reach the ears of God, and judgment shall come for him speedily. He that hateth to be reproved walketh in the trace of a sinner: and he that feareth God will turn to his own heart. He that is mighty by a bold tongue is known afar off, but a wise man knoweth to slip by him. He that buildeth his house at other men's charges, is as he that gathereth himself stones to build in the winter. The congregation of sinners is like tow heaped together, and the end of them is a flame of fire.

Lesson III ~ Ecclus 21:11–16

The way of sinners is made plain with stones, and in their end is hell, and darkness, and pains. He that keepeth justice shall get the understanding thereof. The perfection of the fear of God is wisdom and understanding. He that is not wise in good, will not be taught. But there is a wisdom that aboundeth in evil: and there is no understanding where there is bitterness. The knowledge of a wise man shall abound like a flood, and his counsel continueth like a fountain of life.

Saturday V of August

Lesson I ~ Ecclus 32:1–5

From the book of Ecclesiasticus

Have they made thee ruler? be not lifted up: be among them as one of them. Have care of them, and so sit down, and when thou hast acquitted thyself of all thy charge, take thy place: That thou mayst rejoice for them, and receive a crown as an ornament of grace, and get the honour of the contribution. Speak, thou that art elder: for it becomes thee, To speak the first word with careful knowledge, and hinder not music.

Lesson II ~ Ecclus 32:6–11

Where there is no hearing, pour not out words, and be not lifted up out of season with thy wisdom. A concert of music in a banquet of wine is as a carbuncle set in gold. As a signet of an emerald in a work of gold: so is the melody of music with pleasant and moderate wine. Hear in silence, and for thy reverence good grace shall come to thee. Young man, scarcely speak in thy own cause. If thou be asked twice, let thy answer be short.

Lesson III ~ Ecclus 32:12–17

In many things be as if thou wert ignorant, and hear in silence and withal seeking. In the company of great men take not upon thee: and when the ancients are present, speak not much. Before a storm goeth lightning: and before shamefacedness goeth favour: and for thy reverence good grace shall come to thee. And at the time of rising be not slack: but be first to run home to thy house, and there withdraw thyself, and there take thy pastime. And do what thou hast a mind, but not in sin or proud speech. And for all these things bless the Lord, that made thee, and that replenisheth thee with all his good things.

SUNDAYS OF SEPTEMBER

Sunday I of September

Lesson I - Job 1:1–3

Beginning of the book of Job

There was a man in the land of Hus, whose name was Job, and that man was simple and upright, and fearing God, and avoiding evil. And there were born to him seven sons and three daughters. And his possession was seven thousand sheep, and three thousand camels, and five hundred yoke of oxen, and five hundred she asses, and a family exceeding great: and this man was great among all the people of the east.

Lesson II - Job 1:4–5

And his sons went, and made a feast by houses every one in his day. And sending they called their three sisters to eat and drink with them. And when the days of their feasting were gone about, Job sent to them, and sanctified them: and rising up early offered holocausts for every one of them. For he said: Lest perhaps my sons have sinned, and have blessed God in their hearts. So did Job all days.

Lesson III - Job 1:6–11

Now on a certain day when the sons of God came to stand before the Lord, Satan also was present among them. And the Lord said to him: Whence comest thou? And he answered and said: I have gone round about the earth, and walked through it. And the Lord said to him: Hast thou considered my servant Job, that there is none like him in the earth, a simple and upright man, and fearing God, and avoiding evil? And Satan answering, said: Doth Job fear God in vain? Hast not thou made a fence for him, and his house, and all his substance round about, blessed the works of his hands, and his possession hath increased on the earth? But stretch forth thy hand a little, and touch all that he hath, and see if he blesseth thee not to thy face.

Lesson IV

From the Book of Morals written by Pope St. Gregory

The Holy Scripture is put before the eyes of our mind somewhat after the fashion of a looking-glass, that we may see therein the aspect of our inward man. Therein we see what are our unsightly, and what our beautiful traits, thereby we judge how we are growing and how far yet we are from fullness of stature. The Holy Scripture tells of the doings of the Saints, and stirs up the heart of us weaklings to follow them. While it makes memorial of their victorious deeds, it strengthens our frailty to strive against sin. And so by the words of the Scripture it comes to pass that the soul trembles less at the battle, for that she sees how many times the enemies before her have been beaten by brave men.

Lesson V

And sometimes the Scripture shows unto us, not only how the Saints fought bravely, but also how they fell, that we may see by the example of the mighty, not only what weapons we must take, if we would conquer, but also what snares we must keep clear of, if we would avoid falling. For example, here is Job on the one hand, waxing nobler under trial, and on the other hand, David, tried, and failing utterly. And so the glory of the great strengthens our hope, and the backsliding of the same does stir us up to be watchful and lowly: the one cheering us with gladness and the other putting us on our guard through fear, so that the soul of him which hears of these things may by the one gain sure and certain hope, and by the other, fearfulness and watchfulness, and so neither be rashly puffed up, nor hopelessly cast down, nor may faint under the weight of dread, forasmuch as she is stirred up to trustfulness by the example of him who triumphed.

Lesson VI

"There was a man in the land of Hus, whose name was Job." We are told where this holy man lived, that thereby we may gauge the worth of his bravery. Who knows not that Hus is a place in the countries of the Gentiles? The Gentile world had been so degraded and corrupted by sin, that they had ceased to know that they had a Maker. Therefore is it told us where Job dwelt, that it may redound to his praise that he was good in the midst of the wicked. It is not very praiseworthy to be good among the good, but to be good among the bad. For even as it is more grievous to be bad among the good, so is it right praiseworthy to have remained good among the bad.

Lessons VII, VIII, & IX from the *Sermons for After Pentecost* Section

Monday I of September

Lesson I ~ Job 1:13–16

From the book of Job

Now upon a certain day when his sons and daughters were eating and drinking wine in the house of their eldest brother, There came a messenger to Job, and said: The oxen were ploughing, and the asses feeding beside them, And the Sabeans rushed in, and took all away, and slew the servants with the sword, and I alone have escaped to tell thee. And while he was yet speaking, another came, and said: The fire of God fell from heaven, and striking the sheep and the servants, hath consumed them, and I alone have escaped to tell thee.

Lesson II ~ Job 1:17–19

And while he also was yet speaking, there came another, and said: The Chaldeans made three troops, and have fallen upon the camels, and taken them, moreover they have slain the servants with the sword, and I alone have escaped to tell thee. He was yet speaking, and behold another came in, and said: thy sons and daughters were eating and drinking wine in the house of their elder brother: A violent wind came on a sudden from the side of the desert, and shook the four corners of the house, and it fell upon thy children and they are dead, and I alone have escaped to fell thee.

Lesson III ~ Job 1:20–22

Then Job rose up, and rent his garments, and having shaven his head fell down upon the ground and worshipped, And said: Naked came I out of my mother's womb, and naked shall I return thither: the Lord gave, and the Lord hath taken away: as it hath pleased the Lord so is it done: blessed be the name of the Lord. In all these things Job sinned not by his lips, nor spoke he any foolish thing against God.

Tuesday I of September

Lesson I ~ Job 2:1–5

From the book of Job

And it came to pass, when on a certain day the sons of God came, and stood before the Lord, and Satan came among them, and stood in his sight, That the Lord said to Satan: Whence comest thou? And he answered and said: I have gone round about the earth, and walked through it. And the Lord said to Satan: Hast thou considered my servant Job, that there is none like him in the earth, a man simple, and upright, and fearing God, and avoiding evil, and still keeping his innocence. But thou hast moved me against him, that I should afflict him without cause. And Satan answered, and said: Skin for skin, and all that a man hath he will give for his life: But put forth thy hand, and touch his bone and his flesh, and then thou shalt see that he will bless thee to thy face.

Lesson II ~ Job 2:6–10

And the Lord said to Satan: Behold he is in thy hand, but yet save his life. So Satan went forth from the presence of the Lord, and struck Job with a very grievous ulcer, from the sole of the foot even to the top of his head: And he took a potsherd and scraped the corrupt matter, sitting on a dunghill. And his wife said to him: Dost thou still continue in thy simplicity? Bless God and die. And he said to her: Thou hast; spoken like one of the foolish women: if we have received good things at the hand of God, why should we not receive evil? In all these things Job did not sin with his lips.

Lesson III ~ Job 2:11–13

Now when Job's three friends heard all the evil that had befallen him, they came every one from his own place, Alphas the Themanite, and Baldad the Suhite, and Sophar the Naamathite. For they had made an appointment to come together and visit him, and comfort him. And when they had lifted up their eyes afar off, they knew him not, and crying out they wept, and rending their garments they sprinkled dust upon their heads towards heaven. And they sat with him on the ground seven days and seven nights, and no man spoke to him a word: for they saw that his grief was very great.

Wednesday I of September

Lesson I ~ Job 3:1–5

From the book of Job

After this Job opened his mouth, and cursed his day, And he said: Let the day perish wherein I was born, and the night in which it was said: A man child is conceived. Let that day be turned into darkness, let not God regard it from above, and let not the light shine upon it. Let darkness, and the shadow of death cover it, let a mist overspread it, and let it be wrapped up in bitterness.

Lesson II ~ Job 3:6–10

Let a darksome whirlwind seize upon that night, let it not be counted in the days of the year, nor numbered in the months. Let that night be solitary, and not worthy of praise. Let them curse it who curse the day. who are ready to raise up a leviathan: Let the stars be darkened with the mist thereof: let it expect light and not see it, nor the rising of the dawning of the day: Because it shut not up the doors of the womb that bore me, nor took away evils from my eyes.

Lesson III ~ Job 3:11–16

Why did I not die in the womb, why did I not perish when I came out of the belly? Why received upon the knees? why suckled at the breasts? For now I should have been asleep and still, and should have rest in my sleep. With kings and consuls of the earth, who build themselves solitudes: Or with princes, that possess gold, and All their houses with silver: Or as a hidden untimely birth I should not be, or as they that being conceived have not seen the light.

Thursday I of September

Lesson I ~ Job 4:1–6

From the book of Job

Then Eliphaz the Themanite answered, and said: If we begin to speak to thee, perhaps thou wilt take it ill, but who can withhold the words he hath conceived? Behold thou hast taught many, and thou hast strengthened the weary hands: Thy words have confirmed them that were staggering, and thou hast strengthened the trembling knees: But now the scourge is come upon thee, and thou faintest: it hath touched thee, and thou art troubled. Where is thy fear, thy fortitude, thy patience, and the perfection of thy ways?

Lesson II ~ Job 4:7–11

Remember, I pray thee, who ever perished being innocent? or when were the just destroyed? On the contrary I have seen those who work iniquity, and sow sorrows, and reap them, Perishing by the blast of God, and consumed by the spirit of his wrath. The roaring of the lion, and the voice of the lioness, and the teeth of the whelps of lions are broken: The tiger hath perished for want of prey, and the young lions are scattered abroad.

Lesson III ~ Job 4:12–18

Now there was a word spoken to me in private, and my ears by stealth as it were received the veins of its whisper. In the horror of a vision by night, when deep sleep is wont to hold men, Fear seized upon me, and trembling, and all my bones were affrighted: And when a spirit passed before me, the hair of my flesh stood up. There stood one whose countenance I knew not, an image before my eyes, and I heard the voice as it were of a gentle wind: Shall man be justified in comparison of God, or shall a man be more pure than his maker? Behold they that serve him are not steadfast, and in his angels he found wickedness.

Friday I of September

Lesson I - Job 6:1–4

From the book of Job

But Job answered, and said: O that my sins, whereby I have deserved wrath, and the calamity that I suffer, were weighed in a balance. As the sand of the sea this would appear heavier: therefore my words are full of sorrow: For the arrows of the Lord are in me, the rage whereof drinketh up my spirit, and the terrors of the Lord war against me.

Lesson II - Job 6:5–7

Will the wild ass bray when he hath grass? or will the ox low when he standeth before a full manger? Or can an unsavoury thing be eaten, that is not seasoned with salt? or can a man taste that which when tasted bringeth death? The things which before my soul would not touch, now, through anguish are my meats.

Lesson III - Job 6:8–13

Who will grant that my request may come: and that God may give me what I look for? And that he that hath begun may destroy me, that he may let loose his hand, and cut me off? And that this may be my comfort, that afflicting me with sorrow, he spare not, nor I contradict the words of the Holy One. For what is my strength, that I can hold out? or what is my end that I should keep patience? My strength is not the strength of stones, nor is my flesh of brass. Behold there is no help for me in myself, and my familiar friends also are departed from me.

Saturday I of September

Lesson I - Job 7:1–4

From the book of Job

The life of man upon earth is a warfare, and his days are like the days of a hireling. As a servant longeth for the shade, as the hireling looketh for the end of his work; So I also have had empty months, and have numbered to myself wearisome nights. If I lie down to sleep, I shall say: When shall I arise? and again I shall look for the evening, and shall be filled with sorrows even till darkness.

Lesson II - Job 7:5–8

My flesh is clothed with rottenness and the filth of dust, my skin is withered and drawn together. My days have passed more swiftly than the web is cut by the weaver, and are consumed without any hope. Remember that my life is but wind, and my eyes shall not return to see good things. Nor shall the sight of man behold me: thy eyes are upon me, and I shall be no more.

Lesson III - Job 7:9–12

As a cloud is consumed, and passeth away: so he that shall go down to hell shall not come up. Nor shall he return any more into his house, neither shall his place know him any more. Wherefore I will not spare my month, I will speak in the affliction of my spirit: I will talk with the bitterness of my soul. Am I a sea, or a whale, that thou hast enclosed me in a prison?

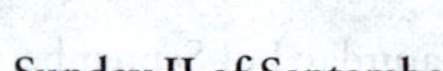

Sunday II of September

Lesson I ~ Job 9:1–5

From the book of Job

And Job answered, and said: Indeed I know it is so, and that man cannot be justified compared with God, If he will contend with him, he cannot answer him one for a thousand. He is wise in heart, and mighty in strength: who hath resisted him, and hath had peace? Who hath removed mountains, and they whom he overthrew in his wrath, knew it not.

Lesson II ~ Job 9:6–10

Who shaketh the earth out of her place, and the pillars thereof tremble. Who commandeth the sun and it riseth not: and shutteth up the stars as it were under a seal: Who alone spreadeth out the heavens, and walketh upon the waves of the sea. Who maketh Arcturus, and Orion, and Hyades, and the inner parts of the south. Who doth things great and incomprehensible, and wonderful, of which there is no number.

Lesson III ~ Job 9:11–17

If he come to me, I shall not see him: if he depart I shall not understand. If he examine on a sudden, who shall answer him? or who can say: Why dost thou so? God, whose wrath no man can resist, and under whom they stoop that bear up the world. What am I then, that I should answer him, and have words with him? I, who although I should have any just thing, would not answer, but would make supplication to my judge. And if he should hear me when I call, I should not believe that he had heard my voice. For he shall crush me in a whirlwind, and multiply my wounds even without cause.

Lesson IV

From the Book of Morals written by Pope St. Gregory

We know that it is so truly, and that a man cannot be justified compared to God. When God is put out of the consideration, a man may be considered to be just, but considered as against God, his righteousness vanishes away. When a man measures himself by his relation to Him, Who is the Author of all good, he does thereby acknowledge that of himself he has no good in him, but has received from God whatsoever he has. He that glorifies himself because of good which has been given him, fights against God with God's own gifts. It is just therefore that the grounds upon which he ought to have been humbled, but upon which he has puffed himself up, should be used to humble his vainglory. But a holy man, because he perceives that the worth of our own good deeds falls short, when he considers his own spiritual man, justly says: If He will contend with him, he cannot answer Him one of a thousand.

Lesson V

In the Holy Scriptures the number one thousand is used to be taken as signifying a generalization. Thus, the Psalmist says "The word which He commanded to a thousand generations," whereas it is notorious that the Evangelist does not reckon more than seventy-and-seven generations between the very beginning of the world and the coming of our Redeemer. What therefore is to be understood here by a thousand? The general ripeness of the old generation to bring forth a new offspring. Hence also it is said by John "And shall reign with Him a thousand years," because the reign of the Holy Church will be over all mankind made perfect.

Lesson VI

Ten times one is ten, and ten times ten is a hundred, and ten times a hundred is a thousand. Observing therefore this connection between one and a thousand, what are we to understand by the one (in the text, connected as it is with the thousand whereby we understand perfection)? Is it not the beginning of a good life, even as the thousand represents perfection? The contending with God (which is spoken of in the text) is the non-acknowledgment of that which is owed to Him, and the vain-glorying instead in our own strength. But a holy man should see, that even if one had received the gifts of perfection, and were to make them the grounds of self-glorification, such a one would thereby lose all that he had received.

Lessons VII, VIII, & IX from the Sermons for After Pentecost Section

Monday II of September

Lesson I ~ Job 27:1–5

From the book of Job

Job also added, taking up his parable, and said: As God liveth, who hath taken away my judgment, and the Almighty, who hath brought my soul to bitterness, As long as breath remaineth in me, and the spirit of God in my nostrils, My lips shall not speak iniquity, neither shall my tongue contrive lying. God forbid that I should judge you to be just: till I die I will not depart from my innocence.

Lesson II ~ Job 27:6–10

My justification, which I have begun to hold, I will not forsake: for my heart doth not reprehend me in all my life. Let my enemy be as the ungodly, and my adversary as the wicked one. For what is the hope of the hypocrite if through covetousness he take by violence, and God deliver not his soul? Will God hear his cry, when distress shall come upon him? Or can he delight himself in the Almighty, and call upon God at all times?

Lesson III ~ Job 27:11–15

I will teach you by the hand of God, what the Almighty hath, and I will not conceal it. Behold you all know it, and why do you speak vain things without cause? This is the portion of a wicked man with

God, and the inheritance of the violent, which they shall receive of the Almighty. If his sons be multiplied, they shall be for the sword, and his grandsons shall not be filled with bread. They that shall remain of him, shall be buried in death, and his widows shall not weep.

Tuesday II of September

Lesson I ~ Job 28:12–16

From the book of Job

But where is wisdom to be found, and where is the place of understanding? Man knoweth not the price thereof, neither is it found in the land of them that live in delights. The depth saith: It is not in me: and the sea saith: It is not with me. The finest gold shall not purchase it, neither shall silver be weighed in exchange for it. It shall not be compared with the dyed colours of India, or with the most precious stone sardonyx, or the sapphire.

Lesson II ~ Job 28:17–22

Gold or crystal cannot equal it, neither shall any vessels of gold be changed for it. High and eminent things shall not be mentioned in comparison of it: but wisdom is drawn out of secret places. The topaz of Ethiopia shall not be equal to it, neither shall it be compared to the cleanest dyeing. Whence then comes wisdom? and where is the place of understanding? It is hid from the eyes of all living. and the fowls of the air know it not. Destruction and death have said: With our ears we have heard the fame thereof.

Lesson III ~ Job 28:23–28

God understandeth the way of it, and he knoweth the place thereof. For he beholdeth the ends of the world: and looketh on all things that are under heaven. Who made a weight for the winds and weighed the waters by measure. When he gave a law for the rain, and a way for the sounding storms. Then he saw it, and declared, and prepared, and searched it. And he said to man: Behold the fear of the Lord, that is wisdom: and to depart from evil, is understanding.

Wednesday II of September

Lesson I ~ Job 31:1–6

From the book of Job

I made a covenant with my eyes, that I would not so much as think upon a virgin. For what part should God from above have in me, and what inheritance the Almighty from on high? Is not destruction to the wicked, and aversion to them that work iniquity? Doth not he consider my ways, and number all my steps? If I have walked in vanity, and my foot hath made haste to deceit: Let him weigh me in a just balance, and let God know my simplicity.

Lesson II ~ Job 31:7–12

If my step hath turned out of the way, and if my heart hath followed my eyes, and if a spot hath cleaved to my hands: Then let me sow and let another eat: and let my offspring be rooted out. If my heart hath been deceived upon a woman, and if I have laid wait at my friend's door: Let my wife be the harlot of another, and let other men lie with her. For this is a heinous crime, and a most grievous iniquity. It is a fire that devoureth even to destruction, and rooteth up all things that spring.

Lesson III ~ Job 31:13–18

If I have despised to abide judgment with my manservant, or my maidservant, when they had any controversy against me: For what shall I do when God shall rise to judge? and when he shall examine, what shall I answer him? Did not he that made me in the womb make him also: and did not one and the same form me in the womb? If I have denied to the poor what they desired, and have made the eyes of the widow wait: If I have eaten my morsel alone, and the fatherless hath not eaten thereof: (For from my infancy mercy grew up with me: and it came out with me from my mother's womb)

Thursday II of September

Lesson I ~ Job 38:1–7

From the book of Job

Then the Lord answered Job out of a whirlwind, and said: Who is this that wrappeth up sentences in unskillful words? Gird up thy loins like a man I will ask thee, and answer thou me. Where wast thou when I laid up the foundations of the earth tell me if thou hast understanding. Who hath laid the measures thereof, if thou knowest? or who hath stretched the line upon it? Upon what are its bases grounded? or who laid the corner stone thereof, When the morning stars praised me together, and all the sons of God made a joyful melody?

Lesson II ~ Job 38:8–13

Who shut up the sea with doors, when it broke forth as issuing out of the womb? When I made a cloud the garment thereof, and wrapped it in a mist as in swaddling bands? I set my bounds around it, and made it bars and doors. And I said: Hitherto thou shalt come, and shalt go no further, and here thou shalt break thy swelling waves. Didst thou since thy birth command the morning, and shew the dawning of the day its place? And didst thou hold the extremities of the earth shaking them, and hast thou shaken the ungodly out of it?

Lesson III ~ Job 38:14–20

The seal shall be restored as clay, and shall stand as a garment. From the wicked their light shall be taken away, and the high arm shall be broken. Hast thou entered into the depths of the sea, and walked in the lowest parts of the deep? Have the gates of death been opened to thee, and hast thou seen the darksome doors? Hast thou considered the breadth of the earth? tell me, if thou knowest all things? Where is the way where light dwelleth, and where is the place of darkness? That thou mayst bring every thing to its own bounds, and understand the paths of the house thereof.

Friday II of September

Lesson I ~ Job 40:1–5

From the book of Job

And the Lord answering Job out of the whirlwind, said: Gird up thy loins like a man I will ask thee, and do thou tell me. Wilt thou make void my judgment and condemn me, that thou mayst be justified? And hast thou an arm like God, and canst thou thunder with a voice like him? Clothe thyself with beauty, and set thyself up on high and be glorious, and put on goodly garments.

Lesson II ~ Job 40:6–11

Scatter the proud in thy indignation, and behold every arrogant man, and humble him. Look on all that are proud, and confound them, and crush the wicked in their place. Hide them in the dust together, and plunge their faces into the pit. Then I will confess that thy right hand is able to save thee. Behold behemoth whom I made with thee, he eateth grass like an ox. His strength is in his loins, and his force in the navel of his belly.

Lesson III ~ Job 42:1–6

Then Job answered the Lord, and said: I know that thou canst do all things, and no thought is hid from thee. Who is this that hideth counsel without knowledge? Therefore I have spoken unwisely, and things that above measure exceeded my knowledge. Hear, and I will speak I will ask thee, and do thou tell me. With the hearing of the ear, I have heard thee, but now my eye seeth thee. Therefore I reprehend myself, and do penance in dust and ashes.

Saturday II of September

Lesson I ~ Job 42:7–8

From the book of Job

And after the Lord had spoken these words to Job, he said to Eliphaz the Themanite: My wrath is kindled against thee, and against thy two friends, because you have not spoken the thing that is right before me, as my servant Job hath. Take unto you therefore seven oxen, and seven rams, and go to my servant Job, and offer for yourselves a holocaust and my servant Job shall pray for you; his face I will accept, that folly be not imputed to you for you have not spoken right things before me, as my servant Job hath.

Lesson II ~ Job 42:9–11

So Eliphaz the Themanite, and Baldad the Suhite, and Sophar the Naamathite went, and did as the Lord had spoken to them, and the Lord accepted the face of Job. The Lord also was turned at the penance of Job, when he prayed for his friends. And the Lord gave Job twice as much as he had before. And all his brethren came to him, and all his sisters, and all that knew him before, and they ate bread with him in his house and bemoaned him, and comforted him upon all the evil that God had brought upon him. And every man gave him one ewe, and one earring of gold.

Lesson III ~ Job 42:12–16

And the Lord blessed the latter end of Job more than his beginning. And he had fourteen thousand sheep, and six thousand camels, and a thousand yoke of oxen, and a thousand she asses. And he had seven sons, and three daughters. And he called the names of one Dies, and the name of the second Cassia, and the name of the third Cornustibil.

And there were not found in all the earth women so beautiful as the daughters of Job: and their father gave them inheritance among their brethren. And Job lived after these things, a hundred and forty years, and he saw his children, and his children's children, unto the fourth generation, and he died an old man, and full of days.

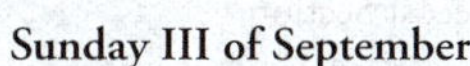

Sunday III of September

Lesson I - Tob 1:1–4

Beginning of the book of Tobias

Tobias of the tribe and city of Nephtali (which is in the upper parts of Galilee above Naasson, beyond the way that leadeth to the west, having on the right hand the city of Sephet). When he was made captive in the days of Salmanasar king of the Assyrians, even in his captivity, forsook not the way of truth, But every day gave all he could get to his brethren his fellow captives, that were of his kindred. And when he was younger than any of the tribe of Nephtali, yet did he no childish thing in his work.

Lesson II - Tob 1:5–10

Moreover when all went to the golden calves which Jeroboam king of Israel had made, he alone fled the company of all, And went to Jerusalem to the temple of the Lord, and there adored the Lord God of Israel, offering faithfully all his firstfruits, and his tithes, So that in the third year he gave all his tithes to the proselytes, and strangers. These and such like things did he observe when but a boy according to the law of God. But when he was a man, he took to wife Anna of his own tribe, and had a son by her, whom he called after his own name, And from his infancy he taught him to fear God, and to abstain from all sin.

Lesson III - Tob 1:11–15

And when by the captivity he with his wife and his son and all his tribe was come to the city of Ninive, (When all ate of the meats of the Gentiles) he kept his soul and never was defiled with their meats. And because he was mindful of the Lord with all his heart, God gave him favour in the sight of Salmanasar the king. And he gave him leave to go whithersoever he would, with liberty to do whatever he had a mind. He therefore went to all that were in captivity, and gave them wholesome admonitions.

Lesson IV

Sermon of St. Leo the Great, Pope.

Well do I know, dearly beloved, that many of you are fervent in your observance of all those practices which belong to the Christian Faith, so that you have no need to be admonished by our exhortations. For what tradition has laid down, and custom well established, is neither unknown to the learned nor neglected by the devout. But because it appertains to the priestly office to exercise the same general care over all the Church's children in all such matters as are profitable alike to the learned and to the simple (both of whom are equally dear to us), we do now exhort the both of you to celebrate, with lively faith, and all due discipline of soul and body, the Quarterly Fast, which the seventh month [that is, September] does once again bring to us in its yearly round.

Lesson V

The Ember Days of fasting are appointed to the four seasons, in order that their quarterly recurrence in the course of the year may teach us how unceasingly we need to be purified, and how, as long as we are tossed about by the changes and chances of this life, we need through fasting and alms-deeds to be cleansed from the stain of that sin which we have contracted by the frailty of our flesh and our concupiscence. Let us diminish a little, beloved, what we are accustomed to use for ourselves, in order that we have somewhat more to use for the relief of the poor and needy.

Lesson VI

The conscience of the generous can thus be made glad by the fruits of their own liberality. Whilst thou art giving happiness thou shalt receive joy. Thy love for thy neighbor is a unity with thy love for God; and he has taught us that in the unity of this twofold charity is to be found the fulfillment of all the Law and the Prophets. Further, if anyone doubt that what is given to man is offered to God, we have the saying of our Lord and Saviour, when he spoke of feeding and helping the poor: "Inasmuch as you have done it unto one of the least of these, my brethren, you have done it unto me." Wherefore, let us fast on Ember Wednesday and Friday; and on Ember Saturday let us also keep vigil at the shrine of blessed Peter the Apostle; by whose merits and prayers we believe that we shall be aided, so that we may please our merciful God in our fasting and prayer.

Lessons VII, VIII, & IX from the Sermons for After Pentecost Section

Monday III of September

Lesson I - Tob 2:1–4

From the book of Tobias

But after this, when there was a festival of the Lord, and a good dinner was prepared in Tobias's house, He said to his son: Go, and bring some of our tribe that fear God, to feast with us. And when he had gone, returning he told him, that one of the children of Israel lay slain in the street. And he forthwith leaped up from his place at the table, and left his dinner, and came fasting to the body: And taking it up carried it privately to his house, that after the sun was down, he might bury him cautiously.

Lesson II - Tob 2:8–12

Now all his neighbours blamed him, saying: Once already commandment was given for thee to be slain because of this matter, and thou didst scarce escape the sentence of death, and dost thou again bury the dead? But Tobias fearing God more than the king, carried off the bodies of them that were slain, and hid them in his house, and at midnight buried them. Now it happened one day, that being wearied with burying, he came to his house, and cast himself down by the wall and slept, And as he was sleeping, hot dung out of a swallow's nest fell upon his eyes, and he was made blind. Now this trial the Lord therefore permitted to happen to him, that an example might be given to posterity of his patience, as also of holy Job.

Lesson III - Tob 2:13–18

For whereas he had always feared God from his infancy, and kept his commandments, he repined not against God because the evil of blindness had befallen him, But continued immoveable in the fear of God, giving thanks to God all the days of his life. For as the kings insulted over holy Job: so his relations and kinsmen mocked at his life, saying: Where is thy hope, for which thou gavest alms, and buriedst the dead? But Tobias rebuked them, saying: Speak not so; For we are the children of the saints, and look for that life which God will give to those that never change their faith from him.

Tuesday III of September

Lesson I - Tob 2:19–21
From the book of Tobias

Now Anna his wife went daily to weaving work, and she brought home what she could get for their living by the labour of her hands. Whereby it came to pass, that she received a young kid, and brought it home: And when her husband heard it bleating, he said: Take heed, lest perhaps it be stolen: restore ye it to its owners, for it is not lawful for us either to eat or to touch any thing that comes by theft.

Lesson II - Tob 2:22–23; 3:1–3

At these words his wife being angry answered: It is evident thy hope is come to nothing, and thy alms now appear. And with these, and other such like words she upbraided him. Then Tobias sighed, and began to pray with tears, Saying: Thou art just, O Lord, and all thy judgments are just, and all thy ways mercy, and truth, and judgment: And now, O Lord, think of me, and take not revenge of my sins, neither remember my offenses, nor those of my parents.

Lesson III - Tob 3:4–6

For we have not obeyed thy commandments, therefore are we delivered to spoil and to captivity, and death, and are made a fable, and a reproach to all nations, amongst which thou hast scattered us. And now, O Lord, great are thy judgments, because we have not done according to thy precepts, and have not walked sincerely before thee: And now, O Lord, do with me according to thy will, and command my spirit to be received in peace: for it is better for me to die, than to live.

Ember Wednesday in September

Lesson I

From the Holy Gospel according to St. Mark (Mark 9:16–28)

At that time, one of the multitude answered and said unto Jesus:

Master, I have brought unto thee my son, which hath a dumb spirit. And so on.

Homily by St. Bede the Venerable, Priest

Concerning this possessed person whom the Lord healed, after He was come down from the mount, Mark says that he was deaf and dumb, and Matthew that he was lunatic. He was a figure of them of whom it is said: A fool changes as the moon. These are they who continue never in one stay, but change now to one sin, and now to another, waxing and waning, dumb in that they confess not the faith, deaf in that they have no ears for the word of truth. They foam at the mouth also, and pine away with folly. For it is the way with idiots, and swooners, and the stupified, to foam their spittle out at their mouths. They gnash their teeth when they are inflamed with the heat of passion. They wither up in the paralysis of sloth and live nerveless lives unbraced by any strong exercise.

Lesson II

The father says: "And I spoke to thy disciples, that they should cast him out, and they could not." Here he makes a sort of accusation against the Apostles. But that cures cannot be wrought is sometimes owing, not to the powerlessness of them that would heal, but to the want of faith in them that are to be healed as says the Lord: "According to your faith be it unto you." He answers him, and says: "O faithless generation, how long shall I be with you?" The meek and lowly One, Who, as a lamb before his shearers is dumb, so opened not His Mouth, was not wearied out of patience, nor did He break out into words of passion, but He spoke as a physician might speak, who saw that the sick man did contrary to his commands. Why should I come unto thine house? How long am I to throw away the exercise of my skill, while I order one thing and thou dost another?

Lesson III

And He said unto them: "This kind can come forth by nothing but by prayer and fasting." While He teaches the Apostles how the very worst kind of devil must be driven out, He gives unto all of us an instruction unto life, that we may know that the most grievous trials, either from unclean spirits, or from men, are to be overcome by fasting and prayer. The wrath of the Lord also, when it is kindled to take vengeance of our sins, can be turned away by this remedy only. To fast, in a general sense, is not only to abstain from meats, but to restrain oneself from all the enticements of the flesh, and from all evil passions. So also, to pray, is not only to call in words for the mercy of God, but also, in all things which we do, in earnestness of faith to worship our Maker.

Thursday III of September

Lesson I ~ Tob 12:1–4

From the book of Tobias

Then Tobias called to him his son, and said to him: What can we give to this holy man, that is come with thee? Tobias answering, said to his father: Father, what wages shall we give him? or what can be worthy of his benefits? He conducted me and brought me safe again, he received the money of Gabelus, he caused me to have my wife, and he chased from her the evil spirit, he gave joy to her parents, myself he delivered from being devoured by the fish, thee also he hath made to see the light of heaven, and we are filled with all good things through him. What can we give him sufficient for these things? But I beseech thee, my father, to desire him, that he would vouchsafe to accept one half of all things that have been brought.

Lesson II - Tob 12:5–10

So the father and the son, calling him, took him aside: and began to desire him that he would vouchsafe to accept of half of all things that they had brought. Then he said to them secretly: Bless ye the God of heaven, give glory to him in the sight of all that live, because he hath shewn his mercy to you. For it is good to hide the secret of a king: but honourable to reveal and confess the works of God. Prayer is good with fasting and alms more than to lay up treasures of gold: For alms delivereth from death, and the same is that which purgeth away sins, and maketh to find mercy and life everlasting. But they that commit sin and iniquity, are enemies to their own soul.

Lesson III - Tob 12:11–17

I discover then the truth unto you, and I will not hide the secret from you. When thou didst pray with tears, and didst bury the dead, and didst leave thy dinner, and hide the dead by day in thy house, and bury them by night, I offered thy prayer to the Lord. And because thou wast acceptable to God, it was necessary that temptation should prove thee. And now the Lord hath sent me to heal thee, and to deliver Sara thy son's wife from the devil. For I am the angel Raphael, one of the seven, who stand before the Lord. And when they had heard these things, they were troubled, and being seized with fear they fell upon the ground on their face. And the angel said to them: Peace be to you, fear not.

Ember Friday in September

Lesson I

From the Holy Gospel according to St. Luke (Luke 7:36–50)

At that time, one of the Pharisees desired that Jesus would eat with him. And He went into the Pharisee's house, and sat down to meat. And so on.

Homily by Pope St. Gregory

Of what is the Pharisee that was exalted by self-righteousness a type, but of the Jewish people? And of what the woman which was a sinner and came and wept at the Lord's feet, but of the conversion of the Gentiles? She brought an alabaster box of ointment, and stood at His feet behind Him weeping, and began to wash His Feet with tears, and did wipe them with the hairs of her head, and kissed His Feet, and anointed them with the ointment. Of us, therefore, even of us, was that woman a type, if after our sins we turn unto the Lord with all our heart, and imitate the example of her repentant grief. And of what is the ointment a type, but of the sweet savor of a good reputation? Whence also Paul says: "In every place we are unto God a sweet savour of Christ."

Lesson II

If therefore we do good works, whereby we gain for the Church the savor of good reputation, what do we do but pour ointment upon the body of the Lord? But the woman stood at the Feet of Jesus, behind Him; we stood opposite to the Feet of the Lord in that time we were in sin, and went contrary unto His ways. But when we turn again, and truly repent of our sins, we stand behind His Feet, for we follow His footsteps against Whom we once contended. The woman washed His Feet with her tears and we do in very deed the same when we show the tenderness of sympathy to any of His humbler members, when we feel with His Saints in their tribulations, when we make their woes our own.

Lesson III

She wipes the Lord's Feet with our hair when we give charity, even out of such things as we have ourselves no need of, to His holy ones, with whom we feel in their trials, insofar as our heart so sympathizes, that the bounty of our hand shows the truth of our compassion. He washes the Feet of the Redeemer but wipes them not with his hair, who feels for the sufferings of his neighbors, but nevertheless relieves them not, even out of such things as he himself has no need for. He weeps but wipes not, who offers words of tenderness, but soothes not sorrow by giving such things as be lacking. The woman kissed the Feet and we do fully the same, if we warmly love those whom out of bounty we support, so that the neediness of our neighbor is not grievous unto us, nor the destitution which we relieve a weariness to us, nor, when the hand is giving what is needful, the heart is untouched by compassion.

Ember Saturday in September

Lesson I

From the Holy Gospel according to St. Luke (Luke 13:6–17)

At that time, Jesus spoke unto the multitudes this parable: A certain man had a fig-tree planted in his vineyard, and he came and sought fruit thereon, and found none. And so on.

Homily by Pope St. Gregory

Our Lord and Redeemer speaks unto us sometimes by words, and sometimes by deeds, sometimes one thing by words, and another by deeds, and sometimes the same thing both by word and deed. In the portion of the Gospel which has this day been read, you have heard, my brethren, two things: the parable of the fig-tree and the history of the woman which was bowed together. In both is a manifestation of the Lord's mercy, but in the one by a parable, in the other by an example. But the barren fig-tree signifies the same thing as does the woman bowed together, and the patience shown to the fig-tree the same thing as does the healing of the woman bowed together.

Lesson II

What is the fig-tree a type, but of mankind? Of what is the woman bowed together by a spirit of infirmity a type, but of the same mankind? Man was originally placed in a garden like the fig-tree, and created upright like the woman, but man fell away by his own willful fault; like the fig-tree he brought forth no fruit, like the woman he ceased to stand straight. When he willfully went into sin because he would not bring forth the fruit of obedience, he lost his uprightness. The nature which had been created in the image of God, continued not in honor, but cast aside the state wherein it had been placed and made. The lord of the vineyard came thrice to the fig-tree, for God has come in hope and in warning, seeking fruit from mankind under three successive dispensations, that is to say, before the law, under the law, and under grace.

Lesson III

It came before the law, in that by natural understanding, He let all know by example of Himself, what and how they should do toward their neighbor. In the law He came teaching. After the law He came by grace, opening, manifesting His merciful Presence. But after all these three years He yet has to complain that He finds no fruit upon the fig-tree, for there are still some degraded minds which the inborn voice of the natural law does not control, which the commandments do not teach, and which the wonders of the Incarnation itself do not convert. Of what is the dresser of the vineyard a type, but of the Episcopacy? For these are they who have the government in the Church, and are therefore truly called the dressers of the Lord's vineyard.

✠

Sunday IV of September

Lesson I ~ Jdt 1:1–4

Beginning of the book of Judith

Now Arphaxad king of the Medes had brought many nations under his dominions, and he built a very strong city, which he called Ecbatana, Of stones squared and hewed: he made the walls thereof seventy cubits broad, and thirty cubits high, and the towers thereof he made a hundred cubits high. But on the square of them, each side was extended the space of twenty feet. And he made the gates thereof according to the height of the towers: And he gloried as a mighty one in the force of his army and in the glory of his chariots.

Lesson II ~ Jdt 1:5–9

Now in the twelfth year of his reign, Nabuchodonosor king of the Assyrians, who reigned in Ninive the great city, fought against Arphaxad and overcame him, In the great plain which is called Ragua, about the Euphrates, and the Tigris, and the Jadason, in the plain of Erioch the king of the Elicians. Then was the kingdom of Nabuchodonosor exalted, and his heart was elevated: and he sent to all that dwelt in

Cilicia and Damascus, and Libanus, And to the nations that are in Carmelus, and Cedar, and to the inhabitants of Galilee in the great plain of Asdrelon, And to all that were in Samaria, and beyond the river Jordan even to Jerusalem, and all the land of Jesse till you come to the borders of Ethiopia.

Lesson III ~ Jdt 1:10–12; 2:1–3

To all these Nabuchodonosor king of the Assyrians, sent messengers: But they all with one mind refused, and sent them back empty, and rejected them without honour. Then king Nabuchodonosor being angry against all that land, swore by his throne and kingdom that he would revenge himself of all those countries. In the thirteenth year of the reign of Nabuchodonosor, the two and twentieth day of the first month, the word was given out in the house of Nabuchodonosor king of the Assyrians, that he would revenge himself. And he called all the ancients, and all the governors, and his officers of war, and communicated to them the secret of his counsel: And he said that his thoughts were to bring all the earth under his empire.

Lesson IV

From the Book upon Elias and Fasting, written by St. Ambrose, Bishop

It is not for kings to drink wine, nor for princes strong drink, lest they drink and forget the law. The rulers drank wine even unto drunkenness, who planned to deliver themselves into the hand of Holofernes, captain of the host of the King of the Assyrians but the woman Judith drank not, who fasted all the days of her widowhood, saving the solemn Feast-days. She went forth in the harness of this abstinence, and overreached the whole army of the Assyrians. By the clear thought of her sobriety she took away the head of Holofernes, kept her chastity, and carried off the victory.

Lesson V

Armed with fasting, she entered the camp of the strangers; he lay soaked in wine, so that he could not feel the blow that slew him. And thus the fast of one woman overthrew the countless armies of the Assyrians. Esther also became fairer by fasting, for the Lord gave favor unto her for her sobriety. She delivered all her nation, that is, the whole people of the Jews, from the fierceness of persecution, so that she brought down the King himself under her will.

Lesson VI

Thus also (Esther) who fasted three days, and washed her body with water, found greater favor, and obtained vengeance, whereas Aman, who boasted himself at the King's table, paid the penalty of his drunkenness, even while yet he was in his cups. Fasting, therefore, is a sacrifice of reconciliation, a means of strength, whereby in the might of grace, women wax manful. Fasting knows not usury, nor the gain of the usurer; the faster's table smells not of usury, but the fast itself gives favor to them that sit at meat. A banquet is all the pleasanter after hunger, whereas by constant use it becomes unattractive, and when it is long carried on it comes to be lightly esteemed. Fasting is a good sauce for meat. The keener the appetite, the more toothsome the food.

Lessons VII, VIII, & IX from the Sermons for After Pentecost Section

Monday IV of September

Lesson I - Jdt 4:1–4

From the book of Judith

Then the children of Israel, who dwelt in the land of Juda, hearing these things, were exceedingly afraid of him. Dread and horror seized upon their minds, lest he should do the same to Jerusalem and to the temple of the Lord, that he had done to other cities and their temples. And they sent into all Samaria round about, as far as Jericho, and seized upon all the tops of the mountains: And they compassed their towns with walls, and gathered together corn for provision for war.

Lesson II - Jdt 4:5–8

And Eliachim the priest wrote to all that were over against Esdrelon, which faceth the great plain near Dothain, and to all by whom there might be a passage of way, that they should take possession of the ascents of the mountains, by which there might be any way to Jerusalem, and should keep watch where the way was narrow between the mountains. And the children of Israel did as the priest of the Lord Eliachim had appointed them, And all the people cried to the Lord with great earnestness, and they humbled their souls in fastings, and prayers, both they and their wives. And the priests put on haircloths, and they caused the little children to lie prostrate before the temple of the Lord, and the altar of the Lord they covered with haircloth.

Lesson III - Jdt 4:9–12

And they cried to the Lord the God of Israel with one accord, that their children might not be made a prey, and their wives carried off, and their cities destroyed, and their holy things profaned, and that they might not be made a reproach to the Gentiles. Then Eliachim the high priest of the Lord went about all Israel and spoke to them, Saying: Know ye that the Lord will hear your prayers, if you continue with perseverance in fastings and prayers in the sight of the Lord. Remember Moses the servant of the Lord, who overcame Amalec that trusted in his own strength, and in his power, and in his army, and in his shields, and in his chariots, and in his horsemen, not by fighting with the sword, but by holy prayers.

Tuesday IV of September

Lesson I - Jdt 8:1–4

From the book of Judith

Now it came to pass, when Judith a widow had heard these words, who was the daughter of Merari, the son of Idox, the son of Joseph, the son of Ozias, the son of Elai, the son of Jamnor, the son of Gedeon, the son of Raphaim, the son of Achitob, the son of Melehias, the son of Enan, the son of Nathanias, the son of Salathiel, the son of Simeon, the son of Ruben: And her husband was Manasses, who died in the time of the barley harvest: For he was standing over them that bound sheaves in the field and the heat came upon his head, and he died in Bethulia his own city, and was buried there with his fathers. And Judith his relict was a widow now three years and six months.

Lesson II - 8:5–8

And she made herself a private chamber in the upper part of her house, in which she abode shut up with her maids. And she wore haircloth upon her loins, and fasted all the days of her life, except the sabbaths, and new moons, and the feasts of the house of Israel. And she was exceedingly beautiful, and her husband left her great riches, and very many servants, and large possessions of herds of oxen, and flocks of sheep. And she was greatly renowned among all, because she feared the Lord very much, neither was there any one that spoke an ill word of her.

Lesson III - Jdt 8:9–11

When therefore she had heard that Ozias had promised that he would deliver up the city after the fifth day, she sent to the ancients Chabri and Charmi. And they came to her, and she said to them: What is this word, by which Ozias hath consented to give up the city to the Assyrians, if within five days there come no aid to us? And who are you that tempt the Lord?

Wednesday IV of September

Lesson I - Jdt 10:1–4

From the book of Judith

And it came to pass, when she had ceased to cry to the Lord, that she rose from the place wherein she lay prostrate before the Lord. And she called her maid, and going down into her house she took off her haircloth, and put away the garments of her widowhood, And she washed her body, and anointed herself with the best ointment, and plaited the hair of her head, and put a bonnet upon her head, and clothed herself with the garments of her gladness, and put sandals on her feet, and took her bracelets, and lilies, and earlets, and rings, and adorned herself with all her ornaments. And the Lord also gave her more beauty.

Lesson II - 10:11–12

And it came to pass, when she went down the hill, about break of day, that the watchmen of the Assyrians met her and stopped her, saying: Whence comest thou? or whither goest thou? And she answered: I am a daughter of the Hebrews, and I am fled from them, because I knew they would be made a prey to you, because they despised you, and would not of their own accord yield themselves, that they might find mercy in your sight.

Lesson III - Jdt 10:16–20

And they brought her to the tent of Holofernes, telling him of her. And when she was come into his presence, forthwith Holofernes was caught by his eyes. And his officers said to him: Who can despise the people of the Hebrews who have such beautiful women, that we should not think it worth our while for their sakes to fight against them? And Judith seeing Holofernes sitting under a canopy, which was woven of purple and gold, with emeralds and precious stones: After she had looked on his face bowed down to him, prostrating herself to the ground.

Thursday IV of September

Lesson I ~ Jdt 12:10–13

From the book of Judith

And it came to pass on the fourth day, that Holofernes made a supper for his servants, and said to Vagao his eunuch: go, and persuade that Hebrew woman, to consent of her own accord to dwell with me. For it is looked upon as shameful among the Assyrians, if a woman mock a man, by doing so as to pass free from him. Then Vagao went in to Judith, and said: Let not my good maid be afraid to go in to my lord, that she may be honoured before his face, that she may eat with him and drink wine and be merry. And Judith answered him: Who am I, that I should gainsay my lord?

Lesson II ~ 13:1–7

And when it was grown late, his servants made haste to their lodgings, and Vagao shut the chamber doors, and went his way. And they were all overcharged with wine. And Judith was alone in the chamber. But Holofernes lay on his bed, fast asleep, being exceedingly drunk. And Judith spoke to her maid to stand without before the chamber, and to watch: And Judith stood before the bed praying with tears, and the motion of her lips in silence, Saying: Strengthen me, O Lord God of Israel, and in this hour look on the works of my hands, that as thou hast promised, thou mayst raise up Jerusalem thy city: and that I may bring to pass that which I have purposed, having a belief that it might be done by thee.

Lesson III ~ Jdt 13:8–11

And when she had said this, she went to the pillar that was at his bed's head, and loosed his sword that hung tied upon it. And when she had drawn it out, she took him by the hair of his head, and said: Strengthen me, O Lord God, at this hour. And she struck twice upon his neck, and out off his head, and took off his canopy from the pillars, and rolled away his headless body. And after a while she went out, and delivered the head of Holofernes to her maid, and bade her put it into her wallet.

Friday IV of September

Lesson I ~ Jdt 15:1–3

From the book of Judith

And when all the army heard that Holofernes was beheaded, courage and counsel fled from them, and being seized with trembling and fear they thought only to save themselves by flight: So that no one spoke to his neighbor, but hanging down the head, leaving all things behind, they made haste to escape from the Hebrews, who, as they heard, were coming armed upon them, and fled by the ways of the fields, and the paths of the hills. So the children of Israel seeing them fleeing, followed after them. And they went down sounding with trumpets and shouting after them.

Lesson II ~ 15:5–7

And Ozias sent messengers through all the cities and countries of Israel. And every country, and every city, sent their chosen young men armed after them, and they pursued them with the edge of the sword until they came to the extremities of their confines. And the rest that were in Bethulia went into the camp of the Assyrians, and took away the spoils, which the Assyrians in their flight had left behind them, and they were laden exceedingly.

Lesson III ~ Jdt 15:9–12

And Joachim the high priest came from Jerusalem to Bethulia with all his ancients to see Judith. And when she was come out to him, they all blessed her with one voice, saying: Thou art the glory of Jerusalem, thou art the joy of Israel, thou art the honour of our people: For thou hast done manfully, and thy heart has been strengthened, because thou hast loved chastity, and after thy husband hast not known any other: therefore also the hand of the Lord hath strengthened thee, and therefore thou shalt be blessed for ever. And all the people said: So be it, so be it.

Saturday IV of September

Lesson I ~ Jdt 16:22–23

From the book of Judith

And it came to pass after these things, that all the people, after the victory, came to Jerusalem to adore the Lord: and as soon as they were purified, they all offered holocausts, and vows, and their promises. And Judith offered for an anathema of oblivion all the arms of Holofernes, which the people gave her, and the canopy that she had taken away out of his chamber.

Lesson II ~ 16:24–27

And the people were joyful in the sight of the sanctuary, and for three months the joy of this victory was celebrated with Judith. And after those days every man returned to his house, and Judith was made great in Bethulia, and she was most renowned in all the land of Israel. And chastity was joined to her virtue, so that she knew no man all the days of her life, after the death of Manasses her husband. And on festival days she came forth with great glory.

Lesson III ~ Jdt 16:28–31

And she abode in her husband's house a hundred and five years, and made her handmaid free, and she died, and was buried with her husband in Bethulia. And all the people mourned for seven days. And all the time of her life there was none that troubled Israel, nor many years after her death. But the day of the festivity of this victory is received by the Hebrews in the number of holy days, and is religiously observed by the Jews from that time until this day.

Sunday V of September

(If not the Sunday closest to Oct 1)

Lesson I - Esth 1:1–4

Beginning of the book of Esther

In the days of Assuerus, who reigned from India to Ethiopia over a hundred and twenty-seven provinces: When he sat on the throne of his kingdom, the city Susan was the capital of his kingdom. Now in the third year of his reign he made a great feast for all the princes, and for his servants, for the most mighty of the Persians, and the nobles of the Medes, and the governors of the provinces in his sight, That he might shew the riches of the glory of his kingdom, and the greatness, and boasting of his power, for a long time, to wit, for a hundred and fourscore days.

Lesson II - Esth 1:5–6

And when the days of the feast were expired, he invited all the people that were found in Susan, from the greatest to the least: and commanded a feast to be made seven days in the court of the garden, and of the wood, which was planted by the care and the hand of the king. And there were hung up on every side sky coloured, and green, and violet hangings, fastened with cords of silk, and of purple, which were put into rings of ivory, and were held up with marble pillars. The beds also were of gold and silver, placed in order upon a floor paved with porphyry and white marble: which was embellished with painting of wonderful variety.

Lesson III - Esth 1:7–9

And they that were invited, drank in golden cups, and the meats were brought in diverse vessels one after another. Wine also in abundance and of the best was presented, as was worthy of a king's magnificence. Neither was there any one to compel them to drink that were not willing, but as the king had appointed, who set over every table one of his nobles, that every man might take what he would. Also Vasthi the queen made a feast for the women in the palace, where king Assuerus was used to dwell.

Lesson IV

From the Book On Duties written by St. Ambrose, Bishop

What did Queen Esther do? Did she not, to save her people from danger (a beautiful and noble object) put herself in jeopardy of death, and face the anger of the cruel King? The King of the Persians, cruel and violent as he was, nevertheless, thought it seemly to show grace unto him that told him of the plot that was made against him, to free the people from bondage, and to deliver them from death, but not to spare him that had persuaded such iniquity. In the end he went up to the gallows, whom he had held second only to himself, and chiefest among all his friends, because he found himself dishonored through his false counsels.

Lesson V

That true friendship, which cares for honor, cares less for riches, or dignities, or power than for itself, but for honor before itself. Such was the friendship of Jonathan, which caused him to risk the anger of his father, and danger to himself. Such was the friendship of Achimelech, who chose to earn death for himself by giving relief to David, rather than to betray the outlaw. But before honor nothing is to be put, and friendship must not be allowed to outrun it, even as we are warned by the Scriptures.

Lesson VI

The Philosophers have started diverse questions whether friendship can or cannot justify disloyalty to a man's own country, whether friendship can, or cannot justify serving a friend at the cost of breach of faith. Scripture indeed says "A man that bears false witness against his neighbor, is a maul, and a sword, and a sharp arrow." But mark that what is here condemned is not witness by itself, but false witness. How if a man be compelled to give such witness, for the sake of God or for the sake of his country? Ought friendship to outweigh religion? Is not to say this, as much as to say that a sinful weakness is to outweigh a duty?

Lessons VII, VIII, & IX from the Sermons for After Pentecost Section

Monday V of September

Lesson I ~ Esth 2:5–7

From the book of Esther

There was a man in the city of Susan, a Jew, named Mardochai, the son of Jair, the son of Semei, the son of Cis, of the race of Jemini, Who had been carried away from Jerusalem at the time that Nabuchodonosor king of Babylon carried away Jechonias king of Juda, And he had brought up his brother's daughter Edissa, who by another name was called Esther: now she had lost both her parents: and was exceeding fair and beautiful. And her father and mother being dead, Mardochai adopted her for his daughter.

Lesson II ~ Esth 2:8–11

And when the king's ordinance was noised abroad, and according to his commandment many beautiful virgins were brought to Susan, and were delivered to Egeus the eunuch: Esther also among the rest of the maidens was delivered to him to be kept in the number of the women. And she pleased him, and found favour in his sight. And he commanded the eunuch to hasten the women's ornaments, and to deliver to her her part, and seven of the most beautiful maidens of the king's house, and to adorn and deck out both her and her waiting maids. And she would not tell him her people nor her country. For

Mardochai had charged her to say nothing at all of that: And he walked every day before the court of the house, in which the chosen virgins were kept, having a care for Esther's welfare, and desiring to know what would befall her.

Lesson III ~ Esth 2:15–17

And as the time came orderly about, the day was at hand, when Esther, the daughter of Abihail the brother of Mardochai, whom he had adopted for his daughter, was to go in to the king. But she sought not women's ornaments, but whatsoever Egeus the eunuch the keeper of the virgins had a mind, he gave her to adorn her. For she was exceeding fair, and her incredible beauty made her appear agreeable and amiable in the eyes of all. So she was brought to the chamber of king Assuerus the tenth month, which is called Tebeth, in the seventh year of his reign. And the king loved her more than all the women, and she had favour and kindness before him above all the women, and he set the royal crown on her head, and made her queen instead of Vasthi.

Tuesday V of September

Lesson I ~ Esth 3:1–3

From the book of Esther

After these things, king Assuerus advanced Aman, the son of Amadathi, who was of the race of Agag: and he set his throne above all the princes that were with him. And all the king's servants, that were at the doors of the palace, bent their knees, and worshipped Aman: for so the emperor had commanded them, only Mardochai did not bend his knee, nor worship him. And the king's servants that were chief at the doors of the palace, said to him: Why dost thou alone not observe the king's commandment?

Lesson II ~ Esth 3:4–6

And when they were saying this often, and he would not hearken to them; they told Aman, desirous to know whether he would continue in his resolution: for he had told them that he was a Jew. Now when Aman had heard this, and had proved by experience that Mardochai did not bend his knee to him, nor worship him, he was exceeding angry. And he counted it nothing to lay his hands upon Mardochai alone: for he had heard that he was of the nation of the Jews, and he chose rather to destroy all the nation of the Jews that were in the kingdom of Assuerus.

Lesson III ~ Esth 3:6–7

And he counted it nothing to lay his hands upon Mardochai alone: for he had heard that he was of the nation of the Jews, and he chose rather to destroy all the nation of the Jews that were in the kingdom of Assuerus. In the first month (which is called Nisan) in the twelfth year a of the reign of Assuerus, the lot was cast into an urn, which in Hebrew is called Phur, before Aman, on what day and what month the nation of the Jews should be destroyed: and there came out the twelfth month, which is called Adar.

Wednesday V of September

Lesson I ~ Esth 4:1–5

From the book of Esther

Now when Mardochai had heard these things, he rent his garments, and put on sackcloth, strewing ashes on his head: and he cried with a loud voice in the street in the midst of the city, shewing the anguish of his mind. And he came lamenting in this manner even to the gate of the palace: for no one clothed with sackcloth might enter the king's court. And in all provinces, towns, and places, to which the king's cruel edict was come, there was great mourning among the Jews, with fasting, wailing, and weeping, many using sackcloth and ashes for their bed. Then Esther's maids and her eunuchs went in, and told her. And when she heard it she was in a consternation: and she sent a garment, to clothe him, and to take away the sackcloth: but he would not receive it. And she called for Athach the eunuch, whom the king had appointed to attend upon her, and she commanded him to go to Mardochai, and learn of him why he did this.

Lesson II ~ Esth 4:6–11

And Athach going out went to Mardochai, who was standing in the street of the city, before the palace gate: And Mardochai told him all that had happened, how Aman had promised to pay money into the king's treasures, to have the Jews destroyed. He gave him also a copy of the edict which was hanging up in Susan, that he should shew it to the queen, and admonish her to go in to the king, and to entreat him for her people. And Athach went back and told Esther all that Mardochai had said. She answered him, and bade him say to Mardochai: All the king's servants, and all the provinces that are under his dominion, know, that whosoever, whether man or woman, comes into the king's inner court, who is not called for, is immediately to be put to death without any delay: except the king shall hold out the golden sceptre to him, in token of clemency, that so he may live. How then can I go in to the king, who for these thirty days now have not been called unto him?

Lesson III ~ Esth 4:12–17

And when Mardochai had heard this, He sent word to Esther again, saying: Think not that thou mayst save thy life only, because thou art in the king's house, more than all the Jews: For if thou wilt now hold thy peace, the Jews shall be delivered by some other occasion: and thou, and thy father's house shall perish. And who knoweth whether thou art not therefore come to the kingdom, that thou mightest be ready in such a time as this? And again Esther sent to Mardochai in these words: Go, and gather together all the Jews whom thou shalt find in Susan, and pray ye for me. Neither eat nor drink for three days and three nights: and I with my handmaids will fast in like manner, and then I will go in to the king, against the law, not being called, and expose myself to death and to danger. So Mardochai went, and did all that Esther had commanded him.

Thursday V of September

Lesson I - Esth 5:1–5

From the book of Esther

And on the third day Esther put on her royal apparel, and stood in the inner court of the king's house, over against the king's hall: now he sat upon his throne in the hall of the palace, over against the door of the house. And when he saw Esther the queen standing, she pleased his eyes, and he held out toward her the golden sceptre, which he held in his hand: and she drew near, and kissed the top of his sceptre. And the king said to her: What wilt then, queen Esther? what is thy request? if thou shouldst even ask one half of the kingdom, it shall be given to thee. But she answered: If it please the king. I beseech thee to come to me this day, and Aman with thee to the banquet which I have prepared. And the king said forthwith: Call ye Aman quickly, that he may obey Esther's will. So the king and Aman came to the banquet which the queen had prepared for them.

Lesson II - Esth 5:9–13

So Aman went out that day joyful and merry. And when he saw Mardochai sitting before the gate of the palace, and that he not only did not rise up to honour him, but did not so much as move from the place where he sat, he was exceedingly angry: But dissembling his anger, and returning into his house, he called together to him his friends, and Zares his wife: And he declared to them the greatness of his riches, and the multitude of his children, and with how great glory the king had advanced him above all his princes and servants. And after this he said: Queen Esther also hath invited no other to the banquet with the king, but me: and with her I am also to dine to morrow with the king: And whereas I have all these things, I think I have nothing, so long as I see Mardochai the Jew sitting before the king's gate.

Lesson III - Esth 5:14

Then Zares his wife, and the rest of his friends answered him: Order a great beam to be prepared, fifty cubits high, and in the morning speak to the king, that Mardochai may be hanged upon it, and so thou shalt go full of joy with the king to the banquet. The counsel pleased him, and he commanded a high gibbet to be prepared.

Friday V of September

Lesson I - Esth 6:1–5

From the book of Esther

That night the king passed without sleep, and he commanded the histories and chronicles of former times to be brought him. And when they were reading them before him, They came to that place where it was written, how Mardochai had discovered the treason of Bagathan and Thares the eunuchs, who sought to kill king Assuerus. And when the king heard this, he said: What honour and reward hath Mardochai received for this fidelity? His servants and ministers said to him: He hath received no reward at all. And the king said immediately: Who is in the court? for Aman was coming in to the inner court of the king's house, to speak to the king, that he might order Mardochai to be hanged upon the gibbet which was prepared for him. The servants answered: Aman standeth in the court, and the king said: Let him come in.

Lesson II - Esth 6:6–9

And when he was come in, he said to him: What ought to be done to the man whom the king is desirous to honour? But Aman thinking in his heart, and supposing that the king would honour no other but himself, Answered: The man whom the king desireth to honour, Ought to be clothed with the king's apparel, and to be set upon the horse that the king rideth upon, and to have the royal crown upon his head, And let the first of the king's princes and nobles hold his horse, and going through the street of the city, proclaim before him and say: Thus shall he be honoured, whom the king hath a mind to honour.

Lesson III - Esth 6:10–13

And the king said to him: Make haste and take the robe and the horse, and do as thou hast spoken to Mardochai the Jew, who sitteth before the gates of the palace. Beware thou pass over any of those things which thou hast spoken. So Aman took the robe and the horse, and arraying Mardochai in the street of the city, and setting him on the horse, went before him, and proclaimed: This honour is he worthy of, whom the king hath a mind to honour. But Mardochai returned to the palace gate: and Aman made haste to go to his house, mourning and having his head covered: And he told Zares his wife, and his friends, all that had befallen him. And the wise men whom he had in counsel, and his wife answered him: If Mardochai be of the seed of the Jews, before whom thou hast begun to fall, thou canst not resist him, but thou shalt fall in his sight.

Saturday V of September

Lesson I - Esth 7:1–4

From the book of Esther

So the king and Aman went in, to drink with the queen. And the king said to her again the second day, after he was warm with wine: What is thy petition, Esther, that it may be granted thee? and what wilt thou have done: although thou ask the half of my kingdom, thou shalt have it. Then she answered: If I have found Favour in thy sight, O king, and if it please thee, give me my life for which I ask, and my people for which I request. For we are given up, I and my people, to be destroyed, to be slain, and to perish. And would God we were sold for bondmen and bondwomen: the evil might be borne with, and I would have mourned in silence: but now we have an enemy, whose cruelty redoundeth upon the king.

Lesson II - Esth 7:5–7

And king Assuerus answered and said: Who is this, and of what power, that he should do these things? And Esther said: It is this Aman that is our adversary and most wicked enemy. Aman hearing this was forthwith astonished, not being able to bear the countenance of the king and of the queen. But the king being angry rose up, and went from the place of the banquet into the garden set with trees. Aman also rose up to entreat Esther the queen for his life, for he understood that evil was prepared for him by the king.

Lesson III ~ Esth 7:8–10

And when the king came back out of the garden set with trees, and entered into the place of the banquet, he found Aman was fallen upon the bed on which Esther lay, and he said: He will force the queen also in my presence, in my own house. The word was not yet gone out of the king's mouth, and immediately they covered his face. And Harbona, one of the eunuchs that stood waiting on the king, said: Behold the gibbet which he hath prepared for Mardochai, who spoke for the king, standeth in Aman's house, being fifty cubits high. And the king said to him: Hang him upon it. So Aman was hanged on the gibbet, which he had prepared for Mardochai: and the king's wrath ceased.

SUNDAYS OF OCTOBER

Sunday I of October

Lesson I ~ 1 Mac 1:1–7

Beginning of the first book of Machabees

Now it came to pass, after that Alexander the son of Philip the Macedonian, who first reigned in Greece, coming out of the land of Cethim, had overthrown Darius king of the Persians and Medes: He fought many battles, and took the strong holds of all, and slew the kings of the earth: And he went through even to the ends of the earth, and took the spoils of many nations: and the earth was quiet before him. And he gathered a power, and a very strong army: and his heart was exalted and lifted up. And he subdued countries of nations, and princes: and they became tributaries to him. And after these things, he fell down upon his bed, and knew that he should die. And he called his servants the nobles that were brought up with him from his youth: and he divided his kingdom among them, while he was yet alive.

Lesson II ~ 1 Mac 1:8–11

And Alexander reigned twelve years, and he died. And his servants made themselves kings every one in his place: And they all put crowns upon themselves after his death, and their sons after them many years, and evils were multiplied in the earth. And there came out of them a wicked root, Antiochus the Illustrious, the son of king Antiochus, who had been a hostage at Rome: and he reigned in the hundred and thirty-seventh year of the kingdom of the Greeks.

Lesson III ~ 1 Mac 1:12–16

In those days there went out of Israel wicked men, and they persuaded many, saying: Let us go, and make a covenant with the heathens that are round about us: for since we departed from them, many evils have befallen us. And the word seemed good in their eyes. And some of the people determined to do this, and went to the king: and he gave them license to do after the ordinances of the heathens. And they built a place of exercise in Jerusalem, according to the laws of the nations: And they made themselves prepuces, and departed from the holy covenant, and joined themselves to the heathens, and were sold to do evil.

Lesson IV

From the Book upon Duties written by St. Ambrose, Bishop

There may perchance be some who are so blinded by the glory of war as to think there is no valor but warlike valor, and that the reason why I have taken up other subjects is that among us there is no warlike valor whereof to speak. But what was the valor of Josue the son of Nun, when in one battle he laid low five nations, and took prisoners their kings when he was fighting against the Gibeonites, and feared lest the closing in of night should cut short his victory, he cried aloud in the greatness of his mind and of his faith? And he said, in the sight of Israel: "Sun stand thou still over against Gibeon, and thou Moon over against the valley of Ajalon" and the sun stood still, and the moon stayed, until the people had avenged themselves upon their enemies. Gideon, with three hundred men, won the victory over the vast people, and the savage enemy. The lad Jonathan waxed valiant in fight.

Lesson V

Shall I speak of the Machabees? But before I speak of them, I will speak of their fathers, even of them who, when they were ready to fight for the Temple of God and for their own rights, were assailed by a trick of their enemies upon the Sabbath day, and were willing rather to offer their bodies naked to the sword than to strike back again and break the Sabbath, and so they gave themselves up gladly to death but when the Machabees bethought them that the whole nation might thus perish, avenged the innocent blood of their brethren even upon the Sabbath day when they were provoked to battle, and afterward, when King Antiochus had been stirred up to make war on them by his generals, even Lysias and Nicanor and Gorgias, he and his Eastern and Assyrian forces were so crushed that forty eight thousand were laid low on the field by three thousand.

Lesson VI

What the valor of Judas the Machabean leader was we may judge by the type of one of his men. When Eleazar saw an elephant bigger than the rest and adorned with the King's harness, he thought that the King was riding thereon, and he threw himself into the midst of the enemy, and cast away his shield and slew on either hand until he was come to the beast, and ran underneath it, and killed it with his sword, and so the beast fell upon Eleazar and crushed him, and he died. What valor was here? To begin with, he feared not to die, and when the enemy surrounded him he cast himself into the midst of their ranks, pierced their column, and becoming all the fiercer through his mockery of death, he threw away his shield and upheld with both hands the huge bulk of the wounded monster beneath which he had gone the better to spite it, so that when he died with it he might well have been said not so much to be crushed as to be swallowed up in victory.

Lessons VII, VIII, & IX
from the Sermons for After Pentecost Section

Monday I of October

Lesson I ~ 1 Mac 1:17–20

From the first book of Machabees

And the kingdom was established before Antiochus, and he had a mind to reign over the land of Egypt, that he might reign over two kingdoms. And he entered into Egypt with a great multitude, with chariots and elephants, and horsemen, and a great number of ships: And he made war against Ptolemy king of Egypt, but Ptolemy was afraid at his presence, and fled, and many were wounded unto death. And he took the strong cities in the land of Egypt: and he took the spoils of the land of Egypt.

Lesson II ~ 1 Mac 1:21–23

And after Antiochus had ravaged Egypt in the hundred and forty-third year, he returned and went up against Israel. And he went up to Jerusalem with a great multitude. And he proudly entered into the sanctuary, and took away the golden altar, and the candlestick of light, and all the vessels thereof, and the table of proposition, and the pouring vessels, and the vials, and the little mortars of gold, and the veil, and the crowns, and the golden ornament that was before the temple: and he broke them all in pieces.

Lesson III ~ 1 Mac 1:24–29

And he took the silver and gold, and the precious vessels: and he took the hidden treasures which he found: and when he had taken all away he departed into his own country. And he made a great slaughter of men, and spoke very proudly. And there was great mourning in Israel, and in every place where they were. And the princes, and the ancients mourned, and the virgins and the young men were made feeble, and the beauty of the women was changed. Every bridegroom took up lamentation: and the bride that set in the marriage bed, mourned: And the land was moved for the inhabitants thereof, and all the house of Jacob was covered with confusion.

Tuesday I of October

Lesson I ~ 1 Mac 2:1–6

From the first book of Machabees

In those days arose Mathathias the son of John, the son of Simeon, a priest of the sons of Joarib, from Jerusalem, and he abode in the mountain of Modin. And he had five sons: John who was surnamed Gaddis: And Simon, who was surnamed Thasi: And Judas, who was called Machabeus: And Eleazar, who was surnamed Abaron: and Jonathan, who was surnamed Apphus. These saw the evils that were done in the people of Juda, and in Jerusalem.

Lesson II ~ 1 Mac 2:7–10

And Mathathias said: Woe is me, wherefore was I born to see the ruin of my people, and the ruin of the holy city, and to dwell there, when it is given into the hands of the enemies? The holy places are come into the hands of strangers: her temple is become as a man without honour. The vessels of her glory are carried away captive: her old men are murdered in the streets, and her young men are fallen by the sword of the enemies. What nation hath not inherited her kingdom, and gotten of her spoils?

Lesson III ~ 1 Mac 2:14–16

And Mathathias and his sons rent their garments, and they covered themselves with haircloth, and made great lamentation. And they that were sent from king Antiochus came thither, to compel them that were fled into the city of Modin, to sacrifice, and to burn incense, and to depart from the law of God. And many of the people of Israel consented, and came to them: but Mathathias and his sons stood firm.

Wednesday I of October

Lesson I ~ 1 Mac 2:19–22

From the first book of Machabees

Then Mathathias answered, and said with a loud voice: Although all nations obey king Antiochus, so as to depart every man from the service of the law of his fathers, and consent to his commandments: I and my sons, and my brethren will obey the law of our fathers. God be merciful unto us: it is not profitable for us to forsake the law, and the justices of God: We will not hearken to the words of king Antiochus, neither will we sacrifice, and transgress the commandments of our law, to go another way.

Lesson II ~ 1 Mac 2:23–26

Now as he left off speaking these words, there came a certain Jew in the sight of all to sacrifice to the idols upon the altar in the city of Modin, according to the king's commandment. And Mathathias saw and was grieved, and his reins trembled, and his wrath was kindled according to the judgment of the law, and running upon him he slew him upon the altar: Moreover the man whom king Antiochus had sent, who compelled them to sacrifice, he slew at the same time, and pulled down the altar. And shewed zeal for the law, as Phinees did by Zamri the son of Salomi.

Lesson III ~ 1 Mac 2:27–30

And Mathathias cried out in the city with a loud voice, saying: Every one that hath zeal for the law, and maintaineth the testament, let him follow me. So he, and his sons fled into the mountains, and left all that they had in the city. Then many that sought after judgment, and justice, went down into the desert: And they abode there, they and their children, and their wives, and their cattle: because afflictions increased upon them.

Thursday I of October

Lesson I ~ 1 Mac 2:49–54

From the first book of Machabees

Now the days drew near that Mathathias should die, and he said to his sons: Now hath pride and chastisement gotten strength, and the time of destruction, and the wrath of indignation: Now therefore, O my sons, be ye zealous for the law, and give your lives for the covenant of your fathers. And call to remembrance the works of the fathers, which they have done in their generations: and you shall receive great glory, and an everlasting name. Was not Abraham found faithful in temptation, and it was reputed to him unto justice? Joseph in the time of his distress kept the commandment, and he was made lord of Egypt. Phinees our father, by being fervent in the zeal of God, received the covenant of an everlasting priesthood.

Lesson II ~ 1 Mac 2:55–63

Jesus, whilst he fulfilled the word, was made ruler in Israel. Caleb, for bearing witness before the congregation, received an inheritance. David by his mercy obtained the throne of an everlasting kingdom. Elias, while he was full of zeal for the law, was taken up into heaven. Ananias and Azarias and Misael by believing, were delivered out of the flame. Daniel in his innocency was delivered out of the mouth of the lions. And thus consider through all generations: that none that trust in him fail in strength. And fear not the words of a sinful man, for his glory is dung, and worms: To day he is lifted up, and to morrow he shall not be found, because he is returned into his earth; and his thought is come to nothing.

Lesson III ~ 1 Mac 2:64–69

You therefore, my sons, take courage, and behave manfully in the law: for by it you shall be glorious. And behold, I know that your brother Simon is a man of counsel: give ear to him always, and he shall be a father to you. And Judas Machabeus who is valiant and strong from his youth up, let him be the leader of your army, and he shall manage the war of the people. And you shall take to you all that observe the law: and revenge ye the wrong of your people. Render to the Gentiles their reward, and take heed to the precepts of the law. And he blessed them, and was joined to his fathers.

Friday I of October

Lesson I ~ 1 Mac 2:70; 3:1–3; 3:5–6

From the first book of Machabees

And he died in the hundred and forty-sixth year: and he was buried by his sons in the sepulchres of his fathers in Modin, and all Israel mourned for him with great mourning. Then his son Judas, called Machabeus, rose up in his stead. And all his brethren helped him, and all they that had joined themselves to his father, and they fought with cheerfulness the battle of Israel. And he got his people great honour, and put on a breastplate as a giant, and girt his warlike armour about him in battles, and protected the camp with his sword. And he pursued the wicked and sought them out, and them that troubled his people he burnt with fire: And his enemies were driven away for fear of him, and all the workers of iniquity were troubled: and salvation prospered in his hand.

Lesson II ~ 1 Mac 3:7–12

And he grieved many kings, and made Jacob glad with his works, and his memory is blessed for ever. And he went through the cities of Juda, and destroyed the wicked out of them, and turned away wrath from Israel. And he was renowned even to the utmost part of the earth, and he gathered them that were perishing. And Apollonius gathered together the Gentiles, and a numerous and great army from Samaria, to make war against Israel. And Judas understood it, and went forth to meet him: and he overthrew him, and killed him: and many fell down slain, the rest fled away. And he took their spoils, and Judas took the sword of Apollonius, and fought with it all his lifetime.

Lesson III - 1 Mac 3:25–28

And the fear of Judas and of his brethren, and the dread of them fell upon all the nations round about them. And his fame came to the king, and all nations told of the battles of Judas. Now when king Antiochus heard these words, he was angry in his mind: and he sent and gathered the forces of all his kingdom, an exceeding strong army. And he opened his treasury, and gave out pay to the army for a year: and he commanded them, that they should be ready for all things.

Saturday I of October

Lesson I - 1 Mac 3:42–45

From the first book of Machabees

And Judas and his brethren saw that evils were multiplied, and that the armies approached to their borders: and they knew the orders the king had given to destroy the people and utterly abolish them. And they said every man to his neighbour: Let us raise up the low condition of our people, and let us fight for our people, and our sanctuary. And the assembly was gathered that they might be ready for battle: and that they might pray, and ask mercy and compassion. Now Jerusalem was not inhabited, but was like a desert: there was none of her children that went in or out: and the sanctuary was trodden down: and the children of strangers were in the castle, there was the habitation of the Gentiles: and joy was taken away from Jacob, and the pipe and harp ceased there.

Lesson II - 1 Mac 3:46–53

And they assembled together, and came to Maspha over against Jerusalem: for in Maspha was a place of prayer heretofore in Israel. And they fasted that day, and put on haircloth, and put ashes upon their heads: and they rent their garments: And they laid open the books of the law, in which the Gentiles searched for the likeness of their idols: And they brought the priestly ornaments, and the firstfruits and tithes, and stirred up the Nazarites that had fulfilled their days: And they cried with a loud voice toward heaven, saying: What shall we do with these, and whither shall we carry them? For thy holies are trodden down, and are profaned, and thy priests are in mourning, and are brought low. And behold the nations are come together against us to destroy us: thou knowest what they intend against us. How shall we be able to stand before their face, unless thou, O God, help us?

Lesson III - 1 Mac 3:54–60

Then they sounded with trumpets, and cried out with a loud voice. And after this Judas appointed captains over the people, over thousands, and over hundreds, and over fifties, and over tens. And he said to them that were building houses, or had betrothed wives, or were planting vineyards, or were fearful, that they should return every man to his house, according to the law. So they removed the camp, and pitched on the south side of Emmaus. And Judas said: Gird yourselves, and be valiant men, and be ready against the morning, that you may fight with these nations that are assembled against us to destroy us and our sanctuary. For it is better for us to die in battle, than to see the evils of our nation, and of the holies: Nevertheless as it shall be the will of God in heaven so be it done.

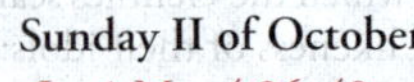

Sunday II of October

Lesson I ~ 1 Mac 4:36–40

From the first book of Machabees

Then Judas, and his brethren said: Behold our enemies are discomfited: let us go up now to cleanse the holy places and to repair them. And all the army assembled together, and they went up into mount Sion. And they saw the sanctuary desolate, and the altar profaned, and the gates burnt, and shrubs growing up in the courts as in a forest, or on the mountains, and the chambers joining to the temple thrown down. And they rent their garments, and made great lamentation, and put ashes on their heads: And they fell face down to the ground on their faces, and they sounded with the trumpets of alarm, and they cried towards heaven.

Lesson II ~ 1 Mac 4:41–46

Then Judas appointed men to fight against them that were in the castle, till they had cleansed the holy places. And he chose priests without blemish, whose will was set upon the law of God: And they cleansed the holy places, and took away the stones that had been defiled into an unclean place. And he considered about the altar of holocausts that had been profaned, what he should do with it. And a good counsel came into their minds, to pull it down: lest it should be a reproach to them, because the Gentiles had defiled it; so they threw it down. And they laid up the stones in the mountain of the temple in a convenient place, till there should come a prophet, and give answer concerning them.

Lesson III ~ 1 Mac 4:47–51

Then they took whole stones according to the law, and built a new altar according to the former: And they built up the holy places, and the things that were within the temple: and they sanctified the temple, and the courts. And they made new holy vessels, and brought in the candlestick, and the altar of incense, and the table into the temple. And they put incense upon the altar, and lighted up the lamps that were upon the candlestick, and they gave light in the temple. And they set the loaves upon the table, and hung up the veils, and finished all the works that they had begun to make.

Lesson IV

From *The City of God* by St. Augustine, Bishop

The Jewish nation no doubt became worse after it ceased to have prophets, just at the very time when, on the rebuilding of the temple after the captivity in Babylon, it hoped to become better. For so, indeed, did that carnal people understand what was foretold by Aggeus the prophet, saying, "The glory of this latter house shall be greater than that of the former." Now, that this is said of the New Testament, he showed a little above, where he says, evidently promising Christ, "And I will move all nations, and the desired One shall come to all nations."

Lesson V

For by such chosen ones of the nations there is built, through the New Testament, with living stones, a house of God far more glorious than that temple was which was constructed by king Solomon, and rebuilt after the captivity. For this reason, then, that nation had no prophets from that time, but was afflicted with many plagues by kings of alien race, and by the Romans themselves, lest they should fancy that this prophecy of Aggeus was fulfilled by that rebuilding of the temple. For not long after, on the arrival of Alexander, it was subdued, when, although there was no pillaging because they dared not resist him, and thus, being very easily subdued, received him peaceably, yet the glory of that house was not so great as it was when under the free power of their own kings.

Lesson VI

Then Ptolemy son of Lagus, after Alexander's death carried them captive into Egypt. His successor, Ptolemy Philadelphus, most benevolently dismissed them; and by him it was brought about, as I have narrated a little before, that we should have the Septuagint version of the Scriptures. Then they were crushed by the wars which are explained in the books of the Machabees. Afterward they were taken captive by Ptolemy king of Alexandria, who was called Epiphanes. Then Antiochus king of Syria compelled them by many and most grievous evils to worship idols, and filled the temple itself with the sacrilegious superstitions of the Gentiles. Yet their most vigorous leader Judas, who is also called Maccabæus, after beating the generals of Antiochus, cleansed it from all that defilement of idolatry.

Lessons VII, VIII, & IX
from the Sermons for After
Pentecost Section

Monday II of October

Lesson I ~ 1 Mac 4:52–55

From the first book of Machabees

And they arose before the morning on the five and twentieth day of the ninth month (which is the month of Casleu) in the hundred and forty-eighth year. And they offered sacrifice according to the law upon the new altar of holocausts which they had made. According to the time, and according to the day wherein the heathens had defiled it, in the same was it dedicated anew with canticles, and harps, and lutes, and cymbals. And all the people fell upon their faces, and adored, and blessed up to heaven, him that had prospered them.

Lesson II ~ 1 Mac 4:56–59

And they kept the dedication of the altar eight days, and they offered holocausts with joy, and sacrifices of salvation, and of praise. And they adorned the front of the temple with crowns of gold, and escutcheons, and they renewed the gates, and the chambers, and hanged doors upon them. And there was exceeding great joy among the people, and the reproach of the Gentiles was turned away. And Judas, and his brethren, and all the church of Israel decreed, that the day of the dedication of the altar should be kept in its season from year to year for eight days, from the five and twentieth day of the month of Casleu, with joy and gladness.

Lesson III ~ 1 Mac 4:60–61

They built up also at that time mount Sion, with high walls, and strong towers round about, lest the Gentiles should at any time come, and tread it down as they did before. And he placed a garrison there to keep it, and he fortified it to secure Bethsura, that the people might have a defence against Idumea.

Tuesday II of October

Lesson I ~ 1 Mac 5:1–5

From the first book of Machabees

Now it came to pass, when the nations round about heard that the altar and the sanctuary were built up as before, that they were exceeding angry. And they thought to destroy the generation of Jacob that were among them, and they began to kill some of the people, and to persecute them. Then Judas fought against the children of Esau in Idumea, and them that were in Acrabathane: because they beset the Israelites around about, and he made a great slaughter of them. And he remembered the malice of the children of Bean: who were a snare and a stumblingblock to the people, by lying in wait for them in the way. And they were shut up by him in towers, and he set upon them, and devoted them to utter destruction, and burnt their towers with fire, and all that were in them.

Lesson II ~ 1 Mac 5:6–9

Then he passed over to the children of Ammon, where he found a mighty power, and much people, and Timotheus was their captain: And he fought many battles with them, and they were discomfited in their sight, and he smote them: And he took the city of Gazer and her towns, and returned into Judea. And the Gentiles that were in Galaad, assembled themselves together against the Israelites that were in their quarters to destroy them: and they fled into the fortress of Datheman.

Lesson III ~ 1 Mac 5:10–13

And they sent letters to Judas and his brethren, saying, The heathens that are round about are gathered together against us, to destroy us: And they are preparing to come, and to take the fortress into which we are fled: and Timotheus is the captain of their host. Now therefore come, and deliver us out of their hands, for many of us are slain. And all our brethren that were in the places of Tubin, are killed: and they have carried away their wives, and their children, captives, and taken their spoils, and they have slain there almost a thousand men.

Wednesday II of October

Lesson I ~ 1 Mac 5:55–58

From the first book of Machabees

Now in the days that Judas and Jonathan were in the land of Galaad, and Simon his brother in Galilee before Ptolemais, Joseph the son of Zacharias, and Azarias captain of the soldiers, heard of the good success, and the battles that were fought. And he said: Let us also get us a name, and let us go fight against the Gentiles that are round about us. And he gave charge to them that were in his army, and they went towards Jamnia.

Lesson II ~ 1 Mac 5:59–62

And Gorgias and his men went out of the city, to give them battle. And Joseph and Azarias were put to flight, and were pursued unto the borders of Judea: and there fell, on that day, of the people of Israel about two thousand men, and there was a great overthrow of the people: Because they did not hearken to Judas, and his brethren, thinking that they should do manfully. But they were not of the seed of those men by whom salvation was brought to Israel.

Lesson III ~ 1 Mac 5:63–67

And the men of Juda were magnified exceedingly in the sight of all Israel, and of all the nations where their name was heard. And people assembled to them with joyful acclamations. Then Judas and his brethren went forth and attacked the children of Esau, in the land toward the south, and he took Chebron, and her towns: and he burnt the walls thereof and the towers all round it. And he removed his camp to go into the land of the aliens, and he went through Samaria. In that day some priests fell in battle, while desiring to do manfully they went out unadvisedly to fight.

Thursday II of October

Lesson I ~ 1 Mac 6:1–6

From the first book of Machabees

Now king Antiochus was going through the higher countries, and he heard that the city of Elymais in Persia was greatly renowned, and abounding in silver and gold. And that there was in it a temple, exceeding rich: and coverings of gold, and breastplates, and shields which king Alexander, son of Philip the Macedonian that reigned first in Greece, had left there. Lo, he came, and sought to take the city and to pillage it: But he was not able, because the design was known to them that were in the city. And they rose up against him in battle, and he fled away from thence, and departed with great sadness, and returned towards Babylonia. And whilst he was in Persia, there came one that told him, how the armies that were in the land of Juda were put to flight: And that Lysias went with a very great power, and was put to flight before the face of the Jews.

Lesson II ~ 1 Mac 6:6–9

And that thy were grown strong by the armour, and power, and store of spoils, which they had gotten out of the camps which they had destroyed: And that they had thrown down the abomination which he had set up upon the altar in Jerusalem, and that they had compassed about the sanctuary with high walls as before, and Bethsura also his city. And it came to pass when the king heard these words, that he was struck with fear, and exceedingly moved: and he laid himself down upon his bed, and fell sick for grief, because it had not fallen out to him as he imagined. And he remained there many days: for great grief came more and more and more upon him, and he made account that he should die.

Lesson III ~ 1 Mac 6:10–13

And he called for all his friends, and said to them: Sleep is gone from my eyes, and I am fallen away, and my heart is cast down for anxiety. And I said in my heart: Into how much tribulation am I come, and into what floods of sorrow, wherein now I am: I that was pleasant and beloved in my power! But now I remember the evils that I have done in Jerusalem, from whence also I took away all the spoils of gold, and of silver that were in it, and I sent to destroy the inhabitants of Juda without cause. I know therefore that for this cause these evils have found me: and behold I perish with great grief in a strange land.

Friday II of October

Lesson I ~ 1 Mac 7:1; 7:4–7

From the first book of Machabees

In the hundred and fifty-first year Demetrius the son of Seleucus departed from the city of Rome, and came up with a few men into a city of the sea coast, and reigned there. So the army slew them. And Demetrius sat upon the throne of his kingdom: And there came to him the wicked and ungodly men of Israel: And Alcimus was at the head of them, who desired to be made high priest. And they accused the people to the king, saying: Judas and his brethren have destroyed all thy friends, and he hath driven us out of our land. Now therefore send some man whom thou trustest, and let him go, and see all the havock he hath made amongst us, and in the king's lands: and let him punish all his friends and their helpers.

Lesson II ~ 1 Mac 7:8–11

Then the king chose Bacchides, one of his friends that ruled beyond the great river in the kingdom, and was faithful to the king: and he sent him, To see the havock that Judas had made: and the wicked Alcimus he made high priest, and commanded him to take revenge upon the children of Israel. And they arose, and came with a great army into the land of Juda: and they sent messengers, and spoke to Judas and his brethren with peaceable words deceitfully. But they gave no heed to their words: for they saw that they were come with a great army.

Lesson III ~ 1 Mac 7:12–17

Then there assembled to Alcimus and Bacchides a company of the scribes to require things that are just: And first the Assideans that were among the children of Israel, and they sought peace of them. For they said: One that is a priest of the seed of Aaron is come, he will not deceive us. And he spoke to them peaceably: and he swore to them, saying: We will do you no harm nor your friends. And they believed him. And he took threescore of them, and slew them in one day, according to the word that is written: The flesh of thy saints, and the blood of them they have shed round about Jerusalem, and there was none to bury them.

Saturday II of October

Lesson I - 1 Mac 8:1–4

From the first book of Machabees

Now Judas heard of the fame of the Romans, that they are powerful and strong, and willingly agree to all things that are requested of them: and that whosoever have come to them, they have made amity with them, and that they are mighty in power. And they heard of their battles, and their noble acts, which they had done in Galatia, how they conquered them, and brought them under tribute: And how great things they had done in the land of Spain, and that they had brought under their power the mines of silver and of gold that are there, and had gotten possession of all the place by their counsel and patience: And had conquered places that were very far off from them, and kings that came against them from the ends of the earth, and had overthrown them with great slaughter: and the rest pay them tribute every year.

Lesson II - 1 Mac 8:17–22

So Judas chose Eupolemus the son of John, the son of Jacob, and Jason the son of Eleazar, and he sent them to Rome to make a league of amity and confederacy with them. And that they might take off from them the yoke of the Grecians, for they saw that they oppressed the kingdom of Israel with servitude. And they went to Rome, a very long journey, and they entered into the senate house, and said: Judas Machabeus, and his brethren, and the people of the Jews have sent us to you, to make alliance and peace with you, and that we may be registered your confederates and friends. And the proposal was pleasing in their sight. And this is the copy of the writing that they wrote back again, graven in tables of brass, and sent to Jerusalem, that it might be with them there for a memorial of the peace and alliance.

Lesson III - 1 Mac 8:23–27

Good success be to the Romans, and to the people of the Jews, by sea and by land for ever: and far be the sword and enemy from them. But if there come first any war upon the Romans, or any of their confederates, in all their dominions: The nation of the Jews shall help them according as the time shall direct, with all their heart: Neither shall they give them, whilst they are fighting, or furnish them with wheat, or arms, or money, or ships, as it hath seemed good to the Romans: and they shall obey their orders, without taking any thing of them. In like manner also if war shall come first upon the nation of the Jews, the Romans shall help them with all their heart, according as the time shall permit them.

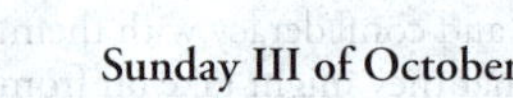

Sunday III of October

Lesson I ~ 1 Mac 9:1–6

From the first book of Machabees

In the mean time when Demetrius heard that Nicanor and his army were fallen in battle, he sent again Bacchides and Alcimus into Judea; and the right wing of his army with them. And they took the road that leadeth to Galgal, and they camped in Masaloth, which is in Arabella: and they made themselves masters of it, and slew many people. In the first month of the hundred and fifty-second year they brought the army to Jerusalem: And they arose, and went to Berea with twenty thousand men, and two thousand horsemen. Now Judas had pitched his tents in Laisa, and three thousand chosen men with him: And they saw the multitude of the army that they were many, and they were seized with great fear: and many withdrew themselves out of the camp, and there remained of them no more than eight hundred men.

Lesson II ~ 1 Mac 9:7–11

And Judas saw that his army slipped away, and the battle pressed upon him, and his heart was cast down: because he had not time to gather them together, and he was discouraged. Then he said to them that remained: Let us arise, and go against our enemies, if we may be able to fight against them. But they dissuaded him, saying: We shall not be able, but let us save our lives now, and return to our brethren, and then we will fight against them: for we are but few. Then Judas said: God forbid we should do this thing, and flee away from them: but if our time be come, let us die manfully for our brethren, and let us not stain our glory. And the army removed out of the camp, and they stood over against them: and the horsemen were divided into two troops, and the slingers, and the archers went before the army, and they that were in the front were all men of valour.

Lesson III ~ 1 Mac 9:12–20

And Bacchides was in the right wing, and the legion drew near on two sides, and they sounded the trumpets: And they also were on Judas' side, even they also cried out, and the earth shook at the noise of the armies: and the battle was fought from morning even unto the evening. And Judas perceived that the stronger part of the army of Bacchides was on the right side, and all the stout of heart came together with him: And the right wing was discomfited by them, and he pursued them even to the mount Azotus. And they that were in the left wing saw that the right wing was discomfited, and they followed after Judas, and them that were with him, at their back: And the battle was hard fought, and there fell many wounded of the one side and of the other. And Judas was slain, and the rest fled away. And Jonathan and Simon took Judas their brother, and buried him in the sepulchre of their fathers in the city of Modin. And all the people of Israel bewailed him with great lamentation, and they mourned for him many days.

Lesson IV

On the duties of the Clergy by St. Ambrose, bishop

But as fortitude is proved not only by prosperity but also in adversity, let us now consider the death of Judas Machabæus. For he, after Nicanor, the general of King Demetrius, was defeated, boldly engaged 20,000 of the king's army with 800 men who were anxious to retire for fear of being overcome by so great a multitude, but whom he persuaded to endure a glorious death rather than to retire in disgraceful flight. "Let us not leave," he says, "any stain upon our glory." Thus, then, engaging in battle after having fought from sunrise till evening, he attacks and quickly drives back the right wing, where he sees the strongest troop of the enemy to be. But while pursuing the fugitives from the rear he gave a chance for a wound to be inflicted. Thus he found the spot of death more full of glory for himself than any triumph.

Lesson V

Why need I further mention his brother Jonathan, who fought against the king's force with but a small troop? Though forsaken by his men, and left with only two, he retrieved the battle, drove back the enemy, and recalled his own men, who were flying in every direction, to share in his triumph. Here, then, is fortitude in war, which bears no light impress of what is virtuous and seemly upon it, for it prefers death to slavery and disgrace. But what am I to say of the sufferings of the martyrs? Not to go too far abroad, did not the children of Machabæus gain triumphs over the proud King Antiochus as great as those of their fathers? The latter in truth were armed, but they conquered without arms.

Lesson VI

The company of the seven brothers stood unconquered, though surrounded by the legions of the king—tortures failed, tormentors ceased; but the martyrs failed not. One, having had the skin of his head pulled off, though changed in appearance, grew in courage. Another, bidden to put forth his tongue, so that it might be cut off, answered: "The Lord hears not only those who speak, for He heard Moses when silent. He hears better the silent thoughts of His own than the voice of all others. Do you fear the scourge of my tongue—and do you not fear the scourge of blood spilt upon the ground?" Blood, too, has a voice whereby it cries aloud to God—as it did in the case of Abel.

Lessons VII, VIII, & IX from the Sermons for After Pentecost Section

Monday III of October

Lesson I ~ 1 Mac 9:28–32

From the first book of Machabees

And all the friends of Judas came together, and said to Jonathan: Since thy brother Judas died, there is not a man like him to go forth against our enemies, Bacchides, and them that are the enemies of our nation. Now therefore we have chosen thee this day to be our prince, and captain in his stead to fight our battles. So Jonathan took upon him the government at that time, and rose up in the place of Judas his brother. And Bacchides had knowledge of it, and sought to kill him.

Lesson II ~ 1 Mac 9:33–36

And Jonathan and Simon his brother, knew it, and all that were with them: and they fled into the desert of Thecua, and they pitched by the water of the lake of Asphar, And Bacchides understood it, and he came himself with all his army over the Jordan on the sabbath day. And Jonathan sent his brother a captain of the people, to desire the Nabutheans his friends, that they would lend them their equipage, which was copious. And the children of Jambri came forth out of Madaba, and took John, and all that he had, and went away with them.

Lesson III ~ 1 Mac 9:37–40

After this it was told Jonathan, and Simon his brother, that the children of Jambri made a great marriage, and were bringing the bride out of Madaba, the daughter of one of the great princes of Chanaan, with great pomp. And the remembered the blood of John their brother: and they went up, and hid themselves under the covert of the mountain. And they lifted up their eyes, and saw: and behold a tumult, and great preparation: and the bridegroom came forth, and his friends, and his brethren to meet them with timbrels, and musical instruments, and many weapons. And they rose up against them from the place where they lay in ambush, and slew them, and there fell many wounded, and the rest fled into the mountains, and they took all their spoils.

Tuesday III of October

Lesson I ~ 1 Mac 12:1–4

From the first book of Machabees

And Jonathan saw that the time served him, and he chose certain men and sent them to Rome, to confirm and to renew the amity with them: And he sent letters to the Spartans, and to other places according to the same form. And they went to Rome, and entered into the senate house, and said: Jonathan the high priest, and the nation of the Jews have sent us to renew the amity, and alliance as it was before. And they gave them letters to their governors in every place, to conduct them into the land of Juda with peace.

Lesson II ~ 1 Mac 12:5–8

And this is a copy of the letters which Jonathan wrote to the Spartans: Jonathan the high priest, and the ancients of the nation, and the priests, and the rest of the people of the Jews, to the Spartans, their brethren, greeting. There were letters sent long ago to Onias the high priest from Arius who reigned then among you, to signify that you are our brethren, as the copy here underwritten doth specify. And

Onias received the ambassador with honour: and received the letters wherein there was mention made of the alliance, and amity.

Lesson III - 1 Mac 12:9–11

We, though we needed none of these things, having for our comfort the holy books that are in our hands, Chose rather to send to you to renew the brotherhood and friendship, lest we should become strangers to you altogether: for there is a long time passed since you sent to us. We therefore at all times without ceasing, both in our festivals, and other days, wherein it is convenient, remember you in the sacrifices that we offer, and in our observances, as it is meet, and becoming to remember brethren.

Wednesday III of October

Lesson I - 1 Mac 12:39–43

From the first book of Machabees

Now when Tryphon had conceived a design to make himself king of Asia, and to take the crown, and to stretch out his hand against king Antiochus: Fearing lest Jonathan would not suffer him, but would fight against him: he sought to seize upon him, and to kill him. So he rose up and came to Bethsan. And Jonathan went out to meet him with forty thousand men chosen for battle, and came to Bethsan. Now when Tryphon saw that Jonathan came with a great army, he durst not stretch forth his hand against him, But received him with honour, and commended him to all his friends, and gave him presents: and he commanded his troops to obey him, as himself.

Lesson II - 1 Mac 12:44–47

And he said to Jonathan: Why hast thou troubled all the people, whereas we have no war? Now therefore send them back to their own houses: and choose thee a few men that may be with thee, and come with me to Ptolemais, and I will deliver it to thee, and the rest of the strong holds, and the army, and all that have any charge, and I will return and go away: for this is the cause of my coming. And Jonathan believed him, and did as he said: and sent away his army, and they departed into the land of Juda: But he kept with him three thousand men: of whom he sent two thousand into Galilee, and one thousand went with him.

Lesson III - 1 Mac 12:48–52

Now as soon as Jonathan entered into Ptolemais, they of Ptolemais shut the gates of the city, and took him: and all them that came in with him they slew with the sword. Then Tryphon sent an army and horsemen into Galilee, and into the great plain to destroy all Jonathan's company. But they, when they understood that Jonathan and all that were with him were taken and slain, encouraged one another, and went out ready for battle. Then they that had come after them, seeing that they stood for their lives, returned back. Whereupon they all came peaceably into the land of Juda. And they bewailed Jonathan, and them that had been with him, exceedingly: and Israel mourned with great lamentation.

Thursday III of October

Lesson I - 1 Mac 13:1–6

From the first book of Machabees

Now Simon heard that Tryphon was gathering together a very great army, to invade the land of Juda, and to destroy it. And seeing that the people was in dread, and in fear, he went up to Jerusalem, and assembled the people: And exhorted them, saying: You know what great battles I and my brethren, and the house of my father, have fought for the laws, and the sanctuary, and the distresses that we have seen: By reason whereof all my brethren have lost their lives for Israel's sake, and I am left alone. And now far be it from me to spare my life in any time of trouble: for I am not better than my brethren. I will avenge then my nation and the sanctuary, and our children, and wives: for all the heathens are gathered together to destroy us out of mere malice.

Lesson II - 1 Mac 13:7–13

And the spirit of the people was enkindled as soon as they heard these words. And they answered with a loud voice, saying: Thou art our leader in the place of Judas, and Jonathan thy brother. Fight thou our battles, and we will do whatsoever thou shalt say to us. So gathering together all the men of war, he made haste to finish all the walls of Jerusalem, and he fortified it round about. And he sent Jonathan the son of Absalom, and with him a new army into Joppe, and he cast out them that were in it, and himself remained there. And Tryphon removed from Ptolemais with a great army, to invade the land of Juda, and Jonathan was with him in custody. But Simon pitched in Addus, over against the plain.

Lesson III - 1 Mac 13:14–19

And when Tryphon understood that Simon was risen up in the place of his brother Jonathan, and that he meant to join battle with him, he sent messengers to him, Saying: We have detained thy brother Jonathan for the money that he owed in the king's account, by reason of the affairs which he had the management of. But now send a hundred talents of silver, and his two sons for hostages, that when he is set at liberty he may not revolt from us, and we will release him. Now Simon knew that he spoke deceitfully to him, nevertheless he ordered the money, and the children to be sent: lest he should bring upon himself a great hatred of the people of Israel, who might have said: Because he sent not the money, and the children, therefore is he lost. So he sent the children, and the hundred talents: and he lied, and did not let Jonathan go.

Friday III of October

Lesson I - 1 Mac 14:16–19

From the first book of Machabees

And it was heard at Rome, and as far as Sparta, that Jonathan was dead: and they were very sorry. But when they heard that Simon his brother was made high priest in his place, and was possessed of all the country, and the cities therein: They wrote to him in tables of brass, to renew the friendship and alliance which they had made with Judas, and with Jonathan his brethren. And they were read before the assembly in Jerusalem. And this is the copy of the letters that the Spartans sent.

Lesson II ~ 1 Mac 14:20–23

The princes and the cities of the Spartans to Simon the high priest, and to the ancients, and the priests, and the rest of the people of the Jews their brethren, greeting. The ambassadors that were sent to our people, have told us of your glory, and honour, and joy: and we rejoice at their coming. And we registered what was said by them in the councils of the people in this manner: Numenius the son of Antiochus, and Antipater the son of Jason, ambassadors of the Jews, came to us to renew the former friendship with us. And it pleased the people to receive the men honourably, and to put a copy of their words in the public records, to be a memorial to the people of the Spartans. And we have written a copy of them to Simon the high priest.

Lesson III ~ 1 Mac 14:24–26

And after this Simon sent Numenius to Rome, with a great shield of gold the weight of a thousand pounds, to confirm the league with them. And when the people of Rome had heard These words, they said: What thanks shall we give to Simon, and his sons? For he hath restored his brethren, and hath driven away in fight the enemies of Israel from them: and they decreed him liberty, and registered it in tables of brass, and set it upon pillars in mount Sion.

Saturday III of October

Lesson I ~ 1 Mac 16:14–17

From the first book of Machabees

Now Simon, as he was going through the cities that were in the country of Judea, and taking care for the good ordering of them, went down to Jericho, he and Mathathias and Judas his sons, in the year one hundred and seventy-seven, the eleventh month: the same is the month Sabath. And the son of Abobus received them deceitfully into a little fortress, that is called Doch which he had built: and he made them a great feast, and hid men there. And when Simon and his sons had drunk plentifully, Ptolemy and his men rose up and took their weapons, and entered into the banqueting place, and slew him, and his two sons, and some of his servants. And he committed a great treachery in Israel, and rendered evil for good.

Lesson II ~ 1 Mac 16:18–21

And Ptolemy wrote these things and sent to the king that he should send him an army to aid him, and he would deliver him the country, and their cities, and tributes. And he sent others to Gazara to kill John: and to the tribunes he sent letters to come to him, and that he would give them silver, and gold, and gifts. And he sent others to take Jerusalem, and the mountain of the temple. Now one running before, told John in Gazara, that his father and his brethren were slain, and that he hath sent men to kill thee also.

Lesson III ~ 1 Mac 16:22–24

But when he heard it he was exceedingly afraid: and he apprehended the men that came to kill him, and he put them to death: for he knew that they sought to take him away. And as concerning the rest of the acts of John, and his wars, and the worthy deeds, which he bravely achieved, and the building of the walls, which he made, and the things that he did: Behold these are written in the book of the days of his priesthood, from the time he was made high priest after his father.

Sunday IV of October

If the Last Sunday of October: Feast of Christ the King instead of October IV

Lesson I ~ 2 Mac 1:1–6

From the second book of Machabees

To the brethren the Jews that are throughout Egypt, the brethren, the Jews that are in Jerusalem, and in the land of Judea, send health, and good peace. May God be gracious to you, and remember his covenant that he made with Abraham, and Isaac, and Jacob, his faithful servants: And give you all a heart to worship him, and to do his will with a great heart, and a willing mind. May he open your heart in his law, and in his commandments, and send you peace. May he hear your prayers, and be reconciled unto you, and never forsake you in the evil time. And now here we are praying for you.

Lesson II ~ 2 Mac 1:18–19

Therefore whereas we purpose to keep the purification of the temple on the five and twentieth day of the month of Casleu, we thought it necessary to signify it to you: that you also may keep the day of Scenopegia, and the day of the fire, that was given when Nehemias offered sacrifice, after the temple and the altar was built. For when our fathers were led in Persia, the priests that then were worshippers of God took privately the fire from the altar, and hid it in a valley where there was a deep pit without water, and there they kept it safe, so that the place was unknown to all men.

Lesson III ~ 2 Mac 1:20–22

But when many years had passed, and it pleased God that Nehemias should be sent by the king of Persia, he sent some of the posterity of those priests that had hid it, to seek for the fire: and as they told us, they found no fire, but thick water. Then he bade them draw it up, and bring it to him: and the priest Nehemias commanded the sacrifices that were laid on, to be sprinkled with the same water, both the wood, and the things that were laid upon it. And when this was done, and the time came that the sun shone out, which before was in a cloud, there was a great fire kindled, so that all wondered.

Lesson IV

From Saint John Chrysostom on the 43rd Psalm

“We have heard with our ears, O God, our fathers have told us, what thou hast done in their time of old." The Prophet speaks thus in the Psalm, yet not in his own person, but in the person of the Machabees, relating and foretelling what events were to happen at the time. For such are the Prophets: they outrun all times, past, present, and future. But in order that our discussion of the subject may be more intelligible, we must first state who were these Machabees, and what they suffered, and what they did. For when Antiochus, surnamed Epiphanes, had invaded Judaea, and laid everything waste, and had forced many who then dwelt there to fall away from the laws of their fathers, the Machabees remained unsullied by these temptations.

Lesson V

And when a serious war broke out, and they could do nothing to help themselves, they hid themselves, as also in aftertimes did the Apostles. For they did not always rush openly into the midst of dangers, but sometimes fled, withdrawing thus to hide. However, after one such short respite, they were like eager animals leaping out of their caves and coming forth from their lairs, and they thereupon resolved for the future, not to win safety for themselves only, but for others, whomsoever they could. And going through all that city and country, they gathered together as many as they found who were still healthy and steadfast; and even many who were weak, and had been corrupted, they persuaded to return to the Law of their fathers.

Lesson VI

For they told them that God is merciful and gracious, and that he has never deprived men of that salvation which is obtained by penitence. And, so saying, they raised a levy of the most valiant men. For they fought not for their wives, their children and servants, or because of the ruin and captivity of their fatherland, but for the Law and the religion of their fathers. Now their leader was God. Therefore, when they arrayed their battle line, and put their lives in jeopardy, they overthrew their adversaries because they trusted not in arms, but considered that the just cause of their war was in itself a good armor. Moreover, when they went forth to the conflict, they uttered no bombast, nor sang battle songs, as some do; nor did they call together musicians, as is done in other armies; but they invoked the help of the Most High God, that He might be with them, and aid them, and strengthen their hand, because that war which they waged was for His glory.

Lessons VII, VIII, & IX from the Sermons for After Pentecost Section

Monday IV of October

Lesson I ~ 2 Mac 2:1–3

From the second book of Machabees

Now it is found in the descriptions of Jeremias the prophet, that he commanded them that went into captivity, to take the fire, as it hath been signified, and how he gave charge to them that were carried away into captivity. And how he gave them the law that they should not forget the commandments of the Lord, and that they should not err in their minds, seeing the idols of gold, and silver, and the ornaments of them. And with other such like speeches, he exhorted them that they would not remove the law from their heart.

Lesson II ~ 2 Mac 2:4–6

It was also contained in the same writing, how the prophet, being warned by God, commanded that the tabernacle and the ark should accompany him, till he came forth to the mountain where Moses went up, and saw the inheritance of God. And when Jeremias came thither he found a hollow cave: and he carried in thither the tabernacle, and the ark, and the altar of incense, and so stopped the door. Then some of them that followed him, came up to mark the place: but they could not find it.

Lesson III ~ 2 Mac 2:7–9

And when Jeremias perceived it, he blamed them, saying: The place shall be unknown, till God gather together the congregation of the people, and receive them to mercy. And then the Lord will shew these things, and the majesty of the Lord shall appear, and there shall be a cloud as it was also shewed to Moses, and he shewed it when Solomon prayed that the place might be sanctified to the great God. For he treated wisdom in a magnificent manner: and like a wise man, he offered the sacrifice of the dedication, and of the finishing of the temple.

Tuesday IV of October

Lesson I ~ 2 Mac 3:1–4

From the second book of Machabees

Therefore when the holy city was inhabited with all peace, and the laws as yet were very well kept, because of the godliness of Onias the high priest, and the hatred his soul had of evil, It came to pass that even the kings themselves, and the princes esteemed the place worthy of the highest honour, and glorified the temple with very great gifts: So that Seleucus king of Asia allowed out of his revenues all the charges belonging to the ministry of the sacrifices. But one Simon of the tribe of Benjamin, who was appointed overseer of the temple, strove in opposition to the high priest, to bring about some unjust thing in the city.

Lesson II ~ 2 Mac 3:5–8

And when he could not overcome Onias he went to Apollonius the son of Tharseas, who at that time was governor of Celesyria and Phenicia: And told him, that the treasury in Jerusalem was full of immense sums of money, and the common store was infinite, which did not belong to the account of the sacrifices: and that it was possible to bring all into the king's hands. Now when Apollonius had given the king notice concerning the money that he was told of, he called for Heliodorus, who had the charge over his affairs, and sent him with commission to bring him the foresaid money. So Heliodorus forthwith began his journey, under a colour of visiting the cities of Celesyria and Phenicia, but indeed to fulfil the king's purpose.

Lesson III ~ 2 Mac 3:9–12

And when he was come to Jerusalem, and had been courteously received in the city by the high priest, he told him what information had been given concerning the money: and declared the cause for which he was come: and asked if these things were so indeed. Then the high priest told him that these were sums deposited, and provisions for the subsistence of the widows and the fatherless. And that some part of that which wicked Simon had given intelligence of, belonged to Hircanus son of Tobias, a man of great dignity: and that the whole was four hundred talents of silver, and two hundred of gold: But that to deceive them who had trusted to the place and temple which is honoured throughout the whole world, for the reverence and holiness of it, was a thing which could not by any means be done.

Wednesday IV of October

Lesson I ~ 2 Mac 3:23–25

From the second book of Machabees

But Heliodorus executed that which he had resolved on, himself being present in the same place with his guard about the treasury. But the spirit of the almighty God gave a great evidence of his presence, so that all that had presumed to obey him, falling down by the power of God, were struck with fainting and dread. For there appeared to them a horse with a terrible rider upon him, adorned with a very rich covering: and he ran fiercely and struck Heliodorus with his fore feet, and he that sat upon him seemed to have armour of gold.

Lesson II ~ 2 Mac 3:26–29

Moreover there appeared two other young men beautiful and strong, bright and glorious, and in comely apparel: who stood by him, on either side, and scourged him without ceasing with many stripes. And Heliodorus suddenly fell to the ground, and they took him up covered with great darkness, and having put him into a litter they carried him out. So he that came with many servants, and all his guard into the aforesaid treasury, was carried out, no one being able to help him, the manifest power of God being known. And he indeed by the power of God lay speechless, and without all hope of recovery.

Lesson III ~ 2 Mac 3:32–24

So the high priest considering that the king might perhaps suspect that some mischief had been done to Heliodorus by the Jews, offered a sacrifice of health for the recovery of the man. And when the high priest was praying, the same young men in the same clothing stood by Heliodorus, and said to him: Give thanks to Onias the priest: because for his sake the Lord hath granted thee life. And thou having been scourged by God, declare unto all men the great works and the power of God. And having spoken thus, they appeared no more.

Thursday IV of October

Lesson I - 2 Mac 4:1–5

From the second book of Machabees

But Simon, of whom we spoke before, and of his country, spoke ill of Onias, as though he had incited Heliodorus to do these things, and had been the promoter of evils: And he presumed to call him a traitor to the kingdom, who provided for the city, and defended his nation, and was zealous for the law of God. But when the enmities proceeded so far, that murders also were committed by some of Simon's friends: Onias considering the danger of this contention, and that Apollonius, who was the governor of Celesyria and Phenicia, was outrageous, which increased the malice of Simon, went to the king, Not to be an accuser of his countrymen, but with a view to the common good of all the people.

Lesson II - 2 Mac 4:6–9

For he saw that, except the king took care, it was impossible that matters should be settled in peace, or that Simon would cease from his folly. But after the death of Seleucus, when Antiochus, who was called the Illustrious, had taken possession of the kingdom, Jason the brother of Onias ambitiously sought the high priesthood: And went to the king, promising him three hundred and sixty talents of silver, and out of other revenues four-score talents. Besides this he promised also a hundred and fifty more, if he might have license to set him up a place for exercise, and a place for youth, and to entitle them, that were at Jerusalem, Antiochians.

Lesson III - 2 Mac 4:10–11

Which when the king had granted, and he had gotten the rule into his hands, forthwith he began to bring over his countrymen to the fashion of the heathens. And abolishing those things, which had been decreed of special favour by the kings in behalf of the Jews, by the means of John the father of that Eupolemus, who went ambassador to Rome to make amity and alliance, he disannulled the lawful ordinances of the citizens, and brought in fashions that were perverse.

Friday IV of October

Lesson I - 2 Mac 5:1–4

From the second book of Machabees

At the same time Antiochus prepared for a second journey into Egypt. And it came to pass that through the whole city of Jerusalem for the space of forty days there were seen horsemen running in the air, in gilded raiment, and armed with spears, like bands of soldiers. And horses set in order by ranks, running one against another, with the shakings of shields, and a multitude of men in helmets, with drawn swords, and casting of darts, and glittering of golden armour, and of harnesses of all sorts. Wherefore all men prayed that these prodigies might turn to good.

Lesson II - 2 Mac 5:5–7

Now when there was gone forth a false rumour, as though Antiochus had been dead, Jason taking with him no fewer than a thousand men, suddenly assaulted the city: and though the citizens ran together to the wall, the city at length was taken, and Menelaus fled into the castle. But Jason slew his countrymen without mercy, not considering that prosperity against one's own kindred is a very great evil, thinking they had been enemies, and not citizens, whom he conquered. Yet he did not get the principality, but received confusion at the end, for the reward of his treachery, and fled again into the country of the Ammonites.

Lesson III ~ 2 Mac 5:8–10

At the last having been shut up by Aretas the king of the Arabians, in order for his destruction, flying from city to city, hated by all men, as a forsaker of the laws, and execrable, as an enemy of his country and countrymen, he was thrust out into Egypt: And he that had driven many out of their country, perished in a strange land, going to Lacedemon, as if for kindred sake he should have refuge there: But he that had cast out many unburied, was himself cast forth both unlamented and unburied, neither having foreign burial, nor being partaker of the sepulchre of his fathers.

Saturday IV of October

Lesson I ~ 2 Mac 6:1–4

From the second book of Machabees

But not long after the king sent a certain old man of Antioch, to compel the Jews to depart from the laws of their fathers and of God: And to defile the temple that was in Jerusalem, and to call it the temple of Jupiter Olympius: and that in Gazarim of Jupiter Hospitalis, according as they were that inhabited the place. And very bad was this invasion of evils and grievous to all. For the temple was full of the riot and revellings of the Gentiles: and of men lying with lewd women. And women thrust themselves of their accord into the holy places, and brought in things that were not lawful.

Lesson II ~ 2 Mac 6:5–9

The altar also was filled with unlawful things, which were forbidden by the laws. And neither were the sabbaths kept, nor the solemn days of the fathers observed, neither did any man plainly profess himself to be a Jew. But they were led by bitter constraint on the king's birthday to the sacrifices: and when the feast of Bacchus was kept, they were compelled to go about crowned with ivy in honour of Bacchus. And there went out a decree into the neighbouring cities of the Gentiles, by the suggestion of the Ptolemeans, that they also should act in like manner against the Jews, to oblige them to sacrifice: And whosoever would not conform themselves to the ways of the Gentiles, should be put to death: then was misery to be seen.

Lesson III ~ 2 Mac 6:10–12

For two women were accused to have circumcised their children: whom, when they had openly led about through the city with the infants hanging at their breasts, they threw down headlong from the walls. And others that had met together in caves that were near, and were keeping the sabbath day privately, being discovered by Philip, were burnt with fire; because they made a conscience to help themselves with their hands, by reason of the religious observance of the day. Now I beseech those that shall read this book, that they be not shocked at these calamities, but that they consider the things that happened, not as being for the destruction, but for the correction of our nation.

In years when October has V Sundays, Oct V is always the Final Sunday of October and thus, is **always** replaced by the Feast of Christ the King.

OUR LORD JESUS CHRIST THE KING ~ Last Sunday of October

In place of the occurring Sunday—be it Oct IV, Oct V, or Nov I

Duplex I Class

Lesson I ~ Col 1:3–8

From the epistle of St. Paul the Apostle to the Colossians

Grace be to you and peace from God our Father, and from the Lord Jesus Christ. We give thanks to God, and the Father of our Lord Jesus Christ, praying always for you. Hearing your faith in Christ Jesus, and the love which you have towards all the saints. For the hope that is laid up for you in heaven, which you have heard in the word of the truth of the gospel, Which is come unto you, as also it is in the whole world, and bringeth forth fruit and groweth, even as it doth in you, since the day you heard and knew the grace of God in truth. As you learned of Epaphras, our most beloved fellow servant, who is for you a faithful minister of Christ Jesus; Who also hath manifested to us your love in the spirit.

Lesson II ~ Col 1:9–17

Therefore we also, from the day that we heard it, cease not to pray for you, and to beg that you may be filled with the knowledge of his will, in all wisdom, and spiritual understanding: That you may walk worthy of God, in all things pleasing; being fruitful in every good work, and increasing in the knowledge of God: Strengthened with all might, according to the power of his glory, in all patience and longsuffering with joy, Giving thanks to God the Father, who hath made us worthy to be partakers of the lot of the saints in light: Who hath delivered us from the power of darkness, and hath translated us into the kingdom of the Son of his love, In whom we have redemption through his blood, the remission of sins; Who is the image of the invisible God, the firstborn of every creature: For in him were all things created in heaven and on earth, visible and invisible, whether thrones, or dominations, or principalities, or powers: all things were created by him and in him. And he is before all, and by him all things consist.

Lesson III ~ Col 1:18–23

And he is the head of the body, the church, who is the beginning, the firstborn from the dead; that in all things he may hold the primacy: Because in him, it hath well pleased the Father, that all fullness should dwell; And through him to reconcile all things unto himself, making peace through the blood of his cross, both as to the things that are on earth, and the things that are in heaven. And you, whereas you were some time alienated and enemies in mind in evil works: Yet now he hath reconciled in the body of his flesh through death, to present you holy and unspotted, and blameless before him: If so ye continue in the faith, grounded and settled, and immoveable from the hope of the gospel which you have heard, which is preached in all the creation that is under heaven, whereof I, Paul, am made a minister.

Lesson IV

From the Encylical Letter
Quas Primas of Pope Pius XI

Since this Holy Year therefore has provided more than one opportunity to enhance the glory of the kingdom of Christ, we deem it in keeping with our Apostolic office to accede to the desire of many of the Cardinals, Bishops, and faithful, made known to Us both individually and collectively, by closing this Holy Year with the insertion into the Sacred Liturgy of a special feast of the Kingship of Our Lord Jesus Christ. This matter is so dear to Our heart, Venerable Brethren, that I would wish to address to you a few words concerning it. It will be for you later to explain in a manner suited to the understanding of the faithful what We are about to say concerning the Kingship of Christ, so that the annual feast which We shall decree may be attended with much fruit and produce beneficial results in the future. It has long been a common custom to give to Christ the metaphorical title of "King," because of the high degree of perfection whereby he excels all creatures. So he is said to reign "in the hearts of men," both by reason of the keenness of his intellect and the extent of his knowledge, and also because he is very truth, and it is from him that truth must be obediently received by all mankind. He reigns, too, in the wills of men, for in him the human will was perfectly and entirely obedient to the Holy Will of God, and further by his grace and inspiration he so subjects our free-will as to incite us to the most noble endeavors. He is King of hearts, too, by reason of his "charity which exceeds all knowledge." And his mercy and kindness which draw all men to him, for never has it been known, nor will it ever be, that man be loved so much and so universally as Jesus Christ. But if we ponder this matter more deeply, we cannot but see that the title and the power of King belongs to Christ as man in the strict and proper sense too. For it is only as man that he may be said to have received from the Father "power and glory and a kingdom," since the Word of God, as consubstantial with the Father, has all things in common with him, and therefore has necessarily supreme and absolute dominion over all things created.

Lesson V

The foundation of this power and dignity of Our Lord is rightly indicated by Cyril of Alexandria. "Christ," he says, "has dominion over all creatures, a dominion not seized by violence nor usurped, but his by essence and by nature." His kingship is founded upon the ineffable hypostatic union. From this it follows not only that Christ is to be adored by angels and men, but that to him as man angels and men are subject, and must recognize his empire; by reason of the hypostatic union Christ has power over all creatures. But a thought that must give us even greater joy and consolation is this that Christ is our King by acquired, as well as by natural right, for he is our Redeemer. Would that they who forget what they have cost their Saviour might recall the words: "You were not redeemed with corruptible things, but with the precious blood of Christ, as of a lamb unspotted and undefiled." We are no longer our own property, for Christ has purchased us "with a great price"; our very bodies are the "members of Christ." Let Us explain briefly the nature and meaning of this lordship of Christ. It consists, We need scarcely say, in a threefold power which is essential to lordship. This is sufficiently clear from the scriptural testimony already adduced concerning the universal dominion of our Redeemer, and moreover it is a dogma of faith that Jesus Christ was given to man, not only as our Redeemer, but also as a lawgiver, to whom obedience is due. Not only do the gospels tell us that he made laws, but they present him to us in the act of making them. Those who keep them show their love for their Divine Master, and he promises that they shall remain in his love. He claimed judicial power as received from his Father, when the Jews accused him of breaking the Sabbath by the miraculous cure of a sick man. "For neither does the Father judge any man; but has given all judgment to the Son." In this power is included the right of rewarding and punishing all men living, for this right is inseparable from that of judging. Executive power, too, belongs to Christ, for all must obey his commands; none may escape them, nor the sanctions he has imposed.

Lesson VI

This kingdom is spiritual and is concerned with spiritual things. That this is so the above quotations from Scripture amply prove, and Christ by his own action confirms it. On many occasions, when the Jews and even the Apostles wrongly supposed that the Messiah would restore the liberties and the kingdom of Israel, he repelled and denied such a suggestion. When the populace thronged around him in admiration and would have acclaimed him King, he shrank from the honor and sought safety in flight. Before the Roman magistrate he declared that his kingdom was not of this world. The gospels present this kingdom as one which men prepare to enter by penance, and cannot actually enter except by faith and by baptism, which, though an external rite, signifies and produces an interior regeneration. This kingdom is opposed to none other than to that of Satan and to the power of darkness. It demands of its subjects a spirit of detachment from riches and earthly things, and a spirit of gentleness. They must hunger and thirst after justice, and more than this, they must deny themselves and carry the cross. Christ as our Redeemer purchased the Church at the price of his own blood; as priest he offered himself, and continues to offer himself as a victim for our sins. Is it not evident, then, that his kingly dignity partakes in a manner of both these offices? It would be a grave error, on the other hand, to say that Christ has no authority whatever in civil affairs, since, by virtue of the absolute empire over all creatures committed to him by the Father, all things are in his power. Therefore by Our Apostolic Authority We institute the Feast of the Kingship of Our Lord Jesus Christ to be observed yearly throughout the whole world on the last Sunday of the month of October—the Sunday, that is, which immediately precedes the Feast of All Saints. We further ordain that the dedication of mankind to the Sacred Heart of Jesus, to be renewed yearly.

Lessons VII

From the Holy Gospel according to St. John (John 18:33–37)

In that time: Pilate said to Jesus: Art thou the king of the Jews? Jesus answered: Sayest thou this thing of thyself, or have others told it thee of me? And so on.

Homily by St. Augustine, Bishop

What great matter was it for the King of all worlds to become King of men? For Christ was not King of Israel for exacting of tribute, or arming a host with the sword, and visibly subduing enemies: but King of Israel that he should rule minds, that he should counsel for eternity, that he should bring unto the kingdom of heaven them that believe, hope, and love. Being then, Son of God, the Word by whom all things were made, that it should be his will to be King of Israel is condescension, not preferment, a betokening of mercy, not an increasing of power. For he who was called on earth King of the Jews is in heaven Lord of the Angels. But is Christ King of the Jews only, or also King of the Gentiles? Yea, of the Gentiles also. For when he said in the prophecy: "But I am set by him as King upon Sion his holy mountain, preaching the precepts of the Lord," lest on account of the Mount Sion, any should say that he was set as King only of the Jews, he has straightway subjoined: "The Lord has said unto me, Thou art my Son: this day I have begotten thee. Ask of me, and I shall give thee the heathen for thy inheritance, and the uttermost parts of the earth for thy possession."

Lesson VIII

Jesus answered: "My kingdom is not of this world: if my kingdom were of this world, then would my servants fight, that I should be delivered to the Jews; but now is my kingdom not from hence." This it is which was the will of our Good Master that we should know: but first we were to be shown the vanity of the opinion concerning his kingdom, entertained by men, whether Gentiles or Jews, from whom Pilate had heard that: as if the reason why he must be punished by death, were that he had affected a kingdom to which he had no right; or because the reigning are wont to look with an evil eye upon those destined to reign; and there were indeed need to beware lest his kingdom should be adverse either to the Romans or the Jews.

Lesson IX

Now the Lord might have answered at once: "My kingdom is not from hence" to the first question put by the governor, "Art thou the King of the Jews?" But in putting a question in return, namely whether he spoke this of himself, or had been told it by others, it was his will to show by Pilate's reply that this had been laid up to him as a crime by the Jews in their conference with the Governor: thus laying open to us, the thoughts of men, which he knew: that they are vain: and to them after Pilate's answer, making a reply which was more reasonable and suitable to Jews and Gentiles: "My kingdom is not of this world."

The readings of the Fifth week of October are omitted if Christ the King is Sunday I of November (the Sunday closest to Nov 1st)

Monday V of October

Lesson I ~ 2 Mac 6:18–22

From the second book of Machabees

Eleazar one of the chief of the scribes, a man advanced in years, and of a comely countenance, was pressed to open his mouth to eat swine's flesh. But he, choosing rather a most glorious death than a hateful life, went forward voluntarily to the torment. And considering in what manner he was come to it, patiently bearing, he determined not to do any unlawful things for the love of life. But they that stood by, being moved with wicked pity, for the old friendship they had with the man, taking him aside, desired that flesh might be brought, which it was lawful for him to eat, that he might make as if he had eaten, as the king had commanded of the flesh of the sacrifice: That by so doing he might be delivered from death: and for the sake of their old friendship with the man they did him this courtesy.

Lesson II ~ 2 Mac 6:23–28

But he began to consider the dignity of his age, and his ancient years, and the inbred honour of his grey head, and his good life and conversation from a child: and he answered without delay, according to the ordinances of the holy law made by God, saying, that he would rather be sent into the other world. For it doth not become our age, said he, to dissemble: whereby many young persons might think that Eleazar, at the age of ninety years, was gone over to the life of the heathens: And so they, through my dissimulation, and for a little time of a corruptible life, should be deceived, end hereby I should bring a stain and a curse upon my old age. For though, for the present time, I should be delivered from the punishments of men, yet should I not escape the hand of the Almighty neither alive nor dead. Wherefore by departing manfully out of this life, I shall shew myself worthy of my old age: And I shall leave an example of fortitude to young men, if with a ready mind and constancy I suffer an honourable death, for the most venerable and most holy laws. And having spoken thus, he was forthwith carried to execution.

Lesson III ~ 2 Mac 7:1–5

It came to pass also, that seven brethren, together with their mother, were apprehended, and compelled by the king to eat swine's flesh against the law, for which end they were tormented with whips and scourges. But one of them, who was the eldest, said thus: What wouldst thou ask, or learn of us? we are ready to die rather than to transgress the laws of God, received from our fathers. Then the king being angry commanded fryingpans, and brazen caldrons to be made hot: which forthwith being heated, He commanded to cut out the tongue of him that had spoken first: and the skin of his head being drawn off, to chop off also the extremities of his hands and feet, the rest of his brethren, and his mother, looking on. And when he was now maimed in all parts, he commanded him, being yet alive, to be brought to the fire, and to be fried in the fryingpan: and while he was suffering therein long torments, the rest, together with the mother, exhorted one another to die manfully.

Tuesday V of October

Lesson I ~ 2 Mac 7:7–12

From the second book of Machabees

So when the first was dead after this manner, they brought the next to make him a mocking stock: and when they had pulled off the skin of his head with the hair, they asked him if he would eat, before he were punished throughout the whole body in every limb. But he answered in his own language, and said: I will not do it. Wherefore he also in the next place, received the torments of the first: And when he was at the last gasp, he said thus: Thou indeed, O most wicked man, destroyest us out of this present life: but the King of the world will raise us up, who die for his laws, in the resurrection of eternal life. After him the third was made a mocking stock, and when he was required, he quickly put forth his tongue, and courageously stretched out his hands: And said with confidence: These I have from heaven, but for the laws of God I now despise them, because I hope to receive them again from him. So that the king, and they that were with him, wondered at the young man's courage, because he esteemed the torments as nothing.

Lesson II ~ 2 Mac 7:13–19

And after he was thus dead, they tormented the fourth in the like manner And when he was now ready to die, he spoke thus: It is better, being put to death by men, to look for hope from God, to be raised up again by him: for, as to thee thou shalt have no resurrection unto life. And when they had brought the fifth, they tormented him. But he looking upon the king, Said: Whereas thou hast power among men, though thou art corruptible, thou dost what thou wilt: but think not that our nation is forsaken by God. But stay patiently a while, and thou shalt see his great power, in what manner he will torment thee and thy seed. After him they brought the sixth, and he being ready to die, spoke thus: Be not deceived without cause: for we suffer these things for ourselves, having sinned against our God, and things worthy of admiration are done to us: But do not think that thou shalt escape unpunished, for that thou attempted to fight against God.

Lesson III ~ 2 Mac 7:20–23

Now the mother was to be admired above measure, and worthy to be remembered by good men, who beheld seven sons slain in the space of one day, and bore it with a good courage, for the hope that she had in God: And she bravely exhorted every one of them in her own language, being filled with wisdom: and joining a man's heart to a woman's thought, She said to them: I know not how you were formed in my womb: for I neither gave you breath, nor soul, nor life, neither did I frame the limbs of every one of you. But the Creator of the world, that formed the nativity of man, and that found out the origin of all, he will restore to you again in his mercy, both breath and life, as now you despise yourselves for the sake of his laws.

Wednesday V of October

Lesson I ~ 2 Mac 7:24–27

From the second book of Machabees

Now Antiochus, thinking himself despised, and withal despising the voice of the upbraider, when the youngest was yet alive, did not only exhort him by words, but also assured him with an oath, that he would make him a rich and a happy man, and, if he would turn from the laws of his fathers, would take him for a friend, and furnish him with things necessary. But when the young man was not moved with these things, the king called the mother, and counselled her to deal with the young man to save his life. And when he had exhorted her with many words, she promised that she would counsel her son. So bending herself towards him, mocking the cruel tyrant, she said her own language: My son, have pity upon me, that bore thee nine months my womb, and gave thee suck three years, and nourished thee, and brought thee up unto this age.

Lesson II ~ 2 Mac 7:28–33

I beseech thee, my son, look upon heaven and earth, and all that is in them: and consider that God made them out of nothing, and mankind also: So thou shalt not fear this tormentor, but being made a worthy partner with thy brethren, receive death, that in that mercy I may receive thee again with thy brethren. While she was yet speaking these words, the young man said: For whom do you stay

I will not obey the commandment of the king, but the commandment of the law, which was given us by Moses. But thou that hast been the author of all mischief against the Hebrews, shalt not escape the hand of God. For we suffer thus for our sins. And though the Lord our God is angry with us a little while for our chastisement and correction: yet he will be reconciled again to his servants.

Lesson III - 2 Mac 7:34–41

But thou, O wicked and of all men most flagitious, be not lifted up without cause with vain hopes, whilst thou art raging against his servants. For thou hast not yet escaped the judgment of the almighty God, who beholdeth all things. For my brethren, having now undergone a short pain, are under the covenant of eternal life: but thou by the judgment of God shalt receive just punishment for thy pride. But I, like my brethren, offer up my life and my body for the laws of our fathers: calling upon God to be speedily merciful to our nation, and that thou by torments and stripes mayst confess that he alone is God. But in me and in my brethren the wrath of the Almighty, which hath justly been brought upon all our nation, shall cease. Then the king being incensed with anger, raged against him more cruelly than all the rest, taking it grievously that he was mocked. So this man also died undefiled, wholly trusting in the Lord. And last of all after the sons the mother also was consumed.

Thursday V of October

Lesson I - 2 Mac 9:1–4

From the second book of Machabees

At that time Antiochus returned with dishonour out of Persia. For he had entered into the city called Persepolis, and attempted to rob the temple, and to oppress the city: but the multitude running together to arms, put them to flight: and so it fell out that Antiochus being put to flight returned with disgrace. Now when he was come about Ecbatana, he received the news of what had happened to Nicanor and Timotheus. And swelling with anger he thought to revenge upon the Jews the injury done by them that had put him to flight. And therefore he commanded his chariot to be driven, without stopping in his journey, the judgment of heaven urging him forward, because he had spoken so proudly, that he would come to Jerusalem, and make it a common burying place of the Jews.

Lesson II - 2 Mac 9:5–7

But the Lord the God of Israel, that seeth all things, struck him with an incurable and an invisible plague. For as soon as he had ended these words, a dreadful pain in his bowels came upon him, and bitter torments of the inner parts. And indeed very justly, seeing he had tormented the bowels of others with many and new torments, albeit he by no means ceased from his malice. Moreover being filled with pride, breathing out fire in his rage against the Jews, and commanding the matter to be hastened, it happened as he was going with violence that he fell from the chariot, so that his limbs were much pained by a grievous bruising of the body.

Lesson III ~ 2 Mac 9:8–10

Thus he that seemed to himself to command even the waves of the sea, being proud above the condition of man, and to weigh the heights of the mountains in a balance, now being cast down to the ground, was carried in a litter, bearing witness to the manifest power of God in himself: So that worms swarmed out of the body of this man, and whilst he lived in sorrow and pain, his flesh fell off, and the filthiness of his smell was noisome to the army. And the man that thought a little to before he could reach the stars of heaven, no man could endure to carry, for the intolerable stench.

Friday V of October

Lesson I ~ 2 Mac 10:1–5
From the second book of Machabees

But Machabeus, and they that were with him, by the protection of the Lord, recovered the temple and the city again. But he threw down the altars, which the heathens had set up in the streets, as also the temples of the idols. And having purified the temple, they made another altar: and taking fire out of the fiery stones, they offered sacrifices after two years, and set forth incense, and lamps, and the loaves of proposition. And when they had done these things, they besought the Lord, lying prostrate on the ground, that they might no more fall into such evils; but if they should at any time sin, that they might be chastised by him more gently, and not be delivered up to barbarians and blasphemous men. Now upon the same day that the temple had been polluted by the strangers, on the very same day it was cleansed again, to wit, on the five and twentieth day of the month of Casleu.

Lesson II ~ 2 Mac 10:24–27

But Timotheus who before had been overcome by the Jews, having called together a multitude of foreign troops, and assembled horsemen out of Asia, came as though he would take Judea by force of arms. But Machabeus and they that were with him, when he drew near, prayed to the Lord, sprinkling earth upon their heads and girding their loins with haircloth, And lying prostrate at the foot of the altar, besought him to be merciful to them, and to be an enemy to their enemies, and an adversary to their adversaries, as the law saith. And so after prayer taking their arms, they went forth further from the city, and when they were come very near the enemies they rested.

Lesson III ~ 2 Mac 10:28–32

But as soon as the sun was risen both sides joined battle: the one part having with their valour the Lord for a surety of victory and success: but the other side making their rage their leader in battle. But when they were in the heat of the engagement there appeared to the enemies from heaven five men upon horses, comely with golden bridles, conducting the Jews: Two of whom took Machabeus between them, and covered him on every side with their arms, and kept him safe: but cast darts and fireballs against the enemy, so that they fell down, being both confounded with blindness, and filled with trouble1 And there were slain twenty thousand five hundred, and six hundred horsemen. But Timotheus fled into Gazara a strong hold, where Chereas was governor.

Saturday V of October

Lesson I - 2 Mac 15:7–11

From the second book of Machabees

But Machabeus ever trusted with all hope that God would help them. And he exhorted his people not to fear the coming of the nations, but to remember the help they had before received from heaven, and now to hope for victory from the Almighty. And speaking to them out of the law, and the prophets, and withal putting them in mind of the battles they had fought before, he made them more cheerful: Then after he had encouraged them, he showed withal the falsehood of the Gentiles, and their breach of oaths. So he armed every one of them, not with defence of shield and spear, but with very good speeches and exhortations, and told them a dream worthy to be believed, whereby he rejoiced them all.

Lesson II - 2 Mac 15:12–16

Now the vision was in this manner: Onias who had been high priest, a good and virtuous man, modest in his looks, gentle in his manners, and graceful in his speech, and who from a child was exercised in virtues, holding up his hands, prayed for all the people of the Jews: After this there appeared also another man, admirable for age, and glory, and environed with great beauty and majesty: Then Onias answering, said: This is a lover of his brethren, and of the people of Israel: this is he that prayeth much for the people, and for all the holy city, Jeremias the prophet of God. Whereupon Jeremias stretched forth his right hand, and gave to Judas a sword of gold, saying: Take this holy sword a gift from God, wherewith thou shalt overthrow the adversaries of my people Israel.

Lesson III - 2 Mac 15:17–19

Thus being exhorted with the words of Judas, which were very good, and proper to stir up the courage, and strengthen the hearts of the young men, they resolved to fight, and to set upon them manfully: that valour might decide the matter, because the holy city and the temple were in danger. For their concern was less for their wives, and children, and for their brethren, and kinsfolks: but their greatest and principal fear was for the holiness of the temple. And they also that were in the city, had no little concern for them that were to be engaged in battle.

SUNDAYS OF NOVEMBER

Sunday I of November

If this Sunday occurs as the last within the calendar month of October, it is replaced by the Feast of Christ the King.

Lesson I ~ Ezech 1:1–4

Beginning of the book of the Prophet Ezechiel

And it came to pass in the thirtieth year, in the fourth month, on the fifth day of the month, when I was in the midst of the captives by the river Chobar, the heavens were opened, and I saw the visions of God. On the fifth day of the month, the same was the fifth year of the captivity of king Joachin, The word of the Lord came to Ezechiel the priest the son of Buzi in the land of the Chaldeans, by the river Chobar: and the hand of the Lord was there upon him. And I saw, and behold a whirlwind came out of the north: and a great cloud, and a fire infolding it, and brightness was about it: and out of the midst thereof, that is, out of the midst of the fire, as it were the resemblance of amber.

Lesson II ~ Ezech 1:5–9

And in the midst thereof the likeness of four living creatures: and this was their appearance: there was the likeness of a man in them. Every one had four faces, and every one four wings. Their feet were straight feet, and the sole of their foot was like the sole of a calf's foot, and they sparkled like the appearance of glowing brass. And they had the hands of a man under their wings on their four sides: and they had faces, and wings on the four sides, And the wings of one were joined to the wings of another. They turned not when they went: but every one went straight forward.

Lesson III ~ Ezech 1:10–12

And as for the likeness of their faces: there was the face of a man, and the face of a lion on the right side of all the four: and the face of an ox, on the left side of all the four: and the face of an eagle over all the four. And their faces, and their wings were stretched upward: two wings of every one were joined, and two covered their bodies: And every one of them went straight forward: whither the impulse of the spirit was to go, thither they went: and they turned not when they went.

Lesson IV

From the Exposition of the Prophet Ezechiel written by Pope St. Gregory

It is the use of the Prophetic writers first to give name, date, and place, and then to begin to unfold the mysteries of the prophecy thus, to give certainty of trustworthiness, a foundation is laid before, and afterward the fruits of the Spirit are set forth by signs and in figures. Thus Ezechiel says concerning the date: "And it came to pass in the thirtieth year, in the fourth month, on the fifth day of the month." And to show the place, he adds further: "When I was in the midst of the captives by the river Chobar, the heavens were opened, and I saw visions of God." Then he defines the time even more exactly, saying "On the fifth day of the month, the same was the fifth year of the captivity of king Joachin." And he who had thus clearly indicated his individuality, goes on farther to state his kin, saying "The word of the Lord came to Ezechiel the priest the son of Buzi."

Lesson V

But the first question which meets us is: Why does the Prophet, having hitherto said nothing, begin with the words: "And it came to pass in the thirtieth year." Now, this word "And" is a conjunction, and we know that it is so called because it conjoins that which comes after it with that which goes before it. Why, then, does he who has hitherto been silent, commence by "And," when there is nothing going before for the conjunction to join to that which comes after? To explain this, we must consider that our senses perceive only things bodily, while those of Prophets perceive also things ghostly, and to them things exist things which to our ignorance seem not to do so. Hence it comes that in the mind of a Prophet, things outer and things inner are so joined that he sees both together, and the word which he hears within him and that which he utters come together.

Lesson VI

It appears plainly, therefore, that he which had hitherto been silent, begins by the words: "And it came to pass in the thirtieth year," because his first utterance was but the continuation of something to which he had already been listening in his own mind. The words which he spoke were merely a continuation of the vision already going on within, and therefore the first are, "And it came to pass." His language is framed as though his inner revelation had been an open one. That it was in the thirtieth year that the word of the Lord came unto Ezechiel, causes us to remark that in the ordinary use of human understanding, men receive not a call to teach until they be of full age. Hence also even the Lord Himself, when He sat in the Temple in the midst of the doctors, in the twelfth year of His age, was pleased to be found, not teaching, but hearing them and asking them questions.

Lessons VII, VIII, & IX from the Sermons for After Pentecost Section

Monday I of November

Lesson I ~ Ezech 2:2–5

From the Prophet Ezechiel

And the spirit entered into me after that he spoke to me, and he set me upon my feet: and I heard him speaking to me, And saying: Son of man, I send thee to the children of Israel, to a rebellious people, that hath revolted from me, they, and their fathers, have transgressed my covenant even unto this day. And they to whom I send thee are children of a hard face, and of an obstinate heart: and thou shalt say to them: Thus saith the Lord God: If so be they at least will hear, and if so be they will forbear, for they are a provoking house: and they shall know that there hath been a prophet in the midst of them.

Lesson II ~ Ezech 2:6–7

And thou, O son of man, fear not, neither be thou afraid of their words: for thou art among unbelievers and destroyers, and thou dwellest with scorpions. Fear not their words, neither be thou dismayed at their looks: for they are a provoking house. And thou shalt speak my words to them, if perhaps they will hear, and forbear: for they provoke me to anger.

Lesson III ~ Ezech 2:8–9

But thou, O son of man, hear all that I say to thee: and do not thou provoke me, as that house provoketh me: open thy mouth, and eat what I give thee. And I looked, and behold, a hand was sent to me, wherein was a book rolled up: and he spread it before me, and it was written within and without: and there were written in it lamentations, and canticles, and woe.

Tuesday I of November

Lesson I ~ Ezech 3:1–4

From the Prophet Ezechiel

And he said to me: Son of man, eat all that thou shalt find: eat this book, and go speak to the children of Israel. And I opened my mouth, and he caused me to eat that book. And he said to me: Son of man, thy belly shall eat, and thy bowels shall be filled with this book, which I give thee. And I did eat it: and it was sweet as honey in my mouth. And he said to me: Son of man, go to the house of Israel, and thou shalt speak my words to them.

Lesson II ~ Ezech 3:5–9

For thou art not sent to a people of a profound speech, and of an unknown tongue, but to the house of Israel: Nor to many nations of a strange speech, and of an unknown tongue, whose words thou canst not understand: and if thou wert sent to them, they would hearken to thee. But the house of Israel will not hearken to thee: because they will not hearken to me: for all the house of Israel are of a hard forehead and an obstinate heart. Behold I have made thy face stronger than their faces: and thy forehead harder than their foreheads. I have made thy face like an adamant and like flint: fear them not, neither be thou dismayed at their presence: for they are a provoking house.

Lesson III ~ Ezech 3:10–13

And he said to me: Son of man, receive in thy heart, and hear with thy ears, all the words that I speak to thee: And go get thee in to them of the captivity, to the children of thy people, and thou shalt speak to them, and shalt say to them: Thus saith the Lord: If so be they will hear and will forbear. And the spirit took me up, and I heard behind me the voice of a great commotion, saying: Blessed be the glory of the Lord, from his place. And the noise of the wings of the living creatures striking one against another, and the noise of the wheels following the living creatures, and the noise of a great commotion.

Wednesday I of November

Lesson I ~ Ezech 7:1–4

From the Prophet Ezechiel

And the word of the Lord came to me, saying: And thou son of man, thus saith the Lord God to the land of Israel: The end is come, the end is come upon the four quarters of the land. Now is an end come upon thee, and I will send my wrath upon thee, and I will judge thee according to thy ways: and I will set all thy abominations against thee. And my eye shall not spare thee, and I will shew thee no pity: but I will lay thy ways upon thee, and thy abominations shall be in the midst of thee: and you shall know that I am the Lord.

Lesson II ~ Ezech 7:5–9

Thus saith the Lord God: One affliction, behold an affliction is come. An end is come, the end is come, it hath awaked against thee: behold it is come. Destruction is come upon thee that dwellest in the land: the time is come, the day of slaughter is near, and not of the joy of mountains. Now very shortly I will pour out my wrath upon thee, and I will accomplish my anger in thee: and I will judge thee according to thy ways, and I will lay upon thee all thy crimes. And my eye shall not spare, neither will I shew mercy: but I will lay thy ways upon thee, and thy abominations shall be in the midst of thee: and you shall know that I am the Lord that strike.

Lesson III ~ Ezech 7:10–13

Behold the day, behold it is come: destruction is gone forth, the rod hath blossomed, pride hath budded. Iniquity is risen up into a rod of impiety: nothing of them shall remain, nor of their people, nor of the noise of them: and there shall be no rest among them. The time is come, the day is at hand: let not the buyer rejoice: nor the seller mourn: for wrath is upon all the people thereof. For the seller shall not return to that which he hath sold, although their life be yet among the living. For the vision which regardeth all the multitude thereof, shall not go back: neither shall man be strengthened in the iniquity of his life.

Thursday I of November

Lesson I ~ Ezech 13:1–6

From the Prophet Ezechiel

And the word of the Lord came to me, saying: Son of man, prophesy thou against the prophets of Israel that prophesy: and thou shalt say to them that prophesy out of their own heart: Hear ye the word of the Lord: Thus saith the Lord God: Woe to the foolish prophets that follow their own spirit, and see nothing. Thy prophets, O Israel, were like foxes in the deserts. You have not gone up to face the enemy, nor have you set up a wall for the house of Israel, to stand in battle in the day of the Lord. They see vain things, and they foretell lies, saying: The Lord saith: whereas the Lord hath not sent them: and they have persisted to confirm what they have said.

Lesson II - Ezech 13:7–10

Have you not seen a vain vision and spoken a lying divination: and you say: The Lord saith: whereas I have not spoken. Therefore thus saith the Lord God: Because you have spoken vain things, and have seen lies: therefore behold I come against you, saith the Lord God. And my hand shall be upon the prophets that see vain things, and that divine lies: they shall not be in the council of my people, nor shall they be written in the writing of the house of Israel, neither shall they enter into the land of Israel, and you shall know that I am the Lord God. Because they have deceived my people, saying: Peace, and there is no peace: and the people built up a wall, and they daubed it with dirt without straw.

Lesson III - Ezech 13:11–14

Say to them that daub without tempering, that it shall fall: for there shall be an overflowing shower, and I will cause great hailstones to fall violently from above, and a stormy wind to throw it down. Behold, when the wall is fallen: shall it not be said to you: Where is the daubing wherewith you have daubed it? Therefore thus saith the Lord God: Lo, I will cause a stormy wind to break forth in my indignation, and there shall be an overflowing shower in my anger: and great hailstones in my wrath to consume. And I will break down the wall that you have daubed with untempered mortar.

Friday I of November

Lesson I - Ezech 15:1–5

From the Prophet Ezechiel

And the word of the Lord came to me, saying: Son of man, what shall be made of the wood of the vine, out of all the trees of the woods that are among the trees of the forests? Shall wood be taken of if, to do any work, or shall a pin be made of it for any vessel to hang thereon? Behold it is cast into the fire for fuel: the fire hath consumed both ends thereof, and the midst thereof is reduced to ashes: shall it be useful for any work? Even when it was whole it was not fit for work: how much less, when the fire hath devoured and consumed it, shall any work be made of it?

Lesson II - Ezech 15:6–8

Therefore thus saith the Lord God: As the vine tree among the trees of the forests which I have given to the fire to be consumed, so will I deliver up the inhabitants of Jerusalem. And I will set my face against them: they shall go out from fire, and fire shall consume them and you shall know that I am the Lord, when I shall have set my face against them. And I shall have made their land a wilderness, and desolate, because they have been transgressors, saith the Lord God.

Lesson III - Ezech 16:1–5

And the word of the Lord came to me, saying: Son of man, make known to Jerusalem her abominations. And thou shalt say: Thus saith the Lord God to Jerusalem: thy root, and thy nativity is of the land of Chanaan, thy father was an Amorrhite, and thy mother a Cethite. And when thou wast born, in the day of thy nativity thy navel was not cut, neither wast thou washed with water for thy health, nor salted with salt, nor swaddled with clouts. No eye had pity on thee to do any of these things for thee, out of compassion to thee: but thou wast cast out upon the face of the earth in the abjection of thy soul, in the day that thou wast born.

Saturday I of November

Lesson I ~ Ezech 19:1–7

From the Prophet Ezechiel

Moreover take thou up a lamentation for the princes of Israel, And say: Why did thy mother the lioness lie down among the lions, and bring up her whelps in the midst of young lions? And she brought out one of her whelps, and he became a lion: and he learned to catch the prey, and to devour men. And the nations heard of him, and took him, but not without receiving wounds: and they brought him in chains into the land of Egypt. But she seeing herself weakened, and that her hope was lost, took one of her young lions, and set him up for a lion. And he went up and down among the lions, and became a lion: and he learned to catch the prey, and to devour men. He learned to make widows, and to lay waste their cities: and the land became desolate, and the fulness thereof by the noise of his roaring.

Lesson II ~ Ezech 19:8–11

And the nations came together against him on every side out of the provinces, and they spread their net over him, in their wounds he was taken. And they put him into a cage, they brought him in chains to the king of Babylon: and they cast him into prison, that his voice should no more be heard upon the mountains of Israel. Thy mother is like a vine in thy blood planted by the water: her fruit and her branches have grown out of many waters. And she hath strong rods to make sceptres for them that bear rule, and her stature was exalted among the branches: and she saw her height in the multitude of her branches.

Lesson III ~ Ezech 19:12–14

But she was plucked up in wrath, and cast on the ground, and the burning wind dried up her fruit: her strong rods are withered, and dried up: the fire hath devoured her. And now she is transplanted into the desert, in a land not passable, and dry. And a fire is gone out from a rod of her branches, which hath devoured her fruit: so that she now hath no strong rod, to be a sceptre of rulers. This is a lamentation, and it shall be for a lamentation.

Sunday II of November

This Sunday and its accompanying week are omitted entirely **except** in years when Nov 5th is a Sunday.

In most years, Week I of November is immediately followed by Week III.

Lesson I ~ Ezech 21:1–5

From the Prophet Ezechiel

And the word of the Lord came to me, saying: Son of man, set thy face toward Jerusalem, and let thy speech flow towards the holy places, and prophesy against the land of Israel: And say to the land of Israel: Thus saith the Lord God: Behold I come against thee, and I will draw forth my sword out of its sheath, and will cut off in thee the just, and the wicked. And forasmuch as I have cut off in thee the just, and the wicked, therefore shall my sword go forth out of its sheath against all flesh, from the south even to the north. That all flesh may know that I the Lord have drawn my sword out of its sheath not to be turned back.

Lesson II ~ Ezech 21:6–11

And thou, son of man, mourn with the breaking of thy loins, and with bitterness sigh before them. And when they shall say to thee: Why mournest thou? thou shalt say: For that which I hear: because it comes, and every heart shall melt, and all hands shall be made feeble, and every spirit shall faint, and water shall run down every knee: behold it comes, and it shall be done, saith the Lord God. And the word of the Lord came to me, saying: Son of man, prophesy, and say: Thus saith the Lord God: Say: The sword, the sword is sharpened, and furbished. It is sharpened to kill victims: it is furbished that it may glitter: thou removest the sceptre of my son, thou hast cut down every tree. And I have given it to be furbished, that it may be handled: this sword is sharpened, and it is furbished, that it may be in the hand of the slayer.

Lesson III ~ Ezech 21:12–15

Cry, and howl, O son of man, for this sword is upon my people, it is upon all the princes of Israel, that are fled: they are delivered up to the sword with my people, strike therefore upon thy thigh, Because it is tried: and that when it shall overthrow the sceptre, and it shall not be, saith the Lord God. Thou therefore, O son of man, prophesy, and strike thy hands together, and let the sword be doubled, and let the sword of the slain be tripled: this is the sword of a great slaughter, that maketh them stand amazed, And languish in heart, and that multiplieth ruins. In all their gates I have set the dread of the sharp sword, the sword that is furbished to glitter, that is made ready for slaughter.

Lesson IV

From the Exposition of the Prophet Ezechiel, written by St. Jerome, Priest

Because he has said above: "they say of me, Does he not speak parables?" But now, as the people asked for something clearer, the Lord does speak more openly that which He had uttered in what is called metaphor, parable, or proverb. He shows how that the forest of the field of Nageb, and Darom, and Theman, are figures of Jerusalem, and the Temple, and the Holy-of-Holies, and of all the land of Judah, and that by the flaming fire which should devour the forest, was to be understood that sword, which should be drawn out of the sheath, and should cut off from the land of

Israel the righteous and the wicked. The righteous and the wicked are figured by the green tree and the dry tree. Whence also the Lord says: "If they do these things in a green tree, what shall be done in a dry?"

Lesson V

The first time He had said: "Set thy face toward the South, and drop thy word toward the South wind, and prophesy against the forest of the South." But forasmuch as this seemed dark, and the people knew not what the Prophet said, it is a second time stated more clearly that the forest of the South is Jerusalem and all its unfruitful trees, unto whose roots the axe is being laid, are to be understood as figures of her inhabitants, and the fire to be kindled in it to be interpreted the sword. A third time is the Prophet commanded that when they should hold their peace, nor ask why he prophesied thus, he should do that by which he should be questioned, and should answer that which the Lord had spoken.

Lesson VI

"Sigh thou," He says, "cry aloud, not softly nor only half sorrowfully, but with the breaking of thy loins, that thy groaning may come from the depth of thy bowels and from the bitterness of thy soul. And this shalt thou do before them." And when they shall ask thee why thou art afflicted with such lamentation, and what evil has befallen thee that thou groanest thus, thou shalt answer them with My word, saying I lament, and am not able to hide the grief of my heart, because that that which hath ever sounded in mine ears will indeed be fulfilled, and comes, even the host of the wrathful Babylonians which threatens you and when it shall have come, and shall have made trenches all round about Jerusalem, then "every heart shall melt, and all hands shall be feeble," and horror shall take hold of the minds of men, and none shall dare to withstand.

Lessons VII, VIII, & IX from the Sermons for After Pentecost Section

Monday II of November

Lesson I - Ezech 33:1–5

From the Prophet Ezechiel

And the word of the Lord came to me, saying: Son of man, speak to the children of thy people, and say to them: When I bring the sword upon a land, if the people of the land take a man, one of their meanest, and make him a watchman over them: And he see the sword coming upon the land, and sound the trumpet, and tell the people: Then he that heareth the sound of the trumpet, whosoever he be, and doth not look to himself, if the sword come, and cut him off: his blood shall be upon his own head. He heard the sound of the trumpet and did not look to himself, his blood shall be upon him: but if he look to himself, he shall save his life.

Lesson II - Ezech 33:6–8

And if the watchman see the sword coming, and sound not the

trumpet: and the people look not to themselves, and the sword come, and cut off a soul from among them: he indeed is taken away in his iniquity, but I will require his blood at the hand of the watchman. So thou, O son of man, I have made thee a watchman to the house of Israel: therefore thou shalt hear the word from my mouth, and shalt tell it them from me. When I say to the wicked: O wicked man, thou shalt surely die: if thou dost not speak to warn the wicked man from his way: that wicked man shall die in his iniquity, but I will require his blood at thy hand.

Lesson III ~ Ezech 33:9–11

But if thou tell the wicked man, that he may be converted from his ways, and he be not converted from his way: he shall die in his iniquity: but thou hast delivered thy soul. Thou therefore, O son of man, say to the house of Israel: Thus you have spoken, saying: Our iniquities, and our sins are upon us, and we pine away in them: how then can we live? Say to them: As I live, saith the Lord God, I desire not the death of the wicked, but that the wicked turn from his way, and live. Turn ye, turn ye from your evil ways: and why will you die, O house of Israel?

Tuesday II of November

Lesson I ~ Ezech 34:1–4

From the Prophet Ezechiel

And the word of the Lord came to me, saying: Son of man, prophesy concerning the shepherds of Israel: prophesy, and say to the shepherds: Thus saith the Lord God: Woe to the shepherds of Israel, that fed themselves: should not the hocks be fed by the shepherds? You ate the milk, end you clothed yourselves with the wool, and you killed that which was fat: but my flock you did not feed. The weak you have not strengthened, and that which was sick you have not healed, that which was broken you have not bound up, and that which was driven away you have not brought again, neither have you sought that which was lost: but you ruled over them with rigour, and with a high hand.

Lesson II ~ Ezech 34:5–9

And my sheep were scattered, because there was no shepherd: and they became the prey of all the beasts of the field, and were scattered. My sheep have wandered in every mountain, and in every high hill: and my flocks were scattered upon the face of the earth, and there was none that sought them, there was none, I say, that sought them. Therefore, ye shepherds, hear the word of the Lord: As I live, saith the Lord God, forasmuch as my flocks have been made a spoil, and my sheep are become a prey to all the beasts of the field, because there was no shepherd: for my shepherds did not seek after my flock, but the shepherds fed themselves, and fed not my flocks: Therefore, ye shepherds, hear the word of the Lord:

Lesson III ~ Ezech 34:10–12

Thus saith the Lord God: Behold I myself come upon the shepherds, I will require my flock at their hand,

and I will cause them to cease from feeding the flock any more, neither shall the shepherds feed themselves any more: and I will deliver my flock from their mouth, and it shall no more be meat for them. For thus saith the Lord God: Behold I myself will seek my sheep, and will visit them. As the shepherd visiteth his flock in the day when he shall be in the midst of his sheep that were scattered, so will I visit my sheep, and will deliver them out of all the places where they have been scattered in the cloudy and dark day.

Wednesday II of November

Lesson I ~ Ezech 40:1–2

From the Prophet Ezechiel

In the five and twentieth year of our captivity, in the beginning of the year, the tenth day of the month, the fourteenth year after the city was destroyed: in the selfsame day the hand of the Lord was upon me, and he brought me thither. In the visions of God he brought me into the land of Israel, and set me upon a very high mountain: upon which there was as the building of a city, bending towards the south.

Lesson II ~ Ezech 40:3–4

And he brought me in thither, and behold a man, whose appearance was like the appearance of brass, with a line of flax in his hand, and a measuring reed in his hand, and he stood in the gate. And this man said to me: Son of man, see with thy eyes, and hear with thy ears, and set thy heart upon all that I shall shew thee: for thou art brought hither that they may be shewn to thee: declare all that thou seest, to the house of Israel.

Lesson III ~ Ezech 40:5–6

And behold there was a wall on the outside of the house round about, and in the man's hand a measuring reed of six cubits and a handbreadth: and he measured the breadth of the building one reed, and the height one reed. And he came to the gate that looked toward the east, and he went up the steps thereof: and he measured the breadth of the threshold of the gate one reed, that is, one threshold was one reed broad.

Thursday II of November

Lesson I ~ Ezech 41:1–3

From the Prophet Ezechiel

And he brought me into the temple, and he measured the fronts six cubits broad on this side, and six cubits on that side, the breadth of the tabernacle. And the breadth of the gate was ten cubits: and the sides of the gate five cubits on this side, and five cubits on that side: and he measured the length thereof forty cubits, and the breadth twenty cubits. Then going inward he measured the front of the gate two cubits: and the gate six cubits, and the breadth of the gate seven cubits.

Lesson II ~ Ezech 41:4–6

And he measured the length thereof twenty cubits, and the breadth twenty cubits, before the face of the temple: and he said to me: This is the holy of holies. And he measured the wall of the house six cubits: and the breadth of every side chamber four cubits round about the house on every side. And the side chambers one by another, were twice thirty-three: and they bore outwards, that they might enter in through the wall of the house in the sides round about, to hold in, and not to touch the wall of the temple.

Lesson III ~ Ezech 41:7–9

And there was a broad passage round about, going up by winding stairs, and it led into the upper loft of the temple all round: therefore was the temple broader in the higher parts: and so from the lower parts they went to the higher by the midst. And I saw in the house the height round about, the foundations of the side chambers which were the measure of a reed the space of six cubits: And the thickness of the wall for the side chamber without, which was five cubits: and the inner house was within the side chambers of the house.

Friday II of November

Lesson I ~ Ezech 43:1–5

From the Prophet Ezechiel

And he brought me to the gate that looked towards the east. And behold the glory of the God of Israel came in by the way of the east: and his voice was like the noise of many waters, and the earth shone with his majesty. And I saw the vision according to the appearance which I had seen when he came to destroy the city: and the appearance was according to the vision which I had seen by the river Chobar: and I fell upon my face. And the majesty of the Lord went into the temple by the way of the gate that looked to the east. And the spirit lifted me up and brought me into the inner court: and behold the house was filled with the glory of the Lord.

Lesson II ~ Ezech 43:6–8

And I heard one speaking to me out of the house, and the man that stood by me, Said to me: Son of man, the place of my throne, and the place of the soles of my feet, where I dwell in the midst of the children of Israel for ever: and the house of Israel shall no more profane my holy name, they and their kings by their fornications, and by the carcasses of their kings, and by the high places. They who have set their threshold by my threshold, and their posts by my posts: and there was but a wall between me and them: and they profaned my holy name by the abominations which they committed: for which reason I consumed them in my wrath.

Lesson III ~ Ezech 43:9–11

Now therefore let them put away their fornications, and the carcasses of their kings far from me: and I will dwell in the midst of them for ever. But thou, son of man, shew to the house of Israel the temple, and let them be ashamed of their iniquities, and let them measure the building: And be ashamed of all that they have done. Shew them the form of the house, and of the fashion thereof, the goings out and the comings in, and the whole plan thereof, and all its ordinances, and all its order, and all its laws, and thou shalt write it in their sight: that they may keep the whole form thereof, and its ordinances, and do them.

Saturday II of November

Lesson I ~ Ezech 47:1–2

From the Prophet Ezechiel

And he brought me again to the gate of the house, and behold waters issued out from under the threshold of the house toward the east: for the forefront, of the house looked toward the east: but the waters came down to the right side of the temple to the south part of the altar. And he led me out by the way of the north gate, and he caused me to turn to the way without the outward gate to the way that looked toward the east: and behold there ran out waters on the right side.

Lesson II ~ Ezech 47:3–5

And when the man that had the line in his hand went out towards the east, he measured a thousand cubits: and he brought me through the water up to the ankles. And again he measured a thousand, and he brought me through the water up to the knees. And he measured a thousand, and he brought me through the water up to the loins. And he measured a thousand, and it was a torrent, which I could not pass over: for the waters were risen so as to make a deep torrent, which could not be passed over.

Lesson III ~ Ezech 47:6–9

And he said to me: Surely thou hast seen, O son of man. And he brought me out, and he caused me to turn to the bank of the torrent. And when I had turned myself, behold on the bank of the torrent were very many trees on both sides. And he said to me: These waters that issue forth toward the hillocks of sand to the east, and go down to the plains of the desert, shall go into the sea, and shall go out, and the waters shall be healed. And every living creature that creepeth whithersoever the torrent shall come, shall live: and there shall be fishes in abundance after these waters shall come thither, and they shall be healed, and all things shall live to which the torrent shall come.

✠

Sunday III of November

Lesson I ~ Dan 1:1–4

Beginning of the book of the Prophet Daniel

In the third year of the reign of Joakim king of Juda, Nabuchodonosor king of Babylon came to Jerusalem, and besieged it. And the Lord delivered into his hands Joakim the king of Juda, and part of the vessels of the house of God: and he carried them away into the land of Sennaar, to the house of his god, and the vessels he brought into the treasure house of his god. And the king spoke to Asphenez the master of the eunuchs, that he should bring in some of the children of Israel, and of the king's seed and of the princes, Children in whom there was no blemish, well favoured, and skilful in all wisdom, acute in knowledge, and instructed in science, and such as might stand in the king's palace, that he might teach them the learning, and the tongue of the Chaldeans.

Lesson II ~ Dan 1:5–9

And the king appointed them a daily provision, of his own meat, and of the wine of which he drank himself, that being nourished three years, afterwards they might stand before the king. Now there were among them of the children of Juda, Daniel, Ananias, Misael, and Azarias. And the master of the eunuchs gave them names: to Daniel, Baltassar: to Ananias, Sidrach: to Misael, Misach: and to Azarias, Abdenago. But Daniel purposed in his heart that he would not be defiled with the king's table, nor with the wine which he drank: and he requested the master of the eunuchs that he might not be defiled. And God gave to Daniel grace and mercy in the sight of the prince of the eunuchs.

Lesson III ~ Dan 1:10–15

And the prince of the eunuchs said to Daniel: I fear my lord the king, who hath appointed you meat and drink: who if he should see your faces leaner than those of the other youths your equals, you shall endanger my head to the king. And Daniel said to Malasar, whom the prince of the eunuchs had appointed over Daniel, Ananias, Misael, and Azarias: Try, I beseech thee, thy servants for ten days, and let pulse be given us to eat, and water to drink: And look upon our faces, and the faces of the children that eat of the king's meat: and as thou shalt see, deal with thy servants. And when he had heard these words, he tried them for ten days. And after ten days their faces appeared fairer and fatter than all the children that ate of the king's meat.

Lesson IV

From the Book addressed To Virgins by St. Athanasius, Pope of Alexandria.

If any should come and say unto thee, "Fast not so often, lest thou injure thine health," believe them not, neither listen to them. They are but the tools of the great enemy to suggest such a thing unto thee. Remember how it is written that when the three children, and Daniel, and the other lads, were led captives by Nabuchodonosor King of Babylon, and it was commanded them to eat of his Royal table, and to drink of his wine, Daniel and those three children would not defile themselves with the King's table, but said unto the eunuch into whose keeping they had been given, "Give us of the fruits of the earth, and we will eat." And the eunuch answered them, "I fear my lord the King, who hath appointed your meat and your drink, lest perchance your faces should appear unto the King worse—liking than the other children, who are fed from his Royal table, and he should punish me."

Lesson V

Then they said unto him "Prove thy servants ten days, and give us herbs." And he gave them pulse to eat and water to drink and, when he brought them in before the King, their countenances appeared fairer than all the children which did eat the portion of the King's meat. Seest thou what fasting does? It heals diseases, it dries up the humors of the body, it scares away devils, it purges forth unclean thoughts, it makes the intellect clearer, it purifies the heart, it sanctifies the body, and in the end it leads a man unto the throne of God. Think not that this is rash talking. Thou hast the testimony of this in the Gospels under the sanction of the Saviour Himself. His disciples asked Him why they could not cast out an evil spirit, and He said unto them "This kind can come forth by nothing but by prayer and fasting."

Lesson VI

If any man therefore be troubled with an unclean spirit, if he bethink him of this, and have recourse to this remedy, namely, fasting, the evil spirit will be forthwith compelled to leave him from dread of the power of fasting. Devils take great delight in fullness, and drunkenness, and bodily comfort. There is great power in fasting, and great and glorious things are wrought thereby. How comes it that men work such wonders, and that signs are done by them, and that God through them giveth health to the sick, unless it be from their ghostly exercises, and the meekness of their souls, and their godly conversation? To fast is to banquet with Angels, and he that fasts is to be reckoned, so far, among the Angelic host.

Lessons VII, VIII, & IX from the Sermons for After Pentecost Section

Monday III of November

Lesson I ~ Dan 2:31–35

From the Prophet Daniel

Thou, O king, sawest, and behold there was as it were a great statue: this statue, which was great and high, tall of stature, stood before thee, and the look thereof was terrible. The head of this statue was of fine gold, but the breast and the arms of silver, and the belly and the thighs of brass: And the legs of iron, the feet part of iron and part of clay. Thus thou sawest, till a stone was cut out of a mountain without hands: and it struck the statue upon the feet thereof that were of iron and of clay, and broke them in pieces. Then was the iron, the clay, the brass, the silver, and the gold broken to pieces together, and became like the chaff of a summer's thrashingfloor, and they were carried away by the wind: and there was no place found for them: but the stone that struck the statue, became a great mountain, and filled the whole earth.

Lesson II ~ Dan 2:36–40

This is the dream: we will also tell the interpretation thereof before thee, O king. Thou art a king of kings: and the God of heaven hath given thee a kingdom, and strength, and power, and glory: And all places wherein the children of men, and the beasts of the field do dwell: he hath also given the birds of the air into thy hand, and hath put all things under thy power: thou therefore art the head of gold. And after thee shall rise up another kingdom, inferior to thee, of silver: and another third kingdom of brass, which shall rule over all the world. And the fourth kingdom shall be as iron. As iron breaketh into pieces, and subdueth all things, so shall that break and destroy all these.

Lesson III ~ Dan 2:41–44

And whereas thou sawest the feet, and the toes, part of potter's clay, and part of iron: the kingdom shall be divided, but yet it shall take its origin from the iron, according as thou sawest the iron mixed with the miry clay. And as the toes of the feet were part of iron, and part of clay, the kingdom shall be partly strong, and partly broken. And whereas thou sawest the iron mixed with miry clay, they shall be mingled indeed together with the seed of man, but they shall not stick fast one to another, as iron cannot be mixed with clay. But in the days of those kingdoms the God of heaven will set up a kingdom that shall never be destroyed, and his kingdom shall not be delivered up to another people, and it shall break in pieces, and shall consume all these kingdoms, and itself shall stand for ever.

Tuesday III of November

Lesson I ~ Dan 3:14–15

From the Prophet Daniel

And Nabuchodonosor the king spoke to them, and said: Is it true, O Sidrach, Misach, and Abdenago, that you do not worship my gods, nor adore the golden statue that I have set up? Now therefore if you be ready at what hour soever you shall hear the sound of the trumpet, flute, harp, sackbut, and psaltery, and symphony, and of all kind of music, prostrate yourselves, and adore the statue which I have made: but if you do not adore, you shall be cast the same hour into the furnace of burning fire: and who is the God that shall deliver you out of my hand?

Lesson II ~ Dan 3:16–19

Sidrach, Misach, and Abdenago answered and said to king Nabuchodonosor: We have no occasion to answer thee concerning this matter. For behold our God, whom we worship, is able to save us from the furnace of burning fire, and to deliver us out of thy hands, O king. But if he will not, be it known to thee, O king, that we will not worship thy gods, nor adore the golden statue which thou hast set up. Then was Nabuchodonosor filled with fury: and the countenance of his face was changed against Sidrach, Misach, and Abdenago, and he commanded that the furnace should be heated seven times more than it had been accustomed to be heated.

Lesson III ~ Dan 3:21–24

And immediately these men were bound and were cast into the furnace of burning fire, with their coats, and their caps, and their shoes, and their garments. For the king's commandment was urgent, and the furnace was heated exceedingly. And the flame of the fire slew those men that had cast in Sidrach, Misach, and Abdenago. But these three men, that is, Sidrach, Misach, and Abdenago, fell down bound in the midst of the furnace of burning fire. And they walked in the midst of the flame, praising God and blessing the Lord.

Wednesday III of November

Lesson I ~ Dan 4:16–19

From the Prophet Daniel

Baltassar answered, and said: My lord, the dream be to them that hate thee, and the interpretation thereof to thy enemies. The tree which thou sawest which was high and strong, whose height reached to the skies, and the sight thereof into all the earth: And the branches thereof were most beautiful, and its fruit exceeding much, and in it was food for all, under which the beasts of the field dwelt, and the birds of the air had their abode in its branches. It is thou, O king, who art grown great and become mighty: for thy greatness hath grown, and hath reached to heaven, and thy power unto the ends of the earth.

Lesson II ~ Dan 4:20–22

And whereas the king saw a watcher, and a holy one come down from heaven, and say: Cut down the tree and destroy it, but leave the stump of the roots thereof in the earth, and let it be bound with iron and brass among the grass without, and let it be sprinkled with the dew of heaven, and let his feeding be with the wild beasts, till seven times pass over him. This is the interpretation of the sentence of the most High, which is come upon my lord the king. They shall cast thee out from among men, and thy dwelling shall be with cattle and with wild beasts, and thou shalt eat grass as an ox, and shalt be wet with the dew of heaven.

Lesson III ~ Dan 4:22–25

And seven times shall pass over thee, till thou know that the most High ruleth over the kingdom of men, and giveth it to whomsoever he will. But whereas he commanded, that the stump of the roots thereof, that is, of the tree, should be left: thy kingdom shall remain to thee after thou shalt have known that power is from heaven. Wherefore, O king, let my counsel be acceptable to thee, and redeem thou thy sins with alms, and thy iniquities with works of mercy to the poor: perhaps he will forgive thy offences. All these things came upon king Nabuchodonosor.

Thursday III of November

Lesson I ~ Dan 5:1–6

From the Prophet Daniel

Baltasar the king made a great feast for a thousand of his nobles: and every one drank according to his age. And being now drunk he commanded that they should bring the vessels of gold and silver which Nabuchodonosor his father had brought away out of the temple, that was in Jerusalem, that the king and his nobles, and his wives and his concubines, might drink in them. Then were the golden and silver vessels brought, which he had brought away out of the temple that was in Jerusalem: and the king and his nobles, his wives and his concubines, drank in them. They drank wine, and praised their gods of gold, and of silver, of brass, of iron, and of wood, and of stone. In the same hour there appeared fingers, as it were of the hand of a man, writing over against the candlestick upon the surface of the wall of the king's palace: and the king beheld the joints of the hand that wrote. Then was the king's countenance changed, and his thoughts troubled him.

Lesson II - Dan 5:13–17

Then Daniel was brought in before the king. And the king spoke, and said to him: Art thou Daniel of the children of the captivity of Juda, whom my father the king brought out of Judea? I have heard of thee, that thou hast the spirit of the gods, and excellent knowledge, and understanding, and wisdom are found in thee. And now the wise men the magicians have come in before me, to read this writing, and shew me the interpretation thereof: and they could not declare to me the meaning of this writing. But I have heard of thee, that thou canst interpret obscure things, and resolve difficult things: now if thou art able to read the writing, and to shew me the interpretation thereof, thou shalt be clothed with purple, and shalt have a chain of gold about thy neck, and shalt be the third prince in my kingdom. To which Daniel made answer, and said before the king: thy rewards be to thyself, and the gifts of thy house give to another: but the writing I will read to thee, O king, and shew thee the interpretation thereof.

Lesson III - Dan 5:25–31

And this is the writing that is written: MANE, THECEL, PHARES. And this is the interpretation of the word. MANE: God hath numbered thy kingdom, and hath finished it. THECEL: thou art weighed in the balance, and art found wanting. PHARES: thy kingdom is divided, and is given to the Medes and Persians. Then by the king's command Daniel was clothed with purple, and a chain of gold was put about his neck: and it was proclaimed of him that he had power as the third man in the kingdom. The same night Baltasar the Chaldean king was slain. And Darius the Mede succeeded to the kingdom, being sixty-two years old.

Friday III of November

Lesson I - Dan 6:11–15

From the Prophet Daniel

Wherefore those men carefully watching him, found Daniel praying and making supplication to his God. And they came and spoke to the king concerning the edict: O king, hast thou not decreed, that every man that should make a request to any of the gods, or men, for thirty days, but to thyself, O king, should be cast into the den of the lions? And the king answered them, saying: The word is true according to the decree of the Medes and Persians, which it is not lawful to violate. Then they answered, and said before the king: Daniel, who is of the children of the captivity of Juda, hath not regarded thy law, nor the decree that thou hast made: but three times a day he maketh his prayer. Now when the king had heard these words, he was very much grieved, and in behalf of Daniel he set his heart to deliver him and even till sunset he laboured to save him. But those men perceiving the king's design, said to him: Know thou, O king, that the law of the Medes and Persians is, that no decree which the king hath made, may be altered.

Lesson II ~ Dan 6:16–20

Then the king commanded, and they brought Daniel, and cast him into the den of the lions. And the king said to Daniel: thy God, whom thou always servest, he will deliver thee. And a stone was brought, and laid upon the mouth of the den: which the king sealed with his own ring, and with the ring of his nobles, that nothing should be done against Daniel. And the king went away to his house and laid himself down without taking supper, and meat was not set before him, and even sleep departed from him. Then the king rising very early in the morning, went in haste to the lions' den: And coming near to the den, cried with a lamentable voice to Daniel, and said to him: Daniel, servant of the living God, hath thy God, whom thou servest always, been able, thinkest thou, to deliver thee from the lions?

Lesson III ~ Dan 6:21–24

And Daniel answering the king, said: O king, live for ever: My God hath sent his angel, and hath shut up the mouths of the lions, and they have not hurt me: forasmuch as before him justice hath been found in me: yea and before thee, O king, I have done no offence. Then was the king exceeding glad for him, and he commanded that Daniel should be taken out of the den: and Daniel was taken out of the den, and no hurt was found in him, because he believed in his God. And by the king's commandment, those men were brought that had accused Daniel: and they were cast into the lions' den, they and their children, and their wives: and they did not reach the bottom of the den, before the lions caught them, and broke all their bones in pieces.

Saturday III of November

Lesson I ~ Dan 9:1–5

From the Prophet Daniel

In the first year of Darius the son of Assuerus of the seed of the Medes, who reigned over the kingdom of the Chaldeans: The first year of his reign, I Daniel understood by books the number of the years, concerning which the word of the Lord came to Jeremias the prophet, that seventy years should be accomplished of the desolation of Jerusalem. And I set my face to the Lord my God, to pray and make supplication with fasting, and sackcloth, and ashes. And I prayed to the Lord my God, and I made my confession, and said: I beseech thee, O Lord God, great and terrible, who keepest the covenant, and mercy to them that love thee, and keep thy commandments. We have sinned, we have committed iniquity, we have done wickedly, and have revolted: and we have gone aside from thy commandments, and thy judgments.

Lesson II - Dan 9:21–24

As I was yet speaking in prayer, behold the man Gabriel, whom I had seen in the vision at the beginning, flying swiftly touched me at the time of the evening sacrifice. And he instructed me, and spoke to me, and said: O Daniel, I am now come forth to teach thee, and that thou mightest understand. From the beginning of thy prayers the word came forth: and I am come to shew it to thee, because thou art a man of desires: therefore do thou mark the word, and understand the vision. Seventy weeks are shortened upon thy people, and upon thy holy city, that transgression may be finished, and sin may have an end, and iniquity may be abolished; and everlasting justice may be brought; and vision and prophecy may be fulfilled; and the saint of saints may be anointed.

Lesson III - Dan 9:25–27

Know thou therefore, and take notice: that from the going forth of the word, to build up Jerusalem again, unto Christ the prince, there shall be seven weeks, and sixty-two weeks: and the street shall be built again, and the walls in straitness of times. And after sixty-two weeks Christ shall be slain: and the people that shall deny him shall not be his. And a people with their leader that shall come, shall destroy the city and the sanctuary: and the end thereof shall be waste, and after the end of the war the appointed desolation. And he shall confirm the covenant with many, in one week: and in the half of the week the victim and the sacrifice shall fall: and there shall be in the temple the abomination of desolation: and the desolation shall continue even to the consummation, and to the end.

✚

Sunday IV of November

Lesson I - Osee 1:1–3

Beginning of the book of the Prophet Osee

The word of the Lord, that came to Osee the son of Beeri, in the days of Ozias, Joathan, Achaz, and Ezechias kings of Juda, and in the days of Jeroboam the son of Joas king of Israel. The beginning of the Lord's speaking by Osee: and the Lord said to Osee: Go, take thee a wife of fornications, and have of her children of fornications: for the land by fornication shall depart from the Lord. So he went, and took Gomer the daughter of Debelaim: and she conceived and bore him a son.

Lesson II - Osee 1:4–7

And the Lord said to him: Call his name Jezrahel: for yet a little while, and I will visit the blood of Jezrahel upon the house of Jehu, and I will cause to cease the kingdom of the house of Israel. And in that day I will break in pieces the bow of Israel in the valley of Jezrahel. And she conceived again, and bore a daughter, and he said to him: Call her name, Without mercy: for I will not add any more to have mercy on the house of Israel, but I will utterly forget them. And I will have mercy on the house of Juda, and I will save them by the Lord their God: and I will not save them by bow, nor by sword, nor by battle, nor by horses, nor by horsemen.

Lesson III ~ Osee 1:8–11

And she weaned her that was called Without mercy. And she conceived, and bore a son. And he said: Call his name, Not my people: for you are not my people, and I will not be yours. And the number of the children of Israel shall be as the sand of the sea, that is without measure, and shall not be numbered. And it shall be in the place where it shall be said to them: You are not my people: it shall be said to them: Ye are the sons of the living God. And the children of Juda, and the children of Israel shall be gathered together: and they shall appoint themselves one head, and shall come up out of the land: for great is the day of Jezrahel.

Lesson IV

From *The City of God* by St. Augustine, Bishop

As to the Prophet Osee, the deeper his meaning, the harder to pierce. But something may be gotten out of him, and, as I promised, I will give it here. He says: "And it shall come to pass that, in the place where it shall be said unto them, 'Ye are not My people,' there it shall be said unto them 'Ye are the sons of the living God.'" This was understood even by the Apostles as a Prophetic witness to the call of the Gentiles, who formerly had not been God's people.

Lesson V

And since the converted Gentiles are the spiritual children of Abraham, and are therefore rightly called Israelites, therefore he goes on, and says: "Then shall the children of Judah and the children of Israel be gathered together, and appoint themselves one head, and they shall come up out of the land." If we went on expounding this, we should water down the flavor of the prophetic draught. Let there be remembered, however, that Corner Stone, and let there be acknowledged those twain walls (which It binds into one), the Jews and the Gentiles, one called the children of Judah and the other the children of Israel, bound together under One Head, and coming up out of the land.

Lesson VI

Concerning them that are now Israelites according to the flesh, that will not now believe in Christ, but shall believe hereafter (that is, their children shall believe, for these shall die, and go to their own place), this same Prophet gives witness, where he says "The children of Israel shall abide many days without a King, and without a Prince, and without a sacrifice, and without an Altar, and without a Priest, and without oracles." To whom is it not manifest that such is the state of the Jews now?

Lessons VII, VIII, & IX from the Sermons for After Pentecost Section

Monday IV of November

Lesson I - Osee 4:1–3

From the Prophet Osee

Hear the word of the Lord, ye children of Israel, for the Lord shall enter into judgment with the inhabitants of the land: for there is no truth, and there is no mercy, and there is no knowledge of God in the land. Cursing, and lying, and killing, and theft, and adultery have overflowed, and blood hath touched blood. Therefore shall the land mourn, and every one that dwelleth in it shall languish with the beasts of the field, and with the fowls of the air: yea, the fishes of the sea also shall be gathered together.

Lesson II - Osee 4:4–6

But yet let not any man judge: and let not a man be rebuked: for thy people are as they that contradict the priest. And thou shalt fall to day, and the prophet also shall fall with thee: in the night I have made thy mother to be silent. My people have been silent, because they had no knowledge: because thou hast rejected knowledge, I will reject thee, that thou shalt not do the office of priesthood to me: and thou hast forgotten the law of thy God, I also will forget thy children.

Lesson III - Osee 4:7–10

According to the multitude of them so have they sinned against me: I will change their glory into shame. They shall eat the sins of my people, and shall lift up their souls to their iniquity. And there shall be like people like priest: and I will visit their ways upon them, and I will repay them their devices. And they shall eat and shall not be filled: they have committed fornication, and have not ceased: because they have forsaken the Lord in not observing his law.

Tuesday IV of November

Lesson I - Joel 1:1–4

Beginning of the Prophet Joel

The word of the Lord that came to Joel the son of Phatuel. Hear this, ye old men, and give ear, all ye inhabitants of the land: did this ever happen in your days, or in the days of your fathers? Tell ye of this to your children, and let your children tell their children, and their children to another generation. That which the palmerworm hath left, the locust hath eaten: and that which the locust hath left, the bruchus hath eaten: and that which the bruchus hath left, the mildew hath destroyed.

Lesson II - Joel 1:5–7

Awake, ye that are drunk, and weep, and mourn all ye that take delight in drinking sweet wine: for it is cut off from your mouth. For a nation is come up upon my land, strong and without number: his teeth are like the teeth of a lion: and his cheek teeth as of a lion's whelp. He hath laid my vineyard waste, and hath pilled off the bark of my fig tree: he hath stripped it bare, and cast it away; the branches thereof are made white.

Lesson III - Joel 1:8–11

Lament like a virgin girded with sackcloth for the husband of her youth. Sacrifice and libation is cut off from the house of the Lord: the priests, the Lord's ministers, have mourned: The country is destroyed, the ground hath mourned: for the corn is wasted, the wine is confounded, the oil hath languished. The husbandmen are ashamed, the vinedressers have howled for the wheat, and for the barley, because the harvest of the field is perished.

Wednesday IV of November

Lesson I - Joel 3:1–3

From the Prophet Joel

For behold in those days, and in that time when I shall bring back the captivity of Juda and Jerusalem: I will gather together all nations, and will bring them down into the valley of Josaphat: and I will plead with them there for my people, and for my inheritance Israel, whom they have scattered among the nations, and have parted my land. And they have cast lots upon my people: and the boy they have put in the stews, and the girl they have sold for wine, that they might drink.

Lesson II - Joel 3:4–7

But what have you to do with me, O Tyre, and Sidon, and all the coast of the Philistines? will you revenge yourselves on me? and if you revenge yourselves on me, I will very soon return you a recompense upon your own head. For you have taken away my silver and my gold: and my desirable and most beautiful things you have carried into your temples. And the children of Juda, and the children of Jerusalem you have sold to the children of the Greeks, that you might remove them far off from their own country. Behold, I will raise them up out of the place wherein you have sold them: and I will return your recompense upon your own heads.

Lesson III - Joel 3:8–12

And I will sell your sons, and your daughters by the hands of the children of Juda, and they shall sell them to the Sabeans, a nation far off, for the Lord hath spoken it. Proclaim ye this among the nations: prepare war, rouse up the strong: let them come, let all the men of war come up. Cut your ploughshares into swords, and your spades into spears. Let the weak say: I am strong. Break forth, and come, all ye nations, from round about, and gather yourselves together: there will the Lord cause all thy strong ones to fall down. Let them arise, and let the nations come up into the valley of Josaphat: for there I will sit to judge all nations round about.

Thursday IV of November

Lesson I - Amos 1:1–2

Beginning of the Prophet Amos

The words of Amos, who was among herdsmen of Thecua: which he saw concerning Israel in the days of Ozias king of Juda, and in the days of Jeroboam the son of Joas king of Israel two years before the earthquake. And he said: The Lord will roar from Sion, and utter his voice from Jerusalem: and the beautiful places of the shepherds have mourned, and the top of Carmel is withered.

Lesson II - Amos 1:3–5

Thus saith the Lord: For three crimes of Damascus, and for four I will not convert it: because they have thrashed Galaad with iron wains. And I will send a fire into the house of Azael, and it shall devour the houses of Benadad. And I will break the bar of Damascus: and I will cut off the inhabitants from the plain of the idol, and him that holdeth the sceptre from the house of pleasure: and the people of Syria shall be carried away to Cyrene, saith the Lord.

Lesson III - Amos 1:6–8

Thus saith the Lord: For three crimes of Gaza, and for four I will not convert it: because they have carried away a perfect captivity to shut them up in Edom. And I will send a fire on the wall of Gaza, and it shall devour the houses thereof. And I will cut off the inhabitant from Azotus, and him that holdeth the sceptre from Ascalon: and I will turn my hand against Accaron, and the rest of the Philistines shall perish, saith the Lord God.

Friday IV of November

Lesson I - Abd 1:1–4

Beginning of the Prophet Abdias

The vision of Abdias. Thus saith the Lord God to Edom: We have heard a rumour from the Lord, and he hath sent an ambassador to the nations: Arise, and let us rise up to battle against him. Behold I have made thee small among the nations: thou art exceeding contemptible. The pride of thy heart hath lifted thee up, who dwellest in the clefts of the rocks, and settest up thy throne on high: who sayest in thy heart: Who shall bring me down to the ground Though thou be exalted as an eagle, and though thou set thy nest among the stars: thence will I bring thee down, saith the Lord.

Lesson II - Abd 1:5–7

If thieves had gone in to thee, if robbers by night, how wouldst thou have held thy peace? would they not have stolen till they had enough if the grapegatherers had come in to thee, would they not have left thee at the least a cluster? How have they searched Esau, how have they sought out his hidden things? They have sent thee out even to the border: all the men of thy confederacy have deceived thee: the men of thy peace have prevailed against thee: they that eat with thee shall lay snares under thee: there is no wisdom in him.

Lesson III - Abd 1:8–11

Shall not I in that day, saith the Lord, destroy the wise out of Edom, and understanding out of the mount of Esau And thy valiant men of the south shall be afraid, that man may be cut off from the mount of Esau. For the slaughter, and for the iniquity against thy brother Jacob, confusion shall cover thee, and thou shalt perish for ever. In the day when thou stoodest against him, when strangers carried away his army captive, and foreigners entered into his gates, and cast lots upon Jerusalem: thou also wast as one of them.

Saturday IV of November

Lesson I ~ Jonas 1:1–4

Beginning of the Prophet Jonas

Now the word of the Lord came to Jonas the son of Amathi, saying: Arise, and go to Ninive the great city, and preach in it: for the wickedness thereof is come up before me. And Jonas rose up to flee into Tharsis from the face of the Lord, and he went down to Joppe, and found a ship going to Tharsis: and he paid the fare thereof, and went down into it, to go with them to Tharsis from the face of the Lord. But the Lord sent a great wind into the sea: and a great tempest was raised in the sea, and the ship was in danger to be broken.

Lesson II ~ Jonas 1:5–7

And the mariners were afraid, and the men cried to their god: and they cast forth the wares that were in the ship, into the sea, to lighten it of them: and Jonas went down into the inner part of the ship, and fell into a deep sleep. And the shipmaster came to him, and said to him: Why art thou fast asleep? rise up, call upon thy God, if so be that God will think of us, that we may not perish. And they said every one to his fellow: Come, and let us cast lots, that we may know why this evil is upon us. And they cast lots, and the lot fell upon Jonas.

Lesson III ~ Jonas 1:8–12

And they said to him: Tell us for what cause this evil is upon us, what is thy business? of what country art thou? and whither goest thou? or of what people art thou? And he said to them: I am a Hebrew, and I fear the Lord the God of heaven, who made both the sea and the dry land. And the men were greatly afraid, and they said to him: Why hast thou done this? (For the men knew that he fled from the face of the Lord: because he had told them.) And they said to him: What shall we do to thee, that the sea may be calm to us? for the sea flowed and swelled. And he said to them: Take me up, and cast me into the sea, and the sea shall be calm to you: for I know that for my sake this great tempest is upon you.

Sunday V of November

Lesson I ~ Mic 1:1–3

Beginning of the Prophet Michæas

The word of the Lord that came to Micheas the Morasthite, in the days of Joathan, Achaz, and Ezechias, kings of Juda: which he saw concerning Samaria and Jerusalem. Hear, all ye people: and let the earth give ear, and all that is therein: and let the Lord God be a witness to you, the Lord from his holy temple. For behold the Lord will come forth out of his place: and he will come down, and will tread upon the high places of the earth.

Lesson II ~ Mic 1:4–6

And the mountains shall be melted under him: and the valleys shall be cleft, as wax before the fire, and as waters that run down a steep place. For the wickedness of Jacob is all this, and for the sins of the house of Israel. What is the wickedness of Jacob? is it not Samaria? and what are the high places of Juda? are they not Jerusalem? And I will make Samaria as a heap of stones in the field when a vineyard is planted: and I will bring down the stones thereof into the valley, and will lay her foundations bare.

Lesson III ~ Mic 1:7–9

And all her graven things shall be cut in pieces, and all her wages shall be burnt with fire, and I will bring to destruction all her idols: for they were gathered together of the hire of a harlot, and unto the hire of a harlot they shall return. Therefore will I lament and howl: I will go stripped and naked: I will make a wailing like the dragons, and a mourning like the ostriches. Because her wound is desperate, because it is come even to Juda, it hath touched the gate of my people even to Jerusalem.

Lesson IV

From the Sermon of St. Basil the Great upon the Thirty-third Psalm.

Whenever the desire to sin comes over thee, I would that thou couldest think of the awful and overwhelming judgment-seat of Christ. There the Judge shall sit upon a throne high and lifted up. Every creature shall stand before Him, quaking because of the glory of His presence. There are we to be led up, one by one, to give account for those things which we have done in life. Presently there will be found, by the sides of those who have in life wrought much evil, dreadful and hideous angels with faces of fire, and burning breath, appointed thereto, and showing their evil will, in appearance like the night, in their despair and hatred of mankind.

Lesson V

Think again of the bottomless pit, the impenetrable darkness, the lightless fire, burning, but not glowing the poisonous mass of worms, preying upon the flesh, ever feeding and never filled, causing by their gnawing unbearable agony, lastly, the greatest punishment of all, shame and confusion for ever. Have a dread of these things, and let that dread correct thee, and be as a curb to thy mind to hold it in from the hankering after sin.

Lesson VI

This fear of the Lord the Prophet has promised to teach. But he has not promised to teach it to all, but only to such as will hear him, not to such as have fallen far away, but to such as run to him, hungry for salvation, not to such as have no part in the promises, but to such as by baptism are born children of adoption, set at peace and oneness with the Word. "Come, children," says he, that is to say, "Draw nigh unto me by good works, all you who by the new birth have become the worthy children of light, hearken unto me, all you who have the ears of your heart opened, I will teach you the fear of the Lord, even the fear of that Being of Whom we have just been speaking."

Lessons VII, VIII, & IX from the Sermons for After Pentecost Section

Monday V of November

Lesson I ~ Nah 1:1–4

Beginning of the Prophet Nahum

The burden of Ninive. The book of the vision of Nahum the Elcesite. The Lord is a jealous God, and a revenger: the Lord is a revenger, and hath wrath: the Lord taketh vengeance on his adversaries, and he is angry with his enemies. The Lord is patient, and great in power, and will not cleanse and acquit the guilty. The Lord's ways are in a tempest, and a whirlwind, and clouds are the dust of his feet. He rebuketh the sea, and drieth it up: and bringeth all the rivers to be a desert.

Lesson II ~ Nah 1:4–6

Basan languisheth and Carmel: and the dower of Libanus fadeth away. The mountains tremble at him, and the hills are made desolate: and the earth hath quaked at his presence, and the world, and all that dwell therein. Who can stand before the face of his indignation? and who shall resist in the fierceness of his anger? his indignation is poured out like fire: and the rocks are melted by him.

Lesson III ~ Nah 1:7–10

The Lord is good and giveth strength in the day of trouble: and knoweth them that hope in him. But with a flood that passeth by, he will make an utter end of the place thereof: and darkness shall pursue his enemies. What do ye devise against the Lord? he will make an utter end: there shall not rise a double affliction. For as thorns embrace one another: so while they are feasting and drinking together, they shall be consumed as stubble that is fully dry.

Tuesday V of November

Lesson I ~ Hab 1:1–4

Beginning of the Prophet Habacuc

The burden that Habacuc the prophet saw. How long, O Lord, shall I cry, and thou wilt not hear? shall I cry out to thee suffering violence, and thou wilt not save? Why hast thou shewn me iniquity and grievance, to see rapine and injustice before me? and there is a judgment, but opposition is more powerful. Therefore the law is torn in pieces, and judgment comes not to the end: because the wicked prevaileth against the just, therefore wrong judgment goeth forth.

Lesson II ~ Hab 1:5–7

Behold ye among the nations, and see: wonder, and be astonished: for a work is done in your days, which no man will believe when it shall be told. For behold, I will raise up the Chaldeans, a bitter and swift nation, marching upon the breadth of the earth, to possess the dwelling places that are not their own. They are dreadful, and terrible: from themselves shall their judgment, and their burden proceed.

Lesson III ~ Hab 1:8–10

Their horses are lighter than leopards, and swifter than evening wolves; and their horsemen shall be spread abroad: for their horsemen shall come from afar, they shall fly as an eagle that maketh haste to eat. They shall all come to the prey, their face is like a burning wind: and they shall gather together captives as the sand. And their prince shall triumph over kings, and princes shall be his laughingstock: and he shall laugh at every strong hold, and shall cast up a mount, and shall take it.

Wednesday V of November

Lesson I ~ Soph 1:1–3

Beginning of the Prophet Sophonias

The word of the Lord that came to Sophonias the son of Chusi, the son of Godolias, the son of Amarias, the son of Ezechias, in the days of Josias the son of Amon king of Juda. Gathering, I will gather together all things from off the face of the land, saith the Lord: I will gather man, and beast, I will gather the birds of the air, and the fishes of the sea: and the ungodly shall meet with ruin: and I will destroy men from off the face of the land, saith the Lord.

Lesson II ~ Soph 1:4–6

And I will stretch out my hand upon Juda, and upon all the inhabitants of Jerusalem: and I will destroy out of this place the remnant of Baal, and the names of the wardens of the temples with the priests: And them that worship the host of heaven upon the tops of houses, and them that adore, and swear by the Lord, and swear by Melchom. And them that turn away from following after the Lord, and that have not sought the Lord, nor searched after him.

Lesson III ~ Soph 1:7–9

Be silent before the face of the Lord God: for the day of the Lord is near, for the Lord hath prepared a victim, he hath sanctified his guests. And it shall come to pass in the day of the victim of the Lord, that I will visit upon the princes, and upon the king's sons, and upon all such as are clothed with strange apparel. And I will visit in that day upon every one that entereth arrogantly over the threshold: them that fill the house of the Lord their God with iniquity and deceit.

Thursday V of November

Lesson I ~ Agg 1:1–2

Beginning of the Prophet Aggeus

In the second year of Darius the king, in the sixth month, in the first day of the month, the word of the Lord came by the hand of Aggeus the prophet, to Zorobabel the son of Salathiel, governor of Juda, and to Jesus the son of Josedec the high priest, saying: Thus saith the Lord of hosts, saying: This people saith: The time is not yet come for building the house of the Lord.

Lesson II ~ Agg 1:3–6

And the word of the Lord came by the hand of Aggeus the prophet, saying: Is it time for you to dwell in ceiled houses, and this house lie desolate? And now thus saith the Lord of hosts: Set your hearts to consider your ways. You have sowed much, and brought in little: you have eaten, but have not had enough: you have drunk, but have not been filled with drink: you have clothed yourselves, but have not been warmed: and he that hath earned wages, put them into a bag with holes.

Lesson III ~ Agg 1:7–10

Thus saith the Lord of hosts: Set your hearts upon your ways: Go up to the mountain, bring timber, and build the house: and it shall be acceptable to me, and I shall be glorified, saith the Lord. You have looked for more, and behold it became less, and you brought it home, and I blowed it away: why, saith the Lord of hosts? because my house is desolate, and you make haste every man to his own house. Therefore the heavens over you were stayed from giving dew, and the earth was hindered from yielding her fruits.

Friday V of November

Lesson I ~ Zach 1:1–3

Beginning of the Prophet Zacharias

In the eighth month, in the second year of king Darius, the word of the Lord came to Zacharias the son of Barachias, the son of Addo, the prophet, saying: The Lord hath been exceeding angry with your fathers. And thou shalt say to them: Thus saith the Lord of hosts: Turn ye to me, saith the Lord of hosts: and I will turn to you, saith the Lord of hosts.

Lesson II ~ Zach 1:4–5

Be not as your fathers, to whom the former prophets have cried, saying: Thus saith the Lord of hosts: Turn ye from your evil ways, and from your wicked thoughts: but they did not give ear, neither did they hearken to me, saith the Lord. Your fathers, where are they? and the prophets, shall they live always?

Lesson III ~ Zach 1:6

But yet my words, and my ordinances, which I gave in charge to my servants the prophets, did they not take hold of your fathers, and they returned, and said: As the Lord of hosts thought to do to us according to our ways, and according to our devices, so he hath done to us.

Saturday V of November

Lesson I ~ Mal 1:1–4

Beginning of the Prophet Malachias

The burden of the word of the Lord to Israel by the hand of Malachias. I have loved you, saith the Lord: and you have said: Wherein hast thou loved us? Was not Esau brother to Jacob, saith the Lord, and I have loved Jacob, But have hated Esau? and I have made his mountains a wilderness, and given his inheritance to the dragons of the desert. But if Edom shall say: We are destroyed, but we will return and build up what hath been destroyed: thus saith the Lord of hosts: They shall build up, and I will throw down: and they shall be called the borders of wickedness, and the people with whom the Lord is angry for ever.

Lesson II ~ Mal 1:5–7

And your eyes shall see, and you shall say: The Lord be magnified upon the border of Israel. The son honoureth the father, and the servant his master: if then I be a father, where is my honour? and if I be a master, where is my fear? saith the Lord of hosts. To you, O priests, that despise my name, and have said: Wherein have we despised thy name? You offer polluted bread upon my altar, and you say: Wherein have we polluted thee? In that you say: The table of the Lord is contemptible.

Lesson III ~ Mal 1:8–11

If you offer the blind for sacrifice, is it not evil? and if you offer the lame and the sick, is it not evil? offer it to thy prince, if he will be pleased with it, or if he will regard thy face, saith the Lord of hosts. And now beseech ye the face of God, that he may have mercy on you (for by your hand hath this been done), if by any means he will receive your faces, saith the Lord of hosts. Who is there among you, that will shut the doors, and will kindle the fire on my altar gratis? I have no pleasure in you, saith the Lord of hosts: and I will not receive a gift of your hand. For from the rising of the sun even to the going down, my name is great among the Gentiles, and in every place there is sacrifice, and there is offered to my name a clean oblation: for my name is great among the Gentiles, saith the Lord of hosts.

SANCTORAL COMMONS

These are the Lessons shared in common by various classes of Saints as particularly delineated in the following section, the Proper of Saints.

What follows always gives way to whatever is noted as proper according to the feast of each Saint.

VIGILS OF APOSTLES

Lesson I

From the Holy Gospel according to St. John (John 15:12–16)

At that time: Jesus said to His disciples: This is my commandment, That you love one another, as I have loved you. And so on.

Homily by Pope St. Gregory

All the holy words of the Lord are full of His commandments. Why, then, does the Lord speak of the commandment to love one another as if He gave no other commandment? "This," says He, "is My commandment, That you love one another." Is it not because love is the one object of all His commandments, and all his commandments are one? For, even as a tree, having but one root, brings forth many branches, so, if the root be love, many virtues do spring therefrom. Neither is the branch of good works green, if it abide not in the root of love.

Lesson II

Therefore the commandments of the Lord are manifold, and yet one. Manifold, indeed, by the diversity of working, but one, as concerning the root of love. And how it behooves us to keep hold on that root of love, we know from Him, Who in sundry places of His holy Scripture, moves us to love our friends in Him, and our enemies for Him. He truly abides in love, who loves his friend in God, and his enemy for God. For there are some who love their neighbor indeed, but by an affection engendered of kinship and of the flesh: such a love the Scripture forbids not: but it is one thing to love our neighbor with that love whereto nature does freely move us, and another thing to love him with that love whereto we are obliged, if we would do whatsoever the Lord commands us.

Lesson III

He, then, that loves his neighbor naturally, loves him indeed, but attains not unto that great reward of love, for he loves him, not after the spirit, but after the flesh. Therefore, when the Lord says: "This is My commandment, That you love one another," He says also, "as I have loved you,"—even as though He said openly, "Love one another, with that aim wherewith I have loved you." And in this matter, dearly beloved brethren, it behooves us to watch; for he that hates us of old time, even while he draws our mind to love the things which are seen and temporal, rouses up against us our neighbor who is weaker than we are, to take from us that which we love.

COMMON OF APOSTLES

Lesson I - 1 Cor 4:1–5

From the First letter of St. Paul the Apostle to the Corinthians

Let a man so account of us as of the ministers of Christ, and the dispensers of the mysteries of God. Here now it is required among the dispensers, that a man be found faithful. But to me it is a very small thing to be judged by you, or by man's day; but neither do I judge my own self. For I am not conscious to myself of any thing, yet am I not hereby justified; but he that judgeth me, is the Lord. Therefore judge not before the time; until the Lord come, who both will bring to light the hidden things of darkness, and will make manifest the counsels of the hearts; and then shall every man have praise from God.

Lesson II - 1 Cor 4:6–9

But these things, brethren, I have in a figure transferred to myself and to Apollo, for your sakes; that in us you may learn, that one be not puffed up against the other for another, above that which is written. For who distinguisheth thee? Or what hast thou that thou hast not received? And if thou hast received, why dost thou glory, as if thou hadst not received it? You are now full; you are now become rich; you reign without us; and I would to God you did reign, that we also might reign with you. For I think that God hath set forth us apostles, the last, as it were men appointed to death: we are made a spectacle to the world, and to angels, and to men.

Lesson III - 1 Cor 4:10–15

We are fools for Christ's sake, but you are wise in Christ; we are weak, but you are strong; you are honourable, but we without honour. Even unto this hour we both hunger and thirst, and are naked, and are buffeted, and have no fixed abode; And we labour, working with our own hands: we are reviled, and we bless; we are persecuted, and we suffer it. We are blasphemed, and we entreat; we are made as the refuse of this world, the offscouring of all even until now. I write not these things to confound you; but I admonish you as my dearest children. For if you have ten thousand instructors in Christ, yet not many fathers. For in Christ Jesus, by the gospel, I have begotten you.

Lesson IV

Sermon by St. Gregory, Pope

It is written: "By His Spirit the Lord has adorned the heavens." Now the ornament of the heavens are the godly powers of preachers, and this ornament, what it is, Paul teaches us thus: "To one is given by the Spirit the word of wisdom, to another the word of knowledge by the same Spirit; to another faith by the same Spirit; to another the gifts of healing by the same Spirit, to another the working of miracles, to another prophecy, to another discerning of spirits, to another diverse kinds of tongues, to another the interpretation of tongues." But in all these works that one and the self-same Spirit, dividing to every man several as He wills.

Lesson V

So much power then as have preachers, so much ornament have the heavens. Wherefore again it is written: "By the word of the Lord were the heavens made." For the Word of the Lord is the Son of the Father. But, to the end that all the Holy Trinity may be made manifest as the Maker of the heavens, that is, of the Apostles, it is straightway added regarding God the Holy Ghost: "you and all the host of them by the Breath of His mouth." Therefore the might of the same heavens is the might of the Spirit, for they had not braved the powers of this world, unless the strength of the Holy Ghost had comforted them. For we know what manner of men the Teachers of the Holy Church were before the coming of this Spirit and since He came we see in Whose strength they are made strong.

Lesson VI

Verily, if we ask of the damsel that kept the door, she will tell us what was the measure of weakness and of strength in that Shepherd of the Church nigh to whose most holy body we are now sitting, before the Spirit came. He was so stricken by the words of one woman, that for fear of death, he denied Life. And we may well remember that Peter denied in captivity Him, Whom the thief confessed, even when He was lifted up upon the Cross. But let us hear what that coward was after the Spirit came. When the rulers and elders were gathered together, the Apostles were beaten, and commanded not to seek at all nor teach in the name of Jesus. And Peter answered with great boldness, "We ought to obey God rather than men."

Lessons VII–IX from Matt 19:27–29 with Homily by St. Jerome: the first set in the Common of Abbots

Other Lessons for Feasts of the Apostles

Second Set

Lesson IV

From the Exposition of Psalm 86 by St. Augustine, Bishop

"Her foundation is in the holy mountains: the Lord loveth the gates of Zion." Why has the city twelve foundations, and in them the names of the Prophets and of the Apostles of the Lamb? Because their authority is the foundation whereon our weakness rests. Why are they the gates? Because through them we enter in unto the kingdom of God, since they have preached the same unto us, and when we enter in through their preaching, we enter in by Christ, Who is Himself The Door. And, whereas it is written that the city has twelve gates, and again, that Christ is the one Door, Christ is all the twelve, for He is in all the twelve: and therefore were twelve Apostles chosen. There lies a great mystery in the signification of this number, Twelve. "Ye shall sit," says the Lord, "upon twelve thrones, judging the twelve tribes of Israel."

Lesson V

If then there be set there twelve thrones of judgment, Paul, in that he is the thirteenth Apostle, has nowhere to sit, nor wherein to judge. Nevertheless, he has said of himself that he will judge not men only, but angels. "Know you not," says he, "that we shall judge angels?"—that is, the fallen angels. Then might they have answered him: "Why boastest thou thyself to be a judge? For where is thy seat? The Lord has said that for the twelve Apostles there shall be twelve thrones: one of the twelve, even Judas, is indeed fallen, but holy Matthias is chosen into his place; for the twelve thrones there are still twelve to sit thereon: first find whereon thou shalt sit, and afterward give thyself out for a judge." Let us see, then, what is the meaning of these twelve thrones. By them is signified in a mystery the whole world, since the Church shall be throughout all the earth, whence this building is called to be built up together in Christ.

Lesson VI

Therefore is it said that there shall be twelve thrones, because from all quarters shall there come men to be judged; even as it is said that the city has twelve gates, because from all quarters shall the nations of them which are saved, enter into it. So, not the twelve only, and the Apostle Paul, but all, as many as shall judge, have part in these twelve thrones, this signifying, that they shall judge all men; even as all that enter into the city, have part in her twelve gates. For there are four quarters of the world, the East, and the West, and the North, and the South: of which four quarters is mention often made in the Scriptures. From the four winds shall the elect be gathered together, as says the Lord in the Gospel: "And He shall send His Angels with a great sound of a trumpet; and they shall gather together His elect from the four winds, from one end of heaven to the other." From the four winds, therefore, is the Church called together; and how are they called? Everywhere are they called in the Trinity; for they are called no otherwise than by baptizing them in the Name of the Father, and of the Son, and of the Holy Ghost. Now four being multiplied by three is twelve.

Lesson VII

From the Holy Gospel according to St. Matthew (Matt 19:27–29)

At that time, Peter said unto Jesus: Behold, we have forsaken all, and followed thee what shall we have therefore? And so on.

Homily by St. Bede the Venerable, Priest

"If thou wilt be perfect," says Christ, "go and sell that thou hast, and give to the poor, and come and follow Me: and thou shalt have treasure in heaven." Yea, treasure that passes not away! Unto such says Jesus, at the questioning of Peter: "Amen I say unto you, that you which have followed Me, in the regeneration, when the Son of Man shall sit in the throne of His glory, you also shall sit upon twelve thrones, judging the twelve tribes of Israel." He taught them, which work for His Name's sake in this life, to look for their reward in another life: that is, in the regeneration. "In the regeneration!"—when we who have been born dying creatures into a dying life, shall in the resurrection be born again into an undying life.

Lesson VIII

And truly, it is a just retribution, that they, who, while they were yet here, have for Christ's sake set no store by being great among men, should there by Christ be singularly glorified to be the assessors of His judgment-seat, even they whom nothing here could turn aside from being the followers of His footsteps. Nevertheless, let there be no man that believes that the twelve Apostles only, among whom Matthias holds that place from which Judas by transgression fell, that they only shall judge, even as the twelve tribes of Israel shall not alone be judged: for then were the tribe of Levi, which is the thirteenth, unjudged.

Lesson IX

Moreover, then, would Paul, who is the thirteenth Apostle, be deprived of all part in the judgment; whereas he says of himself: "Know you not that we shall judge angels? How much more things that pertain to this life?" But it behooves us to know that everyone who has forsaken all and followed Christ, as did the Apostles, shall also come with Him to judgment, even as every man shall stand at His judgment seat. And the Scriptures often use by this number twelve to signify all; by the twelve thrones of the Apostles are signified the thrones of all them that shall judge; and by the twelve tribes of Israel, the whole number of them that shall be judged.

COMMON OF EVANGELISTS

Lesson I - Ezech 1:1–4

Beginning of the book of the Prophet Ezechiel

Now it came to pass in the thirtieth year, in the fourth month, on the fifth day of the month, when I was in the midst of the captives by the river Chobar, the heavens were opened, and I saw the visions of God. On the fifth day of the month, the same was the fifth year of the captivity of king Joachin, The word of the Lord came to Ezechiel the priest the son of Buzi in the land of the Chaldeans, by the river Chobar: and the hand of the Lord was there upon him. And I saw, and behold a whirlwind came out of the north: and a great cloud, and a fire infolding it, and brightness was about it: and out of the midst thereof, that is, out of the midst of the fire, as it were the resemblance of amber.

Lesson II ~ Ezech 1:5–9

And in the midst thereof the likeness of four living creatures: and this was their appearance: there was the likeness of a man in them. Every one had four faces, and every one four wings. Their feet were straight feet, and the sole of their foot was like the sole of a calf's foot, and they sparkled like the appearance of glowing brass. And they had the hands of a man under their wings on their four sides: and they had faces, and wings on the four sides, And the wings of one were joined to the wings of another. They turned not when they went: but every one went straight forward.

Lesson III ~ Ezech 1:10–12

And as for the likeness of their faces: there was the face of a man, and the face of a lion on the right side of all the four: and the face of an ox, on the left side of all the four: and the face of an eagle over all the four. And their faces, and their wings were stretched upward: two wings of every one were joined, and two covered their bodies: And every one of them went straight forward: whither the impulse of the spirit was to go, thither they went: and they turned not when they went.

Lesson IV

From the Exposition of the Book of the Prophet Ezechiel by Pope St Gregory

The Prophet writes very minutely touching the four holy living creatures, whom he saw in the spirit as being to come. He says: "Every one had four faces, and every one had four wings." What signifies the face, save likeness whereby we are known? or wings, save the power to fly? since it is by the face that man is known from man, and by their wings that the birds' bodies are carried up into the air. So the face pertains to certitude, and the wings to contemplation. With certitude we are known of God Almighty Who says: "I am the Good Shepherd, and know My sheep, and am known of Mine." And again: "I know whom I have chosen." And by contemplation, whereby we rise above ourselves, we—as it were—fly heavenwards.

Lesson V

"Every one had four faces"—four faces, that is, and one body. If thou seek to know what Matthew teaches concerning the Incarnation of the Lord, he teaches no other doctrine than teaches Mark, or Luke, or John. If thou seek to know what John teaches, it is beyond all doubt that his doctrine is the doctrine of Matthew, and Mark, and Luke. If thou ask concerning Mark, he has that which has Matthew, and John, and Luke. If thou wilt know of Luke, know that he teaches as does Matthew, and Mark, and John. Therefore every one has four faces, for God knows and sees in them but one faith, which thou mayest see in each and in all.

Lesson VI

"And every one had four wings." For they do all with one accord preach our Lord Jesus Christ, the Son of Almighty God: toward Whose Divinity lifting up the eyes of their mind, they do lift the wings of contemplation, and do fly. In the Evangelists, the face pertains to the Lord's Manhood, and the wings to His Divinity: for they turn their face toward Him Whom they see in bodily shape: but when they say that He is, regarding His Divinity, Incomprehensible, and Incorporeal, the wings of their contemplation do, in a manner, carry them in flight heavenward. Because, then, they have all one faith in the Incarnation, and all equally look by contemplation toward the Deity: it is well written of them, "Every one had four faces, and every one had four wings."

Lesson VII

From the Holy Gospel according to St. Luke (Luke 10:1–9)

At that time: The Lord appointed other seventy-two also, and sent them two and two before His face into every city and place, whither He Himself would come. And so on.

Homily by Pope St Gregory

Dearly beloved brethren, our Lord and Saviour does sometimes admonish us by words, and sometimes by works. Yea, His very works do themselves teach us: for that which He does silently His example still moves us to copy. Behold how He sends forth His disciples to preach by two and two: since there are two commandments to love, that is, a commandment to love God, and a commandment to love our neighbor: and where there are not two, the one, being alone, has nothing wherewith to do the Lord's commandment. And no man can properly be said to love himself: for love tends outward toward our neighbor, if it be the love whereto the Gospel does oblige us.

Lesson VIII

Behold, the Lord sends forth His disciples to preach by two and two: and thus doing, He does silently teach us that whosoever loves not his neighbor, such a one it behooves not to take upon him the office of a preacher. Well also is it said that He sent them before His face into every city and place whither He Himself would come. The Lord follows His preachers: first comes preaching, and then the Lord Himself comes to the house of our mind, whither the word of exhortation has come before: and so comes the truth into our mind.

Lesson IX

Therefore to preachers says Isaias: "Prepare the way of the Lord, make straight a highway for our God." And again the Psalmist says: "Spread a path before Him That rideth upon the West." The Lord rides upon the West; above that from which in death He veiled His glory, He has royally exalted that glory that excels even the glory of His rising again. He rides upon the West, Who, being risen again from the dead, is throned high above the death to which He bowed. Before Him, therefore, That rides upon the West, we spread a path, when we set forth His glory before the eyes of your mind, to the end that He Himself may come after, and Himself enlighten your same minds by His presence and His love.

COMMON OF ONE MARTYR

Lessons I–III for a Martyr-Bishop

Lesson I ~ Acts 20:17–24

From the Acts of the Apostles

And sending from Miletus to Ephesus, he called the ancients of the church. And when they were come to him, and were together, he said to them: You know from the first day that I came into Asia, in what manner I have been with you, for all the time, Serving the Lord with all humility, and with tears, and temptations which befell me by the conspiracies of the Jews; How I have kept back nothing that was profitable to you, but have preached it to you, and taught you publicly, and from house to house, Testifying both to Jews and Gentiles penance towards God, and faith in our Lord Jesus Christ. And now, behold, being bound in the spirit, I go to Jerusalem: not knowing the things which shall befall me there: Save that the Holy Ghost in every city witnesseth to me, saying: That bands and afflictions wait for me at Jerusalem. But I fear none of these things, neither do I count my life more precious than myself, so that I may consummate my course and the ministry of the word which I received from the Lord Jesus, to testify the gospel of the grace of God.

Lesson II ~ Acts 20:25–31

And now behold, I know that all you, among whom I have gone preaching the kingdom of God, shall see my face no more. Wherefore I take you to witness this day, that I am clear from the blood of all men; For I have not spared to declare unto you all the counsel of God. Take heed to yourselves, and to the whole flock, wherein the Holy Ghost hath placed you bishops, to rule the church of God, which he hath purchased with his own blood. I know that, after my departure, ravening wolves will enter in among you, not sparing the flock. And of your own selves shall arise men speaking perverse things, to draw away disciples after them. Therefore watch, keeping in memory, that for three years I ceased not, with tears to admonish every one of you night and day.

Lesson III ~ Acts 20:32–38

And now I commend you to God, and to the word of his grace, who is able to build up, and to give an inheritance among all the sanctified. I have not coveted any man's silver, gold, or apparel, as You yourselves know: for such things as were needful for me and them that are with me, these hands have furnished. I have showed you all things, how that so labouring you ought to support the weak, and to remember the word of the Lord Jesus, how he said: It is a more blessed thing to give, rather than to receive. And when he had said these things, kneeling down, he prayed with them all. And there was much weeping among them all; and falling on the neck of Paul, they kissed him, Being grieved most of all for the word which he had said, that they should see his face no more. And they brought him on his way to the ship.

Lessons I–III for a Martyr Non-Bishop

Lesson I ~ Rom 8:12–19

From the epistle of St. Paul the Apostle to the Romans

Therefore, brethren, we are debtors, not to the flesh, to live according to the flesh. For if you live according to the flesh, you shall die: but if by the Spirit you mortify the deeds of the flesh, you shall live. For whosoever are led by the Spirit of God, they are the sons of God. For you have not received the spirit of bondage again in fear; but you have received the spirit of adoption of sons, whereby we cry: Abba, Father. For the Spirit himself giveth testimony to our spirit, that we are the sons of God. And if sons, heirs also; heirs indeed of God, and joint heirs with Christ: yet so, if we suffer with him, that we may be also glorified with him. For I reckon that the sufferings of this time are not worthy to be compared with the glory to come, that shall be revealed in us. For the expectation of the creature waiteth for the revelation of the sons of God.

Lesson II ~ Rom 8:28–34

And we know that to them that love God, all things work together unto good, to such as, according to his purpose, are called to be saints. For whom he foreknew, he also predestinated to be made conformable to the image of his Son; that he might be the firstborn amongst many brethren. And whom he predestinated, them he also called. And whom he called, them he also justified. And whom he justified, them he also glorified. What shall we then say to these things? If God be for us, who is against us? He that spared not even his own Son, but delivered him up for us all, how hath he not also, with him, given us all things? Who shall accuse against the elect of God? God that justifieth. Who is he that shall condemn? Christ Jesus that died, yea that is risen also again; who is at the right hand of God, who also maketh intercession for us.

Lesson III ~ Rom 8:35–39

Who then shall separate us from the love of Christ? Shall tribulation? or distress? or famine? or nakedness? or danger? or persecution? or the sword? As it is written: For thy sake we are put to death all the day long. We are accounted as sheep for the slaughter. But in all these things we overcome, because of him that hath loved us. For I am sure that neither death, nor life, nor angels, nor principalities, nor powers, nor things present, nor things to come, nor might, Nor height, nor depth, nor any other creature, shall be able to separate us from the love of God, which is in Christ Jesus our Lord.

Lesson IV

Sermon by St. Augustine, Bishop

The illustrious day whereon the blessed Martyr N. conquered, this day comes round to us again: and as the Church does rejoice with him in his glory, so does she set before us his footsteps to be followed. For if we suffer, we shall also reign with him. In his glorious battle we have two things chiefly to consider: the hardened cruelty of the tormentor, and the unconquered patience of the Martyr: the cruelty of the tormentor, that we may abhor it; the patience of the Martyr, that we may imitate it. Hear what the Psalmist says, complaining against sin: "Fret not thyself because of the evil-doers, for they shall soon dry up like the grass." But regarding the patience which is to be shown against the evildoers, hear the word wherewith the Apostle moves us: "You have need of patience, that you may receive the promise."

Lesson V

So the patience of the blessed Martyr was crowned, and the unchastened spite of the tormentor is given over to everlasting torture. Christ's glorious champion looked for this during his battle, and shrank not from prison. Like his Head, he bore reproach, underwent mocking, and feared not for scourges: and as many sufferings as for Christ's sake he bore before he died, so many offerings did he make unto Him of himself. He had drunk in the Apostles' word and kept it deep in him: "The sufferings of this present time are not worthy to be compared with the glory which shall be revealed in us, for our light affliction which is but for a moment, worketh for us a far more exceeding and eternal weight of glory." Being lifted up above earthly things by the love of this promise, and tasting beforehand the sweetness of the heavenly peace, he was unspeakably moved, and said with the Psalmist: "What have I in heaven, and what is there upon earth that I desire beside Thee? My flesh and my heart faileth: Thou art the God of my heart, and God is my portion for ever."

Lesson VI

For he considered, as far as man's weakness is able, through this darkness, to fix the eyes of his mind upon the eternal things, what is the gladness of the city above: and being not able to tell it, he cried out wondering: "What have I in heaven?" As though he would have said: "It passes my strength, it passes the power of my utterance, it goes beyond the reach of my understanding, what is that beauty, what is that glory, what is that exaltation, wherein, when He has hidden us from the troubling of men, in the secret of His presence, our Lord Jesus Christ shall change our vile body, that it may be fashioned like unto His glorious Body!" In sight of this perfect liberty he shrank from no danger, and quailed before no suffering: and if he could have died a thousand times, he would not have thought himself to have bought it at a price high enough.

Lesson VII

From the Holy Gospel according to St. Luke (Luke 14:26–33)

At that time: Jesus said unto the multitudes: If any man come to Me, and hate not his father, and mother, and wife, and children, and brethren, and sisters, yea, and his own life also, he cannot be My disciple. And so on.

Homily by Pope St Gregory

Dearly beloved brethren, if we consider what and how great things are promised unto us in heaven, all things which are upon earth grow poor to our mind. For when this world's goods are reckoned against the gladness above, they are found to be a clog rather than a help. This present life being compared to life eternal, ought rather to be called death than life. For what is the daily failing of our corruption but, as it were, a creeping death? But what tongue is there that can tell, or what understanding that can comprehend how great is the rejoicing in the city above, where they have part with the choirs of Angels, where they stand with the most blessed spirits before the glory of the Creator, where they see the face of God present, where they behold the Incomprehensible Light, where they have no fear of death, and where they rejoice eternally incorruptible?

Lesson VIII

When we hear these things our hearts burn within us; and we long to be already there, where we hope to rejoice for ever. But we cannot attain unto great rewards, save through great labour. Therefore says the excellent preacher Paul: "He is not crowned, except he strive lawfully." The greatness of the reward does delight our mind; let not the throes of the struggle dishearten us. Therefore the Truth says unto every one that comes unto Him: "If any man come to Me, and hate not his father and mother, and wife, and children, and brethren, and sisters, yea, and his own life also, he cannot be My disciple."

Lesson IX

But it may be asked how we are commanded in one place to hate our parents, and them that are near us in the flesh, and in another place to love even our enemies. And, verily, the Truth has said, regarding a wife: "What God hath joined together, let not man put asunder." And Paul says: "Husbands, love your wives, even as Christ also loved the Church." Behold, the disciple commands a man to love his wife, and the Master says: "If any man hate not his wife, he cannot be My disciple." Does the judge, then, order one proclamation, and the crier make another? or can the man both love and hate? If we consider well the force of the commandment, we shall be able in wisdom to do both. Let us love wife, and kindred, and neighbor, as regards their nearness in the flesh; but as regards the way of God, if they withstand us therein, let us not know them, but hate them and flee from them.

Other Lessons for Feasts of One Martyr

Second Set

Lesson IV

From the Exposition of Psalm 118 by St Ambrose, Bishop

"Princes have persecuted me without a cause; but my heart standeth in awe of Thy word." These are rightly the words of a martyr, who bears unjustly the torments of the persecutors, who has robbed no man, who has violently oppressed no man, who has shed the blood of no man, who has imagined to defile the bed of no man, who is debtor to the laws in nothing, and who is punished more grievously than if he were a robber: who speaks righteousness, and there is none that will hear: who speaks salvation, and all men fight against him: who is able to say: "When I spoke unto them, they fought against me without a cause." They fight against him without a cause, who can lay no sin to his charge; they fight against him as an evildoer, who is by their own acknowledgment righteous: they fight against him as a warlock, who glories in the name of the Lord, and who does all things well because he does all things for God's sake.

Lesson V

They fight against him in vain who is accused of ungodliness among the ungodly and the unfaithful, because he teaches Faith. Verily, him that is fought against without a cause it behooves to be strong and patient. Why then says he: "My heart standeth in awe of Thy word?" Awe is the mark of the weak, the timid, and the fearful. But there is also a weakness unto salvation, there is a fear which is a holy fear. "O fear the Lord, all you His Saints." And again: "Blessed is the man that feareth the Lord." And why is he blessed? because he "delighteth greatly in His commandments."

Lesson VI

Think, then, how the martyr stands between two dangers. On the one hand the wild beasts, roaring for his blood, do indeed strike terror; he hears the hissing of the plates of white-hot metal, and sees surging up the flames of the fiery furnace; behind him is the clanking of fetters, and beside him the executioner, stained with fresh blood; think of him there, face to face with the apparatus of death—but think again—of what thinks he? Of the Law of God, of the everlasting fire, of the eternal flames, wherein the unbelieving shall burn for ever, of that torture whereof the agony is for ever new. And then indeed his heart fails for fear, lest by giving way under torment here, he should give himself up to everlasting torment hereafter: then indeed he trembles, when Faith makes to glitter before his eyes the awful sword of the judgment to come. And in this, the faithful trembling of the true-hearted, are there not both unshaken hope of the eternal things, and awe of the things of God?

Lesson VII

From the Holy Gospel according to St. Matthew (Matt 16:24–27)

At that time: Jesus said unto His disciples: If any man will come after Me, let him deny himself, and take up his cross, and follow Me. And so on.

Homily by Pope St Gregory

Our Lord and Redeemer came into the world a new Man, and gave the world new commandments. For against the ways of our old life, brought and bred up in sin, He set the contrast of His new life. It was the old way, according to the knowledge of the carnal man, for every man to keep his own goods, and, if he were able to do it, to take his neighbor's goods also, and, if he were not able to take them, at least to lust after them. But the Heavenly Physician has medicines wherewith to meet all the diseases of sin. For, even, as by the art of the physician, things hot are healed by things cold, and things cold by things hot, so does our Lord set holiness against sin, ordaining purity for the lecherous, munificence for the miserly, meekness for the hot-tempered, and lowliness for the proud.

Lesson VIII

So the Lord, when He would give a new commandment unto them that came to Him, said: "Whosoever he be of you that forsaketh not all that he hath, he cannot be My disciple,"—as though He had said openly: "All you that according to the old man lust after your neighbor's goods, must, according to the zeal of the new man, give away even that which is your own." But let us hear again what He says in this place: "If any man will come after Me, let him deny himself." First He says that we must deny to ourselves that which is our own, and now that we must even deny ourselves to ourselves. Perhaps it is not hard for a man to give up that which is his own, but it is exceedingly hard to give up himself. To deny himself his possessions is little: but to deny himself himself is a denial exceedingly great.

Lesson IX

Yet when we come unto Him the Lord will have us deny to ourselves even ourselves, since as many of us as are entered into the battle of faith, are entered into a contention against evil spirits. But the evil spirits have nothing of their own in this world, and therefore must we wrestle with them, naked with naked. For if he that is clothed, wrestle with him that is naked, he faileth swiftly, because he hath whereon he that is naked taketh hold. And what are all things earthly but things wherewith the soul is clothed upon? whosoever therefore will wrestle with Satan, let him cast away his clothes, lest he be thereby endangered.

Third Set

Lesson VII

From the Holy Gospel according to St. Matthew (Matt 10:26–32)

At that time: Jesus said unto His disciples: There is nothing covered, that shall not be revealed, and hid, that shall not be known. And so on.

Homily by St Hilary, Bishop

The Lord points to the day of judgment, that day wherein the hidden counsels of the hearts shall be made manifest, and those things which are obscure now shall be the subject of all men's knowledge. Therefore He warns us not to fear threats, nor persuasions, nor the power of such as fight against us; since in the day of judgment it will be manifest that all these things are null and void. "And what I tell you in darkness, that speak you in light; and what you hear in the ear, that preach you upon the house-tops." We read not that the Lord's use was to speak by night, or to tell His doctrine in darkness, but that to the carnal all His words were darkness, and to the unbelieving all His discourse night.

Lesson VIII

Therefore, He wills that that which He has spoken, should be freely proclaimed in faith and in confession. Therefore, He commands that that which He has told in darkness shall be spoken in light, and that that which He has made to be heard in the ear should be preached upon the house-tops, that is, with loud and high words. For it behooves us ever to make God known, and to speak in the light of Apostolic preaching the obscure things of the Gospel message, having no fear of them which have power over bodies, but none over our souls, but rather fearing God, Who is able to destroy both body and soul in hell.

Lesson IX

"Fear not them which kill the body." Therefore we need fear nothing which may chance to our bodies, nor sorrow because of the destruction of the flesh, when, according to the laws of our nature and that from whence we are taken, we are unclothed upon, and become a pure spirit. And, since it behooves us who are rooted in such a doctrine, freely and constantly to confess God, even were it only because of the alternative whereby we are bound, He says further: "Whosoever shall confess Me before men, him will I confess also before My Father, Which is in heaven. But whosoever shall deny Me before men, him will I also deny before My Father, Which is in heaven." Such witnesses as He has seen us to have been here to His name before men, such a Witness shall we find Him to be hereafter to our names before His Father Which is in heaven.

COMMON OF ONE or MANY MARTYRS IN PASCHALTIDE

Lessons I–III are Proper to the Feast or the Occurring Scripture

Lesson IV

From the sermon of Saint Ambrose Bishop

Dearly beloved brethren, it is very fitting and right that after the gladness of Easter, which we have celebrated in the Church, we should mingle our own joy with the joy of the holy Martyrs; yea, that we should tell of the glory of the Lord's rising again, to them that have been made partakers of the Lord's sufferings. It truly must needs be that they which have been partakers of His sufferings, should be also of His joy. For thus says the blessed Apostle: "As you are partakers of the sufferings, so shall you be also of the consolation." And again: "If we suffer, we shall also reign with Him." He, therefore, that endures sorrow for Christ, must needs also have glory with Christ.

Lesson V

I say again, let us tell to the holy Martyrs what the grace of the Lord's Passover is: let us tell them that, even as He has opened the bars of His own grave, even so shall their graves also be opened: let us tell them that, even as in His dead Body the Veins grew warm and quick again, even so shall their limbs, that now are cold, flush with the heat of an eternal vigor. That power which brought again our Lord from the dead will bring His Martyrs too. For as they have followed Him in His sufferings, so shall they follow Him also in His newness of life. It is written in the Psalms: "Thou hast shown Me the path of life." This is said of the Resurrection in the Person of the Saviour, as of Him Who, after He died, came up again from hell, and began to have that path of life which was not known before.

Lesson VI

For, before Christ came, that path of life was not known, which none had risen from the dead to tread. But, since the Lord has risen, it is known, and many have trodden it after the Lord. Regarding them, the holy Evangelist says: "Many bodies of the saints which slept arose with Him, and went into the holy city." Therefore, when the Lord rises again and says: "Thou hast shown Me the path of life," we also can now say to Him: "Thou hast shown us the path of life." For He has shown us the path of life, Who has shown us the way that leads unto life. He has shown me the path of life, Who has taught me faith, mercy, righteousness, and chastity; for these are the ways that lead unto life eternal.

Lesson VII

From the Holy Gospel according to St. John (John 15:1–7)

In that time Jesus said to his disciples: I am the true vine; and my Father is the husbandman. And so on.

Homily by St. Augustine, Bishop

Dearly beloved brethren, this passage of the Gospel, wherein the Lord says that He is the vine, and that His disciples are the branches, is to be taken in that sense wherein it is also said, that He is the Head of the Church, and that we are the members of Him Who is the Mediator between God and men, the man Christ Jesus. The vine and his branches are of one and the same nature. Therefore, seeing that He was God, of which nature we are not, He was made man, to the end that He might have in Himself this vine, that is, the manhood, whereof we men can be made branches.

Lesson VIII

Why says He: "I am the true vine"? Regarding this word true, has He not here regard to that other parable of a vine, the like figure whereto He does here apply to Himself? Here is He called a vine, not plainly, but in parable, as also He is called elsewhere a sheep, a lamb, a lion, a rock, a cornerstone, and other things of the like kind. But these things are in themselves that which they seem to be, albeit He is called by their names, not plainly, but in a parable, and herein are they different from that vine, whereof in this place He takes on Him the name. For when He says: "I am the true vine," does He not make distinction between Himself, and that which indeed seemed to be a vine, but to which it is said: "How art thou turned into the degenerate plant of a strange vine unto Me?" For by what title shall that plant be called other than a false vine, whereto they looked that she should bring forth grapes, and she brought forth thorns?

Lesson IX

He says: "I am the true vine, and My Father is the husbandman." Is the vine one with the husbandman? These words then are to be taken in that sense wherein He also says: "My Father is greater than I." In this sense is He the vine, and the Father is the husbandman. But again, in regard to those words: "I and the Father are one," and again and: "My Father is the husbandman," we understand that They are not the vine and the husbandman, after the manner of a vine, and the husbandman that from without does care for and keep it, but after the manner of a vine and Him That from within does make it to bring forth fruit. For neither is he that plants anything, neither he that waters, but God that gives the increase. But Christ is God, for the Word was God. Therefore He and the Father are one: and, albeit the Word was made flesh, which, before, He was not, He ceased not to be still That Which He was.

Other Lessons for Feasts of Martyrs in Paschaltide

Second Set

Lesson IV

From the Epistle of St Cyprian, Bishop and himself Martyr, to the Martyrs and Confessors

How shall I praise you, Martyrs so brilliantly victorious? Can the voice of man's praise add anything to the glory of your manful heart and unshaken faithfulness? You have borne all the hardness of the torment, and have attained unto the excellent height of glory: the tormentors have not worn you out, nay, you rather have worn out the tormentors. When they that kill the body would give you no rest from suffering, you suffered until you gained the crown. And the torment waxing still more dreadful, waxed not to the casting down of your strong faith, but to the sooner sending God's men home to God.

Lesson V

They that stood by looked in wonder at your heavenly conflict, that battle of God, that wrestling of spirit, that combat of Christ. There they saw His servants standing with voice unshaken, with spirit unbroken, strong in God's strength, naked indeed as to the arms of this world, but clothed on with the armor of God, and equipped with the fiery weapons of faith. There the tormented stood braver than their tormentors. Their bruised and mangled bodies overcame the instruments of cruelty that bruised and mangled them. The bloody stripes, so often laid on, could not beat down the impregnable castle of their faith, even when the covering of their bowels was broken, and that which was tormented in God's servants was no longer limbs but wounds. The blood that ran down, ran down to quench the rage of persecution, noble blood, that can put out the flames and fire of hell.

Lesson VI

O what a spectacle was that in the eyes of the Lord! O how noble! O how mighty! O how precious in the sight of God were His soldiers' loyalty and faithfulness! Even as it is written in the Psalms, the Holy Ghost therein at once speaking to us and warning us, "Precious in the sight of the Lord is the death of His Saints." O what a precious death is his, who makes purchase of life that can never die, at the price of his own blood, and seizes on the crown, when courage has no more left to meet! O how joyful was Christ! How gladly fought He in such servants as these, in these how gladly did He triumph, the Keeper of their faith, and, in the end, to them how gladly did He give that reward which no man knows save he that receives it! He it was Who was there when they fought, He it was Who raised them up to be the champions and defenders of His holy Name, He, who gave them the strength, He, Who nerved them. He, That by death has once conquered for us, lives now for ever to conquer in us.

COMMON OF MANY MARTYRS

Lesson I ~ Rom 8:12–19

From the epistle of St. Paul the Apostle to the Romans

Therefore, brethren, we are debtors, not to the flesh, to live according to the flesh. For if you live according to the flesh, you shall die: but if by the Spirit you mortify the deeds of the flesh, you shall live. For whosoever are led by the Spirit of God, they are the sons of God. For you have not received the spirit of bondage again in fear; but you have received the spirit of adoption of sons, whereby we cry: Abba, Father. For the Spirit himself giveth testimony to our spirit, that we are the sons of God. And if sons, heirs also; heirs indeed of God, and joint heirs with Christ: yet so, if we suffer with him, that we may be also glorified with him. For I reckon that the sufferings of this time are not worthy to be compared with the glory to come, that shall be revealed in us. For the expectation of the creature waiteth for the revelation of the sons of God.

Lesson II ~ Rom 8:28–34

And we know that to them that love God, all things work together unto good, to such as, according to his purpose, are called to be saints. For whom he foreknew, he also predestinated to be made conformable to the image of his Son; that he might be the firstborn amongst many brethren. And whom he predestinated, them he also called. And whom he called, them he also justified. And whom he justified, them he also glorified. What shall we then say to these things? If God be for us, who is against us? He that spared not even his own Son, but delivered him up for us all, how hath he not also, with him, given us all things? Who shall accuse against the elect of God? God that justifieth. Who is he that shall condemn? Christ Jesus that died, yea that is risen also again; who is at the right hand of God, who also maketh intercession for us.

Lesson III ~ Rom 8:35–39

Who then shall separate us from the love of Christ? Shall tribulation? or distress? or famine? or nakedness? or danger? or persecution? or the sword? As it is written: For thy sake we are put to death all the day long. We are accounted as sheep for the slaughter. But in all these things we overcome, because of him that hath loved us. For I am sure that neither death, nor life, nor angels, nor principalities, nor powers, nor things present, nor things to come, nor might, Nor height, nor depth, nor any other creature, shall be able to separate us from the love of God, which is in Christ Jesus our Lord.

Lesson IV

Sermon by St. Augustine, Bishop

Dearly beloved brethren, as often as we keep the Feasts of the holy Martyrs, we look to obtain of the Lord, by their intercession, such good things in this life that thereby we, following them, may gain better in that which is to come. For they alone do truly keep Holiday on the Feasts of the Martyrs, who follow after the

Martyrs' example. These Feasts of the Martyrs are the Martyrs' preaching, whereby to stir us up to imitate what we are not loath to honor.

Lesson V

But we, who would eagerly rejoice with the Saints, would not eagerly share with them the persecution of the world. Whosoever will not take example of the holy Martyrs, as far as lies in him, such a one cannot attain unto their beatitude. Thus preaches the Apostle Paul, when he says: "As you are partakers of the sufferings, so shall you be also of the consolation." Yea, the Lord Himself says in the Gospel: "If the world hate you, you know that it hated Me before it hated you." He will not be of the body, who will not be hated with the head.

Lesson VI

But some man will say: "And who is he that can tread in the footsteps of the blessed Martyrs?" To such a one I answer that, by the Lord's help, we are able, if we so will to tread in the footsteps, not of the blessed Martyrs only, but even of the same Lord Himself. Hearken, not to me, but to the same Lord, Who cries unto all men: "Learn of Me, for I am meek and lowly in heart." Hear also with what words the Apostle Peter warns us: "Christ suffered for us, leaving us an example, that we should follow His steps."

Lesson VII

From the Holy Gospel according to St. Luke (Luke 21:9–19)

At that time: Jesus said unto His disciples: When you shall hear of wars and commotions, be not terrified: for these things must first come to pass; but the end is not by and by. And so on.

Homily by Pope St Gregory

Our Lord and Redeemer wills us to know what shall be the signs that the end of the world is at hand, to the end that you may be the less terrified, when comes that whereof you have already had warning. Darts strike less which are seen coming: and the plagues of the earth will be to us more bearable, if we are harnessed against them with the shield of foreknowledge. Behold, how He says: "When you shall hear of wars and commotions be not terrified: for these things must first come to pass; but the end is not by and by." It behooves us to ponder these words of our Redeemer, wherein He warns us of suffering from without and from within. Wars are the work of a foreign enemy, commotions of the citizens. Therefore, that He may let us know that we shall be troubled from within and from without, He shows that our wrestling shall be in part against strangers, and in part against our brethren.

Lesson VIII

But, when these woes come, the end is not immanent. And He says further: "Nation shall rise against nation, and kingdom against kingdom; and great earthquakes shall be in divers places, and pestilences, and famines, and fearful sights and great signs shall there be from heaven." Before the last tribulation comes, shall come many other tribulations: and, by the many woes which shall come first, shall be foreshadowed the everlasting woe which shall come in the end. And therefore, after wars and commotions, the end is not yet nigh: many woes must come first, to give warning of the woe that has no end.

Lesson IX

But, forasmuch as the signs and troubles whereof the Lord speaks are so manifold, we must needs shortly consider each: for, of necessity, we must suffer some things from heaven, some from the earth, some from the powers of nature, and some from men. For where He says: "Nation shall rise against nation"—He speaks concerning the troubling of men: where: "great earthquakes shall be in divers places"—concerning wrath from above: where: "and pestilences"—concerning the frailty of the body: where: "and famines"—concerning the barrenness of the earth: where: "fearful signs from heaven," and tempests—concerning commotions of the air. As, then, all things shall have an end, so, before the end, shall all things be troubled: and we who have sinned and come short in all things, shall in all things be afflicted, that it may be fulfilled that is written: "and the world shall fight with Him against the unwise."

Other Lessons for the Feasts of Many Martyrs

Second Set

Lesson IV

Sermon by St John Chrysostom

Every man knows how, by the good Providence of God, the divers glories of His Martyrs are held in such esteem by His people, that His same Saints in all places receive worthy honor, and before us is set, by the favor of Christ, the noble example of their courage: thus are we stirred up to consider, on the occasion of these Holidays, how great glory does abide them in heaven, whose birthdays are thus kept upon earth: thereby, also, we are roused to strive to be like them, brave, godly, and true: so that, in the strength of Christ, we, like them, may wrestle with, and conquer our enemy, and, when we have gained the same victory that they gained, may with them at last be glorified in the kingdom of heaven.

Lesson V

For what man is there willing to share their reward, that if he do not first lay hold on their steadfastness, follow after the example of their faith, and imitate their brave patience, can either seek or find their glory by likeness to their lives? But whosoever does so follow them, let him not doubt but that, though in very deed he gain not the crown of martyrdom, he is yet able by good works to make himself worthy therefor. For we have a most merciful God, Which either gives Martyrdom unto such as be willing, or, without Martyrdom, does make them joint heirs with the Saints in the kingdom of God.

Lesson VI

For even as afflictions unman the ungodly, so do trials harden the righteous. Even thus did the Saints strive against sin; but the work braced their muscles, and in death they were more than conquerors. Of such as run in a race, no man says that they are strong, unless they run, and none can be crowned, unless he conquer. No soldier prevails against his enemy, unless he fight; or wins the Emperor's favor, unless he have warred. Christian! the needful arms are thine! In thy hands are the strong weapons wherewith thou canst conquer the enemy!

Lesson VII

From the Holy Gospel according to St. Luke (Luke 6:17–23)

At that time: Jesus came down from the mountain, and stood in the plain, and the company of His disciples, and a great multitude of people out of all Judea, and Jerusalem, and from the sea coast of Tyre and Sidon. And so on.

Homily by St Ambrose, Bishop

Mark well how Jesus goes upward with His disciples, and downward to the multitude. How should the multitude behold Christ, save in a lower place? Such go not up to the things which are above; such attain not to the things which are high. And when Jesus comes down, He finds such as are diseased: for such like go not up to the heights. Hence also Matthew says that there were there "all sick people." Of these every man had need of healing, that, when he had received strength, he might eventually go up into the mountain. And therefore, being Himself come down, He heals them in the plain, that is to say, He calls them away from their lust, and frees them of their blindness. He comes down to our wounds, to the end that by a certain use of His nature, and by the abundance thereof, He might make us joint-heirs of the kingdom of heaven.

Lesson VIII

"Blessed be you poor, for yours is the kingdom of God." Saint Luke gives us but four of the Lord's Beatitudes, and Saint Matthew eight: but in those eight are contained these four, and in these four those eight. For in these four are embraced the cardinal virtues: and in those eight they are set forth in a number full of mystery. It is written at the head of more than one of the Psalms that they are "for the octave," and thou hast received the commandment: "Give a portion to seven, and also to eight"—to seven or eight what? Perchance degrees of blessedness. For as this eighth does name the most glorious realization of our hope, so does it also name the most royal exertion of our strength.

Lesson IX

But let us first consider the fuller of the forms of these Beatitudes. "Blessed be you poor, for your's is the kingdom of God." Both of the Evangelists give to this Beatitude the first place. Yea, surely, for poorness, at least in spirit, is the first in order, the mother, and procreatrix of virtues; since he that sets no store by temporal things, wins toward eternal things; neither is any man able to gain the kingdom of heaven, on whom the love of this present world does so press, that he cannot rid himself thereof.

Third Set

Lesson VII

From the Holy Gospel according to St. Luke (Luke 12:1–8)

At that time: Jesus said unto His disciples: Beware of the leaven of the Pharisees, which is hypocrisy. And so on.

Homily by St. Bede the Venerable, Priest

Concerning this leaven the Apostle warns us: "Therefore let us keep the feast, not with old leaven, neither with the leaven of malice and wickedness, but with the unleavened bread of sincerity and truth." For even as a little leaven does infect the whole lump wherein it is put, and the savor thereof does spread all abroad therein, so does hypocrisy, when once it has tainted the soul, drive out from it all sincerity and truth. The meaning, therefore, of this passage is this: "Beware, lest you be as the hypocrites, for yet a little while, and all men shall see that you are good, and they are evil."

Lesson VIII

As regarding what follows: "For there is nothing covered that shall not be revealed, neither hid, that shall not be known. Therefore, whatsoever you have spoken in darkness shall be heard in the light." These words are true, not only as concerning the world which is to come, wherein the secrets of all hearts shall be made manifest, but even as concerning this present world, since now that which the Apostles spoke and suffered in the darkness of persecution, and the gloom of dungeons, is, since that the Church is glorified, told of them for a memorial of them, wherever their acts are read throughout the whole world. "Be not afraid of them that kill the body," for they that persecute the righteous, when they have killed the body, "after that, have no more that they can do." Truly, it is a childish folly which makes such men to cast the dead limbs of the martyrs to birds and beasts, while yet they have no strength to withstand the Omnipotence of God, whereby He will surely quicken the same limbs and raise them up again.

Lesson IX

Of persecutors there are two kinds: first, of such as do openly rage in cruelty against us; and, secondly, of such as do seek, by cunning wiliness and lying, to beguile us. Against both these the Saviour wills to guard and strengthen us, in one place warning us to be not afraid of them that kill the body, and, in another place, to beware of the leaven of the Pharisees: since, when we are dead, neither the cruelty of the one class, nor the falsehood of the other, will be able any more to touch us. "Are not five sparrows sold for two farthings?" If God, says the Lord, if God cannot forget the least of the works of His hands that has life, the little birds that fly hither and thither in the air, if He cannot forget them, why should you, who are made in the image and likeness of your Maker, why should you be afraid of them that kill the body? He that is the careful Lord of the beasts which think not, how much more shall He be careful of man which has a reasonable soul?

COMMON OF CONFESSOR BISHOPS

For One Confessor Bishop

Lesson I - I Tim 3:1–7

From the first epistle of St. Paul the Apostle to Timothy

A faithful saying: if a man desire the office of a bishop, he desireth a good work. It behoveth therefore a bishop to be blameless, the husband of one wife, sober, prudent, of good behaviour, chaste, given to hospitality, a teacher, Not given to wine, no striker, but modest, not quarrelsome, not covetous, but One that ruleth well his own house, having his children in subjection with all chastity. But if a man know not how to rule his own house, how shall he take care of the church of God? Not a neophyte: lest being puffed up with pride, he fall into the judgment of the devil. Moreover he must have a good testimony of them who are without: lest he fall into reproach and the snare of the devil.

Lesson II - Titus 1:7–11

From the epistle to Titus

For a bishop must be without crime, as the steward of God: not proud, not subject to anger, not given to wine, no striker, not greedy of filthy lucre: But given to hospitality, gentle, sober, just, holy, continent: Embracing that faithful word which is according to doctrine, that he may be able to exhort in sound doctrine, and to convince the gainsayers. For there are also many disobedient, vain talkers, and seducers: especially they who are of the circumcision: Who must be reproved, who subvert whole houses, teaching things which they ought not, for filthy lucre's sake.

Lesson III - Titus 2:1–8

But speak thou the things that become sound doctrine: That the aged men be sober, chaste, prudent, sound in faith, in love, in patience. The aged women, in like manner, in holy attire, not false accusers, not given to much wine, teaching well: That they may teach the young women to be wise, to love their husbands, to love their children, To be discreet, chaste, sober, having a care of the house, gentle, obedient to their husbands, that the word of God be not blasphemed. Young men, in like manner, exhort that they be sober. In all things shew thyself an example of good works, in doctrine, in integrity, in gravity, The sound word that can not be blamed: that he, who is on the contrary part, may be afraid, having no evil to say of us.

For Multiple Confessor Bishops

Lesson I - Ecclus 44:1–5

From the book of Ecclesiasticus

Let us now praise men of renown, and our fathers in their generation. The Lord hath wrought great glory through his magnificence from the beginning. Such as have borne rule in their dominions, men of great power, and endued with their wisdom, shewing forth in the prophets the dignity of prophets, And ruling over the present people, and by the strength of wisdom instructing the people in most holy words. Such as by their skill sought out musical tunes, and published canticles of the Scriptures.

Lesson II - Ecclus 44:6–9

Rich men in virtue, studying beautifulness: living at peace in their houses. All these have gained glory in their generations, and were praised in their days. They that were born of them have left a name behind them, that their praises might be related: And there are some, of whom there is no memorial: who are perished, as if they had never been: and are become as if they had never been born, and their children with them.

Lesson III - Ecclus 44:10–15

But these were men of mercy, whose godly deeds have not failed: Good things continue with their seed, Their posterity are a holy inheritance, and their seed hath stood in the covenants. And their children for their sakes remain for ever: their seed and their glory shall not be forsaken. Their bodies are buried in peace, and their name liveth unto generation and generation. Let the people shew forth their wisdom, and the church declare their praise.

For Multiple Confessor Bishops, the following Lessons are all read in the Plural, supplying applicable names where appropriate.

Lesson IV

Sermon by St Maximus, Bishop

It is idle to strive to add anything to the praise of our holy and most blessed Father N., whose Feast is this day kept. The beauty of his life ought not to be the subject of panegyrics, so much as the object of imitation. The Scripture says: "A wise son is the glory of his father," Truly then will he be honored by such as, by doing after his example, show themselves to be his children: "for in Christ Jesus hath he begotten us through the Gospel."

Lesson V

Whatsoever, therefore, of virtue and grace there may be in this holy people, all the bright streams thereof do flow from him, as from a most clear fountain, By his manly chastity, by his sternly noble temperance, by the graceful courtesy which marked him, he drew all men's love to God: and by his eminent ministry in his Bishopric, he has left behind him in his disciples many heirs of his priesthood.

Lesson VI

It is very fitting and right that upon this day, which is made a joyful day for us because it is the day whereon our blessed Father N., passed away to heaven, I say it is very fitting and right that on this day we should sing that verse of the Psalms: "The righteous shall be in everlasting remembrance." His memory is rightly honored among men who is at this present making glad among Angels. The word of God says: "Judge none blessed before his death," as though it were said, "Judge him blessed when life is ended, praise him when he is made perfect." For there are two main reasons why it is better to praise a dead man than a living, since, if thou call him holy and worthy after his death, thou dost it when neither canst thou be corrupted by being a flatterer, nor he by being flattered.

Lesson VII

From the Holy Gospel according to St. Matthew (Matt 25:14–23)

At that time: Jesus spoke unto His disciples this parable: A man, travelling into a far country, called his own servants and delivered unto them his goods. And so on.

Homily by St Gregory, Pope

Dearly beloved brethren, this lesson from the Holy Gospel moves us to take good heed lest we, who are seen in this world to have received more than others, should thereby bring ourselves into greater condemnation from the Maker of this world. To whom much is given, of the same is much required. Therefore, let him that receives much, strive to be all the more lowly, and all the more ready to serve God, for his very gifts' sake, knowing that he will be obliged to give account thereof. Behold, a man, traveling into a far country, calls his own servants, and delivers unto them talents, to the end that they may trade therewith. After a long time, the lord of those servants comes, and reckons with them, and to them that have done well He renders a reward of their labors, but that servant which was careless of his master's work He condemns.

Lesson VIII

Who else, then, is that man traveling into a far country but our Redeemer, Who is gone up from us into heaven in that Flesh Which He had taken unto Himself? For the earth is the home of the Flesh, Which travels into a far country—when our Redeemer gives It a place in heaven. But that man traveling into a far country delivered unto his servants his goods; and so does our Redeemer give spiritual gifts unto His faithful people. "And unto one he gave five talents, to another two, and to another one." There are five bodily senses; that is, sight, hearing, taste, smell, and touch. By the five talents therefore are signified the five senses, that is, outward knowledge. By the two, wit and work. And by the figure of the one talent, understanding, which is alone.

Lesson IX

"And so he that had received five talents, gained other five talents"—for there be some who, while yet they are not able to go on unto things inward and mystic, do yet so desire our Fatherland which is above, that they teach well all whom they can, and of those very outward things which they have received make double gain. These are they which keep themselves clean from the unruly motions of the flesh, and from the lust of the world, and from the delight of things which are seen, and, by their preaching, keep other men also clean from all these things. And some there are who receive, as their two talents, the power to think and the power to work. These are they which inwardly understand obscure things, and outwardly work wonders. And these, since they preach unto others, both through their understanding and their works, gain, as it were, double for the talents which they have received.

Other Lessons for Feasts of Confessor Bishops

Second Set

Lesson IV

Sermon by St Maximus, Bishop

Our Blessed Father N., is safe now, and we may safely praise his great deeds. He that kept such a manful hand upon the tiller of faith, has now cast the anchor of hope in moorings of great calm, and brought his ship, heavy laden with heavenly riches and everlasting merchandise, safe into the haven where he would be. Thus fares it now with him who never fainted, but for so long a time ever held up the shield of the fear of God against all that beset him. What was his whole life but one long fight against an enemy that never slept?

Lesson V

O how many blinded souls there were, that had wandered away from the path of the Truth, and were hanging from the edge of the precipice over the pit, when he gave them sight again, and opened their eyes that they might see Christ! How many deaf ears were there, stopped up with unbelief and condemnation, when he opened them to hear that voice of commandment that speaks from heaven, and gave them that precious hearing that hears God calling us to be forgiven, so that they obeyed, and answered! How many wounded spirits were there, to whom his tongue, persuading them and praying for them like the tongue of an angel, brought health again!

Lesson VI

O how God wrought in him to cleanse and pardon, by discipline and exhortation, many a stricken soul, long distempered, and, as it seemed, incurably foul with sin, covered all over with virulent leprosy! How many souls there were, dwelling in living bodies, but dead, and crushed and buried under the sense of sin, whom he quickened again for God, by calling them to amendment as to light, souls dead to God, in which that great follower of his Lord killed sin by the same Lord's life-giving death.

Lesson VII

From the Holy Gospel according to St. Matthew (Matt 24:42–47)

At that time: Jesus said unto His disciples: Watch, for you know not in what hour your Lord comes. And so on.

Homily by St Hilary, Bishop

To the end that we may know that our ignorance of that day whereof no man knows is not without use, the Lord moves us to watch for the coming of the thief, to be ever instant in prayer, and ever busy in such works as He commands. He shows how the devil is that thief who watches ever how he may spoil our goods, breaking into the house of our body; that, while we are dwelling therein careless and heavy with sleep, he may dig through our walls with the arms of his craft and temptations. Us, therefore, it behooves to be ready, who have ever our ignorance concerning that day to be unto us a reason of watchfulness.

Lesson VIII

"Who then is a faithful and wise servant, whom his Lord hath made ruler over His household?" Although the Lord does move us all in common to weary not in carefulness and watching, He lays more especially upon the rulers of His people, that is, the Bishops, this duty, to look always for His coming. For such a one is that faithful and wise servant, made ruler over his Lord's household, who ever seeks such things as be convenient and useful for the people unto him committed. Such a one, if he hear this word, and do that which he is commanded, that is, if he strengthen by seasonable and sound doctrine such things as be weak, if he bind together that which is sundered, if he make straight again what is become crooked, and give to the household the lively Word which is able to feed them unto life eternal, if such a one do thus, and meanwhile the hour which he knows not comes upon him, he shall obtain glory of the Lord, as a faithful steward and a useful overseer: that is, he shall have glory with God, for in all things he shall have of that which is best.

Lesson IX

But if that servant despise the long-suffering of God, Which waits to give salvation unto all men, and begin to wax wanton against his fellow-servants, and to give himself over to the evil and the vices of this present world, having all his care for the worship of his belly: the Lord of that servant shall come in a day when he looks not for Him, and shall cut him off from the goods wherewith he was entrusted, and appoint him his portion with the hypocrites, in everlasting punishment, because he has disobeyed the commandments, because he has minded the things of this present world, because he has lived the life of a heathen, because being unmindful of the judgment to come, he has afflicted with hunger, and thirst, and stripes, the flock committed to his care.

COMMON OF SUPREME PONTIFFS

All as in the Common of One/ Many Martyrs or Confessor Bishops as befits the feast except the following:

Lesson VII

From the Holy Gospel according to St. Matthew (Matt 16:13–19)

At that time: Jesus came into the quarters of Caesarea Philippi: and he asked his disciples, saying: Whom do men say that the Son of man is? And so on.

Homily by St. Leo, Pope

When the Lord, as we read in the Gospel, asked his disciples who did men, amid their diverse speculations, believe him, the Son of Man, to be, blessed Peter answered and said: "Thou art the Christ, the Son of the living God." And the Lord answered and said unto him: "Blessed art thou, Simon Bar-Jona: for flesh and blood hath not revealed it unto thee, but my Father, which is in heaven: and I say also unto thee: That thou art Peter, and upon this rock I will build my Church, and the gates of hell shall not prevail against it; and I will give unto thee the keys of the kingdom of heaven; and whatsoever thou shalt bind on earth shall be bound in heaven; and whatsoever thou shalt loose on earth shall be loosed in heaven." But the dispensation of truth perdures, and blessed Peter, persevering in the strength of the rock which he has received, has not relinquished the position he assumed at the helm of the Church.

Lesson VIII

In the universal Church it is as if Peter were still saying every day: "Thou art the Christ, the Son of the living God." For every tongue which confesses the Lord is taught that confession by the teaching of Peter. This is the Faith that overcomes the devil and looses the bonds of his prisoners. This is the Faith which makes men free of the world and brings them to heaven, and the gates of hell are impotent to prevail against it. This is the rock which God has fortified with such ramparts of salvation, that the contagion of heresy will never be able to infect it, nor idolatry and unbelief to overcome it. And therefore, dearly beloved, we celebrate today's festival with reasonable obedience, that in my humble person he may be acknowledged and honored who does continue to care for all the shepherds as well as sheep entrusted unto him, and who loses none of his dignity even in an unworthy successor.

Lesson IX

When, therefore, we address our exhortations to your godly ears, believe that you are hearing him speak whose office we are discharging. Yea, it is with his love for you that we warn you. And we preach unto you no other thing than that which he taught, entreating you as did he: "Gird up the loins of your mind; be sober; be ye holy in all manner of living; pass the time of your sojourning here in the fear of God." My disciples, dearly beloved, you are to me as the disciples of the Apostle Paul were to him, namely: "My crown and joy;" if it so be that your faith abides still in all lowliness and holiness, like unto the first times of the Gospel. For although the whole Church, which is in all the world, should indeed abound in all the virtues, it becomes you especially among all others to excel in acts of piety, founded as you be on the very citadel of the Apostolic Rock, you who have not only been redeemed with the rest of men by our Lord Jesus Christ, but who have been instructed by the blessed Apostle Peter far beyond all others.

COMMON OF CONFESSOR NON-BISHOPS

For One Confessor Non-Bishop

Lesson I - Ecclus 31:8–11

From the book of Ecclesiasticus

Blessed is the rich man that is found without blemish: and that hath not gone after gold, nor put his trust in money nor in treasures. Who is he, and we will praise him? for he hath done wonderful things in his life. Who hath been tried thereby, and made perfect, he shall have glory everlasting. He that could have transgressed, and hath not transgressed: and could do evil things, and hath not done them: Therefore are his goods established in the Lord, and all the church of the saints shall declare his alms.

Lesson II - Ecclus 32:18–20; 32:28; 33:1–3

He that feareth the Lord, will receive his discipline: and they that will seek him early, shall find a blessing. He that seeketh the law, shall be filled with it: and he that dealeth deceitfully, shall meet with a stumblingblock therein. They that fear the Lord, shall find just judgment, and shall kindle justice as a light. He that believeth God, taketh heed to the commandments: and he that trusteth in him, shall fare never the worse. No evils shall happen to him that feareth the Lord, but in temptation God will keep him, and deliver him from evils. A wise man hateth not the commandments and justices, and he shall not be dashed in pieces as a ship in a storm. A man of understanding is faithful to the law of God, and the law is faithful to him.

Lesson III - Ecclus 34:14–20

The spirit of those that fear God; is sought after, and by his regard shall be blessed. For their hope is on him that saveth them, and the eyes of God are upon them that love him. He that feareth the Lord shall tremble at nothing, and shall not be afraid for he is his hope. The soul of him that feareth the Lord is blessed. To whom doth he look, and who in his strength? The eyes of the Lord are upon them that fear him, he is their powerful protector, and strong stay, a defence from the heat, and a cover from the sun at noon, A preservation from stumbling, and a help from falling; he raiseth up the soul, and enlighteneth the eyes, and giveth health, and life, and blessing.

For Multiple Confessor Non-Bishops

Lesson I - Ecclus 44:1–5

From the book of Ecclesiasticus

Let us now praise men of renown, and our fathers in their generation. The Lord hath wrought great glory through his magnificence from the beginning. Such as have borne rule in their dominions, men of great power, and endued with their wisdom, shewing forth in the prophets the dignity of prophets, And ruling over the present people, and by the strength of wisdom instructing the people in most holy words. Such as by their skill sought out musical tunes, and published canticles of the Scriptures.

Lesson II ~ Ecclus 44:6–9

Rich men in virtue, studying beautifulness: living at peace in their houses. All these have gained glory in their generations, and were praised in their days. They that were born of them have left a name behind them, that their praises might be related: And there are some, of whom there is no memorial: who are perished, as if they had never been: and are become as if they had never been born, and their children with them.

Lesson III ~ Ecclus 44:10–15

But these were men of mercy, whose godly deeds have not failed: Good things continue with their seed, Their posterity are a holy inheritance, and their seed hath stood in the covenants. And their children for their sakes remain for ever: their seed and their glory shall not be forsaken. Their bodies are buried in peace, and their name liveth unto generation and generation. Let the people shew forth their wisdom, and the church declare their praise.

———

For Multiple Confessor Non-Bishops, the following Lessons are read in the Plural

Lesson IV

Sermon by St John Chrysostom, Patriarch

The blessed N., whose Feast we are this day keeping, does justly call on our tongue to tell what great deeds he wrought. Today did that blessed servant of God pass into that higher life, which is a life of peace, a life where there is no trouble. Today his ship reached that harbor whereafter wreck is to be dreaded no more. He has felt trouble and anguish of spirit for the last time. And why do we marvel that that place is one where the mind is vexed no more, when we remember that Paul says even to men living here in this life: "Rejoice evermore, pray without ceasing"?

Lesson V

Here there are sicknesses, here there are strivings, here there are untimely deaths, here there are lies, here there are jealousies, here there are troubles, here there is anger, here there are lustings, here there are pit-falls unnumbered, here there are daily cares, here one evil follows after another, and all bring vexation. And yet Paul has it that even here a man may rejoice evermore, if he will but raise his head above the flood of earthly things, and order his life aright. How much better shall we fare when we have passed away from all these things, and all these things are taken away from us, when we shall have no ill-health, nor disease, nor matter wherein to sin, when that hard thing, right of property, shall exist no more, whereby all unrighteousness comes into this life, and strifes unnumbered are begotten.

Lesson VI

In this verily do I most chiefly rejoice, for the happiness of that holy servant of God, in that, being taken away hence, and having found here no abiding city, he is become a citizen of that other city, which is the city of the living God: from the Church here he is gone, but he is come unto the Church of the firstborn which are written in heaven; he keeps holiday with us no more, but he is passed to where he holds high festival with Angels. And what be that city, and that Church, and that festival above, Paul bids us know, saying: "Ye are come unto the city of the living God, the heavenly Jerusalem, and unto the Church of the first-born which are written in heaven, and to an innumerable company of Angels."

Lesson VII

From the Holy Gospel according to St. Luke (Luke 12:35–40)

At that time: Jesus said unto His disciples: Let your loins be girded about, and your lights burning. And so on.

Homily by Pope St Gregory

Dearly beloved brethren, the words of the Holy Gospel, which have just been read, lie open before you, and, lest their very plainness should make them seem to some to be hard, we will go through them with such shortness as that neither may they which understand not remain unenlightened, nor they which understand be wearied. The Lord says: "Let your loins be girded about." Now, we gird our loins about, when by continence we master the lustful inclination of the flesh. But, forasmuch as it suffices not for a man to abstain from evil deeds, if he strive not to join thereto the earnest doing of good works, it is immediately added: "And your lights burning." Our lights burn when, by good works, we give bright example to our neighbor; concerning which works the Lord says: "Let your light so shine before men, that they may see your good works, and glorify your Father Which is in heaven."

Lesson VIII

Here, then, are two commandments, to gird our loins about, and to keep our lights burning: the cleanness of purity in our body, and the light of the truth in our works. Whoso has the one and not the other, pleases not thereby our Redeemer; that is, he pleases Him not which does good works, but bridles not himself from the pollutions of lust, neither he which is eminent in chastity, but exercises not himself in good works. Neither is chastity a great thing without good works, nor good works anything without chastity. And if any man do both, it remains that he must look by hope toward our Fatherland above, and not have the love of honor in this present world for his reason wherethrough he turns himself away from vice.

Lesson IX

"And you yourselves like unto men that wait for their lord, when he will return from the wedding: that, when he comes and knocketh, they may open unto him immediately."

The Lord comes at the hour of judgment: He knocks when, by the pains of sickness, He bids us know that death is nigh. To Him open we immediately, if we receive Him in love. Whoso fears to leave this body, will not open to the Judge when He knocks, for he dreads to see that Judge, Whom he knows that he has despised. But whosoever knows that his hope and works are built upon a good foundation, when he hears the Judge knock, opens to Him immediately, for to such a one that coming is blessed. Yea, when the hour of death is at hand, such a one hails with gladness a glorious reward.

Other Lessons for Feasts of Confessor Non-Bishops

Second set

Lesson I ~ Wis 4:7–14

From the book of Wisdom

But the just man, if he be prevented with death, shall be in rest. For venerable old age is not that of long time, nor counted by the number of years: but the understanding of a man is grey hairs. And a spotless life is old age. He pleased God and was beloved, and living among sinners he was translated. He was taken away lest wickedness should alter his understanding, or deceit beguile his soul. For the bewitching of vanity obscureth good things, and the wandering of concupiscence overturneth the innocent mind. Being made perfect in a short space, he fulfilled a long time: For his soul pleased God: therefore he hastened to bring him out of the midst of iniquities:

Lesson II ~ Wis 4:14–19

But the people see this, and understand not, nor lay up such things in their hearts: That the grace of God, and his mercy is with his saints, and that he hath respect to his chosen. But the just that is dead, condemneth the wicked that are living, and youth soon ended, the long life of the unjust. For they shall see the end of the wise man, and shall not understand what God hath designed for him, and why the Lord hath set him in safety. They shall see him, and shall despise him: but the Lord shall laugh them to scorn. And they shall fall after this without honour, and be a reproach among the dead for ever: for he shall burst them puffed up and speechless, and shall shake them from the foundations, and they shall be utterly laid waste: they shall be in sorrow, and their memory shall perish.

Lesson III ~ Wis 4:20–5:5

They shall come with fear at the thought of their sins, and their iniquities shall stand against them to convict them. Then shall the just stand with great constancy against those that have afflicted them, and taken away their labours. These seeing it, shall be troubled with terrible fear, and shall be amazed at the suddenness of their unexpected salvation. Saying within themselves, repenting, and groaning for anguish of spirit: These are they, whom we had some time in derision, and for a parable of reproach. We fools esteemed their life madness, and their end without honour. Behold how they are numbered among the children of God, and their lot is among the saints.

Lesson IV

From the Book of Morals written by Pope St Gregory

The simplicity of the righteous is made a subject of derision. The wisdom of this world hides our true feelings by artifice, and uses language to conceal our thoughts; this is the wisdom which demonstrated the truth of falsehood, and shows the falsehood of the truth. This kind of shrewdness the young acquire by practice, and children pay for the learning of it. Those who are good at this look down upon their neighbors; those who are bad at it are humble and timid, and wonder at it in others; they regard this astuteness too, wrong though it be, with wistful admiration, under softened epithets. Unstraightforwardness is called good breeding. The principles of the world teach those who entertain them, to try and rise to distinction, and when they have attained the bubble of glory which is so soon to pass away, to feel it sweet to have at their feet them on whom they may wreak rich revenge. These principles teach a man, as long as he is strong enough, to give way to nobody else, and, if he has no chance by force, to try and attain his object by diplomacy.

Lesson V

The wisdom of the righteous is the contrary of all this. They seek to avoid deception, to give their thoughts a clear expression in their words, to love the truth because it is the truth, to avoid falsehood, and rather to suffer than to inflict evil. Such are they who seek not to avenge themselves for wrong, and deem it gain to be despised for the truth's sake. Thus their simplicity is made a subject of derision, for such as are wise in this world believe the purity of their virtue to be simple foolery. Whatsoever is done innocently, they consider without a doubt stupid. Such works as the truth approves are idiotic when tried by carnal standards of wisdom. After all, what stupider thing is there in this world than to express our real thoughts in our words, to keep nothing quiet by skillful tact, to repay no injuries, to pray for them which curse us, to seek poverty, to give up property, to strive not with such as take from us, to turn the other cheek to the smiter?

Lesson VI

"A lamp despised in the thoughts of the rich, is ready for the time appointed." It often happens that one of the elect, who is on his way to be happy for ever, is crushed down here by repeated misfortunes. He reposes in no luxury of possessions, no distinction marks him as honorable among men, no admiring followers court him, no rich dress makes comely his bodily appearance. Everybody sees in him a person to be looked down upon, and his reputation is that of one unworthy of the world's favor. And yet, that is a man who, to the eyes of the Judge Who sees in secret, is glorious through virtue, whose life is radiant with worth. He dislikes to be honored, and does not refuse to meet with contempt. He brings abstinence to bear on his body, and his luxury is spiritual richness in love. He tries to keep his feelings patient, and when he has to stand up for righteousness' sake, is glad to be despised. He feels from his heart for the afflicted, and the prosperity of the godly gives him as much pleasure as if it were his own. He is careful inwardly to digest the food of the Holy Word. When he is inquired of, he does not know how to give a double answer.

Lesson VII

From the Holy Gospel according to St. Luke (Luke 12:32–34)

At that time: Jesus said unto His disciples: Fear not, little flock, for it is your Father's good pleasure to give you the kingdom. And so on.

Homily by St. Bede the Venerable, Priest

The elect are called a little flock, perchance because the reprobate are far more in number than they, but, more probably, because they love to be lowly, since it is God's will that however much His Church should grow in numbers, she should grow with lowliness even unto the end of the world, and should enter lowly into that kingdom which is hers by His promise. That kingdom He promises to her here, when He bids her to seek only the kingdom of God, and, to comfort her in her travail, He does so sweetly and so graciously say that her Father will give it to her.

Lesson VIII

"Sell that you have and give alms." Fear not, He says, lest, while you fight for the kingdom of God, you should lack such things as are needful for this life, nay rather, sell even that which you have, and give alms. This he does, whosoever for the Lord's sake leaves all that he has, and then works with his hands so that he may have something to eat and withal to give alms. In this does the Apostle boast himself, saying: "I have coveted no man's silver, or gold, or apparel, as you yourselves know: for these hands have ministered unto my necessities, and to them that were with me. I have showed you all things, how that so labouring you ought to support the weak."

Lesson IX

"Provide yourselves bags which wax not old." That is to say, by almsgiving, the reward thereof remains for ever. Nevertheless, we must not think here that this commandment forbids the Saints to keep money for their own use, and for helping of the poor. The Lord Himself, to Whom Angels ministered, had a bag, and kept therein that which the faithful people gave unto Him to relieve therewith the need of His disciples, and other poor folk. But we are commanded not to serve God for gain, nor to work unrighteousness for fear of poverty.

COMMON OF ABBOTS

Lesson VII

From the Holy Gospel according to St. Matthew (Matt 19:27–29)

At that time, Peter said unto Jesus: Behold, we have forsaken all, and followed thee what shall we have therefore? And so on.

Homily by St. Jerome, Priest

Peter was a fisherman; he was not rich, he earned his bread by his hand and skill, and nevertheless he is so bold, and says confidently: "We have forsaken all." And because it suffices not to forsake only, he adds that which to do is to be perfect: "and followed thee." We have done that which Thou hast commanded us, what reward therefore wilt Thou give us? And Jesus said unto them "Amen I say unto you, that you which have followed Me, in the regeneration, when the Son of Man shall sit in the throne of His glory, you also shall sit upon twelve thrones, judging the twelve tribes of Israel." He said not, "Ye which have forsaken all," for this did even Crates the philosopher, and they which have set nothing by riches are many, but, "Ye which have followed Me." This did the Apostles, and this do believers.

Lesson VIII

"In the regeneration, when the Son of Man shall sit in the throne of His glory, and when the dead shall rise again from corruption incorruptible, you also shall sit upon twelve thrones of judgment, condemning the twelve tribes of Israel, because, when you believed in Me, they would not. And every one that has forsaken houses, or brethren, or sisters, or father, or mother, or wife, or children, or lands, for My Name's sake, shall receive a hundredfold, and shall inherit everlasting life." This place agrees well with that other where the Saviour says "I came not to send peace, but a sword. For I am come to set a man at variance against his father, and the daughter against her mother, and the daughter-in-law against her mother-in-law; and a man's foes shall be they of his own household." Everyone, therefore, that has set no store by affection, and riches, and the pleasures of the world, for Christ's faith's sake, and the preaching of the Gospel, shall receive a hundredfold, and shall inherit everlasting life.

Lesson IX

By reason of these words, "a hundredfold," some will have it that there shall be a thousand years after the resurrection, wherein they that have forsaken all things shall receive a hundredfold of those things which they have forsaken, and shall inherit everlasting life. Such men consider not that though in other things this were worthy, regarding wives it is unseemly: for it becomes us not to think that he that has forsaken one wife in this world, shall receive a hundred wives in that which is to come. But the meaning is this, that every one that has for the Saviour's sake forsaken earthly things, shall receive spiritual things: which things, being rightly weighed against earthly things, are as though a hundredfold were weighed against one.

OR ~ Second set

Lesson VII

From the Holy Gospel according to St. Matthew (Matt 11:25–30)

At that time Jesus answered and said: I thank Thee, O Father, Lord of heaven and earth, because Thou hast hid these things from the wise and prudent, and hast revealed them unto babes. And so on.

Homily by St Augustine, Bishop

"Come unto Me, all you that labour!" And why labor we all, but because we are frail, sickly, dying creatures, burdened with earthen vessels which distress us? But if these fleshly vessels be distressful, let the open expanse of love be free and wide. "Come unto Me, all you that labour!" And why? That we may labor no more. His promise is an instant promise, for He calls such as are laboring. Perchance they will ask Him what their reward shall be? "And I," says He, "will give you rest. Take My yoke upon you, and learn of Me" not how to make the world, not how to create all things visible and invisible, not to work wonders in the earth, nor to raise the dead but "for I am meek and lowly in heart."

Lesson VIII

Wilt thou be great? Begin by being little. Dost thou think to raise up a lofty building? Then lay the foundations thereof in lowliness. The greater and more massive soever be that which any man thinks to build, so much the deeper does he dig his foundation. And when the house is built, it towers heavenward; but he which lays the foundation goes down into the earth. The building, therefore, is low before it is high, and, after it is low, it rises high to the roof.

Lesson IX

What is the roof of the house on which we labour? To where do its spires rise? I answer you at once; to the presence of God. You see how high a thing it is to see God. He that hears and is willing understands what I say. What is promised you is to see God, God the True, God the Supreme. Blessed is he who sees Him by Whom he is seen. Such as worship false gods see them easily, but they see them who have eyes and see not. But unto us it is promised that we shall see that God Who lives and sees.

OR ~ Third set

Lesson VII

From the Holy Gospel according to St. Matthew (Matt 19:27–29)

At that time, Peter said unto Jesus: Behold, we have forsaken all, and followed thee what shall we have therefore? And so on.

Homily by St Bede the Venerable, Priest

In the judgment to come, the elect will be in two classes. One class are they who have forsaken all, and followed the Lord: and these shall judge along with Him. The other class are they who have not equally forsaken all that they had, but who have been careful daily to give alms of their goods to the poor of Christ: these shall be the subjects of judgment, and these are they who shall then hear these words: "Come, you blessed of My Father, possess the kingdom prepared for you from the foundation of the world: for I was hungry, and you gave Me meat: I was thirsty, and you gave Me drink."

Lesson VIII

Of the reprobate also we gather, from the words of the Lord, that there will be two classes. One class are they who, being made partakers in the mystery of Christian faith, have neglected to show their faith by their works: these are they to whom it will be said at the judgment: "Depart from Me, you cursed, into everlasting fire, prepared for the devil and his angels: for I was hungry, and you gave Me no meat." The other class are they who either have never received the faith and mysteries of Christ, or who, having received, have apostatized, and abandoned it: and touching these it is said: "But he that believeth not is condemned already, because he hath not believed in the name of the only-begotten Son of God."

Lesson IX

And now that we have touched for a moment, with fear and just dread, upon these things, let us rather turn our hearing to the right joyful promises of our Lord and Saviour. Let us look to what His so great, beautiful, and fatherly love will give to such as follow Him; not the reward of life everlasting only, but gifts exceedingly precious in this life also. "Every one," says He, "that hath forsaken houses, or brethren, or sisters, or father, or mother, or wife, or children, or lands, for My Name's sake, shall receive a hundredfold, and shall inherit everlasting life." For everyone that shall forsake earthly affections and goods, to go and be Christ's disciple, the further he goes on in Christ's love, the more shall he find who will rejoice to give him a place in their hearts, and to minister to him of their substance.

COMMON OF DOCTORS

Lesson I - Ecclus 39:1–5

From the book of Ecclesiasticus

The wise men will seek out the wisdom of all the ancients, and will be occupied in the prophets. He will keep the sayings of renowned men, and will enter withal into the subtilties of parables. He will search out the hidden meanings of proverbs, and will be conversant in the secrets of parables. He shall serve among great men, and: appear before the governor. He shall pass into strange countries: for he shall try good and evil among men.

Lesson II - Ecclus 39:6–10

He will give his heart to resort early to the Lord that made him, and he will pray in the sight of the most High. He will open his mouth in prayer, and will make supplication for his sins. For if it shall please the great Lord, he will fill him with the spirit of understanding: And he will pour forth the words of his wisdom as showers, and in his prayer he will confess to the Lord. And he shall direct his counsel, and his knowledge, and in his secrets shall he meditate.

Lesson III - Ecclus 39:11–14

He shall show forth the discipline he hath learned, and shall glory in the law of the covenant of the Lord. Many shall praise his wisdom, and it shall never be forgotten. The memory of him shall not depart away, and his name shall be in request from generation to generation. Nations shall declare his wisdom, and the church shall show forth his praise.

Lesson IV

From the Book of Morals written by Pope St Gregory

In the Book of Job, it is written that it is God "which maketh Arcturus, Orion, and Hyades." Now if by the constellation Orion be mystically signified the spiritual constellation of the holy Martyrs, whom can we understand to be named after them under the title of the Hyades, but the Doctors of the Holy Church? When the glorious constellation of the Martyrs had set, and the light of the faith grew stronger, then appeared the constellation of the Doctors in the firmament of the Church, even in that springtime when the winter of unbelief was past, and the Sun of truth rose higher to shine on the hearts of His faithful ones. The storms of persecution were gone, and the long nights of unbelief were over; then rose the Doctors to shine on the Church, when the springtime of belief promised her a brighter year.

Lesson V

It seems well that the holy Doctors be figured by Hyades, for these stars are so styled from the Greek word *hyetos*, and *hyetos* signifies rain. The Hyades are therefore named after rain, because when they rise they undoubtedly bring rain. Well, then, do we apply the name of the Hyades to those who, when they rise to shine in the firmament of the universal Church, make the rain of holy preaching to fall upon the parched ground of man's heart. For if the word of preaching had not been as rain, then had Moses never said: "My doctrine shall drop as the rain," nor had the Truth said by Isaias: "I will also command the clouds that they rain no rain upon it," nor yet these words which we have just quoted: "Therefore the showers were withholden."

Lesson VI

At the same time that the Hyades come bringing rain, the sun daily rises higher in the heavens: thus do we, seeing the learning of the Doctors, and having our minds saturated with the rain of preaching, grow warmer in faith. And when the hot heavens shine fiery over her, the wet earth tends to harvest: thus do we, when the fire of holy learning burns bright in our heart, tend to bring forth the fruit of good works. When, day by day, we learn more of the knowledge of heavenly things, a springtime of inward light is opening within us, a new Sun is irradiating our mind, and, as we know Him better by the words of His Teachers, He does daily Himself shine the more therein. As the end of the world grows nearer, the knowledge of things heavenly will grow greater, and continue to develop with time.

Lesson VII

From the Holy Gospel according to St. Matthew (Matt 5:13–19)

At that time: Jesus said unto His disciples: "You are the salt of the earth; but if the salt lose its savor, wherewith shall it be salted?" And so on.

Homily by St Augustine, Bishop

The Lord shows how such men are to be judged but fools as do so run after temporal things either through lust for abundance, or through dread of lack, as to lose those things which are eternal, which men cannot give nor take away. "If, therefore, the salt lose its savor, wherewith shall it be salted?" This is as much as to say: If you, by whom the stale mass of mankind is to be preserved, through shrinking from the trials of persecutions, which endure but for a moment, do yourselves cast away that kingdom which is everlasting, who will there be to correct your error, seeing as you are they whom God has chosen to correct the errors of others?

Lesson VIII

"It is thenceforth good for nothing, but to be cast out, and to be, trodden under foot of men." He that suffers persecution is not thus trodden underfoot by men but rather he that through fear of persecution, has lost his savor. No man can be trodden upon, unless he be beneath him which treads upon him; but he cannot be beneath his tormentor, who, however grievously he suffers in his body upon earth, still has his heart in heaven.

Lesson IX

"You are the light of the world." They whom the Lord has, just above, called the salt of the earth, the same He now calls the light of the world. By the earth, whereof they were said to be the salt, we have not understood to be signified that earth whereupon we walk with our bodily feet, but the men which dwell upon the earth, or sinners, for the sweetening and correction of whose stinking corruption the Lord has sent His Apostles, as it were, as so much salt. And so here also, by the world we are to understand, not the heavens and the earth, but the men which are in the world, or which love the world for the enlightening of whom the Apostles have been sent. "A city that is set on a hill cannot be hid;" that is, set upon the heights of the same plain and great righteousness, whereof the mountain upon the which the Lord taught was itself a figure.

Second set

Lesson VII

From the Holy Gospel according to St. Matthew (Matt 5:13–19)

At that time: Jesus said unto His disciples: "You are the salt of the earth; but if the salt lose its savor, wherewith shall it be salted?" And so on.

Homily by St Hilary, Bishop

"You are the salt of the earth. But if the salt lose its savor, wherewith shall it be salted? It is thenceforth good for nothing, but to be cast out, and to be trodden under foot of men." There is, I take it, no such thing as salt of the earth. How, then, can the Apostles be called the salt of the earth? But the true meaning of these words will be made plain, when we consider the duty of Apostles, and the nature of salt itself. Now, salt is a compound of the elements of water and fire, out of the which two things in salt there is made one.

Lesson VIII

This thing, therefore, thus made to serve in divers ways the use of men, keeps from corruption the bodies whereon it is sprinkled, and does readily yield to all the senses the perception of its inborn savor. And thus are the Apostles, seeing that they are the preachers of the kingdom of heaven, and in a certain sense the sowers of the seed of life everlasting, since that Word of God which they scatter has power to make this mortal put on immortality. Fittingly then are they called salt, the savor of whose teaching keeps sweet the receiver thereof even unto life everlasting.

Lesson IX

But the nature of salt is to be ever the same and unchanging, and, on the other hand, the nature of man has this weakness to be changeable. He alone is blessed who has continued even unto the end in all the works which God has commanded. Therefore does the Lord warn them whom He calls the salt of the earth, that they are supposed to remain strong in that strength which He has given unto them, lest, becoming themselves savorless, they should be impotent to season others: losing the freshness of their own saltiness, be unable to stop the corruption round about them; and so the Church cast them out of her buttery, and they and those that they should have salted, be together trodden underfoot of such as enter in.

OR ~ Third set

Lesson VII

From the Holy Gospel according to St. Matthew (Matt 5:13–19)

At that time: Jesus said unto His disciples: "You are the salt of the earth; but if the salt lose its savor, wherewith shall it be salted?" And so on.

Homily by St John Chrysostom, Patriarch

Consider how that the Lord says: "You are the salt of the earth," by which figure He shows what a necessity of life is the Gospel. By this figure, He has us know that they unto whom He spoke have an account to render, not of their own life only, but for the whole world. Not unto two cities, says the Lord, nor unto ten, nor unto twenty, nor unto one people, as I sent the Prophets, do I send you. But I send you unto every land and sea, even unto the whole world, lying groaning, as it is, under the burden of divers sins.

Lesson VIII

These words, "You are the salt of the earth," show unto us the whole nature of man as savorless and stinking with the strong corruption of sin. And therefore demands He of His Apostles such qualities as are most needful and useful to furthering the salvation of many. He that is gentle and lowly; tender and just, shuts not up all these good things in his own heart, but opens these bright fountains that they may gush forth for the use of his neighbor. He whose heart is pure, and who seeks peace, suffering persecution for the truth's sake, does still lead a life for the good of the commonwealth.

Lesson IX

Think not, says the Lord, that the struggle is easy whereunto you shall be led, neither shall your reckoning be of light matters. You are the salt of the earth. Have you then salted that which is corrupted? Nay, for it is impossible that that which is once corrupted can be made sound again by the rubbing it with salt. This it is not asked of them to do. But their work is to sprinkle with salt, and to keep fresh thereafter, such things as the Lord has given over into their charge, and which He Himself has made new, and freed from all taint, before giving them. To make sound after the corruption of sin, is the work of Christ's power alone; to preserve from falling away again, is the duty and the toil commanded to the Apostles.

COMMON OF VIRGINS

Lesson I ~ 1 Cor 7:25–31

From first epistle of St. Paul the Apostle to the Corinthians

Now concerning virgins, I have no commandment of the Lord; but I give counsel, as having obtained mercy of the Lord, to be faithful. I think therefore that this is good for the present necessity, that it is good for a man so to be. Art thou bound to a wife? seek not to be loosed. Art thou loosed from a wife? seek not a wife. But if thou take a wife, thou hast not sinned. And if a virgin marry, she hath not sinned: nevertheless, such shall have tribulation of the flesh. But I spare you. This therefore I say, brethren; the time is short; it remaineth, that they also who have wives, be as if they had none; And they that weep, as though they wept not; and they that rejoice, as if they rejoiced not; and they that buy, as though they possessed not; And they that use this world, as if they used it not: for the fashion of this world passeth away.

Lesson II ~ 1 Cor 7:32–35

But I would have you to be without solicitude. He that is without a wife, is solicitous for the things that belong to the Lord, how he may please God. But he that is with a wife, is solicitous for the things of the world, how he may please his wife: and he is divided. And the unmarried woman and the virgin thinketh on the things of the Lord, that she may be holy both in body and in spirit. But she that is married thinketh on the things of the world, how she may please her husband. And this I speak for your profit: not to cast a snare upon you; but for that which is decent, and which may give you power to attend upon the Lord, without impediment.

Lesson III ~ 1 Cor 7:36–40

But if any man think that he seemeth dishonoured, with regard to his virgin, for that she is above the age, and it must so be: let him do what he will; he sinneth not, if she marry. For he that hath determined being steadfast in his heart, having no necessity, but having power of his own will; and hath judged this in his heart, to keep his virgin, doth well. Therefore, both he that giveth his virgin in marriage, doth well; and he that giveth her not, doth better. A woman is bound by the law as long as her husband liveth; but if her husband die, she is at liberty: let her marry to whom she will; only in the Lord. But more blessed shall she be, if she so remain, according to my counsel; and I think that I also have the spirit of God.

For a Virgin Martyr

Lesson I ~ Ecclus 51:1–7

From the book of Ecclesiasticus

I will give glory to thee, O Lord, O King, and I will praise thee, O God my Saviour. I will give glory to thy name: for thou hast been a helper and protector to me. And hast preserved my body from destruction, from the snare of an unjust tongue, and from the lips of them that forge lies, and in the sight of them that stood by, thou hast been my helper. And thou hast delivered me, according to the multitude of the mercy of thy name, from them that did roar, prepared to devour. Out of the hands of them that sought my life, and from the gates of afflictions, which compassed me about: From the oppression of the flame which surrounded me, and in the midst of the fire I was not burnt. From the depth of the belly of hell, and from an unclean tongue, and from lying words, from an unjust king, and from a slanderous tongue.

Lesson II - Ecclus 51:8–12

My soul shall praise the Lord even to death. And my life was drawing near to hell beneath. They compassed me on every side, and there was no one that would help me. I looked for the succour of men, and there was none. I remembered thy mercy, O Lord, and thy works, which are from the beginning of the world. How thou deliverest them that wait for thee, O Lord, and savest them out of the hands of the nations.

Lesson III -Ecclus 51:13–17

Thou hast exalted my dwelling place upon the earth and I have prayed for death to pass away. I called upon the Lord, the father of my Lord, that he would not leave me in the day of my trouble, and in the time of the proud without help. I will praise thy name continually, and will praise it with thanksgiving, and my prayer was heard. And thou hast saved me from destruction, and hast delivered me from the evil time. Therefore I will give thanks, and praise thee, and bless the name of the Lord.

———

Lesson IV

Sermon by St Ambrose, Bishop

This day is a maiden's Birthday. The love of virginity provokes us to say something concerning maidenhood, lest, if we pass thereby, we should seem to cast a slur on that which was her chief strength. Virginity is not to be praised because it is a grace which is poured forth in Martyrs, but because it is a grace which makes Martyrs. But what understanding of man can rightly grasp this excellency which rises above the laws of nature herself? What natural voice can portray a thing which is supernaturally noble? It is a reflection on earth of a glory whose home is in heaven. And it is but that which we may justly look for, when we see her who has her Husband in heaven, live a life whose model is the life of heaven.

Lesson V

It was maidenhood that pierced beyond the clouds, the atmosphere, the Angels, and the stars, and came upon the Word of God in the very bosom of the Father, and sucked Him into her heart. For who, that has once found such blessedness, would leave it again? "For thy name is as ointment poured forth, therefore do the virgins love thee," and draw thee after them. Lastly, it is not I, but the Lord by Whom it is said that they which neither marry nor are given in marriage are as the angels of God in heaven. Let no man therefore marvel that they which be married unto the Lord of angels should be likened themselves to angels.

Lesson VI

Who would deny that this is a life which has come down from heaven, seeing it is a life whereof it is not easy to find an example before God came down to dwell in a Body of clay? Then was it a virgin which conceived Him in her womb, and the Word was made Flesh, that Flesh might be made God. Some will say: Concerning Elias also, we find that he shared not in the lusting after a bodily coming-together. Yea; and therefore is it that he was carried up in a fiery chariot into heaven; therefore is it that he is seen with the Lord amid all the glory of the Transfiguration; therefore it is that he is to come as a Forerunner of the Lord's coming again.

Lesson VII

From the Holy Gospel according to St. Matthew (Matt 25:1–13)

At that time: Jesus said to His disciples: The Kingdom of heaven shall be likened unto ten virgins, which took their lamps, and went forth to meet the Bridegroom and the Bride. And so on.

Homily by Pope St Gregory

Dearly beloved brethren; oftentimes do I warn you to fly corrupt conversation, and to keep yourselves unspotted from the world. But the portion which is this day read from the Holy Gospel does oblige me to say that even to these good things which you do, you must needs take all careful heed. Look well to it, that, when you work righteousness, you do it not as seeking the praise and admiration of men, for if the lust of praise do once creep in, that which seems so fair without, loses its reward within. Behold how the Redeemer speaks of these ten virgins. He calls them all virgins, yet entered not all of them into the door of blessedness, for there were some of them who sought outwardly the honor of virginity, but would take no oil within their vessels with their lamps.

Lesson VIII

But, first of all, it is for us to ask: What is the kingdom of Heaven? And why shall the same be likened unto ten virgins, whereof, albeit five were wise, yet five were foolish? For if the kingdom of heaven be such that there shall in no way enter into it anything that defiles, neither whatsoever works abomination or makes a lie, how can it be like unto five virgins which were foolish? But we must know that, in the word of God, the kingdom of heaven does oftentimes signify the Church as she now is, regarding which the Lord says in another place: "The Son of Man shall send forth His Angels, and they shall gather out of His kingdom all things that offend." In that kingdom of Blessedness, wherein peace shall have her perfect reign, there shall be nothing found that offends for the angels to gather out.

Lesson IX

The body of every man does consist of five senses, and five being doubled, is ten. Forasmuch, therefore, as the whole body of the faithful does consist of two sexes, the Holy Church is likened unto ten virgins. And forasmuch as in the Church the good are for the present mingled with the bad, and the reprobate with the elect, it is rightly said that, of the ten virgins, five are wise and five are foolish. There are many who have self-control, which do keep themselves from lusting after things outward, whose hope bears them to things inward, who chastise the flesh, who long with intense homesickness for their Fatherland which is in heaven, who seek an eternal reward, and who will not to receive for their labors the praise of men. These are they who reckon their glory, not in the mouths of men, but in the testimony of their own conscience. And many there be likewise who afflict the body by self-control, and yet who seek for their self-control applause from men.

Alternate Lessons for Feasts of Virgins

Second set

Lesson IV

From the Book of Saint Cyprian, Bishop & Martyr, on the discipline and habit of Virgins

I am now to address myself to virgins, and as their condition is one of such glorious exaltation, I am the more supposed to be careful. This mass of consecrated virginity is the flower upon the plant of the Church. It is the charm and loveliness of spiritual grace. It is a generation of gladness. It is a work of praise and honor, untouched and uncorrupted. It is the image of God reflecting the holiness of the Lord. It is the brightest portion of the flock of Christ. It is the joy of our holy Mother the Church, and the rich blossom of her glorious fruitfulness, and every addition to the number of her virgins is an increase of her gladness. To these I speak, them I exhort, more in tenderness than in authority. Not that I, who am so worthless, and little, and feel so keenly the lowliness of mine own estate, would speak as finding any fault to reprove, but because when I feel the tenderest care, I feel the most nervous dread of any troubling by the wicked one.

Lesson V

This is not an unreasonable care, nor a groundless dread, which looks to the way of salvation and keeps the life-giving commandments of the Lord, to the end that they, who have consecrated themselves to Christ, who have turned their back for ever upon the pleasure of the flesh, who have vowed themselves God's own in body as well as in mind, may finish the work for which so vast a reward awaits them; that they may desire no more to seem fair and pleasing in any eyes but those of the Lord, from Whose hand they look to receive the wage of their continence, as He Himself has said: "All men cannot receive this saying, save they to whom it is given. For there are some eunuchs which were so born from their mother's womb; and there are some eunuchs which were made eunuchs of men; and there be eunuchs which have made themselves eunuchs for the kingdom of heaven's sake. He that is able to receive it, let him receive it."

Lesson VI

And yet again, the voice of an Angel has proclaimed what is the reward of continence. "These are they which were not defiled with women; for they are virgins. These are they which follow the Lamb whithersoever He goeth." Neither is it to man only that the Lord has promised this glorious reward for virginity. He passes not by women, but, since the woman is made out of the man, and taken and formed from him, God in His Holy Scriptures uses mostly to address Himself to the race in the form wherein He originally created it, for they are two in one flesh, and when mankind is spoken of, womankind also is signified. But if continence be a following of Christ, and virginity have her aim in the kingdom of heaven, what concern have such with earthly finery, or with self-adorning, whereby, while they seek to please men, they offend God?

Lessons VII–IX from the Common of Non-Virgins: "The Kingdom of Heaven is like unto"

OR - Third set

Lesson VII

From the Holy Gospel according to St. Matthew (Matt 19:3–12)

At that time: the Pharisees came unto Jesus, tempting Him and saying unto Him: Is it lawful for a man to put away his wife for any cause? And so on.

Homily by St John Chrysostom, Patriarch

Seeing that to directly exhort them unto virginity was nearly more than they could bear, our Lord seeks to draw them to the desire thereof, taking occasion by the needfulness of a law against divorce. Then He shows that virginity is possible, saying: "There are some eunuchs which were so born from their mother's womb; and there are some eunuchs which were made eunuchs of men; and there be eunuchs which have made themselves eunuchs for the kingdom of heaven's sake." In these words He persuades them indirectly to choose virginity, while He teaches them that such a gift is not so good as to be impossible.

Lesson VIII

Thus His doctrine He establishes as something like this. Supposing that thou hadst been born a eunuch by nature, or hadst been made a eunuch by the cruelty of men, so that thou hadst no sexual enjoyment, and hadst no credit for having none, what wouldest thou do? Give God thanks therefore, that thou dost for a reward and a crown what such others suffer with no reward and no crown: yea, and rather a lighter burden than the same, and not only because thou hast the joy of hope, and of knowing that thou doest well, but also because thou art not so battered by storms of desire as they are.

Lesson IX

When, therefore, He had spoken of such as are eunuchs by nature, or by mutilation, and are eunuchs vainly and uselessly, unless they also bridle their thoughts, and of such as deny themselves for the kingdom of heaven's sake, He added: "He that is able to receive it, let him receive it," that He might make them the readier by showing the very sternness of the work, and, in His unspeakable goodness, He would not include any such precept within the requirements of the law, and, by saying this, shows it to be the more possible, that He might increase the desire of freely choosing it.

COMMON OF NON-VIRGINS

If a Martyr, Lessons I–III from those of a Virgin Martyr

Lesson I ~ Prov 31:10–17

From the Proverbs of Solomon

Who shall find a valiant woman? Far and from the uttermost coasts is the price of her. The heart of her husband trusteth in her, and he shall have no need of spoils. She will render him good, and not evil, all the days of her life. She hath sought wool and flax, and hath wrought by the counsel of her hands. She is like the merchant's ship, she bringeth her bread from afar. And she hath risen in the night, and given a prey to her household, and victuals to her maidens. She hath considered a field, and bought it: with the fruit of her hands she hath planted a vineyard. She hath girded her loins with strength, and hath strengthened her arm.

Lesson II ~ Prov 31:18–24

She hath tasted and seen that her traffic is good: her lamp shall not be put out in the night. She hath put out her hand to strong things, and her fingers have taken hold of the spindle. She hath opened her hand to the needy, and stretched out her hands to the poor. She shall not fear for her house in the cold of snow: for all her domestics are clothed with double garments. She hath made for herself clothing of tapestry: fine linen, and purple is her covering. Her husband is honourable in the gates, when he sitteth among the senators of the land. She made fine linen, and sold it, and delivered a girdle to the Chanaanite.

Lesson III ~ Prov 31:25–31

Strength and beauty are her clothing, and she shall laugh in the latter day. She hath opened her mouth to wisdom, and the law of clemency is on her tongue. She hath looked well to the paths of her house, and hath not eaten her bread idle. Her children rose up, and called her blessed: her husband, and he praised her. Many daughters have gathered together riches: thou hast surpassed them all. Favour is deceitful, and beauty is vain: the woman that feareth the Lord, she shall be praised. Give her of the fruit of her hands: and let her works praise her in the gates.

Lesson IV

From the Book on Widows by St Ambrose, Bishop

I behold the field of the Church, that the same is a fruitful field, sometimes smiling with the brightness of virginity, sometimes golden with the ripe harvest of widowhood, sometimes rich with the crop of marriage. These things be diverse, but they be the fruits of the same field. There are not so many choice lilies as stalks of bearded grain, ears for the harvest, and there are more places in the soil fitted once to receive seed than there are places which, when they have yielded a crop, are fitted again to be plowed. Good, then, is widowhood, which the judgment of an Apostle has so often commended, widowhood, which is the teacher of faith and of purity.

Lesson V

Therefore, they who worship adultery and uncleanness in their gods made celibacy and widowhood punishable. They who lusted after abominations, taxed self-control. The pretense was the desire of fruitfulness, but the aim was to abolish virginity, the resolution of chastity. When a soldier has served his time he lays down his arms, leaves his trade, and retires to his own lands, that as well himself may rest after the toils of life, as that the hope of rest to come may make others the more ready to undergo work. So also the aged laborer leaves it for others to guide the handle of the plow, and withdraws from the weariness of his younger days' labor to essay the task of an old man's thoughtful supervision. It is easier to prune vines, than to stamp them out, to check the first wild outburst of their vigor, and to curtail the wantonness of their young growth, so teaching, even by the example of the vineyard, that chastity, which keeps itself within the bearing of but a few children.

Lesson VI

Like to these is a widow, a veteran retiring to rest upon the earned rewards of her chastity, and who, albeit she lays down the arms of wifehood, still rules the order of all her household; albeit she be at rest from bearing burdens, she is careful in the marriage of her youngsters, and with the wisdom of age chooses what study is the most useful, what fruit is the richest, what wedlock is the worthiest. And so, if the government of the field be given more to the elder than to the younger, why shouldest thou hold that a wife is more useful than a widow? But if they which persecuted the faith persecuted also widowhood, then, surely, in the eyes of them which hold the faith, must widowhood be looked upon as a reward, rather than shrunk from as a punishment.

Lesson VII

From the Holy Gospel according to St. Matthew (Matt 13:44–52)

At that time: Jesus spoke unto His disciples this parable: The kingdom of heaven is like unto treasure hid in a field. And so on.

Homily by Pope St Gregory

Dearly beloved brethren, the kingdom of heaven is likened unto the things of earth, to the end that by means of things which we know, our mind may rise to the contemplation of the things which we know not; by the example of things which are seen, may fix her gaze on things which are not seen; by the touch of things which she uses, may be warmed towards the things which she uses not; by things which she knows and loves, to love also the things which she knows not. For, behold, "The kingdom of heaven is like unto a treasure hidden in a field. Which a man having found, hid it, and for joy thereof goeth, and selleth all that he hath, and buyeth that field."

Lesson VIII

And herein we must remark that the treasure, when once it has been found, is hidden to keep it safe. He who keeps not hidden from the praises of men his eager striving heavenwards, does not enough to keep the same safe from the attacks of evil spirits. In this life we are, as it were, on the way home, and the road is beset by evil spirits, as it were, by highwaymen. He, therefore, invites robbery who carries his treasure glaringly. This I say, not that our neighbor should not see our good works since it is written: "Let your light so shine before men that they may see your good works, and glorify your Father Which is in heaven." Rather we should not seek, by what we do, to gain the praise of men. Let the outward work agree with the inward thought, that by our good works we may give an example to our neighbor, and still, by our intention, directed only to the pleasing God, we may also have sooner that our works were secret.

Lesson IX

The treasure is the desire for heaven; the field wherein it is hidden is the earnest observance wherewith this desire is surrounded. Whosoever turns his back upon the enjoyments of the flesh, and by earnest striving heavenward, puts all earthly lusts under the feet of discipline, so that he smiles back no more when the flesh smiles at him, and shudders no more at anything that can only kill the body—whosoever does thus, has sold all that he had, and bought that field.

Alternate Lessons for Feasts of a Martyr Non-Virgin Second Set

Lesson IV

Sermon by St John Chrysostom, Patriarch

The commemorations which I love and welcome the most are the commemorations of the Martyrs, and, while I love and welcome them all, more especially do I do so when the wrestling set before us is the wrestling of a woman. The weaker the vessel, the stronger the grace, the greater the spoils, the clearer the victory; and that, not because the sex of the wrestler is frail, but because the enemy is now conquered by her through whom he once conquered.

Lesson V

By a woman he overcame, by a woman he is overcome. A woman was once his weapon; a woman is now become the instrument of his defeat; he finds that the weak vessel cannot be broken. The first woman sinned and died; this one died rather than sin. The first, under the delusion of a lying promise, broke the law of God; this one chose rather to keep covenant with her Benefactor, than to keep this present life. What excuse for softness and sloth can men any longer hope to make? or what forgiveness, when women bear themselves so bravely and manfully, and gird themselves up so nobly for the wrestling of godliness?

Lesson VI

She had a weak body, and a sex which is exposed to hurt; but grace came, and made nothing of these frailties. Nothing is stronger than one in whose mind the fear of God is firmly and willfully rooted. The enemy may threaten fire, or iron, or beasts, or anything else, but such a one takes them all for matters not worth consideration. And thus did this blessed woman do.

COMMON OF THE DEDICATION OF A CHURCH

Lesson I ~ 2 Par 7:1–5

From the second book of Paralipomenon

And when Solomon had made an end of his prayer, fire came down from heaven, and consumed the holocausts and the victims: and the majesty of the Lord filled the house. Neither could the priests enter into the temple of the Lord, because the majesty of the Lord had filled the temple of the Lord. Moreover all the children of Israel saw the fire coming down, and the glory of the Lord upon the house: and falling down with their faces to the ground, upon the stone pavement, they adored and praised the Lord: because he is good, because his mercy endureth for ever. And the king and all the people sacrificed victims before the Lord. And king Solomon offered a sacrifice of twenty-two thousand oxen, and one hundred and twenty thousand rams: and the king and all the people dedicated the house of God.

Lesson II ~ 2 Par 7:6–9

And the priests stood in their offices: and the Levites with the instruments of music of the Lord, which king David made to praise the Lord: because his mercy endureth for ever, singing the hymns of David by their ministry: and the priests sounded with trumpets before them, and all Israel stood. Solomon also sanctified the middle of the court before the temple of the Lord: for he offered there the holocausts, and the fat of the peace offerings: because the brazen altar, which he had made, could not hold the holocausts and the sacrifices and the fat: And Solomon kept the solemnity at that time seven days, and all Israel with him, a very great congregation, from the entrance of Emath to the torrent of Egypt. And he made on the eighth day a solemn assembly, because he had kept the dedication of the altar seven days, and had celebrated the solemnity seven days.

Lesson III ~ 2 Par 7:11–16

And Solomon finished the house of the Lord, and the king's house, and all that he had designed in his heart to do, in the house of the Lord, and in his own house, and he prospered. And the Lord appeared to him by night, and said: I have heard thy prayer, and I have chosen this place to myself for a house of sacrifice. If I shut up heaven, and there fall no rain, or if I give orders, and command the locust to devour the land, or if I send pestilence among my people: And my people, upon whom my name is called, being converted, shall make supplication to me, and seek out my face, and do penance for their most wicked ways: then will I hear from heaven, and will forgive their sins and will heal their land. My eyes also shall be open, and my ears attentive to the prayer of him that shall pray in this place. For I have chosen, and have sanctified this place, that my name may be there for ever, and my eyes and my heart may remain there perpetually.

Lesson IV

Sermon by St. Augustine, Bishop

Dearly beloved brethren, as often as we keep the Dedication-Feast of some Altar or Church, if we think faithfully and carefully, and live holily and righteously, that which is done in temples made with hands, is done in our soul by a spiritual building. He at the Dedication of the Temple. lied not who said: "The temple of God is holy; which temple you are," and again: "Know ye not that your body is the temple of the Holy Ghost, Which is in you." And therefore, dearly beloved brethren, since by the grace of God, without any foregoing deserts of our own, we have been made worthy to become the Temple of God, let us work as hard as we can, with His help, that our Lord may not find in His Temple, that is, in us, anything to offend the eyes of His Majesty.

Lesson V

Let the Tabernacle of our heart be swept clean of vices and filled with virtues. Let it be locked to the devil, and thrown open to Christ. Yea, let us so work, that we may be able to open the door of the kingdom of heaven with the key of good works. For even as evil works are so many bolts and bars to close against us the entrance into life, so beyond doubt are good works the key thereto. And therefore, dearly beloved brethren, let each one look into his own conscience, and when he finds the wounds of guilt there, let him first strive by prayers, fasting, or alms deeds to purge his conscience, and so let him dare to take the Eucharist.

Lesson VI

For if he acknowledge his iniquity, and withdraw himself from the Altar of God, he will soon attain unto the mercy of the pardon of God, for, as he that exalted himself shall be abased, so shall he that humbles himself be exalted. He who, as I have said, acknowledging his iniquity, withdraws himself through lowliness from the Altar of the Church, till he have mended his life, need have but little fear that he will be excommunicated from the eternal marriage supper in heaven.

Lesson VII

From the Holy Gospel according to St. Luke (Luke 19:1–10)

At that time: Jesus entered and passed through Jericho. And, behold, there was a man named Zacchaeus, which was the chief among the publicans, and he was rich. And so on.

Homily by St. Ambrose, Bishop

Zacchaeus was little of stature, that is, he was not raised aloft among men by nobility of birth, and, like the most of the world, he possessed few merits. When he heard that the Lord and Saviour, Who had come unto His Own, and Whom His Own had not received, was coming, he desired to see Him. But the sight of Jesus is not easy; to any on the earth it is impossible. And since Zacchaeus had neither the Prophets, nor yet the Law, as a gracious help to his nature, he climbed up into a sycamore tree, raising his feet above the vanity of the Jews, and straightening the crooked branches of his former life, and therefore he received Jesus to lodge within his house.

Lesson VIII

He did well to climb up into a tree, that a good tree might bring forth good fruits, and that the slip of the wild olive, grafted, contrary to nature, into the good olive, might bring forth the fruits of the law. For the root is holy, however unprofitable the branches. Their barren beauty has now been overshadowed by the belief of the Gentiles in the Resurrection, as by a material upgrowth. Zacchaeus, then, was in the sycamore tree, and the blind man by the wayside. For the one, Jesus stood waiting to show mercy, and asked him before He healed him, what he would that He should do for him; being unbidden of the other, He bade Himself to be his Guest, knowing how rich was the reward of receiving Him. Nevertheless, albeit He had heard no words of invitation, yet had He seen how his heart went.

Lesson IX

But lest we should seem haughtily to pass by the poor blind man, and to hurry on to the rich one, let us stand waiting for him, as the Lord stood and waited; let us ask of him, as Christ asked of him. Let us ask because we are ignorant; Christ asked because He knew. Let us ask, that we may know whence he received his cure; Christ asked, that all of us may know from one example where through we are to earn a sight of the Lord. Christ asked, that we might believe that none, save they that confess Him, can be saved.

COMMON OF FEASTS OF THE BLESSED VIRGIN MARY

Lesson I - Prov 8:12–17

From the Proverbs of Solomon

I wisdom dwell in counsel, and am present in learned thoughts. The fear of the Lord hateth evil: I hate arrogance, and pride, and every wicked way, and a mouth with a double tongue. Counsel and equity is mine, prudence is mine, strength is mine. By me kings reign, and lawgivers decree just things, By me princes rule, and the mighty decree justice. I love them that love me: and they that in the morning early watch for me, shall find me.

Lesson II - Prov 8:18–25

With me are riches and glory, glorious riches and justice. For my fruit is better than gold and the precious stone, and my blossoms than choice silver. I walk in the way of justice, in the midst of the paths of judgment, That I may enrich them that love me, and may fill their treasures. The Lord possessed me in the beginning of his ways, before he made any thing from the beginning. I was set up from eternity, and of old before the earth was made. The depths were not as yet, and I was already conceived. neither had the fountains of waters as yet sprung out: The mountains with their huge bulk had not as yet been established: before the hills I was brought forth.

Lesson III - Prov 8:34–36; 9:1–5

Blessed is the man that heareth me, and that watcheth daily at my gates, and waiteth at the posts of my doors. He that shall find me, shall find life, and shall have salvation from the Lord: But he that shall sin against me, shall hurt his own soul. All that hate me love death. Wisdom hath built herself a house, she hath hewn her out seven pillars. She hath slain her victims, mingled her wine, and set forth her table. She hath sent her maids to invite to the tower, and to the walls of the city: Whosoever is a little one, let him come to me. And to the unwise she said: Come, eat my bread, and drink the wine which I have mingled for you.

Lesson IV

Sermon by St John Chrysostom, Patriarch

The Son of God chose for His Mother not a woman of wealth, not a woman of substance, but that blessed maiden whose soul was bright with grace. It was because Blessed Mary had preserved a superhuman chastity, that she conceived the Lord Jesus Christ in her womb. Let us then fly to the most holy maiden, who is Mother of God, that we may gain the help of her patronage. Yea, all you that are virgins, whosoever you be, run to the Mother of the Lord. She will keep for you by her protection your most beautiful, your most precious, and your most enduring possession.

Lesson V

Verily, dearly beloved brethren, the Blessed Virgin Mary was a great wonder. What thing greater or more famous than she, has ever at any time been found, or can be found? She alone is greater than heaven and earth. What thing holier than she has been, or can be found? Neither Prophets, nor Apostles, nor Martyrs, nor Patriarchs, nor Angels, nor Thrones, nor Dominions, nor Seraphim, nor Cherubim, nor any other creature, visible or invisible, can be found that is greater or more excellent than she. She is at once the handmaid and the parent of God, at once virgin and mother.

Lesson VI

She is the Mother of Him Who was begotten of the Father before all ages, and Who is acknowledged by Angels and men to be Lord of all. Wouldst thou know how much nobler is this virgin than any of the heavenly powers? They stand before Him with fear and trembling, veiling their faces with their wings, but she offers humanity to Him to Whom she gave birth. Through her we obtain the remission of sins. Hail, then, O Mother! Heaven! Damsel! Maiden! Throne! Adornment, and glory, and foundation of our Church! Cease not to pray for us to thy Son and our Lord Jesus Christ that through thee we may find mercy in the day of judgment, and may be able to obtain those good things which God has prepared for them that love Him, by the grace and goodness of our Lord Jesus Christ; to Whom, with the Father, and the Holy Ghost, be ascribed all glory, and honor, and power, now, and for ever and ever. Amen.

Lesson VII

From the Holy Gospel according to St. Luke (Luke 11:27–28)

At that time: as Jesus spoke unto the multitudes, a certain woman of the company lifted up her voice and said unto Him: Blessed is the womb that bore Thee. And so on.

Homily by St. Bede the Venerable, Priest

It is plain that this was a woman of great earnestness and faith. The Scribes and Pharisees were at once tempting and blaspheming the Lord, but this woman so clearly grasped His Incarnation, and so bravely confessed the same, that she confounded both the lies of the great men who were present, and the faithlessness of the heretics who were yet to come. Even as the Jews then, blaspheming the works of the Holy Ghost, denied the very Son of God Who is of one substance with the Father, so afterwards did the heretics, by denying that Mary always a Virgin did, under the operation of the Holy Ghost, supply flesh to the Only-begotten One of God, when He was about being born in a human body, even so, I say, did the heretics deny that the Son of Man should be called a true Son, Who is of one substance with His Mother.

Lesson VIII

But if we shall say that the Flesh, Wherewith the Son of God was born in the flesh, was something outside of the flesh of His Virgin Mother, without reason should we bless the womb that bore Him, and the breasts which

He has sucked. But the Apostle says: "God sent forth His Son, made of a woman, made under the law," and they are not to be listened to who read this passage: "Born of a woman, made under the law." He was made of a woman, for He was conceived in a virgin's womb, and took His Flesh, not from nothing, not from elsewhere, but from the flesh of His Mother. Otherwise, and if He had not been sprung of a woman, He could not with truth be called the Son of man. Let us therefore, denying the doctrine of Eutyches, lift up our voice, along with the Universal Church, whereof that woman was a figure, let us lift up our heart as well as our voice from the company, and say unto the Saviour: "Blessed is the womb that bore Thee, and the paps which Thou hast sucked!" Blessed Mother! of whom one has said: Thou art His Mother Who reigns o'er earth and o'er heaven for ever.

Lesson IX

"Yea, rather, blessed are they that hear the Word of God and keep it." How nobly does the Saviour say "Yea" to the woman's blessing, declaring also that not only is she blessed who was worthy to give bodily birth to the Word of God, but that all they who spiritually conceive the same Word by the hearing of faith, and, by keeping it through good works, bring it forth and, as it were, carefully nurse it in their own hearts and in the hearts of their neighbors, are also blessed. Yea, and that the very Mother of God herself was blessed in being for a while the handmaid of the Word of God-made-Flesh, but that she was much more blessed in this, that through her love she keeps Him for ever.

VOTIVE OFFICE OF THE BLESSED VIRGIN MARY ON SATURDAYS

For all Saturdays on which there are no greater Feasts, Vigils, or Octaves—that is, for Saturday Ferias or Simplex Feasts

Lessons I & II are taken from the occurring Scripture in the Proper of Time; by more recent custom, one may append Lesson III's Scripture to that of Lesson II.

Lesson III is taken from the following Lessons according to the corresponding month

NOVEMBER

Lesson III

From the Commentary of St. Basil, Bishop, on the Prophet Isaias

"I went to the prophetess," he says, "and she conceived and bore a son." To see Mary in the prophetess whom Isaias approached by spiritual foreknowledge one need only recall the words Mary uttered when she was inspired by the spirit of prophecy: "My soul magnifies the Lord, and my spirit rejoices in God my Saviour; because He has regarded the lowliness of His handmaid; for behold, henceforth all generation shall call me blessed." In fact, if you bear in mind all that she said, you can only agree that she was indeed the prophetess, since the spirit of Lord came upon her, and the power of the Most High overshadowed her.

DECEMBER

Lesson III

From the Book of Offices of St. Ambrose, Bishop

The good comrade and guardian of chastity is modesty. And this is the first thing that strikes the reader of the Gospel, as he begins to learn about the Mother of our Lord. Her modesty commends her, and like reliable witness, attests that she is worthy of being chosen for so high an office. Alone in her room, she was silent at the Angel's greeting. His entrance had disturbed her, and her countenance reflected the Virgins agitation at seeing this stranger appear in the form of a man. And so, although she was humble, still out of modesty she did not return his greeting, nor did she gave any answer, until she learned that she must agree to becoming the Mother of God, and then she spoke, not to reject his message but to learn how this marvel was to come about.

JANUARY

Lesson III

From the letter of Blessed Ambrose, bishop, to Pope Siricius

How great is the madness of their dismal barkings, that the same persons should say that Christ could not be born of a virgin, and yet assert that women, after having given birth to human pledges, remain virgins? But if they will not believe the doctrines of the Clergy, let them believe the oracles of Christ, let them believe the admonitions of Angels who say,

"For with God nothing shall be impossible." Let them give credit to the Creed of the Apostles, which the Roman Church has always kept and preserved undefiled. Mary heard the voice of the Angel, and she who before had said "How shall this be?," not asking from want of faith in the mode of generation, afterwards replied: "Behold the handmaid of the Lord, be it unto me according to thy word."

FEBRUARY

Lesson III

From the book of St. Jerome, Priest, against Jovian

Christ is virgin, and the mother of our virgin Christ remains forever virgin, the Virgin Mother. For Jesus entered the world, as he entered the upper room, "the doors being closed," and in his sepulcher, which had been hewn out of the hard rock, "no one had yet been laid," nor was anyone else laid in it afterward. "An enclosed garden, a fountain sealed" was Mary. And from that fountain, according to Joel, flows the stream that waters the torrent either of "ropes" or of "thorns." The ropes would be the sins by which we had been bound down; the thorns would be those which choke the householder's seed. Mary is the eastern gate, of which Ezechiel speaks, always closed and luminous, whether concealing in itself or bringing forth from itself the Holy of holies. She is the gate through which the Sun of justice and our High Priest according to the order of Melchisedech goes in and out.

MARCH

Usually impeded by a Lenten Feria or Feast

Lesson III

From the book of St. Irenæus, Bishop & Martyr, Against Heretics

That the Lord should come "unto His own" and that His own creation should bear Him by whom itself was born; that He should make amends through His obedience on the tree of the Cross for the disobedience committed at the tree in Paradise; that He should annul the effects of the seduction by which the virgin Eve, already destined for a husband, was led into evil—all this good news, this true revelation was fittingly brought by an Angel to the Virgin Mary, already espoused to a husband. For, just as Eve was seduced by the words of a fallen angel into turning away from God by disobeying His command, so Mary was evangelized by the words of an Angel, who persuaded her to give birth to God in obedience to His word. One has lured into fleeing from God, the other was persuaded to obey God, that the Virgin Mary might became an advocate for the virgin Eve. Through a virgin mankind was tied to death; so also through a virgin the bonds loosed; the Virgin's obedience balanced the virgin's disobedience.

APRIL

Usually impeded by Passiontide, Holy Week, or the Easter Octave

Lesson III

From the Commentary of St. Jerome, Priest, on the prophet Ezechiel

"This gate is to remain closed it is not to be opened." In a beautiful figure, some persons understand the closed gate which only the Lord, the God of Israel enters: the leader on whose account it has been closed—as a type of the Virgin Mary who remained a virgin both before and after she gave birth. She remained a virgin, while the Angel was speaking to her: "The Holy Spirit shall come upon you and the power of the Most High shall overshadow you; and therefore the Holy One to be born shall be called the Son of God." And when He was born, she remained a virgin, her perpetual virginity confounding those who think, because of the mention in the Gospel of the Saviour's brethren, that after His birth she had children by Joseph.

MAY

Lesson III

From the Treatise of St. Augustine, Bishop, on the Creed, to the Catechumens

Through a woman came death; through a woman, life: through Eve, ruin; through Mary, salvation. The former corrupted, followed the deceiver; the latter uncorrupted, gave birth to the Saviour. Eve willingly accepted the drink offered by the serpent and handed it on to her husband; and by their action both deserved the penalty of death. Mary, filled with heavenly grace from above, brought forth life, by which mankind, already dead, can be revived. Who has worked this miracle, if not the Son of the Virgin and the Spouse of virgin who brought fruitfulness to His mother without taking away her integrity?

JUNE

Lesson III

Sermon of St. Bernard, Abbot

It was indeed a serious injury that one man and one woman inflicted on us, dearly beloved; but thanks to God, it was also by one Man and one woman that all things were restored, and with a great increase of grace too. For "not like the offense is gift." On the contrary, the benefits received are greater than the loss sustained. Yes, that was how the Maker, supreme in good judgment and in kindness, plied His craft: what had been bruised, He did not break. Rather, He remade it completely in such a way as to be in more advantage to us: out of the old Adam He made a new Man; Eve He transformed into Mary.

JULY

Lesson III

From the letter of Blessed Ambrose, Bishop to Pope Siricius

That a man was born from a virgin is not beyond belief, since a fountain of water gushed from a rock, and iron floated on water, and a man walked on the sea. Therefore if the waves bore a man, cannot a virgin give birth to a man, and to that man of whom we read: The Lord shall send them a Saviour, a man, and he shall deliver them, and the Lord shall be known to Egypt? In the Old Testament, a virgin led the Hebrew hosts through the Red Sea; in the New Testament, a Virgin was chosen as the palace of the heavenly Birth, to bring us salvation.

—

AUGUST

Lesson III

From the Commentary of Pope St. Gregory on the books of Kings

"There was a man of Ramathaim-Sophim, of mount Ephraim." The name of this mountain can be taken to designate the Most Blessed Virgin Mary, Mother of God. She is a mountain inasmuch as, among chosen creatures, the dignity of her calling was above that of any others. Surely Mary was the highest of mountains, was she not, when she heaped up merits beyond all the choirs of Angels, to the very throne of God, that she might be worthy to conceive the eternal Word? It was this mountain whose supreme dignity Isaias was prophesying when he said: "In days to come, the mountain of the Lord's house shall be established as the highest mountain." Mary was indeed the highest mountain, since her summit gleamed above those of all the Saints.

—

SEPTEMBER

Lesson III

From the epistle of Pope St. Leo to Pulcheria Augusta

And the fulfillment of the mystery of our atonement, which was ordained from all eternity, was not assisted by any figures because the Holy Spirit had not yet come upon the Virgin, and the power of the Most High had not overshadowed her: so that Wisdom building herself a house within her undefiled body, the Word became flesh; and the form of God and the form of a slave coming together into one person, the Creator of times was born in time; and He Himself through whom all things were made, was brought forth in the midst of all things. For if the New Man had not been made in the likeness of sinful flesh, and taken on Him our old nature, and being consubstantial with the Father, had deigned to be consubstantial with His mother also, and being alone free from sin, had united our nature to Him the whole human race would be held in bondage beneath the Devil's yoke.

—

OCTOBER

Lesson III

A sermon of St. Bernard, Abbot

My brothers, let us cast ourselves at Mary's blessed feet with the most devout supplication. Let us embrace them, let us hold fast to her, and not let go until she blesses us; for she has great power. Like the fleece between the dew and the threshing floor, like the woman between the sun and the moon, so Mary stands between Christ and the Church. But perhaps you wonder, not so much at the fleece covered with dew, but at the woman clothed with the sun. Any relationship between the sun and the woman would be striking enough, but this proximity is indeed something to be marveled at. How can so fragile a nature subsist in that excessive heat? You have a right to wonder, saintly Moses; it is only natural that in your curiosity you should want to look more closely. But "remove the sandals from your feet," put aside the covering of fleshly thoughts, if you wish to draw near.

PROPER OF SAINTS

When a Commemoration or another proper lesson impedes a Lesson from the Lives of the Saints or Occurring Scripture, by recent custom (as in the rubrics of 1961) the impeded Lesson may be appended to the preceding Lesson so as not to omit it altogether.

November 26 ~ St. Silvester

Abbot ~ Duplex

All from Common except what follows

Lessons I–III from the occurring Scripture

Lesson IV

Silvester was born of a noble family at Osimo, in Picenum, and in his childhood was a wonderful example both in regard to letters and good living. When he grew older his father sent him to Bologna to study the law, but God warned him to give himself to divinity, and he thereby incurred the wrath of his father, which he bore with complacency for ten full years. On account of his eminent graces he was elected an honorary canon of the Cathedral of Osimo, in which dignity he ministered to the people by his prayers, his example, and his sermons.

Lesson V

At the funeral of a certain nobleman he perceived in an open grave the disfigured corpse of a kinsman of his own who had been very beautiful in his lifetime, and he said to himself, "I am what he was, and what he is I shall be." Straightway after the funeral he read the words of the Lord, "If any man will come after Me let him deny himself and take up his cross and follow Me." Thereupon he withdrew into the desert to seek after greater perfection, and then gave himself up to watching, praying, and fasting, very often taking no food but uncooked herbs. In order, however, to cut himself off the more from men, he moved from one place to another, and at length came to Mount Fano, which is near Fabriano, but was itself then absolutely uninhabited. Then he built a church in honor of the Saintly Father Benedict, and founded the congregation of Silvestrians, with a rule and dress which were revealed to him in a vision by the very same Saint.

Lesson VI

Satan enviously strove to trouble his monks by diverse terrors, and made a hostile attack by night upon the gates of his monastery, but the man of God so overcame the assault of the enemy that his monks were the more confirmed in their Institute and recognized the holiness of their father. He shone with the spirit of prophecy and other gifts. These things he always preserved by the deepest humility, whereby he so stirred up against him the ill-will of the devil that that evil spirit cast him headlong down the stairs of his oratory, and went near to slay him, but he was restored to soundness by the helpful gift of the Virgin. This help he remembered with an unceasing and singular love toward her until the last breath of his life, which he resigned to God, famous for holiness and miracles, aged almost ninety years, upon the 26th day of November, in the year of salvation 1267. The Supreme Pontiff Leo XIII extended his Office and Mass to the whole Church.

Lessons VII–IX from the first in the Common of Abbots (Homily by St. Jerome)

Lesson IX—Commemoration of St. Peter of Alexandria, Martyr

Peter succeeded that eminent Saint, Theonas, as Pope of Alexandria, and the glory of his holiness and teaching has enlightened not Egypt only, but the whole Church of God. The wondrous patience wherewith he bore the roughness of the times in the persecution under Maximian Galerius caused many to greatly increase in Christian graces. He was the first who cut off Arius, then a Deacon of Alexandria, from the Communion of the faithful on account of his leaning to the Meletian schism. He was condemned to death by Maximian, and was in prison when there came to him the two Priests, Achilles and Alexander, to plead for Arius, but Peter told them that Jesus had appeared to him in the night clad in a rent garment, and when he asked what was thereby signified, had said unto him "Arius has torn My vesture, which is the Church." Also, he foretold to them that they should be Popes of Alexandria after him, and strictly commanded them never to receive Arius into Communion, because he knew him to be dead in the sight of God. That this was a true prophecy the event did shortly prove. At length, in the twelfth year of his episcopacy, upon the 26th day of November in the year of salvation 311, his head being cut off, he went to the martyr's crown.

November 29 ~ Vigil of St. Andrew

Apostle ~ Vigil

Lesson I

From the Holy Gospel according to St. John (John 1:35–51)

At that time again John stood, and two of his disciples. And beholding Jesus walking, he saith: Behold the Lamb of God. And so on.

Homily by St. Augustine, bishop

Since John was the friend of the Bridegroom, he sought not his own glory, but bore witness to the truth. Would he that his disciples should remain with him rather than that they should follow the Lord? Nay, he showed his disciples Whom they should follow. They thought that he himself was the Lamb; but he says: "Why wait ye on me? I am not the Lamb. Behold the Lamb of God!" This was He of Whom he had already said above "Behold the Lamb of God!" And what use to us is the Lamb of God? "Behold the Lamb of God," says John, "Which taketh away the sin of the world." And the two disciples heard him speak, and they followed Jesus.

Lesson II

Let us see what followed. "John stood, and two of his disciples; and looking on Jesus as He walked, he saith Behold the Lamb of God! And the two disciples heard him speak, and they followed Jesus." They followed Him, not yet to cleave unto Him, for it is manifest that they clove unto Him only after He had called them out of the ship. One of the two which heard John speak and followed Him was Andrew, Simon Peter's brother. And we know how it is written in the Gospel of Matthew: "Jesus walking by the sea of Galilee, saw two brethren, Simon called Peter, and Andrew his brother, casting a net into the sea, for they were fishermen. And He saith unto them Follow Me, and I will make you fishers of men. And they straightway left their nets and followed Him."

Lesson III

From that time, therefore, was it that they clove unto Him continuously. Then Jesus turned, and saw them following, and said unto them "What seek ye?" They said unto Him "Rabbi (which is to say, being interpreted, Master), where dwellest Thou?" So they follow Him now, not as to cleave unto Him for ever, but as to know where He dwelt, and to obey that which is written: If thou see a man of understanding, go to him early in the morning, and let thy foot wear the steps of his doors. He says unto them "Come and see." They came and saw where He dwelt, and abode with Him that day. O what a blessed day! O what a blessed night! for it was about the tenth hour. Who shall tell what they heard from the Lord? O let us also build a house in our hearts, where He may come, and teach us, and talk with us!

November 30 ~ St. Andrew the Apostle

Duplex II Class

All from Common except what follows

Lesson I ~ Rom 10:4–9

From the epistle of St. Paul the Apostle to the Romans

For the end of the law is Christ, unto justice to every one that believeth. For Moses wrote, that the justice which is of the law, the man that shall do it, shall live by it. But the justice which is of faith, speaketh thus: Say not in thy heart, Who shall ascend into heaven? that is, to bring Christ down; Or who shall descend into the deep? that is, to bring up Christ again from the dead. But what saith the Scripture? The word is nigh thee, even in thy mouth, and in thy heart. This is the word of faith, which we preach. For if thou confess with thy mouth the Lord Jesus, and believe in thy heart that God hath raised him up from the dead, thou shalt be saved.

Lesson II ~ Rom 10:10–15

For, with the heart, we believe unto justice; but, with the mouth, confession is made unto salvation. For the Scripture saith: Whosoever believeth in him, shall not be confounded. For there is no distinction of the Jew and the Greek: for the same is Lord over all, rich unto all that call upon him. For whosoever shall call upon the name of the Lord, shall be saved. How then shall they call on him, in whom they have not believed? Or how shall they believe him, of whom they have not heard? And how shall they hear, without a preacher? And how shall they preach unless they be sent, as it is written: How beautiful are the feet of them that preach the gospel of peace, of them that bring glad tidings of good things!

Lesson III ~ Rom 10:16–21

But all do not obey the gospel. For Isaias saith: Lord, who hath believed our report? Faith then comes by hearing; and hearing by the word of Christ. But I say: Have they not heard? Yes, verily, their sound hath gone forth into all the earth, and their words unto the ends of the whole world. But I say: Hath not Israel known? First, Moses saith: I will provoke you to jealousy by that which is not a nation; by a foolish nation I will anger you. But Isaias is bold, and saith: I was found by them that did not seek me: I appeared openly to them that asked not after me. But to Israel he saith: All the day long have I spread my hands to a people that believeth not, and contradicteth me.

Lesson IV

The Apostle Andrew was born at Bethsaida, a town of Galilee, and was the brother of Peter. He was a disciple of John the Baptist, and heard him say of Christ, "Behold the Lamb of God," whereupon he immediately followed Jesus, bringing his brother also with him. Some while after, they were both fishing in the Sea of Galilee, and the Lord Christ, going by, called them both, before any other of the Apostles, in the words, "Follow Me, and I will make you fishers of men." They made no delay, but left their nets, and followed Him. After the death and Resurrection of Christ, Andrew was allotted Scythia as the province of his preaching, and, after laboring there, he went through Epirus and Thrace, where he turned vast multitudes to Christ by his teaching and miracles. Finally he went to Patras in Achaia, and there also he brought many to the knowledge of Gospel truth. Ægeas the Proconsul resisted the preaching of the Gospel, and the Apostle freely rebuked him, bidding him know that while he held himself a judge of his fellow men, he was himself hindered by devils from knowing Christ our God, the Judge of all.

Lesson V

Then Ægeas, being angry, answered him, "Boast no more of this thy Christ. He spoke words even such as thine, but they availed Him not, and He was crucified by the Jews." Whereto Andrew boldly answered that Christ had given Himself up to die for man's salvation; but the Proconsul blasphemously interrupted him, and bade him look to himself, and sacrifice to the gods. Then said Andrew, "We have an altar, whereon day by day I offer up to God, the Almighty, the One, and the True, not the flesh of bulls nor the blood of goats, but a Lamb without spot and when all they that believe have eaten of the Flesh Thereof, the Lamb That was slain abides whole and lives." Then Ægeas being filled with wrath, bound the Apostle in prison. Now, the people would have delivered him, but he himself calmed the multitude, and earnestly besought them not to take away from him the crown of martyrdom, for which he longed and which was now drawing near.

Lesson VI

Come a short while after, he was brought before the judgment-seat, where he extolled the mystery of the cross, and rebuked Ægeas for his ungodliness. Then Ægeas could bear with him no longer, but commanded him to be crucified, in imitation of Christ. Andrew, then, was led to the place of martyrdom, and, as soon as he came in sight of the cross, he cried out, "O precious cross, which the Members of my Lord have made so good, how long have I desired thee! how warmly have I loved thee! how constantly have I sought thee! And, now that thou art come to me, how is my soul drawn to thee! Welcome me from among men, and join me again to my Master, that as by thee He redeemed me, so by thee also He may take me unto Himself." So he was fastened to the cross, whereon he hung living for two days, during which time he ceased not to preach the faith of Christ, and, finally, passed into the Presence of Him the likeness of Whose death he had loved so well. All the above particulars of his last sufferings were written by the Priests and Deacons of Achaia, who bear witness to them of their own knowledge. Under the Emperor Constantine the bones of the Apostle were first taken to Constantinople, whence they were afterwards brought to Amalfi. In the Pontificate of Pope Pius II, his head was carried to Rome, where it is kept in the Basilica of St. Peter.

Lesson VII

From the holy gospel according to St. Matthew (Matt 4:18–22)

At that time, Jesus, walking by the sea of Galilee, saw two brethren, Simon who is called Peter, and

Andrew his brother, casting a net into the sea. And so on.

Homily by Pope St. Gregory.

Dearly beloved brethren, you hear how Peter and Andrew, having once heard the Lord call them, left their nets, and followed their Saviour. As yet they had seen none of His miracles, as yet they had received no promise of their exceeding and eternal reward; nevertheless, at one word of the Lord they forgot all those things which they seemed to have. We have seen many of His miracles; we have received many of His gracious chastisements; many times has He warned us of the wrath to come and yet Christ calls and we do not follow.

Lesson VIII

He who calls us to be converted is now enthroned in heaven; He has broken the necks of the Gentiles to the yoke of the faith, He has laid low the glory of the world, and the wrecks thereof, falling ever more and more to decay, He preaches unto us that the coming of that day when He is to be revealed as our Judge is drawing nigh and yet, so stubborn is our mind, that we will not yet freely abandon that which we lose day by day. Dearly beloved brethren, what shall we answer at His judgment-seat, we whom no lessons can persuade, and no stripes can break of the love of this present world?

Lesson IX

Perhaps one perchance will ask in his heart, what Peter or Andrew had to lose by obeying the call of the Lord? Dearly beloved brethren, we must consider here rather the intention than the loss incurred by this obedience. He that keeps nothing for himself, gives up much; he that sacrifices his all, sacrifices what is to him a great deal. Beyond a doubt, we cling to whatever we have, and what we have least, that we desire most. Peter and Andrew therefore gave up much when they gave up even the desire of possessing anything.

FEASTS OF DECEMBER

December 2 ~ St. Bibiana

Virgin Martyr ~ Semiduplex

All from Common except what follows

Lessons I–III from the occurring Scripture

Lesson IV

Bibiana was a Roman maiden, distinguished on account of the nobility of her family, but now far more distinguished for her confession of Christ. In the reign of the foul tyrant, Julian the Apostate, her father Flavian, although he was an ex-Præfect, was branded as a slave and banished to Acquapendente, not far from Rome, where he soon died a martyr for his faith. His wife, Dafrosa, and his two daughters, Bibiana and Demetria, were first imprisoned in their own house, with the idea of starving them to death; but the mother was afterwards taken outside the city and beheaded. Bibiana and her sister Demetria, after the death of their holy parents, were stripped of all they had in the world. Apronianus, the city Prætor who hankered after their property, continued to persecute them, but although they were destitute of all human support, God, Who gives bread to the hungry, fed them, and kept them in health, life, and strength, to the wonder of their enemies.

Lesson V

Apronianus then attacked them, to make them worship the gods of the Gentiles, and promised them the restoration of their property, the favor of the Emperor, and a great marriage for each of them, if they would give way, and, on the other hand, imprisonment, stripes, and death. But neither promises nor threats availed, for they remained firm in the faith, being resolved rather to die than to pollute themselves by doing according to the deeds of the heathen; and, as for the iniquity of the Prætor, they loathed it continually. At length the strength of Demetria gave way, and she fell down suddenly, and died in the Lord, before the eyes of her sister Bibiana. Then Bibiana was put into the hands of an artful woman named Rufina, to seduce her if possible; but she had known the law of Christ from her childhood, and kept the lily of her purity undefiled, triumphing over the efforts of that vile person, and disappointing the lust of the Prætor.

Lesson VI

Then, when Rufina saw that her false words availed not, she took to blows, and scourged Bibiana daily, but the saint was not staggered in her holy resolution. At last the Prætor, mad with baffled lust when he found his labour was thrown away, ordered his lictors to strip her naked, hang her up by the hands to a pillar, and flog her to death with whips weighted with lead. When all was over, her sacred body was thrown out for the dogs to eat. It lay two days in the Forum Tauri, but the animals would not touch it; and at last, a Priest named John, took it, and buried it by night beside the graves of her mother and sister, near the Licinian Palace. This is the place where there is still a church, dedicated in the name of St. Bibiana. When this church was being restored by Urban VIII, the bodies of these three holy women, Bibiana, Demetria, and Dafrosa, were found, and were reburied under the High Altar.

Lessons VII–IX from the first set in the Common of Non-Virgins (Homily by St Gregory)

December 3 ~ St. Francis Xavier

Confessor ~ Major Duplex
All from Common
except what follows

Lessons I–III from the occurring Scripture

Lesson IV

Francis was of noble family, and was born in the castle of Xavier, in the diocese of Pamplona, in the year of our Lord 1506. He was a companion of St. Ignatius at Paris, and one of his earliest disciples. Under his teaching, he learnt to become so wrapt in the contemplation of divine things, that he was sometimes lifted in ecstasy off the ground, which happened to him several times when he was saying Mass in public before large congregations. He earned these refreshments of the soul by the sharpest punishment of the body. He gave up the use not only of meat and wine, but also of wheaten bread; he lived on the vilest food, and ate only once every two or three days. He used an iron scourge till his blood ran freely; he shortened the hours of his rest and lay only on the ground.

Lesson V

The hardness and holiness of his life had made him worthy to be called to be an Apostle, and when John III, King of Portugal, asked Pope Paul III to send to the Indies some members of the then new Society of Jesus, the Pontiff, by the advice of St. Ignatius, sent Francis to enter on that vast field of labour with the powers of Apostolic Nuncio. He arrived in India on the 6th day of May, in the year 1542. When he began his work, it seemed as though God Himself taught him the many and difficult languages of the natives. It even happened that when he preached in one language to a mixed congregation of different nationalities, each one heard him in his own tongue wherein he was born. He travelled over countless districts, always walking, and often barefoot. He introduced the faith into Japan, and six other countries. In India he turned many hundreds of thousands to Christ, and regenerated many chiefs and kings in the holy font. And notwithstanding that he was doing all these great things for God's service, so deep was his humility that when he wrote to St. Ignatius, the General of the Society, he did so on his knees.

Lesson VI

God was pleased to support his zeal for spreading the Gospel with many and great miracles. He gave sight to a blind man. On one occasion the supply of fresh water failed when he was at sea, and five hundred sailors were in danger of perishing by thirst, but the servant of God, by the sign of the Cross, turned salt water into fresh, and they used it for a considerable time. Some of this water was also carried into different countries, and a great number of sick persons were instantaneously cured by it. He called several dead men to life, among whom was one who had been buried the day before, and who was disinterred by command of the saint; and likewise two others who were being carried to the grave, and whom he took by the hand and restored living to their parents. He had the spirit of prophecy, and foretold many things, remote both in place and time. Utterly worn out with his labors, he died full of good works in the Chinese island of Shangchuan, upon the 2nd day of December, in the year of our Lord 1552. His body was buried in quicklime, and, being again taken up, was again buried in the same, but at the end of many months it was found entirely incorrupt, and sweet, and, when cut, blood flowed freely from it. From China it was carried to Malacca, and, as soon as it reached that place, a plague, which was raging there, ceased. At length, when he had become famous throughout the whole world for new and wonderful miracles, Gregory XV added his name to the list of the Saints.

Lesson VII

From the Holy Gospel according to St. Mark (Mark 16:15–18)

In that time, Jesus said to his disciples: Go into the whole world, and preach the gospel to every creature. And so on.

Homily by Pope St. Gregory

By the words "every creature" we may understand every tribe of the Gentiles. Of aforetime it had been said, "Go not into the way of the Gentiles," but now, "Preach the Gospel to every creature," that, since the Jews had proudly rejected the preaching of the Apostles, that might become our gain which was the seal of their condemnation. But when the Eternal Truth sends forth His disciples to preach, what does He but scatter seed over the field of the world? He scatters abroad a few grains for seed, that He may afterward reap an abundant harvest in our faith.

Lesson VIII

The great harvest of faithful souls throughout the whole world would never have sprung up if the hand of the Lord had not first scattered those chosen grains of preachers over the reasonable soil of men's minds. Then is written, "He that believeth and is baptized shall be saved but he that believeth not, shall be damned." Now, perchance, thou sayest in thine heart: "I believe, and therefore I shall be saved." True, if to thy faith thou dost add works. He only has a living faith whose life does not give the lie to his profession. It is of this that Paul speaks, where he says of certain vain believers, "They profess that they know God; but in works they deny Him."

Lesson IX

"And these signs shall follow them that believe: In My name they shall cast out devils, they shall speak with new tongues, they shall take up serpents; and if they drink any deadly thing, it shall not hurt them; they shall lay hands on the sick, and they shall recover." My brethren, these signs do not follow us. Do we, then, not believe? Nay. The truth is, these things were needful when the Church was young. That she might grow by the increase of the faithful, she needed to be nourished with miracles. So we, when we plant a young tree, continually water and tend it, till we see that it has taken firm root in the earth but when once it has taken firm root, it can grow of itself. Hence Paul says of tongues: "Tongues are for a sign, not to them that believe, but to them that believe not."

December 4 ~ St. Peter Chrysologos

Bishop, Confessor, Doctor ~ Duplex

All from Common except what follows

Lessons I–III from the occurring Scripture

Lesson IV

Peter, called in Greek *Chrysologos*, or, of the golden words, on account of his wonderful eloquence, was born of respectable parents at Imola, near Ravenna. He displayed a very early leaning to godliness, and became a disciple of Cornelius of Rome, Bishop of Imola. This Prelate, having experience of his learning and holiness of life, soon ordained him Deacon. On the death of the Archbishop of Ravenna, the people of that place elected a successor, and sent him, according to custom, to Rome, to be confirmed in his appointment by Pope Sixtus III. The Archbishop elect accordingly set forth, along with the ambassadors of the people of Ravenna and Cornelius, Bishop of Imola, attended by Peter the Deacon. While they were yet on the way, the holy Apostle Peter and Apollinaris the Martyr appeared to the Supreme Pontiff in a dream, leading a young man between them, whom they commanded him to make Archbishop. As soon as the embassy arrived at Rome the Pope knew in Peter the young man of his dream, chosen of God to the Archbishopric. Wherefore he set aside him that the people of Ravenna had presented, and preferred Peter to that Metropolitan Church, in the year of our Lord 433. The ambassadors of the people of Ravenna took it ill, till they heard the vision then they gave themselves up to the will of God, and received the new Archbishop with great reverence.

Lesson V

Peter being against his will consecrated Archbishop, arrived at Ravenna, where he was received with great joy by the Emperor Valentinian, the Empress-Mother Galla Placidia, and all the people. And this one thing he asked of them, that, as he, for the saving of their souls, had not refused to bear the heavy weight of the Archbishopric, so they would strive to follow his warnings, and live in submission to the law of God. He took the bodies of the two

Saints, namely, Barbatian the Priest, and Germanus, Bishop of Auxerre, and caused them to be embalmed with rich ointments and honorably buried, and he kept the cowl and haircloth shirt of Germanus for a legacy for himself. At Classis, three miles from Ravenna, he built a Baptistery of extraordinary size, and several splendid churches, in honor of the blessed Apostle Andrew and other Saints. He preached a most severe sermon against the acting and masquerading about New Year time, in which discourse he said among other things, "He that jests with the devil will never rejoice with Christ." By command of Pope Leo I, he addressed an Epistle to the Council of Chalcedon against the heretic Eutyches. He also confuted Eutyches himself in another letter, which is likewise published in the new editions of the Acts of the Council, and is a matter of Church History.

Lesson VI

When he preached in public his vehemence was such that he sometimes became speechless from excitement. This happened to him once when he was preaching on the subject of the woman who had an issue of blood. The congregation on this occasion were so wrought up, that they filled the whole place with tears, cries, and prayers, and Peter afterwards thanked God, Who had turned his failure to the profit of their souls. When he had ruled the Church of Ravenna in holiness for about eighteen years, God gave him knowledge that the end of his labors was at hand, and he returned to his home at Imola to die. When he arrived at Imola, he entered the church of St. Cassian, and offered upon the High Altar a great circlet of gold, set with stones of great price, a golden chalice, and a silver paten. Water poured out of these vessels has often healed hydrophobia and fevers. Some of the people of Ravenna had followed the Archbishop, but he now dismissed them with a charge to use great prudence in their choice of his successor. Then he fell to prayer, that God would mercifully receive his spirit, asking the same likewise for the sake of his patron St. Cassian, and so he passed in peace to a better life, on the 2nd of December about the year of our Lord 450. His holy body was buried, amid the sorrow and veneration of the whole city, near the remains of St. Cassian, where it lies even to this day, guarded with great reverence. One arm was cut off and sent to Ravenna, where it is preserved in the Ursian Church, in a reliquary of gold and precious stones.

Lessons VII–IX from the first set in the Common of Doctors (Sermon by St. Augustine)

December 6 ~ St. Nicolas

Confessor Bishop ~ Duplex

All from Common except what follows

Lessons I–III from the occurring Scripture

Lesson IV

Nicolas was born at the famous city of Patara in Lycia. His parents obtained him from God by prayer, and the holiness of his life was marked even from the cradle. When he was at the breast he never would suck more than once on Wednesdays and Fridays, and that always after sunset, though he sucked freely on other days. This custom of fasting he never broke through during his whole life. While he was still a young man he lost both his father and mother, after which he gave his whole property away to the poor. One particular example is given of his Christian charity. There was a certain needy man in the city who had three marriageable daughters, for whom he could not get husbands, and so thought to make them harlots. When Nicolas heard of it, he went to the house by night and threw in by the window such a sum of money as made a dowry for one of them. This he did a second and a third time, and thus by his charity they were honorably given in marriage.

Lesson V

When he had given himself entirely to God he set forth for Palestine, that he might see the Holy Places, and worship therein. During this pilgrimage he embarked once onboard a ship when the sky was clear and the sea calm, but he foretold a great storm, which afterwards arose and raged until the sailors were afraid; and then the saint by prayer stilled the tempest. After he had returned home, and his holy life was known to all men, God bade him go to Myra, which is the chief city of Lycia, at a time when the Bishop had just died and the Bishops of the Province were called together to choose a successor. While they deliberated, they received a warning from heaven to choose that Nicolas who should first come into the church in the morning. In obedience to that warning, Nicolas was seized at the door of the church, and, with universal consent, consecrated Archbishop. In his great office he was an unceasing model of purity, as he had always been, of gravity, of regularity in prayer, of watching, of abstinence, of charity, of hospitality, of meekness in exhortation, and of sternness in rebuke.

Lesson VI

He was the comforter of widows and orphans by money, by advice, and by labour. He was the deliverer of the oppressed, so mightily, that it is related that the Emperor Constantine once unjustly condemned three Tribunes to death, and these unhappy men called upon Nicolas, though living and absent, to save them, who yet appeared in a vision to the Emperor, and forced him by threats to set them free. When the Emperors Diocletian and Maximian published their edict against Christianity, Nicolas did not cease to preach the truth at Myra, wherefore he was seized by the soldiers of the Emperors, carried away from his See, and thrown into prison, where he remained until the accession of Constantine. This Prince set him free, and he returned to Myra. He betook himself to the first Council of Nicæa, where he was one of the 318 Bishops who condemned the heresy of Arius. He returned thence to his Bishopric, and, not long after, became aware of the approach of death. When his last moment was come, he lifted up his eyes to heaven, and, when he saw the Angels coming to meet him, he began to recite the thirtieth Psalm, "In thee, O Lord, do I put my trust," and when he had said, "Into thy hands I commend my spirit," he passed to the heavenly Fatherland. His body was finally removed to Bari in Apulia, where it is kept with great fame and honor.

Lessons VII–IX from the first set in the Common of Confessor Bishops (Sermon by St. Gregory)

December 7 ~ St. Ambrose

Bishop, Confessor, Doctor ~ Duplex

All from Common except what follows

Lessons I–III from the occurring Scripture

Lesson IV

Ambrose, Bishop of Milan, was the son of another Ambrose, a Roman citizen, and was born when his father was Præfect of Gaul, about the year of our Lord 340. A swarm of bees settled upon his face when he was in his cradle, which was considered an omen of his future eloquence. He received a liberal education at Rome. He was afterwards, under the Præfect Probus, made governor of Liguria and Emilia, and so came with authority to Milan. Auxentius, an Arian, who had been intruded into the Bishopric of Milan, happening to die, the most violent disputes arose about the choice of a successor. Ambrose came to the church in his official capacity, and urged upon the contending factions, in a long and powerful speech, the necessity of keeping the public peace; whereupon a child suddenly cried out, "Ambrose Bishop," and the whole assembly took it up, and unanimously called for his election.

Lesson V

Ambrose refused, and would not yield to their prayers, whereupon they carried their petition to the Emperor Valentinian. It was very pleasing to this Prince that those he had appointed as judges should be chosen Bishops, as also to the Præfect Probus, who had, as it were prophetically, said to him when he appointed him, "Go and govern them more like a Bishop than a Judge." When the will of the Emperor was added to the desire of the people, Ambrose yielded, and received Baptism (for hitherto he was only a Catechumen), Confirmation, and Communion, and then the several Orders on successive days, till on the eighth day, which was the 7th of December in the year 374, the weight of the Episcopate was laid upon his shoulders. Being made Bishop, he showed himself a stout upholder of the Catholic faith, and the discipline of the Church, and turned to the truth great numbers of Arians and other heretics, and, among them, he begat in Christ Jesus that burning and shining light of the Church, Saint Augustine.

Lesson VI

After the murder of the Emperor Gratian in 383, Ambrose was sent as an ambassador to Maximus, by whom he had been slain, and, as he refused to repent, the Bishop renounced his communion. After the massacre which the Emperor Theodosius had commanded at Thessalonica in 390, he refused to permit that Prince to enter a church. The Emperor pleaded that he was no worse than David, who had been guilty of adultery and murder, to which Ambrose answered him, "As thou hast followed him in his sin, follow also in his repentance." Then Theodosius humbly did public penance laid upon him by the Bishop. At length the Saint was worn out with his continual labour and care for the Church, for which also he composed many excellent books, and foretold that the day of his death was at hand, though he had not then fallen into his last sickness. As he lay dying, Honoratus, Bishop of Vercelli, heard a voice from God three times crying to him that the hour of Ambrose's departure was come, whereupon he went to him quickly, and gave him the sacred Body of our Lord. When he had received It, the Saint, still praying, with his hands stretched out in the form of a cross, gave his spirit to God, upon the 4th day of April in the year 397 after the birth of Christ.

Lessons VII–IX from the first set in the Common of Doctors (Sermon by St. Augustine)

December 8 ~ THE IMMACULATE CONCEPTION OF THE BLESSED VIRGIN MARY

Duplex I Class

All from Common except what follows

Lesson I ~ Gen 3:1–5

From the book of Genesis

Now the serpent was more subtle than any of the beasts of the earth which the Lord God made. And he said to the woman: Why hath God commanded you, that you should not eat of every tree of paradise? And the woman answered him, saying: Of the fruit of the trees that are in paradise we do eat: But of the fruit of the tree which is in the midst of paradise, God hath commanded us that we should not eat; and that we should not touch it, lest perhaps we die. And the serpent said to the woman: No, you shall not die the death. For God doth know that in what day soever you shall eat thereof, your eyes shall be opened: and you shall be as Gods, knowing good and evil.

Lesson II ~ Gen 3:6–8

And the woman saw that the tree was good to eat, and fair to the eyes, and delightful to behold: and she took of the fruit thereof, and did eat, and gave to her husband who did eat. And the eyes of them both were opened: and when they perceived themselves to be naked, they sewed together fig leaves, and made themselves aprons. And when they heard the voice of the Lord God walking in paradise at the afternoon air, Adam and his wife hid themselves from the face of the Lord God, amidst the trees of paradise.

Lesson III - Gen 3:9–15

And the Lord God called Adam, and said to him: Where art thou? And he said: I heard thy voice in paradise; and I was afraid, because I was naked, and I hid myself. And he said to him: And who hath told thee that thou wast naked, but that thou hast eaten of the tree whereof I commanded thee that thou shouldst not eat? And Adam said: The woman, whom thou gavest me to be my companion, gave me of the tree, and I did eat. And the Lord God said to the woman: Why hast thou done this? And she answered: The serpent deceived me, and I did eat. And the Lord God said to the serpent: Because thou hast done this thing, thou art cursed among all cattle, and the beasts of the earth: upon thy breast shalt thou go, and earth shalt thou eat all the days of thy life. I will put enmities between thee and the woman, and thy seed and her seed: she shall crush thy head, and thou shalt lie in wait for her heel.

Lesson IV

Sermon by St. Jerome, Priest

Who and what the blessed and glorious Mary was, always a Virgin, has been revealed by God by the message of an Angel, in these words: "Hail, full of grace, the Lord is with thee; blessed art thou among women." It was fitting that a fullness of grace should be poured into that Virgin who has given to God glory and to man a Saviour, who has brought peace to earth, who has given faith to the Gentiles, who has killed sin, who has given law to life, who has made the crooked ways straight. Verily, she is full of grace. To others grace comes measure by measure; in Mary grace dwells at once in all fullness. Verily, she is full of grace. We believe that the holy Fathers and Prophets had grace; but they were not full of grace. But into Mary came a fullness of all the grace which is in Christ, albeit otherwise than as it is in Him. Therefore is it said: "Blessed art thou among women," that is, Blessed art thou above all women. The fullness of blessing in Mary utterly neutralized in her any effects of the curse of Eve. In her praise Solomon writes in the Canticle of Canticles: "Rise up, my dove, my fair one, for the winter is past, the rain is over and gone." And again: "Come from Lebanon, my Spouse, come, thou shalt be crowned."

Lesson V

Not unjustly then is she bidden to come from Lebanon, for Lebanon is so named on account of its stainless and glistening whiteness. The earthly Lebanon is white with snow, but the lonely heights of Mary's holiness are white with purity and grace, brilliantly fair, whiter far than snow, sparkling with the gifts of the Holy Ghost; she is undefiled like a dove, all clean, all upright, full of grace and truth. She is full of mercy, and of the righteousness that has looked down from heaven, and therefore is she without stain because in her has never been any corruption. She has compassed a man in her womb, says holy Jeremias, but she conceived not by the will of fallen man. "The Lord," says the Prophet, "has created a new thing in the earth; a woman shall compass a man." Verily, it is a new thing. Verily, it was a new work of power, greater than all other works, when God, Whom the world cannot bear, and Whom no man shall see and live, entered the lodging of her womb, breaking not the blissful cloister of her virgin flesh. And in her body He was borne, the Infinite inclosed within her womb. And from her womb He came forth, so that it was fulfilled which was spoken of the Prophet Ezechiel, saying: "This gate shall be shut, it shall not be opened, and no man shall enter in by it; because the Lord, the God of Israel, has entered in by it, therefore it shall be shut." Hence also in the Canticle of Canticles it is said of her: "A garden enclosed is my sister, my spouse, a garden enclosed, a fountain sealed, thy perfumes are a garden of delights." Verily a garden of delights, filled with the perfumes of all flowers, rich with the sweet savor of grace. And the most holy Virgin herself is a garden enclosed, whereinto sin and Satan have never entered to sully the blossoms, a fountain sealed, sealed with the seal of the Trinity.

Lesson VI

From the acts of Pope Pius IX

The fact that the Virgin Mother of God had at the moment of her conception triumphed over the foul enemy of man, has ever been borne out by the Holy Scriptures, by the venerable tradition of the Church, and by her unceasing belief, as well as by the common conviction of all Bishops and faithful Catholics, and by marked acts and constitutions of the Holy See. At length the Supreme Pontiff Pius IX, in compliance with the wishes of the Universal Church, determined to publish it as a truth of faith, on his own absolute and unerring authority, and accordingly, on the 8th day of December 1854, in the Vatican Basilica, in presence of a great multitude composed of the Fathers Cardinal of the Holy Roman Church, and Bishops from all parts of the earth, he, with the consent and jubilation of the whole world, declared and defined as follows: That doctrine which declares that the most Blessed Virgin Mary was in the first instant of her Conception preserved, by a special privilege granted unto her by God, from any stain of original sin, is a doctrine taught and revealed by God, and therefore is to be held by all faithful Christians firmly and constantly.

Lesson VII

From the Holy Gospel according to St. Luke (Luke 1:26–28)

In that time, the angel Gabriel was sent from God into a city of Galilee, called Nazareth, to a virgin espoused to a man whose name was Joseph, of the house of David; and the virgin's name was Mary. And so on.

Homily by St. Germanus, Patriarch of Constantinople.

Hail, Mary, full of grace, holier than the Saints, higher than the heavens, more glorious than the Cherubim, more honorable than the Seraphim, and the most worshipful thing that the hands of God have made. Hail, O dove, bearing in thy beak the olive-branch of peace that tells us of salvation from the spiritual flood, dove, blessed omen of a safe harbor, whose wings are of silver, and thy feathers of gold, shining in the bright beams of the Most Holy and Light-giving Spirit. Hail, thou living garden of Eden, planted towards the East by the right hand of the Most Merciful and Mighty God, wherein do grow to His glory rich lilies and unfading roses, for the healing of them that have drunk in death from the blighting and pestilential breezes of the bitter West; Eden, wherein has sprung that Tree of life, Whereof if any man eat he shall live for ever. Hail, stately Palace of the King, most holy, stainless, purest House of the Most High God, adorned with His Royal splendor, open to all, filled with Kingly delights; Palace wherein is that spiritual bridal chamber, not made with hands, nor hung with diverse colors, in which the Eternal Word, when He would raise up fallen man, wedded flesh unto Himself, that He might reconcile unto the Father them who had cast themselves away.

Lesson VIII

Hail, O rich and shady Mountain of God, whereon pastured the True Lamb Who has taken away our sins and infirmities, mountain whereout has been cut without hands that Stone which has smitten the altars of the idols, and become the head-stone of the corner, marvelous in our eyes. Hail, thou holy Throne of God, thou divinest storehouse, thou temple of glory, thou bright crown, thou chosen treasure, thou mercy-seat for the whole world, thou heaven declaring the glory of God. Hail, thou vessel of pure gold, made to hold the manna that came down from heaven, the sweet food of our souls, even Christ. Hail, O purest Virgin, most praiseworthy and most worshipful, hallowed treasury for the wants of all creatures; thou art the untilled earth, the unplowed field; thou art the vine full of flowers, the well overflowing with waters, Maiden and Mother; thou art the Mother that knew not a man, the hidden treasure of guilelessness, and the clear, bright star of holiness; by thy most acceptable prayers, strong from thy motherly mouth, obtain for all estates of men in the Church that they may continually tend unto Him Who is the Lord, and God, and Maker of thee, and of them, and of all, but of thee the Son also, conceived without man's intervention; obtain this, O Mother, pilot them to the harbor of peace.

Lesson IX

Be it thine to clothe God's priests with righteousness, and to make them shout aloud for joy in approved and stainless and upright and glorious faith. Thine be it to guide in peace the scepters of orthodox princes, even of princes who put their trust in thee to be the crown of their Majesty, and the Royal Robe of their greatness, and the firm foundation of their dominion, more than in purple, or fine gold, or pearls, or precious stones; thine be it to put under their feet the unfaithful nations, nations that blaspheme thee, and the God That was born of thee; thine be it to keep in meek obedience the people that are under them, according to the commandment of God. Behold, this is thine own city, which has thee for her towers and her foundations, crown her with victory, gird the house of God with strength, keep undefiled the loveliness of His tabernacles, as for them that praise thy name, be thou their deliverer from strife and bitterness of spirit. Free thou the prisoner, protect the wanderer, and if there be any that has no refuge, be thou to him a consolation. Stretch forth thy hand and help the whole earth; so shall we year by year keep this and all thy feasts, and at last be found with thee in Christ Jesus, Who is Lord of all, and verily our God. To Him, with the Holy Father, Who is the Fountain of Life, and the coeternal Spirit, Three Persons and One Substance, even as there is one Kingdom, be glory and strength, now and for ever. Amen.

December 9 ~ Day 2 within the Octave of the Immaculate Conception

Semiduplex

All from the Feast except what follows

Lessons I–III from the occurring Scripture

Lesson IV

From the Dogmatic Bull of Pope Pius IX.

God Ineffable—whose ways are mercy and truth, whose will is omnipotence itself, and whose wisdom "reaches from end to end mightily, and orders all things sweetly"—having foreseen from all eternity the lamentable wretchedness of the entire human race which would result from the sin of Adam, decreed, by a plan hidden from the centuries, to complete the first work of his goodness by a mystery yet more wondrously sublime through the Incarnation of the Word. This he decreed in order that man who, contrary to the plan of Divine Mercy had been led into sin by the cunning malice of Satan, should not perish; and in order that what had been lost in the first Adam would be gloriously restored in the Second Adam. From the very beginning, and before time began, the eternal Father chose and prepared for his only-begotten Son a Mother in whom the Son of God would become incarnate and from whom, in the blessed fullness of time, he would be born into this world. Above all creatures did God so love her that truly in her was the

Father well pleased with singular delight.

Lesson V

Therefore, far above all the angels and all the saints so wondrously did God endow her with the abundance of all heavenly gifts poured from the treasury of his divinity that this mother, ever absolutely free of all stain of sin, all fair and perfect, would possess that fullness of holy innocence and sanctity than which, under God, one cannot even imagine anything greater, and which, outside of God, no mind can succeed in comprehending fully. And indeed it was wholly fitting that so wonderful a mother should be ever resplendent with the glory of most sublime holiness and so completely free from all taint of original sin that she would triumph utterly over the ancient serpent. To her did the Father will to give his only-begotten Son—the Son whom, equal to the Father and begotten by him, the Father loves from his heart—and to give this Son in such a way that he would be the one and the same common Son of God the Father and of the Blessed Virgin Mary.

Lesson VI

The Catholic Church, directed by the Holy Spirit of God, is the pillar and base of truth and has ever held as divinely revealed and as contained in the deposit of heavenly revelation this doctrine concerning the original innocence of the august Virgin—a doctrine which is so perfectly in harmony with her wonderful sanctity and preeminent dignity as Mother of God—and thus has never ceased to explain, to teach and to foster this doctrine age after age in many ways and by solemn acts. From this very doctrine, flourishing and wondrously propagated in the Catholic world through the efforts and zeal of the bishops, was made very clear by the Church when she did not hesitate to present for the public devotion and veneration of the faithful the Feast of the Conception of the Blessed Virgin. By this most significant fact, the Church made it clear indeed that the conception of Mary is to be venerated as something extraordinary, wonderful, eminently holy, and different from the conception of all other human beings—for the Church celebrates only the feast days of the saints.

Lesson VII

From the Holy Gospel according to St. Luke (Luke 1:26–28)

In that time, the angel Gabriel was sent from God into a city of Galilee, called Nazareth, to a virgin espoused to a man whose name was Joseph, of the house of David; and the virgin's name was Mary. And so on.

Homily by St. Sophronius, Patriarch of Jerusalem.

When this blessed Angel was sent to the most pure virgin what did he say? In what words did he break the happy news of Redemption? "Hail, full of grace, the Lord is with thee." (Now this word Hail is in the Greek *Chaire*, which being interpreted signifies Rejoice.) The messenger of joy in his first word bids her rejoice. He knew well that his message was a message of good tidings of great joy to men, yea, to all creatures, a message of healing to all sicknesses. He knew well that his message was a message of God's light to a dark world. He knew well that it proclaimed the end of error. He knew well that it blunted the sting of death. He knew well that it broke the power of corruption. He knew well that it brought victory over hell. He knew well that it told of salvation to all the fallen children of Adam, groaning under that yoke of malediction which fell on them when they were thrust out of Eden, and banished from that happy home. Therefore, when he began to speak, he spoke in tones of rejoicing, and opened his message with sounds of gladness. Therefore made he the name of joy to herald the tidings of good, which were to be for a joy unto all people, whosoever should believe.

Lesson VIII

And, of a truth, it was fitting that God's proclamation of joy should open with the accents of gladness. And this is the reason why the angel names joy first, because he knew the coming fruits of his message, and that his conversation with the Virgin was to bring joy to the whole world. Can we find any joy or any brightness like the joy and the brightness of that salutation addressed to the Blessed Mother of gladness? Rejoice, O mother of joy more than heavenly! Rejoice, O thou that nourishest joy in the highest! Rejoice, O Lady, full of the joy of salvation! Rejoice, O thou that bringest a joy that passes not away! Rejoice, O mysterious treasury dispensing unspeakable joy! Rejoice, O most blessed fountain, overflowing with unfailing joy! Rejoice, O storehouse of God, filled with the everlasting joy of eternity! Rejoice, O fair tree, bearing fruit of life-giving joy! Rejoice, O Maiden Mother of God! Rejoice, O thou that after childbirth remainest a virgin! Rejoice, O wonder, who, after all wonders, art still the most wonderful!

Lesson IX

Who shall worthily set forth thy glory? Who shall make bold to say what thou art? Who will hold himself able to tell of all thy splendor? Thou art the exaltation of humanity; thou art made much higher than the Angels; thy brightness has thrown the brightness of the Archangels into shadow; thou lookest down upon the lofty seats of the Thrones; thou makest the height of the Dominions to seem low; thy rank takes precedence before the rank of the Principalities; compared with thee the Powers are weakness; thou art a Mighty one mightier than all the Mighty; thine earthly eyes see further than the contemplation of the Cherubim can reach; the Seraphim have six wings, but thy flight is nobler than theirs; in a word, thou hast far excelled every other work of God; thou wast far purer than any other creature; and thou hast conceived the Creator of all creatures, carried Him in thy womb, and brought Him forth; thou hast been chosen, out of all that He has made, to be His mother.

December 10 ~ Day 3 within the Octave of the Immaculate Conception

Semiduplex

All from the Feast except what follows

Lessons I–III from the occurring Scripture

Lesson IV

From the Dogmatic Bull of Pope Pius IX.

Both in her Offices and in the most holy Liturgy the Church hath been accustomed to apply to the creation of Mary the language in which the Holy Scriptures set forth the Eternal Generation of the Uncreated Wisdom, and that, because Mary was predestined in the decree of the Incarnation of the same Wisdom. This practice has been received by the faithful in all quarters, and plainly shows what has been the mind of the Church of Rome, which is the mother and mistress of all Churches, on the subject of the sinless conception of the Virgin. Nevertheless, it is fitting to set forth in greater detail the celebrated acts of this Church, on account of that preeminent rank and power which all other Churches are bound to yield her, because she is the centre of Catholic truth and unity, wherein alone Doctrine is always preserved pure, and from whom all the other Churches must receive the tradition of the Faith.

Lesson V

Thus it has always been one of the most striking features of the Roman Church that she has most powerfully asserted, guarded, promoted, and vindicated the doctrine that the Virgin was conceived without sin. It has been the boast of Our Predecessors that by their authority they instituted in the Roman Church the Feast of the Conception of Mary, and caused it to be observed with an Office and a Mass wherein her privilege of immunity from original sin was openly asserted. Our said Predecessors have done everything in their power to increase the love of the faithful for this doctrine by granting Indulgences in its honor; by giving permission to cities, provinces, and kingdoms to choose for their Patroness the Mother of God, under her title "the Immaculate Conception"; by approving of Guilds, Congregations, and Associations of persons under vows, all instituted in honor of the sinless Conception; by praising the piety of those who have founded Convents, Hospitals, Altars, and Churches named from this belief; and lastly, by encouraging those who have taken an oath to defend this opinion to the utmost of their power.

Lesson VI

Moreover, Our said Predecessors with great joy ordained that the Feast of the said Conception should be observed as of the same rank as that of the Nativity of the Blessed Virgin, and appointed that it should be kept with an Octave throughout the whole Church. They added this Feast to those which are commanded to be kept with solemnity, and ordered that a Solemn Papal High Mass should take place every year on this Feast in our Patriarchal Basilica of our Lady of the Snows. And above all did they rejoice in the hope of strengthening this belief in the minds of the faithful, and stirring them up to love and venerate the Virgin conceived without sin, when they granted permission to add to the Litany of Loreto the invocation, "Queen conceived without original sin," and to insert the word "stainless" into the Preface of the Mass on this Feast, that so the law of prayer might become the law of belief.

Lesson VII

From the Holy Gospel according to St. Luke (Luke 1:26–28)

In that time, the angel Gabriel was sent from God into a city of Galilee, called Nazareth, to a virgin espoused to a man whose name was Joseph, of the house of David; and the virgin's name was Mary. And so on.

Homily by St. Bernard, Abbot

Rejoice, father Adam, and yet more thou mother Eve, you that are the source of all, and the ruin of all, and the unhappy cause of their ruin before you gave them birth. Be comforted both in your daughter, and such a daughter; but chiefly thou, O woman, of whom the first evil came, and who hast cast thy slur upon all women. The time is come for the slur to be taken away, and for the man to have nothing to say against the woman. At the first, when he unwisely began to make excuse, he scrupled not to throw the blame upon her, saying, "The woman whom Thou gavest to be with me, she gave me of the tree, and I did eat." Wherefore, O Eve, betake thyself to Mary Mother, betake thyself to thy daughter; let the daughter answer for the mother; let her take away her mother's reproach; let her make up to her father for her mother's fault for if man be fallen by means of woman, it is by means of woman that he is raised up again.

Lesson VIII

What didst thou say, O Adam? "The woman whom Thou gavest to be with me, she gave me of the tree, and I did eat." These are wrathful words, by which thou dost rather magnify than diminish thine offense. Nevertheless, Wisdom has defeated thy malice. God asked thee that He might find in thee an occasion of pardon, but, in that He found it not, He has sought and found it in the Treasure of His Own mercy. One woman answers for another; the wise for the foolish; the lowly for the proud; for her that gave thee of the tree of death, another that gives thee to taste of the tree of life; for her that brought thee the bitter food of sin, another that gives thee of the sweet fruits of righteousness. Wherefore accuse the woman no more, but speak in thanksgiving, and say, "Lord, the woman whom Thou hast given me, she has given me of the tree of life, and I have eaten; and it is in my mouth sweeter than honey, for thereby hast Thou quickened me." Behold, it was for this that the angel Gabriel was sent to the Virgin, to the most worshipful of women, a woman more wonderful than all women, the restorer of them that went before, and the quickener of them that come after her.

Lesson IX

Was it not of this thy daughter, O Adam, that God spoke when He said unto the serpent, "I will put enmity between thee and the woman"? And if thou wilt still doubt that He speaks of Mary, hear what follows: "She shall crush thy head." Who won this conquest but Mary? She brought to nought the whole wiles of Satan, whether for the pollution of her body or the injury of her soul. Was it not of her that Solomon spoke, where he says, "Who shall find a virtuous woman?" The wise man knew the weaknesses of women, how frail they are in body, and how changeable in mind. But he had read that God had promised that the enemy, who had prevailed by means of a woman, was by a woman to be overthrown, and he believed. But he wondered greatly, and said, "Who shall find a virtuous woman?" That is to say, If our salvation, and the bringing back of that which is lost, and the final triumph over the enemy, is in the hand of a woman, it must be that a virtuous woman be found, worthy to work in that matter.

December 11 ~ St. Damasus I

Confessor Pope ~ Semiduplex

All from Common except what follows

Lessons I–III from the occurring Scripture

Lesson IV

Damasus was a Spaniard, a man of eminence and of great learning in the Scriptures, and was elected to the Chair of Peter in the year of our Lord 381. He convoked the First Council of Constantinople, wherein he crushed the wicked heresy of Eunomius and Macedonius. He confirmed the condemnation of the Assembly, at Rimini, which condemnation had already been pronounced by Liberius. This Assembly of Rimini was that in which, to use the language of St. Jerome, Valens and Ursacius brought about through trickery that the Faith of Nice was abrogated by mob law, and "the world afterwards groaned in amazement to find itself Arian."

Lesson V

This Pope built two Basilicas, first, St. Lawrence's, near Pompey's Theatre, which he magnificently enriched, and endowed with houses and farms; and, secondly, another, over the Catacombs on the Road to Ardea. He also consecrated the Platonia, where the bodies of St. Peter and St. Paul lay for some time, and decorated it with elegant inscriptions in poetry composed by himself. He wrote on the subject of virginity both in prose and verse, and likewise many other poems on various subjects.

Lesson VI

He ordained that false accusers should be punished for the offenses which they had falsely laid to the charge of their neighbors. He established the usage, which already prevailed in many churches, of singing the Psalms, both by day and by night, by alternate choirs, and of adding at the end of each Psalm the words, "Glory be to the Father, and to the Son, and to the Holy Ghost." It was at his command that St. Jerome revised the translation of the New Testament to accord with the Greek text. He ruled the Church for seventeen years, two months, and twenty-six days. He held five Advent ordinations, wherein he ordained thirty-one Priests, eleven Deacons, and sixty-two Bishops for diverse Sees. At length he fell asleep in the Lord, in the reign of Theodosius the Elder, upon the 10th day of December in the year 384, being aged nearly eighty years, and full of righteousness, truth, and judgment. He was buried beside his mother and sister in the Church which he had himself founded on the Road to Ardea. His relics were afterwards taken to the Basilica of St. Lawrence, which is thence sometimes called San Lorenzo in Damaso.

Lessons VII–IX from the Common of Supreme Pontiffs

December 12 ~ Day 5 within the Octave of the Immaculate Conception

Semiduplex

All from the Feast except what follows

Lessons I–III from the occurring Scripture

Lesson IV

From the Dogmatic Bull of Pope Pius IX.

The language used in public worship is the necessary offspring of the teaching which it expresses, and the former can have no safety unless the latter be settled. Wherefore Our Predecessors, the Roman Pontiffs, while encouraging the pious love of the faithful for the Conception of the Blessed Virgin, have taken care ceaselessly to inculcate the sinlessness of the same. They have always particularly insisted that the Feast should be observed not in honor of Mary's sanctification, a false opinion most foreign to the mind of the Church (but which has nevertheless been maintained by some), but in honor of her Conception itself.

Lesson V

Our same Predecessors have likewise resisted the dreams of those who have imagined that in the sinless Conception there were Two Instants, and that the Church celebrates the Second and not the First. Indeed, Our said Predecessors have considered the sinlessness of the First Instant to be as much a truth for their assertion, protection, and promulgation, as the sinlessness of the Conception at all. Hence came those words in which Our Predecessor Alexander VII in a decree declares the mind of the Church, and says, "Christ's faithful people, drawn by love to His most blessed Mother, the Virgin Mary, have of a long time believed that God, at the very First Instant in which He made her soul and joined it to her body, by a special grace and privilege granted to her, through the merits of His dear Son, Christ Jesus, the Saviour of the world, Whose precious death He foreknew, cleansed her from all sin, original as well as actual; and it is in this belief, and no other, that the said faithful of Christ have always kept with devotion and joy."

Lesson VI

It has always been one of the most weighty cares of Our said Predecessors, the Roman Pontiffs, to protect the doctrine of the sinlessness of Mary's Conception from any sort of attack or corruption. Not only have they suffered no one to condemn or change it, but they have gone much further, and in public and repeated declarations have stated that the doctrine by which we profess the Immaculate Conception of the Virgin is on its own merits entirely in harmony with the ecclesiastical veneration; that it is ancient and widespread, and of the same nature as that which the Roman Church has undertaken to promote and to protect, and that it is entirely worthy to be used in the Sacred Liturgy and solemn prayers. Not content with this they most strictly prohibited any opinion contrary to this doctrine to be defended in public or private in order that the doctrine of the Immaculate Conception of the Virgin might remain inviolate. By repeated blows they wished to put an end to such false opinions.

Lesson VII

From the Holy Gospel according to St. Luke (Luke 1:26–28)

In that time, the angel Gabriel was sent from God into a city of Galilee, called Nazareth, to a virgin espoused to a man whose name was Joseph, of the house of David; and the virgin's name was Mary. And so on.

Homily by St. Tarasius, Patriarch

O Mary, where shall I find words to praise thee? Maiden undefiled, virgin unstained, exaltation of women, glory of daughters! Holy Maiden Mother, blessed art thou among women, thy glory is in thy guilelessness, and thy name is a name of purity. In thee the curse of Adam is done away, and the debt of Eve paid. Thou art the clean offering of Abel, chosen out of the firstlings, a pure sacrifice. Thou art the hope of Enos, that firm hope that he had in God, and was not ashamed. Thou art the grace that was in Enoch in this life, and his transit to a better. Thou art the Holy Ark of Noe, and the bond of reconciliation with God in a new regeneration. Thou art the exceeding glory of the kingdom and Priesthood of Melchisedech. Thou art the unshaken trust of Abraham, and his faith in the promise of children that were to-be. Thou art the renewed oblation and the reasonable burnt-offering of Isaac. Thou art the ladder that Jacob saw going up to heaven, and the most noble of all his children throughout the twelve tribes of Israel. According to the flesh thou art the daughter of Judah. Thou art the modesty of Joseph, and the overthrow of the old Egypt, yea, and of the Synagogue of the Jews. O purest! Thou art the book of Moses the Lawgiver, whereon the new covenant is written with the finger of God, for the new Israel, fleeing from the spiritual Egypt, even as the old law was written upon Sinai, for the old Israel, that Israel which was fed in the wilderness upon manna and water from the rock, whereof both were types of Christ, which was yet to come from thy womb, as a bridegroom from his chamber. Thou art Aaron's rod that budded. Thou art David's daughter, all glorious within, clothed in a vesture of gold, wrought about with diverse colors.

Lesson VIII

Thou art the vision of the Prophets and the fulfillment of those things which they foretold. Thou art the gate whereof Ezechiel spoke, when he prophesied, and said, "This gate shall be shut, it shall not be opened, and no man shall enter in by it; because the Lord, the God of Israel, has entered in by it, therefore it shall be shut." Thou art the Rod of Jesse, whereof Isaias spoke, even that Rod whose Flower is Christ, and whose offshoots shall choke out all the seedlings of sin, and fill the earth with plants of grace. Thou art the Covenant foretold by Jeremias when he said: "Behold, the days come, saith the Lord, that I will make a new covenant with the house of Israel, and with the house of Judah, not according to the covenant that I made with their fathers" thereby signifying the coming of thy Son, and calling upon all nations to worship Him for their God, even to the uttermost parts of the earth. Thou art the great mountain spoken of by Daniel, the man greatly beloved, wherefrom is cut without man's hands the cornerstone, that is, Christ, which has smitten in pieces the parti-colored image of the old serpent. I honor thee as the unpolluted fountain, I proclaim that thou art full of grace, I praise thee as the clean and undefiled tabernacle of God. Verily, where sin abounded, grace did much more abound. As by a woman death entered into the world, by a woman came the power to rise again. The serpent gave us to eat deadly fruit, but that fall has ended in the life-giving Bread of Immortality. Eve, our first mother, brought forth Cain the first murderer; thou, O Mary, hast brought forth Christ, the first-fruits of life and of the resurrection. O unheard of wonder! O wonderful novelty! O wisdom to be equaled by no words!

Lesson IX

And now we, the people of God, a holy generation, an acceptable congregation, the nestlings of the dove of peace, children of grace, do with purified minds and unpolluted lips, praise God in the tongues of all nations in this joyful solemnity of the Virgin. This is a noble Feast wherein the Angels keep holiday and men do most rightly offer praise, even a feast wherein we echo with reverence and joy that salutation first spoken by Gabriel. Hail Mary! Hail, thou Paradise of God the Father, whence the knowledge of Him flows in broad rivers to the ends of the earth! Hail, Dwelling-place of God the Son, whence He came forth clothed in flesh! Hail, mysterious Tabernacle of God the Holy Ghost! Hail, thou that art holier than the Cherubim! Hail, thou that art more glorious than the Seraphim! Hail, thou that art nobler than the heavens! Hail, thou that art brighter than the sun! Hail, thou that art fairer than the moon! Hail, manifold splendor of the stars! Hail, light cloud, dropping the dew of heaven! Hail, holy breeze, clearing the air of the vapors of sin! Hail, royal theme of the Prophets! Hail, sound of the Apostles gone out into all the earth! Hail, most excellent confession of the Martyrs! Hail, just hope of the Patriarchs! Hail, peculiar honor of all the Saints! Hail, source of health to dying creatures! Hail, O Queen, ambassadress of peace! Hail, stainless crown of motherhood! Hail, advocate of all under heaven! Hail, restoration of the whole world! Hail, thou that art full of grace, the Lord is with thee, even the Lord that is before thee, and from thee, and that is with us. To Him, with the Father, and the most holy and Life-giving Spirit, be ascribed all praise, now and ever, world without end. Amen.

Commemoration of Our Lady of Guadalupe (United States & Mexico)

In Mexico, on the hill of Tepeyac, in the year 1531, the God-bearing Virgin Mary, as is piously handed down, appeared to the neophyte Juan Diego, and gave him a command for Bishop Juan de Zumarraga, which she urgently repeated, that a church was to be constructed in her name at that location. The bishop, however, requested a sign. Then, while he was seeking the sacraments for his dying uncle far from the place of the apparition, his loving Mother favored the neophyte with a third vision, assured him of his uncle's health, and after he had gathered roses into his cloak that had blossomed out of season, she ordered him to take them to the bishop. The roses having spilled out in the sight of the bishop, an image of Mary, impressed upon the cloak itself, according to the tradition, appeared to those present in a wondrous manner. At first kept in the bishop's chapel, then transferred to a shrine constructed on the hill of Tepeyac, it was finally moved to a magnificent temple, to which Mexicans increasingly began to gather in droves, for reasons of veneration and frequency of miracles. And therefore as an ever-present defense, the Mexican bishops, to the applause of the whole people, chose the Blessed Virgin Mary of Guadalupe as the first Patroness of the Mexican people, which was duly confirmed by the apostolic authority of Benedict XIV. Leo XIII adorned the sacred image with a golden crown on Columbus Day 1895, by the agency of the archbishop of Mexico. And St. Pius X declared the blessed Guadalupan Virgin as the Patroness of all Latin America.

December 13 ~ St. Lucia

Virgin Martyr ~ Duplex

All from the Common except what follows

Lessons I–III from the occurring Scripture

Lesson IV

Lucy was a maiden of Syracuse, the daughter of a noble Christian family. Her mother Eutychia, being afflicted with an issue of blood, went with her to Catania, to pray before the body of the blessed Agatha. Lucy, by her earnest prayers at the grave, obtained her mother's cure through the intercession of Agatha, and then immediately begged her to give to Christ's poor the whole dowry which had been set apart for herself. As soon, therefore, as they returned to Syracuse, they sold the property, and distributed the money among the poor.

Lesson V

When this came to the ears of one to whom her parents had betrothed her against her will, he accused Lucy before Paschasius, the Præfect, of being a Christian. The Præfect could not move her to commit idolatry, either by his entreaties or his threats; nay, the more he strove to persuade her, so much the bolder did she become in her confession. Then, seeing that he could prevail nothing, "words," said he, "will cease when we come to blows." To whom the virgin answered, "God's servants will never want words, for the Lord Christ has said: When you shall stand before kings and governors, take no thought how or what you shall speak, for it shall be given you in that same hour what you shall speak, for it is not you that speak, but the Holy Ghost Which speaks in you."

Lesson VI

Then Paschasius asked her, saying: "Is the Holy Ghost in thee?" Whereto she answered: "They that live in chastity and piety are the temples of the Holy Ghost." "Then," said he, "I will send thee to be prostituted in a brothel, and get the Holy Ghost out of thee." To whom she made reply: "Thou canst not prostitute my will. If thou cause this poor body to be violated, the crown of my soul's purity will be brighter through suffering." Then he bade them take her to the place of shame, but by the power of God it became impossible to move her. Whereupon, being inflamed with anger, he had pitch, resin, and boiling oil poured upon her, and then set on fire. But the fire did not take hold upon her. Therefore he practiced many other cruelties upon her, and at last thrust a sword through her neck. When Lucy had received this wound, she began to speak of the peace of the Church, which it should enjoy after the death of Diocletian and Maximian, and presently returned her soul into the hands of God. She testified on the thirteenth day of December. Her body was buried at Syracuse, but afterwards taken to Constantinople, and lastly to Venice.

Lessons VII–IX from the first set in the Common of Non-Virgins (Homily by St Gregory)

December 14 ~ Day 7 within the Octave of the Immaculate Conception

Semiduplex

All from the Feast except what follows

Lessons I–III from the occurring Scripture

Lesson IV

From the Dogmatic Bull of Pope Pius IX.

It is known to all men, with what care this doctrine of the

sinlessness of the conception of the Mother of God has been handed down, set forth, and defended by the most distinguished Religious Orders, Theologians, Universities, and Doctors skilled in the things of God. All men know likewise how carefully Christian Bishops, even in their public teaching, have professed the doctrine that through the merits of Christ our Lord and Saviour, foreknown by God, the Holy Virgin Mary, Mother of God, was delivered from ever being the victim of original sin, but, on the contrary, had the fruits of redemption applied to her at the very moment of her Conception, and was therefore redeemed in a nobler way than others. But the weightiest fact of all is that the most holy Council of Trent, when, in accordance with the Holy Scriptures, as interpreted by the holy Fathers and the approved Councils, it decreed that all men are conceived in sin, expressly added that it did not mean thereby to say that the blessed and stainless Mary, Mother of God, did not form an exception to the rule. From this declaration of the Fathers of Trent it can clearly be drawn that there is nothing in the Bible, nothing in tradition, and nothing in the Fathers which can rightly be adduced against this prerogative of the most Blessed Virgin; nay, as far as circumstances demanded, they as much as declared her free from the original stain.

Lesson V

In truth, this doctrine upon the Conception of the most Blessed Virgin is day by day more earnestly set forth by the graver thought of the Church, by her teaching, by her care, by her learning, and by her wisdom. It is explained, taught, confirmed, and wonderfully spread among all peoples and nations of the Catholic world. The Church has received it from the Fathers, as a part of the original faith, attested strongly by the most ancient and venerable monuments of both the Eastern and Western Churches. Indeed, the Fathers and Ecclesiastical writers, learned in Holy Scripture, are marked by no more earnest feature than that in all their books and Scriptural Commentaries, written for the confirmation of doctrine, and the edification of the faithful, they do all in divers ways preach and teach the excelling holiness of this Virgin, her dignity, her freedom from any stain of sin, and the glory of her victory over the dark enemy of our race.

Lesson VI

All Commentators on the Book of Genesis remark that passage where God at the very time of the Fall speaks of the Atonement, to the confusion of the lying serpent, and the comfortable hope of man, and says: "I will put enmity between thee and the woman, and between thy seed and her seed," and all the ancients teach that by this passage is meant the most merciful Saviour of mankind, namely, our Lord Jesus Christ, the Only-Begotten Son of God and His most blessed Mother the Virgin Mary, as if the enmity which both He and she felt against the devil was, in a sense, of a kind common to them Both. Christ took our nature upon Him, and is become the Mediator between God and man, blotting out the handwriting that was against us, nailing it to His Cross, and the most Holy Virgin, by that subtle, close, and abiding tie which binds mother to Child, feels along with Him His truceless enmity to the serpent, and He, through His merits, has granted to her that moment of victory wherein her stainless foot bruised the serpent's head.

Lesson VII

From the Holy Gospel according to St. Luke (Luke 1:26–28)

In that time, the angel Gabriel was sent from God into a city of Galilee, called Nazareth, to a virgin espoused to a man whose name was Joseph, of the house of David; and the virgin's name was Mary. And so on.

Homily by St Sophronius, Patriarch

Blessed indeed art thou among women, for thou hast turned the curse of Eve into a blessing; thou hast even brought a blessing upon Adam, when he lay smitten by the first sentence of death. Blessed indeed art thou among women, for thou art the means whereby the Father's blessing has come upon man, and delivered him from the old curse. Blessed indeed art thou among women, for by thee thy fathers have found salvation; the salutation of the Angel tells thee that thou art about to bear them a Deliverer. Blessed indeed art thou among women, for thou, not knowing a man, conceivest a Son through Whom the whole earth shall be blessed, and bring forth thorns and thistles no more. Blessed indeed art thou among women, for thou remainest thyself no more than a woman, and yet art made Mother of God. If That holy Thing Which shall be born of thee be truly God made Man, then art thou truly Mother of God, for God is made thine Offspring.

Lesson VIII

"Fear not, Mary, for thou hast found grace with God"—abiding grace. Thou hast found grace with God—exceeding grace. Thou hast found grace with God—all desirable grace. Thou hast found grace with God—greater grace than any other. Thou hast found grace with God—unfailing grace. Thou hast found grace with God—saving grace. Thou hast found grace with God—immoveable grace. Thou hast found grace with God—invincible grace. Thou hast found grace with God—everlasting grace. Before thee there have been others, many others, made wonderful in holiness, but to none has it been given, as to thee, to be full of grace; to none has it been given, as to thee, to attain to such divine riches; to none, as to thee, to be prevented by purifying grace; to none, as to thee, to shine from the dayspring with light from heaven; to none, as to thee, to be exalted above all things before created.

Lesson IX

And justly; for none has ever drawn so near to God as thou hast;

none has ever been gifted by God with good gifts as thou hast; none has ever received of God's grace as thou hast. Thou art mightier than all things which are called mighty among men; thou hast received more than the goodness of God has conferred on any other. It is indeed because God made His home in thee that thus thou aboundest. There has never been any save thee that has comprehended the Incomprehensible; none save thee that has enjoyed His presence so much; none that He has made so ready therefor; none on whom the uncreated light has shone so clearly; and therefore none who has, like thee, sheltered the Lord God, the Maker and Lord of all, conceived Him in thy womb, and brought Him into the world, to redeem men lying under the Father's sentence, and to offer to them everlasting salvation. Wherefore, O Lady, I have already cried unto thee with the Angel, and I will still cry—"Hail, full of grace, the Lord is with thee! Blessed art thou among women!"

December 15 ~ Octave Day of the Immaculate Conception

Major Duplex

All from the Feast except what follows

Lessons I–III from the occurring Scripture

Lesson IV

From the Dogmatic Bull of Pope Pius IX.

From of old time continual prayers have been offered to this Apostolic See not only by Bishops, Churchmen, and the Regular Orders, but also by Emperors and Kings, beseeching that the sinlessness of the Conception of the Mother of God might be made the subject of a Dogmatic Definition. These prayers have been still more urgently addressed in recent times to Our Predecessor, of happy memory, Gregory XVI, and to Ourselves, by the Bishops, by the Secular Clergy, by the Regular Orders, and by the most eminent Christian Princes and nations. The knowledge of these things has caused Our heart to rejoice, and they have been the serious occupation of Our thoughts ever since, in spite of our unworthiness, the inscrutable Providence of God was pleased to set Us in this supreme Chair of Peter, and to put His Church into Our hands, for Us to govern. Since then, We have had nothing so much at heart as to yield to the desires of the Church in this matter, to the increasing of the veneration of which the most holy Virgin is already the object, and to the setting in a clearer light the singular graces with which God has adorned her, being Ourselves especially drawn to the same by the reverence, love, and affection with which We have been from Our childhood animated towards the same most holy Virgin Mary, Mother of God.

Lesson V

And now We trust in the Lord that the time is come to define as a truth of faith the doctrine of the stainless Conception of the most holy Virgin Mary, Mother of God, that doctrine already set forth by Holy Scripture, by the ancient tradition, by the unbroken belief of the Universal Church, by the one common opinion of the Catholic Episcopate and laity, and by the marked acts and decrees of Our Predecessors. We have weighed everything in Our mind, and We have without ceasing implored the help and light of God's Holy Spirit by earnest prayer, and We are of opinion that it is Our duty no longer to delay, but by Our Supreme Decision to settle and declare that the Virgin was conceived without sin, and thus to satisfy the godly cravings of the whole Christian world, as well as the instinct of Our own love for the said most holy Virgin, and, above all, because she is His Mother, to glorify our Lord Jesus Christ by this act, since whatever we do rightly to honor the Mother must redound to the glory of the Son.

Lesson VI

Therefore, having in all fasting and humbleness of heart continually implored God the Father through His Blessed Son, to hear Our own prayers and those of His whole Church, and to teach and strengthen Our mind by the power of His Holy Spirit, having begged the intercession of the Church Triumphant, and, above all, with groans called on the Holy Ghost the Comforter, We now, moved by Him, for the honor of the Holy and Undivided Trinity, for the greater praise and exaltation of the Virgin Mother of God, the glory of the Catholic Faith, and the good of Christianity, in the name and authority of our Lord Jesus Christ, of the Blessed Apostles Peter and Paul, and in Our own, declare and define that That doctrine which declares that the most blessed Virgin Mary was, in the first instant of her Conception, preserved, by a special grace and privilege granted to her by Almighty God, through the merits of Christ Jesus, Saviour of mankind, which He foreknew, from any stain of original sin, is a doctrine taught and revealed by God, and therefore from this time forward must be held by all faithful Christians firmly and constantly. Wherefore if any one, which God forbid, shall at any time think in his heart any thing contrary to this Our definition, let him know that he is condemned by his own judgment, that he has made shipwreck of the faith, and that he has cut himself off from the body of the Church.

Lesson VII

From the Holy Gospel according to St. Luke (Luke 1:26–28)

In that time, the angel Gabriel was sent from God into a city of Galilee, called Nazareth, to a virgin espoused to a man whose name was Joseph, of the house of David; and the virgin's name was Mary. And so on.

Homily by St. Epiphanius, Bishop

I am at a loss for what words or terms I ought to employ in speaking of this illustrious and holy Virgin. She is raised above all things except God; she was made much higher than the Cherubim and Seraphim, and the whole host of heaven; neither the voices of heaven nor of earth are full enough to set forth her majesty, no, not the voices of Angels. O blessed Virgin! O pure dove and Bride of heaven! O Mary! At once the heaven, the temple, and the throne of God! Mother of the Sun that shines both on heaven and on earth, even Christ! Bright cloud, through which the Son of Man has come as the lightning, that lightens from the East even unto the West! Hail, gate of heaven, full of grace, of whom the Prophet in the Canticle of Canticles openly speaks in the course of his prayer, saying, "A garden enclosed is My sister, My Spouse, a garden enclosed, a fountain sealed."

Lesson VIII

The Virgin is that stainless lily whence has sprung the Rose that fades not, even Christ. O Holy Mother of God! Ewe without spot, that hast borne the Lamb That took flesh of thee, even Christ! O Maiden whose holiness has dazzled the heavenly armies! There has appeared a great sign in heaven, a woman clothed with the sun, and with the Light in her arms; a great sign in heaven, the Virgin's womb the chamber of the Son of God; a great sign in heaven, the Lord of angels made the Virgin's child. The angels accused Eve, but now they praise Mary, who has raised Eve fallen, and restored to heaven Adam banished from Paradise. For Mary is the bridge between heaven and earth, the ambassadress who has reconciled them in her womb.

Lesson IX

We cannot measure the grace bestowed upon this holy Virgin. Hence the salutation addressed to her by Gabriel, Hail, thou glorious heaven, full of grace. Hail, Virgin adorned with many graces, yea, full of grace. Hail, thou vessel of gold that holdest the manna that came down from heaven, full of grace. Hail, thou unfailing fountain, that satisfiest the thirsty soul with sweet waters, full of grace. Hail, holy, sinless Mother of Him That was before thee, even Christ. Hail, thou Queenly purple, mantle of the King of heaven and earth. Hail, thou Book that no man can understand, and yet which the Eternal Word, the Son of the Father, hath opened for earth to read.

December 16 ~ St. Eusebius of Vercelli

Bishop & Martyr ~ Semiduplex

All from the Common except what follows

Lessons I–III from the occurring Scripture

Lesson IV

Eusebius was a Sardinian by birth, first a Lector in the Roman Church, and then Bishop of Vercelli. It seemed specially designed by Providence that he should be called to govern that Church, for the electors, who had never before known him, passed over, with a strange unanimity, all their own fellow-citizens, and chose Eusebius, as soon as they had seen him. He was the first Bishop in the Western Church who established an Order of Regular Clergy, to combine the active with the contemplative life. At this time the storm of Arian blasphemy and sin was sweeping far and wide over the West, and Eusebius set himself to fight against it so manfully, that his unshaken faith brought back Liberius again to life and hope. This Pope, knowing that the Spirit of God was in him, sent him with his Legates to the Emperor Constantius, in the year 354, to plead the cause of the Catholic Faith. His earnestness prevailed with that Prince, so that he obtained all that was asked for, and, among other things, permission for a Council to be summoned.

Lesson V

The year following, the Council met at Milan, and Eusebius, by the invitation of the Emperor, and the desire and command of the Papal Legates, attended. Here the Arians, assembled in a perfect synagogue of Satan, and all furiously raging together against Saint Athanasius, found Eusebius one of the stoutest enemies of their faction. As soon as he entered the Council, he delivered a long harangue, wherein he remarked that, of those there gathered together, some were notoriously defiled with heresy, and therefore he proposed that everyone should first of all subscribe the Nicene Creed, before proceeding to any other business. The Arians, in a violent passion, refused, whereupon he on his part refused to subscribe any proceedings against Athanasius, and even skillfully procured the withdrawal of the signature of the holy martyr Denis, then Bishop of Milan, which they had deceptively procured by preying on his simplicity. The Arians were now entirely enraged, and, after many persecutions, procured a decree of banishment against Eusebius. The Saint shook off the dust of his feet against them, and, defying alike the threats of Caesar and the drawn swords of the soldiery, accepted the sentence as one of the dignities of his office. He was sent to Scythopolis—Bethshan—in the Holy Land, suffering hunger, thirst, stripes, and all manner of violence, but for the Faith's sake he despised this life, and feared not death, but freely delivered his body to the tormentors.

Lesson VI

He wrote a solemn letter from Bethshan, addressed to the clergy and people of Vercelli and that neighborhood, full of constancy, devotion, and piety, describing the frightful cruelty and brazen impudence of the Arians. From this letter we know how completely they failed to scare him by their threats and their inhuman brutality, or to seduce him by their serpentine cunning into receiving their communion. In consequence of his unshaken resolution, he was moved from Bethshan into Cappadocia, and then again, to the deserts of Upper Egypt. He suffered exile until the death of Constantius, in 361, after which he was allowed to return to his flock. First, however, he took care to attend the Council at Alexandria, called to heal the wounds of the Church, and, afterwards, like a skillful physician, he made a progress through all the provinces of the East, strengthening those that were weak in the Faith, and confirming them in Christian doctrine. Then, with the same healthful results, he passed through Illyricum into Italy, who, at his coming, laid aside her garments of mourning. After his return, he published an expurgated edition of Origen's Commentary on the Psalms, and likewise of the works of Eusebius of Caesarea, both which he translated from Greek into Latin. At length, distinguished by all these great works, he passed to that crown of glory which fades not away, promised to them who suffer for the truth. He departed this present life at Vercelli, in 371, in the reign of Valentinian and Valens.

Lessons VII–IX from the second set in the Common of One Martyr (Homily by St. Gregory)

December 21 ~ St. Thomas the Apostle

Duplex II Class

All from the Common except what follows

Lesson IV

The Apostle Thomas, called Didymus, or the Twin, was a Galilean. After the descent of the Holy Ghost, he went into many provinces to preach Christ's Gospel. He gave knowledge of the rules of Christian faith and life to the Parthians, Medes, Persians, Hyrcanians, and Bactrians. He went last to the East Indies. Here he provoked the anger of one of the idolatrous kings, because the holiness of his life and teaching, and the number of his miracles, drew many after him, and brought them to the love of Christ Jesus. He was therefore condemned, and slain with lances. He crowned the dignity of the Apostleship with the glory of martyrdom, on the Coromandel coast, not far from Madras.

Lessons V–VI are Lessons IV–V from the First Set in the Common of Apostles (Sermon by St. Gregory, Pope)

Lesson VII

From the Holy Gospel according to St. John (John 20:24–29)

In that time, Thomas, one of the twelve, who is called Didymus, was not with them when Jesus came. And so on.

Homily by Pope St. Gregory

Dearly beloved brethren, what is it in this passage which particularly claims our attention? Do you think that it was by accident that this chosen Apostle was not with them when Jesus came? or, when he came, heard? or, when he heard, doubted? or, when he doubted, felt? or when he had felt, believed? All these things were not accidental, but Providential. It was a wonderful provision of Divine mercy, that this incredulous disciple, by thrusting his fingers into the bodily Wounds of his Master, should apply a remedy to the spiritual wounds of unbelief in our souls.

The doubts of Thomas have done us more good than the faith of all the disciples that believed. While he feels his way to faith, our minds are freed from doubt, and settled in faith.

Lesson VIII

Even as the Lord before His birth willed that Mary should be espoused, and yet never lose her virginity, so, after His Resurrection, He willed that His disciple should doubt, and yet not lose his faith. For, even as the espoused husband was the keeper of the virginity of the Mother, so was the disciple who doubted and felt, the witness of the truth of the Resurrection. He felt, and cried out: "My Lord and my God!" Jesus says unto him: "Thomas, because thou hast seen Me, thou hast believed." When the Apostle Paul says: "Faith is the substance of things hoped for, the evidence of things not seen," he plainly means that faith is the evidence of things that cannot be seen. When they are seen, there remains not faith, but knowledge.

Lesson IX

Thomas, then, sees and believes. Why is it said to him "Because thou hast seen Me, thou hast believed?" The truth is, he saw one thing, and so believed another. To mortal man it is not given to see God. He therefore saw only the Manhood, and yet had faith in the Divinity: "My Lord and my God!" This he said, seeing and believing, seeing Perfect Man, and yet believing in Perfect God, Whom he could not see. O what a comfort are the words which follow! "Blessed are they that have not seen, and yet have believed." These words are specially meant for us, who have not seen even the Flesh, and who yet do believe. They are specially meant for us if we believe and do not, by our lives, contradict our belief. He alone has a saving faith whose faith bears fruit.

All Feasts of the Saints from December 22 through January 13 inclusive are found in the Proper of Time.

FEASTS OF JANUARY

January 14 ~ St. Hilary of Poitiers

Bishop, Confessor, Doctor ~ Duplex

All from Common except what follows
Lessons I–III from the occurring Scripture.

Lesson IV

This Hilary was born of a noble family in Aquitaine, and excelled in learning and eloquence. He was married in his earlier life, but even then lived the life of a monk and on account of his remarkable holiness, was ultimately made Bishop of Poitiers, about the year 353, in which office he did his duty so as to gain the universal praise of the faithful. At that time the Emperor Constantius was persecuting the Catholics by threats, plundering of their goods, exile, and at length, by every species of cruelty, in order to force them to yield to the Arian heresy. Against the Arians, Hilary set himself up as a brazen wall, and turned upon himself the fierceness of their anger. They assailed him by many artifices, and at last Saturnine, Bishop of Arles, at the Council of Beziers, in 356, procured his banishment to Phrygia. During this exile he raised a dead man to life, and wrote a work in twelve books on the Trinity against the Arians.

Lesson V

In the year 359, the fourth of his exile, was the Council of Seleucia in Isauria, at which Hilary was obliged to be present, but afterwards withdrew to Constantinople. Here he realized more sharply the awful nature of this crisis in the history of Christianity, published three pamphlets in the form of letters to the Emperor, and demanded from that Prince leave to hold a public disputation in his presence. The Arian Bishops Ursacius and Valens, whom Hilary had already confuted in writing, were afraid to meet him in debate, and therefore induced Constantius, under pretense of pardon, to send him back to his Bishopric, in 360. His mother, the Church of Gaul, to use the language of Jerome, received him with open arms on his return from the battle with the heretics. He was followed to Poitiers by Martin, afterwards Bishop of Tours, whose later holiness was a fruit of his teaching.

Lesson VI

Henceforth he ruled the Church of Poitiers in great peace. By his exertions the Church of Gaul was led to denounce the Arian blasphemy. His wonderful learning is seen in his numerous works, of which Jerome writes to Læta that he deems them quite faultless. "One can follow Hilary in his books," says he, "without stumbling once." He passed from earth to heaven upon the thirteenth day of January, in the year of our Lord 369, in the reign of the Emperors Valentinian and Valens. He had already been called an illustrious Doctor of the Church by many Fathers and Councils, and was so styled in the Liturgy in some Dioceses, when at length, in the year 1850, Pope Pius IX, at the prayer of the Synod of Bordeaux, and in accordance with a resolution of the Sacred Congregation of Rites, proclaimed and confirmed the title, and commanded that the Mass and Office of his Feast should be everywhere said as those of a Doctor.

Lessons VII–IX from the second set in the Common of Doctors (Sermon by St Hilary)

Lesson IX—Commemoration of St. Felix of Nola, Priest & Martyr

Felix was a Priest of Nola, who on account of his fiery zeal against idolatry, suffered much persecution from the heathens, and was cast into prison. From thence an angel delivered him by night, and bade him go to Maximian, Bishop of Nola. This Bishop, enfeebled by old age, had at length despaired of power to withstand the torments of the persecutors, and had hidden himself in a wood. Thither came Felix, by the will of God, and found the holy bishop lying half-dead upon the ground. He aided him, and carried him upon his shoulders to the house of a holy widow. On another occasion, Felix, having again provoked the anger of the devil-worshippers, became an object of their pursuit, from which he hid himself in a narrow place between two walls. Hardly had he entered, when some spiders wove their webs across the entrance, which the enemy perceiving, concluded that no man had entered, and passed by. After leaving this hiding-place, Felix lay for three months in the house of a holy woman. After the Lord gave peace to His Church, the Saint returned to Nola, where he turned many to Christ by his life, his preaching, and his miracles. He steadily refused to accept the Episcopacy, fell asleep in the Lord, and was buried at Nola in the place called "The Pines."

January 15 ~ St. Paul the First Hermit

Confessor ~ Duplex

All from Common except what follows

Lessons I–III from the occurring Scripture.

Lesson IV

Paul the first and model of all hermits, was a native of the lower Thebaid in Egypt. At the age of fifteen years he lost both his parents. In order to escape from the persecution of Decius and Valerian, and to serve God in quietness, he betook himself to a cave in the desert. Here there was a palm-tree, on the fruit of which he lived, and of whose leaves he made his raiment until he attained the age of 113 years. At that time, Anthony, being now himself aged 90 years, received a command from God to go and see him. They met without knowing one another's names, and saluted one another, after which they fell straightway into a long discourse concerning the kingdom of God. Now it so happened that a raven had of a long time brought

Paul every day half a loaf, but on this day while they spoke together he brought a whole one.

Lesson V

When the raven had flown away, "Well," said Paul, "the Lord has sent us our dinner. Truly He is gracious; truly He is merciful. It is now sixty years that I have had half a loaf of bread every day, but now that thou art come, Christ gives His soldiers double rations." Then they asked a blessing, and ate together, sitting by a spring. When they were refreshed, they returned thanks, as is the custom, and afterwards spent the whole night praising God. At break of day Paul felt the approach of death, and desired Anthony to bring the cloak which Athanasius had given him, to use for his winding-sheet. While Anthony was on his way back from this journey, he saw in a vision the soul of Paul ascending to heaven, surrounded by choirs of angels, and accompanied by the Prophets and Apostles.

Lesson VI

When Anthony reached the cell of Paul, he found the dead body of the Saint in a kneeling posture, with the head thrown up and the hands stretched out towards heaven. He immediately began to chant the psalms and hymns ordained by Christian tradition, while he wrapped the body in the cloak of Athanasius. He had no spade to dig a grave, but two lions came roaring from the desert, as though to attend the burying, and scratched a hole big enough to hold a man's body, with their paws, showing meanwhile such signs of grief as their nature allows. When they were gone away, Anthony put the holy body in this hole, covered it with earth, and arranged it like a Christian's grave. He took away for himself Paul's tunic, which he had woven out of the palm-leaves somewhat after the manner of basket-work, and this tunic Anthony was in the habit of wearing on the great days of the Passover and Pentecost as long as he lived.

Lessons VII–IX from the second set in the Common of Abbots (Sermon by St Augustine)

Lesson IX—Commemoration of St. Maurus, Abbot

Maurus was born of a noble Roman family, and while he was yet a child was offered to God by his father Eutychius, in the order and under the personal teaching of St. Benedict. In a short while he made such progress in the life of grace that he became a wonder to his master, who often held him up to his other disciples as a pattern of regular observance and all virtues. While he was yet very young, Pope St. Gregory tells a wonderful instance of his obedience. Placid, the monk, having fallen into a lake where he was being swept away by the current, the holy Patriarch called Maurus and bade him run to the rescue, which he did, walking on the water till he reached Placid, whom he took by the hair of the head and dragged to the shore. He was sent by St. Benedict into France, where he founded the celebrated monastery (of Glanfeuil, now called St. Maur-sur-Loire), which he governed for forty years. He was a zealous and successful propagator of monastic discipline. He passed to heaven, famous for holiness and miracles, when he was more than seventy years of age, in the year of Salvation 565.

January 16 ~ St. Marcellus

Pope & Martyr ~ Semiduplex

All from Common except what follows

Lessons I–III from the occurring Scripture.

Lesson IV

This Marcellus was a Roman, and held the supreme Pontificate from the year of our Lord 304, in the reign of Constantius and Galerius, till 310, in that of Maxentius. It was through his persuasion that the Roman lady Lucina left the whole of her property to the Church of God. As the believers increased, he instituted new titles in the City, which he divided after the manner of dioceses for their convenience, and for the baptism and penance of heathens converted to Christianity, and for the burial of the martyrs. These proceedings excited the wrath of Maxentius, who threatened Marcellus with the heaviest punishment, unless he would lay down the Papacy and sacrifice to idols.

Lesson V

The servant of God treated with contempt the mad cries of this man, who accordingly took him and sent him to a menagerie, to take care of the beasts which were fed at the public cost. Marcellus remained at this place for nine months, which he spent in continual fasting and prayer, and, as he could not visit the parishes in person, he wrote letters to them. Some clerics rescued him, and the blessed Lucina hospitably received him into her house, in which he dedicated a Church, which is now called St. Marcellus'. Here the Christians met to pray, and the blessed Marcellus himself preached.

Lesson VI

These proceedings came to the knowledge of Maxentius, who thereupon had the wild beasts brought from the menagerie and located in the church, where Marcellus was made to feed them. The noisomeness of the place and the filthiness of his occupation broke down a constitution already enfeebled by many ailments, and he fell asleep in the Lord. The blessed Lucina buried his body in the cemetery of Priscilla, on the Salarian Way, on the 16th of January. He sat on the throne of Peter for five years, one month, and twenty-five days. He wrote an epistle to the Bishops of the Patriarchate of Antioch on the primacy of the Roman Church, wherein he proves the right of the same Church to be called the head of all the Churches. In this letter he likewise says that no Council can be lawfully gathered together except by the authority of the Roman Pontiff. He ordained at Rome in the month of December twenty-five Priests, two Deacons, and twenty-one Bishops for diverse Sees.

Lessons VII–IX from the Common of Supreme Pontiffs (Homily by St. Leo)

January 17 ~ St. Anthony the Abbot

Abbot ~ Duplex

All from Common except what follows

Lessons I–III from the occurring Scripture.

Lesson IV

Anthony was an Egyptian, the child of noble and Christian parents, whom he lost while yet very young. On one occasion he entered a Church, and heard these words of the Gospel, "If thou wilt be perfect, go and sell that thou hast, and give to the poor." He took these words as if they were addressed to himself personally, for this was the obedience which he thought every word of the Lord Christ should meet with. He therefore sold his whole possessions, and gave the price to the poor. Being thus delivered from worldly entanglements, he set himself to lead on earth the life of an angel. Finding himself, as it were, about to enter the field of battle against Satan, he thought it wisest to add to the shield of faith, which he already possessed, all the rest of the armor of God, wherefore he observed all those who were eminent for any grace, and strove to copy them.

Lesson V

He was excelled by none in watchfulness and self-restraint. He surpassed all in long-suffering, meekness, tenderness, lowliness, perseverance, and continual study of the Holy Scriptures. He had such a loathing of the company and conversation of heretics and schismatics, especially Arians, that he used to say that a faithful Christian ought as far as possible never to come near any such. He took the sleep which was needful for the body lying on the ground. Such was his devotion to fasting, that he took nothing with his bread but salt, and drank only water; he never ate or drank before sunset; he often abstained from food altogether for two days at a time; and very often passed whole nights in prayer. Being so valiant a soldier of God, Anthony was attacked by the devil with diverse temptations, but he overcame them all by prayer and fasting. Nevertheless, these frequent triumphs over Satan did not lull Anthony into security, for he was well aware of the numberless arts of assault possessed by the evil one.

Lesson VI

Then he betook himself into the vast deserts of Africa that lie near Egypt. Day by day he advanced on the path to perfection. Day by day the attacks of the fiends became more violent, but day by day his strength grew greater to strive against them. At length he came to mock at the powerlessness of the devils, against whom he stirred up his disciples to fight, teaching them with what arms to combat. "Believe me, my brethren," he used to say, "Satan is afraid of good men's watchings, and prayers, and fasts, and voluntary poverty, and mercifulness, and lowliness, but above all, of their warm love for Christ our Lord, the mere sign of Whose most holy Cross is enough to undo him and put him to flight." He became such an object of dread to the devils, that many persons throughout Egypt who were tormented by them, were delivered by calling on his name; moreover the fame of his holiness was so spread abroad, that Constantine the Great and his sons wrote to him to commend themselves to his prayers. In the hundred and fifth year of his age, and the fulness of his reputation for piety and miracles, having roused up great numbers to follow his example, he gathered his monks around him, and when he had exhorted them to strive after Christian perfection, he passed to heaven on the 17th day of January, in the year of our Lord 356.

Lessons VII–IX from the first set in the Common of Confessor Non-Bishops (Sermon by Pope St. Gregory)

January 18 ~ Chair of St. Peter at Rome

Major Duplex

All from Common of a Confessor Bishop except what follows

Lesson I ~ 1 Pet 1:1–5

From the first letter of St. Peter the Apostle

Peter, an apostle of Jesus Christ, to the strangers dispersed through Pontus, Galatia, Cappadocia, Asia, and Bithynia, elect, According to the foreknowledge of God the Father, unto the sanctification of the Spirit, unto obedience and sprinkling of the blood of Jesus Christ: Grace unto you and peace be multiplied. Blessed be the God and Father of our Lord Jesus Christ, who according to his great mercy hath regenerated us unto a lively hope, by the resurrection of Jesus Christ from the dead, Unto an inheritance incorruptible, and undefiled, and that can not fade, reserved in heaven for you, Who, by the power of God, are kept by faith unto salvation, ready to be revealed in the last time.

Lesson II ~ 1 Pet 1:6–9

Wherein you shall greatly rejoice, if now you must be for a little time made sorrowful in diverse temptations: That the trial of your faith much more precious than gold which is tried by the fire may be found unto praise and glory and honour at the appearing of Jesus Christ: Whom having not seen, you love: in whom also now, though you see him not, you believe: and believing shall rejoice with joy unspeakable and glorified; Receiving the end of your faith, even the salvation of your souls.

Lesson III ~ 1 Pet 1:10–12

Of which salvation the prophets have inquired and diligently searched, who prophesied of the grace to come in you. Searching what or what manner of time the Spirit of Christ in them did signify: when it foretold those sufferings that are in Christ, and the glories that should follow: To whom it was revealed, that not to themselves, but to you they ministered those things which are now declared to you by them that have preached the gospel to you, the Holy Ghost being sent down from heaven, on whom the angels desire to look.

Lesson IV

Sermon by St. Leo, Pope

When the twelve holy Apostles had received from the Holy Ghost the power to speak all languages, they divided the whole world into districts, which they severally allotted to themselves as fields for their Gospel labors. Then was Peter, the Prince of the Apostles, sent to the capital city of the Roman Empire, that he might cause the light to shine thence throughout the whole body of the civilized nations. At that time what nation was there that had no representative in Rome? What peoples were ignorant of what Rome had learnt?

Lesson V

In Rome were the dreams of an unbelieving philosophy to be destroyed, in Rome were the empty utterances of earthly wisdom to be confuted, in Rome was idolatry to be overcome, in Rome profanity to be put down, even in Rome, where the activity of superstition had gathered together from the whole earth every error which it could find. O most blessed Apostle Peter! this was the city to which thou didst not shrink to come. The Apostle Paul, thy comrade in glory, was yet occupied in founding the Churches, and thou didst enter alone into that forest of wild beasts roaring furiously; thou didst commit thyself to that stormy ocean, more boldly than when thou walkest upon the waters to come to Jesus.

Lesson VI

Thou hadst already taught them of the circumcision who were converted; thou hadst founded the Church of Antioch, the first that bore the noble name of Christian; thou hadst published the law of the Gospel throughout Pontus, Galatia, Cappadocia, Asia, and Bithynia; and thou didst not fear for the hardness of thy work, nor turn back because of thine old age, but didst boldly set up the trophy of the cross of Christ upon those Roman walls, where the Providence of God had appointed the throne of thine honor, and the glorious scene of thy passion.

Lesson VII

From the Holy Gospel according to St. Matthew (Matt 16:13–19)

At that time, Jesus came into the quarters of Cæsarea Philippi: and he asked his disciples, saying: Whom do men say that the Son of man is? And so on.

Homily by St. Hilary, Bishop

The Lord asks His disciples who men say that He is, and He adds, "the Son of Man." Let us ever remember to hold fast this truth of our profession, namely, that the Son of God is the Son of Man also.

Were He one and not the other, then were He no Saviour for us. The Lord then, having heard the various opinions of men, asks, "But Who say ye that I am?" And Simon Peter answered and said: "Thou art the Christ, the Son of the living God." Peter had weighed the questions. The Lord had asked, "Who do men say that I, the Son of Man, am?" That He was Son of Man was sufficiently evident to all who looked upon His Body. But when He spoke of His whole Self, and asked, "Who do you say that I am?" He showed that the mind had something to grasp beyond That Which was seen, for Son of Man He was manifestly. What judgment did He wish them to give? I think it was not that which He had owned concerning Himself. That something more, which He wished them to own, was a hidden thing, whereunto the faith of them that believed in Him was to reach.

Lesson VIII

Peter's confession was followed by a proper reward for having seen the Son of God in the Son of Man. Blessed is this holy Apostle, in whose praise it is said that he saw with more than human eyes That Which was unseen, who gazed upon Flesh and Blood, and by the secret revelation of the Heavenly Father recognized the Eternal Son of God; who was the first thought worthy to acknowledge the Divinity of Christ.

God bless thee, O Peter, thou who by uttering for the first time the title of Divine honor, didst lay the good foundation of the Church! God bless thee, thou worthy rock whereon she is built, forever triumphant over the infernal powers, the gates of hell, and the bands of death! God bless thee, happy doorkeeper of heaven, to whose keeping are given the keys of the everlasting mansions, whose sentences on earth are already confirmed in heaven so that whatsoever thou shalt bind on earth shall be bound in heaven, and whatsoever thou shalt loose on earth shall be loosed in heaven.

Lesson IX - Commemoration of St. Prisca, Virgin Martyr

Prisca was a noble Roman maiden, who at thirteen years of age was accused of Christianity before the Emperor Claudius. By his command she was taken to the temple of Apollo to sacrifice there, and when she refused, was beaten and sent to prison. She was taken out from thence again, but as she still held steadfastly to the faith, they flogged her, poured boiling tallow upon her, and sent her back a second time. She was at last thrown to a lion in the amphitheater, but it quietly lay down at her feet. She was starved for three days in a slaves' prison house, and then tortured upon the rack. Pieces of flesh were next torn from her body with iron hooks, and she was thrown on a burning pile. She marvelously still remained alive, and was accordingly beheaded outside the city. Thus she added the crown of martyrdom to the palm of virginity. The Christians buried her body at the tenth milestone on the road from

Rome to Ostia on the eighteenth of January.

January 19 ~ Sts. Marius, Martha, Audifax, & Abachum

Martyrs ~ Simplex

Lessons I–II from the occurring Scripture.

Lesson III

Marius was a Persian of high rank, who came to Rome in the reign of the Emperor Claudius, with his wife Martha, who was equally noble, and their two sons Audifax and Abachum, to pray at the graves of the Martyrs. Here they comforted the Christians who were in prison, and whom they relieved by their ministrations and alms, and buried the bodies of the Saints. For these acts they were all arrested, but no threats or terrors could move them to sacrifice to idols. They were accordingly mangled with clubs, and drawn with ropes, after which they were burnt by applying plates of red-hot metal to their bodies, and their flesh partly torn off with metal hooks. Lastly their hands were all cut off, and they were fastened together by the neck, in which state they were driven through the city to the thirteenth milestone on the Cornelian Way, a place now called Santa Ninfa, where they were to die. Martha addressed a moving exhortation to her husband and sons to hold out bravely to the last, for the love of Jesus Christ; and was then herself drowned. The other three martyrs were next beheaded in the same sand-pit. Their bodies were thrown into a fire. The lady Felicity of Rome collected the half-burnt remains, and caused them to be buried at her own farm.

January 20 ~ Sts. Fabian & Sebastian

Pope & Martyr ~ Duplex

All from Common except what follows

Lessons I–III from the occurring Scripture.

Lesson IV

Fabian was a Roman, and sat as Pope from the year of our Lord 236, in the reign of the Emperor Maximinus till 250, in that of Decius. He appointed a Deacon to each of the seven districts of Rome to look after the poor. He likewise appointed the same number of Subdeacons to collect the acts of the Martyrs from the records kept by the seven district notaries. It was by him that it was ordained that every Maundy Thursday the old Chrism should be burnt and new consecrated. He was crowned with martyrdom upon the 20th of January, in the persecution of Decius, and buried in the cemetery of St. Callistus on the Appian Way, having sat in the throne of Peter fifteen years and four days. He held five Advent ordinations, in which he ordained twenty-two Priests, seven Deacons, and eleven Bishops for diverse Sees.

Lesson V

The father of Sebastian was of Narbonne, and his mother a Milanese. He was a great favorite of the Emperor Diocletian, both on account of his noble birth and his personal bravery, and was by him appointed captain of the first company of the Prætorian Guards. He was in secret a Christian, and often supported the others both by good offices and money. When some showed signs of yielding under persecution, he so successfully exhorted them, that, for Jesus Christ's sake, many offered themselves to the tormentors. Among these were the brothers Mark and Marcellian who were imprisoned at Rome in the house of Nicostratus. The wife of Nicostratus himself, named Zoe, had lost her voice, but it was restored to her at the prayer of Sebastian. These facts becoming known to Diocletian, he sent for Sebastian, and after violently rebuking him, used every means to turn him from his faith in Christ. But as neither promises nor threats availed, he ordered him to be tied to a post and shot to death with arrows.

Lesson VI

Sebastian was treated accordingly, and left for dead, but in the night the holy widow Irene sent for the body in order to bury it, and then found that he was still alive, and nursed him in her own house. As soon as his health was restored, he went out to meet Diocletian, and boldly rebuked him for his wickedness. The Emperor was at first thunderstruck at the sight of a man whom he believed to have been long dead, but afterwards, frenzied with rage at the reproaches of Sebastian, ordered him to be beaten to death with rods, under which torment the martyr yielded his blessed soul to God, upon the 20th day of January, in the year of our Lord 288. His body was thrown into a sewer, but he appeared in sleep to Lucina, and made known to her where it was, and where he would have it buried. She accordingly found it and laid it in those Catacombs, over which a famous Church has since been built, called St. Sebastian's outside the Walls.

Lessons VII–IX from the second set in the Common of Many Martyrs (Sermon by St. Ambrose)

January 21 ~ St. Agnes

Virgin Martyr ~ Duplex

Lessons I–III from the Common of a Virgin Martyr

Lesson IV

From the Book of St. Ambrose, Bishop, on Virgins

This is a virgin's birthday; let us then follow the example of her chastity. It is a Martyr's birthday; let us then offer sacrifices. It is the birthday of the holy Agnes; let men then be filled with wonder, little ones with hope, married women with awe, and the unmarried with emulation. But how shall I set forth the glory of her whose very name is an utterance of praise? It seems to me that this being, holy beyond her years, and strong beyond human nature, received the name of Agnes, not as an earthly designation, but as a revelation from God of what she was to be. For this name Agnes is from the Greek, and being interpreted, signifies Pure. So that this saintly maiden is known by the very title of Chastity and when I have added thereto the word Martyr,

I have said enough. She needs not the praise which we could utter, but do not. None is more praiseworthy than she for whose praise all mouths are fitted. As many as name her, so many praise her by the noble title of martyr.

Lesson V

We learn by tradition that this holy martyr testified in the thirteenth year of her age. We will pass by the foul cruelty which did not spare her tender years, to contemplate the great power of her faith, whereby she overcame the weakness of childhood, and witnessed a good confession. Her little body was hardly big enough to give play to the instruments of their cruelty, but if they could scarce sheathe their swords in her slight frame, they found in her that which laughed the power of the sword to scorn. She had no fear when she found herself grasped by the bloody hands of the executioners. She was unmoved when they dragged her with clanging chains. Hardly entered on life, she stood fully prepared to die. She quailed not when the weapons of the angry soldiery were pointed at her breast. If they forced her against her will to approach the altars of devils, she could stretch forth her hands to Christ amid the very flames which consumed the idolatrous offerings, and mark on the heathen shrine the victorious Cross of the Lord. She was ready to submit her neck and hands to the iron shackles, but they were too big to clasp her slender limbs. Behold a strange martyr! She is not grown of stature to fight the battle, but she is ripe for the triumph; too weak to run in the race, and yet clearly entitled to the prize; unable from her age to be aught but a learner, she is found a teacher.

Lesson VI

She went to the place of execution a virgin, with more willing and joyful footsteps than she would have gone with to the nuptial chamber as a bride. The spectators were all in tears, and she alone did not weep. They beheld her with wonder, laying down that life of which she had hardly begun to taste the sweets, as freely as though she had drained it to the dregs and was weary of its burden. All men were amazed when they saw her whose years had not made her her own mistress, arise as a witness for the Deity. Consider how many threats her murderer used to excite her fears, how many arguments to shake her resolution, how many promises to bribe her to accept his offers of marriage. But she answered him "It is an insult to Him Whom I have wedded to expect me to comply. He That first chose me, His will I be. Headsman, why waitest thou? Perish the body which draws the admiration of eyes from which I would turn away." She stood, prayed, and then bent her neck for the stroke. Now mightest thou have seen the murderer trembling as though he himself were the criminal, the executioner's hand shake, and the faces of them that stood by turn white at the sight of her position, and all the while herself remain without fear. This one victim brought God a double offering, that of her purity, and that of her faith. She preserved virginity and achieved martyrdom.

Lessons VII–IX from first set in the Common of Virgins (Homily by Pope St. Gregory)

January 22 ~ Sts. Vincent & Anastasius

Martyrs ~ Semiduplex

All from Common of a Confessor Bishop except what follows

Lessons I–III from the Common of a Virgin Martyr

Lesson IV

Vincent was born at Huesca in Aragon in Spain. He was early turned to study, and learned sacred letters from Valerius, Bishop of Saragossa. He was accustomed to deliver discourses for this Prelate, who, owing to a speech impediment, was not able to preach. This coming to the ears of Dacian, Præfect of the province under Diocletian and Maximian, he caused Vincent to be arrested at Saragossa, and brought before him at Valencia in bonds. The saint was scourged, and afterwards tormented on the rack, in presence of numerous spectators, but neither torture, threats, nor fair words could bend his resolution. He was then laid on a grating over hot coals, his flesh mangled with iron hooks, and white-hot plates of metal applied to the wounds. The still breathing remains were taken back to a prison, and laid on broken potsherds, that the agony of his naked body might prevent his sleeping from exhaustion.

Lesson V

As he lay in his dark cell, a glorious light suddenly filled the prison, to the astonishment of all who saw it. The jailor informed Dacian, who caused the martyr to be brought out and cared for in a soft bed, hoping that though he had failed to move him by cruelty, he might seduce him by pretended kindness. But the indomitable soul of Vincent, armed with faith and hope in Christ Jesus, remained unconquered even to the end, and triumphing over the fire, the steel, and the cruelty of the tormentors, passed away to receive the victorious crown of martyrdom in heaven, on the 22nd day of January, in the year of our Lord 304. His body was thrown out unburied. A raven perched upon it and kept off with his beak, claws, and wings both the other birds and a wolf, which came to prey on it. Dacian then had it thrown into the sea, but by the will of God it was washed up again, and the Christians took and buried it.

Lesson VI

Anastasius was a Persian monk who made a pilgrimage to the Holy Places at Jerusalem in the reign of the Emperor Heraclius, during which journey he endured bonds and stripes on account of his confession of Christ at Banias, then called Cæsarea in Palestine. Soon after his return, he was arrested by the Persians for the same cause, and, after enduring diverse torments, he and seventy other Christians were beheaded by order of King Khosrow II. He testified upon the 22nd day of January in the year of our Lord 628. His relics were first carried to Jerusalem, to the monastery in which he had made his monastic profession, and afterwards to Rome, where they were laid in the monastery of Saints Vincent and Anastasius.

Lessons VII–IX from first set in the Common of Many Martyrs (Homily by St. Gregory)

January 23 ~ St. Raymund of Peñafort

Confessor ~ Semiduplex

All from Common except what follows

Lessons I–III from the occurring Scripture

Lesson IV

The blessed Raymond was born at Barcelona, in the year of our Lord 1175, and was of the noble family of the De Peñafuerte. He was early instructed in the Christian religion, and even while he was still a little child, he showed such excellence of mind and body, as filled his friends with strong hopes of his future greatness. As a young man he taught letters in his native place. He afterwards went to Bologna, where he applied himself to works of godliness, and to the study of the Ecclesiastical and Civil Law. He took the degree of Doctor, and lectured with great applause upon the Canon Law. He attained so much celebrity that Berengarius, Bishop of Barcelona, on his way from Rome to his own See, turned aside to visit the Saint at Bologna, and at length persuaded him after many entreaties to return with him to Spain. He was appointed to a Canonry and the Archdeaconry in the Church of Barcelona, in which offices he set both clergy and people a brilliant example of uprightness, modesty, learning, and meekness, and more especially strove, as far as in him lay, to increase the honor and reverence paid to the Virgin Mother of God, whom he venerated with an affection singularly devoted.

Lesson V

When he was about forty-five years of age he solemnly professed in the Order of Friars Preachers, and strove, as a new recruit, to perfect himself in all the duties of his calling, particularly in charity to the poor, and above all to those unhappy Christians who were slaves to the unbelievers. He was the Confessor of St. Peter Nolasco and of James I, King of Aragon, and by his advice St. Peter Nolasco gave up his whole worldly possessions to ransom as many as possible of the wretched captives. At this moment the Most Blessed Virgin appeared simultaneously to St. Raymond, St. Peter Nolasco, and King James, and revealed to them the pleasure of her Only-begotten Son and herself, that they should establish in her honor an order of Religious whose work should be the redemption of Christian slaves from bondage among unbelievers. The three took counsel together, and then founded the Order of the Blessed Mary of Ransom, for the Redemption of Captives. The blessed Raymond himself composed a most appropriate code of rules for the new institution, for which he after some years obtained the express sanction of Pope Gregory IX, and himself on the 10th day of August, in the year 1223, with his own hands clothed St. Peter Nolasco in the habit, and constituted him the first Master General of the Order.

Lesson VI

He was summoned to Rome by Gregory IX in the year 1230, and appointed by him his Chaplain, Penitentiary, and Confessor, and by his orders collected into one volume of the Decretals the ordinances of the Roman Pontiffs, which up to that time were only to be found scattered among the records of diverse Councils and Churches. He firmly refused the Archbishopric of Tarragona, which was offered him by the Pope himself, and, having been chosen Master General of the whole order of Friars Preachers, he discharged the duties of that office in holiness for two years, and then resigned it. It was by his advice that James, King of Aragon, established the Office of the Holy Inquisition in his dominions. He was distinguished by many miracles, the chief of those which are narrated of him is that on one occasion being in the island of Majorca and wishing to go to Barcelona, he spread his cloak upon the sea, and passed over the waters on it, accomplishing the whole distance of sixty leagues in six hours, and finally entering his convent through the closed doors. He attained the age of nearly a hundred years, and fell asleep in the Lord on the 6th day of January, in the year of salvation 1275. His name was enrolled by Clement VIII among those of the Saints.

Lessons VII–IX from first set in the Common of Confessor Non-Bishops (Homily by St. Gregory)

Lesson IX ~ Commemoration of St. Emerentiana, Virgin Martyr

Emerentiana was a Roman maiden, and the foster-sister of the blessed Agnes. While she was still a Catechumen she was inspired by her faith and love to rebuke the fury of the idol-worshippers against the Christians, whereupon a mob assembled, and stoned her so severely that she was only able to drag herself to the grave of holy Agnes, where, while she prayed, she gave up her soul to God, being baptized, not in water, but in her own blood, so freely shed for Christ.

January 24 ~ St. Timothy

Bishop & Martyr ~ Duplex

All from Common
except what follows

Lessons I–III from the
occurring Scripture

Lesson IV

Timothy was a native of Lystra in Lycaonia, born of a Gentile father and a Jewish mother. He embraced the Christian religion when the Apostle Paul came into those parts. The holy Apostle was so struck with the fame of Timothy's sanctity, that he chose him to be the companion of his journeys, and caused him to be circumcised, in order to remove a stumbling-block from the way of those Jews who felt drawn to Christianity. When they came together to Ephesus, the Apostle consecrated him Bishop of that Church.

Lesson V

Two of the Apostle Paul's Epistles are addressed to this Saint, of which one was written from Laodicea, and the other from Rome. These sacred writings so stirred him up to the zealous discharge of his duties as a spiritual shepherd, that he strove to prevent the people of Ephesus from sacrificing to Artemis on her feast day, knowing that sacrifice is due to God alone. The heathens thereupon stoned him till he was well-nigh dead, and although he was rescued by the Christians, and carried to a mountain near the city, he then fell asleep in the Lord, on the 24th day of January.

Lesson VI: from Lesson IV of the first set in the Common of One Martyr (Homily by St. Augustine)

Lessons VII–IX from first set in the Common of One Martyr (Sermon by Pope St. Gregory)

January 25 ~ Conversion of St. Paul

Apostle ~ Major Duplex

All from Common except what follows

Lesson I ~ Acts 9:1–5

From the Acts the Apostles

And Saul, as yet breathing out threatenings and slaughter against the disciples of the Lord, went to the high priest, And asked of him letters to Damascus, to the synagogues: that if he found any men and women of this way, he might bring them bound to Jerusalem. And as he went on his journey, it came to pass that he drew nigh to Damascus; and suddenly a light from heaven shined round about him. And falling on the ground, he heard a voice saying to him: Saul, Saul, why persecutest thou me? Who said: Who art thou, Lord? And he: I am Jesus whom thou persecutest. It is hard for thee to kick against the goad.

Lesson II ~ Acts 9:6–9

And he trembling and astonished, said: Lord, what wilt thou have me to do? And the Lord said to him: Arise, and go into the city, and there it shall be told thee what thou must do. Now the men who went in company with him, stood amazed, hearing indeed a voice, but seeing no man. And Saul arose from the ground; and when his eyes were opened, he saw nothing. But they leading him by the hands, brought him to Damascus. And he was there three days, without sight, and he did neither eat nor drink.

Lesson III ~ Acts 9:10–16

Now there was a certain disciple at Damascus, named Ananias. And the Lord said to him in a vision: Ananias. And he said: Behold I am here, Lord. And the Lord said to him: Arise, and go into the street that is called Straight, and seek in the house of Judas, one named Saul of Tarsus. For behold he prayeth. And he saw a man named Ananias coming in, and putting his hands upon him, that he might receive his sight. But Ananias answered: Lord, I have heard by many of this man, how much evil he hath done to thy saints in Jerusalem. And here he hath authority from the chief priests to bind all that invoke thy name. And the Lord said to him: Go thy way; for this man is to me a vessel of election, to carry my name before the Gentiles, and kings, and the children of Israel. For I will shew him how great things he must suffer for my name's sake.

Lesson IV

Sermon by St. Augustine, Bishop

We have this day heard read out of the Acts of the Apostles how that the Apostle Paul, from being a persecutor of the Christians, was changed into a preacher of Christ. Christ laid low the persecutor, that He might raise him up a teacher of His Church. He smote and healed him, slew him and made him alive again. For the Lord Christ is that Lamb That was Himself slain by the wolves, and That now turns the wolves into lambs. Now was fulfilled in Paul that which was clearly spoken in prophecy by the Patriarch Jacob, when he blessed his children, laying hands indeed on them which then were, but looking forward to the things which were yet for to come. Paul bears witness of himself that he was of the tribe of Benjamin, and when Jacob blessed his sons, and came to bless Benjamin, he said: "Benjamin a ravenous wolf."

Lesson V

What then? Is Benjamin a wolf that shall ravin for ever? God forbid. "In the morning he shall devour the prey, and at night he shall divide the spoil." This is exactly what was fulfilled in the Apostle Paul. If it please you, we will now consider how in the morning he devoured the prey, and at night divided the spoil. Here morning and evening are put for the beginning and the end. So we may read, In the beginning he shall devour the prey, and at the end he shall divide the spoil. First, then, in the beginning, he devoured the prey. So it is written that he received letters from the chief priests and went forth, that wheresoever he should find any Christians, he might bring them bound unto the priests, that they might be punished.

Lesson VI

He went breathing out threatenings and slaughter, yea, truly, devouring the prey. When also they stoned Stephen, the first Martyr that laid down his life for Christ's name's sake, "Saul was consenting unto his death," and, as though it contented him not to stone him, he kept the clothes of all them that did it, urging them on more than if he had joined them. So in the morning he devoured the prey. How in the evening did he divide the spoil? Struck down by the voice of Christ from heaven, ravening no more, he falls upon his face, cast down to be raised up, smitten to be healed.

Lessons VII–IX from the second set in the Common of Apostles (Sermon by the Venerable Bede)

January 26 ~ St. Polycarp

Bishop & Martyr ~ Duplex

All from Common except what follows

Lessons I–III from the occurring Scripture

Lesson IV

From the Book on Ecclesiastical Writers, composed by St. Jerome, Priest

Polycarp was a disciple of the Apostle John, and was consecrated by him Bishop of Smyrna. He was reckoned the chief of all the Christians of Asia, because he had been taught by several of the Apostles, and other persons who had seen the Lord. During the reign of the Emperor Antoninus Pius, and while Anicetus presided over the Church of Rome, Polycarp came thither to discuss some questions regarding the time for observing Easter. He found some heretics at Rome, who had been led astray by the doctrine of Marcion and Valentinus, and brought back many of them to the faith. One day Marcion met him by accident, and said to him: "Do you recognize me?" whereto he replied: "I recognize the devil's eldest son." Some time after, in the reign of Marcus Antoninus and Lucius Aurelius Commodus, during the fourth persecution since Nero, when the Proconsul was ruling in Smyrna, the whole population, being assembled in the theatre, clamored against Polycarp, and he was burnt to please them. He wrote an extremely useful Epistle to the Philippians, which is publicly read in the Churches of Asia even to this day.

Lessons V–VI: from Lessons IV & V of the Second set in the Common of One Martyr (Exposition by St. Ambrose)

Lessons VII–IX from third set in the Common of One Martyr (Sermon by St. Hilary)

January 27 ~ St. John Chrysostom

Bishop, Confessor, Doctor ~ Duplex

All from Common except what follows

Lessons I–III from the occurring Scripture

Lesson IV

John of Antioch, who, on account of the golden stream of his eloquence, is called by the Greeks *Chrysostomos*, or, the golden-mouthed, was a lawyer and man of the world of much eminence, before he turned his great intellect and wonderful industry to the study of things sacred. He took orders, and was ordained a priest of the Church of Antioch, in the year of our Lord 386, and after the death of Nectarius, was forced by the Emperor Arcadius to accept, though sorely against his own will, the Archbishopric of Constantinople. Having received the burden of a shepherd's office, upon the 26th day of February, in the year 398, he set himself zealously to do his duty, struggling against the degradation of public morality and the loose lives of the nobility, and thereby drew upon himself the ill-will of many enemies, especially the Empress Eudoxia, whom he had rebuked on account of the money of the widow Callitropa, and the land of another widow.

Lesson V

Some Bishops being assembled in a Council at Chalcedon, which Council the Saint held to be neither lawful nor public, although he was commanded to go there, he refused. Whereupon Eudoxia, striving earnestly against him, caused him to be sent into exile. Soon after, however, the people of the city rose, and demanded his recall, and he was then brought back again amid great public rejoicings. Nevertheless he ceased not to war against vice, and absolutely forbade the celebration of public games round the silver statue of Eudoxia in the square outside the Church of Holy Wisdom—the Hagia Sophia. Upon this, a party of Bishops, who were enemies to him, banded together, and obtained that he should be banished again, which was done accordingly, on the 20th day of June, 404, amid the lamentations of widows and the poor, who felt as if they were being deprived of a common father. During this exile, it almost passes belief how much Chrysostom suffered, and how many souls he turned to faith in Christ Jesus.

Lesson VI

At this time a Council was assembled at Rome, wherein Chrysostom's restoration to his See was decreed by Pope Innocent I, but meanwhile, he was suffering great hardships and cruelties on his journey at the hands of the soldiers who had him in charge. As he passed through Armenia he prayed in the Church of the holy martyr Basiliscus, and the same night that blessed conqueror appeared to him in a vision and said: "Brother John, tomorrow thou shalt be with me." On the next day, therefore, he received the Sacrament of the Eucharist, and, arming himself with the sign of the cross, resigned his soul to God, it being the 14th of September, in the year of salvation, 407. As soon as he was dead a furious hailstorm took place at Constantinople, and after four days the Empress died. The Emperor Theodosius, the son of Arcadius, brought the body of John Chrysostom to Constantinople with great state, and numerously attended, and on the 27th of January, 438, laid it with magnificent honors in the grave, beside which he prayed for the forgiveness of his own father and mother. The holy body was afterwards taken to Rome, and is now buried in the Vatican Basilica. The number, devoutness, and brilliance of St. John Chrysostom's sermons and other writings, his acuteness in exposition, and the close aptness of his explanations of Holy Scripture, have been and are the object of universal wonder and admiration, and often seem not unworthy to have been dictated to him by the Apostle

Paul, for whom he entertained a wonderful devotion.

Lessons VII–IX from third set in the Common of Doctors (Sermon by St. John Chrysostom)

January 28 ~ St. Peter Nolasco

Confessor ~ Duplex

All from Common except what follows

Lessons I–III from the occurring Scripture

Lesson IV

Peter Nolasco was born of noble parents at Recaudun near Carcassonne in France about the year 1189, and is chiefly distinguished for his great love toward his neighbor. It was considered a foreshadowing of this virtue, that when he was a little child in his cradle, a swarm of bees settled on his right hand, and began to make a honey-comb there. He lost his parents while still young, and in consequence of his horror of the Albigensian heresy, with which France was then plagued, he sold his property there and emigrated to Spain. Here he first discharged a vow which he had made at the sanctuary of the Blessed Virgin of Monserrat, and afterwards went to Barcelona. Here he was so affected by the miserable state of the Christians who were in slavery to the Moors, that he expended his whole fortune in ransoming as many of them as possible, and used to say that he wished he could be sold himself to ransom more, or could himself change places with them.

Lesson V

It came to pass that God showed how agreeable to Him was the charitable zeal of Peter. One night when he was praying, and his mind was much exercised on the means of helping the enslaved Christians, the Blessed Virgin appeared to him in a vision, and gave him to understand that it would be most pleasing to her Son and herself, if he would found in her honor an order of religious men, whose chief duty it should be to effect the redemption of Christian bondsmen out of the hand of the unbelievers. In conformity to this revelation, which had likewise on the same night been made to St. Raymond de Peñafort and King James I of Aragon, he founded the Religious Order of the Blessed Mary of Ransom, for the redemption of captives. The members of this order add a fourth vow to the three essential ones of Poverty, Chastity, and Obedience, namely, that they will be ready if need be to remain as hostages in the hand of the unbelievers for the liberation of others.

Lesson VI

After he took the vow of virginity, he remained with his purity quite unsullied all his life, and was at the same time a bright pattern of long-suffering, humility, temperance, and other virtues. God was pleased to adorn him with the gift of Prophecy, whereby he foretold things to come. Among others, he prophesied to King James that he would take the city of Valencia from the Moors, which he afterwards did. He was refreshed by frequent apparitions of his Guardian Angel and of the Virgin Mother of God. He had lived to a great age, when being quite worn out, and falling into a grievous sickness, he perceived that his end was at hand. He then received the holy Sacraments, and, gathering his brethren around him, exhorted them for the last time to show pity to slaves. After this he began to repeat with great emotion the Psalm: "I will praise thee, O Lord, with my whole heart;" and when he had uttered the words: "He sent redemption unto His people," he resigned his soul to God. This happened at midnight between the 23rd and 24th of December, 1256. Alexander VII extended his feast to the whole Church.

Lessons VII–IX from second set in the Common of Confessor Non-Bishops (Sermon by the Venerable Bede)

Lesson IX ~ Commemoration of St. Agnes's Second Feast

The night when the parents of the blessed Agnes were watching at her grave, she appeared to them in the company of a band of virgins, and said to them: "Father and Mother, weep not for me as though I were dead; for now these virgins and I live together in Him Whose love was my whole life upon earth." Some years afterwards, Constance, the daughter of the Emperor Constantine, being sick of an incurable ulcer, betook herself to said grave, although she was not yet a Christian, and as she lay by it and slept, she seemed to hear the voice of Agnes, saying to her: "Constance, be of good courage; believe in Jesus Christ the Son of God, and He will make thee whole." The Princess, being healed, was baptized, along with many others of the Emperor's family and household, and afterwards built over the grave of the blessed Agnes a Church named in her honor.

January 29 ~ St. Francis De Sales

Bishop, Confessor, Doctor ~ Duplex

All from Common except what follows

Lessons I–III from the occurring Scripture

Lesson IV

Francis was born of godly and noble parents, in the town of Sales, from which his family take their name of de Sales, upon the 21st day of August, in the year of our Lord 1567. In his childish years his innocent and grave demeanor gave promise of his future sanctity. He received a liberal education as he grew up, and afterwards studied Philosophy and Theology at Paris. In order to the complete furnishing of his mind, he took the degree of Doctor of Laws, both Civil and Ecclesiastical, at Padua, with much distinction. He had already bound himself with a vow of perpetual virginity at Paris, and he renewed the same in the Holy House of Loreto. From this path of virtue, neither the temptations of the devil nor the allurements of the world ever induced him to swerve.

Lesson V

He refused to be made Counsellor of the Parliament of Chambery, for which his family had obtained for him patents from the Duke of Savoy, and determined to become a clergyman. He was appointed to the Provostship of the Church of Geneva, and, being shortly afterwards ordained Priest, discharged so admirably the duties of his position, that he was sent by Granier, his Bishop, to preach the word of God in Chablais, and other places in the outskirts of the diocese, where the inhabitants had embraced the Calvinist heresy. He joyfully undertook this mission, in which he suffered much, being often hunted by the Protestants to murder him, and assailed by many calumnies and plots. Amid all these dangers and struggles his constancy remained invincible, and under the blessing and care of God he is said to have recalled seventy-two thousand of these heretics to the Catholic Faith, among whom were many distinguished by rank and learning.

Lesson VI

After the death of Bishop Granier, who had procured his appointment as Coadjutor, he was consecrated Bishop upon the 3rd day of December, 1602. In that office he was truly a burning and a shining light, showing all around a bright example of godliness, zeal for the discipline of the Church, ardent love of peace, tenderness to the poor, and indeed, of all graces. For the greater ornament of God's worship he established a new Order of Nuns, which is named from the Visitation of the Blessed Virgin. These nuns follow the Rule of St. Augustine, but Francis added thereto several additional constitutions distinguished by wisdom, prudence, and tenderness. He enlightened the Church by writings full of heavenly teaching, and pointing out a safe and simple road to Christian perfection. In the 55th year of his age, while on his way from France to Annecy, after saying Mass at Lyons on the Feast of St. John the Evangelist, he was seized with fatal illness, and on the next day passed from earth to heaven, in the year of our Lord 1622. His body was carried to Annecy and honorably buried in the Church of the nuns of the Visitation, where it soon began to be distinguished for miracles. The truth of these having been proved, Alexander VII, the Supreme Pontiff, enrolled his name among those of the Saints, and appointed for his Feast day the 29th of January. And the Supreme Pontiff, Pius IX, on the advice of the Congregation of Sacred Rites, declared him a Doctor of the Universal Church.

Lessons VII–IX from first set in the Common of Doctors (Sermon by St. Augustine)

January 30 ~ St. Martina

Virgin Martyr ~ Semiduplex

All from Common except what follows

Lessons I–III from the occurring Scripture

Lesson IV

Martina was a maiden of a most illustrious Roman family, daughter of a Consul. She lost her parents while still very young, and, being inflamed with Christian zeal, she distributed her wealth, whereof she had abundance, with great profusion among the poor. Under the Emperor Alexander, she was commanded to sacrifice to the imaginary gods, and refused with much boldness to commit this great wickedness. Upon this she was again and again scourged, and mangled with iron prongs and hooks, and pieces of broken pottery. Her limbs were cut off piece by piece with sharp swords, and boiling tallow poured upon the living trunk. Lastly she was sent to be eaten publicly by the wild beasts in the amphitheatre, but by the will of God they would not touch her, and she was then thrown upon a burning pile, but still remained alive.

Lesson V

Some of her tormentors were so moved by the spectacle, that they repented, and, by the grace of God confessing the faith of Christ, through which she remained constant, were themselves tortured and beheaded. Martina herself lay praying, with a brightness on her face, while a matter like milk oozed from her body along with the blood, emitting a soft, sweet smell. She was as it were unconscious of an earthquake and most violent thunderstorm which arose and was raging, and while the lightning struck temples, and melted statues, she seemed in spirit rather to be seated above on a queenly throne, praising God in heaven among the Blessed.

Lesson VI

The judge, being infuriated at what had taken place, and chiefly at her unbending firmness, ordered the head of the martyr to be cut off. At the moment this was done, a peal which shook the city was heard, like a voice calling her home, and so great was the consternation, that it was made the means of conversion for many idolaters. The holy body of Martina, wherein she had suffered in the Pontificate of Urban I, was discovered in the time of Urban VIII in the very old Church called after her, situated at the foot of the Capitoline Hill, near the Mamertine Prison, along with the bodies of the holy martyrs Concordius, Epiphanius, and others. The Church was then altered and restored and handsomely decorated, and then the body was replaced in it, amid public rejoicings, with a solemn ceremony and procession.

Lessons VII–IX from first set in the Common of Virgins (Sermon by St. Gregory)

January 31 ~ St. John Bosco

Confessor ~ Duplex

All from Common except what follows

Lessons I–III from the occurring Scripture

Lesson IV

John Bosco, born in the poor town of Castelnuovo d'Asti, and having lost his father at the age of two, was raised by his mother in a most saintly manner, and from his earliest years gave evidence of an extraordinary future. Docile and pious, he had a remarkable influence over those of his own age, whose fights he soon began to settle, and whose indecent words and improper jokes he stopped. Then he busied himself with drawing them to him by good stories, by including prayers in their games, by repeating in an attractive way the complete sermons he had heard in church, and with persuading them to receive the sacraments of Penance and of the Holy Eucharist without delay and frequently. His unassuming manner, his affability, and his innocence drew everyone to him. Although pressed with difficulties at home, and forced to work hard in his youth, he ardently desired with trust in God to become a priest.

Lesson V

His wish was fulfilled, and he went first to Chieri, and then to Turin, where under the direction of Blessed Joseph Cafasso, he made rapid progress in the science of the Saints and in the learning of moral theology. There moved by divine grace and personal liking he began to take an interest in the youths, whom he taught the rudiments of the Christian religion. Their number increased day by day, and notwithstanding great and persistent difficulties, under divine inspiration he made a foundation for them in that section of the city called the Valdocco, on which he began to spend all his energy. Shortly after, with the help of the Blessed Virgin, who in a vision to him when a boy had revealed his future, John founded the Society of the Salesians, whose principal purpose was to be the saving of youthful souls for Christ. In like manner he founded a new family of nuns, who were called the daughters of St. Mary Auxiliatrix, and who would do for poor girls what the Salesians were doing for boys. To these he finally attached the Third Order of Salesian Cooperators, who by their piety and zeal were to assist in the educational work of the Salesians. And so in a short time he made great contributions both to the Christian and Civil society.

Lesson VI

Filled with zeal for souls, he spared himself no labour and no expense to build recreational centers for the young, orphanages, schools for working children, schools and homes for the training of the young, and churches far and wide throughout the world. At the same time he did not stop spreading the Faith throughout the Subalpine country by word and by example, and throughout the whole of Italy, by writing and editing good books and by distributing the same, and in the foreign missions to which he sent numerous preachers. A simple and upright man, bent on every good work, he shone with all manner of virtue, which was fostered by his intense and ardent charity. With his mind always on God, and showered with heavenly gifts, this holy man of God was not disturbed by threats, nor tired by work, nor overwhelmed by care, nor upset by adversity. He recommended three works of piety to his followers: to receive as frequently as possible the sacraments of Penance and of Holy Eucharist, to cultivate a devotion to St. Mary Auxiliatrix, and to be the most loyal children of the Sovereign Pontiff. It should also be mentioned that John Bosco in very difficult circumstances went to the Pope more than once to console him in the evils coming from laws at that time passed against the Church. With a life of such accomplishments he died on the 31st day of January, 1888. Illustrious for his many miracles, the Supreme Pontiff, Pius XI, beatified him in 1929. Five years later, in the nineteenth centenary of the anniversary of our redemption, he was canonized among a vast gathering come to the Eternal City from every part of the world.

Lesson VII

From the Holy Gospel according to St. Matthew (Matt 18:1–5)

At that time: the disciples came unto Jesus, saying: Who is the greatest in the kingdom of heaven? And so on.

Homily by St. John Chrysostom

Do you see in how many ways the Lord leads us on to the care of our lesser brethren? Therefore do not say: He is only a taxpayer, or a shoemaker, or a farmer, or that he is foolish, that you may in that way look down on him. So that you will not fall into such evil, reflect on how many ways he leads you to act humbly and take care of them. He placed a child in their midst and said: "Become like little children;" and: "Whosoever receives one such little child for my sake, receives me;" and: "Who causes one to sin, will suffer the severest penalties." If therefore God so rejoices over a little one that has been found, why do you despise those for whom God is so solicitous, when you should trade your own life for one of those little ones? So great indeed is God's care for a soul that he did not spare his own Son. Wherefore, I entreat you, the first thing in the morning when we go out of the house, let us have in mind this purpose and this concern, to save someone in danger. I do not speak here of a visible danger, for this is not danger at all, but of danger to the soul, which the devil prepares for men.

Lesson VIII

You say it is hard to tolerate the bad. You should be joined to him in love, to lead him away from vice, to convert him and lead him back to virtue. But he does not follow, you say, nor takes he advice. How do you know this? Have you exhorted him and tried to correct him? I have often exhorted, you will say. How often? Once or twice. Do you call that very often? Even if you were to do it for your whole life, you should neither stop nor despair. Do you not see how God always encourages us through the Prophets, through the Apostles, and through the Evangelists? What follows? Do we act rightly? Do we obey in everything? Not at all. Should there be an end, then, to admonishing?

Lesson IX

There is indeed nothing as precious as a soul. "For what does it profit a man if he gain the whole world, and suffer the loss of his soul?" But love of money has destroyed and cast down everything, it has thrust aside the fear of God, taking possession of the soul as a tyrant occupies a fortress. And so we neglect our own salvation and that of our children. Great is that folly, and our children are worse than servants. Why do I speak of servants? If you have a mule, you take care to give it the best groom, one who is not worthless, nor a thief, nor a drunk, and one not inexperienced in his work. If, however, it is necessary to have a teacher for your son, do you take anyone you may meet by chance and give no thought to selection, although there is no profession greater than this one? What is equal to that profession which is concerned with directing the soul and forming the mind and character of the young? He who has such a task should show more diligence than any painter or sculptor.

FEASTS OF FEBRUARY

February 1 ~ St. Ignatius of Antioch

Bishop & Martyr ~ Duplex

All from Common except what follows

Lessons I–III from the occurring Scripture.

Lesson IV

From the book of saint Jerome, Presbyter, on the Ecclesiastical writers.

Ignatius was the third Bishop of Antioch after the Apostle Peter. When Trajan stirred up his persecution, he was condemned to be devoured by wild beasts, and sent to Rome in chains. When on his journey there he arrived at Smyrna, where Polycarp, the disciple of John, was Bishop, he wrote an Epistle to the Ephesians, another to the Magnesians, a third to the Trallians, and a fourth to the Romans and after leaving Smyrna, he addressed a further Epistle to the Philadelphians, and another to the Smyrnians, along with a private Epistle to Polycarp, to whose care he commended the Church of Antioch. In this last he quotes a passage regarding the Person of Christ from the Gospel, which I have recently translated.

Lesson V

It is fitting that, as we have made mention of a man of so much importance, we should also note briefly the Epistle which he addressed to the Romans. "I am on my way," says he, "from Syria to Rome, and am already fighting with beasts on sea and on land all the way. I may say I am chained day and night to ten leopards, for indeed the soldiers, who have charge of me, are no better. The more courteous I am to them, the worse they use me. But still their wickedness is good schooling for me, though I know that my mere sufferings cannot in themselves gain me justification. I earnestly wish for the beasts which are to devour me; at any rate, I pray they may put me out of pain quickly, and fly on me willingly, that I be not like some other Martyrs, whose bodies the animals have refused to touch. If I find that they will not come on, I will use force, I will urge myself, that I may be devoured. Let me be, my little children I know what is good for me."

Lesson VI

"I feel now that I am beginning to be Christ's disciple; I desire none of those things which are seen, if so be I may find Christ Jesus. I care not that there come upon me fire, or cross, or wild beasts, or breaking of my bones, or sundering of my members, or destruction of my whole body, yea, or all the torments of the devil, if only I may win Christ." When he was brought condemned to the theatre, and heard the roaring of the beasts which were to devour him, he felt so strong an eagerness to suffer, that he cried out "I am Christ's wheat, and so let the beasts' teeth be my mill, that I may be ground, and be found to make good bread." He suffered in the eleventh year of Trajan. What was left of his body lies at Antioch, in the graveyard outside the gate which leads toward Daphne.

Lesson VII

From the Holy Gospel according to St John (John 12:24–26)

In that time Jesus said to his disciples: Amen, amen I say to you, unless the grain of wheat falling into the ground die, Itself remaineth alone. And so on.

Homily by St. Augustine, Bishop

The Lord Jesus was Himself a corn of wheat that was to die and bring forth much fruit; to die by the unbelief of the Jews, and to bring forth much fruit in the faith of the Gentiles. He, exhorting men to follow His steps, says "He that loves his life shall lose it." Now, these words may be understood in two ways. First: he that loves his life shall lose it, that is, If thou love life, thou wilt lose it; if thou wilt live for ever in Christ, refuse not to die for Christ. Or secondly: he that loves his life shall lose it; love not then that which thou shalt lose; love not this present life, so that thou be thereby in jeopardy of losing life eternal.

Lesson VIII

What this second interpretation is the meaning of the Gospel, appears most probably from the words which follow "And he that hates his life in this world, shall keep it unto life eternal." From which we may suppose the sense of the first words to be He that loves his life in this world shall lose it unto life eternal. This is a great and marvelous saying, showing how a man may so love life as to lose life, and so hate life as to keep life. If thou love it too well, then dost thou hate it; if thou hate it with a holy hatred, then dost thou love it. Blessed are they that, lest they should so love it as to lose it, so hate it as to keep it.

Lesson IX

Beware lest thou take these words "He that hates his life in this world shall keep it unto life eternal" as some do, for an approval of suicide. Some evil and perverse men, bloody and guilty murderers of themselves, do indeed throw themselves into the fire, drown themselves in water, and cast themselves down precipices, and so perish. This is not the teaching of Christ, Who, when the devil would have Him cast Himself down from a high place, answered "Get thee behind Me, Satan. It is written, Thou shalt not tempt the Lord thy God." Who also said to Peter, signifying by what death he should glorify God, "When thou wast younger thou didst gird thyself and didst walk where thou wouldst; But when thou shalt be old, thou shalt stretch forth thy hands, and another shall gird thee, and lead thee whither thou wouldst not." From which it is evident that he that would follow Christ's footsteps, must be slain, not by himself, but by another.

February 2 - THE PURIFICATION OF THE BLESSED VIRGIN MARY

Duplex II Class

All from Common of the Blessed Virgin Mary except what follows

Lesson I - Exod 13:1–3; 13:11–13

From the book of Exodus

And the Lord spoke to Moses, saying: Sanctify unto me every firstborn that openeth the womb among the children of Israel, as well of men as of beasts: for they are all mine. And Moses said to the people: When the Lord shall have brought thee into the land of the Chanaanite, as he swore to thee and thy fathers, and shall give it thee: Thou shalt set apart all that openeth the womb for the Lord, and all that is first brought forth of thy cattle: whatsoever thou shalt have of the male sex, thou shalt consecrate to the Lord. The firstborn of an ass thou shalt change for a sheep: and if thou do not redeem it, thou shalt kill it. And every firstborn of men thou shalt redeem with a price.

Lesson II - Lev 12:1–5

From the book of Leviticus

And the Lord spoke to Moses, saying: Speak to the children of Israel, and thou shalt say to them: If a woman having received seed shall bear a man child, she shall be unclean seven days, according to the days of the separation of her flowers. And on the eighth day the infant shall be circumcised: But she shall remain three and thirty days in the blood of her purification. She shall touch no holy thing, neither shall she enter into the sanctuary, until the days of her purification be fulfilled. But if she shall bear a maid child, she shall be unclean two weeks, according to the custom of her monthly courses, and she shall remain in the blood of her purification sixty-six days.

Lesson III - Lev 12:6–8

And when the days of her purification are expired, for a son, or for a daughter, she shall bring to the door of the tabernacle of the testimony, a lamb of a year old for a holocaust, and a young pigeon or a turtle for sin, and shall deliver them to the priest: Who shall offer them before the Lord, and shall pray for her, and so she shall be cleansed from the issue of her blood. This is the law for her that beareth a man child or a maid child. And if her hand find not sufficiency, and she is not able to offer a lamb, she shall take two turtles, or two young pigeons, one for a holocaust, and another for sin: and the priest shall pray for her, and so she shall be cleansed.

Lesson IV

Sermon by St. Augustine, Bishop

In old time it was written: "And of Zion shall it not be said: This and that man was born in her, and the Highest Himself shall establish her?" Blessed be the omnipotence of Him That was born! Blessed the glory of Him That came from heaven to earth! While yet He was borne in His

Mother's womb, He was saluted by John the Baptist; He was presented in the temple, and recognized by that famous, ancient, glorious, and worthy old man Simeon. As soon as he knew Him, he worshipped Him, and said "Lord, now lettest Thou thy servant depart in peace for mine eyes have seen thy Salvation."

Lesson V

He lingered in the world to see the birth of Him Who made the world. The old man knew the Child, and in that Child became a child himself, for in the love wherewith he regarded the Father of all, he felt his own years to be but as of yesterday. The old man Simeon bore the newborn Christ, and all the while, Christ was the old man's Lord. It had been told him by the Lord that he should not taste of death before he had seen the birth of the Lord's Christ. Now Christ is born, and all the old man's wishes on earth are fulfilled. He That came to a decrepit world came to an old man.

Lesson VI

He wished not to remain long in the world, but he longed to see Christ in the world, singing with the Prophet, and saying: "Show us thy mercy, O Lord, and grant us thy salvation." And now at last, that you may know that the cause of his joy was that this prayer was granted, he says: "Now lettest Thou thy servant depart in peace, for mine eyes have seen thy salvation." The Prophets have sung that the Maker of heaven and earth would converse on earth with men, an angel has declared that the Creator of flesh and spirit would come in the flesh; the unborn John, yet in the womb, has saluted the unborn Saviour yet in the womb. The old man Simeon has seen God, a little Child.

Lesson VII

From the Holy Gospel according to St Luke (Luke 2:22–32)

In that time, after the days of her purification according to the law of Moses were accomplished, they carried him to Jerusalem to present him to the Lord, as it is written in the law of the Lord. And so on.

Homily on this passage by St. Ambrose, Bishop

And, behold, there was a man in Jerusalem, whose name was Simeon, and the same man was just and devout, waiting for the consolation of Israel. The birth of the Lord is attested not only by Angels and Prophets, and shepherds, but also by elders and just men. Every age, and both sexes, as well as the miracles of the events themselves, are here to strengthen our faith. A virgin conceives, a barren woman bears, a dumb man speaks, Elizabeth prophesies, the wise man worships, the unborn child leaps, the widow praises, and the just man waites.

Lesson VIII

Well is he called just, who looked not for favor for himself, but for consolation for his people. He desired to be set free from the bondage of this frail body, but he waited to see the Promised One for he knew that blessed are the eyes that see Him. Then took he Him up in his arms, and blessed God, and said: "Lord, now lettest Thou thy servant depart in peace, according to thy word." Behold a just man, confined in the weary prison of the body, desiring to be dissolved and to begin to be with Christ. For to be dissolved and to be with Christ is much better.

Lesson IX

Whosoever will be dissolved and be with Christ, let him come into the Temple, let him come to Jerusalem, let him wait for the Lord's Christ, let him take hold on the Word of God, let him embrace it with good works, as it were with arms of faith and then let him depart in peace, for he shall not see death, who has seen life. Behold how the Lord's Birth overflows with abounding grace for all, and prophecy is not denied to the just, but to the unbelieving. Behold, Simeon prophesies that the Lord Jesus Christ is come for the fall and rising again of many; yea, He shall separate the just from the unjust by their merits, and according as our work shall be, so shall the true and righteous Judge command us to be punished or rewarded.

February 3 ~ St. Blaise

Bishop & Martyr ~ Simplex

Lessons I–II from the occurring Scripture.

Lesson III

Blaise was chosen Bishop of the city of Sebaste in Armenia, in which place he enjoyed a great reputation for virtue. When Diocletian began to make the Christians the objects of his insatiable cruelty, the Saint hid himself in a cave on Mount Argæus, where he lay till he was found by some of the soldiers of Agricolaus the governor, who were out hunting. He was brought before the governor, who commanded him to be thrown into irons. While he was in prison, Blaise healed many of the sick, who were brought to him on account of his reputation of saintliness, and among others a boy who had been despaired of by the physicians, and who was at the point of death, from a fish bone which had become fixed in his throat. Blaise appeared twice before the governor, but neither cajolements nor threats could induce him to sacrifice to the gods. He was first beaten with rods, and afterwards put on the rack, where his flesh was mangled with iron combs. At last his head was cut off, whereby he finished a noble testimony to the faith which is in Christ our Lord. He bore witness on the 3rd day of February, in the year of salvation 316.

February 4 ~ St. Andrew Corsini

Confessor Bishop ~ Duplex

All from Common except what follows

Lessons I–III from the occurring Scripture—in Lent: from the Common

Lesson IV

Andrew was born at Florence, of the noble family of Corsini, upon the 30th day of November, in the year 1302. His birth was a special answer to prayer, and his parents vowed him to the Blessed Virgin. God foreshowed even before his birth what he was to be. While his mother was great with child she dreamt that she brought forth a wolf, which ran to the Carmelite Church and was changed into a lamb as soon as it reached the porch. The lad was brought up in godliness and learning becoming his rank, but turned to bad courses; wherefore his mother often rebuked him. Nevertheless, when he knew how his parents had vowed him to the Maiden Mother of God, the love of God touched his heart, and the vision of his mother moving him, he betook himself to the Institute of the Carmelites. In that place the devil exercised him with many and diverse temptations, but could not break him off from his determination to profess as a friar. He was soon after sent to Paris, where he finished his studies at the University, and took his degree; after which he returned to his own country, and was set over the houses of his order in Tuscany.

Lesson V

The Bishop of Fiesole being dead, the Church in that place chose Andrew Corsini for his successor. He held himself altogether unworthy of that office, and for a long time lay hidden and unknown, till he was betrayed by the voice of a child marvelously speaking, and found outside the city. Then, lest he should seem to resist the Will of God, he took the Bishopric, in the year 1360. Being dignified with this office, he set himself to a more perfect exercise of the virtue of humility, whereof he was already a diligent practicer. He was eminent in watchfulness over the flock committed to his charge, joining thereto great tenderness and liberality towards the poor. He continued instant in prayer and watching. Thus was he so adorned with these and many other virtues, and even with the gift of prophecy, that the fame of his holy life was in the mouths of all men.

Lesson VI

Urban V, moved by these things, sent him as his Legate to quiet disturbances at Bologna. He endured much in the discharge of this duty, calming with great wisdom the angry passions of the citizens, who had broken out into civil war, and when peace was restored, he returned home. Shortly after, he received from the Blessed Virgin a warning of his approaching death, and being worn out with his unceasing toil, and the rigor of his voluntary mortifications, he passed to the kingdom of heaven, upon the 6th day of January, in the year of our Lord 1373, and the 71st of his own age. His name became illustrious for many and great miracles, and Urban VIII enrolled him in the number of the Saints. His body rests at Florence in the Church of his Order, and is looked on with great reverence by the citizens, to whom, even in these days, he has more than once shown himself a protector.

Lessons VII–IX from the first set in the Common of Confessor Bishops (Sermon by St. Gregory)

In Lent: Lesson VII from the Proper of Time is read as a Lesson IX commemoration of the Lenten Feria

February 5 ~ St. Agatha

Virgin Martyr ~ Duplex

All from Common except what follows

Lessons I–III from the Common of Virgin Martyrs (Ecclesiasticus)

Lesson IV

The Maiden Agatha was a Sicilian of noble birth. The citizens of Palermo and Catania dispute as to which city had the honor of being her birthplace. It was at Catania that, during the persecution under the Emperor Decius, she won the crown of a glorious martyrdom. She was equally celebrated for her beauty and her chastity, and Quintianus, Prætor of Sicily, conceived a passion for her. He tried every sort of device to overcome her modesty, and when he found it impossible to make her consent to his wishes, he caused her to be arrested on a charge of Christian superstition, and handed over to a woman named Aphrodisia to be corrupted. The company, however, of this woman had no effect in shaking her constancy in the Christian worship, nor her settled determination to preserve her purity. Aphrodisia therefore reported to Quintianus that she was only throwing away her pains on Agatha. He ordered her to be brought before him. "Thou," said he, "art the daughter of a noble family; dost thou feel no shame in living the degraded and slavish life of a Christian?" Agatha answered him, "The lowliness and bondage of a Christian are far nobler than the estate and pride of a king."

Lesson V

Then the Prætor, being incensed against her, gave her the alternative of either sacrificing to the gods, or being submitted to the torture; and as she remained firm in the faith, she was beaten and sent back to prison. The next day she was brought forth, and, because her resolution was still unshaken, she was stretched on the rack and tortured with pieces of white-hot metal. Then her breasts were cut off. When Agatha received this injury she cried out to Quintianus, "Cruel tyrant, art thou not ashamed to do this to me, having thyself sucked at a mother's breast?" She was remanded again to prison and put in irons. That night an old man, who called himself an Apostle of Christ, came to her, and healed her wounds. The following day she was brought for the last time before the Prætor. Her constancy was unmoved, and she was rolled on sharp potsherds and live embers.

Lesson VI

At that time the whole city was shaken with a great earthquake, and two of the Prætor's dearest friends, Silvinus and Falconius, were killed by falling walls. The townspeople were in an uproar, and Quintianus, in fear of a riot, ordered Agatha, who was half dead, to be carried back to prison quietly. Then she made the following prayer: "O Lord, Who hast been my Keeper from my childhood, Who hast taken from me all love for this present world, Who hast strengthened me so that I am more than conqueror over the cruelty of the executioners, receive my spirit." Having said this, she passed to heaven. She finished her testimony on the 5th day of February, in the year of our Lord 251. Her body was buried by the Christians.

Lessons VII–IX from the final set in the Common of Virgins (Sermon by St. John Chrysostom)

In Lent: Lesson VII from the Proper of Time is read as a Lesson IX commemoration of the Lenten Feria

February 6 ~ St. Titus

Confessor Bishop ~ Duplex

All from Common except what follows

Lessons I–III from the occurring Scripture—in Lent: from the Common

Lesson IV

Titus, bishop of the Cretans, was hardly cultivated by the words of Paul the Apostle in the sacraments and mysteries of the Christian faith, when he was found to have shone with that light of holiness in the wandering Church, so that he deserved to be recruited among the disciples of that same Doctor of the Gentiles. Being taken to share in the work of preaching, he so endeared himself to Paul by his faithfulness and zeal in declaring the Gospel, that the Apostle says: "When I came to Troas to preach Christ's Gospel, and a door was opened unto me of the Lord, I had no rest in my spirit, because I found not Titus my brother, but, taking my leave of them, I went from thence into Macedonia." And again he says: "When we were come into Macedonia, our flesh had no rest, but we were troubled on every side; without were fightings, within were fears. Nevertheless, God, that comforts those that are downcast, comforted us by the coming of Titus."

Lesson V

It was this affection of Paul toward Titus, which had induced him to send him to Corinth upon a Mission which mainly concerned the collection of alms from the charity of the faithful for the relief of the poor Hebrew Church. This mission Titus discharged with such wisdom and gentleness, that he not only strengthened the Corinthians in the faith, but also stirred up in them an earnest desire, a mourning, a fervent mind toward Paul, their earliest teacher. Many were the other journeys by land and sea which Titus undertook in order to sow the seed of God's word among men of diverse nations, tongues, and countries. Filled with bold loyalty to the banner of the Cross, he went with Paul to the island of Crete. Of this Church, the Apostle himself made him the first Bishop; and we may not doubt that, as such, he was what his Teacher bade him be, in all things showing himself a pattern of good works, in doctrine, in integrity, in gravity.

Lesson VI

Like a lamp, he gave forth the light of faith in the midst of men sitting in the darkness of idolatry and falsehood, as in the shadow of death. He is said to have sweated mightily to unfurl the banner of the Cross among the Dalmatians. He was full of days and good works, when, upon a 4th of January, in the 94th year of his age, he died one of those deaths which are precious in the sight of the Lord. He was buried in the Church of which the Apostle had made him the minister. His praises have been mostly written by St. John Chrysostom and St Jerome. The 4th of January is the day upon which his name is read in the Roman Martyrology, but Pope Pius IX assigned for his Festival, to be kept with an Office and Mass by the clergy secular and regular throughout the Catholic world, the first free day afterwards.

Lessons VII–IX from the Common of Evangelists (Sermon by St. Gregory)

Lesson IX ~ Commemoration for St. Dorothy, Virgin Martyr

The maiden Dorothy, of Caesarea in Cappadocia, was betrayed to Apricius, the Præfect, by her two sisters who had denied the faith, Chrysta and Callista, in the hope that he would induce her to do likewise. She was arrested, but it came not to pass as they hoped. On the contrary, she brought them back to the Christian worship, and they received martyrdom. She was long tormented upon the rack, and scourged with palm branches, and in the end was beheaded, receiving the double palm of virginity and martyrdom.

In Lent: Lesson VII from the Proper of Time is read as a Lesson IX commemoration of the Lenten Feria

February 7 ~ St. Romuald

Abbot ~ Duplex

All from Common except what follows

Lessons I–III from the occurring Scripture—in Lent: from the Common

Lesson IV

The holy Abbot Romuald was the son of Sergius, of a noble family of Ravenna. While he was still very young, he went to a neighboring monastery at Classis to do penance. While he was there he heard a discourse by a monk, which stirred him up strongly to aim at godliness of living; and he had afterwards in the Church by night two visions in which the blessed servant of God Apollinaris foretold to him that he should become a monk himself. He accordingly did so; and soon afterwards betook himself to one Marinus, whose holy life and strict discipline were then much celebrated in all the coasts of the Venetians, that he might by his teaching and guidance attain towards the hard and lofty point of perfection.

Lesson V

The more he was assailed by the wiles of Satan and the unkindness of men, the more did he exercise himself in lowliness, with continual fasting and prayer, and rejoice in thinking of heavenly things with abundance of tears. And all the while he bore so bright a face as gladdened all who looked on him. He was held in great honor by princes and kings, and his counsel moved many to leave the blandishments of the world and withdraw to the desert. He had such a burning desire to obtain the crown of martyrdom that he set out for Pannonia on purpose to seek it, but, falling into sickness whenever he went forward though growing strong again whenever he drew back, he thought to return home.

Lesson VI

God worked miracles by him both during his life and after his death, and likewise gave him the gift of prophecy. Like the Patriarch Jacob, he saw a ladder reaching from earth to heaven, and men in white garments ascending and descending upon it, in whom he marvelously knew were represented the monks of the Camaldolese Institute, of which he was the founder. At the age of 120 years, of which he had spent 100 in serving God in great hardness, he passed into His Presence, in the year of Salvation 1027. Five years after his death his body was found incorrupt, and laid in a magnificent grave in the Church of his order at Fabriano.

Lessons VII–IX from the first set in the Common of Abbots (Sermon by the Venerable Bede)

In Lent: Lesson VII from the Proper of Time is read as a Lesson IX commemoration of the Lenten Feria

February 8 ~ St. John de Matha

Confessor ~ Duplex

All from Common except what follows

Lessons I–III from the occurring Scripture—in Lent: from the Common

Lesson IV

John de la Mata, the founder of the Order of the Most Holy Trinity for the Ransom of Prisoners, was born at Faucon, in Provence, upon Midsummer's Day, in the year 1169, and was the child of parents equally distinguished for their rank and their godly life. He went for his education first to Aix and then to Paris. At the University of Paris, where he went through the course of Divinity and took the degree of Doctor, he became eminent for learning and virtue. For this reason the Bishop of Paris ordained him Priest, an honor from which his lowliness caused him to shrink, in the hope that he should induce him to remain at Paris, and be a bright example of wisdom and manners to the students who resorted there. He offered up the Holy Sacrifice to God for the first time in the private Chapel of the Bishop, and in the presence of that Prelate and diverse other persons. In the midst of the ceremony, a vision from God appeared to John. There appeared to him an angel, clad in raiment white and glistering; having sewn on his breast a cross of red and blue. His arms were crossed before him, and his hands were upon the heads of two slaves, one a Christian and the other a Moor. And immediately the man of God was in the spirit, and knew that he was called to the work of ransoming captives from the infidels.

Lesson V

That he might set himself with due forethought to the carrying out of his work, he withdrew into a certain desert, and there, by the will of God, he found Felix de Valois, who had already spent many years in that place. With him he joined company, and they passed three years together in continual prayer, meditation, and all spiritual exercises. It came to pass, one day, when they were sitting on the bank of a spring, that there came to them a stag having between his horns a cross of red and blue. Felix cried out in wonder at that sight, and John then told him of the vision that had appeared to him when he was saying his first Mass. Thenceforth they gave themselves with redoubled fervor to prayer, and, being three times warned in sleep, they determined to go to Rome, and pray the Pope to institute an Order for the ransom of prisoners. They arrived at the time of the election of Innocent III, who received them courteously, and entertained in his mind their petition. While he was in consideration, he went to the Lateran Cathedral on the second Feast of St. Agnes, and there, while Mass was being solemnly sung, at the moment of the elevation of the Sacred Host, there appeared to him an angel, clad in raiment white and glistering, having sewn on his breast a cross of red and blue, and making as though he would free prisoners. Thereupon the Pope founded the Order, commanding that it should be called the Order of the Most Holy Trinity for the Ransom of prisoners, and that they who professed in it should be clad in white raiment, having sewn on their breasts a cross of red and blue.

Lesson VI

The Order being thus established, the holy Founders returned into France, and built their first Convent at Cerfroid, in the diocese of Meaux. Felix remained in charge of this house, and John went back to Rome with several companions. To them Innocent gave the house, Church, and hospital of St. Thomas de Formis on the Cœlian Mount, with great endowments and property. Moreover he gave them a letter of introduction to Miramolin, King of Morocco, and they began with bright hopes the work of ransoming prisoners. John next betook himself to Spain, a great part of which was then oppressed under the yoke of the Saracens, and stirred up the hearts of the kings, princes, and all the faithful to have pity on slaves and the poor. He built Convents, founded Hospitals, and ransomed many bondsmen, to the great gain of souls. At last he returned to Rome, still busied in good works, but worn out by unceasing toil, and weakened by sickness. As he drew near the end of his earthly pilgrimage, his burning love for God and for his neighbor suffered no diminution. He called together his brethren, and earnestly exhorted them to go on with that work of ransom which had been pointed out to them from heaven, and then fell asleep in the Lord, on the 21st day of December, 1213. His body was buried with due honor in the Church of St. Thomas de Formis.

Lessons VII–IX from the first set in the Common of Confessor Non-Bishops (Sermon by St. Gregory)

In Lent: Lesson VII from the Proper of Time is read as a Lesson IX commemoration of the Lenten Feria

February 9 ~ St. Cyril of Alexandria

Confessor & Doctor ~ Duplex

All from Common except what follows

Lessons I–III from the occurring Scripture—in Lent: from the Common

Lesson IV

The praises of Cyril of Alexandria have been celebrated not only by one writer or another, but have even been registered in the acts of the Ecumenical Councils of Ephesus and Chalcedon. He was born of distinguished parents, and was the nephew of Theophilus, Pope of Alexandria. While he was still young he displayed marks of his excellent understanding. After giving a deep study to letters and science he betook himself to John, Bishop of Jerusalem, to be perfected in the Christian faith. After his return to Alexandria, and the death of Theophilus, he was raised to that see. In this office he kept ever before his eyes the type of the Shepherd of souls as it had been laid down by the Apostle; and by ever adhering thereto deservedly earned the glory of a holy Bishop.

Lesson V

Zeal for the salvation of souls was kindled in him, and he undertook all care to keep in the faith and in soundness of life the flock committed unto him, and to preserve them from the poisonous pastures of infidelity and heresy; hence, in accordance with the laws, he caused the followers of Novatian to be expelled from the city, and those Jews to be punished who had been induced by rage to plan a massacre of the Christians. His eminent care for the preservation of the Catholic faith pure and undefiled shone forth especially in his controversy against Nestorius, Patriarch of Constantinople, who asserted that Jesus Christ had been born of the Virgin Mary as man only and not as God, and that the Divinity had been bestowed upon Him because of His merits. Cyril first attempted to convert

Nestorius, but when he found this hopeless he denounced him to the Supreme Pontiff Saint Celestine I.

Lesson VI

As delegate of Pope Celestine I, Cyril presided at the Council of Ephesus where the Nestorian heresy was condemned, Nestorius was deprived of his see, and the Catholic doctrine as to the unity of Person in Christ and the divine Motherhood of the glorious Virgin Mary was laid down amid the rejoicings of all the people, who escorted the bishops to their lodgings with a torchlight procession. For this reason, Nestorius and his followers made Cyril the object of slanders, insults, and persecutions which he bore with profound patience, having all his care for the purity of the faith, and taking no heed to what the heretics might say or try against him. At length he died a holy death, in the year of salvation 444 and of his own episcopate the 32nd. After vast work for the Church of God, and leaving behind him diverse writings directed either against heathens and heretics or to the exposition of the holy Scriptures and of Catholic doctrine, the Supreme Pontiff Leo XIII extended to the Universal Church the Office and Mass of this most eminent champion of the Catholic faith and light of the Eastern Church.

Lessons VII–IX from the second set in the Common of Doctors (Sermon by St. Hilary)

Lesson IX - Commemoration of St. Apollonia, Virgin Martyr

Apollonia was an aged virgin of Alexandria, who, in the year of salvation 249, in the reign of the Emperor Decius, was brought before idols to worship them, but refused, declaring that Christ Jesus is True God, and that to Him worship is due. The cruel executioners beat and pulled out all her teeth, and threatened to burn her alive if she would not deny Christ. She answered to them that for Christ Jesus' sake she was ready to die. Being taken to the place of execution she stood for a few moments as if in doubt, and then, the fire of the Holy Ghost burning up in her heart, she broke from those that held her, and leapt of her own accord into the flames. Her body was quickly consumed, and her soul departed pure to obtain the eternal crown of martyrdom.

In Lent: Lesson VII from the Proper of Time is read as a Lesson IX commemoration of the Lenten Feria

February 10 - St. Scholastica

Virgin - Duplex

All from Common except what follows

Lessons I–III from the occurring Scripture—in Lent: from the Common

Lesson IV

From the Second Book of the Dialogues of Pope St. Gregory

Scholastica, the sister of our Venerable Father Benedict, was hallowed unto the Lord Almighty from the time of infancy. Her custom was to come to see her brother once every year. And when she came, the man of God went down unto her, not far from the gate, but, as it were, within the borders of his monastery. And there was a day when she came, as her custom was, and her venerable brother went down to her, and his disciples with him. Then they passed the whole day together praising God and speaking to each other of spiritual things; and when the night came, they broke bread together. While they were yet at table conversing together on spiritual things, the hour grew late. Then the holy woman, his sister, besought him, saying "Leave me not, I pray thee, this night, but let us speak even until morning of the gladness of the eternal life." He answered her: "What is it that thou sayest, my sister? I can by no means remain out of my cell." Now the firmament was so clear that there were no clouds in the sky. Then the holy nun, when she had heard the words of her brother, that he would not abide with her, clasped her hands on the table, and laid her face on her hands, and besought the Lord Almighty. And it came to pass that when she lifted up her head from the table, there were great thunderings and lightnings, and a flood of rain, insomuch that neither the venerable Benedict nor the brethren that were with him could move as much as a foot over the threshold of the place where they sat.

Lesson V

Now when the holy woman laid her head in her hands upon the table, she wept bitterly, and as she wept, the clearness of the sky was turned to a tempest. As she prayed, immediately the flood followed. And the time was so, that she lifted up her head when it thundered, and when she had lifted up her head, the rain came. When the man of God saw that he could not return to his monastery, because of the lightnings, and thunderings, and the great rain, he was sorrowful and grieved, saying: "Almighty God forgive thee, my sister; what is this that thou hast done?" She answered him: "Behold, I besought thee, and thou wouldest not hear; I besought my God, and He has heard me; if, therefore, thou wilt, go forth, leave me alone, and go thy way to thy monastery." But he could not, and so he tarried in the same place, not willingly, but of necessity. And so it came to pass that they slept not all that night, but fed one another with discourse on spiritual things.

Lesson VI

And when the morning was come, the worshipful woman arose, and went unto her own cell, and the man of God went back to his monastery. And, behold, after three days he was sitting in his cell, and he lifted up his eyes to heaven, and saw the soul of his sister, delivered from the body, fly to heaven in a bodily shape like a dove. Wherefore he rejoiced because of the glory that was revealed in her, and gave thanks to Almighty God in hymns and praises, and made known to the brethren that she was dead. He commanded them also to go and take up her body, and bring it to his monastery, and lay it in the grave which he had made ready for himself. Whereby it came to pass that the two who had always been of one mind in the Lord, even in death were not divided.

Lessons VII–IX from the first set in the Common of Virgins (Sermon by St. Gregory)

In Lent: Lesson VII from the Proper of Time is read as a Lesson IX commemoration of the Lenten Feria

February 11 ~ Apparition of the Blessed & Immaculate Virgin Mary at Lourdes

Major Duplex
All from Common of the Blessed Virgin Mary except what follows

Lesson IV

In the fourth year from the dogmatic definition of the Immaculate Conception of the Blessed Virgin, at the bank of the river Gave near the town of Lourdes of the diocese of Tarbes in France, the Virgin herself in a bend of the rock above the grotto of Massabielle, often showed herself to a certain girl, called in the vernacular tongue Bernadette, indeed most poor but noble and pious, to be seen. The Immaculate Virgin appeared with a young and kind appearance, clothed with a white garment and white veil, and girt with a blue girdle; she adorned her bare feet with a golden rose. On the first day of the apparition, which was the eleventh of February in the year 1858, she taught the girl the sign of the cross to be duly and piously made, and she incited her, by her example, to the recitation of the sacred rosary, turning over with her hand the chaplet, which before was hanging down from her arm: which she supplied also in the other apparitions. And on the second day of the apparition, the girl in the simplicity of her heart, fearing diabolic fraud, flung holy water on the Virgin; but the blessed Virgin, smiling gently, shewed her face more kindly to her. And when she appeared a third time, she invited the girl to the grotto for fifteen days. Thence she often addressed her; then commanded, that it might be declared to the priests, a chapel to be built there, and to be approached there for supplications in a manner of solemnity. Moreover she commanded that from the spring, which thus far was hidden under the sand but now was about to erupt, she might drink the water, and by it cleanse herself. Finally on the feast day of the Annunciation, to the girl earnestly inquiring her name, the Virgin, for whose appearance she was so often deemed worthy, the Virgin, her hands having been moved to her breast and her eyes raised to heaven, answered: "I am the Immaculate Conception."

Lesson V

The fame of favors becoming widespread, which the faithful were said to have received in the sacred grotto, in time the assembly of men increased, whom the sanctity of the place called to the grotto. Therefore the bishop of Tarbes, moved by the fame of the wonders and the purity of the girl, after a juridical inquiry of the happenings, approved by his decree the signs of the apparition to be supernatural, and permitted the worship of the immaculate Virgin in the same grotto. Soon a chapel was built; from that day the almost innumerable crowds of the faithful, for the purpose of prayer and supplication, from France, Belgium, Italy, Spain, and the other provinces of Europe and also from the remote regions of America arrived there in every year, and the name of the Immaculate of Lourdes becomes famous of countries everywhere. The water of the spring, having been carried into all parts of the world, restored health to the sick. And the Catholic world mindful of such great favors, built holy shrines there with wonderful work. Innumerable banners, as if monuments of received benefits, sent there by cities and nations, decorate the shrine of the Virgin with wonderful adornment. In this as if her own seat the immaculate Virgin is continually honored: indeed by day with prayers, religious chant and other solemn ceremonies; and by night with those solemn supplications, by which the almost infinite crowds of pilgrims proceed with candles and lit torches and sing the praises of the blessed Virgin.

Lesson VI

It is known by all for certain the pilgrimages of this sort to have stirred up faith, in a world becoming cold, the soul to have increased to profess the Christian law, and to have spread the worship of the immaculate Virgin in a wonderful manner. In which wonderful profession of faith the Christian people have the priests as leaders, who lead their people thence. The holy Bishops themselves also frequently visit the holy place, lead pilgrimages, and take part in more solemn feasts. Nor indeed is it rare to observe these empurpled fathers of the Roman Church approaching humbly in the manner of pilgrims. Even these Roman Pontiffs, for their piety towards the Immaculate of Lourdes, enhanced the sacred shrine with most noble gifts. Pius IX, with sacred indulgences, distinguished it with the privilege of an arch-confraternity and title of a minor Basilica; and willed the image honored there of the Godbearer, with solemn rite through his apostolic legate in France, to be adorned with a crown. And Leo XIII also conferred innumerable benefits and granted indulgences in the manner of a jubilee in the twenty-fifth year of the Apparition occurring, promoted pilgrimages by his authority and word, and arranged to complete by his name the solemn dedication of the Church under the title of the Rosary. He accumulated the extent of which benefits, when, with the asking of many bishops, he kindly granted a solemn feast to be celebrated under the title of the Apparition of the Blessed Virgin Mary Immaculate with a proper Office and proper Mass. Finally, supreme Pontiff Pius X, for his piety towards the Godbearer, and agreeing to the wishes of many holy Bishops, extended the same feast to the universal Church.

Lessons VII–IX from December 10 ~ Day 3 within the Octave of the Immaculate Conception

February 12 ~ Seven Holy Founders of the Servite Order

Confessors ~ Duplex

All from Common except what follows

Lessons I–III from the occurring Scripture—in Lent: from the Common

Lesson IV

In the thirteenth century, when the more cultured parts of Italy were rent by the dread dissension of the Emperor Frederick II and by bloody civil wars, the mercy of God set forth diverse men eminent for holiness, and among others raised up seven nobles of Florence, who were bound one to another in charity and gave an illustrious example of brotherly love. Their names were Bonfiglio Monaldi, Bonajuncta Manetti, Manetto Antalli, Amadeo de' Amidei, Uguccio de' Uguccioni, Sosteneo de' Sostenei, and Alexis de' Falconieri. Upon the holiday of the Assumption of the Virgin into heaven in the year 1233, they were praying in the oratory of a guild called the Guild of Praise, when the same Mother of God appeared to each one of them, and bade them embrace a life of greater holiness and perfection. These seven men discussed the matter with the Bishop of Florence, and then, considering neither the nobility of their birth nor their wealth, and clad in haircloth under vile and worn-out garments, withdrew into a little house in the country upon the eighth day of September, that they might begin their holier life upon the same day whereon the Mother of God herself had by her birth begun her life of holiness upon earth.

Lesson V

She showed by a miracle how acceptable in His sight should be their manner of life, for a short while after, when these seven men were begging alms from door to door through the city of Florence, it came to pass that some children, among whom was Saint Philip Benizi, who had then scarcely entered the fifth month of his age, called them blessed Mary's servants, by which name they were called ever after. To avoid meeting people, and in the desire to be alone, they all withdrew together to the solitude of Monte Senario, and there began a kind of heavenly life. They lived in caves and upon herbs and water only, while they wore out their bodies with watching and other hardships, while they contemplated unweariedly the sufferings of Christ and the woes of His most sorrowful Mother. One Good Friday, when their thoughts were fixed thereon more than ever, the Blessed Virgin appeared to them twice, and showed them her garments of mourning as those wherein they should clothe themselves. She bade them know that she would take it right well that they should raise up in the Church a new order to recall the memory of the sorrows which she bore beneath the Cross of the Lord. St. Peter, the illustrious martyr of the Order of Friars Preachers, learnt this not only from his familiar conversation with these holy men, but also from a special vision of the Mother of God, and it was on his incitement that they founded the regular Order called that of the Servites, or servants of the Blessed Virgin, which Order was afterward approved by the Supreme Pontiff Innocent IV.

Lesson VI

These holy men, when they had gathered to themselves some companions, began to go through the cities and towns of Italy, and especially of Tuscany, everywhere preaching Christ crucified, stilling contests among the citizens, and calling back almost countless backsliders into the path of grace. Neither did they make Italy only the field of their Gospel labors, but also France, Germany, and Poland. They passed away to be ever with the Lord when they had spread far and wide a sweet savor of Christ, and were famous also for the glory of signs and wonders. As one love of brotherhood and of the monastic life had joined them together upon earth, so one grave held their dead bodies, and one honor was paid them by the people. For this reason the Supreme Pontiffs Clement XI and Benedict XIII confirmed the honor which had for centuries been paid to them individually, and Leo XIII, after proof of their miracles which had been wrought by God on the common invocation of these saints, after their veneration had been sanctioned in the jubilee year of his priesthood, decreed to them the honors paid to Saints, and ordered that their memory should every year be kept throughout the universal Church with an office and Mass.

Lessons VII–IX from the first set in the Common of Abbots (Sermon by St. Jerome)

In Lent: Lesson VII from the Proper of Time is read as a Lesson IX commemoration of the Lenten Feria

February 14 ~ St. Valentine

Priest & Martyr ~ Simplex

Lessons I–III from the occurring Scripture

Lesson III: from Lesson IV of the first set in the Common of One Martyr (Homily by St. Augustine)

February 15 ~ Sts. Faustinus & Jovita

Martyrs ~ Simplex

Lessons I–III from the occurring Scripture

Lesson III

Faustinus and Jovita were brothers, born of a noble family at Brescia. While Trajan's persecution was raging, they were taken about in chains from one city of Italy to another, and exhibited in torture in each. This cruelty utterly failed to silence their confession of Christ, Whom they preached by their sufferings in every place where they were shown. They were afterwards kept for a long time at Brescia, where they were exhibited with wild beasts, and tormented with fire. Being both still alive, they were brought to Milan, without their chains having ever been taken off. At Milan they were tortured again with every invention of cruelty that could be devised. Nevertheless the great power of their faith made them more than conquerors, shining even as gold tried in the furnace. From Milan they were brought to Rome, where they were confirmed by Pope Evaristus, and where they were put to the torture again with extreme barbarity. They were afterwards shown in public at Naples, where the tormentors displayed their skill in diverse ways upon them. Here they were thrown chained into the sea, but the angels delivered them. Their stations of suffering, by their Godlike patience, and the wonderful Power displayed in them, had now turned many souls to Jesus. In the end they were carried back to Brescia, and, when Hadrian took the empire, they were there smitten with the axe, thus accepting the glorious crown of the martyrs.

February 18 ~ St. Simeon

Bishop & Martyr ~ Simplex

Lessons I–III from the occurring Scripture

Lesson III

Simeon, the son of Cleophas, was chosen the second Bishop of Jerusalem, in the year 62, being the first after James. Under the Emperor Trajan he was accused before the Proconsul Atticus, as being both a Christian and a relation of Christ, this being the time when all were arrested that were of the lineage of David. He underwent with great suffering the same things that were inflicted on our Saviour, and all men marveled to see with how great boldness and firmness he endured the grievous torment of the cross at his great age, for he was a hundred and twenty years old.

February 22 ~ Chair of St. Peter at Antioch

Major Duplex

All from Common of a Confessor Bishop except what follows

Lessons I–III as on January 18: Chair of St. Peter at Rome

Lesson IV

Sermon by St. Augustine, Bishop

The solemn Feast of today received from our forefathers the name of that of St Peter's Chair at Antioch, because there is a tradition that it was on this day that Peter, first of the Apostles, was enthroned in a Bishop's Chair. Rightly, therefore, do the Churches observe the first day of that Chair, the right to which the Apostle received for the salvation of the Churches from the Lord of the Churches Himself, with the words: "Thou art Peter, and upon this rock I will build My Church."

Lesson V

It was the Lord Himself Who called Peter the foundation of the

Church, and therefore it is right that the Church should reverence this foundation whereon her mighty structure rises. Justly is it written in the Psalm which we have just heard: "Let them exalt him in the congregation of the people, and praise him in the assembly of the elders." Blessed be God, Who has commanded that the Blessed Apostle Peter should be exalted in the congregation! Worthy to be honored by the Church is that foundation from which her towers rise, pointing to heaven!

Lesson VI

In the honor which is this day paid to the inauguration of the first Bishop's throne, an honor is paid to the office of all Bishops. The Churches testify one to another, that, the greater the Church's dignity, the greater the reverence due to her priests. While I confess how rightly religious custom has exalted this Feast in the estimation of all the Churches, the more do I wonder at the growth of that unhealthy error which at this day causes some unbelievers to lay food and wine upon the graves of the dead, as if souls once rid of the body had any longer any need of bodily refreshment.

Lesson VII

From the Holy Gospel according to St. Matthew (Matt 16:13–19)

At that time, Jesus came into the quarters of Cæsarea Philippi: and he asked his disciples, saying: Whom do men say that the Son of man is? And so on.

Homily by Pope St. Leo

The Lord asked His disciples Who men said that He was, and their answers were human as long as they were the answers of human reason unilluminated by Divine light. At last, when the glimmerings of earthly conjecture were spoken, he whose Apostleship is the first in dignity, was the first to confess his Lord. And Simon Peter answered and said: "Thou art the Christ, the Son of the living God." And Jesus answered and said unto him: "Blessed art thou, Simon Bar-Jona, for flesh and blood hath not revealed it unto thee, but My Father Which is in heaven." That is to say, For this cause art thou blessed, because My Father Himself has taught thee; the opinions of men have not beguiled thee, the voices of angels have not taught thee, not flesh and blood, but He, Whose Only begotten Son I am, has revealed Me unto thee.

Lesson VIII

Thus says the Lord unto Simon Peter: "And I say also unto thee, That thou art Peter." That is to say, Even as My Father has revealed unto thee concerning Me that I am God, even so now will I also reveal unto thee that thou art Peter; I am the sure Rock of defense, the Cornerstone Who makes both one, I am the Foundation besides Which other can no man lay, and thou also art a rock, in My Strength made hard, and those things whereof I by right am Lord, into thy hand do I give them, that thou mayst bear rule over them, for

Me, and with Me. "And upon this rock I will build My Church, and the gates of hell shall not prevail against it." Upon this strength of thine, whereof I am the Strength, I will build My eternal temple, and upon the truth of thy confession of Me I will make to rise My glorious Church whose spires shall pierce to heaven.

Lesson IX

Against this confession the gates of hell shall never prevail, neither shall the bonds of death take hold upon it. Thus says He That is faithful and true. And as this confession has power to lift up to heaven them that make it, so is it able to thrust down to hell them that deny it. Wherefore it is said unto the most blessed Peter: "And I will give unto thee the keys of the kingdom of heaven and whatsoever thou shalt bind on earth, shall be bound in heaven; and whatsoever thou shalt loose on earth, shall be loosed in heaven." This power passed indeed to the other Apostles also; this the Lord's will had effect in them; but it is not in vain that it is written that that was given to one which passed from him to all. To Peter alone were the keys given, and Peter is set as the pattern for all them that bear rule in the Church to follow. There remains therefore the right of Peter, wheresoever his judgment decrees justice. Neither is there anything too hard, or too lax, where there is nothing bound and nothing loosed, save when Peter binds or looses.

February 23 ~ St. Peter Damian

Bishop, Confessor, Doctor ~ Duplex

All from Common except what follows

Lessons I–III from the occurring Scripture—in Lent: from the Common

Lesson IV

The holy Doctor Peter Damian was born of respectable parents at Ravenna, about the year of our Lord 988. While he was still a suckling, his mother, overcome with the care of many children, cast him out to perish, but one of the women servants saved him when he was nigh to death, and fed him until natural affection appeared again in his mother, to whom she then gave him back. After the death of both his parents he lived with a brother who treated him like the lowest slave, and in whose house he underwent a hard bondage. Even while he was in this condition he gave a wonderful proof of his faith toward God and his dutiful love toward his father. It chanced that one day he found a considerable sum of money, but instead of using it to relieve his own poverty, he gave it all to a priest to offer God's sacrifice for the forgiveness of his father's sins. He had happily another brother called Damian, the same from whom he seems afterwards to have taken his surname. By him he was affectionately adopted, and put in the way of being educated. He made such progress in learning as astonished his teachers, and when he had won an eminent name in letters, he began to teach on his own accord with general applause. Meanwhile, lest his body should get the better of his mind, he constantly wore a hair-shirt under his softer clothes, and exercised himself in fasting, watching, and prayer. In the springtime of his age he was grievously tormented by the stings of the flesh; and sometimes, when the rebellions of lust seemed about to get the mastery over him at night, he threw himself into a freezing stream to check them. After this he would go about visiting consecrated places, and repeat the whole book of Psalms. He was most careful in relieving the poor, on whom he would wait with his own hands.

Lesson V

Desiring to attain to perfection of life he betook himself to the convent of Font-Avellano, in the diocese of Gubbio, in Umbria, a house founded by the blessed Ludolph, the disciple of St. Romuald, for the monks of the Holy Cross. He dwelt there not long before he was sent by his Abbot, first to the Abbey of Pomposia, and, secondly, to that of St. Vincent at Pietra Pertusa, both of which brotherhoods he greatly profited by his godly exhortations, discreet rules, and grave manners. After his return home, and the death of his Superior, he was chosen to rule the brethren of Avellano. Here he founded diverse new hermitages, and made the community so to flourish under his saintly direction, that he is esteemed the second Father and chief ornament of that Order. This healthful care of Peter was made a blessing to convents of other Rules than his own, to houses of Canons, and to the people. He was many ways profitable to the diocese of Urbino. He sat with Theuzo the Bishop of that See to judge of a most weighty matter, and led him by his counsel and assistance rightly to administer his Bishopric. He was foremost in contemplation of the things of God, in severity toward his own body, and in other things whereby to set a bright example of godliness. In consideration of these things the Supreme Pontiff Stephen IX, in the year 1057, created him, in spite of his own unwillingness and objections, a Cardinal of the Holy Roman Church, and appointed him Bishop of Ostia. This dignity Peter bore with the most splendid virtues, and adorned with works worthy of a Bishop.

Lesson VI

At the most anxious times he greatly sustained the Church of Rome and the Supreme Pontiffs by his teaching, by missions which he discharged, and by diverse other labors which he undertook on their behalf. He strove manfully even unto death against the heresies of the Nicolaïtans and the Simoniacs, by putting down which evils he reconciled the Church of Milan to that of Rome. He was one of the stoutest opponents of the Antipopes Benedict and Cadalus. He deterred Henry IV, King of Germany, from his wicked scheme for putting away his wife. He recalled the people of Ravenna to their bounden duty to the Bishop of Rome, and restored them to the communion of the Church. He reformed the Canons of Velletri, and brought them to lead more godly lives. There were hardly any Cathedral Churches, especially in the province of Urbino, of which he did not deserve well. In Gubbio, of which he had at one time the management, he abolished many things unseemly. He brought about improvements in many and diverse places, as if each were his special charge. In 1062 he gave up his dignities of Cardinal and Bishop, but he allowed his love toward his neighbors to know no diminution. He was particularly zealous in spreading abroad four devout practices: first, To fast every Friday in honor of the Holy Cross of Jesus Christ; second, To recite the Hours of the Blessed Mother of God, called also her Little Office; third, To sanctify Saturday in her honor; and fourth, and especially, to scourge oneself in punishment for sin committed. At length he departed to be with Christ, at Fænza, on his way back from his mission to Ravenna, on the 22nd of February, in the year 1072, at the height of his reputation for holiness, learning, miracles, and good works. His body is buried in the house of the Cistercians at Fænza, where the people resort often to his grave with great reverence. The citizens of Fænza, to whom he has been found good at need even to this day, have chosen him for their Patron in the presence of God. The supreme Pontiff Leo XII, finding that an Office and Mass in his memory as a Confessor and Bishop was in use in some dioceses and in the Camaldolese Order, by advice of the Sacred Congregation of Rites, added the title of Doctor, and extended the use of said Office and Mass to the whole Church.

Lessons VII–IX from the first set in the Common of Doctors (Sermon by St. Augustine)

In Lent: Lesson VII from the Proper of Time is read as a Lesson IX commemoration of the Lenten Feria

February 24 in Leap Years outside of Lent ~ Vigil of St. Matthias the Apostle

Apostle ~ Vigil

All from Common of the Vigil of Apostles

February 24 (Leap year: Feb 25) ~ St. Matthias the Apostle

Duplex II Class

All from Common of Apostles except what follows

Lesson I ~ Acts 1:15–18

From the Acts of the Apostles

In those days Peter rising up in the midst of the brethren, said: now the number of persons together was about a hundred and twenty: Men, brethren, the Scripture must needs be fulfilled, which the Holy Ghost spoke before by the mouth of David concerning Judas, who was the leader of them that apprehended Jesus: Who was numbered with us, and had obtained part of this ministry. And he indeed hath possessed a field of the reward of iniquity, and being hanged, burst asunder in the midst: and all his bowels gushed out.

Lesson II ~ Acts 1:19–22

And it became known to all the inhabitants of Jerusalem: so that the same field was called in their tongue, Haceldama, that is to say, The field of blood. For it is written in the book of Psalms: Let their habitation become desolate, and let there be none to dwell therein. And his bishopric let another take. Wherefore of these men who have companied with us all the time that the Lord Jesus came in and went out among us, Beginning from the baptism of John, until the day wherein he was taken up from us, one of these must be made a witness with us of his resurrection.

Lesson III ~ Acts 1:23–26

And they appointed two, Joseph, called Barsabas, who was surnamed Justus, and Matthias. And praying, they said: Thou, Lord, who knowest the hearts of all men, shew whether of these two thou hast chosen, To take the place of this ministry and apostleship, from which Judas hath by transgression fallen, that he might go to his own place. And they gave them lots, and the lot fell upon Matthias, and he was numbered with the eleven apostles.

Lesson IV–VI from the Second set in the Common of Apostles (Homily by St. Augustine)

Lessons VII–IX from the second set in the Common of Abbots (Sermon by St. Augustine)

February 27 (Leap year: Feb 28) ~ St. Gabriel of the Sorrowful Virgin

Confessor ~ Duplex

All from Common except what follows

Lessons I–III from the second set in the Common of Confessor Non-Bishops (Wisdom)

Lesson IV

Gabriel, born at Assisi in Umbria of a respectable family, and called Francis in memory of his seraphic fellow-townsman, showed from boyhood an excellent disposition of soul. As a youth, when studying letters at Spoleto, he seemed for a time to be allured by the empty beauty and pomp of the world. But by the gift of the merciful God, who had already called him to the perfection of a Christian life when he had fallen sick, he began to tire of the vanity of the world, and to desire immortal treasures alone. But to quicken his obedience to the call of God, it happened that as he saw the celebrated Image of the Blessed Virgin being carried with solemn pomp outside the precincts of the church of Spoleto, he experienced the flame of divine love, and at the same time decided to enter the Institute of the

Clerks of the Passion of Jesus. Therefore, after overcoming no slight difficulties, he joyfully donned the somber habit in the secluded place of Morrovalle, and chose to be called Gabriel of Our Lady of Sorrows, to recall forever the memory of her joys and griefs.

Lesson V

In the novitiate, day by day he became conspicuous for regular observance and for the exercise of all the virtues, and in a short time he came to be considered a pattern of perfect holiness, not only by his companions and his seniors, but also beyond the confines of the monastery; he became a sweet odor of Christ in every place. An assiduous devotee of the Lord's Passion, he spent days and nights meditating upon it. He was drawn by unbelievable zeal towards the Holy Eucharist, a memorial of that Passion; and when he nourished himself with it, he burned with seraphic ardor. There was nothing more noticeable than his filial piety towards the great Mother of God. He was accustomed to pay her honor for every type of devotion, but especially to contemplate her stricken and afflicted by the sufferings of Jesus, with such sorrow that he shed floods of tears. The sorrowful Virgin was, as it were, the whole reason of his being, and the teacher of the holiness that he had acquired. As a result all his associates shared the one opinion that this servant of God had been inspired from on high so that the cult of St. Mary of Sorrows through his example might receive a great increase.

Lesson VI

Among other virtues, he especially loved Christian humility and obedience; for he considered himself the least of all. He therefore strove eagerly to do all the most menial work of the house, and he most diligently performed, not only the direct commands, but even the unexpressed wishes of his superiors. Curbing his senses, and accustoming himself to a life of austerity, he retained unfaded the flower of his virginity, and completely crucified to the world, he lived to God alone, enjoying an intimate familiarity with his Lord. And so, at Isola in Abruzzi, filling the short span of his life with so many noble virtues, consumed by the fire of charity rather than by disease, and refreshed by the aid of the Mother of God, his soul flew to heaven in a most peaceful journey in the year 1862, at the age of twenty-four. Then, as he had been made illustrious by God through miracles, Pope Pius X added him to the number of the Blessed in heaven. Likewise, the Supreme Pontiff Benedict XV in 1920, two hundred years after the foundation of the Institute of the Passion, on the feast of the Ascension of the Lord, decreed the honors of the Saints to the blessed youth; and Pius XI extended his Office and Mass to the Universal Church.

Lesson VII

From the Holy Gospel according to St. Mark (Mark 10:13–21)

At that time: They brought young children to Jesus, that he should touch them: and his disciples rebuked those that brought them. And so on.

Homily by St. Bede the Venerable, Priest

Jesus said unto his disciples: "Suffer the little children to come unto me, and forbid them not: for of such is the kingdom of God." It is noteworthy that he says: "Of such;" not: "Of these." That is, he is concerned with conduct, not with age; for the reward is promised to all such as are like unto children, not in age, but in innocence and simplicity; as says the Apostle: "Be not children in understanding; howbeit, in malice you are children, but in understanding are men." Verily I say unto you, Whosoever shall not receive the kingdom of God as a little child, he shall not enter therein. A child does not for long remain angry or remember an injury; he takes no lustful pleasure in looking at a beautiful woman; he does not think one thing and say another. In like manner, you also, unless you have this innocence and purity of soul, cannot enter the kingdom of heaven. We are commanded to receive the kingdom of God (that is, the teaching of the Gospel) like as children, because they, when learning, do not contradict their teacher, nor adduce reasons and arguments against them, but trustingly accept what they are taught in respectful silence and obedience. And the Lord took them up in his arms, put his hands upon them, and blessed them. He blesses the children by taking them up in his arms, to show that such as are poor in spirit do merit his blessing, grace, and love.

Lesson VIII

And as he was going forth on his journey, a certain man came running up, and fell on his knees before him, and asked him: "Good Master, what shall I do that I may inherit eternal life?" Doubtless this seeker after eternal life was one of those who had heard the Lord say that whoso shall not receive the kingdom of God as little child shall not enter therein; and therefore, taking the safer course, he asks for himself not in parables, but simply and openly, for teaching concerning the meritorious works by which eternal life is to be gained. Whereupon Christ said: "Thou knowest the commandments." This is the chastity of childlike innocence, which is proposed for our imitation, if we wish to enter the kingdom of God. "But he answering, said unto him: Master, all these have I observed from my youth." This man should not be considered as having asked the Lord with a view to tempting him (as some have thought), or to have lied about his life when he said he had kept the commandments of the law; but that rather he was trying to explain how he had hitherto lived. Because, if he be considered guilty of lies and pretense, it would not have been said of Jesus, who looks on the secrets of the heart, that he, "beholding him, loved him."

—Lesson IX if not Lent—

For the love of the Lord goes out to all those who not only keep the commandments of the law, but have regard even for things which are not of strict precept. Which latter things he who came not to destroy the Law and the Prophets, but to fulfill them, shows forth unto such as would be perfect, saying: "Sell whatsoever thou hast, and give to the poor, and thou shalt have treasure in heaven; and come, follow me." Whosoever would be perfect must sell all (not merely in part, as did Ananias and Sapphira), and thereafter give all to the poor, and thus prepare for himself a treasure in the kingdom of heaven. But contempt for riches is not enough to achieve perfection. He must also follow the Saviour, leaving evil and doing good. For it is easier to spurn the world than the will; and many spurn their riches, but fail thereafter to follow the Lord. Whosoever would follow him must be his imitator, and walk in his footsteps. For whoso says he believes in Christ ought also to walk as Christ walked.

In Lent: Lesson VII from the Proper of Time is read as a Lesson IX commemoration of the Lenten Feria

✠

FEASTS OF MARCH

March 4 ~ St. Casimir

Confessor ~ Semiduplex

All from Common except what follows

Lessons I–III from the occurring Scripture—in Lent: from the Common of Confessor Non-Bishops (Wisdom)

Lesson IV

Casimir was the son of King Casimir III of Poland, by Elizabeth of Austria, his wife, and was born upon the 3rd day of October, in the year 1458. From his childhood he was taught by the best masters, and was trained in all piety and good learning. While he was still a boy he wore rough haircloth, and chastened himself with much fasting. He forsook the softness of his princely bed, and lay upon the hard ground, and on stormy nights he would go out secretly and prostrate himself before the doors of the churches, crying to God for mercy. He was unwearied in contemplating the Passion of Christ, and when he was present at Mass, so profound was his recollection, that he seemed to be altogether beside himself.

Lesson V

He made the propagation of the Catholic faith one of the chief works of his life, and strove hard to abolish the schism of the Ruthenians. He persuaded his father to forbid by law that the schismatics should build any new churches, or repair the existing ones when they fell into decay. So great was his liberality and tenderness toward the needy and the afflicted, that he came to be called the father and guardian of the poor. From his infancy he never soiled his purity, and in his last illness, when his physicians advised him to seek relief from his grievous sufferings by the sacrifice of his chastity, he cheerfully determined rather to die.

Lesson VI

Being perfected in a short time, and full of piety and good works, he foretold the day of his own death, and, gathering round him a choir of priests and monks, he rendered his soul into the hands of God Whom they were praising, upon the 4th day of March, in the year of our Lord 1482, and the 25th of his own age. His body was carried to Vilnius, where many miracles are reputed to have been wrought around it. At his grave a dead girl is said to have received her life again, blind men their sight, cripples the power of walking, and many sick folk health. Moreover, on an occasion when the Lithuanians in scanty numbers were exposed to the shock of a powerful enemy, they believed that he appeared in the air, and gave them the signal victory which they won. On the assurance of these things, Leo X was moved to add his name to those of the Saints.

Lessons VII–IX from the first set in the Common of Confessor Non-bishops (Sermon by St. Gregory)

In Lent: Lesson VII from the Proper of Time is read as a Lesson IX commemoration of the Lenten Feria

March 6 – Sts. Perpetua & Felicitas

Martyrs – Duplex

All from Common except what follows

Lessons I–III from the occurring Scripture—in Lent: from the second set in the Common of Virgins (Ecclus)

Lesson IV

Perpetua and Felicitas were arrested during the persecution of the emperor Severus in Africa, together with Revocatus, Saturninus and Secundulus, and were cast into a dark dungeon, where Satyrus was added to their company. They were yet catechumens but shortly afterwards they were baptized. After a few days they and their companions were led forth from prison to the court, and, after a glorious profession of faith, were condemned by the procurator Hilarion to the beasts. Thereupon they went down to the prison rejoicing, and there they were refreshed with many visions, and fired with longing for the martyr's palm. Neither the repeated prayers and tears of Perpetua's father, a man of extreme old age, nor her motherly love for her baby son still at the breast, nor the atrocity of the torture, could shake her faith in Christ.

Lesson V

As the day of the spectacle came close, Felicitas was afflicted with great sorrow lest it should be put off, since she was eight months with child; and the law forbade expectant mothers to be put to the torture. But at the prayers of her fellow-martyrs her delivery was hastened, and she gave birth to a daughter. While she was groaning in the pains of childbirth, one of the jailers said to her: "What wilt thou do when thrown to the beasts, if thou groanest thus now?" She replied: "Now it is I who suffer; but then Another will be within me, who will suffer on my behalf, seeing that it is for him that I am to suffer."

Lesson VI

At length the noble-hearted women were brought into the amphitheatre, in the sight of all the people, on the 7th day of March, and were first beaten with scourges. Then they were tossed for some time by a ferocious cow, beaten with lashes, and dashed on the ground. Lastly, together with their companions, who had been attacked by various beasts, they were slain with blows of the sword. Pope Pius X raised the feast of these holy Martyrs to the rite of a Duplex for the Universal Church, and ordered it to be kept on March 6th.

Lessons VII–IX from the Common of Non-Virgins (Sermon by St. Gregory)

In Lent: Lesson VII from the Proper of Time is read as a Lesson IX commemoration of the Lenten Feria

March 7 ~ St. Thomas Aquinas

Confessor & Doctor ~ Duplex

All from Common except what follows

Lessons I–III from the occurring Scripture—in Lent: from the Common

Lesson IV

That splendid adornment of the Christian world and light of the Church, blessed Thomas, was the son of Landulph, Earl of Aquino, and Theodora of Naples, his wife, being nobly descended on both sides. He was born in the year of salvation 1226, and even as an infant gave token of the love which he afterwards bore to the Mother of God. He found a little bit of paper upon which was written the Angelic Salutation, and held it firm in his hand in spite of the efforts of his wet-nurse; his mother took it away by force, but he cried and stretched out for it, and when she gave it back to him, he swallowed it. When he was only four years old, he was given into the keeping of the Benedictine monks of Monte Cassino. He was thence sent to Naples to study, and there, while very young, entered the Order of Friars Preachers. This displeased his mother and brothers, and he left Naples for Paris. When he was on his journey his brothers met him, and carried him off by force to the castle of Monte San Giovanni, where they imprisoned him in the keep. Here they used every means to break him of his intention, and at last brought a woman into his room to try to overcome his purity. The lad drove her out with a fire-brand. When he was alone he knelt down before the figure of the Cross, and there he fell asleep. As he slept, it seemed to him that angels came and girded his loins and from this time he never felt the least lustful inclination. His sisters came to the castle to beseech him to give up his purpose of leaving the world, but he so worked on them by his godly exhortations, that both of them ever after set no value on earthly things, and busied themselves rather with heavenly.

Lesson V

Being let down from a window, Thomas escaped out of the castle of Monte San Giovanni, and returned to Naples. Thence he went first to Rome, and then to Paris, in company of Brother John the German, then Master-General of the Friars Preachers. At Paris he studied Philosophy and Theology under Albert the Great Doctor. At the age of twenty-five years he took the degree of Master, and gave public disquisitions on the Philosophers and Theologians with great distinction. He never set himself to read or write till he had first prayed, and when he was about to take in hand a hard passage of the Holy Scriptures, he fasted also. Hence he was wont to say to Brother Reginald, his comrade, that whatever he knew he had learnt, not so much from his own labour and study, as from the inspiration of God. At Naples he was once kneeling in very earnest prayer before an image of Christ Crucified, when he heard a voice which said "Thomas, thou hast written well of Me; therefore, what reward shalt thou accept?" He answered: "Nothing other, O Lord, than thyself." He studied most carefully the works of the Fathers, and there was no kind of author in which he was not well read. His own writings are so wonderful, both because of their number, their variety, and the clearness of his explanations of hard things, that his rich and pure teaching, marvelously consonant with revealed truth, is an admirable antidote for the errors of all times.

Lesson VI

The Supreme Pontiff Urban IV sent for him to Rome, and at his command he composed the Office for the feast of Corpus Christi. The Pope could not persuade him to accept any dignity. Pope Clement IV also offered him the Archbishopric of Naples, but he refused it. He did not neglect the preaching of the Word of God. Once while he was giving a course of sermons in the Basilica of St Peter, during the octave of Easter, a woman who had an issue of blood was healed by touching the hem of his garment. He was sent by blessed Gregory X to the Council of Lyons, but fell sick on his way to the Abbey of Fossanova, and there during his illness he made an exposition of the Canticle of Canticles. There he died on the 7th day of March, in the year of salvation 1274, aged fifty years. He was distinguished for miracles even after his death, and on proof of these Pope John XXII added his name to those of the Saints in the year 1323. His body was afterwards carried to Toulouse by command of blessed Urban V. He has been compared to an angel, both on account of his innocence and of his intellectual power, and has hence been deservedly termed the Angelic Doctor. The use of which title as applied to him was approved by the authority of Saint Pius V. Leo XIII, cheerfully agreeing to the prayers and wishes of nearly all the bishops of the Catholic world, and in conformity with a vote of the Congregation of Sacred Rites, by his Apostolic letters declared and recognized Thomas Aquinas as the heavenly patron of all Catholic schools, as an antidote to the plague of so many false systems, especially of philosophy, for the increase of scientific knowledge, and for the common good of all mankind.

Lessons VII–IX from the first set in the Common of Doctors (Sermon by St. Augustine)

In Lent: Lesson VII from the Proper of Time is read as a Lesson IX commemoration of the Lenten Feria

March 8 ~ St. John of God

Confessor ~ Duplex

All from Common except what follows

Lessons I–III from the occurring Scripture—in Lent: from the Common

Lesson IV

John of God was born of Catholic and pious parents in the town of Montemor in Portugal, in the year 1495. The lot to which God had elected him was foreshown at his birth by a light shining over the house, and by the ringing of a bell untouched by human hands. He fell at one time into a loose habit of life, but was recalled by the grace of God, and began to show tokens of true reformation. By hearing the Word of God, he so felt himself stirred up to strive after nobler things, that he considered not that to which he had already attained, and yearned to be perfect, as our Father in heaven is perfect. He gave away all his property to the poor and prisoners, and became a spectacle to all that knew him, by the strength of his repentance, and the depth of his self-contempt. On this account he was commonly supposed to be mad, and was once shut up in a lunatic asylum. He was only the more filled with schemes of charity, and collected, by begging, funds sufficient to build a large double Hospital in the city of Granada. Here he founded the new Order of Brothers Hospitallers with which he enriched the Church. These Brethren are now spread throughout all parts of the world, and engaged in ministering to the souls and bodies of the sick.

Lesson V

He strove to get for the sick and poor, whom he sometimes brought to the Hospital on his own shoulders, whatever was needful for their souls or bodies. His charity was extended to the poor outside of his institution, and he used to supply food privately to necessitous widows, and more so to young women whose virtue was tempted on account of their poverty. He was most careful in encouraging the virtue of purity in all whom he knew. On one occasion when there was a great fire in the hospital at Granada, John bravely entered the burning house, ran from one part of it to another, carried out the sick on his shoulders, and threw the beds out of the windows, and finally, after passing half-an-hour in the midst of the flames, which were now raging with great violence, by the mercy of God left the building uninjured, to the great wonder of all the citizens; thereby to teach all them that love God that the fire which burnt in his heart gave him strength to risk the fire which threatened him from without.

Lesson VI

He was a marked example of every kind of austerity, of the most lowly obedience, of the deepest voluntary poverty, of the most constant prayer, of spiritual contemplation, and of love towards the Blessed Virgin. He was distinguished for the gift of tears. Being at last seized by deadly sickness, he duly received, with saintly affection, all the Sacraments of the Church. After all strength seemed to have left him, he got out of his bed, put on his own clothes, and knelt down before an image of the Lord Christ hanging on the Cross. Round it he threw his arms and pressed it against his heart, and in this position, as it were in the kiss of the Lord, he died, on the 8th day of March 1550. After his death his body did not leave its grip of the crucifix until it was forcibly taken away, six hours after. During these six hours all the inhabitants of the city came to see it, and noticed an odor of strange sweetness proceeding from it. His name was illustrious as a worker of miracles both before and after his death, and the Supreme Pontiff Alexander VIII added it to those of the Saints, and Leo XIII, at the desire of the Bishops of the Catholic world, and in accordance with a vote of the Congregation of Rites, declared him the patron in heaven of all the sick and those who nurse them, wheresoever dwelling, and ordered that his name should be called upon in the Litany for the dying.

Lesson VII

From the Holy Gospel according to St. Matthew (Matt 22:34–46)

At that time, the Pharisees came unto Jesus, and one of them, which was a lawyer, asked Him a question, tempting Him, saying: Master, which is the great commandment in the Law? And so on.

Homily by St. John Chrysostom

When the Pharisees had heard that Christ had put the Sadducees to silence, they gathered themselves together for a fresh attack just when it behooved them to be quiet, they willed to contend and so they put forward one of themselves who professed skill in the law, not wishing to learn, but to lay a snare. This person therefore proposed the question: "Which is the great commandment in the law?" The first and great commandment is: "Thou shalt love the Lord thy God," but they expected that He would make some exception or addition to this in His Own case, since He made Himself God. With this expectation they asked Him the question, but what said Christ? To show that they had adopted this course, because they were loveless, and sick with envy, He answered: "Thou shalt love the Lord thy God with all thy heart, and with all thy soul, and with all thy mind. This is the first and great commandment. And the second is like unto it: Thou shalt love thy neighbor as thyself."

Lesson VIII

Why is this second commandment like unto the first? Because the first is the second's source and sanction. "For every one that does evil hates the light, nor comes to the light." And again: "The fool has said in his heart There is no God" and there follows: "They are corrupt, and become abominable in their works." And yet again: "The love of money is the root of all evil which while some coveted after, they have erred from the faith." And yet once more: "If ye love Me, keep My commandments," of which commandments the head and root is "Thou shalt love the Lord thy God and thy neighbor as thyself."

—Lesson IX if not Lent—

If therefore, to love God is to love our neighbor (also, it is written: "Simon, son of Jonas, lovest thou Me? Feed My sheep"), and if "love is the fulfilling of the law," justly does the Lord say that "on these two commandments hang all the law and the Prophets." And even as when, before this, being interrogated about the Resurrection, He answered them more than they asked, so, now, being interrogated concerning the first and great commandment, He answers them, of His own accord, regarding that second one also, which is little lower than the first, for "the second is like unto it." Herein He would have them understand that it was hatred that stirred them up to question Him. For "Charity," says the Apostle, "envies not."

In Lent: Lesson IX from the Lenten Feria

March 9 ~ St. Frances of Rome

Widow ~ Duplex

All from Common except what follows

Lessons I–III from the occurring Scripture—in Lent: from the Common

Lesson IV

The noble Roman matron Frances was born in the year 1384 and was a pattern of godliness from her earliest years. As a child she shrank from games, and set no store by the amusements of the world, but delighted to be continually alone and engaged in prayer. At the age of eleven years she desired to consecrate her virginity to God, and to enter a convent, but humbly yielded obedience to the wishes of her parents, and was married to Lawrence de' Pontiani, a young man whose rank was equal to his wealth. As a wife she persevered, as far as she lawfully could, in her determination to lead an austere life; she abstained as much as possible from going to shows, feasts, and such like amusements, dressed plainly in wool, and spent in prayer or the service of her neighbor whatever time she did not occupy with her duties as mistress of her husband's house. She strove earnestly to wean the married women of Rome from the vanities of the world and the frivolities of dress. To this end she founded during her husband's lifetime the Sisterhood of the Oblates, under the rule of the Benedictine congregation called of the Mount of Olives. When it pleased God, in the year 1413, that her husband should be banished, all her goods taken away, and her home ruined, she meekly bowed down before His holy will, often repeating the words of the blessed Job "The Lord gave, and the Lord has taken away; blessed be the name of the Lord."

Lesson V

On her husband's death in 1437, she betook herself immediately to the house of the Oblates, and, with her feet bare and a rope round her neck, threw herself down on the threshold, entreating the sisters with tears to receive her into their number. When she obtained her wish, although she was the mother of them all, she would be among them only as one that served, glorying rather to be called the most degraded of women and a vessel of uncleanness. Her lowly esteem of herself was shown both by her word and example. She passed often through the city from a vineyard in the country carrying a bundle of sticks on her head, or driving a laden ass; she aided the needy, for whom she collected large alms, and visited the sick in the hospitals, ministering to them both food for the body and exhortations healthful for their souls. She strove continually to bring her body into subjection by watchings, fastings, haircloth, the wearing of an iron girdle, and the often use of a scourge. She never ate but once a day, and then only vegetables, and she took no drink but water. These severities she however sometimes relaxed, in obedience to her confessor, on whose word and wishes she framed her customs.

Lesson VI

So great was her mental realization of the things of God, and chiefly of the sufferings of the Lord Christ, and so abundant her tears in contemplating them, that she seemed sometimes about to sink under her grief. Often when she was engaged in prayer, and principally after she had received the Most Holy Sacrament of the Eucharist, her spirit became altogether lifted up to God, and she remained motionless, carried away by the thought of heavenly things. The enemy of man assailed her with diverse reproaches and buffetings to break her off her intent, but she feared him not, and with the help of an Angel whom God gave her to be her familiar friend, she won a noble victory over the tempter. God glorified her with the gifts of healing and of prophecy, whereby she foretold things to come, and saw the secrets of the hearts of men. More than once while her thoughts were busy in God she remained unwet by streams or rain. When there was left only bread enough for three sisters, the Lord at her prayers was pleased so to multiply it, that fifteen had enough, and the basket was filled again with the fragments. In the month of January also, when the sisters were gathering sticks in the country, and were thirsty, she satisfied them abundantly with bunches of fresh grapes from a tree. She departed to be with the Lord, famous for good works and miracles, in the fifty-sixth year of her age, upon the 9th day of March, in the year of our Lord 1440. The Supreme Pontiff Paul V caused her to be numbered among the saints.

Lessons VII–IX from the Common of Non-Virgins (Sermon by St. Gregory)

In Lent: Lesson VII from the Proper of Time is read as a Lesson IX commemoration of the Lenten Feria

---

March 10–22 will always fall in the Season of Lent

March 10 ~ The Forty Holy Martyrs

Semiduplex

All from Common except what follows

Lesson IV

While Licinius was Emperor and Agricolaus Præfect, in the year of our Lord 320, forty soldiers at Sebaste, a city of Armenia, gave a singular instance of faith in Jesus Christ, and bravery under suffering. After being often remanded to a horrid prison, bound in fetters, and their mouths bruised with stones, they were ordered out in the depth of winter, stripped naked, and put upon a frozen pool to die of cold during the night. The prayer of them all was the same: "O Lord, forty of us have begun to run in the race, grant that all forty may receive the crown, let not one be wanting at the last. Behold, is it not an honorable number in thy sight, Who didst bless the fast of forty days, and at the end thy Divine Law came forth to the earth? When also Elias sought thee, Thou, O God, didst reveal thyself unto him when he had fasted for forty days." Even so was their petition.

Lesson V

When the keepers were all asleep and the watchman only was awake, he heard them praying and saw a light shining round about them, and Angels coming down from heaven, as the messengers of the King, bearing thirty-nine crowns, and distributing them to the soldiers. Then he said within himself: "Are not forty here? Where is the crown of the fortieth?" And as he looked he saw one of them whose courage could not bear the cold, come and leap into a warm bath that stood by; and the Saints were grievously afflicted. Nevertheless, God suffered not that their prayer should return unto them void; for the watchman wondered, and called the keepers, and stripped himself of his clothes; and, when with a loud voice he had confessed himself a Christian, he joined the Martyrs. When the servants of the Præfect knew that the watchman also was a Christian, they broke the legs of them all with staves.

Lesson VI

Under this torment died they all, saving Melithon, who was the youngest. Now, his mother stood by, and when she saw that his legs were broken, but that he was yet alive, she cried, and said: "My son, have patience but a little longer. Behold how Christ stands at the door to help thee." When she saw the bodies of all the others put upon carts and taken away to be burned, and that her son was left behind, because the multitude wickedly hoped that being but a lad, if he lived, he might yet be drawn to commit idolatry, the holy mother took him on her own shoulders and bravely followed behind the carts laden with the bodies of the Martyrs. In her arms, Melithon gave up his soul to God, and the mother who loved him so well laid his body with her own hands upon the pile, with those of the other Martyrs, that, as they had all been one in faith and strength, in death they might not be divided, and might enter heaven together. After the burning, what remained of them was thrown into a running stream, but the ashes were all washed together into one place, and being found and rescued, they were laid in an honorable sepulchre.

Lessons VII, VIII from the second set in the Common of Many Martyrs (Sermon by St. Ambrose)

Lesson IX from the Lenten Feria

March 12 ~ St. Gregory I

Pope, Confessor, & Doctor ~ Duplex

All from Common except what follows

Lesson IV

Gregory the Great was a Roman, the son of Gordian the Senator, and was born about the year of our Lord 540. As a young man he studied philosophy, and afterwards discharged the office of Prætor. After his father's death he built six monasteries in Sicily, and a seventh in honor of St. Andrew, in his own house at Rome, near the Church of Saints John and Paul at the ascent of the slope of Scaurus. In this monastery of St. Andrew, he and his masters, Hilarion and Maximian, professed themselves monks, and Gregory was afterwards Abbot. Later on, he was created a Cardinal Deacon, and sent to Constantinople as legate from Pope Pelagius to the Emperor Tiberius Constantine. Before the Emperor he so successfully disputed against the Patriarch Eutychius, who had denied that our bodies shall verily and indeed rise again, that the Prince threw his book into the fire. Eutychius himself also, soon after fell sick, and when he felt death coming on him, he took hold of the skin of his own hand and said in the hearing of many that stood by: "I acknowledge that we shall all rise again in this flesh."

Lesson V

Gregory returned to Rome, and, Pelagius being dead of a plague, he was unanimously chosen Pope. This honor he refused as long as he could. He disguised himself and took refuge in a cave, but was betrayed by a fiery pillar. Being discovered and overruled, he was consecrated at the grave of St. Peter, upon the 3rd day of September, in the year 590. He left behind him many examples of doctrine and holiness to them that have followed him in the Papacy. Every day he brought pilgrims to his table, and among them he entertained not only an Angel, but the very Lord of Angels in the guise of a pilgrim. He tenderly cared for the poor, of whom he kept a list, as well without as within the city. He restored the Catholic faith in many places where it had been overthrown. He fought successfully against the Donatists in Africa and the Arians in Spain. He cleansed Alexandria of the Agnoites. He refused to give the Pall to Syagrius, Bishop of Autun, unless he would expel the Neophyte heretics from Gaul. He caused the Goths to abandon the Arian heresy. He sent into Britain Augustine and diverse other learned and holy monks, who brought the inhabitants of that island to believe in Jesus Christ. Hence Gregory is justly called by Bede, a Priest of Jarrow, the Apostle of England. He rebuked the presumption of John, Patriarch of Constantinople, who had taken to himself the title of Bishop of the

Universal Church, and he dissuaded the Emperor Maurice from forbidding soldiers to become monks.

Lesson VI

Gregory adorned the Church with holy customs and laws. He called together a Synod in the Church of St. Peter, and therein ordained many things; among others, the ninefold repetition of the words *Kyrie eleison* in the Mass, the saying of the word *Alleluja* in the Church service except between Septuagesima inclusive and Easter exclusive, and the addition to the Canon of the Mass of the words "Do Thou order all our days in thy peace." He increased the Litanies, the number of the Churches where is held the Stational observance; and the length of the Ecclesiastical Office. He would that the four Councils of Nice, Constantinople, Ephesus, and Chalcedon should be honored like four Gospels. He released the Sicilian Bishops from visiting Rome every three years, willing them to come instead once every five years. He was the author of many books, and Peter the Deacon declares that he often saw the Holy Ghost on his head in the form of a dove when he was dictating them. It is a marvel how much he spoke, did, wrote, and legislated, suffering all the while from a weak and sickly body. He worked many miracles. At last God called him away to be blessed for ever in heaven, in the thirteenth year, sixth month, and tenth day of his Pontificate, being the 12th day of March, in the year of salvation 604. This day is observed by the Greeks, as well as by us, as a festival, on account of the eminent wisdom and holiness of this Pope. His body was buried in the Church of St. Peter, near the Private Chapel.

Lessons VII, VIII from the Common of Supreme Pontiffs (Sermon by St. Leo)

Lesson IX from the Lenten Feria

March 17 – St. Patrick

Confessor Bishop – Duplex

All from Common except what follows

Lesson IV

Patrick, called the Apostle of Ireland, was born in Great Britain. The name of his father was Calphurnius, and that of his mother Conchessa, who is said to have been a relation of St. Martin, Bishop of Tours. When Patrick was a lad, he was several times taken prisoner by barbarians. While in their hands he was employed as a shepherd and already showed marks of his saintliness to come. His spirit was filled with faith, and love, and fear of God, so that he would rise before the light, in snow, and frost, and rain, to make his prayers to God, being accustomed to address God in prayer a hundred times every day, and a hundred times every night. After being rescued from his third captivity, he was placed among the clergy, and for a long time exercised himself in sacred learning. To this end, he travelled with much labor through Gaul, Italy, and the islands of the Tyrrhenian Sea, but at last being called of God to work for the salvation of the Irish, and, having received from the Blessed Pope Celestine a commission to preach the gospel, and likewise being consecrated a Bishop, he betook himself to Ireland.

Lesson V

In the discharge of his calling it is a marvel with how many evils, with how many sufferings and labors, and with how many adversaries the Apostolic Patrick had to bear. Nevertheless, by the goodness of God, that island, which had up to that time been given over to the serving of idols, was, through the preaching of Patrick, so wrought on that she soon brought forth the fruit which won her the name of the Island of Saints. Patrick caused many of her people to be born again by the washing of regeneration; he ordained many Bishops and clerics; he decreed rules for virgins and widows living in continence. By the authority of the Bishop of Rome, he established the See of Armagh as the Primatial See of all Ireland, and enriched the Church with relics of the Saints brought from Rome. Patrick, moreover, was so eminently adorned with heavenly visions, the gift of prophecy, and with great signs and wonders from God, that the fame of him spread itself abroad more and more, day by day.

Lesson VI

Besides the daily care of all the Churches of Ireland, he never relaxed his spirit from constant prayer. They say that it was his custom to repeat every day the whole Book of Psalms, together with Canticles and Hymns, and two hundred Prayers; that he bent his knees to God in worship three hundred times every day, and that he made on himself the sign of the Cross a hundred times at each of the Seven Hours of the Church Service. He divided the night into three portions; during the first he repeated the first hundred Psalms, and bent his knees two hundred times; during the second he remained plunged in cold water, with heart, eyes, and hands lifted up to heaven, and in that state repeated the remaining fifty Psalms; during the third he took his short rest, lying upon a bare stone. He was a great practicer of humility, and, after the pattern of the Apostle, he always continued to work with his own hands. At last he fell asleep in the Lord in extreme old age, refreshed with the Divine Mysteries, worn out with unceasing care for the Churches, and glorious both in word and work. His body is buried in Down in Ulster. He passed away in the fifth century after the salvation by Christ.

Lessons VII, VIII from the first set in the Common of Confessor Bishops (Sermon by St. Gregory)

Lesson IX from the Lenten Feria

March 18 ~ St. Cyril of Jerusalem

Bishop, Confessor, & Doctor ~ Duplex

All from Common except what follows

Lessons I–III from the Common of Doctors (Ecclus)

Lesson IV

Cyril of Jerusalem was given to the study of the Holy Scriptures from childhood, and so learnt therein that he became an eminent champion of the orthodox faith. He embraced the monastic institute in perpetual continence, and all hardship of living. He was ordained Priest by Saint Maximus, Patriarch of Jerusalem, and undertook with eminent success the task of preaching the word of God to the faithful and of instructing the catechumens. Thus did he compose those truly wonderful Catecheses, wherein he has embraced, clearly and fully, all the teaching of the Church, and stoutly defended every one of her doctrines against the enemies of the faith. His treatment of these subjects was such that he has overthrown therein, not only the heresies which had then come into being, but, by a kind of foreknowledge, even those which were to arise in later times. An example of this is his contention for the real Presence of the Body and Blood of Christ in the wondrous Sacrament of the Eucharist. After the death of Saint Maximus, the bishops of the province chose Cyril in his place.

Lesson V

In his office of Bishop he had for the faith's sake, like his blessed contemporary Athanasius, to endure many wrongs and sufferings at the hands of the Arian sect. The Arians could not bear that Cyril should steadfastly withstand their heresy. They assailed him with calumnies, deposed him in a pretended council, and drove him out of his see. To escape their rage he fled to Tarsus in Cilicia, and as long as Constantius lived he bore the hardships of exile. After his death and the accession to the imperial throne of the Apostate Julian, Cyril was able to return to Jerusalem, where he set himself with burning zeal to deliver his flock from false doctrine and from sin. He was driven into exile a second time under the Emperor Valens. But when peace was restored to the Church by Theodosius the Great, and the cruelty and insolence of the Arians were restrained, Cyril was received with honor by the Emperor as one of Christ's most eminent soldiers, and was restored to his see. With what earnestness and holiness he fulfilled the duties of his exalted office was made manifest by the flourishing state of the church of Jerusalem at that time, of which a picture has been left for us by Saint Basil, who dwelt there for a while when he went to worship at the holy places.

Lesson VI

Tradition has handed down that God Himself crowned with signs from heaven the holiness of this venerable Patriarch. Among these signs is numbered an apparition of a cross, more resplendent than the beams of the sun, which appeared at the beginning of his Patriarchate. Not only Cyril himself, but heathens and Christians alike were eyewitnesses of this marvel, and Cyril first gave thanks to God therefore in the church, and then sent news thereof by letter to the Emperor Constantius. A thing no less wonderful came to pass when the Jews were commanded by the profane Emperor Julian to attempt the restoration of the temple which had been destroyed by Titus. A great earthquake arose, and great masses of fire broke forth from the earth and consumed all the works, so that the Jews and Julian were dismayed and stayed their hand, all the which it can be proved that Cyril had foretold. A little while before his death he was present at the second Council of Constantinople; herein was condemned the heresy of Macedonius, and once more the Arian heresy. After his return to Jerusalem he died a holy death in the 69th year of his age and the 35th of his episcopate. The Supreme Pontiff Leo XIII commanded that his office and Mass should be celebrated throughout the universal Church.

Lessons VII & VIII from May 2nd—St. Athanasius (Homily by St. Athanasius)

Lesson IX from the Lenten Feria

March 19 - ST. JOSEPH, SPOUSE OF THE BLESSED VIRGIN MARY

Duplex I Class

Lesson I - Gen 39:1–5

From the book of Genesis

And Joseph was brought into Egypt, and Putiphar a eunuch of Pharao, chief captain of the army, an Egyptian, bought him of the Ismaelites, by whom he was brought. And the Lord was with him, and he was a prosperous man in all things: and he dwelt in his master's house, Who knew very well that the Lord was with him, and made all that he did to prosper in his hand. And Joseph found favour in the sight of his master, and ministered to him: and being set over all by him, he governed the house committed to him, and all things that were delivered to him: And the Lord blessed the house of the Egyptian for Joseph's sake.

Lesson II - Gen 41:37–40

The counsel pleased Pharao and all his servants. And he said to them: Can we find such another man, that is full of the spirit of God? He said therefore to Joseph: Seeing God hath shewn thee all that thou hast said, can I find one wiser and one like unto thee? Thou shalt be over my house, and at the commandment of thy mouth all the people shall obey: only in the kingly throne will I be above thee.

Lesson III - Gen 41:41–44

And again Pharao said to Joseph: Behold, I have appointed thee over the whole land of Egypt. And he took his ring from his own hand, and gave it into his hand: and he put upon him a robe of silk, and put a chain of gold about his neck. And he made him go up into his second chariot, the crier proclaiming that all should bow their knee before him, and that they should know he was made govenor over the whole land of Egypt. And the king said to Joseph: I am Pharao; without thy commandment no man shall move hand or foot in all the land of Egypt.

Lesson IV

Sermon by St. Bernard, Abbot

Who and what manner of man the blessed Joseph was, we may gather from that title wherewith, albeit only as a deputy, God deemed him fit to be honored as both said and believed to be the Father of God. We may gather it from his very name, which, being interpreted, signifies Increase. Remember likewise that great Patriarch who was sold into Egypt, and know that the Husband of Mary not only received his name, but inherited his purity, and was likened to him in innocence and in grace.

Lesson V

If then, that Joseph who was sold by his brethren through envy and brought down to Egypt, was a type of Christ sold to the Gentiles, the other Joseph, flying from the envy of Herod, carried Christ into Egypt. That first Joseph kept loyal to his master, and would not carnally know his master's wife; that second Joseph knew that his Lady, the Mother of his Lord, was a virgin, and he himself remained faithfully virgin toward her. To that first Joseph was given knowledge in mysteries of dreams; to the second Joseph it was given in sleep to know the mysteries of the kingdom of heaven.

Lesson VI

The first Joseph saved bread, not for himself, but for all people; the second Joseph received into his keeping that Living Bread Which came down from heaven, not for himself only, but for the whole world. There is no doubt that Joseph was good and faithful to whom was espoused: the Mother of the Saviour. Yea, I say, he was a faithful and wise servant, whom the Lord appointed to be the comfort of His own Mother, the keeper of His own Body, and the sole trusted helper in the Eternal Counsels.

Lesson VII

From the Holy Gospel according to St. Matthew (Matt 1:18–21)

When as his mother Mary was espoused to Joseph, before they came together, she was found with child, of the Holy Ghost. And so on.

Homily by St. Jerome, Priest

Why was the Lord conceived not of a simple virgin but rather of one espoused? First, for the sake of the genealogy of Mary, which we have obtained by that of Joseph. Secondly, because she was thus saved from being stoned by the Jews as an adulteress. Thirdly, that Himself and His mother might have a guardian on their journey into Egypt. To these, Ignatius, the martyr of Antioch, has added a fourth reason namely, that the birth might take place unknown to the devil, who would naturally suppose that Mary had conceived by Joseph.

Lesson VIII

"Before they came together, she was found with child of the Holy Ghost." She was found, that is, by Joseph, but by no one else. He had already almost a husband's privilege to know all that concerned her. "Before they came together." This does not imply that they ever did come together; the Scripture merely shows the absolute fact that up to this time they had not done so.

—Lesson IX if not in Lent—

"Then Joseph, her husband, being a just man and not willing to make her a public example, was minded to put her away privately." If any man be joined to a fornicatress they become one body; and according to the law they that are privy to a crime are thereby guilty. How then can it be that Joseph is described as a just man, at the very time he was compounding the supposed criminality of his espoused? It must have been that he knew her purity, and yet understood not the mystery of her pregnancy, but, while wondering at that which had happened, held his peace.

If in Lent: Lesson IX from the Feria

March 21 ~ St. Benedict

Abbot ~ Major Duplex

All from Common
except what follows

Lessons I–III from the
second set in the Common of
Confessor Bishops (Ecclus)

Lesson IV

Benedict was born of a noble family at Nursia, about the year of our Lord 480, and studied letters at Rome. Desiring to give himself altogether to Christ Jesus, he betook himself to a very deep cave at the place now called Subiaco. In this place he lay hid for three years, unknown to all except the monk Romanus, by means of whom he received the necessaries of life. While he was in the cave at Subiaco, the devil one day assailed him with an extraordinary storm of impure temptation, and to get it under, he rolled himself in brambles till his whole body was lacerated, and the sting of pain drove out the sallies of lust. At last the fame of his holiness spread itself abroad from the desert, and some monks came to him for guidance, but the looseness of their lives was such that they could not bear his exhortations, and they plotted together to poison him in his drink. When they gave him the cup, he made the sign of the Cross over it, whereupon it immediately broke, and Benedict, leaving that monastery, retired in solitude.

Lesson V

Nevertheless his disciples followed him daily, and for them he built twelve monasteries, and set holy laws to govern them. Afterwards he went to Cassino, and broke the image of Apollo which was still worshipped there, overturned the altar, and burnt the groves. There, in the year 529, he built the Church of St. Martin and the little chapel of St. John; and instilled Christianity into the townspeople and inhabitants. He grew in the grace of God day by day, so that being endowed with the spirit of prophecy he foretold things to come. When Totila, King of the Goths, heard of it, and would see whether it really were so, he sent his Spatharius before him with the kingly ensigns and attendance, feigning himself to be Totila. But as soon as Benedict saw him he said: "My son, put off that which thou wearest, for it is not thine." To

Totila himself he foretold that he would go to Rome, cross the sea, and die after nine years.

Lesson VI

Some months before he departed this life, Benedict forewarned his disciples on what day he was to die; and he ordered his grave to be opened six days before he was carried to it. On the sixth day, being the 21st of March, in the year 543, he would be carried into the Church, where he received the Eucharist, and then, in the arms of his disciples, with his eyes lifted up to heaven, and rapt in prayer, he gave up the ghost. Two monks saw his soul rising to heaven, clothed in a most precious garment, and surrounded with lights, and One of a most glorious and awful aspect standing above, Whom they heard saying: "This is the way whereby Benedict, the beloved of the Lord, goes up to heaven."

Lessons VII, VIII from the first set in the Common of Abbots (Sermon by St. Jerome)

Lesson IX from the Lenten Feria

March 24 ~ St. Gabriel the Archangel

Major Duplex

Lesson I ~ Dan 9:20–23

From the Prophet Daniel

Now while I was yet speaking, and praying, and confessing my sins, and the sins of my people of Israel, and presenting my supplications in the sight of my God, for the holy mountain of my God: As I was yet speaking in prayer, behold the man Gabriel, whom I had seen in the vision at the beginning, flying swiftly touched me at the time of the evening sacrifice. And he instructed me, and spoke to me, and said: O Daniel, I am now come forth to teach thee, and that thou mightest understand. From the beginning of thy prayers the word came forth: and I am come to show it to thee, because thou art a man of desires: therefore do thou mark the word, and understand the vision.

Lesson II ~ Dan 9:24–25

Seventy weeks are shortened upon thy people, and upon thy holy city, that transgression may be finished, and sin may have an end, and iniquity may be abolished; and everlasting justice may be brought; and vision and prophecy may be fulfilled; and the saint of saints may be anointed. Know thou therefore, and take notice: that from the going forth of the word, to build up Jerusalem again, unto Christ the prince, there shall be seven weeks, and sixty-two weeks: and the street shall be built again, and the walls in straitness of times.

Lesson III ~ Dan 9:26–27

And after sixty-two weeks Christ shall be slain: and the people that shall deny him shall not be his. And a people with their leader that shall come, shall destroy the city and the sanctuary: and the end thereof shall be waste, and after the end of the war the appointed desolation. And he shall confirm the covenant with many, in one week: and in the half of the week the victim and the sacrifice shall fall: and there shall be in the temple the abomination of desolation: and the desolation shall continue even to the consummation, and to the end.

Lesson IV

Sermon by St. Bede the Venerable, Priest

The Angel appeared to Zachary in the sanctuary of the temple at the right side of the altar of incense. This was fitting, thus: he appeared in the sanctuary because he came to proclaim sacrifice; and at the right side thereof, to indicate how joyous was the honor about to be bestowed on mankind by the heavenly gift. The right side is the side of honor, and therefore words indicating a position at the right hand are often used to signify an eternal good, and by the same token, to be at the left side does sometimes signify only present good. As for example where the Book of Proverbs sings thus in praise of wisdom: "Length of days is in her right hand, and in her left hand riches and honor." First of all the Angel comforts the trembling Zachary. "Fear not," says he. For just as it is natural for human frailty to fear spiritual manifestations, so it is natural for Angels to comfort with good words the mortals that be fearful. Contrariwise, when the devil perceives that his audacious manifestations do frighten, he proceeds to frighten as much as he can, and that with an increasing fearsomeness. There is no better way to overcome his workings than by a courageous faith.

Lesson V

Next, the Angel says that the prayer of Zachary was heard, and then straightway promises that the wife of Zachary should bear a child. We are not to understand that he had been praying for the birth of a son whilst he was offering the sacrifice according to the liturgy of that time, for we are told that he had given up hope of a son, and no one prays for that which he has no hope of obtaining. Yea, so hopeless was he of ever having children of his own, because Elizabeth was barren, and they were both now well stricken in years, that he did not even believe the Angel's promise. Therefore the words of the Angel, "Thy prayer is heard," refer to the redemption of the people, for which Zachary had prayed in the pleading of the sacrifice. And the words, "Thy wife shall bear a son," do show the manner of that redemption, for he adds that the son of Zachary shall go before the Redeemer as a herald, to make ready his way amongst the people. Thus, in this saying that the prayer of supplication offered by Zachary was heard of God, the Angel shows in what manner the people can be brought to salvation and perfection; namely, by repentance at the preaching of John, whereby they are to be led to faith in Christ.

Lesson VI

But Zachary hesitates because of the sublime things which have been promised. Wherefore he asks for a sign, that he may believe, albeit the coming of the Angel and his words of promise ought to have been a sufficient sign. Hence he was stricken dumb as a just penalty for his slowness of belief: to be dumb was both a sign to stir him up to the faith which he sought, and the penance which he deserved for his unbelief. We may thus understand that if a man of earth had promised such things, it would be lawful to seek for a sign, but when an Angel is sent from heaven to give God's promise, there should have been no occasion for doubt. And yet the Angel gives the desired sign, so that he who spoke from disbelief may learn from silence to believe. Note that the Angel says: "I am Gabriel, that stand in the presence of God, and am sent to speak unto thee these glad tidings." Doubtless when Angels come to us they fulfill this active and outward ministry in such a way that they yet do always remain in God's presence by contemplation. Wherefore, they stand in his presence even though they be sent from him on a mission. An Angel is a created spirit, and therefore has many limitations. But God has no limitations, and is everywhere. Thus when he sends his Angels from his presence, they yet do stand therein, for wheresoever they go on a mission, they go in him.—This Feast of the Archangel Gabriel was extended to the universal Church by Pope Benedict XV.

Lesson VII

From the Holy Gospel according to St. Luke (Luke 1:26–38)

At that time: The Angel Gabriel was sent from God unto a city of Galilee named Nazareth, to a virgin espoused to a man whose name was Joseph, of the house of David: and the Virgin's name was Mary. And so on.

Homily by St. Bernard, Abbot

Consider that this Angel was not one of lesser rank, even though such are, on one account or another, often sent on embassies to this earth. That he was an Angel of greater rank is indicated by his name which signifies "Strength of God," and by the fact that he was sent, not by some Angel perhaps more excellent than he (as is usual), but from God himself. Therefore for this reason it is said: "From God." Or, it might be for another reason, namely, lest it should be thought that God had discourteously revealed his counsel to any of the blessed spirits, except only the Archangel Gabriel, before he did so to the Virgin. For Gabriel alone was found so eminent among his own as to be held worthy both of such a name and message.

Lesson VIII

Neither do his name and his message disagree. For whom did it more befit to announce Christ, who is the Power of God, than him who is honored by a like name? For what else is power than strength? Neither does it appear to be unbecoming or unseemly that the Lord and his messenger should be known by a like title. Christ is called the power or strength of God in a very different sense from that in which this appellation is given to the Angel. In the Angel it is but a name. In the case of Christ, it is also an eternal attribute.

—Lesson IX if not in Lent—

Christ is called, and is, the Power of God. Stronger than the strong-armed, the Prince of this world, who kept his goods in peace, He came down upon him, waged war against him, and with His own arm bore away the spoils. The angel is called the Strength of God either because he had merited the prerogative of officially announcing the Advent of the Power of God, or in order that he might strengthen and support the Virgin, by nature timid and bashful, whom the novelty of the miracle might terrify and overpower. This he did when he said: "Fear not, Mary, thou hast found grace with God." It is not unreasonable to suppose, though the Evangelist does not mention the angel's name, that this was the same archangel who strengthened and comforted Mary's spouse, a humble and timorous man.

If in Lent: Lesson IX from the Feria

March 25 ~ ANNUNCIATION OF THE BLESSED VIRGIN MARY

Duplex I Class

Lesson I ~ Isa 7:10–15

From the Prophet Isaias

And the Lord spoke again to Achaz, saying: Ask thee a sign of the Lord thy God either unto the depth of hell, or unto the height above. And Achaz said: I will not ask, and I will not tempt the Lord. And he said: Hear ye therefore, O house of David: Is it a small thing for you to be grievous to men, that you are grievous to my God also? Therefore the Lord himself shall give you a sign. Behold a virgin shall conceive, and bear a son, and his name shall be called Emmanuel. He shall eat butter and honey, that he may know to refuse the evil, and to choose the good.

Lesson II ~ Isa 11:1–5

And there shall come forth a rod out of the root of Jesse, and a flower shall rise up out of his root. And the spirit of the Lord shall rest upon him: the spirit of wisdom, and of understanding, the spirit of counsel, and of fortitude, the spirit of knowledge, and of godliness. And he shall be filled with the spirit of the fear of the Lord. He shall not judge according to the sight of the eyes, nor reprove according to the hearing of the ears. But he shall judge the poor with justice, and shall reprove with equity for the meek of the earth: and he shall strike the earth with the rod of his mouth, and with the breath of his lips he shall slay the wicked. And justice shall be the girdle of his loins: and faith the girdle of his reins.

Lesson III ~ Isa 35:1–7

The land that was desolate and impassable shall be glad, and the wilderness shall rejoice, and shall flourish like the lily. It shall bud forth and blossom, and shall rejoice with joy and praise: the glory of Libanus is given to it: the beauty of Carmel, and Saron, they shall see the glory of the Lord, and the beauty of our God. Strengthen ye the feeble hands, and confirm the weak knees. Say to the fainthearted: Take courage, and fear not: behold your God will bring the revenge of recompense: God himself will come and will save you. Then shall the eyes of the blind be opened, and the ears of the deaf shall be unstopped. Then shall the lame man leap as a hart, and the tongue of the dumb shall be free: for waters are broken out in the desert, and streams in the wilderness. And that which was dry land, shall become a pool, and the thirsty land springs of water.

Lesson IV

Sermon by St. Leo, Pope

The Almighty and merciful God, Whose nature is goodness, Whose will is power, and Whose work is mercy, did, at the very beginning of the world, as soon as the devil's hatred had mortally poisoned us with the venom of his envy, foretell those remedies which His mercy had foreordained for our healing. He bade the serpent know that there was to be a Seed of the woman Who should yet bruise the swelling of his pestilential head; this Seed was none other than the Christ to come in the flesh, that God and Man in one Person, Who, being born of a Virgin, should, by His undefiled birth, damn the seducer of man.

Lesson V

The devil rejoiced that by his fraud he had so deceived man as to make him lose the gifts of God, forfeit his privilege of eternal life, bring himself under the hard sentence of death, and find in his misery a certain comfort in the accomplice of his guilt; he rejoiced also that God, in His just anger, was changed towards man, whom He had made in such honor. But, dearly beloved brethren, that Unchangeable God, Whose Will cannot be divorced from His goodness, by His own secret counsel carried out in a mysterious way His original purpose of goodness, and man, who had been led into sin by the wicked craft of the devil, perished not to disappoint that gracious purpose of God.

Lesson VI

Then therefore, dearly beloved brethren, the fullness of that time came, which God had appointed for our Redemption, our Lord Jesus Christ entered this lower world, came down from His heavenly throne, and, while not leaving that Paternal glory, was incarnate by a new order and a new birth; new, in that He Who is Invisible among His own, was made visible among us; He Who is Incomprehensible, willed to be comprehended; He Who is before the ages, began to be in time; the Lord of all shadowed the glory of His Majesty, and took upon Him the form of a servant; the Impassible God vouchsafed to become a man subject to suffering; and the Immortal laid Himself under the laws of death.

Lesson VII

From the Holy Gospel according to St. Luke (Luke 1:26–38)

At that time: The Angel Gabriel was sent from God unto a city of

Galilee named Nazareth, to a virgin espoused to a man whose name was Joseph, of the house of David: and the Virgin's name was Mary. And so on.

Homily by St. Ambrose, Bishop

The mysteries of God are unsearchable, and it is especially declared by a Prophet, that a man can hardly know His counsels. Nevertheless, some things have been revealed to us, and we may gather from some of the words and works of the Lord our Saviour, that there was a special purpose of God, in the fact that she who was chosen to be the mother of the Lord was espoused to a man. Why did not the power of the Highest overshadow her before she was so espoused? Perhaps it was lest any might blasphemously say that she had conceived the Holy One in fornication.

Lesson VIII

"And the angel came in unto her." Let us learn from this Virgin how to bear ourselves, let us learn her modesty, let us learn by her devout utterance, above all let us learn by the holy mystery enacted. It is the part of a maiden to be timid, to avoid the advances of men, and to shrink from men's addresses. Would that our women would learn from the example of modesty here set before us. She upon whom the stare of men had never been fixed was alone in her chamber, and was found only by an angel. There was neither companion nor witness there, that what passed might not be debased in gossip and the angel saluted her.

—Lesson IX if not in Lent—

The message of God to the Virgin was a mystery, which it was not lawful for the mouth of men, but only of angels, to utter. For the first time on earth the words are spoken "The Holy Ghost shall come upon thee." The holy maiden hears and believes. At length she says "Behold the handmaid of the Lord; be it unto me according to thy word." Here is an example of lowliness, here is a pattern of true devotion. At the very moment she is told that she is chosen to be the mother of the Lord she at once declares herself His handmaid. The knowledge that she was Mother of God caused in the heart of Mary only an act of humility.

If in Lent: Lesson IX from the Feria

March 27 ~ St. John Damascene

Confessor & Doctor ~ Duplex

All from Common
except what follows

Lessons I–III from the occurring Scripture—in Lent: from the Common of Doctors

Lesson IV

John, said to be of Damascus, was of noble birth, and studied sacred and profane letters at Constantinople, under the monk Cosmas. At what time Emperor Leo the Isaurian was making a wicked attack upon the honoring of holy images, John, at the desire of the Roman Pontiff, Gregory III, earnestly defended both by his words and his writings, the holiness of this honor. By this he roused against him so great a hatred on the part of Leo, that he, by forged letters, accused John as a traitor to the Caliph of Damascus, whom he was serving as a councillor and minister. John denied the charge, but the Caliph was deceived by it, and caused his right hand to be cut off. He called earnestly for the help of the most holy Virgin, and she manifested the innocence of her servant by reuniting his hand to his arm as though it had never been cut off. This miracle moved John to carry out a design which he had long had in mind. He obtained from the Caliph, albeit with difficulty, leave to go away, distributed all his goods to feed the poor, and freed all his slaves, then visited as a pilgrim the holy places in Palestine, and at length withdrew, along with his teacher Cosmas, to the monastery of St. Sabbas, near Jerusalem. There he was ordained priest.

Lesson V

As a monk, John set a bright example to all the others, especially as regarded humility and obedience. He sought for the lowest offices in the community, as though they were in a peculiar sense his own, and fulfilled them with the greatest care. When he was sent to Damascus to sell baskets made by himself, he welcomed the mockery and jests of the lowest classes in that city where he had before time been charged with the most honorable offices. He was so devoted to obedience that he not only started up to obey every nod of his superiors, but also never thought it right to ask the reason of any duty laid upon him, however difficult or however strange it might be. While thus living he never ceased earnestly to defend the Catholic doctrine as to the honoring of holy images. For this reason he drew upon himself the hatred and persecution of the Emperor Constantine Copronymus, as he had first done that of the Emperor Leo the Isaurian, and this all the more because he freely rebuked the arrogance of these Emperors, who took up matters concerning the faith, and pronounced sentence upon them according to their own judgment.

Lesson VI

It is a marvel how many things John devised both for the protection of the faith, and for the encouragement of piety, and expressed in his writings both in prose and verse. He was worthy of the high praise which was given him by the Second Council of Nicæa. On account of the golden streams of his eloquence, he was surnamed *Chrysorrhoas*, or John of the golden streams. It was not against the enemies of holy images alone that he defended the orthodox faith. He fought stoutly against the Acephali, the Monothelites, and the Theopaschites. He maintained the laws and the power of the Church. He taught with great learning the Primacy of the Prince of the Apostles, and many times calls him the Pillar of the Churches, the unbroken rock, and the Teacher and Ruler of the world. The whole of his writings are not only steeped in learning and teaching, but have a certain savor of simple piety, especially when he is praising the Mother of God, toward whom he was filled with a special reverence and love. But the greatest praise of John is that he was the first who arranged in order a complete course of theology, and prepared the way in which Saint Thomas (Aquinas) has so clearly dealt with the whole body of sacred doctrine. This truly holy man, full of days and good works, fell asleep in the peace of Christ about the year of salvation 754. The supreme Pontiff, Leo XIII, established his office and Mass throughout the universal church, whereof he also gave him the title of Doctor.

Lesson VII

From the Holy Gospel according to St. Luke (Luke 6:6–11)

At that time: It came to pass also on another Sabbath, that Jesus entered into the synagogue, and taught; and there was there a man whose right hand was withered. And so on.

Homily by St. Peter Chrysologus.

This man is a figure of all men. His healing is a type of their healing, and his soundness is a pledge of that soundness for which all have looked so long. The hand of man has withered through the deadness of faith rather than through the drying up of the sinews, and by the fault of the conscience rather than by the weakness of the flesh. The withering up of man's hand has been of old, and a sickness which smote him at the very beginning of the world, and no art or benefit of man could heal that which had been blasted by the wrath of God. That hand had touched the forbidden thing, it had sought that which was unlawful when it had been stretched out to the tree of the knowledge of good and evil. It had need of Him who had made it, not to lay a plaster upon it, but to cancel the sentence which He had uttered, and to loosen by pardon that which He had bound by judgment.

Lesson VIII

This man's healing is a type of the healing of all men, our perfect health is to be found in Christ, then shall our miserable hand be withered no more when there drops thereon the Blood of the Suffering Lord, when it is stretched forth to the Tree of Life, which is the Cross. When it gathers the mighty fruit of His suffering, when it lays hold upon the Tree of Salvation, when the body is so nailed thereto with the nails of the Lord that it can never return again to the tree of lust and barren enjoyment. And He said to the man which had the withered hand, "Rise up, and stand forth in the midst." Rise up and stand forth in the midst, O Thou that dost confess thine own weakness, thou that dost call for pity from on high, thou that canst witness to the power of God; rise up and stand forth in the midst, thou that tellest of the unbelief of the Jews; the power of so many signs has not pierced them, so many works of healing have not beset them; let the pity shown to such misery constrain them and soften them.

—Lesson IX if not in Lent—

"He said unto the man, Stretch forth thine hand, and he did so; and his hand was restored whole as the other." "'Stretch forth thine hand'—the hand which had been blasted by a commandment is by a commandment loosed." "Stretch forth thine hand"—the punishment which had been the work of God was a sufficient testimony of Him Who had been the Judge Who inflicted it, and the pardon was a proof that the Pardoner was the same. Brethren, pray that upon the synagogue only may the shadow of such an affliction fall, and that there may be in the Church no hand which is withered by greed, shrunken by avarice, paralyzed by theft, stricken by selfishness; but if such there be, let him who is so afflicted give his ear unto the Lord, and stretch forth his hand in works of godliness, let him exercise it in mercy, and set it to almsgiving. He that knows not how to lend unto the Lord by giving unto the poor, knows not how to be healed by the Lord.

If in Lent: Lesson IX from the Feria

March 28 ~ St. John of Capistrano

Confessor ~ Semiduplex

All from Common except what follows

Lessons I–III from the occurring Scripture—in Lent: from the Common

Lesson IV

John was born at Capistrano, in the Abruzzi. He was educated at Perugia, and became so expert in letters, both sacred and profane, that on account of his eminent knowledge of law, Ladislaus, King of Naples, set him over several cities. He was seeking in righteousness to bring the affairs of these places out of trouble into peace, when he himself was kidnapped and put in chains. From this captivity he marvelously escaped, and then professed himself a Friar Minor under the rule of Francis of Assisi. Here he went forward in the study of divinity, and had Saint Bernardine of Siena as a teacher, of whom he was one of the most marked followers, especially in spreading abroad the honor paid to the Most Holy Name of Jesus, and to the Mother of God. The bishopric of Aquila was offered to him, but he refused it. He was chiefly known by the hardship of his self-denial, and by the writings which he published in large numbers for the reform of manners.

Lesson V

He devoted himself without ceasing to the preaching of the Word of God, in which work he travelled throughout nearly all Italy, and by the power of eloquence and not a few miracles, he recalled almost countless souls into the path of salvation. Martin V appointed him Inquisitor to stamp out the sect of the Fraticelli. Nicolas V appointed him Inquisitor General in Italy against Judaism and Mohammedanism, and he brought many such infidels to believe in Christ. He did much good work in the affairs of the Eastern Church, and at the Council of Florence, wherein he shone like the sun, he brought back the

Armenians to the Catholic church. The same Pope Nicolas V, at the request of the Emperor Frederick III, sent him into Germany as Nuncio of the Apostolic See, in order that he might bring back the heretics to the Catholic faith and the minds of the princes to peace and agreement. He did wonderful work for God's glory during the six years that he labored in Germany and other countries, and by his teaching of the truth and the striking evidence of his miracles brought back to the bosom of the Church almost countless numbers of Hussites, Adamites, Taborites, and Jews.

Lesson VI

It was mainly at the entreaty of John that Callistus III proclaimed a Crusade, and John hastened about through Pannonia and other provinces, where by his words and his letters he so roused the minds of princes to that holy war, that in a short while seventy thousand Christian soldiers were enrolled. It was mainly through his advice and by his power that victory was gained at Belgrade, when one hundred and twenty thousand Turks were either slain or put to flight. The news of this victory reached Rome upon the sixth day of August, and Pope Callistus thereupon consecrated that day for ever to the solemn commemoration of the transfiguration of the Lord Christ. As John lay sick unto death at Illak, many princes came to see him, and he exhorted them to protect religion. He gave up his soul in holiness to God, upon the 23rd day of October, in the year of salvation 1456. God confirmed his glory by many miracles after his death, and when these had been duly proved, Alexander VIII enrolled his name with those of the saints in the year 1690, and two hundred years after his canonization, Leo XIII extended his Office and Mass to the whole Church.

Lesson VII

From the Holy Gospel according to St. Luke (Luke 9:1–6)

At that time: Jesus called the twelve Apostles together and gave power and authority over all devils and to cure diseases. And so on.

Homily by St. Bonaventure, Bishop

Apostles are so called as a mark of their authority, for this word Apostle signifies sent, and they were sent out to preach, as it is written: "Christ sent me not to baptize but to preach the gospel." They were sent to preach not any small thing but a very great thing, even the Kingdom of God, whereby we may understand the teaching of the truth, as it is said, "The Kingdom of God should be taken from you and given to a nation bringing forth the fruits thereof." The Kingdom of God may also be understood to signify the grace of the Holy Ghost, as it is written: "The Kingdom of God is not meat and drink, but righteousness, and peace, and joy in the Holy Ghost"; as also it was said: "The Kingdom of God is within you." The Kingdom of God may also be understood to signify eternal glory, as it is said: "Amen, I say unto thee, except a man be born again of water and of the Holy Ghost he cannot enter into the Kingdom of God."

Lesson VIII

The Apostles were sent to preach the Kingdom of God in all these three senses, that is to say, as the true teaching, as the grace of God, and as eternal glory. In order to invest their teaching with authority He gave them the power to cure diseases, whence where it is written: "And He sent them to preach the Kingdom of God." It is also said: "And to heal the sick." This power He gave in order to confirm the truth of their preaching, as it is written: "And they went forth, and preached everywhere, the Lord working with them, and confirming the Word with signs following." The sign that a preacher is indeed sent forth by the Spirit of God is that they that hear him should be cured of the disease of sin.

—Lesson IX if not in Lent—

There are three manifest signs which show whether a preacher has been sent by the Lord to preach the gospel. The first is that he should be sent by one having authority to do so, such as is a bishop, and above all the Pope, who is in the place of Peter, yea of Jesus Christ. So that he who is sent by him is sent by Christ. The second sign is a love for souls in the person who is sent, so that he seeks mainly the honor of God and the salvation of souls. The third sign is that his hearers should bring forth fruit and should be converted. By the first sign a preacher is known as being sent by the Father, by the second he is known as being sent by the Son, by the third he is known as being sent by the Holy Ghost. Of the first sign it may be said, "Instead of Thy Father shall be Thy children"; of the second sign it may be said, "We preach not ourselves, but Christ Jesus our Lord"; of the third sign it may be said, "I have chosen you, and ordained you, that you should go and bring forth fruit, and that your fruit should remain." And he who is thus sent forth can say, "The Spirit of the Lord is upon me because He has anointed me to preach the gospel."

If in Lent: Lesson IX from the Feria

FEASTS OF APRIL

April 2 ~ St. Francis de Paula

Confessor ~ Duplex

All from Common
except what follows

Lessons I–III from the
occurring Scripture—in
Lent: from the Common

Lesson IV

Francis was born of humble parents at Paola, a town in Calabria, about the year of our Lord 1416. His parents, who had long been childless, obtained him, after making a vow, by the prayers of blessed Francis. While he was yet a lad, the love of God moved him to withdraw into a desert place, where he lived for six years, hardly as to the body, but sumptuously in meditation on things heavenly. Nevertheless, when the fame of his holy life was noised abroad, and many betook themselves to him, that they might learn godliness, he was drawn out of the desert by love to his neighbor, and built a church near Paola, wherein he laid the first foundations of his Order.

Lesson V

In his words there was a wonderful charm; he kept his virginity always inviolate; he was so great a lover of lowliness that he used to call himself the last of all, and would that his disciples should be called the *Minimi*, which is, being interpreted, the Least of the brethren. His raiment was coarse; he went always barefoot and he slept on the ground. The extreme smallness of the amount of food which he took was extraordinary. He ate only once a day, and that after sunset. Then he took only bread and water, with scarcely any of such condiment as is allowed in Lent. He bound his disciples by a fourth vow, added to those of Poverty, Chastity, and Obedience, to observe the same rule of eating as himself.

Lesson VI

It was the will of God to make the holiness of His servant manifest by many miracles. The most notorious of these is that on one occasion when some seamen refused to take him over the Straits of Messina, he spread his cloak upon the sea, and crossed over on it with his companion. In the spirit of prophecy he foretold many things to come. Louis XI, King of France, held him in great worship, and bade him to his court. At last, at Tours, in the ninety-first year of his age, and the 1507th of our salvation, he departed hence to be buried eleven days after his death, but it not only showed no signs of corruption but even gave forth a sweet savor. Pope Leo X caused him to be numbered among the Saints.

Lessons VII–IX from the
second set in the Common of
Confessor Non-Bishops (Homily
by St. Bede the Venerable)

If in Lent: Lesson IX from the Feria

April 2 ~ St. Isidore of Seville

Bishop, Confessor, &
Doctor ~ Duplex

All from Common except what follows

Lessons I–III from the occurring Scripture—in Lent: from the Common

Lesson IV

Isidore, the admirable teacher, was a Spaniard by birth, being the son of Severian, governor of the Province of Cartagena. He was trained up in all godliness and learning by his holy brethren Leander, Archbishop of Seville, and Fulgentius, Bishop of Cartagena. He was well instructed in the Latin, Greek, and Hebrew letters, and he came from his masters a most eminent scholar in all human knowledge, and a pattern of all Christian graces. While yet he was very young, he attacked with such firmness the Arian heresy, which had of former times polluted the Gothic nation, who then were the chief rulers of Spain, that he was near being murdered by the heretics. After Leander was departed this life, Isidore was chosen to the See of Seville, against his own will, but at the vehement instance of King Reccared, and with the strong assent of the clergy and people. Saint Gregory the Great not only confirmed his election by his own Apostolic authority, and caused him to be adorned, as is the custom, with a Pallium sent from the body of Blessed Peter, but is also stated to have appointed him Vicar of the Apostolic See for all Spain.

Lesson V

When he was Archbishop no tongue can tell how loyal he was, how lowly, and meek, and merciful, how careful to restore the laws of Christianity and the Church, and how unwearied in establishing the same by his word and writings, yea, how brightly he shone in all graces. He was a leading promoter and spreader of monastic institutions throughout Spain. He built many monasteries. He founded colleges in which, when his duty allowed him spare time for sacred study and reading, he taught the many disciples who betook themselves to him from all quarters. Among these, two of the most distinguished were the holy Bishops Ildephonsus of Toledo, and Braulio of Saragossa. He called the Council of Seville, wherein, in a most incisive and eloquent discourse, he shattered and crushed the heresy of the Acephali, by which Spain was then threatened. So great was his fame among all men for the holiness of his life and doctrine, that scarcely sixteen years after his death the whole Council of Toledo, by the acclamation of more than fifty Bishops, among whom was the holy Ildephonsus himself, declared him to be worthy to be called the excellent Teacher, the newest ornament of the Catholic Church, one whose learning would endure to the end of the world, and of worshipful memory. It was the opinion of the holy Braulio that he was not only fit to be compared to Gregory the Great, but also that he was a gift from God to Spain in place of the Apostle James.

Lesson VI

Isidore wrote Books of Etymologies and on Church Offices, and likewise many others, so useful in the administration of Christian and Church Law, that the holy Pope Leo IV felt no scruple in writing to the Bishops of Britain that the sayings of Isidore were worthy to be kept like those of Jerome and Augustine, whenever there is to be done some strange work, wherein the rules of the Canon Law are not enough defined. Many sentences from his writings may also be discovered embedded in the Canon Law of the Church itself. He presided over the Fourth Council of Toledo, the most celebrated that ever met in Spain. Before his death he had purged Spain of the Arian heresy, and publicly foretold his own dissolution and the wasting of the kingdom by the Saracens which was to come. He passed away to heaven, at Seville, where he had ruled his Church for forty years, upon the 4th day of April, in the year of our Lord 636. In accordance with his own commands, his body was first buried between his brother Leander and his sister Florentina, but Ferdinand I, King of Castile and León, bought it for a great price from Enet, the Saracen, who then ruled at Seville, carried it to León, and there built a Church in honor of him, wherein his body lies, illustrious through miracles, and reverenced with great worship by the people.

Lesson VII

From the Holy Gospel according to St. Matthew (Matt 5:13–19)

At that time, Jesus said unto His disciples: "You are the salt of the earth; but if the salt lose its savor, wherewith shall it be salted?" And so on.

Homily by St. Isidore, Bishop

Whosoever is set over the people to teach them and to catechize them in good works, him it behooves in all things to be holy, and in nothing to be held blameworthy. For he which rebukes another for sin, should have no dealings with sin himself. Since with what face can he rebuke them which are under him, if he which is rebuked of him be able to answer him straightway, saying "Begin by teaching thyself to do well?" Verily, whosoever sets himself to teach others to live well, him it behooves first of all to correct his own life, so that in all things he may be able to give his own life for an example, and may provoke all to good living by his works as well as by his words. Likewise also he must be learned in the Scriptures, since if the life of a Bishop be only holy, then is he profitable to himself only. But if he be learned also in his teaching and discourse, he is able to edify his neighbors, both teaching such as are his own, and confounding the gainsayers, who, unless they be confounded and unmasked, are easily able to lead astray the hearts of the simple.

Lesson VIII

Such a one it behooves that his discourse should be pure, plain, open, very weighty, and seemly, full of sweetness and beauty, touching often upon the mystery of Law, the teaching of faith, the manliness of self-control, and the training of righteousness. Such a one it behooves to exhort all men with varying exhortation, according to the profession and way of life of each, that is to say, such a one must know what, to whom, when, and how to speak. His duty is, before all others, to read the Scriptures, to know the Canons, to copy the examples of the Saints, to be instant in watching, fasting, and prayer, to keep peace with his brethren, to separate himself from none of the members of Christ, to condemn no man untried, and to excommunicate no man unheard. Such a one it behooves, as he is the first in authority, so also to be the first in humility, yet ever so, that, by misplaced lowliness, he suffer not nor encourage the sins of those that are under him, nor use his authority hardly and with violence, but as one that is the more careful of the flock committed unto him, as being mindful of that stricter account which he will have to give at the fearful judgment seat of Christ.

—Lesson IX if not in Lent—

Such a one must have firm hold on charity, that gift which surpasses all others, and without which all others are worth nothing. Charity is the keeper of chastity, and that keeper's home is lowly-mindedness. With all other gifts he must needs be eminent for purity, yea, his must be a mind belonging utterly to Christ, clean and free from any fleshly defilement. But these are not all his needful gifts. Besides these, it behooves him to undertake the care of the poor, and to do the same with zeal and likewise with prudence, to feed the hungry, to clothe the naked, to entertain strangers, to ransom prisoners, to be the guardian of the widow and the orphan, to watch over all without ceasing, and to be heedful that his alms be neither foolish nor wasteful. In him hospitality must shine, entertaining all men with courtesy and brotherly love; for if it be the duty of all the faithful to listen to that Gospel which says: "I was a stranger, and you took Me in," how much more is it the duty of Bishops, whose house it behooves to be a home for all men?

If in Lent: Lesson IX from the Feria

April 5 ~ St. Vincent Ferrer

Confessor ~ Duplex

All from Common except what follows

Lessons I–III from the occurring Scripture—in Lent: from the Common

Lesson IV

Vincent was born of respectable parents, at Valencia in Spain, upon the 23rd day of January, in the year of our Lord 1357. Even as a child he had a heart like the heart of an old man. Considering, to the utmost of his young understanding, how fleeting is the course of this dark world, he, in the eighteenth year of his age, took the habit of a Friar in the Order of Preachers. After he had made his solemn profession, he devoted himself to sacred learning, and took the degree of Master in

Divinity with much distinction. He soon after received permission from his superiors to preach the word of God, on which duty he entered with such power and success, striving against the unbelief of the Jews, and overthrowing the errors of the Saracens, that he brought an exceedingly great multitude of unbelievers to believe in Christ, and turned many thousands of Christians from sin to sorrow, and from vice to virtue. He was a chosen vessel unto God to proclaim the tidings of salvation among all nations, and tribes, and tongues, crying out that the last day, that awful day of judgment, is at hand, smiting consternation into the minds of all, as many as heard him, weaning their love from a perishing world, and turning it to God.

Lesson V

While Vincent wrought the Apostolic work of preaching committed to him, he lived ever as follows; Every morning he sang a solemn Mass, and every day he preached in public. He fasted every day, unless prevented by some absolute necessity. He refused to no one his holy and just advice. He never ate meat, nor wore linen. He quieted public disturbances, and negotiated the peace of kingdoms. When the seamless garment of the Church was rent by a horrid schism, he worked his every nerve to unite it again, and keep it one. He was a burning and a shining light of all virtues, walking always in lowliness and simpleness, so that he meekly welcomed and embraced them which spoke evil against him and persecuted him.

Lesson VI

The Power of God confirmed his life and doctrine with many great signs and wonders. He often laid his hands upon the sick and they recovered. He cast out unclean spirits, and made the deaf to hear, the dumb to speak, and the blind to see. He cleansed the lepers, and raised the dead. After passing through many countries of Europe with exceeding profit to souls, worn out with age and disease, but still ever the same unwearied herald of the Gospel, he brought his life and his preaching together to a happy end, at Vannes in Brittany, upon the 5th day of April, in the year of salvation 1419. Pope Callistus III numbered him with the Saints.

Lessons VII–IX from the first set in the Common of Confessor Non-Bishops (Homily by St. Gregory)

If in Lent: Lesson IX from the Feria

April 11 ~ St. Leo I

Pope, Confessor, & Doctor ~ Duplex

All from Common except what follows

Lessons I–III from the occurring Scripture—in Lent: from the Common of Supreme Pontiffs

Lesson IV

Leo I was an Etruscan who ruled the Church at the time

when Attila, king of the Huns, whose surname is the Scourge of God, invaded Italy, and after a siege of three years, took, sacked, and burnt Aquileia. Thence he was hurrying to Rome, on fire with anger, and his troops were already preparing to cross the Po at the place where that river joins the Mincio, when he was met by Leo, moved with compassion at the thought of the ruin which hung over Italy. By his God-given eloquence, Attila was persuaded to turn back, and when he was afterwards asked by his servants why, contrary to his custom, he had so meekly yielded to the entreaties of the Bishop of Rome, he answered that he had been alarmed by a figure dressed like a Priest, which had appeared at the side of Leo while he was speaking, holding a drawn sword, and had made as though to kill the king unless he consented. And so he returned into Pannonia.

Lesson V

While Leo went back to Rome, where he was received with rejoicing by all men. A while later, Genseric entered the city, but Leo, by the power of his eloquence and the authority of his holy life, persuaded him to abstain from fire, insult, and slaughter. When Leo beheld how the Church was assailed by many heresies, and in dire trouble through the Nestorians and Eutychians, to purify the same and establish her in the Catholic Faith, he called the Council of Chalcedon, where, in an assembly of six hundred and thirty Bishops, Nestorius was again condemned along with Eutyches and Dioscorus; the decrees of which Council were confirmed by the authority of Leo.

Lesson VI

After these matters, this holy Pope set himself to the restoration and building of Churches. By his advice, that godly woman Demetria built the Church of St. Stephen upon her farm on the Latin Road, at the third milestone from the city. He himself built another Church upon the Appian Way, which Church is called that of St. Cornelius. He restored likewise many other Churches, and the holy vessels used therein. He built clerical housing at the three Basilicas of Peter, Paul, and Constantine. He built a monastery near the Basilica of St. Peter. He appointed for the graves of the Apostles certain keepers, whom he called the Chamberlains of the Apostles. He ordained that in the action of the Mystery (The Canon of the Mass) should be uttered the words "A holy sacrifice, an offering without spot." He ordered that no nun should have the covering of her head blessed until she had made trial of her virginity for forty years. After doing all these and other illustrious works, and after he had written much that is both godly and easy to be understood, he fell asleep in the Lord on the eleventh day of April, in the year 461. He held the Papal See for twenty years, one month, and thirteen days.

Lessons VII–IX from the Common of Supreme Pontiffs (Homily by St. Leo)

If in Lent: Lesson IX from the Feria

April 13 ~ St. Hermenegild

Martyr ~ Semiduplex

All from Common except what follows

Lessons I–III from the occurring Scripture—in Lent: from the Common of Many Martyrs

Lesson IV

From the Book of Dialogues written by Pope St. Gregory

King Hermenegild, the son of Leovigild, King of the Visigoths, was turned from the Arian heresy to the Catholic Faith by the preaching of the most reverend Leander, Bishop of Seville, the same who was for a long season my own familiar friend. Then his father, being himself an Arian, strove to bring him back to that heresy, first by offering him gifts, and then seeking to awe him by threatening. And when he answered always that, having once had knowledge of the true faith, he never could forsake it, his father was wrathful, and took away his kingdom from him, and plundered him of all his goods. And when not even so could he sap the manliness of his soul, he cast him into a most strait prison, having his neck and his hands in fetters of iron. And so that young King Hermenegild began to hold in little esteem an earthly kingdom, and to long exceedingly for a heavenly. Yea, he clothed himself in sackcloths in the prison, and as he lay bound therein, he poured forth supplications to Almighty God to give him strength. There he lay bound, having suffered the loss of all things, but his suffering made him but to esteem more worthless the glory of this world, which passes away so easily.

Lesson V

But when the day of Paschal festivity came, at dead of night, the unbelieving father sent to his son an Arian Bishop, to offer him, as the price of his favor, to receive at the hands of said Bishop the Communion from a sacrilegious consecration. But when the Arian Bishop came into the prison, the servant of God, remembering that he was not his own but God's man, rebuked the unbeliever as he deserved, and drove him from his presence with just reproaches for though he was weak and bound as touching this outer body, yet was he strong in the mighty castle of his soul. The Bishop, therefore, went away again to that Arian father. And when he came to Leovigild, he waxed exceedingly irate, and sent his servants to kill God's faithful witness where he lay. Such a thing was done for as soon as they came to him into the prison, they cleaved his head with an axe, and freed him from the dying life of this body. And so they did to him all that which they that kill the body are able to do. But God, to make manifest the glory of His servant, was pleased to work signs from heaven, for suddenly the solemn swell of the singing of Psalms was heard in the silence of the night from round about the place where lay the body of the kingly martyr, kingly now in a higher and truer sense than the sense of earthly kingship, since he had witnessed a good confession for the truth, sealing it with his blood.

Lesson VI

Some say, too, that lights were seen there that night. Wherefore it came to pass that the body of the martyr became the rightful object of reverence to all God's faithful people. The unbelieving father, murderer of his own child, was seized with remorse, and repented of what he had done, but he sorrowed not unto salvation. For though he knew that the Catholic faith was true, he stood in fear of his people, and deserved not to attain unto it. He fell sick, and, when he was at the point of death, he made it his duty to recommend King Reccared, his surviving son, to the care of the Bishop Leander, whom before he had grievously persecuted, that though Reccared was now left in heresy, the Bishop might work in him by his exhortations the same change that he had worked in his brother, which when Leovigild had said, he died. After his death, King Reccared took for his example not his unbelieving father but his martyred brother. He forsook the Arian heresy, and brought the whole nation of the Visigoths to believe in the true faith, so that he allowed no man in his kingdom to be an officer, who dared any longer range himself through heresy as an enemy of the Kingdom of God. Neither need we marvel that Reccared was a preacher of the faith, since he had a martyr for his brother, for whose sake Almighty God has helped him to bring back so many to His bosom.

Lessons VII–IX from the first set in the Common of One Martyr (Homily by St. Gregory)

If in Lent: Lesson IX from the Feria

April 14 ~ St. Justin

Martyr ~ Duplex

All from Common except what follows

Lessons I–III from the occurring Scripture—in Lent: from the Common of Many Martyrs

Lesson IV

Justin, the son of Priscus, was a Greek by race, but was born at Nablus in Palestine. He passed his youth in the study of letters. When he became a man he was so taken with the love of philosophy and the desire of truth that he became a student in the schools of all the philosophers and examined the teaching of them all. In them he found only deceitful wisdom and error. The light of heaven was given him, through an old man of worshipful aspect whom he knew not, and he embraced the philosophy of the true Christian faith. Henceforth he had the books of the Holy Scriptures in his hands by day and by night, and by meditating thereon the fire of God was so kindled in his soul that, himself possessing the excellency of the knowledge of Christ Jesus our Lord, he wrote many books, with all the learning which he possessed, to set forth the Christian faith and to spread it abroad.

Lesson V

Among the most famous of the works of Justin are his two Apologies or Defenses of the Christian faith. These he brought before the Senate when the Emperors Antoninus Pius, and his sons, as also Marcus Antoninus Verus and Lucius Aurelius Commodus, were savagely persecuting the followers of Christ, and by their means, and his vigorous disputations in favor of the same faith, he obtained a public edict from the government to stay the slaughter of the Christians. But Justin himself did not escape he had rebuked the life and infamous manners of the Cynic Crescens, and was accused and arrested through that man's schemings. He was brought before Rusticus, the Præfect of Rome, who asked him what were the doctrines of the Christians, whereto he answered, in the presence of many witnesses, with this good confession: "The right dogma which we Christian men do keep with piety is this, that we should believe that there is one God, Who is the Maker and Creator of all things, both those things which are seen and those things which bodily eyes do not see, and that we should confess the Lord Jesus Christ, the Son of God, Who was foretold of ancient days by the prophets, and Who will come to be the Judge of all mankind."

Lesson VI

In order to rebut the slanders of the heathen, Justin had in his first Apology given an open account of how the Christians would gather for divine worship, and what holy Mysteries would have been celebrated therein. The Præfect therefore asked him what was the place where he and Christ's other faithful ones in the city were accustomed to meet. Justin, lest he should betray that which was holy unto God and his brethren, told only where was his own lodging, where he was used to abide and to teach his disciples, near the famous Church of the Shepherd, in the house of Pudens. The Præfect then gave him the choice whether to sacrifice to the gods or to be flogged with scourges over his whole body. The unconquered champion of the faith answered that he had always desired to suffer in the Name of the Lord Jesus Christ, from Whom he looked to receive a mighty reward in heaven. The Præfect thereupon sentenced him to death, and then this excellent philosopher, giving praise to God, was first beaten and afterwards shed his blood for Christ's sake, and so received the crown of a glorious martyrdom. Some of the faithful secretly stole away his body, and buried it in a fitting place. The Supreme Pontiff Leo XIII commanded that his Office and Mass should be used throughout the whole Church.

Lesson VII

From the Holy Gospel according to St. Luke (Luke 12:2–8)

In that time, Jesus said to His disciples: there is nothing covered, that shall not be revealed; neither hid, that shall not be known. And so on.

Homily by St. John Chrysostom

"There is nothing covered, that shall not be revealed; and hid, that shall not be known." It is as though He would say: It is comfort enough for you, if I, your Master and Lord, am a partaker in your reproach. But if it grieve you unto this present to hear these things, bethink you likewise that it is but a little while, and you shall be free from that reproach. For what is it that grieves you? Is it that they call you tricksters and deceivers? Wait but a little while and all men shall call you the preservers and benefactors of the world. In a little while all the things which are obscure now shall be made clear, and the falsehood of them that reproach you and your own goodness shall be shown in the light. For when that which comes to pass shall itself show that you are preservers and benefactors, and filled with all goodness, men will regard not the words of your gainsayers but the truth. They that now speak evil of you will be found out in the slanderers, liars, and calumniators, and you shall be seen to be brighter than the sun; time shall make you known and shall preach you with a voice louder than the voice of a trumpet, and shall bring forward all men as the witnesses of your goodness. Let not, therefore, those things which are now spoken cast you down, but rather let the hope of the good things which are to come lift you up. For the things which regard you cannot be hidden.

Lesson VIII

And when He had freed them from pain, fear, and care, and set them above the reproaches of men, He spoke unto them in due season concerning the freedom of preaching, "What I tell you in darkness, that speak in light and what you hear in the ear, that preach upon the housetops." It was not darkness when He uttered these words, neither was He speaking into their ear. These words were a figure; He was speaking to them alone and in a little corner of Palestine, and therefore He says in darkness and in the ear, as comparing this manner of speech with that boldness of speaking wherewith He was afterwards to inspire them. Preach, He says, not in one nor two nor three cities, but throughout the whole world; go over the earth and the sea, the land that is dwelt in and the land that is not dwelt in; speak all things with great boldness to kings and to peoples, to philosophers and to rhetoricians therefore without any subtlety, but with all freedom. He says, "What I tell you in darkness, that speak in light and what you hear in the ear, that preach upon the housetops."

—Lesson IX if not in Lent—

Commemoration of Sts. Tiburtius, Valerian, & Maximus, Martyrs

Valerian was a Roman, of a family as noble as that of the blessed virgin Cecilia, to whom he was contracted in marriage, in the reign of the Emperor Alexander Severus. At her persuasion he and his brother Tiburtius were baptized by the holy Pope

Urban. When it came to the knowledge of Almachius, the Præfect of the city, that they were become Christians, had given their substance to the poor, and were burying the bodies of the faithful, he sent for them and strongly rebuked them but as they constantly confessed that Christ is God, and that the gods of the heathen are but vain images of demons, he commanded them to be beaten with rods. But, forasmuch as no blows could force them to worship the image of Jupiter, rather they seemed to wax strong in witnessing to the truth of the faith that was in them, they were beheaded at the fourth milestone from the city. One of the chamberlains of the Præfect, named Maximus, who had led them out to die, was so moved at the sight of their courage that he himself, with many other servants of the Præfect, owned to being a Christian; they were sentenced to be scourged to death with whips loaded with lead, under which torment, in a little while, all these, who had once been the devil's ministers, passed away as martyrs of Christ the Lord.

If in Lent: Lesson IX from the Feria

April 17 ~ St. Anicetus

Pope & Martyr ~ Simplex

Lessons I–II from the occurring Scripture—in Lent: Lessons I–III from occurring Lenten sermon

Lesson III

Anicetus was a Syrian who ruled the Church in the time of the Emperor Marcus Aurelius Antoninus. It was his ordinance which forbade the clergy to grow long hair. He held five December ordinations wherein he ordained seventeen Priests, four Deacons, and nine Bishops for divers sees. He lived as Pope eight years, eight months, and twenty-four days. He bore witness to his faith in Christ even unto blood, and, being crowned on the seventeenth day of April, in the year of salvation 173, was buried upon the Appian Way in the Cemetery which has since been called that of St. Callistus.

April 21 ~ St. Anselm

Bishop, Confessor, & Doctor ~ Duplex

All from Common except what follows

Lessons I–III from the occurring Scripture

Lesson IV

Anselm was born of noble and Catholic parents, named Gundulph and Ermenberga, at Aosta, in Piedmont, about the year of our Lord 1033. From his tenderest years his diligence in study and his aspirations to a more perfect state of life gave no indistinct foreshadowing of the holiness and learning to which he afterwards attained. The heat of youth drew him for a while into the snares of the world, but he soon returned to his first courses, and, forsaking his country and his goods, betook himself in 1060 to the monastery of Bec, under the rule of St. Benedict. There he made his profession as a monk, and under the rigid discipline of Herluin, the Abbot, and the learned instruction of the profound Lanfranc, with great zeal of spirit and eager obedience to the Rule, he made such progress in learning and piety, that he shone before all others as an example of holiness of life, and power of doctrine.

Lesson V

Abstinence and purity were his marked characteristics, and by assiduous fasting all taste for food seemed to have died in him. He spent the day in the monastic work, in teaching, and in answering hard questions upon religion, and he took away from sleep during what remained to him of the night, that he might refresh his soul by thoughts of God, wherein he was always comforted by an unceasing flow of tears. When he was chosen Prior of the monastery, he so won over, by his charity, humility, and wisdom, some brethren who looked ill upon him, that from enviers, as he had found them, he turned them into lovers of God and of himself likewise, with exceeding gain to the strictness of observance in that Abbey. After the death of the Abbot, in 1078, Anselm, though against his own will, was chosen to succeed him. In this high place the light of his learning and holiness so shone all round about, that he was reverenced not only by Kings and Bishops, but was taken up by the holy Pope Gregory VII, who, amid the great persecutions which were then trying him, wrote with words of great love to Anselm to recommend himself and the Catholic Church to his prayers.

Lesson VI

After the death of Lanfranc, Archbishop of Canterbury, in 1089, Anselm, whose teacher Lanfranc had formerly been, was driven by William II, King of England, supported by the entreaties of the clergy and people, though sorely against his own wishes to take upon him the government of that Church. Raised to that See upon the 4th day of December, in the year 1093, he straightway set himself to reform the corrupt manners of the people, and, first by his word and example, and then by his writings and the Councils which he held, succeeded in restoring the ancient godliness and discipline of the Church. But when the aforesaid King William tried by force and threats to seize on the rights of the Church, Anselm withstood him as beseemed a Priest, and after that he had suffered the plundering of all his goods and been sent into banishment, he betook himself to Rome to Urban II. There he was received with great worship, and won high praise for that in the Council of Bari, in 1098, he maintained by countless proofs from Scripture and the holy Fathers, against the error of the Greeks, that the Holy Ghost proceeds from the Son also. When William lived no more, his brother Henry I, King of England in the year 1100, recalled Anselm, and there he fell asleep in the Lord, upon the 21st day of April, 1109. His is a name illustrious not for miracles alone, nor for holiness, and indeed he had a wondrous love for his Lord Who had suffered for him, and for the blessed Virgin Mother of our Same Lord, but also for the deep learning which he used for the defense of the Christian Religion and the good of souls. That wonderful knowledge of theology which he had, and which is shown in all the books which he wrote, seems to have been given him from heaven for the teaching of all writers on the same subject, who have used what is called the Scholastic method.

Lessons VII–IX from the second set in the Common of Doctors (Homily by St. Hilary)

April 22 ~ Sts. Soter & Caius

Popes & Martyrs ~ Semiduplex

All from Common except what follows

Lessons I–III from the occurring Scripture

Lesson IV

Soter, a countryman of Fondi in Campania, succeeded the holy martyr Anicetus, in the year 173. It was he who ordained that nuns should not touch the sacred vessels and linens of the Altar, nor serve with the incense in the Church. He ordained likewise, that on the anniversary of the Lord's Supper, everyone should receive the Body of Christ, except those who were forbidden to do so on account of grievous sin. He sat as Pope three years, eleven months, and twenty-eight days. He ordained in the month of December eighteen Priests, nine Deacons, and eleven Bishops for diverse places. He was crowned with martyrdom under the Emperor Marcus Aurelius, in 177, and was buried after the manner of them that had gone before him, in the Cemetery, which was afterwards called that of St. Callistus.

Lesson V

Caius was a Dalmatian and a kinsman of the Emperor Diocletian and succeeded Saint Eutychian in the year 283. It was he who ordained that the following should be the order of degrees in the Church through which all should pass before they be made Bishop: Porter, Lector, Exorcist, Acolyte, Subdeacon, Deacon, Priest. Caius fled from the cruelties practiced by Diocletian against the Christians, and lay hid for a while in a cave, but after eight years, he and his brother Gabinus won the crown of martyrdom upon the 21st day of April, in the year 296. At that time he had sat in the chair of Peter twelve years, four months, and five days, and had ordained in the month of December twenty-five Priests, eight Deacons, and five Bishops. He was buried in the Cemetery of Callistus upon the 22nd day of April. It was Urban VIII who renewed the memorial of him in the city, rebuilt his Church, which had been in ruins, and distinguished it by making it one of those whence the Cardinals take their titles, and of those which are called "Stations," and enriching it with the relics of the Saint.

Lesson VI is Lesson IV from the first set in Common of Martyrs in Paschaltide (Sermon by St. Ambrose)

Lessons VII–IX from the Common of Supreme Pontiffs (Homily by St. Leo)

April 23 ~ St. George

Martyr ~ Semiduplex

All from Common except what follows

Lessons I–III from the occurring Scripture

Lessons IV–VI from the second set in the Common of Martyrs in Paschaltide (Homily by St. Cyprian)

—Lesson IV in England—

The martyr George bears among the Easterns the title of the holy and glorious Archmartyr, George the Triumphant. He suffered a glorious death for Christ's sake, in the persecution under Diocletian. When peace was given to the Church soon after, under Constantine, the memory of the martyr began to be celebrated, and churches were built under his invocation at Lydda in Palestine and at Constantinople. For thenceforth an extraordinary enthusiasm with regard to him grew up among the faithful, first in all parts of the East, and afterwards in the West. In times past, when Christian armies had been about to fight, they have been used to call as patrons upon Sts. George, Maurice, and Sebastian. There had been already special honor paid in England to the holy martyr George, and the supreme Pontiff Benedict XIV declared him the protector of the whole kingdom.

Lessons VII–IX from the Common of Martyrs in Paschaltide (Homily by St. Augustine)

April 24 ~ St. Fidelis of Simaringen

Martyr ~ Duplex

All from Common except what follows

Lessons I–III from the occurring Scripture

Lesson IV

Fidelis was born of the respectable family of Rey in the town of Sigmaringen in Swabia, in the year of our Lord 1577. From his childhood he was adorned with many bright gifts of nature and grace. Intellectually distinguished, and assisted by all the advantages of education, he took at Fribourg the degrees of Philosophy and of Civil and Canon Law, and it was while engaged in these studies, that he began to strive after the height of perfection in the school of Christ, to which end he earnestly trained himself in all the exercises of godliness. He ceased not to exhort to Christian godliness, both by his words and works, the noblemen who made him their companion, and who were drawn from the chief families of diverse parts of Europe. While on his travels, he was careful to mortify the lusts of the flesh by frequent austerities, and so to get the command of himself, that he was never seen under any circumstances to be moved to anger. He was a zealous champion of law and justice, and when he returned into Germany, he won a most distinguished name in his profession as an advocate. After a while, however, in view of the dangers which beset him, he determined to enter on a path safer as regarded his eternal salvation, and, in obedience to an inward call from above, he sought admission into the Seraphic Order, among the Capuchin Friars Minor, in the year 1612.

Lesson V

After he had obtained his holy wish, he showed himself even in his novitiate a singular despiser of the world and of himself, and still more so when with great spiritual joy he had made his solemn profession to the Lord. By his observance of the Rule, he became the wonder and the example of all. He gave himself chiefly to prayer and sacred learning, but he excelled, by a remarkable grace, in the ministry of the Word, and thereby not only stirred up the Catholics to bring forth more fruit, but also drew misbelievers to the knowledge of the truth. He was set at the head of communities of Friars in diverse places, and discharged the duty so laid upon him with great praise for prudence, justice, meekness, wisdom, and lowliness. He was animated by a vehement love of the strictest poverty, and cleansed the convent of whatever was not altogether needful. While he pursued himself with a healthy hatred, and most stern fasts, vigils, and scourgings, he showed to all others a love like the love of a mother for her sons. When a contagious fever made horrid ravages among the Austrian soldiers, he gave himself up with his whole soul to unwearied offices of tenderness toward the helpless sick. In allaying quarrels and relieving the temporal distress of his neighbor, he bore himself with such wisdom and zeal as to earn the name of Father of his country.

Lesson VI

He tenderly and warmly loved the Virgin Godbearer and her Rosary, and he besought God under the patronage of many of His holy servants, but especially under that of the same blessed Mother, to vouchsafe to let him offer his life and his blood together for the sake of the Catholic faith. This burning desire came upon him more and more, day by day, as he celebrated with great ardor of spirit the Holy Liturgy and by the unexpected Providence of God it came to pass that this brave soldier of Christ was chosen Præfect of the Missions which the Congregation for the Propagation of the Faith had at that time just founded for the Grisons. He accepted this hard task with a willing and joyful heart, and discharged it with such zeal, that many heretics were turned to the orthodox faith, and great hope was engendered that the whole of that people would return to the peace of Christ and His Church. Fidelis, who was gifted with the spirit of Prophecy, often foretold the great woes which afterwards came upon the Grisons, and that he himself would be murdered by the heretics. At last, on a certain 23rd of April, some of the heretics, who pretended to be converted, entreated him to come and preach the following day at the Church of a place which is called Sevis. He complied with the treacherous invitation, but, as he knew that plots were being laid against him, he had made himself ready beforehand for the last conflict. On the 24th day of April, in the year 1622, he went to Sevis, and began to preach, but his discourse was interrupted by a riot, and on his way back, he was met by a party of Calvinists, and brutally murdered. By this glorious death, which he suffered with a willing and cheerful heart, he offered to God in his own blood the first-fruits of martyrdom from the aforementioned Congregation. God has since glorified him by many signs and wonders, especially at Chur and Feldkirch, where his relics are kept with much popular veneration.

Lessons VII–IX from the first set in the Common of Martyrs in Paschaltide (Homily by St. Augustine)

April 25 ~ St. Mark

Evangelist ~ Duplex II Class

All from Common except what follows

Lesson IV

From the Book upon Church Writers, by St. Jerome, Priest

Mark was the disciple and interpreter of Peter, and it was from what he had heard Peter tell, that, at the request of the brethren at Rome, he wrote the shortest of the Gospels. When Peter had heard it, he approved it, and gave it to the Church to be read, by his authority. Mark betook himself to Egypt, with the Gospel which he had compiled, and was the first man who preached Christ at Alexandria. There he founded a Church with such teaching and austerity of life, that all who followed Christ were constrained to imitate him.

Lesson V

Last of all, Philo, that most learned Jew, observing that the first Church of Alexandria still kept the law of Moses, wrote a book concerning their customs, as if in praise of his own nation, wherein he says that under the teaching of Mark, the Christians of Alexandria had all things in common, just as Luke tells us was the case with all them that believed at Jerusalem. Mark died in the eighth year of Nero, and was buried at Alexandria, succeeded by Anianus.

Lesson VI is Lesson IV from the Common of Evangelists (Exposition by St. Gregory)

Lessons VII–IX from the Common of Evangelists (Homily by St. Gregory)

April 26 ~ Sts. Cletus & Marcellinus

Pope & Martyr ~ Semiduplex

All from Common except what follows

Lessons I–III from the occurring Scripture

Lesson IV

Cletus was a Roman, the son of Æmilian, of the Fifth Region of the city, and the street called Noble. He ruled the Church in the time of the Emperors Vespasian and Titus. In accordance with the precept of the Prince of the Apostles, He ordained twenty-five Priests for the city. He was the first Pope who made use in his letters of the phrase "Health and Apostolic Benediction." When he had ruled the Church for twelve years, seven months, and two days, and brought it into an excellent state of order, in the reign of the Emperor Domitian, and the second persecution since the time of Nero, he was crowned with martyrdom, and buried on the Vatican mount, near the body of blessed Peter.

Lesson V

Marcellinus was a Roman; he ruled the Church from the year 296 to the year 304, during the savage persecution which was ordered by the Emperor Diocletian. He suffered through the false severity of those who blamed him as being too indulgent toward them who had fallen into idolatry, and for this reason also has been slandered to the effect that he himself burnt incense to idols but this blessed Pope, on account of his confession of the faith, was put to death along with three other Christians, whose names are Claudius, Cyrinus, and Antoninus. At the command of the Emperor their bodies were cast out unburied, and lay so for thirty-six days. At the end of that time St. Peter appeared in a dream to Blessed Marcellus, and in obedience to his command, Marcellus went with Priests and Deacons, singing hymns and carrying lights, and buried these four bodies honorably in the Cemetery of Priscilla upon the Salarian Way. Marcellinus ruled the Church for seven years, eleven months, and twenty-three days. During this time he held two Advent ordinations, and ordained at them four Priests, and five Bishops for diverse Sees.

Lesson VI is Lesson IV from the first set in Common of Martyrs in Paschaltide (Sermon by St. Ambrose)

Lessons VII–IX from the Common of Supreme Pontiffs (Homily by St. Leo)

April 27 ~ St. Peter Canisius

Confessor & Doctor ~ Duplex

All from Common except what follows

Lessons I–III from the occurring Scripture

Lesson IV

Peter Canisius was born at Nijmegen in Gelderland, the Netherlands, in the very year in which Luther openly rebelled against the Church in Germany, and in which Ignatius of Loyola in Spain gave up earthly warfare to fight the battles of the Lord; God thus showed what adversaries he was to encounter, and under whose leadership he was to fight. He made his studies at Cologne, where he took a vow to God of perpetual chastity, and shortly afterwards entered the Society of Jesus. After his ordination as priest, he began at once to defend the Catholic faith against the wiles of the innovators by missions, sermons, and writing books. His eminent wisdom and experience caused the Cardinal of Augsburg and the papal legates to invite him to the Council of Trent, and he was present at its sessions more than once. Moreover, by the authority of the Supreme Pontiff, Pius IV, he was entrusted with the charge of making its decrees known in Germany and carrying them into effect. Paul IV sent him to the Synod of Petrikau, and Gregory XIII entrusted him with the carrying out of other missions, all of which he undertook with an eager spirit, never conquered by any difficulties, and carried the most important affairs of religion through all the crises of this present life to a successful end.

Lesson V

Inflamed with the heavenly fire of charity, which he had once received in the Vatican basilica from the sanctuary of the Heart of Jesus, and intent only on increasing the glory of God, it is almost impossible to describe how, for more than forty years, he took upon himself laborious tasks, and endured hardship, that he might defend very many cities and provinces of Germany from the contagion of heresy, or restore to the Catholic faith those that were infected with heresy. At the Diets of Ratisbon and Augsburg, he exhorted the princes of the Empire to defend the rights of the Church and reform the lives of their subjects. At Worms he reduced the insolent teachers of impiety to silence. St. Ignatius made him Prefect of the province of Upper Germany, where he founded houses and colleges in many places. He used every effort to advance and enlarge the German College founded at Rome; he restored the study of sacred and profane learning in academies, which had fallen into a wretched condition. He wrote two excellent volumes against the Centuriators of Magdeburg; and he edited a summary of Christian doctrine, which has been thoroughly approved by the judgment of theologians and by common use everywhere for three centuries, as well as very many other works useful for public instruction in the vulgar tongue. For all these reasons he was called the Hammer of the Heretics, and the Second Apostle of Germany, and is rightly thought to have been worthy of having been chosen by God to protect religion in Germany.

Lesson VI

In these activities he was accustomed to unite himself to God by frequent prayer and assiduous meditation on heavenly things, often bathed in tears and sometimes with his soul rapt in ecstasy. He was held in great honor by men of rank, or of most distinguished holiness, and by four of the Supreme Pontiffs, but he thought so humbly of himself that he spoke of and held himself as the least of all. He refused the bishopric of Vienna no less than three times. He was most obedient to his superiors, and ready at their mere nod to stop or to undertake all labors, even at the risk of his health and life. He guarded his chastity with perpetual voluntary self-mortification. At length, at Fribourg in Switzerland, where during the last years of his life he had labored much for the glory of God and the salvation of souls, he passed to God on the 21st day of December, 1597, in the seventy-seventh year of his age. This zealous champion of Catholic truth was adorned with the heavenly honors of the blessed by Pope Pius IX; and, as fresh miracles added to his renown, the Supreme Pontiff Pius XI, in the year of the Jubilee, included him among the Saints, and at the same time declared him a Doctor of the Universal Church.

Lesson VII

From the Holy Gospel according to St. Matthew (Matt 5:13–19)

At that time: Jesus said unto his disciples: "You are the salt of the earth; but if the salt lose its savor, wherewith shall it be salted?" And so forth.

Homily by St. Peter Canisius, Priest

I shall always love and reverence the Apostles sent by Christ, and their successors as well, in their work of sowing the Gospel seed. For all such may justly say of themselves: "Let a man so account of us, as of the ministers of Christ, and stewards of the mysteries of God." It was Christ himself, like a watchful and most faithful householder, who wished that the Gospel-lamp should be lit by his ministers and stewards with fire sent down from heaven; and once lit, that it should not be put under a bushel, but set upon a candlestick, so as to spread its brightness far and wide, and put to flight all darkness and error rife among both Jews and Gentiles.

Lesson VIII

It is not enough for the Gospel-teacher to please the people with his speaking. He must also be "the voice of one crying in the wilderness," and so by his eloquence call many to the good life. He must not be "a dumb dog, not even able to bark," as spoken of by the Prophet Isaias. Yea, he should also burn in such a way that, equipped with good works and love, he may adorn his evangelical office, and follow the leadership of Paul. He indeed was not satisfied with bidding the bishop of the Ephesians: "This command and teach: conduct thyself in work as a good soldier of Christ Jesus"; but he unflaggingly preached the Gospel to friend and foe alike, and said with a good conscience to the bishops gathered at Ephesus: "You know how I kept back nothing that was profitable unto you, but have showed you, and have taught you publicly, and from house to house, urging Jews and Gentiles to turn unto God in repentance and to believe in our Lord Jesus Christ."

Lesson IX

Such should be the shepherd in the Church who, like Paul, becomes all things to all men, so that the sick may find healing in him; the sad, joy; the desperate, hope; the ignorant, instruction; those in doubt, advice; the penitent, forgiveness and comfort, and finally, everyone whatever is necessary unto salvation. And so Christ, when he wished to appoint the chief teachers of the world and of the Church, did not limit himself to saying to his disciples: "You are the light of the world:" but also added: "A city that is set on a hill cannot be hidden; neither do men light a candle, and put it under a bushel, but on a candlestick, and it gives light unto all that are in the house." Those churchmen err who imagine that it is by brilliant preaching that they fulfill their office; rather, it is by holiness of life and an ardent charity.

April 28 ~ St. Paul of the Cross

Confessor ~ Duplex

All from Common
except what follows

Lessons I–III from the
occurring Scripture

Lesson IV

Paul of the Cross was sprung of a noble family of the Danei, at Castellazzo, near Alessandria, in the Province of Acqui, in the territory of the then Republic of Genoa, but was born at Ovada, in the same province. The holiness with which he was afterwards to shine was foreshown by a strange light which filled his mother's chamber while she was in labour, and by the remarkable help which was bestowed upon him by the great Queen of Heaven, who delivered him unhurt from certain destruction when he was fallen into a river as a lad. From the first use of reason he burnt with love for Jesus crucified, and began to spend long times in contemplating Him. He chastised his innocent flesh with watching, scourging, fasting, and all severe hardships, and on Friday he drank vinegar mingled with gall. He was seized with a desire for martyrdom, and enlisted in the army which was being raised at Venice to fight against the Turks but in consequence of the Will of God, made known to him while he was in prayer, he left the army in order to serve in a more exalted regiment whose duty it should be to defend the Church and to toil for the eternal salvation of men. When he returned home he refused a very honorable marriage, and also the inheritance which was bequeathed to him by his father's brother, and would eagerly enter upon a straiter way of the cross and be clad by his own Bishop with a rough tunic. By command of the Bishop, on account of his eminent holiness of life and knowledge of the things of God, he began, even before he became a cleric, to toil in the Lord's field with great fruit of souls by the preaching of the Divine Word.

Lesson V

He betook himself to Rome, and when he had there studied a regular course of theology he was ordained Priest in obedience to the command of the Supreme Pontiff Benedict XIII, who also gave him permission to gather comrades around him. He withdrew to the solitude of Mount Argentaro, whither he had been already called by the Blessed Virgin, at which time she also showed him in vision a black habit marked with the emblems of the sufferings of her

Son. At Mount Argentaro, he laid the foundations of his new Congregation, which under the blessing of God, grew quickly through the labors of Paul, and attracted to it eminent men. It received the confirmation of the Apostolic See more than once, with the rules which Paul himself had received from God in prayer and the addition of a fourth vow, that, namely, to promote the blessed remembrance of the sufferings of the Lord. He founded a congregation of holy virgins also, who should dwell constantly upon the overflowing love of the Divine Bridegroom. Amid all these works his untiring love for souls caused him never to weary in the preaching of the Gospel, and he led into the path of salvation men almost countless, among whom were some of the most lost, or those who had fallen into heresy. The greatest and most wonderful power of his preaching was how he told of the sufferings of Christ, so that he himself and his hearers would alike burst into tears, and hardened hearts were rent by repentance.

Lesson VI

The fire of the love of God burnt so in his heart that the part of his undergarment which was next thereto often presented the appearance of having been scorched, and two of his ribs seemed to be raised. He could not withhold his tears, especially when he was saying Mass, and when he was in a state of trance, as oftentimes befell, his body was sometimes seen to be raised into the air, and his face to shine as with light from heaven. Sometimes when he was preaching, a heavenly voice was heard prompting him, or his words became audible at the distance of several miles. He was eminent for the gifts of prophecy, of speaking with tongues, of reading the heart, and of power over evil spirits, over diseases, and over the inanimate elements of nature. The Supreme Pontiffs themselves regarded him as dear and venerable, but he held himself to be but an unprofitable servant, and a sinful wretch upon whom devils might well trample. He held to the bitter hardships of his life, even unto a great age, and passed to Heaven from Rome, upon the 18th day of October, being the day which he had himself foretold, in the year 1775, after he had addressed to his disciples noble exhortations which are as the heritage of his spirit, and had been comforted by the sacraments of the Church, and by a heavenly vision. The Supreme Pontiff Pius IX numbered his name among those of the blessed, and then, after renewed signs and wonders, among those of the Saints.

Lessons VII–IX from the Common of Evangelists (Homily by St. Gregory)

Lesson IX—Commemoration of St. Vitalis, Martyr

Vitalis was a soldier, and the father of the holy Martyrs Gervase and Protase. He went to Ravenna with Paulinus the judge, and there saw the physician Ursicinus led out to die, because he owned to being a believer in Christ. As the torments went on, Ursicinus seemed to waver a little, and Vitalis cried out to him, "Ursicinus! As a physician thou hast been used to heal other men's bodies, take heed lest thou let thine own soul die eternally." These words encouraged Ursicinus, and he endured bravely in his testimony even unto the end but Paulinus was filled with fury, and caused Vitalis to be seized, tormented on the rack, and finally thrown into a pit and buried under an heap of stones. When it was over, a certain priest of Apollo, who had urged on Paulinus against Vitalis, was seized by the devil, and began to cry out, "Vitalis, Vitalis, thou art Christ's Martyr, but thou makest me to burn, thou makest me to burn!" And cast into that frenzy, he threw himself into the river.

April 29 ~ St. Peter of Verona

Martyr ~ Duplex

All from Common
except what follows

Lessons I–III from the
occurring Scripture

Lesson IV

Peter was born at Verona, in the year of our Lord 1205, of parents polluted with the Manichæan heresy, but he himself began his lifelong strife against error when he was but a little child. When he was seven years old he went to school, and was asked by his heretic uncle what he learnt there. He answered that he had learnt the Christian Creed and neither his father nor his uncle were ever able to shake his constancy in the faith, either by cajolements or threats. When he was a young lad he went to Bologna to study, and there he was called by the Holy Ghost to a higher state of life, and entered the Order of Friars Preachers, at fifteen years of age.

Lesson V

He was marked by great perfection as a Friar so watchful was he over the purity of his body and soul, that he never felt himself defiled by a mortal sin. He chastened his body by fasting and watching, and ennobled his soul by the contemplation of the things of God. He was constantly busied in works for furthering the salvation of souls and had a peculiar gift of grace for clearly convincing heretics. Such was his power as a preacher, that countless crowds were drawn together to hear him, and many were moved to repentance.

Lesson VI

The faith which was in him burnt so hotly, that he longed to seal his confession with his blood, and oftentimes he earnestly besought from God the grace to do so. It was but a little while before the heretics murdered him, that he foretold, in preaching, his own approaching death. While he was entrusted with the duties of the Holy Inquisition, he was returning from Como to Milan, when an ungodly ruffian assailed him and wounded him once and again in the head with a sword. Peter, to whom these blows were nearly fatal, began with his last breath to recite that Profession of Faith to which as a little child he had clung with such manly courage, but the murderer thrust the weapon into his side, and he passed away to receive a Martyr's palm in heaven. It was the 6th day of April, in the year of salvation 1252. In the following year, Innocent IV, seeing by how many miracles God had been pleased to glorify him, added his name to the sacred roll of Martyrs.

Lessons VII–IX from the first set in the Common of Martyrs in Paschaltide (Homily by St. Augustine)

April 30 ~ St. Catharine of Siena

Virgin ~ Duplex
All from Common except what follows

Lessons I–III from the occurring Scripture

Lesson IV

This Catharine was a maiden of Siena, and was born of godly parents, in the year 1347. She took the habit of the Third Order of St. Dominic. Her fasts were most severe, and the austerity of her life wonderful. It was discovered that on some occasions she took no food at all from Ash Wednesday till Ascension Day, receiving all needful strength by taking Holy Communion. She was engaged oftentimes in a wrestling with devils, and was sorely tried by them with diverse assaults: she was consumed by fevers, and suffered likewise from other diseases. Great and holy was the name of Catharine, and sick folk, and such as were vexed with evil spirits, were brought to her from all quarters. Through the Name of Christ, she had command over sickness and fever, and forced the foul spirits to leave the bodies of the tormented.

Lesson V

While she dwelt at Pisa, on a certain Lord's Day, after she had received the Living Bread Which came down from heaven, she was in the spirit; and saw the Lord nailed to the Cross advancing towards her. There was a great light round about Him, and five rays of light streaming from the five marks of the Wounds in His Feet, and Hands, and Side, which smote her upon the five corresponding places in her body. When Catharine perceived this vision, she besought the Lord that no marks might become manifest upon her flesh, and straightway the five beams of light changed from the color of blood into that of gold, and touched in the form of pure light her feet, and hands, and side. At this moment the agony which she felt was so piercing, that she believed that if God had not lessened it, she would have died. Thus the Lord in His great love for her, gave her this great grace, in a new and twofold manner, namely, that she felt all the pain of the wounds, but without there being any bloody marks to meet the gaze of men. This was the account given by the handmaiden of God to her Confessor, Raymund, and it is for this reason that when the pious wishes of the faithful lead them to make pictures of the blessed Catharine, they paint her with golden rays of light proceeding from those five places in her body which correspond to the five places wherein our Lord was wounded by the nails and spear.

Lesson VI

The learning which Catharine had was not acquired but inspired. She answered Professors of Divinity upon the very hardest questions concerning God. No one was ever in her company without going away better. She healed many hatreds, and quieted the most deadly feuds. To make peace for the Florentines, who had quarreled with the Church and were under an Ecclesiastical Interdict, she travelled to Avignon in 1376 to see the Supreme Pontiff Gregory XI. To him she showed that she had had revealed to her from heaven his secret purpose of going back to Rome, which had been known only to God and himself. It was at her persuasion, as well as by his own judgment, that the Pope did in the end return to his own See. She was much respected by this Gregory, as well as by his successor Urban VI, who even employed her in their embassies. The Bridegroom took her home, upon the 29th day of April, in the year of salvation 1380, when she was about thirty-three years old, after she had given almost countless proofs of extraordinary Christian graces, and manifestly displayed the gifts of Prophecy and miracles. Pope Pius II enrolled her among the Virgin Saints.

Lessons VII–IX from the first set in the Common of Virgins (Homily by St. Gregory)

FEASTS OF MAY

May 1 ~ Sts. Philip & James

Apostles ~ Duplex II Class

All from Common
except what follows

If this Feast falls during the time when the Catholic Epistle of St. James is read in the occurring Scripture (4th week after Easter), then Lessons I–III are instead taken from the occurring Scripture—otherwise, Lessons I–III are as follows

Lesson I ~ Jas 1:1–6

Beginning of the Catholic Epistle of St. James the Apostle

James the servant of God, and of our Lord Jesus Christ, to the twelve tribes which are scattered abroad, greeting. My brethren, count it all joy, when you shall fall into diverse temptations; Knowing that the trying of your faith worketh patience. And patience hath a perfect work; that you may be perfect and entire, failing in nothing. But if any of you want wisdom, let him ask of God, who giveth to all men abundantly, and upbraideth not; and it shall be given him. But let him ask in faith, nothing wavering.

Lesson II ~ Jas 1:6–11

For he that wavereth is like a wave of the sea, which is moved and carried about by the wind. Therefore let not that man think that he shall receive any thing of the Lord. A double minded man is inconstant in all his ways. But let the brother of low condition glory in his exaltation: And the rich, in his being low; because as the flower of the grass shall he pass away. For the sun rose with a burning heat, and parched the grass, and the flower thereof fell off, and the beauty of the shape thereof perished: so also shall the rich man fade away in his ways.

Lesson III ~ Jas 1:12–16

Blessed is the man that endureth temptation; for when he hath been proved, he shall receive a crown of life, which God hath promised to them that love him. Let no man, when he is tempted, say that he is tempted by God. For God is not a tempter of evils, and he tempteth no man. But every man is tempted by his own concupiscence, being drawn away and allured. Then when concupiscence hath conceived, it bringeth forth sin. But sin, when it is completed, begetteth death. Do not err, therefore, my dearest brethren.

Lesson IV

Philip was born in the town of Bethsaida, and was one of the first of the twelve Apostles who were called by the Lord Christ. Then Philip finds Nathanael, and says unto him: "We have found Him of Whom Moses in the Law, and the Prophets, did write." And so he brought him to the Lord. How familiarly he was in the company of Christ, is manifest from that which is written: "There were certain Greeks among them that came up to worship at the Feast; the same came therefore to Philip, and desired him, saying: Sir, we would see Jesus." When the Lord was in the wilderness, and was about to feed a great multitude, He said unto Philip: "Whence shall we buy bread, that these may eat?" Philip, after he had received the Holy Ghost, took Scythia, by lot, as the land wherein he was to preach the Gospel, and brought nearly all that people to believe in Christ. At the last he came to Hierapolis in Phrygia, and there, for Christ's Name's sake, he was fastened to a cross and stoned to death. The day was the first of May. The Christians of Hierapolis buried his body at that place, but it was afterwards brought to Rome and laid in the Basilica of the Twelve Apostles, beside that of the blessed Apostle James.

Lesson V

James, surnamed the Just, the brother of the Lord, was a Nazarite from the womb. During his whole life he never drank wine or strong drink, never ate meat, never shaved, and used neither oil nor bath. He was the only man who was allowed to go into the Holy of Holies. His raiment was always linen. So continually did he kneel in prayer, that the skin of his knees became calloused, like a camel's knees. After Christ was ascended, the Apostles made James Bishop of Jerusalem and even the Prince of the Apostles gave special intelligence to him after he was delivered from prison by an angel. When in the Council of Jerusalem there was risen a controversy about the law and circumcision, James, following the opinion of Peter, addressed a discourse to the brethren wherein he proved the call of the Gentiles and commanded letters to be sent to such brethren as were absent, that they might take heed not to impose the yoke of the Mosaic Law upon the Gentiles. It is of him that the Apostle Paul says, writing to the Galatians: "Other of the Apostles saw I none, save James the Lord's brother."

Lesson VI

So great was James' holiness of life that men strove one with another to touch the hem of his garment. When he was ninety-six years old, and had most holily governed the Church of Jerusalem for thirty years, ever most constantly preaching Christ the Son of God, he laid down his life for the faith. He was first stoned, and afterward taken up on to a pinnacle of the Temple and cast down from thence. His legs were broken by the fall, and he was well-nigh dead, but he lifted up his hands towards heaven, and prayed to God for the salvation of his murderers, saying: "Lord, forgive them, for they know not what they do." As he said this, one that stood by smote him grievously upon the head with a fuller's club, and he resigned his spirit to God. He testified in the seventh year of Nero and was buried near the Temple, in the place where he had fallen. He wrote one of the Seven Epistles which are called Catholic.

Lesson VII

From the Holy Gospel according to St. John (John 14:1–13)

At that time, Jesus said unto His disciples: "Let not your heart be troubled. You believe in God, believe also in Me. In My Father's house there are many mansions." And so on.

Homily by St. Augustine, Bishop

It behooves us, my brethren, to have our minds more given toward God, if we would that those words of the Holy Gospel which have just sounded in our ears, should become a living reality for our understandings. The Lord Jesus says: "Let not your heart be troubled. You believe in God, believe also in Me." Lest, being but men, their heart should be troubled by the fear of death, He strengthens them, even by the reminder that He is God. He says: "Ye believe in God, believe also in Me," for if you believe in God, you must believe in Me. And this would not be so, if Christ were not God.

Lesson VIII

We believe in God, believe also in Him Who is by nature and not by robbery equal with God, for in that He emptied Himself, He did it not by laying aside the form of God, but by taking upon Him the form of a servant. You fear death for this form of a servant, but let not your heart be troubled, the form of God will raise it up again. But what signifies that which follows? "In My Father's house there are many mansions." Was it not that they had fear on their own account, and needed for themselves to hear Him say, "Let not your heart be troubled" Which of them trembled not when they had heard Him say to Peter, the truest and boldest of them all: "The cock shall not crow this day, before that thou shalt thrice deny that thou knowest Me."

Lesson IX

Rightly were they troubled, for they were about to be scattered from Him; but when they heard Him say, "In My Father's house are many mansions," they had been comforted even if He had not also said, "I go to prepare a place for you," for then they believed and knew, that, when all dangers and all trials were for ever over, they should be for ever with the Lord, with Christ and with God. Yea, though one man be stronger than another, though one be wiser than another, though one be holier than another, yet "in My Father's house are many mansions." That house is a house wherein none are strangers, but every man shall receive a mansion therein according to his merits.

May 2 ~ St. Athanasius

Bishop, Confessor, & Doctor ~ Duplex

All from Common except what follows

Lessons I–III from the occurring Scripture

Lesson IV

The great Athanasius, the greatest soldier that the Catholic Religion perhaps ever had, was an Alexandrian. He was ordained Deacon, in the year 326, by Alexander, Bishop of that city, whom he afterwards succeeded. In 325 he had followed

Alexander to the Council of Nicæa, where he wrestled triumphantly against the blasphemy of Arius. For this reason he was honored with so much hatred by the Arians, that their vindictiveness never forsook him from that time forward. In the year 335, they called together a Council at Tyre, composed for the most part of Arian Bishops, where they suborned a wretched woman to charge Athanasius with having raped her when she had received him as a guest into her house. Athanasius therefore came into the assembly, and with him a certain priest whose name was Timothy. This Timothy arose as though he were Athanasius, and asked her, saying: "Woman, was it not I that was thy guest? Was it I that raped thee?" She cried out indignantly: "Yea, thou it was that didst rape me," which she attested with an oath, and called on the honor of the judges to punish such iniquity. Upon discovery of her perjury, they cast the shameless woman from their presence.

Lesson V

The Arians also accused Athanasius of having murdered the (schismatic) Bishop Arsenius. This Arsenius they kept shut up, and brought into the court a dead man's hand, which they declared had been his, and had been cut off by Athanasius to use in sorcery. But Arsenius escaped in the night, and when he appeared before all the Council whole and sound, this most shameless crime of the enemies of Athanasius was exposed. They nevertheless attributed this to Athanasius being a warlock, and persisted still in their attack on him. He was driven into exile, and banished to Trier in Gaul. Thenceforth, under authority of the Emperor Constantius, that abettor of Arians, he was hunted to and fro with unceasing persecutions. He suffered hardships which defy belief. He was sent wandering all about the Roman world. He was twice more thrust out of his See, and again restored through the authority of Pope Julius of Rome, and with the protection of the Emperor Constans, the brother of Constantius, by decrees of the Councils of Sardica and of Jerusalem. The vindictiveness of the Arians never let him alone. In his third exile so great was the danger of his life from the pursuit of their undying hatred, that he had to lie hid for five years in a dry cistern, unknown to all men, save one of his friends who brought him food.

Lesson VI

After the death of Constantius, Julian the Apostate, who succeeded him, allowed every sort of Bishop who had been banished to return to their own Churches. Athanasius therefore returned to Alexandria, and was received with profound reverence. But it was not long before the same Arians got Julian to hunt him down again, and again it behooved him to flee. A band of soldiers were sent in pursuit of him to kill him, and as he fled up the Nile, their boat pressed hard on his. Athanasius, before they were yet in sight, had his own boat turned round, and went down the stream to meet them. As the vessels passed one another the murderers called out to ask if they knew where Athanasius was, and the servant of God himself cried to them in answer, "You are close to him!" Whereupon they redoubled their exertions to ascend the stream, and Athanasius went peacefully down to Alexandria, and found means of concealment till the death of Julian. Yet once again he had to fly from another persecution at Alexandria, and in this his fifth and last exile he hid himself for four months in his own father's sepulchre. From all these so many and so great dangers did God deliver him, and at last he died in his own bed at Alexandria, upon the 2nd day of May, in the year of salvation 373, in the reign of Valens. He wrote much that is both godly and luminous in explaining the Catholic Faith, and governed the Church of Alexandria in great holiness, amid all changes of weather, for forty-six years.

Lesson VII

From the Holy Gospel according to St. Matthew (Matt 10:23–28)

At that time Jesus said to his disciples: And when they shall persecute you in this city, flee into another. And so on.

Homily by St. Athanasius, Bishop

It is written in the Law, "You shall appoint cities to be cities of refuge for you, that in these cities they which were pursued to put them to death might enter and be safe." And in the latter days when He was come, even that very Word of the Father, Which had spoken before unto Moses, He gave again the same commandment: "When they persecute you in this city, flee into another." And, a while afterward, He said "When you shall see the abomination of desolation, spoken of by Daniel the Prophet, stand in the Holy Place, whoso reads, let him understand, then let them which be in Judaea flee unto the mountains; let him which is on the housetop not come down to take anything out of his house; neither let him which is in the field return back to take his clothes."

Lesson VIII

The Saints, therefore, knowing these words of the Lord, have obeyed them in their lives. What the Lord has now commanded by His Own Mouth He commanded through His Saints before He Himself was come in the flesh, and to obey this commandment works perfection in a man, since whatever God commands is a thing which it behooves man to do. For this cause, that very Word of God Which was made flesh for our sake thought it right when they sought Him, even as at this present time they are seeking us, to hide Himself, and, when they persecuted Him, to fly and escape from their laying in wait for Him although when that time came which He had Himself decreed, and wherein He willed, in the Body, to suffer for us all, He willingly gave Himself up to His enemies.

Lesson IX

Holy men of God, therefore, have learnt to take example from their Saviour, and the Same is and has been the Teacher of all such, whether of old, or in these latter days, and know how it is lawful to baffle their persecutors by flying from them, and by lying hid when they seek them. For since they know not the day nor the hour wherein an all-seeing God has ordained their end, they do not daringly give themselves into the power of such as hate them, but rather, knowing it to be written, "My times are in Thy hand," and that "the Lord kills and makes alive," they "endure unto the end," "they wander about," as says the Apostle, "in sheep-skins and goatskins, being destitute, afflicted, they wander in deserts, and" hide "in dens and caves of the earth," until either their appointed time come, or until more plainly God, the real Appointer of times, speaks unto them, and chains up the persecutors, or manifestly gives them over into the hands of the same, as may be His Own good pleasure.

May 3 ~ Invention of the Holy Cross

Duplex II Class

Lesson I ~ Gal 3:10–14

From the Epistle of St. Paul the Apostle to the Galatians

For as many as are of the works of the law, are under a curse. For it is written: Cursed is every one, that abideth not in all things, which are written in the book of the law to do them. But that in the law no man is justified with God, it is manifest: because the just man liveth by faith. But the law is not of faith: but, He that doth those things, shall live in them. Christ hath redeemed us from the curse of the law, being made a curse for us: for it is written: Cursed is every one that hangeth on a tree: That the blessing of Abraham might come on the Gentiles through Christ Jesus: that we may receive the promise of the Spirit by faith.

Lesson II ~ Phil 2:5–11

From the Epistle to the Philippians

For let this mind be in you, which was also in Christ Jesus: Who being in the form of God, thought it not robbery to be equal with God: But emptied himself, taking the form of a servant, being made in the likeness of men, and in habit found as a man. He humbled himself, becoming obedient unto death, even to the death of the cross. For which cause God also hath exalted him, and hath given him a name which is above all names: That in the name of Jesus every knee should bow, of those that are in heaven, on earth, and under the earth: And that every tongue should confess that the Lord Jesus Christ is in the glory of God the Father.

Lesson III ~ Col 2:9–15

From the Epistle to the Colossians

For in him dwelleth all the fulness of the Godhead corporeally; And you are filled in him, who is the head of all principality and power: In whom also you are circumcised with circumcision not made by hand, in despoiling of the body of the flesh, but in the circumcision of Christ: Buried with him in baptism, in whom also you are risen again by the faith of the operation of God, who hath raised him up from the dead. And you, when you were dead in your sins, and the uncircumcision of your flesh; he hath quickened together with him, forgiving you all offences: Blotting out the handwriting of the decree that was against us, which was contrary to us. And he hath taken the same out of the way, fastening it to the cross: And despoiling the principalities and powers, he hath exposed them confidently in open show, triumphing over them in himself.

Lesson IV

After that famous victory which the Emperor Constantine gained over Maxentius, in the year 312, on the eve of which the banner of the Cross of the Lord had been given to him from heaven, Helen, the mother of Constantine, being warned in a dream, came to Jerusalem, in 326, to seek for the Cross. There it was her care to cause to be overthrown the marble statue of Venus, which had stood on Calvary for about one hundred and eighty years, and which had originally been put there to desecrate and destroy the memorial of the sufferings of the Lord Christ. Similar work Helen did at Bethlehem, by cleansing from an image of Adonis the stable where the Saviour was born, and from an idol of Jupiter, the place where He had arisen from the dead.

Lesson V

Then she had thus cleansed the place where the Cross had stood, Helen caused deep excavations to be made, which resulted in the discovery of three crosses, and, apart from them, the writing which had been nailed on that of the Lord. But which of the crosses had been His was unknown, and was only manifested by a miracle. Macarius, Bishop of Jerusalem, after offering solemn prayers to God, touched with each of the three a woman who was afflicted with a grievous disease. The two first had no effect, but at the touch of the third she was immediately healed.

Lesson VI

Helen, after she had found the life-giving Cross, built over the site of the Passion a Church of extraordinary splendor, wherein she deposited part of the Cross, enclosed in a silver case. Another part which she gave to her son, Constantine, was laid up in the Church of the Holy Cross of Jerusalem, which he built at Rome on the site of the Sessorian Palace. She also gave to her son the nails with which the Most Holy Body of Jesus Christ had been pierced. Constantine established a law abolishing the punishment of crucifixion for all time coming and thenceforth what had hitherto been a hissing and a curse among men, began to be esteemed worshipful and glorious.

Lesson VII

From the Holy Gospel according to St. John (John 3:1–15)

At that time, There was a man of the Pharisees named Nicodemus, a ruler of the Jews. The same came to Jesus by night, and said unto Him

Rabbi, we know that Thou art a Teacher come from God. And so on.

Homily by St. Augustine, Bishop

Nicodemus was one of them which believed in the Name of Jesus, when they saw the signs and wonders which He did. So has John given us to understand a few words before our text: "Now when He was in Jerusalem at the Passover, in the feast-day, many believed in His Name." And why they believed in His Name John tells us immediately: "When they saw the miracles which He did." And now, what says he regarding Nicodemus? "There was a man of the Pharisees, named Nicodemus, a ruler of the Jews. The same came to Jesus by night, and said unto Him Rabbi, we know that Thou art a Teacher come from God." Nicodemus therefore believed in His Name. And why he believed He says: "For no man can do these miracles that Thou doest, except God be with him."

Lesson VIII

Lo, then, Nicodemus was one of the many which had believed in His Name; let us seek to find in Nicodemus why "Jesus did not commit Himself unto them." "Jesus answered and said unto him: Amen, Amen, I say unto thee, except a man be born again, he cannot see the kingdom of God." Jesus therefore commits Himself unto such as be born again. Behold, Nicodemus and they that were with him believed in Jesus, but Jesus did not commit Himself unto them. Just so are all Catechumens; they believe in the Name of Christ, but Jesus has not yet committed Himself unto them.

Now I trust you will be good enough to pay attention, and understand what I am going to say. If you ask of a Catechumen "Dost thou believe in Christ" he says "I believe," and he signs himself with the sign of the Cross. The Cross of his Lord is marked upon his forehead, and he is not ashamed of it. Behold, he believes in the Name of Christ. But let us ask him "Dost thou eat the flesh of the Son of Man" and he knows not what we mean, for Jesus has not yet committed Himself unto him.

Lesson IX—Commemoration of Sts. Alexander I, Eventinus, and Theodulus, Pope and Martyrs, and Juvenal, Confessor Bishop

Alexander was a Roman, who ruled the Church during the reign of the Emperor Hadrian. He turned to Christ a great number of the Roman nobility. He ordained that nothing but bread and wine should be offered at the mystery, but that some water should be mingled with the wine, in memory of the Blood and Water Which flowed from the Side of Jesus Christ. He added to the Canon of the Mass the words "Who, the day before He suffered." He also ordained that blessed water mingled with salt, should be kept always in Churches, and should be used in private rooms to scare away devils.

He sat in the throne of Peter ten years, five months, and twenty days. He has great renown on account of the holiness of his life, and the usefulness of his institutions. He was crowned with martyrdom, in the year 119, together with the Priests Eventius and Theodulus, and was buried beside the Nomentan Way, at the third milestone from the city, in the same place where he had been beheaded. During his Pontificate he held diverse Advent ordinations, and at them ordained six Priests, two Deacons, and five Bishops for diverse places. The bodies of these three Martyrs, Alexander, Eventius, and Theodulus, were afterwards brought into the city, and buried in the Church of St. Sabina. On this day likewise, about the year 367, occurred the blessed death of Juvenal, the saintly Bishop of Narnia, who by the holiness of his life and teaching, became the father in Christ of so many of the dwellers in that city. He fell asleep very peacefully, with great fame for miracles, and was there honorably buried.

May 4 ~ St. Monica

Widow ~ Duplex

All from Common except what follows

Lessons I–III from the occurring Scripture

Lesson IV

Monica was twice the mother of St. Augustine, for, under God, he owed to her both earth and heaven. When her husband was very old she made him a friend of Jesus Christ, and after his death she lived a widow in all purity and constantly occupied in works of mercy. Her son Augustine had fallen into the heresy of the Manichæans, and for his conversion she earnestly pleaded with God for years, with strong crying and tears. She followed Augustine to Milan, and tenderly and constantly besought him to confer with Ambrose the Bishop. This he consented to do, and at last, through the public sermons and private conversations of Ambrose, his eyes were opened to see the truth of the Catholic Religion, and he received baptism at the Bishop's hands, at Easter of the year 387.

Lesson V

The mother and son set out to return to their home in Africa, but after they had reached Ostia at the mouth of the Tiber, she fell into fever. One day as she lay sick, she came to herself after her mind had been long wandering, and said: "Where am I?" Then she saw who were standing by, and said "Let your mother lie here, only, remember me at the altar of the Lord." On the ninth day this blessed lady surrendered her spirit to God. Her body was buried there at Ostia in the Church of St. Aurea, but, long after, in the papacy of Martin V, it was carried to Rome and honorably buried again in the Church of St. Augustine.

Lesson VI—Conf. St. Aug. Bk. 9. ch. 12

Augustine added these words after describing his mother's death:

"For we did not think it fitting to celebrate that funeral with tearful laments and groanings; for in such ways are they mourned who die unhappily, or are altogether dead. But she neither died unhappy, nor did she altogether die. For of this were we assured by the witness of her good conduct, and her faith unfeigned. And then little by little did I bring back my former thoughts of Your handmaid, her devout conduct towards You, her holy tenderness and attentiveness towards us, of which I was suddenly deprived; and it pleased me to weep for her and for me. And if one finds me to have sinned in weeping for my mother during so small a part of an hour—that mother who was for a while dead to my eyes, who had for many years wept for me, that I might live in Your eyes—let him not laugh, but rather, if he be a man of a noble charity, let him weep for my sins against You, the Father of all the brethren of Your Christ."

Lessons VII–IX from Sunday XV after the Octave of Pentecost (Homily by St. Augustine)

May 5 ~ St. Pius V

Pope & Confessor ~ Duplex

All from Common except what follows

Lessons I–III from the occurring Scripture

Lesson IV

Pius was born on the 27th of January, in the year 1504, in a town of the Milanese which they called Bosco, to the noble Ghislieri family of Bologna. At the age of fourteen years he entered the order of Friars Preachers. He was a man marked by wonderful patience, profound humility, greatest austerity of life, an unwavering earnestness in prayer, and a most strong zeal for the perfect observance of the Rule of his Order, and for the greater glory of God. He gave himself to the study of Philosophy and Theology, and was so learned in both, that he discharged for many years with great reputation the duties of a Professor of those sciences. He preached publicly in many places, to the great profit of his hearers. He long did the work of Inquisitor with unflinching spirit, and preserved many cities, not without risk to his own life, from the heresy which was then creeping in everywhere.

Lesson V

Paul IV, to whom his virtues had greatly endeared him, raised him in 1556, to the united Bishoprics of Nepi and Sutri, and after two years he was enrolled among the Cardinal Priests of the Roman Church. Pius IV translated him to the Church of Mondovi in Piedmont, wherein, on his coming, he found that many corruptions had crept in. He reformed the whole of his diocese, and, after settling his affairs, returned to Rome, where his attention was called to matters of the gravest business, in determining which he used Apostolic boldness and firmness. After the death of Pius IV, Pius V was elected to succeed him, on the 7th of January, 1566, to the astonishment of all men.

On becoming Pope he changed his way of life in no respect except as regarded his raiment. The Propagation of Religion was to him the object of unceasing care, the restoration of the Discipline of the Church: of unwearied toil, the uprooting of error: of sleepless watchfulness, the relieving the needs of the poor: of unfailing charity, the maintenance of the rights of the Apostolic See: of adamantine firmness.

Lesson VI

The Turkish Sultan Selim was bloated with many victories, and had got together a huge fleet in the Gulf of Lepanto, but Pius V crushed him, on the 7th of October, 1571, not so much by force of arms as by means of the prayers wherein he pleaded with God. At the hour that the victory was won, Pius knew it by the inward revelation of God, and stated the fact to his servants. He was busied with the preparations for a new expedition against the Turks, when he was laid down by grievous sickness. He bore most sharp sufferings with the gentlest patience, and when the end came, he received the Sacraments as is usual, and with great peace yielded his spirit to God, on the 1st of May, in the year of salvation 1572, and of his own age the 68th, having sat as Pope six years, three months, and twenty-four days. His body is buried in the Basilica of St. Mary, where the Manger from Bethlehem is, and is there held in great respect by the faithful, who have obtained from God by his prayers many evident miracles. Said miracles having been proved by a judicial investigation, Pope Clement XI enrolled his name among those of the Saints.

Lessons VII–IX from the Common of Supreme Pontiffs (Homily by St. Leo)

May 6 ~ St. John before the Latin Gate

Apostle & Evangelist ~ Major Duplex

All from Common except what follows

If this Feast falls during the time when the Apocalypse or Epistles of St. John are read in the occurring Scripture (3rd week after Easter or within the Ascension Octave, respectively), then Lessons I–III are instead taken from the occurring Scripture—otherwise, Lessons I–III are as follows

Lesson I ~ 1 John 1:1–5

From the first letter of St. John the Apostle

That which was from the beginning, which we have heard, which we have seen with our eyes, which we have looked upon, and our hands have handled, of the word of life: For the life was manifested; and we have seen and do bear witness, and declare unto you the life eternal, which was with the Father, and hath appeared to us: That which we have seen and have heard, we declare unto you, that you also may have fellowship with us, and our fellowship may be with the Father, and with his Son Jesus Christ. And these things we write to you, that you may rejoice, and your joy may be full. And this is the declaration which we have heard from him, and declare unto you: That God is light, and in him there is no darkness.

Lesson II ~ 1 John 1:6–10

If we say that we have fellowship with him, and walk in darkness, we lie, and do not the truth. But if we walk in the light, as he also is in the light, we have fellowship one with another, and the blood of Jesus Christ his Son cleanseth us from all sin. If we say that we have no sin, we deceive ourselves, and the truth is not in us. If we confess our sins, he is faithful and just, to forgive us our sins, and to cleanse us from all iniquity. If we say that we have not sinned, we make him a liar, and his word is not in us.

Lesson III ~ 1 John 2:1–5

My little children, these things I write to you, that you may not sin. But if any man sin, we have an advocate with the Father, Jesus Christ the just: And he is the propitiation for our sins: and not for ours only, but also for those of the whole world. And by this we know that we have known him, if we keep his commandments. He who saith that he knoweth him, and keepeth not his commandments, is a liar, and the truth is not in him. But he that keepeth his word, in him in very deed the charity of God is perfected.

Lesson IV

From the Book against Jovinian written by St. Jerome, Priest

The Apostle John was one of the disciples of the Lord. There is a tradition that he was the youngest of the Apostles. He was a virgin when the Faith of Christ found him, and he remained a virgin for ever. This is why he was "the disciple whom Jesus loved" more than any of the others, and why he "leaned on Jesus' Breast." When Peter, who had been married, wished to ask the Lord who it was that was about to betray Him, he dared not ask for himself, but beckoned to John, that he should ask it. After the Resurrection, when "Mary Magdalene came and told the disciples that the Lord was risen, Peter and John ran both together to the sepulchre, but John did outrun Peter." Later on, when the Apostles were on the Sea of Galilee, in a ship, fishing, "Jesus stood on the shore, but the disciples knew not that it was Jesus," till virgin knew Virgin, and that disciple whom Jesus loved says unto Peter "It is the Lord."

Lesson V

John was an Apostle, an Evangelist, and a Prophet. He was an Apostle, for he wrote to the Churches as their Teacher. He was an Evangelist, for he wrote one of the Gospels, the like whereto was not done by any other of the twelve Apostles, save Matthew. He was a Prophet, for when he was on the isle of Patmos, where he had been banished by Domitian on account of his uplifting of his testimony for the Lord, he saw there that Apocalypse which contains such unfathomable mysteries concerning "things which shall be hereafter." Tertullian also says that when he was at Rome, he was put into a vessel of boiling oil, but that he came out cleaner and healthier than he went in.

Lesson VI

There is a great difference between his Gospel and the three others. Matthew begins to write as of a man "The Book of the Generation of Jesus Christ, the Son of David, the son of Abraham." Luke's first words of history relate to the priesthood of Zachary; Mark commences with the prophecies of Malachias and Isaias. The first has the face of a man, with a human genealogy; the second has the face of a calf, being a victim offered by priests; the third has the face of a lion, even "the voice of one crying in the wilderness, Prepare the way of the Lord, make His paths straight;" but the John of whom I write is like a flying eagle, whose kingly flight bears him up above earth-gathered clouds, an eagle that wings his way toward the Father Himself, and which cries: "In the beginning was the Word, and the Word was with God, and the Word was God."

Lesson VII

From the Holy Gospel according to St. Matthew (Matt 20:20–23)

At that time: Then came to him the mother of the sons of Zebedee with her sons, adoring and asking something of him. And so on.

Homily by St. Jerome, Priest

Where had the mother of Zebedee's children gotten her idea of the Lord's kingdom? He had but just said "The Son of man shall be betrayed unto the chief priests and unto the scribes, and they shall condemn Him to death, and shall deliver Him to the Gentiles to mock, and to scourge, and to crucify Him." He had told His trembling disciples of the outrages that awaited Him in His Passion and yet that mother came to Him to ask for her sons a share in the glory of His Triumph. I think it was because the Lord, after He had said all the rest, had said also "And the third day He shall rise again." The woman supposed that after His resurrection His kingdom would immediately be established, and that it would be fulfilled at His first coming which is promised at His second. And so, with womanly haste, she forgets the future, and catches at the present.

Lesson VIII

It was the mother who asked, but the Lord addressed His answer to the disciples, understanding that she had made her prayer in obedience to their wishes. "Can you drink the chalice that I shall drink?" From God's written Word we gather that by this chalice, He meant the Passion, about which we read that He said "O My Father, if it be possible, let this chalice pass from Me!" Likewise is it written in the 115th Psalm: "I will take the chalice of salvation, and call upon the Name of the Lord," and what that life-giving chalice was, the words which soon follow tell us: "Precious in the sight of the Lord is the death of His Saints."

Lesson IX

The question arises, how the two sons of Zebedee, namely James and John, drank of the chalice of martyrdom, seeing that though we know by the Scriptures that "Herod the king killed James the brother of John with the sword," yet John ended his earthly life by a natural death. But if we read the Records of the Church, we shall find there told how that John, on account of his testifying to the truth, was cast into a vessel of boiling oil, and although the holy champion came out unhurt and continued his pilgrimage here for a while longer before he received his crown from Christ's hand, being straightway banished into the isle of Patmos, yet we see that he had the soul of a martyr, and drank the same cup of martyrdom that was drunk by the three children in the burning fiery furnace, albeit the persecutor did not actually shed his blood.

May 7 – St. Stanislaus

Bishop & Martyr – Duplex

All from Common except what follows

Lessons I–III from the occurring Scripture

Lesson IV

Stanislaus was a Pole. He was born of a noble family, on the 26th day of July, in the year of our Lord 1030, at Szczepanow, in the diocese of Krakow. His godly parents, who had been childless for thirty years, obtained him from God by prayer, and from his earliest years he gave token of the holiness of life which afterwards marked him. When he was a young man he applied himself heartily to all useful learning, and was deeply read in the sacred teaching of the Canons and of Theological doctrine. After the death of his parents he inherited great possessions, but he sold them, and distributed the price to the poor, purposing himself to become a monk. However, by the Providence of God, Lampert, Bishop of Krakow, named him Canon of the Cathedral Church of that diocese, and Preacher in the same and afterwards, in 1072, he was elected, against his own will, to succeed to Lampert's place. In this office he was a bright and shining light of all pastoral virtues, especially of mercy toward the poor.

Lesson V

At that time, Boleslaus II was King of Poland, and him Stanislaus grievously offended because he openly rebuked him for his shameless lust. Wherefore, in a solemn Parliament of his kingdom, he made Stanislaus to be brought before him on a false accusation of having taken wrongfully a certain village, which he had bought in the name of his Church. The Bishop could not rebut this charge by documents, and the witnesses were in too great fear to speak the truth. Stanislaus therefore said that in three days he would produce before the judgment-seat one Peter, from whom he had bought the village, and who had been dead three years. His enemies laughed thereat, and closed with his proposal, and the man of God gave himself up to fasting and prayer for three days. On the day which he had promised, after he had offered up the Holy Sacrifice of the Mass, he commanded

Peter to rise from the grave. Peter then immediately came to life, arose, and followed Stanislaus to the King's judgment-seat, where before the King and all others, who were struck dumb with amazement, he bore witness of the sale of the village, and the honest payment of the price by the Bishop, and then again fell asleep in the Lord.

Lesson VI

Stanislaus often rebuked Boleslaus, but when he found it was in vain, he at last cut him off from the communion of Christ's faithful people. Thereupon Boleslaus became frenzied with rage, and on the 8th of May, in the year 1079, sent soldiers to the Church to murder the holy Bishop. This they thrice attempted to do, but God was pleased that they should be held back by some unseen power. In the end, the impious King with his own hand cut off the head of the Priest of God as he was standing at the Altar offering up the immaculate Host. His body was hewn into pieces and strewn about the fields, but the eagles strangely kept the beasts of prey off it. The Canons of the Cathedral of Krakow soon gathered together the mutilated and scattered limbs, which they were enabled to see by a light which overspread the sky at night and they fit them together, each into its place. The relics immediately so joined themselves one to the other, that no marks of wounds remained. Moreover, God was pleased to manifest the holiness of His servant by many wonders after his death, being moved by which, Pope Innocent IV added his name to those of the Saints, and the Supreme Pontiff Clement VIII gave his Feast a place in the Roman Breviary, commanding that the memory of so glorious a Martyr should be everywhere celebrated under the Duplex rite.

Lessons VII–IX from the first set in the Common of Martyrs in Paschaltide (Homily by St. Augustine)

May 8 ~ The Apparition of St. Michael the Archangel

Major Duplex

Lessons I–III from the occurring Scripture

Lesson I ~ Dan 7:9–11

From the Prophet Daniel

I beheld till thrones were placed, and the Ancient of days sat: his garment was white as snow, and the hair of his head like clean wool: his throne like flames of fire: the wheels of it like a burning fire. A swift stream of fire issued forth from before him: thousands of thousands ministered to him, and ten thousand times a hundred thousand stood before him: the judgment sat, and the books were opened. I beheld because of the voice of the great words which that horn spoke: and I saw that the beast was slain, and the body thereof was destroyed, and given to the fire to be burnt:

Lesson II ~ Dan 10:4–8

And in the four and twentieth day of the first month I was by the great river which is the Tigris. And

I lifted up my eyes, and I saw: and behold a man clothed in linen, and his loins were girded with the finest gold: And his body was like the chrysolite, and his face as the appearance of lightning, and his eyes as a burning lamp: and his arms, and all downward even to the feet, like in appearance to glittering brass: and the voice of his word like the voice of a multitude. And I Daniel alone saw the vision: for the men that were with me saw it not: but an exceeding great terror fell upon them, and they fled away, and hid themselves. And I being left alone saw this great vision: and there remained no strength in me, and the appearance of my countenance was changed in me, and I fainted away, and retained no strength.

Lesson III - Dan 10:9–14

And I heard the voice of his words: and when I heard, I lay in a consternation, upon my face, and my face was close to the ground. And behold a hand touched me, and lifted me up upon my knees, and upon the joints of my hands. And he said to me: Daniel, thou man of desires, understand the words that I speak to thee, and stand upright: for I am sent now to thee. And when he had said this word to me, I stood trembling. And he said to me: Fear not, Daniel: for from the first day that thou didst set thy heart to understand, to afflict thyself in the sight of thy God, thy words have been heard: and I am come for thy words. But the prince of the kingdom of the Persians resisted me one and twenty days: and behold Michael, one of the chief princes, came to help me, and I remained there by the king of the Persians. But I am come to teach thee what things shall befall thy people in the latter days, for as yet the vision is for days.

Lesson IV

That the blessed Archangel Michael has oftentimes appeared to men is attested on the authority of the Holy Bible, and also by the ancient traditions of the Saints. For this reason such visions are held in remembrance in many places. As of old did the Synagogue of the Jews, so now does the Church of God venerate Michael as her watcher and defender. But during the papacy of Gelasius I, the summit of Mount Gargano in Apulia, at whose foot lies the town of Siponto, was the scene of an extraordinary apparition of the Archangel Michael.

Lesson V

For it came to pass that from the livestock of a man of Gargano there strayed a bull, which when sought for a long while, was found stuck in the mouth of a cavern. Then one that stood there shot an arrow to slay it, but the arrow turned round and came back against him that had shot it. They therefore that saw it, and all those that heard it, were sorely afraid because of what had happened, so that no man dared any more to draw near to the cavern. But when they had sought counsel of the Bishop of Siponto, he answered that it behoved to seek the interpretation from God, and proclaimed three days of fasting and prayer.

Lesson VI

After three days, the Archangel Michael gave warning to the Bishop that that place was under his protection, and that he had thus pointed out by a sign that he wished that worship should be offered to God there, in commemoration of himself and of the Angels. Then the Bishop and the citizens made haste and came to the cavern and when they found that the form thereof was somewhat after the fashion of a Church, they began to perform the public worship of God therein: which sanctuary has been glorified with many miracles. It was not long after these things that Pope Boniface dedicated the Church of St. Michael at the great circus in Rome, on the 29th day of September, on which day the Church also holds in remembrance All the Angels. But this present day is consecrated to the apparition of the Archangel Michael.

Lesson VII

From the Holy Gospel according to St. Matthew (Matt 18:1–10)

At that time came the disciples unto Jesus, saying: Who is the greatest in the kingdom of heaven? And so on.

Homily by St. Hilary, Bishop

"Unless you become as little children," says the Lord, "you shall not enter into the kingdom of heaven," that is, unless by the uprooting of bodily and mental depravity, we bring our souls to the innocence of childhood. But He gives the name of children to all such as believe by the hearing of faith. Children follow their father, love their mother, know not how to wish evil to their neighbors, are not careful for earthly riches; they insult not, they hate not, they lie not, they believe what they are told, and take for truth what they hear. Us then it behooves to return to the simpleness of little children, for when we are well rooted therein, we shall so far bear about in ourselves an image of the sublime simpleness of the Lord Jesus.

Lesson VIII

Woe unto the world because of offenses. The humility of the Passion is an offense unto the world. Such is the state of stupidity to which man's ignorance has reduced itself, that it turns away from the Lord of Eternal Glory, because of the unsightliness of the Cross. And what is so certain to bring woe unto the world as to turn away from Christ? And therefore He says: "It must needs be that offenses come," because His fulfilling the lowliness of the Passion was the predestined means whereby He was to give us eternal life.

Lesson IX

"Make heed that you despise not one of these little ones that believe in Me." He has laid on us a most fitting tie to constrain us to love one another, especially such as indeed believe in the Lord. "For I say unto you that in heaven their Angels do always behold the face of My Father Which is in heaven. For the Son of Man is come to save that which was lost." From these words we see, first, that the Son of Man saves, secondly, that the Angels do see God, and thirdly, that the Angels of these little ones have custody over the prayers of the faithful. That the Angels have this custody is taught us absolutely. The Angels therefore do every day offer to God the prayers which the saved do make to Him in the Name of Christ. Therefore it is dangerous for a man to despise them, seeing that these are they by whose watchful service and ministry his wishes and requests are presented before the throne of the eternal and unseen God.

May 9 ~ St. Gregory Nazianzen

Bishop, Confessor, & Doctor ~ Duplex

All from Common except what follows

Lessons I–III from the occurring Scripture

Lesson IV

Gregory, to whom, is commonly given, on account of his extraordinary depth of sacred learning, the title of "the Divine," was a noble Cappadocian, born at Nazianzus in that country, and educated at Athens along with St. Basil, with whom likewise, when they had acquired knowledge in diverse branches of earthly learning, he gave himself up to learn the things of God. This they did for some years in a Monastery, framing their opinions, not out of their own heads, but according to the interpretation arrived at by the wisdom and decision of the ancients. They were both distinguished by power of doctrine and holiness of life, they were both called to the duty of preaching the Gospel of truth and, through the Gospel they both begat many sons unto Christ.

Lesson V

Gregory after a while returned home. He was first made Bishop of Sasima, and afterwards administered the Church at Nazianzus. Then he was called to rule the Church of Constantinople. That city, which he found reeking with heresy, he purged and brought again to the Catholic faith. But this, which deserved for him the warmest love of all men, raised up many enemies. Among the Bishops themselves there was a great party against him, and to still their contentions, he, of his own free will, gave up his see, saying with the Prophet Jonas: "Take me up, and cast me forth into the sea; so shall the sea be calm unto you, for I know that for my sake this great tempest is upon you," So he went his way back again to Nazianzus, and when he had seen that Eulalius was set over that Church, he gave himself up altogether to think and write concerning the things of God.

Lesson VI

He wrote much, both in prose and verse, with wonderful godliness and eloquence. According to the judgment of learned and holy men, there is nothing in his writings which anywhere strays from the line of true piety and Catholic truth, and not a single word which any one can justly call in doubt. He was one of the latest champions of the doctrine that the Son is consubstantial with the Father. No one has ever won greater praise for goodness of life, neither was any man more earnest in prayer. During the reign of the Emperor Theodosius, he dwelt in the country after the manner of a monk, and was unceasingly taken up with writing and reading, until, in a good old age, he entered into heavenly life.

Lessons VII–IX from the first set in the Common of Doctors (Sermon by St. Augustine)

May 10 ~ St. Antoninus

Confessor Bishop ~ Duplex

All from Common except what follows

Lessons I–III from the occurring Scripture

Lesson IV

Antoninus was born of respectable parents at Florence, in the year of grace 1389, and the holiness of his later life was foreshadowed in him even as a little child. When he was sixteen years of age he entered the Order of Friars Preachers, and from that time forth he was a burning and shining light to all the godly. He proclaimed a truceless war against idleness. After a short night's rest, he was the first to come to the service of Matins; when they were over he spent the rest of the night in prayer, or at least in reading, or writing out books, or if sleep altogether overcame his weary body, he would rest against the wall with his head bowed down, and then shake off slumber again, and set himself anew with fresh eagerness to his sacred watch.

Lesson V

He required of himself the most unflinching observance of the Rule of his Order, and never ate meat unless he were grievously ill. He slept upon the ground or upon bare boards. He always wore haircloth, and sometimes an iron girdle which bit into his naked skin. His virginity he kept ever undimmed by the least breath or shadow. He was so skillful in giving advice that he gained the common nickname of "Counsel Antoninus." At the same time so beautifully brilliant was his humility, that even when he was at the head of houses and provinces of his Order, he most cheerfully undertook all the most abject duties of the houses where he was. Eugenius IV appointed him Archbishop of Florence, and he took it so poorly, that it was only when awed by the threats of the Apostolic See that he obeyed, and accepted the dignity, in the year 1446.

Lesson VI

As Archbishop it can hardly be told how noble he was, in wisdom, in piety, in love, in meekness, in Priestly zeal. It was wonderful to see how thoroughly he taught himself nearly all the sciences without the help of a master. At last, after much work, and publishing many valuable books on Doctrine, he received the Holy Eucharist and was anointed, and then, clasping the image of his crucified Saviour to his heart, joyfully welcomed death, on the 2nd day of May, in the year 1459. He was remarkable for the working of miracles, both during his life and after his death, and Hadrian VI enrolled his name among those of the Saints, in the year 1523.

Lessons VII–IX from the first set in the Common of Confessor Bishops (Homily by St. Gregory)

Lesson IX ~ Commemoration of Sts. Gordian & Epimachus, Martyrs

Gordian was a judge before whom, in the reign of Julian the Apostate, Januarius the Priest was brought to be condemned. Januarius instructed Gordian in the Christian faith, and he, with his wife and fifty-three other persons of the same household, were all baptized at Rome. On this account the Prætor sent back Januarius, and ordered Clementian the Vicar to cast Gordian into prison. Afterward he caused the same Gordian to be brought before him in chains, and when he found he could not shake him in his deepening faith, he commanded that he should be beheaded. His body was thrown out before the temple of Apollo for dogs to eat, but the Christians buried it at night in the catacombs upon the Latin Way, in the same vault where were already lying the remains of the blessed Martyr Epimachus. These had been brought from Alexandria, in which city Epimachus had long been imprisoned for confessing Christ, and had in the end grasped the crown of his testimony by being burnt alive.

May 12 ~ Sts. Nereus, Achilleus, Domitilla, & Pancras

Virgin & Martyrs ~ Semiduplex

All from Common except what follows

Lessons I–III from the occurring Scripture

Lesson IV

Nereus and Achilleus were brethren, eunuchs belonging to Flavia Domitilla, who were baptized by blessed Peter, along with her and her mother Plautilla. They had advised Domitilla to consecrate her virginity to God, and on this account Aurelian, to whom she was betrothed, accused them of being Christians. They nobly confessed the faith, and were banished to the island of Ponza. Then they were again put to the torture, and after being scourged, were taken to Terracina. At Terracina, Minucius Rufus tormented them with the rack and with fire, but as they constantly affirmed that having once been baptized by the blessed Apostle Peter, no torture could ever make them sacrifice to idols, they were beheaded. Auspicius, their own disciple and the tutor of Domitilla, took their bodies to Rome, where they were buried on the Ardeatine way.

Lesson V

The Virgin Flavia Domitilla was a Roman, the niece of the Emperors

Titus and Domitian, and was veiled by the blessed Pope Clement. Aurelian, son of the Consul Titus Aurelius, to whom she was betrothed, accused her of being a Christian, and the Emperor Domitian banished her into the island of Ponza, where she long suffered and testified in prison. At length she was taken to Terracina, where she again confessed Christ, and as she seemed ever to grow firmer, the judge, under the Emperor Trajan, caused her chamber to be set on fire, and there Domitilla, with her foster-sisters, the maidens Theodora and Euphrosyne, finished the race of faith by grasping the crown of glory on the 7th day of May. Their bodies were found whole, and were buried by the Deacon Cæsarius. This, the twelfth day of May, is that whereon the bodies of Nereus and Achilleus, and that of Domitilla, were carried from the Cardinal Deaconry of St. Hadrian [Sant'Adriano al Foro], and laid in the Church which is properly called by the name of these holy martyrs, but formerly by that of "St. Peter's Bandage."

Lesson VI

Pancras was the son of a noble family of Phrygia. He came to Rome in the reign of the Emperors Diocletian and Maximian, being then a boy of fourteen years of age. There he was baptized by the Bishop of Rome, and brought up in the Christian faith. On this account he was soon after taken, and having constantly refused to sacrifice to the gods, he offered his neck to the executioner with manly courage, and won a glorious crown of martyrdom. The matron Octavilla took his body by night, embalmed it with precious ointments, and buried it on the Aurelian Way.

Lesson VII

From the Holy Gospel according to St. John (John 4:46–53)

At that time, There was a certain nobleman, whose son was sick at Capharnaum. And so on.

Homily by Pope St. Gregory

Why was it that when this nobleman besought the Lord to come down where his child died, the Lord (albeit He healed him) would not come, and yet, when the Centurion prayed Him to heal his servant, albeit not asked to come down, He went with them? He deemed not that the nobleman's son was worthy of His bodily presence, but He refused not to go to help the Centurion's servant. What is this but a rebuke to earthly pride, which makes us to respect in men their honors and riches rather than that Divine image wherein they are created? It was not so with our Redeemer, who would not go to the son of the nobleman, but was ready to come down for the Centurion's servant, to show that to Him the things which are great among men are but of little moment, and the things which are little esteemed among men are not beneath His notice.

Lesson VIII

Our pride then stands rebuked, that pride which makes us forget for the sake of one man that another man is a man at all. This pride, as we have said, looks only at the surroundings of men, not at their nature, and sees not that God is to be honored in a man because he is a man. Behold how the Son of God will not go unto the nobleman's son, but is ready to go and heal the servant. Of myself I know that if anyone's servant were to ask me to go to him, I have a sort of pride which would say to me silently inside my heart: "Go not; thou wilt lower thyself; the Papal dignity will be lightly esteemed; thy exalted station will be degraded." Behold how He Which came down from heaven, does not deem it below Him to go to help a servant, and yet we who are of the earth despise being humbled on earth!

Lesson IX

Think not therefore within yourselves on what you have, but on what you are. Behold, the world which I love is a world which passes away. Those holy servants of God, by whose grave I am standing, ennobled themselves mentally above the world at its fairest. To them was offered length of days, robust health, plenty in possessions, fruitfulness in offspring, comfort under perpetual peace: and yet while the spring-tide of life was unfolding before them, their hearts had already condemned it to an arid winter. Behold, winter in their hearts, spring in mine. Death, and pain, and barrenness occur all around me, I am attacked on all sides, and I feel very bitter, and yet the sting of fleshly lust so blinds me, that I love the bitter feelings, I hunt after that which flees from me, and cling to that which would leave me.

May 13 ~ St. Robert Bellarmine

Bishop, Confessor, &
Doctor ~ Duplex

All from Common
except what follows

Lessons I–III from the
occurring Scripture

Lesson IV

Robert, a native of Montepulciano and of the noble family of Bellarmine, had for his mother the most pious Cynthia Cervini, sister of Pope Marcellus II. From the first he was conspicuous for exemplary piety and most chaste manners, earnestly desiring this one thing, to please God alone and to win souls to Christ. He attended the college of the Society of Jesus in his native town where he was highly commended for his intelligence and modesty. At the age of eighteen he entered the same Society at Rome, and was a model of all religious virtues. Having passed through the course of philosophy at the Roman College, he was sent first to Florence, then to Monreale, later to Padua to teach sacred theology, and afterwards to Louvain where, not yet a priest, he ably discharged the office of preacher. After ordination at Louvain, he taught theology with such success that he brought back many heretics to the unity of the Church, and was regarded throughout Europe as a most brilliant theologian; and St. Charles, Bishop of Milan, and others keenly sought after him.

Lesson V

Recalled to Rome at the wish of Pope Gregory XIII, he taught the science of controversial theology at the Roman College, and there, as spiritual director he guided the angelic youth Aloysius in the paths of holiness. He governed the Roman College and then the Neapolitan province of the Society of Jesus in accordance with the spirit of St. Ignatius. Again summoned to Rome, he was employed by Clement VIII in the most important affairs of the Church, with the greatest advantage to the Christian state; then against his will and in spite of opposition, he was admitted among the number of the cardinals, because, as the Pontiff publicly declared, he did not have his equal among theologians in the Church of God at the time. He was consecrated bishop by the same Pope, and administered the archdiocese of Capua in a most saintly manner for three years; having resigned this office, he lived in Rome until his death, as a most impartial and trusty counsellor to the Supreme Pontiff. He wrote much, and in an admirable manner. His principal merit lies in his complete victory in the struggle against the new errors, during which he distinguished himself as a strenuous and outstanding vindicator of Catholic tradition and the rights of the Roman See. He gained this victory by following St. Thomas as his guide and teacher, by a prudent consideration of the needs of his times, by his unconquered doctrine, and by a most abundant wealth of testimony well-chosen from the Sacred Scriptures and from the very rich fountain of the Church Fathers. He is eminently noted for very numerous short works for fostering piety, and especially for that golden Catechism, which he never failed to explain to the young and ignorant both at Capua and at Rome, although preoccupied with other very important affairs. A contemporary cardinal declared that Robert was sent by God for the instruction of Catholics, for the guidance of the good, and for the confounding of heretics; St. Francis de Sales regarded him as a font of learning; the Supreme Pontiff Benedict XIV called him a hammer of heretics; and Benedict XV proclaimed him the model of promoters and defenders of the Catholic religion.

Lesson VI

He was most zealous in the religious life and he maintained that manner of life after having been chosen as one of the empurpled cardinals. He did not want to any wealth beyond what was necessary; he was satisfied with a moderate household, and scanty fare and clothing. He did not strive to enrich his relatives, and he could scarcely be induced to relieve their poverty even occasionally. He had the lowest opinion of himself, and was of wonderful simplicity of soul. He had an extraordinary love for the Mother of God; he spent many hours daily in prayer. He ate very sparingly, and fasted three times a week. Uniformly austere with himself, he burned with charity towards his neighbor, and was often called the father of the poor. He earnestly strove that he might not stain his baptismal innocence with even the slightest fault. Almost eighty years old, he fell into his last illness at St. Andrew's on the Quirinal hill, and in it he showed his usual radiant virtue. Pope Gregory XV and many cardinals visited him on his deathbed, lamenting the loss of such a great pillar of the Church. He fell asleep in the Lord in the year 1621, on the day [September 17] of the sacred Stigmata of St. Francis, the memory of which he had been instrumental in having celebrated everywhere. The whole city mourned his death, unanimously proclaiming him a Saint. The Supreme Pontiff Pius XI inscribed his name, first, in the number of the Blessed, and then in that of the Saints, and shortly afterwards, by a decree of the Sacred Congregation of Rites, he declared him a Doctor of the universal Church. His body is honored with pious veneration at Rome in the church of St. Ignatius, near the tomb of St. Aloysius, as he himself had desired.

Lesson VII

From the Holy Gospel according to St. Matthew (Matt 5:13–19)

At that time: Jesus said unto his disciples: "You are the salt of the earth; but if the salt lose its savor, wherewith shall it be salted?" And so forth.

Homily by St. Robert Bellarmine, Bishop

Just as in God, whom we venerate as one in Trinity and three in Unity, there are three things in particular which are especially clear: power, wisdom, and goodness; so also God, beloved listeners, that he might make his special friends and children, our fathers and teachers, very like unto himself and, so to be esteemed and admired by all nations, wished them to be in the highest degree powerful, wise, excellent, and holy. First, he furnished them with that power by which they might do many evidently wonderful and extraordinary things, out of the usual course and order of nature in regard to the elements, trees, brute beasts, and even to mankind. Then, he gave them such wisdom that they saw not only the past and present, but they even foresaw the future long before, and predicted it. Finally, he enlarged their hearts with very great and burning charity, enabling them not only to enter whole-heartedly on their labors, but also to influence those whom they were about to convert, as well by their example and holy life, as by their preaching and miracles.

Lesson VIII

And so, the whole world knew how pious, how just, how religious were the preachers of our law, both those who first brought to us the faith and the Gospel, and those whom God thereafter stirred up in every age to confirm or propagate that same faith. First, consider the Apostles. What could be better or more sublime than the Apostles' way of life? Consider next those holy men whom we call Fathers and Doctors, those most shining lights which God has ordained to shine in the firmament of the Church, that all the darkness of heresy might be dispersed, such as Irenæus, Cyprian, Hilary, Athanasius, Basil, the two Gregories, Ambrose, Jerome, Augustine, Chrysostom, and Cyril. Do not their lives and conduct shine forth in the records, which they have left us, as in a special kind of mirror? "For out of the fullness of the heart the mouth speaks."

Lesson IX

Consider, I ask you, the humility, together with the most profound learning, which appears in the books of the holy fathers. What moderation! Nothing offensive there, nothing unseemly, no cunning, nothing assuming, nothing pompous. How the manifold working of the Holy Ghost, who dwelt in their hearts, reveals itself in their pages! Who can read Cyprian attentively without immediately longing for martyrdom? Who can assiduously turn over the pages of Augustine without learning the most profound humility? Who can open Jerome frequently without beginning to love virginity and fasting? The writings of the saints breathe forth religion, chastity, integrity, and charity. Such then are our bishops and pastors (to use the words of heavenly Augustine), learned men, eminent, holy, intelligent, defenders of the truth, who have taken in the Catholic faith as their milk, and have consumed it as food: and have ministered this milk and food to the great and small. Since the Apostles, holy Church has flourished by such planters, waterers, builders, shepherds, and nurses.

May 14 ~ St. Boniface

Martyr ~ Simplex
All from Common
except what follows

Lessons I–II from the
occurring Scripture

Lesson III

Boniface was a Roman citizen who had lived in sin with the noble lady Aglaia. The memory of this intemperance overwhelmed him with exceeding sorrow, so that for penance he gave himself up to look for and bury the bodies of the martyrs. While he was at Tarsus, and apart from his fellow-travelers, he saw a great many persons being tormented in diverse ways because they confessed to believing in Christ. He kissed their chains, and vehemently exhorted them bravely to bear their sufferings, for their short labor was to be followed by eternal rest. For this cause Boniface also was taken, and his flesh torn off him with iron claws. Sharp reeds also were driven between the nails of his hands and the flesh, and molten lead poured into his mouth. In his agony he was only heard to say "I thank thee, O Lord Jesus Christ, Son of God." Afterwards he was cast headlong into a vessel of boiling pitch, and as he was drawn out unharmed, the judge in fury commanded him to be beheaded. At which time, there was a great earthquake whereby many unbelievers were turned to believe in the Lord Christ. The fellow-travelers of Boniface sought him the next day, and when they knew that he had undergone martyrdom, they bought his body for fifty shillings, and after they had embalmed it with spices and wrapped it in linen, they carried it to Rome. The Lady Aglaia, who had herself with great contrition given up her life to godly works, was told by an angel what had come to pass. She therefore went forth to meet the holy body, and built a Church in the name of Boniface, wherein his body was buried upon the 5th day of June next after that 14th of May whereon in the city of Tarsus in Cilicia, under the Emperors Diocletian and Maximian, he had passed away to heaven.

May 15 ~ St. John Baptiste de la Salle

Confessor ~ Duplex

All from Common except what follows

Lessons I–III from the occurring Scripture

Lesson IV

John Baptiste de La Salle, born of an honorable family at Rheims, when still a boy showed by his manners and actions that he was called by destiny to the Lord, and was to be adorned with the excellence of holiness. As a youth he studied literature and the philosophical sciences at the academy at Rheims. During this time, although his mental powers and his lively and pleasant disposition endeared him to all, he nevertheless shrank from the company of his fellows, so that, being inclined to solitude, he might the more easily find time for God. Already having been for some time enlisted in the ranks of the clergy, he was enrolled among the canons of Rheims at the age of sixteen years. He went to Paris to study theology at the university of the Sorbonne, and was admitted to the Sulpician seminary. But he was soon forced to return home because of the death of his parents, and undertook the education of his brothers, which he carried on without meanwhile interrupting his sacred studies and with the greatest success, as was proved by subsequent events.

Lesson V

He was finally ordained a priest, and said his first Mass with the intense faith and ardor of the soul which, throughout his whole life, he brought to those holy Mysteries. Meanwhile, burning with zeal for the salvation of souls, he devoted himself wholly to their service. He undertook the direction of the Sisters of the Infant Jesus, founded for the education of girls; and not only managed them most prudently, but saved their institute from dissolution. From this time onwards, he turned his attention to the education of poor boys in religion and good morals. And God had raised him up for this very end, namely, that he should found in his Church a new family of religious men, and should look after boys' schools, especially of poor boys, with unceasing and efficient care. And, indeed, this duty, entrusted to him by Divine providence, was successfully accomplished, in spite of very much opposition and great hardships, by the foundation of an institute of brothers which he named the Christian Schools.

Lesson VI

His male associates in this great and arduous work he at first received into his own house; and then, establishing them in a more suitable dwelling, thoroughly inspired them with his method and with those wise laws and regulations which were afterwards confirmed by Benedict XIII. Because of humility and love of poverty, he first resigned his canonry and distributed all his property among the poor; and later also, after many unsuccessful attempts to do so, he of his own will resigned the government of the institute which he had founded. But meanwhile his solicitude for the brothers and for the schools which he opened in different places did not lessen, though he began to give himself more diligently to God. Constantly punishing himself with fasts, flagellations, and other hardships, he spent his nights in prayer. At length, conspicuous for every kind of virtue, especially obedience, and zeal for fulfilling the divine will, and love and devotion to the Apostolic See, full of merit, and having devoutly received the sacraments, he fell asleep in the Lord in the sixty-eighth year of his age. The Supreme Pontiff Leo XIII placed him in the list of the Blessed; and, illustrious by new miracles, he was adorned with honors of the Saints in the jubilee year of 1900. Pius XII appointed him the special heavenly patron of all teachers of boys and young men.

Lesson VII

From the Holy Gospel according to St. Matthew (Matt 18:1–5)

At that time: the disciples came to Jesus, saying: Who thinkest thou is the greater in the kingdom of heaven? And so on.

Homily by St. John Chrysostom

"Take heed that you despise not one of these little ones," says the Lord, "for their Angels do always behold the face of my Father which is in heaven." It was as though he had said: "It was for them that I came, because this is the will of my Father." Thus does he make it our duty to be thoughtful and careful for the protection and safety of these little ones. You see what vast ramparts he has built for the protection of the little ones, and how much care and trouble he has taken that they shall not be lost; yea, he pronounces extreme penalties on them that despise them; and for them that undertake to care wholeheartedly for them he promises highest rewards. And all these things of his teaching he does further enforce by his own example and by the example of the eternal Father himself.

Lesson VIII

Let us therefore take to heart what the Lord says, and imitate his example. Let us neglect nothing which it is in our power to do for these our little brothers and sisters. Let us be ready to undertake any work on their behalf, even the most humble and vile. And if there should be some further need of our assistance, even to the point of self-denying and laborious effort on our part, let us render it graciously; and let us do these things the more so when our help is required for one that is tiny and unloved and unwanted. And let us practice ourselves in these things until they become tolerable to us, and even easy, because we do them for the sake of one who is our little brother or sister in Christ. For God has made evident that every soul is worthy of so much diligent care that he spared not his own Son for the sake of such.

Lesson IX

If it be not enough for our salvation that we ourselves live virtuously, but we should desire in very truth the salvation of others; what shall we answer if we do not live right nor teach others? What hope of salvation will remain unto us? What is nobler than to rule minds or to mould the character of the young? I consider that he who knows how to form the youthful mind is truly greater than all painters, sculptors, and all others of that sort.

May 16 ~ St. Ubald

Confessor Bishop ~ Semiduplex

All from Common
except what follows

Lessons I–III from the
occurring Scripture

Lesson IV

Ubald was born of a noble family at Gubbio in Umbria, and well established in piety and learning from his earliest years. When he was a young man, it was often proposed to him to marry, but he never abandoned his determination to preserve his virginity. After he was ordained a Priest, he divided his inheritance among the poor and Churches, and embraced the Institute of Canons Regular of St. Augustine. This Institute he brought to Gubbio, and for some time led therein a most holy life. When the fame of his saintliness had got noised abroad, Pope Honorius II set him, contrary to his own wishes, over the Church of Gubbio, and he was honored with consecration as Bishop by the hands of the Pope himself, in the year of our Lord 1129.

Lesson V

When Ubald came to live as Bishop in Gubbio, he changed his manner of life in no way from that which he had led before, but his virtues began to be more eminent because his word and example were now more able to benefit his neighbors, to whom the shepherd of their souls was a pattern, not by outward showing only, but from his heart. He ate little, dressed simply, and slept upon a hard and very poor bed. He "always bore in the body the dying of the Lord Jesus," while he daily fed his soul in unceasing and earnest prayer. Hence he acquired such wonderful meekness, that when he was most grievously wronged and insulted he not only took it patiently, but, by a strange impulse of love for them, embraced his persecutors with every proof of affection.

Lesson VI

Just the space of two years before Ubald passed away from this present life, he was tried as gold in the furnace by grievous bodily weakness, and, day after day, amid the sharpest sufferings, he never ceased patiently to give thanks to God. He rested in peace on the sacred day of Pentecost, in the year 1160, having for many years governed with great praise the Church which had been entrusted to him, and glorious for good works and miracles. Pope Celestine III numbered him with the Saints. His strength is most chiefly shown in the casting out of evil spirits. His body has remained without corruption for all these ages, and is reverenced greatly in his native town by Christ's faithful people. To them he has more than once shown himself good at need.

Lessons VII–IX from the first set in the Common of Confessor Bishops (Homily by St. Gregory)

May 17 ~ St. Paschal Baylon

Confessor ~ Duplex

All from Common except what follows

Lessons I–III from the occurring Scripture

Lesson IV

Paschal Baylon was the son of poor and godly parents, in the town of Torre Hermosa, in the Diocese of Sagunta in Aragon, in the year of our Lord 1540. From his childhood he gave indications of a holy life. He was naturally of a good disposition, and very wishful to learn about heavenly things. His boyhood and youth he passed in the occupation of a shepherd. This way of life pleased him well, because he thought it one useful and fitted to nourish lowliness and keep innocence. He ate little, and was assiduous in prayer. He had great weight and favor with his fellows and neighbors, whose quarrels he healed, errors he corrected, ignorance he instructed, and from whose idleness he aroused them. They all greatly honored and loved him, as though he were their father and teacher, and even then many called him "Beato," that is "the Blessed."

Lesson V

In a world which was to him "a dry and unwatered land," this flower of the valleys, "planted in the House of the Lord" spread a wonderful fragrance all around. Therefore, when Paschal took upon himself a harder life by entering the Order of Discalced Friars Minor of the strict Observance, "he rejoiced as a strong man to run a race" and gave himself up altogether to serve the Lord, thinking by day and by night only how he might attain more and more to have that mind in him which was also in Christ Jesus. And so it came to pass in a little while, that his very elders set him before them for their model, as a pattern of a man seeking to be perfect in the path of the Seraphic Order. Paschal himself held the lowly place of a lay brother, and deemed himself "the off-scouring of all things." He took most cheerfully, and discharged with the greatest humility and patience, the most arduous and abject duties of the house, as though such were his peculiar right. His flesh would sometimes rebel against his spirit, but he broke it under the yoke of mortification, and brought it into subjection. Day by day the spirit of self-denial waxed stronger in him, and "forgetting those things which were behind, he reached forth unto those things which were before."

Lesson VI

To the Virgin Mother of God he had vowed himself when he was but a little lad, and he paid her every day the services of a son, and trusted her as a mother. It is hard to tell how intense was the love which bound him to the Most Holy Sacrament of the Eucharist, a love which seemed literally stronger than death, for when his dead body was found lying on the bier, its eyes opened and shut twice when the Sacred Host was lifted up, to the amazement of all that were there. When he was among heretics, he suffered much and grievously at their hands for plainly and openly telling the truth about this Sacrament; they often sought after him to murder him, but by the singular Providence of God he was delivered from those wicked men. When he was at prayer he often became utterly insensible, and his soul fainted away with the love of God. During these trances it was believed that he received directly from heaven that knowledge which he had, and which enabled him, although a man altogether rough and unlettered, to answer the hardest questions upon the mysteries of the faith, and even to write some books. At last, full of good works, he joyfully passed away to be ever with the Lord at the hour foretold by himself: the Feast of Pentecost, the 17th day of May, in the year of salvation 1592, on which day also he had been born fifty-two years before. Illustrious for the graces above mentioned, and for the miracles which he worked both during his life and after his death, he was named Blessed by Pope Paul V, and Alexander VIII enrolled him among the Saints.

Lessons VII–IX from the first set in the Common of Confessor Non-Bishops (Homily by St. Gregory)

May 18 ~ St. Venantius

Martyr ~ Duplex

All from Common except what follows

Lessons I–III from the occurring Scripture

Lesson IV

Venantius was a lad of Camerino (in the neighborhood of Ancona), who at fifteen years of age was accused of Christianity before Antiochus, Praefect of Camerino under the Emperor Decius. Venantius therefore appeared before Antiochus at the gate of the city, and when the Praefect had striven with him for a long while, by promises and threats, he commanded him to be scourged and thrown into irons, but an Angel loosed his bonds. He was afterwards burned with lamps, and hung head downwards in smoke. Anastasius the trumpeter was amazed at his constancy under suffering, and when it appeared to him that the Martyr was a second time freed by an Angel, and was walking in white raiment on the smoke, he believed in Christ, and was baptized, with all his house, by the blessed Priest Porphyry, and shortly thereafter they both together earned the palm of martyrdom.

Lesson V

Now Venantius stood before the Praefect, and when he had again vainly tempted him to give up his faith in Christ, he cast him into prison, and sent unto him Attalus the herald. Attalus told him how that he also had been a Christian, but had denied that name, seeing it was a foolish faith which made Christians to throw away present things for a groundless hope of things to come. But Christ's brave champion, knowing well the wiles of our subtle enemy, drove the devil's servant from his presence. When he appeared again before the Praefect, his teeth and jaws were broken, and, so mangled, he was cast out upon a dunghill. But thence also an Angel delivered him, and he stood again before the judge. And there while Venantius was yet speaking, the judge fell from off the judgment-seat, and when he had cried with a loud voice, "True is the God of Venantius, destroy our gods," he died.

Lesson VI

Then they told the Præfect of it, he commanded Venantius to be straightway thrown to the lions. But the beasts were not wild to him, and lay down at his feet. And meanwhile he taught the Christian faith to the people. So they took him away from thence and cast him once more into prison. The next day Porphyry came to the Præfect, and told him how that he had seen in a vision of the night Venantius sprinkling certain ones with water, and they that were sprinkled shone with a marvelous light, yet the Præfect himself remained hidden in deep darkness. Then was the Præfect moved to great anger and commanded forthwith to behead Porphyry. As for Venantius, he bade them drag him about in rough places, full of briars and thistles, until the evening. When it was over, he was left half-dead, but in the morning he stood for the last time before the Præfect, who commanded to cast him down from a steep rock. It pleased God that this should not kill him, and he was dragged again through rough places for about a mile. There the soldiers were thirsty, and Venantius, by the sign of the Cross, made waters to flow from a stone in a gulley near. This is that stone whereon also he left the imprint of his knees, and which can be seen to this day in his Church. By this wonder many were moved to believe in Christ and the Præfect commanded them all, and Venantius with them, to be beheaded in the same place where they were. When it was done, there were great lightnings and earthquakes so that the Præfect fled, but he could not fly from the judgment of God, and but a few days thereafter he died a most shameful death. Meanwhile the Christians took the bodies of Venantius and the others, and buried them in an honorable place, wherein they lie to this day, under the Church at Camerino which is dedicated to Venantius.

Lessons VII–IX from the first set in the Common of Martyrs in Paschaltide (Homily by St. Augustine)

May 19 ~ St. Peter Celestine

Pope & Confessor ~ Duplex

All from Common except what follows

Lessons I–III from the occurring Scripture

Lesson IV

Peter, who is surnamed according to his Papal name of Celestine V, was the son of respectable Catholic parents, and was born at Isernia in Apulia, about the year of grace 1221. He was hardly entered on boyhood, when he withdrew into a desert, in order to keep his soul safe from the snares of the world. In solitude he fed his mind with heavenly meditation, and brought his body into subjection, even by wearing an iron chain next to his bare flesh. He founded, under the Rule of St. Benedict, that congregation which was afterwards known as the Celestines. His light, as of a candle set upon a candlestick, could not be kept hidden, and after the Church of Rome had for a long while been widowed of a shepherd, he was chosen without his knowledge and in his absence, to fill the chair of Peter. The news of his election filled him with as great amazement as it did all others with sudden joy. When, however, he was seated in the exalted place of the Papal dignity, he found that the many cares by which he was beset made it nearly impossible for him to give himself to his accustomed meditations; after four months, of his own free will he resigned the burden and the honor together on the 13th day of December, 1294; and, while he sought to return to his old way of life, on the 19th day of May, 1296, he fell asleep in the Lord. How precious his death was in His sight was gloriously manifested by a Cross which appeared shining in the air before the door of the cell. He was illustrious for miracles both during his life and after his death, and when these had been duly investigated, Clement V, in the eleventh year after his departure hence, enrolled his name among those of the Saints.

Lessons V–VI are Lessons IV & V from the second set in the Common of Confessor Non-Bishops (From the Book of Morals by Pope St. Gregory)

Lessons VII–IX from the Common of Supreme Pontiffs (Homily by St. Leo)

Lesson IX—Commemoration of St. Pudentiana, Virgin

The maiden Pudentiana was the orphan daughter of Pudens the Roman Senator. She was a Christian of eminent piety. She with her sister Praxedes distributed to the poor the money which they obtained by the sale of their inheritance. She gave herself continually to fasting and prayer. By her care the whole of the household, being ninety-six persons, were baptized by Pope Pius I. Whereas the Emperor Antoninus had forbidden the Christians to offer sacrifice in public, Pope Pius used to meet with them in Pudentiana's house, to celebrate the holy rites. She was a gracious hostess to them, and ministered to them in such things as are needful for the body. She thus busied herself in works of Christian godliness until she passed from this present life to a better one. She was buried in her father's sepulchre in the cemetery of Priscilla on the Salarian Way upon the 19th day of May.

May 20 ~ St. Bernardine of Siena

Confessor ~ Semiduplex

All from Common except what follows

Lessons I–III from the occurring Scripture

Lesson IV

Bernardine was born of the noble family of the Albizeschi of Siena, on the 8th of September, in the year 1380. His saintliness began to manifest itself from his earliest years. He was well brought up by a pious father and mother, and even when he was being taught the first rudiments of worldly learning, he used to give up his playtime to occupy himself with devout works, being much drawn to fasting, prayer, and the devotion to the most Blessed Virgin. He abounded likewise in tenderness for the poor. As time went on, that he might the more entirely do these things, it was his will to enroll himself among those who work in the Hospital of Blessed Mary, called "of the Ladder," at Sienna. There, during the raging of a horrible pestilence, he labored with marvelous charity and great bodily suffering in serving the sick. In bodily presence he was a very handsome person, but, with all his other virtues, he kept ever so holy a guard over his purity, that it soon came to pass that no one, however shameless, dared to say an unseemly word in his presence.

Lesson V

He suffered a severe sickness, and when, after bearing it with the utmost patience, he recovered his health, he began to think of embracing some institute of the religious life. To make his way sure, he built a little hut in the outskirts of the city, where he hid himself and led a life of hardships of all kinds, continuing assiduously in prayer to God that He would be pleased to make clear to him what path he should follow. And so it came to pass by God's will that he chose the Order of Blessed Francis. In that Order he shone a bright instance of humility, patience, and every other virtue of a religious man. When the superior of his monastery saw this, and had already considered what his teaching and knowledge of sacred learning were, he laid on Bernardine the duty of preaching. This the Saint humbly accepted, and finding that his usefulness was much impaired by his having a shrill, harsh voice, he betook him to implore the help of God, Who was pleased, not without a miracle, to free him from this impediment.

Lesson VI

Those were times fruitful in vices and crimes and the bloody civil wars which raged in Italy and confounded all things Divine and human. Bernardine went through the cities and towns, and, in the Name of Jesus, that Name which he ever bore upon his lips and in his heart, he prevailed in great measure by his word and example in the restoration of collapsing piety and morality. Illustrious cities demanded him from the Pope as their Bishop, but this was an honor which his unconquerable humility caused him always steadily to refuse. At last the man of God, after untold labors, the working of many and great miracles, and the writing of godly and learned books, in the 67th year of his age, at Aquila in the Abruzzi, rested in a blessed death, upon the 20th day of May 1444. As the fame of new signs and wonders increased day by day, Pope Nicholas V, in the sixth year after his death, added his name to the roll of the Saints.

Lessons VII–IX from the first set in the Common of Abbots (Homily by St. Jerome)

May 25 ~ St. Gregory VII

Pope & Confessor ~ Duplex

All from Common except what follows

Lessons I–III from the occurring Scripture

Lesson IV

Pope Gregory VII, was born Hildebrand at Sovana in Tuscany. By his teaching, holiness, and graces of all kinds, he was a noble light of the Church, whose brightness has shone throughout all lands. When he was a little child without any schooling, he was playing at the feet of a carpenter who was planing wood, and God guided his hand to arrange the shavings which fell into the form of letters, making the inspired words of David, "He shall have dominion from sea to sea," a foreshadowing, as it were, of that wide lordship over the earth which was afterwards his. He was taken to Rome, and brought up under the shelter of St. Peter. As a young man he bitterly sorrowed over the oppression of the freedom of the Church by the laity, and over the corruption of the clergy themselves. He took the habit of a monk in the Abbey of Cluny, which was then in all the glory of the severest observance of the Rule of St. Benedict. There he served God's majesty with such warmth of earnestness that the saintly fathers of the convent chose him to be their Prior. But the Providence of God had greater things in store for him, whereby to make him a source of health to many, and he was brought away from Cluny. He was first elected Abbot of the monastery of St. Paul-outside-the-walls at Rome, and afterwards created a Cardinal of the Roman Church. Under the Popes Leo IX, Victor II, Stephen IX, Nicholas II, and Alexander II, he discharged great offices of trust, and the duties of a Legate, and Blessed Peter Damian, speaking of him at this time, calls him a man of most holy and honest thoughts. When Pope Victor II sent him as his

Legate into France, he, by a miracle, forced the Bishop of Lyons, who was befouled by the pollution of simony, to acknowledge his sin. In the Council of Tours he wrung from Berengarius a second abjuration of his heresy and he prevailed against the schism of Cadolaus, and strangled it.

Lesson V

After the death of Alexander II, Hildebrand, against his own will and to his own grief, was, on the 22nd day of April, in the year of Christ 1073, chosen Pope by one common consent of all. Reigning as Gregory VII, he was as the sun shining upon the Temple of the Most High. Mighty both in word and deed, he toiled for the restoration of Ecclesiastical discipline, for the spread of the Faith, for the defense of the freedom of the Church, for the suppression of error and corruption, so that since the time of the Apostles there is said never to have been a Pope who bore more labour and trouble for the sake of God's Church, or contended more manfully for her liberties. He purged diverse provinces of the pollution of simony. Like a brave soldier he withstood without dread the unrighteous contentions of the Emperor Henry IV, against whom he shrank not from setting himself as a wall of defense for the house of Israel. And when said Henry fell into the depths of sin, he cut him off from the communion of the faithful, and from his kingdom, and loosed the nations that were subject to him from their sworn allegiance.

Lesson VI

While he was celebrating solemn Mass, godly men saw a dove descend from heaven, perch upon his right shoulder, and spread out its wings so as to veil his head, a testimony that it was not by reasonings of man's wisdom, but by the teachings of the Holy Ghost, that he was guided in his rule over the Church. When the armies of the infamous Henry encompassed Rome, and hedged her in on every side, a great fire which the enemy had raised became extinct when Gregory made the sign of the Cross towards it. The Norman Duke, Robert Guiscard, at length delivered Gregory from the hand of Henry, and he departed from Rome, first to the Abbey of Monte Cassino, and thence onward to Salerno, to dedicate the Church of St. Matthew the Apostle at that place. While he was preaching to the people there on a certain day, he was smitten with grievous pains, and fell into a sickness whereof he foresaw that he should never be healed. As he lay on his deathbed, Gregory's last words were "I have loved righteousness and hated iniquity, and therefore I am dying in exile." It is past reckoning how many sufferings he manfully bore, and how much he wisely ordained in many Councils, which he gathered together in Rome. He was a man truly holy, an avenger of crimes, and a most loyal defender of the Church. He had been Pope twelve years, when, on the 25th day of May, in the year of salvation 1085, he went hence to be ever with the Lord. Both during his life and after his death he was marked by signs and wonders not a few. His holy body was honorably buried in the Cathedral Church of Salerno.

Lessons VII–IX from the Common of Supreme Pontiffs (Homily by St. Leo)

Lesson IX—Commemoration of St. Urban I, Pope & Martyr

Urban was a Roman, who, in the reign of the Emperor Alexander Severus, by his teaching and holy life, brought many to believe in Christ. Among others was Valerian, the husband of the blessed Cecilia, and Tiburtius, the brother of Valerian, both of whom afterwards bravely underwent martyrdom. It was Urban I who wrote the following words concerning the property of the Church: "Those things which His faithful ones make offering of unto the Lord, must never be turned to any other use than those of the Church, or of our Christian brethren, or of the poor. They are the free-will offerings of faithful believers, the trespass offerings of sinners, and the inheritance of the poor." He sat in the chair of Peter six years, seven months, and four days, and being crowned with martyrdom, was buried in the cemetery of Praetextatus, on the 25th day of May. He held five ordinations in December, wherein he ordained nine Priests, five Deacons, and eight Bishops for diverse places.

May 26 ~ St. Philip Neri

Confessor ~ Duplex

All from Common except what follows

Lessons I–III from the occurring Scripture

Lesson IV

Philip Neri was born of godly and respectable parents at Florence, on the 23rd day of July, in the year of grace 1515. From his earliest childhood he gave signs of the holiness of life which he afterwards attained. As a young man he gave up the rich inheritance which would have come to him from his uncle, and went to Rome, where, in the study of philosophy and theology, he gave himself altogether to Christ. His self-control was such that he sometimes fasted from all food for three days at a time. He was constant in watching and prayer, and during the frequent pilgrimages which he made to the seven churches of Rome, it was his custom to remain all night in prayer to God in the Catacomb of Callistus. On the 23rd of May, 1551, he became a Priest in obedience to the advice of his Confessor, and afterwards made the salvation of souls the one object of his existence; he heard confessions with unwearied tenderness until his dying day, and became the spiritual father in Christ of many sons, whom it was his beloved work to feed day by day upon the Word of God, upon the frequent reception of the Sacraments, upon assiduous prayer, and upon other godly works: to which end he founded the Congregation of the Oratory.

Lesson V

He was full of the love of God, and his heart was so hot therewith, that it became strained in its place, and the Lord was pleased to ease him by breaking the gristle which joined the fourth and fifth ribs on his left side, and so allowing more play to the internal organs. Sometimes, when he was saying Mass, or more intent than usual in prayer, he was seen to be raised off the ground, and become refulgent with wondrous light. He was ever ready to aid the poor and needy with kindly services, in which works God was pleased to make him worthy once to give alms to an Angel, and again, when once by night he was carrying bread to the hungry, and was fallen into a pit, an Angel drew him out unhurt. He longed to be lowly, and always shrank from honors, and from dignities in the Church, whereof several of the highest were diverse times offered to him, but he always firmly refused them.

Lesson VI

He was illustrious for the gift of prophecy, and had a marked and very wonderful power of reading the thoughts of men's souls. He ever kept his own virginity undefiled, and could distinguish those that were pure by a sort of sweet savor, and the unclean, on the contrary, by a kind of stench. He sometimes appeared to the distant, and brought aid those in peril. He healed many that were sick and dying. He also raised one dead man to life. He was honored by seeing several times heavenly spirits, and likewise the Virgin Mother of God herself. He saw the souls of diverse persons, radiant with glory, ascend to heaven. In the year of salvation 1595, the Feast of Corpus Christi fell upon the 25th day of May. Philip, on that day, said Mass with extraordinary gladness of spirit, and performed the other religious works of the day, and after the hour of midnight, at the time he had himself foretold, he fell asleep in the Lord, in the eighty-second year of his life. Gregory XV, finding that God had glorified him by many miracles, enrolled his name among those of the saints.

Lessons VII–IX from the first set in the Common of Confessor Non-Bishops (Homily by St. Gregory)

Lesson IX—Commemoration of St. Eleutherius, Pope & Martyr

Eleutherius, born at Nicopolis in Greece, deacon of Pope Anicetus, presided over the Church under the Emperor Commodus. To him, at the beginning of his pontificate, was sent a letter from Lucius, king of the Britons, that he and his people may be received into the number of Christians. For this reason he sent Fugatius and Damian, learned and pious men, into Britain, through whom the king and the rest would accept the faith. Bringing another letter to the Pontiff was Irenæus, a disciple of Polycarp, who, coming to Rome, was kindly received by him. In his time, the Church of God enjoyed the greatest peace and quiet; and the faith was propagated throughout the world, especially in Rome. Eleutherius lived in the pontificate fifteen years, twenty-three days. He held three ordinations in the month of December, wherein he ordained twelve Priests, eight Deacons, and fifteen Bishops for diverse places; he was buried in the year of Our Lord 192, at the Vatican, near the body of Saint Peter.

May 27 ~ St. Bede the Venerable

Confessor & Doctor ~ Duplex

All from Common except what follows

Lessons I–III from the occurring Scripture

Lesson IV

Bede, a priest, was born at Jarrow, [in Northumbria] on the borders of Britain and Scotland. At the age of seven years he was placed under the care of holy Benedict Biscop, Abbot of Wearmouth, to be educated. Thereafter he became a monk, and so ordered his life that, whilst he should devote himself wholly to the study of the sciences and of doctrine, he might in nothing relax the discipline of his Order. There was no branch of learning in which he was not most thoroughly versed, but his chief care was the study of Holy Scriptures; and so he might better understand them, he acquired a knowledge of the Greek and Hebrew tongues. When he was thirty years of age he was ordained priest at the command of his Abbot, and immediately, on the advice of Acca, Bishop of Hexham, undertook the work of expounding the Sacred Books. In his interpretations he so strictly adhered to the teaching of the holy Fathers that he would advance nothing which was not approved by their judgment, nay, had the warrant of their very words. He ever hated sloth, and by habitually passing from reading to prayer, and in turn from prayer to reading, he so inflamed his soul that often amid his reading and teaching he was bathed in tears. Lest also his mind should be distracted by the cares of transitory things, he never would take the office of Abbot when it was offered to him.

Lesson V

The name of Bede soon became so famous for learning and piety that Pope St. Sergius thought of calling him to Rome, where, certainly, he might have helped to solve the very difficult questions which had then arisen concerning sacred things. He wrote many books for the bettering of the lives of the faithful, and the defending and extending of the faith. By those he gained everywhere such a reputation that the Saint Boniface, Bishop and Martyr, styled him a Light of the Church; Lanfranc called him The Doctor of the English; and the Council of Aix-la-Chapelle, The Admirable Doctor. But as his writings were publicly read in the churches during his life, and as it was not allowable to already call him a saint, they named him The Venerable, a title which in all times after has remained peculiarly his. The power of his teaching was the greater also, in that it was attested by a holy life and the graces of religious observance. In this way, by his earnestness and example, his disciples, who were many and distinguished, were made eminent, not only in letters and the sciences, but in personal holiness.

Lesson VI

Broken at length by age and labour, he was seized by a grievous illness. Though he suffered under it for more than fifty days, he ceased not from his prayers and his interpreting of the Scriptures; for at that time he was turning the Gospel of John into English for the use of his people. But when, on the Eve of the Ascension, he perceived that death was coming upon him, he desired to be fortified with the last sacraments of the Church: then, after he had embraced his companions, and was laid on a piece of sackcloth on the ground, he repeated the words, "Glory be to the Father, and to the Son, and to the Holy Ghost," and fell asleep in the Lord. His body, very sweet, as it is related, breathing sweet odor, was buried in the monastery of Jarrow, and afterwards was translated to Durham with the relics of St. Cuthbert. Bede, who was already a Doctor among the Benedictines, and in other religious Orders, and venerated in certain dioceses, was declared by Pope Leo XIII, after consulting with the Congregation of Sacred Rites, to be a Doctor of the universal Church; and the Mass and Office for Doctors was ordered to be recited by all on his feast-day.

Lesson VII

From the Holy Gospel according to St. Matthew (Matt 5:13–19)

At that time Jesus said to His disciples: "You are the salt of the earth; but if the salt lose its savor, wherewith shall it be salted?" And so on.

Homily by St. Bede the Venerable, Priest.

The Gospel says, "You are the salt of the earth." In these words the earth signifies human nature, and the salt signifies wisdom. Salt, verily, by its nature renders the earth unfruitful. Hence we read of cities, which in the anger of their victors were sown with salt. And hereto agrees the teaching of the Apostle that by the salt of wisdom the lust of this world is restrained in the earth of human flesh, lest the foulness of vice should sprout up. But what if the salt shall have lost its savor? That is to say: If you, by whom the people are to be seasoned, on account of fear of persecution, or terror, you should lose the kingdom of heaven, are placed outside the Church, there is no doubt that you will incur the taunts of the enemy.

Lesson VIII

"You are the light of the world;" that is to say: You, because you are enlightened by the true light, ought to be the light of them who are in the world. "A city set on a hill cannot be hid;" that is to say: The Apostles' teaching, founded upon Christ; in other words, the Church built upon Christ, out of many nations, in the unity of the faith, and bound together with the cement of love; to those who enter it, a place of safety; to those who go up to it, toilsome; the guardian of those who dwell in it, and excluding every enemy.

"Neither does any man light a candle and put it under a bushel; but upon a candlestick." So he who puts the light under the bushel is he who for his own temporal ends would hide and tamper with the light of doctrine; but upon the candlestick he places it who follows the ministry of God in order that the teaching of the truth may be accounted a greater thing than the service of the body. In another aspect, the Saviour lit the candle when He filled our mortal body with the flame of the Divinity; and He placed it on a candlestick, that is the Church; for He fixed the faith of His incarnation upon our foreheads. The Light which cannot be placed under a bushel; that is to say, it cannot be included within the measures of the law, nor in Judea alone, but has lightened the whole earth.

Lesson IX—Commemoration of St. John I, Pope & Martyr

Pope John I was a Tuscan, who ruled the Church during the reign of the Emperor Justinian. He went to Constantinople to get help from Justinian in the troubles which the heretic King Theodoric was then causing in Italy. It pleased the Lord to mark this journey with wonders. A certain nobleman at Corinth lent to the Pope for his journey a very quiet horse on which his own wife was used to ride. But when the horse was returned to his owner he was found become so vicious, that by his restiveness and plunging he was always throwing off his mistress, as though he were not content to carry the lady after having carried the Vicar of Jesus Christ. When the nobleman and his wife found the beast to be thus worthless, they gave him for a present to the Pope. But a thing much more marvelous was that when the Pope, accompanied by the Emperor, and under the gaze of an immense multitude of people, who had come forth with Justinian to do him honor, was at the entrance of the Golden Gate of Constantinople, he gave sight to a blind man. Even the Emperor fell at his feet to show him respect. When he had arranged his business with Justinian, he returned into Italy and forthwith sent out a letter to all the Bishops of Italy, bidding them to consecrate the churches of the Arians for Catholic worship, and adding these words: "We Ourselves when We were at Constantinople on some matters pertaining to the Catholic Religion and others pertaining to the King Theodoric, consecrated as Catholic all their Churches which We were able to find in those parts." Theodoric took this rule very ill, and, having enticed John by fraud to come to Ravenna, he cast him into prison, wherein, in a few days, he died of filth and hunger. He had sat in the chair of Peter two years, nine months, and fourteen days, within which time he had ordained fifteen Bishops. A little while afterward Theodoric also died. St. Gregory writes that a certain hermit saw him between Pope John and Symmachus the Patrician, whom he had likewise slain, going down into the fiery crater of Lipari, as though they who had been his victims were become the judges of his punishment. The body of John was carried from Ravenna to Rome, and there buried in the Church of St. Peter.

May 28 ~ St. Augustine of Canterbury

Confessor Bishop ~ Duplex

All from Common except what follows

Lessons I–III from the occurring Scripture

Lesson IV

Augustine, a Roman monk of the Lateran monastery, the first Archbishop of Canterbury, and the Apostle of the English, was sent into England with about forty of his confreres by Gregory the Great in the year 597. At that time there was in Kent a most mighty king named Ethelbert, who, when he had heard why the holy man was come, he received him kindly, and bade him and his monastic companions to come to his own capital city of Canterbury, whereupon he liberally granted him the opportunity to remain there and preach Christ. Hence, the holy man built an oratory near Canterbury, where he himself abode for some time, and emulated the apostolic way of life with his followers.

Lesson V

Heavenly doctrine, supported by many miracles, by his preaching and the example of his life, so softened the islanders, that he led most of them to the Christian faith. Finally he purified the king himself with an innumerable company of his companions at the sacred font, to the greatest joy of Bertha, wife of the King, who was herself a Christian. Once, on Christmas Day, when more than ten thousand had been baptized in the channel of the river York, it is remembered that as many of them as had been affected by some disease, with the salvation of their souls they also received health of their bodies. Ordained bishop by order of Gregory, he established the See of Canterbury in the church of the Savior, which he had erected, in which he placed the monks to assist his work; and he built in the suburbs the monastery of St. Peter, which was afterwards called by his name. The same Gregory granted him the use of the pallium with the faculty of establishing an ecclesiastical hierarchy in England, whereupon he also sent a new band of laborers, namely Mellitus, Justus, Paulinus, and Rufinian.

Lesson VI

Having arranged the affairs of his church, Augustine held a synod with the bishops and doctors of the ancient Britons, who had long been at variance with the Roman Church in the celebration of Easter and other rites. But since he could move them neither by the authority of the apostolic see nor by miracles to put an end to these variations, in a prophetic spirit he foretold their ruin. At length, after having endured many difficulties for Christ, and having become noted for miracles, when he had placed Mellitus in charge of the church of London, Justus of Rochester, and Laurence in charge of his own, he passed to heaven on the 26th day of May, in the reign of Ethelbert, and was buried in the monastery of St. Peter, which thereafter became the burying-place of the bishops of Canterbury and of some kings. The English people honored his memory with fervent zeal; and the Supreme Pontiff Leo XIII extended his Office and Mass to the universal Church.

Lessons VII–IX from the Common of Evangelists (Homily by St. Gregory)

May 29 ~ St. Mary Magdalene de Pazzi

Virgin ~ Semiduplex

All from Common except what follows

Lessons I–III from the occurring Scripture

Lesson IV

Mary Magdalene was born of the noble Florentine family of the Pazzi, on the 2nd day of April, in the year of Christ 1566. She was hardly out of her cradle when she set her feet in the path of perfection. At ten years of age she made a vow of perpetual virginity, and at fifteen took the habit of the Order of Mount Carmel, in the convent of Saint Mary of the Angels. In that sisterhood she was in always a pattern to all. She was pure to that degree, that she did not even know of the existence of anything which can hurt modesty. For five years, by the command of God, she lived only upon bread and water, excepting only the Lord's Day, in which she used the food which is taken in Lent. She chastised her body with hair-cloth, scourging, cold, hunger, watching, nakedness, and all manner of hardships.

Lesson V

The love of God was so hot within her, that she was sometimes compelled to bathe her breast with cold water to soothe the agitation. She was oftentimes rapt in the spirit, and most marvelously so, for whole days at a time, during which trances she saw things hidden and heavenly, and was enlightened by God with great gifts. But after all these things she endured a long struggle with the prince of darkness, while God allowed her spirit to remain dry, desolate, abandoned by all, and tormented with diverse temptations. God permitted thus so that she could remain the exemplar of unconquered patience and of the profoundest humility.

Lesson VI

She was very remarkable for her tender love toward her neighbors. Sometimes she went whole nights without sleep, while she was working for the service of the sisters, or waiting upon the sick. She sometimes healed sores even by licking them. That there should be unbelievers and sinners perishing caused her bitter weeping, and she offered herself to God to suffer for their conversion whatsoever He chose.

For many years, therefore, before her death, her heroic virtue made her to freely renounce all the heavenly delights wherewith she had once so overflowed. She had often in her mouth the words: "To suffer, not to die." At length, in the forty-second year of her age, on the 25th day of May, in the year 1607, after a long and grievous sickness, the Bridegroom came, and she entered with Him into the marriage-chamber. Clement IX, finding that God had glorified her by many miracles, both during her life and after her death, enrolled her name among those of the Holy Virgins. Her body, up to the present day, has never shown the least sign of corruption.

Lessons VII–IX from the first set in the Common of Virgins (Homily by St. Gregory)

May 30 ~ St. Felix I

Pope & Martyr ~ Simplex

Lessons I–II from the occurring Scripture

Lesson III

Pope Felix I was a Roman who ruled the Church in the days of the Emperor Aurelian. His father's name was Constantius. His is the ordinance which commands that Mass should be celebrated on the monuments and graves of martyrs. He held two December ordinations, wherein he ordained nine Priests, five Deacons, and five Bishops for diverse places. Having finished his testimony he was buried upon the Aurelian Way, in the Church which he had himself built and dedicated. He lived as Pope two years, four months, and twenty-nine days.

May 31 ~ Blessed Virgin Mary, Queen

Duplex II Class

All from Common except what follows

Lesson IV

Sermon of St. Peter Canisius, Priest

If we follow St. John Damascene, St. Athanasius and others, are we not forced to call Mary Queen, since her father David receives the highest praise in Scripture as a renowned king, and her son as King of kings and Lord of lords, reigning forever? She is Queen, moreover, when compared with the Saints who reign like kings in the heavenly kingdom, co-heirs with Christ, the great King, placed on the same throne with him, as the Scripture says. And as Queen she is second to none of the elect, but in dignity is raised so high above both Angels and men that nothing can be higher or holier than she, who alone has the same Son as God the Father, and who sees above her only God and Christ, and below her creatures other than herself.

Lesson V

The great Athanasius said clearly: "Mary is not only the Mother of God, but also can be properly and truly called Queen and Lady, since in fact the Christ who was born of the Virgin Mother is God and Lord and also King." It is to this Queen, therefore, that the Psalmist's words are applied: "The Queen stood on thy right hand; in gilded clothing." Thus Mary is rightly called Queen, not only of heaven, but also of the heavens, as the Mother of the King of Angels, and as the Bride and beloved of the King of the heavens. O Mary, most august Queen and most faithful Mother, to whom no one prays in vain who prays devoutly, and to whom all mortal men are bound by the enduring memory of so many benefits, again and again reverently I beseech thee to accept and be pleased with every evidence of my devotion to thee, to value the poor gift I offer according to the zeal with which it is offered, and to recommend it to thine all-powerful Son.

Lesson VI

From the Encyclical Letter of Pope Pius XII *Ad cæli Reginam*

From the documents of ancient Christianity, from the prayers of the liturgy, from the innate religious sense of the Christian people, from works of art, from all sides we gather witnesses which assert that the Virgin Mother of God excels in queenly dignity. And we have set forth the reasons which sacred theology deduces from the treasury of divine faith to confirm the same truth. All these witnesses form a sort of chorus, proclaiming far and wide the supreme queenly honor granted to the Mother of God and man, who is above all created things and exalted over the choirs of Angels to reign in heaven. Thus it is that after mature and thoughtful consideration we have been persuaded that great benefits would flow to the Church if, like a light that illumines more brightly when placed in its stand, this solidly proved truth were to shine out more clearly to all, and so, by Our Apostolic Authority, we decree and institute the feast of Mary, Queen, which is to be celebrated every year on the thirty-first day of May throughout the world.

Lesson VII

From the Holy Gospel according to St. Luke (Luke 1:26–33)

In that time: In the sixth month, the angel Gabriel was sent from God into a city of Galilee, called Nazareth, to a virgin espoused to a man whose name was Joseph, of the house of David; and the virgin's name was Mary. And so on.

Homily by St. Bonaventure, Bishop

The Blessed Virgin Mary is the Mother of the great King by reason of a noble kind of conception, according to the message given her by the Angel. "Behold," he said, "thou shalt conceive and shalt bring forth a son;" and again, "the Lord God will give him the throne of David his father, and he shall be king over the house of Jacob forever, and of his kingdom there shall be no end." This is as if to say in so many words, "Thou wilt conceive and bear a son who is King, eternally reigning on the royal throne, and as Queen thou wilt be seated on the royal throne." For if it becomes a son to give honor to his mother, it is also fitting that he share his royal throne with her; and so the Virgin Mary, because she conceived him on whose thigh was written, "King of kings and Lord of lords," was Queen not only of earth but also of heaven as soon as she conceived the Son of God. This is indicated in the Apocalypse where it says: "A great sign appeared in heaven: a woman clothed with the sun, and the moon was under her feet, and upon her head a crown of twelve stars."

Lesson VIII

Mary the Queen outshines all others in glory, as the Prophet clearly shows in the Psalm which particularly concerns Christ and the Virgin Mary. It first says of Christ: "Thy throne, O God, stands forever and ever," and shortly thereafter of the Virgin: "The Queen stands on thy right hand," that is, in the position of highest blessedness, for it refers to glory of soul. It continues: "In gilded clothing," by which is meant the clothing of glorious immortality which was proper to the Virgin in her Assumption. For it could not be that the garment which clothed Christ, the garment completely sanctified on earth by the incarnate Word, should be the food of worms. As it was fitting for Christ to grant the fullness of grace to his Mother at her Conception, so was it fitting that he grant her the fullness of glory at her Assumption. And so we are to hold that the Virgin, glorious in soul and body, is enthroned next to her Son.

Lesson IX

Mary the Queen is also the distributrix of grace. This is indicated in the book of Esther, where it is said: "The little spring which grew into a river and was turned into a light and into the sun." The Virgin Mary, under the type of Esther, is compared to the outpouring of a spring and of light, because of the diffusion of grace for two uses, that is, for action and for contemplation. For the grace of God, which is a healing for the human race, descends to us through her as if through an aqueduct, since the dispensing of grace is attributed to the Virgin not as to its beginning, but because of her position through merit. By position the Virgin Mary is a most excellent Queen towards her people: she obtains forgiveness, overcomes strife, distributes grace, and thereby she leads them to glory.

FEASTS OF JUNE

June 1 ~ St. Angela Merici

Virgin ~ Duplex

All from Common except what follows

Lessons I–III from the occurring Scripture

Lesson IV

Angela Merici was born of godly parents at Decenzano on the western shore of the Lake of Garda, in the diocese of Verona and territory of Venice, on the 21st day of March, about the year of grace 1474. From her earliest years she carefully guarded the lily of her virginity, with the intention of keeping it forever unbroken. She had no taste for women's finery, and purposely marred the exceeding beauty of her face and her sightly hair, as seeking to appear beautiful only in the eyes of Him Who is the Lover of souls. At ten years of age she lost both her father and mother, and thereafter, being eager to take upon her a life of greater hardness, she essayed to retire into a deserted place apart, but this her uncle forbade her to do, and she learn how to practice at home what she was not allowed to attempt in the wilderness. She often used hair-cloth and scourging, never ate flesh-meat except when she was sick, drank wine only on the Feast-days of Christmas and Easter; and many a day took nothing at all. She was constant in prayer. What little sleep she took, she took lying on the ground. The devil strove to beguile her, appearing under the form of an angel of light, but she quickly detected him and put him to flight. At length she added to the glory of virginity that poverty which is commended in the Gospel; she gave up all that she had, and adopted the dress and rule of the Third Order of St Francis.

Lesson V

She left undone no service of kindness which she was able to do to her neighbors. If there remained anything over of the food which was given in alms to herself, she gave that to the poor. She cheerfully waited upon the sick. She journeyed about with a great reputation for holiness, comforting the afflicted, asking forgiveness for the guilty, reconciling the angry, and recalling the wicked from evil. Her only hunger was for the bread of Angels, and she took the Same quite often, and then arose in her vehemence of love bearing her towards God, which oftentimes made her beside herself. She made a pilgrimage, with intense feeling, to the Holy Places in Palestine, during which journey she lost her sight in Crete on her way out, and recovered it at the same place on her way home. In this journey also, God saved her from being made prisoner by the unbelievers and from shipwreck. She went to Rome, in 1525, at once to pray at the immovable Rock of the Church, and to gain the abundant pardons of the Jubilee. Pope Clement VII conversed with her, was edified by her holiness, and highly commended her; nor would he let her leave Rome until he knew that God was calling her elsewhere.

Lesson VI

She went back to Brescia, and there hired a house near the Church of St. Afra, in which house, in obedience to a vision and command from heaven, she founded a new Order of religious women, constituted under certain rules and holy regulations of life. This Order she put under the name and patronage of St. Ursula, the fearless leader of virgins. When Angela was near to death, she foretold that this Order will never cease. She was well-nigh seventy, and full of good works, when, in the night between the 27th and the 28th of January, in the year 1540, she winged her flight heavenward. Her dead body lay unburied thirty days, supple and lifelike. It was laid at last in the Church of St. Afra, where sleep so many more of God's holy children. Diverse miracles forthwith began to be worked at her grave. The fame of these being noised about, she began to be commonly called Blessed, and not only at Brescia and Decenzano and pictures of her were put over Altars. Not many years afterward, Saint Charles Borromeo said openly at Brescia, that she was one whose name the Apostolic See might well enroll among those of holy virgins. The reverence which had of a long time been shown to her memory was approved by the local Ordinaries, confirmed by diverse Papal Indults, and solemnly ratified and established by decree of Pope Clement XIII. As she continued famous for new and proved miracles, Pope Pius VII, at the solemn canonization held in the Vatican Basilica, upon the 24th day of May, in the year 1807, added her name to the list of holy virgins.

Lessons VII–IX from the first set in the Common of Virgins (Homily by St. Gregory)

June 2 ~ Sts. Marcellinus, Peter, & Erasmus

Bishop, Martyrs ~ Simplex

Lessons I–II from the occurring Scripture

Lesson III

Peter was an exorcist, whom, in the reign of the Emperor Diocletian, Serenus the Judge cast into prison at Rome because he confessed the Christian faith. He there set free Paulina, the daughter of Artemius, the keeper of the prison, from an evil spirit which tormented her. Upon this, Artemius and his wife and all their house, with their neighbors who had run together to see the strange thing, would eagerly be made friends with Jesus Christ. Peter therefore brought them to Marcellinus, the Priest, who baptized them all. When Serenus heard of it, he called Peter and Marcellinus before him, and sharply rebuked them, adding to his bitter words threats and terrors, unless they would deny Christ. Marcellinus answered him with Christian boldness, whereupon he caused him to be beaten, separated him from Peter and shut him up naked in a prison strewn with broken glass, without either food or light. Peter also he commanded bound with tightest chains. But when both of them were found to grow from their torments in faith and spirits, they were beheaded, unshaken in their testimony, and confessing Jesus Christ gloriously by their blood. Erasmus [Elmo] was a Bishop in Campania who, in the year 303, in the reign of the Emperors Diocletian and Maximian was beaten with clubs and leaden whips, and afterwards anointed with melted pitch, sulphur, and lead, and boiling resin, wax, and oil. From all this he came forth whole and sound which wonder turned many to believe in Christ. He was remanded again to prison, and straitly bound in heavy iron fetters. But from these he was wondrously delivered by an angel. At last, at Formi, Maximian caused him to be subjected to diverse torments, and then being clad in a coat of red-hot brass, he conquered by the power of God even this torment. In the end he grasped the palm-branch of a glorious testimony, whereby he strengthened many in the faith and turned many to it.

June 4 ~ St. Francis Caracciolo

Confessor ~ Duplex
All from Common
except what follows
Lessons I–III from the
occurring Scripture

Lesson IV

Francis, whose worldly name was Ascanius, was one of the noble family of Caracciolo. He was born in the town of Santa Maria della Villa, in the Abruzzi, on the 13th day of October, in the year of grace 1563. From his earliest years he showed great marks of godliness. When he was a young man he had a severe illness, and on his recovery determined to serve God alone, and bade farewell to the world. He betook himself to Naples, where he was ordained Priest, enrolled himself in a devout guild, and gave himself up altogether to seek after God, and to gain souls for Him, in which work he showed himself an unwearied comforter to such prisoners as were condemned to death. It came to pass that those two great servants of God, Giovanni Agostino Adorno and Fabrizio Caracciolo, wrote a letter to a certain person, wherein they exhorted him to found a new religious Institute. This letter came by a mistake to be delivered to Francis Caracciolo. The newness of the idea and the strange ways of God's Providence took possession of his mind, and he joyfully added himself to their company. They withdrew themselves to the wilderness of the Camaldolese hermits near Naples, and there concerted the Rule of the New Order. Thence they went together to Rome, and obtained the confirmation of their work from Sixtus V, who was pleased that they should be called The Clerics Regular Minor, since they add to the three accustomed vows of Poverty, Chastity, and Obedience, a fourth, binding themselves not to seek preferment in the Church.

Lesson V

Ascanius Caracciolo, moved by a special love and devotion he had to the holy Francis of Assisi, took, when he made his solemn profession, the name of Francis. After two years, Giovanni Adorno departed this life, and Francis, against his own will, was made Head of the Order. In this office he shone a burning light of grace. Devoted to the prosperity of the Institute, he earnestly sought the blessing of God upon it by constant prayer, tears, and stern treatment of his own body. In this work, he thrice travelled into Spain in the guise of a pilgrim, and begging his bread from door to door. In these his journeys he suffered very great hardships, and was most wonderfully helped by the Almighty, especially once while when he was on shipboard and the ship was nigh to perish, but for the work of his prayers. He toiled hard in those countries to attain his wishes, but through the widespread fame of his holy life, and the noble generosity of the Most Catholic Kings Philip II and Philip III, he overcame with his brave perseverance the opposition of all that withstood him, and founded several houses of his Order. This he was also able to do in Italy.

Lesson VI

He excelled in a great pattern of humility, so that when he came to Rome he betook himself to an almshouse, and chose a leper for his familiar friend. Paul V offered him diverse honors in the Church, but he firmly refused them all. He preserved his purity unspotted, and when certain shameless women set themselves to attack his chastity, he took the occasion to gain over their souls for Christ. Toward God's great mystery of the Eucharist he was drawn with passionate tenderness, and would pass almost whole nights without sleep, simply adoring Him. This pious custom he established in his Order, to be kept up therein forever, the peculiar mark thereof. He was a great encourager of the worship of the Virgin God-bearer. He was burning with charity for his neighbor. He was gifted with prophecy, and the discerning of spirits. In the forty-fourth year of his age he was continuing long in prayer in the Holy House of Loreto, when it was made known to him that the end of his earthly life was at hand. He straightway took his way to the Abruzzi, and was there seized with illness while he was with the disciples of St. Philip Neri, in the town of Agnone. He received with great devotion the Sacraments of the Church, and then, upon the 4th day of June, being the Vigil of the Feast of Corpus Christi, in the year 1608, he very peacefully fell asleep in the Lord. His sacred body was honorably laid in the Church of St. Mary Major, where he had laid the first foundations of his Order, and later carried to Naples. As he became distinguished for miracles, Pope Clement XIV enrolled his name, with solemn rites, among those of the Blessed, and Pope Pius VII, in the year 1807, finding his mighty works continue, added it to the list of the Saints.

Lessons VII–IX from the first set in the Common of Confessor Non-Bishops (Homily by St. Gregory)

June 5 ~ St. Boniface

Bishop & Martyr ~ Duplex

All from Common
except what follows

Lessons I–III from the
occurring Scripture

Lesson IV

Winfrid, afterwards called Boniface, was an Anglo-Saxon, and born near Wessex, towards the end of the seventh century. From his very childhood, he turned away from the world, and set his heart upon becoming a monk. His father tried in vain to turn him from his wishes by the beguilements of the world, and he entered a Monastery, where the Blessed Wolphard instructed him in all piety and diverse kinds of learning. At the age of twenty-nine years he was ordained Priest, and became an unwearied preacher of the Word of God, wherein he had a gift which he used with great gain of souls. Nevertheless, his great desire was to spread the kingdom of Christ, and he continually bewailed the vast number of savages who were plunged in the darkness of ignorance and were the servants of the devil. This zealous love of souls increased in him in intensity day by day, till nothing would serve him, but, having implored the blessing of God by tears and prayers, and obtained authority from the head of his monastery to set forth for the coast of Germany.

Lesson V

He set sail from Anglia with two companions in the year 716 and reached the town of Dorestadt in Friesland. A great war being then raging between Radbod, King of the Frieslanders, and Charles Martel, Winfrid preached the Gospel in vain. He went back to Anglia, and betook himself again to his Monastery, whereof he was, against his own will, chosen to be the head. After two years he obtained the consent of the Bishop of Winchester to resign his office, and in 719 went to Rome to seek an Apostolic commission to preach to the heathen. When he arrived at the city he was courteously welcomed by Gregory II, who changed his name from Winfrid to Boniface. He departed thence to Germany, and preached Christ to the tribes in Thuringia and Saxony. Radbod, King of Friesland and bitterest enemy to the Christian name, being dead, Boniface went a second time among the Frieslanders, and there, with his comrade St. Willibrord, preached the Gospel for three years with so much fruit, that the idols were hewn down, and countless churches arose to the true God.

Lesson VI

Willibrord urged upon him to take the office of a Bishop, but he deferred to seek it, that he might the more constantly toil for the salvation of the unbelievers. Advancing into Germany, he reclaimed thousands of the Old Saxons from devil-worship. Pope Gregory sent for him to Rome, whither he came in 723, and after hearing a noble profession of his faith, consecrated him a Bishop. He again returned to Germany, and thoroughly purged Hessia and Thuringia from all remains of idolatry. On account of such great works, Gregory III advanced Boniface to the dignity of an Archbishop, and on the occasion of a third journey to Rome in 738, he was invested by the Sovereign Pontiff with the powers of Legate of the Apostolic See. As such, he founded the four Bishoprics of Erfurt, Paderborn, Würtzburg, and Eichstadt, and held diverse

Synods, among which is especially to be remembered that of Lessines, held in Belgium, in the diocese of Cambrai, wherein he made his strongest endeavours to spread the Faith among the Belgians. By Pope Zachary he was named Archbishop of Mainz, and by command of the same Pope, he anointed Pepin to be King of the Franks. After the death of St. Willibrord, he undertook the government of the Church of Utrecht, at first through Eoban but he afterwards was released from the care of the Church of Mainz and established his see at Utrecht. The Frieslanders having again fallen back into idolatry, he once more betook himself to preach the Gospel among them, and while he was busied in this duty, he grasped the crown of martyrdom, being murdered by some barbarous and impious men, along with his fellow-Bishop Eoban, and many others, in a bloody massacre near the River Born, on the 5th day of June, in the year of our Lord 755, and of his own age the 75th. In accordance with the wish expressed by himself during life, the body of St. Boniface was carried to Mainz, and buried in the monastery of Fulda, of which he had been the founder, and where God has gloriously honored it by the working of many signs and wonders. Pope Pius IX ordered the Office and Mass in his memory to be used throughout the whole Church.

Lesson VII

From the Holy Gospel according to St. Matthew (Matt 5:1–12)

At that time Jesus, seeing the multitudes, went up into a mountain, and, when He was set down, His disciples came unto Him. And so on.

Homily by St. Augustine, Bishop

"Blessed are the pure in heart, for they shall see God." What fools then be they that seek God with their outward eyes, since it is in the heart that He is seen, as it is written elsewhere: "In simplicity of heart seek Him." A simple heart is a pure heart. And even as we cannot see this earthly light, unless the eyes be open, so cannot God be seen, unless that be open which alone can perceive Him. "Blessed are the peacemakers, for they shall be called the children of God." The perfection of peace is the absence of contrariness, and the peacemakers are called the children of God because they offer no resistance against the will of God. As befits children, they have their Father's likeness.

Lesson VIII

They are peacemakers in themselves, who order all the movements of their own mind in obedience to reason, that is, to their intellect and soul, and so doing, taming the lusts of the flesh, become a kingdom for God. In such kingdom all things are so ordered, that the chiefest and noblest part of man rules without contention over those lower things which we have in common with beasts. And just in the same way, must that nobler part of man, that is to say, intellect and reason, needs be put in subjection to what is above it, namely, Truth, the Only begotten Son of God. He only can rule well who has learnt to obey. And this ordering is that peace which is given on earth to men of good will; this is the life of whomsoever is thoroughly and perfectly wise.

Lesson IX

From this most peaceful and most orderly kingdom is cast forth the prince of this world, whose rule is over the perverse and disordered. When once this peace has been proclaimed and established within, whatsoever persecutions he that is cast forth can raise can only augment that glory which is according to God, for nothing of the castle will yield before him, but the yielding of his own siege engines will witness how strong the ramparts are. And therefore comes next: "Blessed are they which are persecuted for righteousness' sake, for theirs is the kingdom of heaven."

June 6 ~ St. Norbert

Confessor Bishop ~ Duplex

All from Common
except what follows

Lessons I–III from the
occurring Scripture

Lesson IV

Norbert, born in the year 1080 of parents of the highest rank, thoroughly educated in his youth in worldly knowledge, and a member of the Imperial court, turned his back upon the glory of the world, and chose rather to enlist himself as a soldier of the Church. Being ordained Priest, he laid aside all soft and showy raiment, clad himself in a coat of skins, and made the preaching of the Word of God the one object of his life. Renouncing his right to rich revenues of the Church and giving to the poor to his ample patrimony, he ate only once a day, and that in the evening, and then his meal was of the fare of Lent. His life was one of singular hardness, and he was used even in the depth of winter to go out with bare feet and ragged garments. Hence came that mighty power of his words and deeds, whereby he was enabled to turn countless heretics to the true faith, sinners to repentance, and enemies to peace and concord.

Lesson V

While at Laon, the Bishop besought him not to leave his diocese, and he therefore made choice of a desert at the place called Prémontré, whither he withdrew himself with thirteen disciples, and thus founded the Order of the Premonstratensians, whereof he, by the will of God, received the Rule, in a vision, from St. Augustine. When, however, the fame of his holy life became every day more and more noised abroad, and great numbers sought to become his disciples, and the Order had been approved by Honorius II, and other Popes, many more monasteries were built by him, and the Order wonderfully extended.

Lesson VI

Being called to Antwerpen, he there gave the death-blow to the shameful heresy of Tanchelm. He was remarkable for the spirit of prophecy and for the gift of miracles. He was created (albeit reluctantly) Archbishop of Magdeburg, and as such he was a strong upholder of

Church discipline, especially contending against the marriage of the clergy. At a Council in Rheims he was a great help to Innocent II, and went with some Other Bishops to Rome, where they stamped out the schism of Peter Pierleoni [Antipope Anacletus II]. It was at last at Magdeburg that this man of God, full of good works and of the Holy Ghost, fell asleep in the Lord, on the 6th day of June, in the year of salvation 1134.

Lessons VII–IX from the first set in the Common of Confessor Bishops (Homily by St. Gregory)

June 9 ~ Sts. Primus & Felician

Martyrs ~ Simplex

Lessons I–II from the occurring Scripture

Lesson III

Primus and Felician were brothers who were accused of Christianity during the persecution by Diocletian and Maximian, and thrown into chains, which an angel broke, and so freed their limbs. In the presence of the Prætor they most earnestly clung to the profession of their faith, and were immediately parted one from the other. Felician's was the steadfastness which was first tried in diverse ways. They, however, that strove to argue him into sin, when they found that words availed nothing, fastened his hands and feet to a post, and left him to hang there three days without food or drink. On the fourth day, the Prætor called Primus before him, and said to him: "Seest thou how much thy brother is wiser than thou? He has obeyed the Emperors, and they have made him honorable. Thou hast only to follow his example to be made partaker of his honors and favors." Primus answered him: "What has befallen my brother I know, for an angel told me. May God grant, seeing as I have the same will that he has, that I may not be divided from him in uplifting of testimony." These words raised the wrath of the Prætor, and to the torments which he had already inflicted on Primus, he added this also, that he had boiling lead put into his mouth, compelling his brother Felician to be present and see it done. After that, he had them led into the theatre and two lions let loose upon them, in the presence of about twelve thousand people who were gathered together to see the show. The lions only fawned upon the knees of the Saints, making friends with them with motions of their heads and tails. This exhibition turned five hundred persons and their households to Christ. The Prætor, then, moved beyond all endurance by what had passed, commanded Primus and Felician to be beheaded.

June 10 ~ St. Margaret of Scotland

Queen & Widow ~ Semiduplex

All from Common except what follows

Lessons I–III from the occurring Scripture

Lesson IV

Margaret, Queen of the Scots, was most noble by birth, uniting in herself, from her father the blood of the Kings of England and from her mother the blood of the Cæsars, but far nobler was she by her Christian virtue. She was born in Hungary, where her father was then an exile, in the year 1046, and had passed a religious childhood, when her uncle Saint Edward, the King of England, recalled him to his own royal home, and she came to England with him in 1054. A few years after, upon the ruin of her family, she was escaping from England by sea, when the violence of the weather, or, to speak more truly, the Providence of God, caused that the ship should take refuge upon the coast of Scotland. There her extraordinary graces of mind and body so attracted King Malcolm III, that by the advice of his mother, he took her to wife in 1070, and of Scotland she deserved exceedingly well for the thirty years of her reign, by the holiness of her life and the abundance of her works of mercy.

Lesson V

In the midst of regal delights, she afflicted her body with hardships and watching, using to spend great part of the night in earnest prayer. Besides other fasts which she imposed upon herself, it was her custom to observe one of forty days before Christmas, concerning which fast she was so rigid, that she would not relax it even under sharp suffering. She took great delight in the public worship of God, and founded or renewed a great number of Churches and convents, which she enriched at great cost with sacred furniture. Her healthy example drew the King her husband to habits of sobriety, and to imitate her in her good works. To all her children she had the happiness of giving a godly education, and several of them, like her mother Agatha and her sister Christina, led notably holy lives. The happiness of the whole kingdom was the object for which she constantly strove, and she successfully rooted out all the vices which had stealthily crept in, and established among the people a standard of living worthy of Christians.

Lesson VI

The most remarkable feature of her life was the tenderness of her charity toward her neighbor, especially the needy. Of these she would not only order whole flocks to be relieved, but was accustomed to give dinner to three hundred of them every day, treating them with the tenderness of a mother, and waiting upon them on her knees like a maidservant. She held it one of the privileges of her rank to wash their feet with her own Royal hands, and to dress, even to kiss, their sores. To meet the expenses of her charities she sold not only her queenly raiment and her precious jewels, but more than once exhausted her funds entirely. Purified by grievous suffering, which she bore with marvelous patience during an illness of six months, she resigned her soul to its Author, upon the 16th day of November, 1093. At the moment of death, the bystanders saw her poor worn face, pale and disfigured by continual suffering, flush again with a beauty to which it had long been unused. After her death she became illustrious on account of great signs and wonders. With the approval of Clement X, she was chosen Patroness of Scotland, and her memory is held in profound reverence throughout the whole earth.

Lessons VII–IX from the Common of Non-Virgins (Homily by St. Gregory)

June 11 ~ St. Barnabas the Apostle

Major Duplex

All from Common except what follows

Lesson I ~ Acts 13:43–47

From the Acts of the Apostles

And when the synagogue was broken up, many of the Jews, and of the strangers who served God, followed Paul and Barnabas: who speaking to them, persuaded them to continue in the grace of God. But the next sabbath day, the whole city almost came together, to hear the word of God. And the Jews seeing the multitudes, were filled with envy, and contradicted those things which were said by Paul, blaspheming. Then Paul and Barnabas said boldly: To you it behoved us first to speak the word of God: but because you reject it, and judge yourselves unworthy of eternal life, behold we turn to the Gentiles. For so the Lord hath commanded us: I have set thee to be the light of the Gentiles; that thou mayest be for salvation unto the utmost part of the earth.

Lesson II ~ Acts 13:48–52

And the Gentiles hearing it, were glad, and glorified the word of the Lord: and as many as were ordained to life everlasting, believed. And the word of the Lord was published throughout the whole country. But the Jews stirred up religious and honourable women, and the chief men of the city, and raised persecution against Paul and Barnabas: and cast them out of their coasts. But they, shaking off the dust of their feet against them, came to Iconium. And the disciples were filled with joy and with the Holy Ghost.

Lesson III ~ Acts 14:1–3

And it came to pass in Iconium, that they entered together into the synagogue of the Jews, and so spoke that a very great multitude both of the Jews and of the Greeks did believe. But the unbelieving Jews stirred up and incensed the minds of the Gentiles against the brethren. A long time therefore they abode there, dealing confidently in the Lord, who gave testimony to the word of his grace, granting signs and wonders to be done by their hands.

Lesson IV

Joseph, who by the Apostles was surnamed Barnabas (which is, being interpreted, the Son of Consolation), a Levite and of the country of Cyprus, having land, sold it, and brought the money, and laid it at the Apostles' feet. When Paul, after his conversion, came to Jerusalem, the disciples were all afraid of him, but Barnabas took him, and brought him to the Apostles. When tidings that a great number believed and turned unto the Lord at Antioch came unto the ears of the Church which was at Jerusalem, they sent forth Barnabas that he should go as far as Antioch. Who, when he came, and had seen the grace of God, was glad, and exhorted them all that with purpose of heart they would cleave unto the Lord. For he was a good man, and full of the Holy Ghost, and of faith, and many people came to the Lord.

Lesson V

Then departed Barnabas to Tarsus for to seek Paul, and, when he had found him, he brought him unto Antioch. And it came to pass that a for whole year they assembled themselves with the Church, and gave to those men the precepts of Christian faith and life even where the worshippers of Jesus Christ were first called Christians. Moreover, the disciples of Paul and Barnabas sent relief unto the brethren which dwelt in Judea, sending money to them through Paul and Barnabas, who, when they had fulfilled their office of charity and summoned John, whose surname was Mark, returned to Antioch.

Lesson VI

Now there were in the Church at Antioch, certain Prophets and teachers and, as Paul and Barnabas, together with them, ministered to the Lord and fasted, the Holy Ghost said: "Set apart for Me Saul and Barnabas for the work to which I have called them." And when they had fasted and prayed, and laid their hands on them, they sent them away. So they, being sent forth by the Holy Ghost, departed unto Seleucia, from thence to Cyprus, and moreover in many other cities and countries, preaching the Gospel with great gain to them that heard them. Nevertheless, at last, Paul and Barnabas departed asunder one from the other. And so Barnabas took Mark and sailed unto Cyprus once more. And there it was that upon a certain elevennth of June, about the seventh year of the reign of Nero, Barnabas crowned the dignity of the Apostolate with the glory of martyrdom. During the reign of the Emperor Zeno, his body was found in its grave in Cyprus; on his breast lay a copy of the Gospel according to Matthew, written by the hand of Barnabas himself.

Lesson VII

From the Holy Gospel according to St. Matthew (Matt 10:6–22)

At that time: Jesus said unto His disciples: Behold, I send you forth as sheep in the midst of wolves. And so on.

Homily by St. John Chrysostom

When the Lord had cleared the minds of His disciples of all care, and had armed them by showing forth His mighty works, and had estranged them from all business of this world, and freed them from all anxiety about temporal things, moulding them into a frame of iron-like, nay, diamond-like, hardness, then at length He told them of the contentions against which they were later to wrestle. By this foretelling of things to come they were much helped. First, they learnt the power of His foreknowledge. Then, they were guarded against all suspicion that these great sorrows flowed from faultiness in their Master. Again, the future sufferers were made safe from all trouble of being taken unawares. Lastly, seeing that they heard these things at a time nigh to His own suffering, they were not over troubled.

Lesson VIII

And now, that they may understand how this is a new kind of warfare, and an unaccustomed manner of doing battle, when He sends them forth unarmed, providing neither gold, nor silver, nor brass in their purses nor scrip for their journey, neither two coats, neither shoes, nor yet staves, left to the hospitality of whosoever would receive them, He makes not here an end to His discourse, but, in manifestation of His unspeakable power, He bids them, so going, to show forth the meekness of sheep, seeing they were about going unto wolves; neither simply unto wolves, but in the very midst of wolves. Neither is it only the meekness of sheep which He bids them have, but also the harmlessness of doves, that He might so much more gloriously display His power, when the sheep overcame the wolves. These are the sheep which albeit they abide in the midst of wolves, and are mangled by many a bite, not only are not destroyed, but do gradually make the wolves change their nature, and become sheep themselves.

Lesson IX

Surely it is a greater and more marvelous thing to change the minds of enemies, and to turn their thoughts round, than to kill them; more especially when the work is to be done by only twelve sheep, and the whole world is full of the wolves. Shame then upon us, whose deeds are so contrary, and who rather run like wolves upon our enemies. For so long as we are sheep we conquer, yea, though a thousand wolves be gathered round about us, we overcome, and are the conquerors; but if we become wolves ourselves, then are we conquered. For then does the Shepherd's help forsake us, Who feeds not wolves but sheep.

June 12 ~ St. John of San Facundo

Confessor ~ Duplex

All from Common except what follows

Lessons I–III from the occurring Scripture

Lesson IV

John was born of a noble race, at Sahagún (or San Facundo) in Spain, on Midsummer Day in the year of grace 1430. His father and mother after long childlessness, obtained him from God by prayers and good works. From his earliest years, he gave clear signs of his later holiness of life. He used to climb up upon a high place to preach to the other little boys, and to exhort them to be good and to worship God, and he made it his work to reconcile their quarrels. While he was still at home he was given in charge to the monks of the Order of Saint Benedict, at San Facundo, to teach him his first lessons. While he was thus busied, his father obtained for him the benefice of the Parish, but no persuasions could induce him to keep this preferment. He became one of the household of the Bishop of Burgos, and that Prelate, seeing his uprightness, took him into his counsels, ordained him Priest, and made him a Canon, heaping upon him many kindnesses. However, that he might serve God more quietly, he left the Bishop's Palace, resigned all his Church income, and betook him to a certain Chapel wherein he celebrated the Holy Liturgy every day, and oftentimes preached concerning the things of God, with great profit to all that heard him.

Lesson V

He went later to Salamanca to study, and there being taken into the celebrated College of St. Bartholomew, he exercised his priestly office, so that he was simultaneously constant to the studies he desired and busy with sermons. Here he had a severe illness, and vowed to take up a sterner way of living. In fulfillment of this vow, he gave to a half-naked beggar the better of the two garments which were all that he had, and then went to a Convent of the friars of St. Augustine, which was then in the richest bloom of rigid discipline. Being admitted therein, he surpassed the most advanced in obedience, lowliness, watchings, and prayer. At the time that he had charge of the table, one small cask of wine abundantly sufficed in his hands for all the friars throughout a whole year. After his year of novitiate, he undertook the duty of preacher at the command of his Superior. At that time, owing to bloody feuds, all things human and divine at Salamanca were in such utter confusion, that murders were committed almost every hour, and the streets and squares, and even the very churches, flowed with the blood of all classes, especially of the nobility.

Lesson VI

It was John, who by public preaching and private conversations, softened the hearts of the citizens so that the town was restored to peace. He grievously offended one of the nobles by rebuking him for his cruelty toward his vassals. This man sent two knights to murder him on the road. They had already come near him when God sent a terror upon them, so that they and their horses stood still, until they cast themselves down before the feet of the Saint, imploring his forgiveness for their sin. The Prince himself, also, smitten with a sudden dread, despaired of his salvation till he had sent for John, who, finding him repentant of his deed, restored him to soundness. Some quarrelsome men, likewise, who sought to give him a cudgeling, found their arms stiffen, nor would their strength come back till they had asked his pardon for their wickedness. Oftentimes when he was celebrating the Holy Liturgy, the Presence of the Lord Christ became sensibly manifest to him, and he drank in heavenly things from their Divine Font Himself. Oftentimes also he could see the secrets of men's hearts, and foretell strange things to come. He raised from the dead his own niece, aged seven years. He foretold the day of his own death, and prepared himself by receiving most devoutly the Sacraments of the Church, and then fell asleep in the Lord, upon the 11th day of June, in the year 1475. God glorified him by many miracles, both before and after his death. These being duly proved, Alexander VIII numbered him among the Saints.

Lessons VII–IX from the first set in the Common of Confessor Non-Bishops (Homily by St. Gregory)

Lesson IX—Commemoration of Sts. Basilides, Cyrinus, Nabor, & Nazarius, Martyrs

Basilides, Cyrinus, Nabor, and Nazarius were Roman soldiers of illustrious birth and distinguished gallantry. Having embraced the Christian Religion, and being found publishing that Christ was the Son of God, they were arrested by Aurelius, Præfect of Rome under the Emperor Diocletian. As they despised his orders to sacrifice to the gods, they were committed to prison. While they were at prayer there, a brilliant light broke forth before the eyes of all that were there, and shone in all the prison. Marcellus, the keeper of the prison, and many others were moved by this heavenly glory to believe in the Lord Christ. Basilides, Cyrinus, Nabor, and Nazarius were afterwards discharged out of the prison. However, in the reign of the Emperor Maximian, when they neglected his command also, and had ever in their mouth that there is but one Christ, one God, and one Lord, they were tormented with scorpions and again cast into chains. Thence, on the seventh day, they were brought out, and set before the Emperor, and there still persisted in mocking the inane gods, and declaring that Jesus Christ is God. They were accordingly condemned to death and beheaded. Their bodies were given to wild beasts to eat, but, as the creatures would not touch them, the Christians took them, and buried them honorably.

June 13 ~ St. Anthony of Padua

Confessor ~ Duplex

All from Common except what follows

Lessons I–III from the occurring Scripture

Lesson IV

Anthony was born of decent parents at Lisbon in Portugal, on the Feast of the Assumption, in the year of grace 1195. They gave him a godly training, and while he was still a young man, he joined an Institute of Canons Regular. However, when the bodies of the five holy martyred Friars Minor, who had just suffered in Morocco for Christ's sake, were brought to Coimbra, the desire to be himself a martyr took a strong hold upon him, and in 1220 he left the Canons Regular and became a Franciscan. The same yearning led him to attempt to go among the Saracens, but he fell sick on the way, and, being obliged to turn back, the ship in which he had embarked for Spain was driven by stress of weather to Sicily.

Lesson V

From Sicily he came to Assisi to attend the General Chapter of his Order, and thence withdrew himself to the Hermitage of Monte Paolo near Bologna, where he gave himself up for a long while to consideration of the things of God, to fasts, and to vigils. Being afterwards ordained Priest and sent to preach the Gospel, his wisdom and fluency were very marked, and drew on him such admiration of men, that the Pope, once hearing him preach, called him "The Ark of the Covenant." One of his chief points was to expend all his strength in attacking heresies, whence he gained the name of "the Perpetual Hammer of Heretics."

Lesson VI

He was the first of his Order who, on account of his excellent gift of teaching, publicly lectured at Bologna on the interpretation of Holy Scripture, and directed the studies of his brethren. He traveled through many provinces. The year before his death he came to Padua, where he left some remarkable records of his holy life. After having undergone much toil for the glory of God, full of good works and miracles, he fell asleep in the Lord upon the 13th day of June, in the year of salvation 1231. Pope Gregory IX enrolled his name among those of the Holy Confessors.

Lessons VII–IX from the first set in the Common of Confessor Non-Bishops (Homily by St. Gregory)

June 14 ~ St. Basil the Great

Bishop, Confessor, & Doctor ~ Duplex

All from Common except what follows

Lessons I–III from the occurring Scripture

Lesson IV

Basil was a noble Cappadocian who studied earthly learning at Athens, in company with Gregory Nanzianzen, to whom he was united in a warm and tender friendship. He afterwards studied things sacred in a monastery, where he quickly attained an eminent degree of excellence in doctrine and life, whereby he gained to himself the surname of "the Great." He was called to Pontus to preach the Gospel of Christ Jesus, and brought back into the way of salvation that country which before had been wandering astray from the rules of Christian discipline. He was shortly united as coadjutor to Eusebius, Bishop of Cæssarea, for the edification of that city, and afterwards became his successor in the see. One of his greatest labors was to maintain that the Son is consubstantial with the Father, and when the Emperor Valens, moved to wrath against him, was willing to send him into exile, he so bent him by way of the miracles which he worked that he forced him to forego his intention.

Lesson V

The chair upon which Valens sat, in order to sign the decree of Basil's ejection from the city, broke down under him, and three pens which he took one after the other to sign the edict of banishment, all would not write and when nevertheless he remained firm to write the impious order, his right hand violently trembled. Valens was so frightened at these omens, that he tore the paper in two. During the night which was allowed to Basil to make up his mind, Valens' wife had a severe stomach-ache, and their only son was taken seriously ill. These things alarmed Valens so much that he acknowledged his wickedness, and sent for Basil, during whose visit the child began to get better. However, when Valens sent for some heretics to see him, he died shortly thereafter.

Lesson VI

The abstinence and self-control of Basil were truly wonderful. He was content to wear nothing but one single garment. In observance of fasting he was most earnest, and so constant in prayer, that he would oftentimes pass the whole night therein. His virginity he kept always unsullied. He built monasteries, wherein he so adapted the institution of monasticism, that he exquisitely united for the monks the advantages of the contemplative and the active life. He was the author of many learned writings, and, according to the witness of Gregory Nanzianzen, no one has ever composed more faithful and edifying explanations of the books of the Holy Scripture. He died upon the 1st day of January, in the year of our Lord 379, at which time so essentially spiritual was his life, that his body showed nothing but skin and bones.

Lesson VII

From the Holy Gospel according to St. Luke (Luke 14:26–35)

At that time: Jesus said unto the multitudes: If any man come to Me, and hate not his father, and mother, and wife, and children, and brethren, and sisters, yea, and his own life also, he cannot be My disciple. And so on.

Homily by St. Basil, Bishop

This is perfect self-renunciation, when we attain to indifference as regards our own lives, and wring from death himself the confession that our trust is not in our own strength. The first step toward this crown of abnegation is to estrange ourselves from outward things, such as property, public reputation, habits of life, and affection for things unnecessary, whereof the immediate disciples of our Holy Lord have left us a fine example; James, for instance, and John, who left their father Zebedee and the boats which were their only means of getting their daily bread, or Matthew, who got up from the receipt of custom, and straightway followed the Lord.

Lesson VIII

But what need have we for our own arguments, or for the examples of holy men to confirm what we say, when we are able to cite the very words of the Lord Himself, and by them to move any earnest soul that loves God? Such were they unto whom He plainly and unhesitatingly declared: "Whosoever he be of you that forsakes not all that he has, he cannot be My disciple." And again, in another place, when He had said: "If thou wilt be perfect, go, and sell that thou hast, and give to the poor" the completion of the sentence was, "And come and follow Me."

Lesson IX

This then, as we have taught, is self-renunciation: to unlock the chains of this earthly life, which passes away, and to set oneself free from the business of men, and so to make ourselves thinner and more worthy to enter on that path which leads to God, and let our reason be more unhampered to gain and to use those things which are far more precious than gold or precious stones. In short, it is to have our heart in heaven and not on earth, so as to be able to say "Our conversation is in heaven." And (which is the great thing) this is the first step towards the attaining to be like Christ, who, though He was rich, yet for our sakes He became poor.

June 15 ~ Sts. Vitus, Modestus & Crescentia

Martyrs ~ Simplex

Lessons I–II from the occurring Scripture

Lesson III

Vitus was a child who was baptized without his father's knowledge. When his father had found out, he used his best endeavors to dissuade his son from the Christian religion, but as he found him persistent in it, he handed him over to Valerian the judge to be whipped. But as he still remained as unshaken as before, he was given back to his father. But while his father was turning over in his mind to what severe discipline to subject him, Vitus, being warned by an Angel, fled out of the country, in company with his foster-parents Modestus and Crescentia. In his new home he gained great praise for holiness, so that the fame of it came to Diocletian, which Emperor sent for him to deliver his own child which was vexed with a demon. Him Vitus delivered, but when the Emperor found that with all his great gifts he could not bring him to worship the gods, he had the ingratitude to cast him and Modestus and Crescentia into prison, binding them in fetters. But when they were found in their prison more faithful than ever to their confession, the Emperor commanded them to be thrown into a great vessel full of melted lead, resin, and pitch. Therein these three, like the three Holy Children in the burning fiery furnace, sang praise to God and upon that they were dragged forth and cast to a lion, but it lay down before them, and licked their feet. Then the Emperor, being filled with fury, more especially because he saw that the multitude that looked on were stirred up at the miracle, commanded Vitus, Modestus, and Crescentia to be stretched upon a block, their limbs crushed, and their bones rent one from the other. While they were dying there came great thunderings, and lightnings, and earthquakes, so that temples of the gods fell down, and many men were killed. As for the remains of the Martyrs, the noble lady Florence took them, and, anointing them with spices, honorably buried them.

June 18 ~ St. Ephræm the Syrian

Bishop, Confessor, & Doctor ~ Duplex

All from Common except what follows

Lessons I–III from the occurring Scripture

Lesson IV

Ephræm was of Syrian descent, and son of a citizen of Nisibis. While yet a young man he went to the bishop by whom he was baptized, Saint James, and he soon made such progress in holiness and learning as to be appointed master of a flourishing school at Nisibis, a city of Mesopotamia. After the death of the bishop James, Nisibis was captured by the Persians, and Ephræm went to Edessa. Here he settled first on the mountain among the monks, and then, that he might avoid the great numbers of men who flocked to him, he adopted the eremitical life. He was ordained deacon of the Church of Edessa, but refused the priesthood out of humility. He was conspicuous with the splendor of every virtue and strove to acquire piety and religion by professing true wisdom. He placed all his hope in God alone, despised all human and transitory things, and always longed for the divine and eternal.

Lesson V

When, led by the Spirit of God, he went to Cæsarea in Cappadocia, there he saw Basil, that mouthpiece of the Church, and both enjoyed mutual companionship in a suitable manner. In order to refute the countless errors which were rife at that time, and which were troubling the Church of God, and in order to expound zealously the divine mysteries of our Lord Jesus Christ, he wrote many studies in Syrian, almost all of which have been translated into Greek. St. Jerome bears witness that he attained such fame, that his writings were read publicly in certain churches after the reading from the Scriptures.

Lesson VI

His works taken as a whole, so infused with the bright light of learning, brought it about that this holy man, while yet alive, was held in great honor, and was even considered a Doctor of the Church. He also composed songs in verse, in honor of the Most Blessed Virgin

Mary and the Saints, and for this reason he was appropriately named by the Syrians "the Harp of the Holy Ghost." He was noted for his great and tender devotion towards the Immaculate Virgin. He died, rich in merits, at Edessa in Mesopotamia on the 18th day of June in the reign of Valens. Pope Benedict XV, at the instance of many Cardinals of the Holy Roman Church, Patriarchs, Archbishops, Bishops, Abbots, and religious communities, declared him by a decree of the Congregation of Sacred Rites to be a Doctor of the universal Church.

Lesson VII

From the Holy Gospel according to St. Matthew (Matt 5:13–19)

At that time: Jesus said unto His disciples: "You are the salt of the earth; but if the salt lose its savor, wherewith shall it be salted?" And so on.

Homily by St. Ephræm the Syrian, Deacon

Clearly it is a good thing to begin and to accomplish, to be acceptable to God and useful to one's neighbor, to please our most high and gracious ruler, Christ Jesus, who says: "You are the salt of the earth and the pillars of the heavens." The burden of your affliction, dearly beloved, is as a sleep; then there follows unspeakable and priceless rest from labor. Therefore, watch thyself carefully, so that while thou followest after neither, wholeheartedly, thou shouldst not lose both the present and the eternal joy. Study rather to attain to the perfect virtue, adorned and stamped by all that God loves. If thou dost strive after this, thou wilt never either anger God nor injure thy neighbor.

Lesson VIII

Moreover this virtue is called special and singular, having within itself the beauty of different virtues. We cannot have a royal diadem without precious stones and gleaming pearls arranged and fitted together; so likewise this single virtue cannot remain without the splendor of other different virtues. For it is, indeed, most like a kingly crown. For as in the latter case, if one stone or one pearl be missing it cannot shine perfectly upon the royal head; so, then, this special virtue cannot be called a perfect virtue, unless it is worthily connected with other virtues. Again, it is like unto very rich food, furnished with exquisite seasonings, but lacking salt. For as those rich dishes cannot be eaten without salt, so this simple virtue may be adorned with the glory and honor of different virtues, but if a man lack the love of God and of his neighbor, he is wholly worthless and contemptible.

Some have adopted this kind of virtue, and wearing it like a royal diadem, they have taken a great deal of ornaments from it. Afterward, however, the grace of each of the meanest things reduced the virtue so illustrious to nothing. For their minds are bound by the cares of earthly things, and virtue hindered by such bonds could not enter heaven. Be vigilant, therefore, my beloved, lest, conquering yourself with these bonds, you open yourself a prey to the enemy; do not lose that wonderful and most brilliant virtue which you have sought with so much effort, do not prevent yourself from entering the heavenly doors, do not stand confused with redness before the chamber, nor allow a single hair to be attached to the ground. Moreover, give yourself free confidence and a loud voice, so that you may enter the chamber rejoicing, and repeat his praises with lofty voice.

Lesson IX—Commemoration of Sts. Mark & Marcellian, Martyrs

Mark and Marcellian were two brothers, Romans, who were arrested by the præfect Fabian for believing in Christ, and fastened to a beam, to which their feet were nailed. The Judge said to them: "Wretched creatures, do think for a moment, and free yourselves from such suffering." But they answered him: "We have never enjoyed any dinner so much as we do what we are now undergoing here for Jesus Christ's sake. We have got ourselves a little fast to His love now. Would that He would let us suffer this as long as we are clad in this corruptible body." Still suffering, they for a day and a night sang the praises of God continually, and in the end were thrust through with darts, and so attained the glory of Martyrdom. Their bodies are buried upon the Ardeatine way.

June 19 ~ St. Juliana Falconieri

Virgin ~ Duplex

All from Common
except what follows

Lessons I–III from the
occurring Scripture

Lesson IV

Juliana was a daughter of the noble family of the Falconieri, and was born in the year 1270. Her father was the same who at his own costs so splendidly built from the foundations the Church of Our Lady of the Annunciation as it now stands at Florence. Her mother's name was Reguardata. They were both well stricken in years, and, until the birth of Juliana, had been childless. From her very cradle she gave tokens of the holiness of life to which she afterwards attained. And from the murmuring of her baby lips was caught the sweet sound of the names of Jesus and Mary. As she entered on her girlhood, she delivered herself up entirely to the pursuit of Christian godliness, and so excellently shone therein, that her uncle, the Blessed Alexius, scrupled not to tell her mother that she had given birth to an Angel rather than to a woman. So modest was her comportment, and so clean her soul from the lightest speck of indiscretion, that she never in her whole life stared a man in the face, and that the very mention of sin made her shiver, and when the story of a grievous crime was told her, she dropped down nearly fainting. Before she had finished her fifteenth year, she renounced her inheritance, although a rich one, and all prospect of an earthly marriage, and made to God a vow of virginity, before Saint Philip Benizi, from whom she was the first to receive the religious habit of what are called the Mantellate sisters.

Lesson V

Juliana's example was followed by most of the women from the nobler families, and her very mother put herself for instruction under her own daughter. Thus in a little while their number increased, and she became the foundress of the Order of Mantellate nuns, to whom she gave a rule of life full of wisdom and godliness. Saint Philip Benizi, having thorough knowledge of her excellence, chose her above all living to whom at his death to leave the care not of the women only but of the whole of the Servite Order, of which he had been the propagator and director. Juliana, who deemed ever lowly of herself, even when she was the mistress of the others, ministered to her sisters in the lowest duties of the work of the house. She passed whole days in incessant prayer, and was often rapt in spirit, and the remainder of her time she toiled to make peace among the citizens, who were at variance together, to recall transgressors from the ways of iniquity, and to nurse the sick, whom to cure she would sometimes even use her tongue to remove the matter that ran from their sores. It was her custom to afflict her own body with whips, knotted cords, iron girdles, vigils, and sleeping upon the ground. Upon Mondays, Tuesdays, Wednesdays, and Thursdays, she ate very sparingly some unpalatable food, upon Fridays she took nothing except the Bread of Angels, and upon Saturdays, besides the Holy Communion, only bread and water.

Lesson VI

The self-inflicted hardships of her life brought upon her a disease of the stomach, whereby, when she was seventy years of age, she was brought to the point of death. She bore the daily sufferings of her illness with a smiling face and a brave heart. The only thing of which she was heard to complain was that, her stomach being so weak that she could not keep down any food, she was withheld by reverence for the Sacrament from drawing near to the Eucharistic Table. Finding herself in these straits she begged the Priest to bring the Bread of God, and, as she dared not take It into her mouth, to put It as near as possible to her heart. The Priest did as she wished, and, to the amazement of all present, the Divine Bread at once disappeared from sight, and at the same instant a smile of joyous peace crossed the face of Juliana, and she gave up the ghost. All were confounded until the virgin body was being laid out after death in the accustomed manner. Then there was found upon the left side of the bosom a mark like the stamp of a seal, reproducing the form of the Sacred Host, the mould of which was one of those that bear a figure of Christ crucified. The fame of this and other wonders got for Juliana a reverence not only from

Florence, but from all parts of the Christian world, which so increased through the course of four hundred years, that Pope Benedict XIII commanded an office in her honor to be said by the whole Order of Servants of the Blessed Virgin Mary, and Clement XII, a munificent Protector of the same Servite Order, finding new signs and wonders shining upon her memory every day, numbered her among Holy Virgins.

Lessons VII–IX from the first set in the Common of Virgins (Homily by St. Gregory)

Lesson IX—Commemoration of Sts. Gervase & Protase, Martyrs

Gervase and Protase were the sons of Vitalis and Valeria, both of whom testified even unto death for the Lord Christ's sake, the father at Ravenna, and the mother at Milan. After the victory of their parents, Gervase and Protase gave all the inheritance to the poor, and set free their slaves. This act of theirs stirred up against them a savage hatred on the part of the heathen priests, and when the præfect Astasius was about setting forth to war, they believed they had got a good occasion for the destruction of the two godly brethren. They persuaded Astasius that their gods had revealed to them that he had no chance of conquering in the war, unless he had first made Gervase and Protase to deny Christ and to offer sacrifice to the gods. Being commanded so to do, they flatly refused, and Astasius then ordered Gervase to be lashed until he died between the stripes, and Protase to be cudgeled and beheaded. A servant of Christ named Philip took away their dead bodies by stealth, and buried them in his own house, and, in after times, St. Ambrose, by God's warning, found them, and bestowed them in a hallowed and honorable place. They suffered at Milan upon the 19th day of June.

June 20 ~ St. Silverius

Pope & Martyr ~ Simplex

Lessons I–II from the occurring Scripture

Lesson III

Silverius was a native of Campania, and succeeded Agapitus in the Papacy in 536. His orthodoxy and holiness shone brightest in his onslaughts upon heretics, and he showed admirable firmness in upholding a sentence by Agapitus. Agapitus had deposed Anthimus from the Patriarchate of Constantinople for defending the Eutychian heresy; when repeatedly asked by the Empress Theodora to restore him, he refused. The woman was enraged at him on this account, and ordered Belisarius to send Silverius into exile. He was accordingly banished to the island of Ponza, whence he is said to have written these words to Bishop Amator: "I am fed upon the bread of tribulation and the water of affliction, but nevertheless I have not given up, and I will not give up, doing my duty." But sickness and the hardships of his exile soon broke his strength, and he fell asleep in the Lord upon the 20th day of June in the year of grace 538. Many miracles shed a lustre upon his grave. He ruled the Church for more than three years, and ordained in the month of December thirteen Priests, five Deacons, and nineteen Bishops for diverse Sees.

June 21 ~ St. Aloysius Gonzaga

Confessor ~ Duplex

All from Common except what follows

Lessons I–III from the occurring Scripture

Lesson IV

Aloysius, eldest son of Ferdinand Gonzaga, Marquess of Castiglione, was so hurriedly baptized on account of danger that he seemed to be born to heaven almost before he was born to earth, and he so faithfully kept that his first grace that he seemed to have been confirmed therein. From his first use of reason, which he employed to offer himself to God, he led a life more holy day by day. At Florence, when he was nine years old, he made a vow of perpetual virginity before the Altar of the Blessed Virgin, upon whom he always looked as in the place of a mother to him, and by a remarkable mercy from God, he kept this vow wholly and without the slightest impure temptation, either of mind or body, during his whole life. As for any other uprisings of the soul, he began at that age to check them so sternly, that he was never more pricked by even their earliest movements. His senses, and especially his eyesight, he so mortified, that he never once looked upon the face of Mary of Austria, whom, when he was for several years one of the Pages of honor of the King of Spain, he saluted almost every day and he even denied himself in part, the pleasure of looking on the face of his own mother. He might indeed have been justly called a man without flesh, or an angel in the flesh.

Lesson V

With this fettering of the senses he added torture of the body. He kept three days as fasts in every week, and that mostly upon a little bread and water. But indeed he as it were fasted every day, for he hardly ever took so much as an ounce weight of food at breakfast. Often also, even thrice in one day, he would bloody himself with cords, or with spiked chains. He sometimes used a dog-whip, instead of a scourge, and the rowels of spurs instead of haircloth. He privately filled his soft bed with pieces of broken plates, that he might find it easier to wake to pray. He passed great part of the night, clad only in a shirt even in the depth of winter, kneeling on the ground, or lying flat on his face when too weak and weary to remain upright, busied with heavenly thoughts. Sometimes he would keep himself thus for three, four, or five hours, until he had spent at least one without any movement of body or any wandering of mind. Such perseverance obtained for him the reward of being able to keep his understanding quite concentrated in prayer without distraction, as though rapt in God in an unbroken ecstasy. Desiring to give himself up to Him alone, he overcame, after a strong opposition for three years, the objections of his father, procured the transfer to his brother of his right to the Marquessate, and on the 25th of November, 1585, joined at Rome the Society of Jesus, to which he had been called by a voice from heaven when he was at Madrid.

Lesson VI

In his very Novitiate he began to be held a master of all virtues. His obedience to even the most trifling rules was absolutely exact, his contempt for the world extraordinary, and his hatred of self implacable. His love of God was so keen that it gradually undermined his bodily strength. Being commanded to give his mind some rest from thinking unceasingly of God, he struggled vainly to distract himself from Him Who met him everywhere. From tender love toward his neighbor, he joyfully ministered to the sick in the public hospitals, during the great plague at Rome in 1591, and in the exercise of this charity he caught a deadly disease. This sickness slowly wore him away, and soon after he had entered on the 24th year of his age, upon the 21st day of June, a day which he had himself foretold, after entreating that he might be scourged, and laid upon the ground to die, he passed away to heaven. What glory he enjoys therein Saint Mary Magdalene de' Pazzi was enabled, by the revelation of God, to behold, and she declared that it was such as she had hardly believed existed even in heaven, and that his holiness and love were so great that she should call him an unknown martyr of charity. On earth God glorified him by many great miracles. These being duly proved, Benedict XIII inserted the name of this angelic lad in the Kalendar of the Saints, and commended him to all young scholars both as a pattern of innocence and purity, and as a patron.

Lesson VII

From the Holy Gospel according to St. Matthew (Matt 22:29–40)

At that time Jesus answered and said unto the Sadducees: Ye do err, not knowing the Scriptures, nor the power of God; for in the resurrection they neither marry nor are given in marriage, but are as the angels of God in heaven. And so on.

Homily by St. John Chrysostom

This I say, that virginity is good. And in this I agree likewise, that it is better than marriage. And I will even add, that it is as much more excellent than marriage, as heaven is more noble than earth, or Angels than men, and indeed, if I must say more, even more so. For if Angels neither marry nor are given in marriage, at least, they are not creatures of flesh and blood, they dwell not upon earth, they are exposed to no restless troublings of desire or lust, they need neither meat nor drink, they are not such that sweet sound, or soft song, or the delight of beauty can charm them; there is nothing of this sort to take hold on them and draw them away.

Lesson VIII

Yet the human nature which strives its utmost to follow them, is not so exalted as that of these blessed intelligences. How Angels marry not nor are given in marriage neither does a virgin. Angels stand ever before God, and serve Him and so does a virgin. But if a virgin, still weighed down with this body, and unable, like the Angels, to ascend to heaven, it does make it his one great comfort here to be holy in body and in spirit, and to open his heart for a home for the King of heaven; dost thou not see wherein a virgin is higher than an Angel? The excellence of virginity in men over virginity in Angels lies in this, that it makes them which are yet earth-dwellers and body-burdened equal to intelligences unshackled by bodies.

Lesson IX

In what respect, I ask, differed Elias, Eliseus, and John, those great lovers of virginity, from Angels? In nothing, except that their faithfulness was exercised in a dying body. For the rest, if we look carefully, their minds were no otherwise than those of the blessed spirits, and their crown of glory is this: that they attained the same honor under conditions less favorable. For consider of what manliness, of what superiority of reason over feeling they must have been possessed, to enable them bravely to fight their way, earth-dwellers and dying creatures as they were, to the bright summit of grace which was theirs.

June 22 ~ St. Paulinus

Confessor Bishop ~ Duplex

All from Common except what follows

Lessons I–III from the occurring Scripture

Lesson IV

Pontius Meropius Anicius Paulinus was born of a most illustrious family of Roman citizens at Bordeaux, in Aquitaine, in the year of the reparation of salvation 353, and was of keen intelligence and graceful manners. With Ausonius as his master, he was honorably distinguished for eloquence and poetry. Being of the higher nobility, and very wealthy, he entered the *cursus honorum* in the flower of his youth, and attained senatorial dignity. Then he went to Italy as consul, where he obtained the province of Campania and fixed his residence at Nola. Here he was struck, as by a ray of the divine light, by the heavenly miracles which were making illustrious the tomb of Felix, Priest and Martyr, and began to adhere more earnestly to the true faith of Christ, which he had long been revolving in his mind. And so he resigned the consular fasces and axe, never defiled by blood, and returned to Gaul, and after suffering various hardships and many toils both by land and by sea he received an injury to the eye; but being restored to health by the blessed Martin, Bishop of Tours, he was washed in the lustral waters of baptism by the blessed Delphinus, Bishop of Bordeaux.

Lesson V

He despised his abundant wealth, sold his property, and gave the money to the poor, and left his wife Therasia, changed his country, broke all natural ties, and retired to Spain, conforming to the more precious poverty of Christ, which he valued more than the whole world. While he was devoutly assisting at Mass in Barcelona on the feast of the Lord's Nativity, he was suddenly seized by force by an admiring crowd, and in spite of his reluctance, ordained priest by the Bishop Lampidius. Then he returned to Italy, and at Nola, where he had been drawn by devotion to St. Felix, he built a monastery near his tomb, and entered upon the monastic life with some companions. This man, already notable for his senatorial and consular dignity, embraced the folly of the cross to the admiration of almost the whole world, and, clothed in a mean garment, in vigils and in fasts, remained for days and nights fixed in constant contemplation of heavenly things. But, as the fame of his sanctity spread, he was elevated to the see of Nola, and entering upon that pastoral office, he gave a wonderful example of piety, wisdom, and above all, of charity.

Lesson VI

Meanwhile he had produced writings full of wisdom, treating of religion and faith, and often also as a recreation, he had celebrated the deeds of the Saints in numerous elegant poems, attaining the highest fame as a Christian poet. All the men living at that time who were preeminent for holiness and learning, he attached to himself with the bonds of friendship and admiration. Very many flocked to him from all parts of the country, as if to a master of Christian perfection. When Campania was laid waste by the Goths, he devoted all his resources to feeding the poor, and ransoming captives, without even leaving for himself the necessities of life. And after that, when the Vandals invaded the same region, a widow begged him to ransom her son who had been captured by the enemy; and as he had spent all his resources in works of piety, he sold himself into slavery in the young man's place, and was taken in chains to Africa. At length he was set at liberty, not without the evident assistance of God, and, returning to Nola, the good shepherd once more saw his beloved flock. There, in a most peaceful end, he fell asleep in the Lord in the seventy-eighth year of his age. His body was buried near the tomb of St. Felix, and later, in the time of the Lombards, was translated to Benevento and, under the Emperor Otto III, to Rome, where it was laid in the basilica of St. Bartholomew on the island in the Tiber. But Pope Pius X ordered the sacred relics of Paulinus to be restored to Nola, and he raised his feast to the rite of a Duplex for the universal Church.

Lesson VII

From the Holy Gospel according to St. Luke (Luke 12:32–34)

At that time: Jesus said unto his disciples: Fear not, little flock; for it is your Father's good pleasure to give you the kingdom. And so on.

Homily by St. Paulinus, Bishop

The Lord who is omnipotent, dearly beloved, might have made all men equally rich, so that no one need ask anything from another. In his infinite goodness, however, the merciful and gracious Lord has planned otherwise, in order to prove your disposition in these matters. He has made misery, that he might discern mercy; he has made the needy, that he might make use of the rich. For your brother's poverty is your material of riches, if you do not understand concerning the needy and the poor, and do not consider as your own what wealth you have received. For God has bestowed upon you your brother's portion in this world, in order that you should offer of your own willing affection something of his gifts to those in need, and that he may enrich you in your turn with that portion in eternity. For now Christ receives through them, and hereafter he will repay for them.

Lesson VIII

Refresh the hungry soul, and you will not fear the wrath to come in the evil day. "For," says he, "Blessed is he that understands concerning the needy and poor; the Lord will deliver him in the evil day." Therefore, brother, work and cultivate this parcel of thy land, that it may bear for you a rich crop, full of the fatness of wheat, bringing to you with great interest the fruit of the seed a hundred times multiplied. In the desire and pursuit of this business or this possession there is a holy and salutary avarice; for such desire which does merit the kingdom of heaven, and does long for eternal goods, is the root of all good. Therefore covet such riches, and take possession of this kind of patrimony, that the creditor may weigh out to you the fruit increased a hundredfold, and you and your heirs may abound in everlasting good things. For this possession is great and precious, which does not burden the owner with earthly wealth, but enriches him with an eternal reward.

Lesson IX

Truly, dearly beloved, by present carefulness and constant just dealing, provide not only that you may seek eternal good things, but that you may deserve to escape innumerable evils. For we require strong helps and protection, and stand in need of many and unceasing prayers for our defense. For our adversary does not rest, and the ever-watchful enemy besets all our ways in order to work our ruin. Moreover, in this world we have many crosses, very numerous struggles, pestilent diseases, fires of fever and stabs of pain do violence to our souls. The flames of lust are kindled; hidden snares are set everywhere, on all sides there bristle drawn swords, life is passed in the midst of ambushes and combats, and we walk through fires craftily buried under ashes. Therefore before you should by your misfortune or your fault rush into any one of such great calamities, hasten to become acceptable and dear to the physician, so that in time of need you may have ready the remedy of salvation. It is one thing when you alone pray for yourself; and quite another when a multitude entreats for you before God.

June 23 ~ Vigil of St. John the Baptist

Vigil

Lesson I

From the Holy Gospel according to St. Luke (Luke 1:5–17)

There was, in the days of Herod the King of Judaea, a certain Priest named Zachary, of the course of Abia; and his wife was of the daughters of Aaron, and her name was Elizabeth. And so on.

Homily by St. Ambrose, Bishop

The Divine Scriptures teach us that we are to praise the lives, not only of those concerning whom we are to speak honorably, but the lives also of their fathers, so as to show that that which we will praise in our subjects was in them a gift inherited from the bright purity of the source from which they came. What other meaning can the holy Evangelist have had in this place but to glorify St. John the Baptist, as well for having been the offspring of such parents, as for his miracles, his life, his gifts, and his sufferings? So likewise is praise ascribed to Anna, the mother of Samuel so also did Isaac draw from his parents that noble godliness which he in his turn bequeathed to his children. Thus it is told not only that Zachary was a Priest, but a Priest of the course of Abia, that is to say, of a family noble among the noblest.

Lesson II

And his wife was of the daughters of Aaron. Thus we see that the noble blood of St. John was inherited not only from parents, but from an ancient ancestry, not illustrious indeed by worldly power, but worshipful for the tradition of a sacred succession. Such were the forefathers whom it well became the forerunner of the Christ to have, that it might manifestly fall to his lot, not as a sudden gift, but as an heirloom, to preach belief in the coming of the Lord. And they were both righteous before God, walking in all the commandments and ordinances of the Lord, blameless. What do they make of this text who, to take them some consolation for their own sins, hold that man cannot exist without oftentimes sinning, and quote to that end that which is written in Job: "Not one is clean, even though his life on the earth be but one day"?

Lesson III

To such we must reply by asking them first to tell us what they mean by a man without sin, whether it be one who has never sinned, or one who has ceased to sin. If they mean by a man without sin one who has never sinned, I myself agree in their position, "for all have sinned and come short of the glory of God." But if they mean to deny that he who has reformed his old crooked ways, and changed his life for a new one, on purpose to avoid sin, cannot avoid sin, I am not able to subscribe to their opinion while I read that "Christ loved the Church and gave Himself for it, that He might sanctify and cleanse it with the washing of water by the word, that He might present it to Himself a glorious Church, not having spot, or wrinkle, or any such thing but that it should be holy and without blemish."

June 24 ~ THE NATIVITY OF ST JOHN THE BAPTIST

Duplex I Class

Lesson I ~ Jer 1:1–5

Beginning of the book of the Prophet Jeremias

The words of Jeremias the son of Helcias, of the priests that were in Anathoth, in the land of Benjamin. The word of the Lord which came to him in the days of Josias the son of Amon king of Juda, in the thirteenth year of his reign. And which came to him in the days of Joakim the son of Josias king of Juda, unto the end of the eleventh year of Sedecias the son of Josias king of Juda, even unto the carrying away of Jerusalem captive, in the fifth month. And the word of the Lord came to me, saying: Before I formed thee in the bowels of thy mother, I knew thee: and before thou camest forth out of the womb, I sanctified thee, and made thee a prophet unto the nations.

Lesson II ~ Jer 1:6–10

And I said: Ah, ah, ah, Lord God: behold, I cannot speak, for I am a child. And the Lord said to me: Say not: I am a child: for thou shalt go to all that I shall send thee: and whatsoever I shall command thee, thou shalt speak. Be not afraid at their presence: for I am with thee to deliver thee, saith the Lord. And the Lord put forth his hand, and touched my mouth: and the Lord said to me: Behold I have given my words in thy mouth: Lo, I have set thee this day over the nations, and over the kingdoms, to root up, and pull down, and to waste, and to destroy, and to build, and to plant.

Lesson III ~ Jer 1:17–19

Thou therefore gird up thy loins, and arise, and speak to them all that I command thee. Be not afraid at their presence: for I will make thee not to fear their countenance. For behold I have made thee this day a fortified city, and a pillar of iron, and a wall of brass, over all the land, to the kings of Juda, to the princes thereof, and to the priests, and to the people of the land. And they shall fight against thee, and shall not prevail: for I am with thee, saith the Lord, to deliver thee.

Lesson IV

Sermon by St. Augustine, Bishop

Outside the most holy Birthday of the Lord, we find celebrated in the Gospel the birth of only one other, namely, that of the blessed Baptist, John. As regards all others among God's holy and chosen ones we know that the day is observed whereon, with their work finished, and the world conquered and finally trampled down, they were born from this into a better life, even one of everlasting blessedness. In others is honored the crowning of the struggle on their last day of dying life, but in John is honored the first day; in him the very beginning is found hallowed. And the reason of this is, without doubt, because he was sent from God to bear witness to the coming of the Light, lest when It came It might take the darkness by surprise, and the darkness might not comprehend It. Now, John was a figure of the Old Testament, and showed in his own person a typical embodiment of the Law; and therefore John heralded beforehand the coming of the Saviour, even as the Law was our schoolmaster to bring us to the grace of Christ.

Lesson V

That he prophesied while yet in the hidden depths of his mother's womb, and while himself lightless bore testimony to the truth: this is to be understood as a figure of how while concealed by a veil and carnal ordinances of the letter, he by the spirit preached unto the world a Redeemer, and testified from the womb that ours is Lord of the law. The Jews were estranged from the womb, that is from the Law, that womb heavy with the Christ; they went astray from the belly, speaking lies; and therefore John came for a witness, to bear witness of the Light, that all men through him might believe.

Lesson VI

For because John had heard in prison the works of Christ, he sent two of his disciples; the Law sends to the Gospel. For John here was a figure of the Law, imprisoned in ignorance, lying in the dark, and in a hidden place, and he was fettered through Jewish blindness within the bonds of the letter. But of him was it said, as is written in the Blessed Evangelist "He was a burning and a shining light" that is to say, that, when the whole world was wrapt in the night of ignorance, this Saint was kindled by the fire of the Holy Ghost, to show before men the light of salvation, and at the hour of the thickest darkness of sin, appeared like a bright morning star to herald the rising of that Sun so most gloriously radiant, the Son of righteousness, Christ our Lord. And this is why John said of himself: "I am the voice of one crying in the wilderness."

Lesson VII

From the Holy Gospel according to St. Luke (Luke 1:57–69)

Elisabeth's fullness of time came that she should deliver, and she brought forth a son. And her neighbors and her cousins heard how the Lord had showed great mercy upon her, and they rejoiced with her. And so on.

Homily by St. Ambrose, Bishop

"Elizabeth's full time came that she should be delivered, and she brought forth a son. And her neighbors rejoiced with her." The birth of a Saint is a joy for many, for it is a good to all. Righteousness is a help to all, and therefore when a righteous man is born it is a heralding of his life, which is still to come, that the helpful excellence of his future should be hailed by the, as it were, prophetic joy of the neighbors. It is well that we should be told concerning the prophet while he was yet in the womb, that we may know how Mary was there; but we hear nothing of his childhood, because, we know that it was safe and strong through the nearness of the Lord, Himself then in that womb which was free from the sorrows of pregnancy. And therefore we read in the Gospel nothing about him save his coming, the annunciation thereof to his father, the leap which he gave in the womb, and his crying in the wilderness.

Lesson VIII

It was not for him to feel childishness, who beyond all use of nature or of his age, when as yet he lay in his mother's womb, leapt at once unto the measure of the stature of the fullness of Christ. It is strange how the Holy Evangelist has judged it right to tell us that they thought to call the child Zachary, after the name of his father, that thou mayest notice that the mother would have none of the names whereby their kindred were called, but only that name which the Holy Ghost had dictated, and which the Angel had told before unto Zachary. The dumb man had certainly not been able to tell his wife by what name to call the child, and Elizabeth must needs have learnt by revelation what she could not have heard from her husband.

Lesson IX

"His name is John;" that is, it is not for us to choose a name now for him to whom God has given a name already. He has a name, which we know, but it is not one of our choosing. To receive a name from God is one of the honors of the Saints. Thus was it that Jacob's name was no more called Jacob but Israel, because he saw God face to face. Thus was it that our Lord Jesus was named before He was born, with a name not given by an Angel, but by the Father. Thou seest that Angels tell that which they have been bidden to tell, not matters of their own choosing. Nor oughtest thou to wonder that Elizabeth named a name which she had not heard, since it had been revealed to her by the same Holy Ghost Who had commanded the Angel to tell it.

June 25 ~ St. William

Abbot ~ Duplex

All from Common
except what follows

Lessons I–III from the
occurring Scripture

Lesson IV

William was born of noble parents at Vercelli in Lombardy. He was but little over fourteen years of age, when, impelled by a strange earnestness for holiness, he undertook a pilgrimage to Compostela, to the far-famed Church of St. James. This journey he made clad in a single garment, wearing an iron girdle wound twofold round his body, and with bare feet. He accomplished his object under the severest hardships of cold and heat, hunger and thirst, and at great danger of his life. After his return to Italy, he undertook a new pilgrimage, this time to the Holy Sepulchre of the Lord. But in the way of fulfilling this, there arose diverse and most grievous obstacles, whereby the hand of God drew the lad to the higher and holier life of a monk. He dwelt in the town of Monte Solicolo for two years, which he passed in constant prayer, watching, sleeping upon the ground, and fasting. At the end of this time, the power of God made him the means to restore a blind man to sight. The fame of this miracle became so noised abroad, that William could no longer remain unknown. His thoughts turned again towards Jerusalem, and he again entered cheerfully on the journey.

Lesson V

He was again hindered by a vision from God, and remained among the Italians to be more useful, and to bring forth more fruit than he would have done among strangers. With extraordinary speed, he built a monastery upon the summit of Monte Vergiliano, ever since named Monte Vergine, between Nola and Benevento. There he called around him, as his comrades, devout men, and schooled them into a way of life most closely following the commands and counsels of the Gospel, in great part by a rule taken from the constitutions of Blessed Benedict, and supplemented by his own words, and the example of his own holy life.

Lesson VI

As other monasteries were raised, the holy life of William became more known day by day, and brought men to him from all quarters, drawn by the sweet savor of his sanctity and the fame of his miracles. At his prayers the dumb spoke, the deaf heard, the withered were strengthened, and they that suffered under diverse and incurable diseases received health. He turned water into wine, and openly worked many other miracles. Among all these things it must be told that a wretched woman sought him to lure him to impurity, but he raked hot embers out upon the floor and cast himself down upon them, and wallowed among them, and escaped unhurt. When this thing came to the knowledge of Roger II, King of Naples, it roused in him the highest reverence for the man of God. At the last, after foretelling his own death to the King and to others, and full of good works and miracles, he fell asleep in the Lord, in the year of salvation 1142.

Lessons VII–IX from the first set in the Common of Abbots (Homily by St. Bede)

June 26 ~ Sts. John & Paul

Martyrs ~ Duplex
All from Common
except what follows

Lessons I–III from the occurring Scripture

Lesson IV

John and Paul were two Roman brethren, the godly and trustworthy servants of Constantia, daughter of Constantine. At her death they spent in feeding Christ's poor the property which she left them. Julian the Apostate asked them to enter his household, but they bravely answered that they would not be servants to one who had run away from the service of Jesus Christ. Julian gave them ten days to consider on their choice, whether, at the end of that time, they would cleave to him, and sacrifice to Jupiter, or most surely die.

Lesson V

This interval they spent in distributing to poor creatures all that remained of their goods, that they might be quite free to depart hence to the Lord, and so aided many by whom they have long since been received into everlasting habitations. On the tenth day, Terentian, Præfect of the Prætorian Cohort, was sent to them, bringing with him the image of Jupiter. He explained to them the command of the Emperor, that they should worship the image or die. They were engaged in prayer, but answered him that for their loyalty to Christ, Whom their understanding acknowledged and their mouths confessed to be God, they felt no hesitation in choosing to suffer death.

Lesson VI

Terentian, to avoid the uproar which might have been caused by their public execution, caused their heads to be cut off at home where they then were. They lifted up their last earthly testimony upon the 26th day of June, in the year of our Lord 362. They were privately buried, and a story set about that they had been sent into exile. The fact of their death was made generally known by the unclean spirits by whom the bodies of many were tormented, and among others that of Terentian's own son, who was possessed with a devil, and delivered by being brought to the grave of the Martyrs. By this miracle he was led to believe in Christ, and so likewise was his father Terentian, who is said to have been the very writer of the life of these blessed Martyrs.

Lessons VII–IX from the third set in the Common of Many Martyrs (Homily by St. Bede)

June 27 – Day 4 within the Octave of St. John the Baptist

Semiduplex

All from Common except what follows

Lessons I–III from the occurring Scripture

Lesson IV

Sermon by St. Basil the Great

"The voice of the Lord is upon the waters." What voice is this? What are these waters? Let us take that which is here said as a prophecy. Thou rememberest how that "this is the record of John, when the Jews ask him, 'Who art thou' And he confessed and denied not, but confessed, 'I am not the Christ.' And they asked him, 'What then? Art thou Elias?' And he says, 'I am not.' 'Art thou the Prophet?' And he answered, 'No.' Then said they unto him, 'Who art thou that we may give an answer to them that sent us.' He said, 'I am the voice of one crying in the wilderness.'" Therefore, John is the voice of the Lord. This is he, of whom it is written, "Behold, I send My messenger before thy face to make ready a people prepared for the Lord." This voice upon the waters was heard upon those of Jordan, wherein he baptized, preaching the baptism of repentance for the remission of sins. Nor was this voice heard upon the waters of Jordan only, but also, in Enon near to Salim, because there was much water there.

Lesson V

The voice of the Lord upon the waters, then, is John upon baptism. Then also the God of glory thunders. "For there came a voice from heaven, saying, 'This is My Beloved Son, in Whom I am well pleased.'" Then also was it true that "The Lord is upon many waters" when He was pleased to come from Galilee to Jordan unto John, to be baptized of him, to fullfil all righteousness which is of the law. The voice of the Lord is powerful, powerful to heal the weaknesses of the people through the baptism of repentance, baptizing through John with water unto repentance. The voice of the Lord is powerful, which says "Do penance, for the kingdom of heaven is at hand," and "Bring forth fruit worthy of repentance."

Lesson VI

"The voice of the Lord breaks the cedars." This may well be said of him who, being sent as a messenger before the face of the Lord, to make ready for Him a prepared people, made the crooked places straight, by breaking down and treading flat the haughty growths of ungodliness that had lifted themselves up to block out the acknowledgment of God. He by whom every valley was exalted, and every mountain and hill was made low, the same was he who broke the cedars, and made straight in the desert a highway for our God, by laying low in repentance the hearts that were haughty, and proud, and lifted up. The Lord availing Himself of that preparation, smote down at His coming every power that withstood Him, which are spoken of under a similitude as the cedars of Lebanon. For the Lord must reign till He has put all enemies under His feet and trodden down these cedars.

Lesson VII

From the Holy Gospel according to St. Luke (Luke 1:57–69)

Elisabeth's fullness of time came that she should deliver, and she brought forth a son. And her neighbors and her cousins heard how the Lord had showed great mercy upon her, and they rejoiced with her. And so on.

Homily by St. Ambrose, Bishop

"And his father Zachary was filled with the Holy Ghost, and prophesied." Behold how good is God, and how ready to forgive sinners! Not only does He give back that which He has taken away, but He adds moreover such and such things, more than either we ask or think. He that had hitherto been dumb, now speaks prophecy. But the greatest grace of God is in this, that he which had denied, now makes profession. Therefore let no man despair, nay, though he knows well what his past

holy Martyrs who, when Marcus Aurelius was emperor, were engaged in a vigorous combat for the true religion) he distinguished himself as an emulator of the testament of Christ.

Lesson V

These very Martyrs, together with the clergy of Lyons, began to be anxious concerning the peace of the churches of Asia, which the faction of the Montanists had disturbed. And so they selected Irenæus, whose person they considered of the greatest importance, as the one before all others whom they should send to Rome to Pope Eleutherius to ask, that, with the condemnation of the new dissidents by the authority of the Apostolic See, the cause of the dissensions might be removed. Already the bishop Pothinus had died a martyr and Irenæus succeeded him. He applied himself so well to the duties of a bishop, that in a short time he saw not only all the citizens of Lyons, but also many of the inhabitants of other cities in Gaul cast aside their superstitions and errors, and enroll themselves in the Christian army. Meanwhile, a dispute had arisen concerning the date of the celebration of Easter. As the bishops of Asia were disagreeing with nearly all their fellow-bishops, the Roman Pontiff Victor had cut them off from the communion of the faithful. Irenæus, however, who was zealous for peace, admonished him in a becoming manner, and urged, by examples of the practice of previous Pontiffs, that he should not suffer so many Churches to be cut off from Catholic unity, on account of a rite which they said they had received from their ancestors.

Lesson VI

He wrote many works, which are mentioned by Eusebius of Caesarea and by St. Jerome, a great part of which have perished through the ravages of time. There are extant five books of his *Adversus Hæreses* [Against the Heresies], written down about the year 180, while Eleutherius was still ruling the Christian commonwealth. In the third book, the man of God, instructed by those who, it is certain, had been hearers of the Apostles, gives to the Roman Church and to the succession of her bishops a testimony surpassing all others in weight and brilliance, when he calls her the faithful, perpetual, and most assured guardian of divine tradition. For he said, that with this Church it is necessary that the whole Church (that is, those in all places who are of the faithful) should agree, because of its more powerful preeminence. At length with almost countless others, whom he had himself brought over to the true faith and its practice, being crowned with martyrdom he passed to heaven in the year of salvation 202. At that time Septimius Severus Augustus had commanded that all those who wished to remain constantly steadfast in the practice of the Christian religion should be condemned to the most cruel torments and to death. The supreme Pontiff Benedict XV extended the feast of St. Irenæus to the universal Church.

Lesson VII

From the Holy Gospel according to St. Matthew (Matt 10:28–33)

At that time: Jesus said unto his disciples: Fear not them which kill the body, but are not able to kill the soul: but rather fear him which is able to destroy both soul and body in hell. And so forth.

Homily by St. Irenæus, Bishop and Martyr

The Lord knew both those who would suffer persecution; and he knew those who would be scourged and slain for his sake. His words are indeed those of exhortation: "Fear not them which kill the body, but are not able to kill the soul." Rather fear him which has power to cast both body and soul into hell, and to preserve whomsoever should confess him. For indeed he has promised to confess before his Father those who should confess his name before men; and to deny those who should deny him, and to be ashamed of those who should be ashamed to confess him. Yet for all this, some have gone so far in audacity, as to scorn even the Martyrs, and to revile those who have been put to death for confessing the Lord, and who endure all that the Lord foretold, and so far endeavor to follow in the footsteps of the Lord's Passion, being made Martyrs of one who was capable of suffering; but these we leave to the Martyrs themselves. For when their blood shall be required, and they shall obtain glory, then all those who have dishonored their martyrdom will be put to confusion by Christ.

Lesson VIII

This also meets the objection of those who say that Christ only appeared to be suffering. For if he did not really suffer, no gratitude is due unto him, when there was no suffering; and when we begin really to suffer, he would seem to be deceiving us, when exhorting us to receive blows and to turn the other cheek, if he himself had not first suffered in reality. And as he deceived them, so as to appear to them what he was not; so also he misleads us, exhorting us to endure things which he himself did not endure. And so we should even be higher than the Master, when we suffer and endure things, which the Master neither suffered nor endured. But, whereas our Lord alone is truly the master, he is also truly the Son of God, good and kind, the Word of God the Father made Son of Man. For he strove, and he conquered; for he was a man contending for his fathers and paying the debt of disobedience by his obedience. For he has bound the strong man, and, he unbinds the weak, and he has given salvation to his creature by destroying sin. Therefore, those who say he is manifested only in appearance, and not born in the flesh, nor really made man, are still under the old condemnation.

Lesson IX—For the Vigil of Sts. Peter & Paul, Apostles

From the Holy Gospel according to St. John (John 21:15–17)

At that time: Jesus said to Simon Peter, Simon, son of Jonas, lovest thou me more than these? And so on.

Homily by St. Augustine, Bishop

To the threefold denial there is now appended a threefold confession, that his tongue may not yield a feebler service to love than to fear, and imminent death may not appear to have elicited more from his lips than present life. Let it be the office of love to feed the Lord's flock, if it was the signal of fear to deny the Shepherd. Those who have this purpose in feeding the flock of Christ, that they may have them as their own, and not as Christ's, are convicted of loving themselves, and not Christ, from the desire either of boasting, or wielding power, or acquiring gain, and not from the love of obeying, serving and pleasing God.

June 29 ~ STS. PETER & PAUL

Apostles ~ Duplex I Class

All from Common
except what follows

Lesson I ~ Acts 3:1–5

From the Acts of the Apostles

Now Peter and John went up into the temple at the ninth hour of prayer. And a certain man who was lame from his mother's womb, was carried: whom they laid every day at the gate of the temple, which is called Beautiful, that he might ask alms of them that went into the temple. He, when he had seen Peter and John about to go into the temple, asked to receive an alms. But Peter with John fastening his eyes upon him, said: Look upon us. But he looked earnestly upon them, hoping that he should receive something of them.

Lesson II ~ Acts 3:6–10

But Peter said: Silver and gold I have none; but what I have, I give thee: In the name of Jesus Christ of Nazareth, arise, and walk. And taking him by the right hand, he lifted him up, and forthwith his feet and soles received strength. And he leaping up, stood, and walked, and went in with them into the temple, walking, and leaping, and praising God. And all the people saw him walking and praising God. And they knew him, that it was he who sat begging alms at the Beautiful gate of the temple: and they were filled with wonder and amazement at that which had happened to him.

Lesson III ~ Acts 3:11–16

And as he held Peter and John, all the people ran to them to the porch which is called Solomon's, greatly wondering. But Peter seeing, made answer to the people: Ye men of Israel, why wonder you at this? or why look you upon us, as if by our strength or power we had made this man to walk? The God of Abraham, and the God of Isaac, and the God of Jacob, the God of our fathers, hath glorified his Son Jesus, whom you indeed delivered up and denied before the face of Pilate, when he judged he should be released. But you denied the Holy One and the Just, and desired a murderer to be granted unto you. But the author of life you killed, whom God hath raised from the dead, of which we are witnesses. And in the faith of his name, this man, whom you have seen and known, hath his name strengthened; and the faith which is by him, hath given this perfect soundness in the sight of you all.

Lesson IV

Sermon by St. Leo, Pope

Dearly beloved brethren, in the joy of all the holy solemnities the whole world is partaker. There is but one love of God, and whatsoever is solemnly called to memory, if it has been done for the salvation of all, must be worth the honor of a joyful memorial at the hands of all. Nevertheless, this feast which we are keeping today, besides that reverence which it merits throughout all the earth, deserves from this city of ours an outburst of gladness altogether special and our own. In this place it was that the two chiefest of the Apostles did so gloriously finish their race. And upon this day whereon they lifted up their last testimony, let it be in this place that the memory thereof receives the chiefest of jubilant celebrations. O Rome, these are the men who brought the light of the Gospel of Christ to shine upon thee! These are they by whom thou, from being the teacher of lies, wast turned into a learner of the truth.

Lesson V

These be thy fathers and truly thy shepherds, who laid for thee, regarding the kingdom of heaven, better and happier foundations, than did they that first planned thine earthly ramparts, wherefrom he that gave thee thy name took occasion to pollute thee with a brother's blood. These are they who have set on thine head this thy glorious crown, that thou art become a holy nation, a chosen people, a city both Priestly and Kingly, whom the Sacred Throne of blessed Peter has exalted till thou art become the Lady of the world, unto whom the world-wide love for God has conceded a broader lordship than is the possession of any mere earthly empire. For although, increased by many victories, thou hast advanced the right of thine empire over land and sea; that which the labor of war has subjected to thee, however, is less than that which Christian peace has subjugated.

Lesson VI

It well suited for the doing of the work which God had decreed that the multitude of kingdoms should be bound together under one rule, and that so the universal preaching of the Gospel should find easier entry into all peoples, since all were governed by the empire of one city. But this city, knowing not Him Who had been pleased to make her great, used her lordship over almost all nations to make herself the minister of all their falsehoods and seemed to herself exceedingly godly because there was no false god whom she rejected. But the tighter that Satan had bound her, the more wondrous was the work of Christ in setting her free.

Lesson VII

From the Holy Gospel according to St. Matthew (Matt 16:13–19)

At that time: Jesus came into the quarters of Caesarea Philippi, and He asked His disciples, saying: Whom do men say that the Son of man is? And so on.

Homily by St. Jerome, Priest

"Whom do men say that the Son of man is?" This question is well put, for they who speak of Him as the Son of man are men, while they that know of Him that He is God are called not men but gods. And they said: "Some John the Baptist, and other some Elias." I marvel that some commentators have thought it worth their while to search into the origin of each of these blunders, and to engage in a discussion of weary length as to why some thought that our Lord Jesus Christ was John the Baptist, some, Elias and others, Jeremias, or one of the Prophets. Their blunders concerning Elias and Jeremias were but of a piece with Herod's concerning John the Baptist; "It is John, whom I beheaded: he is risen from the dead and therefore mighty works do show forth themselves in him."

Lesson VIII

"But whom do you say that I am?" Mark, discreet reader, from the context, that a distinction is here drawn between the Apostles and mere men. The Apostles are called gods. "Who," asks the Lord, "do men say that I am," but, on the other hand, "whom do you say that I am?" They, being but men, deal in human speculations, but you that are gods, who are you persuaded that I am? And then Peter, as the representative of all the Apostles, uttered the testimony: "Thou art the Christ, the Son of the living God." He calls God living, to mark the difference between Him and all other that be called gods, and who are indeed dead.

Lesson IX

And Jesus answered and said unto him: "Blessed art thou, Simon Bar-Jona." The Apostle having testified of the Lord, the Lord in turn testifies of the Apostle. Peter had said: "Thou art the Christ, the Son of the living God," and he received, in return for that his testimony to the truth, the words: "Blessed art thou, Simon Bar-Jona." Why, blessed? "For flesh and blood have not revealed it unto thee, but My Father." What flesh and blood could not reveal, the grace of the Holy Ghost had revealed. Right for him therefore, because of his confession, is his name, as the name of one who has revelation from the Holy Ghost, and therefore is called His son. Bar-Jona is, being interpreted, The-son-of-the-Dove.

June 29 ~ The Commemoration of St. Paul the Apostle

Major Duplex

All from Common
except what follows

Lesson I ~ Acts 13:1–4

From the Acts of the Apostles

Now there were in the church which was at Antioch, prophets and doctors, among whom was Barnabas, and Simon who was called Niger, and Lucius of Cyrene, and Manahen, who was the foster brother of Herod the tetrarch, and Saul. And as they were ministering to the Lord, and fasting, the Holy Ghost said to them: Separate me Saul and Barnabas, for the work whereunto I have taken them. Then they, fasting and praying, and imposing their hands upon them, sent them away. So they being sent by the Holy Ghost, went to Seleucia: and from thence they sailed to Cyprus.

Lesson II ~ Acts 13:5–8

And when they were come to Salamina, they preached the word of God in the synagogues of the Jews. And they had John also in the ministry. And when they had gone through the whole island, as far as Paphos, they found a certain man, a magician, a false prophet, a Jew, whose name was Bar-jesu: Who was with the proconsul Sergius Paulus, a prudent man. He sending for Barnabas and Saul, desired to hear the word of God. But Elymas the magician (for so his name is interpreted) withstood them, seeking to turn away the proconsul from the faith.

Lesson III ~ Acts 13:9–13

Then Saul, otherwise Paul, filled with the Holy Ghost, looking upon him, Said: O full of all guile, and of all deceit, child of the devil, enemy of all justice, thou ceasest not to pervert the right ways of the Lord. And now behold, the hand of the Lord is upon thee, and thou shalt be blind, not seeing the sun for a time. And immediately there fell a mist and darkness upon him, and going about, he sought some one to lead him by the hand. Then the proconsul, when he had seen what was done, believed, admiring at the doctrine of the Lord. Now when Paul and they that were with him had sailed from Paphos, they came to Perge in Pamphylia. And John departing from them, returned to Jerusalem.

Lesson IV

From the Book of St. Augustine, Bishop, on Grace and Free will.

The Apostle Paul was a man, who, when we first hear of him, had not only no merits, but a great many demerits. That man received the grace of God, Who returns good for evil, and let us see in what sort of language, when the hour of his last sufferings was at hand, he wrote to Timothy. He says: "I am now ready to be offered, and the time of my departure is at hand. I have fought a good fight, I have finished my course, I have kept the faith." Here he counts his merits, whereon a crown was immediately to follow, just as grace had followed immediately on his demerits. Listen to what comes next: "Henceforth there is laid up for me a crown of righteousness, which the Lord, the righteous Judge, shall give me at that day." Unto whom would the Lord give a crown as a righteous Judge, if He had not first given grace, as a merciful Father? And how would that crown be a crown of righteousness, if there had not first come grace which justifies the ungodly? How could a reward have been earned unless the power to earn had first been given unearned?

Lesson V

Let us now consider what were the merits of the Apostle Paul, which entitled him to look for a crown of righteousness from the Lord, the righteous Judge, and let us see whether these merits sprang from himself or were God's gifts to him. He says "I have fought a good fight, I have finished my course, I have kept the faith." To begin with, these good works would have been worth nothing, unless they had come from good thoughts. Listen therefore to what this same Paul says concerning good thoughts. He writes to the Corinthians: "Not that we are sufficient of ourselves to think anything, as of ourselves but our sufficiency is of God." Now let us take point by point.

Lesson VI

He says: "I have fought a good fight." I should like to know in whose strength he fought; in his own strength or in strength given him from above? God forbid that this great teacher should be supposed not to have known the Law of his God, Who says in the Book of Deuteronomy: "Say not in thine heart: My power and the might of mine hand has gotten me this wealth. But thou shalt remember the Lord thy God, for it is He That gives thee power to get wealth." And, again, what is the good of a fight unless it end in victory? And who is he that gives victory save He of Whom this very same Paul says: "Thanks be to God, Which giveth us the victory, through our Lord Jesus Christ?"

Lesson VII

From the Holy Gospel according to St. Matthew (Matt 10:16–22)

At that time, Jesus said unto His disciples: Behold, I send you forth as sheep in the midst of wolves. And so on.

Homily by St. John Chrysostom

It is as though He said: "Let not your heart be troubled, although, when I send you forth as sheep in the midst of wolves, I bid you be harmless as doves for, albeit, if I would, I could now make things otherwise, and suffer not that you should have to bear anything grievous, neither be at the mercy of the wolves as are other sheep, but on the contrary, could make you more dreadful to the lions than the lions are to you; nevertheless, thus must it be, and yourselves it will make more glorious, and My power it will wholly show forth." For thus was it that afterwards the Same Lord said unto Paul: "My grace is sufficient for thee, for My strength is made perfect in weakness." It is I that have made you to be what you are.

Lesson VIII

But let us look what wisdom it is which the Lord requires. It is the wisdom of the serpent. The serpent draws all the rest of his body after his head, and it is no matter to him if his body be cut through, so long as he keeps his head unharmed. Thus, O Christian, is it with thee. It is no matter to thee that for thy faith's sake thou shouldest lose all things else money, or body, or, if need be, life itself. Thy faith is thy head, and the root of thy being; hold fast to that, and, as long as thou hast that, although thou shouldest lose all things else, it will only be to receive them back again with interest a hundredfold. And thus it is that the Lord bids us, not to be single-hearted only, nor wise only, but both together, that therefrom we may be strong.

Lesson IX

If thou wilt see how these words were brought to the proof in very deed, read the Book of the Acts of the Apostles. There thou wilt see how that oftentimes the Jewish people rose against the Apostles and gnashed on them with their teeth, but they, with dove-like simplicity, gave them modest answers, and turned away their wrath, and quenched their fury, and stopped their onset. When the Jews said: "Did not we straitly command you, that you should not teach in this Name?" although the Apostles could have worked any miracles they chose, yet they neither said nor did anything sharp, but answered them with all meekness: "Whether it be right in the sight of God to hearken unto you more than unto God, you judge." Here thou hast the simplicity of doves, listen now to the prudence of serpents: "We cannot but speak the things which we have seen and heard."

sins have been, let him never give up hope of a reward from God. If thou knowest how to amend thy crooked ways, God knows how to turn away the judgments of His anger.

Lesson VIII

"And thou, child, shalt be called the Prophet of the Highest." How gracefully, while as he prophesies of the Lord, he turns his address to the Prophet, making mention of this great mercy of the Lord along with the others, lest, while he openly gave thanks for his own benefits, he should seem to keep the silence of unthankfulness regarding those which he knew had been given to his boy. But some will perhaps deem it his folly that he addressed his discourse to a babe of eight days old. Verily, if we call to mind that John heard the voice of Mary's salutation when he was in his mother's womb, we shall understand how much rather he could hear the voice of his father now when he was born.

Lesson IX

Zachary knew well that a Prophet has ears which open under the influence of the Spirit of God, instead of that of advancing age. He that had had sense to leap in the womb for joy, lacked not understanding. At the same time remark unto how many Zachary prophesied, and though both he and his wife were filled with the Holy Ghost, yet all things are done in due order, and the woman studies rather to learn the things of God than to teach them.

June 28 ~ St. Irenæus

Bishop & Martyr ~ Duplex

All from Common except what follows

Lessons I–III from the occurring Scripture

Lesson IV

Irenæus was born in proconsular Asia, not far from the city of Smyrna. There he had already as a boy entrusted himself to the teaching of Polycarp, disciple of John the Evangelist, and bishop of Smyrna. Under such an excellent master, he made remarkable progress in learning and in the precepts of the Christian religion. When Polycarp was taken up to heaven by a glorious martyrdom, although Irenæus was eminently versed in sacred letters, nevertheless, he burned with an incredible zeal to learn what articles of belief the others who were instructed by the Apostles had received, to be preserved in the deposit of faith. For this reason he brought together as many of those men as he could, and whatever things he heard from them, he carefully retained in his mind. Thus he could advantageously bring them to bear in the future against those heresies, which he saw were being diffused more widely day by day to the great detriment of the Christian people, and he diligently planned thoroughly to confute them. Then, having set out for Gaul, he was appointed as a priest of the church of Lyons by Pothinus the bishop. And this office he discharged in such a manner, laboring both by word and by teaching, that (according to the testimony of the

FEASTS OF JULY

July 1 ~ MOST PRECIOUS BLOOD OF OUR LORD JESUS CHRIST

Duplex I Class

Lesson I ~ Heb 9:11–15

From the Epistle of St. Paul the Apostle to the Hebrews

But Christ, being come a high priest of the good things to come, by a greater and more perfect tabernacle not made with hand, that is, not of this creation: Neither by the blood of goats, or of calves, but by his own blood, entered once into the holies, having obtained eternal redemption. For if the blood of goats and of oxen, and the ashes of a heifer being sprinkled, sanctify such as are defiled, to the cleansing of the flesh: How much more shall the blood of Christ, who by the Holy Ghost offered himself unspotted unto God, cleanse our conscience from dead works, to serve the living God? And therefore he is the mediator of the new testament: that by means of his death, for the redemption of those transgressions, which were under the former testament, they that are called may receive the promise of eternal inheritance.

Lesson II ~ Heb 9:16–22

For where there is a testament, the death of the testator must of necessity come in. For a testament is of force, after men are dead: otherwise it is as yet of no strength, whilst the testator liveth. Whereupon neither was the first indeed dedicated without blood. For when every commandment of the law had been read by Moses to all the people, he took the blood of calves and goats, with water, and scarlet wool and hyssop, and sprinkled both the book itself and all the people, Saying: This is the blood of the testament, which God hath enjoined unto you. The tabernacle also and all the vessels of the ministry, in like manner, he sprinkled with blood. And almost all things, according to the law, are cleansed with blood: and without shedding of blood there is no remission.

Lesson III ~ Heb 10:19–24

Having therefore, brethren, a confidence in the entering into the holies by the blood of Christ; A new and living way which he hath dedicated for us through the veil, that is to say, his flesh, And a high priest over the house of God: Let us draw near with a true heart in fulness of faith, having our hearts sprinkled from an evil conscience, and our bodies washed with clean water. Let us hold fast the confession of our hope without wavering (for he is faithful that hath promised), And let us consider one another, to provoke unto charity and to good works:

Lesson IV

Sermon by St. John Chrysostom

Wouldest thou hear the power of the Blood of Christ? Then let us look at the figure thereof, let us call to mind the old type, and narrate the ancient Scriptures. In Egypt, at midnight, God threatened the

Egyptians with a tenth plague, that their firstborn might perish, because they were detaining his firstborn people. But, lest the beloved people of the Jews should perish together with them, because the one place contained them all, a discreet remedy was found. Hence a wonderful example, that you may learn virtue in truth. The wrath of divine indignation was awaited, and the death-bearer circled every house. What then, Moses? "Kill," he says, "a yearling lamb, and line the doors with its blood." What say you, Moses? Is the blood of the sheep supposed to free the rational man? "Very much," he said; "not because it is blood, but because by it is shown the figure of the Lord's blood."

Lesson V

The statues of monarchs, mindless and speechless images though they be, have sometimes been a helpful refuge to men endowed with soul and reason, not because they are made of bronze, but because they bear a kingly image. And just so did this unconscious blood deliver the lives of men, not because it was blood, but because it foreshadowed the shedding of the Blood of Christ. On that night in Egypt, when the destroying Angel saw the blood upon the lintel and on the two side-posts, he passed over the door, and came not in unto the house. Even so now much more will the destroyer of souls flee away when he sees, not the lintel and the two side-posts sprinkled with the blood of a lamb, but the mouth of the faithful Christian, the living dwelling of the Holy Ghost, shining with the blood of the True Messiah. If the Angel let the type be, how shall not the enemy quail before the Reality? Wouldest thou hear more of the power of that Blood? I am willing. Consider from what source it wells, from what fountain it springs. Its fountain is the Heart of the Lord, pierced for us upon the Cross: that side of the Lord which the beginning. One of the soldiers with a spear pierced His Side; the veil of the Temple of His Body was rent in two. O how glorious is the treasure that is laid open to me therein! How noble the riches that it is my joy there to have found!

Lesson VI

And so was it done concerning that Lamb: the Jews killed a sheep, and I have learned the value of the sacrament. From the Side flowed forth Blood and Water. I would not, O my hearer, that thou shouldest pass by the depths of such a mystery as this without pausing; for I have yet a mystic and mysterious discourse to deliver. I have said that the Water and Blood showed forth symbolically baptism and the sacraments. For from these, holy Church was founded by the laver of regeneration, and the renovation of the Holy Ghost. Through baptism, I say, and through the sacraments, which seem to have issued from his Side. It was therefore out of the Side of Christ that the Church was created, just as it was out of the side of Adam that Eve was raised up to be his bride. This is the reason why Paul says, no doubt in allusion to his Side: "We are members of his

Body, and of his bones." For even as God made the woman Eve out of the rib which he had taken out of the side of Adam, so has Christ made the Church out of the Blood and Water which he made to flow for us out of his own Side.—On the occasion of the nineteenth centenary of the accomplishment of the redemption of mankind, as a fitting celebration of this ineffable blessing, Pope Pius XI decreed an extraordinary Jubilee. During that year the Supreme Pontiff, wishing that the fruits of the Precious Blood of Christ, the Lamb without spot, might redound more abundantly upon mankind and that the minds of the faithful be impressed with more vivid recollections of this same Blood as the price of their redemption, elevated the Feast of the Most Precious Blood of our Lord Jesus Christ to the rank of a Duplex of the first class, to be celebrated as such every year by the universal Church.

Lesson VII

From the Holy Gospel according to St. John (John 19:30–35)

At that time: When Jesus had received the vinegar, He said: It is finished. And He bowed His Head, and gave up the ghost. And so on.

Homily by St. Augustine, Bishop

"One of the soldiers with a spear opened His Side, and forthwith came thereout Blood and Water." The Evangelist speaks carefully. He says not that he smote the Side, nor yet that he wounded It, nor yet anything else, but "opened." He opened It, to fling wide the entrance unto life, whence flow the Sacraments of the Church, those Sacraments without which there is no entrance unto the life which is life indeed. That Blood which was shed there was shed for the remission of sins, that Water is the water that mingles in the cup of salvation. Therein are we washed, and thereof do we drink. Of this was it a type when it was said unto Noe: "The door of the ark shalt thou set in the side thereof and of every living thing of all flesh shalt thou bring into the ark to keep them alive." A figure this of the Church. Thus was it that the first woman was made from the side of her husband while he slept, and she was called Life, because she was the mother of all living. This name set forth a great good, before it became associated with the bitter fruit of a great evil. And here we have the Second Adam bowing His Head, and the deep sleep of death falling upon Him upon the Cross, and He sleeps, that the Lord God may take a thing out of His side, and may make thereof a wife for Him. O what a death was His, which revives the dead! What is cleaner than His Blood? What more health-giving than His wounding?

Lesson VIII

Then were men being held bondsmen to the devil, slaves to evil spirits. But they have been redeemed from that bondage. They had been able to sell themselves, but they were not able to redeem themselves. A Redeemer came and paid the price for them. He shed His Blood, and at that cost bought the world. You ask what He bought? Look what He paid, and you shall see what He bought. Christ's Blood was the price. What is His Blood worth? What, but the whole world? What but all men? They are very unthankful for His redemption, or very proud, who say that It is only precious enough to buy the Africans, or that they themselves are so precious that It was shed only for them. Let there be an end to such conceit, an end to such vainglory. What He paid, He paid for all.

Lesson IX

That Blood was his own, and thereby he redeemed us. Yea, it was to this end that he took Flesh and Blood, namely that he might shed his Blood in order to redeem us. If thou wilt accept it, the Blood of thy Lord was given for thee. If thou wilt not accept it, it was not given for thee. For perchance thou sayest: My God had Blood, with which he redeemed me, but now since he has suffered, he has given it all; what has remained to him, that he may also give any of it for me? This is a great thing, because he gave once, and he gave for all. The Blood of Christ is salvation to him that accepts it, punishment to him that does not accept it. Why therefore dost thou hesitate to be set free from the second death, thou who dost not wish to die? By this thou art set free, if thou art willing to take up thy Cross, and follow the Lord; for he took up his Cross and sought his servant.

July 2 ~ Visitation of the Blessed Virgin Mary

Duplex II Class

Lesson I ~ Cant 2:1–7

From the Canticle of Canticles

I am the flower of the field, and the lily of the valleys. As the lily among thorns, so is my love among the daughters. As the apple tree among the trees of the woods, so is my beloved among the sons. I sat down under his shadow, whom I desired: and his fruit was sweet to my palate. He brought me into the cellar of wine, he set in order charity in me. Stay me up with flowers, compass me about with apples: because I languish with love. His left hand is under my head, and his right hand shall embrace me. I adjure you, O ye daughters of Jerusalem, by the roes, and the harts of the, fields, that you stir not up, nor make the beloved to awake, till she please.

Lesson II ~ Cant 2:8–13

The voice of my beloved, behold he comes leaping upon the mountains, skipping over the hills. My beloved is like a roe, or a young hart. Behold he standeth behind our wall, looking through the windows, looking through the lattices. Behold my beloved speaketh to me: Arise, make haste, my love, my dove, my beautiful one, and come. For winter is now past, the rain is over and gone. The flowers have appeared in our land, the time of pruning is come: the voice of the turtle is heard in our land: The fig tree hath put forth her green figs: the vines in flower yield their sweet smell.

Lesson III ~ Cant 2:13–17

Arise, my love, my beautiful one, and come: My dove in the clefts of the rock, in the hollow places of the wall, show me thy face, let thy voice sound in my ears: for thy voice is sweet, and thy face comely. Catch us the little foxes that destroy the vines: for our vineyard hath flourished. My beloved to me, and I to him who feedeth among the lilies, Till the day break, and the shadows retire. Return: be like, my beloved, to a roe, or to a young hart upon the mountains of Bether.

Lesson IV

Sermon by St. John Chrysostom

As soon as our Redeemer was come among us, He went with haste, while as yet He was in His mother's womb, to visit His friend John. And John, in the one womb, becoming conscious of the Presence of Jesus in the other womb, dashed himself impatiently against the narrow walls of his natural prison, as though crying out: "I see the very Lord who has given nature her bounds, and I wait not for the due season of my birth. There is no need for me to linger here till nine months are ended, for He That is Eternal is with me! I will break out of my dark cell; I will proclaim my full knowledge of many wonders. I am the sign. I will show that the Christ is here. I am the trumpet; let me peal forth the news that the Son of God is come in the flesh. Let me sound the trumpet, let me bless my father's tongue, and make it to speak again. Let me sound the trumpet, let me vivify my mother's womb."

Lesson V

Thou seest, O beloved, how new and how strange a mystery is here! John is not born, but by leaping he speaks; he is yet unseen, and he gives warning; he is not yet able to cry, but by his acts he is heard. He draws not yet the breath of life, but he preaches God. He sees not yet the light, but he makes known the Sun! He is not come out of the womb, but he hastens to play the Forerunner in the Presence of the Lord. He cannot restrain himself; he rebells against the bounds set by nature, and struggles to break out of the prison of the belly. His longing is to herald the coming Saviour. He says, as it were: "Behold, the Deliverer comes and am I to remain still bound to abide here? The Word comes, that He may set right all things and am I still to tarry in prison? I will go forth. I will run before Him, and cry aloud to all men: 'Behold the Lamb of God Who takes away the sin of the world.'"

Lesson VI

But do thou tell us, O John, how it came to pass that while thou wast still in the darkness of thy mother's womb, thou didst see and hear? How didst thou behold the things of God? How didst thou leap and bound for joy? "Great," says John, "is the mystery of that which takes place here, far from the understanding of men are these doings. It is fitting that I should do a new thing in nature for the sake of Him Who is making new things which are beyond nature. I see in the womb, because I see the Sun of righteousness in a womb. I hear, because I am coming as the herald of the Great Word. I cry out, because I spy the Only-begotten Son of the Father clad in Flesh. I bound for joy, because I see that He by Whom all things were made, has taken upon Him the form of a servant. I leap, because I think of the Redeemer of the world being made Flesh. I run before His coming, and herald His approach unto you with this, as it were, my confession."

Lesson VII

From the Holy Gospel according to St. Luke (Luke 1:39–47)

And Mary arose in those days and went into the hill-country with haste, into a city of Judah. And entered into the house of Zachary, and saluted Elizabeth. And so on.

Homily by St. Ambrose, Bishop

We must here consider that the greater comes unto the lesser, Mary unto Elizabeth, Christ unto John. And again afterwards, to hallow the baptism of John, the Lord came unto him to be baptized. It was soon that the blessings of the coming of Mary and of the Presence of God were made manifest. Have regard here to the distinction made, and to the special weight of every word. Elizabeth was the first to hear the voice of Mary's salutation, but John was the first to receive grace. She heard naturally, but he leaped mystically. She hailed the coming of Mary, he that of the Lord; Mary and Elizabeth spoke words full of grace, but Jesus and John worked, and commenced their mystery of godliness from their mothers' beginnings, and so by twin miracles the mothers prophesied from the spirit of their unborn offspring. The babe leaped, and the mother was filled with the Holy Ghost. The mother was not filled before the son, but when the son was filled with the Holy Ghost, he filled his mother also.

Lesson VIII

"And whence is this to me, that the Mother of my Lord should come to me?" That is to say, How comes it to pass that so great a good should befall me, that the Mother of my Lord should come to me? I feel the miracle, I acknowledge the mystery: the Mother of my Lord, pregnant with the Word, is full of God. And Mary abode with her about three months, and returned to her own house. It is right to record how Mary showed this kindness, and abode this mystic number of months.

She tarried long, not only for friendship's sake, but also for the good of the Great Prophet. For if the first coming of Mary so blessed him, that even as a babe in the womb he leapt for joy, and his mother was filled with the Holy Ghost, what blessedness must we not deem to have flowed upon him from so long a time in the presence of the Holy Mary? Thus was the Prophet anointed, and trained by exercise like a strong wrestler, in his mother's womb, for his sinews were being braced for a hard battle.

Lesson IX—Commemoration of Sts. Processus & Martinian, Martyrs

At the time when Peter and Paul were kept in the Mamertine Prison, at the foot of the Tarpeian Rock, two of the jailors, named Processus and Martinian, along with forty others, were moved by the preaching and miracles of the Apostles to believe in Christ, and were baptized in a spring which suddenly broke forth out of the rock. These men let the Apostles depart if they willed it. But Paulinus, Præfect of the soldiers, when he heard what was come to pass, strove to turn away Processus and Martinian from their purpose. And when he found that he but wasted time, he ordered their faces to be bruised and their teeth to be broken with stones. Moreover, when he had had them led to the image of Jupiter, and they still boldly answered that they would not worship the idols, he ordered them to be tormented on the rack, and white-hot plates of metal to be put to their flesh, and that they should be beaten with clubs. Whilst they were suffering all these things, they were heard to say only this one word: "Blessed be the Name of the Lord." They were afterwards cast into prison, and in a little while they were taken outside the city, and slain with the axe upon the Aurelian Way. The Lady Lucina buried their bodies upon her own farm, upon the 2nd day of July in the year of Our Lord 67, but they were afterwards brought into the City, and are buried in the Church of the Prince of the Apostles.

July 3 ~ St. Leo II

Pope & Confessor ~ Semiduplex

All from Common except what follows

Lessons I–III from the occurring Scripture

Lesson IV

Leo II was a Sicilian. He was learned in sacred and worldly letters in the Greek and Latin tongues, and was moreover an excellent musician. He rearranged and improved the music of the sacred hymns and Psalms used in the Church. He approved the acts of the sixth general Council which was held at Constantinople under the Presidency of the Legates of the Apostolic See in the presence of the Emperor Constantine the Bearded, the Patriarchs of Constantinople and Antioch, and one hundred and seventy Bishops. Leo also translated the decrees of the Council from Greek into Latin.

Lesson V

It was in this Council that Cyrus, Sergius, and Pyrrhus were condemned for teaching the heresy of the Monothelites, that there is in Christ only one Will and one Working. Leo broke the pride of the Archbishops of Ravenna, who had puffed themselves up under the power of the Exarchs to set at naught the power of the Apostolic See. Wherefore he decreed that the elections of the clergy of Ravenna should be worth nothing until they had been confirmed by the authority of the Roman Pontiff.

Lesson VI

He was a very father to the poor. Not by money only, but by his work, his labors, and his advice he relieved the poverty and loneliness of widows and orphans. He was leading all to live holy and godly lives, not by mere preaching, but by his own life, when he fell asleep in the Lord on the 28th of June, having sat as Pope nine months and twenty-seven days. He was buried in the Church of St. Peter upon the 3rd day of July in the year of Our Lord 683. In the month of June he held one ordination whereat he ordained nine Priests, three Deacons, and twenty-three Bishops for diverse places.

Lessons VII–IX from the Common of Supreme Pontiffs (Homily by St. Leo)

July 4 ~ Day 6 within the Octave of Apostles

Semiduplex

All from Common except what follows

Lessons I–III from the occurring Scripture

Lesson IV

From the Exposition by St. John Chrysostom on the Epistle to the Romans

The Apostle Paul wishes unto us the grace of our Lord Jesus Christ, as the mother of all good, and it remaines for us to show ourselves worthy of the care of such a Protector, that we may not only listen to Paul's voice, while we are here, but when we pass away to the hereafter, may earn a sight of that great soldier of Christ. Yea if we listen to him here, we shall see him there. Not nigh, but from afar off, shall we see him see him standing near the glory of that Kingly throne where the Cherubim glorify God, where the Seraphim are flying, there shall we see Paul along with Peter, a prince and a leader of the army of the saints, and we shall rejoice in his brotherly love.

Lesson V

For if, while he was yet here, he so loved men, that, although he would have eagerly been dissolved and been with Christ, yet he was willing still to tarry for man's sake, much greater is the tender love which he now shows. This is why I love Rome, although if I would, there are many other things for which I might praise her: her greatness, her antiquity, her beauty, her population, her empire, her wealth, or her victories. But all these I pass by, and I call Rome blessed for this cause, that Paul in his lifetime loved her children so well, was so kindly toward them, taught openly there, and at length laid down his life among them. They have there his holy body, and this alone makes that city illustrious more than does aught else. And just as a great and strong body has two bright eyes, so are the bodies of these two Holy Apostles in the city of Rome.

Lesson VI

Not brighter is the sky when the sun does make it all light with his beams, than is the city of Rome darting forth these twin rays of light to the uttermost bounds of the earth. There it is that Paul, there it is that

Peter, will arise, and be caught up to meet the Lord in the air. Think, and thrill at the thought, of what Rome will see then, when she beholds Paul and Peter rising suddenly out of that coffin, to be caught up to meet the Lord. What rose will Rome offer to Christ? What twin crowns are they wherewith that city is adorned withal? What fresh springs has she in her? Therefore it is that I marvel at that city, not because of the abundance of her gold, not because of her pillars, not because of any other loveliness that she has, but because of these two pillars of the Church. Would that I could even now embrace the corpse of Paul, that I could cling to his grave, that I could see the dust of that body, which filled up those things that were behind of the sufferings of Christ which bore about in it the marks of the Lord Jesus and which went everywhere carrying the seed of the Gospel.

Lessons VII–IX from the third set in the Common of Abbots (Homily by St Bede the Venerable, Priest)

July 5 ~ St. Anthony Mary Zaccaria

Confessor ~ Duplex

All from Common except what follows

Lessons I–III from the occurring Scripture

Lesson IV

Anthony Mary Zaccaria was born in 1502 of a noble family, at Cremona, on the Po. Even in his childhood marks of his future holiness became manifest. There shone brightly in him, signs of excellent graces of childlike love toward God and the Blessed Virgin, and more especially of tenderness toward the poor, for the relief of whose needs he was ready more than once to strip off his own costly dress. He studied arts at his own home, philosophy at Ticino, and medicine at Padua, and as he excelled all others in goodness, so did he surpass all his companions in intellectual power. After taking his degree he returned home, and there understood from God that his call was to the healing of souls, rather than to that of bodies. He therefore began earnestly to study theology while he continued in the meantime to visit the sick, to teach Christian doctrine to children, to excite piety among the young, and oftentimes even to exhort the aged to amend their ways. It is said that when he first said Mass after his ordination, a light broke from heaven and he seemed to the astonished bystanders to be surrounded by a circle of angels: from that time forth he labored more earnestly for the salvation of souls, and the struggle against evil living. His fatherly love for strangers, for the needy, and for the afflicted, and the godly exhortations and alms wherewith he entertained them, made his house to become a refuge for the wretched, and earned for himself from his fellow-citizens the title of father of the fatherland and of angels.

Lesson V

While he was at Milan he bethought him that greater Christian good might be done if he gathered round him some fellow-laborers in the Lord's vineyard, and when he had conferred thereon with those noble and holy men Bartholomew Ferrari and James Morigia, he founded the brotherhood of Clerics Regular, to whom on account of his own great love for the Apostle of the Gentiles he gave the name of Clerics Regular of St. Paul [Barnabites]. Under the approbation of the Supreme Pontiff Clement VII and the confirmation of Paul III, this brotherhood was in a short time widely spread abroad. The Congregation of nuns who are called the Angelic Sisters also regard Anthony Mary as their Father and Founder. His own thought of himself was so lowly that he never would be at the head of his own Order. In great long-suffering he bore with patience the violent storms which were raised against his Institute. In the greatness of his charity he never ceased to enkindle the members of religious orders to love toward God, to exhort priests to live Apostolic lives, and to found guilds of married men, to the bringing forth of much fruit. Sometimes he and his disciples would walk through the streets and squares with a Cross carried before them, and there by burning and vehement harangues call to salvation the wandering and the wicked.

Lesson VI

It is to be remembered that in his burning love for Jesus Crucified he reminded all men of the Mystery of the Cross by the sound of a bell every Friday evening, and himself as a true disciple of Paul always bore about in his body the dying of the Lord Jesus. The holy Name of Christ is found everywhere in his writings and was ever in his mouth. He was moved by a singular love toward the Holy Eucharist. He established a custom of receiving it often, and is said to have brought in the practice of exposing the same upon a lofty throne for three days' adoration. Of his earnest modesty the appearance of life which was seen even in his dead body seemed a witness. Together with all these things he possessed the gifts of trance, of tears, of knowledge of things to come, of reading the thoughts of the heart, and of power against the enemy of mankind. He was worn out with toil when he was seized with his last illness at Guastalla, whither he had been called as a peacemaker. He was carried to Cremona amid the tears of his brethren and the embraces of his devoted mother, whose imminent death he foretold. He was comforted by a vision of the Apostles above, and predicted the increase of his Brotherhood. On the 5th day of July, in the year 1539, he died a holy death at the age of thirty-six. Christians forthwith began to honor him for his eminent sanctity and the number of his signs and wonders, which honor the Supreme Pontiff Leo XIII approved and confirmed, and on the Feast of the Lord's Ascension in the year 1897 solemnly enrolled his name among those of the Saints.

Lesson VII

From the Holy Gospel according to St. Mark (Mark 10:15–21)

At that time: Jesus said unto His Disciples: Whosoever shall not receive the Kingdom of God as a little child: he shall not enter therein. And so on.

Homily by St. Augustine, Bishop

That which the Lord commands seems hard and heavy: "If any man will come after Me, let him deny himself, and take up his cross, and follow Me." But neither hard nor heavy is that which He commands when He that commands gives help to fulfill it. That is true which is said, "By the words of Thy lips I have kept me to strait paths." That which is hard in the commandment love makes easy. How great the power of love is, we know. And what signifies this: "let him deny"? Let him put no trust in himself, let him feel that he is man, and let him have regard unto that which was spoken of the prophet, saying, "Cursed be the man that trusts in men." Let him mistrust himself, but not to sink; let him mistrust himself, that he may cleave unto God.

Lesson VIII

To where are we to follow the Lord? Where He is gone, we know. He is risen from the dead, and is gone up into heaven. There we must follow Him. And we must not despair of so doing, not because man is able to do anything, but because He That promised is faithful. Why, then, should we despair, since we are members of His Body, of His Flesh, and of His Bones, Who is the Head of the Church, and He is the Saviour of the body? Good it is to follow Him, but where we are to follow Him we must see. When the Lord Jesus uttered those words bidding us to follow Him, He had not Himself as yet arisen from the dead, He had not as yet suffered, there lay still before Him the cross, shame, mockery, scourging, thorns, wounds, outrages, insults, death. After He uttered those words, His way became very rough. Art thou slothful? Willest thou not to follow Him, but follow Him all the same; for who would not follow unto glory? All men love exaltation, but lowliness is the stairway.

Lesson IX

Take up thy cross, and follow the Lord, and the cross that the Lord commands us to carry after Him, that we may follow Him most speedily, what is it but the death of this flesh? For it is this flesh that crucifies us until death is swallowed up in victory. Therefore must this our own cross itself be crucified and pierced with the nails of the fear of God, lest if it be free it hamper thee, in the carrying of it, and thou canst in no way follow the Lord save in carrying it. For how canst thou follow Him if thou be none of His own? "And they that are Christ's," says the Apostle, "have crucified the flesh with the affections and lusts."

July 6 – Octave Day of the Holy Apostles Peter & Paul

Major Duplex

All from Common except what follows

Lessons I–III from the occurring Scripture

Lesson IV

Sermon by St. John Chrysostom

O blessed Apostles, who have toiled so much for us, what thanks shall we give you? When I remember thee, O Peter, I am lost in amazement; Paul, when I think of thee, my heart overwhelms me, and I weep. When I look at your sufferings I know not what to say or what to speak. How many prisons have you sanctified? How many fetters have you made honorable? How many torments have you endured? How many reproaches have you borne? How have you carried Christ? How have you gladdened the Churches by your preaching? Verily, your tongues were blessed instruments; it was for the Church's sake that your limbs were bloody. You have been made in all things followers of Christ. Your sound is gone out through all the earth, and your words to the ends of the world.

Lesson V

Rejoice, O Peter, who hast been gladdened by the wood of the Cross of Christ. It was a showing forth of thy Teacher that thou didst will to be crucified, not like the Lord Christ, standing upright, but with thine head toward the earth, as one that made a way from earth to heaven. Blessed are the nails which pierced thy holy limbs. With sure and certain hope didst thou commend thy spirit into the hands of the Lord, thou who hadst been a faithful servant to Him and to His Bride the Church, thou who in thy warm heart hadst loved the Lord more loyally than all the Apostles.

Lesson VI

Rejoice also, O blessed Paul, whose head was cut off by the sword, thou whose fearless devotion no words can express. What sword was that which divided thy holy neck, that instrument of the Lord's work, worthy that heaven should wonder at it, and earth worship it? What place was that which drank in thy blood, that appeared like drops of milk upon the raiment of him who smote thee, and made the barbarian and his comrades to become strangely gentle and faithful? Would that I could have that sword for a crown, and the nails of Peter set therein as the jewels of the diadem.

Lesson VII

From the Holy Gospel according to St. Matthew (Matt 14:22–23)

At that time Jesus constrained His disciples to get into a ship, and to go before Him unto the other side, while He sent the multitudes away. And so on.

Homily by St. Jerome, Priest

The Lord commanded His disciples to cross over to the other

side, and constrained them to get into a ship. By these expressions we perceive that they were unwilling to leave the Lord, the love of their Teacher making them desire not to lose a moment of His company. And when He had sent the multitudes away, He went up into a mountain apart to pray. Perchance, if Peter, and James, and John, who had seen Him in the glory of the Transfiguration, had been with Him, they would have gone up into the mountain with Him, but the common herd could not follow Him, save when He taught them on the sea shore, or fed them in the wilderness.

Lesson VIII

He went up into a mountain apart to pray, not as He Who, with five loaves and two fishes, had satisfied about five thousand men, besides women and children, but as He, Who when He heard of the death of John, departed into a deserted place apart. Not that we separate two Persons in the Lord but some of His works He did as God, and some as man. But the ship was now in the midst of the sea, tossed with waves. The Apostles were right to be slow and unwilling to leave the Lord, for, when He was not with them, they were in peril of shipwreck.

Lesson IX

Whilst the Lord abode alone upon the top of the mountain, a contrary wind arose, and the sea raged, and the Apostles were endangered and yet the threatening shipwreck held off until Jesus came. And in the fourth watch of the night, Jesus went unto them, walking on the sea. The watches of soldiers are divided into three. When therefore it is said that the Lord came unto them in the fourth watch, it appears that they had been in peril all night, and that it was at the end of the night, as it will again be at the end of the world, that He came to the rescue of His disciples.

July 7 ~ Sts. Cyril & Methodius

Confessor Bishops ~ Duplex

All from Common except what follows

Lessons I–III from the occurring Scripture

Lesson IV

From the Encyclical Letter of Pope Leo XIII

Cyril and Methodius were brothers born in an honorable position at Thessalonica. As they advanced in years, they went to Constantinople to study letters in the capital of the Eastern world. Both made quick progress, but most chiefly Cyril, who gained such learning that he was called for excellence "the Philosopher." Methodius became a monk, but the Empress Theodora, on the recommendation of the Patriarch Ignatius, deemed Cyril worthy of receiving the task of teaching Christianity to the Khazars who dwelt beyond Cherson. By the grace of God, he so taught them that they laid aside their many superstitions and were joined to Jesus Christ. After properly establishing the new community of Christians, Cyril hastened back to Constantinople where he entered the monastery of Polychron, where Methodius had already withdrawn himself. Rastilav, Prince of Moravia, having heard tell of the good deeds beyond the Crimea, sent to Constantinople to the Emperor Michael III to obtain some Gospel laborers. Cyril and Methodius were sent to him, and gladly received in Moravia, and applied themselves with such power and industry to the work of Christianizing souls that it was not long before that nation also joyfully submitted to Jesus Christ. To this end Cyril found of great use the knowledge of the Slavonic language, which he had already acquired, and much effect was produced by the translation of holy Scripture which he made into the language of the people. Cyril and Methodius were the inventors of the alphabet in which the language of the Slavs is characteristically expressed, and for this reason they have been not unjustly termed the fathers of Slavonic literature.

Lesson V

When the happy tidings of what they had done reached Rome, the Supreme Pontiff Saint Nicholas I commanded these excellent brethren to come to Rome. When they started for Rome they brought with them the relics of the supreme Pontiff Saint Clement I, which Cyril had discovered at Cherson. On hearing of their approach Hadrian II, who had succeeded to the Papacy upon the death of Nicholas, went forth to meet them accompanied by the clergy and people with every sign of honor. Then Cyril and Methodius gave to the Supreme Pontiff in the presence of the clergy an account of the Apostolic office which they had discharged in so holy and toilsome a manner. When it was made blame to them by some enviers that they had used the Slavonic language for the purposes of public worship, they stated their reasons with such clearness and force that the Pontiff and clergy praised and approved them. When they had both taken an oath that they would remain in the faith of blessed Peter and of the Roman Pontiffs, they were consecrated bishops by Hadrian, but it was the Will of God that Cyril, old in grace rather than in years, should close his life at Rome in the year of Our Lord 869. His dead body received a public funeral, and was laid in the tomb which Hadrian had built for himself, but it was afterwards brought to St. Clement's and buried near the ashes of that martyr. As it was carried through the city with joyful psalm-singing, it seemed as though the procession were rather that of a triumph than that of a funeral, and that the Roman people were offering heavenly honor to some eminent saint. Methodius went back to Moravia, and there became from his whole soul a pattern to his flock, and from day to day more zealous in the service of Catholicism. He confirmed the Pannonians, the Bulgarians, and the Dalmatians in the Christian religion, and labored much to bring the Corinthians to the worship of the one true God.

Lesson VI

Methodius was again accused before John VIII, the successor of Hadrian, of unsoundness in faith, and transgression of the traditions of the elders; he was summoned to Rome, and there easily proved, in the presence of John and of some Bishops and clergy of the city, that he had himself always firmly held the Catholic faith, and had carefully taught it to others, and that as regarded the use of the Slavonic language for public worship, he had acted lawfully from certain reasons, and the permission of Pope Hadrian, and in no ways contrary to the holy Scriptures. The Pontiff therefore in this matter concurred with Methodius, and confirmed even in writing his archiepiscopal authority and his mission among the Slavs. Methodius therefore went back to Moravia and resumed more earnestly than before the task committed to him, for which also he cheerfully suffered exile. He converted the Prince of the Bohemians and his wife, and spread the Christian name far and wide among that people. He carried the light of the Gospel into Poland, and according to some writers, after establishing the see of Lvov, went into Muscovia properly so called and established the see of Kiev. At the last he returned into Moravia, and when he felt that he was about to go the way of all flesh he named his own successor, exhorted the clergy and people for the last time to good living, and then most peacefully departed that life which had been to him a path to heaven, in the year of Our Lord 885. As Rome had honored Cyril in his death, so did Moravia honor Methodius with the highest honor. The feast day of these Saints, which had long been observed among the Slav nations, the Supreme Pontiff Leo XIII ordered to be kept throughout the Universal Church with a special office and Mass.

Lessons VII–IX from the Common of Evangelists (Homily by St. Gregory)

July 8 ~ St. Elizabeth of Portugal

Queen & Widow ~ Semiduplex

All from Common except what follows

Lessons I–III from the occurring Scripture

Lesson IV

Elizabeth, daughter of Peter III, King of Aragon, was born in the year of Christ 1271, and it was an omen of her saintly life; that her father and mother, contrary to the usual custom, caused her to be baptized, not by the name of her mother or grandmother, but by that of her mother's aunt, Saintly Elizabeth [of Hungary], Lady of Thuringia. As soon as ever she was born, her destiny of being a peacemaker between kings and kingdoms began to appear, for the joy of her birth put an end to the ruinous quarrels of her father and grandfather. As she grew up, her father, delighted with her disposition, was used to foretell that his Elizabeth would in herself excel all the daughters of the kingly house of Aragon, and that the happiness of his own home and kingdom was all owing to this one damsel, whose heavenly life he venerated for her indifference to bodily finery, her abstinence from pleasures, her many fasts, her constancy in prayer to God, and her activity in doing works of charity. This illustrious maiden was sought in marriage by many princes, and at twelve years of age was wedded with Christian rites to Denis, King of Portugal.

Lesson V

As a wife, she gave herself up as much to the education of her children, as to her own improvement, striving in all ways, next to God, to please her husband. For nearly half the year, she was used to live on bread and water, and once, when she was ill, God changed the water into wine, which the physicians had ordered her to drink, but which she was unwilling to take. Once when she kissed a disgusting ulcer in a poor woman, it was immediately healed. One winter-time when she was giving some money to the poor, and so her husband should not see her alms, the coins changed into roses. She gave sight to a maiden who had been born blind, and healed many other persons of grievous sicknesses by the Sign of the Cross. The miracles of this kind, which she worked, were many. She not only built, but richly endowed convents, schools, and churches. She had a wonderful skill in making peace between kings, and toiled unweariedly to lighten all suffering, whether public or private.

Lesson VI

King Denis died on the 7th day of January, 1325, and Elizabeth, who in her maidenhood had been a pattern to virgins, and in her married life to wives, now, in her loneliness, was an example to widows. Clad in the raiment of the nuns of St. Clare, she faithfully attended at the King's funeral, and soon after went to Compostela, where she offered many precious gifts of silk, and gold, and silver, and precious stones, for the benefit of his soul. Thence she returned home, and spent in holy and godly uses everything that remained to her that was dear and costly, eager to relieve every kind of suffering. She lived, not for herself, but for God, and to be useful to mankind. She finished the convent for nuns, right worthy of a Queen, which she had founded at Coimbra. She fed the poor, defended widows, protected orphans. A war arising between her son Afonso IV of Portugal, and her grandson Alfonso XI of Castile, she resolved to set out to reconcile them, and went to the famous city of Estremoz, upon the borders of the two kingdoms. On the journey, she caught a violent fever, of which, after a vision of the Virgin Mother of God, she died a saintly death on the 4th day of July, in the year 1336. She became illustrious for miracles after her death, especially for the sweetness of the savor of her body, which has remained incorrupt for nearly three hundred years, and she has always been spoken of as the Holy Queen Elizabeth. At length, in the year of our salvation 1625, which was that of the Jubilee, with concord and applause from all of Christendom, Urban VIII formally enrolled her name among those of the Saints.

Lessons VII–IX from the first set in the Common of Non-Virgins (Homily by St. Gregory)

July 10 ~ The Seven Holy Brothers & Sts. Rufina & Secunda

Martyrs & Virgin-Martyrs ~ Semiduplex

All from Common except what follows

Lessons I–III from the occurring Scripture

Lesson IV

In the persecution at Rome under Marcus Aurelius Antoninus, there were seven brethren, sons of Saint Felicity, whom the Præfect Publius first essayed to cajole by kindness, and then to shake by fear, to deny Christ and worship the gods but, by their own bravery and the exhortation of their mother, they remained firm in their confession, and were all put to death in diverse ways. Januarius was lashed to death with leaden whips; Felix and Philip were beaten to death with cudgels; Silvanus was thrown over a precipice; Alexander, Vitalis, and Martial were beheaded. Their mother gained the same palm of martyrdom four months afterwards. The seven Brethren gave up their souls to God upon the 10th day of July.

Lesson V

The virgin sisters, Rufina and Secunda, were Romans. Their parents had betrothed them to Armentarius and Verinus, but they both vowed their virginity to Christ, and refused marriage. They were arrested in the reign of the Emperors Valerian and Gallienus. The Præfect Junius failed to change their minds either by promises or threats, and then ordered Rufina to be scourged. While the lashing was going on, Secunda said to the Judge: "Why dost thou judge my sister to honor and me to dishonor? Be pleased to whip us both together, for we both together declare that Christ is God." The Judge was angered at these words, and ordered them both to be cast into a dark and stinking dungeon but it was presently filled with a bright light and a sweet savor. They were then enclosed in a burning hot hypocaust duct in the bathhouse, but they came forth from it unharmed. Stones were next tied to their necks and they were cast into the river Tiber, but an Angel delivered them therefrom. In the end they were beheaded on the Aurelian Way, at the tenth milestone from the city. The Lady Plautilla buried their bodies upon her own farm, but they were afterwards brought into the city, and laid in the Constantinian Basilica [St. John Lateran], near the Baptistery.

Lesson VI

Sermon by St. Augustine, Bishop

Great is the spectacle, my brethren, which is set before the eyes of our faith. We have heard with our ears, and we see in our thoughts, a mother, with superhuman love, watching her sons leaving this life before her. All men would eagerly depart hence before their children, but she was ready to die last. Departing from her, they were not lost, but gone before. And she looked, not to the life they were ending, but to the life they were beginning. They laid aside a life which must end in death, and began that life wherein they are alive forever. The least of her work was that she was an onlooker; more amazing is it, when we remember that she was their exhortress. Her courage was more fruitful than her womb, and when she saw them contending and conquering, her heart contended and conquered in each.

Lesson VII

From the Holy Gospel according to St. Matthew (Matt 12:46–50)

At that time: While Jesus yet talked to the people, behold, His mother and His brethren stood without, desiring to speak with Him. And so on.

Homily by Pope St. Gregory

Dearly beloved brethren, the gospel which is read this day is but very short, but it is heavy with great mysteries. Here Jesus, our Maker and Redeemer, feigns Himself as though He knew not His Own Mother, and tells who they be who are His mother and brethren, not by fleshly kinship, but by kinship of mind. "Who is My Mother And who are My brethren? Whosoever shall do the will of My Father, Which is in heaven, the same is My brother, and sister, and mother." By which words what are we to understand, save that He gathers together from out of Heathendom many that are willing to obey His commandments, and that He knows not Jewry, whereof, according to the flesh, He is a son?

Lesson VIII

Seeing that both men and women are called to the faith, we marvel not that He says that whosoever shall do the will of His Father, the same is His brother, and sister. But it is startling to hear that the same is also His mother. His faithful disciples He is pleased to call His brethren, where He says "Go, tell My brethren." If then it is by joining His religion that one can become the brother of the Lord, let us see how one can become His mother.

Lesson IX

But we must know that even as one becomes His brother or His sister by believing in Him, so one becomes His mother by preaching Him. Such a one, as it were, gives birth to the Lord by causing Him to be in the hearer's heart, and by words giving His love existence in their neighbor's mind. For an example in point, behold blessed Felicity, whose Birthday we keep today. She was one whose faith made her Christ's handmaid, and whose preaching made her Christ's mother. We read in the corrected edition of her Acts that she dreaded as much to leave her seven sons behind her alive in the flesh, as do worldly mothers to send theirs dead before them.

July 11 ~ St. Pius I

Pope & Martyr ~ Simplex

Lessons I–II from the occurring Scripture

Lesson III

Pius I, the son of Rufinus, was from Aquileia, and was a Priest of the holy Roman Church when he was made Supreme Pontiff; he lived under the Emperors Antoninus Pius and Marcus Aurelius; he held five ordinations in the month of December, wherein he ordained twelve Bishops and eighteen Priests. There remain several eminent ordinances of his, notably that which rules that the Resurrection of the Lord be not observed upon any day of the week except the Lord's Day. He turned the house of Pudens into a church, and on account of its eminence above the other churches, as being that where the Bishop of Rome dwelt, he dedicated it under the name of the Shepherd. Here he often celebrated, and baptized and numbered among the faithful many converts to the faith. While he strove to do the work of a good shepherd he shed his blood for his sheep, and for Christ the chief Shepherd. He was crowned with martyrdom upon the 11th day of July, and buried upon the Vatican Hill.

July 12 ~ St. John Gualbert

Abbot ~ Duplex

All from Common except what follows

Lessons I–III from the occurring Scripture

Lesson IV

John Gualbert was the son of a noble family at Florence. In accordance with the wishes of his father, he became a soldier. While he was in that profession, his only brother, Ugo, was slain by a cousin. On a certain Good Friday, John, armed and accompanied by soldiers, met the murderer, alone and defenseless, in a narrow way, where neither could turn aside. As he was at the point to kill him, the wretch fell on his knees, and stretched out his arms in the form of the Cross, adjuring him, for the sake of that sign, to forgive him and out of reverence for the Cross he had mercy on him and spared his life. After pardoning his enemy, he went into the Church of St. Minias, which was near, to pray. And there he saw the image of Jesus crucified, which had that day received the worship of the faithful, bow its head to him. By this miracle John was so moved, that he laid aside soldiering, even against his father's wishes, cut off his hair with his own hands at the Convent of St. Minias, and clad himself in the garb of a monk. In a short while he so shone with all pious and religious virtues, that he became a pattern of excellence to many. When the Abbot of that house died, the monks all chose John to succeed him. But the servant of God desired to obey, more than to command, and, being kept by God for greater things, he betook himself to one Romuald, a dweller in the hermitage at Camaldoli. Through Romuald he received a revelation from heaven, and forthwith founded an Order of his own under the Rule of St. Benedict, in the valley called Vallombrosa.

Lesson V

Many gathered themselves to him, drawn by the fame of his holy life. Them he took for his comrades, and labored earnestly among them to cleanse the Church in those parts from the pollution of heresy and simony, and spread abroad the Apostolic Faith. He and his had to fight with almost countless hardships. Certain enemies broke by night into the monastery of San Salvi, to destroy John and his monks, set the church on fire, pulled down the huts, and mortally wounded all the monks but the man of God perfectly healed them all by the sign of the Cross. One of his monks named Peter also passed unhurt through a vast and raging fire. At length John and his disciples got the peace which they longed for. He purged Tuscany of the pollution of simony, and restored the faith throughout all Italy to its first purity.

Lesson VI

He entirely built several monasteries, and furnished them and others with buildings. He restored in them the strict observance of the Rule, and gave them holy laws. He sold the furniture of the Church to feed the poor, and found the very elements subject to him to bend stubborn hearts withal. He used the Cross like a sword to drive out devils. In his old age, worn out by abstinence, watching, fasts, prayers, and punishing of the flesh, his strength utterly gave way, and he often repeated the words of David "My soul has thirsted after the strong living God; when shall I come and appear before the face of God?" When he was at the point of death, he gathered his disciples together and exhorted them to love one another, and, after a little while, ordered the following words to be written down, which he wished should be buried with him: "I, John, do believe and confess that Faith which the Holy Apostles preached, and which the Holy Fathers have ratified in the four Councils." At length, at Passignano, where he is held in the highest reverence, after a vision of angels which lasted three days, he passed away to be with the Lord, upon the 12th day of July, in the 78th year of his own age, and in that of salvation 1073. He is illustrious for countless miracles, and Celestine III enrolled his name among those of the Saints.

Lesson VII

From the Holy Gospel according to St. Matthew (Matt 5:43–48)

At that time, Jesus said unto His disciples: You have heard that it has been said, Thou shalt love thy neighbor and hate thine enemy. And so on.

Homily by St. Jerome, Priest

"But I say unto you Love your enemies, do good to them that hate you." There are many who judge of the commandments of the Lord by their own weakness, and not by the strength of His Saints and so deem Him to have commanded things impossible. These are they who think that not to hate their enemies is all that they are able to do and that to command us to love them is to command more than man's nature can bear. It behooves then to know, that this which Christ commands is not impossible, albeit perfect. This is what David did in respect of Saul and Absalom; the martyr Stephen also prayed for his enemies, even while they were stoning him and Paul could wish that himself were accursed from Christ for his persecutors. And this, Jesus Himself did, as well as taught, when He said: "Father, forgive them for they know not what they do."

Lesson VIII

For leaving undone other good works, some excuse can sometimes be given but no man can give an excuse for being loveless. Such and such a one may say to me, "I am not able to fast" but can he say, "I am not able to love"? Such and such a one may say, "I am not able to remain a virgin, I am not able to sell all that I have and give to the poor" but can he say, "I am not able to love my enemies"?

Lesson IX

This is a work wherein the feet are not wearied with running, nor the ears with hearing, neither do the hands fail from labor, that we should set up thereby an excuse to rid us of the duty. It is not said unto us "Go to the East, and search for charity; sail to the West, and you shall find love." It is into our own inner hearts that we are to go, as says the Prophet: "Bring it again to mind, O you transgressors." What is asked of us is not to be found afar off.

July 13 ~ St. Anacletus

Pope & Martyr ~ Semiduplex
All from Common
except what follows

Lessons I–III from the
occurring Scripture

Lesson IV

Anacletus was an Athenian who governed the Church in the time of the Emperor Trajan. He ordained that a Bishop should be consecrated by three Bishops and no less, that clerics should be publicly ordained to Holy Orders by their own Bishop, and that in the Mass, after the Consecration, all should afterwards Communicate. He adorned the grave of Blessed Peter, and ordered a place for burial of the Popes. He held two ordinations in the month of December, wherein he ordained five Priests, three Deacons, and six Bishops. He sat as Pope nine years, three months, and ten days. He received the crown of his testimony, and was buried on the Vatican Hill.

Lessons V–VI: from Lessons IV & V of the Second set in the Common of One Martyr (Exposition by St. Ambrose)

Lessons VII–IX from the
Common of Supreme Pontiffs
(Homily by St. Leo)

July 14 ~ St. Bonaventure

Bishop, Confessor, & Doctor ~ Duplex

All from Common except what follows

Lessons I–III from the occurring Scripture

Lesson IV

Bonaventure was born at Bagnoregio in Tuscany, in the year of our Lord 1221. In his infancy he was dangerously ill, and his mother made a vow that, if he recovered, she would dedicate him to the Order of Blessed Francis. While he was still a young man he entered the Order of Friars Minor by his own wish. Under the teaching of Alexander of Hales he advanced so quickly in learning, that in seven years he lectured publicly at Paris on the Books of the Sentences, with great applause. He afterwards explained the same Books by a brilliant Commentary. And not only by the learning of science, but also by integrity of manners and innocence of life, by humility, meekness, contempt of earthly things, and a wonderful desire for heavenly things; worthy indeed, who was to be regarded as an example of perfection and called a saint by the blessed Thomas Aquinas, to whom he was united with the greatest charity. For he, when he found Bonaventure writing the life of St. Francis said: "Let us leave one Saint to work for the other."

Lesson V

Inflamed with the fire of divine love, he was carried away by a singular affection for the passion of Christ the Lord, which he constantly meditated upon, and for the Virgin Mary, to whom he had devoted himself entirely; a fervor which he strove to arouse in others also by word and example, and to increase by written treatises. Hence that gentleness of manners, grace of speech, and charity poured out upon all, by which he won the hearts of each one very closely to himself. For this reason, barely thirty-five years old, he was elected General Master of his Order by the highest universal consent of Rome; and for twenty-two years he performed the office he undertook with admirable prudence and praise for his sanctity. He established greater regularity in discipline and amplifying the utility of the order; whom, together with the other mendicant orders, he successfully defended against the calumnies of slanderers.

Lesson VI

At the council of Lyons he was summoned by blessed Gregory X and created cardinal-bishop of Albano, and in the arduous affairs of the council he performed an eminent work by which schisms and dissensions were repaired, and ecclesiastical dogmas vindicated. In the course of these labors, in the fifty-third year of his age, in the year of Salvation 1224, he died to the greatest sorrow of all, and was honored by the universal council & the presence of the Roman Pontiff himself, to bury him. Famous for the most numerous and great miracles, Sixtus IV brought him into the number of the Saints. He wrote many things, in which, combining the highest erudition with the ardor of piety, he moves the reader by his teaching: for which reason he was distinguished with the name of Seraphic Doctor by Sixtus V.

Lessons VII–IX from the third set in the Common of Doctors (Homily by St. John Chrysostom)

July 15 ~ St. Henry

Emperor & Confessor ~ Semiduplex

All from Common except what follows

Lessons I–III from the occurring Scripture

Lesson IV

Henry II, surnamed the Pious, became successively Duke of Bavaria, King of Germany, in 1002, and the Emperor of the Romans, in 1014. His hope soared beyond the short enjoyment of a fleeting kingdom, and he aimed at the possession of an unfading crown by living as the loyal servant of the Eternal King. After he became Emperor, he earnestly set himself to the furtherance of the cause of godliness. He restored with new splendor the Churches which had been ruined by the infidels, and enriched them with many offerings and possessions. Monasteries and other godly places he either built himself, or endowed them with allowances. He founded out of his own family inheritance the Bishopric of Bamberg, and made it tributary to Blessed Peter and to the Bishop of Rome. When Benedict VIII, who had set on his head the Imperial crown, was an exile, he hospitably received him, and afterwards restored him to his See.

Lesson V

Then he was struck down with a grievous sickness in the Monastery of Monte Cassino, he was healed by an evident miracle through the intercession of St Benedict. He was a princely benefactor to the Church of Rome, for the defense of which he entered into a war against the Greeks, and took again from them the province of Apulia, which they had long possessed. He never undertook anything until he had made it a subject of prayer. And in battle he once saw the Angel of the Lord and the Holy Martyrs (Laurence, George, and Adrian) his patrons under whose protection he had placed his army, fighting for him in front of his line. With the help of God, he prevailed against the barbarous nations more by prayer than by arms. He gave his sister in marriage to King Stephen of Hungary, whom he induced to be baptized, and so brought all that country to believe in Christ. His marriage with Saint Cunegunda is one of the rare instances of the union of two virgins. When he drew near to death, he gave her back inviolate to her kinsfolk.

Lesson VI

He managed with great wisdom whatever could tend to the honor and utility of the Empire. He left in France, Italy, and Germany, splendid monuments of his godly munificence. The perfume of his saintly life spread its sweetness far and wide, and the glory of his holiness outshone the splendor of his crown. When the work of his life was done, he was called by the Lord to the possession of an eternal kingdom on the 13th day of July, in the year of salvation 1024. His body was buried in the Church of the Blessed Apostles Peter and Paul at Bamberg, and God glorified him by the miracles which began forthwith to take place at his grave. The same being duly proved, Eugenius III numbered him among the Saints.

Lessons VII–IX from the first set in the Common of Confessor Non-Bishops (Homily by St. Gregory)

July 16 ~ The Blessed Virgin Mary of Mt. Carmel

Major Duplex

All from Common except what follows

Lesson IV

It is said that many men who had kept a tradition of the holy Prophets Elias and Eliseus, were prepared by the preaching of John the Baptist to hail the coming of the Messiah, and that, when the Apostles having been filled with the Spirit upon the holy day of Pentecost, spoke with diverse tongues and worked miracles by calling upon the Name of Jesus which is above every other name, these men, seeing and being assured of the truth, straightway embraced the faith of the Gospel, and that on account of their singular love toward the Most Blessed Virgin, whose conversation and friendship they were able to enjoy, they paid her the respect of building her a little Chapel, the first which was ever raised in honor of this same most pure Maiden, and which stood upon that part of Mount Carmel from where Elias had in old days seen that manifest type of the Virgin, the little cloud like a man's hand, arising out of the sea.

Lesson V

Now to this new Chapel they repaired oftentimes every day, and in their sacred ceremonies, prayers, and praises, honored the Most Blessed Virgin as the particular Guardian of their Congregation. For this reason they came to be everywhere called the Brethren of the Blessed Mary of Mount Carmel, and the Supreme Pontiffs have not only confirmed to them the right to use this name, but have granted particular indulgences to all those who so call either the Order itself, or any particular member thereof. Her name and protection are not the only gifts which the most bountiful Virgin has given them yea, she has given them the badge of the Holy Scapular, which she delivered to the Blessed Englishman Simon Stock, even a heavenly garment whereby this Holy Order is marked, and harnessed against all assaults. Moreover, in old times, when this Order was unknown in Europe, and not a few were instant with Honorius III to put an end to it, the most gracious Virgin Mary appeared by night to said Honorius, and flatly commanded him to show kindness to the Order and to the men belonging thereto.

Lesson VI

It is not in this world only that the most Blessed Virgin has marked with her favor this Order which pleases her so well, but in the next world, where her power and mercy have a freer scope than here, they who belong to the Guild of the Scapular, who have practiced an easy abstinence, have been regular in reciting a few prayers enjoined to them, and have kept chastity according to their state of life, are comforted by her motherly love while they are being cleansed in the fire of Purgatory, and by her help are borne forward towards their home in heaven more quickly than others. The Order loaded with so many and so great gifts, has instituted a solemn Commemoration of the Most Blessed Virgin, to be made year after year, in perpetual observance, for the glory of the same Virgin.

Lessons VII–IX from the Common of The Blessed Virgin Mary (Homily by St. Bede)

July 17 ~ St. Alexius

Confessor ~ Semiduplex

All from Common except what follows

Lessons I–III from the occurring Scripture

Lesson IV

Alexius was a member of one of the noblest Roman families. Through his exceedingly great love for Jesus Christ, he received a particular command from God to leave his bride untouched upon his wedding night, and to undertake a pilgrimage to the most famous Churches of the world. For seventeen years he remained occupied in these journeys and utterly unknown. At the end of that time, his name was spoken from an image of the most holy Virgin Mary in the city of Edessa, in Syria, and when he found himself recognized, he took a ship from thence. He landed at Porto near Rome, and fared to the house of his own father, who gave him shelter as a strange beggar. He lived there unrecognized by any for seventeen years more, and then passed away to heaven, in the time of Pope Innocent I. He left behind him a writing giving his name, family, and the story of his life.

Lessons V–VI are Lessons IV & V from the second set in the Common of Confessor Non-Bishops (From the Book of Morals by Pope St. Gregory)

Lessons VII–IX from the first set in the Common of Abbots (Homily by St. Jerome)

July 18 ~ St. Camillus de Lellis

Confessor ~ Duplex

All from Common except what follows

Lessons I–III from the occurring Scripture

Lesson IV

Camillus was a son of the noble family of the Lelli, and was born at

Bacchianico, a town in the Diocese of Chieti, in the Abruzzi, in the year of our Lord 1550. His mother was sixty years of age at the time of his birth. While she was great with child, she dreamed that she brought forth a babe bearing the mark of a Cross upon his breast, and going before a troop of other babes marked likewise. When Camillus was a young man he served as a soldier, and yielded himself for a while to the sins of the world. In the twenty-fifth year of his age light from God broke upon him and in a violent fit of tears he determined to wipe away the evil relics of his past life, and to put on the new man. That very day, being the feast day of the Purification of the Most Blessed Virgin, he ran to the Friars Minor, who are commonly called Capuchins, and implored them to enroll him among them. They granted his wishes, but God was keeping him for greater things, and on this as well as on another occasion when he made the same attempt he was forced to abandon it by the increasing virulence of a loathsome running sore in the leg, with which he was afflicted. He meekly bowed himself to the will of Providence, and conquering his own wishes twice, stripped himself of the habit of the Order, which he had sought and received.

Lesson V

He went to Rome and was received as an inmate in the Hospital for Incurables. In consequence of his eminent good qualities the administration of the Hospital was committed to his charge, and he discharged this office with the most thorough trustworthiness and with a tenderness like a father's. He counted himself the slave of all the patients, and made it a religious duty to make their beds, clean them, dress their sores, and help by godly prayers and exhortations such as were in their last agony. In doing these things he showed himself a bright example of wonderful patience, indomitable firmness, and heroic charity. He became persuaded that a knowledge of letters would make him much more useful as a comforter to the dying, who were his peculiar care, and therefore, at the age of thirty-two years, he humbly went to school again, among little boys learning the first rudiments. After a time he took Priests' orders, and, in company with some companions who joined him, he laid the first foundations of the Congregation of Clerics Regular for Ministering to the Sick, a scheme against which the enemy of man made an unsuccessful struggle. Camillus heard a voice from heaven issue from an image of Christ Crucified, strengthening him, and saw the nailed hands stretched out from the Cross to protect him. He obtained from the Apostolic See an approval of his Institute, the members of which (besides the three vows of Poverty, Chastity, and Obedience), take a fourth and very stern one, by which they bind themselves to serve all sick persons, even those stricken with the plague. Saint Philip Neri, who was Confessor to Camillus, testified that he had often seen Angels prompting the members of this Congregation what they should speak when they were assisting the dying, a proof how well-pleasing in the sight of God, and how useful for the salvation of souls, is this Institution.

Lesson VI

Then he had thus given himself entirely over by these strict ties to the service of the sick, it was wonderful to see with what earnestness Camillus, broken by no weariness, and scared by no danger to himself, watched over their comfort by day and by night as long as life lasted. Becoming all things to all men, he took with cheerful readiness the most repulsive duties, discharging them with the most humble attention, and oftentimes on his knees, as though he saw Christ Himself in His suffering members. That he might be the readier to serve every one's need, he resigned the general government of his own Institute, and denied himself the indulgence in the heavenly refreshment which abundantly poured upon him, when he fixed his mind solely upon God. His tender, fatherly love toward the wretched had its brightest manifestations when Rome was stricken first by a contagious sickness, and then by famine, and Nola in Campagna suffered from a frightful plague. His love to God and to his neighbor was so glorious that he earned the nickname of Angel, and found Angels helping him in the difficulties of his diverse journeyings. He had the gifts of prophecy and healing, and could read the secret thoughts of men's hearts. At his prayer, food was multiplied, and water turned into wine. His want of sleep, fasting, and unceasing work wore him down till he seemed nothing but skin and bones. He suffered from a complication of five different painful and incurable diseases, which he was accustomed to call the Lord's mercies to him, and which he bore bravely. He died at Rome on the day which he had himself foretold, the fourteenth of July, in the year of salvation 1614, and of his own age the 65th. He had received the Sacraments, and fell asleep in the Lord in an attempt to utter the sweet names of Jesus and Mary, while the Priest was reciting the words of the Ritual: "Gentle and joyous may the Countenance of Christ Jesus appear to thee." He was famous for many miracles, and Benedict XIV solemnly enrolled him in the Kalendar of the Saints.

Lesson VII

From the Holy Gospel according to St. John (John 15:12–16)

At that time, Jesus said unto His disciples: This is My commandment, That ye love one another, as I have loved you. And so on.

Homily by St. Augustine, Bishop

What do we think, my brethren? Is this His only commandment, this, That we love one another? Is there not another and a greater, the commandment to love God? Or has God commanded us only to love, so that we need seek to do no more? Surely the Apostle commends three things: "And now abides Faith, Hope, Charity, these three but the greatest of these is Charity." And although in charity, that is, in love, he included the two first and great commandments, and charity he called the greatest, yet is charity not said to be alone. Concerning Faith, concerning Hope, how much is commanded us? Who can gather them all together? Who can reckon them all? And yet let us consider how the same Apostle says: "Love is the fulfilling of the Law."

Lesson VIII

Where, therefore, Charity is, what can be lacking or where Charity is not, what can there be availing? The devil believes and loves not, but there is no one that loves and believes not. Useless though it be, it is still possible for one that loves not, to hope to be forgiven but for one that loves it is impossible to give up hope. Therefore, where love is, there also must faith and hope be, and where there is love toward our neighbor there also must be love toward God. For one that loves not God, how can he love his neighbor as himself, seeing he hates himself, for he is a blasphemous, wicked wretch, and the lover of wickedness is not the lover, but the deadly enemy of his own self.

If we hold fast to this commandment of the Lord which bids us to love one another, we shall do whatsoever else He commands us, for all else is included in this. The difference between this love and the earthly love wherewith men use to love one another, is made, where it is added, "as I have loved you." To what end did Christ love us, but that we may be able to reign with Christ? To this end then let us also love one another, and so with a love different to the love of others, who love not one another to this end, because in this sense they love not at all. But they that love themselves to possess God, love themselves: therefore, they love God, that they may love themselves. This love have not all men: but few love themselves that God may be all in all.

Lesson IX—Commemoration of Sts. Symphorosa & Seven Sons, Martyrs

Symphorosa was a woman of Tivoli, the wife of the martyr Getulius, unto whom she bore seven sons, named respectively, Crescentius, Julian, Nemesius, Primitivus, Justin, Stacteus, and Eugene, all of whom were arrested along with their mother, in the reign of the Emperor Hadrian, for professing the Christian faith. Their love was tried by many and diverse torments, and their mother who had taught them their religion, was their leader to martyrdom. A stone was tied round her neck and she was thrown into the river. Her body was found and buried by her brother Eugene. The next day, being the 18th of July, the seven brethren were tied each to a stake, and all put to death in diverse ways. Crescentius was stabbed in the throat, Julian in the breast, Nemesius in the heart, and Primitivus in the navel. Justin was hacked limb from limb. Stacteus was shot to death with darts. Eugene was cut into two parts across his breast (from the head downwards). Thus were these eight sacrifices of sweet savor offered up to God. Their bodies were thrown into a deep pit, on the road between Rome and Tivoli, at the ninth milestone from Rome, but were afterwards brought to Rome and buried in the Church of the Holy Angels in-the-Fish-market.

July 19 ~ St. Vincent de Paul

Confessor ~ Duplex

All from Common except what follows

Lessons I–III from the occurring Scripture

Lesson IV

Vincent de Paul was a Frenchman by nation, and was born at Puy, not far from Dax in Gascony, upon the 24th day of April, in the year of salvation 1576. From a little child he showed remarkable charity towards the poor. His father removed him from keeping his cattle, in order to give him a school education, and he learnt earthly things at Dax, and theology both at Toulouse and at Saragossa. He took Priest's orders, and a degree in Divinity. In 1605, he was taken prisoner by Mohammedan pirates, who carried him off, and sold him for a slave in Africa. In his slavery he converted his owner, who was an apostate, back to Christ. Under the protection of the Mother of God, Vincent escaped from the Barbary coast. He first visited the thresholds of the Apostles, and afterwards returned to France. He was the saintly Rector first of the Parish of Clichy, and afterwards of that of Châtillon. He was appointed by the King, Chaplain General for the galleys of France, and worked with extraordinary zeal for the health of the souls both of those who commanded and of the convicts who rowed. He was made Superior of the Nuns of the Visitation by St Francis de Sales, and discharged this duty for about forty years, with a wisdom which so approved itself to the judgment of their holy Founder, that he was used to say he knew no worthier Priest than Vincent.

Lesson V

The preaching of the Gospel to the poor, especially peasants, was the work at which he toiled unweariedly, till he was disabled by age. To this special work he bound himself and the members of the Congregation which he founded under the missionary Congregation of Secular Priests, by a perpetual vow approved by the Holy See. How great were his labors for bettering the discipline of the clergy, is attested by the building of Seminaries for the final education of young clerics, the number of meetings of Priests to discuss holy things, and the religious exercises preparatory to Ordination, for which, as well as for pious retreats by laymen, he wished that the houses belonging to his Institute should be always freely open. To spread wider the growth of faith and piety, he sent his Gospel laborers not only into the several provinces of France, but also into Italy, Poland, Scotland, and Ireland, and also to the Berbers and

Indians. He assisted Louis XIII on his deathbed, and the Queen Anne of Austria, mother of Louis XIV, put him upon the young King's Council of Conscience during the Regency, in which position it was his unceasing effort that none but the most worthy should be named to churches and monasteries, that civil contests, duels, and creeping errors, at which he shuddered as soon as he sensed them, should be put down, and that all men should yield the obedience which was due to the decisions of the Apostolic See.

Lesson VI

There was no kind of misery which he did not strive with fatherly tenderness to relieve. Christians groaning in Mohammedan slavery, foundlings, deformed children, young maidens exposed to danger, houseless nuns, fallen women, convicts sent to the galleys, sick foreigners, disabled workmen, lunatics, and beggars without number, all these he relieved, and devoutly housed in diverse charitable institutions which remain to this day. When Lorraine, Champagne, Picardy, and other districts were desolated by plague, famine, and war, he made immense efforts for their relief. He founded many charitable societies, to find and aid the unfortunate. Among these are remarkable that of Matrons, and that of Sisters of Charity which has been so widely spread. By those of the Cross, of Providence, and of St. Genevieve he aimed at bringing up young girls as schoolmistresses. Amid all these and other most anxious business-matters, he remained always looking simply to God, kind to all, true to himself, plain, upright, and lowly. From all honors, riches, and pleasures, he ever shrank, and was heard to say, that nothing gave him any pleasure, except in Christ Jesus, Whom it was his wish in all things to follow. With a body worn out with hardships, work, and old age, he gently fell asleep in the house of St. Lazarus at Paris, the chief house of the Congregation of the Missions, upon the 27th day of September, in the year of salvation 1660, and of his own age the 85th. He was famous on account of his life, his works, and his miracles, and Clement XII inscribed his name among those of the saints, appointing for his feast-day the 19th day of the month of July. Finally, at the earnest prayer of many prelates, Leo XIII proclaimed and established this hero of charity, illustrious for his services to all classes of men, as the patron before God of all charitable societies throughout the whole Catholic world which derive their origin in any way from his institution.

Lessons VII–IX from the Common of Evangelists (Homily by St. Gregory)

July 20 ~ St. Jerome Emiliani

Confessor ~ Duplex

All from Common except what follows

Lessons I–III from the occurring Scripture

Lesson IV

Jerome was born at Venice, of the Patrician family of the Miani, in the year of our Lord 1481. He was trained up to be a soldier, and in 1508, in the most troublesome times of the Commonwealth, he commanded the fortress of Castelnuovo at Quero, in the mountains near Treviso. The citadel having being captured, he was chained hand and foot, and cast into a filthy prison. When all hope of help from man had forsaken him, the Most Blessed Virgin, in answer to his prayers, mercifully came to him, loosed his fetters, and brought him unhurt within sight of Treviso, through the midst of the enemy, who held all the roads. As soon as he entered the city of Treviso, as an acknowledgment of the favor he had received, he hung up his chains, which he had brought away with him, at an Altar of the Mother of God, to whom he had vowed himself. After his return to Venice he gave himself up to godly works. Amid his great tenderness to all the poor, his compassion was chiefly roused by the fatherless little boys who wandered through the city starving and filthy; them he took into a house conducted by himself, where at his own cost he provided them with board, lodging, clothing, and a Christian education.

Lesson V

In those days there came to Venice blessed Cajetan of Tiene, and Peter Carafa, who was afterwards Paul IV. They were pleased with the spirit of Jerome, and with his new Asylum for Orphans, and took him to the Hospital for Incurables, as well to bring up Orphans, as to extend his charity equally to the sick. Soon after, by the advice of the same, he went to the mainland, and built orphanages first at Brescia, then at Bergamo and Como. His chief foundations were at Bergamo, where besides an orphanage for little boys, and another for little girls, he opened a house of Refuge for repentant harlots, being the first institution of that kind in that part of the world. In the end he went to dwell at Somascha, a hamlet in the district of Bergamo, close to the frontiers of the Venetian territory, and there made a house for himself and his disciples, and gave shape to a congregation, which is generally called the Congregation of Somaschans. This congregation grew and spread, and found its work not only in the education of orphans and the service of Churches, but also in a wider usefulness to the Christian Commonwealth, by training up lads in letters and good manners. Saint Pius V enrolled it among the religious Orders, and other Popes have given it diverse privileges.

Lesson VI

Jerome went to Milan and to Ticino to gather orphans together, and in both places he gathered a multitude of little boys for whom the charity of noblemen enabled him to provide board, lodging, clothes, and schooling. He returned to Somascha, and, still making himself all things to all men, refused no toil by which he saw that he could be of any use to his neighbor. He was used to go about in the fields, helping the reapers in their work, and meanwhile teaching them in the mysteries of the faith. He was very patient in cleansing and healing the heads of little boys foul with lice, and proved so successful a physician to the stinking sores of the poor country-folk, that he got a reputation for having the gift of healing. He found a cave in the mountain which hangs over Somascha, and there he would hide himself, passing whole days without food or drink, and oftentimes scourging himself, continuing in prayer long into the night, and taking his short sleep upon the bare rock, in expiation of his own sins and the sins of others. In the far end of this cave, there drips out of the dry stone some water, which is said by an unwavering tradition to have come there at the prayers of the man of God. It drops freely even to this day, and is taken to diverse places at a distance, where it often has a healing effect upon the sick. At length an infectious disorder broke out in all the valley, and Jerome, who nursed the sick and carried the dead to burial on his own shoulders, caught it, and died a precious death, as he had himself foretold, upon the 8th day of February, in the fifty-seventh year of his age, and that of salvation 1537. He was famous for many miracles, both during his life and after his death. Benedict X solemnly enrolled his name among those of the Blessed, and Clement XIII inserted it in the Kalendar of the Saints.

Lesson VII

From the Holy Gospel according to St. Matthew (Matt 19:13–21)

At that time, there were brought unto Jesus little children that He should put His Hands on them, and pray. And so on.

Homily by St. John Chrysostom

Why did the disciples rebuke them that brought them? From a thought of His dignity. What therefore did He? To teach them to be lowly, and to be above the niceness of the world, He took the little children, and embraced them in His Arms, and declared that of such is the kingdom of heaven as also He had said above. And we also, if we would be heirs of the kingdom of heaven, let us seek with great earnestness this virtue. For this is the highest peak of philosophy, to be simple and wise: this is the life of an Angel. The mind of a little child is free from all the diseases of the mind; a little child keeps no remembrance of injuries, but goes unto such as have inflicted them, as if unto friends, and as if nothing had happened. Although his mother give him stripes, yet a little child ever seeks her, and puts her before all.

Lesson VIII

If thou wert to show him a Queen adorned with her crown, he would not prefer her before his own mother, in raiment however faded, and he would rather see her, albeit unkempt, than the Queen in all her glorious apparel. For his use is to account of things whether they be his own, or of others, not by the standard of poverty and riches, but by that of love alone. He seeks no more than he needs. When he is satisfied with milk, he leaves the breast. The things that press upon us, such as the loss of money, and the like, do not press upon him, nor do the same transitory things that please us, please him, neither does he gaze with admiration at loveliness of shape. Therefore Christ said: "of such is the kingdom of heaven," to make us do by force of will what little children do by nature.

Lesson IX

The Pharisees' usual springs of action were spite and vanity; therefore the Lord everywhere commands His disciples to be simple, and in teaching the one, points silently at the other class. Nothing breeds pride so much as princedom and precedence. Since, then, His disciples were to receive much honor throughout all the world, He warns their minds beforehand, and lets them not stumble into the snare of men, nor go seeking for honors from the mob, nor put themselves forward before others. It is true, these may seem little things, but they give occasion for very great evils. It was when they were placed in these positions, that the Pharisees fell into their direst misfortunes; from looking for salutations, and foremost or good places, they got into a keen desire of distinction, and from that into ungodliness.

July 21 ~ St. Praxedes

Virgin ~ Simplex

Lessons I–II from the occurring Scripture

Lesson III

This Praxedes was a maiden of Rome, and the sister of the maiden Pudentiana. When the Emperor Marcus Antoninus was hunting down the Christians, she followed them constantly with money, labour, comfort, and every helpful office of Christian charity. Some she hid in her house, some she exhorted to firmness in professing the faith, of some she buried the bodies. For them that were in prison, and them that were toiling in slavery, she supplied every need. At last the sight of such butchery of Christians was more than she could bear, and she implored God that if it were expedient for her to die, He would release her from such suffering. And so upon the 21st day of July she was called away to receive the reward of her piety in heaven. Pastor the Priest laid her body in the grave of her father (Pudens) and her sister Pudentiana, which was in the cemetery of Priscilla, upon the Salarian Way.

July 22 ~ St. Mary Magdalene

Penitent ~ Duplex

All from Common except what follows

Lesson I ~ Cant 3:1–4

From the Canticle of Canticles

In my bed by night I sought him whom my soul loveth: I sought him, and found him not. I will rise, and will go about the city: in the streets and the broad ways I will seek him whom my soul loveth: I sought him, and I found him not. The watchmen who keep the city, found me: Have you seen him, whom my soul loveth? When I had a little passed by them, I found him whom my soul loveth: I held him: and I will not let him go, till I bring him into my mother's house, and into the chamber of her that bore me.

Lesson II - Cant 8:1–4

Who shall give thee to me for my brother, sucking the breasts of my mother, that I may find thee without, and kiss thee, and now no man may despise me? I will take hold of thee, and bring thee Into my mother's house: there thou shalt teach me, and I will give thee a cup of spiced wine and new wine of my pomegranates. His left hand under my head, and his right hand shall embrace me. I adjure you, O daughters of Jerusalem, that you stir not up, nor awake my love till she please.

Lesson III - Cant 8:5–7

Who is this that comes up from the desert, flowing with delights, leaning upon her beloved? Under the apple tree I raised thee up: there thy mother was corrupted, there she was defloured that bore thee. Put me as a seal upon thy heart, as a seal upon thy arm, for love is strong as death, jealousy as hard as hell, the lamps thereof are fire and flames. Many waters cannot quench charity, neither can the floods drown it: if a man should give all the substance of his house for love, he shall despise it as nothing.

Lesson IV

Sermon by St. Gregory, Pope

Mary Magdalene, who was a sinful woman in the city, through love of the truth, washed away in her tears the defilement of her sins, and the words of the Truth are fulfilled which He spoke: "Her sins, which are many, are forgiven; for she loved much." She who had remained chilly in sin, became fiery through love. When even His disciples went away again unto their own home, Mary still stood without at the sepulchre of Christ, weeping. She sought Him Whom her soul loved, but she found Him not. She searched for Him with tears; she yearned with strong desire for Him Who, she believed, had been taken away. And thus it befell her, that being the only one who had remained to seek Him, she was the only one that saw Him. Indubitably, the strength of a good work is perseverance.

Lesson V

At first when she sought Him, she found Him not; she persevered, so she might find Him; and this was so, that her longing might grow in earnestness, and so in its earnestness might find what it sought. Hence is it that the Bride in the Canticle of Canticles says as representing the Church: "By night on my bed I sought him whom my soul loves." We seek on our bed for Him Whom our soul loves, when, having got some little rest in this world, we still sigh for the Presence of our Redeemer but it is by night that we so seek Him, for though our mind may be on the alert for Him, yet still He is hidden from our eyes by the darkness that now is.

Lesson VI

But if we find not Him Whom our soul loves, it remains that we should rise and go about the city, that is, by thought and questioning, go through the holy Church of the elect, seek Him in the streets, and in the broad ways, that is, walk anxiously looking about us both in the narrow and the broad places, that if we can, we may find His footsteps there; for there are some even of those who live for the world, from whom something may be learnt to be imitated by a godly man. As we thus go wakefully about, the watchmen, that keep the city, find us; the holy Fathers, who are the watchmen of the bulwarks of the Church, come to meet our good endeavors, and to teach us either by their words or by their writings. And it needs but a little to pass from them, but we find Him Whom our soul loves; for albeit our Redeemer in lowliness became a man among men, yet by right of His Divine Nature He is still above men.

Lesson VII

From the Holy Gospel according to St. Luke (Luke 7:36–50)

At that time One of the Pharisees desired Jesus that He would eat with him. And He went into the Pharisee's house, and sat down to meat. And so on.

Homily by St. Augustine, Bishop

You have listened carefully to the Gospel while it was being read, so that the thing told has, as it were, passed before the eyes of your heart. You have seen in your mind's eye, albeit not with bodily sight, the Lord Jesus Christ sitting down to meat in the Pharisee's house, and not refusing when He is bidden of him. You have seen also an infamous woman of the city, one of utterly bad character, a sinner, thrusting herself an uninvited guest, into the banquet where her Healer was sitting, and seeking health at His hands with pious shamelessness; thrusting herself in eager for mercy, as though eager for the feast. She knew under what a disease she labored, and she knew that He unto Whom she came was mighty to cure it.

Lesson VIII

She drew near therefore, not unto the Lord's Head, but unto His Feet. She that had so long walked the paths of sin betook her unto the Feet that went about doing good. She first poured forth heartfelt tears, and washed the Lord's Feet with the humble service of her acknowledgment, wiped them with her hair, kissed them, and anointed them. Her silence cried aloud, next in words but in manifested love. The Pharisee, who had desired the Lord Jesus Christ that He would eat with him, belonged to that class of proud men concerning whom the Prophet Isaias says of people which say, "Stand by thyself, come not near to me; for I am holier than thou." When therefore he saw how this woman touched the Lord's Feet with her tears, her kisses, her hair, and her ointment, he spoke within himself, saying: "This Man, if He were a Prophet, would have known who and what manner of woman this is that touches Him; for she is a sinner."

Lesson IX

O Pharisee, inviter and scorner of the Lord! Thou feedest the Lord, and thou knowest not Him by whom thou are to be fed! From whence dost thou know that the Lord knows not who and what manner of woman this is, save from this, that she is allowed to draw near unto Him, and that He suffers her to kiss His Feet, to wipe them, and to anoint them? Ought not an unclean woman to have been permitted to do these things to clean feet? If such a woman had drawn near to the feet of this Pharisee, he would have said to her what Isaias puts into the mouth of such: "Stand by thyself, come not near to me, for I am holier than thou." But she came unto the Lord unclean that she might go away cleansed, sick, that she might go away healed, with confession, that she might go away with thanksgiving.

July 23 ~ St. Apollinaris

Bishop & Martyr ~ Duplex

All from Common except what follows

Lessons I–III from the occurring Scripture

Lesson IV

Apollinaris came from Antioch to Rome with the Prince of the Apostles, and was by him ordained a Bishop, and sent to Ravenna to preach the Gospel of the Lord Christ. He had already converted a great number of persons to the Christian Faith, when the idolatrous priests caught him and gave him a sharp flogging. A second riot was got up against him on account of one Boniface, a nobleman who had long been dumb, speaking, and his daughter being delivered from an unclean spirit. On this occasion Apollinaris was flogged again, and made to walk barefoot over hot embers. The fire did him no harm, and he was expelled from the city.

Lesson V

Apollinaris lay hid for a while with certain Christians. Thence he went to Emilia, where he restored to life the dead daughter of the Patrician Rufinus, so that the whole household of Rufinus might believe in Jesus Christ. This affair greatly incensed the Præfect, who sent for Apollinaris, and earnestly dealt with him to induce him to cease spreading the Christian Faith in that city. As Apollinaris paid no heed to the Præfect's orders, he was tortured on the rack, boiling water poured on his wounds, and his mouth bruised with a stone, after which he was chained and cast into prison. On the fourth day he was put on board a ship and sent into banishment. The ship was wrecked, and he so came to Mysia, thence to the shores of the Danube, and afterwards into Thrace.

Lesson VI

However, the demon in the temple of Serapis declared that he could not give oracles, while the disciple of the Apostle Peter abode in these parts, and after a long search, Apollinaris was found and commanded again to take ship. Thus he went back to Ravenna, where he was denounced by the same idolatrous priests as before, and given into the keeping of a centurion. This centurion was a secret worshipper of Christ, and in the night he let Apollinaris go. When it became known, some of the officers of justice followed after him, caught him on the road, beat him till they thought he was dead, and left him. Some Christians took him up, but on the seventh day, still exhorting them to stand firm in the Faith, he departed this life with the glorious splendor of martyrdom. His body was buried near the wall of the city.

Lesson VII

From the Holy Gospel according to St. Luke (Luke 22:24–30)

At that time, There was a strife among the disciples, which of them should be accounted the greatest. And so on.

Homily by St. Ambrose, Bishop

"My kingdom," our God has said, "is not of this world." Man, then, must strive, not to be equal with God, but to be like unto God. Christ alone is the full image of God, as being the brightness of His Father's glory, and the express image of His Person. But the righteous man is made after the image of God, insofar as, for the sake of following the example of his God, he, through knowledge of God, sets no esteem upon this world, and looks down upon all carnal motions of the will, through having taken in that Word whereby we are fed unto life everlasting and this is the end whereto we eat the Body of Christ, namely, that we may have eternal life.

Lesson VIII

The reward which is promised unto us is not meat and drink, but a part in that grace and that life which come down from heaven. Neither are the twelve thrones to be understood as meaning chairs for bodies to sit in, but as meaning a dignity like that of God Himself, wherein they that have left all and followed Christ shall judge as Christ does, not by way of cross-examinations, but by simple knowledge of the heart, rewarding the good, and condemning the evil. Thus are the Apostles erected into a spiritual tribunal, for the rewarding of faith and the cursing of unbelief, by their virtue disproving errors, and laying upon blasphemers the just punishment of hatred.

Lesson IX

Let us, then, turn about, and look well to it that there be no strife among us, which of us shall be accounted the greatest. That this strife arose among the Apostles, is not an excuse but a caution for us. If it was only after a while that Peter was converted, Peter who had started up at the first command of the Lord, who can promise himself to be converted forthwith? Beware, then, of boasting; beware of the world. He who was commanded to strengthen his brethren was he who was able to say, "Behold, we have forsaken all, and have followed thee."

July 25 ~ St. James the Apostle

Duplex II Class

All from Common
except what follows

Lesson IV

James, the Son of Zebedee and brother of the Apostle John, was a Galilean, and with his brother one of the first of His Apostles whom the Lord called, whileas they were in a ship with Zebedee their father, mending their nets and they immediately left the ship, and their father, and followed Him. And He surnamed them "Boanerges," which is, "The Sons of Thunder." Peter, and James, and John, were the three Apostles whom the Saviour loved best; them He took and brought up into a high mountain apart, and was transfigured before them; when He went to the house of the ruler of the synagogue to raise his daughter from the dead, He suffered no man to follow Him save Peter, and James, and John; and, at the last, just before the Jews took Him, when He comes unto a place called Gethsemane, and says unto the disciples: "Sit here, while I go and pray yonder." He took with Him Peter and the two sons of Zebedee.

Lesson V

After Jesus Christ was ascended into Heaven, James preached how that He was God, and led many in Judaea and Samaria to the Christian Faith. A while afterward, he went to Spain, and there he brought some to Christ, of whom seven were afterwards ordained Bishops by Blessed Peter, and were the first such sent into that country. From Spain, James went back to Jerusalem, where he taught the Faith to diverse persons, and, among others, to the Magus Hermogenes. Thereupon Herod Agrippa, who had been raised to the kingdom under the Emperor Claudius, to curry favor with the Jews, condemned James to death for his firm confession that Jesus Christ is God. The officer who led James to the judgment-seat, at sight of the courage wherewith he was ready to offer up his testimony, declared himself also to be a Christian.

Lesson VI

As they were being hurried to execution, this man asked pardon of James, and the Apostle kissed him, saying, "Peace be to you." James healed a paralytic, and immediately afterwards both the prisoners were beheaded. The body of the Apostle was afterwards taken to Compostela, in the province of Galicia, in Spain, where his grave is very famous. Multitudes of pilgrims from all parts of the earth betake themselves there to pray, out of sheer piety or in fulfillment of vows. The Birthday of James is kept by the Church upon this day, which is that of the bringing of his body to Compostela. It was around Easter that he bore witness to Jesus Christ with his blood, at Jerusalem, being the first of the Apostles to do so.

Lesson VII

From the Holy Gospel according to St. Matthew (Matt 20:20–23)

At that time, came to Jesus the mother of Zebedee's children, with her sons, worshipping Him, and desiring a certain thing of Him. And so on.

Homily by St. John Chrysostom

Let no man be troubled if we say that the Apostles were still imperfect, for the mystery of the Cross was not yet finished, the grace of the Spirit had not yet been shed abroad in their hearts. If thou wilt behold them in their strength, consider them such as they became after the grace of the Spirit was given them, and thou wilt perceive that they had trodden underfoot every vain desire. This is the reason why their present imperfection is made known unto us, that is, that thou mayest see how great a change could be forthwith wrought by grace. But nevertheless let us now look how they came unto Christ, and what they said. "Master," they said, "we wish that Thou shouldest do for us whatsoever we shall ask." And He said unto them: "What do you wish?" He responded not, surely, that He knew not what their wish was, but that He would make them answer, and so uncover the wound, to lay a plaster upon it.

Lesson VIII

Their wish proceeded from earthly motives, and they were shy and ashamed to express it, and therefore they took Christ aside, and so asked Him. The Evangelist says: "For they were gone apart, that they might not be discovered of them and then they told Him what they sought." To me it seems most likely that they had heard how that the disciples should sit upon twelve thrones; they were eager to obtain for themselves the chiefest places at this enthronement; they knew that the Lord loved them better than the most of the others; but they feared that Peter would still be preferred before them; and therefore they made bold to say: "Say that one may sit at thy right, and the other at thy left." They urged Him, saying: "Say it." And what answered He? To show that they were asking no spiritual gift, nor even knew for themselves what they were asking, nor would have asked it if they had known what it was, Jesus said unto them: "You know not what you ask, you know not how great a thing, how wonderful a thing this is, a thing which even is not Mine to give."

Lesson IX

And He said moreover: "Can you drink of the chalice that I shall drink, and be baptized with the baptism by which I am baptized?" Behold how He turns their thoughts at once another way, speaking to them of things altogether different, as though He said, "You come unto Me treating of honors and crowns, but I speak unto you of wrestling and sweat. This is not yet the time of reward, neither is My glory immediately to be revealed; but now death and danger are present with you." But consider how, by the manner of His questioning, He does both exhort and invite them. He says not "Are you able to bear death? Are you able to shed your blood?" but: "How are you able to drink the chalice?" Whereto He presently invites them, saying: "the chalice that I shall drink of" that He may make them readier for the strife by knowing that it is a strife which they are to share with Him.

July 26 ~ St. Anne, Mother of the Blessed Virgin Mary

Duplex II Class

All from Common of Non-Virgins except what follows

Lesson IV

Sermon by St. John Damascene

The home of Anne is set before us, wherein to see an example both of married and of maiden life, the one in the person of the mother, the other in that of the daughter, whereof the one has but now ceased to be barren, and the other is in a little while destined, beyond the course of nature, to become the Mother of the Messiah by a singular birth, specially designed by God to build up our nature anew. It is with reason then that Anne, filled with the Holy Ghost, with joyful and jubilant spirit sings aloud: "Rejoice with me, for out of my barren womb I have borne the bud of promise, and, as I have longed, I nourish at my breasts the fruit of benediction. I have laid aside the mournful garments of barrenness, and put on the joyful raiment of fruitfulness. Let Anna the adversary of Phenenna make merry with me, and join with me in singing of this new and unhoped-for wonder that is wrought in me."

Lesson V

"Let Sarah be glad that was joyfully pregnant in her old age, and was a shadow cast before of my conception that hitherto have been barren. Let all the barren and fruitless break forth into singing, when they behold in what a wondrous way I have been visited from heaven." Let all mothers likewise, that like Anne are gifted with fruitfulness, say: "Blessed be He That gave their desire unto them that besought Him, That gave fruitfulness unto her that was barren, and That granted unto her that from her should bud forth the joy-bringing Virgin, who, according to the flesh, was Mother of God, and whose womb was a heaven wherein He dwelt Whom no place can contain." Let us also with them offer our praises to her that was called barren, but now is become the mother of a virgin; let us say unto her in the words of the Scripture: "O how blessed is the house of David" from whence thou art sprung, and that womb wherein God has fashioned the ark of His holiness, that is, her, by whom He was Himself conceived without seed.

Lesson VI

Blessed art thou, and thrice blessed, whom God has so blessed as to make thee to bring forth, as His own gift, the infant Mary, whose very name is highly honorable, out of whom Christ, the Flower of life, blossomed a maiden whose rising is glorious, and whose delivery is worth more than the world. We also, O woman most blessed, do wish thee joy. Truly thou hast brought forth what we have all hoped for, and God has given us, namely, the offspring of promise. Blessed indeed art thou, and blessed is the fruit of thy womb. The tongues of all the godly do magnify thy seed, and every glad word is spoken concerning her of whom thou art delivered. Right it truly is, and most worthy to praise her who received a revelation from the goodness of God, and bore for us such and so great a fruit, from whom sweet Jesus sprang.

Lessons VII–IX from the Common of Non-Virgins (Homily by St. Gregory)

July 27 ~ St. Pantaleon

Martyr ~ Simplex

Lessons I–II from the occurring Scripture

Lesson III

Pantaleon was of a noble family of Nicomedia, and was a physician by trade. Hermolaus the Priest taught him well the faith of Jesus Christ, and he was baptized. A little while after, he persuaded his father Eustorgius to become a Christian. He afterwards duly preached the Faith of the Lord Christ at Nicomedia, and exhorted all to embrace His doctrine. For this he was tortured under the Emperor Diocletian, first on the rack, and then by putting red-hot metal to his body. He bore all the bitterness of his torments with a quiet and brave heart, and at last stricken with the sword, grasped the crown of martyrdom.

July 28 ~ Sts. Nazarius & Celsus: Martyrs, Victor I: Pope & Martyr, & Innocent I: Pope & Confessor

Semiduplex

All from Common of Many Martyrs except what follows

Lessons I–III from the occurring Scripture

Lesson IV

Nazarius was baptized by the blessed Pope Linus, and afterwards went to Gaul. There he met with the boy Celsus, whom he instructed in Christian precepts, and baptized. They went together to Trier, and, in the persecution under Nero, were both thrown into the sea, from which they had a marvelous escape. Later on, they came to Milan, where they spread the Faith of Christ, and as they remained firm in declaring that He is God, the Præfect Anolinus had them beheaded. Their bodies were buried outside the Roman gate, and lay long unknown, till, by a revelation from God, Blessed Ambrose found them, spattered with fresh blood, as though they had only a little while before undergone martyrdom. They were taken up from thence, carried into the city, and laid in an honorable sepulchre.

Lesson V

Victor I was by birth an African, and governed the Church in the time of the Emperor Severus. He confirmed the decree of Pius I that the Holy Pascha should be kept upon the Lord's Day. To bring this rule into use, Councils were held in many places, and in the First Synod of Nice it was decided that the Holy Paschal Day should be kept after the 14th day of the month (Nisan), lest the Christians should seem to be copying the Jews. Victor decided that if need be, baptism can be administered with any water, as long as it be natural. He cast out of the Church Theodotus the tanner, of Constantinople, who taught that Christ was nothing but a man. He wrote upon the subject of the Passover, and some other small works. He held two Ordinations in the month of December, wherein he ordained four Priests, seven Deacons, and twelve Bishops for diverse places. He received the crown of his testimony, and was buried at the Vatican on the 28th day of July, in the year of our Lord 197. He sat in the throne of Peter nine years, one month, and twenty-eight days.

Lesson VI

Innocent I of Albano flourished in the time of St. Jerome and St. Augustine. Concerning him, St. Jerome says, writing to Demetrias: "Keep firm hold on the faith of holy Innocent, who is the heir and the child of the Apostolic See, and of Anastasius of blessed memory, and receive not any strange doctrine, how wise and acute soever thou mayest count thyself." Orosius writes that God kept Innocent at Ravenna so he might not see the destruction of the Roman people, even as righteous Lot was withdrawn by God's Providence from being at the annihilation of Sodom. He condemned Pelagius and Cælestius, and, against their heresy, made a decree that little children, even those whose mother was a Christian, must be born again in baptism, that the new birth may wash away in them the stain which they have contracted in their conception. He approved also that a Fast should be kept upon Saturday in memory of the Lord Christ's lying in the grave on that day. He sat in the throne of Peter fifteen years, one month, and ten days. He held four Ordinations in the month of December, and made therein thirty Priests, fifteen Deacons, and forty-four Bishops for diverse places. He was buried in the Catacomb of Pontian, [The Cemetery called "at the Capped Bear"] in the year of Our Lord 417.

Lessons VII–IX from the first set in the Common of Many Martyrs (Homily by St. Gregory)

July 29 ~ St. Martha

Virgin ~ Semiduplex

All from Common except what follows

Lessons I–III from the occurring Scripture

Lesson IV

Martha was the daughter of noble and wealthy parents, but is best known as having been the hostess of the Lord Christ. After He was ascended into Heaven, Martha, along with her brother Lazarus, her sister Mary Magdalene, her waiting-woman Marcella, Maximin, who was one of the seventy-two disciples of the Lord Christ, and who had baptized the whole of the family, and many other Christians, was taken by the Jews, and turned adrift upon the open sea in a ship without sail or oars, to meet with certain wreck, but by the governance of God the ship came to land at Marseilles with all safe.

Lesson V

Through this miracle and the preaching of the Saints, the people of Marseilles first, and then those of Aix, and of the uttermost tribes, believed in Christ, and Lazarus was made Bishop of Marseilles, and Maximin Bishop of Aix. Mary Magdalene, who sat still at Jesus' Feet, being altogether given to prayer and the contemplation of heavenly blessedness, that that good part which she had chosen might not be taken away from her, withdrew herself to a great cave in an exceedingly high mountain, where she lived for thirty years, utterly cut off from all conversation with men, and every day during that time was carried up by Angels into the air, to listen to them that dwell in heaven praising God.

Lesson VI

Martha, by the wondrous holiness and charity of her life, drew upon herself the love and wonder of all the inhabitants of Marseilles. She withdrew herself in company with some other honorable women into a place out of the way of men, where she lived long, with great praise for piety and discretion. She foretold her own death long before, and at last, illustrious for miracles, passed away to be ever with the Lord, upon the 29th day of July. Her body is held in great worship at Tarascon.

Lesson VII

From the Holy Gospel according to St. Luke (Luke 10:38–42)

At that time: Jesus entered into a certain village, and a certain woman, named Martha, received Him into her house. And so on.

Homily by St. Augustine, Bishop

The words of our Lord Jesus Christ which have just been read from the Gospel, give us to wit that there is one thing toward which we are making our way, all the while that we are striving amid the diverse cares of this world. Thitherward we make our way, while we are still strangers and pilgrims, unpossessed as yet of any abiding city, still on the journey, not yet come home, still hoping, not yet enjoying. Still thitherward let us make our way, not slothfully nor by fits and starts, but so that some day we may arrive there. Martha and Mary were sisters, not in the flesh only, but also in godliness; together, they clung unto the Lord; together, with one heart they served the Lord present in the Flesh.

Lesson VIII

Martha received Him into her house. It was just as strangers are received, but it was the handmaiden receiving her Lord, the sick receiving her Saviour, the creature receiving her Creator. She received Him, to give bodily food unto Him by

Whom she herself was to be fed unto eternal life. It had been the Lord's will to take upon Him the form of a servant, to be fed by servants, and in that form of a servant which He had taken upon Him. This was His good pleasure, to offer Himself as a subject for hospitality. He had Flesh, wherein He was sometimes hungry and thirsty; but know you not how that, when He was in the desert and was hungry, angels came and ministered unto Him? Himself it was therefore, That gave unto them of whom He was to be fed, the wherewithal. And what wonder is this if we consider how holy Elias, coming from being fed by the ministry of ravens, asked bread of the widow, and himself gave her the wherewithal to feed him? Had God failed to feed Elias when He sent him unto the widow? God forbid. He did so that He might bless that godly widow for a service rendered unto His servant.

Lesson IX

Thus was that same Lord received as a guest, Who "came unto His own, and His own received Him not, but as many as received Him, to them gave He power to become the sons of God," adopting servants and making them children, redeeming prisoners and appointing them coheirs. Perchance some of you will say: "O how blessed were they who were worthy to receive Christ as a guest into their own home!" But mourn not, neither murmur, for thou hast been born in an age wherein thou canst no more see Christ in the flesh. He has not put the honor of receiving Him beyond thy reach. "Inasmuch," says He, "as you have done it unto one of the least of these My brethren, you have done it unto Me." The above remarks have occurred to me regarding the Lord considered as fed in the flesh, and I shall now touch briefly, as time permits, upon the Same, considered as the Feeder of the soul.

July 30 ~ Sts. Abdon & Sennen

Martyrs ~ Simplex

Lessons I–II from the occurring Scripture

Lesson III

Abdon and Sennen were Persians. In the reign of the Emperor Decius they were accused of interring, on their own farm, the bodies of Christians, which had been thrown out unburied. The Emperor commanded them to be arrested and ordered to sacrifice to the gods. This they refused to do, and persistently preached that Jesus Christ is God, whereupon they were put into strict confinement. When Decius afterwards returned to Rome, he had them led in chains in his triumph. Being thus dragged into the city and up to the idols, they abhorred and spat upon them, for which they were cast to bears and lions; the beasts were afraid to touch them. They were butchered with the sword, and the corpses, with their feet bound together, were dragged before the image of the sun. Thence they were stolen away, and the Deacon Quirinus buried them in his own house.

July 31 ~ St. Ignatius of Loyola

Confessor ~ Major Duplex
All from Common
except what follows

Lessons I–III from the
occurring Scripture

Lesson IV

Ignatius was a Spaniard by nation, and was born of the noble Biscayan family of Loyola, in the year of our Lord 1491. He followed first the Court and then the army of the Most Catholic King. At the siege of Pamplona in the year 1521 he received a severe wound which laid him up with a long and dangerous illness. During this time he chanced to read some godly books, and conceived from them a burning desire to follow in the footsteps of Christ and His saints. He betook himself to Montserrat, and there entered himself for the heavenly warfare, by hanging up his weapons, and watching them for a night before the Altar of the Blessed Virgin. Thence he withdrew to Manresa, clad in sackcloth, for he had before given his costly raiment to a beggar. At Manresa he lived upon bread and water, begging the bread, and fasting every day except the Lord's Day. He mastered his flesh by the use of a sharp chain and hair-cloth, slept upon the ground, and lashed himself to bloodshed with iron scourges. Thus he dwelt for a year, feasted by God with such clear lights, that he was used afterwards to say that even if the Holy Bible had not existed, he would have been ready to die for the faith only on the evidence of those things which the Lord had shown unto him at Manresa. It was at this time that, albeit a man of little education, he put together that wonderful book entitled "The Spiritual Exercises," whose worth has been attested by the judgment of the Apostolic See, and by universal usefulness.

Lesson V

To make himself of greater use for the profit of souls, he determined to improve himself by education, beginning by going through the rudiments among little boys. He left nothing untried that could help towards the salvation of others, and it was marvelous what pain and mockery he cheerfully accepted on all hands, suffering abuse also, imprisonment and stripes almost unto death; but he was willing to suffer them all much more for the greater glory of his Master. At Paris he took to him seven comrades from the members of that University, men of different nations, but who had all taken the Degree of Master of Arts and in Divinity. With these seven he laid the first foundations of the Society of Jesus in the crypt at Montmartre, upon the 15th day of August, in the year of Christ 1534. When he afterwards organized the same Society at Rome, he bound it by the closest bonds to the Apostolic See, adding to the three accustomed vows of Poverty, Chastity, and Obedience, a fourth, concerning Missions. Paul III was the first Pope to receive and confirm the Institute, but it has since been approved by other Popes and by the Council of

Trent. Ignatius, to spread the Faith, sent Saint Francis Xavier to preach the Gospel in the Indies, and others in other parts of the world, and the war, which he thus proclaimed against paganism and heresy, was waged with such success, that it was the general belief, confirmed by the utterance of the Pope, that even as God had in other times raised up holy men specially to meet the needs of their day, so He had raised up against Luther and the heretics of that age, Ignatius and the Society which he had founded.

Lesson VI

But the first care of Ignatius was to renew piety among Catholics. The splendor of Churches, the tradition of the Catechism, the frequency of sermons and sacraments all received from him an increase. He opened schools everywhere to train up boys in godliness and good learning. At Rome he founded the German College, a home for fallen and another for imperiled girls, an orphanage for boys and another for girls, houses for converts under instruction, and other godly institutions. He never wearied in his work of gaining souls for God, and was sometimes heard to say that if he had the choice he would rather live without knowing whether he was to be among the blessed, and meanwhile work for God and the salvation of his neighbors, than know he was going to glory and die forthwith. He exercised an extraordinary power over demons. Saint Philip Neri and others saw heavenly light shining from his face. At last, on the 31st day of July, in the year of our Redemption 1556 and of his own age the sixty fifth, he passed away to the embrace of that Lord Whose greater glory had been the constant theme of his words and aim of all his works. He is very illustrious in the Church on account of his great deeds and miracles, and Gregory XV enrolled him in the Kalendar of the Saints.

Lessons VII–IX from the Common of Evangelists (Homily by St. Gregory)

FEASTS OF AUGUST

August 1 ~ St. Peter the Apostle in Chains

Major Duplex

Lesson I ~ Acts 12:1–5

From the Acts of the Apostles

And at the same time, Herod the king stretched forth his hands, to afflict some of the church. And he killed James, the brother of John, with the sword. And seeing that it pleased the Jews, he proceeded to take up Peter also. Now it was in the days of the Azymes. And when he had apprehended him, he cast him into prison, delivering him to four files of soldiers to be kept, intending, after the pasch, to bring him forth to the people. Peter therefore was kept in prison. But prayer was made without ceasing by the church unto God for him.

Lesson II ~ Acts 12:6–8

And when Herod would have brought him forth, the same night Peter was sleeping between two soldiers, bound with two chains: and the keepers before the door kept the prison. And behold an angel of the Lord stood by him: and a light shined in the room: and he striking Peter on the side, raised him up, saying: Arise quickly. And the chains fell off from his hands. And the angel said to him: Gird thyself, and put on thy sandals. And he did so. And he said to him: Cast thy garment about thee, and follow me.

Lesson III ~ Acts 12:9–11

And going out, he followed him, and he knew not that it was true which was done by the angel: but thought he saw a vision. And passing through the first and the second ward, they came to the iron gate that leadeth to the city, which of itself opened to them. And going out, they passed on through one street: and immediately the angel departed from him. And Peter coming to himself, said: Now I know in very deed, that the Lord hath sent his angel, and hath delivered me out of the hand of Herod, and from all the expectation of the people of the Jews.

Lesson IV

In the year of our Lord 439, in the reign of the Emperor Theodosius the younger, his wife went to Jerusalem in fulfillment of a vow, and there was gifted with many presents. Among other things, they gave her especially an iron chain, adorned with gold and precious stones, which they affirmed to be the same wherewith the Apostle Peter had been bound by King Herod. Eudocia, with godly reverence, afterwards sent this chain to Rome, to her daughter Eudoxia, who brought it to the Pope, and the Pope in return showed to her another chain wherewith the same Apostle had been shackled under the Emperor Nero.

Lesson V

When then the Pope put together the Roman chain and that which had been brought from Jerusalem, it came to pass that they got so entangled the one with the other that they seemed no longer two but one chain. From this wonder these holy fetters began to receive such honor, that Eudoxia's

Church of St. Peter on the Esquiline Mount was dedicated under the name of St. Peter in Chains, and a Feast Day instituted upon the first day of August in memory of it.

Lesson VI

From that time forth the honor which before had used to be paid to the profane festivity of the Gentiles, held in memory of the dedication of the temple of Mars, and of the birth of Claudius, began to be turned to the Chains of Peter, whose very touch healed the sick, and drove out devils. Among other such cases there befell in the year of man's Redemption 969, that of a certain Count, a servant of the Emperor Otto I, who was possessed by an unclean spirit, and tore himself with his own teeth. This man the Emperor ordered to be taken to Pope John XIII, and as soon as he had touched the Count's neck with the hallowed chains, the foul spirit came out of him, and left him free. And thenceforward the reverence for these holy chains greatly increased in the City.

Lesson VII

From the Holy Gospel according to St. Matthew (Matt 16:13–19)

At that time: Jesus came into the quarters of Caesarea Philippi: and he asked his disciples, saying: Whom do men say that the Son of man is? And so on.

Homily by St. Augustine, Bishop

Peter was the only one of the Apostles who was worthy to hear the words "Amen, I say unto thee that thou art Peter, and upon this rock I will build My Church." Worthy indeed must he be, who, when the nations are to be built up into a Temple of God, is chosen as the foundation whereon the building is to stand, the pillar whereby it is to be held up, and the key wherethrough entrance is to be made into the kingdom. Concerning him the Word of God says that "they brought forth the sick into the streets, and laid them on beds and couches, that at the least the shadow of Peter passing by might overshadow some of them." If the shadow of his body then could give help, how much more shall the fullness of his strength give help now? If the very air, as he passed by, was then profitable to such as besought him, how much more shall his favor profit where now he abides? It is with reason that, throughout all the Churches of Christ, the iron chains wherewith he was afflicted are reckoned more precious than gold.

Lesson VIII

If his shadow as a visitor was so healthful, what is his chain now that he binds and looses? If his empty image in the air had healing power, how much power must have been contracted from his body by those chains, whose iron weight sank into his holy limbs during his suffering? If, before he testified, he was so mighty to aid them that called upon him, how much mightier is he now since his victory?

—

Blessed were the links, doomed to be changed from fetters and shackles, into a crown, which by touching the Apostle, made him a Martyr. Blessed were the chains, whose prisoner left them for the Cross of Christ, and which brought him thither, not as the instruments of condemnation, but of sanctification.

Lesson IX—Commemoration of the Holy Machabees, Martyrs

Sermon by St. Gregory Nazianzen

What were the Machabees? For it is under their name that the Festival at which you are this day assembled is kept. It is true that many persons do not hold them in honor, because they fought before the coming of Christ; nevertheless they deserve to be venerated by all men, for they bore themselves bravely and faithfully in defense of the laws and ordinances of their people. They that underwent martyrdom before Christ came, what would not have been their deeds, if they had suffered persecution after He came, and had had before them for a pattern the Death which He embraced for the sake of man's salvation? With no example to lead them, their bravery was what it was; had they had the example before their eyes, would they not have gone down with double nerve to the battle? There is a mystic and subtle idea, which seems very likely to me and to all lovers of God, that none of those who were crowned with martyrdom before Christ came, could have been so, unless they had had faith in Christ.

August 2 ~ St. Alphonsus Mary de Liguori

Bishop, Confessor, Doctor ~ Duplex

All from Common except what follows

Lessons I–III from the occurring Scripture

Lesson IV

Alphonsus Mary de Liguori was born of a noble family, at Marianella, near Naples, on the 26th day of September, in the year of salvation 1696. From his earliest days he gave no obscure signs of holiness. When he was but a babe, his parents carried him to Saint Francis de Geronimo, of the Society of Jesus, and Saint Francis, after long prayer, said that the child would live to ninety years of age, that he would become a Bishop, and that he would be a great blessing to the Church. From his childhood, he had a strong distaste of games, and by his entreaty and example, induced the noble pages of the Court, among whom he served, to conduct themselves with Christian decency. As a young man, he became a member of diverse pious guilds, and made it among his delights to nurse the sick in the hospitals, to spend much time in prayer in the Churches, and often to receive the Holy Sacraments. With his godliness he so joined zeal for learning, that when he was scarcely sixteen years of age he took degrees in Canon and Civil law in the University of Naples. In obedience to the wish of his father, he adopted the profession of an advocate, in which he gained great credit, but, finding dangers in the practice of the law, he entirely gave it up. He declined a very brilliant marriage which was proposed to him by his father, resigned his family inheritance as an eldest son, hung up his sword at the Altar of the Blessed Virgin Mary of Ransom, and surrendered himself altogether to the service of God. He became a Priest, in 1726, and made so zealous an onslaught on sin, running hither and thither in the office of an Apostle, that he accomplished the conversion of multitudes of lost creatures. The poor and the country-folk most chiefly roused his compassion, and in 1742 he founded the Congregation of Priests called that of the Most Holy Redeemer, to follow the Redeemer's footsteps by preaching the Gospel to the poor throughout the fields, villages, and hamlets.

Lesson V

That he might not turn aside from his work, he bound himself by a vow never to waste any time. Inflamed with the love of souls, he toiled to gain them to Christ and to amend their lives, not only by preaching of the word of God, but also by writings full of holy learning and piety. It is a marvel how many hatreds he stilled, and how many backsliders he led again into the paths of salvation. He was eminently devoted to the Mother of God, published a book on her glories, and when he was earnestly speaking thereof in his sermons, it happened more than once that all the people openly saw a strange brightness fall upon him from her image, till all his countenance shone, and he was rapt in an ecstasy. The sufferings of the Lord and the Holy Eucharist were ever before his eyes, and to them he spread abroad a wonderful love. When he was praying before the Altar of the Blessed Sacrament, or celebrating the Holy Liturgy, which he never failed to do every day, through the seraphic violence of his love, he wept burning tears, or shook with strange movements, or became altogether beside himself. He joined a wonderful innocence and purity, which he never polluted by the stain of deadly sin, to a wonderful depth of repentance, and chastised his body with hunger, iron chains, hair-cloth, and flagellation even to bloodshed. Among all these things he was remarkable for the gift of prophecy, the ability to read hearts, bilocation, and other miracles.

Lesson VI

He firmly and perseveringly refused all high places in the Church which were offered him, but in 1762 Pope Clement XIII absolutely commanded him to take the Bishopric of the Church of Santa Agata de Goti. On becoming a Bishop, the only change which he made in the hardness of his life was that of his outer raiment. There remained, too, the same simplicity of food, the same strong zeal for Christian discipline, the same determined will to put down sin and keep out false doctrines, and the same earnestness in all the duties of a shepherd of souls. In his tenderness to the poor, he spent among them all the revenues of his Church, and in a year of famine sold the furniture of his own house to feed his starving people. He was all things to all men and brought nuns to lead a more perfect life, while he saw to it that a monastery was opened for nuns attached to his own Congregation. On account of grievous and continual sickness, he resigned his Bishopric, and poor as when he had left them, poor he returned among his disciples. On the 1st day of August, in the year 1787, he peacefully died at Nocera-dei-Pagani, amid the tears of his followers. He was then ninety years of age; his body was worn out with old age and hard work, and with chronic gout, and other painful maladies, but the freshness of his mind never failed to the last, in talking and writing on heavenly things. In the year 1816 Pope Pius VII, finding him famous on account of his good works and miracles, enrolled his name among those of the Blessed. God still glorified him by new signs and wonders, and on the Feast of the Most Holy Trinity, in the year 1839, Gregory XVI, with solemn rites, numbered him among the Saints of the Church. Lastly, Pope Pius IX, in accordance with a Resolution of the Congregation of Sacred Rites, gave him the title of Doctor of the Universal Church.

Lessons VII–IX from the Common of Evangelists (Homily by St. Gregory)

Lesson IX—Commemoration of St. Stephen I, Pope & Martyr

Stephen was a Roman, and exercised the Pontificate in the reign of the Emperors Valerian and Gallienus. It was his ordinance which forbade Priests and Deacons ever to use their sacred vestments except in the Church. He forbade a re-baptism of such as had been baptized by heretics, writing to St. Cyprian in these words: "Let us have no innovations, but only what has been handed down unto us." He turned many to Christ, and, among them, the Tribune Olympius, with his wife Exsuperia, and his son Theodulus, and the Tribune Nemesius, to whose blind daughter he had given sight, along with all his household. All these were martyrs for Jesus Christ. When the persecution of the Emperors was waxing fiercer and more dread, Stephen gathered together the clergy, and exhorted them to be brave in lifting up their testimony, and himself celebrated Masses and Councils in the Catacombs. He was caught by some infidels, and brought to the temple of Mars, to do sacrifice to that idol, but he boldly said he would never pay to demons an honor which is owed to God alone. As he spoke these words an earthquake made the image of Mars to fall down, and all the temple to tremble. All they that held Stephen fled, and the Pope went back to his own people in the cemetery of Lucina. He there delivered to them a discourse full of the Word of God, and gave them the Sacrament of the Body of Christ. While he was finishing the Mass, the soldiers of the Emperor again broke in upon them, and his head was cut off as he sat in his chair. The relics of the Martyr, along with the chair stained with his blood, were buried by the clergy in the cemetery of Callistus, upon the 2nd day of August, in the year of our Lord 257. He lived as Pope three years, three months, and twenty two days. He held two ordinations in the month of December, and in them ordained six Priests, five Deacons, and three Bishops.

August 3 ~ Invention of St. Stephen, Protomartyr

Semiduplex

All from Common except what follows

Lesson I ~ Acts 7:51–54

From the Acts of the Apostles

You stiffnecked and uncircumcised in heart and ears, you always resist the Holy Ghost: as your fathers did, so do you also. Which of the prophets have not your fathers persecuted? And they have slain them who foretold of the coming of the Just One; of whom you have been now the betrayers and murderers: Who have received the law by the disposition of angels, and have not kept it. Now hearing these things, they were cut to the heart, and they gnashed with their teeth at him.

Lesson II ~ Acts 7:55–58

But he, being full of the Holy Ghost, looking up steadfastly to heaven, saw the glory of God, and Jesus standing on the right hand of God. And he said: Behold, I see the heavens opened, and the Son of man standing on the right hand of God. And they crying out with a loud voice, stopped their ears, and with one accord ran violently upon him. And casting him forth without the city, they stoned him; and the witnesses laid down their garments at the feet of a young man, whose name was Saul. And they stoned Stephen, invoking, and saying: Lord Jesus, receive my spirit.

Lesson III ~ Acts 7:59; 8:1–2

And falling on his knees, he cried with a loud voice, saying: Lord, lay not this sin to their charge. And when he had said this, he fell asleep in the Lord. And Saul was consenting to his death. And at that time there was raised a great persecution against the church which was at Jerusalem; and they were all dispersed through the countries of Judea, and Samaria, except the apostles. And devout men took order for Stephen's funeral, and made great mourning over him.

Lesson IV

In the year of our Lord 415, in the reign of the Emperor Honorius, a Priest named Lucian, dwelling at Caphargamala, about twenty miles from Jerusalem, received a message from God, in consequence of which discovery was made of the bodies of the Saints Stephen the Protomartyr, Gamaliel, Nicodemus, and Abibon, the son of Gamaliel, which had long been lying unknown and unheeded. Lucian was asleep when Gamaliel appeared to him in a dream as a tall handsome old man of worshipful presence, told him where the bodies were lying, and bade him go to John, Patriarch of Jerusalem, and deal with him that they might have more honorable burial.

Lesson V

When the Patriarch of Jerusalem heard it, he called together Bishops and Priests from the neighboring cities, and betook himself to the place, where he found the tombs hewn in the rock, and a sweet savor flowing forth from them. The thing being noised abroad, a great multitude of people came together, and many that were sick and weak of diverse diseases returned home healthy and whole. The sacred body of Saint Stephen was then carried with great solemnity to the Church of Hagia Sion. Under Emperor Theodosius the Younger it was taken to Constantinople, and during the Pontificate of Pelagius I it was brought to Rome, where it has been laid in the sepulchre of St. Lawrence the Martyr in the Veranian Field.

Lesson VI

From *The City of God* by St. Augustine, Bishop

When the Bishop Projectus brought some relics of that most glorious Martyr Stephen to the waters of Tibilis, a great multitude came together and went out to meet the shrine. A blind woman prayed to be led to the Bishop who was bearing the hallowed deposit. She laid on the relics the flowers which she was carrying, took them up again, touched her eyes with them and forthwith saw. She went forward rejoicing, at the head of the amazed procession, choosing her own path, and needing no more that any should lead her. I remember also the shrine of this same Martyr which has been placed in the town of Synica, near this city of Hippo. Lucillus, Bishop of that place, was carrying it, with a multitude going before and following after when, all of a sudden, by bearing this hallowed burden, he was healed of the ulcer, from which he was even then suffering, and which was being treated by a physician, an intimate friend of his, who was about to cut it.

Lessons VII–IX from December 26—St Stephen the Protomartyr (Homily by St. Jerome)

August 4 ~ St. Dominic

Confessor ~ Major Duplex

All from Common except what follows

Lessons I–III from the occurring Scripture

Lesson IV

Dominic was a Spaniard, a son of the noble family of Guzman. He was born at Calaruega, in Old Castile, in the year of our Lord 1170, and was sent to be taught worldly and sacred learning at Palencia. He attained great success in his studies, and became, first, a Canon Regular of the Cathedral Church of Osma, and afterwards Founder of the Order of Friars Preachers. While his mother was great with child, she dreamt that what was in her womb was a little whelp dog with a lighted torch in his mouth, and that when she was delivered of him, he set all the world aflame. By this dream was figured that burning and shining light of holiness of life and power of doctrine, whereby he should enkindle godliness throughout whole nations. The end proved the truth of the image, for this is truly what his work was, a work which he has continued to do through the Brethren of his Order.

Lesson V

But his wisdom and bravery were most chiefly shown in confounding the Albigensian heretics, who were trying, with their pestilential falsehoods, to corrupt the people of the county of Toulouse. In this business he spent seven years. Afterwards he came to Rome to the Fourth Lateran Council, along with the Bishop of Toulouse, that the Order which he had founded might be confirmed by Innocent III. While the matter was under consideration, Dominic, by the advice of the Pope, went home, that he might put his Rule into shape. He returned again to Rome in 1216, and obtained from Honorius III, the immediate successor of Innocent, the confirmation of the Order of Preachers. At Rome Dominic founded two Convents, one for men, and one for women. He raised three dead men to life, and worked many other miracles, through which the Order of Preachers became exceedingly spread abroad.

Lesson VI

By his work convents were already during his life-time established in all countries, and almost countless persons embraced the life of prayer and godliness. In the year of Christ 1221, he fell sick of a fever at Bologna. When he understood that he was about to die, he called together his brethren and disciples, and exhorted them to innocence and integrity. Lastly, he left to them as his legacy, charity, humility, and poverty, and as the brethren were all praying, and the words were being said, "Assist him, ye Saints of God; run to meet him, ye Angels," he fell asleep in the Lord. It was the 6th day of August. Pope Gregory IX afterwards placed his name among those of the Saints.

Lessons VII–IX from the Common of Confessor Non-Bishops (Homily by St. Gregory)

August 5 ~ Dedication of Our Lady of the Snows

Major Duplex

All from Common of the BVM except what follows

Lessons I–III from the occurring Scripture

Lesson IV

In the time of Pope Liberius, there lived a Roman patrician named John and his noble wife, who had no children to whom to leave their substance. Then they vowed that they would make the most holy Virgin Mother of God their heiress, and earnestly besought her in some way to make known to them upon what pious work she willed that the money should be spent. The Blessed

Virgin Mary graciously listened to their prayers and heartfelt earnestness, and by a miracle assured them of her will.

Lesson V

On the 5th day of August, which is that time when the heat of summer waxes greatest in Rome, a part of the Esquiline Hill was covered by night with snow. And on this same night the Mother of God appeared in a dream to John and his wife separately, and told them that on that spot, which in the morning they should see clad with snow, they should build a Church, to be dedicated in the name of the Virgin Mary, for this was the way in which she chose that they should make her their heiress. John went and told it to Pope Liberius, who declared that he also had been visited by a similar dream.

Lesson VI

Therefore he came in a solemn procession of Priests and people to the snow-clad hill, and traced upon that spot the plan of a Church which was built with the money of John and his wife. It was afterwards restored by Sixtus III. At the beginning it was called by diverse names, sometimes the Liberian Basilica, sometimes the Church of St. Mary-at-the-Manger. Howbeit, since there are in Rome many Churches called after the Holy Virgin Mary, and this Church does excel them all, both in honor, and because of the strange sign wherewith it was dedicated, it has come to be called the Church of St. Mary Major. The memory of the dedication thereof is kept every year by a Feast day that takes name from the wonderful snowfall which on this day took place.

Lessons VII–IX from the Common of the BVM (Homily by St. Bede)

August 6 ~ The Transfiguration of Our Lord

Duplex II Class

Lesson I ~ 2 Pet 1:10–14

From the Second Epistle of St. Peter the Apostle

Wherefore, brethren, labour the more, that by good works you may make sure your calling and election. For doing these things, you shall not sin at any time. For so an entrance shall be ministered to you abundantly into the everlasting kingdom of our Lord and Saviour Jesus Christ. For which cause I will begin to put you always in remembrance of these things: though indeed you know them, and are confirmed in the present truth. But I think it meet as long as I am in this tabernacle, to stir you up by putting you in remembrance. Being assured that the laying away of this my tabernacle is at hand, according as our Lord Jesus Christ also hath signified to me.

Lesson II ~ 2 Pet 1:15–17

And I will endeavour, that you frequently have after my decease, whereby you may keep a memory of these things. For we have not by following artificial fables, made known to you the power, and presence of our Lord Jesus Christ; but we were eyewitnesses of his greatness. For he received from God the Father, honour and glory: this voice coming down to him from the excellent glory: This is my beloved Son, in whom I am well pleased; hear ye him.

Lesson III ~ 2 Pet 1:18–21

And this voice we heard brought from heaven, when we were with him in the holy mount. And we have the more firm prophetical word: whereunto you do well to attend, as to a light that shineth in a dark place, until the day dawn, and the day star arise in your hearts: Understanding this first, that no prophecy of Scripture is made by private interpretation. For prophecy came not by the will of man at any time: but the holy men of God spoke, inspired by the Holy Ghost.

Lesson IV

Sermon by St. Leo, Pope

The Lord takes chosen witnesses, and in their presence, reveals His glory. That form of body which He had in common with other men, He so transfigured with light, that His Face did shine as the sun, and His raiment became exceedingly white as snow. Of this metamorphosis the chief work was to remove from the hearts of the disciples the scandal of the Cross. Before their eyes was unveiled the splendor of His hidden majesty, that the lowliness of His freely-chosen suffering might not confound their faith. But nonetheless was there here laid by the Providence of God a solid foundation for the hope of the Holy Church, whereby the whole body of Christ should know with what a change it is yet to be honored. The members of that body whose Head has already been transfigured in light may promise themselves a share in His glory.

Lesson V

For the strengthening of the Apostles and bringing them forward into all knowledge, there appeared unto them Moses and Elias, that is, the Law and the Prophets, talking with Him. Before five witnesses did His glorification take place, as though to fulfill that which is written: "At the mouth of two witnesses, or at the mouth of three witnesses, shall the matter be established." What can be more certain, what can be better attested than this matter, which is proclaimed by the trumpets of both the Old and the New Testaments, and concerning which the witness of ancient testimony unites with the teaching of the Gospel? The pages of either Covenant strengthen one another, and the brightness of open glory makes manifest and distinct Him Whom the former prophecies had promised under the veil of mysteries.

Lesson VI

The unveiling of such mysteries roused the mind of the Apostle Peter to an outburst of longing for the things eternal, which despised and disdained the things worldly and earthly; overflowing with gladness at the vision, he yearned to dwell with Jesus there, where the revelation of His glory had gladdened him. And so he said "Master, it is good for us to be here; if Thou wilt, let us make here three tabernacles, one for thee, and one for Moses, and one for Elias." To this proposal the Lord answered nothing, this signifying, that what Peter wished was not wrong, but out of place, since the world could not be saved but by the death of Christ. And the Lord's example was to call the faith of believers to this, that albeit we are bound to have no doubts concerning the promise of eternal blessedness, yet we are to understand that, amid the trials of this life, we are to seek for endurance before glory.

Lesson VII

From the Holy Gospel according to St. Matthew (Matt 17:1–9)

At that time: Jesus took Peter, and James, and John his brother, and brought them up into a high mountain apart, and was transfigured before them. And so on.

Homily by St. John Chrysostom

Since the Lord had spoken much on dangers, much on His Own sufferings, much on death, and the killing of His disciples, and had laid upon them many hard and grievous things, and since all these were in this present life, and already hanging over them, whereas the good things were matter for hope and waiting as, for example, that whosoever should lose his life for His sake should find it, for that the Son of Man should come in the glory of His Father, and reward every man according to his works. Therefore, to assure them by their own eyes, and show them what the glory is wherein He will come, He manifested and unveiled it to them, as far as in this life they were able to grasp it, lest they and especially Peter should grieve over their own deaths, or the death of their Lord.

Lesson VIII

Behold what He does, when He treats of heaven and hell. Where He says: "Whosoever will save his life shall lose it, and whosoever will lose his life for My sake shall find it;" and again: "He shall reward every man according to his works;" in these words He points at heaven and hell. But although He speaks of both, He gives a glimpse of heaven only and not of hell. To see hell would have profited the brutish and stupid, but His disciples were upright and clear-sighted, and therefore for them it was enough to be strengthened by the better things. This was what suited Him the best. Yet He left not the other altogether undone. Sometimes He set the horrors of hell, as it were, before the eyes, as for instance in the parable of the rich man and Lazarus, and that of him who was eager to wring the hundred pence from his fellow-servant.

Consider with how great calmness Matthew gives the names of the three most honored disciples. This trait also John often shows, where he does most truly and carefully write the praises of Peter. In the fellowship of the Apostles jealousy and vanity had no place. The Apostles whom the Lord took up into the mountain apart were the three chiefest. Why took He only those three? Because they were more excellent than the others. But why did He do it, not at once, but "after six days?" Lest either the other disciples or men in general should be moved; wherefore also He did not give beforehand the names of those whom He was going to take.

Lesson IX—Commemoration of Sts. Sixtus II, Felicissimus, & Agapitus, Pope & Martyrs

Sixtus II was an Athenian, who, from a philosopher, became a disciple of Christ. In the persecution under Valerian he was accused of openly preaching Christ, and was seized and dragged to the temple of Mars, where he was given the choice of death or offering sacrifice to the idol. He firmly refused to commit that impiety, and as he was being led away to seal his testimony, Saint Lawrence ran up to him and in his grief said to him "Father, where goest thou without thy son? Holy Priest, where dost thou hurry without a Deacon?" Sixtus answered him: "I am not leaving thee, my son; there awaits thee for Christ's truth far greater contests than mine; yet three days, and thou shalt follow me, the Deacon behind the Priest, and in the meanwhile, if thou hast anything in the treasury, give it to the poor." Sixtus was accordingly slain upon that day, and with him the Deacons Felicissimus and Agapitus, and the Subdeacons Januarius, Magnus, Vincent, and Stephen. He was buried in the cemetery of Callistus, and they in the cemetery of Prætextatus upon the 6th day of August, in the year of our Lord 258. He sat in the throne of Peter eleven months and twelve days. During that time he held one ordination in the month of December, wherein he made four Priests, seven Deacons, and two Bishops.

August 7 ~ St. Cajetan

Confessor ~ Duplex
All from Common except what follows

Lessons I–III from the occurring Scripture

Lesson IV

Cajetan was born at Vicenza, in the year 1480, of the noble family of the lords of Thiene, and was forthwith dedicated by his mother to the Virgin Mother of God. From his childhood such wonderful innocence shone in him that all called him a Saint. He took the degree of Doctor in Civil and Canon Law at Padua, and afterwards went to Rome, where Julius II gave him a place among the Prelates. Having taken Priest's Orders, he became so full of the fire of the love of God, that he left the Court so he might be free to work entirely for God. He founded hospitals at his own expense, and nursed the sick, even such as were suffering from the plague, with his own hands. He labored with such constant earnestness for the salvation of his neighbors that he got the name of "the Hunter of souls."

Lesson V

From a desire to restore the corrupted discipline of the clergy to the model of the Apostolic life, he founded, in 1524, a Congregation of Clerics Regular, who should give up all care of earthly things, neither keeping any income, nor begging the needful things of life from the faithful, but living only on such alms as might be given them unasked. For this end, and with the approval of Clement VII, Cajetan himself, together with John Peter Carafa, Archbishop of Chieti, afterwards Pope Paul IV, and two other men of eminent godliness, took solemn vows at the High Altar of St. Peter's Church on the Vatican. When the city of Rome was sacked in 1527 by the Imperial Army, Cajetan was most cruelly abused to make him reveal his wealth, which had long before been laid up for him in heaven by the hands of the poor, and he endured with unconquered patience stripes, torture, and imprisonment. He held on bravely in the way of life he had taken up, trusting altogether to the Providence of God, Whose unfailing care of him was sometimes attested by miracles.

Lesson VI

He greatly promoted care in the worship of God, the dignity of the house of God, observance of the the holy rites, and more frequent reception of the most holy Eucharist. The hideous forms and dark convolutions of heresy he more than once unmasked and abolished. He would remain in prayer with abundance of tears as much as eight hours at a time. He was often thrown into trances, and was celebrated for the gift of prophecy. One Christmas night at Rome, when he was praying before the Lord's manger, he was deemed worthy that the Mother of God should lay the Child Jesus in his arms. He sometimes spent the whole night in whipping himself, nor could he ever be persuaded to soften the hardness of his life, but witnessed that he was desirous to die in sackcloth and ashes. In the end he fell ill with grief at the offense against God, which the people of Naples committed by rebelling against the establishment of the Inquisition. Refreshed by a vision from heaven, he departed there on the 7th day of August, 1547. His body lies at Naples in the Church of St. Paul, where it is held in great reverence. Pope Clement X, finding him to have been illustrious for miracles both during his life and after his death, enrolled his name among those of the Saints.

Lessons VII–IX from those for Sunday XIV after Pentecost (Homily by St. Augustine)

Lesson IX—Commemoration of St. Donatus, Bishop & Martyr

Donatus was the child of a father and mother who had both been slain for Jesus Christ's sake. He fled with the monk Hilarinus to Arezzo in Tuscany, of which city he afterwards became Bishop. There the Præfect Quadratian, during the persecution under Julian, commanded both Hilarinus and Donatus to worship idols, and when they both refused to commit such abominable iniquity, Hilarinus was beaten with clubs before the eyes of Quadratian, until he gave up the ghost. Donatus also was savagely tortured, and slain with the sword. The Christians buried their bodies honorably near the city.

August 8 ~ Sts. Cyriacus, Largus, & Smaragdus

Martyrs ~ Semiduplex

All from Common except what follows

Lessons I–III from the occurring Scripture

Lesson IV

Cyriacus the Deacon was long kept in prison with Sisinius, Largus, and Smaragdus, and wrought many wonderful works. Among other things he by his prayers freed Arthemia, a daughter of Diocletian, from a demon and, being sent to Shapur, King of the Persians, also delivered his daughter Jobias from a foul spirit. He baptized the king, her father, and four hundred and thirty others, and afterwards returned to Rome. He was arrested by command of the Emperor Maximian, and dragged in chains before his chariot. Then after four days he was brought forth from prison, had boiling pitch poured upon him, was stretched on a scaffold, and at last was slain with the axe, along with Largus, Smaragdus, and twenty others, at the gardens of Sallust, on the Salarian Way. On this Way were their bodies buried by John the Priest, on the 16th day of March, in the year of our Lord 303, but afterwards, on the 8th of August, Pope Marcellus and the noble lady Lucina took them and wrapped them in linen, and embalmed them with costly ointments, and carried them to the farm belonging to the said lady Lucina, at the seventh milestone from Rome on the road to Ostia.

Lessons V & VI are Lessons IV & V from the second set in the Common of Many Martyrs (Sermon by St. John Chrysostom)

Lessons VII–IX from December 3: St. Francis Xavier (Homily by St. Gregory on Mark 16:15–18)

August 9 ~ St. John Mary Vianney

Confessor ~ Duplex

All from Common except what follows

Lessons I–III from the occurring Scripture

Lesson IV

John Mary Vianney, born of pious peasants in the village of Dardilly in the diocese of Lyons, gave many signs of holiness from his infancy. When, at the age of eight, he was taking care of the sheep, he would sometimes by word and example instruct little boys, kneeling before a statue of the Mother of God, in the use of the Rosary; and at other times, entrusting the flock to his sister or to another child, he was used to seek out a more retired spot, that he might more readily devote himself to prayer before an image of the Virgin. Having a very great love for the poor, he would lead them in crowds to his father's house, and he took a delight in aiding them in every way. That he might be initiated into letters, he was sent to the parish priest of the village of Écully; but as he was very slow to understand, he encountered almost insurmountable difficulties in his studies. Fasting and praying, he entreated the divine assistance, and, with a view to begging for a facility in learning, he approached the tomb of St. Francis Regis, earnestly beseeching him for that gift. Having most laboriously passed through the course of theology, he was found to be sufficiently suitable to receive holy orders.

Lesson V

In the village of Écully, under the guidance of the parish priest, whose assistant he had been appointed, he strove with all his strength to attain to the higher degrees of pastoral perfection. After three years had gone by, he was sent, like an Angel from heaven, to the small village of Ars, which not so long after was included in the diocese of Belley, and in a most brilliant manner he entirely renewed the condition of his neglected and forsaken parish. Continually engaged for many hours daily in hearing confessions and in giving spiritual direction, he introduced the frequent reception of the Eucharist, and organized pious sodalities: and in a remarkable manner he inspired into souls a tender devotion to the Immaculate Virgin. And, deeming that it is the duty of the pastor to expiate the sins of the flock accredited to him, he spared neither prayers, nor vigils, nor mortifications and continual fasts. Since Satan could not endure such great virtues in this man of God, he assailed him, first with mere annoyances, and afterwards in open combat; but John Mary patiently endured the most malevolent injuries.

Lesson VI

He was very often asked by the neighboring priests to labor for the salvation of souls after the manner of the Missionaries, either by preaching sermons, or by hearing confessions, and he was always at hand in every case. Burning with zeal for the glory of God, he brought it about that the pious exercises of Missions were established in more than a hundred parishes arranged in a continuous and permanent series. Meanwhile, as God was rendering his servant famous by miracles and by graces, there began that celebrated pilgrimage, in which, throughout a period of twenty years, nearly one hundred thousand persons of every class flocked to Ars, not only from France and from Europe, but even from the distant regions of America. Worn out by labors rather than by old age, having foretold the day of his death, he went to rest in the embrace of the Lord, on the 4th day of August, in the year 1859, and of his age the seventy-third. After he became illustrious for many miracles, Pius X added him to the number of the Blessed, and Pius XI, in the holy year numbered him with the Saints in heaven and extended his feast to the universal Church, and on the fiftieth anniversary of his own priesthood, appointed him the heavenly patron of all parish priests.

Lessons VII–IX from the first set in the Common of Confessor Non-Bishops (Homily by St. Gregory)

Lesson IX—Commemoration of the Vigil of St. Lawrence: taken from Lesson VII in the second set of the Common of One Martyr (Homily by Pope St. Gregory on Matt 16:24–27)

August 10 ~ St. Lawrence

Martyr ~ Duplex II Class

Lessons I–III from the Common of a Virgin Martyr (Ecclus 51)

Lesson IV

Sermon by St. Leo, Pope

When the fury of the heathen power was raging against Christ's choicest members, in aiming especially at such as were of the Priestly Order, the wicked persecutor turned fiercely on the Levite Lawrence, who was remarkable, not only as a minister of the Sacraments, but also as distributor of the property of the Church, promising himself a double prey by the taking of this one man, namely, to make him betray the consecrated treasure, and apostatize from the true faith. The wretch was thus doubly fired by his greed for money and his hatred of the truth, his greed urging him to seize the gold, and his wickedness to rob a believer of Christ. He demanded of the upright keeper of the sacred treasury, to bring him the wealth of the Church, for which his avarice longed. But the most-chaste Levite showed him where these riches were stored, by bringing before him a great multitude of holy poor, by the feeding and clothing of whom he had laid up all that he had, in such a way that it could be lost no more and was now all the safer, as the way of spending it had been the holier.

Lesson V

The baffled thief chafed, and his hatred for the godliness which had appointed such a use of riches, flaming forth, he attempted the robbery of a dearer treasure from him in whose hands he had found no coin, even to take from him that possession wherein he had holier wealth. He commanded Lawrence to deny Christ, and made ready to assail the immovable firmness of the Levite's soul with appalling tortures, of which the failure of the first was followed by the application of others more fearful still. When his limbs had been mangled and cut by many stripes, his tormentor ordered them to be roasted over a fire. He was laid on an iron grating, the bars of which by the continual fire below, became themselves burning hot, so that by turning and rearranging his limbs upon them, his agony was kept keener, and his suffering made to last longer.

Lesson VI

Thou gainest nothing, and advancest nothing, o savage cruelty! That which can die passes by degrees beyond the reach of thy tortures, and when Lawrence departs to heaven, thou and thy fires are conquered. The love of Christ could not be overcome by the flames, and the glow that scorched the outward man was colder than that which burnt inwardly. Thou didst rage, O persecutor against the Martyr; thou didst rage, but by making keener his agony, thou hast but made nobler his palm. What did thine imagination fail to discover that could minister to the glory of him who conquered thee, since even the means of his execution have turned to the honor of his triumph? Therefore, dearly beloved brethren, let us rejoice with spiritual joy, and make our boast in the Lord, Who is wonderful in His Saints and has given unto us in them a help and an example. Let us, I say, make our boast of the extraordinary happiness of the illustrious Lawrence's end, in that same Lord Who has so glorified the name of His servant throughout the whole world, that from the rising of the sun its setting, wheresoever the constellation of the Levitical lights shine, even as Jerusalem is made glorious by Stephen, so Rome is made famous by Lawrence.

Lessons VII–IX from February 1 – St. Ignatius of Antioch (Homily by St. Augustine on John 12:24–26)

August 11 ~ Sts. Tiburtius & Susanna

Virgin, Martyrs ~ Simplex

Lessons I–II from the occurring Scripture

Lesson III

Tiburtius was son to Chromatius, Præfect of the city of Rome, and was converted to Christianity by Saint Sebastian. On this account he was brought before Fabian the judge, and spoke boldly in his presence many things concerning belief in Christ. Then Fabian broke out in anger and caused the pavement to be spread with live coals. "Now, Tiburtius," said he, "thou must either sacrifice to our gods, or walk barefoot on these coals." Tiburtius armed himself with the sign of the Cross and walked boldly on the coals. "Learn from this," said he, "that there is no God but He whom the Christians worship; for the coals are to me like flowers." For this, being attributed to the magic arts, he was led forth outside the city and smitten with the sword at the third milestone on the Lavican Road, where he was buried by the Christians, in the year 286. On the same day, about the year 295, the noble virgin Susanna, having refused the offer of marriage of Galerius Maximianus, son to the Emperor Diocletian, because she had made a vow of her virginity to God, after diverse torments wherewith her holy resolution was tried, was smitten with the sword in her own house, by order of the Emperor, and passed to heaven to receive the double reward of virginity and martyrdom.

August 12 ~ St. Claire

Virgin ~ Duplex

All from Common except what follows

Lessons I–III from the occurring Scripture

Lesson IV

The noble virgin Claire was born at Assisi in Umbria, in the year 1193. In imitation of her holy fellow-citizen Francis, she distributed all her goods among the poor and needy. She fled from the din of the world, and on the 18th day of March, 1212, betook herself to the Church of St. Mary of the Angels in the fields, where blessed Francis cut her hair. She stoutly resisted the efforts of her family to make her come back, and after a while Francis took her to the Church of San Damiano, where the Lord gathered around her several companions. Thus she founded a holy Sisterhood, which, at the earnest entreaty of Saint Francis, she governed. For forty-two years she directed her monastery with wonderful care and wisdom in the fear of the Lord and the full keeping of the Rule. Her own life was an instruction and teaching for the rest, whence others learnt to order their own.

Lesson V

That she might wax stronger in spirit by keeping the body down, she made her bed on the bare ground, sometimes with little twigs, and with hard wood for a pillow. Her dress was a gown and cloak of poor and rough cloth, and she sometimes wore hair-cloth next the skin. She bridled herself with such abstinence, that for a long time she took no bodily nourishment whatever upon three days in the week. Upon the remaining days she ate so little that the others wondered how she lived. As long as her health allowed it, she kept two Lents every year, during which she fasted upon bread and water. Moreover, she was constant in watching and prayer, wherein she chiefly spent both her days and nights. She suffered from constant illnesses, and when she could not herself rise to bodily work, she sat up with the help of the sisters, and with her back propped, worked with her hands, that she might not be idle even in the midst of her weaknesses. She was an eminent lover of poverty, from which no need ever made her swerve, and she persistently refused the possessions which were offered to the sisters by Gregory IX for their support.

Lesson VI

The power of her holy life shone forth in many and diverse miracles. She restored the use of speech to one of the sisters in her convent, for another she opened a deaf ear; she healed one sick with fever, one swollen with dropsy, one troubled with a hollow oozing ulcer, and others afflicted with diverse ailments. She cured a brother of the Order of Friars Minors of raging madness. Once when all the oil in the house was spent, she took the vessel and washed it, and it was found filled with oil by the goodness of God. She multiplied half a loaf till it was enough to satisfy fifty sisters. When the Saracens (attached to the army of Frederick II) attacked Assisi, in the year 1239, and were going to break into Claire's monastery, she being sick, caused herself to be carried to the door, and likewise the vessel in which was held the Most Holy Sacrament of the Eucharist, and there she prayed, saying: "O Lord, deliver not unto beasts the souls of them that praise thee, but defend thine handmaids whom Thou hast redeemed with thy Precious Blood." Whereupon a voice was heard which said: "I will always defend you." Some of the Saracens took to flight, and others who had mounted the wall became blind, and fell down headlong. When Claire herself was at the point of death she beheld a white multitude of blessed Virgins, with one among them nobler and brighter than the rest. Having received the Holy Eucharist, and a Plenary Indulgence from Innocent IV, she resigned her soul to God upon the 12th day of August, 1253. After her death she became illustrious for very many miracles, and Alexander IV enrolled her name among those of the Holy Virgins.

Lessons VII–IX from the first set in the Common of Virgins (Homily by St. Gregory)

August 13 ~ Sts. Hippolytus & Cassian

Martyrs ~ Simplex

Lessons I–II from the occurring Scripture

Lesson III

Hippolytus was one of those baptized by St. Lawrence. He was arrested in his own house while he was receiving Holy Communion. He was brought before the Emperor Valerian, and, when he was asked by him about his religious profession, he freely confessed that he was a Christian. Therefore he was beaten with clubs, but when his faith was found only the bolder under the blows, he was tempted with promises of gifts and honors. Then when words were found only to be thrown away upon him, he was given over to the Præfect to be put to death. The Praefect went to the house of Hippolytus to take possession of his goods, and there found that all the household were Christians. He strove in vain to awe them into the denial of their faith, and then ordered Concordia, the nurse of Hippolytus, who was encouraging the rest, to be beaten to death with leaden whips, and afterwards the others to be slain outside the gate that leads toward Tivoli. Hippolytus was tied to wild horses which dragged him through rough places full of briars and thistles, until with a mangled body he resigned his soul to God. Justin the Priest buried him along with the others. On the same day, at Imola, the martyr Cassian was put to a most cruel death. He was a schoolmaster, and was given up to his schoolchildren, with his hands bound behind his back, to be stabbed and torn to death with iron pens. Owing to the weakness of the means, the suffering of his martyrdom was very grievous and long, and his palm all the more glorious.

August 14 ~ Vigil of the Assumption of the Blessed Virgin Mary

Vigil

All from Common except what follows

Lesson I

From the Holy Gospel according to St. Luke (Luke 11:27–28)

At that time: It came to pass as Jesus spoke, a certain woman of the company lifted up her voice, and said unto him: Blessed is the womb that bore thee, and the paps which thou hast sucked. And so on.

Homily by St. John Chrysostom

When you give ear to the saying of that woman: "Blessed is the womb that bore thee, and the paps which thou hast sucked:" and to the Lord's reply: "Yea, rather, blessed are they that hear the word of God and keep it:" think not that he made this observation as slighting his Mother, but as wishing to show that it would profit her nothing to be called his Mother, unless she excelled in goodness and faith. Now, if a mother's love would avail Mary nothing without virtue, much less will it avail us to be a good father, brother, mother, or son, unless we are good in ourselves.

Lesson II

For indeed, salvation for anyone, apart from the divine grace, is to be hoped for in nothing else but his own virtues. For if her kinship in itself could have profited Mary, it would also have profited the Jews, for Christ was their kinsman according to the flesh; it would have profited the city in which he was born; it would have profited his brethren. Yet as long as his brethren cared only for their own interests, their relationship to Christ profited them nothing, but they were condemned with the rest of the world.

Lesson III

Then only did they begin to be worthy of admiration, when they shone by their own virtue. His native land, indeed, having gained nothing from its own connection with him, fell and was burnt by fire; his fellow-citizens were put to death and perished miserably; his kindred according to the flesh gained nothing towards their salvation; insofar as all these lacked the protection of virtue. But of them all, the Apostles became the most renowned, since by obedience they joined themselves to him in right and desirable friendship and companionship. From this we learn that we always have need of faith and a life shining with virtues; since this alone will have power to save us.

August 15 ~ THE ASSUMPTION OF THE BLESSED VIRGIN MARY [1950]

Duplex I Class

Lesson I ~ Gen 3:9–15

From the Book of Genesis

And the Lord God called Adam, and said to him: Where art thou? And he said: I heard thy voice in paradise; and I was afraid, because I was naked, and I hid myself. And he said to him: And who hath told thee that thou wast naked, but that thou hast eaten of the tree whereof I commanded thee that thou shouldst not eat? And Adam said: The woman, whom thou gavest me to be my companion, gave me of the tree, and I did eat. And the Lord God said to the woman: Why hast thou done this? And she answered: The serpent deceived me, and I did eat. And the Lord God said to the serpent: Because thou hast done this thing, thou art cursed among all cattle, and beasts of the earth: upon thy breast shalt thou go, and earth shalt thou eat all the days of thy life. I will put enmities between thee and the woman, and thy seed and her seed: she shall crush thy head, and thou shalt lie in wait for her heel.

Lesson II ~ 1 Cor 15:20–26

From the First Epistle of Blessed Paul the Apostle to the Corinthians

But now Christ is risen from the dead, the firstfruits of them that sleep: For by a man came death, and by a man the resurrection of the dead. And as in Adam all die, so also in Christ all shall be made alive. But every one in his own order: the firstfruits Christ, then they that are of Christ, who have believed in his coming. Afterwards the end, when he shall have delivered up the kingdom to God and the Father, when he shall have brought to nought all principality, and power, and virtue. For he must reign, until he hath put all his enemies under his feet. And the enemy death shall be destroyed last.

Lesson III ~ 1 Cor 15:53–57

For this corruptible must put on incorruption; and this mortal must put on immortality. And when this mortal hath put on immortality, then shall come to pass the saying that is written: Death is swallowed up in victory. O death, where is thy victory? O death, where is thy sting? Now the sting of death is sin: and the power of sin is the law. But thanks be to God, who hath given us the victory through our Lord Jesus Christ.

Lesson IV

Sermon by St. John Damascene

This day the holy and animated Ark of the living God, which had held within it its own Maker, is borne to rest in that Temple of the Lord, which is not made with hands. David, whence it sprang, leaps before it, and in company with him the Angels dance, the Archangels sing aloud, the Virtues ascribe glory, the Principalities shout for joy, the

Powers make merry, the Dominations rejoice, the Thrones keep holiday, the Cherubim utter praise, and the Seraphim proclaim its glory. This day the Eden of the new Adam receives the living garden of delight, wherein the condemnation was annulled, wherein the Tree of Life was planted, wherein our nakedness was covered.

Lesson V

This day the Immaculate Virgin, who had been defiled by no earthly lust, but ennobled by heavenly desires, returned not to dust, but, being herself a living heaven, took her place among the heavenly mansions. From her true life had flowed for all men, and how should she taste of death? But she yielded obedience to the law established by Him to Whom she had given birth, and, as the daughter of the old Adam, underwent the old sentence, which even her Son, Who is the very Life Itself, had not refused; but, as the Mother of the living God, she was worthily taken by Him unto Himself.

Lesson VI

From the Acts of Pope Pius XII

Since indeed the universal Church has at all times and throughout the ages manifested faith in the bodily Assumption of the Blessed Virgin Mary, and since the Bishops of the whole world by an almost unanimous agreement have petitioned that this truth, which is enshrined in Sacred Scripture and deeply rooted in the souls of Christ's faithful, and is also truly in accord with other revealed truths, should be defined as a dogma of the divine and Catholic Faith, Pope Pius XII, acceding to the requests of the whole Church, decreed that this privilege of the Blessed Virgin Mary be solemnly proclaimed, and thus, on the first day of November of the year of the Great Jubilee, 1950, at Rome, in the open square before the Basilica of St. Peter, surrounded by a throng of many Cardinals and Bishops of the Holy Roman Church who had come from distant parts of the earth, and before a great multitude of the faithful, with the whole Catholic world rejoicing, proclaimed in these words and with infallible statement the bodily Assumption of the Blessed Virgin Mary into heaven: "Wherefore, having offered to God continual prayers of supplication, and having invoked the light of the Spirit of Truth, to the glory of Almighty God who has enriched the Virgin Mary with his special favor; in honor of his Son, the immortal King of ages and victor over sin and death; for the increase of the glory of the same august Mother, and for the joy and exultation of the whole Church, by the authority of Our Lord Jesus Christ, of the holy Apostles Peter and Paul, and by our own authority, we pronounce, declare and define it to be a divinely revealed dogma that: The Immaculate Mother of God, Mary ever Virgin, was, at the end of her earthly life, assumed body and soul into heavenly glory."

Lesson VII

From the Holy Gospel according to St. Luke (Luke 1:41–50)

At that time: Elisabeth was filled with the Holy Ghost: and she spoke out with a loud voice, and said, Blessed art thou among women. And so on.

Homily by St. Peter Canisius, Priest

The Church frequently and reverently keeps feast days dedicated to the Mother of God, realizing that it is a work pleasing to God and worthy of the faithful if many feasts, with fixed dates and public ceremonies, are celebrated in honor of the most blessed of all the blessed in heaven, the Mother of our Lord and God. Among all these feasts which have been celebrated so devotedly for so many years, even unto the present day, the Feast of the Assumption is considered the greatest and holds chief place. Indeed there was no happier or more joyful day for Mary, if we duly consider the happiness of both body and soul granted to her on that day. Then especially, as never before, her spirit, soul and body rejoiced wondrously in the living God and she could rightfully say: "He has regarded the lowliness of his handmaiden; for behold, all generations shall call me blessed; for he that is mighty has magnified me."

Lesson VIII

O thrice blessed and truly august Mother, it is for this reason that we who love thee and thy Son cannot refrain from congratulating thee with all sincerity upon thine admirable and incomparable happiness, especially since everything that has been said to thee and about thee by the Lord, is brought to a conclusion by thy beautiful passing away from this life, and in every way has been perfectly fulfilled. Blessed art thou who hast not only believed but hast this day attained unto the end of faith and the fruit of all virtue, and now at last hast merited to enjoy the most pleasing sight of him whom thou didst love and desire so greatly. Thyself a guest, thou didst receive Emmanuel who as a guest did enter into thee, as into a mighty fortress in this world; and today, thou in turn art received by him into his royal mansion, and magnificently welcomed with the highest honor, as befits one found worthy to be the Mother of such a Solomon.

Lesson IX

O blessed day which sent so precious a gift from the desert of this world, and carried it to the holy and eternal city, so that universal and unheard of joy no less than admiration welled up in all the blessed in heaven. O blessed day, that fulfilled the long and ardent yearning of the gentle spouse, so that she might find what she had sought, that she might receive what she asked; that what she awaited she might possess securely, resting safely at last in that perfect vision and inward joy of the eternal and all-great Goodness. O blessed day which raised up and so highly exalted this most humble handmaiden of the Lord that she might become the most glorious Queen of Heaven and the mistress of the world. Indeed she could not have risen to more sublime heights since she had been elevated to the very Throne of the heavenly kingdom, and thus was established in glory next after Christ. O blessed and truly honorable is this day which constituted and confirmed for us a Queen and Mother who is at once powerful and merciful in the kingdom of God, that we might have her, who ever remains the Mother of the Judge, as a Mother of mercy protecting us and interceding for us with Christ, unceasingly watching over the work of our salvation.

August 15 ~ THE ASSUMPTION OF THE BLESSED VIRGIN MARY [Pre-1950]

Duplex I Class

Lesson I ~ Cant 1:1–4

Beginning of the Canticle of Canticles

Let him kiss me with the kiss of his mouth: for thy breasts are better than wine, Smelling sweet of the best ointments. thy name is as oil poured out: therefore young maidens have loved thee. Draw me: we will run after thee to the odour of thy ointments. The king hath brought me into his storerooms: we will be glad and rejoice in thee, remembering thy breasts more than wine: the righteous love thee. I am black but beautiful, O ye daughters of Jerusalem, as the tents of Cedar, as the curtains of Solomon.

Lesson II ~ Cant 1:5–9

Do not consider me that I am brown, because the sun hath altered my colour: the sons of my mother have fought against me, they have made me the keeper in the vineyards: my vineyard I have not kept. Show me, O thou whom my soul loveth, where thou feedest, where thou liest in the midday, lest I begin to wander after the flocks of thy companions. If thou know not thyself, O fairest among women, go forth, and follow after the steps of the flocks, and feed thy kids beside the tents of the shepherds. To my company of horsemen, in Pharao's chariots, have I likened thee, O my love. Thy cheeks are beautiful as the turtledove's, thy neck as jewels.

Lesson III ~ Cant 1:10–16

We will make thee chains of gold, inlaid with silver. While the king was at his repose, my spikenard sent forth the odour thereof. A bundle of myrrh is my beloved to me, he shall abide between my breasts. A cluster of cypress my love is to me, in the vineyards of Engaddi. Behold thou art fair, O my love, behold thou art fair, thy eyes are as those of doves. Behold thou art fair, my beloved, and comely. Our bed is flourishing. The beams of our houses are of cedar, our rafters of cypress trees.

Lessons IV–V as above in the 1950 propers

Lesson VI

Eve, who had said yea to the proposals of the serpent, was condemned to the pains of travail and the punishment of death, and found her place in the bowels of the Netherworld. But this truly blessed being who had inclined her ears to the word of God, whose womb had been filled by the action of the Holy Ghost, who, as soon as she heard the spiritual salutation of the archangel, had conceived the Son of God without any sexual pleasure or carnal knowledge by a man, who had brought forth her Offspring without any least pang, who had hallowed herself altogether for the service of God how was death ever to feed upon her? How was the grave ever to eat her up? How was corruption to break into that body into which Life had been welcomed? For her there was a straight, smooth, and easy way to heaven. For if Christ, Who is the Life and the Truth, has said "Where I am, there shall also My servant be" how much more shall not rather His mother be with Him?

Lesson VII

From the Holy Gospel according to St. Luke (Luke 10:38–42)

At that time, Jesus entered into a certain village, and a woman named Martha received Him into her house. And so on.

Homily by St. Augustine, Bishop

When the Holy Gospel was read, we heard how a religious woman hospitably received the Lord into her house, and that this woman's name was Martha. And while Martha herself was encumbered with much serving, a sister of hers, called Mary, sat at the Lord's Feet, and heard His word. The one worked, the other was idle. One ministered, the other was filled. Nevertheless, Martha, working hard in the bustle and business of the serving, came to the Lord, and made complaint of her sister, because she would not help her in her work.

Lesson VIII

But the Lord undertook to answer Martha for Mary; He, Who had been called upon to be her Judge, became her Advocate. And Jesus answered and said unto her "Martha, thou art careful and troubled about many things. But one thing is needful, and Mary has chosen the better part, which shall not be taken away from her." We have heard both the complaint, and the sentence of the Judge, the which sentence replies to the complainant, and shields her whom the Lord had received. Mary was wrapped up in the sweetness of the word of the Lord. Martha was busied how to feed the Lord, and Mary, how to be fed by the Lord. Martha was readying a banquet for that same Lord, at Whose banquet Mary was already reveling.

Lesson IX

When, therefore, Mary was listening in peace and gentleness to those words of unutterable sweetness, and being feasted to the full extent of her heart's power, and Martha came and complained of her to the Lord, how must we imagine that she feared, lest the Lord should say unto her "Arise, and help thy sister?" She was held by that wondrous sweetness which is felt more by the mind than by the belly. She was excused, and she sat all the safer. But on what grounds was she excused? Let us now turn our attention to this point, and thoroughly see into and examine it as far as we can, that we also may be fed.

August 16 ~ St. Joachim, Father of the Blessed Virgin Mary

Confessor ~ Duplex II Class

All from Common except what follows

Lesson IV

Sermon by St. Epiphanius, Bishop

From the Root of Jesse arose King David, and from the stock of King David, the Holy Virgin. Holy I call her, and the daughter of holy men. Her father and mother were Joachim and Anne, who pleased God in their lives, and brought forth an offspring well pleasing to Him, even the Holy Virgin Mary, at once the Temple and the Mother of God. These three, Joachim, Anne, and Mary, clearly offered up unto the Trinity a sacrifice of praise. For the name Joachim being interpreted, signifies "the preparation of the Lord," and out of him was prepared the Temple of the Lord, namely, the Virgin. The name Anne signifies grace, and she and Joachim did indeed receive a grace when, in answer to their prayers, they generated such an offspring, compassing the Holy Virgin. Joachim prayed upon the mountain and Anne in her garden.

Lesson V

Sermon by St. John Damascene

Since it was to be that the Virgin Mother of God should be born of Anne, nature dared not to produce any other child before this child of grace, but humbly waited until grace should have produced hers. It was to be that she should come into the world as a firstborn, who was to bear the Firstborn of all creatures, even Him by Whom all things were made. O blessed couple, Joachim and Anne, unto you is all creation laid under debt, since through you creation has offered to the Creator this noblest of gifts, namely, that chaste mother, who alone was worthy of the Creator.

Lesson VI

Rejoice, O Joachim, from whose daughter a Child has unto us been born, and His name is called "The Angel of Great Counsel," that is, of the salvation of the whole world. Let Nestorius be ashamed, and put his hand upon his mouth. Her Child is God. How then can His Mother be other than Mother of God? Whosoever acknowledges not the Holy Mother of God is far from God. This saying is not mine, although it is mine in all other senses than that of authority. I have received it as a most godly legacy from Father Gregory the Divine. O blessed couple, Joachim and Anne! Christ says in a certain place: "By their fruits you shall know them" and you are known by the fruit of your chaste loins. That that which should be born of you might be worthy and well-pleasing in the sight of God, you ordered your own lives by rule. In the chaste and holy exercise of your natural gift, you produced the treasure of virginity.

Lesson VII

From the Holy Gospel according to St. Matthew (Matt 1:1–16)

The book of the generation of Jesus Christ, the son of David, the son of Abraham. Abraham begat Isaac, and Isaac begat Jacob. And so on.

Homily by St. John Damascene

That Joseph sprang from the lineage of David, the most holy Evangelists Matthew and Luke have clearly shown. There is this difference between them, that Matthew traces the pedigree from David through Solomon, and Luke through Nathan. But both of them pass in silence over the descent of the Holy Virgin. In explanation of this we shall find on investigation that among the Jews, and in the Holy Scriptures, it has never been in use to chronicle the pedigrees of women. But the Law contains a warning against the tribes intermarrying one with another. Joseph was of the same tribe as David, namely Judah, and since he was a just man (this is the praise which the Gospel of God gives him), he would not have espoused the Holy Virgin, unless she had been of the same race, as such a union would not have been in accordance with the commandment of the law. For this reason the Evangelist held it enough to have shown the descent of Joseph.

Lesson VIII

Therefore, from the stock of Nathan the son of David, Levi begat Melchi and Panther and Panther begat Bar-Panther (for so was he called) and Bar-Panther begat Joachim and Joachim begat the Holy Mother of God. Again, from the stock of Solomon the son of David, Mathan of his wife begat Jacob. And after Mathan was dead, Melchi, of the family of Nathan, son to Levi and brother to Panther, took to him in marriage her that had been the wife of Mathan, and was mother of Jacob, and begat of her Heli. So Jacob and Heli were half-brothers, sons of the same mother, but one of the stock of Solomon and the other of the stock of Nathan.

Lesson IX

Then Heli, who was the descendant of Nathan, died, having had no children. Whereupon, Jacob, who was the descendant of Solomon, took to himself the widow of his half-brother Heli, to raise up seed unto his brother, and begat of her Joseph. So Joseph was by nature the son of Jacob the descendant of Solomon, but in the eye of the Law he had for his father Heli the descendant of Nathan. Things being thus, Joachim took to wife that most eminent and praiseworthy woman, Anne. And even as the patient Anna, being stricken with barrenness, by prayer and promise became the mother of Samuel, so likewise this woman also through prayer and promise received from God the Mother of God, that in fruitfulness she might not be behind any of the famous matrons. And thus grace (for such is the signification of the name of Anne) is mother of the Lady (for such is the signification of the name of Mary). And indeed she became the Lady of every creature, since she has been mother of the Creator.

August 17 ~ St. Hyacinth

Confessor ~ Duplex

All from Common except what follows

Lessons I–III from the occurring Scripture

Lesson IV

Hyacinth was a Pole, and was born in the year 1185 of the noble and Christian family of the Counts of Odrowatz, in the town of Kamien, in the diocese of Wratislaw. He was trained up in learning from his youth, and after studying law and theology, became a Canon of Krakow, where he was eminent above his fellows by the singular godliness of his life and the depth of his learning. Being at Rome, in 1218, he was received into the Order of Friars Preachers by the Founder himself, St. Dominic, and kept in holiness to the end of his life the rule of perfect living which he had learnt from him. He remained always a virgin, and loved modesty, long-suffering, lowliness, self-restraint, and all other good graces as his heritage in the life of a Friar.

Lesson V

In the heat of his love for God, he sometimes passed whole nights in pouring forth prayers and chastising his body, to which he never gave rest but in leaning against a stone or lying upon the ground. He was sent back to his own country, and, on the way, founded a very large house of his Order at Friesach and soon afterwards another at Krakow. In other provinces of the kingdom of Poland he founded four others, and it passes belief what success he had with all kinds of men, by his preaching of the Word of God, and the innocence of his life. Not a day passed wherein he did not display some bright gift of faith, piety, or innocence.

Lesson VI

The zeal of this most holy man for the salvation of his neighbors was that which God marked by His greatest miracles. Among these is famous the time when coming to the River Vistula near Visegrad, and finding it in flood, he crossed it without a boat, drawing over also his three companions standing upon the waves upon his outspread mantle. He led a wonderful life for nearly forty years after his profession, and then foretold to his brethren the day of his death. Upon the very day of the Feast of the Assumption of the Virgin, he finished the recitation of the Divine Office, received the Sacraments with the utmost reverence, and then with the words, "Into thy hands, O Lord," gave up his soul to God in the year of salvation 1257. He was illustrious for miracles even after his death, and Pope Clement

VIII numbered him among the saints.

Lessons VII–IX from the first set in the Common of Confessor Non-Bishops (Homily by St. Gregory)

August 18 - Day 4 within the Octave of the Assumption [1950]

Semiduplex

Lesson I - Cant 4:7–9, 12

From the Canticle of Canticles

Thou art all fair, O my love, and there is not a spot in thee. Come from Libanus, my spouse, come from Libanus, come: thou shalt be crowned from the top of Amana, from the top of Sanir and Hermon, from the dens of the lions, from the mountains of the leopards. Thou hast wounded my heart, my sister, my spouse, thou hast wounded my heart with one of thy eyes, and with one hair of thy neck. How beautiful are thy breasts, my sister, my spouse! My sister, my spouse, is a garden enclosed, a garden enclosed, a fountain sealed up.

Lesson II - Cant 6:3, 8–9; 8:5a

Thou art beautiful, O my love, sweet and comely as Jerusalem: terrible as an army set in array. One is my dove, my perfect one is but one, she is the only one of her mother, the chosen of her that bore her. The daughters saw her, and declared her most blessed: the queens and concubines, and they praised her. Who is she that comes forth as the morning rising, fair as the moon, bright as the sun, terrible as an army set in array? Who is this that comes up from the desert, flowing with delights, leaning upon her beloved?

Lesson III - Cant 8:6–7

Put me as a seal upon thy heart, as a seal upon thy arm, for love is strong as death, jealousy as hard as hell, the lamps thereof are fire and flames. Many waters cannot quench charity, neither can the floods drown it: if a man should give all the substance of his house for love, he shall despise it as nothing.

Lesson IV

From the Apostolic Constitution of Pope Pius XII

All these proofs and considerations of the holy Fathers and Theologians are based upon the Sacred Scriptures as the final foundation; they establish the blessed Mother of God before our eyes, as it were, as most closely united to her divine Son and always sharing his lot. Therefore, it seems impossible to think of her who conceived Christ, gave birth to him, gave him milk, held him in her arms, and clasped him to her heart, as being, after her earthly life, separated from him in body if not in soul. Since our Redeemer is the Son of Mary, he could surely not do otherwise, as the most perfect observer of the divine law, than to honor his most beloved Mother in addition to honoring his eternal Father. And, since it was possible for him to give her this great honor, that she might be preserved from the corruption of the grave, we must believe that he really did so.

Lesson V

And this indeed should be borne in mind, that as far back as the second century the holy Fathers represented Mary as the new Eve of a new Adam, and closely joined to him (although dependently upon him) in the fight against the hellish enemy which, as already foretold in the Protoevangelium, would end in complete victory over sin and death, which two phases are always joined in the writings of the Apostle of the Gentiles. Wherefore, just as the essential glory of Christ's resurrection was a part and final trophy of this victory, so also the association of Mary with her Son in this common struggle was to end with the glorification of her virginal body; for as the same Apostle says: "When this mortal shall have put on immortality, then shall be brought to pass the saying that is written, Death is swallowed up in victory."

Lesson VI

Therefore the august Mother of God, from all eternity united in a hidden way with Jesus Christ by one and the same decree of predestination, immaculate in her conception, an inviolate virgin in her divine motherhood, the gracious cooperator of the Divine Redeemer who triumphed completely over sin and its consequences, was finally granted as the supreme crown of her privileges that she should be preserved free from the corruption of the grave, and that, like her own Son, having conquered death, she might be taken up, body and soul, to the exalted glory of heaven, where she sits in splendor at the right hand of her very Son, the immortal King of ages.

Lesson VII

From the Holy Gospel according to St. Luke (Luke 1:41–50)

At that time: Elisabeth was filled with the Holy Ghost: and she spoke out with a loud voice, and said, Blessed art thou among women. And so on.

Homily by St. Peter Damian, Bishop

O Virgin Mother of God, at whose beauty the sun and the moon stand in awe, come to the aid of them that unceasingly call upon thee, O Lady. Turn unto us, o turn unto us, O Sunamitess, turn unto us, o turn unto us that we may behold thee, O blessed, yea more than blessed, turn thou unto us in thy power. He that is mighty has magnified thee, and has given thee all power in heaven and in earth. Nothing is impossible to thee, to whom it is possible to show the most desolate souls the hope of happiness. For how can that Power ignore thy power, when it received its fleshly origin from thy flesh? Thou standest before that golden altar of reconciliation, not only asking, but commanding, as mistress rather than handmaid. Let thy nature move thee, because the more power thou art, the more merciful must thou be. For it does surely redound to the glory of power, to be unwilling to exact vengeance for wrong. Look upon us through love; I know, O Lady, that thou art the most blessed and that thou lovest with an unconquerable love them that in thee and through thee, thy Son and thy God has loved with a great love. Who knows how many times thou didst turn away the anger of the Judge when the virtue of justice went forth from the presence of God?

Lesson VIII

Turn thou unto us through thy very uniqueness. In thy hands are the treasures of the Lord's mercy, and thou alone art the chosen one to whom such great grace is given. Heaven forbid thy hand should ever weaken, for thou wilt never have to seek any occasion of saving the unfortunate or of pouring you thy mercy. Nor does thy glory ever grow less, but it ever increases, for penitents are taken back into favor, and just souls are raised into glory. Turn thou unto us, O Sunamitess, that is, one who was despised, whose soul the sword did pierce and who has been called the spouse of a carpenter. And why do we ask thee to turn unto us? So that we may behold thee. The greatest glory after seeing God is to see thee, to cling to thee, and to dwell in the fastness of thy protection. Hear us, for thy Son does honor thee and denies thee nothing, and he is God who is blessed forever and ever. Amen.

Lesson IX—Commemoration of St. Agapitus, Martyr

Agapitus was a young man of Palestrina, who eagerly accepted martyrdom at the age of fifteen years, under the Emperor Aurelian. On account of his firmness in his religion, the Emperor ordered him first to receive an exceedingly long whipping, and then to be thrown into a foul dungeon, where he remained for four days without food. Being brought out of prison, live embers were put upon his head, but, whereas he still gave God thanks, he was whipped again, and hung up naked by the feet, in such a way that a thick smoke from a fire kindled under his face might pour into his mouth. Afterwards, boiling water was poured upon his belly, and his jaws were broken. Then presently the judge fell from his judgement seat, and shortly after died. Whereupon the Emperor was enraged, and commanded the holy youth to be thrown to wild beasts, but these dared not to touch him, and he was stricken by the sword at Palestrina.

August 18 ~ Day 4 within the Octave of the Assumption [Pre-1950]

Semiduplex

Lesson I ~ Cant 4:1–4

From the Canticle of Canticles

How beautiful art thou, my love, how beautiful art thou! thy eyes are doves' eyes, besides what is hid within. thy hair is as flocks of goats, which Come up from mount Galaad. Thy teeth as flocks of sheep, that are shorn which come up from the washing, all with twins, and there is none barren among them. Thy lips are as a scarlet lace: and thy speech sweet. thy cheeks are as a piece of a pomegranate, besides that which lieth hid within. Thy neck, is as the tower of David, which is built with bulwarks: a thousand bucklers hang upon it, all the armour of valiant men.

Lesson II ~ Cant 4:7–10

Thou art all fair, O my love, and there is not a spot in thee. Come from Libanus, my spouse, come from Libanus, come: thou shalt be crowned from the top of Amana, from the top of Sanir and Hermon, from the dens of the lions, from the mountains of the leopards. Thou hast wounded my heart, my sister, my spouse, thou hast wounded my heart with one of thy eyes, and with one hair of thy neck. How beautiful are thy breasts, my sister, my spouse! thy breasts are more beautiful than wine, and the sweet smell of thy ointments above all aromatical spices.

Lesson III ~ Cant 4:11–15

Thy lips, my spouse, are as a dropping honeycomb, honey and milk are under thy tongue; and the smell of thy garments, as the smell of frankincense. My sister, my spouse, is a garden enclosed, a garden enclosed, a fountain sealed up. Thy plants are a paradise of pomegranates with the fruits of the orchard. Cypress with spikenard. Spikenard and saffron, sweet cane and cinnamon, with all the trees of Libanus, myrrh and aloes with all the chief perfumes. The fountain of gardens: the well of living waters, which run with a strong stream from Libanus.

Lesson IV

Sermon of St. John Damascene

We have received from an ancient tradition that, at the time of the glorious dormition of the blessed Virgin, all the holy apostles, indeed, who were traveling the world for the salvation of the Gentiles, were lifted up in the highest for a moment, and met in Jerusalem. When they were there, an angelic vision appeared to them, and the psalmody of the heavenly Powers was heard; and thus with divine glory she delivered her holy soul into the hands of God. And her body, which received God in an ineffable way, and was exalted by angelic care and apostolic hymnody, was deposited in a coffin in Gethsemane: in that place the song of the angels remained for three consecutive days.

Lesson V

And after three days, when the angelic song had ceased, those who were present of the Apostles opened the tomb as one Thomas, who had received God and wished to adore the body yet who had been absent, came after the third day; but they could by no means find her body when praying at the sacred place. But when they had found only those which had yet to be arranged, they were surrounded with an indescribable fragrance and they closed the tomb. Stunned by the miracle of her mysteries, they could only think of this: that whoever pleased to take flesh from the Virgin Mary, and to become man and to be born, was God the Word and the Lord of glory: he who preserved her virginity uncorrupted after birth, and also it pleased to honor her unstained body, preserved uncorrupted, by translation before the common and universal resurrection.

Lesson VI

The most holy Timothy, the first bishop of the Ephesians, and Dionysius the Areopagite were then present with the apostles, as the blessed Hierotheus himself testifies in those things which he who was also present at the time, wrote to the aforesaid Timothy, thus saying: "when we too, as you know, and many of our holy brethren, had come together to examine the body which gave the beginning of life and received God (and the Lord's brother James and Peter, the highest and most ancient summit of theologians, were also present): and having seen the sacred body, it pleased all, as each was able, to celebrate with hymns the infinite goodness of the divine power."

Lesson VII

From the Holy Gospel according to St. Luke (Luke 10:38–42)

At that time, Jesus entered into a certain village, and a woman named Martha received Him into her house. And so on.

Homily by St. Augustine, Bishop

Of Martha, concerning the body of the Lord, what shall I say, necessity or will? She ministered to mortal flesh. But who was in mortal flesh? "In the beginning was the Word, and the Word was with God, and God was the Word." Behold what Mary heard. "The Word was made flesh and dwelt among us." Behold, Martha ministered unto him. Therefore Mary chose the better part, which would not be taken away from her. For she has chosen this, which will always remain, therefore it will not be taken away from her.

Lesson VIII

Maria wanted to occupy herself with one thing. She was already holding: "But it is good for me to cling to God." She sat at the feet of our head. The lower she sat, the more she took. For the water flows down to the low valley, indicating the swelling of the hill. Therefore the Lord did not criticize the work, but distinguished the office. You are busy with many things: but one thing is necessary. Mary has already chosen this for herself.

Lesson IX—Commemoration of St. Agapitus, Martyr, as given above in the 1950 propers

August 19 ~ St. John Eudes

Confessor ~ Duplex

All from Common except what follows

Lessons I–III from the occurring Scripture

Lesson IV

John was born in the year 1601, of pious and respectable parents, at a village commonly known as Ri, in the diocese of Seez. While still a boy, when he was fed with the bread of Angels, he cheerfully made a vow of perpetual chastity. Having been received at the College of Caen, directed by the Fathers of the Society of Jesus, he was conspicuous for a remarkable piety; and, committing himself to the protection of the Virgin Mary, when still a youth he signed with his own blood, the special covenant he had entered into with her. Having completed his courses of letters and of philosophy with great distinction, and having spurned opportunities of marriage which had been arranged for him, he enrolled himself with the Congregation of the Oratory de Bérulle, and was ordained priest at Paris. He was on fire with a marvelous love towards his neighbor: for he took the most constant pains in caring for both the souls and bodies of those smitten with the Asiatic plague, in many different places. He was made Rector of the Oratorian house at Caen, but since he had been thinking for a long time of educating suitable young men for the ministry of the Church, earnestly asking for the divine assistance, with a brave spirit he most regretfully departed from the associates with whom he had lived for twenty years.

Lesson V

Accordingly, associating five priests with himself, in the year 1643, on the feast day of the Annunciation of the Blessed Virgin Mary, he founded a Congregation of Priests, to whom he gave the most holy names of Jesus and Mary, and opened the first seminary at Caen; and a great many others followed immediately in Normandy and Brittany, also founded by him. For the recalling of sinful women to a Christian life, he founded the Order of Our Lady of Charity; of which most noble tree, the Congregation of the Good Shepherd of Angers is a branch. Furthermore, he founded the Society of the Admirable Heart of the Mother of God, and other charitable institutions. He was the author of many excellent treatises, and labored as an Apostolic Missionary to the very end of his life, preaching the Gospel in very many villages, towns, and cities, and even in the royal court.

Lesson VI

His matchless zeal was very conspicuous in promoting the salutary devotion towards the most sacred Hearts of Jesus and Mary, whose liturgical worship he was the first of all to devise, although not without some divine inspiration. He is therefore held to be the father, the teacher, and the apostle of that cultus. Courageously withstanding the doctrines of the Jansenists, he preserved unalterable obedience towards the Chair of Peter, and he constantly prayed to God, both for his enemies as well as for his brethren. Broken by so many labors, rather than by years, desiring to be freed and to be with Christ, on the 19th day of August, 1680, frequently repeating the sweet names of Jesus and Mary, he died in peace. As he became illustrious by many miracles, Pope Pius X added him to the list of the Blessed, and as he still shone forth with new signs and wonders, Pope

Pius XI, in the holy year and on the day of Pentecost, placed him among the Saints, and extended his Office and Mass to the universal Church.

Lessons VII–IX from the first set in the Common of Confessor Non-Bishops (Homily by St. Gregory)

August 20 ~ St. Bernard of Clairvaux

Abbot & Doctor ~ Duplex

All from Common except what follows

Lessons I–III from the occurring Scripture

Lesson IV

Bernard was born in the year of salvation 1091 at a decent place in Burgundy called Fontaines. On account of extraordinary good looks, he was as an adolescent very much sought after by women, but he could never be turned aside from his resolution to keep chaste. To fly from these temptations of the devil, he determined at twenty-two years of age to enter the Monastery of Citeaux, whence the Cistercian Order took its rise. When this resolution of Bernard's became known, his brothers did all their diligence to change his purpose, but he only became the more eloquent and happy about it. Them and others he so brought over to his mind, that thirty young men entered the same Order along with him. As a monk he was so given to fasting, that as often as he had to eat, so often he seemed to be in pain. He exercised himself wonderfully in watching and prayer, and was a great lover of Christian poverty. Thus he led on earth a heavenly life, purged of all care and desire for transitory things.

Lesson V

He was a burning and shining light of humility, mercy, and benignity. His concentration of thought was such, that he hardly used his senses except to do good works, in which latter he acted with admirable wisdom. Thus occupied, he refused the Bishoprics of Genoa, Milan, and others, which were offered to him, declaring that he was unworthy of so high a sphere of duty. Being made Abbot of Clairvaux in 1115, he built monasteries in many places, wherein the excellent rules and discipline of Bernard long flourished. When Pope Innocent II, in 1138, restored the monastery of Sts. Vincent and Anastasius at Rome, Bernard set over it the Abbot who was afterwards the Supreme Pontiff, Eugene III, and who is also the same to whom he addressed his book upon Consideration.

Lesson VI

He was the author of many writings, in which it is manifest that his teaching was rather given him of God, than gained by hard work. In consequence of his high reputation for excellence, he was called by the most exalted Princes to act as arbiter of their disputes, and for this end, and to settle affairs of the Church, he often went to Italy. He was an eminent helper to Pope Innocent II in putting down the schism of Peter Pierleoni [Antipope Anacletus II] and worked to this end, both at the Courts of the Emperor and of Henry King of England, and in the Council of Pisa. He fell asleep in the Lord, at Clairvaux, on the 20th day of August, in the year 1153, the sixty-third year of his age. He was famous for miracles, and Pope Alexander III numbered him among the Saints. Pope Pius VIII, acting on the advice of the Congregation of Sacred Rites, declared and confirmed St. Bernard a Doctor of the Universal Church. He also commanded that all should use the Mass and Office for him as for a Doctor, and granted perpetual yearly plenary indulgences to all who should visit Churches of the Cistercian Order upon the Feast day of this Saint.

Lessons VII–IX from the first set in the Common of Doctors (Sermon by St. Augustine)

August 21 ~ St. Jane Frances Frémiot de Chantal

Widow ~ Duplex

All from Common except what follows

Lessons I–III from the occurring Scripture

Lesson IV

Jeanne Frances Frémiot de Chantal was born of parents of the highest rank, at Dijon in Burgundy, on the 23rd day of January, in the year 1575. From her earliest childhood she gave no obscure promise of a life of eminent holiness. It is said that when she was scarcely fifteen years of age she confuted with precocious acuteness a Calvinist nobleman, and when he gave her a little present she put it in the fire, saying: "That is how heretics will burn in hell for not believing Christ when He speaks." On the death of her mother, she placed herself under the keeping of the Virgin Mother of God, and discharged a maid who strove to entice her into loving the world. She had nothing youthful about her ways. She shrank from the pleasures of life. She had a strong wish that she might die a martyr. She devoted herself unweariedly to religion and piety. Her father gave her in marriage, at twenty years of age, to the Baron de Chantal, and she strove to excel in all the duties and graces of a wife. She made it her work to see that her children, her servants, and all others under her authority were taught the doctrines of the faith and the practice of good living. She relieved the sufferings of the poor by plentiful almsgiving, for which purposes God not infrequently multiplied her money. And so it came to pass that no one ever asked her for food in Christ's name and was refused it.

Lesson V

When her husband was accidentally killed on the hunt, in her widowhood she determined to embrace the more excellent way, and took a vow not to marry again. She bore her bereavement with resignation to the Will of God, and so far overcame her horror of the gentleman who had fired the shot, that, to show she attributed no blame to him, she stood godmother to his little boy. She was quite content with few servants and plain cookery and dress, and sold her rich wardrobe for the benefit of charities. She received offers of second marriage which would have been both useful and honorable, but never was induced to accept one of them, and to harden herself in her intention of remaining in her widowhood, she renewed her vow to that effect, and branded on her chest with a hot iron the most holy name of Jesus Christ. Her love grew tenderer every day, and she had brought to her the starving, the abandoned, the diseased, and those who were afflicted with the most sickening disorders. Them she not only sheltered, comforted, and nursed, but washed and mended their filthy and ragged garments, and shrank not from putting her mouth to their sores oozing with disgusting matter.

Lesson VI

She used the services of St. Francis de Sales as her spiritual adviser, and when she learnt from him what was the will of God, she scrupled not to disregard the wishes of her own father, brother-in-law, and even of her son, whom she left with calm determination, went forth from her home, and founded the holy Institution of the Sisters of the Visitation of St. Mary, at Annecy, upon Trinity Sunday 1610. She most rigidly kept the rules of this Institute, and loved so well to be poor, that it made her glad to lack even the necessaries of life. She showed herself a model of Christian humility, obedience, and all virtues. Having settled in her heart still to go up higher and higher towards the Temple of the Lord, she bound herself by a most difficult vow always to do that which she should understand to be best. It was chiefly through her labour that the holy Institute of the Visitation became spread far and wide, and she stirred up the sisters to piety and love by her words, by her example, and by writings full of Divine wisdom. She duly received the Sacraments before her death, and then, at Moulins, on the 13th day of December, in the year 1641, departed hence, to be for ever with the Lord. St. Vincent of Paul, who was far distant, in a vision beheld her soul borne to heaven, and St. Francis de Sales coming to meet it. Her body was afterwards taken to Annecy. She was famous for miracles both before and after her death, and Pope Benedict XIV enrolled her among the Blessed, and Pope Clement XIII among the Saints. Pope Clement XIV ordered her Feast day to be kept by the whole Church upon the twenty-first day of August.

Lessons VII–IX from the Common of Non-Virgins (Homily by St. Gregory)

August 22 ~ The Immaculate Heart of Mary—Octave Day of the Assumption

Duplex II Class

All from Common except what follows

Lesson IV

Sermon by St. Bernardine of Siena

What man, unless secure in a divine oracle, may presume to speak with impure, indeed with polluted lips, anything little or great about the true Mother of God and of man, whom the Father before all ages predestined a perpetual Virgin, whom the Son chose as his most worthy Mother, whom the Holy Ghost prepared as the dwelling place of every grace? With what words shall I, a lowly man, give expression to the highest sentiments of the virginal Heart uttered by the holiest mouth, for which the tongues of all the Angels do not suffice? For the Lord says: "A good man brings forth good things from the good treasure of his heart;" and this word can also be a treasure. Among pure mortals who can be conceived of as better than she who was worthy to be the Mother of God, who for nine months had as a guest in her heart and in her womb God himself? What better treasure than the divine love itself, which was burning in the Heart of the Virgin as in a furnace?

Lesson V

And so, from this Heart as from a furnace of divine ardor the Blessed Virgin brought forth good words, that is, words of the most ardent charity. For as from a vessel full of the richest and best wine only good wine can be poured; or as from a furnace of intense heat only a burning fire is emitted; so indeed from the Mother of Christ no word can go forth except of the greatest and most intense divine love and ardor. It is also the mark of a wise woman and matron to speak few words, but words that are effective and full of meaning; and so seven times, as it were, seven words of such wonderful meaning and virtue are read as having been uttered by the Most Blessed Mother of Christ, that mystically it may be shown she was full of the sevenfold grace. To the Angel twice only did she speak; to Elizabeth also twice; with her Son likewise twice, once in the temple, and a second time at the marriage feast; and once to the attendants. And on all those occasions she always said very little; with this one exception that she spoke at length in the praise of God and in thanksgiving, namely, when she said: "My soul magnifies the Lord." But here she did not speak with man, but with God. Those seven words were spoken in a wonderful degree and order according to the seven courses and acts of love; as if they were seven flames from the furnace of her Heart.

Lesson VI—From ecclesiastical documents

The liturgical worship, through which due honor is given to the Immaculate Heart of the Virgin Mary, and for which many holy men and women have prepared the way, the Apostolic See itself first approved in the beginning of the nineteenth century, when Pope Pius VII instituted the feast of the Most Pure Heart of the Virgin Mary, to be piously and reverently celebrated by all the dioceses and religious families who had asked for it. Afterwards Pope Pius IX added an Office and a proper Mass to it. But an ardent desire and longing, which had arisen in the seventeenth century, grew day by day, that namely, the same Feast, given greater solemnity, might be spread to the entire Church. In 1942, Pope Pius XII, graciously acceding to this wish, and during the terrible war then ravaging almost the entire world, pitying the infinite hardships of men, and because of his devotion and confidence in our heavenly Mother, in solemn supplication earnestly entrusted the entire human race to her most generous Heart, and in honor of the same Immaculate Heart, he ordered a Feast to be kept forever with its proper Office and Mass.

Lesson VII

From the Holy Gospel according to St. John (John 19:25–27)

In that time: There stood by the cross of Jesus, his mother, and his mother's sister, Mary of Cleophas, and Mary Magdalene. And so on.

Homily by St. Robert Bellarmine, Bishop

The burden and yoke which our Lord imposed on St. John, that he take care of his Virgin Mother, was indeed a sweet yoke and a light burden. Who indeed would not esteem it a happiness to dwell under the same roof with her, who for nine months had borne in her womb the Incarnate Word, and for thirty years had enjoyed the sweetest and happiest communication of sentiments with him? Who does not envy the chosen disciple of our Lord, who in the absence of the Son of God, was given the presence of the Mother of God? Yet, if I am not mistaken, we can obtain by our prayers that our most kind Lord, who became man for our sakes and was crucified for love of us, should say to us: "Behold thy Mother;" and should say to his Mother for each one of us: "Behold thy son."

Lesson VIII

Our good Lord is not avaricious of his graces, if only we approach the throne of grace with faith and confidence, with a true and sincere but not a false heart. He who desires to have us coheirs in the kingdom of his Father, will certainly not disdain to have us coheirs in the love of his Mother. Nor will the most benign Virgin herself take it amiss to have a countless number of children, since she has a heart capable of embracing all of us, and ardently desires that not even one of those souls should perish whom her divine Son redeemed with his precious Blood, and his still more precious death. And so let us approach with confidence the throne of the grace of Christ, and with tears let us humbly beg of him to say to his Mother for each of us: "Behold thy son;" and to each one of us concerning his Mother: "Behold thy Mother."

How well will it be for us under the protection of such a great Mother? Who will dare to drag us out of its bosom? What temptation will be able to overcome us, trusting in the patronage of the Mother of God and of us? Nor would we be the first in obtaining so great a benefit. Many have preceded us; many, I say, came to the particular and clearly maternal patronage of so great a

Virgin, and no one was left confused or sad, but all were cheerful and rejoicing, relying on the patronage of so great a Mother. For of whom it is written: "She will crush thy head," they trust in her, they also will confidently walk on the asp and the basilisk, and trample the lion and the dragon underfoot. For it is not seen that he can perish, of whom it was said to the Virgin by Christ: "Behold your son," provided he himself does not hear with a deaf ear what Christ said to him: "Behold your mother."

Lesson IX—Commemoration of Sts. Timothy, Hippolytus, & Symphorianus, Martyrs

Timothy came from Antioch to Rome in the time of Pope Melchiades. He had preached the faith of Christ there for a year, when he was thrown into irons by Tarquinius, Præfect of the city. After suffering a long imprisonment he was brought to the idols to offer them sacrifice. He boldly refused to commit this great sin, and was thereupon savagely scourged, and his raw body covered with quicklime. He steadily persisted in his testimony under these and other tortures, and at last was beheaded, in the year 311. His body is buried upon the road to Ostia, near the sepulchre of the blessed Apostle Paul. On the same day, under the Emperor Alexander, and at Ostia, Hippolytus, Bishop of Porto, on account of his illustrious confession of the faith, had his hands and feet bound, and was thrown into a deep pit full of water, and so received the crown of his testimony. The Christians buried him there. Also on the same day, in the year 180, under the Emperor Aurelian, and at Autun, the young lad Symphorian was tortured in diverse ways for professing the same faith. As he was being led to die, he heard his mother crying out to him: "My child, my child think of life eternal; Look to heaven and to Him That reigns there! Thy life is not being taken away, but changed for the better." And so, for Jesus Christ's sake, he bravely offered his neck to the executioner.

August 23 ~ St. Philip Benizi

Confessor ~ Duplex

All from Common except what follows

Lessons I–III from the occurring Scripture

Lesson IV

Philip was a scion of the noble Florentine family of the Benizi, from his very cradle he showed signs of holiness. When he had scarcely entered the fifth month of his life, his cries miraculously assumed the form of words, entreating his mother to give some alms to the servants of the Mother of God. While he was a young man at Paris studying letters, but ever of a fervent piety, he stirred up in many the love of our heavenly Fatherland. After his return to his own country, the most Blessed Virgin appeared to him in a vision, and specially called on him to enter the Order of her Servants, which had then been newly founded. He withdrew himself to a cave on Monte Senario, where he led a rough life as regards the chastisement of the flesh, but sweet with meditation on the agonies of Christ. Thence he came forth and went through nearly all Europe and great part of Asia, preaching the Gospel, founding Guilds everywhere in honor of the Seven Sorrows of the Mother of God, and extending his Order by the wonderful example of his own holy life.

Lesson V

He was forced against his own wishes to undertake the duties of General of his Order, and, in his love of God and of the spreading of the Catholic Faith, sent forth brethren to preach the Gospel of Christ in Russia. He himself went through many cities of Italy, stilled the raging quarrels of the inhabitants, and recalled many of them to their obedience to the Bishop of Rome. He left nothing undone to forward the salvation of his neighbor, and brought the most depraved wretches to leave their sins, do penance, and love Jesus Christ. He was most earnest in prayer, and was often seen to fall into trances while engaged in it. Virginity he so prized that to his very last breath he kept it unsullied by way of self-imposed and stern penances.

Lesson VI

Everywhere appeared in him an extraordinary pity towards the poor, whereof it is a famous instance that at the village of Camiliano in the territory of Siena he gave his own garment to a naked leper who asked him for alms, and as soon as the said leper had cast it about him he was straightway cleansed of his leprosy. The fame of this miracle spread far and wide, and some of the Cardinals who had assembled at Viterbo after the death of Clement IV, to elect a successor to him, cast their eyes upon Philip, with whose heavenly wisdom they were also acquainted. When the man of God found how things stood, lest he should be constrained to take upon him the burden of the Pastoral Office, he went and hid himself on Mount Amiata, until Gregory X had been proclaimed Pope. By his prayers he obtained medicinal powers for the waters in these mountains, which are still called St. Philip's Baths. At length, on the 22nd of August, in the year 1285, he departed this life in a most holy manner at Todi, while embracing the image of Christ hanging upon the Cross, which he called his book. At his grave the blind received their sight, the lame walked, and the dead were raised. Pope Clement X, finding him famous for these and many other great signs and wonders, enrolled his name among those of the Saints.

Lessons VII–IX from the second set in the Common of Confessor Non-Bishops (Homily by St. Bede)

August 24 ~ St. Bartholomew the Apostle

Duplex II Class

All from Common except what follows

Lesson IV

The Apostle Bartholomew was a Galilean. In the division of the world among the Apostles it fell to his lot to preach the Gospel of Jesus Christ in hither India. He went thither and preached to those nations the coming of the Lord Jesus, according to the Gospel of St. Matthew. When he had turned many in that province to Jesus Christ, and had endured many toils and woes, he came into the Greater Armenia.

Lesson V

There he brought to the Christian faith Polymius the King, and his wife, and likewise the inhabitants of twelve cities. This stirred up a great hatred against him among the priests of that nation. They so inflamed Astyages, the brother of King Polymius, against the Apostle, that he savagely ordered Bartholomew to be flayed alive and beheaded; under which martyrdom he gave up his soul to God.

Lesson VI

His body was buried at the town of Albanopolis in the Greater Armenia, where he had suffered. It was afterwards taken to the Island of Lipari, and thence carried to Benevento. Lastly, the Emperor Otto III brought it to Rome, where it was laid in the Church dedicated to God in his name on the Island in the Tiber.

Lesson VII

From the Holy Gospel according to St. Luke (Luke 6:12–19)

At that time Jesus went out into a mountain to pray, and continued all night in prayer to God. And when it was day, He called unto Him His disciples. And so on.

Homily by St. Ambrose, Bishop

All they who go up into the mountain are the great and the aspiring. It is not to every man that the Prophet says: "O thou that tellest good tidings to Sion, get thee up into the high mountain, Thou that tellest good tidings to Jerusalem, lift up thy voice with strength." Not with bodily feet, but by high deeds get thee up into this mountain, and follow Christ, that thou mayest be a mountain thyself. Therefore it is that thou findest in the Gospel that none but His disciples went up into the mountain with the Lord. The Lord therefore prays, not to entreat anything for Himself, but to obtain something for me. For, albeit the Father had given the Son power over all flesh, that He might give eternal life to as many as He had given Him the Son Himself, being found in fashion as a man, thinks well to pray the Father on our behalf, inasmuch as He is our Advocate with the Father.

Lesson VIII

And continued all night in prayer to God. Herein, O Christian, a pattern is set before thee, an example is given thee, after the which thou oughtest to aspire. What does it not behoove thee to do for thy salvation, when Christ spent a whole night in prayer for the same? What does it become thee to do, when thou willest some good work, when Christ prayed before He sent forth

His Apostles? He prayed first, and He prayed alone. Neither, unless I am mistaken, do we anywhere find that He ever joined in prayer with His disciples. He always prayed alone. Human desires cannot grasp the counsel of God, nor can any man, however spiritually minded, share the thoughts of God.

Lesson IX

The Evangelist continues thus: "And when it was day, He called unto Him His disciples and of them He chose twelve whom He sent forth to help the salvation of men by sowing the seed of the faith throughout the whole world." Consider here the counsel of heaven. He chose out for His mission men, not wise, nor rich, nor noble, but fishermen and publicans, lest He should seem to have converted any to His grace by skill, or bought them with money, or drawn them by the power and authority of greatness, and the simple force of the truth, not the charms of argument, might have the victory.

August 25 ~ St. Louis IX

King & Confessor ~ Semiduplex

All from Common except what follows

Lessons I–III from the occurring Scripture

Lesson IV

Louis IX, King of France, was born on the 25th day of April, in the year of our Lord 1215. At the age of twelve years he lost his father. He was brought up under the godly care of his mother, Blanche of Castile. In the twentieth year of his reign he fell grievously sick, and the thought then occurred to him of recovering possession of Jerusalem. On his health being restored, he received a banner from the Bishop of Paris, and crossed the sea with a very great army. In his first battle he put the Saracens to flight, but, a great number of the soldiers perishing by disease, he was himself conquered and taken prisoner.

Lesson V

The King afterwards entered into treaty with the Saracens, and he and his army departed in peace. He remained five years in the East, during which he redeemed great numbers of Christians from slavery among the unbelievers, and also brought many of the unbelievers themselves to believe in Christ. Moreover he rebuilt several cities of the Christians at his own cost. Meanwhile, his mother departed this life, whereby he was constrained to return home, where he gave himself up entirely to works of piety.

Lesson VI

He built many monasteries, and charitable institutions for the poor. By his alms he relieved the needy, and often visited the sick, for whom he not only provided at his own cost, but waited on them with his own hands with such things as they wanted. He wore plain dress and constantly chastised his body with hair-cloth and fasting. In the year 1270 he crossed the sea to Tunis to make war again upon the Saracens. His camp was pitched in sight of the enemy, but he was seized with pestilence, and died uttering the words "I will come into thy house; I will worship toward thy holy temple, and praise thy Name." His body was afterwards carried to Paris, and it is kept and honored in the famous Abbey Church of St. Denis, but his head in the oratory called La Sainte Chapelle. He was renowned for miracles, and Pope Boniface VIII enrolled his name among those of the Saints.

Lesson VII

From the Holy Gospel according to St. Luke (Luke 19:12–25)

At that time, Jesus spoke this parable unto His disciples: A certain nobleman went into a far country to receive for himself a kingdom and to return. And so on.

Homily by St. Ambrose, Bishop

It is well ordered that, being about to call the Gentiles, and to command the destruction of those Jews who would not have Christ to reign over them, He should put forth first this parable; lest it should be said He had given the Jews no means of becoming better. How can they be asked to repay who have received nothing? That is not a piece of silver of little worth, which, when the woman before mentioned in this Gospel has lost, she lights a candle, and sweeps the house, and searches diligently until she finds it.

Lesson VIII

In the end, one made ten pounds from one and another five. Perchance by him which had the five pounds is signified he which practices well, since the body has five senses, and by him which had the ten, that is, double the other, he which is learned and orthodox in the deep things of doctrine, as well as upright in his practical life. Hence also in Matthew we have five talents and two talents, the five talents signifying good practice, and the two talents precept and practice together. So that that which counts as the greater number is but a fraction of the lesser number.

Lesson IX

And here we may also understand by the ten pounds the ten words—or Decalogue, that is, the Commandments, and by the five pounds, the enforcement of their teaching. But I would that a lawyer should be in all things perfect. For the kingdom of God is not in word but in power. Also it is well that in speaking of Jews, Christ should represent only two as bringing in increased capital, for these talents are talents not of money but of grace, and to increase money by usury is a very different thing from improving heavenly revelation by like means.

August 26 ~ St. Zephyrinus

Pope & Martyr ~ Simplex

Lessons I–II from the occurring Scripture

Lesson III

Pope Zephyrinus was a Roman, who was called to govern the Church in the year 202, during the reign of the Emperor Severus. It was he who decreed that they who are to be ordained should be ordained only at a fit time, and in the presence of many clerics and laymen, as was indeed already the custom, and that none but learned men and well known and spoken of should be set apart to that office. He decreed also that when the Bishop celebrated the Holy Liturgy, all the Priests should be present around him. Also he decreed that no Patriarch, Primate, or Metropolitan should pronounce sentence on a Bishop, unless they were charged with the authority of the Apostolic See. He lived as Pope eighteen years. He held four December ordinations, wherein he made thirteen Priests, seven Deacons, and thirteen Bishops for diverse places. He received the crown of his testimony under the Emperor Antonine, and was buried on the Appian Way, near the cemetery of Callistus, upon the 26th day of August, in the year 219.

August 27 ~ St. Joseph Calasanz

Confessor ~ Duplex

All from Common except what follows

Lessons I–III from the occurring Scripture

Lesson IV

Joseph Calasanz, called "of the Mother of God," was born of a noble family at Petralta in Aragon, on the 15th day of September, in the year of Christ 1556. From his tender years he began to show that fondness for children, and that gift of instructing them for which he was afterwards distinguished. He called them around him when he was still but a child himself, and taught them the mysteries of the faith and godly prayers. He was deeply learned in profane and sacred letters, and it was while he was studying theology at Valencia that he bravely overcame the wiles of a noble and powerful lady and, by a brilliant victory, kept untarnished that virginity which he had vowed to God. He became a Priest in consequence of a vow, and was summoned by many Bishops in the kingdoms of New Castile, Aragon, and Catalonia to help them in their work, wherein he surpassed the hopes of all, correcting depraved manners, restoring the discipline of the Church, and marvelously putting an end to hatreds and bloody feuds. But in obedience to a vision from heaven and many warnings from the voice of God, he left Spain and went to Rome.

Lesson V

In Rome he afflicted his body with extraordinary hardness of living, with watching, and with fasting, and so passed his days and nights in prayer, and in the contemplation of heavenly things. He was used to visit the Seven Pilgrim Churches of Rome almost every night, a custom which he kept for many years. Having joined several pious Brotherhoods, it was strange how eagerly he relieved the poor by alms and every sort of kindness, choosing especially the sick and the imprisoned. When the city was ravaged by a pestilence, such was the charitable zeal with which he joined in the labors of St. Camillus de Lellis, that besides the great help which he brought to the sick poor, he would even carry the bodies of the dead on his own shoulders to burial. Having understood from God that his call was to bring up children in godliness and good learning, he founded the Order of the Poor Clerics Regular of the Pious Schools of the Mother of God, who profess as the special object of their Institute a singular care for the teaching of the poor. This Institute received the warm approval of Clement VIII, Paul V, and other Popes, and in a short time obtained a marvelous extension through many provinces and kingdoms of Europe. In this work Joseph Calasanz underwent so many toils, and patiently bore so many griefs, that he was proclaimed by all men a wonder of endurance and a very image of holy Job.

Lesson VI

Then when he was at the head of his whole Order, and toiling with all his might for the salvation of souls, he never ceased to teach children, especially the poor, to sweep out the school-rooms, and to accompany the scholars home. Thus, in spite of broken health, he worked on for fifty-two years with the greatest patience and humility. He won that God should glorify him by many miracles worked in the presence of his disciples, and that the Most Blessed Virgin should appear to him, with the Child Jesus in her arms, blessing them as they prayed. He refused wealthy preferments when they were offered to him. He was eminent for the gift of prophecy, for the power of reading the secrets of the heart, of knowing distant events, and of miracles. The Virgin Mother of God, to whom from his childhood he had a special love, and other heavenly ones, honored him by often allowing him to see them. He foretold the day of his own death, and the restoration and growth of his Order, which seemed at that time to be almost entirely destroyed. He fell asleep in the Lord at Rome, upon the 25th day of August, in the year of salvation 1648, and of his own age the 92nd. A hundred years after his death, his heart and tongue were found whole and incorrupt. God glorified him by many miracles even after his death, and he was first crowned by Benedict XIV with the honors paid to the Blessed, and then solemnly enrolled by Clement XIII among the Saints.

Lessons VII–IX from those for May 15—St. John Baptiste de la Salle (Homily by St. John Chrysostom on Matt 18:1–5)

August 28 ~ St. Augustine of Hippo

Bishop, Confessor, & Doctor ~ Duplex

All from Common except what follows

Lessons I–III from the occurring Scripture

Lesson IV

Augustine was born of honorable parents at Tagaste in Africa, upon the 13th day of November, in the year of our Lord 354. As a boy his great intellectual acuity caused him to far surpass all his companions in learning. When he was living at Carthage as a young man, he fell into the heresy of the Manichæans. He afterwards went to Rome, and was thence sent to Milan to teach Rhetoric. At Milan he often went to hear the sermons of Bishop Ambrose, by whose labors he was drawn to the Catholic Church, and by whom he was baptized on Holy Saturday, 387, at the age of thirty-three. After his return to Africa, in 388, Valerius, the illustrious and saintly Bishop of Hippo, finding him to unite holiness of life with Catholic profession, made him a Priest around the end of 390. At this time he founded a sort of family of pious men, who lived and worshipped in common with him, and whom he earnestly formed upon the model of the Apostolic life and teaching. The Manichæan heresy flaming forth with violence, he began strongly to attack it, and confounded the heresiarch Fortunatus.

Lesson V

Valerius, moved by the godly zeal of Augustine, in December 395, joined him with himself as an assistant in his duties of Bishop; and, dying in the year following, was succeeded by him. He was humble and pure in the highest degree. His furniture and dress were plain, and his food of the commonest sort, which he always seasoned when at table by either reading some religious book, or arguing upon some religious subject. His tenderness to the poor was such that, failing all other resources, he broke up the sacred vessels to relieve their wants. It was his rule not to dwell or be very close friends with any woman, a rule which he did not relax even in the case of his sister and niece, for he was accustomed to say that, although no scandal could arise in the case of such near kinswomen, yet it might arise concerning the women friends who sought their company. He never ceased to preach the Word of God, until he was disabled by heavy sickness. He perpetually pursued after heretics, and by his words and his writings never suffered them to rest anywhere. In great measure, he purged Africa of the Manichæans, Donatists, Pelagians, and other heretics.

Lesson VI

He wrote so much, and that with such godliness and understanding, that he is to be held among the very chiefest of them by whom the teachings of Christianity have been shown forth. He is one of the first of those whom later theologians have followed in method and in argument. He fell sick of a fever what time the Vandals were laying Africa waste, and when they were busy in the third month of besieging Hippo. When he understood that his departure from this present life was at hand, he caused the Psalms of David which most speak the language of repentance to be placed before him, and read them with tears, for he was accustomed to say that even if a man's conscience were to accuse him of no sin, he should not dare to leave this world except as a penitent. His senses remained vigorous to the last, and it was while rapt in prayer, in the presence of the brethren whom he had exhorted to love, piety, and all virtues, that he departed for heaven, upon the 28th of August, 430. He lived 76 years, whereof he had been a Bishop nearly thirty six. His body was first carried to Sardinia, but Luitprand, King of the Lombards, afterwards bought it for a great price, and took it to Ticino, where it is honorably buried.

Lessons VII–IX from the first set in the Common of Doctors (Sermon by St. Augustine)

August 29 – The Beheading of St. John the Baptist

Major Duplex

All from Common of One Martyr except what follows

Lessons I–III from those on June 24—The Nativity of St. John the Baptist

Lesson IV

From the Book by St. Ambrose, Bishop, upon Virgins

We must not hurry by the record of Blessed John the Baptist. We must ask what he was, and by whom, and why, and how, and when he was slain. He was a righteous man murdered by adulterers. The guilty passed upon their judge the sentence of death. Moreover, the death of the Prophet was the fee of a dancing-girl. And lastly, there was a feature about it from which even savages shrink; the order for completing the atrocity was given amid the merriment of a dinner-party. From banquet to prison, from prison to banquet, that was the course run by the servants of the murderer. How many horrors does this simple crime embrace within its details?

Lesson V

Who is there, that, on seeing the messenger hasten from the dinner-table to the prison, would not have forthwith concluded that he carried an order for the Prophet's release? Who, I say, upon hearing that it was Herod's birthday, and that he was giving a great feast, and that he had offered a damsel the choice of whatever she wanted, and that thereupon a messenger had been sent to John's dungeon, would not be thinking about release? If any one, I say, had heard this, what would he have supposed? He would have concluded that the damsel had asked and obtained John's freedom. What have executions in common with dinners, or death with cheer? While the banquet was going on, the Prophet was hurried to death, by an order from the reveler whom he had not troubled even by a prayer for release. He was slain with the sword, and his head was served up in a plate. This was the new dish demanded by a cruelty which the Feast had been powerless to feed.

Lesson VI

Look, most savage King, look at a decoration which suits well with thy banquet. Put out thine hand, so as to lose no part of the luxury of cruelty, and let the streams of the sacred blood run between thy fingers. Thine hunger the dinner has been unable to satisfy, thy cups have not been able to quench thine inhuman thirst. Drink, drink the blood which the still palpitating veins are discharging from the place where the neck has been severed. Look at the eyes. Even in death they remain the eyes of a witness of thy wickedness, but they are closing themselves upon the spectacle of thy pleasures. Those eyes indeed are shutting but it seems not so much from the laws of natural death, as from horror at the scene of thine enjoyment. The golden mouth, whose bloodless lips are silent now, can repeat no more the denunciation which thou couldest not bear to hear, and still thou art afraid of it.

Lesson VII

From the Holy Gospel according to St. Mark (Mark 6:17–29)

At that time Herod had sent forth, and laid hold upon John, and bound him in prison, for Herodias' sake, his brother Philip's wife, for he had married her. And so on.

Homily by St. Augustine, Bishop

The reading of the Holy Gospel has set a scene of cruelty before our eyes: the head of St. John in a charger; a message of death sent forth to discharge the bloody commands of one that hates the truth; a damsel dancing, and a mother rabid; a rash oath sworn in the midst of uncleanness and the revels of a supper, and a wicked fulfillment of the oath so sworn. It befell unto John according to his own saying. For he had said concerning the Lord Jesus Christ: "He must increase, but I must decrease," so John decreased by a head, and Christ's height was made higher upon the Cross. The truth drew hatred. It could not be borne in patience that the holy man of God should utter a rebuke, albeit he sought by his rebuke nothing but the soul's health of them to whom he addressed it. They repaid him evil for good.

Lesson VIII

For what could he say but that whereof he was full? And what could they answer him but that whereof they were full? He sowed wheat, and found thorns. He had said unto the King: "It is not lawful for thee to have thy brother's wife."

Lust had got the better of the King, and he kept a woman whom it was not lawful for him to have, even his brother's wife. But she pleased him, so that his cruelty was lulled. He respected the Saint who had spoken the truth to him. But the horrible woman conceived hatred, and by-and-by brought it forth. When she brought forth, she brought forth a girl, a dancing-girl.

Lesson IX—Commemoration of St. Sabina, Martyr

Sabina was a Roman lady, the wife of a distinguished nobleman named Valentine. The Christian faith was taught to her by a maiden named Seraphia. After the martyrdom of this holy virgin, Sabina gathered together her relics, and buried them with godly service. For this cause she was in a little while arrested, under the Emperor Hadrian, and brought before the Judge Elpidius. "Art thou," said he, "the same Sabina who is so distinguished for her blood and for her marriage?" She answered "I am, but I give thanks to my Lord Jesus Christ for having delivered me through the prayers of His handmaiden Seraphia from the power of demons." Diverse attempts were made to make her change her mind, but when they proved in vain the Præfect passed sentence of death upon her for despising the gods. The Christians laid her body in the same grave in which she had herself laid that of Seraphia, her teacher in the faith.

August 30 ~ St. Rose of St. Mary

Virgin of Lima ~ Duplex

All from Common except what follows

Lessons I–III from the occurring Scripture

Lesson IV

The first flower of holiness which came to full blossom in South America, was the maiden Rose. She was born at Lima, of a Christian father and mother, upon the 20th of April, in the year 1586, and was remarkable from her childhood for marks of saintliness. The occasion of her name was a strange likeness to a rose, which her face assumed when she was a babe. To this name she afterwards added that of the Virgin Mother of God, desiring to be called St. Mary's Rose. At the age of fifteen years she uttered a vow of perpetual virginity. As she grew older, lest her parents should force her to marry, she sheared her head of all her hair, which was very beautiful. She fasted to a degree almost superhuman, passing whole Lents without taking bread, and eating daily only five pieces of lime.

Lesson V

She took the habit of the Third Order of St. Dominic, and then doubled her former severities. She wore a long and very rough hair-cloth, into which she inserted small pins. She wore day and night under her veil a crown, the inner side of which was armed with pricks. In imitation of the hard steps of St. Catharine of Siena, she girded her loins with a threefold iron chain. She made to herself a bed of knotty sticks, and filled the gaps with broken bits of pottery. She built herself a very small hut in the farthest corner of the garden, where she gave herself up to thoughts of heavenly things, and to punishing her body with often scourging, starvation, and sleeplessness. But she waxed strong in spirit, and though she often had to fight with evil ghosts, she conquered them, fearlessly prostrated them, and triumphed over them.

Lesson VI

She suffered greatly from painful illnesses, from the maltreatment of the servants, and from slanderous accusations, but still complained that she did not suffer as much as she deserved. For fifteen years she pined in misery from desolation and dryness of spirit, bravely enduring torments worse than any form of death. After this period she began to overflow with consolation, to be enlightened by visions, and to melt with love like a Seraph's. She attained, by the frequency of visions, to a strange personal familiarity with her Guardian Angel, with St. Catharine of Siena, and with the Virgin Mother of God, and she earned from Christ the words, "Rose of My Heart, be thou My bride." She was famous for many miracles, both before and after she departed hence, and was happily transplanted into the Bridegroom's garden, upon the 24th of August 1617, being aged 31 years. Pope Clement X with solemn rites inscribed her name in the list of holy virgins.

Lessons VII–IX from the first set in the Common of Virgins (Homily by St. Gregory)

Lesson IX—Commemoration of Sts. Felix & Adauctus, Martyrs

Felix was arrested in the reign of the Emperors Diocletian and Maximian, on the charge of having embraced the Christian Faith, and was brought to the temple of Serapis. When he was ordered to offer sacrifice, he spat in the face of the brazen idol, which thereupon fell down. When this happened a second and third time in the temples of Mercury and Diana, he was accused of impiety and magic, and tortured upon the rack. It was not long, however, before he was led out to the second mile-stone upon the road to Ostia, to be smitten with the axe. As they were on the way thither, they chanced to meet a certain Christian, who, when he knew that Felix was going to finish his testimony, said aloud, "I live by the same law as he does; I worship the same Christ Jesus." And therewith he kissed Felix, and they were beheaded together, upon the 30th day of August. What the name of the second person was the Christians never knew, and he is therefore honored under the title of "He-who-was-added"—Adauctus—that is, added to the company of the Holy Martyr Felix in winning of the crown.

August 31 ~ St. Raymund Nonnatus

Confessor ~ Duplex

All from Common except what follows

Lessons I–III from the occurring Scripture

Lesson IV

Raymund is commonly called "the Unborn" (*Non-natus*), because his was one of the rare cases in which the child is not brought into the world in the course of nature, but by a surgical operation after the death of the mother. He was the son of godly and noble parents, at Portell, in the diocese of Urgel in Catalonia. The tokens of his holy later life appeared even in his childhood. The things that delight children, and the attractions of the world, had no charm for him. He was so earnest in piety that all men marveled at his habits of premature old age. As he grew older, he gave himself to the study of letters, but, at the command of his father, turned to farming. He went often to the Chapel of St Nicholas, in the suburbs of Portell, to visit the sacred image of the Mother of God, which is still sought with great tenderness by the faithful. There he poured forth his soul in prayer, and earnestly entreated the Mother of God herself to be pleased to take him for her son, to show him the way wherein it should be safe for him to walk, and to teach him the science of the Saints.

Lesson V

And the most gracious Virgin was not deaf to his prayers. From her he understood that it would please her well, if he would join the Religious Order which had just been founded at her own inspiration, under the title of Mercy, for the Ransom of captives. As soon as he had received this intimation from her, he went to Barcelona, and entered the Institute so nobly dedicated to love for our neighbor. Once enlisted in the Regular Army, he guarded unspotted forever the virginity which he had already consecrated to the Blessed Virgin. But he was a bright and shining light of all other good words and works, especially of tender compassion for Christians who were passing a life of grievous bondage in the possession of unbelieving masters. To free such he was sent into Africa, and delivered many. But his money ran short, and as there were still many in imminent danger of denying the faith, he pawned himself. He was enkindled with a most vehement longing for the salvation of souls, and by his exhortations brought many Mohammedans to Christ. The Moors therefore threw him into close prison, and put him to diverse tortures, at last making holes through his lips and locking them together with an iron padlock, which horrid cruelty he long bore.

Lesson VI

By the account of these, and other brave things that he did, he got the name of a Saint far and wide. Gregory IX was moved thereby to make Raymund a Cardinal of the Holy Roman Church, but in this place of honor the man of God shrank from all outward show, and clung ever tightly to the lowliness that beseems a Religious man. He had started for Rome, in obedience to the command of the Pope, but had only got as far as Cardona, six miles from Barcelona, when he was seized with his last illness, and earnestly called for the strengthening Sacraments of the Church. But his position became critical, and the Priest had not arrived. Then Angels came unto him, clad in the habit of his own Order, and ministered unto him the wholesome Viaticum. When he had taken It, he gave God thanks, and departed hence to be ever with the Lord. It was the last Lord's Day in August, 1240. After his death there was some dispute arose as to where his body should be buried so they shut it up in a box, and laid it upon a blind mule, and the beast was guided by God to carry it to the chapel of St. Nicholas, that he might be buried where he had laid the foundations of his nobler life. There was built there a Convent of his Order, and the faithful come together thither from all parts of Catalonia to honor him, and he is famous for diverse signs and wonders.

Lessons VII–IX from the first set in the Common of Confessor Non-Bishops (Homily by St. Gregory)

FEASTS OF SEPTEMBER

September 1 ~ St. Giles

Abbot ~ Simplex

Lessons I–II from the occurring Scripture

Lesson III

The holy Abbot Giles (Ægidius) was by birth an Athenian, and of Royal lineage. From his youth he showed ever such a love for sacred learning and for works of charity, that he seemed to care for nothing else. When his father and mother were dead, he bestowed his whole inheritance upon the poor. He took off even his own coat, to clothe a poor sick man, and the sick man was healed forthwith as soon as he put it on him. As Giles became famous for working miracles, he fled from glory among men, and betook himself to Arles, in France, to the company of blessed Cæsarius. After the space of two years he departed thence, and went into the desert, for he lived in wonderful holiness for a long while upon the roots of herbs and the milk of a hind, which came to him at regular hours. This hind was chased one day by the King's hounds, and took refuge in Giles's cave. Thereby the King of France was moved earnestly to entreat of him that he would suffer a monastery to be built in the place where this cave was. At the behest of the King, he took the rule of this monastery, albeit himself unwilling, and discharged this duty wisely and piously for some years, until he passed away to heaven.

September 2 ~ St. Stephen of Hungary

King & Confessor ~ Semiduplex

All from Common except what follows

Lessons I–III from the occurring Scripture

Lesson IV

Stephen was the son of Geysa, fourth Duke of the Hungarians, and was born at Gran in the year 977. He it was who first gave to Hungary the faith of Christ and the name of a kingdom. He obtained the Kingly crown from the Bishop of Rome, and being by command of the same anointed King, he made an offering of his kingdom to the Apostolic See. With wonderful devotion and bounty he founded diverse godly houses at Rome, Jerusalem, and Constantinople, and in Hungary the Archbishopric of Gran and ten other Sees. Toward the poor he had the same love and bounty. He greeted them as though they were Christ Himself, and never sent any one away sorrowing and empty. He spent vast sums in relieving their poverty, and also often parted among them with exceeding tenderness even the furniture of his house. Moreover it was his use to wash the feet of the poor with his own hands, and to go in the night, alone and unknown, to the hospitals, and to wait on them that lay there, and show them other deeds of kindness. It was the reward of these good works that, when the rest of his body decayed, his right hand remained uncorrupt.

Lesson V

He passed almost whole nights in earnest prayer, and when totally rapt in the thought of heavenly things, he sometimes became beside himself, and was seen to rise off the ground into the air. In more than one instance he strangely escaped through the power of prayer from rebellion, treason, and the onslaughts of mighty foes. He married Gisela of Bavaria, sister to the Emperor Saint Henry, and begat Emeric, whom he trained up in such manners and piety, as are shown by his also becoming a Saint. To carry on the business of his kingdom, he gathered together from all quarters the most learned and godly men, and took nothing in hand without their advice. Meanwhile he entreated of God by the most lowly supplications, offered up in sackcloth and ashes, that, before he departed this life, he might see all Hungary Catholic. On account of his excellent zeal for the spread of the Faith he is called the Apostle of that nation, and the Bishop of Rome gave to him and to his successors the right to have a Cross carried before them.

Lesson VI

He most ardently venerated the Mother of God and, building a very great Church in her honor, made her Patroness of Hungary. In return, the Virgin received him into heaven, in the year 1038, upon the day of her own Assumption, which the Hungarians, by the example of the holy King, call "the Great Lady's Day." His hallowed body yielded the sweetest savor, and reeked with a heavenly liquid, and amid many and diverse wonders it was removed by command of the Bishop of Rome into a more noble place, and more honorably buried. Pope Innocent XI ordered his Feast to be held upon the 2nd day of September, on account of the famous victory over the Turks which was gained upon this day, in the year 1686, when the army of Leopold I, Emperor-elect of the Romans, and King of Hungary, wrested from them, by the help of God, the city of Buda.

Lessons VII–IX from those found on August 25—St. Louis IX (Homily by St. Ambrose on Luke 19:12–26)

September 3 - St. Pius X

Pope & Confessor - Duplex

All from Common except what follows

Lessons I–III from the occurring Scripture

Lesson IV

Pope Pius X, whose name previously was Joseph Sarto, was born in the village of Riese in the Venetian province, to humble parents remarkable for their godliness and piety. He enrolled among the students in the seminary of Padua, where he exhibited such piety and learning that he was both an example to his fellow students and the admiration of his teachers. Upon his ordination to the priesthood, he labored for several years first as curate in the town of Tombolo, then as pastor at Salzano. He applied himself to his duties with such a constant flow of charity and such priestly zeal, and was so distinguished by the holiness of his life, that the Bishop of Treviso appointed him as a canon of the cathedral church and and made him the chancellor of the bishop's curia, as well as spiritual director of the diocesan seminary. His performance in these duties was so outstanding and so highly impressed Leo XIII, that he made him bishop of the Church of Mantua.

Lesson V

Lacking in nothing that makes a good pastor, he labored particularly to teach young men called to the priesthood, as well as fostering the growth of devout associations and the beauty and dignity of divine worship. He would ever affirm and promote the laws upon which Christian civilization depend, and while leading himself a life of poverty, never missed the opportunity to alleviate the burden of poverty in others. Because of his great merits, he was made a cardinal and created Patriarch of Venice. After the death of Pope Leo XIII, when the votes of the College of Cardinals began to increase in his favor, he tried in vain with supplications and tears to be relieved of so heavy a burden. Finally he ceded to their persuasions, saying "I accept the cross." Thus he accepted the crown of the supreme pontificate as a cross, offering himself to God, with a resigned but steadfast spirit.

Lesson VI

Placed upon the chair of Peter, he gave up nothing of his former way of life. He shone especially in humility, simplicity and poverty, so that he was able to write in his last testament: "I was born in poverty, I lived in poverty, and I wish to die in poverty." His humility, however, nourished his soul with strength, when it concerned the glory of God, the liberty of Holy Church, and the salvation of souls. A man of passionate temperament and of firm purpose, he ruled the Church firmly as it entered into the twentieth century, and adorned it with brilliant teachings. He restored the sacred music to its pristine glory and dignity; he established Rome as the principal centre for the study of the Holy Bible; he ordered the reform of the Roman Curia with great wisdom; he restored the laws concerning the faithful for the instruction of the catechism; he introduced the custom of more frequent and even daily reception of the Holy Eucharist, as well as permitting its reception by children as soon as they reach the age of reason; he zealously promoted the growth of Catholic action; he provided for the sound education of clerics and increased the number of seminaries in their diverse regions; he encouraged every priest in the practice of the interior life; he brought the laws of the Church together into one body; he condemned and suppressed those most pernicious errors known collectively as Modernism; he suppressed the custom of civil veto at the election of a Supreme Pontiff. Finally worn out with his labors and overcome with grief at the European war which had just begun, he went to his heavenly reward on the twentieth day of August in the year 1914. Renowned throughout all the world for the fame of his holiness and miracles, Pope Pius XII, with the approbation of the whole world, numbered him among the Saints.

Lesson VII

From the Holy Gospel according to St. John (John 21:15–17)

At that time: Jesus said to Simon Peter, Simon, son of Jonas, lovest thou me more than these? And so on.

Homily by St. Augustine, Bishop

To the threefold denial there is now appended a threefold confession, that his tongue may not yield a feebler service to love than to fear, and imminent death may not appear to have elicited more from his lips than present life. Let it be the office of love to feed the Lord's flock, if it was the signal of fear to deny the Shepherd. Those who have this purpose in feeding the flock of Christ, that they may have them as their own, and not as Christ's, are convicted of loving themselves, and not Christ, from the desire either of boasting, or wielding power, or acquiring gain, and not from the love of obeying, serving and pleasing God.

Lesson VIII

Against such, therefore, there stands as a wakeful sentinel this thrice inculcated utterance of Christ, of whom the Apostle complains that "they seek their own," not the things that are of Christ Jesus. For what else signify the words: "Lovest thou me? Feed my sheep:" than if it were said: "If thou lovest me, think not of feeding thyself, but feed my sheep as mine, and not as thine own; seek my glory in them, and not thine own; my dominion, and not thine; my gain, and not thine; lest thou be found in the fellowship of them that belong to the perilous times, lovers of their own selves, and all else that is joined on to this beginning of evils."

Lesson IX

With great propriety, therefore, is Peter addressed: "Lovest thou me?" and found replying: "I love thee;" and the command applied to him: "Feed my lambs," and this a second and a third time. We have it also demonstrated here that love (*amor*) and liking (*dilectio*) are one and the same thing; for the Lord also in the last question said not: "Dost thou like me? (*Diligis me?*):" but: "Dost thou love me? (*Amas me?*)" Let us, then, love not ourselves but him; and in feeding his sheep, let us be seeking the things which are his, not the things which are our own. For in some inexplicable way, I know not what, every one that loves himself, and not God, loves not himself; and whoever loves God, and not himself, he it is that loves himself. For he that cannot live by himself will certainly die by loving himself; he therefore loves not himself that loves himself to his own loss of life.

September 5 – St. Lawrence Justinian

Confessor Bishop – Semiduplex

All from Common except what follows

Lessons I–III from the occurring Scripture

Lesson IV

Lawrence was born at Venice, in the year 1380, of the noble family of the Justiniani, and was an exceedingly sober lad even from his childhood. He passed a pious boyhood, and feeling the Divine Wisdom calling him to a pure marriage between his own soul and the Word of God, he began to think of becoming a monk. He therefore tried in private some of the exercises of this new warfare, and, among other afflictions of his body, used to sleep upon the bare boards. As he thus sat weighing on the one hand the pleasures of the world and the marriage which his mother wished to bring about for him, and, on the other, the austerity of the cloister, he turned his eyes upon the Cross of the suffering Christ, and said: "Thou, O Lord, art my trust; there hast Thou made my surest refuge." He entered among the Canons of San Giorgio in Alga, where he devised new tortures and declared war against himself as his own worst enemy. He allowed himself no enjoyment, so that he would not even go into the private garden of the house, neither did he ever go thenceforth into the house of his own father, except when his mother was dying, and he went there with dry eyes to pay her the last offices of a son's duty and affection. His obedience, gentleness, and especially his lowliness were very great. He went out of his way to take the most abject pieces of work about the house. He used to go to the most public places of the city, seeking, not so much for food as for mockery, and bore unmoved and in silence the insults and slanders which were cast upon him. He found his ever-present help in prayer, wherein he became often beside himself and rapt in God, and such was the warmth that burned in his heart, that he stirred up failing comrades to hold bravely on and to love Jesus Christ.

Lesson V

In the year 1433, Eugene IV named him Bishop of Venice, an office which he very earnestly struggled to avoid, and which he discharged with great honor. He changed in no way his mode of living, but kept always to his beloved poverty in his table, his furniture, and his bed. He kept but a small household, saying that he had another very large one in Christ's poor. At what hour soever anyone came to see him, he was always ready to receive them, he helped all with the tenderness of a father, not refusing to charge himself with debts, that he might have wherewith to relieve misery. When he was asked with what hope he incurred these liabilities, he answered: "With hope in my Master, Who can easily meet them for me." And the Providence of God put not his hope to shame, but helped him amply with unexpected funds. He built several Convents of nuns, for whom his watchful care ordered a more perfect way of living. He labored much to wean married women from worldly folly and display, and to reform the discipline of the Church and the lives of all. He was indeed worthy that Eugene should call him in the presence of the Cardinals "the glory and ornament of the Episcopate," and that his successor Nicholas V should transfer the title of Patriarch from Grado, and create him, in 1451, the first Patriarch of Venice.

Lesson VI

He was eminent for the gift of tears, in which he offered up to God every day the Sacrifice of atonement. When he was so doing one Christmas at Midnight, he merited to see Christ Jesus in the form of a little Child exceedingly fair to look upon. Such was his care of the flock committed to his charge, that it was sometime revealed from heaven that the Commonwealth had been saved by the prayers of her Bishop. He was inspired with the spirit of prophecy, and foretold many things which no wit of man could have perceived. By his prayers he often put diseases and devils to flight. Though very ignorant of letters, he wrote books which breathe heavenly teaching and godliness. When he fell into his last deadly sickness, his servants got ready a more comfortable bed for the suffering old man, but he turned away from such ease as so different from the hardness of the Cross upon which his Master had died. He ordered himself to be laid upon the planks to which he was accustomed, and when he knew that the end of his life was come, he looked up to heaven and said: "I come to Thee, O good Jesus" and so fell asleep in the Lord on the 8th day of January, in the year 1455. How precious was his death was attested by this, that some Carthusian monks heard Angels singing and that the hallowed corpse, remaining unburied for two months, was whole and incorrupt, always yielding a sweet smell, and rosy in the face. New miracles took place after his death, whereby Pope Alexander VIII was moved to enroll his name among those of the Saints. Innocent XII appointed for his Feast the 5th day of September, being that upon which he had first been enthroned in his Cathedral Church.

Lessons VII–IX from the first set in the Common of Confessor Bishops (Sermon by St. Gregory)

September 8 ~ The Nativity of the Blessed Virgin Mary

Major Duplex

All from Common except what follows

Lessons I–III from those on August 15—The Assumption of the BVM [Pre-1950 Propers] (Cant 1:1–16)

Lesson IV

Sermon by St. Augustine, Bishop

Dearly beloved brethren, the day for which we have longed, the Feast-day of the Blessed and venerable and

Ever-Virgin Mary, has come. Let our land laugh and sing with merriment, bathed in the glory of this great Virgin's rising. She is the flower of the field on which the priceless lily of the valley has blossomed. This is she whose delivery changed the nature that we draw from our first parents, and cleansed away their offense. At her that dolorous sentence which was pronounced over Eve ended its course; to her it was never said: "In sorrow thou shalt bring forth children." She brought forth a Child, even the Lord, but she brought Him forth, not in sorrow, but in joy.

Lesson V

Eve wept, but Mary laughed. Eve's womb was big with tears, but Mary's womb was big with joy. Eve gave birth to a sinner, but Mary gave birth to the sinless One. The mother of our race brought punishment into the world, but the Mother of our Lord brought salvation into the world. Eve was the foundress of sin, but Mary was the foundress of righteousness. Eve welcomed death, but Mary helped in life. Eve smote, but Mary healed. For Eve's disobedience, Mary offered obedience; and for Eve's perfidy, Mary offered faith.

Lesson VI

Let Mary now strike up the organ, and between its quick notes let the rattling of the Mother's timbrel be heard. Let the gladsome choirs sing with her, and their sweet hymns mingle with the changing music. Hearken to what a song her timbrel will make accompaniment. She says: "My soul magnifies the Lord, and my spirit has rejoiced in God my Saviour. For He has regarded the lowliness of His handmaid, for, behold, from henceforth all generations shall call me blessed; for He That is Mighty has done to me great things." The new miracle of Mary's delivery has effaced the curse of the frail backslider, and the singing of Mary has silenced the wailing of Eve.

Lesson VII

From the Holy Gospel according to St. Matthew (Matt 1:1–16)

The Book of the generation of Jesus Christ, the Son of David, the son of Abraham. Abraham begat Isaac, and Isaac begat Jacob. And so on.

Homily by St. Jerome, Priest

In Isaiah we read: "Who shall declare His generation?" Let us not think that there is any contradiction between the Prophet and the Evangelist, because the Prophet says that this thing cannot be done, and the Evangelist begins by doing it. The one speaks of the generation of the Divine, the other of the Incarnation. Matthew begins with carnal things, that by learning of men we may go on to learn of God. "The Son of David, the son of Abraham." The reversal of the order in these clauses is a needful change. If Abraham had been put first and David afterwards, Abraham would have had to be taken again, in order to marshal the pedigree properly.

Lesson VIII

Matthew first calls Christ the Son of these (Abraham and David) without making mention of the others, because unto these two only was promise of Christ made unto Abraham, where it is said: "In thy seed" that is, in Christ "shall all the nations of the earth be blessed," and unto David, in the words "Of the fruit of thy body will I set upon thy throne." "And Judas begat Phares and Zara of Thamar." It is to be remarked that in the genealogy of the Saviour none of the holy women are named, but those women only are named against whom the Scripture has to say something amiss. He Who came to save sinners was born of sinners, that He might wash away all sin. Afterwards are named Ruth, who was a Moabitess, and Bethsabee, who had been the wife of Urias.

"And Jacob begat Joseph." Julian [the Apostate] Augustus objected in this place with the (apparent) disagreement of the Evangelists: why Matthew the Evangelist called Joseph the son of Jacob, and Luke called him the son of Heli. He does not understand the custom of the Scriptures, that one is his father according to nature, and the other according to law. For we know this through Moses, ordering the precept from God, that if a brother or a relative died without a son, another should take a wife to raise up the seed of his brother or relative. "Joseph, the husband of Mary." When you will have heard "husband," let not nuptials befall your suspicion; but remember the custom of the Scriptures, that the bridegroom is called husband, and the bride wife.

Lesson IX—Commemoration of St. Adrian, Martyr

Adrian was a man who was employed by the Emperor Maximian to persecute the Christians of Nicomedia. The firmness with which they owned their faith and endured their torments oftentimes excited his wonder, and at last so powerfully moved him that he himself turned to Christ. For this he was thrown into prison along with twenty-three other Christians. There he was visited by Natalia his wife, who also herself already had believed in Christ, and by her urged on to lift up his testimony. When he was brought out of prison he was lashed until his bowels fell out. His shins were then broken, and his hands and feet cut off, whereafter, in company with many others, he brought to a happy end the conflict of martyrdom.

Saturday after the Nativity of the Blessed Virgin Mary

Simplex

If there be no occurring feast, all as in the Votive Office of Our Lady on Saturday, with Lessons I & II from the occurring Scripture except for the following:

Lesson III

Sermon by St. Bernard, Abbot

What starry splendor flashes in the birth of Mary? Manifestly, she was a daughter of Kings, a child of the seed of Abraham, a Princess of the lineage of David. But whereas this is but too little, add that she is known to be granted by God to that race, on account of her singular privilege of holiness which the same possesses, to have been promised from heaven long before her fathers were born, to have been foreshadowed by mysterious wonders, and foretold by the utterances of Prophets. She was the rootless rod of Aaron the Priest, which not yet budded, and brought forth buds, and blooms, and blossoms, and yielded almonds. She was the fleece of Gideon, which was put on the floor, and whereon only there was a dew when it was dry upon all the earth besides. She was the gate which Ezechiel saw, which looked toward the East and was shut, and the Lord said unto him: "This gate shall be shut, it shall not be opened, and no man shall enter on by it."

September 9 ~ St. Gorgonius

Martyr ~ Simplex

Lessons I–II from the occurring Scripture

Lesson III

Gorgonius was a native of Nicomedia, and one of the chamberlains of the Emperor Diocletian. He, with the help of a fellow-chamberlain named Dorotheus, brought all the other chamber-servants to believe in Christ. Both of them one day saw a martyr hideously tortured in the presence of Diocletian, and the example of his testimony roused them both up to desire the same, and they both said: "Why, O Emperor, dost thou punish this man only, by condemning an opinion which we share with him? His belief is our belief. Our will is the same." The Emperor thereupon ordered them to be bound and scourged till their bodies were perfectly flayed, and a mixture of vinegar and salt poured into the wounds. Soon after he commanded them to be bound again and grilled on bars over hot coals. Finally, after a variety of tortures, they were hanged. The body of the holy Gorgonius was some time brought to Rome, and buried between the two laurel-trees upon the Latin Way, but, afterwards, during the Pontificate of Gregory IV, it was brought into the Church of the Prince of the Apostles.

September 10 ~ St. Nicholas of Tolentino

Confessor ~ Duplex

All from Common except what follows

Lessons I–III from the occurring Scripture

Lesson IV

Nicholas, surnamed Tolentino because he lived in that town for most part of his life, was born at St. Angelo, a place near Fermo, in the March of Ancona, about the year 1245. His parents were godly people, and in their desire to have children, vowed and made a pilgrimage to the shrine of St. Nicholas at Bari, where they were assured of their wish, and therefore gave the name of Nicholas to the son whom they received. From his childhood the lad gave many good signs, but especially as regarded abstinence. In his seventh year, in imitation of his blessed namesake, he began to fast on several days of the week, which custom he always kept, and was content with only bread and water.

Lesson V

After he reached man's estate, he enlisted himself in the army of the clergy, and was made a Canon. One day he chanced to hear a sermon upon contempt of the world delivered by a preacher of the Order of Hermits of St. Augustine, and was so moved by it that he forthwith entered that Order. As a Friar he was most strictly observant of that way of life. He subdued his body with rough clothing, stripes, and an iron chain. He never ate meat, and seldom any relish to his meals. And he was a burning and shining light of love, humility, patience, and all other virtues.

Lesson VI

He persisted in constant and earnest prayer, notwithstanding many troubles from the assaults of Satan, who sometimes even flogged him. Every night for six months before his death he heard Angels singing with such sweetness that it was a foretaste of the happiness of heaven, and he would often repeat the words of the Apostle: "I have a desire to depart and to be with Christ." Lastly, he foretold to his brethren the day of his death, which was the 10th day of September 1306. After his death also he was famous for miracles, and when due investigation had been made thereof, Pope Eugene IV enrolled his name among those of the Saints.

Lessons VII–IX from the second set in the Common of Confessor Non-Bishops (Homily by St. Bede)

September 11 ~ Sts. Protus & Hyacinth

Martyrs ~ Simplex

Lessons I–II from the occurring Scripture

Lesson III

Protus and Hyacinth were brothers, eunuchs of the blessed Virgin Eugenia, and were baptized along with her by Bishop Helenus. They gave themselves to the study of God's Word, and dwelt for a while in wonderful lowliness and holiness of life in a monastery in Egypt. However, they afterwards followed the holy Virgin Eugenia to Rome, in the reign of the Emperor Gallienus, and were arrested in that city for professing the Christian faith. By no means could they be brought to leave the Christian religion and to worship the gods, and they were therefore severely scourged and beheaded, upon the 11th day of September.

September 12 ~ The Holy Name of Mary

Major Duplex

All from Common of the BVM except what follows

Lesson IV

Sermon by St. Bernard, Abbot

It is said: "And the virgin's name was Mary." Let us speak a few words upon this name, which signifies, being interpreted, "Star of the Sea," and suits very well the Virgin Mother, who may very fittingly be likened unto a star. A star gives forth her rays without any harm to herself, and the Virgin brought forth her Son without any hurt to her virginity. The light of a star takes nothing away from the star itself, and the birth of her offspring took nothing away from the Virginity of Mary. She is that noble star which was to come out of Jacob, whose brightness still sheds luster upon all the earth, whose rays are most brilliant in heaven, and shine even unto hell, lighting up earth midway, and warming souls rather than bodies, fostering good and scaring away evil. She, I say, is a clear and shining star, twinkling with excellencies, and resplendent with example, needfully set to look down upon the surface of this great and wide sea.

Lesson V

Thou, whosoever, that knowest thyself to be here not so much walking upon firm ground, as battered to and fro by the gales and storms of this life's ocean, if thou wouldest not be overwhelmed by the tempest, keep thine eyes fixed upon this star's clear shining. If the hurricanes of temptation rise against thee, or thou art running upon the rocks of trouble, look to the star, call on Mary. If the waves of pride, or ambition, or slander, or envy toss thee, look to the star, call on Mary. If the billows of anger or avarice, or the enticements of the flesh beat against thy soul's barque, look to Mary. If the enormity of thy sins trouble thee, if the foulness of thy conscience confound thee, if the dread of judgment appall thee, if thou begin to slip into the deep of despondency, into the pit of despair, think of Mary.

Lesson VI

In danger, in difficulty, or in doubt, think on Mary, call on Mary. Let her not be away from thy mouth or from thine heart, and that thou mayest not lack the aid of her prayers, turn not aside from the example of her conduct. If thou follow her, thou wilt never go astray. If thou pray to her, thou wilt never have need to despair. If thou keep her in mind, thou wilt never wander. If she hold thee, thou wilt never fall. If she lead thee, thou wilt never be weary. If she help thee, thou wilt reach home safe at the last and so thou wilt prove in thyself how rightly it is said "And the virgin's name was Mary."

[Here ends St Bernard]

Particular honors were already paid to this venerable name in diverse parts of the Christian world, but the Roman Pontiff, Innocent XI, ordered this Feast in honor of it to be held every year throughout the whole Church, within the Octave of the Nativity of the Blessed Virgin Mary, as an everlasting thanksgiving for the great blessing that, under her protection, the brutal Sultan of the Turks, who was trampling upon the necks of the Christian population, was thoroughly beaten before the walls of Vienna in Austria, upon the 12th day of September, in the year 1683.

Lesson VII

From the Holy Gospel according to St. Luke (Luke 1:26–38)

At that time: The Angel Gabriel was sent from God unto a city of Galilee, named Nazareth, to a Virgin espoused to a man whose name was Joseph, of the house of David; and the Virgin's name was Mary. And so on.

Homily by St. Peter Chrysologus

Dearly beloved brethren, you have heard this day how an Angel treated with a woman about the reparation of mankind. You have heard how it was arranged that man should return to life by the same means whereby he had fallen into death. The Angel deals, deals with Mary concerning salvation, because an angel had dealt with Eve concerning destruction. You have heard how an Angel set about to raise with unspeakable building a temple of the Divine Majesty out of the dust of the earth. You have heard how by a mystery which cannot be understood, God got a place on earth and man a place in heaven. You have heard how by a working hitherto unheard of, God and man are joined together in one Body. You have heard how at the message of an angel, the weak nature whereof our flesh is sharer, became strong to bear the whole glory of the Divinity.

Lesson VIII

Then, lest the frail clay of humanity should break down under the weight of God's work, and in Mary the tender stem should snap, which was about to bear the fruit of all mankind, the Angel's first words were a preventive against fear. And the Angel said unto her "Fear not, Mary." Even before the matter is revealed, the exalted station of this Virgin is made clear by her very name, for the name "Mary" is a Hebrew word which in Latin is called *Domina*—that is, "Lady." The Angel therefore greets her as "Lady," that the Mother of the Lord may lay aside the fearfulness of His handmaiden, whom the will of her own Offspring had made to be born and to be called a Lady. "Fear not, Mary, for thou hast found grace." He that has found grace, need fear no more. "Thou hast found grace."

Lesson IX

Blessed is she who first and alone among mankind deserved to hear: "Thou hast found grace." And how much grace? Even as the Angel had said: Full! "Full of grace." Full indeed! Grace like a bountiful shower drenched and soaked her whole being. "For thou hast found grace with God." As he says this, even the Angel does marvel. He marvels that a woman should merit eternal life, that all men should merit it through her. The Angel marvels that the whole Divinity, He to whom the entire universe is small, should enter the narrow womb of a virgin. So he delays. He calls her virgin. That was her right. He hails her as full of grace. Then, with great trepidation he delivers his message, scarcely able to phrase it so that it could be understood.

September 14 ~ The Exaltation of the Holy Cross

Major Duplex

Lesson I ~ Num 21:1–3

From the Book of Numbers

And when king Arad the Chanaanite, who dwelt towards the south, had heard this, to wit, that Israel was come by the way of the spies, he fought against them, and overcoming them carried off their spoils. But Israel binding himself by vow to the Lord, said: It thou wilt deliver this people into my hand, I will utterly destroy their cities. And the Lord heard the prayers of Israel, and delivered up the Chanaanite, and they cut them off and destroyed their cities: and they called the name of that place Horma, that is to say, Anathema.

Lesson II ~ Num 21:4–6

And they marched from mount Hor, by the way that leadeth to the Red Sea, to compass the land of Edom. And the people began to be weary of their journey and labour: And speaking against God and Moses, they said: Why didst thou bring us out of Egypt, to die in the wilderness? There is no bread, nor have we any waters: our soul now loatheth this very light food. Wherefore the Lord sent among the people fiery serpents.

Lesson III ~ Num 21:6–9

The serpents bit them and killed many of them. Upon which they came to Moses, and said: We have sinned, because we have spoken against the Lord and thee: pray that he may take away these serpents from us. And Moses prayed for the people. And the Lord said to him: Make a brazen serpent, and set it up for a sign: whosoever being struck shall look on it, shall live. Moses therefore made a brazen serpent, and set it up for a sign: which when they that were bitten looked upon, they were healed.

Lesson IV

Khosrow II of Persia, having, in the last days of the reign of the Emperor Phocas, overrun Egypt and Africa, in 614, took Jerusalem, where he slaughtered thousands of Christians and carried off to Persia the Cross of the Lord, which Helen had put upon Mount Calvary. Heraclius, the successor of Phocas, moved by the thought of the hardships and horrid outrages of war, sought for peace, but Khosrow, drunken with conquest, would not allow of it even upon unfair terms. Heraclius therefore, being set in this uttermost strait, earnestly sought help from God by constant fasting and prayer, and through His good inspiration gathered an army, joined battle with the enemy, and prevailed against three of Khosrow's chief captains, and three armies.

Lesson V

Khosrow was broken by these defeats, and when in his flight, in 628, he was about crossing the Tigris, he proclaimed his son Medarses partner in his kingdom. Khosrow's eldest son Sheroë took this slight to heart, and formed a plot to murder his father and brother, which plot he brought to effect soon after they had come home. Then he got the kingdom from Heraclius upon certain terms, whereof the first was that he should give back the Cross of the Lord Christ. The Cross therefore was received back after it had been fourteen years in the power of the Persians, and in 629 Heraclius came to Jerusalem and bore it with solemn ceremony unto the Mount whereunto the Saviour had borne it.

Lesson VI

This event was marked by a famous miracle. Heraclius, who was adorned with gold and jewels, was forced to stand at the gateway which leads unto Mount Calvary, and the harder he strove to go forward, the harder he seemed to be held back, whereat both himself and all they that stood by were astonished. Then spoke Zacharias, Patriarch of Jerusalem, saying: "See not, O Emperor, that in carrying the Cross adorned in triumphal vesture thou showest too little of the poverty and humility of Jesus Christ." Then Heraclius cast away his princely raiment and took off his shoes from his feet, and in common garb easily finished his journey, and set up the Cross once more in the same place upon Calvary whence the Persians had carried it away. Therefore, the solemnity of the Exaltation of the Holy Cross became more famous thenceforward because the Cross had been replaced by Heraclius where it had first been planted by the Saviour.

Lesson VII

From the Holy Gospel according to St. John (John 12:31–36)

At that time, Jesus said unto the multitudes of the Jews: Now is the judgment of this world, now shall the prince of this world be cast out. And so on.

Homily by St. Leo, Pope

Dearly beloved brethren, when we gaze upon Christ lifted up upon the Cross, the eyes of our mind see more than that which appeared before the wicked, unto whom it was said through Moses: "And thy life shall hang in doubt before thee, and thou shalt fear day and night, and shalt have no assurance of thy life." They saw in the crucified Lord nothing but the work of their own wickedness, and they feared greatly, not with that faith which gives life by justification, but with that whereby the evil conscience is tortured. But our understanding is enlightened by the Spirit of truth, and with pure and open hearts we see the glory of the Cross shining over heaven and earth, and discern by inward glance what the Lord meant when His Passion was nigh at hand, and He said: "Now is the judgment of this world, now shall the prince of this world be cast out. And I, if I be lifted up from the earth, will draw all things unto Myself."

Lesson VIII

How wonderful is the power of the Cross! O how unutterable is the glory of the Passion, wherein stands the Lord's judgment-seat, and the judgment of this world, and the might of the Crucified! Lord! Thou hast drawn all things unto thee! Thou didst spread out thine Hands all the day unto an unbelieving and gainsaying people, but the world has felt and owned thy Majesty! Lord! Thou hast drawn all things unto thee! All the elements gave one wild cry of horror at the iniquity of the Jews, the lights of the firmament were darkened, day turned into night, earth quaked with strange tremblings, and all God's work refused to serve the guilty. Lord! Thou hast drawn all things unto thee! The veil of the Temple was rent in two from the top to the bottom, the Holy of Holies denied itself as a Sanctuary for the ministration of unworthy Priests, that the shadow might be changed for the substance, prophecy for realization, and the Law for the Gospel.

Lesson IX

Lord! Thou hast drawn all things unto thee! That which was veiled under types and shadows in the one Jewish Temple, is hailed by the love of all peoples in full and open worship. There is now a higher order of Levites, a more honorable rank of elders, a Priesthood with a holier anointing. Thy Cross is a well of blessings for all, and a cause of thanksgiving for all. Thereby for them that believe in thee, weakness is turned into strength, shame into glory, and death into life. The changing ordinance of diverse carnal sacrifices is gone; the one oblation of thy Body and Blood fulfills them all. For Thou art the Very Paschal Lamb, Which takest away the sins of the world, and art in thyself all offerings finished. And even as Thou art the One Sacrifice Which takes the place of all sacrifices, so may thy kingdom be one kingdom established over all peoples.

September 15 ~ The Seven Sorrows of the Blessed Virgin Mary

Duplex II Class

Lesson I ~ Lam 1:2; 1:20–21

From the Lamentations of the Prophet Jeremias

Weeping she hath wept in the night, and her tears are on her cheeks: there is none to comfort her among all them that were dear to her: all her friends have despised her, and are become her enemies. Behold, O Lord, for I am in distress, my bowels are troubled: my heart is turned within me, for I am full of bitterness: abroad the sword destroyeth, and at home there is death alike. They have heard that I sigh, and there is none to comfort me.

Lesson II ~ Lam 2:13, 15–16

To what shall I compare thee? or to what shall I liken thee, O daughter of Jerusalem? to what shall I equal thee, that I may comfort thee, O virgin daughter of Sion? for great as the sea is thy destruction: who shall heal thee? All they that passed by the way have clapped their hands at thee: they have hissed, and wagged their heads at the daughter of Jerusalem, saying: Is this the city of perfect beauty, the joy of all the earth? All thy enemies have opened their mouth against thee: they have hissed, and gnashed with the teeth, and have said: We will swallow her up.

Lesson III ~ Lam 2:17–18

The Lord hath done that which he purposed, he hath fulfilled his word, which he commanded in the days of old: he hath destroyed, and hath not spared, and he hath caused the enemy to rejoice over thee, and hath set up the horn of thy adversaries. Their heart cried to the Lord upon the walls of the daughter of Sion: Let tears run down like a torrent day and night: give thyself no rest, and let not the apple of thy eye cease.

Lesson IV

Sermon by St. Bernard

The Martyrdom of the Virgin is set before us, not only in the prophecy of Simeon, but also in the story itself of the Lord's Passion. The holy old man said of the Child Jesus, "Behold, this Child is set for the fall and the resurrection of many in Israel; and for a sign which shall be contradicted; yea," said he unto Mary, "a sword shall pierce through thine own soul also." Even so, O Blessed Mother! The sword did indeed pierce through thy soul! for nought could pierce the Body of thy Son, nor pierce thy soul likewise. Yea, and when this Jesus of thine had given up the ghost, and the bloody spear could torture Him no more, thy soul winced as it pierced His dead Side. His Own Soul might leave Him, but thine could not.

Lesson V

The sword of sorrow pierced through thy soul, so that we may truly call thee more than martyr, in whom the love that made thee suffer along with thy Son, wrung thy heart more bitterly than any pang of bodily pain could do. Did not that word of His indeed pierce through thy soul, sharper than any two-edged sword, even to the dividing asunder of soul and spirit? "Woman, behold thy son!" O what a change to thee! Thou art given John for Jesus, the servant for his Lord, the disciple for his master, the son of Zebedee for the Son of God, a mere man for Very God. O how keenly must the hearing of those words have pierced through thy most loving soul, when even our hearts, stony, iron, as they are, are wrung at the mere memory thereof!

Lesson VI

Marvel not, my brethren, that Mary should be called a Martyr in spirit. He indeed may marvel who remembers not what Paul says, naming the greater sins of the Gentiles, that "they were without natural affection." Such was far from the heart of Mary, and far may it be from those of her servants! But some man perchance will say: Did she not know that He was to die? Yea, without a doubt she knew it. Did she not hope that He was soon to rise again? Yea, she most faithfully hoped it. And did she still mourn because He was crucified? Yea, bitterly. But who art thou, my brother, or whence hast thou such wisdom, to marvel less that the Son of Mary suffered than that Mary suffered with Him? He could die in the Body, and could not she die with Him in her heart? His was the deed of that Love, greater than which has no man; hers, of a love, like to which has no man, save He.

Lesson VII

From the Holy Gospel according to St. John (John 19:25–27)

At that time: There stood by the Cross of Jesus His Mother, and His Mother's sister, Mary of Cleophas, and Mary Magdalene. And so on.

Homily by St. Ambrose, Bishop

"There stood by the Cross His Mother." Men had forsaken Him, but she stood there fearless. Behold how the Mother of Jesus could break through her shrinking modesty, but could not belie her heart. With the eyes of a mother's love she gazed upon the Wounds of her Son, those Wounds through Which she knew redemption for all mankind was flowing. The Mother, who feared not the executioners, was able to endure the sight of their work. Her Son was hanging upon the Cross, and she braved His tormentors.

Lesson VIII—From 25th Epistle to Vercelli

Mary, the Mother of the Lord, stood by the Cross of her Son. My only informant of this fact is Saint John the Evangelist. Others have written that when the Lord suffered, the earth quaked, the heavens were veiled in darkness, the sun was hidden, and the thief received, after a good confession, the promise of Paradise. John has taught us what the others have not taught us. Upon the Cross He called her Mother. It is reckoned a greater thing that in the moment of triumph over agony, He should have discharged the watchful duty of a Son to His Mother, than that He should have made gift of the kingdom of heaven. For if it be a sacred thing to have forgiven the thief, this so great kindness of the Son to the Mother is to be honored as the outcome of a tenderer and more touching love.

Lesson IX—Commemoration of St. Nicomedes, Martyr

Nicomedes was a Priest who was ordered to be seized during the persecution of the Christians by the Emperor Domitian, because he had buried the body of the Virgin Felicula, who had been slain by Count Flaccus for confessing the Christian Faith. He was led to the statues of the gods, and forasmuch as he stoutly disobeyed the command to sacrifice to them, since sacrifice is due only to the one true God Who reigns in heaven, he was scourged with leaden whips until he sealed his testimony by giving up his spirit to God. The same Count ordered his body to be thrown into the floods of the Tiber, but Justus, cleric to Nicomedes, sought diligently for it until he found it, and buried it honorably upon the Nomentan Way, near the city walls.

September 16 ~ Sts. Cornelius & Cyprian

Pope & Bishop, Martyrs

~ Semiduplex

All from Common of Many Martyrs except what follows

Lesson IV

Cornelius was a Roman who held the Papacy during the reign of the

Emperors Gallus and Volusian. He, and that most holy Lady Lucina, took the bodies of the Apostles Peter and Paul out of the Catacombs and put them in more convenient places. Lucina laid the body of Paul in a farm of her own upon the road to Ostia, near the place where he had received the sword-stroke. Cornelius placed that of the Prince of the Apostles near where he had been crucified. When this was told to the Emperors, and likewise that Cornelius was the means of making many Christians, he was banished to Civitavecchia, where Saint Cyprian, the Bishop of Carthage, comforted him by letters.

Lesson V

They continued thus to write often one to the other, till the Emperors took in bad part these exchanges of Christian love, and sent for Cornelius to Rome. There they commanded him to be lashed with leaden scourges as though he were a traitor, and then to be carried to offer sacrifice before the image of Mars. He firmly refused to commit this great impiety, and was forthwith beheaded, upon the 14th day of September, in the year of our Lord 252. The blessed Lucina, with the help of the clergy, buried his body in the sand-pit on her own farm, near the Cemetery of Callistus. He lived as Pope about two years.

Lesson VI

Cyprian was an African. He was first distinguished as a teacher of Rhetoric. He afterwards became a Christian at the persuasion of the Priest Cæcilius, whose surname he took, and parted all his goods among the poor. It was not long before he was chosen a Priest, and then made Bishop of Carthage. It would be idle to enlarge upon his wit, seeing that his works are as well known as the sun. He suffered under the Emperors Valerian and Gallienus, in the eighth persecution, and upon the same day, though not in the same year, that Cornelius testified at Rome.

Lessons VII–IX from the first set in the Common of Many Martyrs (Homily by St. Gregory)

Lesson IX—Commemoration of Sts. Euphemia, Virgin, Lucy, & Geminian, Martyrs

Euphemia, Lucy, and Geminian were all crowned with Martyrdom in the persecution under Diocletian, upon the same day, though not in the same place. Euphemia was a virgin of Chalcedon, who suffered diverse tortures under the Proconsul Priscus. She endured unflinchingly the rods, the rack, the wheels, and the fire, and in the end was thrown to wild beasts which all licked her feet, save one that gave her holy body such a bite, that she forthwith resigned her immaculate spirit to God. Lucy was a widow at Rome, who was accused by her own son Eutropius, that she had for many years worshipped Christ. She was put into a vessel of hot pitch and lead, but came forth unhurt. As she was being dragged through the city loaded with iron and lead, the sight of her faith and unwavering testimony converted to Christ the nobleman Geminian. He was one of many whom she had brought to the faith, and she had him for a comrade in her glorious martyrdom, for he was diverse ways tormented, and then beheaded. Their bodies were given honorable burial by the Christian lady Maxima.

September 17 ~ The Impression of the Holy Stigmata on St. Francis of Assisi

Confessor ~ Duplex

All from Common except what follows

Lesson I ~ Gal 5:25–26; 6:1–6

From the Epistle of St. Paul the Apostle to the Galatians

If we live in the Spirit, let us also walk in the Spirit. Let us not be made desirous of vain glory, provoking one another, envying on another. Brethren, and if a man be overtaken in any fault, you, who are spiritual, instruct such a one in the spirit of meekness, considering thyself, lest thou also be tempted. Bear ye one another's burdens; and so you shall fulfil the law of Christ. For if any man think himself to be some thing, whereas he is nothing, he deceiveth himself. But let every one prove his own work, and so he shall have glory in himself only, and not in another. For every one shall bear his own burden. And let him that is instructed in the word, communicate to him that instructeth him, in all good things.

Lesson II ~ Gal 6:7–13

Be not deceived, God is not mocked. For what things a man shall sow, those also shall he reap. For he that soweth in his flesh, of the flesh also shall reap corruption. But he that soweth in the spirit, of the spirit shall reap life everlasting. And in doing good, let us not fail. For in due time we shall reap, not failing. Therefore, whilst we have time, let us work good to all men, but especially to those who are of the household of the faith. See what a letter I have written to you with my own hand. For as many as desire to please in the flesh, they constrain you to be circumcised, only that they may not suffer the persecution of the cross of Christ. For neither they themselves who are circumcised, keep the law; but they will have you to be circumcised, that they may glory in your flesh.

Lesson III ~ Gal 6:14–18

But God forbid that I should glory, save in the cross of our Lord Jesus Christ; by whom the world is crucified to me, and I to the world. For in Christ Jesus neither circumcision availeth any thing, nor uncircumcision, but a new creature. And whosoever shall follow this rule, peace on them, and mercy, and upon the Israel of God. From henceforth let no man be troublesome to me; for I bear the marks of the Lord Jesus in my body. The grace of our Lord Jesus Christ be with your spirit, brethren. Amen.

Lesson IV

From the Commentaries of St. Bonaventure, bishop, upon the Life of St. Francis

Francis being indeed a faithful servant and minister of Christ, about the space of two years before he gave back his spirit to heaven, withdrew himself into a high mountain apart, even that mountain which is called Mount Alverno, and began to fast for forty days to the honor of the Archangel Michael. To think of the things above gave him sweeter comfort than he was used to before, and the hot longing for heaven was kindled in him, so that he began to feel that the gifts from above were poured forth upon him in such fullness as he had never felt before. The burning of his desire made his heart rise towards God like the heart of a seraph, and his tender answering love yearned to be changed into the likeness of Him Who has so loved us that He was content to bear the Cross. And it was so that early one morning, about the time of the Feast of the Exaltation of the Holy Cross, he was praying upon the side of the mountain, and there appeared unto him as it had been one of the Seraphim, having six wings, glorious and fiery, flying to him from heaven. It came therefore very swiftly, and stood in the air, near the man of God. He beheld then the appearance thereof that it was not winged only, but crucified also. His hands and feet were stretched forth and nailed to a Cross. Two of his wings were lifted up and joined one to the other over his head, and two were stretched forth to fly withal, and with two he wrapped around his body. When Francis saw it, he was astonished, and his soul was filled with sorrow and gladness, for the eyes of him that appeared were full of strange love and tenderness, so that he conceived great rejoicing thereat, but the nailing to the Cross was so exceedingly dreadful, that as he saw it, a sword of sorrow pierced his soul.

Lesson V

Then He Whom he beheld with his bodily eyes, began to speak silently unto him in his heart, and he understood that albeit the deathless Seraphim cannot suffer or faint, this vision was nevertheless therefore set before him, that he might know that as a friend of Christ he was to be all changed into the likeness of Christ Jesus crucified, not by the martyrdom of the body, but by the fervor of the soul. Then they held together some sweet conversation, as of a man with his friend, and the vision passed from him, but his heart was kindled inwardly with the fire of the Seraphim, and his body was outwardly changed into the likeness of Him Who was crucified, even as wax is softened by the fire and takes the impression of the seal. From thenceforth there were in his hands and feet the marks of the nails. The heads of the nails were seen in the palms of his hands and on the insteps of his feet, and the points came out on the backs of his hands and the soles of his feet. In his right side also was a long raw wound, as though he had been pierced with a spear, from which wound his holy blood oftentimes ran and stained his shirt and breeches.

Lesson VI

Thereafter Francis was a new creature, famous for a new and awful sign. The holy marks of the Lord Jesus, whereon living man for twelve centuries had not been allowed to look, were his adornment. He came down from the mount bearing in himself the form of Jesus Crucified, not portrayed upon tables of stone or wood by the hand of any earthly craftsman, but drawn upon his flesh by the finger of the living God. The dying Seraph knew well that it is good to keep close the secret of a king, and knowing the secret of his King, he strove as far as in him lay to keep the sacred marks hidden from men. Nevertheless, forasmuch as it is the will of the Lord God for His Own glory to make manifest the greatness of His Own works, He openly showed forth diverse wonders through these wounds which He had Himself made in secret, so that the hidden and wondrous power of the marks might become known by the fame of the miracles. The foregoing marvelous but thoroughly witnessed facts, which were already spoken of in Papal documents with special praise and joy, were made, by the pleasure of Pope Benedict XI, the subject of a yearly memorial, which was afterwards extended by Paul V to the whole Church, in the hope of fanning in the hearts of the faithful the love of Christ Crucified.

Lessons VII–IX from the second set in the Common of One Martyr (Homily by St. Gregory)

September 18 ~ St. Joseph of Cupertino

Confessor ~ Duplex

All from Common except what follows

Lesson I ~ 2 Cor 4:6–11

From the Second Epistle of St. Paul the Apostle to the Corinthians

God, who commanded the light to shine out of darkness, hath shined in our hearts, to give the light of the knowledge of the glory of God, in the face of Christ Jesus. But we have this treasure in earthen vessels, that the excellency may be of the power of God, and not of us. In all things we suffer tribulation, but are not distressed; we are straitened, but are not destitute; We suffer persecution, but are not forsaken; we are cast down, but we perish not: Always bearing about in our body the mortification of Jesus, that the life also of Jesus may be made manifest in our bodies. For we who live are always delivered unto death for Jesus' sake; that the life also of Jesus may be made manifest in our mortal flesh.

Lesson II ~ 2 Cor 5:1–8

For we know, if our earthly house of this habitation be dissolved, that we have a building of God, a house not made with hands, eternal in heaven. For in this also we groan, desiring to be clothed upon with our habitation that is from heaven. Yet so that we be found clothed, not naked. For we also, who are in this tabernacle, do groan, being burthened; because we would not be unclothed, but clothed upon, that that which is mortal may be swallowed up by life. Now he that maketh us for this very thing, is God, who hath given us the pledge of the Spirit. Therefore having always confidence, knowing that, while we are in the body, we are absent from the Lord. (For we walk by faith, and not by sight.) But we are confident, and have a good will to be absent rather from the body, and to be present with the Lord.

Lesson III - 2 Cor 12:1–9

If I must glory (it is not expedient indeed), but I will come to visions and revelations of the Lord. I know a man in Christ above fourteen years ago (whether in the body, I know not, or out of the body, I know not; God knoweth), such a one caught up to the third heaven. And I know such a man (whether in the body, or out of the body, I know not: God knoweth), that he was caught up into paradise, and heard secret words, which it is not granted to man to utter. For such a one I will glory; but for myself I will glory nothing, but in my infirmities. For though I should have a mind to glory, I shall not be foolish; for I will say the truth. But I forbear, lest any man should think of me above that which he seeth in me, or any thing he heareth from me. And lest the greatness of the revelations should exalt me, there was given me a sting of my flesh, an angel of Satan, to buffet me. For which thing thrice I besought the Lord, that it might depart from me. And he said to me: My grace is sufficient for thee; for power is made perfect in infirmity. Gladly therefore will I glory in my infirmities, that the power of Christ may dwell in me.

Lesson IV

Joseph was born of godly parents at Cupertino, a small village of the diocese of Nardo, between Brindisi and Otranto, six miles from the coast of the Gulf of Tarento, upon the 17th day of June, in the year of Redemption 1603. The love of God came to him early, and he passed his childhood and youth in great simplicity and innocence. After recovering by the help of the Virgin Mother of God from a long and painful sickness which he bore very quietly, he gave himself altogether to piety and growth in virtue. God called him inwardly to higher things, and to give himself more utterly to His service, he determined in himself to join the Seraphic Order. After diverse failures and changes, he obtained his wish among the Order of Conventual Friars Minor of "La Grotella." He went first as a lay-brother, on account of his ignorance of letters, but God was pleased to allow him afterwards to be taken among the choir brethren. After taking his solemn vows he was ordained Priest, and then set before him to aim at a more perfect life. To this end (as far as in him lay) he thrust from him all earthly affections and all carnal things, even to such as seem almost needful for life. He tormented his body with haircloth, scourging, spiked chains, and every kind of hardship and affliction. He fed his spirit sweetly upon the constant exercise of holy prayer, and gazing upon the highest matters. And so it came to pass that the love of God, which had been enkindled in his heart from his earliest years, burnt forth day by day more strangely and openly.

Lesson V

The chief outcome of this love of God was the strong and marvelous ecstasies whereinto he oftentimes fell. It was, nevertheless, strange to observe that after he had entirely lost his senses he could be called out of the trance by the mere order of his superiors. To be utterly obedient was one of his chief aims, and he was used to say that those who ruled him could lead him about like a blind man, and that it was better to die than not to obey. He so imitated the poverty of the Seraphic Patriarch, that when he was at the point of death, when the Friars use to dispose of anything they have, he was able to tell his Superior that he had absolutely nothing. Thus bearing about in his body the dying of the Lord Jesus, the life also of Jesus was made manifest in his body. When he saw that certain persons had committed a foul sin of impurity, there came from him a strong savor, a proof of that snowy and glorious purity which, in spite of the most hideous temptations whereby the unclean spirit wrestled long to darken it, he kept undefiled, partly by an iron bridling of his senses, partly by the stern punishments he inflicted upon his own body, and partly by the extraordinary protection of the pure Virgin Mary, whom he was used to call his own Mother, whom he honored and worshipped as his most tender Mother in his very heart of hearts, and whom he was eager that all men should honor, because, as he said, "if we have her protection, every good thing comes with it."

Lesson VI

This eagerness on the part of the blessed Joseph was but one outcome from his love for his neighbors. So great was his zeal for souls, that he vehemently sought in all ways for the salvation of all. When he saw his neighbor in any trouble, whether it were poverty or sickness or any other affliction, his tenderness went out toward him, and he helped him as well as he could. They who reviled, and slandered, and insulted himself were not cut off from his love. He was used to welcome such with great long-suffering, meekness, and cheerfulness of countenance and he preserved the same constantly amid many hardships and changes when he was sent hither and thither by command of the Superiors of his Order, and of the Holy Inquisition [on account of his levitations]. People and princes alike marveled at the exceeding holiness of his life, and the spiritual gifts poured upon him from above, but he was so lowly, that he sincerely held himself to be chief among sinners, and earnestly besought God to take away from him the more showy of His gifts. Of men he entreated that after his death they would cast his body somewhere where his memory might soonest perish. But God, Who exalts them of low degree, glorified His servant during life with the gifts of heavenly wisdom, of prophecy, of discerning the hidden thoughts of the heart, of healing, and of other spiritual gifts in marvelous abundance, gave him a precious death, and made the place of his rest glorious. He fell asleep in Jesus upon the very day and at the very place foretold by himself, that is, at Osimo, between Ancona and Loretto, upon the 18th day of September, in the 61st year of his own age, and in that of salvation 1663. He was famous for miracles even after his death, and Benedict XIV enrolled his name among those of the Blessed, and Clement XIII among those of the Saints. Clement XIV, being himself a member of the same Order, extended the use of the Office and Mass in memory of him to the whole Church.

Lesson VII

From the Holy Gospel according to St. Matthew (Matt 22:1–14)

At that time Jesus spoke unto the chief priests and Pharisees by parables, and said The kingdom of heaven is like unto a certain king, which made a marriage for his son. And so on.

Homily by Pope St. Gregory

Dearly beloved brethren, you have already entered, at the Lord's bidding, into the house where the marriage-feast is being held, that is to say, into the Holy Church, and look well to it, that when the King comes in to see the guests, he sees nothing amiss in your soul's wedding-garment. For indeed it is with great searchings of heart that we are bound to consider that which so soon comes. "And when the King came in to see the guests, he saw there a man which had not on a wedding-garment." Dearly beloved brethren, what are we to think is signified by this wedding garment? Is it baptism or is it faith? But without baptism, or without faith, who could be seated at the marriage-feast? He that believes not would still be outside the house. What then, except love, must we understand by the wedding-garment? He who has faith and is in the Holy Church, but has not charity, comes in unto the wedding indeed, but has not a wedding-garment. And charity is well called the wedding-garment, for it is the garment wherewith our Maker decked Himself when He came to wed the Church unto Himself.

Lesson VIII

It was the work of God's love alone that His Only-begotten Son should wed Himself unto the souls of the elect. Whence indeed John says "God so loved the world, that He gave His Only-begotten Son, that whosoever believes in Him should not perish, but have eternal life." He therefore Whom love brought among men, shows that the same love is His wedding-garment. Each one therefore of you who is in the Church and believes in God, has already come in unto the marriage-feast, but if he keeps not the grace of charity, he is come in there not having a wedding garment. In truth, my brethren, if one be asked to an earthly marriage, he changes his attire, to show even by his garments that he rejoices in the joy of the Bride and Bridegroom, and he would be ashamed to appear in unseemly raiment among the guests that are feasting and making merry. We are come unto God's marriage feast, and we make pretense to change the vesture of our hearts. There is joy among the angels when the elect are taken to heaven. With what face shall we look upon this spiritual feast if we come in thither not having charity, the only wedding-garment wherein we can appear beautiful?

Lesson IX

We must know that as every garment is woven upon two beams, an upper and a lower, so love is bound unto two commandments, the one bidding us to love God, and the other to love our neighbor. For thus is it written: "Thou shalt love the Lord thy God with all thy heart, and with all thy soul, and with all thy mind and thy neighbor as thyself." In which we are to see that bounds are set to that love wherewith we are to love our neighbor, for it is said "Thou shalt love thy neighbor as thyself." But to the love wherewith we are to love God are set no bounds, for it is said "Thou shalt love the Lord thy God with all thy heart, and with all thy soul, and with all thy mind." A man is not commanded to what point he is to love God, but from what point, even as it is said, "with all" for he only truly loves God, who leaves nothing for himself. We are bound therefore to keep two commandments regarding love, if we would be seen at the marriage with a wedding-garment.

September 19 ~

Sts. Januarius & Companions

Bishop & Martyrs ~ Duplex

All from the Common of Many Martyrs except what follows

Lessons I–III from the occurring Scripture

Lesson IV

At the time when the Emperors Diocletian and Maximian were furiously raging against Christians, Januarius, Bishop of Benevento, was taken to Nola, to Timothy, Præfect of Campania, on the charge of professing the Christian faith. There his firmness was tried diverse ways, and he was cast into a burning fiery furnace, but came forth thence unhurt, for neither upon his raiment nor upon the hairs of his head did the flame take any hold. Thereupon the wrath of the Præfect was enkindled, and he commanded the martyr to be torn limb from limb. But in the meanwhile Januarius' Deacon Festus and his Lector Desiderius were taken, and the whole three were led in bonds to Puzzuoli in front of the Præfect's carriage, and there thrown into the same prison wherein were already held four other Christians condemned to be devoured by wild beasts, that is to say, Sosius, a Deacon of Miseno, Proculus, a Deacon of Puzzuoli and two laymen, named respectively Eutyches and Acutius.

Lesson V

The next day all seven were exposed to the wild beasts in the amphitheatre, but these creatures forgot their natural fierceness, and lay down at the feet of Januarius. Timothy attributed this to incantations, and commanded the witnesses of Christ to be beheaded. Thereupon he became suddenly blind, until Januarius had prayed for him by which miracle nearly five thousand persons were turned to Christ. But the judge, ungrateful of such a kindness, rather, was enraged by the conversion of such a multitude, and to obey the decrees of the Emperors, he commanded that the holy Bishop and his companions should be smitten with the sword.

Lesson VI

The cities of those coasts strove to obtain their bodies for honorable burial, so as to make sure of having in them advocates with God. By God's will the relics of Januarius were taken to Naples at last, after having been carried from Puzzuoli to Benevento, and from Benevento to Monte Vergine; when they were brought thence to Naples, they were laid in the chief Church there, and there have been famous on account of many miracles. Among these is remarkable the stopping of eruptions of Mount Vesuvius, whereby both that vicinity and also places afar off have been desolated. It is also well known, and is the plain fact, seen even unto this day, that when the blood of Januarius, kept dried up in a small glass phial, is put in sight of the head of the same martyr, it is used to melt and bubble in a very strange way, as though it had but freshly been shed.

Lesson VII

From the Holy Gospel according to St. Matthew (Matt 24:3–13)

At that time As Jesus sat upon the Mount Olivet, His disciples came unto Him privately, saying Tell us when shall these things be? And so on.

Homily by St. Hilary, Bishop

"His disciples came unto Him privately, saying: 'Tell us, when shall these things be and what shall be the sign of thy coming and of the end of the world?'" Here are in one question three distinct points, and the answers are to be understood of three separate times, and by three separate interpretations. "When shall these things be?" And herein He taught them concerning the fall of the city of Jerusalem, whereof He made plain announcement, lest the unlearned might fall a prey to any deceiver. For within the lifetime of His then hearers were to come many, saying: "I am Christ." He gives warning therefore beforehand, lest such pestilential liars should gain any belief.

Lesson VIII

Therefore he strengthens them for the endurance of sufferings, flight, beatings, intimidation, and public hatred against them because of his name. And indeed many are disturbed by these harassments, and are scandalized by so many insurgent evils, and are even roused to mutual hatred. And there will be false prophets (as was Nicholas, one of the seven deacons), and they will pervert the truth with many falsehoods; and, when wickedness abounds, charity will grow cold.

Lesson IX

"But that shall endure unto the end, the same shall be saved. And this Gospel shall be preached in all the world, for a witness unto all nations and then shall the end come." When the knowledge of the heavenly revelation had been carried everywhere, then should come the fall and end of Jerusalem;

then should the punishment of them that had not believed, and the awful example of the city that had been destroyed, bear out the truth of the preacher. When she had stoned, and hunted down, and murdered the Apostles, then should she be consumed by famine, and war, and slavery. And indeed she would then have shown herself unworthy to be any longer, having shown by casting out the preachers of Christ that she was unworthy that any should speak to her of God.

September 20 ~ Sts. Eustace & Companions

Martyrs ~ Duplex

All from Common except what follows

Lessons I–III from the occurring Scripture

Lesson IV

Eustace (Eustachius), whose name before his Baptism was Placidus, was a Roman, well-known on account of his noble birth, his great earthly wealth, and his eminent distinction as a soldier. He gained, under the Emperor Trajan, the post of military commander. Once upon a time he was hunting and following an extraordinarily large stag, when the beast stood still, and Eustace saw between his horns a tall and glorious figure of the Lord Christ hanging upon the Cross, whence came a voice bidding him to follow after life eternal. Thereupon Eustace and his wife Theopista, and their two little sons Agapitus and Theopistus, enlisted themselves as soldiers under the Great Captain, Christ.

Lesson V

In a little while he went back, according as the Lord had commanded him, to the place where he had seen the first vision, and there he heard from God how much he was to bear for His glory. It was not long after that he had great losses and became exceedingly poor, but he bore it very patiently. Then he was constrained to flee secretly, and on the journey was grievously afflicted in that, first, his wife and then his children were parted from him and carried he knew not where. Under the weight of these sorrows he lay hid a long while in a far-off place, working as the steward of a landowner, until the voice of God called him forth, and Trajan sought for him again to make him a captain in his army.

Lesson VI

While he was with the army he found his wife and children once more, by an unexpected happiness, and reentered the City as a conquering soldier amid the loud applause of all men, but thereupon, when he was commanded to offer sacrifices of thanksgiving for the victory to the empty gods, he stoutly refused. They tried him in vain with various artifices to make him deny Christ, but could not, and he and his wife and little ones were thrown to the lions. When these beasts would not touch them, the Emperor's fury was kindled, and he commanded them all to be shut up in the brazen image of a bull, which was heated with fire underneath. There they praised God until their testimony was ended, and they departed hence to be perfectly blessed for ever and ever, upon the 20th day of September. Their bodies were buried whole by the faithful with deep reverence, and were afterwards honorably carried to a Church built in their name.

Lessons VII–IX from the second set in the Common of Many Martyrs (Homily by St. Ambrose)

Lesson IX—Commemoration of the Vigil of St. Matthew

From the Holy Gospel according to St. Luke (Luke 5:27–32)

At that time, Jesus saw a publican, named Levi, sitting at the receipt of custom, and He said unto him: Follow me. And so on.

Homily by St. Ambrose, Bishop

There is a mystery in this calling of the publican, whom He bids to follow Him, not so much by bodily steps as by change of heart. Hitherto Levi had been making greedy gains from merchandise, cruel riches at the cost of sailors' toils and dangers; but now, at the call of a word, he, who had been plundering other men's goods, leaves his own. He leaves that base station, and follows closely after the Lord with all his heart. "And Levi made Him a great feast in his own house." He that welcomes Christ into his home, feasts upon the excellence of all pleasures.

September 21 ~ St. Matthew the Apostle & Evangelist

Duplex II Class

All from Common of Evangelists except what follows

Lesson IV

Matthew, also called Levi, was an Apostle and Evangelist. At Capharnaum, he was sitting at the toll booth and, called by Christ, immediately followed Him whom, with His disciples, he offered a great feast in his own house. After Christ was risen again from the dead, and while he was yet in Judea, before he set forth for that land which had fallen to the lot of his preaching, he wrote the Gospel of Jesus Christ in the Hebrew tongue, for the sake of them of the circumcision who had believed. His was the first written of the four Gospels. Thereafter he went to Ethiopia, and there preached the Gospel, confirming his preaching with many miracles.

Lesson V

Of his miracles, the most notable was that he raised the King's daughter from the dead, and thereby brought her father the King, his wife, and all that region to believe in Christ. After the King was dead, Hirtacus, who came after him, was eager to take his daughter Iphigenia to wife, but by the exhortation of Matthew she had made vow of her virginity to God, and stood firm to that holy resolution, for which cause Hirtacus commanded to slay the Apostle at the Altar while he was performing the mystery. He crowned the dignity of the Apostleship with the glory of martyrdom upon the 21st day of September. His body had been brought to Salerno, where it was afterwards buried in a Church dedicated in his name during the papacy of Gregory VII, and there it is held in great worship and sought to by great gatherings of people.

Lesson VI is Lesson IV from the Common of Evangelists (Exposition by Pope St. Gregory on the Prophet Ezechiel)

Lesson VII

From the Holy Gospel according to St. Matthew (Matt 9:1–13)

At that time, Jesus saw a man, named Matthew, sitting at the receipt of custom; and He saith unto him Follow Me. And so on.

Homily by St. Jerome, Priest

The other Evangelists, out of tenderness towards the reputation and honor of Matthew, have abstained from speaking of him as a publican by his ordinary name, and have called him Levi. Both names were his. But Matthew himself, according to what Solomon says, "the just man is the first to accuse himself," and again, in another place, "declare thou thy sins that thou mayest be justified," does plainly call himself Matthew the publican, to show unto his readers that none need be hopeless of salvation if he will but strive to do better, since he himself had been all of a sudden changed from a publican into an Apostle.

Lesson VIII

Porphyry and the Emperor Julian (the Apostate) will have it that the account of this call of Matthew is either a stupid blunder on the part of a lying writer, or else that it shows what fools they were who followed the Saviour, to go senselessly after any one who called them. But there can be no doubt that before the Apostles believed they had considered the great signs and works of power which had gone before. Moreover, the glory and majesty of the hidden God, which shone somewhat through the Face of the Man Christ Jesus, were enough to draw them which gazed thereon, even at first sight. For if there be in a stone a magnetic power which can make rings and straws and rods come and cleave thereunto, how much more must not the Lord of all creatures have been able to draw unto Himself them whom He called?

Lesson IX

"And it came to pass, as Jesus sat at meat in the house, behold, many publicans and sinners came and sat down with Him." They saw how that a publican who had turned to better things had found a place of repentance, and therefore they also hoped for salvation. It was not, as the Scribes and Pharisees complained, sinners clinging to their sinfulness who came to Jesus, but sinners repenting, as indeed appears from the next words of the Lord, where He says: "I will have mercy and not sacrifice; for I am not come to call the righteous, but sinners to repentance." The Lord went to eat with sinners to the end that He might have occasion to teach, and to break spiritual bread unto them which bade Him.

September 22 ~ St. Thomas de Villanova

Confessor Bishop ~ Duplex

All from Common except what follows

Lessons I–III from the occurring Scripture

Lesson IV

Thomas of Villanova was born of excellent parentage, in the town of Fuenllana, in the Diocese of Toledo in Spain, in the year of our Lord 1488, and was early taught piety, and a special pity towards the needy. Of this grace he gave many examples while he was still a lad, whereof it is an eminent one that he more than once stripped himself of raiment of his own, in order to clothe the naked. He was become a man when the death of his father called him from Alcalá, where he had been sent to work as a student in the great College of St. Alonzo. He gave all the inheritance which fell to him to feed poor unmarried women, and forthwith returned to Alcalá, and finished his course in Theology. He was so eminent in learning that he was commanded to take a Professorship in that University, and delivered remarkable Lectures upon Philosophy and Theology. Meanwhile he ceased not earnestly to entreat of the Lord in prayer the knowledge of the Saints, and to know what was the path of life whereunto he was called. In course of time, by the inspiration of God, he entered the Institute of Hermits of St. Augustine.

Lesson V

In the Order wherein he had professed, he was marked for all that makes a good and edifying Friar, for humility, for patience, for continence, but, above all, for the warmth of his charity. Amid diverse and hard works, he let his spirit never faint from prayer and study of the things of God. On account of his holiness and learning he was bidden to undertake the work of preaching, and, by the help of God's grace, was the means of drawing countless souls out of the mire of sin into the way that leads unto life. Being raised to rule over his brethren, he so joined wisdom, justice, and gentleness with watchfulness and firmness, that he either established or restored in many places the original discipline of his Order.

Lesson VI

He was named to the Archbishopric of Granada, but, with excellent lowliness and firmness, he refused to take so high a place. However, not long after, he was forced by the commands of his superiors to accept the government of the Church of Valencia, which he discharged for nearly eleven years with the reputation of a most holy and watchful shepherd of souls. His elevation changed in no way his manner of life, except to give greater scope to his wonderful charity by placing the revenues of a wealthy Church at his disposal to distribute to the poor. He did not leave himself even a bed that on which he was lying when he was called to heaven, he had only on loan from a person to whom he had shortly before given it as an alms. He fell asleep in the Lord upon the 8th day of September, in the 69th year of his own age, and of our Lord 1555. God was pleased to approve the holiness of His servant by miracles, both during his life and after his death, whereof are specially remarked that when he had utterly emptied his barn by giving away all his corn to the poor, it was suddenly found full again, and that a dead boy was raised to life at his grave. Finding him famous for these signs, and not a few others, Pope Alexander VII enrolled him in the list of the Saints.

Lessons VII–IX from the first set in the Common of Confessor Bishops (Sermon by St. Gregory)

Lesson IX—Commemoration of St. Maurice & Companions, Martyrs

When the Emperor Maximian led his army into Gaul, he stopped at the frontiers of the Seduni to offer a sacrifice. The Theban legion, that they might not be defiled by any share in the unholy rites, withdrew themselves from the rest of his army. Therefore the Emperor sent soldiers unto them to bid them in his name, if they valued their lives, come back into the camp to the sacrifice. They answered that the Christian religion did not allow them. This answer enkindled in him greater wrath than before. He therefore despatched a part of his army to the Thebans with orders to begin by killing one man in every ten of them. By their own will, and at the urgent exhortation of Maurice, they chose rather to endure this martyrdom than to do the commandment of the unrighteous Emperor. At the last, the Emperor, upon the 22nd day of September, bade his whole army fall upon them and slay them all. They confessed Christ bravely even to the end.

September 23 ~ St. Linus

Pope & Martyr ~ Semiduplex

All from Common except what follows

Lessons I–III from the occurring Scripture

Lesson IV

Pope Linus was by birth a native of Velletri in Tuscany, and was the first after Peter who governed the Church. His faith and holiness were such that he not only cast out demons, but also raised the dead. He wrote the acts of Blessed Peter, and especially the history of his strife with Simon Magus. He forbade women to enter the Church without having a veil upon their heads. His own head was cut off, on account of his firmness in confessing Christ, by command of the impious Consul Saturninus, an ungrateful wretch whose own daughter he had delivered from being tormented by a demon. He was buried upon the Vatican Mount, near the grave of the Prince of the Apostles, upon the 23rd day of September. He sat as Pope eleven years, two months, and twenty-three days. He held two December ordinations, wherein he made fifteen Bishops, and eighteen Priests.

Lessons V–VI: from Lessons IV & V of the Second set in the Common of One Martyr (Exposition by St. Ambrose)

Lessons VII–IX from the Common of Supreme Pontiffs (Homily by St. Gregory)

Lesson IX—Commemoration of St. Thecla, Virgin Martyr

This virgin Thecla was the daughter of noble parents at Iconium, and a disciple of the Apostle Paul. She is the subject of extraordinary praises by the holy Fathers. In the eighteenth year of her age, she parted from one Thamiris, to whom she had been betrothed, and her kindred accused her of being a Christian. A pile was set aflame for her, unless she should deny Christ, but she made the sign of the Cross, and willingly entered it, and rain came, and put out the fire. She came to Antioch, where they threw her to wild beasts; and strove to tear her asunder, by tying her to oxen driven different ways; and cast her into a pit with many snakes; but by the mercy of Jesus Christ she was delivered from all. The warmth of her faith and the holiness of her life brought many to Christ. She returned into her own country, and withdrew to be a hermit, alone on a certain mountain, and passed away to be with the Lord, aged ninety years, and famous for many good works and miracles. She was buried at Seleucia.

September 24 ~ Our Lady of Ransom

Major Duplex

All from Common except what follows

Lesson IV

In the early thirteenth century of the era of our Lord, the greatest and fairest part of Spain lay crushed under the yoke of the Saracens, and countless numbers of the faithful were held in brutal slavery, with the most lively danger of being made to deny the Christian faith and of losing everlasting salvation. Amid such sorrows the most Blessed Queen of heaven came mercifully to the rescue, and showed how the greatness of her motherly love was eager for their redemption. Saint Peter Nolasco, in the full bloom of the treasures of godliness as well as rich in earthly wealth, was earnestly pondering with himself how he could aid so many suffering Christians dwelling in bondage to the Moors. To him appeared with gracious visage the Most Blessed Virgin, and bade him know that it would be well pleasing in her own sight, and in the sight of her Only-begotten Son, that an Order of Religious men should be founded in her honor, whose work it should be to redeem prisoners from Mohammedan slavery. Strengthened by this heavenly vision, the man of God began to burn with wonderful charity, nursing in his heart the one desire that he himself and the Order which he should found might exercise that love, greater than which has no man: that a man lay down his life for his friends.

Lesson V

Upon the same night the same most holy Virgin appeared to the Blessed Raymund of Peñafort, and to James, King of Aragon, charging them concerning the founding of the Order, and desiring them to help in raising up so great a work. Peter betook himself forthwith to the feet of Raymund, who was his confessor, and laid the matter before him, whom also he found taught from heaven, and to whose governance he humbly submitted himself. Then came King James, who appointed to carry out this revelation, which himself also had received from the Most Blessed Virgin. The three took counsel together, and all with one consent entered upon the institution of an Order in honor of said Virgin Mother, to be placed under the invocation of St. Mary of Ransom, for the redemption of captives.

Lesson VI

Upon the 10th of August, in the year of our Lord 1218, the same King James decreed the establishment of this Order, thus already conceived by these holy men. The brethren take (in addition to the vows of Poverty, Chastity, and Obedience), a fourth vow, whereby they bind themselves to remain hostage under the power of the pagans, if so required, for the liberation of Christians. The King granted them the right to bear on their breasts his own Royal blazon, and obtained from Gregory IX the confirmation of this Institute and Order so nobly marked by brotherly charity. God Himself, through the Virgin Mother, gave the increase, causing this Institute speedily and prosperously to spread through all the world, and to blossom with holy men, great in love and godliness, to spend in the redemption of their neighbors the alms which are committed to them by Christ's faithful people, to that end, and sometimes to give themselves up for the ransom of many. That due thanks might be rendered to God and to the Virgin Mother for the great blessing of this Institute, the Apostolic See among other nearly countless favors bestowed upon it, permitted that this special Feast day should be kept and this Office said.

Lessons VII–IX from the Common of the Blessed Virgin Mary (Homily by St. Bede)

September 26 ~ Sts. Cyprian & Justina

Virgin, Martyrs ~ Simplex

Lessons I–II from the occurring Scripture

Lesson III

Cyprian was firstly a sorcerer and lastly a Martyr. A certain young man having a violent lust after a Christian maiden named Justina, employed him to excite her to join in this lewdness, by way of incantations and potions. Cyprian thereupon asked counsel of a demon, how he might best gain that end. But the demon answered him that these arts are only thrown away upon true worshippers of Christ. This answer troubled Cyprian, and he began to repent heartily of the course of life he had hitherto led. And then he forsook his magic arts, and gave himself wholly up to the faith of the Lord Christ. For this cause, he and the Virgin Justina were arrested together, beaten with blows and scourging, and cast into prison, if perchance they might change their mind. Being brought out of the prison, but still standing fast in their Christian religion, they were dipped in a vessel full of hot pitch, fat, and wax, and in the end beheaded, at Nicomedia, on the 26th day of September, in the year of our Lord 304. Their bodies were thrown out, and lay unburied for the space of six days, at the end of which time some sailors took them secretly by night aboard a ship and carried them to Rome. They were first buried on the farm of the noble Lady Rufina, but afterwards brought into the city, where they lie near the Baptistery of the Constantinian Basilica [St. John Lateran].

September 27 ~ Sts. Cosmas & Damian

Martyrs ~ Semiduplex

All from Common except what follows

Lessons I–III from the occurring Scripture

Lesson IV

Cosmas and Damian, who were eminent physicians in the time of the Emperors Diocletian and Maximian, were brothers, and Arabs by race, but born in the city of Ægeæ in Cilicia. Not more by their knowledge of medicine than by the power of Christ they healed diseases which had been hopeless for others. When the Præfect Lysias learnt to what faith they belonged, he commanded them to be brought before him, and questioned them as to their way of life, and the confession of their religion; and then, forasmuch as they freely owned themselves Christians and the Christian faith needful to salvation, he commanded them to worship the gods, under threats of torments and a most cruel death.

Lesson V

He bound their hands and feet together, and put them to the sharpest of the question. And he was obeyed, but nevertheless Cosmas and Damian abode still of the same mind. Therefore they were cast into the depth of the sea, bound as they were, but they came forth again, whole and unbound. The Præfect, therefore, who ascribed it the magic arts, cast them into prison. On the morrow he dragged them forth again, and bade cast them upon a great fire, but the flame turned away from them. He was pleased then to have them tormented in diverse and cruel ways, and lastly, smitten with the axe. Thus did they bear witness for Christ Jesus even until they grasped the palm of their testimony.

Lesson VI is Lesson IV from the First Set in the Common of Many Martyrs (Sermon by St. Augustine)

Lessons VII–IX from the second set in the Common of Many Martyrs (Homily by St. Ambrose)

September 28 ~ St. Wenceslaus

Duke & Martyr ~ Semiduplex

All from Common except what follows

Lessons I–III from the occurring Scripture

Lesson IV

Wenceslaus, Duke of Bohemia, was the son of a Christian father, Duke Vratislaus I, and a heathen mother named Drahomíra. He had for his grandmother a most holy woman, named Ludmila, who trained him up in piety. He was a man eminent in all virtues, and one who carefully held his virginity unsullied throughout the whole course of his life. His mother seized the supreme power by the foul murder of Ludmila, and lived foully with her younger son Boleslaus, and the nobles roused thereby to indignation, and wearied with her tyranny and wicked government, cast off the yoke of both of them, and hailed Wenceslaus in the city of Prague as their King.

Lesson V

He ruled his kingdom by his virtues rather than by force. To the orphaned, the widowed, and the destitute he was very charitable, so that sometimes in the winter he carried firewood to the needy on his own shoulders. He helped oftentimes to bury the poor, he set captives free, and went many times to the prisons at the dead of night to comfort with money and advice them that were detained therein. To a Prince of so tender a heart it was a great grief to be bound to condemn any to death, however guilty. For Priests he had a most earnest respect, and with his own hands sowed the wheat and pressed the grapes for the bread and wine which they were to use for the Sacrifice. He would walk round the Church by night with bare feet upon the snow and ice, leaving behind him bloody footprints that warmed the ground.

Lesson VI

For his Bodyguard he had angels. For when Radislaus, Prince of Gurinna, invaded Bohemia, and Wenceslaus, to spare the effusion of his people's blood, went out to meet him in single combat, angels were seen serving him with arms, and heard to say to the adversary "Strike not." Therefore, his enemy was stricken with terror, fell down in reverence before him, and begged his forgiveness. When he went to Germany, the Emperor saw two angels carrying a golden Cross before him as he drew nigh him, and arose from his throne, embraced him in his arms, created him a King, and gifted him with the arm of Saint Vitus. Nevertheless, his godless brother, at the exhortation of their mother, bade him to a feast, given on account of the birth of his son, and when Wenceslaus, with a foreboding of the death prepared for him, went afterwards into the Church, and was praying there, Boleslaus followed him thither together with some accomplices of his crime, and when they had wounded him, dispatched him with his own hand, running him through the body with a lance. He suffered a little after midnight, upon the 28th day of September, in the year of our Lord 938. The stains of his blood may still be seen upon the walls. By the judgment of God, his inhuman mother was swallowed up by the earth, and his murderers, in diverse ways, perished miserably.

Lessons VII–IX from the third set in the Common of One Martyr (Homily by St. Hilary)

September 29 ~ The Dedication of St. Michael the Archangel

Duplex I Class

Lessons I–III from those on May 8—The Apparition of St. Michael the Archangel (Daniel)

Lesson IV

Sermon by St. Gregory, Pope

We say that there are nine orders of Angels, for, by the witness of the holy Word, we know that there be Angels, Archangels, Virtues, Powers, Principalities, Dominions, Thrones, Cherubim, and Seraphim. Nearly every page of the holy Word witnesses that there be Angels and Archangels. The books of the Prophets, as is well known, do oftentimes make mention of Cherubim and Seraphim. Paul, writing to the Ephesians, counts up the names of four orders, where he says: "far above all Principalities, and Powers, and Virtues, and Dominions." And the same, again, writing to the Colossians says: "whether they be Thrones, or Dominions, or Principalities, or Powers." If, then, we add the Thrones to the four orders of which he spoke unto the Ephesians, we have five orders; and when we add unto them the Angels and the Archangels, the Cherubim and the Seraphim, we find that the orders of Angels are beyond all doubt nine.

Lesson V

But we must know that the word Angel is the designation, not of a nature, but of an office. Those holy spirits in the heavenly fatherland are always spirits, but they may in no way be always called Angels, for they are Angels only when they are sent as Messengers. Hence also it is said by the Psalmist: "Who makest spirits thine Angels!" As if it were: "Of them who are always with Him as spirits, He does sometimes make use as Messengers." They who go on the lesser messages are called Angels, they who go on the greater Archangels. Hence it is that unto the Virgin Mary was sent no common Angel, but the Archangel Gabriel. For the delivery of this, the highest message, it was fitting that there should be sent the highest Angel. Their individual names also are so given as to signify the kind of ministry wherein each is powerful. Michael signifies: "Who-is-like-unto-God?" Gabriel, the "Strength-of-God," and Raphael, the "Medicine-of-God."

Lesson VI

As often as anything very mighty is to be done, we see that Michael is sent, that by the very thing, and by his name, we may remember that none is able to do as God does. Hence that old enemy whose pride has puffed him up to be eager to be like unto God, even he who said, "I will ascend unto heaven, I will exalt my throne above the stars of God; I will be like the Most High." This old enemy, when at the end of the world he is about to perish in the last death, having no strength but his own, is shown unto us fighting with Michael the Archangel, even as says John: There was a war with Michael the Archangel. Unto Mary is sent Gabriel, whose name is interpreted the Strength-of-God, for he came to herald the appearance of Him Who was content to appear lowly that He might fight down the powers of the air. Raphael, also, as we have said, signifies the Medicine-of-God, and it is the name of him who touched as a physician the eyes of Tobias, and cleared away his blindness.

Lesson VII

From the Holy Gospel according to St. Matthew (Matt 18:1–10)

At that time came the disciples unto Jesus, saying: Who is the greatest in the kingdom of heaven? And so on.

Homily by St. Jerome, Priest

After the finding of the piece of money in the fish's mouth, after the payment of the tribute, what means this sudden question of the Apostles? "Who is the greatest in the kingdom of heaven?" They had seen that the same tribute-money was paid for Peter as for the Lord, and from this equality of reckoning they gathered that Peter was Prince of all the Apostles, seeing that he had been appraised at the same price as his Master. Therefore they ask, "Who is the greatest in the kingdom of heaven?" And Jesus, seeing their thoughts, and understanding why they erred, is willing to heal the desire of glory by the love of humility.

Lesson VIII

"Therefore, if thy hand or thy foot scandalize thee, cut them off, and cast them from thee. It must needs be that scandals come." Woe to the man who, through his vices, causes that which needed to be done in the world, and to be done in himself. Away, then, with every affection and every kinship, lest thy love should throw a stumbling-block before a single believer. "Be there any," says He, "who is as near to thee as thine hand, thy foot, or thine eye, useful, careful, far-seeing, but who lays a stumbling-block before thee, and whose diverse way of life may draw thee to hell? It is better for thee to lose such a one and thy worldly happiness with him, than to live surrounded by them that are near and needful to thee, and to pile up unto thyself damnation."

Lesson IX

"I say unto you that in heaven their angels do always behold the face of My Father." Above, He had said that every tie of kinship or of convenience which might become a stumbling-block, albeit close and needful as hand, or foot, or eye, was to be cut off, but here He softens the hardness of that precept: "Take heed that you despise not one of these little ones." Austerity, says He, I command not except as teaching tenderness; "Because in heaven their Angels do always behold the face of My Father." Oh, how great is the dignity of souls, whereof every one has from its birth an Angel appointed to guard it! Hence, we read in the Apocalypse of John: "unto the Angel of the Church of Ephesus, write thus." And the Apostle also says: "The woman, in the Church, ought to have a covering on her head, because of the Angels."

September 30 ~ St. Jerome

Priest, Confessor, & Doctor ~ Duplex

All from Common except what follows

Lessons I–III from the occurring Scripture

Lesson IV

Jerome was the son of one Eusebius, and was born at Stridon, (a small town upon the confines) of Dalmatia, in the reign of the Emperor Constantius. He was baptized at Rome when a lad, and studied there, under the instruction of Donatus and other very learned personages. He travelled in Gaul for the sake of improving his mind, and there sought the friendship of diverse godly men learned in the Scriptures, and made with his own hand many copies of the holy books. He afterwards betook himself to Greece, where he attained eminence as a philosopher and orator, in the following of the most famous theologians. At Constantinople, especially, he sat at the feet of Gregory Nazianzen, from whom he professes himself to have learnt his theology. Then, for piety's sake, he went to see the home of the Lord Christ, and so throughout all Palestine. He witnesses that this pilgrimage, wherein he got the help of the most learned of the Jews for the understanding of the Holy Scriptures, did him much good.

Lesson V

He withdrew himself into the wild deserts of Syria, where he passed four years in studying the Holy Scriptures and in considering the blessedness of heaven, afflicting his body by alway denying himself, by bitter tears, and by chastisement of the flesh. He was ordained Priest by Paulinus, Patriarch of Antioch. He went to Rome on account of the quarreling of certain Bishops with Paulinus and Epiphanius, and there helped Pope Damasus I in the writing of his letters upon Church affairs. But the longing for his old solitude came upon him, and he went back to Palestine, where, in the monastery at Bethlehem, built beside the cradle of the Lord Christ by the Lady Paula of Rome, he set himself to enter on earth upon the life of heaven, serving God in reading and writing without ceasing, regardless of the sufferings of a body tormented by diverse diseases and pains.

Lesson VI

Hard questions upon the interpretation of the Holy Scripture were sent to him from all parts of the earth, as to an oracle. He was oftentimes consulted by Pope Damasus and by Saint Augustine upon the meaning of the most obscure passages of the Scripture, because of his extraordinary learning, and that he knew not the Latin and Greek tongues only, but also the Hebrew and Chaldean Aramaic, and, as the same Augustine testifies, had read nearly all writers. He attacked heretics with keen publications, and ever undertook the defense of the godly and Catholic. He translated the Old Testament from Hebrew into Latin, and, at the command of Damasus, reformed, according to the original Greek, the existing version of the New. Upon great part of the Scriptures he wrote commentaries. He translated likewise into Latin the works of many learned men, and himself contributed to the Christian life many monuments of his own wit. He lived to an extreme old age, and passed away to heaven, famous for learning and holiness, in the reign of the Emperor Honorius, upon the 30th day of September, in the year of our Lord 420. His body was buried at Bethlehem, but has since been brought to Rome, where it lies in the Church of St. Mary at the Manger [St. Mary Major].

Lesson VII

From the Holy Gospel according to St. Matthew (Matt 5:13–19)

At that time Jesus said unto His disciples: "You are the salt of the earth; but if the salt lose its savor, wherewith shall it be salted?" And so on.

Homily by St. Jerome, Priest

Apostles and teachers are called salt, for it is by them that the whole mass of mankind is seasoned. "But if the salt have lost his savor, wherewith shall it be salted?" If the teacher has gone astray, by what other teacher is he to be corrected? "It is thenceforth good for nothing, but to be cast out, and to be trodden under foot of men." This is a figure taken from farming. Salt is used to savor food withal, and to preserve meat, but it has no other use. Sure, we read in the Scriptures of some cities which were sown with salt in the fury of their conquerors, that no bud of life might ever spring there again.

Lesson VIII

The teachers and Bishops, then, look well to it, seeing that mighty men shall be mightily tormented. And there is no help for them, but they fall into hell with a greater crash. "You are the light of the world." "A city that is set on a hill cannot be hid." "Neither do men light a candle, and put it under a bushel, but on a candlestick, that it may give light unto all that are in the house." Here He teaches boldness in preaching, lest the Apostles should shrink away from fear, and be like unto candles under a bushel; but contrariwise should come forward with all freedom, and should proclaim upon the housetops that which had been spoken in the ear in closets.

Lesson IX

"Think not that I am come to destroy the Law or the Prophets; I am not come to destroy, but to fulfill." The meaning is, either that He was come to fulfill those things which others had prophesied concerning Him, or that He was come to give the full measure of those things which had been spoken obscurely and imperfectly on account of the weakness of their hearers, making away with anger, forbidding to take eye for eye and tooth for tooth, and condemning the secret lusting of the heart. "Till heaven and earth pass." But there are promised unto us new heavens and a new earth, which the Lord God shall make. And if new things are to be created, old things must pass away.

✠

FEASTS OF OCTOBER

October 1 ~ St. Remigius

Confessor Bishop ~ Simplex

Lessons I–II from the occurring Scripture

Lesson III

Remigius, Archbishop of Rheims, flourished in the time of Clovis, King of the Franks, whom he baptized, and was the first who, by his preaching and miracles, brought the Franks to believe in the Lord Christ. At his prayers, a dead maiden was raised to life. He expounded many books of the Holy Scriptures. He ministered to the Church of Rheims with the utmost acceptance for above seventy years, and the holiness of his life and death were witnessed by many signs and wonders which befell afterwards.

October 2 ~ The Holy Guardian Angels

Major Duplex

Lesson I ~ Exod 23:20–23

From the book of Exodus

Behold I will send my angel, who shall go before thee, and keep thee in thy journey, and bring thee into the place that I have prepared. Take notice of him, and hear his voice, and do not think him one to be contemned: for he will not forgive when thou hast sinned, and my name is in him. But if thou wilt hear his voice, and do all that I speak, I will be an enemy to thy enemies, and will afflict them that afflict thee. And my angel shall go before thee, and shall bring thee in unto the Amorrhite, and the Hethite, and the Pherezite, and the Chanaanite, and the Hevite, and the Jebusite, whom I will destroy.

Lesson II ~ Zach 1:7–11

From the Prophet Zacharias

The word of the Lord came to Zacharias the son of Barachias, the son of Addo, the prophet, saying: I saw by night, and behold a man riding upon a red horse, and he stood among the myrtle trees, that were in the bottom: and behind him were horses, red, speckled, and white. And I said: What are these, my Lord? and the angel that spoke in me, said to me: I will shew thee what these are: And the man that stood among the myrtle trees answered, and said: These are they, whom the Lord hath sent to walk through the earth. And they answered the angel of the Lord, that stood among the myrtle trees, and said: We have walked through the earth, and behold all the earth is inhabited, and is at rest.

Lesson III ~ Zach 2:1–5

And I lifted up my eyes, and saw, and behold a man, with a measuring line in his hand. And I said: Whither goest thou? and he said to me: To measure Jerusalem, and to see how great is the breadth thereof, and how great the length thereof. And behold the angel that spoke in me went forth, and another angel went out to meet him. And he said to him: Run, speak to this young man, saying: Jerusalem shall be inhabited without walls, by reason of the multitude of men, and of the beasts in the midst thereof. And I will be to it, saith the Lord, a wall of fire round about: and I will be in glory in the midst thereof.

Lesson IV

Sermon by St. Bernard, Abbot

"He has given His Angels charge over thee." O wonderful graciousness, and a wonderful outpouring of love! For who has given charge? And what charge? Unto whom? And over whom? Let us carefully consider, my brethren, let us carefully hold in mind this great charge. For who has given this charge? To Whom belong the Angels? Whose commandments do they obey, and Whose will do they do? "He has given His Angels charge over thee, to keep thee in all thy ways," and that not carelessly, for "they shall bear thee up in their hands." The Highest Majesty, therefore, has given charge unto Angels, even His Angels. Unto these beings so excellently exalted, so blessed, so near to Himself, even as His own household, unto these has He given charge over thee. Who art thou? "What is man, that Thou art mindful of him? or the son of man, that Thou visitest him?" Even as though man were not rottenness, and the son of man, a worm. But what charge has He given them over thee? "To keep thee in all thy ways."

Lesson V

What respect, what thankfulness, what trust, ought this word to work in thee! Respect for their presence, thankfulness for their kindness, trust in their safekeeping. Walk carefully, as one with whom are Angels, as in charge that has been laid upon them, "in all thy ways." In every lodging, in every nook, have reverence for thine Angel. Dare not to do in his presence what thou wouldst not dare to do in mine. Or dost thou doubt whether he be indeed present, because thou seest him not? What if thou heardest him? What if thou touchedst him? What if thou smelledst him? Behold, not by sight alone is the presence of things made manifest.

Lesson VI

Let us also, brethren, dearly love His Angels, as them with whom we are one day to be coheirs, and who in the meanwhile are leaders and guardians set over us by the Father. With such guardians, whereof shall we be afraid? They that keep us in all our ways, can neither be conquered nor corrupted, far less can they corrupt. They are trusty, they are wary, they are mighty. Whereof shall we be afraid? Only let us follow them, only let us cleave unto them, and we shall abide under the shadow of the God of heaven. As often then as the gloom of temptation threatens thee, or the sharpness of tribulation hangs over thee, call upon Him That keeps thee, thy Shepherd, thy Refuge in times of trouble, call upon Him, and say: "Lord, save us, we perish."

Lessons VII–IX from those on May 8—The Apparition of St. Michael the Archangel (Homily by St. Hilary)

October 3 ~ St. Thérèse of the Child Jesus

Virgin ~ Duplex

All from Common except what follows

Lessons I–III from the occurring Scripture

Lesson IV

Thérèse of the Child Jesus was born in Alençon in France. Her parents were estimable people, well known for their piety and their love of God. From her earliest childhood, endowed by a special grace of the Holy Ghost, she yearned to enter the religious life. She promised God with the utmost sincerity that she would deny him nothing he might ask of her. She kept this promise faithfully to the end of her life, although she had to suffer a great deal to keep it. Her mother died when Thérèse was but five years old. From then on the child committed herself to the providence of God, under the vigilant care of a most tender father and her elder sisters. Under their teaching Thérèse raced as strong as a giant along the way of perfection. At the age of nine she was sent to school at Lisieux to the Benedictine nuns, where she made remarkable progress in her knowledge of divine things. In her tenth year she was ill for a long time of a serious and mysterious malady. From this, as she herself relates, she was delivered only by the power of God himself, through the intercession of the Blessed Virgin Mary, who appeared to her with a smiling countenance, and to whom under the title of Our Lady of Victories, she was constantly making novenas. Filled with angelic fervor she prepared herself at this time with the utmost care to receive Christ in the sacred banquet of her first Holy Communion.

Lesson V

After being refreshed for the first time with the Eucharistic Bread, Thérèse seemed to develop an insatiable hunger for the celestial food. Then, as if by inspiration, she asked Jesus to turn all her earthly consolation into bitterness. After that she burned with a most tender love for Christ the Lord and for his Church. More than anything in the world she wanted to enter the Order of the Discalced Carmelites, where by self-sacrifice she might assist priests, missionaries and the whole Church, and so gain innumerable souls for Christ Jesus. All this, she promised God would do for her, even when apparently she lay at the point of death. Her extreme youth was an obstacle which hindered her entrance upon the religious life. Even this she overcame by her incredible courage of soul. She happily entered the Lisieux Carmel at the age of fifteen. There God fashioned the heart of Thérèse in a marvelous way, teaching her to ascend to him step by step. Imitating the hidden life of the Virgin Mary like a well-watered garden she bore flowers of every virtue, especially an abiding love of God and neighbor.

Lesson VI

That she might please the most high God to greater degree, when she read in Sacred Scriptures the warning, "Whoever is a little one, let him come unto me," she determined to be a little one in spirit. As such she consecrated herself forever with childlike confidence to God, her most loving Father. The way of spiritual childhood, following the teachings of the Gospel, she taught to others, especially to the novices who, training in the pursuit of religious virtues, she undertook in obedience to her superiors. Overflowing with apostolic zeal she pointed out to a world filled with pride and a love of vanities, the simple way of the Gospels. Meanwhile Jesus, her spouse, inflamed her with a desire to suffer both in soul and in body. Moreover, perceiving that the love of God was everywhere rejected, she became filled with grief and two years before her death, offered herself as a victim of love to the merciful God. She writes that she was then wounded by a flame of fire from heaven, whereupon she became consumed by love, rapt as it were in ecstasy. Repeating over and over again the fervent words, "My God, I love thee," she passed on to her Spouse on the 30th day of September, in the year 1897, at the age of twenty-four years. As she was dying she promised that she would let fall upon earth a ceaseless shower of roses. This promise she has indeed fulfilled in heaven, and her shower of roses has continued to this very day. The Sovereign Pontiff Pius XI added her name to the Virgins declared Blessed and two years later, at the time of the great Jubilee, listed her among the Saints. He also appointed and declared her Patroness of all the missions.

Lesson VII

From the Holy Gospel according to St. Matthew (Matt 18:1–4)

In that time: The disciples came to Jesus, saying: Who thinkest thou is the greater in the kingdom of heaven? And so on.

Homily by St. Leo, Pope

The whole teaching of Christian wisdom consists, dearly beloved, not in an abundance of words, not in skill in disputation, not surely in seeking after praise or glory, but rather in seeking after true and voluntary humility. This was the way which the Lord Jesus Christ chose and taught with all his strength from his Mother's womb to his death on the Cross. When the Lord's disciples, as the Evangelist says, discussed among themselves which should be the greatest in the kingdom of heaven, he called a little child and set him in the midst of them, and said: "Amen, I say to you, unless you be converted, and become as little children, you shall not enter into the kingdom of heaven. Whosoever therefore shall humble himself as this little child, the same is the greatest in the kingdom of heaven." Christ loves childhood, the state which he first took upon himself, both in his soul and in his body. Christ loves childhood, for it is the teacher of humility, the rule of innocence, and the type of meekness. Christ loves childhood, for he forms the character of the grown man on this model, and brings back the latter years of the old to this very state; and he shapes on this way those whom he would raise to the kingdom of heaven.

Lesson VIII

But, that we may be fully able to understand how this marvelous transformation can be accomplished, and by what change we are to return to the state of childhood, let us follow the teaching of the blessed Paul, who says: "Be not children in understanding; howbeit, in malice be you children, but in understanding be men." Hence we are not to return to the pastimes and imperfect beginnings of childhood, but thence are rather to take whatever is suitable to the full-grown: such as the swift passing of excitement; the speedy restoration of peace; the forgetfulness of injuries; the indifference to dignity; the love of the companionship of their comrades; and the natural evenness of temper. It is indeed a great good not to know and not to have a taste for harm; for to do and to return injuries is the wisdom of this world, but to render no man evil for evil is to possess the childhood of Christian goodwill.

Lesson IX

The mystery of this day's festival, dearly beloved, calls you to this imitation of little children. And the Saviour, who was adored by the Magi as a child, recommends to you this pattern of humility. To show what glory he prepares for them that would imitate him, he consecrated by martyrdom those born at the same time as himself. And thus the children born in Bethlehem, where Christ was born, became sharers of his passion by virtue of sharing the age of his infancy. Let the faithful then love lowliness, and shun all arrogance. Let each one prefer his brother to himself. Let him seek not even what is his own, but only that which will profit his brother. The feeling of charity will abound in all; the poison of envy will be found in none. "For he that exalts himself shall be humbled, and he that humbles himself shall be exalted." This is the teaching of our Lord Jesus Christ, who with the Father and the Holy Ghost lives and reigns, God, for ever and ever. Amen.

October 4 ~ St. Francis of Assisi

Confessor ~ Major Duplex

All from Common except what follows

Lessons I–III from the occurring Scripture

Lesson IV

Francis was born at Assisi in Umbria, in the year of our Lord 1182. From his early youth he followed the example of his father, Pietro Bernardone, and busied himself with merchandise. It befell one day that, contrary to his usage, he had thrust from him a beggar, who cried for money for Christ's sake, when, being cut to the heart with regret, he gave him large alms, and promised to God from that day forth never to deny to any that asked of him. He fell after this into a grievous sickness, and from the time that he was healed thereof, he gave himself more earnestly to works of charity for his neighbor in which he ever strove to be more perfect, even as the Lord said in the Gospel, and gave to the poor whatsoever he had. His father would not have it so, and brought him before the Bishop of Assisi, that he might renounce all right to any inheritance. He cheerfully gave up all to his father, even to his clothes, telling them that now he should be able with more utter dependence to say "Our Father, Who art in heaven."

Lesson V

Upon the 24th day of February, in the year 1209, he heard read the words of the Gospel: "Provide neither gold, nor silver, nor brass in your purses, nor scrip for your journey, neither two coats, neither shoes." Thereupon he determined that that should be his rule of living. He took off his shoes, and contented himself with one coat. When he had gathered twelve comrades, he founded the Order of Friars Minor. He went to Rome in the same year, to get from the Apostolic See a confirmation of his Order. When he came, Pope Innocent III thrust him away. Thereafter he dreamt that he saw the Lateran Basilica falling, and he whom he had cast forth bearing it up with his shoulders. He bade therefore that he should be sought for and brought again before him, welcomed him kindly, and approved all the Institutes which he had established. Francis therefore sent his Friars into all quarters of the world to preach the Gospel of Christ. He himself was desirous to find some occasion of martyrdom, and therefore made a voyage into Syria, in the year 1219, but the Sultan treated him with the greatest kindness, offering him many gifts, and, since he could do no good, he returned again to Italy.

Lesson VI

Towards the Feast of the Assumption, in the year 1224, when there had already been built many houses of Friars of his Order, he withdrew himself into a most secret place upon Mount Alverno, and began to fast for forty days in honor of the holy Archangel Michael. Upon the Feast day of the Exaltation of the Holy Cross, as he was praying upon the side of the mountain, he saw a vision of a crucified Seraph, which left holes in his hands and feet with nails therein, and in his side a great wound. St. Bonaventure has left it in writing that he once heard Pope Alexander IV, when preaching, testify that he had himself seen these marks. It was a sign of such love of Christ toward him as stirred up the great wonder of all men. Two years thereafter he fell sick unto death, and wanted to be carried into the Church of St. Mary of the Angels, that he might give up the breath of life in the same place where God had breathed into him the breath of the life of grace. Being there laid on the earth, sprinkled with ashes, and covered with an old habit, he exhorted the Friars to be poor and lowly, and to cleave to the faith of the Holy

Church of Rome. He then asked the Gospel of St. John to be read from chapter 13 to the end, after which he began to recite Psalm 141: "I cried to the Lord with my voice," and in uttering the words, "the just wait for me, until Thou reward me," he gave up the ghost. It was the 4th day of October, in the year 1226. He was famous for miracles, and Pope Gregory IX added his name to the list of the Saints.

Lessons VII–IX from the second set in the Common of Abbots (Homily by St. Augustine)

October 5 ~ Sts. Placid & Companions

Martyrs ~ Simplex

Lessons I–II from the occurring Scripture

Lesson III

Placidus was the son of Tertullus, one of the noblest persons of Rome. He was offered to God by his father when a child of only seven and given over to Saint Benedict, in whose teaching and Rule of monks he so profited that he was reckoned among the chiefest of his disciples. By him he was sent into Sicily, where he founded near the Port of Messina a Church and monastery in honor of St. John the Baptist, and lived therein with his monks in wonderful holiness. Thither there came to see him his brothers Eutychius and Victorinus and his virgin sister Flavia, and while they were together, there landed there a certain brutal pirate, named Manucha, who took the monastery, and when he could in no way prevail upon Placidus and the others to deny Christ, he commanded him, his brothers, and his sister to be cruelly murdered. With them Donatus, Firmatus the Deacon, Faustus, and thirty other monks brought the conflict of testimony to the blessed end of martyrdom, upon the fifth day of October, in the year of salvation 539.

October 6 ~ St. Bruno

Confessor ~ Duplex

All from Common except what follows

Lessons I–III from the occurring Scripture

Lesson IV

Bruno, the founder of the Carthusians, was born at Cologne, about the year of our Lord 1030. From his earliest years he was a very grave child, turning away from childish things, and that so manifestly, that by the grace of God the tokens of holiness already pointed him out as a Father of monks, and a restorer of the life of hermits. His parents, who were eminent for rank and goodness, sent him to Paris, where he studied so well in Philosophy and Theology, that he took the degree of Doctor in both faculties; and a short while after, for his famous virtues, he was made a Canon of Rheims.

Lesson V

After some years, he and six comrades, forsook the world and betook themselves to Saint Hugh, Bishop of Grenoble, who, when he learned the reason of their coming, and believing them to have been figured by seven stars which he had seen that night in a dream falling at his feet, gave them a grant of land in some very wild mountains in his Diocese, which are called the Chartreuses. There Bruno and his companions, together with Hugh, withdrew themselves, in the year 1084, and led for some years the life of hermits. Pope Urban I., who had formerly been his disciple at Rheims, commanded him to come to Rome, in 1089, and amid the afflictions which then scourged the Church, held him for some time as his counsellor. But at last Bruno, who had refused the Archbishopric of Reggio, got his leave to go away.

Lesson VI

In his love of the wilderness, he betook himself to a certain deserted place in the Diocese of Squillaci, in the uttermost coasts of Calabria, where he went in 1090. He was praying there one day in a cave, when the hounds of Roger, Sovereign Earl of Sicily and Calabria, who was out hunting, came and bayed at its door. Thus was he found by this Prince, who was moved by his holiness, and began to cherish him and his comrades, and treat them very kindly. The Earl's goodness was rewarded, for when he was one time laying siege to Capua, and one Sergius, who was first groom of his bedchamber, had made a plot to betray him, Bruno, who was still living in the desert above mentioned, appeared to him in a dream, and delivered him from the danger which was hanging over him. At length Bruno, full of virtues and merits, and famous for piety not less than for doctrine, fell asleep in the Lord, upon the 6th day of October, in the year 1101, and was buried in the monastery of St. Stephen, founded by the same Earl Roger, where he is still held in great honor.

Lessons VII–IX from the first set in the Common of Confessor Non-Bishops (Homily by St. Gregory)

October 7 ~ The Most Holy Rosary of the Blessed Virgin Mary

Duplex II Class

All from Common except what follows

Lesson I ~ Ecclus 24:11–16

From the book of Ecclesiasticus

And in all these I sought rest, and I shall abide in the inheritance of the Lord. Then the creator of all things commanded, and said to me: and he that made me, rested in my tabernacle, And he said to me: Let thy dwelling be in Jacob, and thy inheritance in Israel, and take root in my elect. From the beginning, and before the world, was I created, and unto the world to come I shall not cease to be, and in the holy dwelling place I have ministered before him. And so was I established in Sion, and in the holy city likewise I rested, and my power was in Jerusalem. And I took root in an honourable people, and in the portion of my God his inheritance, and my abode is in the full assembly of saints.

Lesson II ~ Ecclus 24:17–22

I was exalted like a cedar in Libanus, and as a cypress tree on mount Sion. I was exalted like a palm tree in Cades, and as a rose plant in Jericho: As a fair olive tree in the plains, and as a plane tree by the water in the streets, was I exalted. I gave a sweet smell like cinnamon. and aromatical balm: I yielded a sweet odour like the best myrrh: And I perfumed my dwelling as storax, and galbanum, and onyx, and aloes, and as the frankincense not cut, and my odour is as the purest balm. I have stretched out my branches as the turpentine tree, and my branches are of honour and grace.

Lesson III ~ Ecclus 24:24–31

I am the mother of fair love, and of fear, and of knowledge, and of holy hope. In me is all grace of the way and of the truth, in me is all hope of life and of virtue. Come over to me, all ye that desire me, and be filled with my fruits. For my spirit is sweet above honey, and my inheritance above honey and the honeycomb. My memory is unto everlasting generations. They that eat me, shall yet hunger: and they that drink me, shall yet thirst. He that hearkeneth to me, shall not be confounded: and they that work by me, shall not sin. They that explain me shall have life everlasting.

Lesson IV

When the Albigensian heresy was making headway against God in the County of Toulouse, and striking deeper roots every day, Saint Dominic, who had but just laid the foundations of the Order of Preachers, threw his whole strength into the travail of uprooting these blasphemies. That he might be fitter for the work, he cried for help with his whole soul to that Blessed Virgin, whose glory the falsehoods of the heretics so insolently assailed, and to whom it has been granted to trample down all heresies throughout the whole earth. It is said that he had from her a word, bidding him preach the Rosary among the people, as a strong help against heresy and sin, and it is wonderful with how stout a heart and how good a success he did the work laid upon him. This Rose-garden (or Rosary) is a certain form of prayer, wherein we say one-hundred-and-fifty times the Angelic salutation, and the Lord's Prayer between every decade, and, each of the fifteen times that we say the Lord's Prayer, and repeat tenfold the salutation, think of one of fifteen great events in the history of our Redemption. From that time forth this form of pious prayer was extraordinarily spread about by Saint Dominic, and grew common. That this same Dominic was the founder and prime mover thereof has been said by Popes in diverse letters of the Apostolic See.

Lesson V

From this healthy exercise have grown up innumerable good fruits in the Christian Commonwealth. Among these deserves well to be named that great victory over the Sultan of Turkey, which the most holy Pope Saint Pius V, and the Christian Princes whom he had roused, won at Lepanto, on the 7th day of October, the first Lord's Day in the month, in the year of our Lord 1571. The day whereon this victory was gained was the very one whereon the Guilds of the Most Holy Rosary, throughout the whole world, were used to offer their accustomed prayers and appointed supplications, and the event therefore was not unnaturally connected therewith. This being the avowed opinion of Gregory XIII, he ordered that in all Churches where there was, or should be, an Altar of the Rosary, a Feast, in the form of a Major Duplex, should be forever kept to give unceasing thanks to the Blessed Virgin, under her style of Queen of the Most Holy Rosary, for that extraordinary mercy of God. Other Popes also have granted almost numberless Indulgences to those who say the Rosary, and to those who join its Guilds.

Lesson VI

In the year 1716, Charles VI, Emperor-Elect of the Romans, won a famous victory over countless hordes of Turks, near Timisoara, in the kingdom of Hungary, upon the day when the Feast of the Dedication of the Church of St. Mary of the Snows was being kept, and almost at the very moment when the Guilds of the Most Holy Rosary were moving through the streets of Rome in public and solemn procession, amid vast multitudes, all filled with the deepest enthusiasm, calling vehemently upon God for the defeat of the Turks, and entreating the Virgin Mother of God to bring the might of her aid to the help of the Christians. A few days later, upon the Octave of the Assumption, the Turks raised the siege of Corfu. These mercies Clement XI devoutly ascribed to the helpful prayers of the Blessed Virgin, and that the memory and the sweetness of such a blessing might for all time coming endure gloriously, he extended to the Universal Church the observance of the Feast of the Most Holy Rosary. Benedict XIII commanded the record of all these things to be given a place in the Roman Breviary; and Leo XIII, in the most troublous times of the Church and the cruel storm of long pressing evils, by fresh Apostolic letters vehemently urged upon all the faithful throughout the earth the frequent recitation of the Rosary of the Blessed Virgin Mary, raised the dignity of the yearly festival, added to the Litany of Loreto the invocation "Queen of the Most Holy Rosary," and granted to the whole Church a special Office for this solemn occasion. Let us all then be earnest in honoring the Most Holy Mother of God in this form which she likes so well, that even as the entreaties of Christ's faithful people, approaching her in her Garden of Roses, have so often won her to scatter and destroy their earthly foes, so she may likewise gain for them the victory over their infernal ones.

Lesson VII

From the Holy Gospel according to St. Luke (Luke 1:26–38)

At that time the angel Gabriel was sent from God into a city of

Galilee, called Nazareth, to a virgin espoused to a man whose name was Joseph, of the house of David; and the virgin's name was Mary. And so on.

Homily by St. Bernard, Abbot

To commend His Own love towards us, and to bring to nought the wisdom of men, God was pleased to take flesh of a woman, albeit a virgin, that He might bring like against like, heal by opposites, pluck out the poisonous thorn, and blot out mightily the handwriting of our sin that was against us. Eve was a thorn, Mary is a rose. Eve is a thorn that pierces, Mary is a rose that charms all the senses. Eve was a thorn that fixed death into all, Mary is a rose that brings health to all. Mary was a white rose through her virginity, and a red rose through her love. She was white in her flesh, red in her mind; white in that she followed the path of grace, red in that she trod down sin; white by the purity of her affections, red by the mortification of her body; white by her love for God, red by her compassion for her neighbor.

Lesson VIII—Sermon on the Aqueduct

The Word was made flesh, and dwells even now among us. He dwells in our memory. He dwells in our thought. He has come down even unto our imagination; and how, sayest thou, does he so? By lying in the manger, by nestling in His mother's breast, by preaching upon the mountain, by remaining all night in prayer to God, by hanging upon the Cross, by turning pale in death, by going down free among the dead and triumphing in hell, by rising again the third day, by showing to the Apostles the places of the nails, the marks of his victory, by ascending up into heaven while they all beheld Him, of which of these things think we not with truth, with piety, with holiness?

If I think of any of these, I think of God, and He is my God through them all. To think of these things I have decreed to be wisdom, and to set forth the memory of their sweetness I have judged to be prudence. The rod of Aaron the Priest brought forth buds, and bloomed blossoms, and yielded almonds; but these things are the almonds of that Rod which came forth out of the stem of Jesse, the Rod whereof sprang the flower, a Rod which was raised in Mary into places higher than the earthly tabernacle, higher indeed, even into places higher than angels, since she received the Word into herself out of the very heart of the Eternal Father.

Lesson IX—Commemoration of St. Mark, Pope

Mark was a Roman, who sat as Pope in the reign of the Emperor Constantine the Great. He ordained that the Bishop of Ostia, by whom the Roman Pontiff is consecrated, should use the Pallium. He built two Churches, one in the city and the other on the Ardeatine Way, which Constantine enlarged and richly gifted. Mark lived as Pope eight months, and was buried in the Cemetery of Balbina.

October 8 ~ St. Bridget of Sweden

Widow ~ Duplex

All from Common except what follows

Lessons I–III from the occurring Scripture

Lesson IV

Bridget was the daughter of princely and godly parents, and was born in Sweden, in the year of our Lord 1304. Her life was a very holy one. When she was still in the womb, her mother was for her sake saved from shipwreck. When she was ten years old, she heard a sermon upon the sufferings of the Lord, and the following night she saw Jesus on the Cross, covered with fresh Blood, and heard Him speaking to her of His same sufferings. From that time forth the thought of them touched her so keenly, that she could never again call them to mind without weeping.

Lesson V

When she was given in marriage to Ulf, Prince of Nericia, she moved her husband to pious works, as well by her noble example as by her earnest words. She expended the most motherly care upon the upbringing of her children. She opened a hospital, in which she carefully tended the poor, especially the sick, and would wash and kiss their feet. She made a pilgrimage with her husband to Compostela, to visit the grave of Saint James the Apostle. On their way back, Ulf fell grievously sick at Arras, and St. Denis appeared in the night to Bridget, to tell her that her husband would be healed, as well as diverse other things to come.

Lesson VI

In the year 1344, her husband died after having become a Cistercian monk. Bridget, having heard the voice of Christ in a dream, took upon herself a harder way of life. During her life God made known to her many hidden things. She founded the monastery of Vadstena, under the Rule of the Holy Saviour, a Rule which she had received from the Lord Himself. By the command of God she went to Rome, where she stirred up many by her example to seek the love of God. Thence she went to Jerusalem, and then returned again to Rome. From this pilgrimage she caught a fever, of which she lay sick a whole year in sharp sufferings, and then, laden with good works, and after foretelling the day of her own death, she departed from earth to heaven, upon the 23rd day of July, in the year 1373. Her body was taken to the monastery of Vadstena. She was famous for miracles, and Boniface IX enrolled her name among those of the Saints.

Lessons VII–IX from the Common of Non-Virgins (Homily by St. Gregory)

October 9 ~ St. John Leonardi

Confessor ~ Duplex

All from Common
except what follows

Lessons I–III from the
occurring Scripture

Lesson IV

John Leonardi was born of pious and respectable parents in the town of Diecimo, not far from the city of Lucca. From very early boyhood he showed himself mature and serious, with an inclination to solitude and prayer. When he was twenty-six years old God called him to enlist among the soldiers of the Church. John renounced immediately all his worldly interests. At first he had to study elementary Latin with little boys, but he soon advanced in a knowledge of literature, philosophy and theology. After a scant four years, at the command of his superior, he was ordained to the priesthood. Soon afterward he and a group of noble youths, alike inflamed with high ideals, earnestly set about attaining perfection in virtue. The following year they formed the Congregation of the Clerics Regular of the Mother of God, a name chosen because of their intense devotion to her. John and his companions labored with such diligence in their care of souls, that before long a change of attitude was brought about. In the city-state of Lucca, where through the perfidious wiles of the heretics, hateful passion turned fiercely among the citizens, where morals were corrupted, in a very short space of time the primitive piety of the Christians seemed to revive.

Lesson V

In his work for the salvation of souls John met most bitter insults from wicked men who tried in every way to destroy the newly gathered family. But the man of God, bearing all things cheerfully and serenely, defended pertinaciously the fruit of his apostolic labors by securing from the Supreme Pontiff, Gregory XIII, papal approbation of his Congregation. Many bishops about to undertake difficult enterprises sought his advice and aid. Even the Holy Father delegated to him the solution of intricate litigation and the reform of religious societies. He stood in support of Saint Joseph Calasanz when his society was on the verge of collapse. Scarcely less arduous were the hours John devoted to the affairs of the Hospital of the Holy Spirit in the English section of Rome, and to those of the convent of Saint Frances of Rome.

Lesson VI

Greatly saddened that so many peoples in far distant places were without the light of the Gospel, John burned with a desire to journey to those countries to spread the light of the true Faith. But when Saint Philip Neri, who called John a true reformer, showed him that he and his Congregation were destined to educate the Italian people, John acquiesced to the will of God. He did not, however, refrain so completely that he did not try to do some work for the infidels. He is therefore, very rightly credited along with the most pious pioneer [Cardinal] Vivès with being the founder of the movement among the bishops to send well-qualified young men to distant, alien lands for the Propagation of the Faith. Wherefore he is very properly regarded as the author of that most illustrious institute [*Propaganda Fide*] which augments the work of the Sovereign Pontiffs and serves to spread the Catholic faith throughout the world. John wrote many works on theology and morality, well adapted to the men of that day. Finally, in sackcloth and ashes, lacking nothing in his sacred ministry, he passed to the Lord in Rome on the 9th day of October, 1609, at the age of sixty-six. He was so famous for sanctity and miracles that Pius IX, the Supreme Pontiff, named him on the Kalendar of the Blessed. In 1938, on the solemn Feast of Easter, Pius XI enrolled him among the Saints.

Lessons VII–IX from the Common of Evangelists (Homily by St. Gregory)

Lesson IX—Commemoration of Sts. Dionysius, Bishop, Rusticus & Eleutherius, Maryrs

Dionysius (Denis) was an Athenian, one of the Judges of the Court of the Areopagus, and a man of varied and deep learning. Whilst still immersed in the errors of the pagans, and seeing the unnatural eclipse of the sun on the day when the Lord Christ was nailed to the Cross, Dionysius (it is said) exclaimed: "Either the God of nature is suffering, or the framework of the world is breaking up." But when Apostle Paul had announced Christ in the Areopagus, Dionysius embraced the Christian faith, and was set over the Athenian church by the same Apostle.

[What follows is a different St. Denis]

Afterwards, it is said that He came to Rome, and was sent by Pope Clement into Gaul, to preach the Gospel. There followed him to Paris one Rusticus a Priest, and Eleutherius a Deacon. There all who preached Christ were seized by the Præfect Fescennius, crucified with various tortures, and finally struck with an axe upon the 9th day of October. This is that Denis concerning whom the old story is told that after his head was cut off he took it in his hands and walked two thousand paces, carrying it all the while.

October 10 ~ St. Francis Borgia

Confessor ~ Semiduplex

All from Common except what follows

Lessons I–III from the occurring Scripture

Lesson IV

Francis, fourth Duke of Gandia, was the son of Juan Borgia, and of Juana of Aragon, daughter of Alfonso, natural son to Ferdinand V the Catholic, King of Aragon. He was born at Gandia, in the kingdom of Valencia, in the year of our Lord 1510. He passed his boyhood at home in great innocence and godliness, and was still more remarkable for his Christian graces and the austerity of his living, at the Court of the Emperor Charles V, and as Viceroy of Catalonia. On May the 1st, 1539, the Empress Isabella died, and Francis, as her master of horse, was commanded to attend her body to Granada, where it was to be buried. At Granada the coffin was opened, in order that he might swear to the magistrates of the city that it was indeed the body of the late Empress, and the sight of the awful change which death had made in her countenance so shocked him with the thought of our mortality and corruption, that he bound himself by vow, as soon as he lawfully might, to give up all things, and to serve the King of kings alone. From that time he so advanced in Christian virtues, that he was called the Prince of Miracles, showing, in the midst of a vast mass of business, an image of perfection attained in a cloister.

Lesson V

His wife, Eleanora de Castro, died on the 27th of March, 1546, and in 1551 he entered the Society of Jesus, that therein he might hide himself more safely, and bar the path to dignities by the obligation of a vow. He was the worthy leader of many princes who have embraced a life of hardship, and Charles V himself when he resigned the Empire did not deny that he had been moved and shown the way by Francis. In his struggle after austerity, Francis, by fasting, by iron chains, by the roughest of haircloth, by long and bloody flagellations, and by denying himself any but very little sleep, reduced his body to the last degree, but would still spare no toil to overcome himself and to save souls. Thus full of spiritual strength, he was appointed by Saint Ignatius, in the year 1554, Commissary-General of the Society in Spain, Portugal, and the Indies, and on the 2nd of July, 1565, notwithstanding all the precautions he could take to prevent it, he was chosen by the general Congregation of the Society to be General, being the third who held that office. In this position his wisdom and holiness of life greatly endeared him to Princes and Popes, and besides founding or enlarging very many houses in divers places, he sent brethren into the kingdom of Poland, into the islands of the Ocean, and into the provinces of Mexico and Peru, and into other lands also Apostolic men who spread the Roman Catholic faith by their preaching, their sweat, and their blood.

Lesson VI

He thought so little of himself that he gave himself the nickname of Francis the sinner. By the Popes he was oftentimes offered the dignity of Cardinal of the Roman Church, but the lowly firmness with which he refused it could never be overcome. In his cheap esteem of the world and of himself his chief pleasures were to clean the house, to beg for food from door to door, and to wait upon the sick in hospitals. He spent many hours every day, oftentimes eight and sometimes ten, in prayer and meditation. A hundred times every day he worshipped God upon his knees. He never missed the opportunity of offering the Holy Liturgy, and the fire from God which burnt within him sometimes shone forth in his countenance when he was elevating the Sacred Host, or preaching. By an inward power given him from God he could tell where the most Holy Body of Christ, under the Eucharistic veils, was kept. In 1570, the year before the victory of Lepanto, the blessed Pius V sent Francis with Cardinal Alexandrini on an embassy into France, Spain, and Portugal, to unite the Christian Princes against the Turks. His vital strength was then nearly worn out, but, through obedience, he undertook the toil of the journey. He became much worse during the traveling, and on his return brought the pilgrimage of this life to a blessed end at Rome, as had been his desire, a little before midnight between the last day of September and the first of October, in the sixty-second year of his own life, and that of salvation 1572. Saint Teresa of Avila, who used his advice, called him a holy man, and Gregory XIII, a faithful servant. He was famous for many and great miracles, and Clement X at last numbered him among the Saints.

Lessons VII–IX from the first set in the Common of Abbots (Homily by St. Jerome)

October 11 – Maternity of the Blessed Virgin Mary

Duplex II Class

All from Common except what follows

Lesson I – Ecclus 24:5–11

From the book of Ecclesiasticus

I came out of the mouth of the most High, the firstborn before all creatures: I made that in the heavens there should rise light that never faileth, and as a cloud I covered all the earth: I dwelt in the highest places, and my throne is in a pillar of a cloud. I alone have compassed the circuit of heaven, and have penetrated into the bottom of the deep, and have walked in the waves of the sea, And have stood in all the earth: and in every people, And in every nation I have had the chief rule: And by my power I have trodden under my feet the hearts of all the high and low: and in all these I sought rest, and I shall abide in the inheritance of the Lord.

Lesson II – Ecclus 24:12–16

Then the creator of all things commanded, and said to me: and he that made me, rested in my tabernacle, And he said to me: Let thy dwelling be in Jacob, and thy inheritance in Israel, and take root in my elect. From the beginning, and before the world, was I created, and unto the world to come I shall not cease to be, and in the holy dwelling place I have ministered before him. And so was I established in Sion, and in the holy city likewise I rested, and my power was in Jerusalem. And I took root in an honourable people, and in the portion of my God his inheritance, and my abode is in the full assembly of saints.

Lesson III - Ecclus 24:17–23

I was exalted like a cedar in Libanus, and as a cypress tree on mount Sion. I was exalted like a palm tree in Cades, and as a rose plant in Jericho: As a fair olive tree in the plains, and as a plane tree by the water in the streets, was I exalted. I gave a sweet smell like cinnamon. and aromatical balm: I yielded a sweet odour like the best myrrh: And I perfumed my dwelling as storax, and galbanum, and onyx, and aloes, and as the frankincense not cut, and my odour is as the purest balm. I have stretched out my branches as the turpentine tree, and my branches are of honour and grace. As the vine I have brought forth a pleasant odour: and my flowers are the fruit of honour and riches.

Lesson IV

Sermon by St. Leo, Pope

His Mother was chosen a Virgin of the kingly lineage of David, and when she was to grow heavy with the sacred Child, her soul had already conceived him before her body. She learned the counsel of God announced to her by the Angel, lest the unusual events should alarm her. The future Mother of God knew what was to be wrought in her by the Holy Ghost, and that her modesty was absolutely safe. For why should she, unto whom was promised all sufficient strength through the power of the Highest, have felt hopeless merely because of the unexampled character of such a conception? She believes, and her belief is confirmed by the attestation of a miracle which has already been wrought. The fruitfulness of Elizabeth, before unhoped for, is brought forward that she might not doubt that he who had given conception unto her that was barren, would give the same unto her that was Virgin. And so the Word of God, the Son of God, who was in the beginning with God, by whom all things were made, and without whom was not anything made that was made, to deliver man from eternal death, was made man.

Lesson V—Sermon 2 on the Nativity of the Lord

Our Lord Jesus Christ, descending from his throne in heaven, but leaving not that glory which he has with the Father, comes into this lower world by being born after a new order and in a new birth. He comes after a new order, in that he who is unseen among his own, was seen among us; the Incomprehensible was willing to be comprehended, and he that is from everlasting to everlasting began to be in time. He was the Offspring of a new birth; conceived of a virgin, without the passion of any fleshly father, without any breach of his Mother's virginity, since such a birth beseemed the coming Saviour of mankind, who was to have in him the nature of man's being, and to be free of any defilement of man's flesh. Though he sprung not as we spring, yet is his nature as our nature; we believe that he is free from the use and custom of men; but it was the power of God which wrought that a virgin should conceive, that a virgin should bring forth, and yet abide a virgin still.

Lesson VI

From the Acts of Pope Pius XI

In the year 1931, amid the applause of the whole Catholic world, solemn rites were celebrated to mark the completion of the fifteen centuries which had elapsed since the Council of Ephesus, moving against the Nestorian heresy, had acclaimed the blessed Virgin Mary, of whom Jesus was born, as Mother of God. This acclamation had been made by the Fathers of the Church under the leadership of Pope Celestine. Pius XI, as Supreme Pontiff, wished to commemorate the notable event and give lasting proof of his devotion to Mary. Now there had existed for many years in Rome a grand memorial to the proclamation of Ephesus, the triumphal arch in the basilica of Saint Mary Major on the Esquiline Hill. This monument had already been adorned by a previous pontiff, Sixtus III, with mosaics of marvelous workmanship, now falling to pieces from the decay of the passing ages. Pius XI, therefore, out of his own munificence, caused these to be restored most exquisitely and with them the transept of the basilica. In an Encyclical Letter, Pius set forth also the true history of the Council of Ephesus, and expounded fervently and at great length the doctrine of the prerogatives of the Blessed Virgin Mary as Mother of God. He did this that the doctrine of this lofty mystery might sink more deeply into the hearts of the faithful. In it he set forth Mary, the Mother of God, blessed among women, and the most holy Family of Nazareth as the exemplars to be followed above all others, as models of the dignity and holiness of chaste wedlock, as patterns of the holy education to be given youth. Finally that no liturgical detail be lacking, he decreed that the feast of the Divine Maternity of the Blessed Virgin Mary be celebrated annually on the 11th day of October by the universal Church with a proper Mass and Office under the rite of a Duplex of the second class.

Lesson VII

From the Holy Gospel according to St. Luke (Luke 2:43–52)

In that time, having fulfilled the days, when they returned, the child Jesus remained in Jerusalem; and his parents knew it not. And so on.

Homily by St. Bernard, Abbot

"Son, why hast thou thus dealt with us?" Mary called God, the Lord of Angels, her son. Which of the angels would have dared to do so? It is enough for them, and they reckon it is a great thing, that, being naturally spirits, they should receive the grace of being made and called angels, as witnesses David: "Who makes spirits his angels." But Mary, knowing herself to be his Mother, does boldly apply the word Son to that Majesty whom the angels do serve with awe; neither does God despise to be called what he has made himself. For a little after, the Evangelist says: "And he was subject unto them." Who to whom? God to men. I say that God, unto whom the angels are subject, and who is obeyed by the Principalities and Powers, was subject to Mary.

Lesson VIII

Marvel thou at both these things, and choose whether to marvel most at the sublime condescension of the Son, or at the sublime dignity of Mary. Either is amazing, either marvelous. That God should obey this woman, is a humility without parallel; that this woman should rule over God, an exaltation without match. In praise of virgins, and of virgins only, is it sung that "These are they which follow the Lamb wheresoever he goes." Of what praise then thinkest thou that she must be worthy who even leads the Lamb? O man, learn to obey. O earth, learn to submit. O dust, learn to keep down. It is of thy Maker that the Evangelist says: "And he was subject unto them." Blush, O proud ashes. God humbles himself; and dost thou exalt thyself? God is subject unto men; and wilt thou, by striving to rule over men, set thyself before thy Maker?

Lesson IX

O happy Mary, lowly and virgin; and wondrous virginity, which motherhood destroyed not, but exalted; and wondrous lowliness, which the fruitful virginity took not away, but ennobled; and wondrous motherhood, which was both virgin and lowly. Which of them is not wondrous? Which of them is not unexampled; and which of them does not stand alone? The wonder would be if thou wert not puzzled at which to wonder most: motherhood in a virgin, or virginity in a mother; a motherhood so exalted, or lowliness in such exaltation? But indeed more marvelous than any one of these things is the combination of them all, and without all comparison, it is more excellent and more blessed to have received them all, than to have received any one of them alone. What wonder is it that God, of whom we see and read, that He is wonderful in his holy places, should have shown himself wonderful in his Mother? O you that be married, honor this incorruption in corruptible flesh; O holy virgins, gaze in wonder at fruitfulness in a virgin; O, all mankind, take pattern by the humility of the Mother of God.

October 13 ~ St. Edward the Confessor

King & Confessor ~ Semiduplex

All from Common except what follows

Lessons I–III from the occurring Scripture

Lesson IV

Edward, surnamed the Confessor, was the nephew of the Sainted King Edward the Martyr, and himself the last Anglo-Saxon King. That he should succeed to the Kingdom was shown by the Lord in a trance to a most holy man named Brithwald. When he was ten years old the Danes, who were ravaging England, sought him to put him to death, and he was driven into exile to dwell with his mother's brother, Richard II, Duke of Normandy, at whose Court he lived among all the allurements of vice a life of such uprightness and innocence as made all men to marvel. He was a burning and shining light for love of God and the things of God, very gentle-hearted, and quite free from any lust for power. Of him the saying is preserved, that he "would rather not be a King than win a kingdom through slaughter and blood."

Lesson V

When the Danish tyrants, who had robbed his brothers Edmund and Alfred of life and kingdom, were passed away, Edward was called back into his own country and with the hearty good-will and rejoicing of all, took the kingdom in the year 1042, being then about forty years old. He set himself to repair the breaches which wars had made, and began with the things of God. Of the Churches of the Saints, he built some altogether, and renewed others and gifted them with incomes and privileges, being chiefly desirous that religion should rise from the low estate whereinto it had fallen. He was brought by the nobles of his Court to marry, but it is constantly said by all writers that in matrimony he remained a virgin with a virgin bride. So great was his love toward Christ, and so strong his faith, that sometimes during Mass, he merited to see Him, with a countenance graceful and refulgent with Divine light. By reason of the abundance of his charity he was styled everywhere the father of orphans and of the poor, and he was never happier than when he had spent upon the needy the whole of his kingly treasures.

Lesson VI

He was famous for the gift of prophecy, and foretold by inspiration from heaven many things that were to befall England. Of this gift the following is a remarkable instance. Sweyn, King of the Danes, was embarking on shipboard with the mind to invade England, when he fell into the sea and was drowned, and God made known his death to Edward at the very same moment that it happened. He had a wonderful love toward John the Evangelist, so that he was used never to refuse anything for which he was asked in his name. The Evangelist appeared to him once while in tattered raiment, and, in his own name, asked him for an alms. It befell that the King had no money, wherefore he took a ring from off his finger and gifted him therewith. Not long afterward, the Evangelist sent the same ring back to him by a pilgrim, with a message concerning his death, which was then at hand. The King therefore commanded that prayers should be made for him, and then fell blessedly asleep in the Lord, upon the very day which had been foretold to him by the Evangelist, that is to say, upon the 5th day of January, in the year of salvation 1066. He was famous for miracles, and in 1161 Pope Alexander III numbered him among the Saints. But Innocent XI commanded that his memory should be celebrated with a public Office throughout the whole Church, upon the 13th day of October, being that day whereon in the year 1102 his body had been translated, and found incorrupt and sweet of scent.

Lessons VII–IX from the first set in the Common of Confessor Non-Bishops (Homily by St. Gregory)

October 14 ~ St. Callistus I

Pope & Martyr ~ Duplex

All from Common except what follows

Lessons I–III from the occurring Scripture

Lesson IV

Callistus was a Roman, and ruled the Church in the time of the Emperor Antoninus Heliogabalus. He confirmed the institution of the Ember Days, the fast which has been received by tradition from the Apostles. He built the Church of St. Mary-beyond-the-Tiber [Santa Maria in Trastevere], and enlarged the old cemetery on the Appian Way, wherein are buried so many saintly Priests and Martyrs, and which has since been called, on account of this enlargement, the Cemetery of Callistus.

Lesson V

It was by his reverence that the body of the blessed Priest and Martyr Calepodius, which had been cast into the Tiber, was carefully looked for, and, when it had been found, honorably buried. He baptized Palmatius, of Consular, and Simplicius, of Senatorial rank, and likewise Felix and Blanda, all of whom in the end underwent martyrdom. On this account he was thrown into prison, where he wonderfully healed a soldier named Privatus, who was full of sores, and so gained him to Christ; and this Privatus had hardly received the faith, before he was lashed to death with leaden scourges.

Lesson VI

Callistus sat as Pope five years, one month, and twelve days. He held five Ordinations in the month of December, wherein he ordained sixteen Priests, four Deacons, and eight Bishops. After being long starved, and repeatedly flogged, he was pitched headlong down a well, and so crowned with martyrdom, under the Emperor Alexander. His body was carried to the Cemetery of Calepodius on the Aurelian Way, at the third milestone from the city, upon the 14th day of October, but was afterwards taken to the Church of Santa Maria in Trastevere, which had been built by himself. There it lies beneath the High Altar, and is held in great reverence of all men.

Lessons VII–IX from the Common of Supreme Pontiffs (Homily by St. Leo)

October 15 ~ St. Teresa of Avila

Virgin ~ Duplex

All from Common except what follows

Lessons I–III from the occurring Scripture

Lesson IV

The virgin Teresa was born the daughter of a father and mother, equally honorable on account of their birth and of their godliness, at Avila in the kingdom of Old Castile in Spain, on the 28th day of March, in the year of our Lord 1515. She was brought up from the dawn of her life in the fear of God, and when still only seven years old she gave a startling forecast of the holy earnestness of her later years. The reading of the acts of the holy martyrs so inflamed and excited her imagination, that she ran away from her father's house, with the design of going to Africa and the hope there to lay down her life for the glory of Christ Jesus and the salvation of souls. She was met by an uncle and brought back to her mother, and was eager to slake her thirst for martyrdom by giving to the poor all the alms she could, and by other pious exercises, though still ever bewailing with tears that the highest prize had been snatched from her. In the twelfth year of her age, her mother died, and she besought the Most Blessed Virgin to be a mother to her in her stead. This she gained; thenceforth she lived always as a daughter under the shelter of the Mother of God. In the twentieth year of her age she withdrew herself among the nuns of St. Mary of Mount Carmel. There she dwelt for twenty-two years, tormented by grievous sicknesses and diverse temptations, and so bravely served her time in the hardest ranks of Christ's army, starved even of that comforting knowledge of God's reconciled love, wherein His holy children are so commonly used even upon earth to rejoice.

Lesson V

Strengthened in the virtues of an angel, the wideness of her love embraced in its tender care the salvation of other souls as well as of her own. To this end, under the blessing of God, and the approbation of Pius IV, she set, first before women and then before men, the observance of the stern Rule of the Old Carmelites. The blessing of the Almighty and merciful Lord did indeed rest most evidently upon this design. This penniless virgin, helped by no man, and in the teeth of many that were great in this world, was enabled to build thirty-two houses. The darkness of unbelievers and misbelievers drew from her unceasing tears, and she willingly gave up her own body to God to be tortured, to soften the fury of His indignation against them. His own love so blazed in her heart that she attained to see an Angel run her through with a fiery spear, and Christ Himself take her by the hand, and to hear Him say "Henceforth, as a true bride, thou shalt be zealous for Mine honor." At His inspiration she took the extremely difficult vow to do always that which should seem to her to be most perfect. She wrote much, full of heavenly wisdom, whereby the minds of the faithful are enkindled to long for the Fatherland above.

Lesson VI

Earnest as were the examples of graces which she had shown,

and grievous as was the state of her body, afflicted by disease, she still burnt with the desire of tormenting it. She tortured it with sackcloth, chains of spikes, handfuls of nettles, and heavy scourging. She rolled herself sometimes among thorns, and was used to cry to God "Lord! to suffer or to die." As long as she remained exiled from the heavenly Fountain of eternal life, her life was to her a lingering death. She was eminent for the gift of prophecy, and God did indeed so pour forth His bounties upon her, that she often cried to Him in entreaty not to bless her so as to make her forget her sins. It was worn out rather by the fever of her love than by the wasting of disease that she sank upon her deathbed at Alba. She foretold the day of her own death, received the Sacraments of the Church, and exhorted her disciples to peace, love, and strictness in observing the Rule, and then her soul, like a pure dove, winged its flight to rest with God, on the 15th day of October in the year 1582, being then 67 years of age. At her death she had a vision of Christ Jesus surrounded by Angels; a dead tree near the cell instantly broke into foliage. Her body is untouched by corruption even unto this day, and lies in a sort of perfumed oil, regarded with pious reverence. She was famous for miracles both before and after her death, and was numbered by Gregory XV among the Saints.

Lessons VII–IX from the first set in the Common of Virgins (Homily by St. Gregory)

October 16 ~ St. Hedwig

Widow ~ Semiduplex

All from Common except what follows

Lessons I–III from the occurring Scripture

Lesson IV

Jadwiga (Hedwig), a Princess, in whom the splendor of her family was outshone by the radiant innocence of her life, was the daughter of Berthold and Agnes, Marquess and Marchioness of Moravia, and maternal aunt to Saint Elizabeth of Hungary. From her earliest childhood she was a very grave child, and had already done with childish things when, at twelve years of age, she was given in marriage by her father and mother to Henry, Grand Prince of Poland. In marriage she kept the bed in all fidelity, and brought up in the fear of God the children that were therein begotten of her. After the birth of her sixth child, she was desirous to give herself more continually to God, and induced her husband to agree to a mutual vow of separation of bed-fellowship. After his death in 1238, by the inspiration of God, whom she besought in unceasing prayer, she clad herself for piety's sake in the habit of a Cistercian nun in the monastery at Trebnitz in 1219. She continued absorbed in God. She remained engaged in the Divine Office and hearing Masses from sunrise till noon, and trod mightily underfoot the old enemy of man.

Lesson V

She could not bear to hear talk of worldly things, unless they had to do with the things of God or the salvation of souls. She was very wise in business, not doing too much, nor unseasonably, and withal courteous and gentle toward all men. She got a great victory over herself by weakening her flesh with fasting, watching, and rough clothing. She was an example of the higher Christian graces and of a godly nun, by the wisdom of her counsels, and the straightforwardness and peacefulness of her mind. It was her use to rank herself after all others, and cheerfully to undertake lower offices than those of the other nuns. She ministered to the poor even upon her knees, and washed and kissed the feet of lepers, having such command over herself as not to recoil from their sores oozing with matter.

Lesson VI

Her patience and endurance were very marvelous, especially when her son Henry, Duke of Silesia, to whom she bore a mother's love, was killed by the Tartars in 1241. His death drew from her thanksgiving to God rather than tears for him. She died upon the 15th day of October, in the year 1243. She was famous for miracles. One while, being called on, she restored to life a boy who had fallen into the water, been dashed against the wheels of a mill, and wholly crushed. This and the like being duly proved, Clement IV numbered her name among those of the Saints, and allowed her Feast day to be kept in Poland, in which country, being Patroness, she has most honor, upon the 15th of October; which permission was given to the whole Church by Innocent XI.

Lessons VII–IX from the Common of Non-Virgins (Homily by St. Gregory)

October 17 – St. Margaret Mary Alacoque

Virgin – Duplex

All from Common except what follows

Lessons I–III from the occurring Scripture

Lesson IV

Margaret Mary Alacoque was born of a respectable family in a village in the diocese of Autun. From her earliest years she gave signs of holiness. Filled with a burning love of the Virgin Mother of God, and of the august mystery of the Eucharist, while still a young girl she dedicated her virginity to God. Above all else she strove to realize in her life the performance of Christian virtues. She delighted to spend continuous hours in prayers and in meditation upon the things of heaven. She was humble, and patient in adversity. She practiced bodily penance. She was charitable towards her neighbors, especially the poor. By every means within her power she strove diligently to imitate the most holy example left by our divine Redeemer.

Lesson V

Margaret entered the Order of the Visitation. There her life became immediately a shining example to others. God endowed her highly with the gift of prayer. He gave her other favors, such as frequent visitations. The most famous of these was that one when Jesus appeared to her as she knelt in prayer before the Blessed Sacrament. Opening his breast, He revealed his divine Heart glowing with flames and encircled with a crown of thorns. He bade her in return for his excessive love and in atonement for the insults of ungrateful men, to seek to have established public adoration of his Heart. This devotion he promised to enrich with treasures of heavenly grace. When, out of humility, she hesitated to undertake so great a task, the loving Saviour encouraged her. At the same time he pointed out Claude de la Colombière, a man of great holiness, as one who could guide and help her. Our Lord also comforted her with the assurance that very great blessings would accrue afterwards to the Church from the worship of his divine Heart.

Lesson VI

Margaret strove ardently to fulfill the Redeemer's command. Vexations, even bitter insults, were her portion from some who maintained that she was subject to mental aberrations. She not only bore these sufferings patiently, she even profited by them, offering herself in anguish and reproach as a victim acceptable to God, bearing all things as a more sure means of accomplishing her purpose. Renowned for her religious perfection, becoming each day more closely united with her divine spouse by contemplation of celestial things, she took flight to him in the forty-third year of her age, and in the year of restored salvation 1690. She became famous for miracles. Benedict XV added her to the list of the saints; Pius XI extended her office to the universal Church.

Lesson VII

From the Holy Gospel according to St. Matthew (Matt 11:25–30)

At that time: Jesus answered and said: I thank thee, O Father, Lord of heaven and earth, because thou hast hid these things from the wise and prudent, and hast revealed them unto babes. And so on.

Homily by St. Francis de Sales, Bishop

There is no other true knowledge given but that which is given by the Holy Ghost. And this is granted only to the humble. Have we not known great theologians who spoke marvelously of the virtues but did not practice them? Have we not seen, on the contrary, many women who did not know how to discourse on the virtues, practice the works of virtue worthily? The Holy Spirit has made these wise because they had fear of the Lord, piety, and humility.

Lesson VIII

Our Lord is the great and excellent physician of all our infirmities. Before he came into the world he announced openly to his prophets, "I will bind up that which was broken, and I will strengthen that which is weak." Finally with his own lips he invited us, saying, "Come unto me, all you that labor and are burdened, and I will give you rest." What wonder is it, then, if we see him surrounded by the sick, by sinners, and by publicans. Is it not the glory of the physician to be sought out by the sick?

Lesson IX

The Lord bears our miseries and ennobles them. He lays our miseries to his Heart; he shows his side. It is right then, that we should make some return to him, lest he who now shows us his wounds out of love, may one day show them with wrath and indignation. Grant, O good Jesus, that we may receive the peace which thou dost offer and let us see thy wounds. Since there remain faith, hope, and charity, grant that, rooted in faith, rejoicing in hope, glowing in charity, we may await thy coming in the blessed expectation that we may see thee as the Lamb upon the right, and not as the lion on the left. May clear sight take the place of hope, and, to our imperfect charity may there succeed that perfect charity in which we may rejoice forever and ever. Amen.

October 18 ~ St. Luke the Evangelist

Duplex II Class

All from Common of Evangelists except what follows

Lesson IV

From the Book by St. Jerome, Priest, on Ecclesiastical Writers

Luke was a physician of Antioch, who, as his writings indicate, was not ignorant of the Greek language. He was a follower of the Apostle Paul, and his fellow traveller in all his wanderings. He wrote a Gospel, whereof the same Paul says: "We have sent with him the brother, whose praise is in the Gospel throughout all the Churches." Of him, he writes unto the Colossians: "Luke, the beloved physician, greets you." And again, unto Timothy: "Only Luke is with me." He also published another excellent book entitled *The Acts of the Apostles*, wherein the history is brought down to Paul's two years sojourn at Rome, that is, until the fourth year of Nero. From this we gather that the book was composed in that same city.

Lesson V

Therefore we reckon among Apocryphal books *The Acts of Paul and Thecla*, and the whole story about the baptism of Leo. For why should the fellow traveller of the Apostle, who knew other things, be ignorant only of this? At the same time there is against these documents the statement of Tertullian, almost a contemporary writer, that the Apostle John convicted a certain Priest in Asia, a great admirer of the Apostle Paul, of having written them, and that said Priest confessed that he had been induced to compose them through his admiration for Paul, and that he was consequently deposed. There are some persons who suspect that when Paul in his Epistles uses the phrase: "According to my Gospel," he means the Gospel written by Luke.

Lesson VI

However, Luke learned his Gospel not from the Apostle Paul

only, who had not companied with the Lord in the flesh, but also from other Apostles, as he himself declares at the beginning of his work, where he says: "They delivered them unto us, which from the beginning were eyewitnesses and ministers of the word." According to what he had heard, therefore, did he write his Gospel. As to the Acts of the Apostles, he composed them from his own personal knowledge. He lived eighty-four years, having no wife. He is buried at Constantinople, where his bones were brought from Achaia in the twentieth year of Constantine, together with the relics of the Apostle Andrew.

Lessons VII–IX from the Common of Evangelists (Homily by St. Gregory)

October 19 ~ St. Peter of Alcantara

Confessor ~ Duplex

All from Common except what follows

Lessons I–III from the occurring Scripture

Lesson IV

Peter was born of noble parents at Alcantara, in Spain, in the year of our Lord 1499. The holiness of his life was foreshadowed from his earliest years. In the sixteenth year of his age he entered the Order of Friars Minor, wherein he showed himself a pattern to all. He undertook the work of preaching in obedience to his Superiors, and thereby brought many to turn away from sin to true repentance. He conceived a great desire to restore the Ancient and most exact observance of the Rule of St. Francis, and to that end, supported by God's help, and armed with the approval of the Apostolic See, he founded in the year 1555 a new sterner and poorer house near Pedraso, from which the more austere way of life, therein happily begun, spread marvelously through diverse Provinces of Spain even to the Indies. He was a helper to Saint Teresa, with whom he was likeminded, in bringing about the Reformation of the Carmelites. She was taught by God that no one should ask anything in the name of Peter without being heard, and used to ask him to pray for her, and to call him a Saint while he was yet alive.

Lesson V

He humbly excused himself from accepting the courtesies of princes, by whom his advice was sought as that of an oracle, and declined to become Confessor to the Emperor Charles V. He was a very careful keeper of poverty, and contented himself with a single tunic than which none was worse. Purity he carried to such a point that when he was lying sick of his final illness, he would not allow the brother who ministered to him to touch him, howsoever lightly. He brought his body into bondage by unceasing watching, fasting, scourging, cold, nakedness, and all manner of hardships, having made it a promise never to allow it any rest in this world. The love of God and his neighbor, which was shed abroad in his heart, sometimes burnt so that he was compelled to run from his cell into the open air to cool himself.

Lesson VI

The grace of contemplation was admirable in him; by which, when his spirit was constantly refreshed, it sometimes befell that he neither ate nor drank for the space of several days. He was oftentimes seen to rise into the air, shining with an unearthly glory. He passed dry-shod over torrents. When his brethren were in the last state of need, he fed them with food from heaven. A staff which he fixed in the earth grew presently into a green fig tree. Once while he was traveling by night in the midst of a heavy snowstorm, and took refuge in a ruined and roofless house, the falling snow then made a roof over him lest he should be overwhelmed. Saint Teresa bears witness that he had the gift of prophecy and of the discernment of spirits. At length, in the 63rd year of his own age, and of salvation 1562, at the hour which he had himself foretold, upon the 18th day of October, he passed away to be forever with the Lord, cheered in his last moments by a wonderful vision and by the presence of Saints. At the instant of his death, blessed Teresa, then afar off, saw him carried to heaven. He appeared to her afterwards, and said "O what happy penance, to have won for me such glory!" After his death he became famous for very many miracles, and Clement IX inscribed his name among those of the Saints.

Lessons VII–IX from the second set the Common of Confessor Non-Bishops (Homily by St. Bede)

October 20 ~ St. John Cantius

Confessor ~ Duplex

All from Common except what follows

Lessons I–III from the occurring Scripture

Lesson IV

John was the son of pious and respectable parents named Stanislaus and Anne, and was born in the year of our Lord 1397, in the town of Kęty, a place in the diocese of Krakow in Poland, from which he took the Latin name of *Cantius*. By his gentleness, innocence, and seriousness, he gave great hopes even from his childhood. He studied Philosophy and Theology in the University of Krakow, wherein he rose step by step to be a Professor and teacher of those sciences wherein he lectured many years, not only enlightening the minds of his hearers, but stirring up in them all piety, instructing them by example as well as by word. Having taken Priests' orders, he ceased not to busy himself with letters, but added thereto the striving after Christian perfection. He grieved exceedingly that God should be offended so much, and offered up to Him, day by day, not without many tears, the Unbloody Sacrifice for a propitiation for himself and for his people. He was for some years a faithful Parish Priest at Ilkusi, but after a while gave it up for fear of the danger of souls, and accepted the call of the University to take up again his Professorship.

Lesson V

What time was left him over from his work, he gave up partly to the profit of his neighbor, especially in preaching, and partly in prayer, wherein he is said sometimes to have had heavenly visions and messages. The sufferings of Christ took such hold upon him, that he sometimes passed whole nights without sleep in thinking thereon, and that he might more keenly realize them, he made a pilgrimage to Jerusalem. There he was seized with such a passionate longing to be a martyr, that he preached Christ crucified even to the Turks. He went four times to Rome to the thresholds of the Apostles, on foot, and laden with a wallet, partly to do honor to the Apostolic See, for which he had a great reverence, and partly (to use his own expression) that he might clear off the pains of his own purgatory by use of the Pardons for sin which are there daily offered. In one of these journeys he was set upon by highway robbers, who plundered him, and having asked him if he had any more, whereto he denied, left him and fled. Then he remembered that he had some gold pieces sewn up in his clothes. So he ran after the robbers with shouts, and offered them these also, but they were so amazed at the simplicity and charity of the holy man, that they gave him back even that which they had already taken. So that none should detract from the reputation of others, he wrote certain short verses upon the walls, after the example of Saint Augustine, to be an unceasing warning to himself and others. He gave his own bread to the hungry, and clothed the naked, not with bought raiment only, but by stripping himself of his own garments and shoes, himself meanwhile letting down his own cloak to trail upon the ground, lest any should see that he returned home barefoot.

Lesson VI

He slept very little, and that upon the ground; his clothing was enough only to clothe his nakedness, and his food to keep him alive. He kept his virgin purity guarded like a lily among thorns by rough hair-cloth, scourging, and fasting. For about thirty-five years before his death he never tasted flesh-meat. At length, when he was full of days and good works, he felt that death was near, and made himself ready to meet it by a long and careful preparation, and to be the freer, he gave to the poor everything that was left in his house. Strengthened by the Sacraments of the Church, and having a desire to depart, and to be with Christ, he took flight to heaven upon the 24th day of December, in the year of our Lord 1473. He was famous for miracles both before and after his death. His body was carried into the University Church of St. Anne, near his dwelling, and there honorably buried. The popular reverence and the crowds around his sepulchre grew greater day by day, till he has come to be held in honor as one of the chiefest holy defenders of Poland

and Lithuania. At the glory of more wonders, Pope Clement XIII, upon the 16th day of July, in the year 1767, with solemn rites, enrolled his name among those of the Saints.

Lessons VII–IX from the first set the Common of Confessor Non-Bishops (Homily by St. Gregory)

October 21 ~ St. Hilarion

Abbot ~ Simplex

Lessons I–II from the occurring Scripture

Lesson III

Hilarion was born of heathens at Tabatha in Palestine, about the year of our Lord 291. He was sent to study at Alexandria, where he bore a fair name for life and wit. There he embraced the religion of Jesus Christ, and made wonderful headway in faith and love. He went oftentimes to Church, was careful in fasting and prayer, and set no price upon the pleasures and lusts of the world. When the name of Anthony became famous in Egypt, Hilarion made a journey into the desert on purpose to see him. There he dwelt with him two months, to the end that he might learn all his way of life, and then returned home. After the death of his father and mother, he gave all that he had to the poor. Before he had completed the fifteenth year of his age, he went into the desert, and built there a little house, scarcely big enough to hold him, and wherein he was used to sleep on the ground. The piece of sackcloth wherewith alone he clad himself he never washed and never changed, saying that hair-cloth was a thing not worth the trouble of cleanliness. He took great interest in reading and meditating on the Holy Scriptures. His food was a few figs and some porridge of vegetables, and this he ate not before set of sun. His self-control and lowliness were beyond belief. By these and other arms he overcame diverse and fearful attacks of the devil, and drove out countless demons from the bodies of men in many parts of the world. He had built many monasteries, and was famous for miracles, when, in the eightieth year of his age, he fell sick. When he was gasping for his last breath, he said "Go out, what dost thou fear? Go out, my soul! Why dost thou waver? Thou hast served Christ nearly seventy years and art thou afraid of death?" And so with these words he gave up the Ghost.

October 24 ~ St. Raphael the Archangel

Major Duplex

Lesson I ~ Tob 12:1–4

From the book of Tobias

Then Tobias called to him his son, and said to him: What can we give to this holy man, that is come with thee? Tobias answering, said to his father: Father, what wages shall we give him? or what can be worthy of his benefits? He conducted me and brought me safe again, he received the money of Gabelus, he caused me to have my wife, and he chased from her the evil spirit, he gave joy to her parents, myself he delivered from being devoured by the fish, thee also he hath made to see the light of heaven, and we are filled with all good things through him. What can we give him sufficient for these things? But I beseech thee, my father, to desire him, that he would vouchsafe to accept one half of all things that have been brought.

Lesson II ~ Tob 12:5–13

So the father and the son, calling him, took him aside: and began to desire him that he would vouchsafe to accept of half of all things that they had brought. Then he said to them secretly: Bless ye the God of heaven, give glory to him in the sight of all that live, because he hath shewn his mercy to you. For it is good to hide the secret of a king: but honourable to reveal and confess the works of God. Prayer is good with fasting and alms more than to lay up treasures of gold: For alms delivereth from death, and the same is that which purgeth away sins, and maketh to find mercy and life everlasting. But they that commit sin and iniquity, are enemies to their own soul. I discover then the truth unto you, and I will not hide the secret from you. When thou didst pray with tears, and didst bury the dead, and didst leave thy dinner, and hide the dead by day in thy house, and bury them by night, I offered thy prayer to the Lord. And because thou wast acceptable to God, it was necessary that temptation should prove thee.

Lesson III ~ Tob 12:14–22

And now the Lord hath sent me to heal thee, and to deliver Sara thy son's wife from the devil. For I am the angel Raphael, one of the seven, who stand before the Lord. And when they had heard these things, they were troubled, and being seized with fear they fell upon the ground on their face. And the angel said to them: Peace be to you, fear not. For when I was with you, I was there by the will of God: bless ye him, and sing praises to him. I seemed indeed to eat and to drink with you: but I use an invisible meat and drink, which cannot be seen by men. It is time therefore that I return to him that sent me: but bless ye God, and publish all his wonderful works. And when he had said these things, he was taken from their sight, and they could see him no more. Then they lying prostrate for three hours upon their face, blessed God: and rising up, they told all his wonderful works.

Lesson IV

Sermon by St. Bonaventure, Bishop

Raphael means "Medicine of God," and we should observe that the way out of evil lies through three blessings bestowed on us through Raphael's healing. For Raphael the Healer leads us forth from weakness of soul and brings us into the bitterness of contrition; whence in the book of Tobias, Raphael says: "When thou enterest into thy house, anoint his eyes with gall." He did so, and he saw. Why could not Raphael do this himself? Because an Angel does not bestow compunction, but he shows the way to it. By gall, the bitterness of contrition is to be understood, for it heals the inner eyes of the mind. The Psalmist says: "He heals those that are broken in heart." This is the best eye salve. In the second chapter of the Book of Judges it is written that an angel came up to the place of the weepers, and said to the people: "I made you to go up out of Egypt; I have done all of these good things for you: and all the people wept, so that the place was called the Place of the Weepers." Dearly beloved, all day long the Angels are telling us of God's blessings, and recalling them to our minds: "Who has created thee? Who has redeemed thee? What hast thou done? Whom hast thou offended? When thou considerest this, thine only remedy is to weep."

Lesson V

Secondly, Raphael brings us forth from our slavery to the devil, by recalling Christ's Passion to our mind. There is a figure of the Passion in the sixth chapter of Tobias, where it is said that if a piece of the heart is put on the embers, its smoke will drive out all kinds of devils. It is said in the eighth chapter of Tobias that Tobias put a piece of the heart on the embers, and Raphael bound the devil in the utmost parts of Egypt. What does this mean? Was Raphael unable to bind the devil unless the heart was put on the embers? Surely a fish's heart could not give such strength to an Angel? By no means! It would be impossible unless there was a mystery in this. We are to understand that nothing so frees us from the devil's slavery as the Passion of Christ, which issued from the root of his heart, or of his love. For the heart is the fountain, or hot centre, of all life. Therefore if thou puttest the heart of Christ, that is the Passion, that he underwent, issuing from the root of charity and the fountain of heat, on the embers, that is, on the flame of memory: then immediately the devil will be bound, and he will be unable to hurt thee.

Lesson VI

Thirdly Raphael delivers us from God's displeasure, which we incur by transgressing against God; he does this by leading us to constant prayer: and this is what Raphael said to Tobias in the twelfth chapter: "When thou didst pray with tears, I did bring your prayers before the Lord." For the Angels reconcile us to God, as far as they are able. The devils are accusers before God, but the angels excuse us, when they offer our prayers, and when they urge us to pray devoutly. In the eighth chapter of the Apocalypse it is said: "The smoke of the incense ascended up before God out of the Angel's hand." This sweet smelling incense is the prayer of the saints. Does thou wish to appease God, whom thou hast offended? Then pray devoutly. They offer thy prayer, so that they may reconcile thee to God. It is said in the Gospel of St. Luke, that Christ being in an agony, prayed more earnestly, and there appeared an Angel of the Lord strengthening him. And all of this was done for our sake: for he had no need of strengthening, but it was to show that the Angels willingly assist those who pray devoutly, and help and strengthen them, and bring their prayers before God.

Lesson VII

From the Holy Gospel according to St. John (John 5:1–4)

At that time: There was a feast of the Jews, and Jesus went up to Jerusalem. And so on.

Homily by St. John Chrysostom

What manner of mystery is this? What does it reveal? For it is not written without a purpose: but the future is foretold in figure and similitude lest the unexpected occurrence of a wondrous event should in any way disturb the faith of the hearers. What, then is here described? In the future a baptism was to be given, full of power and of the greatest grace, a baptism that would wash away all sin, that would restore life to dead men. These facts then are depicted figuratively, in the pool and in all the other circumstances. And first in this figure the water is set forth, which washes away stains of the body, and those things that are not actually dirty, though they were thought to be so, such as coming in contact with a corpse, or a leper, and such like: it is to be seen that many things under the old law are cleansed by water, in accordance with this idea.

Lesson VIII

But let us now return to the subject. First defilements of the body are washed out, and then God heals various infirmities by means of water. For because God would bring us nearer to the grace of baptism, he not only cleanses defilements but heals diseases. For those figures which come nearest to the reality, in baptism, the Passion, and others are seen more clearly than the older ones. For it is the same with those who form a king's bodyguard: they are more splendidly appareled than those at the other end of his forces. And the angel came down and troubled the water, and imbued it with healing power; so that the Jews might learn that the Lord of Angels had far more power to heal all the diseases of the soul. But just as here it was not simply the natural property of the water that healed, (otherwise it would have always have done so) but it happened through the work of the Angel: so it is not simply water that works on us, but after the water has received the grace of the Spirit, then it looses us from all sin.

Lesson IX

Around this pool lay a great multitude of impotent folk, of blind, lame, withered, waiting for the moving of the water. But then those who wished for healing were prevented by infirmity from receiving it, while now everyone is able to come forward. For the Angel does not trouble the water, but the Lord of Angels brings all things to come to pass. We may no longer say, "While I am coming, another steps down before me." But even should the whole world come, the grace would not be used up, neither would its power nor effectual working come to an end. For as the sun's rays shine forth each day without burning out, and as they spread abroad without losing any of their light: far less is the operation of the Spirit diminished by the multitudes who receive it. Now this miracle took place so that as men learned that could heal bodily diseases, and as they become accustomed to this fact over a period of time: so they might they more readily believe that it could also heal diseases of the soul.

The Last Sunday of October is the Feast of Christ the King, which may be found in the Proper of Time

---

October 25 ~ Sts. Chrysanthus & Daria

Martyrs ~ Simplex

Lessons I–II from the occurring Scripture

Lesson III

Chrysanthus and Daria were husband and wife, of noble birth, but glorious rather for their faith, which the wife learnt from the husband. They brought to Christ a great number of persons at Rome, she women, and he men. Therefore the Præfect Celerinus caused them to be taken, and gave them over to Claudius the Tribune, who bade Chrysanthus to be tormented by the soldiers, all bound as he was, but all his bonds broke, and so likewise the shackles wherein his feet were afterwards fastened. Then was Chrysanthus sewn up in an ox-hide and set in the full heat of the sun, and thereafter chained hand and foot and cast into a dark prison, but the chains dropped off from him, and the place was filled with light. Meanwhile Daria was taken to a brothel, but God kept her from insult, a lion guarding her, and herself always rapt in prayer. Lastly they were both of them led to a sand-pit upon the Salarian Way, where they were thrown alive into a hole, and buried with stones, and so were not divided in winning the victory of Martyrdom.

October 26 ~ St. Evaristus

Pope & Martyr ~ Simplex

Lessons I–II from the occurring Scripture

Lesson III

Evaristus was by birth a Greek Jew, and held the Pontificate in the reign of the Emperor Trajan. He it was who divided among the Priests the Titular Churches in the city of Rome, and commanded that seven Deacons should attend the Bishop when he was executing his office of preaching the Gospel. He it was who commanded, in accordance with Apostolic tradition, that matrimony should be celebrated publicly, and that a Priestly blessing should be invoked thereon. He ruled the Church for nine years and three months. He held four Ordinations in the month of December, wherein he ordained seventeen Priests, two Deacons, and fifteen Bishops. Having finished his testimony, he was buried upon the Vatican, near the grave of the Prince of the Apostles, upon the 26th day of October, in the year of our Lord 112.

October 27 ~ Vigil of Sts. Simon & Jude

Vigil

Lessons I–III from the Common of Martyrs in Paschaltide (Homily by St. Augustine)

October 28 ~ Sts. Simon & Jude

Apostles ~ Duplex II Class

Lesson I ~ Jude 1:1–4

Beginning of the Catholic Epistle of St. Jude the Apostle

Jude, the servant of Jesus Christ, and brother of James: to them that are beloved in God the Father, and preserved in Jesus Christ, and called. Mercy unto you, and peace, and charity be fulfilled. Dearly beloved, taking all care to write unto you concerning your common salvation, I was under a necessity to write unto you: to beseech you to contend earnestly for the faith once delivered to the saints. For certain men are secretly entered in (who were written of long ago unto this judgment), ungodly men, turning the grace of our Lord God into riotousness, and denying the only sovereign Ruler, and our Lord Jesus Christ.

Lesson II ~ Jude 1:5–8

I will therefore admonish you, though ye once knew all things, that Jesus, having saved the people out of the land of Egypt, did afterwards destroy them that believed not: And the angels who kept not their principality, but forsook their own habitation, he hath reserved under darkness in everlasting chains, unto the judgment of the great day. As Sodom and Gomorrha, and the neighbouring cities, in like manner, having given themselves to fornication, and going after other flesh, were made an example, suffering the punishment of eternal fire. In like manner these men also defile the flesh, and despise dominion, and blaspheme majesty.

Lesson III ~ Jude 1:9–13

When Michael the archangel, disputing with the devil, contended about the body of Moses, he durst not bring against him the judgment of railing speech, but said: The Lord command thee. But these men blaspheme whatever things they know not: and what things soever they naturally know, like dumb beasts, in these they are corrupted. Woe unto them, for they have gone in the way of Cain: and after the error of Balaam they have for reward poured out themselves, and have perished in the contradiction of Core. These are spots in their banquets, feasting together without fear, feeding themselves, clouds without water, which are carried about by winds, trees of the autumn, unfruitful, twice dead, plucked up by the roots, Raging waves of the sea, foaming out their own confusion; wandering stars, to whom the storm of darkness is reserved for ever.

Lesson IV

Simon the Canaanite, called also *Zelotes*, went through Egypt preaching the Gospel, while the like was done in Mesopotamia by Thaddeus, also called Jude the brother of James in the Gospel, and the writer of one of the Catholic Epistles. They met together afterwards in Persia, where they begat countless children in Jesus Christ, spread the faith far and wide in those lands, amid raging heathens, and glorified together by their teaching and miracles, and, in the end, by a glorious martyrdom, the most holy name of Jesus Christ.

Lessons V–VI are Lessons IV–V from the First Set in the Common of Apostles (Sermon by St. Gregory, Pope)

Lesson VII

From the Holy Gospel according to St. John (John 15:17–25)

At that time, Jesus said to his disciples: These things I command you, that you love one another. If the world hate you, know ye, that it hath hated me before you. And so on.

Homily by St. Augustine, Bishop

In the reading from the Gospel, the last before this, the Lord had said: "you have not chosen Me, but I have chosen you, and ordained you, that you should go, and bring forth fruit, and that your fruit should remain; that whatsoever you shall ask of the Father in My Name, He may give it you." And here He says: "These things I command you, that you love one another." And by this it is that we must understand what fruit from us it is, whereof He says: "I have chosen, that you should go, and bring forth fruit, and that your fruit should remain," and so the words added "That whatsoever you shall ask of the Father in My Name, He may give it you." He will give unto us when we love one another, since this mutual love is itself the gift of Him Who has chosen us when as yet we were fruitless, since it has not been we who have chosen Him, but He Who has chosen us, and ordained us, that we should go, and bring forth fruit, that is to say, should love one another.

Lesson VIII

Love then, is the fruit which we should bring forth, and the Apostle Paul tells us that this love is love "out of a pure heart, and of a good conscience, and of faith unfeigned." This is the love wherewith we love our neighbor, the love wherewith we love God, for we do not really love our neighbor unless we love God. For if any man love God, he loves his neighbor as himself, since he that loves not God loves not himself. For on these two commandments hangs all the law and the Prophets. Love, then, is the fruit which we should bring forth. And concerning this fruit, the Lord gives us this commandment: "These things," says He, "I command you, that you love one another." Hence also the Apostle Paul when he is about praising up the fruits of the Spirit as opposed to the works of the flesh, says first of all: "The fruit of the Spirit is love." And from that as the beginning he draws out a string of other fruits, as thence begotten and thereto bound, namely, joy, peace, long-suffering, gentleness, goodness, faith, meekness, temperance, chastity.

Lesson IX

Who is really joyful that loves not the cause of his joy? Who can really be at one with another, unless he loves that other? Who is cheerful under long toil for a good work, unless he loves the aim? Who is kind, unless he love the object of his tenderness? Who is good, unless by the persuasion of love? Who is truly faithful, unless by the faith which works by love? Who is gentle to any use, unless love move him? Who turns away from baseness unless he love honor? Well, then, does the Good Master so often command us to love, as though that commandment were all-sufficient, for love is that gift without which all other good things avail nothing, and which cannot be without having every other good gift which makes a good man good.

October 31 ~ Vigil of All Saints

Vigil

Lessons I–III from the second set in the Common of Many Martyrs (Homily by St. Ambrose)

FEASTS OF NOVEMBER

November 1 ~ ALL SAINTS

Duplex I Class

Lesson I ~ Apoc 4:2–8

From the book of the Apocalypse of St. John the Apostle

And behold there was a throne set in heaven, and upon the throne one sitting. And he that sat, was to the sight like the jasper and the sardine stone; and there was a rainbow round about the throne, in sight like unto an emerald. And round about the throne were four and twenty seats; and upon the seats, four and twenty ancients sitting, clothed in white garments, and on their heads were crowns of gold. And from the throne proceeded lightnings, and voices, and thunders; and there were seven lamps burning before the throne, which are the seven spirits of God. And in the sight of the throne was, as it were, a sea of glass like to crystal; and in the midst of the throne, and round about the throne, were four living creatures, full of eyes before and behind. And the first living creature was like a lion: and the second living creature like a calf: and the third living creature, having the face, as it were, of a man: and the fourth living creature was like an eagle flying. And the four living creatures had each of them six wings; and round about and within they are full of eyes. And they rested not day and night, saying: Holy, holy, holy, Lord God Almighty, who was, and who is, and who is to come.

Lesson II ~ Apoc 5:1–8

And I saw in the right hand of him that sat on the throne, a book written within and without, sealed with seven seals. And I saw a strong angel, proclaiming with a loud voice: Who is worthy to open the book, and to loose the seals thereof? And no man was able, neither in heaven, nor on earth, nor under the earth, to open the book, nor to look on it. And I wept much, because no man was found worthy to open the book, nor to see it. And one of the ancients said to me: Weep not; behold the lion of the tribe of Juda, the root of David, hath prevailed to open the book, and to loose the seven seals thereof. And I saw: and behold in the midst of the throne and of the four living creatures, and in the midst of the ancients, a Lamb standing as it were slain, having seven horns and seven eyes: which are the seven Spirits of God, sent forth into all the earth. And he came and took the book out of the right hand of him that sat on the throne. And when he had opened the book, the four living creatures, and the four and twenty ancients fell down before the Lamb, having every one of them harps, and golden vials full of odours, which are the prayers of saints:

Lesson III ~ Apoc 5:9–14

And they sung a new canticle, saying: Thou art worthy, O Lord, to take the book, and to open the seals thereof; because thou wast slain, and hast redeemed us to God, in thy blood, out of every tribe, and tongue, and people, and nation. And hast made us to our God a kingdom and priests, and we shall reign on the earth. And I beheld, and I heard the voice of many angels round about the throne, and the living creatures, and the ancients; and the number of them was thousands of thousands, Saying with a loud voice: The Lamb that was slain is worthy to receive power, and divinity, and wisdom, and strength, and honour, and glory, and benediction. And every creature, which is in heaven, and on the earth, and under the earth, and such as are in the sea, and all that are in them: I heard all saying: To him that sitteth on the throne, and to the Lamb, benediction, and honour, and glory, and power, for ever and ever. And the four living creatures said: Amen. And the four and twenty ancients fell down on their faces, and adored him that liveth for ever and ever.

Lesson IV

Sermon by St. Bede the Venerable, Priest

Today, dearly beloved, we keep, with one great cry of joy, a Feast in memory of all Saints; at whose presence Heaven exults; whose prayers are a blessing to earth; whose victories are the crown of the Holy Church; whose testifying is the more glorious in honor, as the agony in which it was given was the sterner in intensity, for as the greater grew the battle, so the grander grew the fighters, and the triumph of martyrdom waxed the more incisive by the multiplicity of suffering, and the heavier the torment the heavier the prize. And it is our Mother, the Catholic Church, spread far and wide throughout all this planet, it is she that has learnt, in Christ Jesus her Head, not to fear shame, nor cross, nor death, but has strengthened more and more, and, not by fighting, but by enduring, has breathed into all that noble band who have come up to the bitter starting-post the hope of conquest and glory which has warmed them manfully to accept the race.

Lesson V

Verily thou art blessed, O my Mother the Church! The blaze of God's mercy beats full upon thee; thine adornment is the glorious blood of victorious Martyrs, and thy raiment the virgin whiteness of untarnished orthodoxy. Thy garlands lack neither roses nor lilies. And now, dearly beloved brethren, let each one of us strive to gain the crown of either the glistening whiteness of purity, or the red dye of suffering. In the army in heaven peace and war have both wreaths of their own with which to crown the soldiers of Christ.

Lesson VI

Moreover, to this also has the unutterable and boundless goodness of God seen, that He spreads not the time of working and wrestling, neither makes it long, nor everlasting, and, as it were, but for a moment, so that in this short and scanty life there is wrestling and working, but the crown and the prize is in a life which is eternal. So the work is soon over, but the wage is paid forever. And when the night of this world is over, the Saints are to see the clarity of the essential light, and to receive a blessedness outweighing the pangs of any torment, as testifies the Apostle Paul, where he says: "The sufferings of this present time are not worthy to be compared with the glory which shall be revealed in us."

Lesson VII

From the Holy Gospel according to St. Matthew (Matt 5:1–12)

At that time: Jesus, seeing the multitudes, he went up into a mountain, and when he was seated, his disciples came unto him. And so on.

Homily by St. Augustine, Bishop

If it be asked what is signified by the mountain, the mountain may well be understood to figure the higher and greater commandments of righteousness, since those that have been given to the Jews are the lesser. The one God, in an excellent order of times, gave, by His holy Prophets and servants, His lesser commandments unto the people whom it still befitted to be bound by fear, but by His Son He gave the greater unto the people whom it now beseemed to set free by love. But whether it be the lesser to the lesser, or the greater to the greater, all are alike the gift of Him Who alone knows what is in each epoch the seasonable medicine of mankind.

Lesson VIII

Neither is it a marvel that the greater commandments be given about the kingdom of heaven, and the lesser about a commonwealth upon earth, since both are alike the gifts of that one God Who is the Maker of heaven and earth alike. The higher and greater righteousness, then, is that whereof the Prophet says: "Thy righteousness is like the mountains of God." Thus is that Teacher, Who alone can give such teaching, mystically represented as teaching upon a mountain. "And when He was seated." The attitude of sitting while teaching appertains to the majesty of His instruction. His disciples came unto Him nearer in the body, to hear those precepts, by the fulfillment of which they should be nearer in spirit. "And He opened His Mouth, and taught them," saying these words appear redundant to the sense. It may possibly be that this circumlocution is adopted on account of the exceptional length of the discourse to follow. But it may also be that these words are not really redundant, but the pointed declaration that He now opened His Own Mouth, Who, under the Old Law, had been used to open the mouths of the Prophets.

Lesson IX

And now, what says He? "Blessed are the poor in spirit, for theirs is the kingdom of heaven." We have read where it is written concerning the lusting after temporal things: "The wandering of the desire is vanity and presumption of spirit." Presumption of spirit signifies rashness and pride. We are used to say of proud people that they are "men of high spirit," and we say well, since "spirit" is only one of the Latin names for "wind." It is so used, for instance, in "Fire, hail, snow, ice, stormy wind." Who has not heard the proud spoken of as puffed up, as if they were blown out with wind? Hence, alas, the Apostle says: "Knowledge puffs up, but charity edifies." By the poor in spirit, who are here called blessed, are rightly to be understood such as are lowly and fear God, that is, have not got minds puffed up with windy vanity.

November 2 ~ Commemoration of All the Faithful Departed

If on a Sunday, transfer to November 3

Duplex

Lesson I ~ Job 7:16–21

Spare me, for my days are nothing. What is a man that thou shouldst magnify him? or why dost thou set thy heart upon him? Thou visitest him early in the morning, and thou provest him suddenly. How long wilt thou not spare me, nor suffer me to swallow down my spittle? I have sinned: what shall I do to thee, O keeper of men? why hast thou set me opposite to thee, and I am become burdensome to myself? Why dost thou not remove my sin, and why dost thou not take away my iniquity? Behold now I shall sleep in the dust: and if thou seek me in the morning, I shall not be.

Lesson II ~ Job 14:1–6

Man born of a woman, living for a short time, is filled with many miseries. Who comes forth like a flower, and is destroyed, and fleeth as a shadow, and never continueth in the same state. And dost thou think it meet to open thy eyes upon such a one, and to bring him into judgment with thee? Who can make him clean that is conceived of unclean seed? is it not thou who only art? The days of man are short, and the number of his months is with thee: thou hast appointed his bounds which cannot be passed. Depart a little from him, that he may rest, until his wished for day come, as that of the hireling.

Lesson III ~ Job 19:20–27

The flesh being consumed. My bone hath cleaved to my skin, and nothing but lips are left about my teeth. Have pity on me, have pity on me, at least you my friends, because the hand of the Lord hath touched me. Why do you persecute me as God, and glut yourselves with my flesh? Who will grant me that my words may be written? Who will grant me that they may be marked down in a book? With an iron pen and in a plate of lead, or else be graven with an instrument in flint stone. For I know that my Redeemer liveth, and in the last day I shall rise out of the earth. And I shall be clothed again with my skin, and in my flesh I will see my God. Whom I myself shall see, and my eyes shall behold, and not another: this my hope is laid up in my bosom.

Lesson IV

From the book by St. Augustine, Bishop, on the Care for the Dead

The management of the funeral, condition of the interment, the procession of the funeral rites are more to comfort the living, than to bring relief to the dead. Yet it follows not that the bodies of the departed are to be despised and flung aside, above all those of just and faithful men, whose bodies have been used by their spirits as instruments and tools for doing all their good works. For just as the greater the affection one has for his parents, the more treasured are the father's clothing and ring and all such things to those who survive him, in the same way the bodies themselves should not be neglected, since we wear them and are joined to them more closely than anything which we ourselves put on. For our bodies are not some ornament or aid which is added from outside, but belongs to the very nature of man. So also in ancient times the funerals of just men were arranged with dutiful piety, and their funerals were celebrated, and burials provided for, and while they were still alive they gave instructions to their sons about their burial or even about moving their bodies to another place.

Lesson V

And when this affection is exhibited to the departed by faithful men who were most dear to them, there is no doubt that it profits them who while living in the body merited that such things should profit them after this life. But even if some necessity should through absence of faculty not allow bodies to be interred, or in sacred places interred, yet should there be no omitting of supplications for the souls of the dead; supplications which the Church undertakes to offer for all the dead in Christian and Catholic society, even without mentioning their names, so that they who lack parents or sons or whatever kindred or friends, may have these offices afforded unto them by the one pious mother which is common to all. But if these supplications, which are made with right faith and piety for the dead, were lacking, I account that it should not profit their souls a whit, howsoever in holy places their lifeless bodies should be deposited.

Lesson VI

Which things being so, let us not think that to the dead for whom we have a care, any thing reaches save what by sacrifices either of the altar, or of prayers, or of alms, we solemnly supplicate: although not to all for whom they are done are they profitable, but to them only by whom while they live it is obtained that they should be profitable. But forasmuch as we discern not who these are, it is fitting to do them for all the regenerate, that none of them may be passed by to whom these benefits may and ought to reach. For better it is that these things shall be superfluously done to them whom they neither hinder nor help, than lacking to them whom they help. More diligently however does each man these things for his own near and dear friends, in order that they may be likewise done unto him by his. But as for the burying of the body, whatever is bestowed on that, is no aid of salvation, but an office of humanity, according to that affection by which "no man ever hates his own flesh." Whence it is fitting that he take what care he is able for the flesh of his neighbor, when he is gone that bore it. And if they do these things who believe not the resurrection of the flesh, how much more are they beholden to do the same who do believe; that so, an office of this kind bestowed upon a body, dead but yet to rise again and to remain to eternity, may also be in some sort a testimony of the same faith?

Lesson VII ~ 1 Cor 15:12–22

From the first letter of St. Paul the Apostle to the Corinthians

Now if Christ be preached, that he arose again from the dead, how do some among you say, that there is no resurrection of the dead? But if there be no resurrection of the dead, then Christ is not risen again. And if Christ be not risen again, then is our preaching vain, and your faith is also vain. Yea, and we are found false witnesses of God: because we have given testimony against God, that he hath raised up Christ; whom he hath not raised up, if the dead rise not again. For if the dead rise not again, neither is Christ risen again. And if Christ be not risen again, your faith is vain, for you are yet in your sins. Then they also that are fallen asleep in Christ, are perished. If in this life only we have hope in Christ, we are of all men most miserable. But now Christ is risen from the dead, the firstfruits of them that sleep For by a man came death, and by a man the resurrection of the dead. And as in Adam all die, so also in Christ all shall be made alive.

Lesson VIII ~ 1 Cor 15:35–44

But some man will say: How do the dead rise again? or with what manner of body shall they come? Senseless man, that which thou sowest is not quickened, except it die first. And that which thou sowest, thou sowest not the body that shall be; but bare grain, as of wheat, or of some of the rest. But God giveth it a body as he will: and to every seed its proper body. All flesh is not the same flesh: but one is the flesh of men, another of beasts, another of birds, another of fishes. And there are bodies celestial, and bodies terrestrial: but, one is the glory of the celestial, and another of the terrestrial. One is the glory of the sun, another the glory of the moon, and another the glory of the stars. For star differeth from star in glory. So also is the resurrection of the dead. It is sown in corruption, it shall rise in incorruption. It is sown in dishonour, it shall rise in glory. It is sown in weakness, it shall rise in power. It is sown a natural body, it shall rise a spiritual body.

Lesson IX ~ 1 Cor 15:51–58

Behold, I tell you a mystery. We shall all indeed rise again: but we shall not all be changed. In a moment, in the twinkling of an eye, at the last trumpet: for the trumpet shall sound, and the dead shall rise again incorruptible: and we shall be changed. For this corruptible must put on incorruption; and this mortal must put on immortality. And when this mortal hath put on immortality, then shall come to pass the saying that is written: Death is swallowed up in victory. O death, where is thy victory? O death, where is thy sting? Now the sting of death is sin: and the power of sin is the law. But thanks be to God, who hath given us the victory through our Lord Jesus Christ. Therefore, my beloved brethren, be ye steadfast and unmoveable; always abounding in the work of the Lord, knowing that your labour is not in vain in the Lord.

November 3 – Day 3 in the Octave of All Saints

Semiduplex

Lessons I–III from the occurring Scripture

Lesson IV

Sermon by St. Bede the Venerable, Priest

Never shall there be discord anywhere there, but all things in harmony. For everywhere there, things are in such concord that all the Saints are at unity with each other in one peace and joy; all things are tranquil and quiet. Perpetual is the splendor there; not like unto the sunlight which we know here, but a light which is the brighter, as it is the more blessed. For that city, as says Scripture, needs not the light of the sun, because the Lord Almighty does enlighten it by the Lamb which is the Light thereof. There the Saints shall shine like as the brightness of the firmament, and they that have turned many to righteousness, as the stars, for ever and ever.

Lesson V

And so there is no night there, no darkness, no gathering of clouds, no asperity of heat or cold. But such is the nature of things there as no eye has seen, nor ear heard, neither has it entered into the heart of man, except of those only who have been found worthy to enjoy it, whose names are written in the book of life; and who have washed their robes in the blood of the Lamb, and are before the throne of God, serving him day and night. There is no old age anywhere there, nor misery of old age, for all are come to perfect manhood, to the measure of the stature of the fullness of Christ.

Lesson VI

But far above all these things is the fellowship there. That is, to enjoy the companionship of the heavenly citizens: to look upon the choirs of Angels and Archangels, of Thrones and Dominions, Principalities, Powers, and all the heavenly Virtues on high: and to behold the army of the Saints shining more gloriously than the stars; of the Patriarchs glowing with faith; of the Prophets rejoicing in hope; of the Apostles judging the world reformed into twelve tribes of the new Israel; of the Martyrs resplendent in their ruddy crowns of victory; and of the Virgins wearing garlands of the purest white.

Lesson VII

From the Holy Gospel according to St. Matthew (Matt 5:1–12)

At that time: Jesus, seeing the multitudes, he went up into a mountain, and when he was seated, his disciples came unto him. And so on.

Homily by St. Augustine, Bishop

"Blessed are the pure in heart, for they shall see God." How foolish therefore be they that seek God with their outward eyes, since it is in the heart that he is seen. Thus it is written elsewhere: "In simplicity of heart seek him." For a pure heart is one that has the simplicity of single-mindedness. And just as light can be seen only insofar as the bodily eyes have clear vision, so God can be seen only insofar as the heart is clear by reason of its single-mindedness of purpose. "Blessed are the peacemakers for they shall be called the children of God." Peace is perfect where there is no strife. And the children of God are peacemakers because there is nothing in them which withstands God. And surely children ought to be like unto their father.

Lesson VIII

Peacemakers are all those that have peace within themselves. That is, those who have set all the passions of their souls in order. This they do by subjecting their passions to reason, namely, to the mind and spirit. Thus, by conquering their fleshly desires, they have made of themselves a little kingdom of God. In this kingdom, everything is ordered into a harmonious whole, by virtue of the fact that the element which chief and preeminent in man (namely, mind or reason) rules, without resistance, over the elements which we have in common with the beasts. And in this fashion, the element of mind or reason, which is preeminent in man, is made subject to something preeminent to itself, namely, the Truth, even the Only-Begotten Son of God. For no one is able to govern unless he be subject unto the higher powers. Now, herein we have set forth the peace which is given on earth to men of good-will. This is the life of one who is thoroughly and completely wise.

Lesson IX

From a kingdom such as this, which is a state of complete peace and order, the prince of this world is cast out. For he is one that can rule only through perversity and disorder. When this peace has been inwardly established and confirmed, then whatever persecutions the prince of this world, who is now cast out, shall stir up from without, he only increases the glory which redounds to God. For he is unable to tear down anything in that which is so upbuilt. And by the failure of his machinations, he does but make manifest the strength with which it has been inwardly built. Hence it follows: "Blessed are they that are persecuted for righteousness' sake, for theirs is the kingdom of heaven."

November 4 ~ St. Charles Borromeo

Confessor Bishop ~ Duplex

All from Common except what follows

Lessons I–III from the occurring Scripture

Lesson IV

Charles, of the noble family of Borromeo, was born on the 2nd day of October, in the year of our Lord 1538, at the Castle of Arona, near Milan. In foretoken of his holy life, God caused a bright light to shine by night over the chamber where his mother lay in travail. As soon as his age would allow him, he received the tonsure. When he was twelve years old, he was made Abbot of the rich Benedictine Abbey of Sts. Gratinian and Felin, but reminded his father that the revenues thereof were not to be used as mere family property. His father, to whom the administration of these revenues fell, still gave them forthwith over to him, and whatever was left over, he gave to the poor. While he was young he studied letters at Pavia. He kept his purity thoroughly, so that he scared away the unclean women, of whom many were set upon him, to overthrow his self-control. In the twenty-third year of his age, his uncle Pius IV made him a Cardinal, in which dignity he was a burning and shining light of piety and all virtues before the whole of the Sacred College. About forty days afterwards the same Pope created him Archbishop of Milan. As such it was his great desire to order the Church committed to his charge in accordance with the requirements of the most holy Council of Trent, which was in great part by his labors brought to a conclusion. To raise up the degraded lives of the people, he oftentimes held Synods, but himself set an example of deep piety. He worked earnestly to purge the parts about the Alps and borders of Switzerland of heresy, and brought many of the heretics to the Christian faith.

Lesson V

Charity was the brightest mark of his life. His principality of Oria, in the kingdom of Naples, he sold for forty thousand crowns, and gave the whole sum to the poor in one day. Twenty thousand crowns being left him as a legacy, he gave the whole sum to the poor. The incomes of the benefices wherewith he had been loaded by his uncle, he spent upon the needs of the poor, except what he used for himself. When the plague grievously raged in Milan, he gave up to the sick poor the furniture of his own house, even to his own bedding, and thenceforward slept upon the boards. He constantly visited the sick, cheered them by his fatherly kindness, and wonderfully comforted them, ministering to them with his own hands the Sacraments of the Church. At the same time he drew near to plead for them with God in lowly entreaty, and ordered a public Procession wherein he walked carrying a Cross himself, with a rope halter round his neck, and his bare feet bleeding from the stones, and eager to turn away the Divine wrath by offering himself as a scapegoat for the sins of his people. He was a stout defender of the freedom of the Church. But in the Church he was an earnest reformer of discipline, and once, when he was engaged in prayer, some conspirators took a shot at him with a blunderbuss, but, though the ball struck him, the power of God kept him unharmed.

Lesson VI

He was remarkable for his abstinence. He very often fasted upon nothing but bread and water, and sometimes nothing but lupin beans. He tamed his body by depriving himself of sleep, by very rough haircloth, and by constant scourging. He was an earnest practicer of humility and meekness. However much he was taken up with business, he never gave himself relaxation from prayer and from preaching the word of God. He built many Churches, convents, and schools. He wrote much matter, useful more especially for the good of Bishops. The publication of the Parish Priests' Catechism [The Roman Catechism] was due to his care. In October, 1584, he withdrew himself, for the purpose of making a retreat, to the Sacro Monte of Varallo, a hill whereon the incidents of the Lord's sufferings are represented in life-size groups of colored figures. On Oct. 24 he was taken ill of a fever, but concealed it, and lived there for some days a life of torture by voluntary suffering, but of sweetness by thoughts of Christ's woes. After his return to Milan, which he reached in a litter upon All Souls' Day, his sickness became hopeless, and early in the night between the 3rd and 4th days of November, in the 47th year of his own age, and in that of our Lord 1584, covered with ashes and sackcloth, and with his eyes fixed upon the image of Christ crucified, he exchanged earth for heaven. He was famous for miracles, and Pope Paul V numbered him among the Saints.

Lessons VII–IX from the first set in the Common of Confessor Bishops (Homily by St. Gregory)

Lesson IX—Commemoration of Sts. Vitalis & Agricola

Vitalis and Agricola, a slave and his master, were arrested at Bologna in the persecution under Diocletian and Maximian, for preaching Jesus Christ. Vitalis, the more he was implored and threatened to change his mind so much the more proclaimed himself a worshipper and servant of Christ, and after bravely bearing a course of diverse tortures, gave up his soul in prayer to God. The execution of Agricola had been put off, in the hope that the agonies of his servant might scare him into denying Christ; but the sight only hardened him. He was therefore crucified, and so became sharer and fellow with his slave Vitalis in the glory of testimony. Their bodies were laid in the Jews' burying-place, where they were found by St. Ambrose, who removed them to a hallowed and honorable sepulchre.

November 5 ~ Day 5 in the Octave of All Saints

Semiduplex

Lessons I–III from the occurring Scripture

Lesson IV

Sermon by St. Bede the Venerable, Priest

Therefore, may it be our delight to go on unto this prize of good living. Freely and cheerfully let us strive in the race, running under the eyes of God and of Christ. We have already taken a station above floating and earthly things, and let us allow no love for things fleeting to hamper our running. If the last day shall find us lithe and speedy in the race of good living, we shall never have to complain that our Master is a scanty rewarder of our works.

Lesson V

He that gives a red crown for suffering under persecution, gives a white crown to them that under peace, prevail in battles of righteousness. Neither Abraham, nor Isaac, nor Jacob, were slain, and nevertheless in honor for faith and righteousness, they have gained the first place among the Patriarchs, and it is to sit down with them in the kingdom of God that are gathered the faithful, the righteous, and the praiseworthy. We must remember that it is God's will, and not our own will, that we must do, for he that does His will abides forever, even as He abides forever.

Lesson VI

Therefore, dearly beloved brethren, with mind clear, faith firm, courage true, love thorough, let us be ready to do whatever God wills, keeping stoutly all the commandments of the Lord, having innocence in simplicity, concord in charity, modesty in lowliness, diligence in ministry, watchfulness in helping them that toil, mercy in helping the poor, firmness in standing up for the truth, sternness in keeping of discipline, lest we be found wanting in any good work. These are the steps which the Saints who have already gone home have left marked for us, that we may be able to keep in their footprints, and so to follow them into their joy.

Lesson VII

From the Holy Gospel according to St. Matthew (Matt 5:1–12)

At that time: Jesus, seeing the multitudes, he went up into a mountain, and when he was seated, his disciples came unto him. And so on.

Homily by St. Augustine, Bishop

Thirdly, "Blessed are they that mourn." They that are blessed under this third head, having knowledge, do mourn that they possess not yet the Highest Good, which possession belongs unto the end of their course. But in the fourth place, "Blessed are they which do hunger and thirst after righteousness." Here there is that earnest striving, wherewith the mind does struggle to tear herself away from those things whose deadly sweetness would make her want to cling unto them. Here is hungering and thirsting after righteousness, and there is sore need of firmness, for what it is a joy to have, it must be a grief to lose. But the fifth head is the declaration that "Blessed are the merciful," and in these words a door of comfort and reward is opened unto the toiling. Entangled in such straits a man can be of no use to himself, unless One That is stronger than he help him; and if he be helped of the Stronger, it is but just that he in turn should help such as is weaker than himself. And so, "Blessed are the merciful," for, in their turn, they shall obtain mercy from God.

Lesson VIII

"Blessed are the pure in heart." This sixth benediction is pronounced upon those hearts which by pure, clear consciousness of good works are able to look to that Highest Good, Which only the clear, calm mind can perceive. Lastly comes in the seventh place that "Blessed are the peacemakers," that is to say, blessed are they who cultivate wisdom, which is the contemplation of the Truth, since it is the fruit of this contemplation of the Truth to produce profound and utter internal peace in man, and to catch the reflection of the Divine, this being the idea which is expressed in the words: "Blessed are the peacemakers, for they shall be called the children of God." The eighth phrase is a return to the first, since it shows lowliness of spirit in its aspect of completion and crowning; and thence the kingdom of heaven is the reward mentioned in both places. "Blessed are the poor in spirit, for theirs is the kingdom of heaven." "Blessed are they which are persecuted for righteousness' sake, for their's is the kingdom of heaven."

Lesson IX

Paul says: "Who shall separate us from the love of Christ? Shall tribulation, or distress, or persecution, or famine, or nakedness, or peril, or sword?" There are therefore seven things which bring to perfection, for the eighth is the glorification and manifestation of that which is perfected, that from this head others again may begin, and be finished. It seems to me also that these heads and sayings have some connection with the seven gifts of the Holy Ghost whereof Isaias speaks. But there is a difference of order, for there the highest is taken first, but here the lowest; there the wisdom of God, but here the fear of God, but "the beginning of wisdom is fear of the Lord."

November 6 ~ Day 6 in the Octave of All Saints

Semiduplex

Lessons I–III from the occurring Scripture

Lesson IV

Sermon by St. Bernard, Abbot

Dearly beloved brethren, since we keep on this day the memory of all the Saints, that memory so joyous and so worthy of all our thoughts, it seems worthwhile to me, the Holy Ghost helping me, to address to your kind indulgence some remarks upon that happiness which they are all enjoying in blessed restfulness, and that final consummation they are awaiting. It is a faithful saying, and worthy of all acceptation, that if we thus solemnly honor them, we should follow the example of their conduct; if we proclaim them so blessed, we should strive our best to reach the same blessedness; if we are well pleased to hear them praised, we should be bettered by their prayers.

Lesson V

What is it to the Saints that we should praise them? What to them that we should glorify them? What is this our Feast to them? What are honors on earth to them whom, according as the Son has faithfully promised, His Father is honoring? What are our eulogies to them? They are full. Verily, dearly beloved brethren, of our goods the Saints have no need, and our devotion toward them does nothing for them. Our honoring their memory has to do with ourselves and not with them. Would you know what it has to do with us? In me I confess that at their remembrance I feel kindled a vehement longing, yea, a threefold longing.

Lesson VI

It is a common saying that what the eye does not see, the heart does not ache. The memory is a kind of sight, and to think of the Saints, is to call them up before the mind's eye. Such is our portion in the land of the living, but it is not a little portion, if love, as it ought to do, be joined with remembrance; it is in such sense that we must say that our conversation is in heaven. Very differently to what is theirs. For they are there actually, where we are only in desire; they in very presence, we only in thought.

Lesson VII

From the Holy Gospel according to St. Matthew (Matt 5:1–12)

At that time: Jesus, seeing the multitudes, he went up into a mountain, and when he was seated, his disciples came unto him. And so on.

Homily by St. Augustine, Bishop

Therefore, if we reckon up the Beatitudes as ascending steps, the first is the fear of God; the second, godliness; the third, knowledge; the fourth, fortitude; the fifth, counsel; the sixth, understanding; the seventh, wisdom. The fear of God pertains unto the lowly, as it is said "Blessed are the poor in spirit, for theirs is the kingdom of heaven," that is, it is for them that are not puffed up, for them that are not proud, as also says the Apostle: "Be not high-minded, but fear," that is, Be not puffed up. Piety pertains unto the meek; for he that seeks after a pious sort, honors the Holy Scripture, and when he finds therein that which he does not yet understand he blames not the Scripture, nor resists. And this is to be meek. Therefore is it said here: "Blessed are the meek, for they shall inherit the earth."

Lesson VIII

Knowledge pertains unto them that mourn, who have already learnt from the Scriptures amid what ills they are entangled, even in those things which once in their ignorance they affected as being good and useful. Of such is it said "Blessed are you that weep now." Firmness pertains unto such as hunger and thirst after righteousness. These are they who toil bravely, animated by the longing for that joy which is caused by real blessedness, and striving therefore to wean their love away from so-called joys whose origin is merely earthly and fleshly. Of them is it said "Blessed are they which do hunger and thirst after righteousness." Counsel pertains unto the merciful, for our only way of escape from the horrors of our own guilt's punishment is that we should forgive even as we hope to be ourselves forgiven, and should help others as much as we can, even as we would eagerly be helped in that wherein we can ourselves do nothing. And of such as do so, it is said "Blessed are the merciful, for they shall obtain mercy from God."

Lesson IX

Understanding pertains unto the pure in heart, for these are they whose clear eye can see that which the fleshly eye has not seen, neither the ear heard, neither has it entered into the heart of man to conceive; and therefore of them it is said: "Blessed are the pure in heart, for they shall see God." Wisdom pertains unto the peacemakers, even unto them in whom all things are well ordered, and passion no longer makes insurrection against reason, but all things are subject unto human common sense, even as the same again is made subject unto God. And of such is it said: "Blessed are the peacemakers." But for all these forms of blessedness there is one and the same reward, although diversely named, and that reward is the kingdom of heaven.

November 7 – Day 7 in the Octave of All Saints

Semiduplex

Lessons I–III from the occurring Scripture

Lesson IV

Sermon by St. John Chrysostom

He that wonders with reverential love at the mighty deeds of the Saints, he that has oftentimes on his tongue praises for the glory of the righteous, let such a one copy their holy lives and their righteousness; for if any take pleasure in the work of a Saint, he ought to take pleasure in serving God as that Saint served Him. If he praises the Saint, he ought to imitate him, and if he is not ready to imitate him, he ought not to praise him. Let him that praises another make himself worthy of like praise, and if he be in admiration of the Saints, let his own admirable life reflect the holiness of theirs. If we love the just and faithful because they are just and faithful, let us not forget that we can be what they are, by doing as they did.

Lesson V

It ought not to be hard for us to copy others, when we see what they of old did without any examples before them, so that in them who copied not others, but set example for others to copy, and in us who copy them, and in them which take example by us, Christ may be glorified in His holy Church. Thus from the very beginning of the world there have been the harmless: Abel, who was slain, Enoch, who, pleasing God, was taken, Noe, who was found righteous, Abraham, who was tried and found faithful, Moses, who was the meekest of men, Josue the chaste, David the gentle, Elias the accepted, Daniel the holy, and the three Children who were victorious.

Lesson VI

The Apostles, the disciples of Christ, are held the teachers of believers. Confessors taught of them fight manfully, the noble martyrs triumph, and the Christian army armed with the armor of God, ever prevails in warfare against the army of the devil. All these have been men of like loyalty, diverse warfares, and glorious victories. And thou, O Christian, art but an effeminate soldier, if thou thinkest to conquer without a fight, to triumph without a struggle. Nerve thyself, strive manfully, hit hard in the press. Consider thine engagement, look to thy state, know thine arm, even the engagement which thou hast taken, the state wherein thou art come, and the arm wherewith thou hast enrolled thyself a soldier.

Lesson VII

From the Holy Gospel according to St. Matthew (Matt 5:1–12)

At that time: Jesus, seeing the multitudes, he went up into a mountain, and when he was seated, his disciples came unto him. And so on.

Homily by St. Augustine, Bishop

At the first step in blessedness is set forth, as was proper, the kingdom of heaven, the realization of the perfect and highest wisdom of the reasonable soul. Thus is it said "Blessed are the poor in spirit, for theirs is the kingdom of heaven," as though it were said "The fear of the Lord is the beginning of wisdom." Then unto the meek is given an inheritance, as the legacy of a father to dutiful children. "Blessed are the meek, for they shall inherit the earth." Thirdly, there is comfort for such as mourn, knowing what they have lost, and what encompasses them. "Blessed are they that now mourn, for they shall be comforted." Fourthly, the hungry and thirsty are promised that they shall be filled, a refreshment for the strugglers for life, and for the weary. "Blessed are they which do hunger and thirst after righteousness, for they shall be filled."

Lesson VIII

Mercy is proclaimed unto the merciful, as unto them who have taken the true and best counsel how to obtain from Him That is Mightier than they what they that are weaker than they obtain from them. "Blessed are the merciful, for they shall obtain mercy from God." Unto the pure in heart it pertains to see God, for their eye is clear to take in the things eternal. "Blessed are the pure in heart, for they shall see God." To the peacemakers it is given to be in the likeness and image of God, for these are the perfectly wise, created anew in the image of God, by the regeneration of the new man. "Blessed are the peacemakers, for they shall be called the children of God." The foregoing are forms of blessedness which we believe can be thoroughly attained in this life. The Apostles, for instance, did, we believe, attain them. As for that entire change into the likeness of Angels, which is promised us when this life is done, no words can set it forth.

Lesson IX

"Blessed are they which are persecuted for righteousness' sake, for theirs is the kingdom of heaven." In this eighth word, which returns back again to the fountainhead and sets forth the perfect crown of human blessedness, is contained perchance a connection with the fact that it was upon the eighth day that the old Law commanded that circumcision should be performed, and that it was upon the day next after the Sabbath that the Lord rose again, the day whereon He so rose being thus the eighth day, and the first day. There is perchance also a connection with the fact that we observe eight days in honor of the creation of the new man. And yet again there is perchance a connection with the number contained in the Feast of Pentecost. For this number of fifty days is reckoned by counting seven multiplied by seven, which is forty-nine, and thereto adding one, which joined with seven makes eight, and so making full fifty. And thus borne backward to our fountainhead, the day whereon the Holy Ghost was sent down, we are borne unto the kingdom of heaven, and inherit the earth, and are comforted, and are filled, and obtain mercy, and are made pure, and are set at peace. And when we have thus been perfected within, we bear for truth's and righteousness' sake any troubles that may come upon us from without.

November 8 ~ Octave Day of All Saints

Major Duplex

Lessons I–III from the occurring Scripture

Lesson IV

From the Book upon Death by Saint Cyprian, Bishop and Martyr

Dearly beloved brethren, we should keep well in our mind and thoughts that we are living here meanwhile as strangers and pilgrims. Let us hail that day which will see us each at home in one of the many mansions, which will see us delivered hence, and disentangled from the nets and snares of things temporal, and put us back into the Garden of Eden, and into the kingdom of heaven. Is there any in a far country who is but quick to make his way to his Fatherland? Was any ever in haste to make his voyage homeward, but longed for a fair wind, that he might the sooner embrace his loved ones?

Lesson V

We reckon Paradise to be our home; already we begin to have the Patriarchs for our kinsmen. Why should we not make haste and run, to see our home, and to greet our kinsfolk? There are a great many of those we love waiting for us there: father, and mother, and brothers, and children, there in great company they await us, they who are sure now never to die any more, but not yet sure of us. O, when we come to see them and to embrace them, what gladness will it be both for us and for them! O, what will be the brightness of life in that heavenly kingdom where there is no more fear of death, but the certainty of living everlastingly! O, what highest and perpetual happiness!

Lesson VI

There is the glorious company of the Apostles, there is the exultant number of the Prophets, there is the countless army of Martyrs crowned for victory in strife and in suffering. There triumph the virgins who by noble continence have tamed the desires of the flesh and body. There the merciful are repaid with mercy, who by feeding and gifting the needy, have wrought righteousness, have kept the commandments of the Lord, and have exchanged heritages upon earth for treasures in heaven. Thitherward, dearly beloved brethren, let us eagerly run, with such as these soon to be, unto Christ soon to come, let us be eager.

Lesson VII

From the Holy Gospel according to St. Matthew (Matt 5:1–12)

At that time: Jesus, seeing the multitudes, he went up into a mountain, and when he was seated, his disciples came unto him. And so on.

Homily by St. Augustine, Bishop

"Blessed are you," says the Lord, "when men shall revile you, and persecute you, and shall say all manner of evil against you falsely, for My sake. Rejoice, and be exceedingly glad, for great is your reward in heaven." If any be seeking under the name of a Christian the pleasures of this world and the possession of temporal goods, let him bethink him that our blessedness is inward, even as the mouth of the Prophet says concerning the soul of the Church: "The King's daughter is all glorious within." Without, she is reviled, and persecution and evil report are her promised portion. And yet for these very things, great is her reward in heaven, as indeed is felt in the hearts of the sufferers, at least of such as are able already to say: "But we glory also in tribulations; knowing that tribulation works patience; and patience, trial; and trial, hope; and hope confounds not; because the charity of God is poured forth in our hearts by the Holy Ghost, Who is given to us."

Lesson VIII

To suffer such things is not in itself fruitful; what is fruitful, is to bear them for Christ's Name's sake not calmly only but gladly. There are a great many heretics who mislead souls under the name of Christians, and they suffer such things plentifully, but they are cut out from the reward, for it is not said only "Blessed are they which are persecuted," but "Blessed are they which are persecuted for righteousness' sake." Where there is not sound faith there cannot be righteousness, for the just shall live by faith. Neither let schismatics promise themselves any of that reward, for as righteousness cannot exist where there is no faith, so neither can it exist where there is no charity. And schismatics have no charity, for charity works no ill to his neighbor, and if they had it, they would not tear the Body of Christ, which is the Church.

Lesson IX—Commemoration of the Four Crowned Martyrs (Sts. Severus, Severian, Carpophorus, & Victorinus)

In the persecution under Diocletian four brothers named Severus, Severian, Carpophorus, and Victorinus, boldly refused to worship the gods, and were lashed with leaden whips until they gave up their lives for Christ's Name's sake under the strokes. Their bodies were thrown out to be eaten by the dogs, but as they remained untouched after a long while, the Christians took them away, and buried them in a sand-pit upon the Lavican Way at the third milestone from the City, near the grave of the holy martyrs Claudius, Nicostratus, Symphorian, Castorius, and Simplicius, who had suffered under the same Emperor, because, being excellent sculptors, they could in no way be brought to make statues of idols, and when they were brought to the image of the Sun to do reverence to it, they had said they would never worship the works of men's hands. For this reason they were thrown into prison, and when after many days they were still found of the same mind, they were first lashed with scourges armed with hooks, and then soldered up alive in leaden coffins and thrown into the river. There is in the City of Rome a Church called that of the Four Holy Crowned, whose names were long unknown but afterwards made manifest by God. In this Church are honorably buried the bodies of these former four, and also those of the latter five; and a Festival is held in their honor upon the 8th day of November.

November 9 ~ Dedication of the Archbasilica of the Most Holy Savior

Duplex II Class

All from the Common of the Dedication of a Church except what follows

Lesson I ~ Apoc 21:9–11

From the book of the Apocalypse of St. John the Apostle

And there came one of the seven angels, who had the vials full of the seven last plagues, and spoke with me, saying: Come, and I will shew thee the bride, the wife of the Lamb. And he took me up in spirit to a great and high mountain: and he shewed me the holy city Jerusalem coming down out of heaven from God, Having the glory of God, and the light thereof was like to a precious stone, as to the jasper stone, even as crystal.

Lesson II ~ Apoc 21:12–15

And it had a wall great and high, having twelve gates, and in the gates twelve angels, and names written thereon, which are the names of the twelve tribes of the children of Israel. On the east, three gates: and on the north, three gates: and on the south, three gates: and on the west, three gates. And the wall of the city had twelve foundations, and in them, the twelve names of the twelve apostles of the Lamb. And he that spoke with me, had a measure of a reed of gold, to measure the city and the gates thereof, and the wall.

Lesson III - Apoc 21:16–18

And the city lieth in a foursquare, and the length thereof is as great as the breadth: and he measured the city with the golden reed for twelve thousand furlongs, and the length and the height and the breadth thereof are equal. And he measured the wall thereof a hundred and forty-four cubits, the measure of a man, which is of an angel. And the building of the wall thereof was of jasper stone: but the city itself pure gold, like to clear glass.

Lesson IV

The Rites whereof the Church of Rome makes use for the consecration of Churches and Altars were first instituted by the blessed Pope Sylvester. From the very time of the Apostles there had been places set apart for God, where assemblies took place upon the first day of every week, and where the Christians were used to pray, to hear the word of God, and to receive the Eucharist, which places were by some called "Oratories" and by others "Churches." But these places were not dedicated with so solemn a form, nor did they set up therein an Altar for a pillar, and pour chrism thereon for a figure of our Lord Jesus Christ, Who is Himself our Altar, our Victim, and our Priest.

Lesson V

But when the Emperor Constantine had by the Sacrament of Baptism received health both of body and soul, then first in a law by him published was it allowed to the Christians throughout the whole world to build Churches, to which holy building he exhorted them by his example as well as by his decree. He dedicated in his own Lateran Palace a Church to the Saviour, and built near it a Cathedral in the name of St. John the Baptist, upon the place where he had been baptized by Saint Sylvester and cleansed from his leprosy. This Cathedral was consecrated by the same Pope upon the 9th day of November. It is this consecration, the memory whereof is still celebrated upon this day, the first whereon the public consecration of a Church ever took place in Rome, and the image of the Saviour was seen by the Roman people painted upon the wall.

Lesson VI

The Blessed Sylvester afterwards decreed, when he was consecrating the Altar of the Prince of the Apostles, that Altars were thenceforward to be made of stone only, but notwithstanding this the Lateran Cathedral has the altar made of wood. This is not surprising. From St. Peter to Sylvester the Popes had not been able, by reason of persecutions, to abide fixedly in one place, and they celebrated the Holy Liturgy in crypts, in cemeteries, in the homes of pious persons, or wherever need drove them, upon a wooden altar made like an empty box. When peace was given to the Church, Saint Sylvester took this box, and to do honor to the Prince of the Apostles, who is said to have offered sacrifice thereon, and to the other Popes who thereon had been used to execute the mystery even unto that time, set it in the first Church, even the Lateran, and ordained that no one but the Roman Pontiff should thereafter celebrate the Liturgy thereon. The original Lateran Cathedral, cast down and destroyed by fires, pillages, and earthquakes, and renewed by the constant care of the Popes, was at last rebuilt afresh, and solemnly consecrated by Pope Benedict XIII, of the Order of Preachers, upon the 28th day of April, in the year 1726, the memory of which Festival he ordained to be kept upon this day. In the year 1884, Leo XIII took in hand a work which had received the sanction of his predecessor Pius IX. The great sanctuary, the walls of which were giving way with age, was lengthened and widened, a task of immense labor. The ancient mosaic had been renewed previously in several places; it was now restored according to the original design, and transferred to the new apse, the embellishment of which was carried out with great magnificence. The transept was redecorated, and its ceiling and woodwork repaired. A sacristy, a residence for the canons, and a portico connecting with the baptistry of Constantine, were added to the existing buildings.

Lessons VII–IX from the Common of the Dedication of a Church (Homily by St. Ambrose)

Lesson IX—Commemoration of St. Theodore, Martyr

Theodore was a Christian soldier, who was arrested in the reign of the Emperor Maximian for having set fire to a temple of idols. The Commander of the Legion offered him pardon if he would profess repentance and curse the Christian faith, but, as he persevered in the confession of the faith, he was cast into prison. There he was flayed with iron claws. As his ribs were stripped, he joyfully sang the 33rd Psalm: "I will bless the Lord at all times." Thereafter he was thrown upon a heap of burning wood, and there, still praying and praising God, he gave up his soul to Christ, upon the 9th day of November, in the year of salvation 304. The Lady Eusebia wrapped his body in a winding-sheet, and buried it on her own farm.

November 10 ~ St. Andrew Avellino

Confessor ~ Duplex

All from Common except what follows

Lessons I–III from the occurring Scripture

Lesson IV

Andrew Avelino, who before was called Lancelot, was born at Castro Nuovo, a small town in Lucania, in the kingdom of Naples, in the year of our Lord 1520. From his earliest childhood he gave no obscure signs of the holiness of his later life. When as a lad he was away from home at school, he so passed the slippery paths of that age, as ever keeping before his eyes, amid the pursuit of earthly knowledge, the true beginning of wisdom, which is the fear of the Lord. He was exceedingly handsome, but withal careful in purity, and thereby escaped oftentimes the shameless proposals of women, and sometimes even resisted open violence. He had already become a cleric when he went to Naples to study law. There he was ordained a Priest, and also took his degree in Jurisprudence. He undertook cases only in the Church Courts, and for certain private persons, according to the rules of the Sacred Canons. Once in pleading a cause, in a matter indeed which was of no weight, a lie escaped him. Almost forthwith thereafter, in reading the Holy Scriptures, he came upon the words: "The mouth that lies kills the soul," and so great was the grief and remorse which he felt for his sin that he made up his mind to leave that way of life. He therefore gave up his law business, and set himself altogether to mind the worship of God and the execution of his holy ministry. The eminent pattern which he gave of all the virtues proper to a Churchman moved the Archbishop of Naples to commit to him the care of a certain nunnery in that city. The holy man's zeal stirred up the malice and rage of certain wicked men in the city. He once narrowly escaped death, with which they threatened him; and another time received three wounds in his face from a bully. These injuries he bore with thorough meekness. Out of an earnest desire of more readily attaining to a perfect disengagement of his heart from all earthly things, he humbly sought and in 1556 obtained to be admitted into the Order of Clerics Regular, called Theatines, and on this occasion, out of the love he bore to the Cross, he entreated that his name might be changed from Lancelot to Andrew.

Lesson V

He entered manfully and cheerily upon the harder life, set to work to better himself therein, and to that end made two very grim vows, the first, perpetually to fight against his own will, the second, always to advance to the utmost of his power in Christian perfection. Of the discipline of his Order he was a stern defender, and when he was set over others the observance thereof was his great care. Whatever time the duties of his work and his institute left him, he gave to prayer and the salvation of souls. His godliness and wisdom in hearing of confessions were beautiful. He went many times through the farthest lanes and suburbs of Naples, bringing Gospel ministry with great gain of souls. The greatness of his love toward his neighbor God was pleased to crown even by signs and wonders. One stormy night he was coming home from hearing a sick man's confession, when the rain and wind put out the light which was carried before him, but he and they that were with him not only came dry through the thickest of the rain, but there came also a strange light out of his body and showed them the way in the deepest of the darkness. He was a wonderful instance of self-control, long-suffering, lowliness, and contempt of self. He bore with stillness the murder of his nephew, held in the passion of his kinsfolk to take revenge, and even asked pity for the assassins from the judges.

Lesson VI

He spread in many places the Institute of Clerics Regular, and founded their houses at Milan and Piacenza. The Cardinal Saint Charles Borromeo, and the Cardinal Paul of Arezzo, being himself a Cleric Regular, men by both of whom he was well liked, used his help in their care for souls. Toward the Virgin Godbearer he was constant in an extraordinary love and reverence. He won the conversation of Angels, whom he said he used to hear singing when he was praising God. He set an example of heroic virtue, even to the gift of prophecy, whereby he saw into men's hearts and knew things afar off or even yet to come. Full of years and worn out with work, he was beginning the Liturgy, when, having repeated thrice the words, "I will go unto the Altar of God," he was felled by a stroke of apoplexy, and, duly fortified by the Sacraments, in the arms of his friends, most peacefully gave up his soul to God, upon the 10th day of November, in the year 1608. The crowds which flock to his grave in the Church of St. Paul at Naples are still as great as they were when his body was first laid there. He was famous for signs and wonders both during his life and after his death, and Pope Clement XI solemnly enrolled his name among those of the Saints.

Lessons VII–IX from the first set in the Common of Confessor Non-Bishops (Homily by St. Gregory)

Lesson IX—Commemoration of Sts. Tryphon, Respicius, & Nympha, Virgin, Martyrs

In the reign of the Emperor Decius one Tryphon strove by preaching the faith of Jesus Christ to bring all men to worship Him. For this cause he was taken by the servants of Decius. He was first tormented upon the rack, and flesh stripped from him with iron claws; then red-hot nails were driven into his insteps, he was beaten with cudgels and scorched with lighted torches. The sight of the courage wherewith he bore all, brought the Præfect Respicius to believe in the Lord Christ, and he forthwith declared himself a Christian. He also was diverse ways tormented, and then led along with Tryphon before the statue of Jupiter. When Tryphon prayed, the statue fell down. Then were both Tryphon and Respicius savagely lashed with leaden whips, until they grasped the crown of a most glorious testimony, upon the 10th day of November. Upon the same day a certain maiden named Nympha, having openly confessed that Jesus Christ is very God, added the palm of martyrdom to the crown of virginity.

November 11 – St. Martin of Tours

Confessor Bishop – Duplex

All from Common except what follows

Lesson I – 1 Tim 3:1–7

From the First Letter of St. Paul the Apostle to Timothy

A faithful saying: if a man desire the office of a bishop, he desireth a good work. It behoveth therefore a bishop to be blameless, the husband of one wife, sober, prudent, of good behaviour, chaste, given to hospitality, a teacher, Not given to wine, no striker, but modest, not quarrelsome, not covetous, but One that ruleth well his own house, having his children in subjection with all chastity. But if a man know not how to rule his own house, how shall he take care of the church of God? Not a neophyte: lest being puffed up with pride, he fall into the judgment of the devil. Moreover he must have a good testimony of them who are without: lest he fall into reproach and the snare of the devil.

Lesson II – Titus 1:7–11

From the Letter of St. Paul the Apostle to Titus

For a bishop must be without crime, as the steward of God: not proud, not subject to anger, not given to wine, no striker, not greedy of filthy lucre: But given to hospitality, gentle, sober, just, holy, continent: Embracing that faithful word which is according to doctrine, that he may be able to exhort in sound doctrine, and to convince the gainsayers. For there are also many disobedient, vain talkers, and seducers: especially they who are of the circumcision: Who must be reproved, who subvert whole houses, teaching things which they ought not, for filthy lucre's sake.

Lesson III – Titus 2:1–8

But speak thou the things that become sound doctrine: That the aged men be sober, chaste, prudent, sound in faith, in love, in patience. The aged women, in like manner, in holy attire, not false accusers, not given to much wine, teaching well: That they may teach the young women to be wise, to love their husbands, to love their children, To be discreet, chaste, sober, having a care of the house, gentle, obedient to their husbands, that the word of God be not blasphemed. Young men, in like manner, exhort that they be sober. In all things shew thyself an example of good works, in doctrine, in integrity, in gravity, The sound word that can not be blamed: that he, who is on the contrary part, may be afraid, having no evil to say of us.

Lesson IV

Martin was born around the year 336 at Sabaria in Pannonia. When he was ten years old he went to the Church, in the spite of his heathen parents, and by his own will was numbered among the Catechumens. At fifteen years of age, he joined the army and served as a soldier, first under Constantius II and then under Julian. Once, at the gate of Amiens, a poor man asked him for an alms for Christ's name's sake, and since he had nothing to his hand but his arms and his clothes, he gave him half of his cloak. In the night following, Christ appeared to him clad in the half of his cloak, saying to the angels: "While Martin is yet a Catechumen, he has clad Me in this garment."

Lesson V

At eighteen years of age he was baptized. He gave up thereupon the life of a soldier, and betook himself to Hilary, Bishop of Poitiers, by whom he was placed in the order of Acolytes. Being afterwards made Bishop of Tours, he built a monastery wherein he lived in holiness for a while in company of eighty monks. At last he fell sick of a grievous fever at Cande, a village in his diocese, and besought God in constant prayer to set him free from the prison of this dying body. His disciples heard him and said: "Father, why wilt thou go away from us? Unto whom wilt thou bequeath us in our sorrow?" Their words moved Martin, and he said: "Lord, if I be still needful to thy people, I refuse not to work."

Lesson VI

When his disciples saw him in the height of the fever, lying upon his back and praying, they entreated him to turn over and take a little rest upon his side while the violence of his sickness would allow him. But Martin answered them: "Suffer me to look heavenward rather than earthward, that my spirit may see the way whereby it is so soon going to the Lord." At the moment of death he saw the enemy of mankind, and cried out: "What are you come here for, you bloody brute? You murderer, you'll find nothing in me." With these words on his lips, he gave up his soul to God in the year 397, being aged eighty-one years. He was received by a company of Angels, who were heard praising God by many persons, especially by Saint Severinus, Bishop of Cologne.

Lesson VII

From the Holy Gospel according to St. Luke (Luke 11:33–36)

In that time: Jesus said to his disciples: No man lights a candle, and puts it in a hidden place, nor under a bushel; but upon a candlestick, that they that come in, may see the light. And so on.

Homily by St. Ambrose, Bishop

In that which goes before, Christ has set the Church before the synagogue, and He exhorts us rather to trust in the Church. The candle is faith, even as it is written "thy word is a lamp unto my feet, and a light unto my path." Our faith is the word of God. The word of God is light. Faith is the candle. It is written concerning the Word of God, that "That was the true Light, Which lightens every man that comes into this world." But a candle cannot shine, unless it be lit from some other fire.

Lesson VIII

Also it is written: "What woman, having ten pieces of silver, if she lose one piece, does not light a candle, and sweep the house, and seek diligently till she find it?" And here the candle lit to find the lost piece is the strength in our understandings and affections. Let no man therefore seek faith under the law. For the law is by measure, but grace without measure; the law overshadows, but grace enlightens. And therefore let no man shut up his faith within the measure of the law, but give it unto the Church, the Church, wherein shines the sevenfold grace of the Spirit, and whereon the Divine glory of the Great High Priest strikes from heaven, lest the shadow of the law should rest any more at all upon her.

Under the old law there was the sevenfold lamp which the Priest of the Jews lit every morning and every evening, and this was as it were a candle put under a bushel. That Jerusalem which is on earth, that Jerusalem which killed the Prophets, lies hid, as it were, in a dark place in the valley of tears. But that Jerusalem which is in heaven, whereof by faith we are soldiers, is a city set upon the highest of all mountains, even upon Christ. Her the darkness and tempests of earth cannot hide, but she blazes with the glory of the Eternal Sun, and makes to fall upon us the light of spiritual grace.

Lesson IX—Commemoration of St. Mennas, Martyr

Mennas was a Christian Egyptian soldier who had withdrawn himself into a desert place to do penance, but one day, during the persecution under the Emperors Diocletian and Maximian, upon the Emperors' birthday, when the people were gathered together at a great show, stood forth in the theatre, and reviled with a loud voice the idolatries of the Gentiles. Thereupon he was arrested, and being bound at Cotyasus, the chief city of Phrygia, under the authority of the Præfect Pyrrhus, was first savagely lashed with thongs, then racked, then scorched with fire applied to his naked body, then had his wounds lacerated by rubbing with haircloth, then dragged through thorns and iron spikes with hands and feet tied, then lashed again with whips loaded with lead, and lastly slain with the sword, and thrown into a fire. The Christians saved his body thence and buried it, and it has since been translated to Constantinople.

November 12 ~ St. Martin I

Pope & Martyr ~ Semiduplex

All from Common except what follows

Lessons I–III from the occurring Scripture

Lesson IV

Martin was born at Todi in Tuscany. At the beginning of his Pontificate, in the year 649, he was careful to send a legate with letters to Paul, Patriarch of Constantinople, to call upon him to return to the truth of the Catholic faith from the nefarious heresy of the Monothelites. But Paul, being backed up by the heretic

Emperor Constans II, had become so rabid, that he exiled the legates of the Apostolic See into diverse places in the islands. This crime moved the Pope to gather together at Rome a council of one-hundred and five Bishops, by whom Paul was condemned.

Lesson V

Thereupon Constans sent Olympius into Italy as Exarch, straightly commanding him either to slay Pope Martin, or else to bring him into his Imperial presence. Olympius therefore came to Rome and bade a lictor to kill the Pope while he was solemnly celebrating the Liturgy in the Basilica of St. Mary-at-the-Manger. But when the lictor went there, he was suddenly struck blind.

Lesson VI

From that time forth many evils befell the Emperor Constans; but he repented not. He sent the Exarch Theodore Calliopas to Rome, with command to lay hands on the Pope. By him Martin was treacherously taken on the 17th day of June, 653, and brought to Constantinople, where he was kept in prison till he was sent to Cherson on the 15th of May, 655. There his sufferings for the Catholic faith utterly broke him down, and he left this life for a better one, upon the 12th day of November, in the same year. He was famous for miracles. His body was afterwards brought back to Rome and buried in the Church dedicated under the names of Sts. Silvester and Martin (of Tours). He ruled the Church for six years, one month, and twenty-six days. He held two ordinations in the month of December, wherein he made eleven Priests, five Deacons, and thirty-three Bishops for diverse places.

Lessons VII–IX from the Common of Supreme Pontiffs (Homily by St. Leo)

November 13 ~ St. Didacus

Confessor ~ Semiduplex

All from Common except what follows

Lessons I–III from the occurring Scripture

Lesson IV

Didacus (Diego) was a Spaniard, and was born at the little town of San Nicola-del-Porto, in the diocese of Seville. From his childhood he learnt a holier life under a godly Priest, a hermit in a lonely Church, and so served his apprenticeship. Afterwards, being eager to be more utterly God's only, he professed himself as a lay brother under the Rule of St. Francis in the convent of the Friars Minor (called Observants) of Arruzafa. There he cheerfully bore the yoke of the lowliest obedience and the strictest observance. He was much given to contemplation, and a wonderful light from God shone in him, so that, though he was untaught, he could speak miraculously yet plainly about heavenly things.

Lesson V

In the Canary Islands, where he was warden of the brethren of his Order, he underwent much, earnestly willing to be a martyr, and by his word and example brought many unbelievers to Christ. He came to Rome in the year of the Jubilee, being that of our Lord 1450, in the reign of Pope Nicolas V, and there was set to tend the sick in the Convent of Ara Cœli, which work he did with such love, that although the city was plagued with a famine, the sufferers scarcely lacked anything needful. He was a burning and shining light of faith, and had the gift of healing, taking the oil from the lamp which burned before the image of the most blessed Mother of God, to whom he was earnestly devoted, and anointing the sick therewith, whereupon many were marvelously cured.

Lesson VI

He was at Alcalá when he understood that the end of his life was at hand. Clothed in a ragged cast-away habit, he fixed his eyes upon the Cross, and said with extraordinary earnestness "Sweet the nails, sweet the iron, Sweet the Weight That hung on thee, thou that wast chosen to bear the Lord, the King of heaven," and so he gave up his soul to God, upon the 12th day of November, in the year of our Lord 1463. To satisfy the pious wishes of the multitude, his body was kept unburied for not a few months, and lay in a sweetest savor, as though the corruptible had already put on incorruption. He was famous for many and great miracles, and Pope Sixtus V enrolled him in the number of the Saints.

Lessons VII–IX from the second set in the Common of Confessor Non-Bishops (Homily by St. Bede)

November 14 ~ St. Josaphat

Bishop & Martyr ~ Duplex

All from Common except what follows

Lessons I–III from the occurring Scripture

Lesson IV

Josaphat Kuntsevych was born of noble Catholic parents at Vladimir in Volhynia. Once as a child, as he listed to his mother tell the story of the Passion, a dart came forth from the side of Christ on the crucifix and wounded the boy in the heart. Set on fire with love of God, he devoted himself to prayer and works of charity with such zeal that he became the admiration and the model for youths far older than he. When Josaphat was twenty years old he was professed among the cloistered followers of the monastic rule of Saint Basil. Almost at once he made remarkable progress in evangelical perfection. He went barefoot, even in the severe winters of that country. He never ate meat, and drank wine only when obliged to do so under obedience. He disciplined his body by wearing rough hair-shirts until the day of his death. He kept unspotted the flower of chastity which in his youth he had dedicated to the Virgin Theotokos. He became so celebrated for virtue and learning that, despite his youth, he was made superior of the monastery at Byten, and the Archimandrite of Vilnius. Finally much against his will, but to the very great joy of the Catholic people, he was made Archeparch of Polotsk.

Lesson V

In the years following the promotion to this dignity, Josaphat did not relax in any way his austere mode of living. Nothing was so close to his heart as service to God and the salvation of the flock entrusted to his care. He was a vigorous champion of Catholic unity and truth. He labored to the utmost of his ability to win back schismatics and heretics to unity with the See of blessed Peter. Both by preaching and writing he defended the Supreme Pontiff and the doctrine of the Pope's plenitude of power. He directed these works, full of piety and learning against most shameful calumnies and the errors of wicked men. Josaphat vindicated episcopal rights and restored ecclesiastical property seized by laymen. He won back an incredible number of heretics to the bosom of holy Mother Church. How successfully he labored to reestablish communion between the Greek and Latin Churches is told in Papal commendations. He gladly spent the revenues set aside for his maintenance to rebuild God's house, to erect convents for consecrated virgins, and to carry on other charitable works. So generous was Josaphat towards the poor that in one instance, when he did not have money enough to supply the needs of a certain widow, he pawned his *omophorion*, that is, his episcopal pallium.

Lesson VI

Such great advances of the Catholic faith excited so much hatred among certain wicked enemies that they conspired to murder this athlete of Christ. In a sermon he foretold to his people what was about to happen. As he was setting out for Vitebsk on a pastoral visit, these enemies broke into the episcopal palace, attacking and wounding everyone they found. Undaunted, this most kindly man hurried out to the assassins of his own free will and addressed them mildly. "My little children," he said, "why do you strike my servants? If you have any complaint against me, I am here." Thereupon they rushed at him, overwhelmed him with blows and pierced him through with spears. Finally they slew him a stroke of a great axe and threw his body into the river. This happened on November 12th, 1632, when he was forty-three years old. Later his body, surrounded by a marvelous light, was raised from the deepest part of the river. The blood of this Martyr benefited first of all those murderers of their spiritual father. Sentenced to die for their crime, almost all abjured their schism and repented of their crime. Because this wonderful high priest became famous after his death for many miracles, the Supreme Pontiff, Urban VIII, honored him with the title of Blessed. On the 29th of June, 1867, during the solemn observance of the centenaries of the Princes of the Apostles, in the presence of the college of cardinals, of about five hundred others, patriarchs, metropolitans, and bishops of every rite from all parts of the world, assembled in the Vatican basilica, with all solemn ceremonies, Pius IX canonized the first eastern Christian to uphold the unity of the Church. The Supreme Pontiff, Leo XIII, extended his Mass and Office to the universal Church.

Lessons VII–IX from those on December 29—St. Thomas of Canterbury (Homily by St. John Chrysostom on John 10:11–16)

November 15 ~ St. Albert the Great

Bishop, Confessor, & Doctor ~ Duplex

All from Common except what follows

Lessons I–III from the occurring Scripture

Lesson IV

Albert, called the Great because of his extraordinary learning, was born in Swabia, at Lauingen on the Danube, and very carefully educated from boyhood. To further his higher studies he left his native country and went to Padua. At the urging of blessed Jordan, Master General of the Order of Preachers, he asked admission into the family of the Dominicans, in spite of the futile protests of his uncle. After his election to membership among the brethren, Albert was dedicated in all things to God, and was conspicuous for his piety, his strict observance of the rule, and especially for his tender and filial devotion to the Blessed Virgin Mary. Always before study he spent some time in prayer. After his profession of apostolic religion, he so regulated his schedule of life that he became an accomplished preacher of the word of God and an efficient instrument for the salvation of souls. Soon the Order sent Albert to complete his studies at Cologne, where he made such progress in every branch of secular science that he surpassed all his contemporaries in scholarship and achievement. In the meantime, as Alexander IV testifies, he drank so deeply of the health-giving waters of doctrine, sprung forth from the fountain of the divine law, that his soul was flooded with their abundance.

Lesson V

That others might share the rich treasure of his learning, Albert was appointed professor at Hildesheim, then Freiburg, Ratisbon and Strasbourg successively. He became the marvel of all. During the period when he taught sacred theology in the famous University of Paris, he became world-famous, and received the degree of Master of Theology. Examining the teachings of pagan philosophers in the light of sound reason, he demonstrated clearly that they were in fundamental accord with the tenets of the faith. He expounded most brilliantly the thesis on the extent of the power of human understanding to comprehend divine mysteries. How great was his genius, how brilliant his intellect, how zealously he applied himself to study until he had become learned in every branch of scholarship, especially sacred theology, is best shown by his numerous writings. These encompass every known subject. Albert returned to Cologne to become president of the university conducted by his Order. He was so successful that he became ever more widely acknowledged as an authority by the schools; his reputation for learning increased. Among his pupils was his beloved Thomas Aquinas; Albert was first to recognize and acclaim the greatness of that intellect. He had a deep devotion towards the Blessed Sacrament of the Altar and composed some magnificent works upon it. He also pointed out wider fields for the study of the mystical things of the soul. He succeeded so well that the zeal of this great master spread far and wide in the Church.

Lesson VI

Amid so many very important duties Albert shone as an exemplar of the religious life. His brethren, therefore, selected him to be prior of the Teutonic province. He was summoned to Anagni, in the presence of the Supreme Pontiff, Alexander IV, to refute that William who had been impiously and arrogantly attacking the mendicant orders. Soon after this, the Pope appointed Albert Bishop of Ratisbon. As Bishop, Albert devoted himself almost entirely to the care of his flock. Yet he retained meticulously his humility and love of poverty. Up to the time he resigned his see, Albert was prompt and energetic in fulfilling the duties of his episcopal office. He ministered to the spiritual needs of souls throughout Germany and the neighboring provinces. He was careful that the advice he gave to those who sought his counsels was wise and salutary. So prudent was he in settling disputes that at Cologne he was called "the peacemaker." From far distant places, prelates and princes invited him to act as an arbiter to resolve differences. Saint Louis IX, King of France, presented him with some relics of the sacred Passion of Christ, and Albert cherished them devoutly all his days. In the second Council of Lyons he was instrumental in bringing to a successful conclusion several weighty matters. He taught until he was worn out with age. His last days were spent in holy contemplation. In the year 1280 he entered into the joy of his Lord. By the authority of the Roman Pontiffs, the honors of the altar had long since been conferred upon Albert in many dioceses and in the Order of Preachers, when Pius XI, gladly accepting the recommendations of the Congregation of Sacred Rites, extended his Feast to the universal Church, and conferred the title of Doctor. Pope Pius XII appointed him the heavenly patron with God of all those who study the natural sciences.

Lessons VII–IX from the first set in the Common of Doctors (Sermon by St. Augustine)

November 16 ~ St. Gertrude

Virgin ~ Duplex

All from Common except what follows

Lessons I–III from the occurring Scripture

Lesson IV

Gertrude was born of a noble family at Eisleben, in Saxony, about the year of our Lord 1264. At five years of age she offered her virginity and herself to Jesus Christ, in the Benedictine convent at Rodalsdorf. From that time forth she was utterly estranged from earthly things, ever striving for things higher, and began to lead a kind of heavenly life. To learning in human letters she added knowledge of the things of God. In the thought thereof she earnestly desired, and soon reached, the perfection of a Christian soul. Of Christ, and of the things in His life, she spoke oftentimes with movings of spirit. The glory of God was the one end of all her thoughts, and to that her every longing and her every act were given. Though God had crowned her with so many and noble gifts both of nature and of grace, her belief regarding herself was so humble that she was used to number as among the greatest of the wonders of His goodness that He had always in His mercy borne with one who was so utterly unworthy.

Lesson V

In the thirtieth year of her age she was elected Abbess of Rodalsdorf, where she had professed herself in the religious life, and afterwards of Heldelfs. This office she bore for forty years in love, wisdom, and zeal for strict observance, so that the house seemed like an ideal example of a sisterhood of perfect nuns. To each one she was a mother and a teacher, and yet would be as the least of all, being as in all lowliness among them as she that served. That she might be more utterly God's only, she tormented her body with sleeplessness, hunger, and other afflictions, but withal ever true to herself, stood forth a pattern of innocence, gentleness, and long-suffering. The salvation of her neighbors was her constant earnest endeavor, and her godly toil bore abundant fruit. The love of God oftentimes threw her into trances, and she was given the grace of the deepest contemplation, even to union of spirit with God.

Lesson VI

Christ Himself, to show what such a bride was to Him, revealed that He had in the heart of Gertrude a pleasant dwelling-place. The Virgin Godbearer she ever sought with deep reverence as a mother and caretaker whom she had received from Jesus Himself, and from her she had many benefits. Toward the most Divine Sacrament of the Eucharist, and the sufferings of the Lord, her soul was moved with love and gratitude, so that she sometimes wept abundantly. She helped with daily gifts and prayers the souls of the just condemned to the purifying fire. She wrote much for the fostering of piety. She was glorified also by revelations from God, and by the gift of prophecy. Her last illness was the wasting of home-sickness to be with God rather than decay of the flesh, and she left this life upon the 17th day of November, in the year of our Lord 1292. God made her illustrious with miracles both during her life and after her death.

Lessons VII–IX from the first set in the Common of Virgins (Homily by St. Gregory)

November 17 ~ St. Gregory Thaumaturgus

Confessor Bishop ~ Semiduplex

All from Common except what follows

Lessons I–III from the occurring Scripture

Lesson IV

Gregory, Archbishop of Neocæsarea, in Pontus, is famous indeed for his holiness and doctrine, but much more so on account of the signs and wonders which he wrought, the number and character of which were so extraordinary that they have earned him the name of *Thaumatourgos*, which being interpreted from the Greek, is "Wonder-worker." Saint Basil compares him with Moses, with the Prophets, and with the Apostles, and testifies that by his prayers he moved a mountain that stood in the way of the building of a Church. Moreover, he dried up a marsh, which was a cause of strife between brothers. Also, when the River Lycus overflowed and wasted the fields, he set his walking-stick on the bank (which forthwith grew into a green tree), and confined the stream within its bed, so that it never more passed that place again.

Lesson V

He oftentimes cast out demons either from heathen idols or from the bodies of men, and did many other marvelous things, whereby he drew countless numbers to believe in Jesus Christ. He also had the spirit of prophecy, and foretold things to come. When he was at the point of death, he asked how many unbelievers were left in the city of Neocæsarea and when they answered seventeen, he gave God thanks, and said: "Just as many were the faithful when I took the Episcopate." He wrote a great deal, whereby, as well as by his wonders, he has enlightened the Church of God.

Lesson VI is Lesson IV from the second set in the Common of Confessor Bishops (Sermon by St. Maximus)

Lesson VII

From the Holy Gospel according to St. Mark (Mark 11:22–24)

And Jesus answering, saith to them: Have the faith of God. Amen I say to you, that whosoever shall say to this mountain, Be thou removed and be cast into the sea, and shall not stagger in his heart, but believe, that whatsoever he saith shall be done; it shall be done unto him. And so on.

Homily by St. Bede the Venerable, Priest

The heathen, who have written blasphemies against the Church, are used to taunt that we have not full faith in God, since we have never been able to move mountains. Such should be answered that we do not possess records of everything that has come to pass in the Church, any more than, the Scripture being witness, we possess records of all the doings of our Lord Christ Himself. Mountains may have been removed and cast into the sea, in case of need; a like case, indeed, as we read, was that which came to pass at the prayers of the Blessed Father Gregory, Archbishop of Neocæsarea in Pontus, that man remarkable for merits and virtues, when a mountain was moved from one place on earth to another, as the dwellers in the city had need.

Lesson VIII

Gregory was desirous to build a Church in a suitable place, but the site was too narrow, being wedged in between a mountain on the one side and a precipice going down into the sea on the other. He came therefore by night to the place, kneeling down, and reminded the Lord of His promise, calling upon Him to remove the mountain. And in the morning, when he came there again, he found that the mountain had been moved back and left as much room for the builders of the Church as they needed. This man therefore would have been able, and any other man of like grace would have been able, if need were, to obtain of the Lord, by the force of his faith, that even a mountain should be removed, and be cast into the sea.

Lesson IX

Mystically, however, by a mountain is sometimes signified the devil, on account of the pride whereby he lifts himself up against God, and would want to be like unto the Most High. And when holy teachers, strong in faith, do preach the Word, this mountain is removed, and cast into the sea, that is to say, the unclean spirit is removed out of the hearts of such as are foreordained unto eternal life, and sent free to exercise the wild rage of his tyranny in the riotous and embittered minds of the unfaithful.

November 18 ~ Dedication of the Basilicas of Sts. Peter & Paul

Major Duplex

All from the Common of the Dedication of a Church except what follows

Lesson I ~ Apoc 21:18–20

From the book of the Apocalypse of St. John the Apostle

And the building of the wall thereof was of jasper stone: but the city itself pure gold, like to clear glass. And the foundations of the wall of the city were adorned with all manner of precious stones. The first foundation was jasper: the second, sapphire: the third, a chalcedony: the fourth, an emerald: The fifth, sardonyx: the sixth, sardius: the seventh, chrysolite: the eighth, beryl: the ninth, a topaz: the tenth, a chrysoprasus: the eleventh, a jacinth: the twelfth, an amethyst.

Lesson II ~ Apoc 21:21–23

And the twelve gates are twelve pearls, one to each: and every several gate was of one several pearl. And the street of the city was pure gold, as it were transparent glass. And I saw no temple therein. For the Lord God Almighty is the temple thereof, and the Lamb. And the city hath no need of the sun, nor of the moon, to shine in it. For the glory of God hath enlightened it, and the Lamb is the lamp thereof.

Lesson III - Apoc 21:24–27

And the nations shall walk in the light of it: and the kings of the earth shall bring their glory and honour into it. And the gates thereof shall not be shut by day: for there shall be no night there. And they shall bring the glory and honour of the nations into it. There shall not enter into it any thing defiled, or that worketh abomination or maketh a lie, but they that are written in the book of life of the Lamb.

Lesson IV

Among the hallowed places which have from of old been held in honor among Christians, the most famous and sought after were those where the bodies of the Saints were buried, or where there was some trace or token of the Martyrs. Among these spots so hallowed has been ever among the most noteworthy that place on the Vatican Hill which is called the Confession of St. Peter. There do Christians come from all parts of the earth as unto the rock of faith and the foundation of the Church, and surround with pious reverence and love the spot hallowed by the grave of the Prince of the Apostles.

Lesson V

There came the Emperor Constantine the Great upon the eighth day after his Baptism, and, taking off his crown, cast himself down upon the ground, and wept abundantly. Then he took a spade and pickaxe, and began to break up the earth, whereof he carried away twelve baskets-full in honor of the twelve Apostles, and built a Church upon that spot, appointed for the Basilica of the Prince of the Apostles. This Church was consecrated by Pope Saint Sylvester upon the 18th day of November, in like manner as he had consecrated the Church of the Lateran upon the 9th day of the same month. In this Church did the Pope set up an altar of stone, and pour ointment thereon, and ordain that from thenceforth no altars should be set up, save of stone. The same Emperor Constantine likewise built a very stately Church upon the road to Ostia, in honor of the Saint Paul the Apostle, which Church also was dedicated by the blessed Sylvester. These Churches the Emperor enriched by grants of much land, and adorned with exceedingly rich gifts.

Lesson VI

The Basilica of St. Peter upon the Vatican fell in course of time to ruins, and having been rebuilt from the foundations, enlarged and garnished, by the zeal of many Popes, was solemnly consecrated anew by Urban VIII, upon the same day, in the year 1628. The Basilica of St. Paul upon the road to Ostia was almost entirely consumed by fire in the year 1823, but was rebuilt in a more splendid form and, as it were, raised from the dead, by the unwearied zeal of four successive Popes. Pius IX seized the happy occasion when the doctrine concerning the Immaculate Conception of the

Virgin Mary, which he had just set forth, had drawn together to Rome a great multitude of Cardinals and Bishops from all quarters of the Catholic world, solemnly to dedicate this new Church in their presence upon the 10th day of December in the year 1854; but he decreed that the yearly Feast in honor of that dedication should be kept upon this day.

Lesson VII

From the Holy Gospel according to St. Luke (Luke 19:1–10)

At that time: Jesus entering in, he walked through Jericho. And behold, there was a man named Zacchæus, which was the chief among the publicans, and he was rich. And so on.

Homily by Pope St. Gregory

If we would be truly wise, and behold wisdom herself, we must humbly acknowledge ourselves to be fools. Let us cast away harmful wisdom, and learn praiseworthy folly. For this reason indeed is it written: "God has chosen the foolish things of the world, to confound the wise." And again it is said, "If any man among you seems to be wise in this world, let him become a fool, that he may be wise." And unto this does the very Gospel bear witness, wherein it is said that "Zacchæus sought to see Jesus, Who He was; and could not for the crowd, because he was little of stature. And running before, he climbed up into a sycamore tree to see Him; for He was to pass that way." For this name Sycamore, being interpreted, signifies the Foolish Fig.

Lesson VIII

Little Zacchæus therefore accepted the humiliation of having recourse to the sycamore and saw the Lord. They who humbly choose to be fools in the estimation of the world, have a deep insight into the wisdom of God. The crowd stands in our way, on account of our little stature, when we are eager to see the Lord; for the toilsome din of worldly business torments our weak minds, so as to hinder our perceiving the light of the truth. But we climb up wisely into the sycamore tree, if we willingly give up our minds to that folly which God gives unto us. What can be more utter folly than not to seek for that we have lost, to leave that whereof we have been robbed in the hands of our despoilers, to take no revenge for wrongs which have been done us, yea, even to offer to him that takes away our cloak, our coat also, and be patient?

Lesson IX

The Lord bids us, as it were, to climb up into the sycamore, where He says: "Of him that takes away thy goods, ask them not again." And again: "Whosoever shall smite thee on thy right cheek, turn to him the other also." From the boughs of this sycamore tree, the Lord is seen passing by. He may indeed, as yet, not be seen face to Face, but by this wise folly the inward eye may see the Wisdom of God, as it were, passing by, even that Wisdom Which they that are wise in their own conceit cannot see. They are mixed up in the overbearing crowd of their own imaginations, and have not yet found the sycamore tree into which to climb, if they would see the Lord.

November 19 ~ St. Elizabeth of Hungary

Widow ~ Duplex

All from Common except what follows

Lessons I–III from the occurring Scripture

Lesson IV

Elisabeth, daughter of Andrew II, King of Hungary, was born in the year 1207. She began to fear God even as a little child, and grew in grace as she grew in years. In her fourteenth year she was married to Ludwig IV, Landgrave of Hesse and Thuringia, and thenceforth gave herself up to the things of her husband, with as much zeal as to the things of God. She rose in the night to make long prayers. She consecrated herself to works of mercy. She waited continually on widows and orphans, the sick and the needy. When a sore famine came in the year 1225, she provided corn bountifully from her own house. She founded a house of refuge for lepers, and would even kiss their hands and feet. She built also a great hospital for the suffering and starving poor.

Lesson V

After her husband died on his way to the Crusade, Elizabeth, more utterly to be God's alone, then laid aside all the garments of earthly state, clad herself in poor raiment, and entered the Third Order of St. Francis, wherein she was a burning and shining light of patience and humility. Her brother-in-law stripped her and her three little children of all their goods, and turned them out of their own house. She was deserted by all, and assailed with insults, mockeries, and calumnies, but she bore it all with patience, yea, even rejoicing that she suffered such things for God's sake. She gave herself to the lowest services toward the poor and sick, and sought for them the necessities of life, while she lived herself only on herbs and vegetables.

Lesson VI

In these and many other holy works she prayerfully passed the rest of her life, till in the twenty-fourth year of her age, the end of her earthly pilgrimage came, as she had already foretold to her servants. With her eyes fixed on heaven, absorbed in the thought of God, by Him wondrously comforted, and strengthened by the Sacraments, she fell asleep in the Lord, upon the 19th day of November, in the year of salvation 1231. Forthwith many miracles were wrought at her grave, which being known and duly proved, Gregory IX numbered her name among those of the Saints.

Lessons VII–IX from the Common of Non-Virgins (Homily by St. Gregory)

Lesson IX—Commemoration of St. Pontian, Pope & Martyr

Pontian was a Roman who ruled the Church in the reign of the Emperor Alexander. This Emperor banished him into the Island of

Sardinia, along with the Priest Hippolytus, on account of their profession of the Christian faith. There he endured many hardships because of his belief in Christ, and departed this life upon the 19th day of November, in the year of our Lord 235. His body was brought to Rome by Pope Fabian and his clergy, and buried in the cemetery of Callistus, upon the Appian Way. He sat in the seat of Peter four years, four months, and twenty-five days. He held two Ordinations in the month of December, wherein he made six Priests, five Deacons, and six Bishops for diverse places.

November 20 ~ St. Felix of Valois

Confessor ~ Duplex

All from Common except what follows

Lessons I–III from the occurring Scripture

Lesson IV

Hugo de Valois, who afterwards took the name of Felix, was born in the year 1127 of the same Royal family of the Valois. From his earliest childhood he gave tokens, especially by his pity toward the poor, of the holiness of his coming life. When he was still a little lad he distributed money to the poor with his own hand, with the seriousness of an old man. When he was a little bigger he used to send them dishes from the table, and took special delight in treating poor children with the most toothsome of sweets. As a boy he took clothes off his own back, more than once, to cover the naked. He begged and obtained from his uncle Theobald, Earl of Champagne and Blois, the life of a felon condemned to death, foretelling to him that this reprobate cutthroat would yet become a man of most holy life which did indeed come to pass as he had said.

Lesson V

After a praiseworthy boyhood, he began to think of withdrawing from the world in order to be alone with heavenly thoughts. But he first wished to take orders, to the end that he might clear himself of all expectation of succeeding to the crown, to which, in consequence of the Salic Law, he was somewhat near. He became a Priest, and said his first Mass with deep devotion. Then, in a little while, he withdrew himself into the wilderness, where he lived in extreme abstinence, fed by heavenly grace. There, by the inspiration of God, came Saint John de Matha, the Doctor of Paris, and found him, and they led a holy life together for several years, until they were both warned by an Angel to go to Rome and seek a special Rule of life from the Pope. Pope Innocent III, while he was solemnly celebrating the Liturgy on the 28th day of January, 1198, received in a vision the revelation of the Order and Institute for the Ransom of Captives, and he forthwith clad Felix and John in white garments marked with a cross of red and blue, made after the likeness of the raiment wherein the Angel had appeared. This Pope also willed that the new Order should bear, as well as the habit of three colors, the name of the Most Holy Trinity.

Lesson VI

When they had received the confirmation of their rule from Pope Innocent, John and Felix enlarged the first house of their Order, which they had built a little while before at Cerfroi, in the diocese of Meaux, in France. There Felix wonderfully devoted himself to the promotion of Regular Observance and of the Institute for the Ransom of Captives, and thence he busily spread the same by sending forth his disciples into other provinces. Here it was that he received an extraordinary favor from the blessed Virgin Mother. On the night of the Nativity of the Mother of God, the brethren lay all asleep, and, by the Providence of God, woke not to say Matins. But Felix was watching, as his custom was, and came on time into the Choir. There he found the Blessed Virgin in the midst of the Choir, clad in raiment marked with the Cross of his Order, the Cross of red and blue; and with her a company of the heavenly host in like garments. And Felix was mingled among them. And the Mother of God began to sing, and they all sang with her and praised God; and Felix sang with them; and so they finished the Office. So now that he seemed to have been already called away from glorifying God on earth, to glorify Him in heaven, an Angel told Felix that the hour of his death was at hand. When therefore he had exhorted his children to be tender to the poor and to slaves, he gave up his soul to God upon the 4th day of November in the year of Christ 1212, in the time of the same Pope Innocent III, being eighty-five years old, and full of good works.

Lessons VII–IX from the second set in the Common of Confessor Non-Bishops (Homily by St. Bede)

November 21 ~ The Presentation of the Blessed Virgin Mary

Major Duplex

All from Common except what follows

Lesson IV

From the Book by St. John Damascene on the Orthodox Faith

Joachim took to wife that most eminent and praiseworthy woman, Anne. And even as the ancient Anna, being stricken with barrenness, by prayer and promise became the mother of Samuel, so likewise this woman also through prayer and promise received from God the Mother of God, that in fruitfulness she might not be behind any of the famous matrons. And thus grace (for such is the signification of the name of Anne) is mother of the Lady (for such is the signification of the name of Mary). And indeed she became the Lady of every creature, since she has been mother of the Creator. She first saw the light in Joachim's house, near the Pool of Bethesda, at Jerusalem, and was carried to the Temple. There planted in the Lord, the dew of His Spirit made her to flourish in the courts of her God, and like a green olive she became a tree, so that all the doves of grace came and lodged in her branches. And so she raised her mind utterly above the lust of life and the lust of the flesh, and kept her soul virgin in her virgin body, as became her that was to receive God into her womb.

Lesson V

From the Book by
St. Ambrose, Bishop, on Virgins

Such was Mary that her single life offers an example to all. If then the doer displease us not, let us applaud the deed; if any other woman seek like reward, let her follow after like works. In the one Virgin how many glorious examples do shine forth! Hers was the hidden treasure of modesty, hers the high standard of faith, hers the self-sacrifice of earnestness, hers to be the pattern of maidenhood at home, of companionship in ministry, of motherhood in the Temple. O to how many virgins has she been helpful, how many has she taken in her arms and presented unto the Lord, saying: "Here is one who, like me, has kept stainlessly clean the wedding-chamber, the marriage-bed of my Son!"

Lesson VI

Why should I go on to speak of the scantiness of her eating, or of the multiplicity of her work, how her labour seemed above human capacity, and her refreshment insufficient for human strength, her toil never missing a moment, her fasting taking two days together? And when she was desirous to eat, she took not delicacies, but whatsoever food came first to hand that would keep body and soul together. She would not sleep till need was, and even then, while her body rested, her soul watched, for she often talked in her sleep, either repeating things that she had read, or going on with what she was doing before sleep interrupted her, or rehearsing things executed, or talking of things projected.

Lessons VII–IX from the Common of the Blessed Virgin Mary (Homily by St. Bede the Venerable)

November 22 ~ St. Cecilia

Virgin ~ Duplex
All from Common
except what follows

Lesson IV

Cecilia was a Roman virgin of noble birth, trained up from her earliest years in the teaching of the Christian faith, and who by vow consecrated her virginity to God. She was afterwards given in marriage, against her will, to Valerian. On the first night she said to him: "Valerian, I am under the wardship of an Angel, who keeps me always a virgin. Therefore do nothing unto me, lest the anger of God should be aroused against thee." Valerian was moved at her words, and dared not to touch her. Also he added even this, that he would believe in Christ, if he could see the Angel. Cecilia answered him that that could not be unless he were first baptized, and for the sake of seeing the Angel he was willing. So she bade him go unto Pope Urban, who was hiding in the sepulchre of the Martyrs on the Appian Way on account of the persecution. And he went unto him and was baptized.

Lesson V

Whence he came back to Cecilia, and found her praying, and the Angel with her, shining from the glory of God. As soon as he had recovered from the shock of wonder and fear, he brought his brother Tiburtius, and Cecilia taught him Christ, and he was baptized by the same Pope Urban, and he also was vouchsafed to see the Angel whom his brother had seen. A little while after, both of them bravely suffered martyrdom under the Præfect Almachius, who then caused Cecilia to be taken, and asked of her, first of all, where the property of Tiburtius and Valerian was.

Lesson VI

To him the Virgin answered that all their goods had been given to the poor. Thereupon he was filled with fury, and commanded her to be taken home, and burnt in the bath. She was in that place a day and a night, but the fire had not harmed her. Then was sent the executioner, who gave her three strokes of the axe, and, as he could not cut off her head, left her half-dead. Three days thereafter, upon the 22nd day of November, in the reign of the Emperor Alexander Severus, she winged her flight for heaven, glorified with the two palms of virginity and martyrdom. Her body was buried in the cemetery of Callistus by the aforementioned Pope Urban, who also consecrated a Church in her name in her own house. Her relics were brought into the city by Pope Paschal I, along with those of Tiburtius, Valerian, and Maximus, and all laid together in the same Church of St. Cecilia.

Lesson VII

From the Holy Gospel according to St. Matthew (Matt 25:1–13)

In that time, Jesus said to his disciples: Then shall the kingdom of heaven be like to ten virgins, who taking their lamps went out to meet the bridegroom and the bride. And so on.

Homily by St. John Chrysostom

Why does the Lord set forth this parable under the figure of virgins, and not make it easily acceptable for all men? He had spoken great things about virginity, saying "There be eunuchs, which have made themselves eunuchs for the kingdom of heaven's sake. He that is able to receive it, let him receive it." He knew also that virginity is a thing which is held in great honor among men, being indeed a thing higher than nature, as is plain from this, that under the Old Testament even the Patriarchs and Saints did not practice it, and that under the New Testament it is not enjoined by any commandment of necessity; for the Lord did not make it binding, but left it open to the free choice of the faithful. Whence also Paul says: "Concerning virgins I have no commandment of the Lord; yet I give my judgment, as one that has obtained mercy of the Lord to be faithful." I suppose therefore that this is good for the present distress, that it is good for a man so to be. But and if thou marry, thou hast not sinned, and if a virgin marry, she has not sinned.

Lesson VIII

Virginity then, being a thing in itself so great and so much esteemed among many, lest any man having attained unto it, and kept it undefiled, should think that he has done all, and so leave the rest undone, the Lord puts forth this parable, in order to show that if virginity, though it have all else, lack mercy, its owner will but have his portion without, among the fornicators, among whom Christ does justly place the heartless and pitiless celibate. The fornicator is entangled in lust after bodies, the other in lust after money. The lust for bodies and the lust for money are two very different things, whereof the fleshly is by far the keener and stubborner appetite. They that strive with the weaker enemy are therefore much less excusable if they fall. Therefore the Lord has called such virgins foolish, for having first won the stern battle, and then been destroyed in the light one.

Lesson IX

By the lamps spoken of in this parable, the Lord signifies the actual gift of virginity and holy continence, and by the oil: gentleness, almsgiving, and helpfulness toward the needy. While the Bridegroom tarried, they all slumbered and slept. His disciples hoped that His kingdom was to come forthwith. To call them away from this hope, to lead them away from this thought, He shows them the time of waiting for the Bridegroom to be no very short one. "They all slumbered and slept." He calls death a sleep. "And at midnight there was a cry made, Behold, the Bridegroom comes, go out to meet Him." This "midnight" is either a continuation of the parable, and so signifies the awaking of the dead, or else means that the Resurrection to come will actually take place in the night. Of the cry Paul also makes mention, where he says: "The Lord Himself shall descend from heaven with a shout, with the voice of the Archangel, and the trumpet of God."

November 23 ~ St. Clement I

Pope & Martyr ~ Duplex

All from Common except what follows

Lessons I–III from the occurring Scripture

Lesson IV

Clement, the son of Faustinus, was a Roman, from the quarter of the Cœlian Mount. He was a disciple of the blessed Peter, and is the same concerning whom Paul says, writing to the Philippians: "And I entreat thee also, my sincere companion, help those women who have labored with me in the gospel, with Clement and the rest of my fellow laborers, whose names are in the book of life." He succeeded Cletus as Roman Pontiff. He it was who divided the seven quarters of the city among seven scribes, one to each, whose duty it was to search out most carefully, and record in writing the sufferings and acts of the Martyrs. He himself also wrote much, and that most accurately and healthily, whereby he clearly explained the Christian Religion.

Lesson V

His teaching and the holiness of his life brought many to believe in Christ, and he was therefore exiled by the Emperor Trajan to Cherson, where he found two-thousand Christians, who had been condemned by the same Trajan. There they all worked in the marble quarries. During their labour they suffered for want of water, and Clement prayed then went up a hill near, on the top whereof he saw a Lamb standing, touching with its right foot a flowing spring of sweet waters. Therewith they all quenched their thirst, and by this miracle many unbelievers were brought to believe in Christ, and began to honor the holiness of Clement.

Lesson VI

These things moved Trajan to send someone to tie an anchor about Clement's neck, and cast him into the depths of the sea. After it had been done, while the Christians were praying on the shore, the sea receded by three miles, and when they followed it, they found a grotto of marble, in form like a temple, and therein a stone coffin wherein was laid the body of the Martyr, and, nearby, the anchor wherewith he had been sunk. Then were the countryfolk moved to receive the faith of Christ. The body of Clement was afterwards brought to Rome, in the time of Pope Nicholas I, and buried in his own Church. A Church was also built in the place where God had made the water to break forth. Clement lived as Pope nine years, six months, and six days. He held two Ordinations in the month of December, wherein he made ten Priests, two Deacons, and fifteen Bishops for diverse places.

Lessons VII–IX from the Common of Supreme Pontiffs (Homily by St. Leo)

Lesson IX—Commemoration of St. Felicitas, Martyr

Sermon by St. Gregory, Pope

Blessed Felicity, whose Birthday we are keeping today, had as much dread of leaving her seven sons living after her in the flesh, as have carnal-minded mothers of seeing them go dead before them. When she was taken in the strong pains of persecution, she braced up the hearts of her children by bidding them cleave to the Fatherland above, and became their mother for the spiritual life, as she had before been for the fleshly one, bringing them forth for God by her exhortation, as she had brought them forth for the world by her body. And shall I not call this woman a Martyr? Nay, more than Martyr. The seven whom she trusted to God were seven children sent before her to death. She suffered first and triumphed last.

November 24 ~ St. John of the Cross

Confessor & Doctor ~ Duplex

All from Common except what follows

Lessons I–III from the occurring Scripture

Lesson IV

John of the Cross was born of pious parents at Fontibere, near Avila, in Spain, in the year of our Lord 1542. It began soon to appear that he was foreordained to be an acceptable servant unto the Virgin Mother of God. At five years of age he fell into a well, but the hand of the same Godbearer took him up, and saved him from all harm. So burning was his desire to suffer that when he was nine years old he gave up any softer bed, and used to lie on potsherds. In his youth he devoted himself as a servant in the hospital for the sick poor at Medina del Campo, and embraced with eager charity the meanest offices there, his readiness likewise exciting others to imitate him. In 1563 he obeyed the call to higher things, and entered the Order of the Blessed Virgin Mary of Mount Carmel, wherein, by command of his Superiors, he received Priestly Orders. By their leave and his own strong desire for the sternest discipline and the strictest life, he adopted the primitive Rule. Full of the memory of what our Lord suffered, he declared war against himself as his own worst enemy, and carried it on by depriving himself of sleep and food, by iron chains, by whips, and by every kind of self-torture. And in a little while he had crucified the flesh, with the affections and lusts thereof. He was indeed worthy that Saint Teresa should say of him that he was one of the purest and holiest souls by whom God was then enlightening His Church.

Lesson V

The singular austerity of his life, and the might of his virtues, joined to the unceasing concentration of his mind on God, had the effect of oftentimes subjecting him to daily and extraordinary trances. So burning was his love of God that the fire sometimes could not be kept bound within, and broke forth, so that his face shone. The salvation of his neighbors was one of his dearest longings, and he was unwearied in preaching the Word of God, and in administering the Sacraments. As strong in so many good works, and glowing with zeal to make discipline harder, he was given by God to be a helper to Saint Teresa, and he aided her to set up again the primitive observance among the brethren of the Order of Mount Carmel, as she had already done among the sisters. In doing God's work, he and God's handmaid together went through toils that cannot be numbered. No discomforts or dangers held him back from going throughout all Spain to visit all and each of the convents which the care of that holy Virgin had founded, and in them, and in very many others erected by her means for spreading the renewed observance, he strengthened it by his word and example. He is indeed worthy to be reckoned second only to Saint Teresa as a professor and founder of the Order of Discalced Carmelites.

Lesson VI

He remained a perpetual virgin, and when some shameless women tried to beguile his modesty, he not only foiled them, but gained them for Christ. In the judgment of the Apostolic See he was as much taught of God as was Saint Teresa for explaining God's hidden mysteries, and he wrote books of mystical theology filled with heavenly wisdom. Christ once asked him what reward he would have for so much work; whereto he answered: "Lord, that I may suffer, and be disesteemed for thy sake." He was very famous for his power over demons, whom he oftentimes scared out of men's bodies, for discernment of spirits, for the gift of prophecy, and for eminent miracles. He was extraordinarily humble, and oftentimes entreated of the Lord that he might die in some place where he was unknown. In accordance with his prayer, he was sent to Ubeda, where for three months the Prior imprisoned and cruelly abused him during his last sickness. To crown his love of suffering, he bore uncomplainingly five open sores in his leg, running with water. At last, upon the 14th day of December, in the year 1591, being the day and the hour foretold by himself, after having in godly and holy ways received the Sacraments of the Church, hugging the image of that crucified Saviour of Whom his heart and his mouth had been used to be full, he uttered the words: "Into thy hands I commend my spirit," and fell asleep in the Lord. As his soul passed away it was received into a glorious cloud of fire. His body yielded a sweetest savor, and is still incorrupt where it lies, held in great honor, at Segovia. He was famous for very many miracles both before and since his death, and Pope Benedict XIII numbered his name among those of the Saints.

Lessons VII–IX from the first set in the Common of Doctors (Sermon by St. Augustine)

Lesson IX—Commemoration of St. Chrysogonus, Martyr

Chrysogonus was imprisoned at Rome in the reign of the Emperor Diocletian. There he lived for the space of two years upon the alms of Saint Anastasia. She was suffering much persecution from her husband Publius for Christ's Name's sake, and was used to write to Chrysogonus to ask for the help of his prayers, and he in return comforted her by his epistles. Presently the Emperor wrote to Rome commanding the rest of the Christians who were in prison there to be put to death, and Chrysogonus to be sent to himself at Aquileia. When he was brought there, he said unto him: "I have sent for thee, O Chrysogonus, that I may increase thine honors, if only thou wilt bring thy mind to worship the gods." Thereto Chrysogonus answered: "With my mind and with my prayers I worship Him Who is God indeed, but such gods as are nothing but images of demons; them I hate and curse." Then was the Emperor kindled to fury at this answer, and commanded Chrysogonus to be beheaded at Aquæ Gradatæ upon the 24th day of November. His body was cast into the sea, but found a little while afterwards washed up upon the shore, and the Priest Zoilus took it and buried it in his own house.

November 25 ~ St. Catherine of Alexandria

Virgin & Martyr ~ Duplex

All from Common except what follows

Lessons I–III from the occurring Scripture

Lesson IV

Catherine was a noble maiden of Alexandria, who from her earliest years joined the study of the liberal arts with fervent faith, and in a short while came to such a height of holiness and learning, that when she was eighteen years of age she prevailed over the chiefest wits. When she saw many diversely tormented and dragged to death by command of Maximinus Daja, because they professed the Christian religion, she went boldly unto him and rebuked him for his savage cruelty, bringing forward likewise most sage reasons why the faith of Christ should be needful for salvation.

Lesson V

Maximinus marveled at her wisdom, and bade to keep her, while he gathered together the most learned men from all quarters and offered them great rewards if they would confute Catherine and bring her from believing in Christ to worship idols. But the event fell contrariwise, for many of the philosophers who had come to dispute with her were overcome by the force and skill of her reasoning, so that the love of Christ Jesus was kindled in them, and they were content even to die for His sake. Then did Maximinus strive to beguile Catherine with fair words and promises, and when he found it was lost pains, he caused her to be scourged, and bruised with leaden whips, and so cast into prison, and neither meat nor drink given to her for the space of eleven days.

Lesson VI

At that time Maximinus's wife and Porphyry, the Captain of his host, went to the prison to see the damsel, and at her preaching believed in Jesus Christ, and were afterwards crowned with martyrdom. Then was Catherine brought out of prison, and a wheel was set, wherein were fastened many and sharp blades, so that her virgin body might thereby be most dreadfully cut and torn in pieces, but in a little while, as Catherine prayed, this machine was broken in pieces, at which marvel many believed in Christ. But Maximinus was hardened in his godlessness and cruelty, and commanded to behead Catherine. She bravely offered her neck to the stroke and passed away hence to receive the twin crowns of virginity and martyrdom, upon the 25th day of November. Her body was marvelously laid by angels upon Mount Sinai in Arabia.

Lessons VII–IX from the first in the Common of Virgins (Homily by St. Gregory)

November 26—30

As found in the beginning of the Proper of Saints.